CANON LAW
A Text and Commentary

CANON LAW

A Text and Commentary

by

T. LINCOLN BOUSCAREN, S.J.

LL.B., S.T.D., Mag. Agg., Professor of Canon Law,
West Baden College, West Baden Springs, Indiana;
formerly Professor of Canon Law, Pontifical Gregorian
University, Consultor to the Sacred Congregation for the
Propagation of the Faith

and

ADAM C. ELLIS, S.J.

M.A., J.C.D., Professor of Canon Law, Saint Mary's
College, Saint Marys, Kansas; formerly Professor of
Canon Law, Pontifical Gregorian University, Consultor
to the Sacred Congregation of Religious

THE BRUCE PUBLISHING COMPANY
Milwaukee

Imprimi potest: LEO D. SULLIVAN, S.J.
Nihil obstat: SYLVESTER F. GASS, I.C.D., censor deputatus
Imprimatur: ✠ MOYSES E. KILEY, Archiepiscopus Milwaukiensis
Die 18 Novembris, 1947

(Second Printing — 1948)

TO THE MOST PURE HEART OF MARY

"Thy law in the midst of my heart." — *Ps. 39:9.*

PREFACE

A few remarks to introduce our book to those who may wish to use it. The problem of teaching canon law in seminaries is not a lack of erudition or of learned commentaries. Professors may be well versed in the law, and have a choice of several excellent commentaries both in Latin and in English. But the problem is *lack of time*. The years of theology are crowded with courses, of which several, notably dogmatic and moral theology and Sacred Scripture, outrank canon law in importance. The problem is how to use the relatively little time that is available for canon law in such a way that the student will learn as much as possible of the Code of Canon Law itself. The years of teaching experience have led the authors to the conviction that this objective can best be attained with a text which combines three features: first, the use of the vernacular; second, outline surveys of as much as possible of the Latin text of the Code; third, a judicious use of examples, cases, and questions.

Accordingly we have tried to produce, not the most learned commentary, but a practical book for seminaries and priests. The Latin text of the Code always remains the fundamental text, to which reference must constantly be made, and from which neither the textbook nor the professor can afford to become detached. Latin may be used as the medium for the lectures and quizzes if desired; nothing prevents it. We are studying the Code, but the Code needs to be cracked open to make it quickly available. For the relatively speedy absorption of the Latin Code itself, nothing helps the English-speaking student so much as a preview in English. The seminary course in canon law — we are not speaking of graduate study — is necessarily a rather streamlined preview. The best that can be hoped from it is that it will impart a sound understanding of certain essentials, plus a thirst for deeper drafts of learning. We are convinced that this can be done with a good English text, kept in close co-ordination with the Code.

This book is designed to be used in the closest co-ordination with the Latin text of the Code of Canon Law. The outlines and exposition follow the order of the Code and embrace those parts of it which one may hope to teach in the course of canon law in seminaries: a summary of Book I, the general norms; a summary of nearly all of Book II, persons, clerics and the hierarchy, religious; in Book III, indulgences, the sacraments of marriage and orders (only), sacred places and times, divine worship, the teaching office of the Church (including the censure and prohibition of books), and the acquisition and administration of Church property; finally, a practical summary of Book V, crimes and penalties. We hope that few will condemn us for the almost complete omission of Book IV, *De Processibus*. Procedure is a professional subject calling for mature judgment and an accurate knowledge of a multiplicity of rules. We believe it should not be, and we know that commonly it is not, attempted in a seminary course.

The cases and questions which occur here and there in the text will, we believe, prove their usefulness in actual practice. Readers like concrete illustrations of principles. It is possible to spend much time on the text of the Code and the best commentaries, and then find that one can still learn much that is quite elementary about the law by applying it to a concrete practical case. As far as possible the principle involved, but not the full solution, is suggested in the questions by a reference to canons by number.

We hope that the book may also find a place on the desk of the busy priest, pastor and curate, who may find in it some guidance to the solution of his practical problems.

Very special thanks are due to the Reverend Francis J. O'Boyle, S.J., of West Baden College, Indiana, and to the Reverend James E. Risk, S.J., of Weston College, Weston, Massachusetts, for their careful and painstaking reading of the manuscript and for many useful suggestions. The Reverend Owen M. Cloran, S.J., of Saint Mary of the Lake Seminary, Mundelein, Illinois, has also kindly helped the authors at various times with valuable criticism and suggestions. Finally, the authors wish also to express their sincere thanks to several other friends who have made incidental contributions: to the Reverend Richard E. Tischler, S.J., for the chart of the organization of the Church; to the Reverend John Markoe, S.J., for the chart of the cycle of true time; and to the Reverend William C. Doyle, S.J., for checking the table of the time equation.

THE AUTHORS

West Baden Springs, Indiana
Feast of the Annunciation, April 9, 1945

CONTENTS

PART SEVEN. CRIMES AND PENALTIES
(*Bouscaren*)

INTRODUCTION

•

THE STUDY OF CANON LAW

---

1. History of Canon Law Before the Code.
2. The Making of the Code of Canon Law.
3. The Task of Official Interpretation.
4. Physical Make-up of the Code.
5. Books Used in the Study of Canon Law.
6. Guide to the Study of Sources in the *Corpus Juris*.

1. History of Canon Law Before the Code. The history of canonical legislation before the Code is too long and complicated to be dealt with adequately in these outlines. A good account of it is given in Latin in Cardinal Gasparri's Preface to the *Code of Canon Law;* and an excellent detailed account in English will be found in Archbishop Cicognani's *Canon Law,* pages 131–435. We shall give the barest outline — only what is absolutely necessary as a background before beginning the study of canon law in the Code. The history of canon law before the Code is usually divided into three periods:

1. from Apostolic times to the time of Gratian, A.D. 1140;
2. from Gratian to the Council of Trent, A.D. 1545;
3. from the Council of Trent to the Code.

From Apostolic Times to the Time of Gratian. Beginning with St. Clement, about the year A.D. 97, the Bishops of Rome carried on ecclesiastical government largely by means of correspondence, deciding cases submitted to them and settling points of general discipline. Many of these decisions acquired the force of law either immediately or in the course of time. Moreover, other Bishops enacted for their own dioceses such regulations as local conditions required. These regulations were not of themselves general; but sometimes they spread from one diocese to another, and ended by gaining universal recognition and thus becoming part of the general law. In the fourth century, A.D. 325, the

First Council of Nicaea, first of a series of twenty ecumenical councils, was held. These councils, of which the Second Council of the Lateran, A.D. 1139, held about Gratian's time, was the tenth, not only defined points of faith under the leadership and with the approval of the Popes, but also enacted numerous disciplinary laws for the whole Church. The development of law became particularly rapid when, after the Edict of Constantine at Milan, A.D. 313, the Church became free to develop her own organization. The principal sources of ecclesiastical legislation remained of the same general nature, that is, letters of the Popes and decisions of councils, but these now became more frequent.

Early collections of laws. One of the most interesting features of this growth of canon law was the attempt to keep the growing mass of legislation in order. There appeared an almost endless series of collections of laws: collections which were called apostolic, mostly apocryphal, that is, not authentic; Greek collections dating from before the Council of Chalcedon, A.D. 451; collections from Italy, Spain, France, Africa, and even from England and Ireland. The authorship of many of these collections was unknown; and many of them have since been proved not to have been authentic. The most famous of these latter is the so-called Pseudo-Isidorian Collection, or the "false decretals," which we now know to have been made in France about the middle of the ninth century. It contained a number of forged documents, many of which were accepted as genuine for more than six hundred years. The influence of this particular collection upon the growth of canon law has, however, been much exaggerated.

It may well be imagined that by the middle of the twelfth century canon law must have been in a rather confused condition. It was difficult to know which of the laws currently accepted were genuine; and still more difficult to discover whether they had been repealed either expressly or because they could not be reconciled with later laws.

From Gratian to the Council of Trent. At this time, about A.D. 1140, a learned Italian Camaldolese monk, named Gratian, performed a monumental work. He collected and attempted to put in order the entire mass of ecclesiastical legislation which had accumulated up to his time. He called his book *Concordantia Discordantium Canonum,* but it came to be called *Gratian's Decree.* Although unofficial, it was so useful that it soon became the best-known book of canon law. After the author's death, about A.D. 1158, the *Decretum Gratiani* was supplemented by several later collections of church laws, some authentic, others private. Let us briefly notice five of these which were later incorporated together with Gratian's Decree in the *Corpus Iuris*.

The Decretals of Gregory IX (A.D. 1234) were the first authentic collection of the Church's laws, composed by the famous canonist, St. Raymond of Pennafort, O.P., and promulgated by order of the Supreme Pontiff. It was made up mostly of earlier laws, adding some which were new. Whatever was contained in it, including the chapter headings, had the force of law. It was at first called *Liber Extravagantium*, from the fact that it was outside the *Decretum*, and is still designated in the footnotes of the Code by the sign, "X."

Boniface VIII issued an authentic collection of laws in 1298, which was known as the *Liber Sextus* because it was an addition to the five books of the Decretals of Gregory IX. It is designated by the sign, "in VI°."

John XXII, in 1317, promulgated a body of laws taken mostly from the Constitutions of Clement V in the Council of Vienne (A.D. 1311–1312), which is known as the *Clementinae*, recognized in citations by the sign, "in Clem."

Finally, in 1500, a learned canonist, John Chapuis, edited all the previously mentioned laws and added to them two more collections, namely, the *Extravagantes* of John XXII and the *Extravagantes communes*. These contained the decretals of several Popes from Boniface VIII (d. 1303) to Sixtus IV (d. 1484). His entire work, containing the *Decretum Gratiani*, the Decretals of Gregory IX, the *Liber Sextus*, the *Clementinae*, the *Extravagantes* of John XXII, and the *Extravagantes communes*, became known as the *Corpus Iuris Canonici*. It is the chief source for the study of ante-Tridentine legislation. The sixth section of this introduction gives a key for deciphering the references to this famous old book in the footnotes of the Code.

Authors who commented upon or explained Gratian's Decree are called decretists; those who explained the decretals are known as decretalists, though this distinction is not always strictly observed. In explaining the *Corpus Iuris* in the schools, professors of canon law wrote in it marginal and interlinear notes which are called the *gloss;* the authors of the gloss are called *glossators*.

From the Council of Trent to the Code. The Council of Trent, A.D. 1545–1563, the nineteenth of the general or ecumenical councils, is a landmark in the history of the Church and of canon law. Besides defining many points of faith which had been attacked by the Reformation, it enacted many disciplinary measures. Thanks to the invention of printing by the Catholic Johann Gutenberg, in 1444, not only the decrees of the Council of Trent but the enactments made since then by the successive Popes have been preserved more easily than was formerly possible, and by the beginning of the twentieth century constituted a considerable mass of new canonical legislation.

2. The Making of the Code of Canon Law. By the beginning of the twentieth century the laws of the Church were once more in a state of considerable confusion. No general codification had been even attempted for the past seven hundred years, and even the one which had been made by Gratian was not entirely authentic, and contained many errors. In the meantime new laws, some general and some particular, had been enacted; many of these had been repealed; those that remained in force were not easy to find; and the whole mass of legislation was further confused by the unofficial and not always judicious commentaries of various canonists and moralists. Canon law at that time resembled an ancient ruin buried beneath the drifting sands and accumulated debris of a thousand years. The work of bringing order out of this chaos was seen to be necessary; many Bishops present at the Vatican Council had demanded that a revision be undertaken, but the task was so stupendous that it appeared to be beyond the power of anything short of a general council of the Church.

Some hope was derived from the fact that partial codifications had been attended with success. Pius IX had clarified and arranged the law of the Church regarding censures by his Constitution, *Apostolicae Sedis,* of 12 October, 1869; and Leo XIII, by his Constitution, *Officiorum,* of 25 January, 1897, had promulgated a clear and complete piece of legislation on the prohibition and censure of books. But the codification of all the laws of the Church was an immensely greater task.

Nevertheless, Pius X dared to announce, on the Feast of St. Joseph, 1904, that he was determined to have a complete and orderly codification of all extant ecclesiastical laws, with the obsolete and outdated ones eliminated, and all others brought into conformity with modern conditions. The encyclical in which this announcement was made began with the words *"Arduum sane munus,"* an arduous task indeed!

The work of preparing the Code of Canon Law started immediately. It is well described in Cardinal Gasparri's Preface. Briefly, the steps in the production of the Code were as follows.

A Commission of Cardinals was appointed for the work. The Holy

Father himself assumed the chairmanship of this Commission, with Cardinal Gasparri as Secretary.

On March 25, 1904, all Archbishops throughout the world were asked to confer with their Suffragans and within four months to send word as to which laws in their opinion required amendment. Collaborators of various kinds were employed. The Commission divided itself into two committees, one sitting on Sunday, the other on Thursday. Every Bishop had the right to keep a representative in Rome to attend the meetings.

When a tentative draft had been drawn up, it was not only submitted again to the expert canonists who acted as consultors, but moreover all the Bishops and those superiors of religious orders who are entitled to attend a general council were invited to express their opinions on it. These replies were collected by the Secretary, and were considered and discussed by the Commission. It is estimated that every canon of the Code was discussed from five to twelve times before being finally adopted.

While this work was in progress World War I broke out. It seemed impossible that anything final should be accomplished until the restoration of peace. Yet the work went right on. Pius X died, and the new Pope, Benedict XV, was soon able to announce that the work of building the Code of Canon Law, for which he modestly gave all the credit to his predecessor, was completed.

The new Code of Canon Law was promulgated on Pentecost, May 27, 1917, to become effective on Pentecost, May 19, 1918. A few canons, however, went into effect at once.

3. Official Interpretation of the Code. By the *Motu proprio* of September 15, 1917, a wise provision was made for the purpose of keeping the admirable order which had been produced at such great cost from going back to confusion. The document, which is printed after the Preface in most editions of the Code, makes three important provisions.

First, a Commission of Cardinals is created with power to give authentic interpretations of the Code. The title of this Commission is *Pontificia Commissio ad Codicis Canones Authentice Interpretandos*. We shall hereafter refer to it as the Code Commission. Cardinal Gasparri acted as its president.

Second, the Roman Congregations were thereafter to issue no new general decrees, unless some great need of the Church should require it. It was declared that their function will be rather to issue Instructions which shall both throw light on the provisions of the Code and provide efficaciously for their observance.

Third, in case any new general decree becomes necessary, it shall be drawn up by the proper Congregation; and if it is not in accord with the Code, the Congregation shall inform the Holy Father of that fact. After the decree shall have been approved by the Supreme Pontiff, the same Sacred Congregation shall present it to the Commission, whose office it shall then be to draw up a new canon or canons to be inserted in the Code. These new canons, however, shall be so numbered as not to interfere with the consecutive numbering of the present canons. The new canons are to be designated with the number of the preceding canon and the addition, *bis,* or *ter,* "so that no canon of the Code shall ever lose its place, nor the series of numbered canons be in any way confused."

4. Physical Make-up of the Code. The Code of Canon Law consists of an analytical index, printed at the beginning, a number of canons numbered successively from 1 to 2414, and nine documents printed immediately thereafter and numbered from I to IX. These parts are authentic; that is, they belong to the Code in the strictest sense as parts thereof. The Preface written by Cardinal Gasparri, the footnotes, or *Fontes,* which are references to former laws and which are printed as aids to historical study in some editions of the Code, and the alphabetical index, which was compiled by an expert canonist, Father Ojetti, S.J., of the Gregorian University, are not strictly authentic parts of the Code; that is, they have not the authority of a law promulgated by the Supreme Pontiff.

Division of the canons. The canons are divided into five books; and the major divisions of each book are called parts. The parts are sometimes further subdivided into sections, titles, and chapters. Here is a topical plan of the five books and their principal parts.

Topical Plan of the Five Books of the Code

Book I.   General Rules (Canons 1–86)
Book II.   Persons (Canons 87–725)
        Part I.   Clerics
        Part II.   Religious
        Part III. Lay Persons

Book III. Things (Canons 726–1551)
        Part I.   Sacraments
        Part II.   Sacred Places and Times
        Part III. Divine Worship

Value of the Code. About eight hundred years ago a great juristic scholar gave his life to the codification of the laws of the Church. He brought order out of chaos, and his work, applauded by the whole world, has come down to our own time. Yet Gratian's Decree was not an official codification; it remained of strictly private authority. Nor did later authentic collections entirely remedy the disorder. The Code of Canon Law has brought order out of an even greater mass of confused legislation; and it is absolutely authentic.

The Council of Trent is remembered as the great reform of Church discipline from within. Yet it was not complete; it covered only a part of the field of legislation. The Code is a complete system.

Thanks to the makers of the Code, we have a well-ordered system of laws in place of a confused mass of legislation; a complete and harmonious system instead of a patchwork of fragments; clear and definite provisions in place of obscure and doubtful ones; laws accommodated to the modern world instead of antiquated medieval decrees; finally, we have a succinct Code whose every word is loaded with sense, instead of the old rambling discussions where the state of the question was often obscured beneath a mass of words. We have a Code which settles authoritatively in a few words many important questions of moral theology about which experts disputed for centuries. And all this has come to us within the past thirty years. If one gives but the barest thought to these facts, there is but one conclusion: the Code of Canon Law merits our best efforts to get acquainted with it.

5. Books Used in the Study of Canon Law. Besides the Code itself, there are two types of books which are useful or necessary in the study of canon law; namely, commentaries, which explain or comment on the canons, and source books, in which the text of laws or decisions is given. It is not at all necessary to give a complete list of these books. We will indicate merely a few which seem best adapted to our present purpose.

Commentaries. There are commentaries on the Code in English by Augustine and Woywod; and on several distinct parts of the Code by Ayrinhac. An excellent commentary on the first eighty-six canons is the book entitled *Canon Law* by Archbishop Cicognani, Apostolic Delegate to the United States. In Latin a great number of commentaries have been begun, but relatively few have been finished. Of the latter, probably the most serviceable for our purpose are: Beste, *Introductio in Codicem,* in one volume; Vermeersch-Creusen, *Epitome Iuris Canonici,* in three volumes; Cappello, *Summa Iuris Canonici,* in four volumes; a Coronata, *Institutiones Iuris Canonici,* in five volumes. Besides there are several excellent Latin commentaries on special parts of the Code.

Source books. In an elementary course in canon law there is not much opportunity for the study of any sources other than the text of the Code itself. However, it will be well at least to indicate two distinct problems that may arise regarding the study of sources; namely, how to find sources before the Code and since the Code.

a. Before the Code. All general laws which were enacted before the Code are rendered practically obsolete unless they are also contained in the Code itself (c. 6). Hence the Code is now properly called "the only source book of canon law." Still, the laws before the Code retain a historical interest; and besides their study is often useful, not to say necessary, for a thorough understanding of the present law. For this reason, Cardinal Gasparri, who for years acted as the Secretary to the Commission which drew up the Code, assisted by Cardinal Serédi, kept note of the references to former laws which have any relation to the laws of the Code. This was in itself an immense task, as some of the laws go back to the tenth century or earlier. Moreover, in the printed edition of the Code, they took care to have these references inserted as footnoes under the respective canons which they chiefly concern.

The study of the documents to which these footnotes refer is rather difficult without a little guidance, but it becomes easier when the fog of mystery which surrounds them is lifted. We shall therefore attempt to explain the significance of these footnotes.

We must begin by distinguishing between various classes of references which occur. We may divide them broadly into three classes. First, there are many references to the *Corpus Iuris Canonici.* These present special difficulties, and must be dealt with in a special note, in section 6 of this Introduction. Putting these aside for the moment, we have, second, references to declarations of the Council of Trent, and third, references to decrees or decisions of later date. Those of the Council of Trent are available in several editions of the acts of the Council; but the later ones, until Cardinal Gasparri and his aides took hold of the problem, were very difficult to find, for they were scattered in a great many records of various offices of the Roman Curia, and some of them had never been published at all. Thanks to Cardinals Gasparri and Serédi, at least the footnotes annexed to the various canons of the Code now indicated that there existed an earlier official document dealing with the same subject as the canon. We repeat that these old documents are no longer law; they are only the historical background of the law; but still they are interesting and sometimes necessary for purposes of comparison and criticism. The references, therefore, were very valuable. The next problem was how to find the documents themselves in order to read and study them.

Cardinals Gasparri and Serédi therefore proceeded to collect the documents themselves to which the footnotes referred, and had them published in a work entitled *Codicis Iuris Canonici Fontes,* of which six volumes appeared before the death of Cardinal Gasparri, and three more volumes have since been edited by Cardinal Serédi.[1] The total number of documents included in the first eight volumes is 6464. The ninth volume consists of very elaborate indices. The order and arrangement of this monumental work must be studied by examining the work itself. It is here that one must look for the later documents which are cited in the footnotes to the Code. Some of them are also published in *Collectanea Sacrae Congregationis de Propaganda Fide.*[2] To sum up, therefore, we may say that the *Corpus Iuris Canonici,* the records of the Council of Trent, and the *Codicis Iuris Canonici Fontes* are the most essential source books for the study of the sources *before the Code.*

b. Since the Code. The official documents which have been issued since the Code are of more immediate practical importance. They are of various kinds: rescripts and decisions in particular cases; instructions regarding the application of the law; authentic interpretations made

---

[1] Vatican Press, 1939.
[2] Two Volumes, Polyglot Press, 1907.

by the Code Commission. These last have the force of law, as have also declarations or decrees made by the Roman Pontiff himself or by some branch of the Roman Curia with *specific,* instead of merely general, pontifical approval. It will be seen that the study of these recent sources is not merely a matter of erudition. It is a real necessity, because these decisions affect the law as it now is, and yet they are nowhere explicitly contained in the Code.

Where will we find these documents? Officially, they are published in the commentary of the Holy See, *Acta Apostolicae Sedis,* which began in 1909 and reached volume 36 in 1944. As it would be difficult in practice, however, to search through thirty-odd volumes of the *Acta* for these documents, several collections have been made in which the documents are arranged either chronologically or in the order of the canons which they affect. The most important of these collections are probably the following:

1. The official collection, *Codicis Iuris Canonici Interpretationes Authenticae,*[3] of which later editions have since appeared;

2. *Enchiridion Canonicum,* by Sartori, which gives the principal documents in Latin, arranged in the order of the canons;

3. The *Canon Law Digest.*[4]

The last named of these collections is the one to which we shall most frequently refer in the text because it is convenient to read the documents in English.

6. Guide to the Study of Sources in the *Corpus Iuris*. a. Make-up of the Book. The *Corpus Iuris Canonici* is made up of distinct parts or books, as follows:

1. Gratian's Decree; Parts I, II and III (A.D. 1140);
2. The Decretals of Gregory IX (A.D. 1234);
3. The so-called *Liber Sextus,* promulgated by Boniface VIII (A.D. 1298);
4. The Constitutions of Clement V, called *Clementinae,* promulgated by John XXII (A.D. 1317);
5. The *Extravagantes* of John XXII (A.D. 1499–1502);
6. The *Extravagantes communes* (A.D. 1499–1502).

b. Method of citation. The method of citing the *Corpus Iuris* dates from medieval times, and is unfortunately very different from the modern way. When we wish to cite a book, we give the name of the book, and then the page on which the citation is to be found.

---

[3] Vatican Press, 1935.
[4] Two volumes: Bruce, Milwaukee, 1934–1943.

The citations to the *Corpus Iuris* do not mention the name of the book. They vary according to which of the eight parts of the *Corpus Iuris* mentioned above is referred to; but even the part referred to is not mentioned by name; it must be deciphered from certain rather cryptic signs. Without going into lengthy explanations, it will perhaps be sufficient to give the following key, in which an example of a citation is first given, and then the explanation of what the citation means.

Key to Citations of the *Corpus Iuris*

1. *a.* The first Part of Gratian's Decree is divided into Distinctions and subdivided into canons. Thus, c. 7, D. I is a reference to Gratian's Decree, Part I, Distinction I, canon 7. The example is taken from the footnote to canon 2205, § 4, in the Code.

b. The second Part of Gratian's Decree is divided into Causes, which are subdivided into questions, and further into canons. Thus c. 116, C. I, q. 1 is a reference to Gratian's Decree, Part II, Cause I, question 1, canon 116. See the footnote to canon 728 in the Code.

Note: Special attention must be paid to citations from Cause XXXIII of this book. In this Cause, questions I, II, IV, and V are divided and cited in the manner above indicated; for example, c. 1, C. XXXIII, q. 1, in the footnote to canon 1068, § 1, in the Code. But question III of this Cause XXXIII has a distinctive title and is differently subdivided and differently cited. It is subdivided into Distinctions and canons, and is cited by the title, *de poenit.*— variously spelled, of course — with an indication of the Distinction and canon. Thus c. 6, D. I, *de poenit.* is a reference to Gratian's Decree, Part II, Cause XXXIII, question III, Distinction I, canon 6. See the footnote to canon 2353 in the Code. Note that the title *de poenit.* identifies not only the book, Gratian's Decree, Part II, but also the Cause XXXIII, and the question, III.

c. The third Part of Gratian's Decree is divided into Distinctions and subdivided into canons. The sign of this book in citations is *de cons.* which stands for *de consecratione,* the title to the entire book. Thus c. 18, D. I, *de cons.* means the third Part of Gratian's Decree, Distinction I, canon 18; it is the footnote to canon 1199, § 1, in the Code.

2. The Decretals of Gregory IX, always recognized by the sign, "X," consist of five books, which are subdivided into titles and finally into canons. Thus c. 13, X, I, 2 means the Decretals of Gregory IX, book I, title 2, canon 13; it is in the footnote to canon 10 in the Code.

3. *Liber Sextus,* the Decretals of Boniface VIII, always recognized

by the sign, "in VI°," is divided into five books, which are subdivided
into titles and finally into canons. Thus c. 5, I, 3, in VI° means the
Decretals of Boniface VIII, book I, title 3, canon 5; it is cited in the
Code under canon 86.

4. The Constitutions of Clement V, or *Clementinae,* always recognized by the sign, "in Clem.," are divided into five books and subdivided into titles and canons. Thus c. 2, III, 7, in Clem. means the
Constitutions of Clement V, book III, title 7, canon 2; cited under
canon 874, § 1, in the Code.

5. The *Extravagantes* of John XXII are divided into titles and subdivided into canons. Thus c. un., title VII, in Extravag. Ioan. XXII
means the single canon of title 7 of this book. See footnote to
canon 81.

6. The *Extravagantes communes* are divided into five books, subdivided into titles and canons. Thus c. 3, V, 7, in Extravag. com.
means Book V, title 7, canon 3 of the *Extravagantes communes.* See
footnote to canon 2395 in the Code.

Note: A slight further difficulty occurs, which however can be
easily obviated. Frequently, in addition to the number of the canon,
its Latin title is given; e.g., c. 3, *de privilegiis,* V, 7, in Extravag. com.,
the example already given under n. 6 above. This is done quite
regularly in the footnotes of the Code, whereas the Latin titles are
omitted in the citations as given in the index volume of Serédi's
Fontes. For practical purposes, provided the number of the canon is
given, the Latin titles may be disregarded unless they are *de poenit.*
(see note above under 1, b), or *de cons.* (see 1, c, above).

The *Regulae Iuris. Regulae Iuris,* or rules of law, occur in two places
in the *Corpus Iuris.* The more important set of these rules is at the
end of *Liber Sextus.* They are cited as follows: Reg. 13, R. J., in VI°.
See footnote to canon 16, § 1. The few rules which occur at the end
of the Decretals of Gregory IX (Book V, title 41) are cited in the
same way as the other parts of that book. See n. 2, above.

It may now be useful to give a condensed key in which the various
parts of the *Corpus Iuris* are listed successively, and after each is given
merely the sign by which the book can be recognized. After the book
is identified it will not be difficult to find the part which is referred
to. Thus we shall be able, when it becomes necessary, to consult these
old sources without hesitation or confusion.

Condensed Key

Books of the *Corpus Iuris*	Sign
1. *a. Decretum Gratiani,* Part I..........	c. D.
b. Decretum Gratiani, Part II.........	c. C. q.
But if the citation is to question III of Cause XXXIII of this book, the sign is.....................	*de poenit.*
c. Decretum Gratiani, Part III.......	*de cons.*
2. Decretals of Gregory IX..............	X
3. *Liber Sextus* (Decretals of Boniface VIII)	in VI°
4. *Clementinae*	in Clem.
5. *Extravagantes* of John XXII.........	in Extravag. Ioan. XXII
6. *Extravagantes communes*.............	in Extravag. com.

Note that the first two Parts of Gratian's Decree are the only books of the *Corpus Iuris* which have no *unique* distinctive sign; these must be recognized by the names of the larger divisions, D., meaning Distinction, for Part I, and C., meaning Cause, for Part II. All the other books of the *Corpus Iuris* are immediately recognizable by a unique sign in their citation. Thus what seemed to be a very confused matter becomes really simple.

PART ONE: GENERAL RULES

CHAPTER I

GENERAL NORMS

Section 1. Scope of the Code of Canon Law (cc. 1–7)

PRELIMINARY SURVEY

Oriental Catholics (c. 1)
Liturgical Laws (c. 2)
Concordats (c. 3)
Vested Rights, Privileges, Indults (c. 4)
Customs (c. 5)
Earlier Ecclesiastical Laws (c. 6)
Meaning of the Term Apostolic See (c. 7)

Oriental Catholics. The division of the Church into Eastern and Western, or Oriental and Latin, is of political origin; it followed the division of the Roman Empire made by Diocletian at the end of the third century. The Oriental Churches were those which belonged to the Eastern division of the Empire.[1] All of these at various times fell away by schism from the Catholic Church. Some of them remained in schism, and now go by the name of Orthodox. But, as is well known, many of the Oriental Churches have returned to the true fold, acknowledge the supremacy of the Pope, and are Catholic in the full sense of the word, just as truly as are those of the Latin rite. They are sometimes called Uniates to indicate their union with the See of Rome; but are more properly called Eastern or Oriental Catholics. They have for a long time retained, without objection from

---

[1] The division between the Eastern and Western Empire was first made by Diocletian (284–305) and was confirmed by the sons of Theodosius (Arcadius in the East, 394–408, Honorius in the West, 395–423).

Rome, their traditional government and discipline. The Code, by this first canon, confirms that traditional policy.

It may be useful to present a synoptical summary of the Catholic Oriental Rites.

Oriental Catholic Rites

Original Rites	Subdivisions
Alexandrian	Coptic or Egyptian
	Ethiopian or Abyssinian
Syrian or Antiochine	Maronite
	Pure Syrian
Armenian	Armenian
Greek or Byzantine	Albanian
	Bulgarian
	Georgian
	Pure Greek
	Italo-Albanian
	Serbian
	Melkite
	Rumanian
	Russian
	Ruthenian
	Hungarian
Chaldean	Pure Chaldean
	Malabar
	Malenkar

Orientals: General Principle. The Code, as a general rule, does not affect the Oriental Church (c. 1).

Exceptions: There are some matters in which it affects also the Oriental Church and Oriental Catholics; for example: (1) canons which express dogmatic truths, as canon 218; (2) canons which declare the divine law, as canons 228, § 2; 542, 2°; 1255; (3) canons which mention the Orientals explicitly, as canons 622, § 4; 1099, § 1, 3°.

Authentic Declarations. The following authentic documents will be of interest.

1. Orientals are bound by the decrees of the Holy Office as regards the *prohibition of books*.[2]

2. Orientals may gain all general *indulgences*.[3]

3. Orientals may under certain conditions be admitted to the *noviceship* in religious institutes of the Latin rite.[4]

4. Orientals are subject to the jurisdiction of the *Sacred Penitentiary* for the internal forum.[5]

5. The *four censures* most specially reserved to the Holy See apply also to Orientals.[6]

6. A *Code of Canon Law* for the Oriental Church is in process of preparation; a permanent Commission has been appointed.[7]

7. A private reply on the extent to which *Maronites in the United States* are bound by the laws of the Code is too complex to be summarized here.[8]

8. Oriental *clerics* outside their territories are subject to special regulations especially as to begging alms.[9]

9. Orientals may be invested in the *scapular medal* instead of cloth scapulars.[10]

10. *Dignities* conferred by Oriental Prelates on priests of another rite do not carry with them the faculties annexed to the dignity.[11]

11. The *jurisdiction* of the Sacred Oriental Congregation was notably enlarged in 1938.[12]

12. There are two replies on *jurisdiction for confessions* in a church of another rite.[13]

Greek Ruthenians in the United States and Canada. There are two large groups of Greek Ruthenians in the United States and one in Canada, for whom three national dioceses have been established. In

---

[2] S. C. Or., 26 May, 1928; *AAS*, 20–195; *Digest*, I, p. 685.

[3] S. Paen., 7 July, 1917; *AAS*, 9–399; *Digest*, I, p. 42; S. Paen., 21 July, 1935; *AAS*, 27–379; *Digest*, II, p. 7.

[4] Code Com., 10 Nov., 1925; *AAS*, 17–583; *Digest*, I, p. 298.

[5] S. C. Or., 26 July, 1930; *AAS*, 22–394; *Digest*, I, p. 174.

[6] Holy Office, 21 July, 1934; *AAS*, 26–550; *Digest*, II, p. 577.

[7] S. C. Or., 17 July, 1935; *AAS*, 27–306; *Digest*, II, p. 7.

[8] See S. C. Or., 19 Dec., 1928; *Digest*, I, p. 4.

[9] Cf.: S. C. Or., 2 Apr., 1928; *AAS*, 20–107; *Digest*, I, p. 6; S. C. Or., 23 Dec., 1929; *AAS*, 22–99; *Digest*, I, p. 17; S. C. Or., 7 Jan., 1930; *AAS*, 22–106; *Digest*, I, p. 24; S. C. Or., 7 Jan., 1930; *AAS*, 22–108; *Digest*, I, p. 27; S. C. Or., 26 Sept., 1932; *AAS*, 24–344; *Digest*, I, p. 39; S. C. Or., 20 July, 1937; *AAS*, 29–342; *Digest*, II, p. 3; S. C. Or., 16 Nov., 1938; *AAS*, 31–169; *Digest*, II, p. 5.

[10] S. C. Or., 25 Mar., 1935; *AAS*, 27–145; *Digest*, II, p. 8.

[11] S. C. Or., 11 June, 1940; *AAS*, 32–303; *Digest*, II, p. 6.

[12] See Pius XI, *Motu proprio*, 25 Mar., 1938; *AAS*, 30–154; *Digest*, II, p. 111.

[13] See S. C. Or., 26 Aug., 1932; *Digest*, II, p. 218, and S. C. Prop. Fid., 2 Dec., 1932; *ibid*.

the United States the Ordinary for the Greek Ruthenians from Galicia, also called Ukrainians, resides in Philadelphia, while the Ordinary for those from Podocarpathia resides in Pittsburgh. The Ruthenian Bishop of Canada has his headquarters in Winnipeg. Many practical matters of discipline are regulated by two decrees of the Sacred Oriental Congregation.[14]

Question. Are the Orthodox Orientals bound by the laws of the Code? Being baptized, they are bound by ecclesiastical laws in general, according to canons 12 and 87. But they are, equally with the Catholic Orientals, outside the scope of the Latin Code of Canon Law. Their obligation is rather to accept the discipline of the proper Oriental Catholic rite.

Liturgical Laws. The Code, as a general rule, does not purport to make or revise liturgical laws. Hence these laws, as contained in approved liturgical books, remain generally unchanged (c. 2).

Exceptions. By way of exception, some liturgical regulations are found in the Code; for example, canons 748, 755, 776, regarding baptism; canon 947 on extreme unction; canon 1265 on the custody of the Blessed Sacrament, etc.

Liturgical Books. The principal liturgical books are the Roman Missal, the Roman Breviary, the Martyrology, the Pontifical, the Bishops' Ceremonial, the Roman Ceremonial, the Roman Calendar, the Roman Ritual, the Memorial of Rites, the Clementine Instruction for the Forty Hours' Devotion, and the Collection of Decrees of the Sacred Congregation of Rites.

Liturgical Rulings and Decrees. Liturgical rulings too numerous to mention have been made even since the Code. References to these will be found in a special index in *Digest* I, p. 42, and in volume II, p. 9.

Concordats. There are three theories regarding the nature of concordats:

1. A concordat is merely a civil law by which the state grants certain favors to the Church. This theory is evidently false. The Church has certain rights by divine institution, independently of the state.

2. It is merely a grant by the Holy See of certain privileges to the state. This theory was formerly held by some Catholics, but it is no longer probable and should be abandoned. The state also has rights which are independent of the Church.

---

[14] S. C. Or., 1 Mar., 1929; *AAS*, 21–152; *Digest*, I, p. 6; S. C. Or., 24 May, 1930; *AAS*, 22–346; *Digest*, I, p. 29; S. C. Or., 23 Nov., 1940; *AAS*, 33–27; *Digest*, II, p. 6.

3. It is a true contract between the Holy See on the one hand and a nation on the other, as mutually independent powers. This theory is supported by several pontifical documents, and is the true one.

General Principle. Concordats are not affected by the Code. They remain in effect no matter how contrary to the Code their provisions may be (c. 3).[15]

Vested Rights. In order that a right may become vested, or fully acquired, two conditions are necessary: first, that some norm of law exist by virtue of which the specific right in question *can be acquired;* second, that a juridical fact have taken place, by which the right *has been actually acquired.* Let us illustrate by an example. If I am a citizen of a state I may have a so-called right to acquire land in that state, whereas aliens may be by law incapable of owning land. My general capacity, determined by law, may be loosely called a right, but it is not a vested right. It satisfies the first requisite mentioned above, but not the second. It is an existing norm of law by virtue of which a vested right can be acquired, but that is all. If, however, while my general capacity under the law remains unchanged, I make a contract of purchase, pay the price, and receive the title deed to a specific piece of land, I acquire a perfect right in the land. This is a vested or acquired right in the sense of the canon. My purchase of the land is the juridical fact which satisfies the second requisite.

Privileges. A privilege may be defined as a special right granted through benevolence to a certain person or persons, *per se* perpetually.

Indults. The word *indult* means *granted by way of indulgence.* It designates either the act by which some favor is granted, or the favor itself. The favor may be a faculty, a permission, a dispensation, etc.; but an indult usually denotes a favor granted only for a time.

General Principle. Vested rights acquired by persons, as well as privileges and indults granted by the Holy See before the Code and not revoked but still in use at the time of the enactment of the Code, remain in effect unless expressly revoked by the Code (c. 4). There is no question of the power to revoke even such vested rights and privileges; but the Holy See declares by this canon that it does not intend to revoke them except in the cases where it expressly so states. When a canon contains the clause *"revocato quolibet contrario privilegio,"* as does, for example, canon 460, § 2, the privilege in

---

[15] The study of concordats is a difficult specialty. The texts of many modern concordats may be studied in Restrepo, *Concordata Pio XI Inita,* and Perugini, *Concordata Vigentia.* For Portugal, see *Digest,* II, p. 11.

question is revoked. Where no such clause is expressly enacted, the privilege in question remains in effect even though it be contrary to the Code.[16]

Customs. The question answered by **Canon 5** is, what is the status of customs which existed up to the time of the Code. Are they revoked?

Principles. 1. Customs which are *not contrary* to the Code remain in effect. This is presupposed, though not stated.

2. Customs which are not only contrary to the Code but also *expressly reprobated* in it are revoked without exception.

3. Customs which are contrary to the Code but *not expressly reprobated* are revoked if they are of less than one hundred years' standing. Even if they are centenary they should be discouraged but may be tolerated if the Ordinary deems it imprudent to attempt to suppress them at once.

Explanation. A centenary custom is one which has been in existence for a hundred years. An immemorial custom is one to whose beginning "the memory of man runneth not." Such a custom is proved when witnesses at least fifty-four years old state that they have personally seen the custom in operation for forty years, and have heard from their parents that it was in existence as long as they can remember. Practically, the phrase "centenary and immemorial" is equivalent to "centenary or immemorial" because an existence of one hundred years is sufficient to give a custom the special consideration which the canon gives to those which are "centenary and immemorial." Canon 1180, however, speaks only of immemorial custom.

Many canons in the Code contain the clause *reprobata contraria consuetudine* or some equivalent expression; for example, canons 346, 409, § 2, 418, § 1, 818, 1006, § 5, 1181, etc.[17] Customs so referred to are expressly reprobated.

Problem. Draw a figure or chart illustrating graphically the various classes of customs mentioned in canon 5 and the fate of each class after the Code.

Laws Existing Before the Code. Canon 6 determines the status of laws which were in effect before the Code. Do they or do they not remain in effect? It will be seen that numbers 2, 3, and 4 are rules

---

[16] The alphabetical index at the end of the Code, under the title, **Privilegia**, enumerates the privileges which are revoked by express provision.

[17] For a list of the canons which contain clauses expressly reprobating certain customs, see the alphabetical index at the end of the Code, under the title **Consuetudo.**

of interpretation. If we leave these aside for the moment, we have the following general principles.

General Principles. 1. Laws *contrary to the Code* are revoked, whether they be universal or even particular, unless these latter be expressly protected by a saving clause **(c. 6, 1°).** The clause *salvo iure particulari,* as in canon 1236, saves a particular law contrary to the Code from revocation.

2. *Penal laws,* even though not contrary to the Code, are revoked unless they are mentioned in the Code itself **(c. 6, 5°).** This provision, however, applies only to universal penal laws, not to particular ones. Particular penal laws, such as that of the Third Plenary Council of Baltimore, n. 124, providing a censure of excommunication for persons who marry after obtaining a civil divorce, remain in effect, provided they be not contrary to the Code.

3. *Disciplinary laws other than penal* are also revoked unless they be implicitly or explicitly contained in the Code **(c. 6, 6°).** This provision also applies only to universal, not to particular laws. Thus, a particular diocesan law forbidding beards to the clergy was upheld after the Code, although not contained in it.[18]

Exceptions. Liturgical laws are excepted from these provisions, as are also all divine laws, positive or natural, since the latter are beyond modification or repeal by ecclesiastical authority.

Principles of Interpretation. 1. Canons which *re-enact the old law without change* are in reality nothing more than the old law; and hence are subject to the same interpretation **(c. 6, 2°).**

2. Canons which *agree in part with the old law* carry into the Code the interpretations of that part of the old law which they re-enact **(c. 6, 3°).**

3. *In doubt* whether the law has been changed or not, the presumption is against the change; hence the old law with its interpretations may be relied on **(c. 6, 4°).**

Question. What is the status of general pre-Code legislation which is of a temporary and special nature, and which is not contrary to the Code though in no way contained in it? No special principle governing such cases is laid down. However, in several instances such laws have been authentically declared still in effect after the Code; for example, the pre-Code prescription regarding the Council of Vigilance and the oath against Modernism, and also a pre-Code decree regarding religious in military service. These are not mentioned in

---

[18] Cf. S. C. Conc., 11 Jan., 1920; *AAS,* 12–43; *Digest,* I, p. 123.

the Code because they are of their nature temporary provisions; yet, since the circumstances which called them into existence still persist, they are not revoked.[19]

Meaning of Apostolic See. It is usual to speak of a decision or instruction of the Holy See even when it was given not by the Holy Father himself but by some department of the Roman Curia (cf. cc. 7, 242). The reason is that the various Tribunals, Congregations, and Offices of the Roman Curia are agencies for doing the work of the Holy See. This usage is expressly sanctioned and adopted in **canon 7.** To what extent the acts of the Roman Curia need the approval of the Supreme Pontiff is stated in canon 244.

CASES AND QUESTIONS

1. What is your notion of a vested right (*ius quaesitum*)? A concordat? A concordat made in 1910 contains provisions directly contrary to the Code. Is the entire concordat nullified by the Code? Are the provisions which are contrary to the Code revoked? (C. 3).

2. A religious order received a privilege from the Holy See by communication before the Code. The privilege is contrary to the provisions of the Code. Is it revoked? (C. 4, c. 613, § 1; *Digest*, II, p. 172). How is a pre-Code privilege revoked in the Code? (Cf. cc. 460, § 2, 522, 876, § 1, etc.)

3. Bishops in the United States received an indult from the Holy See before the Code. Are its provisions, which are contrary to the Code, revoked since 1918? (C. 4).

4. From what source do customs obtain the force of law? (C. 5). Do all legally established pre-Code customs remain in effect since the Code? Are they all revoked? State the rule with the necessary distinctions (c. 5).

5. The Third Plenary Council of Baltimore (n. 281) made special provisions regarding priests' salaries. These provisions are not contained in the Code. Are they thereby revoked? (C. 6).

Readings:

Duskie, *The Canonical Status of the Orientals in the United States,* Catholic University, 1928 (n. 48); Roelker, *Principles of Privilege According to the Code of Canon Law,* C.U., 1926 (n. 35); Neuberger, *Canon 6 or the Relation of the Codex Iuris Canonici to the Preceding Legislation,* C.U., 1927 (n. 44); Barrett, *A Comparative Study of the Third Plenary*

---

[19] Cf. Holy Office, 22 March, 1918; *AAS*, 10–136; *Digest*, I, p. 50; and S. C. Rel., 15 July, 1919; *AAS*, 11–321; *Digest*, I, p. 51.

Council of Baltimore and the Code, C.U., 1932 (n. 83); *Ecclesiastical Review,* Vol. 97, p. 448 (Schmal, on the Ruthenian question); *Periodica,* Vol. 17, p. 136* (Vermeersch, on caution needed in arguing from old law).

Section 2. Ecclesiastical Laws (cc. 8–24)

PRELIMINARY SURVEY

Laws in General: Promulgation (c. 8)
Promulgation of Papal Laws: Period of Suspension (c. 9)
Principle of Nonretroactivity (c. 10)
Invalidating Laws (c. 11)
Subject of Ecclesiastical Laws (c. 12)
General and Particular Laws (c. 13)
Obligation of Nonresidents: *Peregrini: Vagi* (c. 14)
Doubt of Law or Fact (c. 15)
Ignorance of Law or Fact (c. 16)
Authentic Interpretation (c. 17)
Doctrinal Interpretation (c. 18)
Broad or Strict Interpretation (c. 19)
Supplementary Norms (c. 20)
Application to Particular Cases (c. 21)
Revocation of Prior Laws (cc. 22, 23)
Particular Precepts (c. 24)

Law is defined by St. Thomas as an ordinance of reason for the common good, promulgated by the one who has charge of the community.

Promulgation means the official publication of a law, which makes it possible for the people to learn of it. It is disputed as a merely academic question whether promulgation belongs to the essence of the law. What is certain is that without promulgation the law is not fully established. It is erroneous to state, as some commentators do, that "laws become effective when they are promulgated." Canon 8 does not say this; and canon 9 says something quite different. Papal laws, do not regularly become effective until three calendar months after their promulgation (c. 9).

Territoriality. The distinction between territorial and personal laws concerns particular laws rather than general ones. For the present it may be sufficient to define a *personal* law as one which binds the residents of a particular territory even while they are absent from the territory; and a *territorial law* as one which binds only persons who are present in the territory. In short, *a personal law follows the person wherever he goes; a territorial law is limited to the territory* for which it was enacted.

General Principles. 1. Laws are not completely established until they are promulgated (c. 8, § 1).

2. Laws are presumed to be territorial unless the contrary is proved (c. 8, § 2).

Exceptions. There are no exceptions to the requirement of promulgation; but there are exceptions to the presumption of territoriality. Some personal laws exist. The Code itself supposes the existence of personal laws, and provides moreover that certain laws are to be binding on residents of the territory even while they are absent from it (c. 14, 1°). Some episcopal laws are of this kind; for example, that of the Third Diocesan Synod of Chicago n. 61, forbidding diocesan priests to attend operas.

Suspension or Vacation of the Law. Even after the promulgation of a law it does not usually become effective at once. Commonly there intervenes a period of suspension for the purpose of giving the people time to learn the law. **Canon 9** fixes, for papal laws, both the manner of official promulgation — publication in the *Acta Apostolicae Sedis* — and the regular period of suspension, three calendar months from the date of the issue in which they are printed. This period is computed according to canon 34, § 3, 2°. Thus, if the date of a number of the *Acta* in which a certain law appears is March 20, 1935, that law will become effective at midnight before the twentieth day of June, 1935. As regards episcopal laws, canon 335, § 2, provides that in the absence of special provision, they become effective immediately upon promulgation.

Nonretroactivity. The laws of the Code are not retroactive (c. 10).

Exception. Explicit provision may be made, so that a law will operate retroactively.

It must be observed that no law can be retroactive as regards the primary effect of law; that is, so as to produce a moral obligation in the past. This would be absurd; for an act is judged morally according to the law at the time the act was performed. As regards the external forum, however, various effects of a law may be produced retroactively; that is, the legislator may declare that an act performed before the law existed shall now have certain effects by virtue of the new law which it would not have had under the old law. Such effects may be the validity or invalidity of an act, in so far as that depends upon positive law, or even a penalty for an act which was culpable when performed, although it was not then forbidden or made punishable by positive law. Even these retroactive effects, however, are outlawed by this canon except where they are expressly provided for.

Applications. The applications of this principle are varied and sometimes difficult. We shall merely list a number of authentic cases which may be studied for illustration.

1. Legal disqualifications of ex-religious under the Code apply to the case of a religious who was secularized before the Code.[20]

2. A marriage invalidly contracted before the Code is not validated by the mere abrogation of the impediment which made it null; a marriage validly contracted before the Code is not invalidated by the enactment of a new impediment which would have applied to the case.[21]

3. Canon 460 which forbids a plurality of pastors in the same parish applies since the Code, even to parishes established before the Code.[22]

4. Spiritual relationship contracted before the Code continues to exist, but it is no longer operative as an impediment to marriage, except within the limits prescribed by the Code.[23]

5. No retroactive penalties exist, unless the act when committed was of peculiar gravity, or has given scandal (c. 2222, § 1). On the other hand, the Code provides for a certain retroactive leniency by giving the culprit the benefit of the milder penalty in case of a change in the law (c. 2226, § 2).

Invalidating Laws. Many laws occur in the Code forbidding certain acts or procedure. But not every law which forbids an act renders that act null when performed contrary to law. We must clearly distinguish between a merely prohibitory law and one which is invalidating. Strictly speaking, a law is invalidating if it directly provides that the act is null; it is incapacitating if it directly provides that the person is incapable. In both cases the effect is the same; the act will be null in either case. Consequently the distinction between invalidating and incapacitating laws is relatively unimportant. The important thing to determine is whether a law does or does not render an act void in either of these ways. The Code, therefore, gives us this general criterion.

---

[20] Code Com., 24 Nov., 1920; *AAS*, 12–575; *Digest*, I, p. 327.
[21] Code Com., 3 June, 1918; *AAS*, 10–346; *Digest*, I, p. 496.
[22] Code Com., 14 July, 1922; *AAS*, 14–527; *Digest*, I, p. 250.
[23] Code Com., 3 June, 1918; *AAS*, 10–346; *Digest*, I, p. 344.

General Principle. Laws do not render acts invalid unless they expressly or equivalently so state (c. 11).

Applications. Apply this criterion to the following canons: 53, 56, 84, 642, 1036, 1074, 1094, 1147, 1148, 1312, 1680.

Subject of Ecclesiastical Laws. Who are bound by laws that are merely ecclesiastical? **Canon 12** gives the answer in negative form, by enumerating the persons who are not bound. We may formulate a positive principle as follows.

General Principle. In order 'that a person be bound by merely ecclesiastical law, three conditions must concur: he must be baptized, have attained the use of reason, and have finished his seventh year (c. 12).

Exceptions. 1. Canons 854, § 2, and 940, § 1, regarding the reception of the sacraments in danger of death, canon 859, § 1, containing the precept of Easter Communion, and canon 906 on the annual confession, expressly provide otherwise; that is, they declare the church law in these matters binding on baptized persons having the use of reason, regardless of the actual completion of the seventh year. This is confirmed by a reply of the Code Commission.[24] The law of fasting (c. 1254, § 2) binds only after the completion of the twenty-first year.

2. Persons who are habitually insane are to be considered as infants under seven (c. 88, § 3). Hence, although in matters of divine law they are bound while they have the actual use of reason, that is during occasional lucid intervals, yet they are not usually bound even during such intervals by purely ecclesiastical laws.

3. Canon 1099 explicitly exempts non-Catholics, in their own marriages, from the law regarding the form of marriage; and canon 1070 exempts them from the impediment of disparity of cult.

Questions. 1. Are Protestants, schismatics, excommunicated persons, bound by ecclesiastical laws? In general, the answer must be yes (cc. 12, 87), unless they are expressly exempted, as in cc. 1070 and 1099. However, as regards persons who in good faith belong to a non-Catholic sect, there are sound reasons for holding them, for all *practical* purposes, excused from certain laws, such as those of fast and abstinence. Cf. Cicognani, *Canon Law,* p. 570. This is not an exemption but an excuse due to ignorance.

2. What if a person's baptism is doubtful? In the internal forum, the rule, *lex dubia non obligat,* excuses from the obligation. In the external forum (with which we are here concerned) a distinction is

---

[24] Code Com., 3 Jan., 1918; *Digest,* I, p. 53.

appropriate. If the fact of baptism itself is doubtful, there is no certain ground of obligation. If the baptism is certain but its validity in doubt, the presumption favors validity, and the person is bound until the contrary is proved. Canon 1070, § 2 states an exception to this rule.

General and Particular Laws. *A general law* is one which is not limited to a particular territory; it is a universal law of the Church. This does not mean that it is binding on all Catholics. It may be enacted for a special class of persons, or for certain peculiar circumstances. Hence canon 13 states that such laws are binding everywhere, without territorial limitation, but only upon the persons for whom they are made.

A particular law is one which is made for a particular territory. Here the applicability of the law will depend on the relation of the person to that particular territory. This relation may be of two kinds; either having a more or less permanent residence in the territory, or actually stopping there, or both. If neither of these relations exist, the person has no relation to the territory, and cannot be bound by its laws. If both relations exist, the person is bound by the ordinary laws of the territory. The terms *domicile* and *quasi-domicile* will be accurately explained under canon 92; for the present both terms may be taken in their common and general sense, as a more or less permanent residence in a certain territory.

General Principle. Canon 13 states the principle that the ordinary laws of a particular territory, territorial laws in the ordinary sense as explained under canon 8, are binding only on persons who are both resident and actually stopping in the territory.

Exceptional Laws. There are two classes of exceptional laws, which bind respectively where either one or the other of the two relations above mentioned, either residence or actual presence, but not both, exists. These laws are dealt with in canon 14; canon 13 calls attention to them by a reference in the last clause.

Nonresidents. Canon 14 uses two technical terms: *peregrini,* which we translate as "strangers," and *vagi,* which we translate as "vagrants." Exact definitions of these terms are given in canon 91. A stranger is a person who has a domicile or quasi-domicile somewhere, but is now absent from that place; a vagrant is one who has no domicile or quasi-domicile anywhere. The question is: What laws are applicable to such persons? Are they bound by general laws? By the particular laws of their own territory? By the particular laws of the place where they are? The canon provides definitely for every case.

As regards general laws, there is little difficulty. All are bound by general laws, provided these are in effect in the place where they are. Even a general law may, by special indult, be inoperative in a certain territory. In that case it binds no one there. Thus, strangers or vagrants sojourning in the United States are not bound to observe those four of the ten holydays of the Church (cf. c. 1247, § 1) which, by indult, are not observed in the United States. In Canada no one is obliged to observe the Feast of the Assumption. If, however, the law is in effect there, the fact that it is not in effect in the home territory from which a stranger comes does not exempt him from the general law. A Canadian residing in the United States must observe the Feast of the Assumption.

As regards particular laws, it will help toward an understanding of the rules to remember that we are now dealing with cases where only one of the relations of person to territory exists — either residence or presence, not both.

Principles. 1. The stranger who is absent from his home territory is not bound by its particular laws because, according to canon 13, § 2, both presence and residence in the territory are required in order that a person be bound by particular territorial laws. But **canon 14** declares some *exceptions* to that rule. If the laws are personal, they bind the resident even while he is away from home. That is the definition of a personal law, given under canon 8. The present canon, moreover, declares that laws are equivalently personal, so as to bind residents even while away from home, if the transgression of the laws would work harm in the home territory.

2. The stranger is not bound by the particular laws of the territory where he is, for the same reason: one of the requisite relations of person to territory is wanting (c. 13, § 2); he is not a resident of the territory. But again **canon 14** declares the *exceptional* cases. Laws which concern the public order bind even strangers, for public order must be protected regardless of the status of persons. The same is true of laws which prescribe legal formalities of acts, for the validity of acts must be readily ascertainable without inquiry into the status of persons. These exceptional laws may be called territorial in the full or extreme sense: they are binding on everyone within the territory.

3. Vagrants, having no permanent residence, are capable of only one relation to a particular territory, actual stopping there. Hence, they are rightly bound by all laws which are in effect there. For, otherwise they would escape all legal control by particular law.

Questions and Applications. 1. Visiting clerics in Rome are bound by the local regulations forbidding clerics to attend cinema performances in public theaters.[25]

2. Would a stranger in the United States be bound to abstain on Wednesdays during Lent? On Saturdays during Lent? On either Wednesdays or Saturdays? The last was the solution officially given in a parallel case.[26]

3. Strangers are bound, in confession, by the reservations on the powers of confessors, which are in effect in the place where they are. Is this an application of this canon, or rather of canon 893?[27]

Effect of Doubt. Various circumstances are discussed as excusing persons from the observance of laws; for example, doubt, ignorance, moral impossibility. Moralists deal with doubt under the head of probabilism; and hence they mention in this place only ignorance and moral impossibility. The Code deals with doubt and ignorance, leaving the discussion of moral impossibility to the moralists.

Doubt. Doubt is the suspension of the mind between contradictory acts, when it neither affirms nor denies a proposition. Doubt is *positive* when assent is withheld because there is reason on both sides; *negative,* when it is withheld because there is no reason on either side. Mere ignorance produces negative doubt; but this canon deals with positive doubt only. Ignorance is the subject of the next canon. A doubt *of law* is a doubt about either the existence or the meaning of a law; a doubt *of fact* is a doubt about the existence of some concrete fact.

General Principles. 1. In a *positive doubt of law,* ecclesiastical laws are not binding. This is true as regards the moral and legal obligation, on the principle of probabilism; but the canon moreover declares that it is also true as regards the validity of acts. Even invalidating and incapacitating laws are not binding if a positive doubt of law exists (**c. 15**).

2. In a *positive doubt of fact,* the canon, instead of declaring the law inoperative, grants to Ordinaries (cf. c. 198) the power to dispense, provided the law is one from which the Holy See usually dispenses.

Application. An ingenious explanation of a difficult decision by means of this canon 15 is given by Maroto.[28]

---

[25] *Vicariatus Urbis,* 25 May, 1918; *AAS,* 10–300; *Digest,* I, p. 54.

[26] See S. C. Conc., 9 Feb., 1924; *AAS,* 16–94; *Digest,* I, p. 54.

[27] See Code Com., 24 Nov., 1920; *AAS,* 12–575; *Digest,* I, p. 415.

[28] See *Digest,* I, p. 544, note explaining reply of Code Com., 25 July, 1931; *AAS,* 23–388.

Exercise. Compare canon 15 with canon 81, and state the power of dispensation given to Ordinaries by the two canons together.

Ignorance. *Ignorance* is the want of due knowledge; *error* is a false judgment of the mind. Error may result from ignorance, but is not identified with it. Ignorance is *invincible* if it cannot be cured by the use of that degree of diligence which is due under the circumstances; it is vincible if it could be so cured, but adequate means are not taken. Vincible ignorance is further divided: it is *simply vincible* if some means of curing it have been used, short of due diligence; it is *crass*. or *supine,* if no diligence whatever is used; it is *affected,* if it is directly desired and preserved.

State of the Question. Canon 16 deals only ·with invalidating or incapacitating laws; it says nothing of the others. For them, we must supply the doctrine from the common teaching of the moralists, which is as follows: *invincible* ignorance excuses from the observance of all laws other than invalidating or incapacitating ones, because it makes their violation involuntary and hence inculpable; *vincible* ignorance diminishes guilt, unless it be *affected,* in which case it rather increases it.

General Principles. 1. In the case of invalidating or incapacitating laws, no ignorance excuses from them, unless the law expressly so state **(c. 16).** The reason is that the validity of acts is a matter which concerns the public good, and cannot be allowed to depend on the subjective state of persons.

2. Ignorance is sometimes presumed and sometimes not. A presumption is "a probable conjecture of something which is uncertain" (c. 1825). It takes the place of proof, where proof is wanting. Ignorance is presumed regarding things as to which it commonly exists: facts not notorious, which do not concern oneself. It is not presumed regarding things as to which it commonly does not exist: one's own affairs, or the affairs of others which are notorious. As regards the law, ignorance is never presumed.

Connected Questions. 1. What is the effect of fear? As regards ecclesiastical crimes and penalties, grave fear commonly excuses from both, with some exceptions (cc. 2205, 2229). As regards the validity of acts done through fear, these are usually valid, with some exceptions, but rescindable (c. 103, §2).

2. Moral impossibility, or too great difficulty, commonly excuses from the observance of laws which are merely ecclesiastical. The rule is understood in this sense: when, in order to observe a merely eccle-

siastical law in a concrete case, one would have to undergo a relatively grave difficulty — that is, grave in consideration of the purpose and importance of the law — and one which is only accidentally, and not regularly, connected with the law's observance, one is excused from observing the law. The application of this principle to *invalidating* laws is difficult and disputed.[29]

Interpretation of Law. The whole of **canon 17** refers to *authoritative* interpretation; that is, interpretation given with official authority, as opposed to doctrinal interpretation, which is given privately by anyone who knows the law. Authoritative interpretation is of two kinds, according to the way in which it is given. It may be given as law; or as either a judicial decision or a rescript. In the first case only is it of general application; in the latter two cases it is of particular application, but still authoritative, since the decision or rescript is an official one.

General Principles. 1. Authoritative interpretation is made by the legislator or his successor in office. The legislator means:

a. For the whole Church, the Supreme Pontiff (cc. 218, 227);

b. For several provinces, the plenary council (cc. 281);

c. For one province, the provincial council (c. 283);

d. For a diocese, the Bishop in the synod or out of it (c. 335);

e. For a vacant see, the Vicar Capitular (cc. 431, 432), or, where chapters do not exist, the Administrator appointed by the diocesan consultors (cf. c. 427).

2. Authoritative interpretation may also be made by anyone to whom these have given authority. For the laws of the whole Church, such authority has been given:

a. To the Code Commission exclusively, at least where there is question of formal interpretation of a canon of the Code, to be given as law.[30]

b. To the Tribunals of the Roman Curia acting according to law in the judicial decision of particular cases, and to the Sacred Congregations and Offices which are competent to give official rescripts or replies in particular cases.

---

[29] Cf. V-C, *Epit.*, I, n. 114. It is conceivable, however, that such extreme difficulty in observing the law might exist together with such urgent necessity that even an invalidating law would cease to be operative, by a kind of *epikeia.* Cf. Cappello, *De Matrimonio*, n. 199.

For a good discussion of the question, see Werts, "the Cessation of Invalidation in Grave Difficulty," in *Theological Studies*, Vol. IV (1943), p. 223.

[30] *Motu proprio*, 15 Sept., 1917; *AAS*, 9–483; *Digest*, I, p. 55.

3. Authoritative interpretation given as law is of general application, as is the law itself. Moreover:

a. It is retroactive and needs no promulgation, in one case only; namely, when it merely declares the sense of words which were already certain in their meaning. The reason is that in that case the interpretation introduces nothing new; it does no more than declare the sense of the law which was already known and promulgated in exactly the sense in which it is now interpreted.[31]

b. It is not retroactive and needs promulgation in three cases: when it explains a real doubt,[32] and when it restricts[33] or extends[34] the law. The reason is that in these cases the interpretation amounts to a new law.

4. Authoritative interpretation by particular decision or rescript directly affects only the persons and things concerned in the case.

Question. What is the force of the Instructions issued from time to time by the Sacred Congregations? Benedict XV declares in the *Motu proprio* by which he created the Code Commission, that the Sacred Congregations are henceforth to issue no new general decrees. Strictly speaking, therefore, they are not invested with legislative power; nor have they the function of formally interpreting the law, since that is given exclusively to the Code Commission. Are the Instructions of the Sacred Congregations, then, mere pious exhortations? Certainly not. In the same *Motu proprio,* His Holiness declares that one of the ordinary functions of the Sacred Congregations will be to issue Instructions "whereby the prescriptions of the Code may be more fully explained and appropriately enforced." He calls such Instructions "complements to the canons." It is undeniable that they are authoritative; and, since they explain the canons, they are interpretations of a sort. Yet, strictly speaking, they are rather to be regarded as administrative regulations and explanations than as formal interpretations. They are binding, either as precepts or directions, according to their terms.[35]

---

[31] The Code Commission has issued several authentic interpretations which astonished not a few canonists. Yet none of its replies has hitherto been officially declared to have been extensive or restrictive of the law. Cf. Code Com., 25 July, 1931; *AAS,* 23–388; *Digest,* I, p. 544.

[32] Cf. for example the interpretation of the words of canon 556, *quacumque ex causa,* Code Com., 13 July, 1930; *AAS, 22*–365; *Digest,* I, p. 301.

[33] Cf. the interpretation of the words of canon 542, *qui sectae acatholicae adhaeserunt,* Code Com., 16 Oct., 1919; *AAS,* 11–477; *Digest,* I, p. 298.

[34] Cf. the interpretation of the words of canon 522, *confessio in qualibet ecclesia vel oratorio,* etc., Code Com., 24 Nov., 1920; *AAS,* 12–575; *Digest,* I, p. 295.

[35] Cf. V-C, *Epit.,* I, nn. 132, 360.

Moreover, the Sacred Congregations give replies on matters within their competency. These are authoritative, but usually involve mere applications of the canons to particular cases. When any real question of interpretation is involved, the Sacred Congregations often consult the Code Commission, and add to their reply the phrase, "having heard the opinion of the special Commission." This would seem to make the reply equivalent to one made by the Code Commission itself. The phrase *facto verbo cum Sanctissimo* added to replies of the Sacred Congregations denotes the approval of the Supreme Pontiff *in forma communi*. Certain other clauses, e.g., *ex motu proprio, ex certa scientia,* mean that the reply is approved by the Holy Father, not merely *in forma communi,* but *in forma specifica;* and that it has the authority of the Supreme Pontiff himself.[36]

General Principles of Interpretation. 1. If the words of the law in the text and context are clear, they are the sole norm of interpretation **(c. 18).** The proper or true meaning of the words is to be considered, whether it be the ordinary meaning or a technical one. Where a word has a technical juridical meaning defined in the Code, there is a general presumption that that word, in any law of the Code, is used in that sense; yet this is not always the case. The text and context may make certain dictionary meanings of words, or even their technical meaning, evidently inapplicable.

2. Only in case the text remains obscure may recourse be had to the other norms of interpretation. These are:

a. Parallel passages of the Code; that is, where the Code treats of the same matter under another aspect. Thus canon 2341 is a parallel passage to canon 120, § 2.

b. The purpose and circumstances of the law. Here historical study of the sources of the law and the circumstances of its enactment are of great value. Read Gasparri, *De Matrimonio,* n. 1217, and see what light he throws on canon 1139 by reporting the deliberations of the Commission on the reply of the Holy Office of 2 March, 1904.

c. The mind, or intention, of the legislator.

Epikeia. *Epikeia* is an interpretation exempting one from the law contrary to the clear words of the law and in accordance with the mind of the legislator. It is evidently a very exceptional thing. It may be used with prudent discretion, and is justified, only in a particular

---

[36] Cf. Choupin, *Valeur des décisions doctrinales et disciplinaires du S. Siège,* p. 75.

case where: (*a*) the strict interpretation of the law would work a great hardship; and (*b*) in view of the usual interpretation it may be prudently conjectured that, in this particular case, the legislator would not wish the law to be strictly applied.

The *general* and *habitual* interpretation of a law contrary to its clear terms is not epikeia, but an evident abuse.

Strict, or Narrow, Interpretation (c. 19). To interpret a law strictly here means to interpret it narrowly; that is, so as to narrow rather than enlarge its application. The rule is stated for three classes of laws:

a. Laws establishing a penalty. *"In poenis, benignior interpretatio"* (c. 2219, § 1). *"Odiosa restringuntur."*

b. Laws limiting the free exercise of rights. This is another liberal principle, easily understood. The exercise of rights is in accord with God-given liberty, and is for the common good.

c. Laws which contain an exception to the law. The general norm of law is favored; the exception is narrowly interpreted, so as to infringe as little as possible on the general law. It is not always easy to determine which laws are to be regarded as exceptional. A few examples may help.

Exceptional Laws. 1. General norm: Mass is to be celebrated in a church or oratory (c. 822, § 1). Exception: The Ordinary may permit Mass outside a church or oratory (c. 822, § 4). The Code Commission has held that this exception is to be strictly interpreted.[37]

2. General norm: exemption of religious Orders (c. 615). Exceptions: various matters expressly mentioned (cc. 612, 874, 1261, 1334, etc.).

3. General norm: no begging by religious without permission of the Ordinary (c. 622). Exception: mendicant Orders, in places where they have a house, may do so by permission of their own Superiors (c. 621). The Code Commission has interpreted this exception strictly.[38]

Supplementary Norms. The Code, in **canon 20,** is no longer treating of the interpretation of law; the question now is, what if there is no law either general or particular governing the matter. Obviously a norm of action must be drawn from somewhere.

Principle. The canon indicates four sources:

a. Laws enacted in similar matters. The reference is to laws of the Church. Civil law provides no regular norm for the interpretation of canon law.

b. General principles of law, applied with canonical equity. Canonical equity may be defined as a certain human moderation with which

---

[37] Code Com., 16 Oct., 1919; *AAS,* 11–478; *Digest,* I, p. 384.
[38] Code Com., 16 Oct., 1919; *AAS,* 11–478; *Digest,* I, p. 323.

canon law is tempered, so that the text may be prudently and even benignly applied to concrete cases.

c. The usage and practice of the Roman Curia. The Code here uses two technical terms, *"a stylo et praxi."* *Stylus Curiae* is the usage with particular reference to procedure; *praxis* is the practice in general. These must be learned from the study of cases and decisions or from actual association with the work of the Curia.

d. Finally, the common and constant teaching of learned authorities still must guide us in points where the Code does not go into detail. For example, canon 1248 docs not state what causes are sufficient to excuse from attending Mass on Sunday. The *common* opinion of reliable moralists is a safe guide.

Exception. Where there is question of applying penalties, no supplementary norm of action is needed; for if the law is silent, no penalty exists (cf. c. 6, 5°).

Cessation of the Law. A law may cease to bind in two ways: either by repeal, which is called extrinsic cessation, or by becoming inoperative without repeal, which is called intrinsic cessation. It is common doctrine that a law ceases to bind without repeal in two cases: first, if the circumstances are such that the law has become positively harmful or unreasonable; second, if the purpose of the law has entirely ceased for the entire community. But what if the purpose of the law has ceased, not for the entire community, but for the particular case in question? Does the law cease to bind in that case? This is the question which **canon 21** answers.

Principle. A law passed to guard against a common danger remains binding even for individual cases in which the danger does not exist **(c. 21).** Two reasons may be cited for this rule: in the first place, there is always danger of illusion in judging that the common danger does not exist; second, the relaxation of the rule by private exemption in particular cases would tend to general relaxation.

Question. What if, in an individual case, not only has the purpose of the law ceased, but its application would be positively harmful? Apply the principle of *epikeia,* as explained under canon 18.

Abrogation by Later Law. Canon 22 deals with the *extrinsic* cessation of law: namely, repeal or revocation.

Principles. 1. If the later law is equally general or equally particular with the former one, then the later law repeals the former one in only three cases: (*a*) if it contains an explicit statement to that effect, a repealing clause; (*b*) if it is directly contrary to the former law, so that it is evidently impossible for the two to stand together; (c) if it deals with the entire subject matter of the former law. In all other cases, or if the matter is doubtful (c. 23), the two laws stand together, and are to be reconciled as far as possible.

2. If the later law is particular and the former law general, the later law prevails, for the particular place or persons to whom it applies. This is a general principle not stated in the canon, but understood.

3. If the later law is general and the former one particular, no repeal is effected, unless the later general law expressly repeals the former particular one.

Exception. The rule stated in canon 6, 1°, is an exceptional case falling under the third principle. The Code, a later general law, expressly states in canon 6, 1°, that it wishes to repeal former laws which are contrary to it, even if those former laws be particular ones.

Doubtful Revocation. In doubt, the revocation of the former law is not presumed, but later laws are to be considered in connection with the earlier ones, and are as far as possible to be reconciled with them (c. 23).

The reason for this rule is that law is for the common good, and hence the repeal of law is considered an odious thing, not to be presumed, nor admitted without proof.

A Precept means an order given by a superior. A precept is *general* if it is given to a whole community for the common good; it is *particular* if it is given to individuals. Canon 24 treats of particular precepts only. A precept differs from a law in three respects:

1. It may proceed either from the power of jurisdiction or from dominative power; whereas a law strictly requires the power of jurisdiction or government.

2. A precept usually concerns directly the private rather than the public good.

3. It is personal, while a law is usually territorial.

Principles. 1. Particular precepts are binding everywhere, because they are personal and not territorial (c. 24).

2. If such precepts have been imposed by a legal document or before two witnesses, they can be enforced judicially, because they are then capable of strict judicial proof; in that case also they do not cease with the expiration of the authority of the person who imposed them. But if they were imposed without either a legal document or two witnesses, they are binding only as long as the authority of the superior who imposed them lasts, and they cannot be *judicially* enforced (c. 24).

Problem. A Bishop imposed upon one of his diocesan priests the precepts: first, never to assist at a public theatrical performance; second, to make a six days' retreat every year. The second precept was imposed in the presence of witnesses; the first was without document or witnesses. May the priest licitly attend a public theatrical performance outside the diocese? May he do so within the diocese after the Bishop's death? Can he be punished *judicially* if he violates the first precept? Is he still obliged, after the Bishop's death, to make the annual six days' retreat according to the precept?

CASES AND QUESTIONS

1. Can a law be completely established without promulgation? (C. 8, § 1). Can it be completely established without being presently binding on the community? (C. 9). How are papal laws promulgated, and when do they become effective? (C. 9).

2. What do you understand by a personal law? A territorial law? An invalidating law? Does a law which forbids an act necessarily render the act invalid? (C. 11).

3. What persons are bound by the laws of the Church? (C. 12).

4. Can a person be bound by particular territorial laws though he have no permanent residence in the territory? (C. 14). What do you mean by a *peregrinus?* A *vagus?*

5. A, an administrator of ecclesiastical property, does an act which is expressly forbidden by canon law. He is concerned about the validity of his action. On further study, he learns that it is regarded as valid by some good canonists, invalid by others. Is the act to be regarded as valid? Is this certain or only probable? (C. 15).

6. Y married while under a diriment impediment (cf. c. 1036, § 2) of which he was ignorant. Is the marriage valid? (C. 16). Later the law is changed so that a marriage under the same circumstances may be validly contracted. Is Y's marriage thereby validated? (C. 10).

7. State carefully the rule which determines when replies of the Code Commission are to be regarded as retroactive (c. 17).

8. "A strict interpretation of the law results in greater individual liberty." In what sense, if any, is this statement true? (C. 19).

Readings:

McCloskey, *The Subject of Ecclesiastical Law According to Canon 12,* Catholic University, 1942 (n. 165); Hammill, *The Obligations of the Traveler According to Canon 14,* C.U., 1942 (n. 160); Schmidt, *The Principles of Authentic Interpretation in Canon 17 of the Code of Canon*

Law, C.U., 1941 (n. 141); *Irish Ecclesiastical Record,* Vol. 41, p. 422 (gravity of obligation of ecclesiastical laws); Vol. 43, p. 113 (*peregrini* and local laws); Vol. 45, p. 645 (Browne, on authentic interpretation); *Ius Pontificium,* Vol. 15, pp. 160–190, 298–313; Vol. 16, pp. 78, 217–256; *The Jurist,* Vol. 2, p. 105 (Roelker, on the traveler and local laws); Vol. 3, p. 480 (McCloskey, on obligation of heretics to observe ecclesiastical laws); Vol. 4, p. 491 (Roelker on acquired rights and the retroactivity of laws); *The Clergy Review,* Vol. 21, p. 357 (Mahoney, on the binding force of Instructions of the Sacred Congregations).

Section 3. Custom (cc. 25–30)

PRELIMINARY SURVEY

Consent of Superior Always Necessary (c. 25)
Extent of Practice as Basis for Custom (c. 26)
Custom Against the Law (c. 27)
Custom Beside the Law (c. 28)
Custom According to Law (c. 29)
Revocation of Customary Law (c. 30)

Custom. Custom may be considered in two ways, as a fact, and as a law. As a *fact,* custom means a practice or way of acting which is common in a certain community — *consuetudo facti.* As a *law,* it means a legal norm or law introduced by such a practice — *consuetudo iuris.* Can custom, then, truly become law? Yes; for law may be written or unwritten. The unwritten law is of two kinds. It may be an ordinance proceeding entirely from the will of the superior, and differing from a formal written law only in the fact that it is unwritten; or it may be what is called customary law; that is, founded upon the common practice in the community and approved by the superior. It is evident that this customary unwritten law is nothing else than custom considered as law — *consuetudo iuris.* Hence, custom in this sense is law.

General Principles. 1. Custom can ôbtain the force of law in the Church **(c. 25).**

2. It can do so, however, only on one condition; that it receive the consent of the competent ecclesiastical superior **(c. 25).** Competent here means having power of jurisdiction or government which would enable him to enact a law on the matter in question. The reason is that only the consent of such a superior can make a law effective.

Three different ways in which the superior's consent to a custom may be given, expressly, tacitly, and legally, are explained under canon 27.

Corollaries. From the general principle that custom is law, there follow immediately several conclusions which are stated in succeeding canons, but which can be understood now.

1. A custom, in order to have the force of law, must be reasonable (c. 27).

2. It can never contradict the divine law (c. 27).

3. Any community which is capable of receiving a law, though it be incapable of enacting a law, can introduce a custom which may obtain the force of law (c. 26).

Extent of Practice Which May Form Basis of Customary Law. The question is how general must a practice be in order to form the foundation for a custom which may obtain the force of law. It must, of course, be a common practice; but in how large a community? Is it necessary that the community in which the practice prevails be a lawmaking unit; that is, that its *immediate* superior be endowed with legislative power, or is it sufficient that the community, though unable to make a law, be capable of receiving a law? If the latter is true, then any community which has some organization which enables it to be recognized as one body, and which has a certain stability and permanence, can furnish the factual foundation for a custom. This is the question which **canon 26** purports to answer.

General Principle. A practice which is common in any community capable of receiving a law, though incapable of making a law, is sufficiently general to form the foundation upon which, through the consent of the superior who is competent to make a law for that community, a lawful custom may be erected.

Examples. Communities capable of introducing customs which may become lawful are: the Church, a diocese, a religious order or congregation, an ecclesiastical province, etc.

Question. Is a custom which is common in a *parish* sufficiently general to obtain the force of law? This question is disputed, most authors answering in the negative. We should rather say yes.[39] The immediate superior of the parish is the pastor; he has no legislative power, hence his consent would be ineffective to make the custom lawful. The consent of the Bishop would be necessary, we concede. But that is not the question. The question is, is a parish such a community

---

[39] Cf. V-C, *Epit.*, I, n. 138.

as is capable of *receiving* a law. If so, it is capable, not indeed of establishing a custom which *has of itself* the force of law, but of "introducing a custom which *may obtain* the force of law." These are the very words of canon 26.

Custom Against Law. Canon 27 deals with custom which is contrary to law, and declares how such a custom can obtain the force of law by prescription. We shall explain prescription, which is a legal term, and also the division of custom, according to law, beside the law, contrary to law.

1. Custom is said to be *according to law* when it contains nothing that is not in the law itself, although it may specify the manner of the law's observance. In this sense canon 29 declares that custom — that is, custom according to law — is the law's best interpreter.

2. Custom *beside the law* is custom which induces a new obligation, not indeed contrary to law, but in addition to it. Canon 28 deals with this division of custom.

3. Custom *contrary to law* is custom which establishes a right or an obligation contrary to law.

Prescription is a legal method of acquiring a right or freeing oneself from an obligation, by a use or possession continued for a certain period of time under certain conditions (cf. c. 1508). It has many applications both in civil and canon law. For example:

a. The possession of land, under certain conditions, for the required period of time, may confer title, which in the old English common law was called "title by adverse possession."

b. The use of a way or road through another's land, maintained under the required conditions for the required period of time, confers a right of way through the land.

c. The nonuse of a right may lead, by prescription, after a stated period of time, to the loss of the right.

d. A custom may obtain the force of law, supposing the other required conditions to be present, by uninterrupted practice for a required period of time. Such uninterrupted practice is called prescription as applied to custom.

General Principles. 1. Custom contrary to the divine law, positive or natural, avails nothing (c. 27, § 1). The reason is that the divine law is not subject to modification by man.

2. Custom contrary to ecclesiastical law may prevail under the following conditions (c. 27, § 1):

a. The custom must be reasonable;

b. It must be lawfully prescribed; that is, it must be in use continuously and under the required conditions for the prescribed time, which is forty years usually, and one hundred years in the case of laws which contain a clause forbidding future contrary customs.

3. Custom which is expressly reprobated in the law is not reasonable (**c. 27, § 2**). The clause *reprobata contraria consuetudine* occurs in several canons of the Code; for example, canons 343, 346, 396, 403, 409, 418, 433, 455, 460, 774, 818, 978, 1006, 1041, 1056, 1181, 1356, 1408, 1492, 1525, 1576. The effect of such a clause *as regards the past* is expressed in canon 5; *as regards the future*, it is decreed by canon 27.

Questions. 1. Is the consent of the superior required in order that a custom contrary to law may obtain the force of law? And if so, how is it given? The consent of the superior is always required, according to canon 25. There is no exception from that rule. But the consent may be given in three ways: (*a*) *expressly,* by explicit words or signs; (*b*) *tacitly,* by such conduct as implies consent; or (*c*) *legally,* through laws which in advance give the consent of the superior to customs which shall have endured for the prescribed time under the required conditions. In these cases the consent of the superior is given legally, and it is sufficient. Neither express nor tacit consent is required.

2. The term "lawfully prescribed" is explained as including other conditions besides the practice of the custom for the required time. What are those other conditions? In canon law, they are chiefly these, that the custom must be practiced continuously, openly, and peaceably —"*neque clam neque vi, per annos continuos.*" Good faith, though required for prescription in general (c. 1512), is certainly not required in prescription of a custom contrary to law.[40]

3. When is prescription required in order to give legal effect to a custom? It may be said in general that prescription is required only when it is necessary as a means of supplying the consent of the superior. Hence:

a. In customs which are according to law, prescription is never required.

b. When the express consent of the superior has been given to a custom, prescription is never required.

c. When only the tacit consent of the superior has been given, prescription is not required for a custom which is against the law, but it is required for a custom that is beside the law. The reason is

---

[40] Cf. Michiels, *Normae Generales,* II, pp. 65–69.

that tacit consent is sufficient to free from an existing obligation, but scarcely sufficient to impose a new one.

d. When neither express nor tacit consent of the superior has been given, and the custom is one which is either beside the law or against the law, legal consent must be obtained by the continuance of the custom under the required conditions for the prescriptive period.[41]

Custom Beside the Law can become law under the following conditions (c. 28):

1. It must be *reasonable;*
2. It must have been observed by the community *knowingly;* that is, with knowledge that no obligation already exists;
3. With the *intention* of creating an obligation;
4. It must have been *legitimately prescribed* for forty years; that is, practiced openly and peaceably, continuously for forty years.

Question. Is the consent of the superior required in this case? Yes; but it need not be given expressly nor even tacitly; it is given *legally* upon the fulfillment of the conditions required by this canon.

Custom According to Law is the law's best interpreter (c. 29). This canon is almost the shortest in the Code, consisting of five words, while canon 436 has only four. It applies only to custom which is according to law. As long as custom does not detract from nor add to the law, it may serve as a guide to the true meaning of the law; in fact, it is of all interpreters the best. Better even than the official interpreter? Yes; because of its clearness and suave efficacy. If all about us observe the law, it is impossible to misunderstand its meaning, and it is a pleasure to observe it with them. In this case the custom is the law, observed by the people.

Revocation of Customary Law. Canon 30 deals with the revocation of customs which have obtained the force of law. It mentions only customs which are against the law or beside the law, because customs which are according to law are really not distinct from the law itself, and hence their revocation is governed by canon 22 which deals with the revocation of laws as such.

Principles (c. 30): 1. A particular law revokes particular customs which are contrary to it.

2. A particular custom revokes a contrary custom.

3. A general law does not revoke a particular custom unless it expressly mentions it, except as provided in canon 5. The reason is

---

[41] Cf. Cappello, *Summa,* I, n. 115.

that the legislator is not presumed to have had the particular custom in mind.

4. A law, general or particular, does not abrogate customs which are centenary or immemorial, without express mention, except as provided in canon 5.

Exceptions. Canon 5 provides exceptions to principles 3 and 4; for it provides:

1. That the Code, although it is a general law, revokes even particular customs which are contrary to it; and

2. That the Code abrogates even centenary and immemorial customs which are contrary to it, unless the Ordinaries judge that such customs cannot prudently be removed.

CASES AND QUESTIONS

1. Can a custom which is contrary to law be considered reasonable? Can it be so considered if it is reprobated in the law? (C. 27).

2. Explain the term "prescription" with reference to custom.

3. "A custom contrary to law may become law under certain conditions without the express or tacit consent of the superior." Is this true? (C. 27, § 1). How is this consistent with canon 25?

4. In a certain diocese a *general* custom prevails which is contrary to a diocesan regulation. It is known that the Bishop (cf. c. 335, § 1) has expressly permitted the practice. Can it be licitly followed before it has been in use continuously for forty years? (C. 27). Would the same be true if the custom were contrary to a general law of the Church? (C. 25). Who is meant by the "competent superior" in canon 25?

Readings:

Guilfoyle, *Custom,* Catholic University, 1937 (n. 105); Vermeersch-Creusen, *Epitome Iuris Canonici,* I, nn. 137–143; Cappello, *Summa Iuris Canonici,* I, nn. 108–121; *Irish Ecclesiastical Record,* Vol. 36, p. 646 (Kinane, on consent of superior); Vol. 37, p. 521 (Kinane, on community capable of introducing custom); Vol. 39, p. 78 (revocation of custom); *The Clergy Review,* Vol. 23, p. 83 (Mahoney, on custom and the superior's consent).

Section 4. The Reckoning of Time (cc. 31–35)

PRELIMINARY SURVEY

Scope of This Title: Liturgical Laws Excepted (c. 31)
Definition of Day, Week, Month, Year (c. 32)
Computation of Time of Day: Time for Fulfilling Contractual
Obligations (c. 33)
Rules for Computing Stated Periods of Time (c. 34)
Available Time (c. 35)

Exception Made for Liturgical Laws. Liturgical laws are excepted from the rules laid down for the reckoning of time, because they have their own peculiar way of reckoning time, which the Code desires to leave unchanged, in accordance with the general policy announced in canon 2 **(cf. c. 31).**

Time is an important element in the observance of laws. Hence the Code in **c. 32** gives exact definitions of the common divisions of time, day, week, month, and year. To these official definitions we prefix a common working definition of an hour.

Definitions. 1. An *hour* is a period of time consisting of sixty minutes. Clocks are so constructed that the hour is up when the clock *begins* to strike.

2. A *day* consists of twenty-four hours, counted continuously from midnight **(c. 32, § 1).** Exceptions to this rule are introduced by canon 34, § 2, which speaks of cases where the day is counted "from moment to moment." In those cases the day is counted continuously, not however from midnight, but from any moment of one day to the corresponding moment of another day. Parts of the day are not counted.

3. A *week* consists of seven days **(c. 32, § 1).** It need not begin with Sunday, nor need the days be continuous. This is clear from the last part of c. 34, § 2, which provides for computing time by weeks of seven days, even when the time is intermittent and not continuous.

4. A *month* consists of thirty days, unless it is to be taken as it is in the calendar **(c. 32, § 2).** In the latter case it may consist of twenty-eight, twenty-nine, thirty, or thirty-one days.

5. A *year* consists of three hundred and sixty-five days, unless it is to be taken as it is in the calendar **(c. 32, § 2).** The cases in which a month and a year are to be taken as they are in the calendar are determined by canon 34.

Time in General. Time is commonly measured from the moment when the sun crosses the meridian at any given place. The meridian is a great circle of the celestial sphere passing through its poles and the zenith of a given place. The number of meridians is, of course, indefinite; only certain meridians are marked on maps as lines of longitude.

True Sun Time. The moment when the sun crosses the meridian is called noon. But days measured from noon to noon according to the passage of the sun across the meridian are not of equal length; such days vary in length according to the seasons of the year. Two reasons are given for this variation: first, the eccentricity of the earth's orbit; second, the obliquity of the ecliptic. Into these reasons we cannot enter here. They are briefly and clearly explained in an article by Hugh C. Mitchell, in the *Ecclesiastical Review,* Vol. 84, p. 495 (May, 1931).

Mean Time. In order to divide time into days of equal length, mean time has been devised. Mean time gives us days of equal length according to the clock, not according to the sun. It is measured by a perfect clock so constructed and regulated as to mark noon on January 1, 1944, when the sun crosses the meridian, and noon again when the sun crosses the meridian on January 1, 1945. Since the time when the sun crosses the meridian depends upon longitude (the meridian being a line of longitude), it is evident that both true sun time and mean time will vary according to the longitude of the place. Neither of them will be the same for different places, except for places which lie exactly on the same meridian line. For this reason, both of these times are called local; the Code designates them by the phrase "local time, either true or mean" (c. 33, § 1).

Standard Time. Canon 33 also refers to "legal time, either regional or extraordinary." What we call standard time is legal regional time, because it is fixed by law for a certain region. For the sake of uniformity of time within a given area, it was desirable to establish a time that would not vary within a certain zone. A step in this direction was taken by the establishment of "railroad time" by a railroad agreement in 1883. In 1919, the Interstate Commerce Commission was empowered by Act of Congress to fix the zones for standard time. There are four zones in the United States. A fifth zone includes only Alaska. The boundaries of the various zones have been modified from time to time; but in a general way each zone represents a strip of territory running north and south, fifteen degrees of longitude in width; so that the three hundred and sixty degrees of the earth's longitude are theoretically[42] divided into twenty-four time zones, one zone for each hour of the sun's apparent transit around the earth. Within each of these zones, the standard time for all points is determined by the mean time at one meridian line passing through the zone. Thus, in the central time zone, the mean time of the ninetieth meridian (which passes through Wisconsin and Illinois west of Milwaukee and Chicago) is the standard time for the entire zone. Eastern time is fixed by the mean time of the seventy-fifth meridian; mountain time, by that of the one hundred and fifth meridian; Pacific time, by that of the one hundred and twentieth; while the standard time of the Alaska zone is the mean time of the one hundred and fiftieth meridian, two hours away from Pacific time.

Extraordinary Legal Time. This means any sort of zone time differing from standard time, *provided it be legally established*. Daylight-saving time, which is legally established for certain seasons in many places, is obtained by adding one hour to standard time; wartime, by adding one hour to prewar standard time everywhere in the United States. By Act of Congress, January, 1942, wartime is legal until six months after the duration of the war.

In exercising the option which the Code gives between various systems of time, one will practically have to begin with standard time; and the problem will be how to compute local mean time, true sun time, or any extraordinary legal time.

How to Compute Local Mean Time From Standard Time. Standard time in any given zone is the mean time of the meridian which has been arbitrarily selected as the standard for that zone. Hence, at all points along the ninetieth meridian mean time is the same as central standard time. At all points east of the ninetieth meridian, within the central time zone, when the sun is on the ninetieth meridian, it *has already passed* the longitude of points east; that is, it is *later* at those points by mean time than it is by standard time;

---

[42] The exact uniformity of the 24 time zones is theoretical only. *In fact,* the legally established boundaries of the various zones conform often enough to state boundaries instead of following the meridian of longitude which should theoretically mark their boundaries. It is the boundaries *as actually fixed by law* which must govern. For it must be noted that what we call standard time is called by the Code *legal regional* time; and the necessity of a norm of law fixing it has been insisted on in a reply of the Code Commission, 10 Nov., 1925; *AAS,* 17–582; *Digest,* I, p. 59. Hence, if a point lies outside the only legally established limits of the central time zone, one may not use central time there on the theory that the place "ought to be" in that zone. On the other hand, if any legal authority, even local, has adopted central time, it becomes legal and may be used for the acts mentioned in canon 33, § 1.

hence one must *add* to standard time to get the mean solar time of those places. Conversely, at all points west of the ninetieth meridian, when the sun is on the ninetieth meridian, it *has not yet reached* the longitude of points west; that is, it is *earlier* at those points by mean time than it is by standard time; therefore one must *subtract* from standard time to get the mean solar time of those places.

Regional Difference. The amount of time that must thus be added to or subtracted from standard time to arrive at local mean time may be called the regional difference. We shall designate as "plus," all regional differences for points east of the standard meridian; these must be added to standard time. And we shall designate as "minus," all regional differences for points west of the standard meridian; these must be subtracted from standard time to obtain local mean time.

Amount of Regional Difference. How much must one add or subtract? That depends on the difference in longitude between the point in question and the standard meridian of the zone. Since the width of the zone, 15 degrees of longitude, equals one hour or sixty minutes of time, each degree equals four minutes. Hence the amount of the regional difference is four minutes for each degree of longitude between the point in question and the standard meridian, to be added to, or subtracted from, standard time, according as the place in question lies east or west of the standard time meridian. The table of Regional Differences on page 48 will supply some illustrations.

How to Calculate True Sun Time From Standard Time. True sun time is very difficult to determine, and for that reason is not of very much use canonically. However, it may occasionally be serviceable. It is a local time which varies from local mean time according to the seasons of the year, the variations being in two cycles which are illustrated by the figure on page 49 drawn by the Reverend John Markoe, S.J., from data obtained from the *American Nautical Almanac 1942*. Fractional differences from one year to another, are practically negligible. The straight line represents local mean time, constant throughout the year. The curve represents true sun time. The parts of the curve which are above the line represent additions which must be made to local mean time to obtain true local sun time; the parts below the line represent subtractions from mean time. The scale figures on the vertical line represent minutes; and the amount of the variation of true time from mean time is thus represented by the distance of any point on the curve above or below the line. Successive dates in the year are indicated by distances from left to right along the straight line.

Table of Regional Differences

Baltimore (E.T.)	minus	6.5
Boston (E.T.)	plus	16
Buffalo (E.T.)	minus	15.5
Chicago (C.T.)	plus	9
Cincinnati (E.T.)	minus	38
Cleveland (E.T.)	minus	26.5
Denver (M.T.)		0.0
Detroit (E.T.)	minus	32
Edmonton (M.T.)	minus	34
Kansas City (C.T.)	minus	18
Key West (E.T.)	minus	27
Los Angeles (P.T.)	plus	7.5
Los Gatos (P.T.)	minus	8
Milwaukee (C.T.)	plus	8.5
Montreal (E.T.)	plus	6
Mundelein (C.T.)	plus	8
New Orleans (C.T.)	minus	0.5
New York (E.T.)	plus	4
Nome (Standard 150th meridian)	minus	61
Omaha (C.T.)	minus	23.5
Philadelphia (E.T.)	minus	0.5
Phoenix (M.T.)	minus	28.5
Pilgrim Springs (Standard 150th meridian)	minus	60
Pueblo (M.T.)	plus	1
Quebec (E.T.)	plus	15
Saint Louis (C.T.)	minus	1
Saint Marys (C.T.)	minus	24.5
San Francisco (P.T.)	minus	8.5
Tampa (E.T.)	minus	30
Toledo (E.T.)	minus	36
Toronto (E.T.)	minus	17
Vancouver (P.T.)	minus	12
Washington (E.T.)	minus	8
West Baden (C.T.)	plus	13
Weston (E.T.)	plus	15
Winnipeg (C.T.)	minus	28
Woodstock (E.T.)	minus	7.5
Wrangel (Standard 150th meridian)	plus	71.5

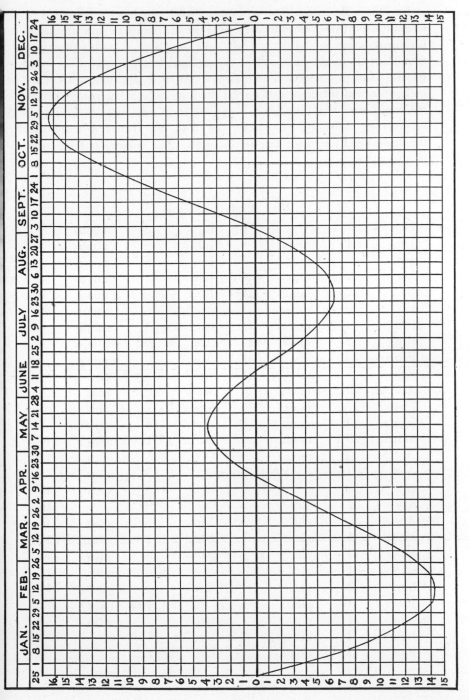

The Time Equation. The amount of time which must be added to or subtracted from local mean time to obtain local true sun time may for convenience be called the time equation. Note that this modification must be made, not directly to standard time, but to mean time for the place in question. The reason is that true sun time is a strictly local time, and therefore varies with the longitude of the place. Hence, to obtain true sun time from standard time one must first add or subtract the regional difference for the place, and then add or subtract the time equation according to the date. The following table may be of service.

Time Equation Table

Dec.	25		0	July	2	minus	4
Jan.	1	minus	4	July	9	minus	5
Jan.	8	minus	8	July	16	minus	6
Jan.	15	minus	10	July	23	minus	6
Jan.	22	minus	12	July	30	minus	6
Jan.	29	minus	13	Aug.	6	minus	6
Feb.	5	minus	14	Aug.	13	minus	5
Feb.	12	minus	14	Aug.	20	minus	3
Feb.	19	minus	14	Aug.	27	minus	1
Feb.	26	minus	13	Sept.	3	plus	1
March	5	minus	12	Sept.	10	plus	3
March	12	minus	10	Sept.	17	plus	5
March	19	minus	8	Sept.	24	plus	8
March	26	minus	6	Oct.	1	plus	10
Apr.	2	minus	4	Oct.	8	plus	12
Apr.	9	minus	2	Oct.	15	plus	14
Apr.	16		0	Oct.	22	plus	15
Apr.	23	plus	2	Oct.	29	plus	16
Apr.	30	plus	3	Nov.	5	plus	16
May	7	plus	4	Nov.	12	plus	16
May	14	plus	4	Nov.	19	plus	15
May	21	plus	3	Nov.	26	plus	13
May	28	plus	3	Dec.	3	plus	10
June	4	plus	2	Dec.	10	plus	7
June	11	plus	1	Dec.	17	plus	4
June	18	minus	1	Dec.	24		0
June	25	minus	2	Dec.	25		0

Explanation

Quantities marked *plus* are minutes *to be added* to local mean time, and quantities marked *minus* are minutes *to be subtracted* from local mean time, in order to obtain local true time. Quantities for dates between those given in the table may be approximated by dividing the sum of the two quantities for adjoining dates before and after. The figures are computed from the *American Nautical Almanac* for 1942. The quantities will vary slightly from year to year, but the table for 1942 will be on the average as nearly accurate as that for any other year; and the variations are so slight as to be practically negligible for canonical purposes. In using this or any other table for the acts mentioned in canon 33, it will be advisable to leave a margin of safety of one or two minutes.

Summary of Practical Rules. 1. Always begin with standard time.

2. Mean time is local; that is, it varies for different places according to longitude; but it is constant throughout the year. It is obtained from standard time by adding or subtracting the regional difference.

3. True sun time is also local, and moreover varies with the season. It is obtained from standard time by adding or subtracting first the regional difference for the place, then the time equation for the date.

4. Daylight-saving time is obtained from standard time by adding one hour. Whether this addition is to be made to prewar standard time or to wartime depends on the terms of the local law defining daylight-saving time. Extraordinary legal time cannot be modified by the regional difference nor by the time equation. If used at all, it must be used as it stands.

Canonical Principles. 1. In general, the common usage of the place, as regards time, is to be observed.

2. In certain acts, an option is given to follow any of the four kinds of time which have been explained above, even if they are different from the common usage. The acts in which this option is given are:

a. The private celebration of Mass. A private Mass in this connection is any Mass, even a solemn high Mass, which is not attached to an office which must be publicly exercised.[43] Practically the only Masses which are public in this *juridical* sense are the capitular or conventual Mass and the parish Mass. According to canon 821 Mass may not be begun earlier than one hour *before dawn* nor later than one hour *after*

---

[43] Cf. V-C, *Epit.*, I, n. 148; Cappello, *Summa*, I, n. 179; Michiels, *Normae Generales*, II, p. 137.

noon. Since dawn has a fixed relation to sunrise (one hour and three quarters earlier), it remains invariable for a certain place and date of the same year; but noon is actually a different point of time according to the system by which it is reckoned.

b. The private recitation of the canonical hours. This is always private except when done in choir by those bound to choir duty.

c. The reception of Holy Communion.

d. The observance of the law of fast or abstinence.

3. As regards the time for fulfilling contractual obligations, the civil law governs, in the absence of express agreement to the contrary (c. 33, § 2).

Questions. 1. May one choose different kinds of time for fulfilling different obligations in which the option is given? Yes; there is both sound reason and solid authority for allowing such choice.[44] We do not see on what principle the option clearly given by the Code can be limited. There is no duty to be consistent in the reckoning of time. Hence I may lawfully choose daylight-saving time for beginning my Eucharistic fast, standard time for beginning my Mass and beginning and finishing my office, and true sun time for beginning and ending the full day of fast or abstinence. But since the day of fast or abstinence, or both, is by law a day of twenty-four hours, I may not shorten it by computing the beginning and the end according to different kinds of time.

2. A large religious (clerical exempt) community is situated in the country, with only small villages in the neighborhood. The village and territory of which the community forms a part, use only central standard time. The community, by order of the superior, in order to accommodate itself to the time of the nearest large city, or for some other reason of convenience, uses daylight-saving time during part of the year for all community exercises. Under these circumstances is daylight-saving time permitted to individual members of the community for the acts mentioned in canon 33?

At first blush two reasons might seem to permit an affirmative answer.

a. May not the *large* religious community under these circumstances be considered a *locus* in the sense of canon 33, so that, not only

---

[44] This is controverted by some good authorities. For the view given in the text we may cite Michiels, *Normae Generales*, II, pp. 140–149; V-C, *Epit.*, I, n. 148; De Meester, *Compendium*, I, n. 286; Coronata, *Institutiones*, I, n. 51. For a complete discussion, see Michiels, *loc. cit.*

the acts mentioned in the canon, but all acts may be regulated by it under the fundamental rule, *standum est communi loci usui?* We dare not admit this. *Communis loci usus* certainly means the common usage of the place or territory as opposed to particular houses in it. To allow particular houses to substitute for this established norm a particular usage of their own would simply nullify the law instead of being an application of it.

b. May not the rector of the house, or at least the Provincial, be considered a legislator, so that the use of daylight-saving time by his authority would make that time *tempus legale regionale?* Again we think not. The Provincial, and even the local superior in an exempt clerical institute, have true jurisdiction (c. 501, § 1), and are legislators *within their sphere;* but the establishment of legal time zones is beyond their sphere. They may, of course, regulate the time of religious exercises in houses under their jurisdiction, subject to the common law of the Church. But according to that law, in our humble judgment, *tempus legale regionale* means time established by civil law for a region of the country, and cannot be stretched to include the order of exercises prescribed for a religious community.

3. Can a Bishop establish for his diocese, for the fulfillment of the acts mentioned in c. 33, a *legal regional time* different from that established by law for the territory. We think not, for the reason given above in the case of the superior of clerical exempt religious.

Computation of Time. Canon 34 demands rather close attention. The text of that canon is as follows:

§ 1. If the month and year are designated by name or equivalently, as for example, the month of February, next year, they are to be taken as they are in the calendar.

§ 2. If the starting point is neither explicitly nor implicitly assigned; for example, suspension from celebrating Mass for a month, or for two years, three months of vacation in the year, etc., the time is to be counted from moment to moment; and if it is continuous, as in the first example, the months and years are to be taken as they are in the calendar; if it is interrupted, a week shall be taken as seven days, a month thirty, a year three hundred and sixty-five.

§ 3. If the time consists of one or more months or years, one or more weeks, or more than one day, and the starting point is assigned either explicitly or implicitly:

1° The months and years are to be taken as they are in the calendar;

2° If the starting point coincides with the beginning of the day, for example, two months of vacation from the fifteenth of August, the first day is to be counted, and the time is up at the beginning of the last day of the same number;

3° If the starting point does not coincide with the beginning of the day, for example, the fourteenth year of age, the year of noviceship, eight days after the episcopal see becomes vacant, ten days for appeal, etc., the first day is not to be counted, and the time is up when the last day of the same number ends;

4° If the month has no day of the same number, for example, one month from the thirtieth of January, then the time is up at the beginning or end of the last day of the month, as the case may be;

5° If there is question of renewing at stated times acts of the same kind, for example, three years for the perpetual profession after the temporary, three years or any other period of time for making a new election, etc., the time is up when the same day from which it started comes round again, but the new act can be placed at any time during that entire day.

If we leave aside for the moment the last two sections (§ 3, 4° and 5°) which provide for special cases, we shall see that this canon answers three practical questions regarding the computation of periods of time. We shall take them up in order, following the provisions made in the text.

1. The first question refers to the *duration* of months and years (cf. c. 32, § 2). When are they to be taken as they are in the calendar? From a careful study of the text it will be clear that months and years are to be taken as they are in the calendar in every case except where the time is intermittent and the starting point is neither explicitly nor implicitly assigned (c. 34, § 2 at end).

2. The next question refers to the *starting point* of the time. When is time to be counted "from moment to moment"? As already explained, this means to count the day as beginning, not at midnight, but at any other moment of the day, and ending at the corresponding moment of the next day. The canon states that time is to be counted from moment to moment when the starting point is not specified explicitly or implicitly (§ 2). The reason for this rule is probably this: no starting point being specified, there will be an option to begin the period at any moment, or the starting point will be determined by circumstances; the moment so determined will most probably be some moment other than midnight, and so the day will begin at that moment and end at the corresponding moment twenty-four hours later.

It might be thought that time should be counted from moment to moment also when the starting point is specified, but does not coincide with midnight. The canon, however, provides otherwise. For reasons, probably, of convenience and certainty, it decrees that in that case the first day, or rather part of a day, shall not be counted at all. Practically, therefore, the period begins at the following midnight, and runs to midnight; and there is no need to count from moment to moment.

3. The third question relates to the *close of the period*. When is the time up? There will be three classes of cases:

a. If the starting point is not specified (by the law or the terms of the precept or document in question), we have seen that the time is computed from moment to moment; that is, it begins at a moment chosen by the person or determined by circumstances, and it ends at the corresponding moment of a future day. The duration of the months and years will be as in the calendar if the time is continuous; and respectively thirty and three hundred and sixty-five days, if the time is intermittent.

b. If the starting point is specified and coincides with the beginning of the day (midnight), then the entire first day is counted, and the period ends at midnight *preceding* the corresponding day designated as the term.

c. If the designated starting point does not coincide with the beginning of the day, the part of the first day is not counted at all, and consequently the period ends at midnight *following* the corresponding day designated as the term.

Special Cases. In § 3, 4° and 5°, two special cases are provided for:

1. Suppose the day which should be the term of the period happens to be a date which is wanting in that month, as Feb. 29, 30, or 31, or the 31 of April, June, September, or November, what is to be done? For convenience the Code specifies that in those cases the last day of the month be considered as the term, and the period closes at midnight, either preceding or following that day, as determined by the rules already given.

2. Acts of the same kind which are to be renewed at stated periods have this special privilege, that they can be lawfully renewed at any time during the day.

Official Decisions and Applications. See *Digest,* I, p. 59.

Available Time. *Tempus utile* means *available* time, time which is at the disposal of a person, for the exercise or prosecution of his right, on such terms that if the person is ignorant of his right or is unable to act, the time does not run; *tempus continuum* means time which does not suffer interruption (c. 35).

Examples of *Tempus Utile:* Canons 155, 161, 647 (cf. *Digest,* I, p. 328), 1432, 1465, § 1, 1881, 1884, § 2, 1885, § 1, 2153, § 1, 2146 (cf. *Digest,* I, p. 837).

Cases on the Computation of Time. 1. Canon 1067 requires for valid marriage that the man have completed his sixteenth year. John was born at 6 a.m. on 4 March, 1917; he contracts marriage at 9 a.m. 4 March, 1933. Is the marriage valid? The marriage is invalid; apply canon 34, § 3, 3°. In reality he completed his sixteenth year on his sixteenth anniversary at the hour corresponding to that at which he was born. Canonically, however, the day of his birth being only part of a day is not counted at all, and consequently he is of canonical age only at midnight following his anniversary.[45]

2. A priest of the Chicago Archdiocese has the privilege of anticipating the office beginning at 1 p.m. May he begin earlier in Mundelein?

3. What is the latest moment, standard time, at which a person in Nome, Alaska, on February 15, may begin the Eucharistic fast? Consult the table of regional differences, p. 48, and the time equation curve, p. 49, or the time equation table, p. 50.

Readings:

Dubé, *The General Principles for the Reckoning of Time in Canon Law,* Cath. University, 1941 (n. 144).

---

[45] Cf. Cappello, *De Matrimonio,* n. 335.

Section 5. Rescripts (cc. 36–62)

PRELIMINARY SURVEY

Who May Receive Benefit of Rescripts (cc. 36, 37)
Date When Effective (c. 38)
Essential Conditions (c. 39)
Truth of Recitals (cc. 40–42)
Favors Previously Refused (cc. 43, 44)
Effect of Clause *Motu Proprio* (c. 45)
Invalid Rescripts (c. 46)
Nonessential Errors in Rescripts (c. 47)
Contradictory Rescripts (c. 48)
Interpretation (cc. 49, 50)
Presentation (cc. 51, 52)

Execution (cc. 53–59)
Revocation of Rescripts (c. 60)
Effect of Vacancy of See (c. 61)
Rescripts Containing Privilege or Dispensation (c. 62)

Rescripts. The word *rescript* means a writing back. A rescript is a reply in writing from the Holy See or from another Ordinary, either granting some favor or dispensation, or giving a decision or information upon request. The effect of rescripts under the Code is limited to the parties concerned (c. 17, § 3).

Classification. Rescripts are divided as follows:

1. Rescripts of *justice* (concerning judicial controversies), of *favor* (granting some favor), and *mixed* rescripts (containing both elements).

2. Rescripts *according to law, contrary to law,* or *beside the law.*

3. Rescripts *in forma gratiosa* (granting a request directly), and *in forma commissoria* (committing the granting of the request to an intermediary or "executor"). The latter is further subdivided: it is *in forma commissoria libera* if the matter is left to the discretion of the executor; and *in forma commissoria necessaria,* if the executor is without discretionary power.

4. *Special* rescripts (limited to a certain case or person) and *general* rescripts (not so limited).

Form of Rescripts in Practice. The only way to determine what kind of rescript one is dealing with, in what form it is, etc., is to read the rescript carefully. It will be useful, however, to have in advance a general knowledge of the practice of the Holy See and of the Bishops in granting various rescripts. In general, rescripts affecting the *internal* forum are given *in forma commissoria,* the confessor being the executor. Rescripts for the *external* forum, from the Holy See, are also usually *in forma commissoria.* An exception to this rule is the rescript granting the dissolution of a nonconsummated marriage; this comes *in forma gratiosa,* but must be presented to the Ordinary.[46] Rescripts for the *external* forum, from Ordinaries, are usually *in forma gratiosa.*

Who May Petition for Rescripts? **Canon 36** answers: all who are not prohibited. This answer must be explained in the light of many other provisions of law.

1. Persons under censure are declared capable, with four exceptions; namely: an excommunicated person who is *vitandus,* a person who has

---

[46] Cf. S. C. Sacr., 7 May, 1923, n. 102; *AAS,* 15–389; *Digest,* I, p. 791.

been *declared* or *condemned* as excommunicated (c. 2265, § 2), or as under a *personal interdict* (c. 2275, 3°), or suspension (c. 2283).

2. Heretics and schismatics are theoretically capable of obtaining a rescript unless they are *notoriously* members of such a sect.[47]

For Another. A rescript may be obtained for another, even without his consent; and, though the latter is not obliged to make use of the favor granted by the rescript, the rescript is nevertheless valid even before his acceptance thereof, unless the contrary appear from its clauses **(c. 37).**

Date When Effective. Rescripts by which a favor is granted without the intervention of an executor, are effective from the moment when the letter was issued; other rescripts are effective from the time of their execution **(c. 38).**

Conditions in rescripts are regarded as essential to their validity only when they are expressed by the particles, *si, dummodo,* or some other particle of the same meaning **(c. 39).**

Truth of Recitals. In all rescripts, the condition: *si preces veritate nitantur,* is to be understood even though it be not expressed, without prejudice to the provisions of canons 45, 1054 **(c. 40).** The condition, *si preces veritate nitantur,* means "provided that the recitals of the petition are true." Truth is therefore an essential condition for the validity of every rescript. This must, however, be understood in connection with canon 42, which states what degree of truth is regarded as essential. Canon 45, moreover, makes an exception in favor of rescripts granted with the clause, *motu proprio.* Canon 1054 provides that a dispensation from a minor matrimonial impediment, granted by rescript, is valid in spite of any concealment or falsehood in the petition.

Moment When Recitals Must Be True. Since the circumstances may change, it is evidently important to determine at what precise moment the essential condition mentioned in canon 40, "provided that the recitals of the petition are true," must be verified. **Canon 41** states that the moment at which the recitals must be true is, for rescripts without an executor, the time when the rescript is given, for those with an executor, the time of their execution. In other words, the recitals of the petition must be true at the moment when, according to canon 38, the rescript becomes effective.

Effect of Omission and Falsehood. The withholding of truth, or

---

[47]Cappello, *Summa,* I, n. 143.

subreptio, in the recitals of the petition, does not prevent the rescript from being effective and valid, provided that what is required for validity according to the *stylus Curiae* has been expressed **(c. 42, § 1)**. Neither does *obreptio,* or the statement of falsehood, impair the effectiveness or validity of the rescript, provided that either the only reason proposed be true, or at least one motivating cause of several that are proposed be true **(c. 42, § 2)**. The defect of *obreptio* or *subreptio* occurring in only one part of a rescript does not impair another part thereof, in case several favors are granted together by the rescript **(c. 42, § 3)**. This canon states *what degree of truth* is essential in the petition. It modifies canon 40, which makes truth an implied essential condition of every rescript.

The *stylus Curiae,* as explained under canon 20, means the rules established by precedent in the procedure of the Roman Curia.

A *motivating* reason, as distinguished from a merely *persuasive* one, is a reason which moves the superior to grant the favor.

Favors Previously Refused. A favor which has been refused by one Sacred Congregation or Office of the Roman Curia cannot be validly granted by another Sacred Congregation or Office, nor by the Ordinary of the place, even though he have the power, unless the consent of the Sacred Congregation or Office with which the matter was first taken up be obtained, without prejudice to the right of the Sacred Penitentiary as regards the internal forum **(c. 43)**.

No one shall ask of another Ordinary a favor which has been refused by his own Ordinary, without mentioning the fact of such refusal; and even if the fact of refusal be mentioned, the Ordinary shall not grant the favor without having learned from the first Ordinary the reasons for his refusal **(c. 44, § 1)**.

A favor which has been refused by the Vicar General, and afterward, without mention of such refusal, has been obtained from the Bishop, is invalid; and a favor which has been refused by the Bishop cannot thereafter be validly obtained from the Vicar General without the Bishop's consent, even though the former refusal of the Bishop were mentioned **(c. 44, § 2)**.

Effect of Clause *Motu Proprio*. Whenever the clause, *motu proprio,* is appended to rescripts which are granted upon any one's petition, these are valid even though in the petition some truth which otherwise must necessarily be expressed is withheld; but they are not valid if their final cause, and the only one proposed, be false, without prejudice to the provision of canon 1054 **(c. 45)**. The clause, *motu proprio,* added to a rescript, therefore, strengthens it to this extent, that no *subreptio,* or omission of otherwise necessary recitals, will then impair it. But the clause does not protect the rescript from the effect of essential falsehood, or *obreptio,* according to canon 42, § 2. The usual exception in favor of a rescript granting a dispensation from a minor matrimonial impediment (c. 1054) is again provided for.

Invalid Rescripts. Rescripts, even with the clause, *motu proprio,* granted to a person who according to the common law is incapable of obtaining the favor in question, also such rescripts issued in contravention of a legitimate local custom or particular law, or against a right already acquired by another person, are not sustained unless an express derogatory clause be appended to the rescript **(c. 46)**.

Error. Rescripts are not invalidated by error in the name of the person to whom or by whom they are granted, nor in the name of the place in which the person lives, nor of the subject matter of the rescript, provided that, in the judgment of the Ordinary, there be no doubt regarding the person nor regarding the matter **(c. 47)**.

Contradictions. If it happens that two contradictory rescripts are obtained in regard to one and the same thing, the particular one prevails over the general, as regards those things which are expressed in particular **(c. 48, § 1)**. If the two rescripts are equally particular or equally general, the one which is first in order of time prevails over the later, unless the later one contains express mention of the earlier, or unless the first grantee failed to use his rescript through guile or notable negligence **(c. 48, § 2)**. In case the rescripts were issued on the same day and it does not appear which of the grantees is prior, both rescripts are void, and if the occasion warrants a new recourse must be made to the one who gave the rescripts **(c. 48, § 3)**.

Interpretation. Rescripts are to be understood according to the proper meaning of the words and common usage, and are not to be extended to other cases than those expressed in them **(c. 49)**.

In case of *doubt,* rescripts which concern litigation, or which impair rights vested in other persons, or which contravene the law in the interest of private parties, or finally which were obtained for the purpose of securing an ecclesiastical benefice, are interpreted strictly; all others, broadly **(c. 50)**.

Presentation. A rescript of the Holy See in which there is no executor need be presented to the Ordinary only when that is required in the rescript itself, or when public matters are involved, or when it is necessary to prove certain conditions **(c. 51)**.

Rescripts for whose presentation no time is prescribed may be presented to the executor at any time, provided there is no fraud or deception (c. 52).

Execution. The executor of a rescript performs that function invalidly before he has received the rescript and has satisfied himself of its authenticity and integrity, unless advance information of the rescript has been sent him by authority of the grantor (c. 53).

If a rescript merely commits to the executor the task of executing it, such execution cannot be refused unless it is clearly evident that the rescript is void for concealment or falsehood, or unless it is clear to the executor that conditions appended to the rescript have not been fulfilled, or unless the person who obtained the rescript appears, in the judgment of the executor, so unworthy of the favor that its concession would be a cause of offense to others; in the case last mentioned the executor, without executing the rescript, shall immediately notify the grantor (c. 54, § 1).

If a rescript commits to the executor the granting of the favor, he must use his prudent and conscientious discretion in granting or refusing it (c. 54, § 2).

The executor must proceed according to his instructions, and unless he fulfills the essential conditions mentioned in the rescript and follows substantially the proper form of procedure, the execution is invalid (c. 55).

The execution of rescripts which concern the external forum is to be made in writing (c. 56).

The executor of rescripts may in his prudent discretion substitute another person for himself, unless such substitution is prohibited or limited to certain persons (c. 57, § 1). But if the executor has been chosen for his personal qualifications, he may commit to another only the steps preliminary to the execution (c. 57, § 2).

All rescripts can be executed by the executor's successor in the dignity or office, unless the executor was chosen for his personal qualifications (c. 58).

In case the executor has made any mistake in the execution of rescripts, he may execute the same a second time (c. 59, § 1). As regards taxes for the execution of rescripts, let the prescription of canon 1507, § 1, be observed (c. 59, § 2).

Note that a mistake in execution, even an essential mistake such as renders the *execution* invalid and ineffective, does not invalidate the *rescript itself*. Hence the remedy is to execute the same rescript a second time.

Canon 1507, § 1, provides that a uniform schedule of taxes for the execution of papal rescripts must be drawn up for the entire ecclesiastical province, by the provincial Council or the assembly of Bishops.

Revocation. A rescript which has been revoked by a special act of the superior remains valid until the revocation has been made known to the person who obtained the rescript **(c. 60, § 1).**

Rescripts are never revoked by a contrary law, unless the law itself so provides, or unless the law is passed by the Superior of the grantor of the rescript **(c. 60, § 2).**

Vacancy of See. A rescript of the Holy See or of an Ordinary is not invalidated by the vacancy of the Holy See or of the diocese, unless the clauses appended to the rescript so provide, or unless the rescript confers upon someone the power to grant a favor to definite persons named therein, and the matter is still uncompromised **(c. 61).**

If a rescript contains a privilege or dispensation instead of a simple favor, the prescriptions of canons 63–86 are moreover to be observed **(c. 62).**

CASES AND QUESTIONS

1. What is a rescript?

2. Explain the terms: *in forma gratiosa; in forma commissoria;* free execution; necessary execution.

3. How can one tell what kind of rescript one has?

4. In what form are rescripts usually given: (*a*) for the interior forum? (*b*) for the exterior forum, by the Holy See? (*c*) for the exterior forum by the Ordinaries?

5. State the practical consequences of the form in which a rescript is given: (*a*) as regards the time when the rescript takes effect (c. 38); (*b*) as regards the time at which the recitals of the petition must be true (c. 41); (*c*) as regards the necessity of waiting until the rescript, or official notice of the same, is received (c. 53); (*d*) as regards the necessity of presenting the rescript (c. 51).

6. In general, when is the fulfillment of any required condition in a rescript, necessary for its validity? (Cc. 39, 40).

7. Explain the meaning and effect of the condition, *si preces veritate nitantur* (cc. 40, 42). How is this clause modified by the presence of the clause, *motu proprio*? (C. 45). What is its effect upon rescripts granting a dispensation from a minor matrimonial impediment? (C. 1054).

8. Explain the terms, *subreptio, obreptio, causa motiva* (c. 42).

9. When is the execution of a rescript invalid? (Cc. 53, 55). What is the effect of an invalid execution? (Cc. 59, 38). How can it be cured?

10. When does the express revocation of a rescript take effect? (C. 60).

11. Are rescripts revoked: (*a*) by laws contrary thereto? (C. 60); (*b*) by the vacancy of the see which granted the rescript? (C. 61).

12. Must the execution of rescripts be in writing? When is this required by law? Is it then required for the validity of the rescript? For the validity of the execution? (C. 56, 11).

Readings:

O'Neill, *Papal Rescripts of Favor,* Catholic University, 1930 (n. 57).

Section 6. Privileges (cc. 63–79)

PRELIMINARY SURVEY

Manner of Acquiring Privileges (c. 63)
Communication of Privileges (cc. 64, 65)
Habitual Faculties (c. 66)
Interpretation (cc. 67, 68)
No Obligation to Use Privileges (c. 69)
Presumption of Perpetuity (c. 70)
Revocation (c. 71)
Renunciation (c. 72)
Expiration (c. 73)
Cessation of Privileges (cc. 74–77)
Deprivation of Privileges (c. 78)
Privileges Granted Orally (c. 79)

Definition and Division of Privilege. Privilege in the broad sense means some special provision of the common law which gives special rights to certain persons; such as the privileges of clerics (cc. 119–123), of Cardinals (c. 239), of Bishops (c. 349), etc. *In the strict sense,* privilege means a special disposition lawfully made by competent authority granting to some person or persons a right which is contrary to or beyond the common law. Taken either in the broad or in the strict sense, a privilege may be considered under two aspects, objectively and subjectively. Objectively, it is the disposition of lawful authority which creates a special right; subjectively, it is the special right thus created. The Code, in canons 63–79, is dealing with privilege *in the strict sense* considered *both* as an *objective grant* and as a *subjective right* created thereby. Privileges in the strict sense are classified in a number of ways, of which the principal ones are:

1. With regard to the relation which its object bears to the common law, a privilege is either *beside the law* or *contrary to law*.

2. With regard to its immediate subject, it is *personal,* if granted immediately to a person or persons; *real* if granted to a thing; *local* if granted to a place. Real privileges include local ones. Strictly speaking, a right can reside only in persons; hence, even real and local privileges become operative only when they redound to the benefit of a person. The point of the classification is that these privileges do this only indirectly, that is, through the thing or place to which the privilege is attached; whereas personal privileges confer rights on persons directly.

3. With regard to its effect upon the rights of other persons, it is *merely favorable* if it confers a favor which involves no burden or disadvantage to others; *odious,* if it places a burden on others or contravenes a right granted them by the common law.

4. With regard to the motive of the grant, a privilege is *gratuitous* if granted through pure liberality; *remuneratory* if given as a reward; *onerous* if it imposes obligations upon the grantee.

5. With regard to the manner in which it is acquired, a privilege is *by direct grant* in the person to whom it is directly given; *by communication* in those to whom it is communicated (cf. c. 64); *by custom* if acquired through custom; *by prescription* if acquired by prescription.

Further obvious divisions of privileges are: *positive* and *negative, absolute* and *conditional, written* and *unwritten,* etc.

General Principles. 1. The methods of acquiring privileges are: direct grant by the competent authority, communication, legitimate custom, and prescription **(c. 63, § 1).**

2. A direct grant is presumed from a possession which has endured for a hundred years or from time immemorial **(c. 63, § 2).** This is a presumption of law, which yields to contrary evidence (c. 1826).

Methods of Acquiring Privileges. 1. A privilege may be acquired by *direct grant* from the competent authority; that is, from the ecclesiastical superior who has legislative power in the matter of the privilege over the person to whom it is granted, if the privilege is contrary to law, or over other persons whose rights it may affect, if the privilege is beside the law.

2. *Communication* means an act of competent ecclesiastical authority extending to certain persons privileges which have already been granted to others. This may be done by general law or by particular acts. In either case the privilege may be communicated in two forms:

in forma accessoria, and *in forma aeque principali.* In the former case the privilege in the new grantee is and remains accessory to the original privilege, in this sense, that it will increase, diminish, or cease entirely in the new grantee if and when such changes of the privilege occur in the original grantee. If the communication is *in forma aeque principali* it is and remains independent of any changes which may affect the same privilege in the original grantee. The form of a privilege must be determined from its terms. Thus Pius V, by the Constitution, *Ex supernae,* of 16 Aug., 1567, extended or communicated *in forma aeque principali,* to all religious orders of regulars, the privileges which had theretofore been granted to any of them.[48] *Future* communications of privileges between religious orders is prohibited by canon 613; and communication is further restricted by canon 64.[49]

3. *Lawful custom,* since it has the force of law, may confer a privilege.

4. *Prescription* as a means of acquiring rights has been briefly explained under canon 27 in connection with custom. It is governed by canons 1508–1512. Upon fulfillment of the requisite conditions; namely, provided the matter concerned is capable of prescription, and that possession be maintained continuously, in good faith, and for the time required by law, prescription may give rise to a privilege.

Communication of Privilege. By the communication of privileges even *in forma aeque principali,* only such privileges are conferred as had been granted to the first grantee directly, perpetually, and without special relation to any certain place, or thing, or person; and moreover the capacity of the person to whom the communication is made must be taken into account **(c. 64).** Cf. Matulenas, *Communication, a Source of Privileges,* Catholic University, 1943.

When privileges are acquired by communication *in forma accessoria,* they are *ipso facto* increased, diminished, or lost, whenever they increase, diminish, or cease to exist in the first possessor of the privilege; this is not the case when privileges are acquired by communication *in forma aeque principali* **(c. 65).**

Faculties. Habitual faculties granted perpetually, or for a definite time, or for a certain number of cases, are considered as privileges beside the law **(c. 66, § 1).**

Unless the grantee has been chosen for his personal qualifications, or express provision to the contrary has been made, habitual faculties

---

[48] Cf. *Fontes,* n. 122, I, p. 220.
[49] Cf. Code Com., 30 Dec., 1937; *AAS,* 30–73; *Digest,* II, p. 172.

granted by the Holy See to a Bishop or to the other persons mentioned in canon 198, § 1, do not expire with the expiration of the authority of the Ordinary to whom they were granted, even though he has begun to make use of them, but they pass to the Ordinary who succeeds him in the government; likewise such faculties granted to the Bishop belong also to the Vicar General (c. 66, § 2).

The grant of a faculty carries with it also other powers which are necessary for its use; hence the faculty to dispense includes also the power to absolve from ecclesiastical penalties, if there are any that stand in the way, but only for the purpose of getting the dispensation (c. 66, § 3).

The practical application of these provisions to the quinquennial faculties of Bishops is important.[50] These quinquennial faculties are habitual; as privileges beside the law, they receive a broad interpretation; in the absence of express limitation, they may be used not only by the Bishop but by the Vicar General; they do not expire when the see becomes vacant, but pass even to the Bishop's temporary successor.

Interpretation. A privilege is to be interpreted according to its tenor, and may not be extended or restricted (c. 67).

In case of *doubt,* privileges are to be interpreted according to the rule of canon 50; but the interpretation must always be such that the persons who have the privilege may receive some favor from the benevolence of the grantor (c. 68).

Various Provisions. No one is obliged to use a privilege which was granted exclusively in his favor, unless there is an obligation to do so on some other ground (c. 69).

A privilege is to be regarded as perpetual unless the contrary appear (c. 70).

Privileges contained in the Code are revoked by a general law; as regards other privileges, the prescription of canon 60 is to be observed (c. 71).

Privileges cease by renunciation which has been accepted by the competent superior (c. 72, § 1).

Any private person can renounce a privilege which is established in his favor exclusively (c. 72, § 2).

---

[50] For the formula, 1939–1944, see *Digest,* II, p. 30. For the latest formula of faculties from the Holy Office, cf. *The Jurist,* Vol. 6, p. 535. For the new triennial faculty to dispense night workers from the Eucharistic fast on certain conditions, cf. *The Jurist,* Vol. 6, p. 538. For the new triennial faculty to dispense hospitalized patients so that they may take drink and medicine before Communion, cf. *The Jurist,* Vol. 6, p. 423.

If a privilege is granted to a community, a dignity, or a place, private persons may not renounce it (c. 72, § 3).

Even the community itself, or the group, is not free to renounce a privilege if it was granted by way of law or if the renunciation would work harm to the Church or to other persons (c. 72, § 4).

Privileges do not lapse with the expiration of the authority of the grantor, unless they were granted with the clause, *ad beneplacitum nostrum*, or some other equivalent one (c. 73).

A personal privilege follows the person and expires with the person (c. 74).

Real privileges cease upon the absolute destruction of the thing or place; but local privileges revive if the place is restored within fifty years (c. 75).

Privileges which are not burdensome to others do not lapse through non-use or through contrary use; but those which impose a burden on other persons do lapse if legitimate prescription or tacit renunciation takes place (c. 76).

A privilege also ceases if in the course of time circumstances have so changed that, in the judgment of the superior, the privilege has become harmful, or its use has become illicit; it ceases likewise by the lapse of time or the completion of the number of cases for which it was granted, without prejudice to the provision of canon 207, § 2 (c. 77). The exception provided for in canon 207, § 2, is in favor of the internal forum; namely, when faculties of jurisdiction for the internal forum have been granted, and acts of such jurisdiction are performed *by inadvertence* after the time has expired or the number of cases for which the faculties were given is exhausted, such acts are nevertheless valid.

One who abuses a power which has been granted to him by privilege deserves to be deprived of the privilege itself; and if any one gravely abuses any privilege granted by the Holy See, the Ordinary must not fail to notify the Holy See of the fact (c. 78).

Although privileges which have been obtained orally from the Holy See may be used by the petitioner in the forum of conscience, yet no one can claim the use of any privilege against any person in the external forum, unless he is able to furnish legal proof that the privilege was granted to him (c. 79). In this connection one of the privileges of Cardinals may be recalled. In virtue of canon 239, § 1, 17°, they can by their bare word sustain even in the external forum the fact of an oral grant made by the Holy Father.

Section 7. Dispensations (cc. 80–86)

PRELIMINARY SURVEY

Definition and Source of Dispensation (c. 80)
Dispensing Power of Ordinaries of Places (cc. 81, 82)
Dispensing Power of Pastors (c. 83)
Necessity of Reasonable Cause for Dispensation (c. 84)
Interpretation (c. 85)
Cessation of Current Dispensation (c. 86)

General Principle. He who makes the law can dispense from the law; as can also his successor or superior, and any person to whom any of these may give the faculty (cf. c. 80).

The *maker of the law,* or legislator is:

1. For the universal Church, and for any particular territory in which the law has been enacted directly by the Holy See (cf. c. 82) the Pope, who acts through the various departments of the Roman Curia (cc. 218, 227, 244);

2. For several provinces, the plenary council (c. 281);

3. For a single province, the provincial council (cc. 283, 291);

4. For a diocese, the Bishop in the synod or out of it (c. 335);

5. For a vacant see, the Vicar Capitular (cc. 431, 432); or, where chapters do not exist, as in the United States, the Administrator appointed by the diocesan consultors (c. 427).

Dispensing Power of Ordinaries. Canon 81 contains an important grant of power to *Ordinaries* (cf. c. 198); namely, to dispense from *general laws* of the Church in cases where three conditions occur together, to wit: (1) recourse to the Holy See to obtain the faculty is difficult; (2) the delay occasioned by such recourse will *probably* result in grave damage; (3) the dispensation is one which the Holy See not only can but usually does grant.

1. *Recourse* to the Holy See is regarded as *difficult* if for any reason without fraud and deceit it involves grave inconvenience.

a. It is difficulty of recourse *to the Holy See itself* that is considered. This may exist though it might be easy to have recourse to the Apostolic Delegate *as such,* or to someone else who has the faculties. See, however, the letter of the Most Reverend Apostolic Delegate of 1 Jan., 1942, *Digest,* II, p. 44.

b. The difficulty concerns *ordinary means* of recourse, e.g., by mail.

Recourse by telegraph, telephone, rail or air travel, is not considered, these being extraordinary means of communication for this purpose.

c. The difficulty need not amount to *moral impossibility*. It may depend upon the distance, the time required for an answer, the scarcity of opportunity for communication by mail, etc.

2. *Danger of grave harm in delay* exists when, everything considered, a probable danger of grave harm is prudently feared. The harm may be private or public, physical or moral, or economic and financial. It must be grave, but need not be extreme nor very grave. It is left to the prudent discretion of the Ordinary to decide whether such danger exists. If the necessity arises after the dispensation has been asked of the Holy See, the power of canon 81 may still be used, but the Holy See should then be notified (c. 204, §§ 1 and 2).

3. Dispensations which are *usually granted* by the Holy See must be known from the law and the practice of the Roman Curia.

a. The Holy See *does not dispense* from sacred orders in the case of Bishops, nor from consanguinity where there is doubt whether it is of the first degree in the collateral line (c. 1076, § 3), nor from the impediment of crime when notorious and involving murder.

b. The Holy See dispenses *only for the gravest reasons* from other major orders; *most rarely and with great difficulty* from affinity in the direct line when the marriage was consummated (cf. c. 1043), and from the impediments of want of age and abduction; only *for just and proportionate reasons* (hence not *usually*) from consanguinity in the second degree mixed with the first.

Ordinaries include major superiors of *clerical exempt religious* institutes in regard to provisions of the general law which may be embodied in the constitutions, but not in regard to provisions peculiar to the institute and approved by the Holy See. In the latter case the dispensing power of the superior depends on the constitutions of the order.

Dispensing Power of Ordinaries of Places. Bishops and other Ordinaries of places can dispense in diocesan laws, and in laws of a provincial and plenary council according to canon 291, § 2; not, however, in laws which the Roman Pontiff has specially enacted for that particular territory, except in accordance with canon 81 **(c. 82).**

Combining the provisions of canons 15, 81, 82 with certain others, we may now present a complete synopsis of the dispensing power of *Ordinaries of places* (cf. c. 198, § 2).

1. In *diocesan* laws, the power of Ordinaries of places is complete and generally unrestricted (c. 82). A just cause is required for *licitness* (c. 84) in all cases, and for *validity* if the dispensing Ordinary is inferior to the legislator of the law in question; e.g., a Vicar General (c. 366).

2. In laws of a *provincial or plenary Council,* they can dispense only as provided in canon 291, § 2; that is, in particular cases and for just cause (c. 82). The just cause is required for validity, since the individual Bishop or other Ordinary is inferior to the council which made the law (c. 84).

3. In *general laws* of the Church, or in laws for a particular place *enacted by the Roman Pontiff,* Ordinaries of places may have the power to dispense given them: (*a*) in the Code itself; the power is then one of ordinary jurisdiction (c. 197), or (*b*) in special faculties; the power is then one of delegated jurisdiction.

a. In the Code itself, Ordinaries of places are given the following power to dispense:

1) Where the conditions mentioned in canon 15 concur; namely: there is a doubt of fact affecting the application of the law, and the law is one from which the Holy See usually dispenses.

2) Where the conditions of canon 81 concur; namely, (*a*) difficulty of recourse; (*b*) danger in delay; and (*c*) a law which is usually dispensed from by the Holy See.

3) From the observance of feasts, fasts, and abstinence, they may dispense individuals or families subject to them; that is, their own subjects even outside the diocese and others within it; and in case of a peculiar great concourse of people or for reasons of public health, they may dispense the entire diocese from fast and abstinence (c. 1245).

4) From nonreserved vows, in accordance with canon 1313.

5) From promissory oaths, in accordance with canon 1320.

6) From the observance of the legal intervals between ordinations, as provided in canon 978.

7) From the banns of marriage, as provided in canon 1028.

8) From the form of marriage and certain marriage impediments, in danger of death and in urgent cases, as provided in canons 1043, 1045.

9) From irregularities, according to canon 990.

10) From certain penalties, according to canon 2237.

11) From the law prohibiting books, only as provided in canon 1402; that is, for certain books, in urgent cases.

12) From the examination required of a candidate for a parish, as provided in canon 459.

b. Special faculties include the regular quinquennial faculties.[51] and any special indults which may be extant.

Pastors can dispense neither from the general nor from the particular law, unless this power has been expressly given them **(c. 83)**.

Dispensing Power of Pastors. *From the Code,* pastors have the power to dispense:

1. From the observance of feasts, fasts, and abstinence, in accordance with canon 1245, § 1; that is, in the case of individuals or families within the parish, or their own subjects anywhere.

2. In marriage: (*a*) for both occult and public cases, when the Ordinary cannot be reached and there is danger of death, according to canon 1044; (*b*) for occult cases only, when the impediment is discovered when all is ready for the marriage and the Ordinary cannot be reached at all, or not without danger of violating the secret, according to canon 1045.

The power given to pastors by the Code (c. 899, § 3) to *absolve* during Paschal time from diocesan reserved cases, is not a power to *dispense.*

From the diocesan pagella, pastors as such sometimes receive special faculties. For example, in the Archdiocese of Chicago pastors have received power to dispense from one publication of the banns of marriage.

Powers of Confessors.[52] 1. *From the Code:*

a. To commute works for gaining indulgences (c. 935).

b. To dispense from irregularities *ex delicto occulto* except those resulting from homicide or abortion, but only in urgent occult cases where the Ordinary cannot be reached and there is danger of grave harm or infamy, and only for the purpose of enabling the penitent to exercise orders already received (c. 990).

c. To suspend the obligation of observing a vindictive penalty *latae sententiae,* under the conditions of canon 2290; that is:

1) In urgent occult cases where the observance of the penalty would expose the penitent to infamy and scandal;

2) The faculty must be exercised in the sacramental forum;

3) The penitent must be enjoined to have recourse within a month

---

[51] See *Digest,* II, p. 30, and note 50, this chapter.
[52] Though not all of these are strictly dispensing powers, they are grouped here for convenience.

to the Sacred Penitentiary or to a Bishop endowed with the faculty to deal with the case, and to abide by their instructions.

d. In an extraordinary case, where the recourse mentioned under *c* is impossible, to dispense entirely from the penalty in accordance with canon 2254, § 3; that is, enjoining a special penance which the penitent must perform within the prescribed time under pain of losing the benefit of the dispensation.

e. To dispense from certain marriage impediments under special circumstances and conditions (cc. 1044, 1045).

f. To absolve from censures in urgent cases (c. 2254).

2. *From the diocesan pagella,* confessors may also receive certain powers. For example, in the Archdiocese of Chicago, all approved confessors have power to dispense from the observance of feasts, fast, and abstinence, in the internal sacramental forum; also, in the parish or church where the Forty Hours' devotions or the services of a mission are going on, to absolve, during such devotions or mission, from all censures which are reserved to the Ordinary.

Confessors who are members of regular orders have by privilege the faculty to dispense from nonreserved, and sometimes even from reserved private vows, and to absolve from censures reserved by common law to the Ordinary.

As regards all these faculties of confessors, when it is not stated that they must be used in confession, they may be used out of confession (c. 202, § 2), but always in favor of their penitents. Anyone whom a confessor has here and now the power to hear and absolve is his penitent.[53]

Simple Priests have certain powers under canons 882, 1098, 1044, and 1045.

Just Cause. A dispensation from the ecclesiastical law should not be given without just and reasonable cause, taking into consideration the gravity of the law from which the dispensation is given; otherwise the dispensation, if given by an inferior, is both illicit and invalid (c. 84, § 1).

In doubt as to the sufficiency of the reason, it is allowed to ask for a dispensation, and it can be licitly and validly granted (c. 84, § 2).

A just cause is always required for a dispensation; but the question is: will the entire and certain absence of a just cause render the dispensation *invalid* as well as illicit. It will, if the dispensation is

---

[53] See V-C, *Epit.*, I, n. 194.

given by an *inferior*. An inferior is one who, though he has the power to dispense, is inferior to the maker of the law from which he dispenses. Such, for example, is the Vicar General with regard to diocesan laws, the Bishop or Metropolitan with regard to laws of a provincial or plenary council.

Interpretation. Not only the dispensation itself, according to canon 50, but also the faculty to dispense, if granted for a certain case, is subject to a strict interpretation (**c. 85**). As regards the quinquennial faculties of Bishops, recall the rule stated under canon 66. Even when granted for a limited number of cases, they are habitual faculties, and enjoy a broad interpretation. But a grant of the faculty to dispense in a single case must be strictly interpreted.

Cessation of Dispensation. A dispensation which is capable of successive applications expires in the same way as does a privilege (cf. cc. 71–78), and also by the certain and entire cessation of the motivating reason for which it was granted (**c. 86**).

Examples. A dispensation from fasting or from reciting the Breviary is therefore good only as long as the cause for which it was given continues to exist. It is commonly supposed that a dispensation from fasting "is good for the whole year." This is true provided the chief and sufficient reason in view of which the dispensation was given continues to exist throughout the year. But as soon as it is *certain* that this reason has *entirely* ceased, the dispensation ceases.

CASES AND QUESTIONS

Privileges. 1. Define privilege in the strict sense; in the broad sense. Explain the objective and subjective aspects of privilege.

2. What are the principal means of acquiring privileges? (C. 63).

3. What is meant by communication? Explain the effect of the two chief forms of communication (cc. 64, 65).

4. What rule is stated in the Code (c. 4) regarding the continuance of privileges which were in effect before?

5. What restrictions affect the communication of privileges in the future; that is, since the Code? (Cc. 64, 613).

6. Are the Bishop's quinquennial faculties regarded as privileges? Of what kind? What is the practical consequence of this classification? May faculties granted to Bishops be used by their Vicars General? Do they pass to the Bishop's successor? Even to the Administrator during the vacancy of the see? Do they lapse when the Holy See becomes vacant? (Cc. 61, 66, 73).

7. Is a privilege valid if it has been obtained orally from the Holy See? What are then the restrictions on its use? (C. 79).

Dispensations. 1. Define a dispensation. Who can grant it?

2. Who is the lawmaker: (*a*) for the Church; (*b*) for a group of ecclesiastical provinces; (*c*) for a single province; (*d*) for a diocese; (*e*) for a diocese during the vacancy of the see?

3. What two general powers of dispensing from the general laws of the Church are given to Ordinaries in the Code? (Cc. 15, 81).

4. Name some of the special powers of dispensing which are given to Ordinaries of places in the Code. What further powers to dispense from general laws do Bishops usually receive? Where are these to be found?

5. What power have Bishops to dispense from their own diocesan laws? From the laws of a provincial or plenary council? (C. 82).

6. What is the rule regarding the power of pastors to dispense from general laws? From particular laws? Name some special matters in which the Code gives them a limited power.

7. Have confessors, as such, any special powers given them in the Code? Name some of them.

8. What is the rule regarding the necessity for a just cause for a dispensation? Would a dispensation given without cause be valid: (*a*) if given from the general law, by the Supreme Pontiff; (*b*) from a diocesan law, by the Bishop; (*c*) from a diocesan law, by the Vicar General; (*d*) from a general law, by the Bishop; (*e*) from a law of the Third Plenary Council of Baltimore, by a Bishop in the United States? (C. 84).

9. When is a faculty to dispense to be interpreted strictly?

10. Why is a dispensation from fasting usually good for the whole year? Is this necessarily true? (C. 86).

Readings:

Roelker, *Principles of Privilege According to the Code of Canon Law,* Catholic University, 1926 (n. 35); Matulenas, *Communication: A Source of Privileges,* C.U. (n. 183); Motry, *Diocesan Faculties According to the Code of Canon Law,* C.U., 1922 (n. 16); Reilly, *The General Norms of Dispensation,* C.U., 1939 (n. 119), *The Clergy Review,* Vol. 10, p. 229 (dispensing powers of pastors); Vol. 6, p. 498 (Episcopal faculties); *Irish Ecclesiastical Record,* 1930, p. 295 (Kinane, on Bishop's power to dispense *peregrini*); *Australasian Catholic Record,* 1935, p. 162 (validity of dispensation when cause not known to exist); *The Jurist,* Vol. 2, p. 182 (means of communicating with the Holy See).

PART TWO: CLERICS

CHAPTER II

PERSONS AND CLERICS IN GENERAL

Section 1. Persons in General (cc. 87-107)

PRELIMINARY SURVEY

Physical Persons (cc. 87-98; 107)
The *Title* by Which a Person Is Constituted a Member
of the Church (c. 87)
Qualities Which Have Juridical Consequences (cc. 88-98)
Age, Use of Reason, Sex, Puberty (c. 88)
Subjection to Parental Control (c. 89)
Origin (c. 90)
Domicile, Quasi-domicile (cc. 91-95)
Consanguinity, Affinity (cc. 96, 97)
Rite (c. 98)
Classification of Physical Persons (c. 107)
Moral Persons (cc. 99-102; 105)
Definition and Classification (c. 99)
How Constituted (c. 100)
Requisites for Action (c. 101)
Duration (c. 102)
Consent or Consultation Required by Law (c. 105)
Acts of Physical and Moral Persons (cc. 103-106)
Force, Fear, Fraud (c. 103)
Error (c. 104)
Acts of a Superior (c. 105)
Precedence Among Persons (c. 106)

Persons as Members of the Church. A person in a juridical sense means a subject of rights; correlatively a person will also be the subject of duties. Rights and duties belong to persons as members of a

75

society. By creation all human beings are made members of human society, and have at least radically all the *natural rights* of human persons, independently of merit or personal qualifications. They are moreover capable of becoming members of other societies, and of acquiring thus a new juridical personality, that is, new rights and duties as members of these other societies. The Church is a society established by Jesus Christ with divine authority for all mankind. Hence human beings can become members of the Church, and as such they acquire a new juridical personality. Baptism of water has been established by Christ as the external sign and effective cause of membership in His Church. It is therefore the title by which a human person, already endowed by creation with natural rights, acquires a new personality juridically; that is, becomes the subject of new rights, and correspondingly also of new duties, as a member of the Church.

General Principle. Baptism of water constitutes a human being a person in the Church of Christ, with all the rights and duties of Christians **(c. 87).**

Exception. As regards the rights, two things impair their free exercise; namely, "an obstacle which impairs the bond of ecclesiastical communion, or a censure imposed by the Church" **(c. 87).**

1. *Obstacle.* A Christian can *voluntarily withdraw* from the visible communion which unites him with the other members of Christ's Church. By so doing he places an obstacle which impairs the bond of ecclesiastical communion; namely, heresy, or schism.

2. *Censure.* On the other hand, the Church, for certain grave crimes including heresy or schism, can *cut off the guilty person* from her external communion by pronouncing a censure against him. Censures, especially the most important of them, excommunications (c. 2257), will be explained in their place.

3. It is noteworthy that the canon declares these exceptions only as regards the *rights.* It would seem to follow that neither membership in a non-Catholic sect nor any censure directly excuses a Catholic from the *duties* which he has as a member of the Church. This is in fact the common general interpretation of this canon.

Questions. 1. Are heretics and schismatics generally bound by merely ecclesiastical laws? In general, yes. See discussion under canon 12.

2. Are non-Catholics subject to the matrimonial impediments of the Code? In general, they are; and this is confirmed by the practice of the Rota. Some canons, however, explicitly exempt non-Catholics;

e.g., canon 1070 on disparity of cult, canon 1099 on the form of marriage where both parties are non-Catholics.

3. Has a non-Catholic the privilege of acting as plaintiff in the ecclesiastical courts? Not as a rule, without special permission.[1] This rule applies also to apostates.[2]

4. Is an excommunicated person bound to hear Mass on Sundays and holydays? The old authors answered in the negative because as they said, an excommunicated person is forbidden to assist at divine services, and hence cannot be bound thereto.[3] Even before the Code, however, several noted authors denied that an excommunicated person is *forbidden* to hear Mass.[4] The Code seems to confirm this view (cf. c. 2259, §1: *caret iure assistendi*).[5] Yet, since the obligation is doubtful, it cannot be urged under pain of sin. It is commonly admitted that an excommunicated person sins mortally if, without sufficient excuse, he fails to seek absolution from his censure and so remains culpably excluded from annual confession and Paschal Communion.

Classification of Persons as to Age. A person who has completed the twenty-first year of age is a major; under that age, a minor (c. 88, §1).

A minor male is regarded as having attained puberty from the completion of the fourteenth year, a female from the completion of the twelfth (c. 88, §2).

A person before puberty who has not yet completed the seventh year is called an infant, a child, or a little one, and is regarded as incompetent; after the completion of the seventh year, however, he is presumed to have the use of reason. All persons who are habitually without the use of reason are juridically in the same class as infants (c. 88, §3).

Whereas the term *infant,* in American law, is usually equivalent to *minor,* designating all persons before the age of majority, in canon law it means only a person *before the age of reason.* The age of majority in civil law, varying in different States, is sometimes the same for males and females, sometimes different. In canon law it is invariably twenty-one for males and females alike. The presumption that

[1] Cf. Holy Office, 27 Jan., 1928; *AAS*, 20–75; *Digest*, I, p. 762; 22 March, 1939; *AAS*, 31–131; *Digest*, II, p. 533.

[2] Cf. Holy Office, 27 Feb., 1937; *Digest*, II, p. 530; 15 Jan., 1940; *AAS*, 32–52; *Digest*, II, p. 534.

[3] Cf. Cappello, *De Censuris*, n. 108.

[4] Cf. D'Annibale, *Summula*, I, p. 362, note 12.

[5] Cf. also Hyland, *Excommunication*, Cath. U. Canon Law Studies, 1928.

the use of reason has been attained at seven is rebuttable by evidence, which may show that it has been attained earlier or not until a later age.

Rights of Minors. A major person has the full exercise of his rights; a minor in the exercise of his rights remains subject to the power of his parents or guardians, except as regards those matters in which the law frees minors from parental control **(c. 89).**

Even minors, since they are human persons, have human rights, and if they are baptized they have also the rights of members of the Church. However, the exercise of these rights is to some extent restricted by parental control. Certain rights are by the natural law, independent of parental control, for example, the right to embrace the true religion. The canon presupposes these truths on the general principle that the natural law is not subject to change by canonical legislation. But, where the full and free exercise of rights is not guaranteed to minors by the natural or divine law, the canon law may declare them subject to parental control, and does so declare by this canon, except as regards certain specified matters.

Exceptions. Exceptions to this general principle are made either explicitly or implicitly in other parts of the Code.

1. Explicitly. Minors after puberty may freely choose a church for their funeral services and a place of sepulture (c. 1223, § 2); and after the age of reason they may, without the consent of their parents, act as parties in spiritual causes (c. 1648, § 3).

2. Implicitly, the Code exempts minors from parental control by the canons which declare the conditions for first tonsure or for entrance into a religious novitiate, without requiring parental consent (cc. 976, § 1, 555, § 1).

Puberty. 1. *Formerly* persons before puberty were forbidden to enter religion (cf. now c. 555), and could not validly marry (cf. now c. 1067, § 1).

2. *Under the Code* the effects of puberty are chiefly concerned with capacity to incur irregularities (c. 994, § 1), free choice of place of funeral services and sepulture (c. 1223, § 2), and capacity to incur penalties *latae sententiae* (c. 2230).[6]

Origin means the juridical relation of a person to the place where he is regarded as having originated. It has certain consequences on the competency of the Bishop for ordination (c. 956) and of the pastor for solemn baptism (cc. 462, 738). The rules stated by **canon 90** are

---

[6] Cf. Michiels, *De Personis*, pp. 37, 38.

declared applicable even to neophytes. This special mention emphasizes the change made by the Code; before the Code it was the place of baptism alone which determined the origin of a person.

Principles. 1. If the child is neither illegitimate nor posthumous, his origin is the place where his *father* had a domicile or quasi-domicile (cf. cc. 91–93) at the time of his birth (**cf. c. 90, § 1**).

2. If the child is illegitimate or posthumous, his origin is the place where his *mother* had a domicile or quasi-domicile at the time of his birth (**cf. c. 90, § 1**).

3. If neither father nor mother had at that time a domicile or quasi-domicile, he is *filius vagorum,* and his origin is the place of his birth (**cf. c. 90, § 2**).

4. If only the father is a *vagus* (cf. c. 91), whereas the mother has a domicile or quasi-domicile, and the child is neither illegitimate nor posthumous, it seems that the mother's domicile or quasi-domicile determines his origin, just as it does under rule 2 in the case of all illegitimate or posthumous children.

5. If only the mother is a *vaga,* and the child is illegitimate or posthumous, it seems reasonable to consider the child as *filius vagorum.* Hence his origin will again be the place of his birth (cf. c. 90, § 2).

6. The origin of a foundling is the place where he is found (**cf. c. 90, § 2**). Since this rule seems to be merely a last resort, it is probable that if the parents or either of them acknowledge the child, rules 1 to 5 should be applied in preference to rule 6.[7]

Classification of Persons as to Residence. A person is called an *incola* in the place where he has a domicile; an *advena* in the place where he has a quasi-domicile; a *peregrinus* (stranger) if he is outside the place of the domicile or quasi-domicile which he still retains; a *vagus* (vagrant) if he has neither domicile nor quasi-domicile anywhere (c. 91).

We retain the terms *incola* and *advena* because it seems impossible to find really equivalent terms in English. *Peregrinus* and *vagus* may be rendered by stranger and vagrant respectively provided the technical meaning is understood.

Domicile and Quasi-domicile. *Domicile* has the general meaning of a more or less settled and permanent place of residence. In law, strictly speaking, it refers less to the place than to the juridical status of the person which arises from his relation to the place. The degree

---

[7] Cf. V-C, *Epit.*, I, n. 210.

of permanence required is further specified by law. *Quasi-domicile* is slightly less permanent and settled than domicile.

There are two important classifications of domicile.

1. It is *voluntary* if acquired by voluntary choice of a place of residence or by actual residence (c. 92); it is *necessary* or *legal* if imposed by law (c. 93).

2. It is *parochial* if acquired within a parish or quasi-parish (cf. c. 216, § 3); it is *diocesan* if acquired within a diocese, vicariate, or prefecture (cf. c. 293, § 1), but not within a parish or quasi-parish (c. 92, § 3). The latter case supposes that all the conditions for acquiring a domicile are not fulfilled as regards any one parish or quasi-parish, but are fulfilled as regards the larger territory.

The above divisions apply equally to quasi-domicile, except that it is disputed whether *legal quasi-domicile* (cf. c. 93) is imposed by law as legal domicile is. The present canon applies only to *voluntary* domicile and quasi-domicile.

Principles. *Domicile* may be acquired in two ways: (1) by staying in the place (parish, diocese, etc.) with the intention of remaining permanently unless called away: and (2) by a stay which is actually protracted to fully ten years **(c. 92, § 1)**.

Quasi-domicile, likewise may be acquired in two ways: (1) by staying in the place with the intention of remaining beyond six months unless called away; and (2) by a stay which is actually protracted beyond six months **(c. 92, § 2)**.

Questions. 1. What is meant by "staying" in a place? Is it the same as merely being present? The Code uses the term *commoratio.* The term does not of itself connote any particular duration of time, but rather a manner of presence. One may be present in a place as if passing through, or as staying there. An air passenger flying over a city, or a railroad passenger waiting at the station between trains, is present but not staying; whereas a homeseeker coming to a place to establish his residence there may be said to be *staying* from the moment of his arrival. This would be equally true though his stay was intended to be of very short duration.[8]

2. What is meant by *menstrua commoratio?* It means a month's residence, and is mentioned only in canon 1097 in connection with the licitness of assistance at marriages.

3. Must the required time of actual residence (six months, ten

---

[8] Cf. *Irish Eccl. Rec.,* Vol. 47, p. 79.

years) be absolutely continuous? No; moral continuity is enough. Hence brief absences will not interrupt it.[9]

Necessary Domicile. A *necessary* or *legal* domicile is imposed by law on three classes of persons: (1) on a wife who is not legally separated from the husband, the domicile of the husband; (2) on an insane person, the domicile of his guardian; (3) on a minor, the domicile of the parent or guardian to whose control he is subject (c. 93, § 1).

These same persons are also declared capable of acquiring voluntary domiciles or quasi-domiciles, as follows: (1) a *wife* who is *not legally separated* can acquire a voluntary quasi-domicile; (2) a *wife* who *is legally separated* can acquire a domicile; (3) a *minor over seven years of age* can acquire a quasi-domicile (c. 93, § 2).

Questions. 1. Can a person have several domiciles or quasi-domiciles? Evidently this canon allows at least a voluntary quasi-domicile concurrently with a necessary domicile. Vermeersch-Creusen and others hold that a person may have several voluntary domiciles or quasi-domiciles.[10]

2. Are the above necessary domiciles the only ones recognized by law? Probably not. Ojetti and others point out that the enumeration made in this canon is not exclusive, and that other persons, e.g., Cardinals, holders of benefices, and religious, may have legal domiciles.[11]

3. Do the rules for legal domicile apply also to quasi-domicile? This is disputed. Some hold that they do;[12] others distinguish as follows: *per se,* a quasi-domicile is not imposed by canon 93, since it is not mentioned; but in the absence of domicile or quasi-domicile of any kind, this canon should be applied by analogy, to prevent the person from being regarded as a *vagus*.[13]

4. Is a wife who has been wrongfully deserted by her husband regarded as "legally separated"? The Code Commission answered this: In the negative, unless she has obtained a decree of separation.[14]

5. What of a wife who leaves her husband because of adultery on his part? Since such separation is contemplated and allowed by law

---

[9] Cf. V-C, *Epit.*, I, n. 212.

[10] A Coronata, *Institutiones,* I, n. 127; V-C, *Epit.*, I, n. 212; Claeys-Simenon, *Manuale,* I, n. 242. As to several quasi-domiciles, see also Maroto, *Institutiones,* I, n. 413.

[11] Cf. Ojetti, *Commentarium,* II, p. 53, note 3. On the necessary domicile of religious, cf. V-C, *Epit.*, I, n. 217; a Coronata, *Institutiones,* I, n. 128.

[12] Cf. Maroto, *Institutiones,* I, n. 413; Wernz-Vidal, *De Personis,* n. 12; Claeys-Simenon, *Manuale,* I, n. 245.

[13] V-C, *Epit.*, I, n. 214.

[14] Code Com., 14 July, 1922; *AAS,* 14–526; *Digest,* I, p. 83.

(c. 1130), some affirm that the woman is legally separated and can acquire a domicile;[15] but this has never been officially recognized and we incline to the contrary opinion.[16]

The Proper Pastor and Proper Ordinary of a person are: (1) if the person has a parochial domicile or quasi-domicile: (*a*) the Ordinary of the diocese, and (*b*) the pastor of the parish; (2) if the person has no domicile or quasi-domicile: (*a*) the Ordinary of the place where he is staying, and (*b*) the pastor of that same place; (3) if the person has only a diocesan, but not a parochial domicile or quasi-domicile: (*a*) the Ordinary of the diocese in which he has the domicile or quasi-domicile, and (*b*) the pastor of the place where he is actually staying (cf. c. 94).

As a person may have more than one domicile or quasi-domicile, so, too, he may have more than one proper Ordinary and pastor.

Juridical Effects of Domicile and Quasi-domicile. 1. Before the 19th of April, 1908, when the *Ne temere* decree became effective, the assistance of the *proper* Ordinary or pastor (or a delegate of either) was required for the *validity* of marriages, in those places where the *Tametsi* decree of the Council of Trent was in force. Since that date the assistance of the Ordinary or pastor *of the place* where the marriage is celebrated (or a delegate of either) has been required for validity.

2. But many consequences still attach to the domicile and to the proper Ordinary and pastor; e.g., relating to the *licitness* of assistance at marriage (c. 1097); the right of burial (c. 1230); the right to ordain (c. 956); subjection to particular laws (cc. 13, 14); the competency of judges in matrimonial trials (c. 1964), etc.

Loss of Domicile and Quasi-domicile. Domicile and quasi-domicile are lost by departure from the place with the intention not to return (c. 95). Of course, this intention need not be adamantine or irrevocable; it is merely a general intention.

Exceptions. Those persons who, according to canon 93, "necessarily retain" a legal domicile, cannot lose that domicile by departure even with the intention never to return.

A domicile or quasi-domicile is not lost by mere absence, however protracted, as long as an intention to return exists. Nor is it necessarily lost by acquiring a new domicile or quasi-domicile.

Consanguinity. Consanguinity is a relation between persons, based on carnal generation. It exists in the *direct* line, if one of the persons

---

[15] Cf. V-C, *Epit.*, I, n. 212.
[16] Cf. *Instruction on Matrimonial Procedure*, S. C. Sacr., 15 Aug., 1936; *AAS*, 28–313; *Digest*, II, p. 474.

is the direct ancestor of the other; in the *indirect* (*oblique, transverse,* or *collateral*) line, if neither person is the direct ancestor of the other, but both are descended from a common ancestor.

Divisions of Consanguinity. Consanguinity may be:

1. *Direct* or *collateral* as explained above.

2. *Legitimate* or *illegitimate,* according as the carnal generation was legitimate or illegitimate. Canonically there is little practical difference.

3. Of the *full blood* or of the *half blood.* This distinction applies to collateral relationships. Two brothers, for example, may have both parents in common or only one parent. Normally, the relationship will be of the full blood, the "ancestor" being in reality double, including both father and mother; but as regards canonical effects there is little practical difference between the full blood and the half blood.

4. *Simple* and *multiple.* This distinction will be explained under canon 1076.

5. Of various *degrees* in either line. The degrees are computed:

a. In the direct line, according to the number of generations, or, what comes to the same thing, according to the number of persons in the line, without counting the ancestor (c. 96).

b. In the collateral line, according to the number of generations in one branch, if the branches are equal, in the longer branch if the two are unequal (c. 96). Collateral consanguinity where the two branches are unequal can therefore be denominated simply according to the longer line (the more remote degree). But it can also be more accurately expressed, for example, as "in the second degree touching the first" or "in the third degree mixed with the second." If collateral consanguinity in the second degree touches also the first in one branch, as in the case of uncle and niece, this must be expressed, and special reasons are required for a matrimonial dispensation.[17]

Affinity may be defined as a relation between two persons of whom one is joined by a valid (or valid and sacramental) marriage to a blood relative of the other. This definition is derived tentatively from **canon 97, §§ 1, 2,** subject to the disputed interpretation indicated in the parenthesis.

Foundation. It will be seen that the basis of affinity is twofold: (1) a valid marriage; (2) consanguinity between one party to the marriage and other persons. Thus when Thomas marries Anne, he incurs affinity with Anne's blood relatives, and vice versa. But the

---

[17] See Instruction of S. C. Sacr., 1 Aug., 1931; *AAS,* 23-413; *Digest,* I, p. 514.

relatives of the one have no affinity to those of the other (cf. c. 97, § 2).

Degrees of Affinity are computed, both in the direct and in the collateral line, in exactly the same way as degrees of the consanguinity on which the affinity is based (cf. c. 97, § 3).

Canonical Effect. The chief canonical effect of affinity is that it constitutes a diriment impediment to marriage, up to the second degree inclusive of the collateral line, and in all degrees of the direct line (c. 1077, § 1).

Change Introduced by the Code. Before the Code, the impediment of affinity arose, not from valid marriage, but from carnal copula, whether that were licit or illicit. Now it arises from valid marriage, whether that is consummated by carnal copula or not. Some canonists express this change by saying that formerly the union of bodies alone was considered; now, the union of spirits.

Disputed Interpretation. The words "affinity arises from a valid marriage, whether it is merely *ratum* or *ratum et consummatum*," are obscure and have given rise to a dispute among canonists. The difficulty is that a marriage may be valid and yet be neither *ratum* nor *ratum et consummatum*. For *ratum,* which literally means ratified, approved, confirmed, is defined in canon 1015 as applying to a marriage between baptized persons. Practically, therefore, it means a sacramental marriage. A marriage between infidels is certainly not sacramental; and even a marriage in which only one of the parties is baptized is almost certainly not sacramental, and hence not *ratum*. And yet it may well be valid. The disputed question is whether affinity arises from every *valid* marriage or only from a *sacramental* marriage.

Some canonists hold that every *valid* marriage, even though not sacramental, produces affinity. Among these are Noldin, Ojetti, Wernz-Vidal.

Others, including De Smet, Cerato, Cappello, Chelodi, Vermeersch-Creusen, hold that affinity arises only from a *sacramental* marriage.

Still others, such as Tanquerey, Michiels, take a middle ground, admitting affinity from a marriage in which one party is baptized, denying it if both are unbaptized.

There is no authentic decision and no moral certainty one way or the other. Hence there is a doubt of law, and one may *certainly* (cf. c. 15) act upon the principle that affinity, at least as an impediment to marriage, arises only from a *sacramental* marriage, that is, a valid marriage between *two validly baptized Christians*.

Rite as a Juridical Quality. Rite has three meanings: (1) the ceremonies used in public worship; (2) the group of the faithful who observe these ceremonies; (3) the juridical bond by which a person belongs to one of these groups. **Canon 98** deals with rite in the last sense, that is, the juridical quality of persons as belonging to one ritual group rather than to another, within the Catholic Church. Its application is limited to cases where membership in one of the Latin rites is being determined, or where there is question of transferring from one Latin rite to another, or from a Latin to an Oriental rite, or vice versa. Where *only* Oriental rites are concerned, the matter is excluded from the general scope of the Code (cf. c. 1). The Oriental rites are enumerated under canon 1; the Latin rites are the Roman, the Ambrosian or Milanese, the Mozarabic, and some rites peculiar to certain religious orders.

Principles and Applications. 1. A person belongs to the rite according to whose ceremonies he was baptized, with certain exceptions (cf. c. 98, § 1).

a. A child should be baptized in the rite of its parents, or, if they belong to different rites, in that of its father (c. 756, § 1). For Greek-Ruthenians in the United States and Canada, the same rule is stated.[18]

b. The Code itself (c. 98, § 1) mentions three exceptional cases, in which rite is not determined in the usual way; namely, where baptism is conferred by a minister of a *foreign* rite (other than the rite of the child's parents); (1) through fraud, or (2) in case of necessity, or (3) with a dispensation. A fourth exception results from a decision of the Code Commission. Where, contrary to the provisions of canon 756, a child is, at the request of the parents, baptized by a minister of a rite other than their own, the child belongs, not to the rite in which he was actually baptized, but to that in which he should have been baptized according to canon 756.[19]

2. Clerics must abstain from *inducing* persons to transfer from the Latin to the Oriental rite or vice versa (c. 98, § 2).

3. Voluntary transfer from one rite to another requires the permission of the Holy See (c. 98, § 3). This permission was formerly obtainable from the Apostolic Delegate except in the case of priests.[20] It has recently been reserved exclusively to the Holy See.[21]

---

[18] See the respective Instructions: for the United States, *AAS*, 21–152; *Digest*, I, p. 16, Art. 41; for Canada, *AAS*, 22–346; *Digest*, I, p. 38, Art. 47.
[19] Code Com., 16 Oct., 1919; *AAS*, 11–478; *Digest*, I, p. 85.
[20] Cf. S. C. Or., 6 Dec., 1928; *AAS*, 20–416; *Digest*, I, p. 85.
[21] Cf. S. C. Or., 23 Nov., 1940; *AAS*, 33–28; *Digest*, II, p. 50.

4. A woman can change to the rite of her husband at the time of the marriage or during its continuance, and after its dissolution (by death or otherwise) can return to her former rite on her own authority (c. 98, § 4).[22]

5. The practice of receiving Holy Communion in another rite, even for a long time, does not produce a change of rite (c. 98, § 5).

a. Formerly Communion in another rite than one's own was unheard of. Benedict XIV in his Constitution, *Etsi pastoralis,* of 26 May, 1742, does not even mention it.

b. Leo XIII in his Constitution, *Orientalium dignitas,* of 30 Nov., 1894, permitted it by way of exception.

c. Pius X in his Constitution, *Tradita ab antiquis,* of 18 Oct., 1912, revoked the old prohibitions.

d. The Code (c. 866) permits it, merely counseling that the Paschal Communion be received in one's own proper rite.

Moral Persons. A moral person means a juridical entity, a subject of rights, distinct from all physical or natural persons. Such a person comes into being only when constituted by public authority (c. 99). This will be further explained under canon 100.

Division. *a.* A moral person is called *collegiate* if it is made up of a "college" or group of natural physical persons. Thus a religious order is made up of its members, a chapter of its canons, a board or committee of its individual members. These are collegiate moral persons. It must be noted that even in these cases the moral person is a legal entity distinct from the physical persons who compose it. A religious order has rights distinct from the sum of the individual rights of its members. It is a distinct legal entity.

b. A moral person is *noncollegiate* if it consists, not of physical persons, but of property and resources which are separated from the ownership and control of other persons and dedicated to some religious or charitable purpose. Churches, seminaries, benefices, are moral persons in this sense (cf. c. 99).

Constitution of Moral Persons. 1. There are two moral persons that exist by divine institution. They are the Catholic Church, established on earth by Jesus Christ, true God, and the Apostolic See, established by the same divine authority (cf. c. 100, § 1). The distinction between these two moral persons is a *real, inadequate* distinction; one is

---

[22] A woman of the Latin rite thus transferring to the Oriental rite of her husband at marriage remains bound to observe the juridical form of marriage as provided in canon 1099, § 1, 3°. Code Com., 29 Apr., 1940; *AAS,* 32–212; *Digest,* II, p. 49.

part of the other. The Apostolic See, in this connection, does *not* include the departments of the Roman Curia (cf. c. 7).

2. Inferior moral persons are constituted by ecclesiastical law for religious or charitable purposes in two ways: by provision of law, and by special decree (cf. c. 100, § 1).

a. By provision of law, expressly or equivalently, we have: the College of Cardinals (cc. 231, 241), the diocesan Curia (c. 363), the Roman Curia (c. 242), etc.

b. By formal decree: new dioceses are constituted by the Holy See (c. 248, § 2), new parishes by the Bishop (c. 216, § 1), etc.

3. Before the Code, parishes could acquire legal entity without a formal decree of erection; and such parishes continue, after the Code, to be true parishes.[23]

Other Rules. Collegiate moral persons must consist of at least three physical persons (c. 100, § 2).

All moral persons, collegiate and noncollegiate, are declared to be in the same class as minors — *minoribus aequiparantur* (c. 100, § 3); that is, they are to enjoy the same protection under the law. The reason is that all their rights are in the hands of physical persons whose negligence or prodigality might otherwise cause them serious loss.

Acts of Moral Persons. Since moral persons are by nature incapable of acting for themselves, they must of necessity act through physical persons; either through individuals endowed with authority to act for them, or through a group as such, similarly authorized. **Canon 101** deals partly with both forms of action; but the action through individual superiors is governed also by canon 105.

Principles. 1. *Collegiate* moral persons, unless specially prohibited by law, can validly determine their action by vote, according to the following rules:

a. In estimating a majority, absolute or relative, invalid votes are not considered (cf. c. 101, § 1, 1°). Thus, where four out of nine members of a chapter voted for one candidate, no other effective votes being cast, the four votes constituted an absolute majority.[24] For a valid action on the first or second ballot an absolute majority is required; seven valid votes out of thirteen, eleven out of twenty, etc. (cf. c. 101, § 1, 1°).

b. If two inconclusive ballots have been taken, the third ballot may be decided upon a relative majority; that is, a vote for one party larger

---

[23] See S. C. Conc., 5 March, 1932; *AAS*, 25–436; *Digest*, I, p. 151.
[24] S. C. Conc., 10 June, 1922; *AAS*, 14–459; *Digest*, I, p. 87.

than for any of the others singly, though less than all others taken together. Thus, if three candidates receive respectively nine, seven, and four, out of twenty valid votes, the first will be elected (cf. c. 101, § 1, 1°).

c. If there is a deadlock after the third ballot, the chairman should break the deadlock by voting (cf. c. 101, § 1, 1°), even if he would not otherwise be entitled to vote. Maroto holds that the chairman may refuse to vote. *In an election,* all agree that he is not obliged to use his right of suffrage. Hence,

d. In an election, if the deadlock is not broken after the third ballot by the vote of the chairman, seniority determines the election as between candidates having equal votes. The seniority considered is first, seniority in (sacred) orders; second, by first profession; third, in age (*ibid*). The words of canon 101, § 1, 1° *"post tertium scrutinium"* do not mean that a fourth ballot is taken, but that the chairman alone may immediately cast the deciding vote.

Exception. Measures which concern all *as individuals* must be approved by a unanimous vote (c. 101, § 1, 2°). This provision applies only to such measures as, if imposed upon dissenting individuals by a mere majority, would do them an injustice either by depriving them of a vested right or imposing an inequitable burden. Hence, an election by compromise must be provided for by unanimous consent (c. 172).

2. *Noncollegiate* moral persons are governed, as regards their action, by the provisions of the common law or particular statutes (c. 101, § 2).

a. The common law has provisions governing the acts of superiors in general (c. 105), and of particular kinds of noncollegiate moral persons, such as parishes, seminaries, etc.

b. Particular statutes may exist for certain moral persons; as, for example, *statuta* approved by the Holy See for Pontifical Seminaries.

Perpetuity of Moral Persons. A moral person is by nature perpetual; it expires, however, if it is suppressed by lawful authority, or if it has been out of existence for one hundred years (**c. 102, § 1**).

If even one member of a collegiate moral person survives, the rights of all are united in him (**c. 102, § 2**).

Since moral personality is distinct from that of all physical persons, there is nothing surprising in this provision that it may endure after all the physical persons who belonged to it are departed. Created by public authority, it is extinguished by public authority. An Apostolic Letter of Pius XI, suppressing a religious order appeared in *AAS,* Vol. 27, p. 482.

Acts of Physical and Moral Persons may be affected by force, grave fear, deceit, or error.

Force From Without which cannot be resisted is physical compulsion, and renders the act involuntary and void by the law of nature (cf. c. 103, § 1).

Grave Fear on the other hand may or may not have this effect. If it is so overpowering as to deprive the agent of all voluntary choice, the act done under its influence is void by the natural law. But this is not usually the case. Canon 103 deals with grave fear which intimidates but does not destroy freedom of choice. Fear is defined as trepidation of mind because of impending evil. It is grave if it arises from a grave danger which is, or is believed to be imminent. It is *unjustly applied* if it is inspired by an external free agent in a manner contrary to justice. What is the effect of such fear, grave and unjustly applied?

a. Acts done under the influence of such fear are *valid,* unless the law provides otherwise **(c. 103, § 2).** The law has special provisions regarding fear as affecting marriage (c. 1087); noviceship (c. 542); religious profession (c. 572); vows (c. 1307); resignation from an office (c. 185); obligations of sacred orders (c. 214).

b. Such acts are, however, *rescindable* according to law, as provided in canons 1684–1689, either at the suit of the injured party or *ex officio* **(c. 103, § 2).**

Deceit is any artifice to deceive. Its effect is declared to be the same as that of grave fear unjustly inspired *(ibid)*. Hence:

a. Acts done in consequence of it are generally valid; but special provisions exist governing the noviceship (c. 542); religious profession (c. 572); resignation from office (c. 185), which are invalid if induced by fraud.

b. Such acts are, however, rescindable.

c. Deceit may also produce substantial error, which invalidates an act according to canon 104.

Error means a false judgment of the mind. Ignorance and inadvertence, though not identical with error, have the same juridical effect.

a. Error is *substantial* if it affects the substance of an act; otherwise it is accidental. But a circumstance which does not of its nature affect the substance of a transaction, for example, the age of a horse in a contract of sale, may by the express stipulation of the parties be made a condition *sine qua non*. In that case it is substantial, not by nature, but by express agreement.

b. Error is said to be the cause of the contract (*dans causam con-*

tractui) if, but for the error, the contract would not have been entered into; otherwise it is *non dans causam contractui*. Note that an error may be the cause of the contract and yet not be substantial either by nature or by stipulation.

c. Error is *of law* if it concerns the existence or meaning of the law; *of fact* if it concerns any other fact.

Principles. 1. Error of law or of fact, if it is *substantial,* renders an act null and void **(cf. c. 104).**

2. The same is true if the error, though not substantial by nature, is made so by a condition *sine qua non* (*ibid.*).

3. Any other error leaves the act valid, unless the law provides otherwise (c. 104), as it does, for example, regarding one quality of the person in marriage (c. 1083, § 2, 2°).

4. In contracts, error may give rise to an action for rescission according to law (c. 104; cf. c. 1684, § 2).

When Consent or Counsel Required. Canon 105 applies to acts of both natural persons and moral persons, for a superior may act in either capacity. It frequently happens that the law gives to a superior a power with the specific limitation that it is to be used with the consent or upon the advice of certain other persons. For example:

1. An Ordinary is to appoint parish assistants after *hearing from* the pastor (c. 476, § 3);

2. A Vicar Capitular cannot grant letters of excardination and incardination except after one year from the vacancy of the episcopal see and *with the consent* of the chapter (c. 113);

3. A Bishop may remove one of the diocesan consultors, with the *advice* of the others (c. 428);

4. He may make a removable pastor irremovable, upon the *advice* of the cathedral chapter (c. 454);

5. He can dispense a candidate for a parish from the examination, in certain cases, with the *consent* of the examiners (c. 459, § 3, 3°);

6. He can appoint a new removable pastor, *after hearing from* the chapter (c. 454, § 3);

7. He may not, outside the Synod, reserve to himself the absolution of special sins, without having *consulted* the cathedral chapter (c. 895);

8. He is to draw up a schedule of taxes, with the *advice* of the chapter (c. 1234, § 1); etc.

The chief practical question is whether the consent or counsel when thus required by law, is required for *validity*.

Principles. 1. If *consent* is required, it is required for *validity* of the superior's action.

2. If only *counsel* is required, then "it is enough for valid action that the superior hears the persons named" (c. 105, 1°). The obscurity of this provision must be acknowledged. It amounts to saying that if only counsel is required, then nothing more than counsel is required. Some canonists, including Maroto, Ojetti, Ferreres, a Coronata, think the canon indicates that the counsel is a requisite for validity. It is true the canon says "it is *enough* for valid action," but it does not say "it is *required* for valid action." Hence others, such as Vermeersch-Creusen, Van Hove, Boudinhon, Vidal hold that the counsel is not a requisite for valid action. This opinion gains some support from canon 11. There is no authentic decision on the point. It is a good example of *dubium juris;* and hence the act of the superior even without the advice required by law may *certainly* be regarded as valid under the rule of canon 15, until a contrary authentic interpretation is made.[25]

3. If only consultation is required, the superior is not bound to accede to the opinion of those consulted even if it be unanimous, but he should show great deference to their unanimous judgment, and should not depart from it without some paramount reason to be estimated according to his own judgment (c. 105, 1°).

4. If the consent or counsel, not merely of one or two but of several together, is required, they must be lawfully summoned, without prejudice, however, to the provisions of canon 162, § 4, and they must state their mind. The superior may, according to his prudent discretion and the importance of the matter, require them to take an oath of secrecy (c. 105, 2°).

5. All who are asked for their consent or counsel must state their opinion with due reverence, confidence, and sincerity (c. 105, 3°).

Application in the United States. 1. The Third Council of Baltimore, nn. 17–22, provided that as long as it remained impossible to establish cathedral chapters, diocesan consultors should be appointed to take their place.

2. The Code (c. 423) makes the same provision, and further provides (c. 427) that whatever powers for the government of a diocese the Code gives to the cathedral chapter belong *ipso facto* to the board of diocesan consultors.

---

[25] Cf. V-C, *Epit.*, I, n. 229.

3. Hence it is the diocesan consultors whose consent or counsel is required in the United States in all matters where the Code requires the consent or counsel of the cathedral chapter (cf. canons 113, 454, 895, 1234, etc.).

4. How many diocesan consultors are required by law? See c. 425. How many are there in your diocese? See Catholic Directory.

Rules of Precedence Between Persons (c. 106). As regards precedence between various persons, physical or moral, the following rules are to be observed, without prejudice to special rules which will be given in their proper place:

1. A person who is taking the place of another takes his precedence from that other; but those who are present at councils or at such other meetings in a representative capacity sit beneath those of the same grade who are present in their own name;

2. One who has authority over physical or moral persons has the right of precedence over them;

3. As between different ecclesiastical persons of whom none have authority over others, those who belong to a higher grade precede those of a lower grade; as between persons of the same grade but not of the same order, one who has a higher order precedes those who are of a lower order; finally, if they belong to the same grade and to the same order, the one who was first promoted to the grade has precedence; if they were promoted at the same time, the senior in order precedes, unless the junior was ordained by the Roman Pontiff; if they received orders at the same time, the senior in age has precedence;

4. In precedence, diversity of rites makes no difference;

5. As between various moral persons of the same kind and grade, that one has precedence who is in peaceful quasi-possession thereof; and if this cannot be determined, then that one which was first established in the place where the question arises; as between the members of a certain college, the right of precedence is determined by their own legitimate constitutions; otherwise by lawful custom; in default of that, it is determined by the common law;

6. It belongs to the Ordinary of the place in his diocese to establish the precedence between his subjects, taking into consideration the principles of the common law, the legitimate customs of the diocese, and the functions committed to the persons; also to settle in urgent cases all controversies regarding precedence, even as regards exempt religious whenever these are to appear as a college with other groups,

nor is there any appeal with suspensive effect from his decision; but this, without prejudice to the right of any person;

7. As regards persons who belong to the Pontifical Household, precedence is to be regulated in accordance with the special privileges, rules, and traditions of the said Pontifical Household.

Authentic Documents. 1. The privilege of precedence in favor of "Apostolic Missionaries" is revoked.[26]

2. Precedence among suffragan Bishops in the provincial council, etc., is governed by seniority according to the date of proclamation or election to the episcopacy.[27]

3. On the precedence of the Vicar General, see canon 370 and two decisions of the Sacred Congregation of the Council.[28]

4. The privileges of members of the Pontifical Household have been revised and are now governed exclusively by the Constitution, *Ad incrementum,* of 15 Aug., 1934; *AAS,* 26–497.

5. An archconfraternity has precedence over a confraternity.[29]

Clerics, Laity, Religious. By divine institution there are in the Church *clerics* distinct from the *laity,* although not all clerics are of divine institution; both clerics and laity may be *religious* **(c. 107).**

The Church is by divine institution a *hierarchical society.*[30] Hence the distinction between *clerics,* who participate in the powers of order and jurisdiction, and the *laity,* who do not, is of divine origin; but not all orders of clerics are of divine institution.

The *religious* state is a stable mode of common life in which the faithful, besides observing the commandments, undertake to observe also the evangelical counsels by the vows of poverty, chastity, and obedience. This state "is to be held in honor by all" (c. 487). Although very ancient and very important in the life of the Church, the religious state does not form part of the constitution of the Church, as does the clerical order at least in its higher grades. Nor is the religious state a new division distinct from the clerical and lay divisions of the faithful; on the contrary, it is recruited from both.

---

[26] S. C. Prop. Fid., 16 Jan., 1924; *AAS,* 16–243; *Digest,* I, p. 88.

[27] Code Com., 10 Nov., 1925; *AAS,* 17–582; *Digest,* I, p. 88.

[28] S. C. Conc., 18 May, 1919; *AAS,* 11–349; *Digest,* I, p. 215 and 15 Dec., 1923; *AAS,* 16–371; *Digest,* I, p. 216.

[29] S. C. Conc., 13 Apr., 1935; *AAS,* 29–33; *Digest,* II, p. 177.

[30] *Conc. Trid., Sess.* XXIII, *De Ordine,* can. 6.

CASES AND QUESTIONS

1. X's family emigrated from Ireland to settle in Kentucky. The mother went first with one of her brothers and a son, while her husband remained to settle some business which detained him ten months. X was born on the high seas during the voyage. What is his place of origin? What if he had been born in Kentucky before his father left Ireland? (C. 90).

2. S, 19, whose home is in St. Louis, enters a college in Connecticut as a freshman. One month later, what is his domicile? His quasi-domicile? (Cc. 92, § 2, 93, §§ 1, 2).

3. A married woman whose home is in Louisville and whose husband is in military service overseas, goes to Indianapolis to work in a war plant; remains 9 months. What is her domicile? Her quasi-domicile? (Cc. 92, 93).

4. K, whose home is in England, went to India on government business; stayed ten years. What are his domiciles? (Cc. 92, § 1, 95).

5. State exactly in canonical terms the relationship of a man to his brother's daughter; of a woman to her husband's brother; of a girl to her stepfather (Cc. 96, 97).

6. N, an unmarried man, travels constantly on business, living in hotels. Arrives in Chicago for a week's stay, stopping at the Blackstone. Who is his proper Ordinary? His proper pastor? (C. 94, § 2).

7. Wife to her husband, soon after marriage: "If I had known you were such a drunkard I would never have married you." Was there substantial error on her part in the marriage contract? Did it invalidate the marriage? (Cc. 104, 1083, § 2).

8. A Bishop appoints an assistant to a parish without consulting the pastor. Is his action proper? (C. 476, § 3). Is the appointment valid? (Cc. 11, 105, 1°).

Readings:

Costello, *Domicile and Quasi-domicile,* Catholic University, 1930 (n. 60); Brown; *The Canonical Juristic Personality, With Special Reference to Its Status in the United States of America,* Cath. U., 1927 (n. 39); *Irish Eccl. Rec.,* Vol. 29, p. 293 (proper pastor of a *vagus*); Vol. 35, pp. 79, 290, 514 (domicile of a teacher); Vol. 37, p. 627 (of insane person); Vol. 47, p. 632 (of servant girl); Vermeersch-Creusen, *Epit.,* I, n. 217 (domicile of religious); *Periodica,* Vol. 9, p. 7 (Vermeersch on domicile of religious); Vol. 24, p. 1* (concept of moral person); Vol. 25, p. 99* (Ellis, on election of Superior General); Vol. 17, p. 138* (effect of fear); *The Jurist,* Vol. 4, p. 405 (Dooley on persons and juridical personality in the Code).

Section 2. Clerics, Incardination (cc. 108–117)

PRELIMINARY SURVEY

The Hierarchies of Order and of Jurisdiction (c. 108)
Source of Power in Each Hierarchy (c. 109)
Prelates (c. 110)
Incardination (c. 111)
Formal Excardination and Incardination (cc. 112, 113)
Virtual Excardination and Incardination (c. 114)
Excardination by Religious Profession (c. 115)
Rules Governing Excardination (c. 116)
Rules for Licit Incardination of Cleric From Other Diocese (c. 117)

Clerics and the Hierarchy. Those who are dedicated to the divine ministry at least by first tonsure are called clerics (c. 108, §1). They are not all of the same grade, but there is a sacred hierarchy among them, some being subordinated to others (c. 108, §2). By divine institution, the sacred hierarchy as regards order consists of Bishops, priests, and ministers; as regards jurisdiction, it consists of the supreme pontificate and the subordinate episcopate; other grades have been added to these by ecclesiastical institution (c. 108, §3).

Hierarchy, which literally means sacred government, is taken in two senses: (1) the power of the Church as a whole, and (2) the series of persons who participate in it. Taken in either sense, it consists of two distinct divisions. As the power of the Church is twofold, consisting of the power of order and the power of jurisdiction, so, too, these distinct powers may be vested in distinct persons. Often, however, the powers will be found united.

The power of *order* is the power to sanctify the faithful by sacred rites; the power of jurisdiction is the power to govern the faithful for the attainment of the supernatural end for which the Church is established.

An intimate *relationship* exists between these two powers:

1. Both are of divine institution, for a supernatural end;

2. The general end of both is the same — eternal salvation;

3. Jurisdiction presupposes order (c. 118), and moderates its exercise (c. 879, §1).

They are *distinguished* by the following differences:

1. Their *immediate origin* is different. Order is conferred by a

sacred rite of ordination (c. 109); jurisdiction, except in the case of the Supreme Pontiff, by canonical mission (cc. 109, 147, § 1). The Supreme Pontiff obtains the primacy of jurisdiction by divine right (cc. 160, 219).

2. Their *particular end* is different. Order is to sanctify; jurisdiction, to govern.

3. They have different *qualities*. Order, based on a supernatural mark or character, is irrevocable; jurisdiction, consisting in a moral relationship, is subject to change.

Among the various degrees in each hierarchy, the highest are of divine institution, the lower of ecclesiastical origin.

Hierarchy of Order		Hierarchy of Jurisdiction
Bishop		Supreme Pontiff
Priest	(By divine law)	Subordinate Episcopate
Deacon		
Subdeacon	(By ecclesiastical	Various ecclesiastical
Minor clerics	institution)	officers.

First Tonsure is not an order but a preparation for orders. It is, however, recognized as the entrance into the clerical state (c. 108, § 1); and is classed with orders, the rite by which it is conferred being called ordination (c. 950). Like the orders, it is *never* repeated.

Title or Source of Power in the Hierarchy (c. 109). (1) It is not the popular will nor the secular power. This was one of the errors of the Reformation, condemned by the Council of Trent.[31] (2) For the power of order, it is sacred ordination. (3) For the power of jurisdiction, it is canonical appointment, with the single exception of the Supreme Pontificate, in which the primacy of power comes by divine law, upon the acceptance of the office by one who has been legitimately elected.

Ordination is a sacred rite which confers the power of order. It is certainly a sacrament in the case of Bishops, priests, and deacons. Almost certainly it is not a sacrament, but a sacramental, in minor orders, and most probably also in the ordination of subdeacons.[32]

Canonical mission means either the conferring of an ecclesiastical office by a competent ecclesiastical superior according to law (c. 147), or the grant of jurisdiction in some other way.

Prelacy. 1. A prelate *in the strict sense* is a cleric who has ordinary

---

[31] *Conc. Trid., Sess.* XXIII, *De Ordine,* can. 7.
[32] Cf. Gasparri, *De Sacra Ordinatione,* nn. 14, 33; Cappello, *De Ordine,* nn. 91–98.

jurisdiction (cf. c. 197, § 1) in the external forum (c. 110). He may be either a religious or secular cleric. But religious superiors as such have only dominative power over their subjects (c. 501, § 1) except in *clerical exempt* religious societies, in which they have true jurisdiction in both the internal and external fora. Religious superiors are therefore prelates only in clerical exempt religious institutes. Prelates in the strict sense are: resident Bishops, but not merely titular ones, since these have no ordinary jurisdiction (cf. c. 348); Prelates *nullius;* Vicars and Prefects Apostolic; Vicars General; superiors in clerical exempt religious societies. Pastors are usually not classed as prelates, in spite of the undeniable fact that they have a certain very limited jurisdiction in the external forum (cf. cc. 1044, 1045, 1245, § 1). The reason perhaps is that this jurisdiction is practically negligible in this connection.

2. Prelates *honoris causa* are clerics who have been honored with a prelatial title by the Holy See, but without jurisdiction. Outside the Roman Curia, in which there are prelates of both classes, both with and without jurisdiction, honorary prelates are graded as follows: (*a*) Prothonotary Apostolic (Right Reverend Monsignor); (*b*) Domestic Prelate (Right Reverend Monsignor); (*c*) Papal Chamberlain (Very Reverend Monsignor). The privileges of all prelates and members of the Roman Curia are now governed exclusively by the Constitution, *Ad incrementum,* of 15 Aug., 1934.[33]

Incardination means the affiliation of a secular cleric to his diocese. From very early times the custom became recognized that clerics be not ordained except for definite service in a certain territory. Unattached clerics were denominated *acephali,* or headless, and were forbidden to exercise the sacred ministry. Bishops were forbidden to dismiss their clerics and thus render them headless. During the middle ages, however, there was a considerable number of unattached clerics, not without some scandal and detriment to the Church. The Council of Trent[34] decreed that "no one hereafter be ordained who is not attached to the church or pious place for whose necessity or benefit he is received." The same provision is made in the Code (c. 111, § 1). Religious clerics are affiliated by membership to their order or congregation, but this relationship is not called incardination.

Principle and Applications. By first tonsure a cleric becomes in-

---

[33] *AAS,* 26–497. For an excellent classification of minor prelates, see Lydon, *Ready Answers in Canon Law,* p. 430.
[34] *Conc. Trid., Sess.* XXIII, *De Reformatione,* cap. 16.

cardinated in the diocese for whose service he was promoted to the clerical state (c. 111, § 2).

1. One must be ordained by his own proper Bishop, or upon a dimissorial letter from him (c. 955). It is illicit for another Bishop to ordain without such a dimissorial letter.[35]

2. The proper Bishop for ordination in the case of nonreligious candidates is the Bishop of the place where the candidate has a domicile and origin, or a domicile without origin; in the latter case an oath to the candidate's intention to remain permanently in the diocese is usually required (c. 956).

3. A Bishop usually ordains his own subject for the service of his own diocese. Other cases, however, are possible.

4. If a Bishop confers tonsure upon one of his own subjects, intending him for the service of another determined diocese, by agreement with the Bishop of that diocese, the candidate is immediately incardinated in the other diocese.[36]

5. If a Bishop ordains his own subject, intending him for the service of some other diocese not yet determined, canon 969, § 2 is applicable; and the cleric is incardinated by first tonsure in the diocese of the ordaining Bishop, but will later be transferred to another diocese by formal excardination and incardination.[37]

6. Where the candidate by first tonsure is immediately incardinated in another diocese, as in the case described above under n. 4 the proper Bishop for the higher orders is the Bishop of the diocese in which he is incardinated.[38]

Formal Excardination and Incardination. Except in the cases dealt with in canons 114 and 641, § 2, in order that a cleric of another diocese be validly incardinated, he must obtain from his Ordinary a letter of perpetual and absolute excardination signed by the Ordinary, and from the Ordinary of the new diocese a letter of incardination, likewise perpetual and absolute and signed by the Ordinary (c. 112).

The general requisites for the *validity* of formal excardination and incardination are stated in this canon. The two exceptions provided for are:

1. Virtual excardination and incardination (c. 114); and

---

[35] Code Com., 17 Feb., 1930; *AAS*, 22-195; *Digest*, I, p. 91.

[36] Code Com., 17 Aug., 1919; *Digest*, I, p. 89; and 24 July, 1939; *AAS*, 31-321; *Digest*, II, p. 52.

[37] Cf. Vermeersch, in *Periodica*, Vol. 12, p. 75.

[38] Cf. Code Com., 7 Dec., 1931; *Digest*, II, p. 51; and 24 July, 1939; *AAS*, 31-321; *Digest*, II, p. 237.

2. The incardination of an ex-religious who requires no excardination since he belongs to no diocese (c. 641, § 2).

Conditions for the *licitness* of these same acts may be summarized as follows:

1. A just cause for excardination (c. 116);

2. Necessity or advantage of the diocese in which he is to be incardinated (c. 117);

3. Testimonials of excardination, character, etc. (c. 117);

4. An oath on the part of the cleric that he wishes to remain permanently affiliated to the new diocese (c. 117).

Competency. The Vicar General cannot grant excardination and incardination without a special mandate, and neither can the Vicar Capitular except after one year from the vacancy of the episcopal see and with the consent of the chapter (c. 113).

The Vicar General has ordinary jurisdiction for the government of the diocese, subject to the Bishop (c. 366), and is an Ordinary of the place (c. 198); but in several matters his power is limited by the clause that he cannot act without a special mandate (c. 368, §1).

The Vicar Capitular is a cleric appointed by the cathedral chapter to govern a vacant diocese until a new Bishop is appointed (c. 432, § 1). He is also an Ordinary of the place (c. 198). In the United States, the Administrator appointed by the diocesan consultors exercises the power of the Vicar Capitular.

Virtual Excardination and Incardination is effected in two ways (cf. c. 114): (1) by obtaining a residential benefice (c. 1411, 3°) from the Ordinary of another diocese, with the written consent of one's own Ordinary; (2) by obtaining such a benefice with the written permission of one's own Ordinary to leave the diocese permanently.

The residential benefice which is required in both cases must probably be a permanent one.[39] All the conditions stated in this canon, including the written consent or written permission, seem to be requisite for the validity of the excardination and incardination.[40]

Excardination of Religious. In case a religious was, before entering religion, incardinated in a diocese, he remains so incardinated until he takes *perpetual* vows, whether solemn or simple (c. 585). He is, of course, tentatively affiliated to the religious society immediately upon entering, and again more definitely by the temporary vows; but this

---

[39] Cf. Wernz-Vidal, *De Personis*, n. 64.
[40] Cf. V-C, *Epit.*, I, n. 238. See also S. C. Conc., 11 July, 1925; *AAS*, 18–48; *Digest*, I, p. 91.

affiliation is not final until it becomes so by the perpetual vows, which also excardinate him from his former diocese (cf. c. 115).

Connected Questions. 1. What if, *before* taking perpetual vows, such a religious returns to the world?

a. If he has sacred orders (subdiaconate), he must return to the diocese in which he remains incardinated, and the Bishop must receive him (c. 641, § 1).

b. If he has only minor orders, and was dismissed from religion in accordance with canon 647, he is *ipso facto* reduced to the lay state (c. 648); if he was not dismissed, but left legitimately in some other way, he should return to his diocese in which he is still incardinated.

2. What if a religious returns to the world *after* taking perpetual vows? Such a religious is excardinated and hence is not bound to return to his diocese, nor is his former Bishop bound to receive him. The ex-religious is either dispensed from his vows or not:

a. If he is *not dispensed,* he is under obligation to amend his life and return to his religious society, to which he is still bound (cc. 669, 671, 672).

b. If he is *dispensed* from his vows (but has sacred orders), he must find a Bishop who is willing to receive him. No Bishop is obliged to receive him; but any Bishop may take him according to canon 641, § 2; that is, either absolutely, in which case he is incardinated at once, or on trial for one or two three-year periods, at the end of which time, unless dismissed earlier, he becomes incardinated permanently.

3. Can a diocesan cleric enter religion?

a. Usually such admission is both valid and licit. Courtesy is usually observed on both sides; religious superiors will ask the consent of the Bishop, although it is not legally required, and the Bishop will graciously consent.

b. In some cases the consent of the Bishop is required, though not for validity. Admission to the noviceship is *valid but illicit* if the cleric is in sacred orders and is received either without consulting the Ordinary or in spite of the latter's objection on the ground that the departure of the cleric will occasion grave spiritual harm which cannot otherwise be avoided (c. 542, 2°).

c. A cleric who *by ordinance of the Holy See* is bound by oath to the service of his diocese or mission *cannot validly* be admitted to the noviceship while the obligation of the oath continues (c. 542, 1°). This refers to the oath which is required by *special* ordinance of the Holy See in certain ecclesiastical seminaries; it does not refer to the oath regularly required before ordination where the canonical title for ordination is the service of the diocese (cf. c. 981, § 1).

Rules Governing Excardination. (1) It may not be done without a *just cause.* This is required *ad liceitatem* only. (2) Its effect is suspended until incardination in some other diocese has been effected. The purpose of this wise provision is to prevent the cleric from being *acephalus* or headless during the interval between excardination from one diocese and incardination in another. (3) The Ordinary who receives and incardinates the cleric must as soon as possible notify the Ordinary who excardinated him (c. 116).

Conditions for Licit Incardination. An Ordinary must not incardinate a cleric from another diocese:

Unless the necessity or advantage of his diocese requires it, with due regard to the requirements of law regarding a canonical title for ordination (c. 117, 1°).

Unless he is satisfied from an authentic document that lawful excardination has been obtained, and unless he has moreover from the dismissing Curia, under secret if need be, the required testimonials regarding the cleric's birth, life, moral character, and studies, especially if the cleric in question is of a different language and nationality; and the dismissing Ordinary is bound by a grave obligation in conscience to see to it that these testimonials are truthful (c. 117, 2°).

Unless the cleric himself shall have declared under oath before the Ordinary or his delegate that he desires to be ascribed permanently to the new diocese according to the sacred canons (c. 117, 3°).

As to the canonical title for ordination, see cc. 974, 1, 7°; 979–982. The oath on the part of the cleric refers to his *present intention* to remain permanently affiliated to the new diocese. It is not a promise.

Priests coming to America from Europe may be incardinated only upon the fulfillment of special conditions.[41]

Orientals are governed by the special decrees cited under canon 1.

Readings:

McBride, *Incardination and Excardination of Clerics,* Catholic University, 1941 (n. 145); *Australasian Catholic Record,* 1933, p. 50 (Nevin, on right of priest to means of livelihood); *Periodica,* Vol. 17, p. 50* (Vermeersch, on exclaustration and secularization of religious priest); Vol. 25, p. 53* (Ellis, case on incardination of ex-religious).

---

[41] Cf. S. C. Consist., 30 Dec., 1918; *AAS,* 11–39; *Digest,* I, p. 93.

Section 3. Rights and Privileges of Clerics (cc. 118–123)

PRELIMINARY SURVEY

Rights of Clerics (c. 118)
Privileges:
  Privilegium canonis (c. 119)
  Privilegium fori (c. 120)
  Privilegium immunitatis (c. 121)
  Privilegium competentiae (c. 122)
Loss of Privileges (c. 123)

Capacity. Clerics alone are capable of obtaining the power of order or of ecclesiastical jurisdiction, and ecclesiastical benefices and pensions **(c. 118).** What are here called rights are merely certain general capacities which are declared exclusive to clerics.

1. The power of *order* is the power to sanctify the faithful by sacred rites. It is a necessary foundation for the power of jurisdiction (cf. c. 948), except that, were a layman to be elected Pope, he would on acceptance, receive supreme jurisdiction at once, by divine law (c. 219).

2. The power of *jurisdiction* is the power to govern the faithful for the supernatural end for which the Church is established (cf. c. 196).

3. An ecclesiastical *benefice* is a juridical entity established in perpetuity by competent ecclesiastical authority and consisting of a sacred office together with the right to receive the revenue from an endowment attached thereto (c. 1409). A benefice is a noncollegiate moral person (c. 99).

4. A *pension* is the right to receive part of the revenue of a benefice for a time.

Religious, unless they are also clerics, do not share in these *rights;* but even lay religious and novices have the *privileges* mentioned in canons 119–123 (cf. c. 614).

Privilegium Canonis. All the faithful owe reverence to clerics according to their various grades and offices; and they commit a sacrilege if they do a real injury to a cleric **(c. 119).**

This privilege derives its name from canon 15 of the Second Council of the Lateran (A.D. 1139), *si quis suadente diabolo.* That canon declared a penalty of excommunication against anyone who should "lay violent hands" upon a cleric. Such an act was one form of the so-called personal sacrilege, the other two forms being sexual violation of any consecrated person (cleric or religious), and hailing such a person before a civil court. Canon 119 does not concern itself with the penalty (cf. c. 2343), but merely declares the privilege and the nature of the sin committed by one who *culpably* violates it. The sin is sacrilege, mortal or venial according to its gravity.

1. *Real injury* is opposed to merely verbal injury. It means any unjust act by which the person suffers violence; such as assault, imprisonment, etc.

2. The *penalty* varies with the grade and office of the person attacked (cf. c. 2343).

Privilegium Fori, of very ancient origin in the Church, has a certain remote sanction in Holy Scripture (1 Cor. 6:1).

In all contentious or criminal cases clerics are to be summoned before an ecclesiastical judge, unless lawful provision to the contrary has been made for particular places (c. 120, § 1).

Cardinals, Legates of the Holy See, Bishops even though merely titular, Abbots and Prelates *nullius,* the highest superiors of religious societies of pontifical law, and the major officials of the Roman Curia in matters pertaining to their office, may not be summoned before a lay judge without permission of the Holy See; other clerics who have the privilege of the forum may not be so summoned without permission of the Ordinary of the place where the case is in progress; the Ordinary, however, shall not refuse such permission without a just and grave reason, especially if the plaintiff is a layman, and more especially after he shall have tried in vain to effect a compromise between the parties (c. 120, § 2).

In case clerics are nevertheless summoned by parties who have not the necessary permission, they may through necessity and to prevent greater evils obey the summons, but they must notify the superior from whom permission ought to have been obtained (c. 120, § 3).

1. What is forbidden is to *summon* the person *as defendant* in a contentious case or *as accused* in a criminal case, without the necessary permission. Summoning as a witness is not forbidden.

2. The *permission* required is that of the Holy See or of the Ordinary of the place of trial, according to the dignity of the person summoned. The words "in matters pertaining to their office" most probably apply only to those immediately preceding; namely, "major officials of the Roman Curia." Vermeersch-Creusen[42] give rather good reasons for

---

[42] V-C, *Epit.,* I, n. 242.

this interpretation, though the official text of this canon carries a comma after the word *Curiae* in paragraph 2. Besides other reasons, they point out that this comma is omitted in the exactly parallel structure of canon 2341, dealing with the penalty (cf. c. 18).

3. The *penalty* for violation varies with the dignity of the person (cf. c. 2341).

Questions. 1. Is this privilege revoked or abandoned in the United States? Since it is a matter merely of ecclesiastical law, the Church can renounce it; and it is subject to modification by concordat. But there is no evidence that the Church has renounced it in the United States. On the contrary she seems to rely on a spirit of mutual forbearance and liberality to adapt it to the conditions of various countries without compromise of her independence or injury to the state. The penalty of canon 2341 was declared by the Sacred Congregation of the Council against those who signed the complaint against the Bishop of Providence in the school and language controversy in 1928.[43]

2. Is the *culpable* violation of this canon a *sacrilege?* Some dispute this, but we see no reason for supposing a change in the law. It was certainly regarded as a sacrilege before the Code; and according to canon 6, 2°, the same interpretation should apply to this canon, since it merely repeats the former law without change. The *nature of the sin* could not be changed by mere silence in the Code. There is no question in this canon, of the *penalty,* which is dealt with in canon 2341.

Privilegium Immunitatis consists in the immunity of clerics from military service and from public civil offices which are foreign to the clerical state **(cf. c. 121).** As to what civil offices are of this sort, the Code is not very specific. There will be little practical difficulty in the United States where it is not usual for clerics to stand for public offices of any kind. As regards military service, the recent practice of our country has been to recognize this immunity at least in part. The Selective Service Draft law of 1917 was upheld by the United States Supreme Court in Arver vs. the United States, 245 U. S., 366. The Selective Service Act of 1940 provides that ordained ministers of religion must register, but are not to be called to service. Many European countries, however, have flagrantly violated the immunity of the Church in this matter, and the Holy See has not failed to protest.[44] Special regula-

---

[43] S. C. Conc., 1928; *AAS,* 20–146; *Digest,* I, p. 855.
[44] See the preamble to the Decree of the S. C. Consist., 25 Oct., 1918; *AAS,* 10–481; *Digest,* I, p. 99.

tions for clerics in military service have accordingly been necessary.[45]

Privilegium Competentiae. Clerics who are obliged to satisfy their creditors are entitled to reserve from execution as much as, in the prudent judgment of an ecclesiastical judge, is necessary for their decent support, without prejudice, however, to their obligation to satisfy their creditors as soon as possible (c. 122).

This ancient privilege, allowing clerics a certain immunity from execution upon their property for debt, to the extent of what is necessary for their decent support, is not recognized by law in the United States, nor has it been necessary in practice for the Church to insist on it.

Loss of Privileges. These privileges cannot be renounced because they are not established for the private benefit of the individual (cf. c. 72, §2). They cease, however, when the state to which they are attached ceases, as when a cleric has been legally reduced to the lay state (c. 213, § 1); and also when a deposed cleric has been punished with perpetual privation of the clerical dress (c. 2304). The privileges are regained when the clerical state is restored or the penalty remitted (cf. c. 123).

Section 4. Obligations of Clerics (cc. 124–144)

PRELIMINARY SURVEY

Positive Obligations:
  Holiness of Life (c. 124)
  Exercises of Piety (c. 125)
  Spiritual Exercises (c. 126)
  Obedience to the Ordinary (cc. 127, 128)
  Sacred Studies (c. 129)
  Junior Clergy Examination (c. 130)
  Diocesan Conferences (c. 131)
  Chastity (c. 132)
  External Safeguards (cc. 133, 134)
  The Breviary (c. 135)
  Ecclesiastical Dress (c. 136)
Negative Obligations:
  Standing as Surety, Forbidden (c. 137)
  Unbecoming Occupations (c. 138)
  Occupations Foreign to the Clerical State (c. 139)
  Unbecoming Shows (c. 140)
  Military Service, Public Disturbances, Etc. (c. 141)
  Commerce, Trade (c. 142)
  Unlawful Absence (cc. 143, 144)

---

[45] Cf. documents reported in *Digest,* I, pp. 98–109.

Holiness of Life. Clerics must live both interiorly and exteriorly a holier life than lay people, and must excel them in giving the example of virtue and good deeds **(c. 124).**

This is the primary and fundamental obligation of clerics and especially of priests. Their example will be more powerful than their preaching. Their holiness must be *interior and exterior.* Ecclesiastical law directly prescribes exterior acts; but it does not prescind from interior dispositions, which in this matter are essential, for without them exterior observance would be mere hypocrisy.

Documents. It would be impossible to cite all the documents by which the Apostles and the Supreme Pontiffs have urged this obligation. The following are only a few among the most notable:

1. St. Paul: 1 Tim. 3 and 4; 2 Tim. 4; Tit. 1:7;

2. The Council of Trent: *Sess.* XXII, *De Reformatione,* cap. 1; *Sess.* XXV, *De Reformatione,* cap. 1;

3. Pius X, Exhortation to the Clergy, 4 Aug., 1908; Gasparri, *Codicis Iuris Canonici Fontes,* n. 683, Vol. III, p. 736.

4. Pius XI, Encyclical on the Priesthood; *AAS* 28–5; *The Catholic Mind,* Feb. 8, 1936.

Exercises of Piety (c. 125). Directly, the obligation is imposed on Ordinaries of places to require certain observances of the clerics under their charge. Indirectly, the law affects the clerics themselves in as much as it manifests the mind of the Church.

1. *Frequent confession* is prescribed, without any exact determination of the interval **(c. 125, 1°).** A directive norm may be drawn from canons 1367, § 2, and 595, § 1, 3°, which prescribe weekly confession for seminarians and religious respectively.

2. *Daily* exercises: meditation, visit to the Blessed Sacrament, the Rosary, the examen of conscience **(c. 125, 2°).** Plenary indulgences may be gained: *toties quoties* for the recitation of five decades of the Rosary before the Blessed Sacrament;[46] once a week for a daily visit to the Blessed Sacrament in which six Our Father's and Hail Mary's are recited;[47] and once daily for the recitation of the Breviary before the Blessed Sacrament.[48] Elsewhere, *daily Communion* is recommended, to religious (c. 595), to seminarians (c. 1367), and to the laity (c. 863).

3. The *celebration of Mass,* not mentioned in canon 125 is *directly* prescribed for all priests several times a year, *indirectly,* at least on all

---

[46] Pius XI, 4 Sept., 1927; *AAS,* 20–376; *Digest,* I, p. 450.
[47] Pius XI, 3 June, 1932; *AAS,* 24–231; *Digest,* I, p. 109.
[48] S. Paen., 23 Oct., 1930; *AAS,* 22–493; *Digest,* I, p. 121.

Sundays and feast days of obligation (c. 805). The most solid reasons of faith and piety urge the celebration of daily Mass.

4. The *monthly recollection* is not mentioned in the Code. Its observance is strongly counseled by all spiritual guides, and may be prescribed by particular law. It is fervently urged by His Holiness Pius XI, in the Encyclical on the Priesthood.[49]

The Clergy Retreat. All secular priests must at least every three years make a spiritual retreat for a time to be fixed by their own Ordinary, in some pious or religious house designated by him; and no one shall be excused from it, except in a particular case, for just cause, and by express permission of the said Ordinary **(c. 126).**

1. *Frequency* of the retreat: (*a*) for all secular priests, at least every three years; (*b*) for secular priests in the United States, at least every two years;[50] (*c*) for religious (c. 595) and seminarians (c. 1367, § 4) every year. The Encyclical on the Priesthood urges periods of spiritual retreat upon all priests as necessary means of sanctity, to be eagerly sought, even beyond the strict requirements of law.

2. *Duration* and *place,* to be determined by the Ordinary.

3. *Method,* not prescribed. The Spiritual Exercises of St. Ignatius have been recommended in several pontifical documents as the best, most effective, and most highly approved in the Church.[51]

4. *Exemption* from the clergy retreat must be express, individual, and for a just cause.

Obedience. All clerics, but especially priests, are bound by a special obligation to show reverence and obedience each to his own Ordinary **(c. 127).**

Source of the obligation. 1. For clerics in general, this obligation arises from their incardination, by which they have a proper Ordinary who has jurisdiction over them.

2. Priests have made a special promise of obedience in their ordination: "*Promittis mihi et successoribus meis reverentiam et obedientiam?*" "*Promitto.*"[52]

3. For those whose title for ordination was the service of the diocese, there is an obligation of justice.

Extent of the obligation. The legal or canonical obligation of

---

[49] *AAS,* 28–50; *The Catholic Mind,* Feb. 8, 1936.
[50] *Conc. Balt.* III, n. 75.
[51] Pius XI, 3 Dec., 1922; *AAS,* 14–627; *Digest,* I, p. 110; 20 Dec., 1929; *AAS,* 21–689; *Digest,* I, p. 110.
[52] *Roman Pontifical, Ordination to the Priesthood.*

obedience has the same limits as the power or authority of the superior. Hence:

1. It *includes*: (*a*) whatever is already obligatory by either the common or the particular law; (*b*) whatever is lawfully imposed by precept, even beyond the law, for the good of the Church.

2. It *excludes* things that are merely private, or purely temporal, or in which the law itself gives the inferior a choice. Even these may, of course, be laudably performed in a spirit of obedience, and thus the virtue of obedience will be practiced; but they are not within the strict juridical obligation of obedience which the canon defines.[53]

The scope of the Bishop's authority "can by no means be limited to strictly religious matters, but extends to questions of whatever nature which concern directly or indirectly the welfare of the Church and the salvation of souls. Hence it extends to ecclesiastical administration, to the education of Catholic youth, and to the relations of the faithful with non-Catholics in civil life."[54] Bishops cannot, however, by their laws prohibit anything that is expressly and undoubtedly permitted by the general law, unless the general law itself gives them this power.[55]

Clerical Duties. As often and as long as, in the judgment of their own Ordinary, the needs of the Church require it, clerics, unless they are lawfully excused by some impediment, must accept and faithfully execute the duty which shall be entrusted to them by the Bishop (c. 128).

The canonical duty of obedience is now further defined by declaring what duties or employments must be accepted and performed when assigned by the Ordinary. Clerical employments are divided into two classes; some are regarded as ordinary, others as extraordinary, in view of the law and custom of various places.

1. *Ordinary* duties or employments may be imposed, even without necessity, provided they are, in the judgment of the Ordinary, *useful* for the good of the Church.

2. *Extraordinary* employments can be imposed only when *necessary;* but the decision as to their necessity rests with the Ordinary.

3. In either case, the priest or cleric is excused from accepting the office or employment by any "lawful impediment"; that is, whenever its imposition would be a grave burden, even taking into consideration the needs of the Church. Such a lawful excuse would be, for example,

---

[53] Cf. Cappello, *Summa*, I, n. 229.
[54] Benedict XV, Letter, 15 Oct., 1921; *AAS*, 14–7; *Digest*, I, p. 114.
[55] Cf. S. C. Conc., 19 Feb., 1921; *AAS*, 13–228; *Digest*, I, p. 399.

serious ill health, or another office or employment lawfully held, from which he could not be released, etc.

Studies After the Priesthood. After receiving the priesthood clerics must not desist from their studies, especially sacred studies; and in the sacred subjects they must follow that solid doctrine which has been handed down by the fathers and is commonly received by the Church, avoiding profane novelties of expression and the science which is falsely so called (c. 129).

1. His Holiness, Pius XI, in the Encyclical on the Priesthood, after stating that the priest, "even among the absorbing tasks of his charge, and ever with a view to it, should continue his *theological studies* with unremitting zeal," continues: "Yet even more is required. The dignity of the office he holds and the maintenance of a becoming respect and esteem among the people, which helps so much in his pastoral work, demand *more than purely ecclesiastical learning*. The priest must be graced by no less knowledge and culture than is usual among well-bred and well-educated people of his day. This is to say that he must be healthily modern, as is the Church, which is at home in all times and all places, and adapts itself to all; which blesses and furthers all healthy initiative and has no fear of the progress, even the most daring progress of science, if only it be true science."[56]

2. The Third Council of Baltimore, n. 76, has provisions similar to those of the Code, and especially condemns the waste of precious time by priests in reading worthless magazines and novels.

3. The attendance of clerics at *secular universities* is forbidden except under special conditions laid down in a decree of the Sacred Consistorial Congregation.[57]

4. Priests *teaching in public schools* are also subject to special regulations.[58]

Junior Clergy Examination. After finishing their course of studies, all priests, even though they have obtained a parochial or canonical benefice, shall, every year for at least three years, unless they are exempted therefrom for just cause by the Ordinary of the place, be examined in the manner to be determined by the said Ordinary, in various subjects of the sacred sciences which shall have been duly designated in advance (c. 130, § 1).

In the conferring of ecclesiastical offices and benefices, consideration

---

[56] Cf. *The Catholic Mind*, Feb. 8, 1936, p. 64.
[57] S. C. Consist., 30 Apr., 1918; *AAS*, 10–237; *Digest*, I, p. 115.
[58] S. C. Conc., 22 Feb., 1927; *AAS*, 19–99; *Digest*, I, p. 116.

shall be given to those who, other things being equal, have made the best showing in these examinations (c. 130, § 2).

The following points may be noted:

1. This canon applies to *secular priests only;* religious are bound to a similar examination for five years (c. 590).

2. The Third Council of Baltimore, nn. 186-188, imposed the obligation for *five years.* This particular law, not contrary to the Code, would seem to be still effective in the United States (c. 6).

3. The obligation can be urged by suitable *penalties* (c. 2376).

4. The junior clergy examination *does not take the place* of the examination required by canon 459 for appointment to a parish.[59]

5. *Religious pastors and vicars* having the care of souls are supposed to take the examination provided for in canon 590; even if this is not done, the Ordinary cannot require them to be examined before him, but must refer the matter to the Sacred Congregation of Religious.[60]

6. A special examination *in preaching* may be prescribed by particular law.[61]

Diocesan Conferences. In the episcopal city and in the various rural deaneries, several times a year on days to be fixed in advance by the Ordinary of the place, meetings or so-called conferences on moral and liturgical subjects shall be held; to which may be added other exercises which the Ordinary may deem helpful toward the advancement of clerical learning and piety (c. 131, § 1).

In case it is difficult to hold the meetings, discussions of the questions proposed shall be submitted in writing, according to regulations which shall be made by the Ordinary (c. 131, § 2).

All secular priests, and religious even though exempt who have the care of souls, and, if a conference is not held in their house, also other religious who have obtained from the Ordinary the faculty of hearing confessions, are obliged to be present at the conference, or in default of a conference are obliged to submit written solutions of the cases proposed, unless they shall have obtained express exemption from the Ordinary in advance (c. 131, § 3).

1. *Three classes of persons* are bound: (*a*) secular priests; (*b*) religious priests having the care of souls; (*c*) other religious who have diocesan faculties for confessions, if no conference is held in their

---

[59] Code Com., 24 Nov., 1920; *AAS,* 12–574; *Digest,* I, p. 119.
[60] Code Com., 14 July, 1922; *AAS,* 14–526; *Digest,* I, p. 119.
[61] Cf. *Norms for Sacred Preaching,* S. C. Consist., 28 June, 1917, n. 14; *AAS,* 9–328; *Digest,* I, p. 626.

house, as it should be according to canon 591. Religious priests having
the care of souls do not include such priests who are merely catechists,
but include religious assistant pastors and chaplains in hospitals and
other pious houses if, according to canon 476, § 6, they are taking the
place of the pastor and helping him in the entire parochial ministry.[62]

2. The Third Council of Baltimore, n. 192, specifies the *frequency*
of these meetings: four times a year in cities, twice a year in rural
districts.

3. *Penalties* against those deliberately refusing this duty may be
imposed by the Ordinary; if the guilty persons are religious with
diocesan faculties, the Ordinary may suspend them from hearing the
confessions of seculars (c. 2377).

Clerical Celibacy and Chastity. Clerics who are in major orders are
prevented from marrying and are so bound to observe chastity that if
they sin against it they are guilty also of sacrilege, without prejudice
to the provision of canon 214, § 1 (c. 132, § 1).

Minor clerics can contract marriage, but, unless the marriage is null
because of force or fear applied to them, they fall *ipso iure* from the
clerical state (c. 132, § 2).

A married man who without apostolic dispensation receives major
orders, even in good faith, is forbidden to exercise those orders
(c. 132, § 3).

1. The law of clerical celibacy, which dates back to the Council
of Elvira early in the fourth century, has frequently been referred to
by the Supreme Pontiffs as "one of the chief ornaments of the Catholic clergy." Benedict XV declared: "We solemnly testify that the
Holy See will never in any way mitigate, much less abolish, this most
sacred and salutary law."[63] Pius XI, in the Encyclical on the Priesthood, calls it "one of the purest glories of the Catholic priesthood."

2. The canonical obligation begins with *major orders,* of which the
subdiaconate is the lowest.

3. The *substance* of the obligation consists in: (*a*) celibacy, or
refraining from marriage, which is invalid if attempted (c. 1072); and,
(*b*) chastity; that is, abstaining from all acts of impurity, *interior or
exterior,* which are forbidden by divine law to unmarried persons;
i.e., *interior* acts by the ninth commandment, *exterior* acts by the sixth.
There is no doubt whatever that even interior acts of impurity are
sacrilegious; for the canon makes no distinction between interior and

[62] Code Com., 12 Feb., 1935; *AAS*, 27–92; *Digest*, II, p. 53.
[63] Allocution, 16 Dec., 1920; *AAS*, 12–585; *Digest*, I, p. 121.

exterior acts, declaring them all sacrilegious; and the authorities on this point are in accord.[64]

4. There is a theoretical dispute as to the *source* of the obligation; namely, whether it arises merely from ecclesiastical law or from a vow implied in accepting the subdiaconate. We may hold, with Wernz, Lehmkuhl, Vermeersch, and others, that: (*a*) the immediate source of the obligation is the *vow* which, though no longer express, is implied in the ordination of subdeacons; (*b*) if the ordinand expressly declines the vow, he is bound by the *law*. This opinion, which is the common one, is adopted in a recent decision of the Rota.[65]

5. The *exception* provided for in canon 214 refers to the case of ordination under the influence of grave fear. It will be studied when that canon is reached.

6. *Minor clerics* can validly marry; but they are by that very fact legally reduced to the lay state and forbidden to exercise their orders.

7. As regards a man *already married:* (*a*) he is under a simple impediment which makes it illicit for him to receive major orders (c. 987, 2°); (*b*) without a dispensation, the ordination would be valid but illicit, and the exercise of the orders would be forbidden; (*c*) with a dispensation such a man may be licitly and validly ordained, but he is then forbidden to use the marriage rights, though the marriage remains valid.

8. The practice of the *Oriental Church* varies slightly. In most of the Oriental rites: (*a*) prospective deacons and priests may validly and licitly marry *before their ordination,* and may afterward use the rights of marriage while exercising their orders; (*b*) Bishops, however, must be either celibates or widowers, or men whose wives, by mutual agreement, have given up the use of marriage to enter religion.[66]

Cohabitation With Women. Clerics must be careful not to have in their houses nor to associate habitually with women who might be objects of suspicion (c. 133, §1).

They may live in the same house only with women who are beyond all suspicion of evil by reason of close relationship, such as mother, sister, or aunt, or who are above suspicion because of irreproachable character joined to a rather advanced age (c. 133, §2).

The decision as to whether living in the same house or habitual asso-

---

[64] Cf. Lehmkuhl, *Theol. Mor.,* II, n. 780; Vermeersch, *Theol. Mor.,* III, n. 30; Cappello, *Summa,* I, nn. 234, 235; Cappello, *De Matrimonio,* nn. 432, 433.

[65] S. R. Rota, 13 Jan., 1928; *Decisiones,* Vol. 20, p. 1; *Digest,* II, p. 554.

[66] Cf. V-C, *Epit.,* I, n. 251.

ciation with women, even with those who ordinarily are not under suspicion, may in a particular case be an occasion of scandal or a danger to chastity, belongs to the Ordinary of the place, and it is his business to forbid clerics such cohabitation or association (c. 133, § 3).

Clerics who are contumacious in this regard are presumed to be guilty of concubinage (c. 133, § 4).

Cohabitation in the wide sense means either to live in the same house with, or to frequent a person, that is, frequently to visit or to receive visits from him or her. The reasons for the prohibition to clerics of such relations with women are obviously: (*a*) to safeguard the chastity to which the priest is dedicated, and (*b*) to guard against even the appearance of evil.

1. *Near relatives* are by that very fact, ordinarily at least, free from all suspicion.

2. *In other cases,* the combination of two qualities makes the proximity of a woman relatively free from scandal or danger; namely: (*a*) an entirely irreproachable character, and (*b*) a rather advanced age. The canonical age in this connection has changed at various times. In this country today it is about forty.

3. The Third Council of Baltimore especially prohibits the habitual presence in the rectory of the families of the priest's relatives, and of young women who may be related to the assistant priest of the parish (n. 81).

4. The *decision* as to the propriety of cohabitation in all cases, even where the woman is by natural standards and according to this canon above suspicion, belongs entirely to the Ordinary.

5. *Contumacy* consists in failing to obey an authoritative warning (c. 2242, § 2); such priests are presumed to be guilty of the grave crime of concubinage, and are subject to its penalties (cf. cc. 2176–2181; 2359). The Church cannot afford to trifle in so sacred and serious a matter.

The Common Life. The practice of the common life for clerics is to be praised and favored; and where it already exists it is as far as possible to be continued (c. 134).

The common life among clerics; that is, living together and sharing a common table, is an aid to piety, a safeguard of chastity, and a mutual advantage in the work of the ministry. Hence, where already established, it is to be observed as far as possible; elsewhere, it cannot be imposed. The custom prevalent in the United States of having curates live with their pastors is a form of the common life (cf. c. 476, § 5).

The Breviary. Clerics who are in major orders, except those mentioned in canons 213 and 214, are bound to recite the canonical hours daily in their entirety according to the proper approved liturgical books **(c. 135).** The obligation of daily reciting the Breviary begins with major orders — subdiaconate.

Exceptions. 1. A cleric in major orders who has been legally reduced or has lawfully returned to the lay state, is free from this obligation, although this is not explicitly stated in the canon referred to (c. 213).

2. Clerics who received the order under the influence of grave fear may be reduced to the lay state by a special procedure, and are then free from the obligation (c. 214).

The *day* for fulfilling this obligation may be reckoned in any of the ways permitted in canon 33, if the recitation is private.

There is a plenary indulgence for reciting the entire office before the Blessed Sacrament.[67]

Clerical Dress. All clerics must wear a decent ecclesiastical dress in accordance with the legitimate local customs and the regulations of the Ordinary of the place, must wear the clerical tonsure or *corona* unless the accepted custom of the country is to the contrary, and must wear their hair in a simple style **(c. 136, § 1).**

They shall wear no ring unless the right to do so has been given them by law or by apostolic privilege **(c. 136, § 2).**

Minor clerics who on their own authority and without lawful reason lay aside the clerical dress and tonsure, and after being warned by the Ordinary fail to amend within a month, fall *ipso iure* from the clerical state **(c. 136, § 3).**

1. The importance which the Church attaches to this law is emphasized by a recent decree of the Sacred Congregation of the Council.[68] There can be no question but that the law binds in conscience. It may be urged by severe penalties (c. 2379).

2. The Third Council of Baltimore, n. 77, decreed that priests must wear the cassock while at home or in the church, and that on the street they must wear a black coat reaching to the knees. Both in and out of doors they are strictly enjoined to wear the Roman collar. No mention is made of the tonsure; and it is certainly not customary in

---

[67] S. Paen., 23 Oct., 1930; *AAS*, 22–493; *Digest*, I, p. 121.
[68] S. C. Conc., 28 July, 1931; *AAS*, 23–336; *Digest*, I, p. 123.

the United States. Few priests wear a coat reaching to the knees. Probably the *general* practice of wearing a shorter coat is by this time of sufficient duration to effect a mitigation in the law (c. 27). The same cannot be said of the style of gray clothes affected by a *few*.

External Appearance. 1. The *hair* is to be dressed in a simple style. The meaning undoubtedly is that there must be no sign of vanity. This provision is both very ancient and very modern; it is urged in some recent diocesan synods. If the Church thus prescribes a neat, plain, and manly exterior appearance for her priests, the use of perfumes and ointments that savor of effeminacy is evidently against the spirit of the law as well as contrary to good taste.

2. The use of a *wig* is unobjectionable, except perhaps during Mass. That a special permission is then needed may be argued from the fact that Apostolic Delegates are especially empowered to grant it.[69]

3. *Beards,* though neither forbidden nor sanctioned by the common law, are not customary in the United States, and may be forbidden by diocesan regulations.[70]

4. A *ring* is not to be worn unless allowed by law (cf. cc. 325, 1378) or by apostolic privilege.

Standing as Surety. A cleric is forbidden to give bail even upon the security of his own property, without consulting the Ordinary of the place **(c. 137).** This is forbidden also by the Third Council of Baltimore, n. 82.

Unbecoming Activities. Clerics must abstain completely from all activities which are unbecoming to their state: they must not engage in indecorous occupations, nor habitually indulge in gambling for money, nor carry weapons unless upon occasion there is reasonable cause for such precaution; they must not habitually be given to hunting, and must never hunt with a pack of hounds; they must not enter saloons or other similar places without necessity or some other just cause approved by the Ordinary of the place **(c. 138).**

The following activities are forbidden as unbecoming: (1) *indecorous occupations,* of which tavernkeeping is the stock example; (2) *habitual gambling* for money; (3) *carrying weapons,* unless reasonably necessary; (4) *habitual hunting,* and all noisy hunting with hounds; (5) entering *taverns.*

The Third Council of Baltimore, nn. 79 and 80, expressly forbade attendance at *horse races,* and entering or frequenting saloons.

---

[69] See *Faculties of Apostolic Delegate,* n. 35; *Digest,* I, p. 182. Cf. however, V-C, *Epit.,* I, n. 254.
[70] S. C. Conc., 11 Jan., 1920; *AAS,* 12–43; *Digest,* I, p. 123.

Venatio clamorosa means riding to hounds; it is this that is entirely forbidden. Ordinary shooting is allowed, unless it becomes habitual or excessive. In a case which arose in Poland, the Sacred Congregation of the Council declared that, while the Ordinary might entirely prohibit hunting by his clerics, still it is inadvisable to be too severe in this matter.[71]

Activities Foreign to the Clerical State (cf. c. 139). The general rule is that all such activities should be avoided. Some of them, however, may be practiced only with the permission of the Holy See, others with the permission of the Ordinary.

1. Those that require an indult from the *Holy See* are: (*a*) to practice medicine or surgery; (*b*) to exercise the office of notary public, except in the ecclesiastical Curia; (*c*) to accept any public office involving the exercise of lay jurisdiction or administration (c. 139, § 2).

2. Those that require permission of the cleric's *own Ordinary* are: (*a*) to undertake the administration of property which belongs to lay persons, or to assume secular offices which involve the duty of rendering an account. In the United States, we think the executor or administrator of a will is included here. The Code Commission has corrected a pre-Code decree which required permission to be obtained from the Holy See;[72] (*b*) to act as procurator or advocate, except in an ecclesiastical court, or in a civil court in one's own case or that of one's own church; (*c*) to take any part, even that of witness except in case of necessity, in a lay criminal trial where a grave personal penalty is involved (c. 139, § 3).

3. As regards running for or accepting *legislative offices:* (*a*) in places where there is a special papal prohibition, clerics may not do so without the permission of the Holy See; (*b*) in other places, the permission both of their own Ordinary and of the Ordinary of the place where the election is held is required.

Notes. 1. As regards running for *legislative offices,* Ordinaries should be strict rather than easy in granting the required permission. Cardinals, Archbishops, and Bishops, require the permission of the Holy See, except in places where, by the Constitution of the country and with the approval of the Holy See, they are *ex officio* senators.[73]

2. *Political action* on the part of the clergy, while not absolutely prohibited, is always subject to the direction of the Holy See and of

---

[71] S. C. Conc., 11 June, 1921; *AAS,* 13-498; *Digest,* I, p. 125.
[72] Code Com., 3 June, 1918; *AAS,* 10-344; *Digest,* I, p. 126.
[73] Code Com., 25 Apr., 1922; *AAS,* 14-313; *Digest,* I, p. 127.

the Ordinary, since it is not supposed to be undertaken except where the interests of the Church are concerned.[74]

3. *Catholic action,* defined as the participation of the laity in the apostolate of the hierarchy, must be promoted actively by all priests, religious as well as secular, for the general' ends outlined by the Holy Father and seconded by the Bishops in various countries. Some pontifical documents on this vital subject will be found in the *Canon Law Digest,* Vol. I, pp. 126–137, and Vol. II, pp. 56–74.[75]

4. Membership in *Rotary Clubs* is not expedient for clerics.[76]

Amusements and Public Shows. They shall not be present at spectacles, dances, and pageants which are unbecoming to them, or at which it would be scandalous for a cleric to be, especially in public theaters **(c. 140).** The word *pompa,* which occurs in this canon, may mean a parade or any form of public pageantry either in connection with worship or with occasions of a very different sort. The propriety of the presence of the clergy depends on the nature of the spectacle and the occasion, and therefore much is left to prudent discretion. The same is true of amusements within the field left open by the Code and its official interpretations.

1. *Shows in public theaters* were simply prohibited to the clergy by the Third Council of Baltimore, n. 79, a provision which is still effective throughout the United States. The Third Diocesan Synod of Chicago, n. 61, extended the prohibition to *operas,* declaring at the same time that it applied even outside the Archdiocese. Although some particular Councils in Europe[77] have forbidden their clergy all attendance at *public moving picture shows,* it seems that the more or less general interpretation in the United States (by individual Bishops) has been to exempt these performances from the general prohibition against attendance at public theaters. But the so-called "stage shows" or vaudeville performances which are given in regular movie houses are, in our opinion, already forbidden by the terms of the canon itself as, to say the least, "unbecoming" to clerics; certainly there is no reason

---

[74] Cf. Bénedict XV, 7 June, 1918; *AAS,* 10–440; *Digest,* I, p. 126; 12 Mar., 1919; *AAS,* 11–122; *Digest,* I, p. 126; 10 Feb., 1921; *AAS,* 13–127; *Digest,* I, p. 127; 16 July, 1921; *AAS,* 13–424; *Digest,* I, p. 127; Pius XI, 2 Feb., 1926; *AAS,* 18–175; *Digest,* I, p. 127; S. C. Conc., 15 March, 1927; *AAS,* 19–138; *Digest,* I, p. 128; Conc. Balt. III, n. 83.

[75] For further study, the following books are recommended: *The Call to Catholic Action* (Jos. Wagner: N. Y.); Civardi-Martindale, *A Manual of Catholic Action* (Sheed and Ward); Will-Hennrich, *Catholic Action Handbook* (Jos. Wagner: N. Y.); Guerry, *L'Action Catholique* (Desclée de Brouwer: Paris).

[76] S. C. Consist., 4 Feb., 1929; *AAS,* 21–42; *Digest,* I, p. 617.

[77] E.g., *Conc. Mechlinen.* IV, 1920, n. 136.

to exempt them from the general prohibition. Attendance at *horse races* is proscribed in general by the Third Council of Baltimore, n. 79.

2. *Parish picnics and dances* have given occasion to the following official documents:

a. The Third Council of Baltimore, n. 290, laid down some regulations for picnics, and added: "We also order that priests abolish the abuse by which *dinners with dances* are arranged in order to promote pious works."

b. The Sacred Consistorial Congregation, by decree of 31 March, 1916, urged the above regulations, and added that clerics should not even *attend dances.*

c. The same Sacred Congregation, by a declaration of 10 Dec., 1917, confirmed this last prohibition and declared it applicable even to dances held during the day or in the early evening, even without dinner, or in connection with picnics.[78] These prohibitions are still in effect, but, as Vermeersch wisely remarks, they are to be observed and enforced with prudence.[79]

3. Priests on *summer vacations* should pay careful attention to the recent decree of the Sacred Congregation of the Council on that subject.[80] Its rather severe provisions were addressed to all Ordinaries and should be observed everywhere.

Military Service, Etc. We have already seen that this is quite alien to the clerical state (c. 121). *Volunteering* is therefore out of the question except where, with the permission of the Ordinary, it might be done as a means of being sooner freed from compulsory service (c. 141, § 1). The penalty for violation of this provision by a *minor cleric* is automatic lapse from the clerical state (c. 141, § 2). Much more is *internal warfare* and the promotion of *public disturbances* forbidden.

Business and Trade. Clerics are forbidden to conduct business or trade, either personally or through agents, either for their own benefit or that of other persons (c. 142). Since this prohibition is taken without change from the older law, it is subject to the same interpretations which were accepted before the Code.

Business (negotiatio) in general means any transactions made for the sake of gain; while *trade (mercatura)* is buying and selling merchandise — one kind of business. Since business is the broader term, the specification of what business is licit or illicit for clerics will be

---

[78] Cf. *Digest,* I, p. 137.
[79] Vermeersch, *Theol. Mor.,* III, n. 18 f.
[80] S. C. Conc., 1 July, 1926; *AAS,* 18–312; *Digest,* I, p. 138.

sufficient; as every form of trade will be found included somewhere in the classification. It should be noted that the canon refers only to *habitual* transactions; single isolated instances do not fall under the prohibition.

Negotiatio, or business, may be divided as follows:

1. It is called *quaestuosa,* or profit seeking, when it consists in buying merchandise with the intention of selling it unchanged at a profit. This is *trade* in the strict sense. It has some special forms:

a. Cambium, or money changing, where the matter bought and sold is money itself;

b. Speculation, where stocks, bonds, or commodities are bought and sold with a view chiefly to immediate profit without expectation of permanent ownership.

2. Business is called industrial (*negotiatio industriosa*) if it consists in buying materials, changing them, and selling them for profit. This is further subdivided:

a. It is *strictly industrial,* where the change of the material is done by hired labor;

b. It is industrial *in the broad sense,* where it is done by one's own or domestic labor.

3. *Economic* or domestic business consists in the profitable manipulation of more or less permanent investments.

Principles. 1. *Profit-seeking* business and *strictly industrial* business are forbidden.

2. *Industrial* business *in the broad* sense and *economic* business are not forbidden.

Excusing Causes. Engaging in forbidden business may be excused by the following causes:

1. *Necessity* of the cleric himself or his family; in which case it is well to secure the permission of the Ordinary;

2. *Inheritance* or *succession* to a going business which cannot be laid aside without loss; in which case the permission of the Holy See should be obtained to continue it.

Practical Cases. 1. A priest is in charge of an industrial trade school. The products of the pupils' work may be sold, even though a slight wage be paid to the pupils.

2. To sell books to students in connection with a school, or pious articles to pilgrims in connection with a shrine, is not profit-seeking business, provided it is reasonably conducted and is really not for profit but for the convenience of the buyers.

3. A priest may make investments in stocks and bonds, provided the investments are really economic and not speculative.

4. Products manufactured from one's own materials, such as butter, wine, chocolate, beer, cheese, liqueurs, may be sold with a profit.

5. To take a lease on property for the express purpose of subletting it at a profit, is forbidden. But if one has taken the lease for other purposes and finds himself unable to use the property, to sublet it with profit would be an economic measure, quite allowable.

Religious are bound by all the canons (cc. 124-142) on the common obligations of clerics (cf. c. 592).

Residence. Clerics, even though they have no residential benefice or office, must not absent themselves from their diocese for any notable time without at least the presumed permission of their Ordinary **(c. 143).**

One who, with the permission of his own Ordinary, has gone to another diocese, remaining incardinated in his own, can be recalled for just cause and with due regard for natural equity; and the Ordinary of the other diocese also, unless he has conferred a benefice upon him, can for just cause refuse him permission to remain longer in his territory **(c. 144).**

1. *All clerics* are bound to residence in their diocese even though they have no residential benefice or office; that is, a benefice (c. 1411, 3°), or office (c. 465), to which a special duty of residence is attached.

2. A *notable time* has been defined in a private authentic document in this connection as a period exceeding one month.[81]

3. *Presumed permission* means permission not actually given expressly nor tacitly, but which would be given if it were asked. Three conditions are required for its legitimate use: (*a*) that the person who is to give the permission cannot be approached here and now; (*b*) that the person who wishes the permission honestly thinks that it would be given; (*c*) that he notify the superior afterward. See Risk, *The Presumed Permission,* in *Review for Religious,* Vol. I, p. 196. Permission to leave the diocese on a vacation should be *asked expressly* in accordance with the recent letter of the Sacred Congregation of the Council.[82]

Recall of Absent Priest. This is a right of the Ordinary, since the absent cleric is still incardinated in his diocese. A just cause is required,

---

[81] S. C. Consist., 7 Mar., 1925; *Il Monitore Ecclesiastico,* 1925, p. 97; V-C, *Epit.,* I, n. 261.

[82] S. C. Conc., 1 July, 1926; *AAS,* 18–312; *Digest,* I, p. 138.

since permission was originally given for the absence. Natural equity may require forbearance in the exercise of the strictly legal right of recall; for example, where the poverty of the priest would make an immediate change of residence a hardship.

Exclusion From Territory. A just cause is required, because this is in the nature of a penalty (c. 2298, 7°). If a benefice has been lawfully obtained, the right of residence has been acquired.

Readings:

Brunini, *The Clerical Obligations of Canons 139 and 142,* Catholic University, 1937 (n. 103); *Ecclesiastical Review,* Vol. 87, p. 409 (on business forbidden to clerics); Vol. 93, p. 360 (Monsignor Kerby, on priest's meditation); Vol. 97, p. 191 (Schaaf, on attendance at diocesan conferences by religious in parish work); *Irish Ecclesiastical Record,* 1937, p. 499 (Fallon, on obligation to wear clerical dress on vacation); *Periodica,* 1934, p. 218* (Lopez, on vow of chastity in major orders).

CHAPTER III

ECCLESIASTICAL OFFICES; JURISDICTION; REDUCTION TO THE LAY STATE

Section 1. Ecclesiastical Offices (cc. 145-195)

PRELIMINARY SURVEY

Definition and Division of Offices (cc. 145, 146)
Canonical Provision (c. 147)
Various Forms of Canonical Provision (c. 148)
Free Conferring (cc. 152-159)
Election (cc. 160-178)
Postulation (cc. 179-182)
Loss of Ecclesiastical Offices (cc. 183-195)

Ecclesiastical Office is a term to be taken in the strict sense unless the contrary appear **(c. 145, § 2)**. It includes the following elements **(cf. c. 145, § 1)**.

1. It must be *permanently established,* in the sense that the office itself is permanent; if the incumbent loses the office, the office itself does not cease to exist; it merely becomes vacant.

2. It must be *established by law,* divine or ecclesiastical. The papacy is an office established by divine law; as is also the episcopate in general. The offices of Vicar General, pastor, are established by ecclesiastical law.

3. It must be *conferred according to law.* The legal manner of conferring offices is governed by canons 147-182.

4. It must *carry with it some participation in ecclesiastical power* either of order or of jurisdiction. If the power is that of jurisdiction, it must be ordinary, that is, attached by the law itself to the office (c. 197). However, Vermeersch-Creusen (*Epitome,* II, n. 742) hold that delegated jurisdiction is sufficient. If the power is that of order, it must be distinct from that which is conferred by ordination, because what is now required is a power *attached to the office* as such. For examples of such powers, see canons 294, § 2; 310.

Examples. Bishop, pastor, rural dean, Vicar General, all have offices in the strict sense. A confessor as such has not, because his power of jurisdiction is delegated, not ordinary (c. 874). Priest, deacon, subdeacon, as such, have no ecclesiastical office.[1]

Benefice is defined in canon 1409 as a juridical entity (moral person) permanently established or created by competent ecclesiastical authority, consisting of a sacred office and the right to receive the revenues attached to the office by endowment. Offices which are also benefices are governed also by the canons (cc. 1409–1494) on benefices **(c. 146).**

Parishes in the United States are both offices and benefices.[2]

Canonical Provision of Offices. An ecclesiastical office cannot be validly obtained without canonical provision **(c. 147, § 1).**

Canonical provision means the grant of an ecclesiastical office by competent ecclesiastical authority, made according to the sacred canons **(c. 147, § 2).**

Provision of an ecclesiastical office is made by way of free conferring by the legitimate superior; or by investiture by the same superior in case there has been a presentation of the candidate by a patron, or the nomination of the candidate; or by confirmation or admission by the same superior, in case there has been an election or a postulation; or finally by simple election and the acceptance thereof by the person elected, in case the election does not need to be confirmed **(c. 148, § 1).**

As regards the provision of offices by investiture, the prescriptions of canons 1448–1471 are to be observed **(c. 148, § 2).**

The law uses five terms to designate as many different forms of canonical provision: *free conferring, investiture, confirmation, admission,* and *acceptance* of an election. These, however, are only the final steps; it appears that some of them are preceded by other steps toward the acquisition of the office; for example, investiture is preceded by presentation or nomination; confirmation is preceded by election; admission, by postulation. In order to grasp the meaning of these terms clearly, we must distinguish three successive stages which may occur in the full enjoyment of an office.

Stages in Full Acquisition of Office. (1) The first stage is the designation of the person. At most such designation confers, not the *ius in re,* that is, the office itself, but only the *ius ad rem,* that is, the right

---

[1] Cf. Cappello, *Summa,* I, n. 271.
[2] Letter of Apostolic Delegate, U. S., 10 Nov., 1922; *Digest,* I, p. 149. Cf. also S. C. Conc., *Principis Alberten. et Saskatoonen.,* 5 March, 1932; *AAS,* 25–436; *Digest,* I, p. 151.

to obtain the office. (2) The second stage is the actual grant of the office to the person so designated, who thereby acquires the office (*ius in re*). (3) In the case of *benefices* and of certain offices, there is moreover required a canonical entry into possession. This may be required even for the *validity* of official acts. Thus canon 1095 requires it for the validity of a pastor's or Bishop's assistance at marriages in his territory. Our present canon does not deal with this third stage in the full enjoyment of an office but only with the first two stages by which the office is acquired.

Preliminary Steps. 1. *Presentation* is the designation of the person for an ecclesiastical office, made by virtue of the right of patronage in the strict sense as governed by canons 1448–1471.

2. *Nomination* is the designation of the person, made by virtue of some privilege other than the strict right of patronage.

3. *Election,* when it needs to be confirmed by the superior, is merely a preliminary step, designating the person.

4. *Postulation* means the designation of a person who is legally ineligible for the office; it amounts to a request on the part of the electors, asking the superior to dispense from the ineligibility (c. 179).

Final Steps. 1. *Free conferring* is the granting of an office by the ecclesiastical superior *freely;* that is, without the intervention of any preliminary action by a privileged person. It both designates the person and confers the office (*ius in re*).

2. *Investiture* is the act of the superior granting the office to a person previously designated either by presentation or nomination.[3]

3. *Confirmation* is the act of the superior granting the office to a person previously designated by an election which needs confirmation.

4. *Admission* is the act of the superior conferring the office on an ineligible candidate who has previously been designated by postulation.

5. *Acceptance* is the act of the candidate himself accepting an office which has previously been proffered him in an election which needs no confirmation. In this case the will of the superior expressed in the law confers the office automatically upon its acceptance. In the single case of the election of the Supreme Pontiff, the power connected with the office comes directly by divine law (c. 219).

---

[3] Cf. S. C. Conc., 12 Nov., 1921; *AAS*, 14–459; *Digest*, I, p. 140.

Canonical Provisions of Ecclesiastical Offices

No right	Ius ad rem	Ius in re	Full possession
1.	....	Free conferring	
2.	Presentation	Investiture	(Canonical entry
3.	Nomination	Investiture	when required.)
4.	Election	Confirmation	
5. Postulation	....	Admission	
6.	Election	Acceptance	

Fitness for an ecclesiastical office means the sum of all the qualities required by law, not merely for the validity but also for the propriety of the appointment. It is to be judged by the candidate's own Ordinary, unless the appointment is being made by the Supreme Pontiff himself; and in judging it the Ordinary may require an examination (cf. c. 149).

Qualifications required by law are generally presumed *not* to be required for *validity,* unless it is so stated (c. 153, § 3).

1. Since clerics alone are capable of ecclesiastical jurisdiction (c. 118), *tonsure* or some valid *order* is, by ecclesiastical law, a prerequisite for the validity of any office, except as provided in c. 219.

2. The *priesthood* is a prerequisite for the validity of all offices which involve the care of souls (c. 154).

Vacancy of an office means the want of a legitimate titular or of an actual incumbent. An office is: (1) vacant both *de iure* and *de facto* if it lacks both a legitimate titular and an actual incumbent; (2) it is vacant *de iure* only, if it lacks a legitimate titular but has an actual incumbent; (3) it is vacant *de facto* only, if it lacks an actual incumbent but has a legitimate titular.

Principles. 1. Appointment to an office which is not vacant *de iure* is null; and the subsequent vacancy of the office does not make it valid (c. 150, § 1). The ways in which an office becomes vacant *de iure* are enumerated in canon 183, § 1.

2. The promise of an office which is not vacant *de iure* is void of juridical effect (c. 150, § 2).

3. Appointment can be made to an office which is vacant *de iure* though there is an unlawful incumbent in possession, provided, (*a*) that the illegitimacy of the occupation has been declared, and (*b*) that the said declaration is mentioned in the letter of appointment (c. 151).

Free Conferring is the principal manner of promotion to ecclesiastical offices. It is dealt with in detail in canons 152–159. We shall call attention summarily to these provisions.

1. The Ordinary of the place usually has the right of conferring offices in his territory (c. 152).

2. The candidate must be a cleric and have the qualifications required by law. The office should be given to the most worthy candidate. The requisite qualifications are not *ad validitatem* unless the law so states (c. 153).

3. Offices involving the care of souls cannot be validly conferred on one who is not a priest (c. 154).

4. Incompatible offices must not be conferred on one and the same person (c. 156).

5. Appointments to all offices should be committed to writing (c. 159).

Election is the subject of canons 160–178. The election of the Supreme Pontiff is regulated exclusively by the Apostolic Constitution, *Vacantis Apostolicae Sedis,* which abrogates earlier documents.[4] A brief summary of the manner of electing the Supreme Pontiff will be given later.[5] The provisions of the Code governing elections in general may be summarized as follows:

An election by a college must be held within three months from notice of the vacancy of the office; otherwise the appointment devolves upon the superior who had the right to confirm the election or who has the right to appoint in default of election (c. 161).

Convocation of the college must be made according to law;[6] if a member was absent because not legally called, the election is valid but may be set aside at his instance; if more than a third of the electors failed to be convoked, the election is invalid; but failure to convoke has no effect if the person was nevertheless present; in an election to an office which is to be held for life, convocation made before the vacancy (*de iure*) of the office is of no effect (c. 162).

After legal convocation the right to elect belongs to those present at the time and place designated in the call, there being no right to vote by letter or by proxy unless it is granted by particular law (c. 163).[7]

---

[4] Cf. *AAS,* 38–65.

[5] In connection with canon 218.

[6] The right to determine the place where the general chapter shall be held in a diocesan religious congregation which has spread to several dioceses belongs to the superioress general, and the right to preside belongs to the Ordinary of the place where the election is held. S. C. Rel., 2 July, 1921; *AAS,* 13–481; *Digest,* I, p. 279.

[7] On exclusion of votes by letter or by proxy see S. C. Conc., 15 March, 1930; *AAS,* 25–315; *Digest,* I, p. 709.

Even though one have the right to vote in his own name on several grounds, he has but one vote (c. 164).

No stranger may be allowed to vote (in the absence of duly acquired privilege) under pain of nullity of the election (c. 165).

An election is void if the lay power interferes effectively to the detriment of canonical liberty (c. 166).

The following are incapable of voting: (1) persons incapable of a human act; (2) those who have not attained puberty (cf. c. 88, § 2); (3) those who are under censure,[8] or legal infamy (cf. c. 2293, § 2), after a declaratory or condemnatory sentence; (4) those who have joined or publicly adhered to a heretical or schismatical sect; (5) those who are deprived of active voice either by lawful sentence of a judge or by general or particular law. If any of these are allowed to vote, their vote is null, but the election is valid unless it is clear either that the number of valid votes was insufficient to elect or that the vote of a person excommunicated by declaratory or condemnatory sentence was knowingly admitted (c. 167).

Special provision is made for taking the vote of an elector who is present in the house but is unable to attend the election because of illness (c. 168).

A vote is invalid unless it is (1) free (hence it is invalid if obtained by grave fear or fraud); (2) secret, certain, absolute, and determinate. All conditions attached to a vote before the election are regarded as null (c. 169).

No one can validly vote for himself (c. 170).

The details of the election (appointment of tellers, counting the votes, etc.) are governed by canon 171.

Election by compromise may be agreed upon by unanimous vote, and must be conducted in accordance with canons 172, 173.

The number of votes required to elect is determined by canon 101, § 1, 1°; the person so elected must be announced by the one who presides (c. 174); and must moreover be notified; he must within eight days declare whether he accepts or renounces it; otherwise he loses all right he may have acquired from the election (c. 175).[9]

If the person elected renounces his right, he loses it, even though he later change his mind; but he can be elected again; and the college

---

[8] I.e., excommunication, *personal* interdict, or *general* suspension. Cf. cc. 2278, § 2, 2279, 2280; Wernz-Vidal, *De Personis*, p. 265.
[9] The right in this case is a *ius ad rem,* since *ius in re* (the office itself) is never acquired through election without acceptance.

should proceed to a new election within a month from notice of the renunciation. By acceptance, if no confirmation is required, the person elected immediately acquires the full right (*ius in re*); otherwise, only the *ius ad rem*. Before confirmation he may not interfere in any way in the office, and any acts so placed are null (c. 176).

If the election needs to be confirmed, the elect must ask for confirmation within eight days; otherwise he loses his right, unless he proves that he was prevented by some just reason. The superior, if he finds the elect duly qualified, and if the election was made according to law, may not refuse to confirm it. The confirmation should be given in writing. Upon confirmation the elect acquires the full right in the office, unless the law provide otherwise (c. 177).

In case the election is not held within the prescribed time, or if the college is penally deprived of the right to elect, the free conferring of the office devolves upon the superior who should have confirmed the election or who has the next right of appointment (c. 178).

Summary of Causes Which Make an Election Void.[10] 1. If more than a third of the electors were absent *because* they were not called (c. 162, §§ 3, 4).

2. If, in the absence of special privilege, a stranger was admitted to vote (c. 165). A member of the college who has no right to vote is not a stranger.

3. If the lay power interfered with the canonical liberty of the election (c. 166).

4. If the person failed to receive a sufficient number of votes, not counting votes that are invalid (cc. 167, § 2, 101).

5. If a person excommunicated by sentence was *knowingly* admitted to vote (c. 167, § 2).

6. If the number of votes exceeds the number of electors (c. 171, § 3).

Postulation is explained in canons 179–182. If the person whom the electors consider better qualified and whom they prefer for the office, is ineligible by reason of some impediment which can be and usually is dispensed, they may by their votes *postulate* that candidate, even for an office in which the person elected needs no confirmation (c. 179, § 1). Postulation, however, confers no right on the candidate until he receives the office by *admission* on the part of the superior. Postulation always requires at least a majority, and requires a majority of two thirds when it "concurs with an election" (c. 180, § 1), i.e., when in

---

[10] Cf. V-C, *Epit.*, I, n. 288. This summary does not include elections by compromise.

the same election in which an ineligible candidate is postulated, some eligible candidate is voted for.[11]

Loss of Ecclesiastical Offices. Canon 183 enumerates the various ways in which ecclesiastical offices may be lost: (1) by resignation (cc. 184–191); (2) by privation (c. 192); (3) by removal (cc. 2401; 2147; 2157); (4) by transfer (cc. 193, 194; 2162–2167); (5) by expiration of the prescribed time (c. 183, § 1). But unless the law provides otherwise, the titutlar can *validly* exercise his office even after the lapse of time, until his successor is appointed.

An office is *not* lost by the expiration of the authority of the superior who conferred the office, unless the law so state, or the appointment contain the clause "during our good pleasure" or some equivalent clause (c. 183, § 2).

Resignation: Validity. Any person of sound mind can, for a just cause, resign an ecclesiastical office, unless there is some special prohibition against it (c. 184). A resignation made through grave fear unjustly induced, or through fraud, or substantial error, or simony, is null and void (c. 185). In order that a resignation be valid it must be made personally either in writing or orally before two witnesses, or it can also be made by a proxy who has a special mandate; a written record of the resignation should be kept in the Curia (c. 186).

Generally speaking, a resignation, in order to be valid, must be made to the person by whom it is to be accepted, or, if it requires no acceptance, to the person from whom the holder received his office, or that person's representative. Hence, if an office was conferred by confirmation, admission, or investiture, the resignation must be made to the superior who has according to the common law the right to confirm or invest (c. 187).

Tacit Resignation. There are certain causes which effect the tacit resignation of an office, which resignation is accepted in advance by operation of law, and hence is effective without any declaration (c. 188). These causes are: (1) If the holder of the office has pronounced religious vows, except as provided in canon 584 regarding benefices; (the latter become vacant only three years later, or in the case of parishes, one year later); (2) if after his appointment he has failed to assume the office within the prescribed time; (3) if he has accepted another office incompatible with the first, and has taken peaceful possession of the same; (4) if he has publicly fallen away from the

---

[11] For an interesting application of this provision, see Code Com., 1 July, 1922; *AAS*, 14–406; *Digest*, I, p. 142.

Catholic faith; (5) if he has contracted marriage, even a merely "civil" one; (6) if he has volunteered for secular military service against the provision of canon 141, § 1; (7) if he has laid aside the clerical dress on his own authority without just cause, and after having been warned by the Ordinary, has failed to resume it within one month from the warning; (8) if he has illegitimately departed from the residence to which he was bound, and, after having received warning from the Ordinary, and without any legitimate excuse, has failed either to appear or to reply within a suitable time fixed by the Ordinary.

Acceptance of Resignation: Effects. Superiors should not accept resignations without a just and proportionate cause. An Ordinary of a place must either accept or reject a resignation within one month (c. 189).[12]

When a resignation has been made and accepted according to law, and the acceptance thereof has been made known to the person who resigned, the office becomes vacant. The person resigning should continue in the office until he has received certain notice of the superior's acceptance **(c. 190).**

Once a resignation has been made according to law, there is no longer any room for changing one's mind,[13] but the person who resigned may obtain the office by some other title. The acceptance of a resignation must be made known in due time to those who have any right in regard to the conferring of the office **(c. 191).**

Deprivation of Office. A person may be unwillingly deprived of, or removed from, an office, either by operation of law or by an act of the lawful superior **(c. 192, § 1).** Deprivation and removal are not mutually exclusive terms.

1. Deprivation is effected *by operation of law:* (*a*) in the cases of *tacit resignation* enumerated above under canon 188; (*b*) in certain cases where the law declares privation from office as a penalty: e.g., upon *sentence* of excommunication, in the case of a *vitandus* (c. 2266), upon deposition (c. 2303), degradation (c. 2305), and in certain other cases (cf. cc. 2396–2398).

2. It may be done *by an act of the lawful superior.* This may be

---

[12] The Ordinary can validly accept a resignation after the lapse of a month, unless the person who resigned has, before the acceptance of the resignation, withdrawn it and given notice of the withdrawal to the Ordinary. Code Com., 14 July, 1922; *AAS,* 14–526; *Digest,* I, p. 143.

[13] One can, however, withdraw his resignation at any time before it has been accepted. Code Com., 14 July, 1922; *AAS,* 14–526; *Digest,* I, p. 143.

either *penal* or *administrative*. It is penal, only if a crime has been committed for which deprivation of office is the legal penalty, not incurred *ipso facto,* but upon judicial sentence or particular precept. It is administrative when the superior deprives a person of an office, according to the law, yet not as a penalty for crime, but in the course of the administration of the Church's government.

Irremovable Offices. Offices are classed as *removable* (if the removal of the incumbent is relatively easy) or *irremovable* (if it is more difficult). No office is absolutely irremovable.

In the case of an irremovable office, the Ordinary cannot deprive the cleric of the office without *due process of law* (c. 192, § 2). This due process may be either judicial or administrative. In certain penal cases a strictly judicial process may be required (cf. c. 1933 *et seq.*). In other cases, penal or nonpenal, even in the case of irremovable offices, the due process may be merely administrative. For example, administrative process is provided for proceeding against nonresident clerics (cc. 2168–2175), and against those guilty of concubinage (cc. 2176–2185). Likewise for the removal of pastors, both removable and irremovable, the process is administrative; and it is certain that even irremovable pastors may be removed without being charged with any crime (cf. cc. 2147–2156).

Removable Offices. In the case of removable offices, deprivation can be decreed by the Ordinary for any reasonable cause according to his prudent judgment, even without crime on the part of the incumbent, but with the observance of natural equity. In these cases the Ordinary is not bound to follow any prescribed procedure, except as provided in the canons regarding the removal of removable pastors (i.e., cc. 2157–2161). However, the deprivation does not become effective until it has been declared by the superior; and a recourse, without suspensive effect, may be taken to the Holy See from the decree of the Ordinary (c. 192, § 3).

Transfer. Transfer from one office to another can be effected only by the person who has the right both to accept a resignation from and to remove from the first office, and to appoint to the second. If a transfer is made with the consent of the cleric (who has the office), any just cause is sufficient for it; if it is done against his will, it requires about the same cause and the same process as deprivation from office, except as provided in canons 2162–2167 regarding the transfer of pastors (c. 193).

In a transfer the first office becomes vacant when the cleric takes canonical possession of the second, unless the law or the legitimate superior has provided otherwise. The person transferred receives the income of the first office until he is in possession of the second (c. 194).

Persons who may have elected, postulated, or presented a cleric for an office have no power to deprive him of it, or to recall or remove him from it, or to transfer him to another office (c. 195).

CASES AND QUESTIONS

1. A pastor, after his appointment but before taking possession of the parish, assists officially at a marriage in the parish. Is the marriage valid? (Cc. 461, 1095, 1444, § 1).

2. A Bishop requests the resignation of a removable pastor, X; the pastor refuses to resign, but departs when the Bishop appoints Y as pastor in his place. Thereafter the proceedings for the canonical removal of X are completed (cf. cc. 2157–2161). Is Y now the lawful pastor? (C. 150, § 1).

3. In the election of a superioress in a religious congregation of women, A received 29 votes on the first ballot, B 17 votes, and C 3 votes. It was learned that the chaplain had cast a vote for C. Is A lawfully elected? (Cc. 101, 165).

4. Shortly after B took possession of the parish of St. Agnes upon appointment by the Bishop, the Bishop died. Does B need to be confirmed as pastor by the new Bishop of the diocese? (C. 183, § 2).

5. After orally resigning from his parish in a private interview with the Bishop, pastor X changes his mind. When he informs the Bishop of this, the latter says: "It is too late now; I have just appointed Y as your successor." Who is the lawful pastor? (Cc. 183, § 1, 186, 150, § 1).

6. In August, L is appointed by his Bishop as pastor of St. Michael's parish (which is vacant), with instructions to take possession before October 1. L neglects to do anything until October 10. The Bishop has in the meantime (on October 2) declared the parish again vacant and has appointed another pastor. Has L any recourse? (Cc. 188, 2°, 1444, § 2). What if L can show that he was prevented by serious illness from taking possession before? (Cc. 188, 2°, 35).

7. Q wrote to his Bishop resigning his office as pastor. A month later, having received no reply, he wrote that he had changed his mind and now wished to remain as pastor. The next day he received a letter from the Bishop accepting his resignation. Is he still the lawful pastor? (Cc. 189, § 2, 190, § 1, *Digest*, I, p. 143).

Reading:
Parsons, *Canonical Elections*, Catholic University, 1939 (n. 118).

Section 2. Jurisdiction (cc. 196–210)

PRELIMINARY SURVEY

Jurisdiction. The power of jurisdiction or government which is in the Church by divine institution, is divided into that of the external forum and that of the internal forum, or the forum of conscience; and the latter is either sacramental or extra-sacramental (c. 196).

Jurisdiction is the *power to govern* the faithful for the supernatural end for which the Church was established by Christ. This power is in the Church by *divine institution,* because Christ with divine authority placed it there (cf. c. 108). Its chief classifications are: (1) jurisdiction in the *external* and *internal fora* (c. 196); (2) *ordinary* and *delegated* jurisdiction (c. 197); (3) *judicial* and *voluntary* jurisdiction (c. 201).

Forum means in general a place for the transaction of official business, judicial or administrative. In the present connection it designates rather a field or province of action than a physical place.

1. The *external* forum is the forum of the Church's external government. Jurisdiction in the external forum: (*a*) concerns actions whereby the faithful are innocent or guilty in the eyes of the Church as members of the Church; and (*b*) it is exercised publicly, and has juridical effects.

2. The *internal* forum is the forum of conscience. Jurisdiction in the internal forum: (*a*) concerns actions whereby the faithful are innocent or guilty before God; and (*b*) it is exercised privately, and has no juridical effects, unless these are specially provided for. Thus canon 2251, by way of exception, provides for certain juridical effects of an absolution from a censure given in the internal forum.

Jurisdiction in the internal forum is *sacramental* when it must be exercised in the Sacrament of Penance or in connection with it (cf. cc. 1044, 2250, 2254, 2290); it is *extra-sacramental* when not subject to this limitation.

Examples. To which forum do the following acts of jurisdiction pertain:

1. Dispensation from consanguinity for marriage?

2. Sacramental absolution from a censure of excommunication?

3. Dispensation, given outside of confession, from an occult matrimonial impediment? (Cf. c. 1037).

Ordinary Jurisdiction has two essential qualities: (1) it must be *attached to an office in the strict sense* (cf. c. 145); (2) it must be attached to that office *by the law* (c. 197, § 1); that is, either by the common law or a particular law, either by written law or lawful custom.

Delegated Jurisdiction is any which has not these two qualities; it is merely *given to a person* (c. 197, § 1). This may be done in either of two ways:

1. The *law itself* may grant the jurisdiction in certain circumstances; as canon 882 grants to all priests jurisdiction to absolve from all sins and censures in danger of death. This is called jurisdiction *delegated by law*. It is not ordinary because it is not attached to an office in the strict sense. The priesthood is not such an office.

2. The jurisdiction may be expressly granted by a *special act* of the superior. Such jurisdiction is delegated, whether the person be chosen for personal qualifications or by reason of the office which he holds. Thus the quinquennial faculties of Bishops, though in a certain sense attached to the office (cf. c. 66), are not ordinary jurisdiction because they are not attached to the office *by law,* but are merely given to the person who holds the office.

Ordinary jurisdiction is *proper* if it is exercised by one who has it in his own name; it is *vicarious* if exercised in the name of another. Thus the Bishop in the government of the diocese exercises *ordinary proper* jurisdiction; but the jurisdiction of many officers who are denominated as "vicars" in the Code; e.g., Vicar General (c. 366), Vicar Capitular (c. 432), *vicarius oeconomus* (c. 473), is *ordinary* because attached to their office by law, but *vicarious* because it is exercised in the name of another.

Examples. Specify the kind of jurisdiction exercised by:

1. A confessor with diocesan faculties (c. 874, § 1);

2. A pastor as regards confessions in his parish (c. 873, § 1);

3. An assistant (*vicarius co-operator*) in the general work of the parish; (this is a difficult question whose considerations may perhaps be postponed until it is met with again under canon 476);

4. A priest absolving in danger of death by virtue of canon 882;

5. A Bishop using his quinquennial faculties (c. 66);

6. A Bishop granting permission to say Mass outside a church (c. 822);[14]

7. A Vicar General acting within his regular powers in diocesan government (c. 366, § 1);

8. A Vicar Delegate appointed by Ordinaries in mission countries;[15]

9. A Coadjutor (c. 352) or Auxiliary Bishop (c. 350, § 3; 351, §§ 1, 2);

10. A Vicar Apostolic or Prefect Apostolic (c. 294, § 1).

Ordinaries. **Canon 198** is of very great practical consequence because the Code frequently attributes certain powers to Ordinaries or to Ordinaries of places and it is essential to define clearly who these are.[16]

Ordinaries, besides the Roman Pontiff, are:

1. *For their respective territories:* (*a*) a *residential Bishop,* not however a merely titular Bishop, nor an Auxiliary, unless he is also Vicar General;[17] (*b*) an *Abbot* or *Prelate nullius* (cc. 319, 323); (*c*) a *Vicar General* (c. 366); (*d*) an *Apostolic Administrator* (cc. 312, 313, 315); (*e*) a *Vicar Apostolic* (c. 293) and *Prefect Apostolic* (c. 293); (*f*) those who, in default of any of the above, temporarily succeed to the government, either according to law or by virtue of approved religious constitutions **(c. 198, § 1);** for example, a Vicar Capitular (cc. 427, 432).

---

[14] Cf. S. C. Sacr., 5 Jan., 1928; *AAS,* 20–79; *Digest,* I, p. 391.

[15] Cf. S. C. Prop. Fid., 8 Dec., 1919; *AAS,* 12–120; *Digest,* I, p. 144.

[16] See the summary of dispensing powers under c. 82.

[17] At the present writing (1944) an Auxiliary Bishop holds the office of Vicar General in the following archdioceses: Baltimore-Washington, Cincinnati, Detroit, Philadelphia. In the following, the Auxiliary Bishop is not the Vicar General: Boston, Chicago, Los Angeles, Newark, New York, Saint Louis, San Francisco; and in the dioceses of Brooklyn and Buffalo.

2. *For their own subjects, major* superiors (c. 488, 8°) in *clerical* religious institutes (c. 488, 4°) which are *exempt* (c. 615).

Ordinaries of a place or of places are all the aforesaid except the religious superiors (c. 198, § 2). The reason is that the jurisdiction of the religious superiors attaches to the person of their subjects without direct dependence upon territory; whereas all the others above mentioned have jurisdiction over their subjects by reason of their domicile or quasi-domicile within the territory (c. 94, § 1), and over other persons by reason of their staying within the territory. Hence also, the latter are called Ordinaries *for their respective territories,* whereas the religious superiors are called Ordinaries only *for their own subjects.* It is only in *exempt clerical* institutes that religious superiors as such have true ecclesiastical jurisdiction; in others they have only dominative power (c. 501, § 1).

Delegation and Subdelegation. One who has ordinary power of jurisdiction can delegate it in whole or in part to another, unless the law expressly provide otherwise **(c. 199, § 1).**

Also the power of jurisdiction delegated by the Holy See can be subdelegated, either by way of act, or even habitually, unless the person receiving the delegated power was chosen for his personal qualifications, or subdelegation was forbidden **(c. 199, § 2).**

Power *ad universitatem negotiorum,* delegated by one who has ordinary power but beneath the Roman Pontiff, can be subdelegated in individual cases **(c. 199, § 3).**

In other cases delegated power of jurisdiction can be subdelegated only in case the power to subdelegate has been expressly granted; but delegated judges can, even without express commission, subdelegate an incidental non-jurisdictional act **(c. 199, § 4).**

No subdelegated power of jurisdiction can be again subdelegated unless the power to do so has been expressly granted **(c. 199, § 5).**

Explanation of Terms. Only two terms here need explanation:

1. Power is *ad universitatem negotiorum* if it is given for all cases or for all cases of a certain class. Thus a delegation to dispense in all dispensable marriage impediments would be *ad universitatem negotiorum.*[18]

2. *Articulus nonjurisdictionalis* means an incidental nonjurisdictional act; that is, an act incidental to a trial but not requiring cognizance of the case itself; for example, administering an oath to a witness.

---

[18] Cf. V-C, *Epit.,* I, n. 318.

Applications. 1. Pastors have *ordinary* jurisdiction for confessions (c. 873); certain other priests have *universal delegated* jurisdiction. Yet none of these can delegate or subdelegate their jurisdiction without special authority to do so from the Ordinary of the place.[19] Perhaps the reason is that canon 874, § 1, at least implicitly forbids it.

2. The power to assist at marriages, though not strictly jurisdiction, follows these rules regarding delegation.[20]

3. A special question can arise in connection with paragraph 3 and 5. Suppose a curate or assistant (*vicarius co-operator*) has by the diocesan pagella (therefore by delegation from the Ordinary) *general* power to assist at marriages in the parish to which he is assigned. This power can be subdelegated by him to a determinate priest for a determinate marriage.[21] But, can it be so subdelegated by him, with power to subdelegate again? Canon 199, § 5 does not explicitly answer this question. The answer is no, because the general rule, drawn from the old law and not contrary to the Code, is that only one having ordinary power, which he can "use as his own," can delegate it and at the same time grant power to subdelegate it.[22]

Interpretation. 1. Ordinary power of jurisdiction and delegated power *ad universitatem negotiorum* are to be broadly interpreted; all others, strictly; but one who has delegated power is understood to have also whatever other powers are necessary for the exercise of the power he has received (c. 200, § 1).

2. Whoever claims to have delegated power has the burden of proving the delegation (c. 200, § 2).

Applications. 1. The quinquennial faculties of Bishops, even though granted for a limited time or for a definite number of cases, are to be broadly interpreted (cf. cc. 66, 68, 50).

2. Power to absolve a heretic, though subject to strict interpretation under this canon, yet includes the power to receive his abjuration, since that is necessary for the exercise of the power granted.

Judicial and Voluntary Jurisdiction. *Judicial* jurisdiction means that which is exercised in tribunals including the tribunal of penance; *voluntary* jurisdiction means simply nonjudicial.

Principles. 1. Jurisdiction can be exercised directly upon subjects only (c. 201, § 1). Indirectly, it may reach other persons; for example,

---

[19] Code Com., 16 Oct., 1919; *AAS*, 11–477; *Digest*, I, p. 410.
[20] For many authentic applications, see *Digest*, I, p. 540.
[21] Code Com., 28 Dec., 1927; *AAS*, 20–61; *Digest*, I, p. 541.
[22] Cf. Ojetti, *Commentarium*, IV, p. 178.

when it attaches by reason of a thing situated within the territory or a crime committed there. Subjects are determined generally and in the strict sense by domicile and quasi-domicile (c. 94); but several canons expressly give power over all persons within the territory (cf. cc. 1043, 1245, etc.), thus making them equivalently subjects.

2. *Judicial* jurisdiction cannot be exercised for one's own benefit, nor outside the territory, except as provided in cc. 401, § 1, 881, § 2, and 1637 **(c. 201, § 2).**

Exceptions to this rule are: (*a*) Those who have ordinary power to absolve, such as local Ordinaries, canons penitentiary, pastors and parochial vicars with full parochial powers (cc. 401, § 1, 873, 451, § 2), can absolve their own subjects anywhere (c. 881, § 2); (*b*) a judge who has been expelled by force or prevented from exercising his office in the territory, can do so outside, with notice to the Ordinary (c. 1637).

3. *Voluntary* jurisdiction, unless the contrary is evident from the nature of the case or from the law, can be exercised for one's own benefit, or while one is outside one's own territory, or upon a subject who is outside the territory **(c. 201, § 3).**

Examples. Thus a Bishop or pastor can dispense himself from laws of fast and abstinence; a Bishop can dispense his subjects from matrimonial impediments while he is outside the territory, or while they are outside; a Bishop and pastor can do the same regarding laws of fast and abstinence.

External and Internal Forum. An act of the power of jurisdiction whether ordinary or delegated, which was conferred for the external forum, is valid also for the internal; but the converse is not true **(c. 202, § 1).**

The power conferred for the internal forum can be exercised even in the internal extra-sacramental forum, unless the sacramental forum is required **(c. 202, § 2).**

If the forum for which the power was granted was not expressed, the power is understood as granted for both fora, unless the contrary is clear from the nature of the case **(c. 202, § 3).**

Applications. 1. Canon 1044 grants the power to dispense from certain matrimonial impediments, to *pastors* without limitation as to forum, to *confessors* for the internal sacramental forum only.

2. The power of confessors as such is limited usually to the sacramental forum. Sacramental absolution from a censure extends in a

limited degree to the external forum by virtue of special provisions of canon 2251.[23]

Use of Power. One having delegated powers, who exceeds the limits of his mandate either as regards the matter or the persons, acts invalidly **(c. 203, § 1).**

However, he is not deemed to have exceeded those limits, merely because he has done the things which he was delegated to do in a manner other than that desired by the person delegating, unless the manner itself was prescribed as a condition by the person delegating **(c. 203, § 2).**

The fact that one has recourse directly to the superior, passing over the inferior, does not suspend the inferior's voluntary power, whether that is ordinary or delegated **(c. 204, § 1).**

Still, the inferior must not interfere in a matter which has been referred to the superior, unless there is a grave and urgent reason for doing so; and in that case he must at once notify the superior thereof **(c. 204, § 2).**

This is a rule of courtesy and common sense, very easy to understand. Its violation would not affect the validity of the act. The rule applies only to voluntary jurisdiction. As regards the suspension of judicial jurisdiction by appeal, see canon 208.

Delegation to Several Persons. If several persons have obtained delegated jurisdiction for the same business, and a doubt arises whether the delegation was made *in solidum* (to each) or *collegialiter* (to all together), it is presumed to have been made *in solidum* in a voluntary matter and *collegialiter* in a judicial matter **(c. 205, § 1).**

In case several have received delegation *in solidum,* the one who first takes up the business excludes the others therefrom, unless he be afterward prevented from proceeding further in the matter, or be unwilling to do so **(c. 205, § 2).**

In case several have been delegated *collegialiter,* it is required for validity that all act together in the matter, unless their mandate provide otherwise **(c. 205, § 3).**

If several persons have been successively delegated, that one whose mandate was prior in time and has not been expressly revoked by a later rescript must conduct the business **(c. 206).**

Canon 205 deals with delegation made to several persons at the same time; canon 206, with delegation made to several in succession.

---

[23] Cf. Cappello, *De Censuris,* nn. 96–98.

The rule in the second case is in accord with the general principle regarding successive rescripts, as given in canon 48.

Cessation of Delegated Power. Delegated power expires: (1) when the business for which it was given is finished; (2) when the time has expired or the number of cases is exhausted; with the exception noted below; (3) when the motivating cause of the delegation has ceased; (4) by revocation, upon direct notice thereof to the delegate; (5) by renunciation directly communicated and accepted **(c. 207, § 1).**

It *does not expire* with the expiration of the authority of the person who made the delegation, except in the two cases mentioned in canon 61; namely: (1) where it is so limited by clauses attached to the delegation, such as "during our good pleasure"; (2) where there is question of granting a favor to determinate persons, and the matter is still uncompromised **(c. 207, § 1).**

When power has been granted *for the internal forum,* an act placed through *inadvertence* after the lapse of the time or the completion of the number of cases, is valid **(c. 207, § 2).**

Power delegated to several corporately (*collegialiter*) expires if one of the persons drops out, unless the contrary appear from the terms of the delegation **(c. 207, § 3).** This is in perfect accord with canon 205, § 3.

Expiration of Ordinary Jurisdiction. In accordance with canon 183, § 2, ordinary power does not expire with the expiration of the authority of the person who conferred the office to which it is annexed; but it expires when the office is lost; and it is suspended by appeal made according to law, unless the appeal happen to be without suspensive effect, without prejudice to the provision of canons 2264 and 2284 **(c. 208).**

Since ordinary jurisdiction is attached by law to an office, it expires only with the loss of the office itself; and by canon 183, § 2, an office does not usually expire with the expiration of the authority of the person who conferred it.

Suspension of ordinary jurisdiction by appeal is the usual thing, because appeals as a rule have a suspensive effect (*in suspensivo*); but if, by way of exception, an appeal is merely *in devolutivo,* it does not suspend the jurisdiction from which the appeal is taken.

Special Provisions govern the acts of persons excommunicated or suspended from jurisdiction:

1. An *excommunicated person* who still holds an office to which ordinary jurisdiction is attached, acts *illicitly* but *validly* until a

condemnatory or declaratory judgment has been passed upon him; thereafter he acts *invalidly* (c. 2264).

2. A person who is *suspended from jurisdiction* similiarly, acts illicitly but validly before, but invalidly after a condemnatory or declaratory judgment (c. 2284).

When Jurisdiction Is Supplied by the Church. In common error or in positive and probable doubt of law or fact, the Church supplies jurisdiction for both the external and internal forum (c. 209).

State of the Question. To supply jurisdiction means to give it *in the very acts* which are placed without jurisdiction from any other source. Hence when jurisdiction is supplied by the Church, the person acting is entirely without jurisdiction both before and after the act in question; he has jurisdiction, supplied by the Church, only in the act itself. The Church thus supplies jurisdiction in two *entirely distinct* cases: (1) in common error; (2) in positive and probable doubt of law or of fact.

Common Error. Error is a false judgment of the mind; and the error with which we are here concerned is error regarding the existence of jurisdiction. The person is erroneously believed to have jurisdiction, whereas he has not. *Common* error is opposed to *private* error, and means in general an error which is in some sense common to the people of the place (diocese, parish, chapter, religious community) where the act is placed. The circumstances required to constitute common error are nearly all disputed by some one. We shall state those which, according to solid reason and authority, are certainly sufficient in practice, without going deeply into the theory and without discussing disputed opinions.

1. In a certain sense, the error must be *common;* that is, must affect, not merely a private party, but the people of the locality as a class. Taken alone, this criterion is of almost no practical value. It requires further definition.

2. It is not required that the majority of the persons of the place *actually elicit a false judgment* regarding the fact of the existence of jurisdiction. It is sufficient that they be in a *state* of error; that is, such a state of mind that, if asked, they would reply erroneously on that question. Hence it is certainly not required that several or many persons in actual error successively approach the person lacking jurisdiction, before the Church supplies it. The impossibility of applying such a criterion is shown by Cappello[24] and others.

---

[24] Cappello, *De Poenitentia*, n. 490.

3. Before the Code, a classical dispute existed as to whether a "color of title" (*titulus coloratus*) was required in the person who was erroneously believed to have jurisdiction. *Titulus coloratus* means a title which is not valid, but is based on an invalid act of the competent superior. For example, the competent superior confers an office, but confers it invalidly; the incumbent has a *titulus coloratus* to the office, and hence apparently has the jurisdiction attached to the office. It is now certain that this *titulus coloratus* is not necessary to make a case of common error.

4. Must there be at least some *probability* of the existence of jurisdiction? Here we must distinguish: if the common error is purely an error of *fact,* it need not be probable; but if the mistaken conclusion on the fact results from an error of *law,* the error is not sufficient unless it has some probability. If it has probability, the title for the supplying of jurisdiction is not common error, but "positive and probable doubt of law."[25]

5. The theory of *interpretative common error* may be outlined as follows. Interpretative common error means common error whose existence is determined, not by strict proof, but by a sort of reasonable presumption. Instead of a plebiscite to learn whether the people as a class were actually in error regarding the existence of jurisdiction (this impossible course would seem to be the only means of strict proof if *actual* error were required), the common error is presumed to exist in all cases where there exists a *public* circumstance or set of circumstances (and these can be strictly proved), from which all reasonable persons, *without any error of law,* would naturally conclude that jurisdiction existed. Thus a priest sitting publicly in a confessional in a public parish church may be presumed to have received general faculties for confession. If the fact is that he has not, yet the *public circumstance* would be a sufficient *reasonable foundation* for interpretative common error; and the Church would supply the jurisdiction for each and every confession heard in these circumstances, regardless of the number of persons who are in the church, and still more regardless of the number who actually went to that priest, or were preparing to do so.[26]

---

[25] Cf. D'Annibale, I, n. 79; V-C, *Epit.,* I, n. 322; Wernz-Vidal, *De Personis,* n. 381.

[26] A priest may be said to be *publicly* engaged in hearing confessions when he is *regularly* so engaged in a public church; or if he has been *publicly announced* as a confessor or missionary; or if any other public circumstance exists, from which it must be supposed he is a confessor. Is the mere fact that he is actually in the confessional in a public church sufficient? We answer, yes, though some who admit the theory of inter-

It should be noted that common error in this case is entirely independent of any *error of law*. People will fall into the error even if they know the law, and precisely because they know it; for the law is that confessors usually receive *general* jurisdiction for confessions, and do not need special delegation for individual penitents. But the mere fact that an unknown priest, not officially connected with the church, is seen to be assisting at the marriage of a couple there, is no sufficient foundation for the inference that he is authorized to marry any other couple. For assistance at marriage by one other than the Ordinary of the diocese, or the pastor of the parish or an assistant who has received general delegation, requires special delegation for each individual case, and thus differs from jurisdiction for confessions, which is usually granted generally. It is doubtless true that the people commonly do not know this; they are in a state of common error or ignorance regarding the law, and would therefore probably erroneously infer that the priest has power to assist at other marriages. But this error, precisely because it rests on an *error of law,* is not supported by a sufficient *reasonable foundation* to constitute *interpretative* common error for the supplying of jurisdiction.[27] If, however, *actual common error* exists regarding the fact of delegation for a particular marriage, it would be sufficient for the supplying of jurisdiction by the Church.

Is the above theory of interpretative common error supported by sufficient reason and authority to make it practically safe? We answer unhesitatingly, yes. It is true, as pointed out by Kearney,[28] and Miaskiewicz,[29] that this is a comparatively recent theory on common error. It is also true that theoretically it is open to some objections. However, the reasons in its favor seem convincing, and it is supported by a sufficient array of high authorities to give it extrinsic as well as intrinsic probability. Practically, therefore, it may *certainly* be adopted without scruple.[30]

---

pretative common error would deny this. (Cf. Vermeersch, *Theol. Mor.*, III, n. 421.) We think the foundation for interpretative common error is public in this case, and therefore sufficient, because a church is a public place, under the vigilance and authority of the Church. The people commonly would judge that any priest hearing confessions there has faculties, whether his name has been publicly announced or not. The same would *not* be true of a priest hearing confessions in a private place.

[27] Cf. *Periodica*, Vol. 22, pp. 113, 191. For an interesting case of common error in a marriage performed by a putative army chaplain, see Rota, 22 Nov., 1927; *S. R. Rotae Decisiones seu Sententiae*, Vol. 19, p. 453; *Digest*, II, p. 76.

[28] Kearney, *The Principles of Delegation*, 1929; Cath. U. Canon Law Studies, n. 55.

[29] Miaskiewicz, *Supplied Jurisdiction According to Canon 209*, 1940; Cath. University Canon Law Studies, n. 122.

[30] V-C, *Epit.*, I, n. 322; D'Annibale, I, n. 79; Wernz-Vidal, *De Personis*, n. 381; Cappello, *De Poenitentia*, n. 490; *De Matrimonio*, n. 663.

Positive and Probable Doubt. 1. *Doubt* means a state of mind in which the mind suspends assent or remains undecided between assent and denial.

2. Doubt is *positive* if there is a serious reason for assenting to a proposition; yet the prudent fear of error is not entirely excluded. A merely *negative* doubt exists if there is no reason, or at least no really serious reason for assent.

3. A doubt is *probable* if there is a solid and probable reason in favor of a proposition, which, however, is not certain.

4. A doubt *of law* means a doubt concerning the existence or meaning of the law; a doubt *of fact* is a doubt concerning the existence of any concrete fact other than the existence of the law.

Principles Summarized. 1. In *common error,* not of law but of fact, the Church supplies jurisdiction. Here the *want* of jurisdiction, until the Church supplies it, is *certain.*

2. In *positive and probable doubt,* either *of law* or *of fact,* the Church supplies jurisdiction. Here the *existence* of jurisdiction, even before the Church supplies it, is *probable;* after the Church supplies it, it is *certain.*

3. As regards the *licitness of the use* of jurisdiction which is merely supplied by the Church: (*a*) in a positive and probable *doubt of law,* the use is simply licit; (*b*) in a positive and probable *doubt of fact,* at least *no grave reason* is required, and in practice the use is licit without inquiring for a reason; (*c*) in *common error* the use is *illicit* without a *grave reason,* which may often be prudently conjectured.[31]

Transmission of the Power of Order. The power of order, either attached by the legitimate superior to an office or entrusted to a person, cannot be transferred to others unless the power to do so is expressly granted by law or indult **(c. 210).**

The power of order is the power to sanctify the faithful by sacred rites. It is conferred by ordination, which, in the case of the episcopacy, the priesthood, and the diaconate, is a sacrament, in the case of the subdiaconate and minor orders, a sacramental.[32] Among the powers usually attached to a certain order, for example to the episcopacy, some are essentially connected with the sacramental character, and hence belong inseparably to that order by divine law, whereas others are attached to the order only by ecclesiastical law, and these can, with

---

[31] Cf. Cappello, *De Poenitentia,* nn. 493, 499; *Summa,* I, nn. 267, 269; Arregui, *Summarium,* n. 602; Noldin, *Theol. Mor.,* III, n. 347.

[32] Cf. Cappello, *De Ordine,* nn. 37, 70, 78, 91, 99.

ecclesiastical authorization, be exercised by a person who has not that same order. This canon deals only with the latter class of powers, since only these are "attached by a legitimate superior to an office or entrusted to a person."

Principles. 1. Powers which are *by divine law* annexed to a certain order, are by divine law nontransferable. The canon does not state, but presupposes this principle.

2. Powers of order which are either attached to an office or entrusted to a person *by a legitimate ecclesiastical superior* (hence by purely ecclesiastical authority) are by ecclesiastical law nontransferable unless their transfer is expressly permitted either by law or indult.

Applications. 1. Though a Bishop alone is the *ordinary minister* of Confirmation (c. 782, § 1), of minor orders (c. 951), and of consecrations (c. 1147, § 1), yet these powers are not attached by divine law to the episcopal character, and they may therefore be attached by ecclesiastical authority to an office held by a simple priest, for example to the office of Vicar or Prefect Apostolic (c. 294, § 2), Abbot or Prelate *nullius* (c. 323, § 2). In such a case the law itself (c. 310, § 2) permits the use of these powers by the person (even a simple priest) who succeeds to the government of the prefecture in accordance with canon 309, § 4. Hence, immediately upon taking possession, he could validly and licitly confirm, confer minor orders, consecrate chalices, etc.

2. Bishops have by their quinquennial faculties power to depute priests to consecrate altars, chalices, etc. In the priests so deputed, these would be "powers of order entrusted to a person."

3. Delegation of the blessing of sacred vestments, etc., is governed by canon 1304.

4. A thorough discussion of the grant to simple priests of the power to confirm, appeared in *L'Ami du Clergé,* Vol. 58, p. 308 (7 May, 1936).

CASES AND QUESTIONS

1. Are the following cases of *ordinary* or *delegated, judicial* or *voluntary* jurisdiction?

a. An Ordinary of a place dispensing one of his subjects from fast and abstinence (c. 1245);

b. A pastor dispensing from the form of marriage in danger of death (c. 1044);

c. A confessor dispensing from a matrimonial impediment when all is ready for the marriage (c. 1045);

d. A pastor giving sacramental absolution to one of his subjects outside the parish (cc. 873, § 1, 881, § 2, 201, § 2);

e. A confessor giving absolution from a reserved censure *in casu urgentiori* (c. 2254);

f. A confessor dispensing from a vindictive penalty in confession (c. 2290, § 2).

2. Can the Quinquennial Faculties of the Ordinary be used by his successor without a new grant? (C. 66, § 2). Why are they not considered ordinary jurisdiction? (C. 197, § 1). To what extent can they be subdelegated? (C. 199, § 2).

3. If an assistant in a parish has received from the pastor general delegation to assist at marriages, can he subdelegate to a particular priest the power to assist at a particular marriage? (Cc. 199, § 3, 1095, § 2, 1096, § 1; *Digest,* I, p. 541).

4. Is the local superior in a clerical exempt religious order an Ordinary? (C. 198, § 1). Has he ordinary jurisdiction? (C. 501, § 1). Is the Provincial in such an order an *Ordinarius loci?* (C. 198, § 2).

5. A confessor with diocesan faculties for the year is in the confessional on Dec. 31 until long after midnight, forgetting that his faculties have expired. Are the confessions heard after midnight validly absolved? (C. 207, § 2).

6. A board of five judges, delegated by the Ordinary, is hearing a matrimonial case for nullity. One of them dies. Can the others go on with the case? (C. 205, §§ 1, 3).

7. A parish mission has been announced, with Father X as preacher and confessor. The pastor, who was to get faculties for him, has neglected to do so, and the Bishop cannot now be reached. Can X validly and licitly hear confessions on the opening night of the mission? (Cc. 874, § 1, 209; *Periodica,* Vol. 17, pp. 52*, 90*).

8. Y has obtained delegation from the pastor of St. Monica's to assist at a marriage there. Before the marriage takes place, the pastor dies. Is Y's delegated power still good? (Cc. 207, § 1, 61; *Irish Cath. Rec.,* Vol. 47, p. 521).

Readings:

Keene, *Religious Ordinaries and Canon 198,* Catholic University, 1942 (n. 135); Kearney, *The Principles of Delegation,* Cath. U., 1929 (n. 55); Miaskiewicz, *Supplied Jurisdiction According to Canon 209,* Cath. U., 1940 (n. 122); *Australasian Catholic Record,* 1937, p. 143 (Nevin, on common error as applied to assistance at marriage); 1936, p. 60 (Nevin, on competent Ordinary to grant dispensation from matrimonial impediment); *The Jurist,* Vol 2, p. 170 (Hannan, on supplied jurisdiction for marriage).

Section 3. Reduction of Clerics to the Lay State (cc. 211–214)

PRELIMINARY SURVEY

Return to the Lay State (c. 211)
Readmission of Laicized Person to the Clerical State (c. 212)
Effects of Reduction to the Lay State (c. 213)
Sacred Orders Received Under Compulsion or Fear (c. 214)

Reduction to the Lay State. Clerics are those who have been ordained, at least by first tonsure. Any ordination, once validly received, cannot become void (c. 211, § 1). In those ordinations which are sacraments, this is because of divine law; in the others, because of the ecclesiastical law expressed in this canon. Nevertheless clerics can be reduced to the lay state; that is, they can, by operation of law or by the act of lawful ecclesiastical authority, lose the rights and privileges which belong to the clerical state. As regards the obligations, provision will be made in canon 213.[33]

A Major Cleric is reduced to the lay state: (1) by *rescript* of the Holy See;[34] (2) by *judicial decree* in accordance with canon 214; (3) by the penalty of *degradation* (c. 211, § 1). This penalty is inflicted for several grave crimes: (*a*) giving grave scandal after deposition or privation of the clerical dress (c. 2305, § 2); (*b*) public adherence to a non-Catholic sect (c. 2314, § 1, 3°); (*c*) violence to the person of the Roman Pontiff (c. 2343, § 1, 3°); (*d*) voluntary homicide (c. 2354, § 2); (*e*) an aggravated case of solicitation (c. 2368, § 1); (*f*) persistence in a state of unlawful marriage after sacred orders or, in the case of minor clerics, with a woman who is bound by solemn vows in religion (c. 2388, § 1). Degradation does not *per se* relieve the culprit of the obligation of celibacy and the Breviary.[35]

A Minor Cleric is reduced to the lay state: (1) *ipso facto* for the reasons mentioned in the law. These are: (*a*) laying aside the clerical dress and tonsure, and failing to amend after warning (c. 136, § 3); (*b*) volunteering for military service without lawful reason (c. 141, § 2); (*c*) freely marrying (c. 132, § 2); (*d*) dismissal from religion (cc. 648, 669, § 2); (*e*) having his religious profession declared void for

---

[33] Celibacy is clearly provided for; as to the Breviary, see notes 35 and 38.
[34] A recent example is in *AAS*, 30–274; *Digest*, II, p. 77.
[35] V-C, *Epit.*, III, n. 499. *Contra* (as to Breviary), Wernz-Vidal, *De Personis*, p. 138.

fraud on his part (c. 2387); (2) upon his own motion, with notice to the Ordinary; (3) by decree of the Ordinary, for just cause, namely, if the Ordinary, everything considered, prudently judges that the cleric cannot be promoted to sacred orders with honor to the clerical state (c. 211, § 2).

Readmission to the Clerical State. This is possible, but requires, for minor clerics, the permission of the Ordinary of the diocese in which he was incardinated, to be granted only after a careful examination of his conduct, and a suitable period of probation; for major clerics, the permission of the Holy See (c. 212). Ordination is never repeated, not even first tonsure.[36]

Effects of Return to the Lay State (c. 213). 1. As to *rights:* (a) the cleric loses all ecclesiastical offices, benefices, rights, and privileges of clerics. Hence he loses all jurisdiction, even delegated, since according to canon 118, he has become incapable of it. He can still validly, though illicitly, exercise the powers of order which he has;[37] (b) he may no longer wear the clerical dress and tonsure.

2. As to *obligations:* (a) in general, the obligations attached to the clerical state cease, except as hereafter noted; (b) a major cleric remains bound by the law of celibacy, except as provided in canon 214; (c) a major cleric who has suffered degradation remains bound also to recite the Breviary, unless expressly exempted therefrom.[38]

Action to Be Freed From Obligation of Sacred Orders. A cleric who received sacred orders under the compulsion of grave fear, and did not afterward, when the fear was removed, ratify the said ordination at least tacitly, by exercising the order with the intention in such act of subjecting himself to the clerical obligations, may be reduced to the lay state by judicial judgment upon legal proof of the compulsion and of the want of ratification, without the obligations of celibacy and the canonical hours (c. 214, § 1).

But the compulsion and the want of ratification must be proved according to canons 1993–1998 (c. 214, § 2).

State of the Question. Grave fear is understood here with the usual qualifications; that is, inspired by a free external agent. Grave fear might have either of two effects on the ordination: first, if it was so overpowering as to destroy the freedom of the will so that the cleric had no genuine human intention of receiving the order, the ordination

---

[36] Cf. Wernz-Vidal, *De Personis,* n. 393; Carbone, *Praxis Ordinandorum,* n. 41.
[37] Cf. Cappello, *Summa,* I, n. 252.
[38] Cf. V-C, *Epit.,* III, n. 499. *Contra,* Wernz-Vidal, *De Personis,* p. 138.

would be invalid; secondly, if the fear did not destroy the intention
to receive orders, the ordination would be valid (c. 103, § 2); nor
could it ever become void (c. 211); but the cleric could be reduced
to the lay state according to the procedure indicated in this canon.
Either or both questions; that is, either entire want of intention due
to grave fear, or compulsion by grave fear without subsequent ratification, or both, may be tried in these cases.

Notes. 1. The procedure is governed by canons 1993–1998, and by
a long Instruction of the Sacred Congregation of the Sacraments.[39]
The procedure is similar to that prescribed in cases or non-consummated marriage.

2. Not only the fact of grave fear, but also the want of ratification
must be positively and fully proved.

3. The effect of a favorable judgment is to release from the two
major obligations of sacred orders; namely, celibacy and the recitation
of the Breviary.

4. Several cases have recently been decided by the Rota.[40]

---

[39] S. C. Sacr., 9 June, 1931; *AAS*, 23–457; *Digest*, I, p. 812.
[40] *S. R. Rotae Decisiones*, Vol. 20, pp. 1, 347; *Digest*, II, p. 554; and Vol. 20, p. 127;
Digest, II, p. 555.

CHAPTER IV

THE SUPREME PONTIFICATE AND THE
HIERARCHY OF THE CHURCH

Section 1. Territorial Divisions in the Church (cc. 215–217)

PRELIMINARY SURVEY

Larger Territorial Divisions (c. 215)
Parishes and Quasi-parishes (c. 216)
Deaneries (c. 217)

Provinces, Dioceses, Etc. It belongs exclusively to the supreme ecclesiastical authority to erect ecclesiastical provinces, dioceses, abbacies or prelacies *nullius,* vicariates and prefectures apostolic, as also to change their boundaries, divide, unite, or suppress them **(c. 215, § 1).**

In law, the term "diocese" includes also abbacy or prelacy *nullius,* and the term Bishop includes an Abbot or Prelate *nullius,* unless the contrary appear from the nature of the case or from the context **(c. 215, § 2).**

State of the Question. Before treating of the various grades of clerics in particular, the Code has a few canons on the various territorial divisions whose government may be entrusted to clerics. Canon 215 deals with the larger territorial divisions, the following canons with smaller ones.

History. In apostolic times the Apostles themselves and their helpers and successors consecrated Bishops and placed them in charge of the "churches" or dioceses established in various parts of the known world. The jurisdiction of the various Bishops was acknowledged by the Supreme Pontiff. It was probably not until the fourth century that the Roman pontiffs began to take part in the actual erection of dioceses. In the ninth century, they reserved this right to themselves exclusively. Pius IX in the Syllabus (Denzinger-Bannwart, n. 1751) again vindicates this right for the Supreme Pontiff.

Terms. A *diocese* is a territory over which a Bishop rules as its proper and ordinary pastor.

A *province* is a territory made up of several dioceses.

An *abbacy* or *prelacy nullius* is a territory set apart from any diocese; that is, belonging to none (*nullius dioecesis*), and where the clergy and people are subject to an Abbot or to a Prelate.

A *vicariate* or *prefecture apostolic* is a territorial division in mission countries, governed by a Vicar or Prefect in the name of the Holy See. These have the same jurisdiction as Bishops (cc. 293, 294); as regards *orders,* Vicars usually have, Prefects usually have not the episcopal character; but both have certain powers of order in virtue of their office (cf. c. 294, § 2).

All of these divisions of territory are noncollegiate *moral persons;* hence they must be erected by ecclesiastical authority (c. 99). **Canon 215** reserves to the Supreme Pontiff the right to erect, modify, divide, unite, or suppress them. Note that in law the term "diocese" includes an abbacy or prelacy *nullius,* and the term "Bishop" includes an Abbot or Prelate *nullius,* unless the contrary appear.

Parishes and Quasi-parishes. The territory of every diocese is to be divided into distinct territorial parts; to each part is to be assigned its own church with a definite part of the population, and its own rector as the proper pastor of that territory is to be put in charge for the necessary care of souls **(c. 216, § 1).**

Vicariates and prefectures apostolic are to be divided in the same way where it can conveniently be done **(c. 216, § 2).**

The parts of a diocese mentioned in § 1 are *parishes;* the parts of a vicariate or prefecture apostolic, if their own rector has been assigned them, are called *quasi-parishes* **(c. 216, § 3).**

Distinct parishes for the people of various tongues or nationalities dwelling in the same city or territory, and for certain families or persons, cannot be created without special apostolic indult; as regards such parishes already in existence, no change is to be made without consulting the Holy See **(c. 216, § 4).**

Parishes and quasi-parishes are to have: (1) distinct territorial limits and a distinct part of the population; (2) their own proper church; (3) their own proper rector or pastor. These three elements are fully realized in a perfectly organized *territorial* parish or quasi-parish. The fourth paragraph of the canon, however, supposes the existence of some parishes that are not purely territorial. Hence, to include all parishes, we need a broader definition.

A Parish may be defined as a community of the faithful to which has been assigned its own rector with ordinary power in the internal forum for the care of souls. It may or may not have its own exclusive church and exclusive territorial limits. The same definition will include a quasi-parish. We may distinguish three kinds:

1. A *territorial* parish is a subdivision of a diocese, with its own proper church, pastor, and people.

2. A *personal* parish is one without territorial limits, having its pastor and its church, and a definite population determined by personal qualities alone without respect to territory; for example, the people of a certain clan or family.

3. A *mixed* parish (partly territorial and partly personal) is one whose population is determined by both territorial and personal criteria; for example, all Italians within a certain territory. Most of the so-called "national" parishes in the United States are of this type. The Code manifests a certain disfavor toward the *future* establishment of such parishes; the plain territorial parish is the preferred type because its government is less subject to confusion and difficulties. Yet existing national parishes preserve under the Code all their rights and privileges, and in fact enjoy a peculiar protection in as much as no change is to be made in their status without consulting the Holy See.

Notes and Documents. 1. The prohibition against the erection of new national parishes applies even to parishes for people using one of the official languages of the country.[1]

2. Distinct territorial parts of dioceses in the United States, each having its boundaries, its resident pastor, and endowment or resources of some kind, are canonical parishes in the strict sense, and also canonical benefices.[2]

3. Rules for the erection of parishes in dioceses which formerly belonged to mission territory were given by the Sacred Consistorial Congregation.[3]

4. Rules for the division of mission territory into quasi-parishes and parishes were given in two documents of the Sacred Congregation of Propaganda.[4]

5. A formal decree of erection is not always necessary *ad validitatem* to constitute a parish. Hence *de facto* parishes existing before the Code

---

[1] Code Com., 20 May, 1923; *AAS*, 16–113; *Digest*, I, p. 151.
[2] Letter of 10 Nov., 1922, from Apostolic Delegate, U. S., reporting replies of Code Commission of 26 Sept., 1921; *Digest*, I, p. 149.
[3] S. C. Consist., 1 Aug., 1919; *AAS*, 11–346; *Digest*, I, p. 146.
[4] S. C. Prop. Fid., 25 July, 1920; *AAS*, 12–331: *Digest*, I, p. 147; and 9 Dec., 1920; *AAS*, 13–17; *Digest*, I, p. 149.

without any formal decree of erection, upon the promulgation of the Code became strictly canonical parishes.[5]

6. Foreign-born Catholics in the United States who belong to national parishes, and their children born in the United States, are not bound to remain affiliated to, or to join, the national parish; they have the right to affiliate with the American (English-speaking) territorial parish in which they have their domicile, but not with any other parish in which the English language may be spoken.[6]

Deaneries. The Bishop is to divide his territory into regions or districts consisting of several parishes, and which are called *forane vicariates, deaneries, arch-presbyteries,* etc. (c. 217, § 1).

If such division, in view of the circumstances, seems impossible or inopportune, the Bishop shall consult the Holy See, unless provision by the latter has already been made (c. 217, § 2).

Notes. 1. The duties of *rural deans,* or *vicars forane* as they are sometimes called, are enumerated in canons 445–450.

2. A similar grouping of quasi-parishes is counseled in vicariates and prefectures apostolic.[7]

Readings:
Connolly, *The Canonical Erection of Parishes,* Catholic University, 1938 (n. 114); *Ecclesiastical Review,* Vol. 108, p. 382 (Bastnagel: is a parish for colored people a "national" parish?).

Section 2. The Ecclesiastical Hierarchy From the Supreme Pontiff to the Bishops (cc. 218–328)

PRELIMINARY SURVEY

The Roman Pontiff (cc. 218–221)
The Oecumenical Council (cc. 222–229)
The Cardinals of the Holy Roman Church (cc. 230–241)
The Roman Curia (cc. 242–264)
Legates of the Roman Pontiff (cc. 265–270)
Patriarchs, Primates, and Metropolitans (cc. 271–280)
Plenary and Provincial Councils (cc. 281–292)
Vicars and Prefects Apostolic (cc. 293–311)
Apostolic Administrators (cc. 312–318)
The Lower Prelates (cc. 319–328)

---

[5] Cf. S. C. Conc., 5 March, 1932; *AAS,* 25–436; *Digest,* I, p. 151.
[6] Cf. Circular Letter, Apostolic Delegate, U. S., 17 Feb., 1938; *Digest,* II, p. 78.
[7] Cf. S. C. Prop. Fid., 25 July, 1920; *AAS,* 12–331; *Digest,* I, p. 148.

Plan of This Section. Although these canons of the Code, describing and regulating the ecclesiastical hierarchy, are of very great importance, the purpose and scope of this book require that we content ourselves with a general outline. It is expected that this brief survey will be supplemented by the study of the canons in the official Latin text of the Code.

The Roman Pontiff. 1. As successor of St. Peter, the Roman Pontiff has the *primacy* not merely of honor but *of jurisdiction* over the universal Church (c. 218).

2. After being lawfully elected, immediately upon his acceptance, he *obtains by divine law* the full power of supreme jurisdiction (c. 219).

3. In case he should resign, the validity of his *resignation does not depend upon its acceptance* by the Cardinals or by any one else (c. 221).

The Election of the Pope. The election of the Roman Pontiff is now regulated exclusively by the Constitution of Pius XII, *Vacantis Apostolicae Sedis,* of 8 Dec., 1945 (*AAS,* 38 pp. 65–99). This Constitution explicitly abrogates all other previous ordinances on the subject. Because of its extraordinary importance we shall give, under successive heads corresponding to its Titles and Chapters, a bare summary of its principal provisions.

The Vacancy of the Apostolic See. 1. During the vacancy of the See the Cardinals have not the power of jurisdiction which belonged to the Pope. They cannot change the Church's laws; but can provide for an emergency, and decide all doubts concerning the meaning of this Constitution (nn. 1–5).

2. Two special Congregations of Cardinals, one general and one particular, are to meet periodically to transact routine business and to arrange for the Conclave. In the general Congregation, this Constitution is read, and the Cardinals present, as well as those who may later enter the Conclave, take an oath to observe it faithfully. Arrangements are made for the obsequies of the deceased Pontiff, and for the Conclave (nn. 6–11).

3. The Cardinals *Camerarius,* Major Penitentiary, Chancellor, Vicar of Rome, and the Legates, Nuncios and Apostolic Delegates, and papal Almoner retain their powers. As had already been provided by Pius XI,[8] the Cardinal Major Penitentiary has, during the vacancy of the Holy See, *for urgent cases,* all powers which pertain in any way to the forum of conscience, even such as are beyond his power at other times. The office of the Secretary of State expires, his place being

---

[8] *AAS,* 27–112; *Digest,* II, p. 114, ref.

taken by the Secretary of the Sacred College. The Vatican State is governed by the Sacred College (nn. 13–23).

4. The Sacred Congregations have no powers which during the lifetime of the Pope they could exercise only *verbo facto cum Sanctissimo,* or *ex audientia Sanctissimi,* etc.; but faculties which they have by special letters, and those which are regarded as proper to the Congregations themselves (cf. c. 244, § 2) are retained. Even in the latter case, however, more important matters should if possible be deferred until the new Pope is elected (nn. 22–25). The Tribunals of the Rota and the Signatura retain their jurisdiction (nn. 24–28).

5. Funeral services for the deceased Pope are held for nine days, the last three being especially solemn. On the last day the oration *De Pontifice defuncto* is pronounced (nn. 29–31).

The Election. 1. The right to elect belongs exclusively to the Cardinals, in no case to an oecumenical council. If such a council is in session, it is *ipso iure* suspended. There is to be no interference from civil authority. Excommunicated Cardinals are not disfranchised; but Cardinals who have been deposed or have resigned may not be reinstated even for the purpose of voting. The Cardinals present are to wait fifteen days for absentees to arrive, and this time may be extended three more days. Cardinals who arrive late are to be admitted, provided the new Pope has not yet been elected. All Cardinals, unless lawfully excused, are bound to attend the Conclave, and if present, are bound under pain of excommunication to respond to the summons when called to the balloting (nn. 32–42).

2. Each Cardinal is entitled to two attendants, lay or clerical, but only one, a layman, may enter the Conclave with him. Special provisions, however, are made for the sick. Other persons to be admitted to the Conclave are enumerated. These include the Secretary of the Sacred College, the Sacristan of the Apostolic Palace, the Master of Apostolic Ceremonies, a religious as confessor, two physicians, a surgeon, etc. (nn. 43–49).

3. After the completion of the nine days' funeral services for the deceased Pontiff, all the Cardinals attend a solemn Mass of the Holy Ghost, celebrated by the Dean of the Sacred College, at St. Peter's. An oration is pronounced warning the Cardinals of the sacredness of their duty. They enter the Conclave on the same day. This Constitution is again read; the Cardinals again take an oath to observe it; other oaths are administered to various officials. All who are to remain in the Conclave are then carefully identified, all others are excluded,

the Conclave is closed within and without, and its closure is duly certified (nn. 50–56).

4. The election is to take place with strict observance of the enclosure of the Conclave. Violations of the enclosure, however, would not invalidate the election. No one is to be admitted except in the presence of the prelates who have the custody of the Conclave. All communications coming in or going out except communications between the Sacred Penitentiary and the Cardinal Major Penitentiary, are to be inspected by the Secretary of the Sacred College and by the prelates who have the custody. News bulletins to the outside are prohibited under pain of excommunication. All are bound to the strictest secrecy regarding the election and everything which happens in the Conclave; and this also under pain of excommunication. The nine excommunications provided for in this Constitution are so reserved that they cannot be absolved even by the Major Penitentiary, nor by any one but the Roman Pontiff, except in danger of death. They are referred to in canon 2330 and in this Constitution, n. 61.[9] For the better preservation of secrecy, instruments of all kinds such as telegraphs, telephones, microphones, radios, cameras, moving-picture machines, are forbidden (nn. 57–64).

5. On the morning after the enclosure of the Conclave the Cardinals either celebrate Mass or receive Holy Communion; after which they proceed to the election. Three forms of election are possible, all others being invalid: first, *per inspirationem,* a unanimous *viva voce* choice; second, *per compromissum,* a choice by three, five, or seven delegates unanimously chosen in advance, all agreeing to abide by their decision; and third, *per scrutinium,* by ballot, which is the ordinary way. In this, a vote of two thirds plus one is required for election. This new provision makes it unnecessary to inquire whether the elect voted for himself. The form of the ballots, which is simpler than formerly, is illustrated in the Constitution. There are three stages in the voting: the *ante-scrutinium,* the *scrutinium* and the *post-scrutinium,* in each of which each step is minutely prescribed.

The voting is done as follows: Each voter simply writes on the ballot the name of the person he votes for, and folds the ballot without signing or sealing it. Then each Cardinal, in the order of precedence, holding his folded ballot between the first two fingers of his right hand, carries it up to the altar, on which a large chalice and paten

---

[9] For a fuller explanation of these extraordinary censures, see Cappello, *De Censuris,* Appendix I, p. 493.

are placed. There, after kneeling for a moment in prayer, he rises, and in a loud voice pronounces the following solemn oath: "I call to witness Jesus Christ, who will judge me, that I am electing him who before God I judge should be elected." Thereupon he places his ballot on the paten and slides it into the chalice. When all have voted, including the sick, for whom special provisions are made, the ballots are counted. If their number does not correspond to the number of Cardinals, all are immediately burned. The three tellers at the altar record and announce the votes cast for each candidate. The ballots are then strung together with a needle and thread passing through the word *"Eligo,"* are tied thus, and laid aside; after which the votes are again counted by the tellers and checked by the reviewers. If any candidate has been elected by two thirds of the vote plus one, as soon as that fact has been duly certified the ballots are immediately burned; if not, they are reserved to be burned with those of the second ballot, which in that case follows immediately. These provisions are to be followed also in case the vacancy of the Holy See occurs through the resignation of the reigning Pontiff (nn. 65–91).

6. Simony in the election is severely condemned under pain of excommunication; it would not however, invalidate the election. Manipulations or promises, made during the lifetime of the Pope and without consulting him, looking to the election of his successor, are punished by excommunication. All are forbidden under pain of excommunication to accept for transmission to the Sacred College or to any member thereof, a so-called *Veto* or *Exclusiva* from any civil government. Promises to vote for or against any particular candidate are void and are punished by excommunication. Pre-election pledges, if any have been made by the successful candidate, are void. All over the world, as soon as the death of the Pope is learned, clergy and people must pray earnestly for the speedy, unanimous, and worthy election of his successor. Finally, the person elected is urged not to be deterred from accepting the burden (nn. 92–99).

7. The consent or acceptance of the person elected is asked by the Dean of the Sacred College in the name of all. Immediately upon his acceptance, he acquires by divine law the full supreme power of jurisdiction (c. 219). Hence, all acts thereafter are valid, even before his coronation. If the elect is not a priest or Bishop, he is to be ordained or consecrated, or both, by the Dean of the Sacred College. Thereafter his coronation, by the senior Cardinal Deacon, takes place (nn. 100–108).

The Oecumenical Council. The oecumenical council is governed by **canons 222–229**. It cannot be convened without a call from the Roman Pontiff, who presides at its sessions in person or through a representative, and confirms its decrees (c. 222). Subject to this essential dependence on the Pope, the council has supreme power over the entire Church; but there is no appeal from the Pope to the council (c. 228). If the Pope dies while the council is in session, it is *ipso iure* suspended until the new Pope reconvenes it (c. 229).

The Twenty Oecumenical Councils

Number	Name	Date	
1	Nicaenum I	325	(Nicea)
2	Constantinopolitanum I	381	(Constantinople I)
3	Ephesinum	431	(Ephesus)
4	Chalcedonense	451	(Chalcedon)
5	Constantinop. II	553	(Constantinople II)
6	Constantinop. III	680–681	(Constantinople III)
7	Nicaenum II	787	(Nicea)
8	Constantinop. IV	869–870	(Constantinople IV)
9	Lateranense I	1123	(Lateran I)
10	Lateranense II	1139	(Lateran II)
11	Lateranense III	1179	(Lateran III)
12	Lateranense IV	1215	(Lateran IV)
13	Lugdunense I	1245	(Lyons I)
14	Lugdunense II	1274	(Lyons II)
15	Viennense	1311–1312	(Vienne)
16	Constantiense	1414–1418	(Constance)
17	Florentinum	1438–1445	(Florence)
18	Lateranense V	1512–1517	(Lateran V)
19	Tridentinum	1545–1563	(Trent)
20	Vaticanum	1869–1870	(Vatican)

The Cardinals of the Holy Roman Church. These constitute the senate of the Roman Pontiff, and assist him as his chief counselors and helpers in governing the Church (c. 230). The Sacred College is divided into three orders: Cardinal Bishops, Cardinal priests, and Cardinal deacons. The Cardinal Bishops are the Bishops of the so-called suburbicarian sees: Ostia, Palestrina, Porto e Santa Rufina, Albano, Velletri, Frascati, and Sabina e Poggio Mirteto. Though there are seven suburbicarian sees, there are only six Cardinal Bishops, because the Dean of the Sacred College always has the see of Ostia in addition to his other suburbicarian see. The full quota of the Cardinal priests is fifty; of the Cardinal deacons, fourteen (c. 231), bringing the full College up to seventy members. The Cardinals are all appointed by the Roman Pontiff, and must be priests of outstanding learning, piety, judgment, and ability (c. 232). The Dean of the Sacred College is the senior of the Cardinal Bishops (c. 237). The many privileges of Cardinals are enumerated in canon 239. During the vacancy of the Apostolic See, the Sacred College has only the powers which are defined in the Constitution, *Vacante Sede Apostolica* (c. 241).

A slight modification, enlarging the powers of the Cardinal Major Penitentiary, for urgent cases only, during the vacancy of the Apostolic See, was introduced by Pius XI.[10]

The Roman Curia: General Provisions. The Roman Curia consists of the Sacred Congregations, Tribunals, and Offices which are enumerated and described in the Code (c. 242). The procedure for the transaction of business in the various units is governed by general and particular rules enacted for them by the Roman Pontiff; and all persons belonging to the Sacred Congregations, Tribunals, or Offices are bound to secrecy as provided in their respective rules (c. 243). No important or extraordinary business may be transacted unless it has previously been made known to the Roman Pontiff. All favors and resolutions need the approval of the Pope, except those for which special faculties have been granted to the Presidents of the respective Congregations, Tribunals, or Offices, and excepting also the decisions of the Rota and the Supreme Signatura (c. 244). The competency of the various units is determined by law; and in case a controversy arises thereon, it is to be decided by a committee of Cardinals specially designated for each such occasion by the Roman Pontiff (c. 245). Several such decisions have been rendered.[11]

The Sacred Congregations. The origin of the Sacred Congregations dates, remotely, from the fourth century — proximately, from a much more recent date. Their present status was approached by Pius X in the Constitution, *Sapienti consilio*, of 29 June, 1908. Their individual organizations have varied much since their origin, and have even been modified in some respects since the Code.

---

[10] Pius XI, Apostolic Const., 25 March, 1935, n. 12; *AAS*, 27–112; *Digest*, II, p. 114, ref. The new Constitution, *Vacantis Apostolicae Sedis*, 8 Dec., 1945, *AAS*, 38–65, now supplants the earlier one.
[11] See *Digest*, I, p. 155, references under c. 245.

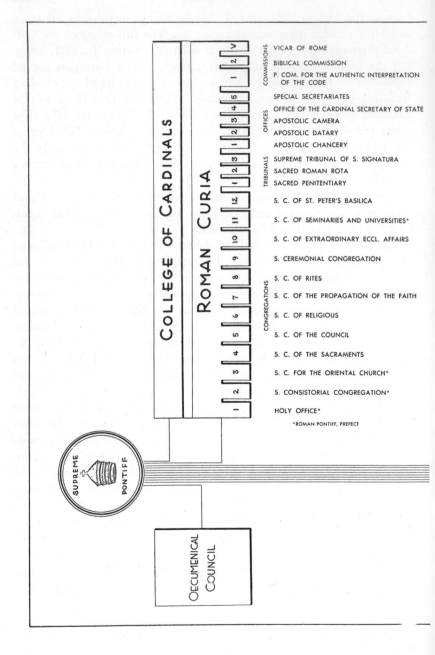

COLLEGE OF CARDINALS

ROMAN CURIA

COMMISSIONS

2 V
1

VICAR OF ROME

BIBLICAL COMMISSION

P. COM. FOR THE AUTHENTIC INTERPRETATION OF THE CODE

OFFICES

5 4 3 2 1

SPECIAL SECRETARIATES

OFFICE OF THE CARDINAL SECRETARY OF STATE

APOSTOLIC CAMERA

APOSTOLIC DATARY

APOSTOLIC CHANCERY

TRIBUNALS

3 2 1

SUPREME TRIBUNAL OF S. SIGNATURA

SACRED ROMAN ROTA

SACRED PENITENTIARY

CONGREGATIONS

12 11 10 9 8 7 6 5 4 3 2 1

S. C. OF ST. PETER'S BASILICA

S. C. OF SEMINARIES AND UNIVERSITIES*

S. C. OF EXTRAORDINARY ECCL. AFFAIRS

S. CEREMONIAL CONGREGATION

S. C. OF RITES

S. C. OF THE PROPAGATION OF THE FAITH

S. C. OF RELIGIOUS

S. C. OF THE COUNCIL

S. C. OF THE SACRAMENTS

S. C. FOR THE ORIENTAL CHURCH*

S. CONSISTORIAL CONGREGATION*

HOLY OFFICE*

*ROMAN PONTIFF, PREFECT

SUPREME PONTIFF

OECUMENICAL COUNCIL

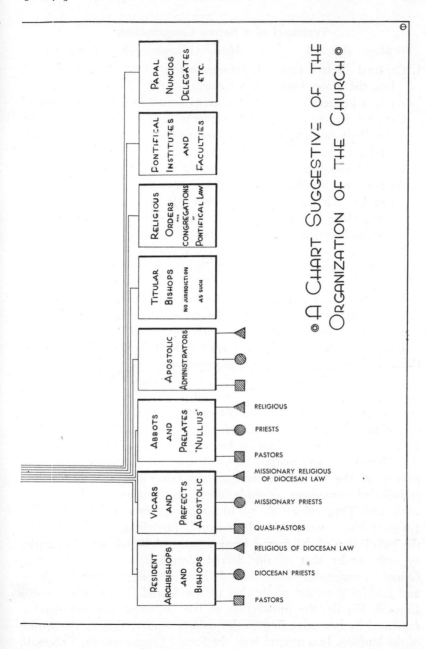

A Chart Suggestive of the Organization of the Church

PAPAL NUNCIOS DELEGATES ETC.

PONTIFICAL INSTITUTES AND FACULTIES

RELIGIOUS ORDERS AND CONGREGATIONS OF PONTIFICAL LAW

TITULAR BISHOPS NO JURISDICTION AS SUCH

APOSTOLIC ADMINISTRATORS

ABBOTS AND PRELATES "NULLIUS"
- RELIGIOUS
- PRIESTS
- PASTORS

VICARS AND PREFECTS APOSTOLIC
- MISSIONARY RELIGIOUS OF DIOCESAN LAW
- MISSIONARY PRIESTS
- QUASI-PASTORS

RESIDENT ARCHBISHOPS AND BISHOPS
- RELIGIOUS OF DIOCESAN LAW
- DIOCESAN PRIESTS
- PASTORS

Personnel of a Sacred Congregation

Major Officials	Minor Officials	Consultors
1. Cardinal Prefect (unless the Pope himself is Prefect) Cardinal Secretary (if the Pope himself is Prefect)	1. *Informatores* 2. *Scriptores* 3. Archivists 4. Accountants (*Computistae*)	(Learned men of both secular and religious clergy,
2. Cardinal members	5. Messengers (*Cursores*)	whose counsel may be asked.)
3. Assessor or Secretary (an Archbishop, when there is not a Cardinal Secretary)	6. Door keepers (*Ianitores*)	
4. Subsecretary (a Monsignor)		

The extent of the jurisdiction of the Sacred Congregations is in some cases limited *territorially*. Thus, the Sacred Congregation of Propaganda is competent only in mission territories other than those assigned to the Sacred Oriental Congregation; the Sacred Consistorial Congregation and the Sacred Congregation of the Council, only outside mission territories; the Sacred Congregation of the Sacraments is competent as regards marriage everywhere, as regards other matters, everywhere except in mission territory, etc. The Sacred Oriental Congregation has territorial jurisdiction (for persons of all rites) in certain defined territories; elsewhere, it has jurisdiction only over persons of the Oriental rite and matters in which they are concerned, even with persons of the Latin rite, with certain reservations.[12] Second, their jurisdiction sometimes depends upon the quality of the *persons* concerned. Thus, subject always to the prerogatives of the Holy Office (in everything concerning faith or morals), religious as such fall under the jurisdiction of the Sacred Congregation of Religious; missionaries as such, under that of the Sacred Congregation of Propaganda; Orientals, under that of the Sacred Oriental Congregation; the clergy and faithful generally under that of the Sacred Congregation of the Council. Finally, the jurisdiction of the respective Congregations is regulated by law according to the *subject matter;* that is, the nature of the business. In a general way, the Sacred Congregations, Tribunals,

---

[12] Cf. Pius XI, *Motu proprio*, 25 March, 1938; *AAS*, 30–154; *Digest*, II, p. 111.

and Offices are distinguished by the nature of the power they exercise: the Congregations exercise administrative and executive power; the Tribunals, judicial power; and the Offices, ministerial duties. However, the separation of these various powers is not absolute. The Holy Office, for example, besides the administrative jurisdiction of a Congregation, has in certain matters also the judicial functions of a Tribunal; the Sacred Congregation of Rites acts as a Tribunal under special procedure in causes of beatification and canonization.

Each Congregation is presided over by a Cardinal Prefect, or, in case the Roman Pontiff himself presides over it, it is directed by a Cardinal Secretary; and consists moreover of such Cardinals as the Roman Pontiff shall assign to each, with other necessary assistants (c. 246). The Pope himself is President of the following Congregations: the Holy Office, the Sacred Consistorial Congregation, the Sacred Oriental Congregation, and the Sacred Congregation of Seminaries and Universities.[13]

The following enumeration of the Sacred Congregations, to each of which is appended a bare statement of one or two of its principal functions or matters of competency, must be supplemented by a study of the individual canons, and of some examples of the work done by each Congregation since the Code.

1. The Supreme Sacred Congregation of the *Holy Office* has the guardianship of faith and morals; jurisdiction over certain crimes; the Pauline privilege; dispensations for mixed marriages; the condemnation of books; the Eucharistic fast for priests, etc. (c. 247).

2. The *Sacred Consistorial Congregation* prepares the agenda for the Sacred Consistories, and in places outside mission territories erects and divides dioceses, and supervises their government, proposes candidates for Bishops, Auxiliaries, etc. (c. 248).

3. The *Sacred Congregation of the Sacraments* has for its province the *discipline,* as distinguished from the *doctrine* and the *rites,* of the *Sacraments;* cases on the non-consummation of marriage, on the validity of sacred orders, etc. (c. 249). This Sacred Congregation has not the general right to intervene in cases for the nullity of marriage, which have already been instituted in diocesan tribunals. Its rights in these cases are strictly limited.[14]

4. The *Sacred Congregation of the Council* is in charge of the

---

[13] Cf. Pius XI, 3 Sept., 1937; *AAS,* 29–381; *Digest,* II, p. 110, ref.
[14] Cf. Code Com., 24 July, 1939; *Digest,* II, p. 547, and 8 July, 1940; *AAS,* 32–317; *Digest,* II, p. 105.

discipline of clergy and people in general: pastors, canons, associations of the faithful, Mass stipends, ecclesiastical property, diocesan taxes, the holding of councils and Bishops' meetings, except in mission territories, etc. (c. 250).

5. The *Sacred Congregation of Religious* has exclusive jurisdiction over matters which relate to the government, discipline, studies, property, and privileges of religious, subject to the rights of the Sacred Congregation of Propaganda, the Holy Office, and the Sacred Congregation of the Council (c. 251).[15]

6. The *Sacred Congregation for the Propagation of the Faith* is limited in its jurisdiction to places where the sacred hierarchy is not yet established and where the conditions of mission lands still prevail, and to places other than those recently placed under the jurisdiction of the Sacred Oriental Congregation.[16] In those places its jurisdiction is rather comprehensive; it does not, however, include matters of faith, matrimonial cases, nor ritual matters; and over missionaries who are also religious it exercises jurisdiction as missionaries only leaving their government as religious to the Sacred Congregation of Religious (c. 252).

7. The *Sacred Congregation of Rites* takes care of whatever concerns rites and ceremonies in the Latin Church. It acts as a tribunal under special rules in causes for beatification and canonization (c. 253), including, for this purpose, a historical section, since 1930.[17]

8. The *Sacred Ceremonial Congregation* regulates the ceremonies of the papal chapel and sacred functions performed by Cardinals in Rome; and also decides matters of precedence involving either Cardinals or Ambassadors to the Holy See (c. 254).

9. The *Sacred Congregation for Extraordinary Ecclesiastical Affairs* handles certain matters which require negotiations with civil governments, and at the request of the Secretary of State examines special matters which may arise relating to concordats (c. 255). The organization and competence of this Sacred Congregation were slightly modified by a Letter of Pius XI, 5 July, 1925.[18]

10. The *Sacred Congregation of Seminaries and Universities* is in general charge of studies and of papal seminaries and universities (c. 256). Its jurisdiction has been further defined and enlarged by the

---

[15] See decisions of the Special Commission of Cardinals, *Digest,* I, pp. 159, 161, 162.
[16] See note 12, this chapter.
[17] Cf. Pius XI, *Motu proprio,* 6 Feb., 1930; *AAS,* 22–87; *Digest,* I, p. 166.
[18] Cf. *AAS,* 18–89; *Digest,* I, p. 168.

Constitution, *Deus scientiarum Dominus,* 24 May, 1931.[19] The Holy Father himself is Prefect of this S. Congregation.[20]

11. The *Sacred Congregation for the Oriental Church* has charge of all matters which relate to the persons, the discipline, or the rites of the Oriental Churches, even when persons or matters belonging to the Latin Church are also involved, subject however to the rights of the Holy Office (c. 257). In the internal forum, jurisdiction over Orientals belongs to the Sacred Penitentiary.[21]

By a *Motu proprio* of Pius XI, this S. Congregation was given territorial jurisdiction (over all persons) in certain defined territories in and near the Orient, which were formerly under the jurisdiction of the S. C. of Propaganda.[22]

The Tribunals. There are three Tribunals: for the internal forum, the Sacred Penitentiary; and for the external forum, the Sacred Roman Rota, and the Supreme Tribunal of the Apostolic Signatura.

The Sacred Penitentiary consists of the Cardinal Major Penitentiary, a Regent, and five other prelates, namely, a Theologian, Datary, *Corrector, Sigillator,* and Canonist. These compose the *Signatura* or main body (not, of course, to be confused with the Apostolic Signatura, an entirely separate tribunal), which has also a Secretary, but without a vote. Besides the Secretary there are other minor officials. This sacred tribunal has jurisdiction for the internal forum only. It grants dispensations, absolutions, faculties, and decides questions of conscience; it is also in charge of matters pertaining to indulgences, unless questions of faith are involved (c. 258). The *minor penitentiaries* are groups of priests in three of the principal churches of Rome (the Vatican, St. John Lateran, and St. Mary Major), who depend upon the Cardinal Major Penitentiary and have special privileges and faculties, but do not strictly form part of the Sacred Penitentiary. The powers of the Cardinal Major Penitentiary continue during the vacancy of the Apostolic See, and are even enlarged during that time, for urgent cases only.[23]

The Sacred Roman Rota is the ordinary court of appeal for judicial cases appealed to the Holy See. It was established in 1424, and many published decisions of the old Rota are still extant. In 1870 it went almost completely out of existence, but was restored by the Constitution,

[19] *AAS,* 23–241; *Digest,* I, p. 172.
[20] Cf. Pius XI, Chirograph, 3 Sept., 1937; *AAS,* 29–381; *Digest,* II, p. 110.
[21] See S. C. Or., 26 July, 1930; *AAS,* 22–394; *Digest,* I, p. 174.
[22] Cf. Pius XI, *Motu proprio,* 25 March, 1938; *AAS,* 30–154; *Digest,* II, p. 111.
[23] Cf. Pius XI, 25 March, 1935, n. 12; *AAS,* 27–112; *Digest,* II, p. 114.

Sapienti consilio, of Pius X, in 1908. It consists of a number of *Auditores* or judges who sit as a corporate tribunal, not all in all cases, but a number of different judges in each, according to a pre-determined rotation. Its constitution and procedure were revised with papal approval in 1934.[24] The *Auditores* are appointed by the Pope; they must be priests, and must have at least the *laurea utriusque iuris* (c. 1598). Its jurisdiction may be summarized as follows:

1. *Major cases* are excluded from its competency entirely (c. 1600). These are cases which by reason of their importance are, either by their nature or by positive law, reserved to the Pope (c. 220). In the judicial field such are, for example, criminal cases against a Bishop or Cardinal, and all cases to which the prince or chief magistrate of a nation is a party.

2. It has no jurisdiction in *appeals from administrative decrees* issued by Bishops in the course of their government of their dioceses (c. 1601), not even in an action for damages claimed to have resulted from such decrees.[25]

3. It has jurisdiction as a trial court *in the first instance:* (*a*) in *contentious judicial* cases to which a resident Bishop is a party (except as provided in canon 1572, § 2; i.e., where the rights or property of the Bishop himself or of the diocesan Curia are in issue);[26] (*b*) in cases in which one party is a diocese, an exempt religious order, or some other ecclesiastical corporation which has no superior beneath the Roman Pontiff; and (*c*) in any other cases reserved to the Pope which he may entrust to it (cc. 1599, § 2; 1557, § 2).[27] In all these cases the Rota also acts, on appeal, as a court of second or third instance (c. 1599, § 2).

4. It has jurisdiction as an appellate court *in the second instance* in cases decided judicially by diocesan courts and appealed to Rome (c. 1599, § 1, 1°). A matrimonial case may be appealed from the diocesan court of first instance, either to another diocesan court established as a court of appeal according to canon 1594, or directly to the Rota.[28]

---

[24] Rota, 29 June, 1934; *AAS*, 26–449.

[25] Cf. Code Com , 22 May, 1923; *AAS*, 16–251; *Digest*, I, p. 739; and Rota, 30 Apr., 1923; *AAS*, 15–296; *Digest*, I, p. 746.

[26] Thus the Rota declared itself competent in a suit on a contract to which a resident Bishop was a party. Cf. Rota, 30 Jan., 1923; *AAS*, 15–124; *Digest*, I, p. 744.

[27] The Rota may be designated by the Holy Father as a court of first instance at the request of the parties. Cf. c. 1599, § 2, and Rota, 28 Feb., 1917; *AAS*, 12–85.

[28] Cf. Instruction on Matrimonial Procedure, S. C. Sacr., 15 Aug., 1936, Art. 216, § 1; *AAS*, 28–313; *Digest*, II, p. 523.

5. It has jurisdiction as a court of *last appeal* in cases appealed according to law either from diocesan tribunals to it, or from one *turnus* (or panel) of the Rota itself to another (c. 1599, § 1, 2°).

The **Apostolic Signatura** is the supreme tribunal of the Church, endowed with ordinary vicarious jurisdiction to act in the name of the Holy Father himself. It consists of eight Cardinals, of whom one is appointed Prefect or President. There are also a secretary, a notary, a custodian of records, and two subsidiary colleges or boards, one *a Votantibus* who act as consultors, the other *a Referendariis,* who perform secondary judicial functions.[29] The procedure of the Signatura is governed by papal ordinances dating from before the Code.[30]

It has *ordinary jurisdiction:* (1) of cases of violation of secret, or of damages caused by the judges of the Rota through invalid or unjust acts; (2) of the exception of suspicion against any judge of the Rota; (3) of complaints of nullity against a judgment of the Rota; (4) of petitions for the extraordinary remedy of *restitutio in integrum* from a judgment of the Rota which has become *res iudicata;* (5) of recourses from judgments of the Rota in matrimonial cases which the Rota has refused to admit to retrial; (6) of disputes as to competency between inferior judges (c. 1603, § 1).

It has delegated jurisdiction of petitions addressed to the Holy See asking that particular cases be assigned to the Rota (c. 1603, § 2).

The Offices. The *Apostolic Chancery* has charge of sending certain apostolic letters and bulls, by order of the Sacred Consistorial Congregation or of the Roman Pontiff (c. 260).

The *Apostolic Datary* takes charge of certain business relating to nonconsistorial benefices (c. 261).

The *Apostolic Camera* takes care of the property and temporal rights of the Holy See (c. 262).

The Office of the *Secretary of State* has charge of transactions between the Holy See and civil powers, and other special matters (c. 263).

The *Secretariates of Briefs to Princes and of Latin Letters* prepare letters to princes and the Latin composition of documents of the Supreme Pontiff at his direction (c. 264).

Commissions, Etc., Not Mentioned in the Code. A Sacred Congregation not mentioned in the Code is the *Congregation of the Venerable Edifice of St. Peter's,* which has the care of the Basilica,

---

[29] Cf. a Coronata, III, n. 1137.
[30] Cf. *Regulae servandae in iudiciis apud Supremum Signaturae Apostolicae Tribunal,* 6 March, 1912, in Wernz, *Ius Decretalium,* V, Appendix IV, p. 211.

and, together with the Sacred Congregation of the Council, the faculty of reducing Mass obligations.[31] The *Commission for Russia,* which was formerly subordinate to the Sacred Oriental Congregation, was later made an entirely independent unit, and still more recently has been annexed to the S. C. for Extraordinary Ecclesiastical Affairs.[32] The *Pontifical Commission for the Authentic Interpretation of the Canons of the Code* was established by the *Motu proprio* of 15 Sept., 1917.[33] The *Biblical Commission,* created by Leo XIII, 30 Oct., 1902, has for its province the study and interpretation of Scripture.[34] The two Commissions last named are not usually regarded as belonging strictly to the Roman Curia. The *Vulgate Commission* was a Commission of Benedictine monks charged by Pius X and Benedict XV with the task of revising the translation of the Vulgate. The Benedictines are still in charge of this important work; but the Commission has been merged in the new monastery of St. Jerome established in Rome.[35] The *Vicariatus Urbis,* or Vicariate of Rome, includes the Cardinal Vicar who administers the diocese of Rome as Vicar of the Pope, and the various persons and offices of his administration. A special Vicar General is now in charge of Vatican City.[36]

Legates of the Roman Pontiff. A Legate *a latere* is a Cardinal bearing this title and representing the Pope as his *alter ego,* with such powers as may be given him (c. 266). Legates with the title of Nuncio or Internuncio are sent to countries having diplomatic relations with the Holy See. Their office is to promote these friendly relations and to observe and report to the Pope on the state of the Church. They have moreover special delegated faculties. Legates with the title of Apostolic Delegate are sent to countries which do not have diplomatic relations with the Holy See. Their office is almost purely supervisory; and they too have certain delegated faculties (c. 267).[37] The faculties and office of Legates do not as a rule expire on the vacancy of the Holy See (c. 268). Legates do not interfere with the government and jurisdiction exercised by Ordinaries of places (c. 269).

---

[31] Cf. V-C, *Epit.,* I, n. 373.

[32] Made independent by Pius XI, *Motu proprio,* 6 Apr., 1930; *AAS,* 22–153; *Digest,* I, p. 172; annexed to the S. C. Neg. Extr. by Pius XI, *Motu proprio,* 21 Dec., 1934; *AAS,* 27–65; *Digest,* II, p. 110.

[33] Printed at the beginning of the Code; also in *AAS,* 9–483, and, in English, in *Digest,* I, p. 55.

[34] See *Digest,* I, pp. 618, 672.

[35] Cf. Pius XI, 15 June, 1933; *AAS,* 26–85.

[36] Cf. *ASS,* 21–309.

[37] For the latest available schedule of these regular faculties, see *Digest,* I, p. 175.

Patriarchs, Primates, Metropolitans. Patriarch and Primate are titles of honor, without special jurisdiction (c. 271). The Metropolitan or Archbishop is in charge of an ecclesiastical province consisting of several dioceses united to his own archdiocese. In his own archdiocese he has the full powers of a Bishop; but his jurisdiction over the suffragan sees of his province is limited to the few matters specified in canon 274.

The Pallium is the insignia of the authority of the Metropolitan.

History and symbolism. At one time the pallium, symbol of the Pope's protective power over the faithful, was worn by the Pope himself. In the sixth century he first conferred it as a mark of distinction on individual Metropolitan Archbishops. Gradually it became the insignia of their office, as the ring, crozier, and pectoral cross are the insignia of a Bishop's. By the ninth century, so well established was its symbolic significance that it became obligatory for Archbishops to petition the Holy See for its use. Finally in the eleventh century, the pallium was designated in papal bulls as the symbol of *plenitudo pontificalis officii,* the fullness of the pontifical office.

Like all the great Christian symbols, the pallium derives from Christ; it suggests the Lamb of God. It is made from the wool of two lambs, emblems of innocence and sacrifice, which are brought into the Church of St. Agnes in Rome, each year on January 21, her feast. Resting on damask cushions, their legs tied in red and blue ribbons, they are laid upon the altar at the conclusion of the high Mass, when the Abbot of the Canons Regular of the Lateran blesses them. They are then delivered to the Master of Ceremonies of the Lateran Basilica, who presents them to the Pope in the Vatican. The Holy Father sends them to the Sisters of St. Cecilia in Trastevere, who care for them. About Easter they are shorn of their fleece, which is sent to the Pope to be woven into pallia. These pallia are blessed on the vigil of the Feast of Ss. Peter and Paul, and are then placed in an urn in the Confession of the Vatican Basilica over the tomb of St. Peter. There they remain until they are conferred on a new Metropolitan Archbishop by the Holy Father himself.

Legal provisions. A Metropolitan is obliged to ask for the pallium within three months of his consecration, or, if he was already consecrated, within three months of his appointment in the Consistory (c. 275). Because it is the symbol of his authority, before its imposition he would perform illicitly acts of metropolitan jurisdiction or of the power of order in which its use is required by liturgical laws (c. 276).

The Metropolitan may wear the pallium in any church in his province, even an exempt one, during solemn Mass, on the days mentioned in the Roman Pontifical and others which he may have been allowed by privilege; but never outside his province, even with the consent of the Ordinary of the place (c. 277). If he loses his pallium, or is transferred to another archiepiscopal see, he must ask for a new pallium (c. 278). It can neither be lent, nor given, nor bequeathed at death, but all the pallia which a Metropolitan has received must be buried with him (c. 279).

Precedence. A Patriarch precedes a Primate; a Primate, an Archbishop; an Archbishop, a Bishop; except as provided in canon 347; i.e., that, in his own territory, the resident Bishop precedes all Bishops and Archbishops except Cardinals, Papal Legates, and his own Metropolitan (c. 280).

Plenary and Provincial Councils. A plenary council is a council of the Ordinaries of several ecclesiastical provinces, such as was the Third Council of Baltimore. It is convened by the Roman Pontiff, who also presides through his representative (c. 281). A provincial council is convened by the Metropolitan, and should be held in each province every twenty years. The membership of both plenary and provincial councils is regulated by law (cc. 282, 286). Laws of both plenary and provincial councils must be sent to Rome, and may not be promulgated until they have been considered and approved by the Sacred Congregation of the Council. The manner of their promulgation and the time when they are to become effective are determined by the council itself; and the laws are thereafter obligatory in the entire territory. Ordinaries of places can dispense from them only for just cause and in particular cases (c. 291). **Canon 292** provides for Bishops' meetings to be held every five years in every ecclesiastical province to deliberate on expedient measures and prepare them for proposal to the next provincial council.

Vicars and Prefects Apostolic. Vicars and Prefects Apostolic appointed by the Holy Father, govern territories not yet erected into dioceses (c. 293, § 1). They have the same ordinary powers of jurisdiction as have resident Bishops, unless the Holy See makes some reservations (c. 294, § 1). Vicars generally have, Prefects generally have not, the episcopal character; but both are empowered by law to give episcopal blessings, to consecrate chalices, etc., to confirm, and confer tonsure and minor orders (c. 294, § 2). They have jurisdiction over the missionaries as such, even though they are religious, but must not interfere in what pertains strictly to their religious discipline. Their relations with the religious superiors are regulated by law (c. 296, § 2) and by a careful Instruction of the Sacred Congregation of Propaganda, 8 Dec., 1929.[38] They are obliged to make the *ad limina* visit every five or ten years (cc. 299, 341), and a quinquennial report on the state of their vicariate or prefecture every five years (c. 300). A new formula for this report is prescribed.[39] They are obliged to reside in their territory and to make canonical visitations thereof when necessary (c. 301). They must appoint a council consisting of at least three of the more experienced missionaries (c. 302), and moreover call a meeting of the principal missionaries every year (c. 303). They must keep archives (c. 304, § 1), offer the Mass *pro populo,* but only on eleven days of the year (c. 306). They are under a grave obligation in conscience to see to the proper training and ordination of a native clergy (c. 305). They may not, without consulting the Holy See, expel missionaries assigned to the territory by the Holy See, nor permit them to leave the vicariate or prefecture permanently, or to transfer to another; but they may in case of public scandal remove missionaries, even religious, immediately notifying the Holy See (c. 307). In case they are not Bishops, their honorary privileges are the same as those of Prothonotaries Apostolic *de numero participantium* (c. 308). They must immediately appoint a Pro-vicar or Pro-prefect, who becomes by law their temporary successor in the administration of the territory should their office become vacant or embarrassed as provided in canon 429 (c. 309). Either the Pro-vicar or Pro-prefect or some other cleric may be appointed Vicar Delegate, with the same jurisdiction as have Vicars General of Bishops.[40] The Pro-vicar or Pro-prefect is without ordinary jurisdiction while the Vicar or Prefect is in charge, but on the latter's demise or incapacitation according to canon 429, succeeds to both his ordinary and delegated jurisdiction (c. 309, § 2).

Apostolic Administrators. The government of a canonically erected diocese, either while the see is occupied or while it is vacant, may, for serious and special reasons, be entrusted by the Holy See either permanently or for a time to an Apostolic Administrator (c. 312). The duties, rights, and jurisdiction of an Apostolic Administrator are regulated by law and by special provisions in his appointment. A recent

[38] Cf. *AAS,* 22–111; *Digest,* I, p. 637.
[39] Cf. Letter, S. C. Prop. Fid.; *AAS,* 14–287; *Digest,* I, p. 192.
[40] Cf. Letter, S. C. Prop. Fid., 8 Dec., 1919; *AAS,* 12–120; *Digest,* I, p. 144.

example is the appointment of an Apostolic Administrator for the Basilica and town of Loretto.[41]

Inferior Prelates. The inferior prelates dealt with in this chapter of the Code are Abbots and Prelates *nullius,* and the minor prelates who constitute the Household of the Roman Pontiff. As to the latter, canon 328 simply states that all members of the Pontifical Household, whether they have the title of Prelate or not, are subject to the privileges, rules, and traditions of the Pontifical Household. The entire subject is now regulated exclusively by the new Constitution, *Ad incrementum,* of 15 Aug., 1934.[42]

Abbots and Prelates nullius, that is, of no diocese, are Abbots and Prelates who govern a territory which is not included in any diocese. Their ordinary powers and obligations are the same as those of Bishops within their territory (**c. 323**); in fact they or their territories are *prima facie* included when the term Bishop or diocese is used in the Code (**c. 215, § 2**). Their appointment (**c. 320**) and honorary privileges (**c. 325**) are regulated by law; as is also the succession to the temporary government of a vacant abbacy or prelature until their permanent successor is appointed (**c. 327**).

Readings:

McDonough, *Apostolic Administrators,* Catholic University, 1941 (n. 139); Winslow, *Vicars and Prefects Apostolic,* Cath. U., 1924 (n. 24); Benko, *The Abbot Nullius,* Cath. U. (n. 173); *Ecclesiastical Review,* Vol. 95, p. 576 (Lallou, on the Apostolic Delegate); *Periodica:* Vol. 26, p. 396 (Pauwels, on the honorary privileges of Vicars Apostolic); Vol. 19, p. 63* (Vermeersch, on membership of the "Pontifical Household"; cf. also *Digest,* II, p. 122); *Digest,* I, pp. 146-154 (on the erection of parishes); *Digest,* I, pp. 175-187 (faculties of the Apostolic Delegate); *Digest,* I, pp. 155-159, and II, pp. 96-100 (moral and canonical decisions of the Holy Office).

---

[41] Cf. S. C. Consist., 11 Oct., 1935; *AAS,* 28–71; *Digest,* II, p. 122, ref.

[42] Cf. *AAS,* 26–497. See also *Irish Eccl. Rec.,* May, 1939, pp. 532–534; V-C, *Epit.,* I, n. 442, and Lydon, *Ready Answers in Canon Law,* pp. 430–432.

Section 3. Bishops and the Government of Dioceses (cc. 329–450)

PRELIMINARY SURVEY

Appointment and Tenure of Resident Bishops. 1. Bishops are the successors of the Apostles and by divine institution are placed over particular churches which they govern with ordinary jurisdiction under the authority of the Roman Pontiff. They are freely appointed by the Roman Pontiff (c. 329). The meaning of this first provision is merely that Bishops, as successors of the Apostles appointed by the

Roman Pontiff, constitute an element of the Church's constitution which is of divine origin.

2. Before anyone is raised to the office of Bishop his fitness must be proved in the manner determined by the Holy See **(c. 330)**. In the United States the names of worthy candidates are proposed to the Holy See through the Apostolic Delegate after having been suggested, discussed, and voted on at meetings of the Bishops of each province held every two years.[43]

3. The qualities required are defined in **canon 331:** legitimacy, thirty years of age, five years in the priesthood, good moral character, piety, zeal, prudence, and solid learning in theology and canon law.

4. Even though a civil government may (under the provisions of a concordat) have the privilege of presenting a candidate, investiture is granted exclusively by the Holy See **(c. 332)**.

5. A Bishop-elect must receive consecration within three months from the receipt of his letter of appointment, and within four months must proceed to his diocese **(c. 333)**.

6. A resident Bishop is the ordinary and immediate pastor of his diocese; but he can in no way interfere in its government until he has taken canonical possession. If before his appointment as Bishop he held the office of Vicar Capitular, *officialis,* or administrator, he may exercise the duties of that office after his designation as Bishop. Canonical possession is taken by showing the letter of appointment to the chapter of the cathedral church in the presence of the secretary of the chapter or the Chancellor of the diocese **(c. 334)**. In the United States, the board of diocesan consultors takes the place of the chapter **(c. 427)**.

Rights of Resident Bishops. 1. They have the right and duty to govern the diocese both in temporal and spiritual matters, with legislative, judicial, and coercive power, to be exercised according to law. Episcopal laws become effective immediately on their promulgation unless they provide otherwise. The manner of promulgation is determined by the Bishops themselves **(c. 335)**. Even in the diocesan Synod, the Bishop is the sole legislator **(c. 362)**. His judicial power may be used in person or delegated **(c. 1572)**.

2. He has a right of precedence regulated by canon 347.

3. Both resident and titular Bishops, from the moment when they receive notice of their appointment, have certain privileges and in-

---

[43] Cf. S. C. Consist., 25 July, 1916; *AAS,* 8–400; *Digest,* I, p. 194. See also Lydon, *Ready Answers in Canon Law,* p. 77.

signia. As regards the insignia, full details are given in a series of replies of the Sacred Congregation of Rites.[44] Residential Bishops, from the time of taking canonical possession of their sees, have moreover the right to receive the episcopal revenues, to grant indulgences of one hundred days, and to erect a throne and baldachin in all the churches of their diocese (c. 349, and S. Paen., 20 July, 1942; *AAS*, Vol. 34, p. 240; *Digest*, II, p. 221).

4. Resident Bishops may exercise pontifical functions as provided in **canon 337.**

Obligations of Resident Bishops. 1. Before his canonical appointment the candidate must make the *profession of faith* according to canons 1406–1408 and take the oath of fidelity to the Holy See **(c. 332, § 2).**

2. The Bishop's primary duties are to *govern the diocese,* see to the observance of the laws of the Church, prevent abuses, safeguard the purity of faith and morals, and promote Catholic education and Catholic Action **(cc. 335, 336).** He must also *preach* the word of God in person unless lawfully excused, and appoint suitable preachers in addition to the pastors (cc. 336, § 3, 1327). The duty to promote Catholic Action is not mentioned in the Code, but has been insisted on in official pronouncements of the Holy Father for the past twenty years.

3. He is bound by the law of *residence,* and the extent and time of his vacation are regulated by law **(c. 338).**

4. He is bound to apply the Mass *pro populo,* that is, for the people of his diocese, according to the norm of **canon 339,** about eighty-eight times a year. The details of this important obligation, which is exactly the same as that of pastors, will be explained in connection with canon 466.

5. He must make a quinquennial *report* to the Holy See *upon the state of his diocese.* The five years of each quinquennial period for the fulfillment of this duty are determined for the Bishops of various parts of the world, the Bishops of the United States having the periods ending with four and nine (1944, 1949, etc.). This report follows a formula prescribed by the Sacred Consistorial Congregation, 4 Nov., 1918.[45] Special provision is made for Bishops who assume the government of the diocese within two years of the beginning of the year upon which the report is due; these need not report until the next time the obligation recurs **(c. 340).**

---

[44] Cf. S. C. Rit., 26 Nov., 1919; *AAS*, 12–177; *Digest*, I, p. 204.
[45] Cf. *AAS*, 10–487; *Digest*, I, p. 202.

Other reports nowhere mentioned in the Code are due as follows: (*a*) on *catechetical instruction,* every five years, concurrently with the report on the diocese;[46] (*b*) on the *seminary,* every three years;[47] (*c*) on *matrimonial cases,* every year;[48] (*d*) on the observance of the S. C. Sacr. on *canonical investigations before marriage* (*AAS,* 33–297; *Digest,* II, p. 253), every year; (*e*) on the *extraordinary administration of confirmation* (S. C. Sacr., Decr., 3 Oct., 1946, n. 9; *AAS,* 38–353), every year; (*f*) on *modesty in dress.*[49] This report was originally prescribed to be made every three years, concurrently with the report on catechetical instruction. Now that the latter has been changed from a triennial to a quinquennial report, it seems that the report on modesty in dress need be rendered only quinquennially.

6. Resident Bishops, not however merely titular ones, must make a visit *ad limina* every five years for dioceses situated in Europe, every ten years for others (**c. 341**). As the years coincide with those on which the diocesan report is due, it is on this occasion that they present the report. They may fulfill this duty through a Coadjutor if they have one, or, with the permission of the Holy See, through another representative, who must be a priest of the diocese (**c. 342**).

7. They must make an *official visitation* of their diocese, partial or complete, yearly, completing the rounds at least every five years. In the United States, the Third Council of Baltimore (n. 14) requires that this visitation be completed at least every three years. The purpose of the visitation is to preserve sound doctrine, to protect right morals and correct evils, to promote peace, piety, innocence, and discipline among people and clergy, and otherwise to provide for the welfare of religion. The Bishop may perform this duty personally or through a Vicar General or other representative. If the Bishop does it in person, he may be accompanied by two clerics (**c. 343**). Not only persons but also things and places devoted to pious uses within the diocese, even though they be exempt, are subject to the ordinary episcopal visitation, unless it can be proved that a special exemption has been granted by the Holy See.[50] Exempt religious, however, may

---

[46] Cf. S. C. Conc., 12 Jan., 1935; *AAS,* 27–145; *Digest,* II, p. 412.
[47] Cf. S. C. Stud., 2 Feb., 1924; *AAS,* 17–547; *Digest,* I, p. 658.
[48] Cf. S. C. Sacr., 1 July, 1932; *AAS,* 24–272; *Digest,* I, p. 801.
[49] Cf. S. C. Conc., 12 Jan., 1930; *AAS,* 22–26; *Digest,* I, p. 212.
[50] In *churches of exempt regulars* in his diocese, the Bishop may not make the regular quinquennial visitation. He may make the visitation provided for in canon 1261, § 2, only in as far as he has positive information that the particular laws enacted by him are not being observed. Cf. Code Com., 8 Apr., 1924; *Digest,* II, p. 374. See also O'Brien, *The Exemption of Religious in Church Law,* p. 118; Slafkosky, *The Canonical Episcopal Visitation of the Diocese,* Cath. University, 1941.

be visited by the Bishop only in the cases expressly provided for in the law (c. 344). The manner of the visitation is paternal; there is a right of recourse, without suspensive effect, from the precepts and decrees made in connection with the visitation (c. 345). Unnecessary delays and the imposition of serious annoyance or burdens in connection with the visitation are to be avoided; no gift may be accepted, but board, lodging, and traveling expenses may be furnished according to local custom (c. 346).

Titular Bishops. 1. They can exercise no powers in their titular diocese, and do not even take possession of it. They are encouraged to offer the Mass *pro populo* occasionally for their titular see through motives of charity, but there is no obligation to do so (c. 348).

2. Titular Bishops enjoy the same privileges and insignia as resident Bishops, except that they cannot receive the episcopal revenues, nor grant indulgences, nor erect a throne and baldachin (c. 349). For a list of the titular sees, between six and seven hundred, see the *Annuario Pontificio* for the current year.

Bishops' Coadjutors and Auxiliaries. Coadjutors fall into three classes: first, Coadjutors given to the person of the Bishop with right of succession; second, Coadjutors given to the person of the Bishop without right of succession; and third, Coadjutors given to the episcopal see (c. 350). Those of the first class succeed the Bishop in the government of the diocese after his death; those of the second class, strictly called Auxiliary Bishops, lose their office immediately on the vacancy of the see; those of the third class neither lose their office nor succeed to the see, but they remain in the same subordinate position to the administrator of the diocese and to the new Bishop.

1. The Roman Pontiff has the exclusive right to appoint a Coadjutor for a Bishop. Usually a Coadjutor is given to the person of the Bishop with right of succession; sometimes, however, he is given to the diocese. A Coadjutor given to the person of the Bishop without right of succession is specifically called an Auxiliary (c. 350).

2. The rights of a Coadjutor given to the person of the Bishop are to be learned from the Apostolic letter by which he was appointed. Unless the letter provides otherwise, a Coadjutor given to a Bishop who is entirely incapacitated has all the episcopal rights and duties; others have only such power as the Bishop grants them. The Bishop shall not habitually delegate to another any work which the Coadjutor is able and willing to do. Whenever his Bishop requests him to do so, the Coadjutor, unless he is prevented by some lawful impedi

ment, must perform the pontifical and other functions which the Bishop himself would otherwise be bound to perform (c. 351).

3. A Coadjutor given to the diocese can exercise within the territory the functions which belong to the episcopal order, with the exception of sacred ordination; in other matters he has whatever power has been committed to him by the Holy See or by the Bishop (c. 352).

4. Every Coadjutor, in order to take canonical possession of his office, must necessarily show the apostolic letter containing his appointment to the Bishop if the latter is *sui compos*. A Coadjutor with the right of succession and a Coadjutor given to the diocese must moreover show the letter to the chapter or to the diocesan consultors according to canons 334, § 3, and 427. If the Bishop is in such condition that he is incapable of a human act, all Coadjutors take possession by merely showing the letter to the chapter or diocesan consultors as above provided (c. 353).

5. Every Coadjutor is obliged, as is the Bishop himself, to reside in the diocese, and outside of vacation time chosen according to canon 338, he may not absent himself except for a short time and with the permission of his Bishop (c. 354).

6. A Coadjutor with the right of succession, as soon as the episcopal see becomes vacant, immediately becomes the Ordinary of the diocese for which he was appointed, provided that he had lawfully taken possession of his office according to canon 353 (c. 355).

7. The office of an Auxiliary expires with that of the Bishop unless the Apostolic letter provides otherwise. If a Coadjutor was given to the diocese, his office continues even after the see becomes vacant (c. 355). To a query involving this last provision, the Sacred Consistorial Congregation replied: his office continues, always however keeping its character of dependence upon the person who shall obtain the government of the diocese.[51]

The Diocesan Synod. The diocesan synod is a consultative body which according to law is to be called by the Bishop every ten years, to consider measures for the welfare of the clergy and people of the diocese (c. 356). It is convened and presided over by the Bishop, and is usually held in the cathedral church (c. 357). Those who must be called to and must attend the synod are: the Vicar General, the canons of the cathedral church or the diocesan consultors, the rector of at least the major seminary, the rural deans, a deputy from each

---

[51] See S. C. Consist., 9 Jan., 1920; *AAS*, 12–41; *Digest*, I, p. 211.

collegiate church, the pastors of the city where the synod is held, at least one pastor from each rural deanery, and governing abbots and one superior from every clerical religious institute in the diocese. In addition to these, the Bishop may invite others also to the synod, with the same consultative vote unless the invitation provide otherwise (c. 358). Members of the synod may not be represented by proxy (c. 359). The agenda may be prepared in advance by committees appointed by the Bishop. Copics of proposed measures are given to the members before the meetings (c. 360). The measures are to be freely discussed in the synod (c. 361). But the Bishop is the sole legislator in the synod, the others having only a consultative vote; he alone subscribes to the synodal constitutions, and these, if promulgated in the synod, become obligatory at once unless express provision be made to the contrary (c. 362).

The Diocesan Curia. The diocesan Curia consists of those persons who assist the Bishop in the government of the diocese. Hence it includes the Vicar General, the *officialis,* the Chancellor, the promoter of justice, the defender of the bond, the synodal judges and examiners, the pastor consultors, auditors, notaries, couriers and constables (c. 363). These appointments are all made by the Bishop, and must be in writing. The appointees must take an oath before the Bishop to fulfill their office faithfully; must transact all business according to law under the authority of the Bishop; and must keep secrecy in confidential matters according to law (c. 364).

Organization and Personnel of the Diocesan Curia

Bishop

Administrative Officers	Judicial Officers	Archives
1. Vicar General	1. *Officialis*	1. Chancellor
2. Diocesan consultors	2. *Vice-officialis* (in	2. Vice-chancellor
3. Pastor consultors	large dioceses)	3. Notaries
4. Synodal (or pro-	3. Promoter of	
synodal) examiners	justice	
	4. Defender of the	
	bond	
	5. Synodal (or pro-	
	synodal) judges	
	6. Auditors	
	7. Couriers	
	8. Constables	

The **Vicar General** is appointed by the Bishop, who also has power to remove him at will **(c. 366)**. The Vicar General is an Ordinary of the place (c. 198), and assists the Bishop with ordinary power in the entire territory. Only one is to be appointed, unless more are needed; but when he is absent or incapacitated the Bishop can appoint another to take his place **(c. 366)**. His qualifications are: he must be a priest of the secular clergy unless the diocese is in the care of a religious institute, in which case he may be a member thereof; he must be at least thirty years of age, truly learned in theology and canon law, a man of sound doctrine, high character, prudence and experience in administration; not a brother, nephew, or uncle of the Bishop; nor, except in case of necessity, a pastor or one having the care of souls; but he may be chosen from the diocese itself **(c. 367)**. His jurisdiction is the same as that of the Bishop except in matters which the Bishop has reserved to himself or which according to law require a special mandate of the Bishop. He can as a rule execute rescripts of the Holy See which are sent to the Bishop or to a former ruler of the diocese, and in general he has also the habitual faculties which are granted by the Holy See to the Ordinary of the place (cc. 66, 368).

Matters which according to law are beyond the jurisdiction of the Vicar General without a special mandate are:

1. To grant excardination and incardination (c. 113);
2. To fill ecclesiastical offices (c. 152);
3. To convene the synod (c. 357, § 1);
4. To appoint pastors (c. 455, § 3);
5. To remove parochial vicars (c. 477, § 1);
6. To erect pious associations (c. 686, § 4);
7. To reserve sins (c. 893, § 1);
8. To grant dismissorial letters (c. 958, § 1, 2°);
9. To permit marriages of conscience (c. 1104);
10. To consecrate places (c. 1155, § 1);
11. To give permission for building a church (c. 1162, § 1);
12. To authenticate relics (c. 1283, § 2);
13. To permit the public veneration of ancient relics whose authentication has been lost (c. 1285, § 1);
14. To fix a legal charge for the celebration of Mass by outside priests in poor churches (c. 1303, § 3);
15. To establish benefices (c. 1414, § 3);
16. To unite (c. 1423, § 1), or to confer benefices (c. 1432, § 2);
17. To grant canonical investiture (c. 1466, § 2);

18. To permit the exchange of benefices (c. 1487, § 1);

19. To act as Ordinary in causes of beatification and canonization (c. 2002);

20. To inflict ecclesiastical penalties (c. 2220, § 2);

21. To remit a penalty imposed by himself as judge (c. 2236, § 3);

22. To absolve apostates, heretics, or schismatics from excommunication (c. 2314, § 2).

The power of the Vicar General to act without special mandate in the administrative removal of pastors (cf. cc. 2147 seq.) is disputed by some authors. But the Code does not mention any such limitation. Cf. O'Connor, *The Administrative Removal of Pastors,* pp. 81, 82.

When the Vicar General acts in any of the above matters with a special mandate as required by law, it is disputed whether he is using merely delegated or ordinary jurisdiction. The dispute is not extremely practical because even if the power in such cases be considered as delegated, it would be *ad universitatem negotiorum* and hence could be subdelegated in individual cases (c. 199, § 3).[52]

The Vicar General must refer the principal acts of the Curia to the Bishop, and must notify him of measures which have been or are to be taken to safeguard the discipline of clergy and people. He must not use his powers in any way contrary to the mind and will of the Bishop, and cannot validly grant a favor which has been denied by the Bishop, except with his consent (cc. 369, 44, § 2). He has the right of precedence over all other clerics of the diocese, unless the other cleric has the episcopal character and the Vicar General has not. In case he is himself a Bishop he has all the honorary privileges of titular Bishops; otherwise, he is entitled, for the duration of his office, to the privileges and insignia of a Prothonotary Apostolic (c. 370). In some of the dioceses of the United States, the Vicar General is a titular Bishop (Auxiliary); in others, he is without the episcopal character. The jurisdiction of the Vicar General expires by his resignation according to canons 183–191, by his recall made known to him by the Bishop, or by the vacancy of the episcopal see; it is suspended whenever the episcopal jurisdiction is suspended (c. 371).

Validity of Acts Done by the Vicar General After Vacancy of the See. In case the see becomes vacant by the death of the Bishop, all

---

[52] Cf. Wernz-Vidal, *De Personis,* n. 640. In favor of delegated jurisdiction, see Hilling, in *Archiv für Katholisches Kirchenrecht,* 1924, p. 199; Toso, in *Ius Pontificium,* 1927, p. 143; in favor of ordinary jurisdiction, a Coronata, *Institutiones,* I, n. 421; V-C, *Epit.,* I, n. 479; Wernz-Vidal, *De Personis,* n. 640. Cf. Roelker, *The Vicar General and the Special Mandate* in *The Jurist,* Vol. 2, p. 346.

acts except the conferring of benefices or ecclesiastical offices, which have been done by the Vicar General before he received certain notice of the Bishop's death, are valid (c. 430, § 2); if the see becomes vacant by the resignation, transfer, or removal of the Bishop, acts done by the Vicar General thereafter, except the conferring of benefices or offices, are valid up to the time when he learns that the Holy See has accepted the resignation, or has transferred or removed the Bishop (c. 430, § 2). In the latter case (resignation, transfer, or removal) the same is true of acts done by the Bishop himself before he receives notice of the action of the Holy See (*ibid.*).

The *officialis* is a diocesan officer appointed by the Bishop with ordinary judicial power. He may have one or more assistants, called *vice-officiales*. All must be priests, learned in canon law, and not less than thirty years of age. They are appointed by the Bishop, and removable by him (c. 1573).

The Chancellor, the Notaries, and the Archives. The Chancellor is a priest appointed by the Bishop to take care of the records of the Curia in the archives; in case of need he may be given an assistant, called the vice-chancellor or vice-recorder. The Chancellor is a notary by virtue of his office **(c. 372).**

The office of notaries is minutely described in the Code (cc. 374, 1585); but may here be taken as sufficiently known from its name.

The custody of the diocesan archives is also regulated by a series of admirable provisions **(cc. 375–384)** for which the official text had better be consulted.

The Promoter of Justice and the Defender of the Bond. These are judicial officers appointed by the Bishop. They must be priests of good reputation, of tried prudence and zeal for justice, learned in canon law (c. 1589). The duties of the promoter of justice are concerned with criminal trials and with contentious cases which, in the judgment of the Ordinary, may involve the public welfare. The duties of the defender of the bond concern cases in which the bond of marriage or of sacred orders is at stake (c. 1586).

The Synodal Judges. In every diocese there are to be not more than twelve judges appointed by the Bishop, with delegated judicial power. They must be priests of good character, learned in canon law, and may be from outside the diocese. If appointed in the diocesan synod, they are called synodal judges; if appointed outside the synod, they are called prosynodal judges; in either case their jurisdiction is the same, depending entirely on delegation by the Bishop (c. 1574).

Synodal Examiners. 1. *Appointment and tenure.* The Code provides that both synodal examiners and pastor consultors are to be appointed in the synod; however, between two synods, or in case a synod is not held, the Bishop may make the appointments upon consultation with the cathedral chapter (cc. 385, 386), or with the diocesan consultors (c. 427). Examiners so appointed are called prosynodal. Examiners and pastor consultors cannot be removed by the Bishop except for grave cause and after consultation with the chapter (c. 388) or diocesan consultors (c. 427). Their tenure of office is minutely regulated by **canon 387.**

2. *Functions.* Examiners have two rather distinct functions: first, to conduct certain examinations for the Bishop; second, to advise him in the course of proceedings for the removal and transfer of irremovable pastors (c. 389). The examinations in which they are principally employed are those prescribed by canon 459, § 3, 3°, for candidates for parishes; in the examination of candidates for orders, of applicants for faculties to hear confessions or to preach, and of the junior clergy (cf. c. 130), the Bishop may call upon the regular examiners or upon other persons specially appointed (c. 389).

Their duties in connection with the administrative removal of pastors will be explained under canon 454 (see p. 194).

Pastor Consultors. Their appointment, removal, and tenure have been described above, with those of the examiners. Their duties are entirely advisory in connection with the removal of irremovable pastors (see c. 454, p. 194) and the transfer of removable pastors.

Auditors. An auditor is one who draws up the record of a trial; however, he is more than a mere notary or court recorder. He has charge, if we may use the expression, of "steering" the trial. He is called *actorum instructor,* a term which may be translated as "marshal of the proceedings" (c. 1580). The Ordinary may appoint one or two auditors either for regular service or for individual cases; if none are thus provided, the judge may appoint one for the case before him (c. 1580). Auditors are usually selected from among the synodal judges (c. 1581). It is their duty to summon and hear witnesses, and draw up the record of the case, but not to decide it (c. 1582). The functions of the auditor in diocesan matrimonial trials for the nullity of marriage are fully described in the recent Instruction of the Sacred Congregation of the Sacraments.[53]

---

[53] S. C. Sacr., 15 Aug., 1936; *AAS,* 28–313; *Digest,* II, p. 471.

Couriers are court messengers; **constables** or **apparitors** are officers whose duty it is to execute the sentence or judgment of the court.

The Council of Vigilance. A branch of the diocesan Curia which is nowhere mentioned in the Code is the Council of Vigilance, to be established in every diocese to watch against the growth of Modernism. This provision was first made by a *Motu proprio* of Pius X, 1 Sept., 1910, and it remains in effect notwithstanding its omission from the Code.[54] The Council of Vigilance is further charged with the duty of considering ways and means of providing for modesty in women's dress.[55]

Chapters of Canons. A chapter of canons is a corporation, or collegiate moral person (cf. c. 99), consisting of canons, and having as its principal duties the care of solemn functions in the church to which they are attached, and certain services to be rendered to the Bishop. They are divided into cathedral and merely collegiate chapters. The cathedral chapter has certain advisory functions toward the Bishop in connection with the government of the diocese; and in case of the vacancy of the see it takes over the government until a new Bishop is appointed, but must appoint a Vicar Capitular for the actual government of the diocese. Since cathedral chapters have not yet been established in the United States, these consultative and administrative functions of the cathedral chapter fall to the board of diocesan consultors (c. 427), and will be explained under the next two titles.

Diocesan Consultors. These are priests of high character, noted for piety, learning, and prudence, to be appointed by the Bishop in dioceses where cathedral chapters have not yet been established or restored (c. 423). There are to be six, or, in dioceses of few priests, at least four, and they are to be appointed by the Bishop for three-year terms (cc. 425, 426). None of them is to be removed during his term of office except for grave reason and after consultation with the other consultors (c. 428). The board of diocesan consultors takes the place of the cathedral chapter as adviser to the Bishop; hence whatever powers and duties for the government of the diocese, either while the see is occupied or while it is embarrassed or vacant, the Code gives to the cathedral chapter, the same are to be understood also of the board of diocesan consultors (c. 427).

The Government of the Diocese When the See Is Vacant or Embarrassed: the Vicar Capitular. When the see is so *embarrassed* by the captivity, relegation, exile, or incapacity of the Bishop that he

---

[54] Holy Office, 22 March, 1918; *AAS*, 10–136; *Digest*, I, p. 50.
[55] S. C. Conc., 12 Jan., 1930; *AAS*, 22–26; *Digest*, I, p. 212.

cannot communicate with his diocesans even by letter, the government of the diocese, unless the Holy See shall provide otherwise, shall be in the hands of the Vicar General or of some other ecclesiastic delegated by the Bishop. In such case the Bishop can, for grave reasons, delegate several persons who shall succeed one another in the office. In case these persons are all unavailable or embarrassed as above described, the chapter of the cathedral church shall appoint its Vicar who shall assume charge of the diocese with the powers of a Vicar Capitular. Whoever assumes the government of the diocese as above provided shall as soon as possible inform the Holy See of the fact that the see is embarrassed and that he has taken charge (c. 429). The case provided for here is far from being an imaginary one; it has occurred repeatedly in the history of the persecuted Church of Christ, in Mexico, Poland, Ireland, Spain, Russia, Germany, and elsewhere. It may be noted that in the absence of any special delegation made by the Bishop, the Vicar General takes charge in the capacity of Vicar Capitular. It is only in case he or the person delegated by the Bishop becomes unavailable that the chapter has any right of delegation. A further special provision is made in canon 429 for the rare case in which the Bishop is under excommunication, interdict, or suspension.

An episcopal see becomes *vacant* by the death of the Bishop, by his resignation accepted by the Roman Pontiff, by his transfer, and by the privation of his office after he is notified thereof. Nevertheless, with the exception of the conferring of benefices or ecclesiastical offices, all acts are valid which have been done by the Vicar General up to the time when the latter received certain notice of the Bishop's death, or by either the Bishop or the Vicar General up to the time when notice of the above-mentioned acts of the Holy See reaches them. Within four months of receiving certain notice of his transfer, the Bishop must go to the diocese to which he has been transferred and assume canonical possession thereof according to canons 333 and 334; and from the day of such taking possession the diocese from which he was transferred is fully vacant; but in the meantime the Bishop in the said diocese: (1) has the powers of a Vicar Capitular and is bound by the same obligations, all the powers of the Vicar General expiring forthwith; (2) retains the honorary privileges of residential Bishops; (3) receives the full income of the *mensa episcopalis* according to canon 194, § 2 (c. 430). The *mensa episcopalis* means that part of the episcopal income which is legally destined for the Bishop's support.

When the see is vacant, unle'ss there is an Apostolic Administrator or some other provision has been made by the Holy See, the government of the diocese devolves upon the chapter of the cathedral church, which must, within eight days from the receipt of notice of the vacancy, appoint a Vicar Capitular who shall govern the diocese in its stead (cc. 431, 432).

If by special disposition of the Holy See in any particular place, the Archbishop or another Bishop designates the Administrator of a vacant diocese, the latter has all the faculties, and those only, which belong to a Vicar Capitular, and is subject to the same obligations and penalties (c. 431).

There is now no general provision allowing a Bishop or Archbishop to appoint an Administrator for a vacant diocese in the United States. The provisions of the Second Council of Baltimore on this matter (nn. 96–99), which had been continued in effect by the Third Council of Baltimore, are revoked by the Code, and the provision of canon 427 is to be observed; that is, the government of the diocese devolves upon the board of diocesan consultors, who must appoint an Administrator to govern the diocese during the vacancy.[56] Special temporary provision was made for the appointment of an Administrator in dioceses where there are not at least five or six diocesan consultors. The Administrator, by whomsoever lawfully appointed, has the rights and duties of a Vicar Capitular (c. 431).

The Code further provides that in case the chapter fails to appoint the Vicar within the eight days prescribed by law, the appointment devolves upon the Metropolitan, or in certain special cases on another Bishop (c. 432, §§ 2 and 3); it also provides for the appointment of one or more subsidiary administrators if necessary to administer the revenues of the diocese during the vacancy (c. 432, § 1); it prescribes the qualifications required in the Vicar, some of which (the priesthood, thirty years of age) are required for the validity of the appointment (c. 434); defines his jurisdiction, which is in general that of a Bishop, with certain exceptions (cc. 435–437); defines his duties, compensation, etc. (cc. 438, 440, 441); defines the manner in which he may be removed or may resign from the office (c. 443); and how he is to account for his administration to the new Bishop (c. 444).

Vicar Forane. A vicar forane, or rural dean, is a priest who is placed by the Bishop in charge of a deanery such as is mentioned in canon 217 (c. 445). He is usually a pastor, is always appointed by the

---

[56] Cf. Code Com., and S. C. Consist., 22 Feb., 1919; *AAS*, 11–75; *Digest*, I, p. 242.

Bishop, and is removable by him at will (c. 446). His duties, prescribed in detail (c. 447), are chiefly to exercise a certain supervision over the pastors of his district, for which purpose he must visit them officially at times prescribed by the Bishop. Also, in case of serious illness of any of these pastors, he must see to it that they have spiritual and material assistance, etc., and in case of their death, must see that they have proper burial and that the papers and belongings of the parish be not disturbed. The dean also presides at the meetings or conferences mentioned in canon 131, for his district (c. 448), and reports once a year to the Bishop (c. 449). His duty of residence is prescribed in canon 448, § 2, in case he is not already bound to residence as a pastor; and his right of precedence is defined by canon 450.

Readings:

Ryan, *Principles of Episcopal Jurisdiction,* Catholic University, 1939 (n. 120); Slafkosky, *The Canonical Episcopal Visitation of the Diocese,* Cath. U., 1941 (n. 142); Donnelly, *The Diocesan Synod,* Cath. U., 1932 (n. 74); Dugan, *The Judiciary Department of the Diocesan Curia,* Cath. U., 1925 (n. 26); Prince, *The Diocesan Chancellor,* Cath. U., 1942 (n. 167); Louis, *Diocesan Archives,* Cath. U., 1941 (n. 137); Connolly, *Synodal Examiners and Parish Priest Consultors,* Cath. U., 1943 (n. 177); Klekotka, *Diocesan Consultors,* Cath. U., 1920 (n. 8); Jaeger, *The Administration of Vacant and Quasi-vacant Episcopal Sees in the United States,* Cath. U., 1932 (n. 81); *Irish Eccl. Rec.,* Vol. 39, p. 641 (Bishops cannot impose obligations against general laws of Church); Vol. 37, p. 632 (powers of Vicar General in administrative removal of pastor); *The Jurist,* Vol. 3, p. 567 (Prince, on the Chancellor as delegate of the Bishop).

CHAPTER V

PASTORS, PAROCHIAL VICARS, AND RECTORS OF CHURCHES

Section 1. Pastors (cc. 451-470)

PRELIMINARY SURVEY

Pastor: History. The word "parish," which means neighborhood, was formerly synonymous with diocese. The Bishop was the sole pastor, his priests being at his command for the care of souls in the episcopal city. As the number of the faithful grew, priests from the city were delegated by the Bishop for the care of souls in outlying places; but it was not until the fifth century that these priests began

188

to reside regularly at the seat of their labors. The beginning of the country parish as a regular institution dates from the sixth century, the development of city parishes, from about the tenth. The law of pastors and parishes in approximately its present form dates only from the Council of Trent (1545–1563).[1]

Definition. Canon 451 defines a pastor as "a priest or moral person upon whom a parish is conferred in his own right with the care of souls to be exercised under the authority of the Ordinary of the place." Some elements of this definition call for explanation.

1. If a pastor is a natural or physical person he must be a *priest*. According to canon 154, no cleric who is not yet a priest can validly receive an office to which the care of souls is attached. The same provision is made specifically for pastors **(c. 453).**

2. But a pastor may be, not a physical person, but a moral person; that is, an ecclesiastical corporation, a chapter, or a religious order. It is to be noted that this implies a full union of the parish to the moral person concerned, and such a union can be effected only by apostolic indult **(c. 452, § 1)**; even in such a case, the moral person is merely the nominal or titular pastor, the actual care of souls being entirely in the hands of a priest designated as vicar (cc. 452, § 2, 471).

3. A pastor has a parish in his own right (*in titulum*); and he is thus distinguished from parochial vicars who, even when they have full parochial powers, have the parish only *in administrationem;* that is, they have the administration of the parish but not the title to the office of pastor in the strict sense.

4. The *care of souls* essentially implies jurisdiction in the internal forum only. Hence all pastors have ordinary jurisdiction to hear confessions (c. 873), and also to absolve, during the paschal time, from all cases which the Bishop has reserved to himself (c. 899, § 3). By special provision of law, pastors have also a very limited jurisdiction in the external forum; namely, to dispense from certain matrimonial impediments in danger of death and in special urgent cases as provided in canons 1044 and 1045; to dispense in accordance with canon 1245, § 1, from the common law regarding the observance of feasts, fast, and abstinence; to assist validly at marriages within their territory (c. 1094), which is, however, not strictly an act of jurisdiction. The care of souls also implies what is called "domestic" power; that is, a certain disciplinary and administrative power by virtue

---

[1] See Cappello, *Summa*, II, n. 487, note.

of which the pastor, like a good father, watches over his subjects, administers his parish both spiritually and temporally, gives counsels and precepts, urges right conduct, corrects the erring, relieves the poor, teaches Christian doctrine, and promotes domestic peace and order.[2]

5. The *subjects* of a pastor, in the ordinary territorial parish, are persons who have a domicile or quasi-domicile in the parish (c. 94, § 1); also, as long as they are staying in the parish, persons who either have no domicile or quasi-domicile (*vagi,* c. 94, § 2); or have only a diocesan one (c. 94, § 3). In certain matters, however, the power of the pastor extends to visitors who are domiciled elsewhere (*peregrini*) as long as they are within his parish (cf. cc. 1044, 1045, 1245).[3]

Classifications. 1. A pastor is both *titular* and *actual* if he has not only the title of pastor but also the actual care of souls. He is *merely titular* (habitual, nominal) if he has only the title of pastor while the actual care of souls belongs, in law and in fact, to a vicar. This is the case when a moral person is the titular pastor. *Merely actual* pastors are: the vicar of a moral person who is titular pastor; the vicar of a priest pastor who is entirely incapacitated; and the administrator of a vacant parish.

2. Pastors are *removable* or *irremovable* according as they can easily or with difficulty be removed from office **(c. 454).**

3. They are *territorial, personal,* or *mixed,* according as their parish belongs to one or the other of these classifications, as explained under canon 216.

4. They are *secular* pastors if secular priests, *religious pastors* if they belong to a religious order, congregation, or society without vows.[4] Note that a religious pastor may, by apostolic indult, be in charge of a secular parish, as will be explained under canon 452.

Quasi-pastors and Parochial Vicars. 1. *Quasi-pastors* are those in charge of quasi-parishes, as described in canon 216, § 3; that is, territorial divisions of vicariates or prefectures apostolic. They have full parochial powers, and are declared equivalent to pastors in rights, obligations, and in name **(c. 451, § 2, 1°).** Their obligation as regards the Mass *pro populo* is slightly different in extent (cf. c. 466).

2. *Parochial vicars* are declared equivalent to pastors if they have full parochial powers **(c. 451, § 2, 2°).** There are five kinds of parochial vicars:

---

[2] Cf. Cappello, *Summa,* II, n. 503.
[3] For the rule regarding affiliation to national parishes in the United States, see Letter, Ap. Del., U. S., 17 Feb., 1938; *Digest,* II, p. 78.
[4] Cf. V-C, *Epit.,* I, n. 573.

a. The *vicar* (for a moral person who has the title of pastor) has full parochial powers (c. 471).

b. The *administrator* (*vicarius oeconomus*) of a vacant parish has full parochial powers (c. 472).

c. The *substitute* or *supplying priest* (*vicarius substitutus*) has full parochial powers unless the Ordinary or the pastor has made some reservation (cc. 465, 474).

d. The *coadjutor* (*vicarius adjutor*) may or may not have full parochial powers, according to canon 475.

e. The *assistant* or *curate* (*vicarius co-operator*) has not full parochial powers as a rule (c. 476, § 6).

Military Chaplains. These are governed by special regulations of the Holy See. Such special regulations have been made in recent years for the French navy;[5] for the Italian forces on land and sea;[6] for the military forces of Germany;[7] for the military forces of the United States.[8]

Union of Parish to Moral Person. In accordance with canon 1423, § 2, a parish cannot, without an indult of the Apostolic See, be united completely (*pleno iure*) to a moral person; that is, on such terms that the moral person itself shall be the pastor **(c. 452, § 1).**

The moral person to which a parish is completely united can retain only the habitual care of souls, observing as regards the actual care of souls the provision of canon 471 **(c. 452, § 2).**

State of the Question. To understand what is meant by "joining a parish to a moral person," we must remember that a parish is usually a benefice, and one to which the care of souls is attached (cf. c. 1411, 5°). As a benefice, it is itself a noncollegiate moral person (c. 99). A parish is therefore in a certain sense united or joined to a moral person when it is joined to another parish or to any other benefice. This is called the union of benefices, a rather complicated matter which is dealt with in canons 1419–1430, but with which we are not now directly concerned. In the present connection, we are concerned rather with the union of a parish to some *collegiate moral person,* such

---

[5] Cf. *AAS*, 10–238; *Digest*, I, p. 245.
[6] Cf. *AAS*, 18–42; *Digest*, I, p. 245.
[7] Cf. *AAS*, 27–367; *Digest*, II, p. 76, ref.
[8] The Most Reverend John F. O'Hara, C.S.C., D.D., Titular Bishop of Milasa, was appointed by the Holy See, Military Delegate of the Armed Forces of the United States, 11 Dec., 1939, and was consecrated on the 15th of January, 1940. For the faculties of Military Vicars themselves, see S. C. Consist., 8 Dec., 1939; *AAS*, 31–710; *Digest*, II, p. 141. For the faculties delegated to the chaplains of the armed forces of the United States, see *Digest*, II, p. 586.

as a chapter, or a religious order or congregation. This may be done in two ways: first, completely, or *pleno iure,* when the union is such that the moral person itself (the chapter or religious society) becomes the titular pastor of the parish and governs the parish through its vicar; or, second, incompletely; that is, as to temporal matters only (*minus pleno iure*), in which case the pastor remains unchanged, and receives a compensation for his services, while the revenues of the parish go to the moral person to whom the parish has been annexed. In the first case, if the moral person concerned is a religious society, the parish becomes a religious parish; in the latter case, it remains a secular parish, and the pastor is a secular priest (cf. c. 1425).

It is possible for a pastor to be a religious, even in a secular parish, and without any union of the parish to the religious society of which the pastor is a member. This is the case when, by apostolic indult, the government of a parish is entrusted either to a certain religious priest or to a religious community, under terms of agreement between the Bishop and the religious society concerned.[9]

Since we have as yet no chapters in the United States, the moral persons to whom parishes may be united, or to whom parishes may be entrusted without any canonical union, will be chiefly religious orders or congregations. It is pleasant, and may be useful, to quote in this connection the beautiful words of the Third Council of Baltimore, n. 86:

"We joyfully and gratefully testify and openly declare that that holy spirit of concord which was earnestly recommended by His Holiness, Pius IX, in the Encyclical, *Ubi primum* — that harmony between the secular clergy and the numerous religious orders which by the blessing of God are increasing and rendering such signal services to our churches in the care of souls and in the education of youth — has hitherto been preserved inviolate in this broad land of ours, through the pious moderation and temperance of all concerned. And with good reason we confidently expect and predict that this same brotherly cooperation and harmony will continue to the end."

Principles. 1. The *complete union* of a parish to any collegiate moral person; that is, such a union that the moral person itself becomes the titular pastor of the parish, can be effected only by an indult of the Holy See (cc. 452, § 1; 1423, § 2).

2. In such case, the moral person has *only the habitual care of souls;*

---

[9] Cf. Wernz-Vidal, *De Religiosis,* n. 414.

the entire actual care of souls being committed to a vicar in accordance with canon 471.

3. An *incomplete union,* as to temporal matters only (*minus pleno iure*) of a parish to a collegiate or cathedral church within the territory of the parish, may be made by authority of the Bishop (c. 1423, § 2); but even such a union of a parish to a religious house or community, or to any other moral person, requires an apostolic indult (cc. 1423, § 2, 1425).

4. *Religious pastors,* in either religious or secular parishes, remain subject to the Ordinary of the place in everything which concerns the government of the parish (c. 630).

5. The *union of two parishes,* or of a parish to another benefice, is governed by canons 1419–1425.

Qualifications of a Pastor. 1. The priesthood is required for the validity of the appointment **(c. 453, § 1).** This rule applies to all offices to which the care of souls is attached (c. 154).

2. Other requisite qualities, whose absence, however, usually would not affect the validity of the appointment, are: good moral character, learning, zeal, prudence, and all other qualifications which are prescribed either by the Code or by particular law **(c. 453, § 2).** The particular law in this connection includes: diocesan regulations; the so-called "law of the foundation"; that is, any legitimate conditions which are incorporated in an endowment; and lawful customs.

Classification of Pastors as to Stability of Tenure. Canon 454 deals with the stability of pastors, dividing them, in this respect, into three classes: irremovable; removable; and religious, who are most easily removed. It must be noted that as between removable and irremovable pastors, their stability is determined by their parish; that is, the quality of removability or irremovability attaches primarily to the parish, so that any pastor occupying such a parish shares the degree of stability which the parish has. On the other hand, a religious pastor has his quality of "high removability," if we may use the expression, from his personal character as a religious.

The Code evidently favors the higher degree of stability, since it provides that parishes may be declared irremovable by the Bishop, after consulting the chapter, and that newly erected parishes are to be irremovable; whereas it requires the permission of the Holy See to make an irremovable parish removable. The provision that new parishes are to be irremovable is not absolute but permits exceptions in the prudent discretion of the Bishop after hearing from the chapter.[10]

Irremovable Pastors can be removed for any cause which renders their ministry inefficacious (c. 2147); but their removal is governed by canons 2148–2156, which require the observance of the following procedure:

1. The Ordinary must consider the matter with two of the synodal examiners before inviting the pastor to resign, and must state in such invitation the reason therefor and the evidence sustaining it (c. 2148).

2. If the pastor neither resigns within the stated time, nor asks for an extension of time, nor makes any representations against the reason alleged for his resignation, the Ordinary may, upon verifying certain facts, proceed to remove him, and will not then be bound by the provisions of canon 2154, which require him to provide for a removed pastor (c. 2149).

3. If the pastor resigns, the Ordinary declares the parish vacant. The pastor can resign for a reason other than that stated in the invitation. He may also resign conditionally, provided the condition be one which the Ordinary can lawfully accept, and the provisions of canon 186 be observed (c. 2150).[11]

4. The pastor can ask for further time to contest the allegations of the Ordinary (c. 2151).

5. When the pastor produces his reasons for refusing to resign, the Ordinary must listen to the advice of the same two synodal examiners who advised him regarding the invitation; he must consider the value of the alleged reasons, decide the matter, and embody his decision in a decree (c. 2152).

6. If the decree is for removal, the pastor can within ten days interpose a recourse, to the same Ordinary for a rehearing. The Ordinary must then, under pain of acting invalidly, consult two of the pastor consultors and re-examine the entire case including new representations which the pastor may file within ten days. At this hearing the pastor may adduce the two or three witnesses allowed by canon 2145, if he was prevented from adducing them at the first hearing. The decision shall be embodied in a decree and communicated to the pastor (c. 2153). Canon 2154 concerns the method of making provision for a pastor after his removal.

---

[10] See also S. C. Consist., 1 Aug., 1919; *AAS*, 11–346; *Digest*, I, p. 146.

[11] A Bishop may provide for a resigning pastor even by pension, not exceeding one third of the revenues of the parish. Cf. c. 1429, § 2, and S. C. Conc., 11 Nov., 1922; *AAS*, 15–454; *Digest*, I, p. 838.

An irremovable pastor cannot be *transferred* against his will, without special permission of the Holy See (c. 2163, § 1).

Removable Pastors, who are not religious, can be removed according to canons 2157–2161. Briefly the steps are these:

1. The pastor is paternally urged to resign, the reason for the request being stated (c. 2158).

2. If the pastor neither resigns within the stated time, nor asks for an extension of time, nor controverts the reasons assigned for his resignation, the Ordinary may remove him, as provided above in the case of irremovable pastors. If the pastor refuses to resign, he must state his reasons in writing, and the Ordinary, under pain of acting invalidly, must consider them together with two synodal examiners (c. 2159).

3. If the Ordinary is not convinced by the pastor's answer, he repeats his paternal exhortation to the pastor, threatening to remove him if he does not resign within a suitable stated time (c. 2160).

4. At the expiration of the time, which may be extended, the Ordinary may issue a decree of removal. He is bound (except as provided in canon 2149) to provide for a pastor who has resigned or been removed, in accordance with canons 2154–2156 (c. 2161).

A removable pastor may be *transferred,* even against his will, observing the procedure of canons 2164–2167.

Quasi-pastors are all removable **(c. 454, § 4).**

Religious Pastors may be removed without any procedure, either by the Ordinary with notice to the superior, or by the superior with notice to the Ordinary, neither one being obliged to account to the other for his action, nor even to state the reason for it **(c. 454, § 5).** It is supposed, of course, that the cause must be a just one; however, it need not involve any fault, and much less any delict, on the part of the pastor. Recourse to the Holy See is allowed, without suspensive effect **(c. 454, § 5).** It must be noted that the term "religious pastor" in this connection does not include a religious society (moral person) which, by indult of the Holy See, may be the titular pastor. Such a pastor is, of course, entirely irremovable by the Ordinary. As to the removal of the vicar who in such a case exercises all the actual care of souls, see canon 471, § 3.

Appointment of Pastors. Let us recall in this connection the various ways of making provision for ecclesiastical offices, as explained under canon 148. **Canon 455** states who has the right to appoint and invest pastors.

Principles. 1. The Ordinary of the place has the right to appoint pastors outright, or to invest them in case someone else has the privilege of election, presentation, or nomination. All contrary customs are reprobated **(c. 455, § 1).**

Exceptions. Parishes *reserved to the Holy See* are withdrawn from this appointing power of the Ordinary **(c. 455, § 1).** These are:

a) Parishes annexed to a dignity in a chapter (c. 396);

b) Parishes annexed to a consistorial benefice (cf. c. 1411, 1°);

c) Parishes rendered vacant by the death, promotion, removal, or transfer of a Cardinal, Legate, major official of the Roman Curia, or member of the Pontifical Household (c. 1435). All grades of *monsignori* in the United States[12] are included in the last-mentioned group.[13] As to the norms to be observed in providing pastors for reserved parishes, see the Instruction of the Apostolic Datary, 11 Nov., 1930.[14]

d) Certain other special cases, mentioned in canon 1435.

2. When the see is either vacant or embarrassed as described in canon 429, the Vicar Capitular, or whoever is in lawful charge of the diocese, can make outright appointments to vacant parishes, only after the see has been vacant for a full year **(c. 455, § 2, 3°).** We think the same power of appointment would belong to the person in charge under canon 429 after the see has been *embarrassed* for a full year. Appointments made before the lapse of the year would be invalid (c. 1432, § 2).[15] Moreover, without any limitation as to time, the Vicar Capitular (or Administrator), or the person in charge of a diocese which is embarrassed as described in canon 429, can appoint those parochial vicars who are mentioned in canons 472–476; namely, all except a permanent vicar for a moral person; and can also confirm the election or accept the presentation of a pastor, and grant him investiture **(c. 455, § 2, 1° and 2°).**

3. The Vicar General may be the person in charge of an embarrassed diocese (cf. c. 429); if so, he can act in that capacity as above outlined; otherwise, however, that is, in his capacity as Vicar General, he cannot act in this matter without a special mandate from the Ordinary **(c. 455, § 3).**

Parishes Entrusted to Religious. For parishes which are entrusted

---

[12] Cf. Lydon, *Ready Answers in Canon Law*, p. 430.
[13] Cf. a Coronata, *Institutiones*, II, p. 385, note.
[14] *AAS*, 22–525; *Digest*, I, p. 220.
[15] Cf. V-C, *Epit.*, I, n. 541.

to religious, the superior to whom this right belongs according to the constitutions presents a priest of his institute to the Ordinary of the place, and the latter grants investiture to the candidate, observing the prescription of canon 459, § 2 (c. 456).

The parishes here referred to will fall into two classes: (*a*) parishes which are *completely united* to a religious order, house, or community, so that the moral person itself is the titular pastor, and there is question of appointing only a vicar or actual pastor; and (*b*) parishes which are *not united* to the religious order or house, but merely *entrusted* to it in pursuance of an agreement with the Bishop and an indult of the Holy See; here the person to be appointed is the pastor himself, titular and actual, and he will be a religious even though the parish is a secular one. A third case comes to mind; namely, that of an *incomplete union* of a parish to a religious order. But such a union concerns temporal matters only, and is not touched by this canon. It is clear from canon 1425, § 1, that in that case the pastor is not a religious but a secular priest, proposed by the religious superior and approved and invested by the Ordinary. The present canon, therefore, cannot intend to deal with that case; if it did, it would contradict canon 1425 as to the character of the appointee, though not as to the manner of his appointment.[16]

Principles. 1. In parishes *fully united* to a religious order or house, the vicar who has the actual care of souls is a religious presented by the superior, and invested by the Ordinary of the place if the latter finds him duly qualified in accordance with canon 459, § 2. This provision is in perfect accord with canons 471, § 2, and 1425, § 2.

2. In parishes merely *entrusted* to a religious order or house, *without any union* even as regards temporal matters, the same method is followed; namely, presentation of a religious by the superior, and investiture by the Ordinary.

3. Parishes which are *united merely as regards temporal matters* to a religious order or community are not "entrusted to religious," and do not come under this canon. In that case the pastor is a secular priest, presented by the superior and invested by the Ordinary (c. 1425, § 1).

Quasi-pastors. As a general rule quasi-pastors as well as pastors should be secular and not religious priests, because parochial benefices are presumably secular ones, and as such should be conferred upon seculars. However, the Bishops of missions have special authority to

---

[16] Cf. V-C, *Epit.*, II, n. 752; Claeys-Simenon, III, n. 212; *contra*, Augustine, *A Commentary on Canon Law*, II, p. 525.

appoint regulars to parishes or quasi-parishes, for the reason that there are not enough priests among the secular clergy who are available for such appointments.[17] The practice, therefore, as regards quasi-parishes, is to appoint either secular priests or religious priests. **Canon 457** speaks only of the appointment of secular quasi-pastors.

Appointment of Quasi-pastors. 1. Quasi-pastors *from the secular clergy* are appointed outright by the Ordinary of the place after hearing from the council composed of three of his elder and more experienced missionaries whom, according to canon 302, he is required to consult in important matters (c. 457).

2. Quasi-pastors *from the regular clergy* are appointed in the same way as are religious pastors; that is, they are presented by the religious superior, and invested by the Ordinary (cc. 451, § 2, 1°, 456).[18]

Time of Appointment. The general rule stated in canon 155 is that appointment to ecclesiastical office should never be deferred beyond six months of available time (*tempus utile*) from the receipt of notice of the vacancy. **Canon 458** mitigates the rule slightly in the case of a parish by permitting the Ordinary to defer the appointment in his prudent discretion if he deems it advisable to do so because of special circumstances. If the Ordinary abuses this discretion by deferring the appointment beyond the six months permitted by canon 155, without having genuine reasons therefor, so that the delay is really due to grave negligence, he loses the right to appoint, and it devolves upon the Holy See (c. 1432, § 3).[19]

Appointments to Parishes (c. 459). Without any favoritism, the Ordinary must confer a vacant parish on the person whom he judges best qualified for that particular parish. This is a grave obligation in conscience. In deciding upon the candidate's fitness the Bishop must consider his learning, but also the other qualities mentioned in canon 453. In particular he must examine his record in the documents which may be in the archives, and he may seek information also elsewhere. He must consider the candidate's record in the junior clergy examination, though that alone does not determine the appointment. He must subject the candidate to an examination to determine his fitness, unless he dispenses him from it according to law. In countries where a competitive examination, either general or special, is in use, it is to be retained until the Holy See provides otherwise (c. 459).

---

[17] Cf. S. C. Prop. Fid., 9 Dec., 1920; *AAS*, 13–17; *Digest*, I, p. 149.
[18] Cf. Cappello, *Summa*, II, n. 495, 5.
[19] Cf. V-C, *Epit.*, I, n. 541.

Competitive Examination. 1. *Concursus* means a competitive examination. This had two forms, general and special.

2. The *general* form was for determining fitness for the parochial office in general, without special relation to any particular parish.

3. The *special* form to determine fitness for a particular parish was ordered by the Council of Trent (*Sess.* XXIV, *de ref.,* cap. 18), and further developed by the Constitution, *Cum illud.,* of Benedict XIV, 14 Dec., 1742, which is reprinted as Document IV at the end of the Code.

4. In the *United States:* The Third Council of Baltimore, nn. 36–59, had decreed that this special form of *concursus* should be used in appointments of irremovable pastors, except in the first appointment. But this provision was expressly declared abrogated, and it was decreed that thereafter all appointments to vacant parishes be made in accordance with canon 459, § 3.[20]

5. Even in places where the *concursus* is still in effect, it is not required: first, in a *transfer* made in accordance with canon 2162 and the following canons,[21] or, second, in the *first appointment* made to a newly erected parish.[22]

Noncompetitive Examination. This is required by the Code and is now required in the United States. The following points regarding the application of the law have been officially decided:

1. A pastor who is transferred at the instance of the Ordinary need not undergo a new examination; but he must, if the transfer is made at his own request, unless the Ordinary with the synodal examiners decide that his fitness, as shown in the examination for the former appointment, still continues and is sufficient for the new parish.

2. A pastor who, after having been removed from one parish, is being transferred to another, need not undergo an examination.

3. A pastor who is being transferred *ex officio* in accordance with canons 2162–2167 need not undergo an examination.

4. In case pastors whom the Ordinary regards as fit refuse to undergo an examination, recourse is to be had to the Sacred Congregation of the Council.

5. The examination in theology which candidates for sacred orders are required to undergo (cf. c. 996, §§ 2 and 3), even if it is held before the Ordinary and the synodal examiners, does not suffice for the

---

[20] Cf. S. C. Conc., 24 June, 1931; *Digest,* I, p. 249.
[21] Cf. S. C. Conc., 21 June, 1919; *AAS,* 11–318; *Digest,* I, p. 247.
[22] Cf. Code Com., 25 June, 1932; *AAS,* 24–284; *Digest,* I, p. 250.

appointment to the first parish, unless it includes also all the matter upon which a candidate for a parish should be examined.

6. The junior clergy examination (cf. c. 130), even if taken before the Ordinary and synodal examiners, does not suffice for appointments to parishes, though its results are to be considered.[23]

One Parish: One Pastor. In accordance with canon 156, a pastor is to have in his own right (*in titulum*) only one parish, unless there is question of parishes which are united on equal terms (*aeque principaliter*) (c. 460, § 1).

In one and the same parish there is to be but one pastor who exercises the care of souls, and all customs to the contrary are reprobated and every contrary privilege revoked (c. 460, § 2).

One Parish. Canon 156 provides that no one is to receive two offices which are incompatible. **Canon 460** applies that rule specifically to parishes. Two parishes held by the same pastor would be incompatible, at least as regards residence (cf. c. 465). The rule applies only to parishes held by the pastor *in his own right*. Nothing prevents a pastor's having one parish in his own right and another, at least temporarily, *in administrationem;* that is, for a charge, but not for a title.

An exception is made for parishes which are "united on equal terms." This phrase refers to canon 1419, 2°, which states that the union of two benefices is *aeque principalis,* or made on equal terms, when the two remain as they are, neither benefice being subjected to the other. But what is meant by one benefice "not being subjected to the other" is not immediately evident. According to some,[24] the meaning is merely that each parish retains its legal personality or entity. But the text of canon 1419, 3° states clearly that this is true even when the benefices are united *minus principaliter.* Consequently we think that a union on equal terms implies more than the mere retention of legal personality or existence. It implies further that the two parishes remain independent though united; that each retains its own distinct and equal rights and privileges, for example, its equal right to the services of the pastor, etc.[25] Since Ordinaries of places have power to unite two parochial benefices on equal terms (c. 1423), it is possible for one pastor to have, even in his own right, more than one parish.

---

[23] All these points, 1–6, were decided by the Code Com., 24 Nov., 1920; *AAS*, 12–574; *Digest*, I, p. 248.

[24] Woywod, *A Practical Commentary,* I, n. 336.

[25] See Cappello, *Summa,* II, n. 870; V-C, *Epit.*, II, n. 752.

One Pastor. Much more strictly is it enjoined that there shall be but one actual pastor in charge of any parish; for here no exception is allowed, contrary customs are reprobated, and even privileges to the contrary are expressly revoked. The prohibition is against more than one *actual* pastor; it does not forbid a habitual or nominal pastor simultaneously with an actual vicar (cf. c. 471), nor several parochial vicars under the direction of the pastor (cf. c. 476). It has been officially decided, first that this prohibition applies to parishes erected before the Code; and second, that it applies also to parishes in which the plurality of pastors was introduced by particular law.[26]

The confused conditions regarding parochial jurisdiction, which existed in the United States in the early days, and to some extent even until the Code, are described in a very enlightening way by Ayrinhac in *The Constitution of the Church,* n. 241.

Taking Canonical Possession. The pastor obtains the care of souls from the moment of taking possession according to canons 1443–1445; and before or in the act of taking possession he shall make the profession of faith mentioned in canon 1406, § 1, n. 7 **(c. 461).**

1. It has already been observed that for the full possession of certain offices, notably those which are also benefices, a canonical entry into possession is required. Now, parishes are usually benefices, and are so even in the United States.[27] Hence we are quite prepared for this provision declaring that the care of souls is obtained only from the moment when the pastor takes possession.

2. It is analogous to the provision that residential Bishops must not interfere in the government of their diocese until they shall have taken canonical possession thereof (c. 334, § 2).

3. This taking possession canonically may be required for the validity of official acts. For example, assistance at marriages in their territory, either by residential Bishops or by pastors, is invalid before they have taken possession of the benefice, in accordance with canon 334, § 3, in the case of Bishops, and canon 1444, § 1, in the case of pastors (c. 1095, §1, 1°).

4. The manner of taking possession is not prescribed by the general law. Canon 1444, § 1, simply states that it must be done as prescribed by particular law or custom, unless the Ordinary dispenses therefrom expressly and in writing, in which case the dispensation amounts to the taking of possession.

---

[26] Code Com., 14 July, 1922; *AAS,* 14–527; *Digest,* I, p. 250.
[27] Cf. Letter, Ap. Del. U. S., 10 Nov., 1922; *Digest,* I, p. 149.

5. Since in the United States no particular formalities are prescribed by law, the manner would seem to be left to be determined by the customs or regulations of each diocese. Park, in the *Homiletic and Pastoral Review,* Vol. 35, p. 579, rightly contends that some act of taking possession is required for the validity of the pastor's acts. This does not seem necessarily to contradict the contention of Schaaf, in the *Ecclesiastical Review* for December, 1934, that in the absence of special regulations this requirement is fulfilled if the Bishop, in the decree appointing the pastor, designates a day on which he is to enter into possession of the parish.[28]

6. The formula for the profession of faith is given at the beginning of the Code.

Reserved Functions. Unless other provision is made by law, the functions which are reserved to the pastor are the following:

1° To confer baptism solemnly;

2° To carry the Most Blessed Eucharist publicly to the sick in his own parish;

3° To carry the Most Blessed Eucharist as Viaticum, publicly or privately, to the sick, and to administer extreme unction to those in danger of death, without prejudice to the provisions of canons 397, n. 3, 514, 848, § 2, 938, § 2;

4° To announce sacred ordinations and nuptial banns; to assist at marriages, and to impart the nuptial blessing;

5° To perform funeral services in accordance with canon 1216;

6° To bless homes in accordance with liturgical books on Holy Saturday or another day according to local custom;

7° To bless the baptismal font on Holy Saturday, to lead a public procession outside the church, to give blessings outside the church with pomp and solemnity, unless the church is a capitular one and the chapter performs these functions (c. 462).

Functions here mean ecclesiastical ministrations; they are said to be reserved to the pastor in the sense that the pastor has the exclusive right to perform them; no one else may do so without his permission. Under numbers corresponding to the divisions of the canon, we shall group some remarks on the subject, with reference to other connected matters.

1. **Solemn Baptism.** *a. Solemn baptism* is reserved; but to which pastor?

b. The pastor *of the place* has the right to baptize solemnly in his

[28] See also Fanfani, *De Iure Parochorum,* n. 95.

parish all persons except those who have a domicile or quasi-domicile in another parish and can be brought to their own parish easily and without delay. As to his own subjects this is stated in canon 738, § 1; as to persons without domicile or quasi-domicile, it follows from canon 94, § 2; as to persons domiciled in another parish, this is the rule given in canon 738, § 2.

c. The pastor *of the person* may not baptize even his own subjects in another pastor's territory, without the permission either of the Ordinary or of the pastor of the place (c. 739).[29]

d. In *danger of death* any priest or deacon may baptize solemnly anywhere (cc. 741, 759); and any person may baptize privately (c. 742).

e. The *baptism of adults* should be referred to the Ordinary where this can conveniently be done, so that he may, if he choose, confer it with special solemnity either personally or by a delegate (c. 744). General permission is sometimes given in the diocesan pagella.

f. In places where *parishes or quasi-parishes are not yet established* local regulations or customs must make it clear what priests besides the Ordinary have the right to baptize (c. 740).

g. Conditional baptism, if conferred privately, is not reserved to the pastor.[30]

h. Is the *supplying of ceremonies* reserved? Authorities do not quite agree. To us it seems clear that this function partakes of the nature of solemn baptism and as such is reserved to the pastor.[31]

2. Carrying the Blessed Eucharist Publicly. *a.* To carry the Most Blessed Eucharist *publicly* to the sick in his own parish, is reserved to the pastor of the place, whether the persons be his own subjects or domiciled elsewhere (c. 848); other priests may do so only in case of necessity or with his presumed permission.

b. Publicly means by passing through public places and in a public manner; that is with candles, acolytes, etc.[32]

c. The Blessed Eucharist should be carried publicly unless a *just cause* makes the contrary advisable (c. 847). The just cause is to be estimated by the Ordinary; but he should not be so strict in this regard as to interfere with the frequent and even daily Communion of the sick.[33] Whenever there is a just cause allowing the carrying of Holy Communion *privately,* any priest may do so without consulting

---

[29] Cf. *Eccl. Rev.,* Vol. 87, p. 304.
[30] Cf. Cappello, *Summa,* II, n. 508, 8.
[31] Cf. V-C, *Epit.,* II, n. 22.
[32] Cf. Fanfani, *De Iure Parochorum,* n. 285.
[33] Cf. S. C. Sacr., 19 Dec., 1927; *AAS,* 20–81; *Digest,* I, p. 404.

the pastor (c. 849). In the United States, the general and approved custom is certainly a just cause for carrying it privately as a rule, at least outside of a religious house.

d. As to the private *First Communion* of children, the decision as to their readiness for it belongs primarily to the confessor and to the parents; the pastor has, however, the duty and the right to exercise a certain vigilance to see that children do not approach the Holy Table without sufficient preparation (c. 854, §§ 4 and 5). The pastor need not necessarily be consulted before First Communion in individual cases; neither can he legislate in a general way so as to require an examination by himself before First Communion; nor refuse Communion to a child who approaches with reverence, on the mere suspicion that he may be unprepared.[34] Even solemn First Communion is not a reserved function by common law, though it can be made so by diocesan statutes.

e. Paschal Communion may validly and licitly be received outside the parish church, with notice to the pastor; but it is recommended that it be made in the parish church (c. 859, § 3).

3. Viaticum and Extreme Unction. *a.* To carry the Most Blessed Eucharist by way of Viaticum either *publicly or privately,* and to administer extreme unction, belong exclusively to the pastor *of the place,* whether the persons concerned be his subjects or not (cc. 850, 938).

b. Exceptions: The highest dignitary of the chapter has the right to minister to the Bishop (c. 397, 3°); in a clerical religious society, the superior has the right as to all who live in the religious house night and day; in a monastery of nuns, the ordinary confessor; in any other lay religious society, the pastor or the chaplain whom the Ordinary may have placed in charge in accordance with canon 464, § 2, has the right (c. 514); in a seminary, the rector or his delegate (c. 1368); in case of necessity, any priest (cc. 848, § 2; 938, § 2).

c. Taken in its *strictest sense,* Viaticum means only the Communion which is prescribed by divine and ecclesiastical law in danger of death (c. 864, § 1). In a broader sense, any Communion received without the Eucharistic fast by a person who is still in danger of death (c. 864, § 3) is received "by way of Viaticum." It is held with good reason that only Viaticum in the strict sense is reserved to the pastor. Hence, either before or after the "last sacraments" which are reserved to the pastor,

---

[34] Cf. V-C, *Epit.,* II, n. 118; Cappello, *Summa,* II, n. 520.

any priest may bring Communion privately to persons in danger of death.[35]

4. Announcements, Marriages, etc. *a.* To *announce candidates for sacred orders* is a function reserved to the proper pastor of the person ordained, except in the case of religious with perpetual vows (c. 998).

b. Publication of *banns for marriage* belongs to the pastor of both parties (c. 1023).

c. To *assist at marriage* is the right of the proper pastor of either of the parties in the sense of canon 1097; though the validity of the marriage depends on the assistance of or delegation by the Ordinary or pastor of the place (cc. 1094, 1095).

d. To impart the *nuptial blessing* belongs to the priest who can licitly and validly assist at the marriage (c. 1101, § 2).

5. Funeral Services. *a.* In *general* these include bringing the remains to the church, celebrating the funeral services according to the ritual, and the services at the grave (c. 1204). *Per se* this right belongs to the proper pastor of the deceased in his proper parish (cc. 1216, 1230).

b. This general rule holds also even if the deceased died outside the parish, provided the remains can conveniently be brought to his parish church; otherwise, the proper church and pastor for the burial are those of the parish where he died (cc. 1218, 1230, § 2).

c. All persons, except religious and those who have not reached puberty, have the right to choose the church for their funeral and the cemetery for their burial (cc. 1223, 1224).

d. Whenever the services are held elsewhere than in the deceased's own parish church, the proper pastor of the deceased is entitled to his parochial portion (*quarta funeralium*), unless the deceased died outside the parish and could not conveniently be brought there for burial (c. 1236). Privileges and customs to the contrary are, however, permitted.[36]

e. Several *cases* involving parochial rights in this matter are reported in the *Canon Law Digest*, I, pp. 569–582.

6. Blessing of Homes. This beautiful rite is performed on Holy Saturday in Catholic countries.[37] It is only the special blessing on Holy Saturday that is reserved.

7. Baptismal Font, Processions, Blessings. *a.* The blessing of the

---

[35] Cf. V-C, *Epit.*, II, n. 114; Vermeersch, in *Periodica*, Vol. 21, p. 123.
[36] For fuller doctrine on this difficult subject, see V-C, *Epit.*, II, nn. 524–544; Cappello, *Summa*, II, nn. 740–758; Ferry, *Stole Fees*, Cath. U. Canon Law Studies, n. 59, pp. 78–94.
[37] Cf. *Roman Ritual*, Tit. VIII, cap. 4.

baptismal font on Holy Saturday is a function reserved to the pastor. The Roman Missal prescribes a similar blessing also on the vigil of Pentecost. Hence, two questions arose in a recent case: first, whether the blessing on the vigil of Pentecost is abrogated, since it is not mentioned in the Code; second, if not, whether it is also reserved to the pastor. The Sacred Congregation of the Council replied that it is not abrogated, and intimated that it is also reserved.[38]

b. Public processions are defined in canon 1290, § 1. They include processions through the streets within the parish even though they do not start from the parish church. These are reserved to the pastor. But nonparochial churches may have processions within the church in connection with solemn services (c. 482); and all churches may have them even in public within the octave of Corpus Christi, except on the feast itself, when only one should be conducted from the principal church of the place, and that one should be attended by all (c. 1291). Except as provided above and by canon 1293 (where the Bishop gives permission), the pastor has the right to conduct public processions even of exempt religious outside their churches.[39]

c. Blessings given outside the church *with pomp and ceremony* are reserved to the pastor.

The rite of the *churching of women* is not reserved by common law; nor is the blessing of candles, ashes, or palms.[40]

Stole Fees and Offerings. The pastor has a right to the offerings which are awarded him by either approved custom or lawful tax provision made in accordance with canon 1507, § 1 (c. 463, § 1).

If he exacts fees in excess thereof, he is bound to restitution (c. 463, § 2).

Even though a parochial function has been performed by another, the offerings nevertheless go to the pastor, unless the contrary will of the offerers is certain as regards the amount in excess of the tax (c. 463, § 3).

A pastor must not refuse gratuitous service to those who are not able to pay (c. 463, § 4).

According to a very ancient practice, offerings are made by the faithful on the occasion of certain sacred functions and of the administration of some sacraments and sacramentals. These offerings were at first entirely voluntary; some of them, however, have in the course

[38] S. C. Conc., 10 June, 1922; *AAS*, 15–225; *Digest*, I, p. 252.
[39] Cf. Code Com., 10 Nov., 1925; *AAS*, 17–582; *Digest*, I, p. 252.
[40] Cf. Cappello, *Summa*, II, n. 518.

of time become so sanctioned by custom or by particular law that they are now obligatory. We must therefore distinguish between voluntary and obligatory offerings. The term "stole fees" may be applied in a general sense to both; strictly, only to the latter. It must be noted that the payment of stole fees is not made obligatory by the Code. The present canon merely states that such offerings as are assigned to the pastor either by custom or by law in accordance with canon 1507, § 1, belong to him as of right. The law referred to in canon 1507, § 1, is that of a provincial council to be approved by the Holy See, or, in the case of funeral taxes, a diocesan regulation (c. 1234). The fact is that schedules of taxes or obligatory offerings for various parochial functions, notably for baptisms, marriages, funerals, may be enacted, usually in recognition of long-standing customs, or custom alone may determine the obligation and amount of the offerings in connection with these same functions. As we shall see, the local law or custom may also determine the disposal of these offerings. In the supposition that they are assigned to the pastor, canon 463 provides that he has a strict right to the offerings so prescribed; yet that he may not refuse his free service to persons who are unable to make the offering. It has always been recognized that the offerings are not a *quid pro quo* or payment for the services.[41]

General Principles. 1. In the case of offerings which are strictly *obligatory;* that is, whose amount is prescribed either by lawful custom or by lawful tax provision in accordance with canons 1507 and 1234, there is question of a strict right (*ius*). The pastor can therefore demand these of persons able to pay (cf. cc. 736, 2349). But he cannot demand more, under pain of being bound to restore the excess, and of being, moreover, subject to a severe fine (c. 2408). Even where he has a strict right, delicacy or forbearance in urging it will often be the better part, and will sometimes be dictated by special circumstances.

2. *Voluntary* offerings made in connection with functions which are *strictly reserved* to the pastor, are also his by right as against other persons. This is not stated here, but it follows from canon 462. Since the pastor has *per se* the exclusive right to perform these functions, he has also the right to receive voluntary offerings, though not, of course, to demand them. If a *reserved function* is performed by another priest, two special cases may arise: (*a*) a *purely voluntary* offering is made, there being no law or custom prescribing any offering;

---

[41] For a fuller account, especially of the historical development of stole fees, see Ferry, *Stole Fees,* Cath. U. Canon Law Studies, n. 59.

or, (*b*) an offering is made which may be considered *partly voluntary* in as much as it exceeds the amount prescribed by law or custom. Our canon provides clearly for the second case, but not for the first. In the second case, the entire amount goes to the pastor, unless it is certain that the donors intended the voluntary part of the offering as a personal gift to the priest officiating; in which case the latter may retain the excess. By analogy, we may offer a similar solution of the first case. The offering, being connected with a reserved function, presumably goes to the pastor; yet, since it is entirely voluntary, the will of the donors, if certainly established in favor of the officiating priest, should prevail. Hence, in this case also, the offering goes to the pastor, unless it is certain that the donors intended it as a gift to the officiating priest, in which case the latter may retain it. If, however, a priest other than the pastor is acting *in a case of necessity,* several authorities hold that he retain whatever offering is made, whether it be obligatory or voluntary.[42]

3. As to *other offerings,* which are neither obligatory nor connected with reserved functions, the law may be stated as follows:

a. The pastor has a *general presumptive right* (*intentio in iure fundata*) to all offerings made in his parish, unless the case is proved exceptional by custom, the intention of the donors, or the law.

b. Exceptions made by law are the following. The pastor has no right to offerings made by the faithful in churches belonging to religious, to confraternities, or which are independent of the parish church (cf. cc. 485, 691, § 2, 1182, § 2).

c. Exceptions resulting from the *presumed intention* of the faithful: the pastor has no right to offerings made for specific designated purposes; e.g., for the poor, for the foreign missions, for the altar, etc.

d. In case *another priest is officiating* at a function not reserved to the pastor, Ferry says, that "the obligation to refund the fee cannot be urged."[43] Even in this case, however, the pastor would seem on general principles to have the better right to the fee, unless the donor's intention to the contrary is clear.

4. The *effect of permission* given by the proper pastor of the parties to another pastor or priest to *assist at a marriage,* will be considered, under canon 1097.

Notes. 1. Stole fees may or may not constitute part of the *endow-*

---

[42] Cf. Ferry, *Stole Fees,* p. 53.
[43] Cf. Ferry, *Stole Fees,* p. 54.

ment of the parish according to canon 1410. This will depend on the decree of the Bishop (cf. cc. 1414, § 2; 1415, § 1; 1418). But even if they are part of the endowment, they will go to the pastor, since he is entitled to the fruits of the benefice, subject to the obligation of expending *superfluous* revenues for the poor and for religion (c. 1473).[44]

2. Canon 1536 provides that unless the contrary appear, the presumption is that *donations* made to the rector of a church are *made to the church*. This, however, does not apply to stole fees simply because these are more specifically regulated by canon 463 as above explained.

3. Canon 736 creates a difficulty. It seems to exclude any stole fees, at least in connection with the administration of the sacraments, unless they are sanctioned by canon 1507, § 1; that is, unless they are established by a provincial council, and *approved by the Holy See*. The difficulty is very practical, because in many provinces of the United States no provincial council has been held, and the Baltimore Councils did not fix the amounts of stole fees. Probably this provision must be considered as modified by canon 463, so that at least *long-standing customs* are to be recognized even when they fix stole fees in connection with the reception of certain sacraments.[45]

Stole Fees, Etc., in the United States. 1. *Funeral* fees are usually regulated by diocesan schedules in accordance with canon 1234.

2. All others must either be determined by custom or by law which is uniform throughout an ecclesiastical province. Such law frequently does not exist, and hence the matter often depends upon custom alone. In general, fees are customary in connection with baptism and marriage; utterly out of place in connection with confession and Holy Communion.[46] In connection with extreme unction there is no customary fee, though the priest may accept reimbursement for the expense of a long journey.[47] Confirmation and Holy Orders concern the Bishop rather than pastors.[48]

3. It must be noted once more that the common law does not absolutely require that stole fees go to the pastor. Hence, custom or particular law may dispose of stole fees, or part of them, otherwise than by assigning them to the pastor. In fact, both the Second Plenary Council of Baltimore (n. 94) and the Third (n. 294) recommended

---

[44] Cf. Golden, *Parochial Benefices*, 1921, Cath. U. Canon Law Studies, n. 10, p. 66.
[45] Cf. V-C, *Epit.*, II, n. 827; S. C. Conc., 10 June, 1896, in *C. I. C. Fontes*, n. 4298, Vol. VI, p. 757.
[46] Cf. *Conc. Balt. II*, n. 289.
[47] Cf. Kenrick, *Tract 12*, n. 66.
[48] Cf. Kenrick, nn. 63, 67; *Conc. Trid., Sess.* XXI, *de ref.*, cap. 1.

that diocesan regulations be enacted governing the distribution of stole fees among the priests resident in the same house. This recommendation has doubtless been followed in the various dioceses according to local needs. In Chicago the Third Diocesan Synod (1905) provided (n. 91): "The money received on the occasion of the administration of baptism and marriage goes to the pastor, who is obliged to meet the expenses of keeping up the rectory and the support of his assistants." Hence the right of an assistant pastor to participate in stole fees depends upon custom, diocesan law, or the will of the pastor. In some parishes the pastor allows assistants to keep the fees received at functions in which the assistant officiates.

4. Regarding *salaries,* the Third Council of Baltimore provided that the Bishops, in the synod or with the advice of their consultors, should determine the salaries of pastors; that the salary should be supplied by the people of the parish and not by the Bishop, unless the pastor without fault of his own be in want of the bare necessities of life; that the yearly salary, unless collected or at least formally demanded before the end of the current year, is to be regarded as donated by the pastor to the church; finally, that all collections belong to the church, unless the Bishop provides otherwise.[49]

The Care of Souls. A pastor is bound by virtue of his office to exercise the care of souls toward all his parishioners who are not lawfully exempt **(c. 464, § 1).**

The Bishop can for just and grave cause withdraw from the care of the pastor religious communities and houses of piety which are located in the territory of the parish and are not exempt by law **(c. 464, § 2).**

1. This primary charge of the pastor has been explained above under canon 451. It involves chiefly *domestic* power and *jurisdiction in the internal forum;* also, a very limited jurisdiction in the external forum.

2. The specific obligations attached to the care of souls will be explained in the canons which follow.

3. Non-Catholics in the parish are commended to the care of the pastor, who has a general duty to strive for their conversion (c. 1350, § 1).

Exemptions. 1. Exempt *by law* are regulars (cf. c. 488, 2° and 7°) together with their houses and churches (c. 615).

---

[49] *Conc. Balt. III,* nn. 273, 281. Cf. also *Third Diocesan Synod, Chicago,* nn. 87–92.

2. Moreover the *Bishop may withdraw* from the pastor's care other religious houses, not exempt by law, and houses of piety, placing them under the care of chaplains.

Residence. This is an obligation attached to the office. Regularly it must be in the parish residence, which must be near the church (c. 465, § 1).

Vacation and Other Absences. 1. *Vacation* is regularly allowed for two months, continuous or interrupted, not counting the time of the annual retreat (c. 465, §§ 2, 3). The time is computed "from moment to moment"; that is, from any hour of one day to the corresponding hour of another; and the months are counted according to the calendar if the time is uninterrupted; otherwise, as thirty days (c. 34, § 2).

2. The Bishop may for grave reason either *extend or shorten* the time (c. 465, § 2).

3. The Bishop's *written permission* is required for any absence beyond a week, unless it is for an unforeseen and grave cause (c. 465, § 4).

Provision During Absence. 1. *Always* the needs of the parish must be provided for (c. 465, § 6). This obligation is of divine law.[50]

2. For an absence of *more than a week,* a substitute must be left in charge.

3. If the absence is *foreseen* the substitute's appointment depends for its validity upon the approval of the Bishop, but not upon that of the religious superior in the case of a substitute for a religious pastor. A substitute so approved can delegate to a particular priest the power to assist at a particular marriage.[51]

4. If the absence is sudden and *unforeseen,* the substitute is appointed outright by the departing pastor, and the Bishop's approval is not required; but the Bishop must be notified. The Code Commission, in the first of the two replies above referred to, decided that *after the Bishop has been notified* of the name of the substitute so left in charge, the substitute may act validly without a positive approval by the Bishop. Whether the same is true even before the Bishop is notified, has not been decided. But we think it is the mind of the Code that the substitute acquire his jurisdiction immediately upon being appointed by the pastor in the emergency.[52]

---

[50] Cf. V-C, *Epit.,* I, n. 552.

[51] Cf. Code Com., 14 July, 1922; *AAS,* 14–527; *Digest,* I, p. 539, and 20 May, 1923; *AAS* 16–114; *Digest,* I, p. 540.

[52] Cf. Bouuaert, *De Vicarii Substituti Constitutione ac Munere* (reprint of article in *Ius Pontificium*).

5. If the absence of the pastor is for *only a week or less,* it is to be noted that the priest who takes his place is not mentioned among the *vicarii paroeciales* even as a *substitutus* (canon 474 refers only to priests supplying for *more than a week*). It follows that he receives no jurisdiction whatever from the Code. The delegation which he may receive from the pastor *ad universitatem negotiorum* is ineffective to confer jurisdiction for confessions (cf. c. 874, §1), though some authors hold it effective to confer general delegation for marriages (cf. c. 1096, § 1). Consequently such a substitute should obtain jurisdiction for confessions from the Ordinary, and at least *ad cautelam,* delegation for particular marriages from the Ordinary or the pastor.[53]

The Mass *Pro Populo* (c. 466). This is a Mass which pastors and others must celebrate, applying it for the intention of the people committed to their care. It is regulated by canons 306, 339, and 466. We offer a general summary of the obligation, with references to the canons involved.

Persons Bound. 1. In accordance with canon 339, the following are bound to say the Mass *pro populo* on about eighty-eight days of the year:

a. Resident Bishops (c. 339). Titular Bishops have no obligation, though it is right that they occasionally apply a Mass for their titular see (c. 348, § 2).

b. Abbots and *Prelates nullius* (c. 323, § 1).

c. Vicars Capitular or *Administrators* during the vacancy of the see (cc. 431, § 2, 440).

d. Pastors (c. 466) and all *parochial vicars* who have full parochial powers (c. 451, § 2, 2°). Hence: the *vicar* acting for a moral person is certainly bound (c. 471, § 4) as is also the *administrator* of a vacant parish (c. 473, § 1); the *vicar coadjutor* is certainly not bound (c. 475, § 2); nor is the *vicar assistant* (c. 476, § 6). As regards the *vicar substitute,* although canon 474 seems to leave the obligation upon him, yet in consideration of canon 466, § 5, it is held that he is not bound in the absence of a special arrangement with the pastor, who is presumed to attend to the matter himself.

2. In accordance with canon 306, the following are obliged to apply the Mass on the eleven days mentioned in that canon:

---

[53] Cf. Fanfani, *De Iure Parochorum,* n. 251, B, 4, p. 231; Goyeneche, *Iuris Canonici Summa Principia,* p. 379, note 10. Coronata, *Institutiones,* I; n. 490, p. 593, note 7, thinks general delegation of the care of the parish would include power to assist at marriages.

a. Vicars and *Prefects Apostolic* (c. 306).

b. Quasi-pastors (c. 466).

Nature of the Obligation. 1. The obligation is *attached to the office,* and hence it is not excused by want or scarcity of revenue.

2. It is *attached to the day* (cc. 339, § 4, 466, § 3), so that *per se* it must be fulfilled on the day itself; yet if it is not fulfilled on that day, it remains urgent and must be fulfilled as soon as possible thereafter (c. 339, § 6).

3. It is *personal,* in the sense that it must be fulfilled personally unless some lawful reason permits its deputation to another (cc. 339, § 4, 466, § 5).

4. It is *real,* in the sense that if a personal fulfillment is impossible it must be fulfilled through another (cc. 339, § 4, 466, § 5).

5. It is *local,* in the sense that as a rule it should be fulfilled in the parish church (c. 466, § 4).

Days Prescribed by Law. 1. For *Bishops* and others who are bound according to canon 339, the days are:

a. All Sundays of the year	52
b. Holydays of obligation (c. 1247)	10
c. Suppressed feasts of obligation	24
d. Legally established feasts of patrons	2
	88

See the list issued by the Sacred Congregation of the Council.[54]

2. For *Vicars* and *Prefects Apostolic* and others who are bound according to canon 306, the days are:

a. Nine days of obligation; namely, all those mentioned in canon 1247, except the Circumcision	9
b. Easter and Pentecost	2
	11

General and Particular Rules. 1. *Multiplicity of parishes* or of dioceses does not multiply the obligation (c. 339, § 5, 466, § 2).

2. *Coincidence of feasts* on the same day does not multiply the obligation (c. 339, § 2).

3. When a *feast is transferred,* the obligation is transferred if the obligations of hearing Mass and abstaining from servile work are transferred together with the celebration of the feast; otherwise not (c. 339, § 3).

---

[54] Cf. S. C. Conc., 28 Dec., 1919; *AAS,* 12-42; *Digest,* I, p. 254.

4. In case of *conflict between various circumstances* of the obligation, the following norms must be borne in mind:

a. All are obliged to offer the Mass personally and on the prescribed day; if this is impossible they must apply it *on the prescribed day,* by another (c. 339, § 4).

b. If even this cannot be done, let them apply it on another day *as soon as possible,* personally or through another (c. 339, § 4).

c. A pastor may, *with the permission of the Ordinary,* apply it on some other day (c. 466, § 3).

d. A pastor should apply it *in the parish church* unless circumstances make the contrary advisable (c. 466, § 4).

e. A pastor who is *legitimately absent* may either apply it personally in the place where he is, or in the parish through the one who is in charge there (c. 466, § 5).

f. Even when the prescribed day is passed, the obligation continues urgent until it is fulfilled (cc. 306, 466, 339, § 6).[55]

Other Pastoral Duties. The pastor must celebrate the divine services, administer the sacraments to the faithful as often as they lawfully ask for them, know his parishioners, prudently correct those who go astray, embrace in his paternal charity the poor and distressed, and employ the greatest care in the Catholic education of children **(c. 467, § 1).**

The faithful are to be admonished to come frequently to their parish churches when they can conveniently do so, there to assist at the divine services and hear the word of God **(c. 467, § 2).**

To Celebrate Divine Services. Divine services are defined as "functions of the power of order which are established by Christ or by the Church for divine worship and which are to be performed by clerics alone" (c. 2256, 1°). Hence they include Mass, Vespers, Benediction with the Blessed Sacrament, etc.

To Administer the Sacraments. The chief duties of the pastor in this connection are:

1. Regarding *baptism:* (*a*) to see that infants are baptized as soon as possible (c. 770); (*b*) to see that the faithful are instructed how to confer baptism in case of necessity (c. 743); (*c*) to see that abortive fetuses receive baptism (c. 747); (*d*) to see that worthy sponsors are chosen (cc. 765, 766).

2. Regarding *confirmation:* to see that the faithful receive it in due

---

[55] Several official documents on the Mass *pro populo* will be found reported in *Digest,* I, pp. 149, 253–257. Cf. also Donnellan, *The Obligation of the Mass Pro Populo,* Cath. University, 1942.

time (c. 787). By general indult (S. C. Sacr., 3 Oct., 1946; *AAS,* 38–349), pastors have the power to administer confirmation to all persons, even infants, in their territory, who are in danger of death from illness, if no Bishop is available. They have also the duty to do so when reasonably requested (cf. c. 785, § 2).

3. Regarding the *Most Blessed Eucharist:* (*a*) to see that children properly disposed receive the divine Bread as soon as possible (c. 854); (*b*) to exhort the faithful to receive frequently, and even daily (c. 863); (*c*) to see that Holy Viaticum for the sick be not too long deferred (c. 865).

4. Regarding *penance:* they are under a grave obligation in justice to hear the confessions of their subjects whenever they ask reasonably (c. 892).

5. Regarding *extreme unction:* to see that the sick receive it while they are in full possession of their faculties (c. 944).

6. Regarding *order:* to announce the names of those to be ordained to major orders (c. 998).

7. Regarding *matrimony:* (*a*) the pastor must not fail to give the people appropriate instruction (c. 1018); (*b*) before an individual marriage he must carefully investigate to see if there is any impediment (c. 1020); (*c*) he must announce the banns (c. 1022); (*d*) he must not assist at the marriage of persons who have no domicile or quasi-domicile without consulting the Ordinary (c. 1032); (*e*) he must do his best to deter the faithful from mixed marriages (c. 1060); (*f*) he must instruct the parties as to the duties of married life (c. 1033).

Paternal Care of His Parishioners. (1) First of all, he must *know* them; the parish census (*liber de statu animarum*) is the primary means toward this (c. 470); (2) he must *prudently correct* the erring, and; (3) embrace the *poor and distressed* with special paternal charity.

Catholic Education. The pastor must exert the highest diligence in the Catholic education of children. It is not sufficient that there be instruction in the parochial school, but classes in catechism must be established also for Catholic children who do not attend the parochial school, and for this work the services of lay catechists should be used as far as is necessary and appropriate.[56]

Preaching and Catechetical Instruction. These duties of the pastor are dealt with in canons 1327–1351.

Obligation of the Faithful. They are to be *admonished* that when

[56] Cf. *Decree on Catechetical Instruction,* S. C. Conc., 12 Jan., 1935; *AAS,* 27–145; *Digest,* II, p. 412.

they can conveniently do so, they must frequently (not exclusively) attend their parish church, there to assist at the divine services and hear the word of God.

Duties to the Sick and Dying. The pastor must with zealous care and abundant charity assist those in his parish who are ill, especially those who are near death, solicitously comforting them with the sacraments and commending their souls to God (c. 468, § 1).

The pastor or other priest who calls upon the sick has the faculty of imparting to them the apostolic blessing with a plenary indulgence at the hour of death, according to the form given in approved liturgical books; and he should not fail to do so (c. 468, § 2).

The *formula* for the apostolic blessing at the hour of death is in the Roman Ritual, Tit. 5, cap. 6, and in the vernacular rituals after extreme unction. The form is required for validity. The blessing may not be repeated in the same danger of death.[57]

Vigilance. The pastor must watch with care that nothing contrary to faith and morals be taught in his parish, especially in the public and private schools; and he must foster or establish works of charity, faith, and piety (c. 469).

Catholic Action. According to repeated declarations of His Holiness, Pius XI, the energetic promotion of Catholic Action is one of the duties of pastors under the leadership of the Bishops. Consider the documents cited under canon 139.

Parish Registers. 1. Those required to be kept are registers of baptisms, confirmations, marriages, deaths, and the parish census or *liber de statu animarum* (c. 470, § 1).

2. In the baptismal register, besides the baptism of the person, certain special entries must later be made as occasion arises; namely, the confirmation, marriage, sacred orders, or solemn vows of the person baptized (c. 470, § 2). In case the marriage is what is called a marriage of conscience, secrecy is required; hence the entry in that case is not made in the usual marriage record nor in the baptismal register, but in a special secret record (c. 1107). Marriages, sacred orders, and solemn

---

[57] *Cards of the Apostolate for the Dying.* For dying non-Catholics, the necessary truths of faith and the necessary acts of the will on the part of the dying person in regard to God have been put in very attractive form on ornamented gift cards, intended for presentation to the dying person in cases where nothing more can be done for him, by the Right Reverend Raphael J. Markham (St. Clare Convent, Hartwell, Ohio). The Reverend John R. Bowen (St. Joseph's Mercy Hospital, Dubuque, Iowa), who has further developed the Apostolate for the Dying, particularly among nurses, has a similar card in a somewhat different form. Both of these cards can be obtained from their respective authors; and both are earnestly recommended to pastors and hospital chaplains.

vows, constitute diriment impediments to subsequent marriage; and the purpose of requiring these facts to be registered and to be included in testimonials of baptism is precisely that these impediments may be known from the baptismal record which is called for as a preliminary to marriage (cf. c. 1021).

3. Copies of the parish records, except the parish census, must be sent at the end of every year to the Bishop's Curia (c. 470, § 3).

4. The pastor must make use of a parish seal, have a registry or archives where the above-named books are to be kept together with the letters of the Bishop and other papers which it is necessary or useful to preserve; and he must religiously see to it that these documents, all of which are to be inspected by the Ordinary or his delegate at the time of the annual visitation or at some other suitable time, do not fall into the hands of outsiders (c. 470, § 4).

5. A recent letter of the Apostolic Delegate urges upon Bishops the greatest zeal in requiring pastors to be diligent in taking the parish census. See *Digest*, II, p. 147.

CASES AND QUESTIONS

1. In a city parish there is a nonreligious maternity hospital frequented by Catholic mothers from all parts of the city. The babies are often kept for several weeks after birth, for incubation or special care. May the pastor baptize these babies without the permission of the parents' proper pastor? (C. 738, §§ 1, 2). Could the parents' pastor baptize the babies? (C. 739). Where should these baptisms be recorded? (Cc. 777, § 1, 778).

2. X, a religious priest, assists at a marriage in St. Martha's church, by delegation of the pastor but without any permission from the proper pastor of either party. Does he violate any right? (C. 1097, § 1, 3°, and § 3).

3. A priest visiting in his parents' parish wishes to bring Holy Communion privately to his mother who is in danger of death but who has already received the last sacraments from her pastor. May he do so without the pastor's permission, although she receives without fasting? (C. 462, 3°; *Periodica*, Vol. 21, p. 123*; Vol. 22, p. 213*).

4. Y, rector of the seminary, assists at a marriage of intimate friends in St. John's church, with delegation and permission from the pastors concerned. The groom offers him $100. What disposal should he make of this offering? (C. 463, § 3).

5. Pastor Z marries a couple in his church without obtaining the requisite permission of the proper pastor of either party. They make a customary offering. To whom does it belong? (C. 1097, § 3).

6. B has obtained the requisite delegation and permission to assist at a marriage in St. John's church. May he, if the parties so desire, perform the marriage himself but appoint another priest to say the nuptial Mass and give the nuptial blessing? (C. 1101, § 2).

7. A pastor takes a month's vacation, leaving his first assistant in charge. Nothing is said about the Mass *pro populo*. On whom does the obligation primarily rest? (C. 466, § 5).

8. Pastor Q is unpopular with his parishioners, many of whom go to neighboring parishes for the Sunday Mass. Has he any recourse? (C. 467, § 2).

Readings:

Golden, *Parochial Benefices in the New Code*, Catholic University, 1921 (n. 10); Koudelka, *Pastors, Their Rights and Duties According to the New Code of Canon Law*, Cath. U., 1921 (n. 11); Coady, *The Appointment of Pastors*, Cath. U., 1929 (n. 52); Ferry, *Stole Fees*, Cath. U., 1930 (n. 59); Drumm, *Hospital Chaplains*, Cath. U. (n. 178); Reilly, *Residence of Pastors*, Cath. U., 1935 (n. 97); Donnellan, *The Obligation of the Mass Pro Populo*, Cath. U., 1942 (n. 155); O'Rourke, *Parish Registers*, Cath. U., 1934 (n. 88); *Ecclesiastical Review*, Vol. 89, pp. 432, 627 (appointments to reserved parish benefices), Vol. 87, p. 304 (rights of pastor as regards baptism), Vol. 91, p. 627 (Schaaf on pastor's forfeiture of arrears of salary), Vol. 95, p. 380 (parish registration as an aid to taking parish census); *Clergy Review*, Vol. 9, p. 338 (induction of pastors), Vol. 17, p. 366 (parish registers); *Irish Ecclesiastical Record,* 1932, p. 406 (O'Neill, on obligation of Mass *pro populo*); *Periodica,* Vol. 21, p. 240* (delegation of supplying priest *ad universitatem negotiorum,* for absence not exceeding one week); *Clergy Review*, Vol. 21, p. 82 (McCann, on parishes served by religious); *The Jurist,* Vol. 1, p. 329 (Hannan, on the juridical status of parishes of religious); Vol. 3, p. 117 (Dooley, another view on same subject).

Section 2. Parochial Vicars and Rectors of Churches (cc. 471–486)

PRELIMINARY SURVEY

The Perpetual Vicar (c. 471)
The Vicar Administrator: His Appointment (c. 472)
The Vicar Administrator: His Powers and Duties (c. 473)
The Vicar Substitute (c. 474)
The Vicar Coadjutor (c. 475)
The Vicar Assistant (c. 476)
Removal of Parochial Vicars (c. 477)
Precedence Among Parochial Vicars (c. 478)
Rectors of Churches (c. 479–486)

The Perpetual Vicar. As we have seen (c. 451) a moral person may be a titular or habitual pastor, only when the parish has been completely united to the moral person by indult from the Holy See; and in that case a vicar must be appointed, who is to have the entire care of souls. This actual pastor is called a perpetual vicar, *vicarius curatus,* or simply vicar. The manner of his appointment and removal, and his rights and obligations, are defined by canon 471.

Appointment. 1. The *regular manner* of appointment is by presentation and investiture; that is, the moral person who is the titular pastor has by common law the right to present a candidate; and the Bishop, after observing the requirements of law to determine the candidate's fitness for the office, confers it upon him by institution or investiture (c. 471, § 2).

2. *By way of exception,* other methods of appointing the vicar are possible: (*a*) If a lawful *privilege* or *custom* determines the appointment, it is to be followed; (*b*) If the Bishop has *endowed* the office and *reserved* to himself the right of appointment, so as to exclude the right of presentation by the titular pastor, the vicar is appointed outright by the Bishop (c. 471, § 2).

Removal. 1. If the vicar is a religious he can be removed either by his superior or by the Bishop as provided for the removal of religious pastors (c. 454, § 5).

2. If not, he is removable in the same way as a nonreligious pastor, with notice to the moral person who presented him. The moral person has no voice in removing him, nor can it prevent his removal by the Bishop (c. 471, § 3).

Rights and Obligations. 1. In general his rights and duties are those of a pastor: he has the entire actual care of souls, the ordinary jurisdiction of a pastor, and all a pastor's obligations, including that of the Mass *pro populo.*

2. The compensation of the vicar consists in a suitable portion of the income of the parish, assigned to him by the Bishop. The moral person, as titular pastor, remains entitled to the income of the benefice and to the stole fees.[58] In addition to his assigned compensation, the vicar may receive for himself whatever offerings or gifts are made to him *intuitu personae,* unless he is a religious (cf. c. 630, § 3); but in the absence of proof, gifts to him other than personal offerings on the occasion of his ministrations, will be presumed to be intended for the church (cf. c. 1536, § 1).

---

[58] Cf. Ferry, *Stole Fees,* p. 44.

3. If he is a religious with solemn vows, whatever he would other-wise receive for himself, such as his salary, personal gifts, stipends, etc., belong to his religious institute or house; if he has only simple vows, he acquires the title to personal gifts (c. 580, § 2); in all cases, what-ever is given for the parish belongs to the parish, and the general pre-sumption is that donations are intended for the church (cf. cc. 630, § 3; 1536, § 1).

4. A religious vicar, just as a religious pastor, is subject to the Ordinary of the place in everything which concerns the government of the parish (c. 630).

The Administrator or *Vicarius Oeconomus.* 1. A parish may be-come vacant by the death of the pastor, by his resignation accepted by the Bishop, by his transfer to another parish, by his removal as an administrative measure (cc. 2147, 2157), or as a penalty for non-residence or other crimes (cf. cc. 2168, 2173, 2174, 2298).

2. During such vacancy the parish is to be governed by an admin-istrator, to be appointed as soon as possible by the Bishop or Ordinary of the place, with an assigned part of the income as his compensation, and in case he is a religious, with the consent of his superior (c. 472, 1°).

3. Until such time as the administrator is appointed someone must take temporary charge. If the parish is one which is entrusted to reli-gious, the superior takes charge; otherwise, the assistant; if there are more than one, the senior in office; if there are none, the nearest neighboring pastor, to be determined in case of doubt according to a schedule to be made out in advance for all parishes by the Ordinary. Whoever takes charge in this way must immediately notify the Ordinary; he has the same powers and duties as a regular admin-istrator, until the latter arrives and takes possession (c. 472, 2° and 3°).

Rights and Duties of the Administrator. 1. As to *spiritual matters* the administrator has the entire care of souls, with *ordinary* jurisdiction (c. 473, § 1). He is obliged to offer the Mass *pro populo,* but only one on any prescribed day, even though he have charge of several parishes.[59] He can validly and licitly assist at marriages in the parish, and may delegate to a particular priest the power to assist at a particular marriage.[60]

2. As to *temporal matters,* compensation, etc., he is in the same position as a perpetual vicar; i.e., he is entitled to a fixed compensation which normally should consist of a *designated part of the income* of

---

[59] Cf. Code Com., 14 July, 1922; *AAS,* 14–528; *Digest,* I, p. 255.
[60] Cf. Code Com., 20 May, 1923; *AAS,* 16–114; *Digest,* I, p. 540.

the parochial benefice (c. 472, 1°). Is he entitled to the stole fees? We must distinguish. If the stole fees are included in the compensation so assigned to him, yes. Otherwise, no; but in this case the stole fees, with the rest of the income accruing during the vacancy of the parish, are to be divided according to canon 1481, i.e., after deducting all expenses and the administrator's compensation, half the net income goes to the endowment of the benefice, and the other half to the church fund or altar fund.[61]

3. *Special provisions:* (*a*) He may not do anything that might prejudice the rights of the pastor or of the benefice; (*b*) he must turn over to his successor, in the presence of the rural dean or other delegate of the Bishop, the key to the archives, an inventory of the parish books and papers, and an account of receipts and expenditures during his administration (c. 473, § 2).

The Vicar Substitute. A vicar substitute who is appointed according to canon 465, §§ 4 and 5, and canon 1923, § 2, takes the place of the pastor in everything which relates to the care of souls, unless the Ordinary of the place or the pastor have made some exceptions (c. 474).

Three sets of circumstances under which a substitute may be appointed are mentioned here, two of which have already been dealt with in canon 465. The three are: (1) when a pastor, *foreseeing* an absence of more than a week, appoints a substitute who must be *approved* by the Bishop (c. 465, § 4); (2) when a pastor, *suddenly called away* for an absence of more than a week, appoints a substitute and *notifies* the Bishop (c. 465, § 5); (3) when a pastor has been *deprived of his office* by judicial decree, and has appealed to the Holy See, thus preventing the execution of the decree; and the Ordinary designates a substitute to take his place pending the appeal (c. 1923, § 2).

Powers and Duties of the Substitute. 1. In all these cases, provided the appointment is legal, the substitute takes the place of the pastor in everything that relates to the care of souls, unless the Ordinary or the pastor has made some exceptions. Hence, in the absence of any special restrictions by either, he has the full and *ordinary jurisdiction* of a pastor, provided he is taking his place for more than a week.

2. A special question arises regarding the obligation of the Mass *pro populo:*

a. Canon 474 seems to place the obligation on the substitute.

---

[61] Cf. c. 1481, and Fanfani, *De Iure Parochorum,* nn. 433 A, 158 E.

b. On the other hand, canon 466, § 5, seems to leave it on the pastor even during his absence.

c. Most authorities deny the obligation of the substitute, in the absence of a special agreement.[62]

d. In practice it is recommended that definite arrangements be made as to who is to say the Mass *pro populo*. In the absence of such an agreement, the pastor and not the substitute will be bound.

3. As to *assistance at marriages,* several replies of the Code Commission must be noted:

a. The substitute appointed according to canon 465, § 4, can validly and licitly assist at marriages, and can delegate to a particular priest the power to assist at a particular marriage, after the approval of his own appointment by the Ordinary, but not before such approval.[63]

b. The substitute appointed according to canon 465, § 5, can both assist and delegate as above, even before the approval of the Ordinary, "as long as the Ordinary who has been notified of the designation of the substitute has not provided otherwise."[64] It is probable that the same would be true even if the departing pastor failed to notify the Ordinary, or the Ordinary failed to receive the notice, of the designation of the substitute.[65]

4. The priest taking the pastor's place *for a week or less* should obtain delegation for particular marriages from the Ordinary or the pastor.

The Vicar Coadjutor. 1. The *occasion* for his appointment is some *permanent* disability of the pastor, such as old age, mental incapacity, want of learning, blindness, or some other permanent cause (c. 475, § 1).

2. His *appointment* is made by the Ordinary, either outright, or upon presentation by the religious superior if the parish is entrusted to religious (c. 475, § 1).

3. His *compensation* is to be provided for in the appointment by assigning him a portion of the income of the parish, unless other provision has been made (c. 475, § 1).

4. His *powers and obligations* depend upon the circumstances: if he takes the place of the pastor in everything, he has all a pastor's *ordinary*

---

[62] Cf. V-C, *Epit.,* I, n. 553; Cappello, *De Sacramentis,* I, n. 638; Fanfani, *De Iure Parochorum,* n. 362.

[63] Code Com., 14 July, 1922; *AAS,* 14–527; *Digest,* I, p. 539; and 20 May, 1923; *AAS,* 16–114; *Digest,* I, p. 540.

[64] *Ibid.*

[65] Cf. Cappello, in *Periodica,* Vol. 19, p. 5.

jurisdiction and all his duties except that of applying the Mass *pro populo;* if he is to supply for the pastor only in part, his powers and duties must be defined in his letter of appointment (c. 475, § 2). As to marriage, the Code Commission refused to enlarge upon the text of this canon defining the powers of the coadjutor.[66]

5. He remains *subject to the authority of the pastor* if the latter is mentally competent.

6. If the welfare of souls cannot be provided for through a coadjutor, the removal of the pastor according to cc. 2147-2161 is indicated (c. 475, § 4).

Appointment of the Vicar Assistant. 1. The *occasion* for his appointment is that the pastor needs help, usually because of the growth of the parish. One or more may be appointed, according to the need of the parish (c. 476, § 1).

2. The *appointment is made* by the Ordinary, outright in the case of a secular assistant, and upon presentation by the superior in the case of a religious (c. 476, §§ 3 and 4). In either case the pastor is to be consulted. The custom of appointing assistants without consulting the pastor is contrary to the Code, and can be tolerated temporarily only if it is centenary.[67]

Obligations. 1. *In general,* in the absence of special provision to the contrary, the assistant must help the pastor in the entire work of the parish, except the Mass *pro populo* (c. 476, § 6).

2. He may, however, be appointed for work only in a *part of the parish* (c. 476, § 2).

3. Moreover, his obligations may be *more specifically defined* in his letter of appointment, in the diocesan regulations, or in the instructions he receives from his pastor (c. 476, § 6).

4. His obligation to *reside in the parish* may be further modified by diocesan regulations, custom, or the instructions of the Bishop. It is recommended that the Ordinary prudently provide for his residence in the parish rectory (c. 476, § 5).

5. His *subjection to the pastor* involves a certain duty of obedience and docility in regard to the parochial work. It also imposes on the pastor the duty of paternal vigilance and direction in his regard (c. 476, § 7).

Rights and Jurisdiction. 1. His *compensation* should be suitably provided for (c. 476, § 1). The Third Council of Baltimore, n. 273,

---

[66] Cf. Code Com., 20 May, 1923; *AAS,* 16–114; *Digest,* I, p. 540.
[67] Cf. S. C. Conc., 14 Nov., 1920; *AAS,* 13–43; *Digest,* I, p. 262.

provided that each Bishop should, with the advice of his consultors, fix definite salaries for the pastors of his diocese, and this provision is understood as applying also to assistants.

2. The assistant is not mentioned as receiving ordinary jurisdiction for confessions as the pastor does (c. 873); hence his jurisdiction is *delegated* (c. 874).

3. His quasi-jurisdiction to assist at *marriages* is also *delegated;* but he may receive general delegation for all marriages in the parish.[68] In some dioceses, this general delegation is given with his appointment.[69]

4. The question whether assistants have any *ordinary jurisdiction* or not was formerly a disputed one. Fanfani,[70] contends for an affirmative answer; and Stocchiero has an interesting monograph published by *Ius Pontificium* which gives the arguments pro and con. But since the reply of the Code Commission referred to above, it has become difficult to concede the probability of the affirmative opinion.[71]

If the spiritual welfare of souls cannot be properly provided for through assistants, the Bishop shall provide for it in the manner described in canon 1427, that is, by the division of the parish (c. 476, § 8).

Removal of Parochial Vicars. 1. The removal of a *vicar for a moral person* has already been provided for in canon 471, § 3.

2. *All other* parochial vicars, if their office is not also a benefice as defined in canon 1409 (and it usually is not), are removable: (*a*) if they are secular, at the will of the Bishop or Vicar Capitular, but not of the Vicar General without a special mandate; (*b*) if they are religious, at the will either of the superior or of the Ordinary, as provided for the removal of religious pastors in canon 454, § 5 (c. 477, § 1).

3. The only parochial vicar whose office *may be a benefice* is an assistant, in case there is an endowment of which he receives the income. In that case the benefice will be according to its constitution, either a removable or an irremovable one; and the removal of the incumbent will be governed accordingly by canons 2157 and those following if it is removable, and by canons 2147 and those following if it is irremovable. In either case, the legal reasons for the removal of pastors (c. 2147) are applicable, but in addition to these the serious

---

[68] See c. 1096, and Code Com., 13 Sept., 1933; *Digest*, II, p. 333.
[69] See *Chicago Diocesan Pagella*, n. XII.
[70] Fanfani, *De Iure Parochorum*, n. 308.
[71] Cf. V-C, *Epit.*, I, n. 571; Cappello, *Summa*, II, n. 558.

want of due subjection to the pastor in the performance of his duties will be sufficient reason for the removal of an assistant.

Precedence. Just as the pastor of the cathedral church has precedence over all other pastors or parochial vicars of the diocese, so too has the vicar of the cathedral chapter; the right of precedence of the vicar administrator is governed by the rules laid down in canon 106 (c. 478, § 1).

Vicar substitutes and vicar coadjutors, as long as they hold the office, precede vicar assistants; the latter precede other priests who are attached to the parish church (c. 478, § 2).

Rectors of Churches. 1. *Scope of the term.* This term as used in cc. 479–486, refers to priests who have charge of churches which are neither parochial nor capitular nor annexed to the house of a religious community which takes care of the services there (c. 479, § 1). Chaplains of religious women, or of members of a lay religious society of men, or of a confraternity or other lawful association, are governed by special canons (cf. cc. 529, 698), so that they too are outside the general scope of the present canons (c. 479, § 2).

2. *Appointment.* Rectors of churches are appointed freely by the Ordinary of the place; or, in case any one has the right according to law to present or elect, they are approved or confirmed after such presentation or election, by the Ordinary. This approval is necessary even if the church belongs to an exempt religious institute whose superior proposes the candidate. In case the church is connected with a seminary or other college under the care of clerics, the superior of the seminary or college is *ipso facto* rector of the church unless the Ordinary provides otherwise (c. 480).

3. *Rights and obligations.* Parochial reserved functions (cf. c. 462) are not within the competency of the rector (c. 481). But he may celebrate even solemn services in the church in accordance with the terms of legal foundations and without prejudice to parochial rights; in doubt as to the latter condition, the Ordinary of the place is to decide, and may regulate the matter by appropriate rules (c. 482). The rector has the right to give and the responsibility according to law for giving permission to say Mass in the church (cf. c. 804), or to administer the sacraments or perform divine services there. These permissions should be given or denied according to law. As regards preaching, the provisions of canons 1337–1342 are to be observed (c. 484). If the church is so distant from the parish church that, in the judgment of the Ordinary, it is a serious inconvenience for the

people of the neighborhood to attend the parish church, the Ordinary of the place may regulate the hours of divine services so that they will be convenient for the people, and may require the rector, even under severe penalties, to hold the services at such hours, to announce feast days and fast days, and to give catechetical instructions and explanations of the Gospel. The pastor of the parish has, moreover the right to take the Most Blessed Sacrament from the church (in case it is lawfully kept there in accordance with canon 1265) to bring Communion to the sick (c. 483). The rector is responsible according to law, under the authority of the Ordinary and with due regard to lawful regulations and vested rights, for the proper celebration of divine services in the church, for the fulfillment of obligations, for the due administration of the church property, and the care of the building with its appurtenances and furnishings; and he must see to it that nothing take place there which is in any way unbecoming the house of God (c. 485).

4. *Removal.* The rector, even though he was presented by some one else, is removable for just cause at the will of the Ordinary of the place; if he is a religious, the provision of canon 454, § 5, regarding the removal of religious pastors, is to be applied (c. 486).

CASES AND QUESTIONS

1. A religious priest who is pastor of a nonreligious parish, receives:

a. A donation of $500 from a parish society, without any designation of the purpose for which it is intended (cf. c. 1536, § 1);

b. Stole fees amounting to $200;

c. A salary of $400;

d. A personal gift of $100;

e. A donation of $300 for the parish school.

How should he dispose of these sums? (Cc. 471, § 1; 580, § 2; 582; 630, § 3).

2. A parish has, by apostolic indult, been united *pleno iure* to a religious house. The vicar is a religious of simple vows. Who is entitled to the stole fees he receives? (Cc. 471, § 1; 451, § 1; 452, § 1; 463, § 1; 630, § 1).

3. A pastor has as his guest a priest from another diocese who is on his vacation. Suddenly called away for about ten days, he asks his guest to take charge of the parish during his absence, but fails to notify the Bishop (cf. c. 465, § 5). Has the visiting priest any jurisdiction for confessions? (C. 874, § 1; *Digest,* I, p. 410); for marriages? (C. 1096, § 1; *Digest,* I, p. 540, n. 4). What should he do?

4. Has an assistant in a parish any ordinary jurisdiction? (Cf. text, c. 476).

5. Among the various kinds of parochial vicars, which, if any, are obliged to say the Mass *pro populo*? (Cc. 471; 473, § 1; 474; 466, § 5).

Readings:

Bastnagel, *The Appointment of Parochial Adjutants and Assistants,* Catholic University, 1930 (n. 58); *Periodica,* Vol. 19, p. 1* (Cappello on powers of *vicarius substitutus* and *sacerdos supplens*); *Ecclesiastical Review,* Vol. 97, p. 76 (administrator of parish); Vol. 95, p. 196; Vol. 95, p. 534 (Schaaf on powers of *vicarius substitutus*); *Irish Ecclesiastical Record,* Vol. 71, p. 636 (Browne on marriage performed by assistants in pastor's absence); *Clergy Review,* Vol. 11, p. 248 (dispensing power of assistant).

PART THREE: RELIGIOUS

CHAPTER VI

GOVERNMENT OF RELIGIOUS

Section 1. The Religious State: Terminology (cc. 487–491)

PRELIMINARY SURVEY

The Religious State (c. 487)
Use and Meaning of Terms (c. 488)
  Religious Institute
  Order
  Pontifical Institute
  Clerical Institute
  Religious House
  Province
  Religious
  Major Superiors
Relation of Rules and Constitutions to the Code (c. 489)
Precedence Among Religious (c. 491)

Art. 1. The Religious State. Four elements make up the religious state: (1) a fixed or stable manner of life; (2) in common; (3) in which the evangelical counsels are observed; (4) by means of the vows of obedience, chastity, and poverty (c. 487).

1. *A fixed or stable mode of life:* Stability or permanency belongs to the very nature of a state. A person who enters into such a state is no longer free to give it up. Such are the married state, the clerical state, the religious state.

2. *Common life:* This means two things: (*a*) membership in a society which enjoys moral personality under a determined superior and a definite rule; (*b*) dwelling together under a common roof,

sharing common lodging and board with others. Common life is essential to the religious state only in the first sense. Formerly hermits were true religious, and even today a religious who has been promoted to the episcopal dignity and lives outside his community remains a religious. Common law, however, today demands community life as the general rule. Thus c. 606 forbids superiors to allow their subjects to dwell outside the religious house for more than six months, except for the purpose of studies.

3. *The observance of the evangelical counsels:* namely, poverty, chastity, and obedience. For the religious state is a state of Christian perfection, not indeed to be *exercised,* as in the case of bishops, but to be *acquired,* that is, members of the religious state may not have *actually* acquired perfection, but they are being taught and trained in the way of obtaining Christian perfection. Now, the normal state of acquiring religious perfection demands the removal of *all,* not merely of some of the impediments to Christian perfection, which arise from the threefold concupiscence. This is obtained by the practice of the evangelical counsels, which are required and are sufficient for the purpose.

It will be well to remark here that the state of Christian perfection is to be clearly distinguished from *Christian perfection itself,* or perfect charity, which may be attained *outside* the state of Christian perfection, as is clearly shown in the case of many saints who lived in the world and arrived at morally continuous perfect charity. Conversely, one may be in the *state* of Christian perfection, although far removed *actually* from Christian perfection.

4. *By means of the vows of obedience, chastity, and poverty:* For the vows give firmness to the observance of the evangelical counsels. They are a bond which binds the person striving after perfection to the *perpetual observance* of the three counsels, and thus they provide the permanency required in the religious state.

Canon 487 prescribes that the religious state, as described above, *is to be held in honor by all.* For the religious state owes its origin to Christ Himself who by word and example exhorted His followers to the observance of the evangelical counsels, and granted His Church the power to establish and govern religious orders whose members bind themselves by vow to strive after perfection by the observance of the three counsels. This approval of religious orders on the part of the Supreme Pontiff or of an oecumenical council is an exercise of the prerogative of infallibility which they enjoy. Moreover, the purpose for which the religious state was instituted is the most useful and excellent after which man can strive. Finally, members of the religious state have brought honor and glory to the Church during the centuries by the sanctity of their lives, by the beneficence of their good works, and by their contribution to the development of the arts and sciences.[1]

Art. 2. The Use and Meaning of Terms in the Treatise on Religious (c. 488). *Religious institute (Religio)* — The Latin term *"religio"* retains its canonical meaning in two English phrases. We speak of "entering religion," and of "the vows of religion." In common parlance the word "religion" in English means religious belief, a system of faith and worship, or the virtue whereby man exercises such worship. Hence we shall use the term "religious institute" or simply, "institute" wherever the Latin term *"religio"* occurs in the canons, as is done in the Authorized (but not official) English Translation of the canons of the Code regarding religious.[2]

1. A *religious institute* as defined practically by canon 488, 1°, is a society approved by legitimate ecclesiastical authority, the members of which strive after evangelical perfection according to the laws proper to their society, by the profession of public vows, either perpetual or temporary, the latter to be renewed after fixed intervals of time. A *society* is a body of physical persons striving after a common purpose, by using the same means under the direction of legitimate authority. Such a society must be *approved by legitimate ecclesiastical authority* — for there is question here of a *moral collegiate person* which can come into being only by public authority by means of a formal decree of erection (c. 100, § 1). *Laws proper to the society* are required — namely rules and constitutions by which the members are bound to strive after evangelical perfection. *Public vows* are those which, according to c. 1308, § 1, are accepted in the name of the Church by a legitimate ecclesiastical superior. Private vows, on the contrary, are taken without being accepted by the Church. Public vows may be *perpetual* or *temporary*. In the latter case, however, they are to be renewed on the day on which they end (c. 577, § 1), otherwise the stability required for the religious state would be absent.

2. An *order* is an institute in which solemn vows are taken; a *congregation* is an institute in which only simple vows are taken,

---

[1] See Apostolic Letter of Pius XI, *Unigenitus Dei Filius*, March 19, 1924, *AAS*, 16–133; *Digest*, I, p. 265.
[2] Published by the Vatican Press under the title: *Canonical Legislation Concerning Religious.*

either perpetual or temporary; a *monastic congregation* is a confederation (union) of a number of independent (*sui iuris*) monasteries. Thus the monasteries of the Order of St. Benedict are united into fifteen congregations, two of which, the American-Cassinese and the Swiss-American, include most of the Benedictine monasteries in the United States. An *exempt institute* is an institute of either solemn or simple vows which has been withdrawn from the jurisdiction of the local Ordinary.

3. A *pontifical institute* (*iuris pontificii*) is an institute which has received the approbation or at least the *decree of praise* (*laudis decretum*) from the Apostolic See (see p. 234); a *diocesan institute* (*iuris dioecesani*) is an institute erected by a local Ordinary which has not as yet obtained the decree of praise.

4. A *clerical institute* is an institute the majority of whose members receive the order of priesthood; otherwise it is a *lay institute*.

5. A *religious house* is a general term for the house of any institute; a *house of regulars* (*domus regularis*) is any house of an order; a *formal house* (*domus formata*) is any religious house in which at least six professed religious dwell; in the case of a clerical institute four of the six members must be priests.

6. A *province* is the union of a number of religious houses under one and the same superior, constituting a part of the same institute.

7. *Religious* are persons who have taken vows in an institute; religious *with simple vows,* those who have taken vows in a religious *congregation; regulars,* those who have taken vows in an *order; sisters* are religious women with *simple* vows; *nuns,* religious women with *solemn* vows; unless the contrary be certain from the nature of the case or from the context, the term *nuns* applies likewise to those religious women whose vows by reason of their institute are solemn, but which, by order of the Apostolic See, are only simple in certain countries.

8. *Major superiors* are, the Abbot Primate, the Abbot Superior of a monastic congregation, the Abbot of an independent monastery, even though it belong to a monastic congregation, the superior general of an entire institute, the provincial superior, the vicars of all the afore-mentioned, likewise all others having powers equivalent to those of provincials.

The statutes of the Code which concern religious even though expressed in the masculine gender apply to religious women as well, unless the contrary appear from the context or from the nature of the case **(c. 490).**

Art. 3. Relation of Rules and Constitutions to the Code. The rules and particular constitutions of individual institutes which are not contrary to the canons of the Code retain their force; those, however, which are contrary to the canons are repealed **(c. 489).** Particular constitutions which are stricter than the canons of the Code are not necessarily contrary to the Code; neither are contrary privileges, indults, centenary or immemorial customs which are not expressly repudiated by the Code (cf. cc. 4 and 5).

Art. 4. Precedence Among Religious. Religious have precedence over the laity; clerical institutes over lay institutes; canons regular over monks; monks over other regulars; regulars over religious congregations; pontifical congregations over diocesan congregations; religious in the same class should observe the prescriptions of canon 106, n. 5. The secular clergy, however, have precedence over both laity and religious, outside the latter's own churches, and even in their own churches in the case of lay institutes; but a cathedral or other collegiate chapter takes precedence over religious everywhere **(c. 491).**

Section 2. The Foundation and Suppression of Religious Institutes, Provinces, and Houses

PRELIMINARY SURVEY

Foundation and Suppression of a Religious Institute (cc. 492–493)
Foundation and Suppression of Provinces (c. 494)
Foundation of Houses (cc. 495–497)
Effect of Canonical Foundation of Religious House (c. 497, § 2)
Change of Religious House to Other Uses (c. 497, § 4)
Suppression of Religious Houses (c. 498)

Art. 1. The Foundation and Suppression of a Religious Institute. Bishops only (exclusive of the vicar capitular and the vicar general) have the power to found religious congregations. They may not, however, found or allow such congregations to be founded without consulting the Holy See. In the case of tertiaries living in common,[3]

---

[3] E.g., Sisters of the Third Order of St. Francis or of St. Dominic, etc.

aggregation to the first order by act of the superior general is likewise required (c. 492, § 1).

A congregation founded by a Bishop is and remains a *diocesan* congregation even though in the course of time it be extended to other dioceses, and it remains entirely subject to the Ordinaries in whose dioceses it exists, according to the prescriptions of the law, until such time as it receives pontifical approbation, or at least the decree of praise (c. 492, § 2).

Neither the name nor the habit of an institute already in existence may be taken by those who are not legitimate members of the same, nor by a new institute (c. 492, § 3).

A Bishop who wishes to found a religious congregation should apply to the Congregation of Religious for the requisite permission. His application should also present the following information: who is the originator of the congregation, and what motive impelled him; what are the name and title of the congregation; what are the form, color, material of the habit to be worn by novices and by the professed; what good works the new congregation wishes to engage in; what is the means of support; whether there are any similar congregations in the diocese.[4] After receiving permission to found a new congregation, the Bishop should establish it by a formal decree in writing, copies of which are to be kept in the archives of the institute and of the diocese. A copy is likewise to be sent to the Congregation of Religious.[5] It may be noted in passing that the S. Congregation of Religious is loath to grant permission for the foundation of new institutes, especially in dioceses in which other religious congregations are already established. The S. Congregation for the Propagation of the Faith, however, encourages the foundation of new missionary congregations especially for natives in missionary countries (see Instruction of March 19, 1937, *Digest,* II, p. 156 ff.).

It is the mind of the Church that after a diocesan congregation has developed its membership and spread to other dioceses, and has given satisfaction in its pursuit of good works, it may apply to the Holy See for pontifical approbation and thus become a pontifical institute. The steps to be taken and the documents required will be found in the *Normae.*[6]

The establishment of a religious *order* is reserved to the Holy See

---

[4] S. C. Rel., March 16, 1921, *Normae,* Cap. I, nn. 3–5; *AAS,* 13–313.
[5] S. C. Rel., Nov. 30, 1922, *AAS,* 14–644; *Digest,* I, p. 269.
[6] Cap. I, nn. 6–12; see footnote 4.

(c. 220). The last order approved by the Holy See was the Order of Penance in 1792.

The Holy See alone can suppress a religious institute, even though it consists of only one house. It is likewise reserved to the Holy See to dispose of the temporal goods of a suppressed or extinct institute, in which case the wishes of founders and benefactors will be respected (c. 493).

Art. 2. The Foundation and Suppression of Religious Provinces. There is no provision made in the Code for the establishment of provinces in a diocesan congregation. Since such a demand would imply the spread of the congregation over several dioceses, and since in that case no change may be made in the constitutions of a diocesan congregation without the consent of all the Ordinaries in whose territory the congregation has houses (c. 495, § 2), the establishment of provinces would seem to demand the consent of all the Ordinaries in whose territory the congregation has houses. A happier solution would be for the congregation to apply to the Holy See for pontifical approval.

In the case of a religious order or of a pontifical congregation, the permission of the Holy See is required to establish provinces in an institute which did not have them before, as well as to unite provinces already existing, or to change their boundaries, as well as to erect new provinces, or to suppress those already in existence. Likewise the Holy See reserves to itself the power to separate an independent monastery from the monastic congregation of which it is a member, and of joining it to another (c. 494, § 1). The disposal of the temporal goods of an extinct province is determined first of all, by the constitutions; if these contain no provisions, it is left to the general chapter, or, outside the time of the general chapter, to the superior general and his council. The laws of justice, and the will of any founders must be safeguarded (c. 494, § 2). As a general rule, the S. Congregation of Religious will not grant permission to divide an institute into provinces unless four provinces can be erected with at least four houses with twelve members in each province.[7] Because of difficult circumstances, such as the establishment of houses in distant countries, and among different nationalities, exceptions are sometimes made.

Art. 3. The Foundation and Suppression of Religious Houses. For the establishment of any religious house, four things are required:

1. There must be at least three religious to form a community,

---

[7] Schaefer, *De Rel.* ed. 3, n. 78, 4.

otherwise there can be no question of erecting a moral collegiate person (cf. c. 100), and when the Code speaks of the founding of a religious house, it means, not the physical dwelling, but the establishment of a religious community, even though it dwell in a rented house.

2. No religious house should be established, unless it can be prudently foreseen that the housing and support of the members of the community will be assured from its own revenue, or from customary alms, or from some other means (c. 496).

3. The establishment of a religious house should be made by a formal decree of erection issued in writing by the proper *religious superior* (c. 100, § 1).

4. For the establishment of any religious house, the authority of the proper *ecclesiastical authority* is also required as follows: (a) For the erection of any religious house in a territory subject to the S. Cong. of the Propagation of the Faith, permission must be obtained from the Holy See; (b) elsewhere, in the case of a *diocesan* congregation it suffices to obtain the written consent of the Ordinary of the place in which the house is to be established, as well as the written consent of the Ordinary of the place in which the mother house is located (c. 495, § 1). The latter's consent would seem to be required only for the *first* house to be established in another diocese; (c) for the establishment of an *exempt* religious house, whether formal or not, the approval of the Holy See as well as the written consent of the Ordinary of the place are required; (d) for the establishment of a monastery of *nuns,* the approval of the Holy See and the written consent of the Ordinary of the place are necessary, even in the case of a monastery of nuns who by reason of apostolic decree, take simple vows only;[8] (e) for the establishment of a house of a nonexempt pontifical congregation, the written permission of the local Ordinary is required and suffices, except in the case of a novitiate house, which requires the consent of the Holy See as well (c. 554, § 1); (f) to build and open a school, hospice, or any similar house at a distance (i.e., not on the same grounds) from the religious house, even though it be exempt, the special written permission of the local Ordinary is necessary and sufficient (c. 497, § 3).

Art. 4. Effect of Canonical Erection of a Religious House (c. 497, § 2).

---

[8] S. C. Rel., Oct. 11, 1922, *AAS*, 14–554; *Digest*, I, p. 266.

1. The religious house or community acquires a moral collegiate personality (c. 100, § 1);

2. *In a clerical institute* the permission to establish a new house carries with it the right to have a church or public oratory in connection with the religious house, but the local Ordinary must give permission for its location (c. 1162, § 4); nonclerical religious need a special permission of the local Ordinary to open a church or oratory in connection with the new religious house (cc. 1162, 1191, 1192); religious clerics may celebrate the sacred functions in their churches or public oratory in conformity with the requirements of law, that is, with due regard to parochial rights (cf. cc. 1171, 1191, § 2);

3. *For all institutes,* the permission to open a house carries with it the right to perform all the good works proper to the institute, with due regard to any conditions agreed upon when the permission was granted.

Art. 5. **Change of Religious House to Other Uses (c. 497, § 4).** Such a change may be *internal,* affecting the religious only, or it may be *external,* affecting the faithful at large. If it be merely internal, e.g., a house of studies added to a novitiate, no new permission is required; if the change be external, e.g., changing a school for extern pupils into a house of studies for religious, it is equivalent to a new foundation and requires the same permission as a new house.

Art. 6. **Suppression of Religious Houses (c. 498).** To suppress a religious house: (1) of an *exempt institute* — whether formal or not — requires an apostolic indult; (2) of a *nonexempt pontifical institute* — requires the consent of the superior general and of the local Ordinary; if the latter wishes to suppress such a religious house, he must obtain an apostolic indult if the superior general objects to the suppression; (3) of a *diocesan institute* — the local Ordinary need only consult the superior general; the latter may appeal to the Holy See *in suspensivo,* if he objects to the suppression. If the house in question be the only house of the institute, its suppression would be tantamount to the suppression of the institute, and the permission of the Holy See would be required (c. 493).

N.B. All that has been said in this title regarding religious institutes, applies as well to societies of persons living in common but without public vows (c. 674).

Section 3. Superiors and Chapters (cc. 499–517)

PRELIMINARY SURVEY

Ecclesiastical Superiors (cc. 499–500)
Religious Superiors (cc. 501–505)
Elections Held in Chapter (cc. 506–507)
Obligation of Superiors (cc. 508–517)
Councilors and Bursars (c. 516)
Procurator General (c. 517)

Note: Since religious are members both of the Church and of a particular society, they are subject to a *twofold hierarchy.* The first is external to their institute, and is made up of superiors of the Church, whom we shall designate as *ecclesiastical superiors;* the second is internal, and is made up of the *religious superiors.* Within the institute the authority is held collectively by the general chapter or general congregation, and individually by religious superiors who have their councilors whose advice they must frequently ask, and sometimes are bound to follow.

Art. 1. Ecclesiastical Superiors (cc. 499–500). 1. *The Sovereign Pontiff:* All religious are subject to the Sovereign Pontiff as their highest superior, and they are bound to obey him not only as members of the Church, but also by reason of their vow of obedience (c. 499, § 1). In the government of the Church the Holy Father employs the aid of groups of Cardinals who make up the various Roman Congregations. Among these the *Sacred Congregation of Religious* is immediately in charge of all matters regarding religious. Hence all questions concerning religious whose solution requires the intervention of the Holy See must be submitted to this Congregation.

2. *The Cardinal Protector:* Religious orders generally have a Cardinal Protector. Congregations approved by the Holy See may also ask for and obtain a Cardinal Protector. He possesses no jurisdiction by law over the institute or over any of its members, but his only concern is to promote the welfare of the institute by his counsel and patronage. Hence he may not interfere in the internal discipline of the institute nor in the management of its temporal goods (c. 499, § 2).

3. *The local Ordinary:* Religious are subject also to the local Ordinary, but in different degrees (c. 500, § 1): (*a*) *exempt religious, and*

nuns who by their constitutions are subject to the jurisdiction of regular superiors, are subject to the local Ordinary only in the cases expressly defined by law **(c. 500, § 2); (*b*) *members of nonexempt pontifical institutes* are subject to the local Ordinary as clerics or as members of the faithful, but not as religious; hence they depend on their religious superiors for everything which has to do with religious discipline properly so called (c. 618); (*c*) *members of diocesan congregations* are subject to the local Ordinary as religious, though this dependence is limited by common law and by the approved constitutions. A diocesan institute is a moral person, directed by its own religious superiors, conformably to the law. Hence the local Ordinary may not interfere with acts dealing with internal government, and which are reserved by law or the constitutions to superiors. He may not, for example, admit or dismiss postulants, novices, or professed religious; nor may he appoint local superiors or remove them from office. (*d*) Without a special apostolic indult, no male institute can have a religious congregation of women subject to it, or retain, as specially confided to it, the care and direction of such religious **(c. 500, § 3)**. By apostolic privilege the Lazarists have the exclusive direction of the Daughters of Charity of St. Vincent de Paul.

Art. 2. Religious Superiors (cc. 501–505). The powers of religious superiors are defined in the constitutions and in the common law. All religious superiors have *dominative power* over their subjects. In a *clerical exempt institute,* superiors and chapters have *ecclesiastical jurisdiction* as well, both in the internal and external forum **(c. 501, § 1)**, (cf. pp. 133–136). All religious superiors are strictly forbidden to interfere in any way in cases pertaining to the Holy Office **(c. 501, § 2)**. An abbot primate as well as the superior of a monastic congregation does not enjoy full power and jurisdiction granted by law to major superiors, but his power and jurisdiction is to be gathered from the proper constitutions and the special decrees of the Holy See. For his judicial powers, see canons 655 and 1594, § 4 **(c. 501, § 3)**. *The Superior General* has authority over all the houses, provinces, and members of the institute, to be exercised, however, according to the constitutions. All other superiors have authority within the limits of their office **(c. 502)**. Major superiors in exempt clerical institutes have the power to appoint notaries, but only for ecclesiastical affairs of their own institute **(c. 503)**.

Term of office: Major superiors shall be temporary, hence cannot be appointed for life unless the constitutions determine otherwise. This prohibition applies to founders of congregations as well. *Minor local superiors* (that is, all local superiors except the superior of an independent monastery) are not to hold office for more than three years; on the expiration of this term they may be reappointed to the same office if the constitutions permit it, but not immediately for a third term in the same religious house **(c. 505)**.

Qualities required in superiors: The *valid* choice of a superior supposes that the candidate possesses those qualities which the common law and the constitutions of the institute require *under pain of nullity;* all other prescriptions of the Code and special regulations of each institute are required for *licit* choice.

For the *valid* choice of a *major* superior the common law of the Church requires: (1) at least *ten* years of religious profession in the same institute; (2) *legitimate* birth (canonical legitimation suffices, see cc. 1116, 1117); (3) *forty* years of age for the superior general, or the superior of a monastery of nuns; *thirty* years for other major superiors. The Code has no special provision regarding the qualities required for minor local superiors **(c. 504)**.

Art. 3. Elections Held in Chapter (cc. 506–507). In all elections held in chapter, the common law set forth in canons 160–182 shall be observed (see pp. 126–128), as well as the constitutions of the institute not contrary to the common law. All must abstain from seeking votes either directly or indirectly, for themselves or for others. Postulation can be admitted in an extraordinary case only, provided the constitutions do not forbid it **(c. 507)**.[9]

1. *In male institutes,* before proceeding to the election of major superiors, all and each of the members of the chapter shall promise under oath to elect those whom, before God, they judge should be elected **(c. 506, § 1)**.

2. *In monasteries of nuns subject to the local Ordinary,* he or his delegate without entering the enclosure presides over the assembly which is to elect the superior, assisted by two priests (ordinary confessors of the nuns excluded) who act as tellers (*scrutatores*); in *monasteries of nuns not subject to the local Ordinary but to the regular superior,* the latter presides over the election of the superior; but even in this case the local Ordinary is to be informed of the day and hour of the election, and if he assist, he *may* preside, either in person or by delegate **(c. 506, § 2)**; that is, either he or his delegate

---

[9] S. C. Rel., Letter March 9, 1920, *AAS*, 12–365; *Digest,* I, p. 276.

governs the election, not the regular superior who must also be present.[10]

3. *In congregations of sisters* the election of the *mother general only* shall be presided over by the Ordinary of the place in which the election is held, or by his delegate; hence the Ordinary of the mother house has no right to preside over the election when it is held in another diocese, even in the case of a diocesan congregation.[11] In the case of a diocesan congregation, however, the Ordinary who presides has full power to confirm or annul the result of the election as his conscience dictates (c. 506, § 4). In case of annulment, however, he may not appoint a superior, but another election must be held.

Art. 4. Obligations of Superiors (cc. 508–517). 1. *Obligation of residence:* All superiors must habitually reside in the house which is assigned to them, and must not absent themselves except for the reasons and for the time allowed by the constitutions (c. 508).

2. *Making known decrees of the Holy See:* Superiors should make known to their subjects all decrees of the Holy See pertaining to religious, and see that they are carried out (c. 509, § 1). This pertains not only to decrees imposing an obligation, but to those granting favors to religious as well, for instance, the granting of indulgences, and the like. Sometimes the Holy See prescribes that certain decrees be read publicly in each community every year. This was the case before the Code with the decree about the account of conscience (*Quemadmodum*), regarding confessions of religious (*Cum de Sacramentalibus*), and regarding frequent Communion (*Sacra Tridentina Synodus*). Since the matter contained in these decrees has been incorporated into the canons of the Code, they need no longer be read in public, and should not be read as existing laws of the Church because their content has been modified in the Code. At present there is only one decree which must be read at the beginning of each year to the *clerical students* of all religious clerical institutes and societies. This is the instruction *Quantum Religiones* issued by the S. Congregation of Religious on December 1, 1931, by order of Pope Pius XI.[12]

3. *The constitutions proper to each institute* must be read at least once a year in public on fixed days. *Catechetical instruction* should be

---

[10] Code Com., Nov. 24, 1920, *AAS*, 12-252; *Digest*, I, p. 279.

[11] S. C. Rel., July 2, 1921, *AAS*, 13-481; *Digest*, I, p. 279.

[12] *AAS*, 24–74; *Digest*, I, 473; Creusen-Ellis, *Religious Men and Women in the Code*, Appendix II.

given twice a month to the lay brothers as well as to the domestic servants. Besides, especially in lay institutes a *pious exhortation* should be given twice a month to all the members of the household (c. 509, § 2, 2°). After having completed the novitiate all religious who are to be employed in teaching Christian doctrine must be given special training both in the catechism itself and in the method of teaching it to children.[13]

4. *Report to Holy See:* Every five years, or oftener, if the constitutions so prescribe, the abbot primate, the superior of every monastic congregation, the superior general of every pontifical institute must send to the Holy See a written account of the state of the institute, signed by themselves and by the members of their council, and in the case of a congregation of women, by the Ordinary of the place where the mother general resides with her council (c. 510).[14]

5. *Canonical visitation:* Most religious are subject to a twofold canonical visitation, one on the part of their own religious superior, the other on the part of the local Ordinary.

a. Major religious superiors of all institutes designated to this office by the constitutions shall visit, either in person, or by others if they themselves are legitimately impeded from doing so, all the houses subject to their jurisdiction, at the times defined by the constitutions (c. 511).

b. The local Ordinary must every five years, either personally or by delegate, conduct a canonical visitation of: (1) *all monasteries of nuns* immediately subject to himself or to the Holy See; likewise all monasteries of nuns subject to regular superiors, but ordinarily only regarding those matters which pertain to the law of enclosure; if, however, the regular superior has not visited the monastery within the past five years, the local Ordinary will conduct a full, canonical visitation as in monasteries subject to himself; (2) *all houses of pontifical clerical congregations,* even though exempt, but only concerning those matters which pertain to the church, sacristy, public oratory, and the confessional; (3) *all houses of pontifical lay congregations,* not only in those matters indicated in the preceding number, but likewise in matters pertaining to internal discipline, in accordance, however, with the terms of canon 618, § 2, 2°; (4) *all houses of diocesan congregations,*

---

[13] S. C. Rel., Nov. 25, 1929, *AAS*, 22–28; *Digest*, I, p. 280.

[14] The manner of carrying out this obligation has been outlined in an instruction of the S. C. Rel., March 8, 1922, *AAS*, 14–161; *Digest*, I, p. 282, and a formula of questions to be answered for the report was given March 25, 1922, *AAS*, 14–278; the official English text is given in *AAS*, 15–459; *Digest* I, p. 284; Creusen-Ellis, Appendix III.

which, being fully under his jurisdiction, he may visit as often as he sees fit, and in all matters, unless the constitutions which have been fully approved by him, should place certain limits to his powers of visitation (c. 512).

6. *Rights and duties of the canonical visitor:* The canonical visitor has the right and obligation of questioning the religious whom he deems it well to hear, and of informing himself on such matters as pertain to the visitation; all religious, on their part, have an obligation of answering truthfully, and it is unlawful for superiors to divert them in any way from this obligation, or otherwise to impede the purpose of the visitation. Appeal may be made against the decrees of the canonical visitor but not with suspensive effect unless the visitor has proceeded in judicial form (c. 513).

7. *Holy Viaticum and Extreme Unction:* In every *clerical* institute, superiors have the right and duty in case of sickness, to administer personally or by delegate, both Holy Viaticum and Extreme Unction to the professed, to novices, as well as to other persons dwelling day and night in the religious house by reason of employment, education, hospitality, or health (c. 514, § 1). When one of these persons becomes seriously ill outside the religious house, the religious superior has the right to administer Holy Viaticum and Extreme Unction to the *professed religious and novices;* all others (postulants, boarders, etc.) should receive these sacraments from the local parish priest.[15]

8. *Merely honorary titles* of dignity or of office are forbidden to religious; the titles of major offices which the religious have actually held in their own institute, are alone tolerated, if the constitutions permit them by positive decree (c. 515). This prohibition does not apply to *academic* titles such as doctor, master, or lector.

Art. 5. Councilors and Bursars (c. 516): The superior general of every institute or monastic congregation, as well as the provincial and local superior of at least every formal house shall have their councilors, whose consent or advice they must seek according to the norms of the constitutions and of the sacred canons. These councilors are usually four in number, though more are allowed; two will suffice in small houses. Bursars are also required for the administration of temporal goods; a *general* bursar who administers the property of the entire institute, a *provincial* bursar for the property of the province, and a *local* bursar for each house; all these exercise their office under the

---

[15] Code Com., July 16, 1931, *AAS*, 23-353; *Digest*, I, p. 294.

direction of their respective superiors. A superior may not hold the office of general or provincial bursar; although it is preferable to have even the local bursar distinct from the superior, the latter may hold this office in case of necessity. If the constitutions do not prescribe the manner of choosing bursars, they shall be chosen by the major superior with the *consent* of his council.

Art. 6. The Procurator General: Every order and pontifical congregation *of men* shall have a procurator general chosen according to the constitutions, who shall take care of the business of his institute with the Holy See. He should reside in Rome,[16] and may not be removed from office before the expiration of the time prescribed by the Constitutions, without consulting the Holy See **(c. 517)**. While theoretically every religious has a right to deal directly with the Holy See, in practice it is the mind of the Church that in ordinary affairs, such as obtaining of indults, etc., they are to act through their procurator general. This practical rule does not apply to matters of conscience, nor to the appeal granted religious against a decree of dismissal. Religious women deal with the Holy See through their diocesan chancery or through their Cardinal Protector, if they have one.

Section 4. Confessors and Chaplains (cc. 518–530)

PRELIMINARY SURVEY

Confessors of Religious Men (cc. 518, 519, 528)
Confessors of Religious Women (cc. 520–523)
Appointment and Qualities of Confessors of Religious
  Women (cc. 524–527)
Chaplains and Preachers (c. 529)
Account of Conscience (c. 530)

Art. 1. Confessors of Religious Men (cc. 518, 519, 528).

1. *In clerical institutes:* In each house several (at least two) legitimately approved confessors are to be appointed, according to the size of the community **(c. 518)**. Such confessors must also be given the power to absolve from cases reserved in their institute.[17] In nonexempt institutes such confessors must be *approved* by the local Ordinary,

---

[16] S. C. Rel., June 4, 1920, *AAS*, 12-301; *Digest*, I, p. 294.
[17] Reserved cases refer to certain sins and censures which may be reserved only in an exempt clerical institute; cf. cc. 893 and 896.

that is, they must receive jurisdiction from him (c. 874). They are then *appointed* as confessors of the community by their own superior according to the constitutions. In exempt clerical institutes their own superiors may *approve* them (that is, confer delegated jurisdiction upon them) (c. 875) and then appoint them according to the constitutions.

2. *In lay institutes:* Each community should have at least one ordinary and one extraordinary confessor, *approved and appointed* by the local Ordinary in the case of nonexempt institutes, *proposed* by the superior but to be *approved* by the local Ordinary in the case of an exempt institute (cf. cc. 874, § 1, 875, § 2). Should any religious ask for a special confessor, the superior shall grant him this favor without in any way inquiring about the reason thereof, or showing displeasure (c. 528).

3. *Every male religious* may, for his peace of conscience, confess to any confessor *approved* by the local Ordinary even though he be not listed among the appointed confessors, and the confession thus made is valid and licit, all contrary privileges being revoked; and this confessor can absolve him likewise from sins and censures reserved by the institute (c. 519).

4. For the confessors of *novices,* see canon 566, §2.

Art. 2. Confessors of Religious Women (cc. 520–527).

1. *The ordinary confessor:* Every religious community of women, no matter how small, should have *one* ordinary confessor, appointed by the local Ordinary. This ordinary confessor should hear the confessions of the entire community. The Bishop may, however, appoint more than one, provided the large number of religious or some other just cause (e.g., language) warrant it (c. 520, §1). It is probable that in the case of small communities which have no chapel of their own, but receive the sacraments of penance and Holy Communion in a neighboring church, no ordinary confessor need be appointed. The sisters are then free to choose their ordinary confessor from among those who hear confessions in the church. The purpose of having only one confessor for each community is evidently unity of direction.

2. *The special confessor:* An individual religious, for the peace of her conscience and for her greater progress in the spiritual life, may request a special confessor or spiritual director from the local Ordinary, and he shall grant the request without difficulty, watchful, however, lest any abuse arise from this concession (c. 520, §2). The superiors may not interfere, but must notify the Ordinary should any abuse arise. When the peculiar circumstances requiring a special confessor

have ceased, the religious should return to the ordinary confessor of the community for confession and spiritual direction.[18]

3. *The extraordinary confessor:* To every community of religious women shall be given an extraordinary confessor who, at least four times a year, shall go to the religious house, and to whom all the religious shall present themselves, at least to receive his blessing (c. 521, § 1). The religious are not obliged to go to confession to the extraordinary, but they must at least enter the confessional and ask for his blessing. It is customary for the extraordinary confessor to present himself during the ember weeks. Custom may also allow the retreat master to act as extraordinary confessor for that occasion, so that the extraordinary need not present himself that quarter.

4. *The supplementary confessor:* Ordinaries who have religious communities of women in their territory shall designate for each house some priests, to whom in particular cases the religious may easily have recourse for the sacrament of penance, without having to apply to the Ordinary on each occasion (c. 521, § 2). The purpose of the supplementary confessor is to satisfy a particular need, hence he is not to become a special confessor of an individual religious without the consent of the Ordinary (see n. 2 above). A particular need would arise also in case the ordinary confessor were sick or absent; the superior could then call one of the supplementary confessors to hear the confessions of the entire community.

When any religious asks for one of these confessors (extraordinary or supplementary) no superior, either personally or through others, either directly or indirectly, may seek to know the reason of the petition, or show opposition to it by word or deed, or in any way manifest displeasure at it (c. 521, § 3). Should abuses arise, the superior should inform the Ordinary. If the supplementary confessor sees that there is no sufficient reason for calling him, he should call the attention of the religious to the fact and prudently but courteously refuse his spiritual ministration.

5. *The occasional confessor:* Any religious, for the peace of her conscience, may have recourse to any confessor approved by the local Ordinary to hear the confessions of women; this confession is valid and lawful when made in any church or oratory, even a semipublic oratory, or in any place *lawfully* designated for the hearing of women's confessions;[19] nor may the superior prohibit it or make any inquiry

---

[18] S. C. Rel., Feb. 3, 1913; *AAS*, 5-63; *Fontes*, n. 4416, Vol. VI, p. 1018.
[19] Code Com., Nov. 24, 1920; *AAS*, 12-575; *Digest*, I, p. 295.

concerning it, even indirectly; and the religious are under no obligation to inform the superior in the matter (c. 522).

Four conditions are laid down in this canon: (*a*) *For peace of conscience:* This condition is not required for validity and should be interpreted broadly. Any sincere desire to purify one's conscience is sufficient. Confessions made from merely human motives, such as mere convenience, should be discouraged. (*b*) *May have recourse to any confessor.* The initiative must be taken by the religious, not by the confessor. In practice, a religious may go to confession to any priest who is hearing confessions in a church, public or semipublic oratory. She may likewise invite a priest who happens to be in the convent (on a visit, or to say Mass, or to give an instruction) to go to the confessional and hear her confession, provided he has diocesan faculties.[20] (*c*) *To a priest approved* by the local Ordinary to hear *confessions of women:* since it is not customary in the United States to approve confessors for men only, any priest who has diocesan faculties to hear confessions satisfies this demand. It is likewise probable that it suffices if the priest be approved only for a particular group of women (whether religious or secular women), e.g., a retreat master. (*d*) *A place approved for the hearing of confessions of women:* This condition is required for validity, hence a confession made by a religious woman outside of a church, public or semipublic oratory, or other place lawfully approved for hearing the confessions of women, is *not only illicit, but also invalid.*[21] The confessions of women should ordinarily be heard in a confessional, placed in an open and conspicuous place in a church, public or semipublic oratory, and provided with a grating or screen (c. 909). The local Ordinary may designate some other place for the hearing of women's confessions. Thus, for instance, during time of retreat when the chapel is much used, or if the chapel is small, he may designate the sacristy, or a parlor, or a classroom as the place for hearing confessions. This, then, becomes an *approved place* within the meaning of the canon, whether it be designated for the confessions of religious women or of women of the world. Such a place may be approved habitually, or by way of act. Finally, an approved place is one chosen by the confessor and the penitent in conformity with canon 910, § 1 which states that "women's confessions are not to be heard outside of a confessional except in case of illness or of *some other real necessity,* in which case precautions

[20] Code Com., Dec. 28, 1927, II; *AAS*, 20–61; *Digest*, I, p. 296.
[21] Code Com., Dec. 28, 1927, I; *AAS*, 20–61; *Digest*, I, p. 296.

prescribed by the Ordinary as opportune are to be observed."[22] Regarding the place, therefore, the following rule holds: a priest having diocesan faculties only, may validly and licitly hear the confession of a religious woman, in any place in which he could licitly hear the confession of a laywoman.

The spirit of the Church's legislation regarding these various classes of confessors for religious women may be summed up by saying that both superiors and subjects are expected to observe the law in its integrity: superiors by not interfering or showing themselves displeased in any way; subjects by using the privilege accorded to them with prudence and moderation; thus tranquillity and harmony will prevail in the community, and the purpose of the legislation, peace and liberty of conscience, will be attained.

6. *The confessor of sick religious:* All religious women, when seriously ill even though not in danger of death, may, as often as they wish during their serious illness, invite any priest whatever to hear their confession, provided that he be approved to hear the confessions of women, even though he be not designated to hear the confessions of religious women; nor may the superior either directly or indirectly hinder them from doing so (c. 523). *Serious illness* includes any sickness which by its nature or by reason of special circumstances considerably lessens the strength of the sick person, or which may bring on dangerous complications. In this matter the judgment of the doctor or of an experienced nurse may be taken as to the seriousness of the sickness, as well as to the beginning of convalescence. It is according to the spirit of the law to interpret both in a wide sense. On the other hand, the mere fact that a religious is obliged to remain in her room by reason of a sprain, for example, is not sufficient, since the Code specifies persons who are *seriously* ill. Such a person, however, could make use of the permission granted in canon 522.[23]

The ordinary, extraordinary, special, and supplementary confessor, as well as the confessor summoned by a sick religious may enter the papal cloister of nuns for the purpose of hearing her confession. The *occasional* confessor of canon 522 is not accorded this privilege.[24]

Art. 3. **Appointment and Qualities of Confessors of Religious Women** (cc. 524–527).

---

[22] Code Com., Feb. 12, 1935; *AAS*, 27-92; *Digest*, II, p. 161; *Eccl. Review*, 1935, v. 92, p. 506.
[23] Cf. 5, d, p. 247, last paragraph.
[24] S. C. Rel., Feb. 6, 1924; *AAS*, 16–96, III, 2, g; *Digest*, I, p. 318.

The local Ordinary freely chooses and appoints all classes of confessors of religious women in his diocese (c. 876), except in the case of a monastery of nuns subject to a regular superior. In this case the superior has the right to *present* both ordinary and extraordinary confessors for monasteries of nuns subject to him to the local Ordinary who then *approves* them, and the Ordinary may also appoint them should the regular superior neglect to do so (c. 525).

The Ordinary may choose all classes of confessors for religious women from the secular or from the religious clergy with the permission of their superiors; they should be priests outstanding in prudence and moral repute. The *ordinary* and *extraordinary* confessors should be *forty* years old, but the Ordinary may dispense in this matter of age for a just reason (c. 524, § 1). These confessors should have no authority in the external forum over the religious whose confessions they are to hear, nor should they interfere in any way with the internal or external government of the community (c. 524, § 3).

The *ordinary* confessor, as a general rule, should be appointed for a period of three years only, nor should he be appointed as extraordinary confessor, or reappointed as ordinary confessor to the same community until one year after the completion of his office (c. 524, § 2). However, in certain cases the Ordinary may confirm him in office for a second and even a third triennium: (1) if he cannot make other provisions because of a dearth of priests capable of fulfilling this office; (2) *or* if the greater part of the community, counting all its members, even the lay sisters, by secret ballot request the reappointment of the same confessor; for those who dissent other provision must be made, if they so desire (c. 526); (3) by reason of his quinquennial faculties,[25] the Ordinary may confirm the ordinary confessor in his office for a fourth, or even a fifth triennium, *provided* that the consent of the community be obtained by secret ballot as explained in 2 above, and other provision be made for those who dissent, if they so desire.

Observing the norms laid down in canon 880, the Ordinary may, for a grave reason, remove both the ordinary and the extraordinary confessor from office, even though the monastery of nuns be subject to regulars, and the confessor himself be a regular; he must, however, inform the regular superior, if the nuns are subject to the latter, but he need give no reason for the removal to anybody, except to the Holy See if it should so require (c. 527).

---

[25] *Digest,* II, p. 36.

Art. 4. Chaplains and Preachers. In the case of *nonexempt* lay religious institutes, the local Ordinary has the right to appoint chaplains, and to approve preachers. Since nonexempt lay religious are under the pastoral care of the local parish priest, it is not absolutely necessary to appoint separate chaplains. One of the assistants may act as such. When the Ordinary deems it advisable to appoint chaplains, especially for large communities, he may, if he so wishes, withdraw the community from the care of the parish priest, and grant the chaplain those parochial powers for the community (cf. cc. 464, § 2, 514, §§ 3 and 4, 1230, § 5).

In the case of *exempt* lay religious institutes, the regular superior appoints both chaplains and preachers, who then exercise full pastoral care over the community, independently of the parish priest. Preachers appointed by the regular lay superior, either before or after their appointment, obtain faculties to preach from the local Ordinary, in conformity with the prescriptions of canon 1338, § 3. Should the regular superior neglect to appoint chaplains and preachers for the exempt lay religious communities, then the Ordinary will provide (**c. 529**).

N.B. No chaplain or preacher may preach to a lay religious community, even though it be exempt, before he has received faculties to preach in the diocese from the local Ordinary (cf. c. 1338, § 3).

Art. 5. Account of Conscience. *All superiors* are strictly forbidden to induce their subjects, in any way whatever, to make a manifestation of conscience to them. *Subjects,* on the other hand, are not forbidden to open their souls freely and spontaneously to their superiors; indeed, it is desirable that they go to their superiors with filial confidence, and, if the superiors be *priests,* expose their doubts and troubles of conscience likewise (**c. 530**).[26]

Section 5. Temporal Goods and Their Administration (cc. 531–537)

PRELIMINARY SURVEY

Temporal Goods (c. 531)
Administration of Temporal Goods (cc. 532–533)
Financial Account to Be Rendered (c. 535)
Alienation of Temporal Goods (c. 534)
Responsibility for Debts Incurred (c. 536)
Gifts and Donations (c. 537)

---

[26] For a detailed explanation of this delicate subject, read Creusen-Ellis, *Religious Men and Women in the Code,* ed. 3, pp. 94–99.

Art. 1. Temporal Goods. All material things which possess an economic value, that is, a value in use or exchange which can be computed in money.

1. *Ecclesiastical goods* are temporal goods owned by any *moral* person in the Church, destined for the use and purposes proper to that moral person (cf. c. 1497, § 1). It may be stated here once and for all that the canons on temporal goods do not apply to the property, whether real or personal, owned by *individual* religious. Such property is not *ecclesiastical* property but is governed by the canons relating to the vow of poverty (cf. cc. 569, 580 sqq.).

2. *Ownership of temporal goods:* Not only every religious institute, but every province and house as well, is capable of acquiring and possessing property with fixed revenues, unless the capacity to do so be excluded or limited by the rules and constitutions **(c. 531).** As far as the general law of the Church is concerned, every religious house or community has the right to acquire and possess property. In some institutes the ownership of the smaller houses, according to the constitutions, is vested in the mother house, but at least the larger houses should be economically independent according to the mind of the Church. The constitutions will determine what amount of the net income is to be contributed each year by the individual houses toward the support of the province, by the provinces toward the support of the general institute. The constitutions may allow the general chapter to determine this amount.

Art. 2. Administration of Temporal Goods. The property of the institute, of the province, and of the house is to be administered conformably to the constitutions. Besides superiors, those officials who are empowered by the constitutions can, within the limits of their office, validly incur expenses and perform the juridical acts necessary for ordinary administration **(c. 532).** In addition to the norms laid down by the constitutions, administrators of ecclesiastical property belonging to religious communities will find further directions in canons dealing with the administration of ecclesiastical property in general (cc. 1518–1528).

1. *Investment of money:* To invest money means to exchange it for non-consumable and productive goods, such as real estate, stocks, bonds, etc. Money deposited in a bank at call is not considered as invested. It is the duty of every administrator of ecclesiastical goods to invest money left over after all expenses are paid (and not needed for ordinary running expenses) for the advantage of the community and with the consent of the proper authority (c. 1523, 4°).

2. *Permissions required to invest money: a. In religious orders of men:* (1) permission of the local Ordinary is required for the investment of money given to a parish or mission, or to an individual religious for the benefit of a parish or mission, as well as for *every change* in the investment of such funds **(c. 533, § 1, 4°)**; (2) for all other investments the permission of their own major superiors according to the constitutions is required and suffices.

b. In monasteries of nuns and in diocesan congregations: permission of the local Ordinary is required for *every* investment of money, as well as for *every change* in investment. Furthermore, nuns require the permission of the regular superior as well, if they be subject to him **(c. 533, § 1, 1°).**

c. In pontifical congregations of men: permission of the local Ordinary is required for the investment of trust funds given to a religious *house* for the benefit of local divine worship or for local charities, as well as for the investment of money given to a parish or mission, or to an individual religious for the benefit of a parish or mission **(c. 533, § 1, 4°)**; this permission must be obtained anew for *every change* of investment in the above-mentioned cases **(c. 533, § 2)**. In all other cases the permission of major superiors according to the constitutions is required and suffices.

d. In pontifical congregations of women: permission of the local Ordinary is required for the investment (*a*) of the dowries of the professed **(c. 533, § 1, 2°)**; (*b*) of trust funds for local divine worship or for local charities **(c. 533, § 1, 3°)**; (*c*) for *every change* of investment in both cases **(c. 533, § 2)**. For all other investments the permission of their own major superiors according to the constitutions is required and suffices.

Art. 3. Financial Account to Be Rendered. 1. *To the Holy See:* The Abbot Primate, the superior of a monastic congregation, as well as the superior general of every *pontifical* institute (order or congregation) must render a financial account every five years as part of the quinquennial report **(c. 510).**[27]

2. *To the local Ordinary:* (*a*) superiors of *all clerical religious* must give an account, as often as requested to do so, regarding money given to a parish or mission, as well as that given to an individual religious for the benefit of a parish or mission; (*b*) superiors of *pontifical congregations of religious men* must give an account, as often as requested

---

[27] See questions 44–64 of quinquennial report; cf. footnote 14, p. 242.

to do so, regarding trust funds given to the religious *house* for local divine worship or for local charities (c. 535, § 3, 2°); (*c*) *all superiors of religious women* must, at the time of the ecclesiastical visitation, or oftener if required, render an account of the dowries of the professed (c. 535, § 2) as well as of trust funds given for local divine worship, or for local charities (c. 535, § 3, 2°); (*d*) superiors of *all monasteries of nuns,* even though exempt, must render an account of all the goods of the monastery *once a year,* or more frequently if thus prescribed by the constitutions (c. 535, § 1, 1°); (*e*) *local superiors in diocesan congregations* must render an account of all the goods of the house *as often as required* (c. 535, § 3, 1°).

Art. 4. Alienation of Temporal Goods (c. 534). (1) Before defining alienation, it will be well to explain briefly the various ways in which *money* is used: (*a*) it may be *consumed* by donation, or by exchange for other nonproductive goods, or in payment of a debt. It is then said to be *spent;* (*b*) it may be *capitalized,* that is, converted into permanent investments of equal value which are productive of revenue, e.g., real estate, stocks, bonds, etc. Such money thus becomes *invested capital.* (2) It may be *saved,* when strictly, or at least morally speaking, it remains in the possession of the owner, or can be obtained by him in a short time, e.g., a bank deposit which can be withdrawn at will, or after six months or a year. (3) Money is termed *free capital* before it is invested. The Code of Canon Law is not concerned with the expenditure of free capital. It may be used freely to pay off debts, to purchase necessary supplies, or it may be set aside for definite future uses, e.g., building fund, etc. In the latter case, however, it may be used only for the purpose for which it is destined. While it is the duty of every administrator to invest the free capital which is left over at the end of the year after all current expenses have been paid, and which is not needed for running expenses or for the payment of debts, nevertheless, until such surplus money is actually invested, it remains free capital, and does not come under the prescriptions of the Code regarding alienation. Provisions of the constitutions regarding the use of free capital must, of course, be observed.

1. By *alienation,* then, is meant any act by which the right of ownership of property representing invested capital is transferred to another, either in whole or in part. Such acts are, for instance, sale, free gift, exchange, mortgage, etc.

2. *Certain conditions must be observed* in the alienation of ecclesiastical goods owned by any moral person in the Church: (*a*) *a written*

appraisal of the property to be alienated must be obtained from reliable experts; (*b*) there must be a just cause for the alienation; (*c*) permission of the legitimate superior; (*d*) the property must be sold to the person offering the highest price (all things considered); (*e*) the money obtained from the alienation must be invested in a prudent, safe, and useful investment (cc. 1530, 1531). These conditions will be explained in greater detail under the canons mentioned. Here there is question of the *permission* required to alienate. Since the same permissions are required for religious to contract debts, they will be stated under one head.

3. *Conditions required to contract debts:* (*a*) permission of legitimate superior (see Art. 5); (*b*) written statement of all debts and obligations burdening the moral person at the time of petition; otherwise the permission obtained will be invalid (**c. 534, § 2**); (*c*) assurance that interest on debt can be met from current revenue; (*d*) plan for sinking fund which will pay off the capital debt within reasonable time (**c. 536, § 5**).

Art. 5. Permissions Required to Alienate Property and to Contract Debts (*under pain of invalidity*).[28]

1. *Permission of the Holy See is required:*

a. To alienate: (1) any *precious* object as defined in canon 1497 which is worth more than $200 (c. 534); (2) other property of any kind worth *more than* $6,000 (c. 534); (3) *votive offerings* of any value whatsoever;[29] (4) *notable* relics or images (c. 1281); (5) other relics or images *in great veneration* among the faithful (c. 1281).

b. To contract debts amounting to more than $6,000 (c. 534). According to the present practice of the S. Congregation of Religious, all religious in the United States who wish to contract a debt of over $6,000 must first obtain the written approval of the local Ordinary or (and) of the Apostolic Delegate, to be forwarded with the petition for the indult to contract the debt.

c. To lease property at *more* than $6,000 per annum, *and* for *more* than nine years (c. 1541, § 2, 1°).

2. *Permission of major religious superiors is required:* to alienate property worth *up to* $6,000, or to contract debts *up to* $6,000. The constitutions will determine which superiors may grant such permissions, but in all cases the superior must first obtain the consent

---

[28] Values indicated mean values in gold. See p. 770.
[29] S. C. Conc., July 13, 1919; *AAS*, 11-416, *Digest*, I, p. 729.

of his council or chapter by secret vote (c. 534). Superiors have a grave obligation to inform their council or chapter with all sincerity about the management of temporal affairs, and to submit such matters to the deliberative vote of their council or chapter when this is prescribed. Councilors and chapter members, on their part, have a grave obligation to exercise that control in the management of temporal affairs which is entrusted to their vigilance by the common law of the Church and by their constitutions.

3. Besides the above permissions, *the permission of the local Ordinary is required:* to alienate property worth less than $6,000, or to incur debts amounting to less than $6,000 in the case of *nuns and of diocesan religious;* moreover, nuns require the further permission of the regular superior if their monastery be subject to him. In all these cases the permission is to be given in writing (c. 534).

Art. 6. Responsibility for Debts Incurred. The moral person contracting debts and obligations, whether it be an institute, a province, or a house, is itself alone responsible for them (c. 536, § 1). The fact that the superiors have given the necessary permission to contract such debts, does not make them responsible. This fact should be made known to creditors at the time the debt is contracted in order to avoid misunderstandings. Should an institute wish to assume responsibility for the debts of a province or house, it may do so provided the consent of the proper authorities is obtained according to the constitutions.

1. If a *religious with solemn vows* contracts a debt with the permission of his superiors, that moral person whose superior gave the permission is responsible, that is, either the institute in the case of the superior general, or the province in the case of the provincial superior, or the house in the case of the local superior, the reason being that the religious in question has lost the right of ownership by reason of his solemn vow of poverty (c. 536, § 2).

2. If *a religious with simple vows* contracts a debt, he alone is responsible, unless he was doing business for the institute with the superior's permission.

Should a religious contract debts without any permission of superiors whatsoever, he alone is responsible, not the institute, nor the province or house. In this case a religious with simple vows would have to pay the debt out of his own patrimony, a religious with solemn vows, by the fruits of his labor, since he owns nothing (c. 536, § 3).

It is a fixed rule, however, that suit may be brought against the person (moral or physical) who has profited by the contract entered into (c. 536, § 4), since no one is allowed to enrich himself at the expense of another.

Art. 7. Gifts and Donations. Gifts may not be bestowed from the goods of a house, province, or institute. Exception is made for alms and for other causes when given with the consent of the proper superior and in conformity with the constitutions (c. 537). Superiors, therefore, may and ought to give alms in proportion to the resources of the community; they may likewise on occasion present gifts to benefactors and friends of the community or institute to show their gratitude and appreciation of favors received.

CASES AND QUESTIONS

1. How does a religious institute (*religio*) differ from a society of men or women living in common? (Cc. 488, 1° and 673, § 1).

2. What is the difference between: order and congregation? Nun and sister? Solemn vow and simple vow? (Cc. 488, 2°, 7°; 579).

3. The mother superior of a diocesan congregation wishes to establish a house in a diocese different from that in which the mother house is located. What permissions does she need? (Cc. 495, § 1; 497, § 1).

4. The superior general of a pontifical congregation wishes to close a house in a certain diocese. What permissions does he need? (C. 498).

5. In the election of the mother general held in chapter, may the Bishop or his delegate allow *postulation* merely because the majority of the sisters wish to have the same mother general for a third consecutive term? (See Letter of S. Cong. of Religious, March 9, 1920, *AAS*, 12 [1920], 365; *Digest*, I, p. 276).

6. A novice of a clerical religious institute is dying in a hospital. Who has the right to administer Viaticum and Extreme Unction? The religious superior or the pastor in whose parish the hospital is located? (C. 514, § 1).

7. Are sisters obliged to go to confession to the *extraordinary* confessor? (C. 521, § 1).

8. The *ordinary* confessor is sick. May the sister superior call in the *supplementary* confessor to hear the confessions of the community? May she ask a visiting priest who has diocesan faculties only to take the place of the ordinary confessor? (Cc. 521, § 2; 522).

9. The chaplain of a large convent is also a *supplementary* confessor, and generously provides the sisters with the opportunity for daily confession. May the sisters who use this privilege abstain regularly from confessing to the *ordinary* confessor, or are they obliged to confess to him also every week? (Cc. 520, § 1; 521, § 2).

10. Is a sister obliged to ask permission from her superior to leave the house in order to go to confession to the *occasional* confessor provided by canon 522? (See private answer of Secy. of S. C. Rel., Dec. 1, 1921, *Digest*, I, p. 296).

11. In connection with the occasional confessor of canon 522, what is meant by the phrase, "in a place approved for the confessions of women"? (See Code Com., Feb. 12, 1935, *AAS*, 27 [1935], 92; *Digest*, II, p. 161).

12. Father Peregrinus, a priest having diocesan faculties in his home diocese in California, is visiting his sister who is a religious in a convent in Wisconsin. While there a sister who is seriously ill asks him to hear her confession. May he do so validly and licitly? (Cc. 523; 874, § 1).

13. The Religious of Our Lady of Studies wish to add a wing to their popular finishing school. This wing is to cost $25,000. The sisters have $10,000 cash on hand. The *alumnae* pledge themselves to raise another $10,000. The religious will have to borrow the balance from the local bank where they can get the cash without giving any security. What permissions do they need to build the new wing? (C. 534, § 1).

14. Father Paternus, provincial of a religious congregation approved by the Holy See, is confronted with the payment of a mortgage due February 1 amounting to $6,500. He has only $1,500 cash on hand, so he decides to sell two pieces of property, one worth $4,000, the other, $2,000. He gets the consent of his councilors and pays off the mortgage with the cash on hand and the proceeds of the sale of the two pieces of property. Were his actions valid and licit? (C. 534, § 1).

Readings:

Browne, *Manifestation of Conscience*, IER., 71 (1935) 415–419; Clancy, *The Local Religious Superior*, C.U., 1943; Ellis, *General Chapter of Elections*, RfR. 1 (1942), 146–156; *General Chapter of Affairs*, RfR. 1 (1942), 253–258; *Bursar General of a Religious Institute*, RfR. 3 (1944), 329–334; *General Councilors of a Religious Institute*, RfR. 4 (1945), 13–21; *Care of Sick Religious*, RfR. 3 (1944), 167–174; *Superiors and Manifestation of Conscience*, RfR. 2 (1943), 101–108; Farrell, *Rights and Duties of Local Ordinary Regarding Congregations of Women Religious of Pontifical Approval*, C.U., 1941; Flanagan, *Canonical Erection of Religious Houses*, C.U., 1943; Gallik, *Rights and Duties of Bishops Regarding Diocesan Sisterhoods*, St. Paul, 1939; Lewis, *Chapters in Religious Institutes*, C.U., 1943; Mahoney, *Confessions of Religious Women in Exceptional Cases*, AER. 74 (1926), 33-44; McCormick, *Confessors of Religious*, C.U., 1926; Orth, *Approbation of Religious Institutes*, C.U., 1931; Parsons, *Canonical Elections*, C.U., 1939; Reilly, *Visitation of Religious*, C.U., 1938.

AER. — American Ecclesiastical Review; C.U. — Published by The Catholic University of America, Washington, D. C.; IER. — Irish Ecclesiastical Record; RfR. — Review for Religious.

CHAPTER VII

MEMBERSHIP

Any Catholic who is not debarred by a legitimate impediment, and is prompted by a right intention, and is fit to bear the burdens of the religious life, may be admitted into religion (c. 538). In these concise terms the legislator sums up the essential conditions and the sufficient signs of vocation to the religious life. Legitimate impediments are those listed in the Code (c. 542) and in the constitutions; the will to serve God more perfectly by the practice of the evangelical counsels constitutes a right intention; while the mental, moral, and physical qualities necessary to bear the burdens and fulfill the offices of the religious life, make one fit for that life.

Section 1. The Postulantship (cc. 539–541)

By postulantship is meant a time of probation which is preliminary to the taking of the habit. It is intended to give superiors an opportunity to observe the candidates, and the candidates an opportunity of becoming acquainted with the general obligations of the religious life.

A postulantship of at least six entire months is required: (1) in all institutes with perpetual vows: (*a*) of all religious women; (*b*) in male institutes, of *lay brothers only* (that is, lay religious devoted exclusively to manual labor; hence not all religious brothers are lay brothers, *conversi,* in the canonical sense). (2) In institutes with temporary vows only, it is left to the constitutions to determine the necessity and duration of the postulantship. The major superior may prolong the time prescribed for the postulantship, but not beyond another term of six months (c. 539).

The postulantship must be made in the novitiate house, or in some other house of the institute where the religious discipline prescribed by the constitutions is faithfully observed. In this latter case the postulant is to be under the special care of an experienced religious (c. 540, § 1).

As to dress, the postulants need not wear a uniform, but should be modestly clothed. They may not wear the habit of the novices. In monasteries of nuns, they are bound by the law of enclosure (c. 540, §§ 2, 3).

Before beginning the novitiate, postulants must make a spiritual retreat of at least eight entire days, and, according to the discretion of the confessor, a general confession of their past life (c. 541). As to the nature of the retreat, see canon 595, § 1.

Section 2. The Novitiate (cc. 542–571)

PRELIMINARY SURVEY

Conditions Required for Entrance (cc. 542–546)
Documents Required of Aspirants (c. 544)
The Dowry (cc. 547–551)
Canonical Examinations (c. 552)
Training of Novices (cc. 553–558; 564–567)
Master of Novices (cc. 559–563)
Second Year of Novitiate (Instruction)
Confessors of Novices (c. 566)
Novices and Their Temporal Goods (cc. 568–570)
Termination of the Novitiate (c. 571)

Art. 1. Conditions Required for Entrance to the Novitiate (cc. 542–552).

1. *Superior competent to admit:* The right of admitting candidates to the novitiate belongs to major religious superiors, designated by the constitutions. Major superiors must, moreover, have the consent of the council or chapter, or at least consult the same, as the constitutions require (c. 543). Hence the local Ordinary no longer enjoys the right to admit novices to a diocesan congregation, as he did before the Code.

2. *Impediments to valid admission* (c. 542, 1°): The following persons cannot be *validly* admitted to the novitiate:

a. Catholics who have voluntarily joined a *non-Catholic* or *atheistic* sect.[1] Hence converts to the Catholic faith are not included in this impediment.

b. Those who have not completed their fifteenth year (c. 555).

c. Those who enter religion under the influence of *violence, grave*

---

[1] Code Com., Oct. 16, 1919, *AAS*, 11-477, n. 7; *Digest*, I, p. 298; July 30, 1934, *AAS*, 26-494; *Digest*, II, p. 286.

fear, or *fraud:* also those whom the superior received by reason of the same influences. Hence if a postulant while being examined for admission concealed a disease or a family condition which *he knew or suspected* would certainly have caused his exclusion, his admission is invalid, and any subsequent profession would also be invalid.

d. Married persons, as long as the marriage bond lasts. The Holy See dispenses very rarely, and only in the case of elderly persons.

e. Those who are, or have been, bound by the vows of *religious profession.* Whoever, therefore, has left a religious institute after taking vows, cannot validly re-enter the same institute, nor be admitted validly to any other institute, without an indult from the Holy See.

f. Those who are *liable to punishment* because they have committed a grave crime of which they have been or can be accused. Every crime supposes a grave fault, hence this impediment requires a crime of *special* gravity, and would not include the violation of some police regulation, or other merely penal law. Liability supposes the probability of denunciation and of an unfavorable judgment. The good name of the religious state nevertheless requires caution in such cases. The violation of an *unjust* law would not create this impediment.

g. A *Bishop,* whether residential or titular, even though merely nominated by the Roman Pontiff, and not yet consecrated.

h. Clerics who by a disposition of the Holy See are bound by oath to devote themselves to the service of their diocese or of the missions, for that period of time for which their oath binds them. The terms employed in this canon seem to imply a *special* provision of the Holy See which creates a transient obligation, such as that assumed by students of certain ecclesiastical colleges who are ordained with a promise under oath to devote themselves for a fixed time to the service of some diocese or mission;[2] hence the impediment does not seem to refer to the *general* promise made under oath according to the provisions of canon 981, § 1, since no reference is made to this canon in our text, although such references are common in the Code.

N.B. Ignorance of the above-mentioned impediments does not excuse from the law (see c. 16).

3. *Impediments to licit admission* (c. 542, 2°): Though their admission would be valid, it is *unlawful* to admit to the novitiate:

a. Clerics in sacred orders, without *consulting* the local Ordinary, or *against his will* if his objection be based on the serious harm to

---

[2] The Pontifical College Josephinum, Worthington, Ohio, is an example.

souls that the withdrawal of such clerics would cause, when this loss cannot be avoided by any other means.

b. Persons who are *in debt and insolvent*. If the debt be small and the institute be willing to pay it, the impediment ceases.

c. Persons *charged with the administration* of temporal affairs which might cause the institute to be involved in lawsuits or other difficulties.

d. Children who are *obliged to support* their parents or grandparents who are in *grave* need; likewise *parents* (father or mother) whose help is needed for the support and education of their children.

e. Those who in religion would be *destined for the priesthood,* from which, however, they are debarred by an irregularity or other canonical impediment.

f. Those who *belong to an Oriental rite* may not enter an institute of the Latin rite without the written permission of the Sacred Congregation for the Oriental Church. This permission is not needed for such persons to enter the novitiate in religious institutes of the Latin rite, provided they are being trained for the establishment of religious houses and provinces of the Oriental rite.[3] Nuncios, Internuncios, and Apostolic Delegates, however, had special faculties to permit Catholics of Oriental rites (but not priests) who live in their territory to change to the Latin rite under certain circumstances. These faculties have recently been withdrawn.[4] The permission is usually granted only temporarily at first, for the period of the novitiate, and permanently only upon admission to the religious profession. Hence two petitions will have to be made to the Holy See.

g. Those who have *left a seminary*. This impediment is contained in a decree issued jointly by the S. Congregation of Religious and the S. Congregation of Seminaries and Universities, July 25, 1941. The term "has left" is to be taken strictly; hence superiors may receive a seminarian who leaves a seminary in order to enter a religious institute (cf. *Digest,* II, pp. 426 and 166).

N.B. The Holy See alone can dispense from the impediments listed above. Besides these canonical impediments, individual institutes may have other impediments listed in their constitutions, from which the superior general of a pontifical institute can usually dispense with the approval or advice of his council. In case the constitutions do not grant him this power, he will have to obtain such dispensations from the

---

[3] Code Com., Nov. 10, 1925, ad VI, *AAS*, 17-583; *Digest*, I, p. 298.
[4] S. C. Or., Dec. 6, 1928, *AAS*, 20-416; *Digest*, I, p. 85; Nov. 23, 1940, *AAS*, 33-28; *Digest*, II, p. 50.

Holy See. In diocesan congregations the local Ordinary can grant dispensations from impediments contained in the constitutions, since he first approved them.

The Code does not require the consent of parents, but allows anyone who has completed fifteen years of age to enter the novitiate. It will, however, at times be a duty of charity or obedience to wait for this consent, at least until the candidate is of age according to civil law; prudence may dictate that superiors do not admit minors to the novitiate without the consent of their parents.

Art. 2. Documents Required of Aspirants (c. 544). In every institute, all aspirants, before being admitted to the novitiate, must present:

1. a certificate of their *baptism and confirmation;*

2. *testimonial letters:*

a. All male aspirants must furnish testimonial letters from the Ordinary of the place of origin (c. 90), as well as from the Ordinary of any other place in which, after completing their fourteenth year, they have lived for more than a year morally continuous, all customs to the contrary being abolished. Drawing a parallel from the morally continuous year required for a valid novitiate (c. 556) canonists consider that more than a month's absence during the year would break its moral continuity. Hence boys who attend a boarding school, but return home for the summer vacations, would not be required to obtain testimonial letters from the Ordinary in whose territory the school is located.

b. For those who have been in a seminary or *ecclesiastical* college testimonial letters must also be furnished by the rector of the seminary or college, after consultation with the local Ordinary;

c. For those who have been in the postulantship or novitiate of another religious institute, testimonial letters must be had from the major religious superior.

d. For *clerics* (at least tonsured, c. 108), besides the certificate of ordination, testimonial letters from the Ordinaries in whose dioceses they have spent more than a year morally continuous after ordination are required, together with the letters mentioned in *b.* above.

e. For a professed religious who is transferred to another institute by apostolic indult, the testimonial of the major superior of the institute which he has left suffices.

f. Besides these testimonial letters required by law, superiors who are empowered to admit aspirants to religion have a right to demand other testimonials which they may consider to be necessary or opportune.

g. For female aspirants, besides the testimonials required in *c.* above, careful investigation should be made regarding their character and conduct before they are received.

Qualities required in testimonial letters: (c. 545). 1. All testimonial letters mentioned above are to be given, signed and sealed, not to the aspirants themselves, but to the religious superiors, within three months, and gratuitously. In the case of those mentioned in *b.* and *c.* on page 262, the superior giving them must confirm them by oath.

2. If, for grave reasons, those who are to issue such testimonial letters, judge that they cannot answer the request, they must make their reasons known to the Holy See within three months.

3. Should they reply that the aspirant is not sufficiently known to them, the religious superior must supply the information needed by other careful, trustworthy investigation; should no reply be forthcoming, the superior who requested the information, shall inform the Holy See.

4. After having made a diligent investigation, even by secret inquiries, Ordinaries and superiors must give information in their testimonial letters (the accuracy of which they are under a grave obligation in conscience to assure) regarding birth, conduct, character, life, reputation, circumstances, and knowledge of the aspirant; whether he be under inquiry (c. 1939) or under any censure, irregularity, or any canonical impediment; whether his family has need of his help; finally, the reasons for dismissal or for voluntary leaving in the case of those who have been in a seminary, postulantship, or novitiate of another institute.

5. All superiors receiving the foregoing information are strictly obliged to keep secret not only the information itself, but the names of the persons who gave it (c. 546). Superiors, however, should remember that these testimonial letters contain information, not direction. Ultimately superiors will decide whether to admit a candidate or not, after having read the testimonial letters.

Art. 3. The Dowry (cc. 547–551). Dowry is capital (personal or real property) entrusted to the institute by a new member so that the revenues derived therefrom may serve for her support. The dowry will naturally be larger in a contemplative order than in an institute whose works (teaching, nursing), will certainly provide a part of the resources needed to support the community.

1. *Amount of dowry: a. In monasteries of nuns* the amount of dowry is determined by the constitutions or by lawful custom. It must be given to the monastery before the taking of the habit, or it should at least be guaranteed at that time by some document which is binding in civil law, and, in this case, it must be handed over at least before profession (c. 547, §§ 1, 2).

b. In institutes of simple vows the constitutions are to be observed regarding the dowry and the manner in which it shall be made up (c. 547, § 3). Frequently the constitutions provide that a *professional* diploma or a teacher's certificate shall supply, at least in part, the lack of a dowry.

c. Only the Holy See can dispense entirely or in part from the dowry prescribed by the constitutions of pontifical institutes; in diocesan congregations, however, the local Ordinary may dispense (c. 547, § 4).

2. *Administration of dowry: a. During the lifetime* of the religious her dowry is absolutely untransferable and inalienable; it may not even be used to put up a building or to pay debts (c. 549);

b. After the first profession of the religious, the superioress with her council, and with the consent of the local Ordinary (and of the regular superior if the monastery be subject to him) must put the dowry into a safe, lawful, and productive investment (c. 549);

c. The dowry must be prudently and honestly administered in the monastery, or in the house in which the superior general or the provincial superior habitually resides (c. 550, § 1); Ordinaries of places must carefully watch over the administration of dowries, and demand an account of them especially in their visitation (c. 550, § 2);

d. If, from whatever cause, a professed religious with either solemn or simple vows leaves the institute, her dowry must be returned to her intact, but not the interest already derived therefrom (c. 551, § 1);

e. If, by virtue of an apostolic indult, a professed religious is transferred to another institute, during her new novitiate the interest on the dowry, and after her profession, the dowry itself must be given to the latter institute; if the religious passes to another monastery of the same order, the dowry is to be given it on the day of transfer (c. 551, § 2);

f. The dowry becomes the absolute property of the monastery or institute on the death of the religious, even though she had made profession of temporary vows only (c. 548).

Art. 4. Canonical Examination (c. 552). At least two months before the date of admission to the novitiate, and again two months before profession of both temporary and perpetual vows whether simple or solemn, the superior of religious women, even though exempt, must inform the local Ordinary, so that he may, either personally or by delegate, conduct the canonical examination to be held at least one month before each of these ceremonies. The sole purpose of this examination is to make certain that the postulant, novice, or professed sister is acting with full *knowledge* of the case and with full *liberty*. Questions may, therefore, be asked her about the essential obligations of the three vows of religion, and the essential points of the constitutions, but neither the Ordinary nor his delegate is to examine her as to her vocation, or to approve her admission. These latter points are to be determined by the confessor and the religious superior. While the Ordinary or his delegate may not demand any fee for this examination, it is not forbidden to accept traveling expenses.

Art. 5. Training of Novices (cc. 553–571).

1. *Novitiate house:* The novitiate begins with the reception of the habit, or in any other manner prescribed by the constitutions (c. 553). It must be made in a novitiate house, established according to the constitutions, and with the permission of the Holy See in the case of a pontifical institute. Only one novitiate is allowed in each institute, or in each province if it be divided into provinces. A special indult of the Holy See is required for the establishment of a second novitiate house in the same institute or province. In the novitiate house duly established superiors shall allow only such religious to live as are exemplary in their zeal for regular observance (c. 554).

2. *Requirements for a valid novitiate* (cc. 555–556): Besides freedom from impediments enumerated in canon 542, the novitiate, in order that it be *valid,* must be made: (*a*) after the fifteenth year has been completed (see c. 34, § 3, 3°); (*b*) in the novitiate house; (*c*) for an entire and uninterrupted year: this so-called *canonical year* is interrupted and must be begun over again: (1) if the novice leaves the novitiate house after being dismissed by the superior; (2) or if he leaves of his own accord without the permission of the superior, with the intention of not returning. The intention of not returning must be manifested externally either by the declaration of the interested party or by his way of acting; (3) or if he has actually been absent from the novitiate house for a period of *more than thirty days,* whether continuous or interrupted, for any reason whatsoever, even with the permission of superiors, and with the intention of returning (c. 556,

§ 1); if the novice, with the permission of superiors or constrained by force, has passed *more than fifteen* but not more than thirty days even interruptedly outside the precincts of the novitiate house but under the obedience of the superior, it is necessary and sufficient that he supply the number of days so passed outside; if the entire period of absence did not exceed fifteen days, superiors may prescribe that this period be supplied, though it is not required for validity (c. 556, § 2).

It is a solidly probable opinion which may be followed in practice that days of absence from the novitiate are to be counted from midnight to midnight, according to canon 32, § 1. Parts of the days are not counted.

Superiors must not allow novices to remain outside the precincts of the novitiate (even though not outside the novitiate house, e.g., in a hospital or school) except for a just and grave reason.

Transfer to another novitiate does not interrupt the novitiate, although the days spent in traveling from one novitiate to another must be counted as days of absence.[5]

Where there are two classes of members in an institute (clerics, choir religious, teaching or nursing sisters, etc., and lay religious destined for the housework) the novitiate made for one class is not valid for the other (c. 558). Should a novice, especially by reason of lack of intellectual capacity, ask or agree to pass from one class to the other after having made the greater part of his novitiate, it will be expedient to apply to the Holy See for a dispensation.

While the division into two classes mentioned above is common in the older orders and congregations, many modern congregations, though made up of lay religious (teaching brothers, nursing and teaching sisters), have no such provision in their constitutions. In such institutes this requirement for two classes in the novitiate would not hold, even though it be foreseen that certain novices will, after profession, be employed exclusively in the occupations usually reserved for lay brothers and lay sisters.

3. *The habit* prescribed for novices by the constitutions must be worn throughout the entire period of the novitiate, unless local circumstances determine otherwise (c. 557). The wearing of the habit, however, is not necessary for the validity of the novitiate.

Art. 6. Master of Novices. He must be at least *thirty-five* years old, professed for at least ten years from the date of his first vows, and eminent in prudence, charity, piety, and fidelity to regular observ-

---

[5] Code Com., July 13, 1930, *AAS*, 14-661; *Digest*, I. p. 301.

ance. In a clerical institute he must be a priest. If the large number of novices or some other just reason make it expedient to give him an assistant, the latter person must be at least *thirty* years old, and professed five years from the date of his first profession; he, like-wise, must be a priest in a clerical institute, and be endowed with other qualities needed and suitable for this office. Both should be free from all occupations which could hinder them in the care and guid-ance of the novices (c. 559). The constitutions will determine the manner of appointing the master of novices and his assistant, and if they prescribe a definite term of office, neither should be removed during that term without grave cause, and both may be reappointed indefinitely (c. 560).

Novices are subject to the authority of the master of novices and of the superior of the institute, and are obliged to obey them. The formation of the novices and the direction of the novitiate belong exclusively to the master of novices, and no one may interfere under any pretext whatsoever, except superiors in cases provided for by the constitutions. This restriction evidently does not apply to visitors, since they are delegates of the major superiors. As regards the general discipline of the religious house, the master of novices, his assistant, and the novices are subject to the local superior (c. 561).

The novitiate shall be, as far as possible, separated from that part of the house inhabited by the professed religious. No communication may be had between the novices and the professed except for special reason, and then only with the permission of the superior *or* of the master of novices. A separate place must be assigned to the lay-novices (c. 564).

The time of novitiate has for its object the forming of the mind of the novice by means of study of the rule and constitutions, by pious meditations and assiduous prayer, by instruction on those matters which pertain to the vows and the virtues, by exercises suitable for the rooting out of the germs of vice, for regulating the emotions of the soul, and for acquiring virtues. The lay-novices are to receive besides weekly conferences on Christian doctrine (c. 565, §§ 1, 2).

During the year of novitiate it is forbidden to *employ* the novices in the external duties of the institute, or in the ministry (preaching or hearing confessions), or in studies properly so called; the lay-brother novices may be employed in the duties of their state, but only within the religious house, in a subordinate capacity, and to that extent only which will not interfere with the exercises of the novitiate prescribed for their formation (c. 565, § 3). Since a serious study of our holy religion enters very naturally into the formation of the religious life, the S. Congregation of Religious deemed it opportune to issue an instruction[6] which prescribes that in all congregations of brothers and of religious women, all postulants and novices be given courses in religion, and that no one shall be admitted to profession without having passed an examination showing that he understands and knows how to explain the Christian doctrine satisfactorily.

During the course of the canonical year of novitiate, the master of novices must give the chapter or the major superior a report concerning the conduct of each of the novices. The constitutions will furnish further details about this obligation (c. 563).

Art. 7. Second Year of Novitiate. The S. Congregation of Religious has issued an instruction for the second year of novitiate[7] which is required by the constitutions of a large number of institutes, and all superiors are obliged to carry out the provisions of this instruction. The principal points are as follows: (1) even during the second year of novitiate, the spiritual formation of the novices shall be considered before every other duty; (2) the novices may be employed in the works of the institute if this is prescribed by the constitutions and, if their training demand it, the novices may be sent to other houses of the institute to be employed in the works of the institute, but only in a secondary capacity and under the direction and supervision of an older religious. The fact that there are not sufficient religious in some houses to carry on the works of the institute is never to be considered as a sufficient cause for sending the novices out of the novitiate; (3) two months before the time for profession the novice must put aside all exterior works so as to have leisure to prepare for this great act in the novitiate house itself.

Art. 8. Confessors of Novices (c. 566). (1) *In institutes of religious women,* the novices are governed by the general prescriptions of the Code regarding confessors for religious women (cc. 520–527); (2) *in institutes of men:* (a) there shall be one or more ordinary confessors, according to the number of novices, but the master of novices, his assistant, and the superior of the house may not hear the confessions of the novices unless they, of their own accord, and for a grave and urgent reason ask them to do so in particular cases (c. 891); in a clerical institute, the ordinary confessors of the novices must live in the novitiate

---

[6] S. C. Rel., Nov. 25, 1929, *AAS,* 22–28; *Digest,* I, p. 280.
[7] S. C. Rel., Nov. 3, 1921, *AAS,* 13–539; *Digest,* I, p. 302.

house; in a lay institute, they should at least visit the novitiate house frequently to hear the confessions of the novices; (*b*) besides the ordinary confessors, some other confessors are to be appointed to whom the novices may freely go in particular cases, and the master of novices is not to show that he is displeased if they do so; (*c*) at least four times a year the novices are to be given an extraordinary confessor to whom all must go, at least to receive his blessing; (*d*) all the novices enjoy the privilege accorded religious men in canon 519.

Privileges of novices: Novices enjoy all privileges and spiritual favors granted to the institute, and should they die during the course of the novitiate, they are entitled to the same suffrages as the professed (c. 567, § 1). They also enjoy the privileges of clerics (c. 614). During the novitiate, novices may not be promoted to orders (c. 567, § 2).

Art. 9. Novices and Their Temporal Goods. 1. *Disposition of property.* Novices may not renounce any benefices or dispose of any temporal goods they possess; should they do so before taking their vows, or put any encumbrances upon their property, such a renunciation or encumbrance is not only illicit, but null and void by law (c. 568).

2. *Cession of administration and income of temporal goods:* (*a*) at the end of the novitiate, before taking his first simple vows, whether temporary or perpetual, each novice must *cede the administration* of his property to whomsoever he wishes for the entire period during which he will be bound by simple vows; (*b*) unless the constitutions provide otherwise, he must also dispose freely of the use and usufruct or income of his property. Constitutions *approved before the Code* which restrict the freedom of the novice in the disposition of his revenues, are not contrary to the Code[8] (c. 569, § 1). The novice may turn over the administration and likewise the income of his property to his institute, if he wishes to do so. But if, before taking his vows he disposed of it in favor of other parties, he may not afterward change this disposition in favor of the institute later on (c. 580, § 3); (*c*) the novice need not comply with the regulations contained in (*a*) and (*b*) if he does not possess any property when he takes his first vows. Should he acquire property *after* profession of simple vows, he must then make the cession and disposition regarding this newly acquired property as described above, even though he had already made the same at the time of his first profession (c. 569, § 2).

3. In every religious *congregation* each novice, before making profession of temporary vows, shall *make a will* in which he freely disposes

---

[8] Code Com., Oct. 16, 1919, *AAS*, 11–478; *Digest*, I, p. 304.

of all the property he actually possesses or may subsequently possess (c. 569, § 3). This does not mean that the novice is to give his property away here and now; it means that he makes a *will* in the ordinary sense of that term: that is, he determines and indicates the person or persons whom he wishes to come into possession of his property *after his death. All* novices in a congregation are obliged to make a will, even though they be *minors,* and even though they possess no property at the time of their first profession.

4. *Expenses of the novitiate:* Superiors may require the payment of an amount prescribed by the constitutions, or by formal agreement, to defray the expenses incurred for food and clothing during the postulancy or the novitiate; no other compensation may be demanded. Should the postulant or novice leave the institute before the time of profession, all the things which he brought with him and which have not been consumed by use, must be returned to him (c. 570).

Art. 10. Termination of the Novitiate. (1) During the course of the novitiate the novice is free (canonically) to leave the institute at any time; (2) he may be dismissed by the superior or chapter, as the constitutions determine, for any just cause which need not be made known to him; (3) upon the completion of the novitiate, the novice, if judged suitable, should be admitted to the religious profession, otherwise he is to be dismissed; (4) should a doubt arise as to his fitness, the major superior may prolong the period of probation, but not beyond six months; (5) before pronouncing his vows, the novice must make a *spiritual* retreat of eight entire days. This retreat need not necessarily end on the very eve or on the day of the profession (c. 571).

Section 3. Religious Profession (cc. 572–586)

PRELIMINARY SURVEY

Art. 1. Religious Profession is the act by which a person embraces the religious state by taking the three public vows of poverty, chastity, and obedience, thus entering upon an agreement made with the institute, which, when accepted by the competent superior, creates a whole series of reciprocal rights and obligations between the institute and the religious.

Art. 2. Requirements for the Validity of Every Religious Profession (c. 572).

1. That he who makes it be of lawful age, that is, *sixteen* years completed for the temporary profession, *twenty-one* years completed for perpetual profession (**c. 573**); profession made on one's sixteenth or twenty-first birthday, respectively, would be invalid (c. 34, § 3, 3°).

2. That he be *admitted* to profession by the *lawful superior* according to the constitutions (**c. 572, § 1, 2°**). The council or chapter, according to the constitutions, will have a *deliberative* vote in the admission to the first temporary profession, but only a *consultative* vote for the perpetual profession, whether solemn or simple (**c. 575, § 2**).

3. That he shall have completed a *valid novitiate* according to the requirements of c. 555;

4. That the profession be made *without violence, grave fear,* or *fraud;*

5. That the profession be *expressed in formal terms;* hence tacit profession formerly tolerated in orders of men, is no longer valid. Even now a written formula is not required by the Code, although the attestation of the act of profession must be made in writing (**c. 576, § 2**).

6. That the profession shall be *received by the lawful superior* according to the constitutions, either personally or by his representative. It may be well here to note the difference between *admitting* to profession and *receiving* the profession: to admit to profession means to grant permission to make the profession; to receive the profession means to accept it in the name of the Church, either by virtue of one's own power, or as representative of the lawful superior. The priest who says the Mass during which profession is usually made in lay institutes does not receive the profession, but acts simply as a witness to the ceremony. It is the superior or his delegate who receives the profession in the name of the Church. In some congregations, however, the constitutions prescribe that the profession be received, not by the superior, but by the Bishop or his delegate. In this latter case, the Bishop must delegate the priest to receive the profession, otherwise it would be invalid.

Art. 3. For the Validity of Perpetual Profession (solemn or simple), it is also required that a period of *at least three years* of temporary vows precede the perpetual profession (c. 572, § 2). This temporary profession is imposed by the Code on all orders and congregations in which perpetual vows are taken, and is to be made at the end of the novitiate in the novitiate house. It is made for a period of three years, unless the constitutions prescribe an annual profession during three years, or if the novice will not have completed his twenty-first year within three years, he will make the temporary profession for the length of time which intervenes between his first temporary profession and his twenty-first birthday. The lawful superior may prolong the duration of the temporary profession by directing the religious to renew it at the end of three years, but such prolongation may not be extended beyond a second period of three years (c. 574). The superior who has thus prolonged the period of temporary vows for one, two, or three years in order further to test the candidate for perpetual profession, may always, if he judge it fitting, allow the perpetual profession to be made sooner.

When the period of temporary vows has expired, the religious shall either make his perpetual profession (simple or solemn according to the constitutions) or he shall return to the world (c. 637); however, should he prove unworthy, he may be dismissed by the lawful superior, at any time during the period of temporary profession, according to the norms laid down in c. 647 (c. 575).

Art. 4. The Rite Prescribed in the constitutions shall be observed in every religious profession. The profession may be made anywhere within the religious house. When it is made during Mass, it should take place after the Communion of the priest.[9] In the constitutions of certain congregations approved by the Holy See it is prescribed that the profession be made after the Gospel of the Mass.

A written document attesting to the act of profession is to be drawn up, and signed by the professed himself and at least by the superior or his delegate who has received the profession in the name of the Church. This document is to be kept in the archives of the institute. In the case of profession of solemn vows, the superior who has received the vows must notify the parish priest of the parish in which the professed was baptized who will record the same in the baptismal record as prescribed by c. 470, § 2 (c. 576).

---

[9] S. C. Rit., *Decr. Auth.*, nn. 3836 and 3912 in which details are given.

Art. 5. Renewal of Vows. There are two kinds of renewal of vows, one of obligation, the other of devotion.

1. The *obligatory renovation* required by the Code is a new profession of temporary vows which will soon expire. No interval of time may be allowed to pass between the expiration of previous vows and the renewal. The latter must be made, at the latest, on the anniversary day of the former profession. For a just cause, however, superiors may allow the renewal to be anticipated, but not earlier than one month before the day on which the vows expire (c. 577). In case of anticipated renewal, however, the obligation assumed begins only on the day on which the previous vows expire, and runs for the full time for which the vows were renewed.

2. The *renewal of devotion,* usually prescribed by the constitutions, has for its purpose the renewal of fervor with which each religious should observe the temporary or perpetual vows which are still in force. It in no wise affects the period of time for which the vows were taken, nor can it validate a profession which was invalid (c. 586, § 1).

Art. 6. Status of Religious Professed of Temporary Vows (c. 578).

1. They share in all the indulgences, privileges, and spiritual advantages which are enjoyed by the professed of perpetual vows (whether solemn or simple); should they die during the period of temporary vows, they have a right to the same suffrages;

2. They are bound by the same obligation to observe the rules and constitutions; those who are not in sacred orders are not bound by the *private* recitation of the divine office in institutes which are bound by the obligation of choir, unless the constitutions expressly declare otherwise.

3. They do not enjoy either active voice (the right to vote in chapter), or passive voice (the right to be eligible for office) unless the constitutions expressly so declare; the time, however, required by the constitutions to obtain these rights is to be counted from the time of the first temporary profession, unless the constitutions direct otherwise.

4. The obligation arising from *private* vows made before entering or before the first religious profession is suspended as long as he who made such private vows remains in religion (c. 1315).

Art. 7. Effects of the Profession of Simple Vows. The profession of simple vows, whether temporary or perpetual, makes acts contrary to the vows unlawful, but not invalid, unless the constitutions state the contrary; solemn profession makes them invalid (c. 579).

Art. 8. Special Effects of the Simple Vow of Poverty.

1. Every professed of simple vows keeps the ownership of his property, and the rights to acquire more property, unless the constitutions explicitly state the contrary (c. 580, § 1).

2. Should he acquire new property, he must again cede the administration of it, and dispose of its use and usufruct as explained in canon 569, page 269.

3. A professed religious may *change* the cession and disposition of his property made in accordance with c. 569, not indeed of his own accord, unless the constitutions allow this, but with the express permission of his superior general. *Nuns,* however, must have the authorization of the local Ordinary, as well as that of the regular superior if they be subject to him. This *change* of the cession and disposition of property may never be made so as to give the institute a notable part (a fourth, or certainly a third) of the revenues. In case the religious leaves his institute, he recovers complete control of his property, and the arrangements mentioned above cease to have any effect (c. 580, § 3).

4. Whatever the religious acquires by his industry or personal activity, or in behalf of the religious institute, becomes the property of the institute (c. 580, § 2). Such would be, for example, offerings given for the exercise of the sacred ministry; fees and royalties paid to authors; salaries of professors and teachers. A religious receives *in behalf of his institute* whatever is given for the community church or chapel, for the repair of the religious house, for the support of the novices, for the library, and the like. Besides, a religious is said to acquire in behalf of his institute whatever is given to him *because he is a religious,* for example, money given to buy a new habit, or to buy books which will be helpful to him in the exercise of the sacred ministry. Small gifts given to religious on special occasions such as feast days or jubilee days, or at Christmas time to a teacher by his pupils, are presumed to be given to the religious because he is a religious, not for personal reasons, unless the contrary is proved to be the case (cf. c. 1536, § 1).

5. In religious *congregations* it is forbidden the professed: (*a*) to abdicate gratuitously the dominion over their property by a voluntary deed of conveyance (*per actum inter vivos*) (c. 583, § 1), that is to give, sell, pledge, or loan property (whether real or personal) without compensation or equivalent consideration; (*b*) to change the will made before profession without the permission of the Holy See. In

urgent cases, however, the major superior, or if recourse cannot be had to him, the local superior may authorize him to change his will (c. 583, § 2).

6. One year after profession of any kind in religion, parochial benefices held by the professed are vacated; all other benefices are vacated after three years of profession[10] (c. 584). A religious who has made profession of *perpetual* vows, whether simple or solemn, loses his proper diocese which he had in the world (c. 585). Excardination from his diocese likewise follows upon perpetual profession (c. 115).

Art. 9. Special Effects of the Solemn Vow of Poverty.

1. By the solemn vow of poverty the professed religious loses his right to own or possess temporal goods; hence,

2. Within sixty days (but not before, under pain of invalidity) preceding the solemn profession, the professed of simple vows must renounce in favor of whomsoever he wishes, all the property which he actually possesses, on condition, however, of his solemn profession subsequently taking place. After the solemn profession has been made, all necessary measures must be taken at once to make the renunciation effective in civil law (c. 581).

3. All property which may come to the religious in any manner whatsoever after his solemn profession accrues to the order, province, or house, according to the constitutions; if the order cannot acquire or own such property, it becomes the property of the Holy See (c. 582) which not infrequently allows the order to administer it.

Art. 10. Invalid Profession. (1) A religious profession which is invalid by reason of an *external* impediment is not validated by any subsequent act (e.g., renewal of vows) but either a sanation must be obtained from the Holy See, or the profession must be renewed after the religious becomes aware that the former profession was null and void, and the impediment which caused it to be so, has either ceased or been dispensed from; (2) if the profession was null and void because of a *purely internal* defect of consent, it becomes validated by the giving of that internal consent, provided that the institute has not meanwhile revoked its own consent; (3) if serious arguments against the validity of the religious profession should arise, and the religious in question refuses, as a measure of precaution, either to renew his profession or to petition for its sanation, the matter shall be referred to the Holy See (c. 586).

---

[10] The S. C. Conc. solved an interesting case, April. 19, 1940, *AAS*, 32-374; *Digest*, II, p. 167.

CASES AND QUESTIONS

1. Are converts barred from entering religion? May a candidate enter the novitiate validly on his sixteenth birthday? (Cc. 542, 1°; 34, § 3, 3°; Code Com. Oct. 16, 1919, ad 7, *AAS*, 11 [1919], 477; *Digest*, I, p. 298).

2. A Syrian girl, belonging to a Maronite parish and attending the public school, goes to a school every Sunday afternoon to attend the catechetical instruction given by the good sisters for public school children. She becomes very much attached to the sisters and, at the age of seventeen, joins the congregation, makes her postulancy, novitiate, and first profession of vows in due form and time. Everything valid and licit? (C. 542, 2°).

3. A postulant's mother is very ill. The postulant goes home and remains there for forty days. Is the *postulantship* interrupted in such a way that it must be begun over again? (C. 539, § 1).

4. Who can dispense from the dowry? May the dowry be spent during the lifetime of the religious who brought it? (Cc. 547, § 4, 549).

5. John enters the novitiate on September 8, 1945, at 8:00 a.m. According to canon law, can he validly pronounce his first temporary vows on September 8, 1946, at 9:00 a.m.? (Cc. 555, § 1, 2°; 34, § 3, 3°).

6. Martha enters the novitiate on August 1, 1944. On September 1 she is taken to a hospital for an appendectomy; she returns to the novitiate on September 18. On December 5 she is called home because of the death of her father. She returns to the novitiate on December 16. Because of her delicate health she is transferred to another novitiate in Florida, leaving on March 1 and arriving there on March 6. What is **the total number of days Martha has lost? What is the earliest date on** which she can validly pronounce her first vows? (Cc. 556, §§ 1 and 2; 32).

7. On August 15, 1945, the sisters of a certain congregation celebrated their diamond jubilee. In order to have all the solemnities possible on this memorable day, Reverend Mother allowed:

   a) the novices who received the habit on August 15, 1944, to take their first temporary vows for one year (cc. 555, § 1, 2°; 34, § 3, 3°);

   b) the sisters who took temporary vows for one year on September 8, 1944, to renew their temporary vows for one year (c. 577, § 2);

   c) the sisters who took their first temporary vows on August 15, 1942, to make their profession of perpetual vows (cc. 574, § 1; 34, § 3, 5°).

   Were these acts valid and licit?

8. May a superior prolong the three year period of temporary vows? May a superior anticipate the profession of perpetual vows?

9. Which are the three acts which every novice must place regarding his personal property before taking his first vows in a religious congregation? (C. 569).

10. Does a religious who has made profession of simple vows retain the ownership of his property? (C. 580, § 1).

11. What is the meaning of the phrase in canon 569, § 3, as found in the authorized English translation: "the novice . . . *shall freely dispose by will* of all the property he actually possesses or may subsequently possess"? Does it mean that he may give away his property during his lifetime? (See explanation in text.)

12. What is meant by the clause "whatever the religious acquires . . . in respect to his institute" in canon 580, § 2? (See explanation in text.)

13. Brother Raymond is obliged to leave his institute at the expiration of three years of temporary vows in order to take care of his aged parents who are left alone in the world by the death of his brother. After five years, both parents having died in the meanwhile, Brother Raymond asks to be readmitted to his old institute. What permissions must be obtained? Must he repeat his novitiate? Take temporary vows again? (Cc. 542, 1°; 640, § 2).

14. On August 15, 1944, Sister Fervorosa, then only 20 years old, is admitted to profession of perpetual vows. Neither she nor her superior advert to the lack of age. Sister celebrates her twenty-first birthday on December 20. On Christmas Day the entire community renew their vows by way of devotion. Does this renewal of devotion validate the previous profession? (C. 586, § 1).

15. Sister Poverella has none of this world's goods when she takes her first vows. Hence she omits the cession and disposition of property required by canon 569, § 1, but makes her will according to the prescriptions of § 3. Three years later a rich uncle dies and leaves her $5,000. May she accept it? What must she do about it? Was she obliged to make her will when she did? May she change it now? (Cc. 569, §§ 2 and 3; 583, 2°).

16. Brother Pious, who owns a big ranch, has taken temporary vows in an order; he made the cession and disposition required by canon 569 before doing so, but he did not make a will. Should he have done so? Might he have done so? Now his superior tells him that after three months, at the expiration of his temporary vows, he will be allowed to take perpetual solemn vows. What disposition must he make of his property before he takes his solemn vows? After he has taken his solemn vows his parents die and leave him their entire estate. To whom does it go? (Cc. 569, § 3; 581, 582).

17. In a certain congregation the second year novices are sent out to teach or to work in a hospital; some, "because they are needed"; the rest, "to give them an idea of the kind of work they will do later on." Is this in conformity with the instruction of the S. Congregation of Religious regarding the second year of novitiate? (See Instruction II and III, *AAS*, 13 [1921], 539; *Digest*, I, p. 303.)

18. John Jones, a wealthy oil man, sustained a fractured leg when a

derrick fell upon it. He was taken to a Catholic hospital for treatment. He had never met a sister before, and during the weeks of recuperation learned to admire them very much. The day he left the hospital he handed Sister Jane an envelope containing $5,000 worth of oil stocks saying, "Sister, here is a little present for having taken such good care of me." Do the oil stocks belong to Sister Jane personally or to the community? (C. 580, § 2).

Readings:

Browne, *Validity of Solemn Profession*, IER. 70 (1934), 424–425; Ellis, *Dowry of Religious Women*, RfR. 3 (1944), 224–239; *Vow of Poverty in the Code*, RfR. 1 (1942), 15–26; *Supplying Days of Absence from Novitiate*, RfR. 1 (1942), 322–326; *Studies During the Novitiate*, RfR. 2 (1943), 255–262; *Profession of Novice in Danger of Death*, RfR. 1 (1942), 117–122; Frey, *Act of Religious Profession*, C.U., 1931; Gearin, *Confessor and the Vow of Religious Poverty*, AER. 61 (1919), 136–153; *A Form for Application for Admission to Religious Institutes of Women*, *The Jurist*, Vol. 3, p. 493; Kealy, *Dowry of Religious Women*, C.U., 1941; Risk, *Admission to the Religious Life*, RfR. 2 (1943) 25–34; Turner, *The Vow of Poverty*, C.U., 1929.

CHAPTER VIII

OBLIGATIONS AND PRIVILEGES OF RELIGIOUS

Section 1. Studies in Clerical Religious Institutes (587–591)

PRELIMINARY SURVEY

Houses of Studies (cc. 587–588)
Courses of Studies (c. 589)
Examinations After Completion of Studies (c. 590)
Cases of Conscience (c. 591)
Religious Attending Secular Universities

This title of the Code deals not with the special studies religious must make in order to qualify for the special works of the institute to which they are to devote their lives, but rather with those studies which are a necessary preparation for the reception and exercise of Holy Orders. These studies will be substantially the same as those required for other clerics in the canons on seminaries (cc. 1364–1366). Hence presupposing those general norms, this title contains special provisions for religious regarding houses of studies, the spiritual care of the students, the studies to be taken up, and, finally, ways and means of preserving and even increasing the wealth of knowledge acquired during the regular curriculum. An excellent commentary on these canons as well as other valuable suggestions and prescriptions may be found in the Letter of Pius XI, *Unigenitus Dei Filius,* addressed to all superiors general of religious men, March 19, 1924.[1]

Art. 1. Houses of Studies. Every clerical religious institute should have its houses of studies, approved by the general chapter or by superiors, in which only such religious should be allowed to dwell as are exemplary in their zeal for regular observance. In these houses of studies perfect common life must flourish (c. 594), otherwise the students may not be promoted to orders (c. 587, §§ 1, 2). Hence, those superiors who present candidates for orders are bound in conscience to see that these conditions are fulfilled (c. 995, § 1), and the ordain-

---

[1] *AAS*, 16-133; *Digest*, I, p. 670.

ing prelate may refuse to ordain candidates for orders who have been trained in a house which he is certain is deficient in the above-mentioned qualities. If the institute or province has no properly equipped house of studies, or if, in the judgment of superiors, it is difficult to send their subjects to them, they should send their students to a properly equipped house of studies of some other province or institute, or to the classes of the diocesan seminary, or to a Catholic university (c. 587, § 3). Canon 606, § 2 allows religious under these conditions to dwell outside a house of their institute for a period more than six months without the permission of the Holy See. Such religious, however, as are outside their own religious house, may not live in private homes, but must take up their abode either in some other house of their institute, or if that cannot be, in the house of some other male institute, or in a seminary, or at least in a pious house in charge of men in sacred orders, and which has the approval of ecclesiastical authority (c. 587, § 4).

During the entire period of their studies, religious students should be entrusted to the care of a spiritual director who shall train their souls in the spiritual life by seasonable admonitions, instructions and advice. The spiritual director should possess those qualities which are required for a master of novices by canon 559, §§ 2, 3. The spiritual director may also be one of the confessors of the religious students. Superiors should see to it that the regulations prescribed for all religious in canon 595 be observed perfectly in houses of studies (c. 588).

Art. 2. Course of Studies. After being properly trained in the lower studies, religious students shall spend at least two years in the diligent study of philosophy and at least four years in that of theology, adhering to the doctrine of St. Thomas as prescribed by canon 1366, § 2, and in conformity with the instructions[2] issued by the Holy See (c. 589, § 1). The main points of these instructions are as follows:

1. Candidates should not be allowed to begin their novitiate until they have completed the course in humanities, as it is called (four years of high school, two years of college); exceptions may be made for a grave cause,[3] but in such cases the course of humanities must be completed before the study of philosophy is begun.[4]

---

[2] Pius XI, *Encycl. on St. Thomas,* June 29, 1923; *AAS,* 15-309; *Digest,* I, p. 669; *Unigenitus,* cf. note 1; S. C. Rel., Dec. 1, 1931, cf. note 4.
[3] Pius XI, *Unigenitus,* as above in note 2.
[4] S. C. Rel., *Instr.,* Dec. 1, 1931; *AAS,* 24-76; *Digest,* I, p. 476 sq.; Creusen-Ellis, *Religious Men and Women in the Code,* ed. 3, pp. 287–297.

2. The school term consists of a period of *nine months* of each year of twelve months, nor may classes be held during vacations in order to finish the course sooner; hence, the theological course must extend over a period of forty-five months, including three summer vacations.[5]

3. These studies may not be made privately, but must be made in an approved house of studies; otherwise the religious may not be presented as a candidate for orders. In the case of an individual religious who for extraordinary reasons has not been able to attend classes, a convalidation may be obtained from the S. Congregation of Religious, provided that the individual has studied diligently and proved his diligence by passing his examination successfully; testimony to this effect sworn to by the examiners, must be presented to the S. Congregation with information regarding the time spent in private study, and the results of the examinations.

If there be question of only one or other accessory branch studied privately for a grave reason by an individual religious, the superior general with the deliberative vote of his council may grant the required convalidation after having received the sworn testimony of the examiners as required above.[6] In both cases mentioned above, it is sufficient for the individual who has studied privately to pass the regular examinations given at the end of the year to those who have attended class, but he must take an examination in each branch which he has studied privately.[7]

4. The Congregation of Religious, being asked whether those religious students who, through no fault of their own, were forced (e.g., by reason of illness or of military duty) to interrupt their studies, were obliged to repeat the year thus interrupted or shortened, gave the following answer: The superior general with the deliberate vote of his council may dispense, provided: (*a*) the interruption or shortening of studies did not exceed three months in its entirety; (*b*) the studies thus lost were made up in private classes; (*c*) that the examiners testify that the person in question has shown in his examination that he has really learned the matter he missed in class.[8]

5. During the period of studies it is forbidden to impose upon professors or students occupations which would in any manner what-

---

[5] S. C. Rel., Sept. 7, 1909, ad III; *AAS*, 1–701; *Fontes*, n. 4397, Vol. VI, p. 993; May 31, 1910, ad 3; *AAS*, 2–449; *Fontes*, n. 4402, Vol. VI, p. 999; S. C. Consist., March 24, 1911, ad 1; *AAS*, 3–181; *Fontes*, n. 2081, Vol V, p. 50.

[6] S. C. Rel., Sept. 7, 1909, ad VI; *AAS*, 1–701; *Fontes*, n. 4397, Vol VI, p. 993.

[7] S. C. Rel., March 1, 1915, ad II; *AAS*, 7–123; *Fontes*, n. 4423, Vol. VI, p. 1030.

[8] S. C. Rel., March 1, 1915, ad I; *AAS*, 7–123; *Fontes*, *loc. cit.*

ever form an obstacle to their studies or to attendance at classes. Superiors may even dispense them from certain common observances, even from choir, especially from the night office, as often as they judge such dispensation to be necessary for the success of their studies (c. 589, § 2).

6. The Holy See has granted to many clerical institutes the privilege of ordination to the priesthood after the third year of theology. Such religious must always complete the fourth year of theology in an approved house of studies, and superiors are not allowed to employ these young priests *habitually* either in the sacred ministry (confessions or preaching), or in the exterior works of the institute (teaching, etc.). These restrictions are always supposed, even though the dispensation was given personally by the Sovereign Pontiff, and the obligation they impose on superiors has been declared to be grave.[9]

Art. 3. Examinations After Completion of Studies. After having finished their clerical studies, all religious priests shall undergo an examination on the different parts of theology to be assigned in advance each year for at least five years, before learned and grave fathers. Those only are excepted who are professors of theology, of canon law, or of scholastic philosophy, as well as those whom major superiors may exempt for a grave reason (c. 590).

Art. 4. Cases of Conscience. In at least every formed house a discussion on moral and liturgical cases must be held not less often than once a month (at least nine each school year), to which the superior may add a conference on dogmatic theology or kindred subjects; all those in the house who are studying or who have completed the study of theology must assist at these conferences unless the constitutions direct otherwise (c. 591). Religious who are assistant pastors, as well as chaplains who exercise parochial functions in religious or pious houses, are also bound to assist at the diocesan conferences prescribed by canon 131.[10] If, for some special reason, these conferences are not held in the religious house, all religious, even though exempt, who have diocesan faculties to hear confessions, must attend the diocesan conferences (c. 131, § 3).

Art. 5. Religious Attending Secular Universities. The S. Consistorial Congregation, in its Decree of April 30, 1918,[11] regulated the attendance of both secular and religious *clerics* at secular (i.e., non-

---

[9] S. C. Rel., Oct. 27, 1923; *AAS*, 15-549; *Digest*, I, p. 483.
[10] Code Com., Feb. 12, 1935; *AAS*, 27-92; *Digest*, II, p. 53.
[11] *AAS*, 10-237; Digest, I, p. 115.

Catholic) universities. It confirmed former legislation,[12] and added some new provisions.

1. Clerical religious, therefore, are bound to observe the following regulations in this matter: (a) The superior general alone of an order or congregation engaged in teaching can give the required permission, but only for that number of his subjects which is necessary and sufficient to satisfy the needs of their colleges and schools;[13] (b) only *priests* may be allowed to attend secular universities,[14] but not if they be novices;[15] (c) such priests are not excused from the quinquennial examinations prescribed by canon 590; but these are to be required even more rigorously of them.[16]

2. No provisions are made in the general law of the Church for the attendance of nonclerical religious (brothers and sisters) at secular universities. Hence it would seem that they must obtain permission of the local Ordinary, and abide by his instructions.

Section 2. General Obligations of Religious (cc. 592–612)

PRELIMINARY SURVEY

Life of Perfection (c. 593)
Common Life (c. 594)
Exercises of Piety (c. 595, § 1)
Regarding Holy Communion (c. 595, § 2)
Wearing the Habit (c. 596)
Papal Cloister (cc. 597–603)
Episcopal Cloister (cc. 604–607)
Relations Between Religious and Diocesan Clergy
    (cc. 608–609)
Obligation of Choir (c. 610)
Correspondence of Religious (c. 611)
Public Prayers and Services (c. 612)

---

[12] S. C. EE. et RR., *Instr.* July 21, 1896; *Fontes,* n. 2031, Vol. IV, p. 1078; Pius X, *Encycl., Pascendi,* Sept. 7, 1907; *Fontes,* n. 680, Vol. III, p. 690; Pius X, *Motu Proprio, Sacrorum Antistitum,* Sept. 1, 1910; *Fontes,* n. 689, Vol. III, p. 774.
[13] S. C. EE. et RR., July 21, 1896, n. 3; *Fontes,* n. 2031, Vol. IV, p. 1078.
[14] S. C. Consist., Decree, Apr. 30, 1918, *AAS,* 10-37, *Digest,* I, p. 115, n. 1.
[15] S. C. EE. et RR., July 21, 1896, n. 3; *Fontes,* n. 2031, Vol. IV, p. 1078.
[16] S. C. Consist., Instr., n. 3; *Digest,* I, p. 115.

The obligations of religious result from their state of life, from their vows, from their rules and constitutions, and from the special laws of the Church.

Since they are consecrated to God, all religious are subject to the common obligations of clerics (cc. 124–142), taking into account, however, the exceptions and modifications arising from the condition of persons, from the nature of things, and from special provisions of the law (c. 592).

Art. 1. Life of Perfection. Each and every religious, superior as well as subject, is bound not only to observe faithfully and entirely the vows of which he has made profession, but also to order his life according to the rules and constitutions of his institute, and thus *tend* to the perfection of his state (c. 593). A religious who observes his vows and his religious rule faithfully, fulfills his obligation to strive after perfection. In this canon the Code does not impose a *new* obligation upon religious regarding the observance of the vows of religion and of the rules and constitutions, but it simply recalls to mind the obligations already accepted in their religious profession.

Art. 2. Common Life. In every religious institute common life must be exactly observed by all, even in those things which pertain to food, clothing, and furniture. Whatever is acquired by religious, including superiors, according to the norms of cc. 580, § 2, and 582, 1°, must be incorporated in the goods of the house, or of the province, or of the institute; and all money and securities (*tituli*) shall be deposited in the common safe (c. 594). Common life in the strict sense as described in the canon is a special manner of practicing religious poverty. It does not exclude common life in the wider sense as described above (see p. 229) but it presupposes it.[17]

Art. 3. Exercises of Piety. The Code imposes upon religious superiors the obligation of providing their subjects both the time and the opportunities to attend to mental and vocal prayer, as well as for the frequent reception of the sacraments of Penance and of the Holy Eucharist. It imposes *no new* obligation upon subjects beyond what is already contained in the constitutions. Hence superiors should see

---

[17] The following "Constitution on Common Life" (n. 7) was contained in the agenda of the Vatican Council: "Since perfect common life consists in this that religious turn in to the religious family in their entirety all goods, income, emoluments, and whatever else they may receive [as religious], and in turn receive in common from their religious house both food, clothing, and all other necessities, superiors should not refuse anything which is necessary to the religious, and the latter should not ask for anything superfluous; hence charity and solicitude are recommended to superiors, religious moderation to subjects" (*Coll. Lacen.*, v. 7, col. 676).

to it that all religious: (1) make a retreat each year; (2) assist at Holy Mass daily, unless legitimately impeded; (3) make their daily meditation; (4) perform the other exercises of piety prescribed by the rules and constitutions; (5) go to confession at least once a week (c. 595, § 1).

Art. 4. Regarding Holy Communion. Superiors should promote frequent and even daily reception of Holy Communion among their subjects, and every properly disposed religious must be allowed freely to approach the Most Holy Eucharist frequently, and even daily (c. 595, § 2). This is a matter for the individual religious to determine after seeking advice of his confessor or spiritual guide. If, however, a religious has, since his last sacramental confession, given grave scandal to the community, or committed a *serious and external* fault, the superior may forbid him to receive Holy Communion until he shall have gone to confession again (c. 595, § 3). The number and the days fixed in the rules and constitutions or in directories and custom books for the reception of Holy Communion have only a directive value (c. 595, § 4).

Religious should carefully avoid watching how often other members of the community receive Holy Communion, and must avoid forming any judgment regarding their occasional abstention, since such occasional abstention gives evidence of freedom, and of a timorous and delicate conscience. To make it easier for those religious who may desire occasionally to abstain from receiving Holy Communion, it will be advisable to avoid having the members of the community approach the Holy Table according to seniority or any other strictly determined order.[18] Religious who are sick should be given every opportunity to receive Holy Communion, even daily, according to their pious desire.

Art. 5. Wearing of the Habit. Religious must wear the habit proper to their institute both inside and outside the house. Major superiors, or in case of urgency, the local superior may dispense from this obligation (c. 596). Some institutes of religious clerics have no distinctive habit; for them the habit consists in the garb worn by clerics according to canon 136, § 1.

Art. 6. Papal Cloister. 1. Cloister may be understood either materially or formally: in the *material* sense cloister means that part of the religious house from which certain persons from the outside world are excluded, and which religious may not leave without authorization.

---

[18] S. C. Sacr., Dec. 8, 1938, *Private Instruction; Digest*, II, p. 208.

In the *formal* sense cloister is taken to mean the laws of the Church which have to do with this double prohibition. Papal cloister is that enclosure which was imposed upon regulars and nuns from the fourteenth century onward by papal constitutions, from which the Holy See alone can dispense, and which is sanctioned by special punishments in papal legislation (c. 2342).

2. Papal cloister *must be observed* in every house of regulars, whether men or women, which has been canonically erected, even though the community does not number six professed religious (c. 597, § 1). This law does not apply to monasteries of nuns in which, by order of the Holy See, only simple vows are taken,[19] although such nuns usually observe strict cloister by reason of their constitutions. Hence a person who would violate the cloister of nuns with simple vows only, would not incur excommunication.

All that part of the house inhabited by the community is subject to the cloister, together with the gardens and orchards access to which is reserved to the religious. The church, however, with the adjoining sacristy, is not in cloister, nor are the guests' rooms and the parlor which should, as far as possible, be located near the main entrance of the house (c. 597, § 2).

3. *In orders of men* it is the duty of the major superior or of the general chapter according to the constitutions, to determine the limits of the cloister exactly, or to change them for good reasons, and these limits must be clearly indicated. In the case of a monastery of nuns, this duty falls upon the local Ordinary (c. 597, § 3).

Under penalty of excommunication reserved to the Holy See, it is forbidden to women and girls of whatever age, class, or condition, to enter the cloister of *orders of men,* under any pretext whatsoever. Those who bring them in or allow them to enter incur the same penalty. The wives of sovereigns and of rulers of states, with their retinue, are exempt from this law (cc. 598, § 2; 2343, 2°).

When the house of an order of men (male regulars) has annexed to it a house for boarding pupils, or for other work proper to the institute, a separate part of the house at least should, if possible, be reserved for the habitation of the religious, and be subject to the law of cloister (c. 599).

There is no special provision of the general law of the Church in regard to religious men leaving the cloister; canon 606 merely obliges superiors to the observance of the constitutions on this point.

---

[19] Code Com., *AAS,* 13–177 ad 2; *Digest,* I, p. 306.

4. *The cloister of nuns* is distinguished in two ways from that of male regulars:

a. No person of whatever class, condition, sex, or age, may be admitted to the cloister of nuns without the permission of the Holy See. Some exemptions, however, are made by the Code: (1) the local Ordinary or the regular superior or other canonical visitors delegated by them, may enter the enclosure when making the canonical visitation, but only for the purpose of inspection, and on condition that they be accompanied by at least one cleric or male religious of mature age; (2) the confessor, or his substitute, may, with due precautions, enter into the cloister in order to administer the sacraments to the sick, or to assist the dying; (3) rulers of states with their wives and retinues, as well as Cardinals with their retinues may enter the cloister; (4) after taking due precautions, the superior may permit the doctor, the surgeon, as well as others whose work is necessary (carpenters, plumbers, etc.) to enter the cloister, after having previously obtained at least the habitual approval of the local Ordinary; but if urgent necessity does not allow time to seek this approval, she may presume his permission (c. 600).

b. No nun, after profession, may, under whatever pretext, leave the monastery even for a short time without a special indult of the Holy See, except in case of imminent danger of death or other serious evil. This danger must be recognized as such by the local Ordinary in writing, if time permits (c. 601). By reason of their quinquennial faculties, local Ordinaries may allow nuns to leave the cloister to undergo a surgical operation, even though there be no danger of death.[20]

The cloister of the monastery of nuns should be protected on every side in such a manner as to prevent, so far as possible, those within from being seen by outsiders, or from seeing them (c. 602).

The cloister of nuns, even those subject to regular superiors, is under the vigilance of the local Ordinary, who can correct and coerce, even with penalties and censures, all delinquents, male regulars not excepted. The regular superior to whom nuns are subject has the same duty of vigilance, and can likewise inflict penalties on the nuns or on his male subjects if they be found guilty in this matter (c. 603).

On February 6, 1924, the S. Cong. of Religious issued a detailed instruction definitely explaining the nature and obligations of the

[20] S. C. Rel., n. 9; *Digest*, II, p. 37.

cloister of nuns.[21] All priests having any spiritual care or ministration of nuns should read this instruction carefully.

Art. 7. Common or Episcopal Cloister. The Code imposes cloister on all religious congregations likewise, but less rigidly. In all houses of religious congregations, there must be a part reserved exclusively for the religious. Persons of the other sex are not to be admitted there, with the exception of those mentioned above (see p. 286), as well as others whom the superior considers may be admitted for just and reasonable motives (c. 604, § 1). Superiors of religious congregations do *not* need the permission of the local Ordinary to allow anyone to enter the cloister in cases where they judge this opportune. Classrooms, workshops, etc., shall be separated as much as possible from the parts of the house reserved for the religious (c. 604, § 2). Permission to enter there may be given more readily than to enter the religious house proper, but even there not without a just reason. The Bishop is to watch over the exact observance of this cloister. In special circumstances and for a grave motive he may punish those who violate it, even by imposing censures, but not in the case of an *exempt clerical* congregation (c. 604, § 3).

All those who have the care of the cloister entrusted to them shall carefully see to it that useless conversations with outsiders do not relax discipline and weaken the religious spirit (c. 605). The constitutions usually prescribe detailed regulations in regard to visitors received by religious.

While all male religious, as well as sisters and nuns not bound by papal enclosure, may leave the religious house on occasion, superiors must see to it that the constitutions be faithfully observed regarding the going out of subjects, and regarding visits which they may pay to outsiders. Superiors may not allow their subjects to remain outside a house of their own institute except for a just and grave cause, and for as brief a period as possible according to the constitutions; but for an absence of more than six months, except by reason of studies, the permission of the Holy See is always required (c. 606).

Superiors of religious women as well as local Ordinaries shall see to it that sisters do not go out alone, except in case of necessity (c. 607). A secular woman or a girl may serve as companion.

Art. 8. Relations Between Clerical Religious and the Diocesan Clergy.

---

[21] *AAS*, 16–95; *Digest*, I, pp. 314–320.

Canons 608 and 609 are intended to foster mutual concord and co-operation between the clergy in their apostolic labors for souls.

Religious superiors must see to it that their priests, destined by them for outside work shall when requested to do so by local Ordinaries or pastors willingly give their help in the sacred ministry whenever they are needed, not only in their own churches and oratories, but in others as well, especially in the diocese in which they live. Religious discipline, however, should not suffer from such outside work.

Local Ordinaries and pastors likewise, shall willingly avail themselves of the help of religious priests, especially of those who live in the diocese, in the sacred ministry, and especially in the administration of the sacrament of Penance (c. 608).

When the church attached to a religious community is, at the same time, a parish church, the prescriptions of canon 415 are to be carried out. This canon regulates in detail the relations between the pastor and the community in matters connected with the parish and the church. A parish may not be established in the church of religious women (either of solemn or of simple vows). Superiors shall see to it that the celebration of the divine services in their own churches in no wise interfere with the catechetical instruction and the explanation of the holy Gospel in the parish church (c. 609).

Art. 9. Obligation of Choir. By virtue of their constitutions, most religious *orders* of both men and women as also some religious congregations are obliged to the public recitation of the divine office *in common*. The Code prescribes that in these institutes, whether of men or women, the divine office must be daily recited in common in every house in which there are at least four religious who are bound to choir and who are not lawfully impeded, and even in those houses where there are fewer, if the constitutions so prescribe it (c. 610, § 1). The obligation of choir is incumbent on the *community as such,* not on the religious as individuals. The professed of solemn vows, however, who have not been present in choir, are bound to recite the divine office privately (c. 610, § 3). The professed who have taken simple temporary vows only are not bound to recite the divine office privately, if they have been absent from choir, unless they are in major orders, or are explicitly obliged to do so by the constitutions (c. 578, 2°). Novices and lay religious are not obliged to choir by the general law of the Church. The obligation of reciting the divine office which binds the community is certainly fulfilled if *four* religious are present; it would seem to be fulfilled likewise if only two professed religious were present in choir, or if the divine office were recited by novices only.[22]

The prescriptions of canon 610 do not apply to any of the communities of religious who are bound by their constitutions to the recitation of the little Office of the Blessed Virgin, even though it is to be recited in common.

The conventual Mass: The Mass corresponding to the divine office of the day (c. 413, § 2), according to the rubrics, must be celebrated daily in all institutes of men, and likewise, where possible, in institutes of women **(c. 610, § 2).** This canon applies not only to nuns with solemn vows, but likewise to all houses of religious women who have only simple vows but who are obliged by their constitutions which have been approved by the Holy See to the recitation of the divine office.[23] Religious who are bound by the obligation of choir are not obliged to celebrate more than one conventual Mass on those days on which the general rubrics of the Roman Missal prescribe or allow several conventual Masses in or out of choir.[24] On such days, however, if only one Mass is celebrated, it must be the Mass of the feria or vigil which has a proper Mass, not that of a feast (double major or minor, or semidouble) which may fall on that day.[25] The obligation resting upon the community to be present at the conventual Mass is satisfied if four members who are obliged to choir are present, and probably if only two such members are present, as in the case of the divine office mentioned above.

Art. 10. Correspondence of Religious. The constitutions of nearly all religious institutes impose upon their members the obligation of not sending or receiving letters without general or special permission. The majority of religious institutes grant superiors the right to read the correspondence of their subjects. The right of control over the correspondence of religious is limited by the Code as follows: All religious may freely send letters, exempt from all control, to the Holy See; to the Apostolic Delegate; to their Cardinal Protector; to their major superiors; to their local superior when he is absent; to the local Ordinary, and to the regular superior upon whom they depend. Conversely, the letters of all these persons when sent to religious, must be given to the persons to whom they are addressed, and may not be opened by anyone **(c. 611).** Superiors who have the right to

---

[22] Schaefer, *De Rel.,* ed. 3, n. 366, 2, p. 743.
[23] Code Com., May 20, 1923 ad III; *AAS,* 16–113; *Digest,* I, p. 320.
[24] S. C. Rit., May 2, 1924; *AAS,* 16-248; *Digest,* I, p. 321.
[25] S. C. Rit., Feb. 28, 1925; *AAS,* 17–159.

read the correspondence of their subjects are bound in conscience to keep the contents of such letters secret. They must follow the rule laid down in moral theology relative to professional secrets. Should a religious superior authorize the sending or receiving of "letters of conscience," he is not allowed to read them.

Art. 11. Public Prayers and Services. If the local Ordinary prescribes the ringing of bells, or certain prayers or sacred ceremonies for a public cause, all religious, even though exempt, must obey, without prejudice, however, to the constitutions and privileges of each institute **(c. 612).** The same rule applies to any instructions issued by the local Ordinary with regard to sermons, homilies, or talks on Christian Doctrine to be given in all churches of the diocese during the Masses on Sundays and holydays of obligation (c. 1345).

Section 3. Privileges of Religious (cc. 613–625)

PRELIMINARY SURVEY

Acquisition of Privileges (cc. 613–614)
Privilege of Exemption (cc. 615–620)
Privilege of Begging (cc. 621–624)
Blessing of Abbots (c. 625)

A privilege is a particular law, granting a favor to an individual or to a community. It either accords an exemption from the common law (privilege against the law), or it adds a special favor to the common law (privilege beside the law).

Art. 1. Acquisition of Privileges. Each institute enjoys those privileges which are contained in the Code, or may have been granted to it directly by the Holy See; every communication of privileges is *henceforth* excluded. The privileges which a regular order enjoys belong also to the nuns of that same order, in so far as they are capable of enjoying them **(c. 613).** Privileges acquired by religious institutes according to the law and of which they were in peaceful possession *before the Code,* are not revoked by this canon.[26] All religious, even lay religious and novices, enjoy the privileges of clerics enumerated in canons 119–123 **(c. 614).**

Art. 2. Privilege of Exemption. Regulars, both men and women, including novices (except those nuns who are not subject to superiors

---

[26] Code Com., Dec. 30, 1937; *AAS,* 30–73; *Digest,* II, p. 172.

of regulars) are exempt together with their houses and churches from the jurisdiction of the local Ordinary, except in the cases provided for by law (c. 615). Exemption for regulars, therefore *is the rule,* and exceptions have to be proved. Postulants do not enjoy the privilege of exemption. Much less do lay people who happen to be in a house of exempt religious. The exceptions or limitations to exemption laid down in the Code have been carefully arranged by Vermeersch-Creusen, in their *Epitome,* I, n. 775, pp. 570–572, as follows:

What a local Ordinary can do with relation to exempt religious:

1. In the churches of exempt religious he may preach (c. 1343, § 1), exercise pontifical functions (c. 337, § 1), and administer the sacrament of confirmation (c. 792).

2. He may make a canonical visitation: (*a*) of their churches and public oratories to enforce any special statutes which he has enacted concerning divine worship (c. 1261, § 2; see commentary on this canon); (*b*) of their schools (with the exception of those for the professed students of the institute), oratories, recreational centers, etc., concerning matters pertaining to religious and moral instruction (c. 1382).

Things to be left to the local Ordinary:

1. The consecration (not the blessing) of sacred places (c. 1155), of bells (c. 1169, § 5), and of immovable altars (c. 1199, § 2);

2. Judgments: (*a*) in cases pertaining to the Holy Office (c. 501, § 2; 1555); (*b*) in controversies between physical or moral persons of different religious institutes (c. 1579, § 3); (*c*) in more urgent cases of controversy regarding collegiate precedence (c. 106, 6°);

3. The examination of postulants or sisters before beginning the novitiate, and before the profession of first temporary as well as of perpetual vows (c. 552).

Things which exempt religious must do at the command of the local Ordinary:

1. Recite prayers when ordered for a public cause (c. 612);

2. Recite collects (*orationes imperatas*) prescribed for Mass, and name the Bishop in the canon of the Mass (liturgical law);

3. Celebrate prescribed sacred solemnities (c. 612);

4. Obey prescriptions concerning the ringing of bells for a public cause (c. 612);

5. Give catechetical instruction to the faithful especially in the churches of their institute (c. 1334);

6. Give a brief explanation of the Gospel or of Christian doctrine on feast days (c. 1345);

7. Observe prescriptions concerning divine worship (c. 1261);

8. Participate in public processions, according to the provisions of canons 1291 and 1292;

9. Observe regulations regarding manual Mass stipends (c. 831, § 3), but not for Mass foundations (c. 1550);

10. Refrain from holding divine services which, in the judgment of the local Ordinary, would interfere with the catechetical instruction or with the homily on the Gospel in the parochial church (c. 609, § 3);

11. Contribute to the seminary tax, unless they live solely by alms or conduct educational institutions for the common good (c. 1356); and, as beneficiaries, pay the charitable subsidy, that is, an extraordinary but moderate contribution for some special pressing need of the diocese (c. 1505).

Things which exempt religious cannot do without the intervention or consent of the local Ordinary:

1. Establish a religious house in the diocese; or convert to other uses a house already established, unless the alteration be of such a nature that, without prejudice to the conditions of the foundation, it affects only the internal regime and the religious discipline; or build or open an edifice separated from the religious house (c. 497);

2. Erect a church or public oratory in a certain specified place (cc. 497, and 1162, § 4);

3. Hear the confessions of the laity or of religious women including novices (cc. 874 and 876);

4. Preach to the laity or to other religious not of their institute (cc. 514, § 1, 1338, and 1339);

5. Reserve the Blessed Sacrament in the principal oratory of a religious house (c. 1265, § 1, 2°);

6. Expose the Blessed Sacrament in a monstrance, or give Benediction with the Blessed Sacrament exposed in a monstrance (c. 1274, § 1);

7. Place or cause to be placed unusual images in churches or sacred places (c. 1279, § 1);

8. Recite prayers or conduct exercises of piety which are not approved, in churches or public oratories (c. 1279, § 1);

9. Designate the rector of a church not attached to a convent (c. 480, § 2);

10. Divulge new indulgences granted to a church, but which have not been promulgated in Rome (c. 919, § 1);

11. Receive minor or major orders if their own superiors are not competent to ordain (cc. 956–959; 964);

12. Establish pious associations among the faithful (cc. 686, §§ 2–4; 703, § 2); prescribe the special garb which members of pious associations are to wear at sacred functions, or make a change in the habit of a confraternity (cc. 713, § 2; 714); appoint a member of the secular clergy as chaplain or moderator of an association erected in the church of an exempt institute (c. 698, § 1);

13. Conduct public processions outside the bounds of their church, except during the octave of Corpus Christi (c. 1291, § 2);

14. Publish books, periodicals, or write for secular daily papers (cc. 1385, 1386);

15. Make the profession of faith (and take the oath against Modernism) as confessors, preachers, and beneficiaries (c. 1406, § 1, 7°);

16. Beg alms, unless they belong to a mendicant order (cc. 621 and 622);

17. Invest money given to a parish or mission, or to an individual religious for the benefit of a parish or mission (c. 533, § 1, 4°, and § 2);

18. Receive property in trust for a pious cause, or for a church or for the benefit of the faithful of the place or of the diocese (c. 1516, §§ 1 and 3).

N.B. Individual religious institutes enjoy special exemptive privileges which free them from some of the limitations expressed in the law as enumerated above. For a thorough explanation of each of the limitations listed above, see O'Brien, *The Exemption of Religious in Church Law,* Bruce, Milwaukee, 1943.

Regulars who are unlawfully absent from their religious house do not enjoy exemption. They may be punished by the local Ordinary for any serious fault committed outside their religious house (whether absent lawfully or not) if their superior, duly informed, does not himself punish them **(c. 616).**

The local Ordinary has the right to watch over every religious house which is not formed (see p. 232) and, in case of abuse which would be a source of scandal to the faithful, he may take provisional measures. The local Ordinary has no duty of watching over the formed houses of exempt religious. Should abuses arise, whether in the house or church, he must inform the superior. He may not, however, intervene directly, even to make good the negligence of the superior. In such a case he has only the right and the duty to inform the Holy See as soon as possible **(c. 617).**

Congregations of Religious Not Exempt: Institutes with simple vows *do not* enjoy the privilege of exemption, unless it has been specially granted to them (c. 618, § 1). General exemption is rarely granted to religious congregations. The Congregation of the Most Holy Redeemer (Redemptorist Fathers), and the Congregation of the Passion (Passionist Fathers) enjoy this privilege. Other congregations enjoy exemption only in the cases laid down in the law. They are as follows: (*a*) in institutes approved by the Holy See, the local Ordinary may not make any changes in the constitutions, nor inquire into the administration of temporalities, except in the cases mentioned in canons 533-535; (*b*) in these same institutes he may not interfere in the internal government and discipline, except in the cases expressed in the law; (*c*) nevertheless, in regard to *non-clerical institutes* (brothers and sisters), the local Ordinary during the canonical visitation (c. 512, § 1, 3°) can and must inquire: whether discipline is maintained conformably to the constitutions, whether sound doctrine and good morals have suffered in any way, whether there have been any violations of the law of enclosure, whether the reception of the sacraments is regular and frequent; and if superiors, after having been warned of the existence of grave abuses have failed to duly remedy them, the Ordinary himself shall provide; if, however, something of greater importance which will not suffer delay, occur, the Ordinary shall decide immediately, but he must report his decision to the Holy See (c. 618, § 2).

In all matters in which religious are subject to the local Ordinary, he may coerce them, even by penalties (c. 619). On the other hand, all religious living in the diocese, whether exempt or not, may avail themselves of every indult lawfully granted by the local Ordinary dispensing from the obligation of the common law (for example, a dispensation from fast or abstinence), without prejudice, however, to the vows and particular constitutions of their own institute (c. 620).

Art. 3. Privilege of Begging. 1. *To beg in the canonical sense,* means to go from house to house seeking alms indiscriminately from all. A visit to the special benefactors of a community for the purpose of making known the needs of the community is not begging in the technical sense. Nor are appeals for help made in writing included. This does not mean, however, that religious should not be reserved and discreet in such appeals. When abuses occur, the local Ordinary may intervene.

2. *Regulars* who by their institute bear the name of *mendicants* and

who are such in fact, may beg from door to door in the diocese in which their religious house is established, without any special authorization of the local Ordinary; outside the diocese they need the written permission of the Ordinary in whose territory they wish to beg. Local Ordinaries, especially those of neighboring dioceses, should not, without grave and urgent reasons, refuse or revoke this permission if the religious house cannot possibly subsist on the alms collected in the diocese in which it is situated (c. 621).

3. *All other religious* who are members of congregations approved by the Holy See are forbidden to seek alms, without a special privilege from the Holy See; those who may have obtained this privilege require, in addition, the written permission of the local Ordinary, unless the contrary be expressly stated in the privilege (c. 622, § 1). *Religious of diocesan congregations* may never seek alms without the written permission of the Ordinary of the place in which their house is located, as well as of the Ordinary in whose territory they wish to beg (c. 622, § 2). Local Ordinaries shall not grant to the religious mentioned above in this paragraph the permission to seek alms, especially in places where there are convents of regulars who are mendicants, unless they have satisfied themselves as to the real need of the house or pious work, and the impossibility of otherwise obtaining help; and if it be possible to provide for this necessity by seeking alms within the locality, the district, or the diocese in which these religious live, the Ordinaries shall not grant them further authorization (c. 622, § 3).

4. *Orientals seeking alms and Mass stipends:* Ordinaries of the Latin rite must not permit *any Oriental of whatever order or dignity* to collect money in their territory without an authentic and recent rescript of the S. Oriental Congregation, nor may they send any of their subjects to Oriental dioceses for the same purpose without a similar document (c. 622, § 4). In order to avoid abuses and deceptions which have arisen in this matter, the S. Oriental Congregation issued a special decree[27] stating that information regarding such permission when granted would be forwarded to the Ordinary directly or through the Apostolic Delegate, and that no Ordinary may grant any Oriental permission to beg or to collect Mass stipends until he has been so personally informed, even though said Oriental present documents from the S. Congregation itself. Nor may Orientals collect alms or Mass stipends in the territory of an Ordinary thus informed without the express

---

[27] S. C. Or., Jan. 7, 1930; *AAS*, 22-108; *Digest*, I, p. 27; July 20, 1937, *AAS*, 29-342; *Digest*, II, p. 3.

consent of said Ordinary. Finally Ordinaries are requested to inform their clergy and all religious in the diocese, and even the faithful at large if they think it necessary, regarding this decree. Thus far the decree. Religious, therefore, should never give alms or Mass stipends to any Oriental without first demanding a recommendation from the local Ordinary written in the vernacular.

Religious superiors who have permission to beg must entrust the collection of alms only to professed subjects of mature age and character, especially in the case of religious women; religious who are still in their studies may never be thus employed (c. 623). As to the method to be followed in seeking alms and the manner in which religious who seek them must conduct themselves, religious of both sexes must follow the instructions given by the Holy See on this subject (c. 624).[28]

Art. 4. Blessing of Abbots. Regular Abbots who have been legitimately elected must, within three months after their election, receive the blessing of the Bishop of the diocese in which the monastery is situated (c. 625). Ordinarily this blessing may not be given without an apostolic mandate. In the case of all Abbots of the Order of St. Benedict, the Holy See, through Pope Benedict XV, granted a general or common mandate, *semel pro semper,* directed to the respective diocesan Bishop, whereby they may receive this blessing without further mandate, either from the local Ordinary, or from any Bishop in communion with the Holy See, whenever the episcopal see is vacant, or whenever written proof exists that the diocesan Bishop is either legitimately impeded from giving the blessing himself, or has consented that it be given by another.[29] After receiving the afore-mentioned blessing Abbots enjoy the following privileges: (1) They may confer the tonsure and minor orders on those religious who are subject to them at least by reason of simple profession (c. 964, 1°); (2) they enjoy the privileges of Prelates and Abbots *nullius,* enumerated in canon 325, with the exception of the violet *zucchetto* (c. 625).

Section 4. Status of Religious Cardinals, Bishops, Pastors (cc. 626–631).

Without the permission of the Holy See, no religious may be pro-

---

[28] The principal decrees are as follows: *Singulari quidem* (for religious women), March 27, 1896; *ASS,* 27–555; *Fontes,* n. 2029, Vol. IX, p. 1071; *De eleemosynis colligendis* (for religious men), Nov. 21, 1908; *AAS,* 1–153; *Fontes,* n. 4391, Vol. VI, p. 938; both decrees may also be found in Vermeersch, *De Rel.,* ed. 4, 1910, v. II, pp. 401–404.
[29] Benedict XV, Letter, June 19, 1921; *AAS,* 13–416; *Digest,* I, p. 321.

moted to any dignity, office, or benefice not in keeping with the religious state. A religious who is lawfully elected to an office or dignity by some college may not assent to the election without the permission of his superior. If such a religious, duly elected, be bound by vow not to accept any such dignity, a special dispensation from the Holy Father is required (c. 626).

Art. 1. Religious Cardinals and Bishops. A religious who has been appointed a Cardinal or a Bishop (either residential or titular) remains a religious, and continues to share in the privileges of his institute, as well as to be bound by his vows and other religious obligations, except such as he prudently judges not to be compatible with the dignity he has received. He is released, however, from the authority of his superiors, and remains subject, by reason of his vow of obedience, to the Roman Pontiff alone (c. 627).

Regarding temporalities (c. 628): A religious raised to the episcopal dignity or to some other *outside his own order* has either lost his right to ownership, or not, by reason of his religious profession:

If he has lost his right to ownership, upon taking possession of his dignity he receives the use, usufruct, and administration of all temporal goods which may come to him *intuitu personae* after receiving his dignity; the proprietorship of such goods a residential Bishop acquires for his diocese, a Vicar or Prefect Apostolic for his vicariate or prefecture respectively. All other prelates acquire the ownership of such personal goods for their own order or for the Holy See, in accordance with the norms laid down in canon 582, and with the exception mentioned in canon 239, § 1, n. 19 (c. 628, 1°).

If he has not lost his right of ownership, he recovers the use, usufruct, and administration of whatever temporal goods he may have possessed; whatever comes to him *intuitu personae,* he acquires entirely for himself (c. 628, 2°).

In either case he must dispose of everything which does not come to him *intuitu personae* according to the mind of the donors (c. 628, 3°).

Should a religious resign his cardinalate or bishopric, or complete the work entrusted to him by the Holy See outside his institute, he is obliged to return to his institute; a religious Cardinal or Bishop, however, may choose any house of his institute in which to live; but he remains deprived of active and passive voice for the rest of his life (c. 629).

Art. 2. Religious Pastors. A religious who rules a parish under the title of parish priest or vicar remains bound to the observance of his vows and constitutions, inasmuch as their observance is compatible with the discharge of his office (c. 630, § 1). Hence: (1) in matters pertaining to religious discipline, he remains subject to his religious superior who alone has the right to make inquiries regarding his religious observance, and to correct him if necessary. He is not subject to the local Ordinary as a religious (c. 630, § 2); (2) all property coming to him in the name of the parish he acquires for the parish; all other things he receives as do other religious (c. 630, § 3); (3) notwithstanding his vow of poverty, when they are offered in any manner whatever, he may gather and receive alms destined for the good of his parishioners or for Catholic schools or pious institutions connected with the parish; he administers alms thus received or collected, and, according to his prudent judgment, applies them, always keeping in mind any special wish of the donors; in all these transactions he is subject to the vigilance of his religious superior; (4) as regards alms and donations given for the building, upkeep, restoration, and adornment of the parish church, the religious superior has the right to receive, collect, keep, and administer such funds if the church belongs to the religious community; otherwise these rights rest with the local Ordinary (c. 630, § 4).

Every religious who is a pastor or vicar is immediately subject to the entire jurisdiction, visitation, and correction of the local Ordinary, as are secular pastors, even though he exercise his ministry in a house or place which is the ordinary residence of his major superior; matters of religious observance only are excepted (c. 631, § 1). Hence, the local Ordinary may issue opportune decrees and impose penalties which have been deserved when he finds that the religious parish priest or vicar has been wanting in his office; the religious superior, likewise, has the same rights as the local Ordinary; should the Ordinary and the superior issue contrary orders, the decree of the Ordinary must prevail (c. 631, § 2). Either the Ordinary or the religious superior may remove the religious parish priest or vicar from his office without having to give any reasons to the other (c. 454, § 5). Finally the religious parish priest or vicar must obtain the previous consent of the Ordinary before investing money of the parish (c. 533, § 1, 4°), and give a financial account to the Ordinary of all such funds (c. 535, § 3, 2°).

CASES AND QUESTIONS

1. What previous studies are normally required before a postulant may be licitly admitted to the novitiate of a clerical institute? If exceptions

are made for grave reasons, must these studies be made up before beginning the study of philosophy? (See text under c. 589, § 1, and documents referred to.)

2. Would it be in accordance with canon law for superiors in a clerical congregation to engage their young religious who are in studies (e.g., philosophy or theology) as prefects in a boarding school? As teachers? (C. 589, § 2).

3. Are religious *obliged* to receive Holy Communion on the days indicated in the calendar or custom book of their institute as "communion days"? (C. 595, § 4).

4. Who are forbidden to enter the cloister in houses belonging to an *order* of men? Of *nuns?* Are the houses of religious *congregations* subject to the law of cloister? (Cc. 600; 604).

5. Is it against common life as prescribed by canon 594 to serve special dishes in the refectory to religious who are on a diet? To allow religious who receive money from home or friends for a new habit, to purchase goods of a better quality than that used for the habits of the community? To allow a religious to take a trip merely because relatives or friends are paying for it? (C. 594 and comment in text).

6. What is meant by the privilege of exemption? Who enjoy it by law? What degree of exemption is allowed by law to pontifical congregations? (Cc. 615, 618).

7. The Sisters of St. Francis are obliged by rule to abstain from meat on all Wednesdays of the year. Decoration Day falls on Wednesday of Ember week. The Bishop dispenses his diocese from fast and abstinence for this day. May the sisters avail themselves of this indult? (C. 620).

8. What is meant by begging in the canonical sense of the term? From whom must permission to beg be obtained by a pontifical congregation? By a diocesan congregation? (Cc. 621, 622).

9. A religious with solemn vows is raised to the episcopal dignity and is made the Ordinary of a diocese. He receives a personal gift of $1,000. To whom does it go? If he had only simple vows in a congregation, to whom would the money go? (C. 628).

10. Father Benignus, a religious priest who has taken simple vows in a congregation, is the pastor of St. Roch's church. He receives the following amounts of money: (*a*) $10 for Masses; (*b*) $500 as a legacy in the will of his deceased brother; (*c*) $100 for the poor; (*d*) $250 for his quarterly salary; (*e*) $25 "for you, Father"; (*f*) $100 "in honor of St. Roch"; (*g*) $300 for the missions. What must he do with the money in each case? (Cc. 580, §§ 1 and 2; 630, § 4).

11. Brother Mark becomes ill. The doctor diagnoses his case as incipient tuberculosis. He assures the superior that a year of rest in a sanatorium will restore the good brother's health completely. May the superior give Brother Mark permission to go to the sanatarium without more ado? (C. 606, § 2).

12. A mother superior wishes to send three sisters to the Catholic University in Washington for a year of study. They will live in the Sisters' Hall there. Does she need anybody's permission to allow them to live outside a house of their own community for ten months? (C. 606, § 2).

Readings:

Barry, *Violation of Cloister*, C.U., 1942; Ellis, *Common Life and the Spirit of Poverty*, RfR. 2 (1943), 4–13; O'Brien, *Exemption of Religious,* Bruce, Milwaukee, 1943; Schaaf, *The Cloister*, C.U., 1921; Shuhler, *Privileges of Religious to Absolve and Dispense*, C.U., 1943; Smith, *Penal Law for Religious*, C.U., 1935.

CHAPTER IX

LEAVING THE RELIGIOUS LIFE

Section 1. Voluntary Leaving (cc. 632-645)

PRELIMINARY SURVEY

Transfer to Another Institute (cc. 632–636)
Leaving After Temporary Vows (c. 637)
Exclaustration (cc. 638–639)
Secularization (cc. 638–643)
Apostasy From the Religious Life (cc. 644–645)
Flight From the Religious Life (cc. 644–645)

Art. 1. Transfer to Another Institute. 1. No religious is allowed to transfer to another institute, even though it be of stricter observance, nor from one independent monastery to another of the same order, without the permission of the Holy See **(c. 632).** This canon applies to all religious. Even *nuns* in monasteries in which only *simple vows* are taken by order of the Holy See may not pass from one monastery to another of the same order merely upon the authority of the local Ordinary; nor may the Ordinary permit a nun to transfer *even temporarily* to another monastery of the same order, but the permission of the Holy See must be obtained in each individual case.[1] A religious who thus passes from one institute to another does not cease to be a religious, but merely leaves one form of the religious life to enter another form of the same state.

2. A religious who passes to another institute must make a new novitiate, during which he remains bound by the vows he took in the first institute; but all other obligations and particular rights are suspended; he is obliged to obey the superiors and the master of novices of the new institute, by reason of his vow of obedience **(c. 633, § 1).** During the novitiate he shall wear the same habit as the other novices.[2] If the religious does not make his profession in the new insti-

---

[1] S. C. Rel., Nov. 9, 1926; *AAS*, 18–490; *Digest*, I, p. 324.
[2] S. C. Rel., May 14, 1923; *AAS*, 15-289; *Digest*, I, p. 325.

tute, he is obliged to return to his first institute, unless the period for which he has taken temporary vows has meanwhile expired (c. 633, § 2).

A religious who transfers from one *independent monastery* to another of the same order, does not make a new novitiate or a new profession of vows (c. 633, § 3).

3. A religious with *perpetual* vows, whether solemn or simple, who has transferred to another institute having perpetual vows, whether solemn or simple, shall, at the end of the novitiate, be admitted immediately to the profession of perpetual vows (either solemn or simple, as the case may be) in the new institute (omitting the temporary profession prescribed by canon 574, since this was already made in the old institute), or he shall return to his former institute. The superior, however, has the right of extending the time of probation, but not beyond *one year* after the completion of the novitiate (c. 634).

4. From the day of transfer from one independent monastery to another of the same order, and from the day of profession made in a new institute: (*a*) the religious thus transferred loses all rights and is freed from all obligations contracted in the former monastery or institute, and assumes the rights and duties of the new institute or monastery (c. 635, 1°); (*b*) the monastery or institute which the religious has left keeps all goods to which it has acquired a right through the religious who has transferred, except the dowry, which is to be handed over to the new monastery on the day of transfer, or to the new institute on the day the religious makes his profession therein; during the novitiate the *income* of the dowry should be given to the new institute, as prescribed in canon 551, § 2; unless some other arrangement has been made in accordance with canon 570, § 1 (c. 635, 2°).

5. The *solemnity* of the vows of a religious who, after a transfer made in conformity with the regulations enumerated above, has lawfully made a new profession of simple vows in a religious congregation, is annulled by this new profession, unless there is an express provision to the contrary in the papal indult allowing the transfer (c. 636).

6. Finally, it should be noted that the Church does not favor such transfers, and is loath to grant permission for them, except in the rare case in which an individual better suited for the contemplative life, has entered an institute devoted to the active life, and vice versa.

Art. 2. Leaving After Temporary Vows. A religious who has taken temporary vows may freely (that is, juridically) leave the institute when the period of time for which he took his vows has expired **(c. 637)**. Should a person who has thus left the religious state desire, later on, to enter another institute, or return to the one he left, an indult would have to be obtained from the Holy See (c. 542) and he would have to make a new novitiate.

Art. 3. Exclaustration. By exclaustration is meant the permission to leave the institute *temporarily* **(c. 638)**. It may happen that a religious who has taken vows (whether temporary or perpetual) has grave reasons for leaving his institute in order to live in the world *for a time*. Such a person remains a religious, hence he is still bound by his vows and by such obligations of the religious life as he can observe in the world. He must, however, lay aside the religious habit, but if he is a cleric, he must wear the clerical dress prescribed by c. 136, § 1. During his sojourn in the world he is deprived of both active and passive voice, but retains the purely spiritual privileges of his institute. During the period of exclaustration he is not subject to his superiors but to the Ordinary in the place in which he resides, even under his vow of obedience **(c. 639)**. For special reasons, provided there be no scandal, the Ordinary who has granted the exclaustration may allow the religious to wear the religious habit.[3] Exclaustration must be clearly distinguished from permission to live outside the religious house (c. 606, § 2), even when such permission is granted by the Holy See.

2. Only the Holy See can grant an indult of exclaustration to a religious who is a member of a pontifical institute; the Ordinary of the place in which the religious *lawfully* resides[4] may grant it to a member of a diocesan institute **(c. 638)**.

Art. 4. Secularization. By secularization is meant the permission to leave the religious institute *permanently* **(c. 638)**. It is, therefore, a total and permanent release from the religious life, granted at the request of a religious who wishes to return to the world for good. Only the Holy See can grant such an indult to a member of a pontifical institute, while the local Ordinary may grant it to a member of a diocesan institute lawfully residing in his territory **(c. 638)**. The religious who has asked for an indult of secularization, whether from the Holy See or from the local Ordinary, is free to refuse the indult or dispensation when he receives notice of it from his local superior, even though the superior general has already issued the decree executing the rescript

---

[3] Code Com., Nov. 12, 1922, ad III; *AAS*, 14-622; *Digest*, I, p. 326.
[4] Code Com., July 24, 1939; *AAS*, 31-321; *Digest*, II, p. 173; Schaefer, *De Rel.*, Ed. 3, n. 549, p. 958; Jone, *Gesetzbuch*, p. 563.

in accordance with c. 56. Should superiors have grave reason to the contrary, they should refer the matter to the S. Congregation of Religious.[5]

2. *Effects of secularization:* A religious who has obtained an indult of secularization and left his institute: (*a*) is completely separated from his institute; he must put off the religious habit and must conduct himself as a secular in all that concerns Holy Mass, the divine office, the use and administration of the Sacraments; (*b*) he is dispensed from his vows, keeping however the obligations connected with major orders, but he is no longer bound to recite the divine office by reason of his former profession, nor is he bound by the other rules and constitutions of the institute which he has left; (*c*) should he later obtain an apostolic indult permitting him to enter the religious life once again, he must make a novitiate and in due time take his vows, but his rank among the professed dates from the day of his new profession (**c. 640**).

3. *A religious in major orders* who is secularized, or who leaves his institute at the expiration of the period of his temporary vows, must return to his diocese, if he has not lost it by perpetual profession (c. 585), and his Bishop must receive him; if he has lost his diocese by reason of profession of perpetual vows, he may not exercise his sacred orders until he has found a Bishop willing to receive him, or the Holy See has made other provisions (**c. 641, § 1**). A Bishop may receive a secularized religious who is in major orders and who has lost his diocese by reason of his former profession in one of two ways: (*a*) he may receive him unconditionally, in which case the latter is *ipso facto* incardinated into the diocese, or; (*b*) he may receive him for a period of three years by way of experiment. In this latter case the Bishop may extend the period of probation, but not beyond another period of three years. At the end of six years of trial, the religious becomes incardinated into the diocese *ipso facto,* unless he has been dismissed before the six years of trial have expired (**c. 641, § 2**).[6] This

---

[5] S. C. Rel., Aug. 1, 1922; *AAS*, 14-501; *Digest*, I, p. 326.

[6] According to the present practice of S. Congregation of Religious (*Formulae Facultatum* 11 and 12-A), an indult of secularization is granted to a religious in major orders in one of the two following ways: (1) The Bishop who is willing to receive such a religious *unconditionally* is granted the power to issue an indult of secularization. He must do so by a formal executorial decree which has the effect of releasing the religious from his vows and of incardinating him in the diocese of said Bishop. Until this executorial decree is issued, the religious may not leave his institute, nor may the Bishop receive him into his diocese. Copies of the executorial decree must be sent to the S. Congregation of Religious as well as to the superior general in question. (2) The Bishop who is willing to receive a religious in major orders *by way of experiment or trial,* is granted the power to issue an *indult of exclaustration,* valid only for the period

automatic incardination after six complete years of trial or probation does not take place in the case of a cleric in major orders who was a member of a society of men living in common without (public) vows (c. 673, § 1), since he was not a religious according to the definition of canon 488, 7°. Members of such societies are governed in this matter by the same laws as are the secular clergy.[7]

4. *Disabilities of secularized religious:* A secularized religious who has taken *perpetual* vows and who is in major orders, may exercise those major orders in conformity with the norms laid down in canon 641, as we have just seen, but he is prohibited from obtaining the following benefices and offices without a new and special indult of the Holy See: (*a*) from any benefice of whatever kind in a major or minor basilica, or in a cathedral church; (*b*) from any professorship or office in any major or minor seminary, or in any college in which *clerics* are being educated, or in any university or institute enjoying an apostolic privilege of granting academic degrees; (*c*) from any office or position in a diocesan Curia, or in any religious house, whether of religious men or women, even in a diocesan congregation (c. 642, § 1). These same disabilities apply to religious in major orders who are *dismissed* either with temporary vows or with perpetual vows (cf. cc. 648 and 672, § 2).

These disabilities are likewise incurred by those who, after being bound for six years by temporary vows, or by an oath of perseverance or other special promises according to the constitutions (in societies of men living in common) have obtained a dispensation from them (c. 642, § 2). Hence those who are dispensed from the above-mentioned obligations *before* six years have elapsed are certainly not subject to these disabilities; those who leave voluntarily or by request *at the expiration* of such obligations, even though they extended over a period of six years or more, are probably not subject to the disabilities in question, since they *have not been dispensed from the obligations.*

---

of trial, which permits the religious to live and work in said Bishop's diocese, wearing the clerical dress prescribed by canon 136, § 1. Should the Bishop, after informing the superiors of the religious, dismiss the latter from his diocese during the period of trial, the religious must return to his institute at once. If, however, the Bishop is willing to receive the religious *definitely* into his diocese, either at the end of the period of trial, or even before, he must proceed as above in n. 1, that is, issue the indult of secularization by an executorial decree under the conditions and with the effects mentioned above. For formulae of S. Congregation of Religious see: Schaefer, *De Rel.,* ed. 3, p. 963; *Periodica,* v. 21 (1932), p. 183.

[7] S. C. Conc., July 15, 1933; *AAS*, 26–234; *Digest,* II, p. 173.

5. *Financial status of secularized religious:* (*a*) A religious who has left his institute at the expiration of the period of time for which he took temporary vows, or one who has obtained an indult of secularization, or one who has been dismissed, may not demand any financial remuneration for services rendered to the institute (c. 643, § 1). This provision of the canon law is readily understood by the civil courts in the case of religious who have received their education or training in a religious institute; but it is not understood by them in the case of lay-religious, that is, those who have been employed in the household duties. Hence it is advisable to have all lay-novices sign an agreement containing the provisions of this canon before admitting them to first profession. (*b*) In the case of a religious woman who leaves at the expiration of temporary vows, or who obtains an indult of secularization, or who is dismissed, and who has been received without a dowry, and who cannot provide for herself out of her own resources, the institute should in charity give her what is necessary for her to return safely and becomingly to her home, and provide her for a special period with the means of support. This amount is to be determined by mutual consent or, in case of disagreement, by the local Ordinary, in accordance with natural equity (c. 643, § 2). In case the subject dismissed had been received with a dowry which does not amount to as much as the reasonably estimated charitable subsidy, the religious institute is bound to supply the amount which is wanting.[8]

Art. 5. Apostasy From the Religious Life. A religious having perpetual vows (solemn or simple) who *unlawfully leaves* the religious house *with the intention of not returning,* or who, though he has left the religious house legitimately, does not return to it because he intends to withdraw himself from religious obedience, is called an *apostate from the religious life* (c. 644, § 1). The perverse intention mentioned here is a presumption in canon law whenever the religious does not return within a month, or does not manifest his intention of returning to his superior within the same space of time (c. 644, § 2). Three elements, therefore, are required for the crime of apostasy from the religious life: (1) a religious with *perpetual* vows; (2) leaving the institute or house without permission, or not returning at the proper time when absent with permission; (3) the intention of not returning. This intention must be certain in the external forum; for instance, the culpable religious has manifested it by a clear statement in word or

---

[8] S. C. Rel., March 2, 1924. *Digest,* I, p. 300.

writing, or has placed an act which can admit of no other interpretation, e.g., by accepting secular employment or entering upon a civil marriage, etc. The prolongation of the unlawful absence beyond a month without any manifestation of the intention to return establishes a presumption of law, that is, the religious may and should be treated as an apostate, until he proves that he had the intention of returning. The penalty of apostasy from the religious life is excommunication reserved to the major superior in a clerical exempt institute, or to the local Ordinary in all other cases (c. 2385).

Art. 6. Flight From the Religious Life. A religious (whether of temporary or perpetual vows) who deserts the religious house without the permission of his superior, but with the intention of returning to his institute, is called a *fugitive* in canon law (c. 644, § 3). He differs from an apostate only in his intention of returning. He wishes to be free from the restraints of the religious life, to throw off the yoke of obedience, and to be his own master for a while without having to attend community exercises. All commentators are agreed that two or three days of unlawful absence are required to constitute a fugitive in the canonical sense. A religious who leaves his religious house without permission and remains away for less than three days might sin gravely and would be punished accordingly by his superior, but he would not incur the legal penalties of a fugitive, namely privation of office, and suspension reserved to his own major superior if he be a cleric in major orders (c. 2386).

A religious with temporary vows who deserts his religious house with the intention of *not returning,* sins gravely no doubt, but he is neither an apostate, since he does not have perpetual vows, nor a fugitive, since he does not intend to return. Although some commentators hold that such a religious is to be considered as a fugitive, and would, consequently, apply the penalties of the law in his case, the better opinion seems to be that, since we are dealing with penalties, the law must be interpreted strictly. All are agreed that such a religious remains bound by the obligations of the rules and constitutions, and is obliged to return to his institute without delay; if he does not do so, his superiors would have ample cause to dismiss him by reason of canon 647, § 2.

Obligations of Apostates and Fugitives. Both remain bound by the obligation of the rules and constitutions, and of their vows, and must return to their institute without delay (c. 645, § 1).

Obligations of Superiors. Superiors must earnestly seek for them and, if possible, bring them back to the institute. In case of an apostate or fugitive nun, this duty falls upon the local Ordinary and upon the regular superior upon whom the monastery depends. After their return superiors must inflict the punishments laid down by the constitutions for such offenses according to the gravity of the fault (c. 645, § 2; cc. 2385–6).

Section 2. Involuntary Leaving (cc. 646–672)

PRELIMINARY SURVEY

Exclusion From Perpetual Vows (c. 637)
Dismissal by the Law Itself (c. 646)
Dismissal of Religious With Temporary Vows (cc. 647–648)
Dismissal of Religious With Perpetual Vows in Non-Exempt
    Clerical, and in All Lay Institutes (cc. 649–652)
Dismissal of Religious With Perpetual Vows in a Clerical
    Exempt Institute (cc. 654–668)
Juridical Condition of Religious Dismissed With Perpetual
    Vows (cc. 669–672)

Art. 1. Exclusion From Renewal of Vows. For just reasons superiors may refuse to allow a religious to renew his temporary profession or to make his profession of perpetual vows. Lack of health, however, is not a sufficient motive, unless the professed has fraudulently hidden or dissimulated his state of health before his profession (c. 637). A serious lack of intellectual and moral qualities required to carry on the work of the institute would be a sufficient reason to refuse a religious the permission to renew temporary profession or to bar him from profession of perpetual vows. Superiors are not allowed to admit a novice whose health is not good to temporary profession as an experiment, on condition that he will be sent away later if his health does not improve. Such a condition would be contrary to the prescriptions of the Code. A religious who becomes mentally afflicted during the period of his temporary vows *must be kept* in the religious institute. He continues to be a member in the state in which he was at the moment the malady manifested itself.[9]

N.B. The fact that a religious is not allowed to renew his temporary vows or to make his profession of perpetual vows is not to be

---

[9] S. C. Rel., Feb. 5, 1925; *AAS*, 17–107; *Digest*, I, p. 309.

considered the same as dismissal. The two cases are quite distinct. The canonical effects of dismissal (see c. 669) are not incurred.

Art. 2. Dismissal by the Law Itself. The commission of certain very grave crimes has the effect of expelling the culpable religious *ipso facto,* that is, the religious is dismissed by the law itself. The terms of this canon are to be interpreted strictly, that is, all the conditions laid down must be actually present before such a grave penalty can be said to be incurred. Three major crimes are punished by dismissal *ipso facto:*

1. *A religious who has publicly apostatized from the Catholic faith* **(c. 646, § 1, 1°):** *Apostasy* is defined in canon 1325, § 2, as the *complete abandonment of the Christian faith.* Our canon, however, says: one who has publicly apostatized from the *Catholic* faith. Hence it would, at least more probably, include a religious who would join a non-Catholic Christian sect (heretic) as well as one who joined a schismatic church. The apostasy from the Catholic faith must be *public,* which means, according to canon 2197, 1°, that either the fact is already known by a large number of people, or that the circumstances of the apostasy are such that one must prudently judge that it will easily become known.

2. *A religious who runs away with a person of the opposite sex* **(c. 646, § 1, 2°):** In order to incur dismissal in this case it is required: (*a*) that the religious run away from the religious house with or without the intention of returning; (*b*) that the person of the opposite sex either accompany the religious from the religious house (a rare case), or meet the religious by previous agreement after the religious has left the house; (*c*) it is a probable opinion, to be followed in practice that near relatives (father, mother, sister, brother) are not included in the term "persons of the opposite sex."

3. *A religious who attempts or contracts marriage,* even a so-called civil marriage (**c. 646, § 1, 3°).** This crime supposes the mutual giving of consent, even though the ceremony be invalid.

4. *Declaration of fact by the religious superior:* Should any one of these three cases occur, the major superior with his chapter or council, according to the constitutions, must make a written declaration of the fact, and must take care to preserve in the archives (register) of the house the evidence collected to prove the fact **(c. 646, § 2).** This declaration of fact, however, is not required for the valid dismissal of the religious by the law itself.[10] The religious who has incurred dis-

---

[10] Code Com., July 30, 1934 ad I; *AAS,* 26-494; *Digest,* II, p. 175.

missal by reason of one of these three crimes is still bound by his vows in accordance with canon 669, § 1, but the religious institute is not bound to take him back even though he fulfill the conditions of canon 672, § 1.[11]

Art. 3. Dismissal of Religious With Temporary Vows (cc. 647–8). 1. *Superior competent to dismiss:* (*a*) *in orders and papal congregations:* the superior general acting with the *consent* of his council, manifested by secret vote; (*b*) *in diocesan congregations:* the local Ordinary in whose territory the religious to be dismissed resides. Hence, not necessarily the Ordinary of the mother house, unless the religious in question actually resides in his territory. The Ordinary, however, may not act in this matter of dismissal without the knowledge of, or against the just opposition of the religious superiors (**c. 647, § 1**). Should he do so, the superiors have the right and the duty to appeal to the Holy See. Such appeal, however, would have no suspensive effect.

2. *Reasons for dismissal:* By the profession of vows the religious has acquired a right to remain a member of the institute. Hence superiors may not dismiss him except for reasons laid down in the law, which they are bound in conscience to observe: (*a*) *the reasons for the dismissal must be grave* (**c. 647, § 2, 1°**); hence, something more than the just and reasonable cause required by canon 637 for the refusal to allow a religious to renew temporal vows or to take perpetual vows; (*b*) these reasons may exist either: (1) *on the part of the religious institute* — in those rare cases in which the good of the individual must yield to the good of the institute, though there be no fault on the part of the individual, e.g., if the financial condition of the institute were such that it could no longer support the religious with temporary vows, and there were no hope of aid being received; otherwise it would be sufficient to allow the religious to live with their relatives for the duration of the financial stress; (2) *on the part of the religious* — the Code does not give a list of such causes. It is left to the prudent judgment and conscience of superiors to decide. Such unfitness on the part of religious may arise from moral or intellectual defects. *Moral defects:* the Code mentions only one, perhaps by way of example: a lack of religious spirit which is a source of scandal to others (**c. 647, § 2, 2°**). Such a lack of religious spirit would be shown by a religious who manifests neither love of, nor interest in the religious life, who frequently omits common exercises without reason, who violates the

---

[11] Code Com., July 30, 1934 ad II; *AAS*, 26-494; *Digest*, II, p. 175.

prescriptions of the rule and of the constitutions without scruple, who obeys the commands of his superiors reluctantly, etc. This lack of religious spirit must be a source of scandal to others, i.e., to members of the community. Such is the case when members of the community begin to imitate the bad example given, or to complain against superiors who tolerate such conduct. *Intellectual defects:* the religious may show a lack of the talent necessary to complete the course of studies or training which is required to fit himself for the work of the institute; or he may manifest a spirit of levity (want of responsibility) which renders him unfit to fulfill the obligations of his state; similarly a lack of common sense which makes him a burden to the community and a source of disturbance. These would be sufficient causes for dismissal of a religious with temporary vows, provided: (*a*) they are not caused *directly by ill health* which afflicts the religious after his profession, or (*b*) superiors were not perfectly aware of these defects or unfitness before when they admitted the professed to his vows. As mentioned above (p. 309) ill health is not a cause for dismissal, unless it be proved with certainty that it had been fraudulently concealed or dissimulated *before* profession.

3. *Procedure to be followed in dismissal* (c. 647, § 2, 3°). (*a*) The superior must be certain of the existence of the reasons for dismissal. This does not mean that a judicial process must be held, but the proofs of the existence of the defects of the subject for which he is to be dismissed must be recorded in writing, so that they may be forwarded to the S. Cong. of Religious in case the religious appeals to the Holy See from the decree of dismissal. (*b*) The reasons for the dismissal must be made known to the culprit, who must be allowed to answer the charges brought against him. These answers should also be recorded in writing, either by having the subject write out his answers to the charges brought against him, or by taking down the answers given orally, which the subject should first read, correct if necessary, and finally sign with his name. Should he refuse to do so, this fact should be attested to in writing. (*c*) *In the case of a lack of religious spirit,* it must be evident that there is no hope of reform because a twofold admonition has produced no effect, and salutary penances joined to the admonitions were likewise ineffective (c. 647, § 2, 2°). (*d*) *Vote of the council:* After the second admonition has proved of no avail the superior shall lay before his council the proofs of the reasons for dismissal, that the admonitions and salutary penances were given, that they were of no avail, and the answers of

the religious to be dismissed. Having carefully studied these matters, the council will take a secret vote. The majority vote will decide. If dismissal is decided upon, the religious will be so informed.

4. *Right of appeal:* The religious against whom a decree of dismissal has been issued has a right to appeal within ten days from the time that he has been informed of his dismissal (c. 647, § 2, 4°). Since this time begins to run only after the religious knows of his right to appeal, it is advisable that the superior inform him of this right when he makes the decree of dismissal known to him.[12] In case the religious appeals to the Holy See against the decree of dismissal, it is suspended until confirmed by the Holy See, the person dismissed remains a religious, hence retains all rights and obligations of the religious state, e.g., he must live in the religious house and obey superiors, etc., until the Holy See decides the case.

5. *Effects of dismissal:* The religious with temporary vows who accepts the decree of dismissal or who, after appeal, is obliged to accept such a decree, is, *ipso facto,* freed from his vows and from all the obligations of the religious life. A cleric in major orders retains his obligations arising therefrom, that is, celibacy and the recitation of the divine office, and he is subject to the disabilities listed in canon 642, § 1; a cleric in minor orders is *ipso facto* reduced to the lay state (c. 648). In the case of a religious woman who is dismissed, her dowry must be returned to her (c. 647, § 2, 5°), or a charitable subsidy given in place of it (c. 643, § 2), or both, if necessary (see p. 307).

Art. 4. Dismissal of Religious Who Have Taken Perpetual Vows in a Non-exempt Clerical Institute or in a Lay Institute (cc. 649, 653).

In congregations of men: a. reasons for dismissal: (1) three grave, external offenses against the general law of the Church or against the special law for religious, (2) which in spite of repeated admonitions and threats of dismissal, (3) are not corrected, so that there is no hope of amendment (c. 649).

1. *Three grave external offenses:* There must be at least three offenses of the same species or, if they are of different species, of such a nature that when taken together they manifest the perversity of the will resolved on evil; one *continuous* offense which is not corrected after repeated admonitions is virtually equivalent to three offenses (c. 657). These three offenses must be grave and external. Frequent venial faults would not suffice, nor would intellectual or physical defects. These

---

[12] S. C. Rel., July 20, 1923; *AAS,* 15-457; *Digest,* I, p. 328.

causes must be moral causes, grave either in themselves, or because of the circumstances, such as violations of general or particular laws of the Church to which a canonical penalty is attached; violations of a formal and grave precept; violations of the vows or constitutions which would be especially grave, or which would give rise to grave scandal either in the community or to outsiders.

2. *Repeated admonitions:* The admonition must be given by the immediate major superior, either personally, or through another who is delegated by him; delegation given for the first admonition holds for the second likewise **(c. 659).** The superior shall not proceed to the admonition unless the grave external offense is publicly known, or the culprit has made an extrajudicial confession of the same, or other sufficient proofs are at hand from the previous inquiry **(c. 658).** *Two* admonitions must be given: either after each of two distinct grave external offenses, or in the case of one and the same grave external offense persisted in, the admonitions must be separated by at least three entire days **(c. 660).**

Threat of dismissal: To each admonition must be added a threat of dismissal. Besides, the superior should exhort the culprit to amend his ways, and impose other suitable penal remedies which may help the culprit to amend his ways and may serve to repair the scandal given. The superior is obliged to remove the occasion of relapses from the culprit, even, if that be necessary, by transferring him to another house, where it will be easier to watch him and the occasion of sinning will be more remote **(c. 661).**

3. *Lack of amendment:* The guilty religious who has been admonished and threatened with dismissal must be given the opportunity to defend himself and answer the charges brought against him **(c. 650, § 3).** His statement (defense) should be made in writing and signed by him, or, if given orally, should be written down and signed by him in the presence of two witnesses. Should he refuse to sign his oral defense, this fact should be put in writing and signed by witnesses. The religious is considered not to have amended himself if, after the second admonition, he has committed a new serious external fault, or persisted in the same fault without any essential change. After the second admonition six days must elapse before the superior takes any further steps in the case **(c. 662).**

b. Procedure to be followed: When the facts explained above are evident, the superior general with his council will consider all the testimony, and finally take a vote on the question: "should the religious be dismissed?" If the greater number of votes are cast for dismissal: (1) if the guilty religious be a member of a diocesan congregation all the documents must be transferred to the Ordinary of the place in whose territory he resides; (2) if he be a member of a pontifical institute, the superior general will draw up a decree of dismissal, but this will have no effect until *confirmed by the Holy See;* hence all the documents in the case should be forwarded to the Sacred Congregation of Religious **(c. 650).**

    c. Right of appeal: (1) In the case of a religious dismissed by the local Ordinary from a *diocesan* congregation, he may appeal to the Holy See with *suspensive* effect; (2) in the case of a religious dismissed from a *pontifical* congregation, there is no formal right of appeal, since such an appeal is already included in the acts of the case. The S. Congregation will not ratify a decree of dismissal if the acts do not include the answers, and therefore, the defense of the religious who is to be dismissed.

    In congregations of women **(c. 651):** 1. *Reasons for dismissal* must be grave and external. Frequent venial faults would not suffice. Intellectual and physical defects are not sufficient causes. External moral causes, grave either in themselves, or because of their circumstances, are required. One grave external cause, by reason of its continuance, would be sufficient, e.g., formal disobedience.

    2. *Procedure to be followed:* (*a*) The superior must have *certain* evidence of the grave external fault, before she can proceed to the admonitions. (*b*) The superior must then admonish the religious to correct the grave, external fault, and help her to do so, by imposing suitable penances, and by removing the occasions of the fault, e.g., by transferring her to another house, or by changing her office or work. Though not strictly of obligation by law, it will always be advisable to add a threat of dismissal to the admonitions. If the sister persists in her fault, or commits another grave, external fault, a second admonition should be given as above, again accompanied by a threat of dismissal. Both the admonitions and the threat of dismissal should be given in writing, or in the presence of two witnesses. The constitutions will decide which superior has the right to give these admonitions. (*c*) The sister who is admonished and threatened with dismissal must be given the opportunity to defend herself, and to answer the charges brought against her. Her statement should be made in writing and signed by her, or, if given orally, should be taken down and signed by the sister after she has read the answers and corrected them. Should

she refuse to sign, a written testimony of this fact should be made. (*d*) Should the sister persist in one grave external fault or commit another grave external fault after a twofold admonition and threat of dismissal, the superior general will collect proof of this, and then collect all the acts and documents of the case. Though the Code does not prescribe that she consult her council before sending the case to the Congregation of Religious, yet this should always be done. Frequently the constitutions will demand the deliberative or at least the consultative vote of the council. In practice the S. Congregation of Religious wishes to know what the vote of the council was.

In the case of a congregation approved by the Holy See, the superior general will transmit all the documents in the case to the S. Congregation of Religious, who in turn will decide whether the sister is to be dismissed or not. *In the case of a monastery of nuns,* the superior will transmit the documents to the local Ordinary, who after he has studied the case, will add his *votum,* and that of the regular superior, if the monastery be subject to regulars, and transmit them to the S. Congregation of Religious. *In the case of a diocesan congregation,* the superior general will transmit all the documents to the Ordinary of the place in whose territory the sister to be dismissed resides. The Ordinary will then consider the case, and if he sees fit, issue the decree of dismissal. In this latter case the sister so dismissed has a right of appeal to the S. Congregation of Religious. During the appeal, the decree has no effect (c. 652).

Art. 5. Judicial Process for the Dismissal of Religious Who Made Profession of Perpetual Vows Whether Solemn or Simple in an Exempt Clerical Institute (cc. 654–668).

1. The *procedure* to be followed is the legal element by which the dismissal of these religious is essentially distinguished from that of other professed bound by perpetual vows. The formalities of the canonical process must be observed, every contrary privilege being revoked **(c. 654).**

2. The *competent tribunal* is made up of the superior general of the institute, or of the monastic congregation, acting as presiding judge, together with the special council of the superior, composed of at least *four* councilors; if one or more of these be absent, the presiding judge appoints with the approbation of the others as many religious as are needed to make up the tribunal with himself; he also names the religious who is to act as prosecutor with the consent of the tribunal **(c. 655).**

3. *The process:* (*a*) The process of dismissal may not be begun before the incorrigibility of the religious who is gravely culpable shall be established in a certain manner. The immediate major superior, therefore, will send all the documents in the case to the superior general, six days after he has fulfilled all the requirements of cc. 656–662 as explained above. (*b*) The promoter of justice, that is, the religious who acts as prosecutor, shall receive the documents from the superior general. He will decide whether it be necessary to complete the records by a new act of accusation (**c. 664, § 1**). (*c*) The accused has the right to choose his own advocate; if he does not do so, the superior general will appoint someone for this office (c. 1655). A religious who acts as notary either habitually or by special appointment will discharge the office of secretary or recorder (cc. 503; 1585). (*d*) The investigation of the judges, the defense of the religious, and the accusation of the promoter of justice must all be directed to three things: (1) Were there three offenses or was there one offense equivalent to three? (2) Was the admonition or warning given twice and with a threat of dismissal each time, and was it given after the interval of time fixed by law? (3) Were proofs of amendment lacking? The details of this procedure are described in Book IV of the Code.

4. *The sentence:* After making a serious examination of the case (**c. 665**), the tribunal pronounces sentence by a majority vote, that is to say, at least three out of five (c. 1577, § 1). If the sentence be for dismissal, this sentence together with all the records of the trial are to be forwarded to the S. Congregation of Religious. The execution of the sentence is suspended until it is confirmed by the Holy See (**c. 666**).

5. *In distant lands:* Superiors general, with the consent of their council or chapter, may delegate the power of dismissal by formal trial to upright and prudent religious, at least three in number, who will observe all the steps of the process and sentence as described above (**c. 667**). Lands may be distant physically or morally (in time of war or persecution). Such delegation, however, should not be given if, under normal circumstances, communication with the superior general by letter is not difficult. Either the entire process may be delegated, or only certain acts of the process. If the entire process be delegated, the local delegated court will pass a true sentence of dismissal, which needs only the confirmation of the S. Congregation to be put into effect. It will be very advisable, however, to send all the records, together with the sentence, to the superior general, so that he may

verify the requirements of law before presenting the case to the S. Congregation for confirmation.

Art. 6. Dismissal in Urgent Cases. In case of grave external scandal or of very serious imminent injury to the community, the religious may be *sent back to the world* immediately by his major superior with the consent of his council or even, if there be danger in delay and time does not admit of recourse to the major superior, by the local superior with the consent of his council *and of the local Ordinary* (c. 653).

1. *In case of grave external scandal:* e.g., the religious has committed a grave crime, either within or outside the religious house, and this fact is already known by many persons outside the community, or it is impossible to keep it from becoming known. This case supposes that the guilty religious must necessarily lose the respect of good people.

2. *In case of very serious imminent injury to the community:* such injury: (*a*) may be spiritual or temporal; e.g., danger of the loss of reputation for a teaching or hospital community, danger of the suppression of the community by the civil authority, danger of financial loss, fines, or lawsuits; (*b*) must be imminent, that is, morally certain to occur if the religious is not sent away; (*c*) must threaten the *community,* not merely one or other person in the community. It is not necessary that the religious who causes the threat of grave injury to the community be guilty of a *moral fault* in doing so. Such serious injury may arise from merely political or civil or other circumstances.

3. The sending away of the religious *must be the only means of avoiding* either the scandal or the injury which threatens the community. If it were sufficient to send the religious to another house, then he may not be sent back to the world. Hence, it must be at least probable that the sending away of the religious will either avert or notably diminish the scandal or the injury threatening the community.

4. *Mode of procedure in an urgent case:* (*a*) Certain proof of the grave external scandal or of the threat of serious injury to the community must be gathered; if possible, the guilty subject must be heard. (*b*) The major superior must propose the case to his council which will then decide by a majority vote, whether the religious is to be sent away or not. (*c*) If there be danger in delay and the major superior cannot be reached, the local superior may act with the consent of his council. If the council decides to send the guilty religious away, the

consent of the local Ordinary must be obtained before any action may be taken. (*d*) The guilty religious must put off the religious habit and leave at once. He may appeal to the Holy See if he thinks that he has been treated unjustly. (*e*) The major superior, or the local Ordinary, as the case may be, must immediately submit the case without delay to the Holy See. The S. Congregation of Religious, having studied the case will issue the decree of dismissal (c. 653).

5. Canon 653 may be invoked also during that period of time when the experiment of incorrigibility is being made according to canon 660, or while waiting for the decision of the Holy See if the decree of dismissal has already been sent to the Holy See for confirmation according to the terms of canons 652 and 665 (c. 668). This canon may also be invoked against a religious who has taken only temporary vows. Ordinarily, however, the power granted superiors in canon 647 will suffice to handle such an urgent case, that is, the superior can issue a decree of dismissal at once.

6. *Effects of being sent away in an urgent case:* The guilty religious who has been sent back to the world remains a member of the institute until the Holy See has issued the decree of dismissal. If the religious is a cleric in major orders, he is not suspended by reason of canon 671, 1° until the Holy See issues the decree of dismissal.

Art. 7. Condition of a Religious Dismissed With Perpetual Vows (cc. 669–672).

1. The dismissed religious remains bound by the vows he took in religion, unless the constitutions or the Holy See ordain otherwise (c. 669, § 1). Thus the S. Congregation of Religious when confirming the decree of dismissal may grant an indult of dispensation in single instances. It is nearly always advisable to ask for such an indult in the case of a non-clerical religious who is dismissed.

2. A *cleric in minor orders* is reduced to the lay state by a decree of dismissal (c. 669, § 2):

3. A *cleric in major orders* who has been dismissed by reason of one of the crimes enumerated in c. 646, or who has been dismissed by reason of a crime which the general law of the Church punishes with *infamy* (*infamia iuris,* cf. cc. 2314, § 1, n. 2, 2320, 2328, 2343, § 1, n. 2, § 2, n. 2, 2351, § 2, 2356, 2357, § 1, 2359, § 2), or with *deposition* (cc. 2303, 2314, § 1, n. 2, 2320, 2322, n. 1, 2328, 2350, § 1, 2354, 2, 2359, § 2, 2379, 2394, n. 2, 2401) or *degradation* (cc. 2305, 2314, § 1, n. 3, 2343, § 1, n. 3, 2354, § 2, 2368, § 1) is perpetually forbidden to wear the ecclesiastical garb (c. 670). This privation carries with it the prohibition

to exercise any ecclesiastical ministry whatsoever, as well as the privation of all clerical privileges (c. 2300). The religious institute has no obligation to give temporal assistance to such a dismissed religious.

4. A *cleric in major orders* who is dismissed for lesser crimes than those mentioned in n. 3, page 319:

a. is suspended *ipso facto* until he receives absolution from the Holy See; for effects of suspension see c. 2278 **(c. 671, 1°)**;

b. The Congregation of Religious *may,* if it sees fit, order the dismissed to wear the garb of the secular clergy, and reside in a certain diocese; in which case it will inform the Bishop of the reasons for the dismissal of the cleric **(c. 671, 2°)**;

c. If the dismissed religious does not obey the order mentioned in *b.* the institute has no obligation to him, and he is deprived, *ipso facto,* of the right to wear the ecclesiastical garb **(c. 671, 3°)**;

d. The Ordinary to whose diocese the dismissed religious has been sent will either send him to a religious house to do penance, or submit him to the care and watchfulness of a pious and prudent priest; and if the religious refuses to obey the injunction of the Ordinary, the effects mentioned in *c.* will follow **(c. 671, 4°)**;

e. The institute from which the religious was dismissed will supply him, through the hands of the Ordinary, with means for the necessities of life, unless he can provide for himself from other sources **(c. 671, 5°)**;

f. If, during the space of a year, or even less according to the judgment of the Ordinary, the dismissed religious does not live a life worthy of an ecclesiastical person, he is to be expelled from the house of penance, deprived of his subsidy on the part of the institute, and deprived by the Ordinary of his right to wear the ecclesiastical garb. The Ordinary shall inform both the Holy See and the institute of these facts **(c. 671, 6°)**;

g. If, on the other hand, during the time mentioned above, the dismissed religious has conducted himself so well that he may rightly be considered to have reformed, the Ordinary will recommend the petition of the religious to the Holy See asking for absolution from the censure of suspension, and, upon receiving the same, may permit him to say Mass, with proper provisions and limitations, and may allow him some other sacred ministry according to his prudent judgment, which will enable him to live decently, in which case the subsidy granted by the institute may be discontinued. If there is question of a deacon or subdeacon, the case is to be referred to the Holy See (c. 671, 7°).

5. The religious who has been dismissed without being dispensed from his vows is obliged to return to the cloister; and if he has proved over a space of three years that he is entirely reformed, the institute is bound to take him back; if grave reasons against his return exist either on the part of the institute or on the part of the religious, the case is to be submitted to the judgment of the Holy See (c. 672, § 1). This canon does not apply to religious who were dismissed *ipso facto* according to the provisions of canon 646.[13] If the religious returns to the institute, he immediately resumes his rank among the professed, but those of his rights which depend on his seniority are counted only from the day of his return.

6. In the case of a religious who is dismissed with a *dispensation from his vows,* and who has found a Bishop willing to receive him, he is to remain under his jurisdiction and special care, observing however, the prescriptions of c. 642 (see art. 3, n. 4, pp. 306–307); otherwise his case is to be referred to the Holy See (c. 672, § 2).

CASES AND QUESTIONS

1. Sister Delicata had her first temporary vows postponed on account of her poor health. Finally the superior said, "I will allow you to take your temporary vows for three years on condition that you will be admitted to perpetual vows if your health improves." The time for perpetual vows is now at hand, and sister's health is no better. May the superior refuse to admit her to perpetual vows and send her back to the world merely because of a lack of good health? (C. 637).

2. What is the difference between an indult of exclaustration and one of secularization? (C. 638).

3. Sister Clementia wishes to be dispensed from her vows and return to the world for a very good reason. She is stationed in Wyoming. The mother house of her diocesan congregation is in Nevada. To which Bishop should she apply for an indult of secularization? (Cc. 638; Code Com. July 24, 1939, *AAS,* 31 [1939], 321; *Digest,* II, p. 173).

4. Sister Inconstantia leaves her convent unlawfully after two years of temporary vows, being still bound by them for another year. She does not intend to return. Is she to be considered as an apostate, and therefore excommunicated? After three months she is married by a priest who

---

[13] Code Com., July 30, 1934 ad II; *AAS,* 26-494; *Digest,* II, p. 175.

does not know of her condition. She is *ipso facto* dismissed by reason of canon 646, 3°. Is she thereby released from her vows? (Cc. 644; 579; 648).

5. Brother Henry, an ardent follower of the pigskin, steals out at night to see a football game, and then spends the night at the home of a friend, returning unobserved in the morning in time for Mass. Is he a fugitive? (C. 644, § 2, and explanation in text).

6. Frater Flighty receives tonsure during the period of his temporary vows; at the expiration of these vows he is not allowed to take perpetual vows but is sent away. Does he incur the penalty laid down in canon 669, § 2? (See explanation in text under cc. 637, 648, 669, § 2.)

7. Sister Dolorosa remains in the convent Saturday afternoon when the other sisters go to the neighboring church for May devotions. She phones her brother and asks him to come and get her and take her home, as she is tired of religious life. He comes, and she goes back home with him, intending never to return to the convent. What is her canonical status? What should sister's superior do in this case? (Cc. 644, 645).

8. Brother Hasty has a quarrel with his superior and demands that the latter obtain an indult of secularization for him. By the time the indult arrives Brother has cooled off and pleads with his superior to be allowed to remain in the community. Is he obliged to accept the indult of secularization? (See Code Com., Aug. 1, 1922, *AAS*, 14 [1922], 501; *Digest*, I, p. 326.)

9. Must a mother superior give warnings to a delinquent subject before proceeding to dismiss her: in the case of a sister with temporary vows? With perpetual vows? (C. 647, § 2, 2°; 651, and explanation in text.)

10. Father Pertinax has asked for and obtained an indult of secularization, but can find no benevolent Bishop who is willing to take him on trial. He finally leaves his monastery and goes to live with his brother who is a diocesan priest. May the Bishop give Father Pertinax permission to say Mass and hear confessions in his brother's parish church? (C. 641, § 1).

11. Brother Simplex becomes weary of the religious life and, taking French leave, returns to his ancestral home. After some days his superior discovers his whereabouts, and sends another brother there to bring him back. Brother Simplex returns sobbing and repentant. The superior promptly dismisses him on the score that he had already decided to send him away at the expiration of his temporary vows. Did the superior act validly and licitly? (C. 645, § 2).

12. Is a religious freed from his vows by the fact that he has been dismissed? (Cc. 648, 669, § 1).

Readings:

Fallon, *Appointment of Religious to Certain Offices in the Diocesan Curia*, IER. 52 (1928), 507–510; Michalicka, *Judicial Procedure on Dis-*

missal of Clerical Exempt Religious, C.U., 1923; O'Leary, *Religious Dismissed After Perpetual Profession,* C.U., 1943; O'Neill, *Dismissal of Religious in Temporary Vows,* C.U., 1942; Riesner, *Apostates and Fugitives,* C.U., 1942.

APPENDIX

Societies of Men and Women Living in Common Without (Public) Vows (cc. 673–681).[14]

1. These societies are composed of those who imitate the religious life by living in common under the authority of superiors according to their constitutions, but either without any vows, or at least without *public* vows. Hence these societies are not, properly so called, religious institutes, nor are their members religious in the strict sense of the word **(c. 673, § 1).** This does not prevent them from following the evangelical counsels, even by reason of one or more vows, but such vows are not *public,* that is, are not received by the superior in the name of the Church (c. 1308, § 1).

· These societies are divided like religious institutes into clerical and lay, papal or diocesan according to the norms of canon 488, nn. 3 and 4 **(c. 673, § 2).**

2. *Erection and suppression:* In the erection and suppression of such institutes, of their provinces and houses, these societies are governed by the canons for religious on this subject **(c. 674).**

3. *Government:* The government of each society is determined by its own constitutions, and by the prescriptions of canons 499–530 **(c. 675).**

4. *Administration of temporalities:* These societies as well as their provinces and houses are capable of acquiring and possessing temporal goods; the administration of such goods is governed by the prescriptions of cc. 532–537. Whatever individual members of these societies receive because they are members, is acquired for the society; other goods may be kept, acquired, and administered by the members themselves according to the constitutions **(c. 676).**

5. *Admission of candidates:* The constitutions are to be observed, as also the prescriptions of canon 542 **(c. 677).**

6. *Studies and ordination:* In the matter of clerical studies and promotion to orders, members of these societies are governed by the

---

[14] For a thorough explanation of these canons read: Stanton, *De Societatibus in Communi Viventium sine Votis,* Halifax, 1936.

same laws as secular clerics, besides any special regulations prescribed by the Holy See (c. 678).

7. *Obligations:* All members of such societies are bound by the obligations common to clerics (unless the contrary is evident from the context or from the nature of things), by the obligations common to religious as laid down in canons 595–612, unless the constitutions declare otherwise, finally by the obligations laid down in their own proper constitutions. They must also observe cloister as prescribed in the constitutions, under the vigilance of the local Ordinary (c. 679).

8. *Privileges:* All members of these societies, both clerical and lay, enjoy the privileges of clerics (cc. 119–123) as well as other privileges granted to the society directly; they do not, however, enjoy the privileges of religious, except by special indult (c. 680).

9. *Separation from the society:* First of all, the prescriptions of the constitutions are to be observed. Besides, as regards transfer to another society or to a religious institute canons 632–635 are to be observed; likewise canon 645 regarding apostates and fugitives; finally, canons 646–672 regarding dismissal (c. 681). If, therefore, the bond binding members of a society without vows is temporary, the canons dealing with the dismissal of religious of temporary vows are to be observed; if the bond is perpetual, the canons dealing with the dismissal of religious of perpetual vows.[15]

Readings:

Acken, van, *Handbook for Sisters* (St. Louis: Herder); Augustine, *Commentary on New Code* (St. Louis: Herder), Vol. III, pp. 1–420; Creusen, *Religious Men and Women in the Code* (Milwaukee: Bruce); Geser, *Canon Law Governing Communities of Sisters* (St. Louis: Herder); Lanslots, *Handbook of Canon Law for Congregations of Women Under Simple Vows* (New York: Pustet); Woywod, *Practical Commentary on the Code* (New York: Wagner), Vol. I, pp. 177–301.

---

[15] Code Com., *AAS,* 13–177; *Digest,* I, p. 331.

PART FOUR: INDULGENCES: ORDERS

CHAPTER X

INDULGENCES

Section 1. The Granting of Indulgences (cc. 911–924)

PRELIMINARY SURVEY

Definition of Indulgences (c. 911)
Power to Grant Indulgences (cc. 912, 913)
The Papal Blessing (cc. 914, 915)
Privileged Altars (cc. 916–918)
Publication of Indulgences (c. 919)
Duty to Notify Sacred Penitentiary of Papal Concessions
(c. 920)
Meaning of Certain Grants of Indulgences (c. 921)
Transfer of Indulgences With Transfer of Feast (c. 922)
Time for Visiting Church if Such Visit Is Prescribed
(c. 923)
Cessation of Indulgences (c. 924)

Indulgences Defined. An indulgence is the remission before God of the temporal punishment due for sins whose guilt has already been forgiven, granted by ecclesiastical authority from the treasury of the Church, by way of absolution for the living and by way of suffrage for the departed (cf. c. 911).

1. This remission is effective *before God,* not merely before the Church. This was declared against the errors of Martin Luther,[1] and the Synod of Pistoia.[2]

2. The *temporal punishment* due for sin (in the next life), not the guilt of sin, is remitted. It is necessary that the guilt be already forgiven before the temporal punishment can be remitted by an indulgence.

---

[1] Cf. Denzinger-Bannwart, *Enchiridion,* n. 759.
[2] *Ibid.,* n. 1540.

3. Granted by *ecclesiastical authority from the treasury* of the Church. This authority is contained in the power of the keys; the treasury consists in the inexhaustible merits of Christ and of the Blessed Virgin and the Saints in union with Him.[3]

4. *By way of absolution for the living.* This remission of temporal punishment is a true act of jurisdiction in their regard, and gives them an absolute title, infallibly effective.

5. *By way of suffrage for the departed.* These have passed out of the Church's jurisdiction, but if they died in the state of grace they are still her suffering members through the Communion of Saints. Hence, though she cannot juridically determine the application of it, she implores God to accept a designated share of her treasury and apply it to the departed soul. Is the effect in this case infallible? Many hold that, since the Church represents Christ, *some* effect is infallible, that is, that God will certainly accept the satisfaction so offered and apply it to some soul, not necessarily to the soul designated nor in the measure specified. Others hold that all rests in the inscrutable dominion and mercy of God.[4] If not infallible, how does such an application of indulgences by the Church differ from the ordinary prayers of the faithful? To ask this question is to answer it. In one case it is the Church herself imploring God and offering the merits of Christ; in the other it is mere man offering a supernatural prayer more or less imperfect. Their manner of operation is similar (both are suffrages or intercession); but their power is unequal, that of the Church is far more effective.[5]

Classification. 1. Indulgences are *plenary* or *partial*. *Plenary* is one which, so far as the intention of the authority granting it is concerned, remits all the temporal punishment due to sin in the next life; *partial* is one which remits only a part of it. The reason for the qualification in the definition of plenary indulgence is that it may be only partially gained (c. 926). Partial indulgences are expressed in periods of time which designate the equivalent of the temporal punishment remitted, in terms of the canonical penances formerly practiced in the Church. Thus an indulgence of 7 years is a remission of the temporal punishment equivalent to the canonical penances performed for 7 full years (including Lent). Formerly, the addition of "7 quarantines" indicated an additional remission equivalent to that of the canonical penances

---

[3] *Ibid.*, n. 757.
[4] Cf. Cappello, *De Poenitentia*, n. 956.
[5] Cf. Sixtus IV, cited by Hagedorn, *General Legislation on Indulgences*, p. 63.

performed during 7 periods of Lent (during which they were more severe). In the latest authentic collection, however,[6] there is no mention of quarantines; partial indulgences are given in days and years. Since the severity of the old canonical penances varied in different places, a partial indulgence is necessarily somewhat indefinite.

2. *Personal, real, mixed, local.* An indulgence is *personal* if granted directly to persons (physical or moral) independently of any particular place or thing. It is *real* if attached to some object or thing which must be used by a person in gaining the indulgence. It is *mixed* if it can be gained only by a designated class or quality of person (e.g., one enrolled in a certain confraternity), by the use of a certain thing (e.g., a blessed scapular). It is *local* if directly attached to a place (e.g., church, shrine, or image located there), which must be visited to gain the indulgence. Things to which indulgences may be attached must be of a specified quality, and not of "tin, lead, glass or any similar material which can be easily broken or worn out."[7] But solid glass may be used for rosary beads.[8] Medals must bear the image of a saint who is canonized or in the Martyrology.[9] The indulgence of a crucifix is attached to the figure of Christ; hence the cross may be changed without losing the indulgence.[10] Several indulgences may be attached to the same place or thing (c. 933).

3. *Perpetual* or *temporary.* It is *perpetual* if its concession is without limit of time, *temporary* if limited in time, e.g., during the year of the jubilee.

4. Applicable to the *deceased only,* or to the *living only,* or to *both* the living and the departed (that is, to *either* the one or the other). Thus the indulgence for visiting a cemetery and offering prayers for the dead during the octave of All Souls' Day is for the deceased only.[11] An indulgence for the living cannot be applied to any other living person than the one who gains it (c. 930). Nevertheless, the indulgence of a privileged altar for the dying is applicable to the dying person for whom the Mass is offered; and such an indulgence is *for the living by way of absolution,*[12] effective at the moment of death. All

---

[6] *Preces et Pia Opera Indulgentiis Ditata,* Vatican Press, 1938, hereafter cited as *Preces et P. O.*

[7] S. Paen., 17 Feb., 1922; *AAS,* 14–143; *Digest,* I, p. 422.

[8] S. C. Indulg., 29 Feb., 1820, ad 2; *Decr. Auth.,* n. 249; and S. Paen., 21 Dec., 1925; *AAS,* 18–24; *Digest,* I, p. 422.

[9] S. C. Indulg., 22 Dec., 1710; *Decr. Auth.,* n. 32.

[10] S. C. Indulg., 11 Apr., 1840; *Decr. Auth.,* n. 281.

[11] Cf. S. Paen., 31 Oct., 1934; *AAS,* 26–606; *Digest,* II, p. 226.

[12] Cf. Holy Office, 9 Nov., 1922; *Digest,* I, p. 449.

indulgences granted by the Holy Father are applicable to the deceased, unless the contrary is proved (c. 930). Any indulgence gained by a person who has made the Heroic Act is applicable to the deceased, even though it was granted only for the living.[13]

5. Indulgences are called *toties quoties* if they can be gained anew each time the prescribed work is performed (cf. c. 928).

Ordinary Power to Grant Indulgences. Besides the Roman Pontiff, to whom the dispensing of the entire treasury of the Church has been entrusted by Christ Our Lord, ordinary power to grant indulgences belongs only to those persons to whom it has been expressly granted by law (c. 912). According to the canons, as modified by a decree of the Sacred Penitentiary, of 20 July, 1942 (*AAS*, 34–240; *Digest*, II, p. 221):

1. *Cardinals* have ordinary power to grant indulgences of 300 days, even *toties quoties*, in places or institutes and for persons subject to their jurisdiction or protection; and also in other places, but to be gained only by those present on the respective occasions (c. 239, § 1, 24°).

2. *Metropolitans:* 200 days, throughout the Province, even outside the time of visitation, in the same way as in their own archdiocese (c. 274, 2°).

3. *Residential Bishops:* 100 days, within their jurisdiction (c. 349, § 2, 2°); even to exempt religious or in their churches.[14]

4. *Vicars and Prefects Apostolic,* even without being consecrated Bishops: 100 days, within their territory and during their office (c. 294, § 2).

5. *Abbots and Prelates nullius:* the same power as residential Bishops, i.e., 100 days (c. 215, § 2).

Delegated Power. 1. *Apostolic Delegates, Nuncios, Internuncios* have rather broad delegated powers, extending even to granting plenary indulgences on certain occasions, and declaring them applicable to the Souls in Purgatory.[15]

2. *Priests who assist the dying* have power delegated by law according to canon 468, § 2.

Competency Regarding Indulgences. The concession and use of indulgences are under the jurisdiction of the Sacred Penitentiary, while dogmatic questions relating to them are reserved to the Holy Office

---

[13] S. C. Indulg., 20 Nov., 1854, *Urbis et Orbis; Rescripta Auth.*, n. 392; Cappello, *De Poenitentia*, n. 1002.

[14] Cf. c. 927; Code Com., 6 Dec., 1930; *AAS*, 23–25; *Digest*, I, p. 210; II, p. 221.

[15] Cf. *Faculties of Apostolic Delegate; Digest*, I, p. 179.

(c. 258, § 2). Orientals of whatever rite are to have recourse to the Sacred Penitentiary for everything that concerns indulgences.[16] Before the Code the matter was successively under the jurisdiction of various Congregations: first the Sacred Congregations of the Inquisition and of the Council; then the S. C. of Indulgences and Relics; then a special section of the S. C. of Rites; and a special section of the Holy Office.[17]

Power to Bless Articles and Attach Indulgences to Them. 1. Certain *religious orders and congregations* have received from the Holy See privileges by which the members, upon ordination to the priesthood, can attach certain indulgences to articles in blessing them. The existence of such privileges is recognized and continued in the Decree of the Sacred Penitentiary of 20 March, 1933.[18]

2. Certain associations of the faithful had received the power to grant to their members and to individual priests similar faculties of blessing and attaching indulgences; but their power to do this after April 1, 1933, was revoked by the same decree. Among the associations which had such power are the Society for the Propagation of the Faith, the Pious Union of the Death of St. Joseph, the Pious Union of the Clergy for the Missions, the Near East Association, etc. Many other privileges remain to them, but not this.

3. Individual priests who received the power in question before April 1, 1933, retain it; but thereafter priests can receive the power only from the Holy See directly, or, if they are members of a privileged religious institute, from that institute. *Clerics* who joined such pious associations before the publication of the decree but received the priesthood only after its publication, do not have the faculties. *Priests,* even though not approved for confessions, who joined the associations before the publication, can enjoy all the faculties except those of annexing the Apostolic indulgences and the plenary indulgence *in articulo mortis;* these can be exercised only after the approval for hearing confessions has been obtained (S. Paen., 2 March, 1937; *AAS,* 29–58; *Digest,* II, p. 220).

4. This power is often limited by the term *in forma Ecclesiae consueta.* This means simply that the blessing can be given and the indulgence attached by a simple sign of the cross over the object. No words are required in this case.[19]

---

[16] Cf. S. C. Or., 21 July, 1935; *AAS,* 27–379; *Digest,* II, p. 7, ref.
[17] Cf. Hagedorn, *General Legislation on Indulgences,* p. 78.
[18] Cf. *AAS,* 25–170; *Digest,* I, p. 418.
[19] Cf. S. C. Indulg., 7 Jan., 1843; *Decr. Auth.,* n. 313.

Limitations on Power of Persons Inferior to Roman Pontiff. Persons inferior to the Roman Pontiff cannot: (1) commit to others the faculty of granting indulgences, unless expressly permitted to do so by apostolic indult; nor (2) grant indulgences applicable to the departed; nor (3) attach further indulgences to the same object, act of piety, or association to which indulgences have already been granted by the Apostolic See or by any other authority, unless new conditions are prescribed (c. 913). Priests of the Society of Jesus who have power to confer the papal blessing at the end of missions or retreats can subdelegate another priest to give the blessing to persons in an overflow meeting, who heard the mission by megaphone.[20]

The Papal Blessing. 1. The papal blessing with a plenary indulgence according to the prescribed formula can be imparted by *Bishops* in their respective dioceses three times a year, that is, on Easter Sunday and on two other solemn feast days of their own choice, even if they assist only at the solemn Mass. *Abbots and Prelates nullius* and *Vicars and Prefects Apostolic,* even without the episcopal dignity, can do the same in their respective territories on only two of the solemn days of the year (c. 914). They cannot delegate this faculty;[21] nor can they transfer the Easter blessing to another day.[22]

2. *Regulars* who have the privilege of imparting this papal blessing not only are obliged to observe the prescribed formula, but cannot use this privilege except in their own churches and in the churches of the nuns or tertiaries legitimately aggregated to their order; but not on the same day and in the same place where the Bishop gives it (c. 915). The prescribed formula is that given in the Roman Ritual, Tit. VIII, c. 32.

3. *This same papal blessing,* when given *in virtue of special indult by any priest,* secular or regular, is given with the same formula.[23]

4. We have now to notice two other papal blessings or Apostolic benedictions which are different from the above and from each other, using different formulas. They are:

a. The papal blessing given by privilege *at the close of missions or retreats.* The formula for this blessing is given in the Roman Ritual, Appendix, *Benedictiones Reservatae,* II, n. 4. It consists in the sign

---

[20] S. Paen, 13 Apr., 1935; *Digest,* II, p. 227, note.

[21] S. Paen., 25 Apr., 1922; *Digest,* I, p. 419.

[22] Code Com., 17 Feb., 1930; *AAS,* 22–195; *Digest,* I, p. 419. The faculty given to these prelates by canon 914 was enlarged by the Sacred Penitentiary, 20 July, 1942. Cf. *Digest,* II, p. 221.

[23] S. C. Rit., 12 March, 1940; *AAS,* 32–200; *Digest,* II, p. 222.

of the cross made over the people with the crucifix while saying the words: *Benedictio Dei omnipotentis, Patris, et Filii, et Spiritus Sancti, descendat super vos, et maneat semper.* (R.) *Amen.* It is clear that this formula was not changed by the reply of the S. C. of Rites cited in the last note above, since that referred explicitly to a different blessing and a different formula. The present blessing is not restricted by canon 915, which does not apply to it.[24]

b. The Apostolic blessing with a plenary indulgence given *in articulo mortis* by any priest who is ministering to the sick (c. 468, § 2). This formula differs from all those given above. It will be found in the Roman Ritual, Tit. V, cap. 6.

Privileged Altars. An altar may, either in its own right, or because of the priest who celebrates, or the time when the Mass is said, have the privilege of a plenary indulgence for the departed soul for whom the Mass is offered. Designation of an altar as privileged in its own right must be according to canon 916. Or the priest celebrating may have a personal privilege: this is true of all priests who have made the Heroic Act;[25] also, priests of the Society of Jesus have this personal privilege whenever they say Mass at any altar for a member of Our Lady's Sodality or a person who shares the indulgences of the Sodality.[26] All Masses are privileged as if said at a privileged altar, on All Souls' Day **(c. 917, § 1)** and during the octave.[27] All the altars of a church in which the Forty Hours' Adoration is being celebrated are privileged **(c. 917, § 2)**.

Conditions. The person must, of course, have died in the state of grace; the Mass must be applied exclusively for his soul; it need not be in black.

Power to designate. Bishops, Abbots or Prelates *nullius*, Vicars and Prefects Apostolic, and major superiors of a clerical exempt religious institute can designate and declare one daily perpetual privileged altar, provided there is no other such, in their cathedral, abbatial, collegiate, conventual, parochial, quasi-parochial churches, but not in public or semipublic oratories unless these are attached to the parish church or subsidiary to it **(c. 916).**

Indication: Stipend. As an indication that an altar is privileged, no other inscription shall be made than: *altare privilegiatum perpetuum*

---

[24] Cf. *Compendium Privilegiorum S. I.,* nn. 72, 73.
[25] *Preces et P. O.,* n. 547.
[26] Cf. *Compendium Privilegiorum S. I.,* n. 350.
[27] Cf. *Digest,* II, p. 226; *Preces et P. O.,* n. 545.

or *ad tempus, quotidianum* or not, according to the terms of the grant
(c. 918, § 1). For Masses which are to be celebrated at a privileged
altar, one may not, under pretext of the privilege, require a larger
stipend (c. 918, § 2).

Publication of Indulgences. New indulgences, even those granted to
the churches of regulars, if they have not been promulgated in Rome,
are not to be made public without consulting the Ordinary of the
place (c. 919, § 1). In the publication of books, booklets, etc., in which
are recorded grants of indulgences for various prayers or pious works,
the provision of canon 1388 is to be observed (c. 919, § 2). For the
provision of canon 1388, see p. 708.

Notification of the Sacred Penitentiary. Persons who have obtained
from the Supreme Pontiff grants of indulgences for all the faithful
are bound under pain of nullity of the favor received to send authentic
copies of the grants to the Sacred Penitentiary (c. 920).

Meaning of Certain Grants of Indulgences. 1. *For feasts of Our
Lord or the Blessed Virgin.* A plenary indulgence granted for feasts
of our Lord Jesus Christ or for feasts of the Blessed Virgin Mary, is
understood as granted only for feasts which are in the universal
calendar (c. 921, § 1).

2. *For feasts of the Apostles.* An indulgence, plenary or partial,
granted for feasts of the Apostles, is understood as granted only for
their natal feast, i.e., the day of their death or martyrdom (c. 921, § 2).

3. *Plenary quotidiana or ad tempus.* A plenary indulgence granted
as *quotidiana perpetua* or *ad tempus* to those who visit some church
or public oratory is to be so understood that it can be gained by any
of the faithful on any day of their choice, but only once in the year,
unless the decree expressly provides otherwise (c. 921, § 3).

Transfer of Indulgence With Feast, Novena, etc. Indulgences which
are attached to feasts or supplications or prayers of nine, seven, or
three days, offered before or after the feast or during its octave, are
understood to be transferred to the day to which such feasts are lawfully transferred, if the feast in question has an office and Mass without solemnity and external observance, and is transferred permanently, or if the solemnity and external observance are transferred
permanently (c. 922). Thus when a feast to which an indulgence is
attached is transferred temporarily and without external celebration
because it falls on Good Friday, the indulgence remains attached to
the day, even though it be Good Friday.[28]

---

[28] S. Paen., 18 Feb., 1921; *AAS*, 13–165; *Digest*, I, p. 420.

Indulgence Attached to Day: Time for Visit to Church. To gain an indulgence which is attached to a certain day, if a visit to a church or oratory is required, it may be made from noon of the preceding day to the midnight which terminates the day named (c. 923). When a visit to a sacred image or altar is prescribed, the same conditions are required as for a visit to a church or oratory.[29]

Cessation of Indulgences. 1. *When attached to a church which is destroyed.* In accordance with canon 75, indulgences which are attached to a certain church do not cease if the church, after being completely destroyed, is rebuilt within fifty years in the same or almost the same place and under the same title (c. 924, § 1).

2. *When attached to objects.* Indulgences attached to rosaries or other objects cease only when the rosaries or other objects are entirely destroyed or sold (c. 924, § 2). Objects blessed even with the Apostolic indulgences may now be loaned or given on request to other persons for the purpose of communicating the indulgences.[30]

QUESTIONS ON THE GRANTING OF INDULGENCES

1. Explain the difference between indulgences for the living and those for the departed as regards their manner of operation (c. 911).

2. In general when are indulgences applicable to the Souls in Purgatory? (Cc. 930, 913, 2°).

3. Explain the expression "an indulgence of five years."

4. What is a *toties quoties* indulgence?

5. Who, besides the Holy See, have ordinary power to grant indulgences? Who have delegated power? What are the limitations on these powers? (C. 912).

6. Which department of the Roman Curia has charge of granting indulgences? (C. 258, § 2).

7. Can the power to grant indulgences be delegated? (Cc. 199, § 1, 913, 1°).

8. Has an indulgence gained by a living person for himself an infallible effect? Can the same be said of one gained for the departed? (Cf. Cappello, *De Poenitentia*, nn. 954–957).

9. Is a plenary indulgence always plenary in its effect? (C. 926).

10. Can an indulgence be gained for another living person? (C. 930). What kind of an indulgence is that of a privileged altar applied to a dying person? (*Digest*, I, p. 449).

---

[29] *Preces et P. O.*, p. XIII, note 1.
[30] Cf. S. Paen., 18 Feb., 1921; *AAS*, 13-164; *Digest*, I, p. 421.

11. Can an indulgence which is only for the living ever be applied to the Souls in Purgatory? (Yes, by one who has made the Heroic Act.)

12. Can indulgences be attached to statues, crosses, beads, etc., which are made of fragile or perishable material? (*Digest,* I, p. 422).

13. Distinguish three different papal blessings (cc. 914–915; 468; *Compendium Privilegiorum, S. I.,* nn. 72, 73; Roman Ritual: Tit. VIII, c. 32; Appendix, *Benedictiones Reservatae,* II, 4; Tit. V, cap. 6).

14. Who besides the Holy See can declare an altar privileged? Under what conditions? (C. 916).

15. What is the connection between All Souls' Day and privileged altars? Between the Forty Hours' Devotion and privileged altars? (C. 917).

16. What is meant by a plenary indulgence *quotidiana perpetua* or *quotidiana ad tempus?* (C. 921).

17. Can a priest not otherwise empowered give the papal blessing with plenary indulgence at the hour of death? (C. 468, § 2).

18. Is any special formula required in attaching indulgences to rosaries, medals, etc.? If a special formula is prescribed, as for the Dominican indulgences of the rosary, it must be used (c. 1148, § 2). If the faculty is given to bless the object and attach the indulgences *in forma Ecclesiae consueta,* a simple sign of the cross, without words, would seem to be sufficient. Yet, until this has been officially declared, it is safer to use the words: *"In nomine Patris et Filii et Spiritus Sancti. Amen."*

19. Can a priest with this ordinary faculty to attach indulgences to rosaries, thus attach them to his own rosary? Yes, unless the faculty is limited to certain persons (S.C. Indulg., 16 July, 1887, ad 7; *Fontes,* VII, p. 683).

20. What is the rule regarding the transfer of indulgences attached to feasts, when the feast is transferred? (C. 922).

21. If a visit to a church is prescribed for an indulgence attached to a certain day, when must the visit be made? (C. 923).

22. Do indulgences attached to a church cease if the church is destroyed by fire? Do indulgences attached to a rosary cease if several beads are lost? If the beads are restrung in a different order? If the rosary is lent or given to another? If it is sold? (C. 924).

Section 2. The Gaining of Indulgences (cc. 925–936)

PRELIMINARY SURVEY

General Requisites for Gaining Indulgences (c. 925)
Proportionate Gaining of Plenary Indulgence (c. 926)
Subjects Who May Gain Bishops' Indulgences (c. 927)
How Often Daily May Indulgences Be Gained? (c. 928)

Subjects Capable of Gaining Indulgences. In order to be capable of gaining indulgences for himself a person must be baptized, not excommunicated, in the state of grace at least at the end of the prescribed works, and a subject of the one who grants the indulgence **(c. 925, §1).**

1. Baptism of water is necessary to make a person a visible member of the Church (c. 87); hence only the baptized can share in the treasury of the Church through indulgences.

2. Excommunication cuts one off from the rights and privileges of membership in the Church (c. 87); an excommunicated person is explicitly declared incapable of gaining indulgences (c. 2262, § 1). Even heretics and schismatics who are in good faith, though not excommunicated, are commonly held incapable.

3. The state of grace is required at least at the completion of the prescribed works, in order to gain an indulgence *for oneself.* The canon avoids settling the long controversy whether the same is true of indulgences for the departed. There is solid theological opinion on both sides.[31]

4. The person must be a subject of the grantor; but this is modified by canon 927, so that a Bishop's indulgences may be gained not only by absent subjects, but also by all visitors in the territory, and even exempt religious. Orientals can gain all general indulgences.[32]

Conditions for Actually Gaining Indulgences. In order that a capable subject actually gain indulgences he must have at least a general intention of gaining them and must perform the prescribed works at the appointed time and in the proper manner according to the terms of the grant **(c. 925, § 2).**

1. An *intention* to gain indulgences, at least habitual, that is, once

---

[31] Cf. Cappello, *De Poenitentia,* nn. 968, 969; Hagedorn, *General Legislation on Indulgences,* p. 88.
[32] S. Paen., 7 July, 1917; *AAS,* 9–399.

actually made and not revoked, is required. Practically it is recommended that the intention to gain all available indulgences and apply them to the Souls in Purgatory be frequently renewed. The intention may be general, that is, without reference to any particular indulgences, and even without knowing what they are.

2. *The prescribed works* must be done *personally,* except alms, which may be given by another in one's name with one's consent. They must be performed fully, and in the manner and within the time prescribed. Any substantial omission of or divergence from the prescribed conditions, even though it be excused by ignorance or impossibility, ordinarily impairs the indulgence. But a negligible omission would not do so; *parum pro nihilo reputatur.* Probably the omission of two *Aves* of the rosary would be a negligible omission.

3. Can probability be of any use in gaining indulgences? A disputed question. Several solid authorities can be cited for the affirmative; they hold that the Church can supply for a merely probable deficiency, and that she intends to do so.[33]

Plenary Indulgence Partially Gained. A plenary indulgence is understood as granted on such terms that if one is unable to gain it fully he may nevertheless gain it partially in proportion to his dispositions (**c. 926**). Since an indulgence is a remission of temporal punishment due for sin *whose guilt is forgiven,* it is impossible for a person to gain for himself an indulgence which is absolutely plenary in its effect, as long as he remains guilty of any slightest venial sin. In such case the Church declares her intention that the indulgence be gained in proportion to the dispositions of the subject. Vermeersch explains this to mean that all temporal punishment is remitted except that which is due for the venial sin whose guilt is still unforgiven. This explanation agrees with the opinion of St. Alphonsus, and is as good as may be found.[34]

Who May Gain Episcopal Indulgences? Unless the contrary appears from the tenor of the grant, indulgences granted by a Bishop may be gained by his subjects outside the territory, and by *peregrini, vagi* (cf. c. 91), and all exempt persons who are in the territory (**c. 927**). This modifies the rule of canon 925, § 1, that the person must be *subditus concedentis.*

---

[33] Cf. Cappello, *De Poenitentia,* n. 978; Vermeersch, *Theol. Mor.,* III, n. 599; Ballerini-Palmieri, *Opus Theol. Mor.,* V, n. 778.
[34] Cf. St. Alphonsus, *Theol. Mor.,* ed. Gaudé, VI, n. 534, 19°; Vermeersch-Creusen, *Epit.,* II, n. 201; Hagedorn, *General Legislation on Indulgences,* p. 65.

How Often Daily May Indulgences Be Gained? 1. *Plenary indulgences.* A plenary indulgence, unless express provision to the contrary is made, can be gained only once a day, even though the prescribed work is performed several times (**c. 928, § 1**). By express provision, the plenary indulgence for reciting the rosary (5 decades) before the Blessed Sacrament, and the plenary indulgence for the Way of the Cross, can be gained as often as the work is performed even on the same day.[35] The same is true of the indulgence of the Portiuncula,[36] and of that for visiting any church, etc., on All Souls' Day or on the following Sunday, with the usual conditions.[37]

2. *Partial indulgences.* A partial indulgence, if there is no express provision to the contrary, can be gained several times a day upon repetition of the same work (**c. 928, § 2**).

For Whom Can Indulgences Be Gained? No one gaining indulgences can apply them to other living persons; but all indulgences granted by the Roman Pontiff are applicable to the Souls in Purgatory unless the contrary is evident (**c. 930**).

Notes on Some Prescribed Conditions. 1. *The usual conditions.* See following paragraph.

2. *Work already obligatory or prescribed as penance.* A work which one is obliged to perform by law or precept under pain of sin cannot serve for the gaining of an indulgence, unless the grant expressly states that it can; but if a work is enjoined as a sacramental penance and happens also to be enriched with indulgences, a person by doing it can at the same time satisfy the penance and gain the indulgences (**c. 932**).[38] The recitation of community prayers which are not prescribed under pain of sin, but only by rule, may serve to gain indulgences. Easter Communion satisfies the requirement of Communion for an indulgence.[39]

3. *Several indulgences attached to the same object or place, or to the same work.* Several indulgences can be attached to one and the same object or place, from various sources; but several indulgences cannot be gained by one and the same work to which indulgences from various sources have been attached, unless the prescribed work be confession or Communion, or unless the contrary has been expressly

---

[35] Cf. *Preces et P. O.*, n. 360 (rosary); n. 164 (Way of the Cross).
[36] Cf. *Preces et P. O.*, n. 648.
[37] Cf. *Preces et P. O.*, n. 544, and S. Paen., 2 Jan., 1939; *AAS*, 31–23; *Digest*, II, p. 230.
[38] S. C. Indulg., 29 May, 1841; *Decr. Auth.*, n. 291, ad 2.
[39] Cf. Beringer, *Les Indulgences*, I, p. 66.

provided **(c. 933)**. The contrary has been expressly provided in granting the Apostolic indulgences. Both Pius XI and Pius XII graciously
made exceptions to this rule, declaring that "the granting of the
Apostolic indulgences in no way derogates from the indulgences
which may at other times have been granted by the Supreme Pontiffs
for the prayers, pious exercises, or works, which are mentioned." This
means that, by doing the prescribed work once, a person would gain
both the Apostolic indulgences and those attached to the work from
other sources.[40]

The Usual Conditions. When the conditions for gaining an indulgence are expressed by the clause, under the usual conditions (*suetis
conditionibus*), they are confession, Communion, a visit to a church
or public oratory (or semipublic oratory for those legitimately using
the same according to canon 929), and prayers according to the intention of the Holy Father. When all these conditions are not required,
those that are required are stated.[41]

Confession. 1. *Sacramental* confession is required, that is, confession
in ordine ad absolutionem; but absolution is not required.[42]

2. Such confession must be made *within eight days immediately
preceding the day* to which the indulgence is attached, or *on the day
itself,* or within the following octave, that is on *one of the seven days
following* the day **(c. 931, § 1).**[43]

3. If the indulgence is attached to prayers or services conducted
during successive days, the confession may be made also at any time
during the *seven days following* the close of the exercises **(c. 931, § 2).**

4. The faithful who are accustomed, unless lawfully prevented, to
go to confession at least twice a month, or to receive Holy Communion in the state of grace and with a right and devout intention
daily, even though they may abstain from its reception once or twice
a week, can gain all indulgences, even without the actual confession
which would otherwise be required to gain them, except indulgences
of an ordinary or extraordinary jubilee, or those which are classified
as jubilee indulgences **(c. 931, § 3).** An ordinary jubilee is that of the
Holy Year, recurring every quarter of a century. Extraordinary
jubilees are those declared on special occasions, as was that of 1929 to

---

[40] Cf. S. Paen., 14 June, 1922; *AAS*, 14–394; *Digest*, I, p. 450 (Pius XI); S. Paen.,
11 March, 1939; *AAS*, 31–132; *Digest*, II, p. 224 (Pius XII).

[41] Cf. *Preces et P. O.*, p. VIII, *Praenotanda*, n. 4.

[42] *Decr. Auth.*, pp. 214, 253, 359.

[43] Cf. Anler-Bonzelet, *Pastoral Companion*, ed. 1943, p. 128.

celebrate the fiftieth anniversary of the priesthood of His Holiness Pius XI, and that of 1933, for the nineteenth centenary of the Redemption. Indulgences are sometimes announced as *ad instar iubilaei,* that is, subject to the same rules.

5. One confession may satisfy the requirements for several indulgences **(c. 933).**

Holy Communion. 1. Likewise one Communion may satisfy for several indulgences **(c. 933).**

2. The time for the prescribed Communion is the eve of the day, or the day itself, or any of the seven days following it, or following the close of the exercises **(c. 931, §§ 1, 2).**

Visit to Church or Public Oratory. 1. By a visit to a church or oratory is meant going thither at least with some general or implicit intention of honoring God in Himself or in His Saints, and making some prayer, the one prescribed if any has been imposed by the one who granted the indulgence, otherwise any prayer, oral or even mental, according to each one's piety and devotion.[44]

2. Any church or any public oratory (cf. c. 1188, § 2, 1°) is sufficient if none in particular is designated.

3. If a special church is designated the visit must be made there. The *parish church* means one's own, or that of the place where one is. The *church of the regulars* includes also a church not owned by them, provided it has been assigned to them perpetually according to law for divine worship and unrestricted use.[45]

4. The faithful of either sex who, for the pursuit of religious perfection, or for education, or for health's sake, live a common life in houses established with the consent of the Ordinaries, but which have no church or public chapel, and likewise all persons who live in the same place for the purpose of ministering to them, whenever a visit to any unspecified church or public oratory is prescribed for gaining indulgences, may make the visit in the chapel of their own house where they can legitimately satisfy the obligation of hearing Mass, provided that they duly perform the other works prescribed **(c. 929).**[46]

5. If one is *unable actually to enter* the church because it is closed or access to it is *for any reason* obstructed, it will be enough to say the

---

[44] S. Paen., 10 Sept., 1933; *AAS,* 25–446; *Digest,* I, p. 458.
[45] Cf. Mocchegiani, *Collectio Indulg.,* pp. 428, 429.
[46] Cf. *Preces et P. O.,* p. VIII, *Praenotanda,* 4.

prayers at the door or on the steps, but the visit even in that case must be pious and devout.[47] This special provision repeatedly made for jubilee visits is now regarded as general.[48]

6. Cardinals (c. 239, § 1, 11°), Archbishops, and Bishops, even merely titular (c. 349, § 1, 1°), and members of their household, may make the visits to their own chapels even though they are prescribed to be made to some public church of the place where they are.

7. The time for making the visit for an indulgence attached to a certain day is from noon of the day before to midnight of the day itself (c. 923).

8. When a plenary indulgence is designated as *quotidiana perpetua* or *ad tempus* and a visit to some particular church is prescribed, it means that the visit may be made on any day, but the indulgence can be gained only once a year (c. 921, § 3).

9. When the visit for indulgences is prescribed to be made to *a sacred image or altar,* the same rules apply as for a church.[49]

Prayers. 1. If for the gaining of indulgences *prayer in general according to the intention of the Supreme Pontiff* is prescribed, merely mental prayer does not suffice; but the vocal prayer may be selected at the choice of the faithful, unless some particular prayer is assigned (c. 934, § 1). The intentions of the Supreme Pontiff are the exaltation of the Church, the extirpation of heresy, the propagation of the faith, the conversion of sinners, peace and concord among Christian rulers. But it is sufficient to have the general intention to pray for the intention of the Pope, or for the intention prescribed, even without knowing specifically what it is.[50]

2. The clause to *pray according to the intention of the Holy Father* is quite fulfilled by adding to the other prescribed works the recitation, according to his intention, of *one Pater, Ave, and Gloria;* each of the faithful, however, remaining free to recite any other prayer according to his piety and devotion toward the Holy Father.[51]

3. Indulgences attached to *ejaculatory prayers* may be gained by reciting them *mentally.*[52] It is difficult to give a definition of ejaculatory prayers. The official collection (*Preces et P. O.*) lists the *Anima Christi* as an ejaculatory prayer (n. 105).

---

[47] Cf. S. Paen., *Monita* for Jubilee of 1925, n. XV; *AAS,* 16–337; *Digest,* I, p. 428; and for Jubilee of 1933, n. XII, 3; *AAS,* 26–149; *Digest,* I, p. 877.
[48] Cf. Vermeersch-Creusen, *Epit.,* II, n. 218.
[49] Cf. *Preces et P. O.,* p. XIII, note.
[50] Cf. S. C. Indulg., 12 July, 1847, ad 3; *Decr. Auth.,* n. 344.
[51] S. Paen., 20 Sept., 1933; *AAS,* 25–446; *Digest,* I, p. 458.
[52] S. Paen., 7 Dec., 1933; *AAS,* 26–35, *Digest,* II, p. 233, ref.

4. For all plenary indulgences *toties quoties* for which a visit to a church is enjoined, it is necessary and sufficient to recite in each visit *six Paters, Aves, and Glorias*.[53]

5. If a particular prayer has been assigned, the indulgences can be gained by reciting that prayer in any language, provided the correctness of the translation be certain from a declaration of the Sacred Penitentiary or of one of the Ordinaries of places where the language in which the prayer is translated is commonly used; but the indulgences cease entirely by reason of any addition, subtraction, or interpolation (c. 934, § 2). This provision was softened by a reply of the Sacred Penitentiary, *facto verbo cum Sanctissimo*, to the effect that *only a substantial change* impairs the indulgence.[54] The single exception to the rule that any language will serve is that the indulgences for the *public* recitation of the Little Office of the Blessed Virgin are gained only if it is recited in Latin.[55]

6. Kneeling is not required unless prescribed; and even if prescribed (as for the prayer *Sacrosanctae* after the Breviary),[56] it can be omitted without loss of the indulgences if it is *impossible owing to illness*,[57] or *si aliquod obstet impedimentum*.[58]

7. All indulgences for the gaining of which the recital of prayers is enjoined together with some bodily act (e.g., genuflection, sign of cross, etc.) which mutilated persons are unable to perform, may be gained by the latter merely by the recital of the prayers.[59]

8. In order to gain indulgences it is sufficient to recite the prayer alternately with a companion, or to follow it mentally while it is recited by another person (c. 934, § 3).

9. Deaf-mutes can gain indulgences attached to public prayers, if together with the rest of the faithful who are praying in the same place, they raise their minds and pious affections toward God; and in the case of private prayers it is sufficient that they recall them mentally, or say them in signs, or merely read them ocularly (c. 936).

10. Pious exercises are said to be done *publicly* only when they are

---

[53] S. Paen., 5 July, 1930; *AAS*, 22–363; *Digest*, I, p. 457.

[54] S. Paen., 26 Nov., 1934; *AAS*, 26–643; *Digest*, II, p. 236; cf. *Preces et P. O.*, p. XVI, note 1.

[55] S. C. Indulg., 28 Aug., 1903; *Fontes*, VII, p. 717. As to meaning of *public*, see *Preces et P. O., Praenotanda 7, p. VIII*, or text, this paragraph, n. 10.

[56] Cf. *Preces et P. O.*, n. 679, and note.

[57] S. C. Indulg., 26 July, 1855; *Decr. Auth.*, n. 368.

[58] *Preces et P. O.*, n. 679, which is evidently broader than the decree of 1855 last cited.

[59] S. Paen., 22 Oct., 1917; *AAS*, 9–539; *Digest*, I, p. 423.

done in common in churches or public oratories, or (for those legitimately using them) in semipublic oratories; in all other cases they are considered as done *privately*.[60]

Notes on Other Prescribed Works and Conditions. 1. Rosaries blessed with indulgences and crucifixes blessed with the indulgence of the Way of the Cross *need not be carried in the hand,* if either manual labor or any other reasonable cause prevents this; but it is sufficient in order to gain the indulgences that the faithful, during the recitation of the prayers in question, carry with them in any way the rosary or the crucifix.[61]

2. The plenary indulgence *toties quoties* attached to a crucifix does not mean that a plenary indulgence can be gained by the same person as often as he kisses such a crucifix, but that any one of the faithful who is at the point of death, even if the crucifix does not belong to him (therefore successive dying persons with the same crucifix) may gain the indulgence. The conditions are: kissing the crucifix or touching it in any way; confession and Communion if possible, otherwise contrition of heart; invoking the Name of Jesus by pronouncing it if possible, otherwise devoutly and internally; patiently accepting death as the wages of sin.[62]

3. The formula *corde saltem contrito,* which often occurs in the grant of indulgences, is not a condition, but a disposition.[63] Therefore an act of contrition is required only if it is necessary in order to regain the state of grace.

4. Can an indulgence be gained by devoutly listening by radio to the blessing which imparts it? In general, no.[64] But in the case of the Pontifical blessing *Urbi et Orbi* given by the Supreme Pontiff on solemn occasions together with a plenary indulgence, both those who are present and those who are absent at any distance but who nevertheless with pious and devout mind receive the blessing, can gain the plenary indulgence on the usual conditions.[65]

5. Persons who heard a mission through an amplifier, in an overflow meeting, can gain the indulgence attached to the papal blessing

---

[60] Cf. *Preces et P. O., Praenotanda,* 7, p. VIII.
[61] S. Paen., 9 Nov., 1933; *AAS,* 25-502; *Digest,* I, p. 445.
[62] S. Paen., 23 June, 1929; *AAS,* 21-510; *Digest,* I, p. 434. The S. Paen., 22 Sept., 1942, again declared that the indulgence is not gained *toties quoties* by kissing the crucifix. Cf. *The Jurist,* Vol. 3, p. 331.
[63] S. C. Indulg. et Reliq., 17 Dec., 1870; *Decr. Auth.,* n. 427.
[64] Cf. S. Paen., 4 March, 1932; *Digest,* II, p. 226.
[65] S. Paen., 15 June, 1939; *AAS,* 31-277; *Digest,* II, p. 231.

at the end of the mission, supposing the blessing itself to be duly given to them.[66]

6. Clerics who joined pious associations before the *publication* (1 Apr., 1933) of the decree of 20 March, 1933, but received the order of the priesthood later, do not enjoy the faculties mentioned in the decree. But priests who joined before that date, even though not approved for confessions, can enjoy all the faculties except those of annexing the Apostolic indulgences and the plenary indulgence *in articulo mortis,* which is to be exercised only after the faculty to hear confessions has been obtained.[67]

Power of Confessors to Commute Prescribed Works. Confessors have the power to commute the pious works, which have been enjoined for gaining indulgences, to other works, for persons who are unable to perform them because of some lawful impediment (c. 935). Confessor here means any priest who is approved for confessions. It is not required that the person actually go to confession; the confessor's power is not limited to the time of confession.[68] Confessors can so commute the visit to a particular church, even for the indulgences known as the *toties quoties* and of the Portiuncula.[69]

QUESTIONS ON THE GAINING OF INDULGENCES

1. Can Protestants gain indulgences? Can Oriental Catholics? What intention is necessary? Is the state of grace required? (C. 925).

2. Can a visitor from New York gain an indulgence in Chicago, if it is granted by the Archbishop of Chicago? If granted by the Archbishop of New York? (C. 927).

3. When prayers are prescribed, must they be said orally? Kneeling? What provision is made for deaf-mutes? (Cc. 934, 936).

4. Does a prescribed visit to a church require prayer? Mental or vocal? If prayers are prescribed in addition to the visit, will mental prayer suffice? (Cf. *Digest,* I, p. 458; c. 934, § 1).

5. What prayers must be said in visits for *toties quoties* indulgences? For other indulgences? (*Digest,* I, pp. 457, 458).

6. What is meant by the usual conditions for gaining indulgences?

7. Can one gain several indulgences by the same work? (C. 933). Can one gain several indulgences in one day by repeating the prescribed work?

---

[66] S. Paen., 13 Apr., 1935; *Digest,* II, p. 227.
[67] S. Paen., 2 March, 1937; *AAS,* 29–58; *Digest,* II, p. 220.
[68] Cf. Hagedorn, *General Legislation on Indulgences,* p. 108.
[69] Code Com., 19 Jan., 1940; *AAS,* 32–62; *Digest,* II, p. 237.

(C. 928). Can several indulgences be attached to the same work or to the same object or place? (Cc. 933, 913, 3°).

8. When may confession and Communion be made for gaining an indulgence which is attached to a certain day or to services held on successive days? (C. 931).

9. Can a plenary indulgence be gained partially? (C. 926).

10. How may nuns whose chapel is only semipublic gain an indulgence when a visit to a church or public oratory is prescribed? (C. 929).

11. What classes of persons, without going to confession, can gain an indulgence for which confession is prescribed? What indulgences are excepted from this provision? (C. 931).

12. What provision is made for cripples who cannot perform bodily acts which are prescribed together with prayers? (*Digest*, I, p. 423).

13. Who has power to commute the works prescribed? On what conditions? (C. 935).

14. Must oral prayers, when prescribed, be actually pronounced in order to gain indulgences? (C. 934, § 3).

15. What changes are considered substantial in the words of the rosary or the Litany of Loretto? (Cf. *Digest*, I, pp. 451-457).

16. Must a rosary be carried in the hand while reciting it? Not if any reasonable cause prevents it. (*Digest*, I, p. 445).

17. Can one gain the indulgence attached to a blessed rosary by using it to recite the *Paters* and *Aves* that occur in the Divine Office? (C. 932).

18. If an indulgence can be gained on Sept. 8, on what dates may confession be made and Holy Communion be received? (C. 931, § 1).

19. When several visits are required to the same church on the same day, must one actually leave and then re-enter the church between the visits? Yes. (Claeys-Bouuaert, *Manuale I. C.*, II, n. 167; Vermeersch-Creusen, *Epitome*, II, n. 218; Cappello, *De Poenit.*, n. 972, 6).

Section 3. Notes on Some Special Indulgences and Practices

PRELIMINARY SURVEY

Gregorian Altars and Masses
Scapulars
Rosaries
The Way of the Cross
Apostolic Indulgences
Indulgences for the Dying
Indulgences of All Souls' Day
The Heroic Act of Charity
The Portiuncula Indulgence
Little Treasury of Plenary Indulgences for Priests and
    Religious

Gregorian Altars and Masses. A very ancient tradition attributes special efficacy for the relief of the suffering souls in Purgatory to Masses celebrated at the altar in the Church of Saint Gregory on the Coelian Hill in Rome, on the site of the old monastery of Saint Andrew, where Saint Gregory the Great was Abbot at the time of his election to the papacy in A.D. 590. This is the primary *Gregorian altar*. The S. C. of Indulgences declared in 1884 that this confidence on the part of the faithful has the approval of the Church.[70] The Holy Office has declared it a privileged altar.[71] In the course of time the Supreme Pontiffs granted the privileges of the Gregorian altar to certain other altars in and out of Rome; these are called Gregorian altars *ad instar*. Some of these altars still exist and retain their privilege; but the privilege is now no longer granted.

Gregorian Masses are a series of thirty Masses celebrated for a particular departed soul on thirty successive days without interruption. While it is not certain that an indulgence has been attached to the practice, it has the full approval of the Church.[72] These Masses need not be said at a privileged altar, nor by the same priest, nor in black; but they must be applied for the soul of the deceased person. The suspension of the series for Thursday, Friday, and Saturday of Holy Week is not considered a fatal interruption, provided the series be continued and finished on the days which follow. Some authorities[73] would not oblige the priest to begin the series anew if an involuntary interruption occurs near the end of the series when only two or three Masses remain. Others[74] would oblige the priest to repeat the entire series after an involuntary interruption at any point, only if he received an extra stipend.

Scapulars. Of the sixteen approved scapulars, the best known are the red scapulars of the Passion (Lazarists); the white of the Most Holy Trinity (Trinitarians); the blue of the Immaculate Conception (Theatines); the brown of Mount Carmel (Carmelites); and the black of the Seven Dolors (Servites). These are frequently worn together and are called the Five Scapulars. The scapulars must be of woven wool material of the respective colors, rectangular in form.[75] The

---

[70] Cf. *ASS*, 16–500.
[71] Holy Office, 12 Dec., 1912; *AAS*, 5–33.
[72] *Ibid.*
[73] Arregui, *Summarium Theol. Mor.*, n. 561.
[74] Noldin, *De Sacr.*, n. 327; Marc, *Theol. Mor.*, II, n. 1622. For critical discussion, see *Eccl. Rev.*, Vol. 82, p. 75.
[75] S. C. Indulg., 18 Aug., 1868; *Decr. Auth.*, n. 423.

black has on one side the picture of Christ crucified, on the other the Sacred Heart of Jesus and the Immaculate Heart of Mary; the white has the red and blue cross of the Trinitarians. The connecting bands may be of any material or color except that for the red scapular they must be of red wool; hence if the scapular of the Passion is joined to the others, the band must be of red wool. The different scapulars must be distinguishable; hence they may be sewn together only on one side, and joined by a band common to all. The so-called indulgences of the *six Paters, Aves, and Glorias,* are attached to the blue scapular of the Immaculate Conception;[76] and the so-called *Sabbatine Privilege,* to the brown scapular of Mount Carmel. All the scapulars must be so worn that one part hangs before the breast, the other between the shoulders.[77]

Blessing, imposition, enrollment. The scapulars must be blessed and imposed by the same authorized priest, faculties having been obtained from the respective orders or from the Holy See.[78] The proper formula must be used. The *Roman Ritual (Benedictiones Propriae,* nn. 3, 6, 7, 8, 11, 12, 13) gives separate formulas for each of the five scapulars, and also (n. 14) a short formula for the five together. Imposition of the scapular is done by placing it around the neck or on one shoulder so that one part hangs behind and the other in front; the same blessed scapular may be used for the imposition upon many persons successively; special faculties are required for imposing the scapular on many together (e.g., from the pulpit) without separate investing of each person. The first scapular worn must be blessed, after which any new scapular worn by the person enrolled need not be blessed. Enrollment, that is, recording and sending the names to a canonically erected confraternity of the respective scapular is required for validity in the case of the white, black, and brown scapulars (cf. c. 694, § 2), unless the Holy See has dispensed from it.

The Quinquennial Faculties of Ordinaries from the Sacred Congregation of Rites, nn. 6 and 7 *(Digest,* II, p. 37) give to Ordinaries the power: to bless and impose the five scapulars with a single formula, with power to subdelegate; and to bless and impose the five scapulars without recourse to the competent Ordinaries or religious congregations, and without the obligation of recording the names in cases of

---

[76] Schneider, *Rescripta Authentica necnon Summaria Indulgentiarum,* p. 577; but cf. S. Paen., 22 Apr., 1933; *AAS,* 25-254; *Digest,* I, p. 448.

[77] S. C. Indulg., 12 Feb., 1840; *Decr. Auth.,* n. 277.

[78] Cf. *as regards the Society of Jesus,* S. C. Relig., Rescript of 9 Aug., 1927, and 9 Aug., 1929.

a great concourse of people during the time of spiritual exercises and missions, with power to subdelegate.

The Military Faculties, Part I, n. 28, give to military chaplains the power to bless and invest with the five scapulars under one formula without recourse to the competent Ordinaries or religious congregations, and in the case of large gatherings at the time of spiritual exercises or missions, without the obligation of enrollment (*Digest,* II, p. 603).

During the present war, military chaplains have, by subdelegation from the Military Vicar for the armed forces of the United States, the power to attach to *medals* prescribed for this purpose the *individual blessings of the scapulars* so that those who wear them may gain the graces and indulgences of the scapulars without having been previously enrolled in the cloth scapulars (Military Faculties, Part II, n. 21, *Digest,* II, p. 615).

The scapular medal may take the place of any or all of these scapulars, not for the imposition and enrollment, but for use by a person duly invested in the scapular. The medal must bear on one side an image of our Lord showing His Sacred Heart, on the other an image of the Blessed Virgin. The medal must be blessed with distinct signs of the cross corresponding to each of the scapulars which it is to represent; no formula of words is required; the faculty required is that of blessing and imposing the respective scapulars themselves.[79] In blessing medals for the five scapulars together it would be well to determine once for all the order of the blessings, so that each sign of the cross be joined to an intention to bless one of the five in particular.

Rosaries. The rosary of five decades can be blessed with the Apostolic, the Crozier, and the Dominican indulgences, and also with the Brigittine indulgences, although the Brigittine rosary usually consists of six decades.[80] The Apostolic indulgences are attached by the Holy Father to articles which he personally blesses, and by priests having the faculty. The Crozier indulgences (500 days for *each Pater or Ave,* without the need of finishing the rosary or meditating on the mysteries) are attached by the Canons Regular of the Holy Cross, popularly known as the Crozier Fathers, or by priests having the faculty. The Dominican indulgences are attached by the Dominican Fathers, or by

---

[79] Cf. Holy Office, 16 Dec., 1910; *AAS,* 3–22; 5 June, 1913; *AAS,* 5–303; 11 May, 1916; *AAS,* 8–175.

[80] Cf. Cappello, *De Poenitentia,* n. 992.

other priests having the faculty. To gain the Dominican indulgences it is required to meditate on the mysteries. The decades may be separated, but the five must be recited on the same day. It is not altogether clear whether the Apostolic and Brigittine indulgences are lost by the separation of the decades or not.[81] The Brigittine indulgences can be gained (even on a rosary of five decades properly blessed) without meditating on the mysteries, but the rosary must be said according to the Brigittine rite, that is, adding a *Credo* to each of the five decades. The Apostolic, Crozier, and Brigittine indulgences can be attached to rosaries, by a priest having the respective faculties, by a single sign of the cross without words, but with the intention of attaching all three indulgences. The Dominican indulgences require the use of a special formula, which is in the *Roman Ritual, Benedictiones Propriae,* n. 36. The Crozier, Apostolic, and Dominican indulgences can be gained cumulatively by one recitation of a rosary which has the three blessings.[82] To gain the indulgences, the rosary need not be carried in the hand, if any reasonable cause prevents this; but it must be carried on one's person.

There is a *plenary indulgence toties quoties* for reciting five decades before the Blessed Sacrament. For this no beads and no blessing are necessary; nor is it necessary to leave the church or chapel and re-enter in order to gain the plenary indulgence repeatedly. No other prayers for the intention of the Pope are required. One Communion suffices for several plenary indulgences, according to canon 933.[83]

The Way of the Cross. This pious exercise is performed by passing from one to the other of all the fourteen stations legitimately erected, and meditating briefly on the Passion of Our Lord. When it is performed *publicly,* that is, *in common* in a church, if it might cause confusion for the whole crowd to attempt to pass from station to station, it is sufficient for the people to remain in their places, while the priest, with two clerics or choristers (or perhaps also alone), goes from station to station, pausing at each station and reciting some prayers concerning the Passion, to which the people respond.[84] Another priest

---

[81] Cf. Cappello, *De Poenitentia,* n. 992; *Preces et P. O.,* n. 360, note 1.

[82] *Preces et P. O.,* n. 360, note 2. Cf. S. C. Indulg. et Reliq., 12 June, 1907; *Periodica,* Vol. 3, p. 167; Vermeersch-Creusen, *Epit.,* II, n. 215.

[83] These conclusions are clear to us from the terms of the grant and from *Preces et P. O.,* n. 360, taken in conjunction with *Praenotanda,* 4, p. VIII. Cf. also *Digest,* I, p. 450, and *Indulgenzie Plenarie (Estratto del Calendarium Assistentiae Italiae S. I.)* 1940, p. 15.

[84] S. C. Indulg., 6 Aug., 1757; *Decr. Auth.,* n. 210. The Sacred Penitentiary declared on 20 March, 1946 (*AAS,* Vol. 38, p. 160) that *this decree* does not apply to religious making the stations in their oratories.

may read the prayers from the pulpit instead of having them read by the one who moves from station to station.[85] In oratories of religious men or women, if for lack of space all the religious cannot without disturbance move from station to station, it is sufficient that one religious make the round reciting the usual prayers at each station, the others remaining in their places and rising and kneeling there for each station. Men and women who live in common according to canon 929, that is, in pursuit of perfection, or for study or education, or as patients, in houses erected with the consent of the Ordinary but which have no church or public chapel, as well as all who live there for their care, may gain the indulgences if one man or woman as the case may be makes the round of the stations and recites the accustomed prayers.[86]

Erection of the Stations. This faculty is no longer limited by a multiplicity of conditions, but it is sufficient that it be obtained from the Sacred Penitentiary. All Bishops, resident or titular, after receiving notice of their appointment, have the faculty (cc. 349, § 1, 1°; 239, § 1, 6°). It is fitting, though not required for validity, that the permission of the Ordinary of the place be obtained; this may be legitimately presumed if he cannot be reached. All erections of the Way of the Cross which were done before March 12, 1938, and which were *for any reason* invalid, are validated.[87] The Sacred Penitentiary, May 19, 1942, granted to the Military Vicar for the armed forces of the United States, the faculty to erect the stations, either personally or through others (*Digest,* II, p. 627).

Indulgences of the Way of the Cross. These indulgences, formerly incalculable and therefore uncertain, were made perfectly definite and certain by Pius XI in 1931. They are:

1. A *plenary indulgence each time* for all the faithful who, at least with contrite hearts, either singly or in groups, perform the Way of the Cross, with stations lawfully erected. To gain this plenary indulgence *toties quoties,* no special prayers are prescribed, nor is it necessary to leave and re-enter the church in order to gain it repeatedly.

2. Another plenary indulgence for those who receive Holy Communion on the same day on which they have performed the said pious exercise, or within a month from the time when they have completed it ten times.

---

[85] Cf. Cappello, *De Poenitentia,* n. 990.
[86] Cf. S. Paen., 20 March, 1946; *AAS,* 38–160.
[87] S. Paen., 12 March, 1938; *AAS,* 30-111; *Digest,* II, p. 229. Cf. *The Jurist,* Vol. 2, p. 162, *Erection of the Way of the Cross* (Hannan).

3. A partial indulgence of ten years for each of the stations, in case, having begun the exercise, they failed for any reasonable cause to finish it.[88]

The Station Crucifix. A crucifix (not necessarily of bronze, but of any nonfragile material)[89] may be blessed for the indulgences of the Way of the Cross, by any priest having the faculty, with a single sign of the cross.[90] The conditions for gaining the indulgences of the Way of the Cross with a crucifix so blessed are these:

1. Persons *impeded* from visiting the stations *by other causes than sickness*[91] must hold the crucifix in their hands,[92] or, if any reasonable cause prevents this, must carry it with them in some way,[93] and must moreover recite *twenty Paters, Aves, and Glorias* (fourteen for the stations, five for the five wounds, and one for the intention of the Holy Father).

2. The *sick who cannot visit the stations* may of course gain the indulgences as above described, but if they are unable without grave inconvenience to fulfill those conditions they can gain *all the indulgences of the Way of the Cross* if with a loving and contrite heart they either kiss or even only look at any crucifix which has been blessed for this purpose, and which is shown to them either by a priest or by any other persons, and recite some short prayer or ejaculation in memory of the Passion and death of our Lord Jesus Christ.[94]

The Apostolic Indulgences are those which are gained by a person who carries on his person or keeps in a suitable way at home an object (beads, rosary, cross, crucifix, small statue or medal) made of suitable material and blessed by the Holy Father or by some priest having the faculty, and performs any of the works enjoined for these indulgences. The works so enjoined are published by the Holy Father at the beginning of his reign.[95] Although an elenchus of these indulgences may not be published without special permission of the Holy See (c. 1388, § 2), it is allowed to speak of them in general and to mention some of them. The more important *plenary* indulgences among them are:

1. A plenary indulgence to be gained on *any or each of 27 named*

---

[88] S. Paen., 20 Oct., 1931; *AAS*, 23–522; *Digest*, I, p. 436; *Preces et P. O.*, n. 164. Note that this *partial* indulgence, originally declared as of *ten years and ten quarantines*, is mentioned in the official collection as simply of *ten years*.

[89] Cf. S. C. Indulg., 8 Aug., 1859; *Decr. Auth.*, n. 387, ad 2; *Digest*, I, p. 437.

[90] However, in the absence of an authentic declaration, it is safer to use the words: "In nomine Patris et Filii et Spiritus Sancti. Amen."

[91] It seems that the impediment must be for a *whole day*. Cf. *Indulgenzie Plenarie (Estratto del Calendarium Assistentiae Italiae, S. I.)*, 1940, p. 14.

[92] Cf. S. C. Indulg., 8 Aug., 1859; *Digest*, I, p. 437.

[93] S. Paen., 9 Nov., 1933; *AAS*, 25–502; *Digest*, I, p. 445.

[94] S. Paen., 25 March, 1931; *AAS*, 23–167; *Digest*, I, p. 438.

[95] For those of Pius XII, see *AAS*, 31–132.

feasts, on the usual conditions, that is, confession, Communion, prayers according to the intention of the Holy Father (without any prescribed visit to a church), provided that, in addition to fulfilling these conditions and keeping the blessed object, the person also:

a. Habitually recites at least a third part of the rosary, or hears Mass, once a week;

b. Or, in the case of priests, that they habitually celebrate Mass daily unless lawfully prevented;

c. Or, in the case of all who are bound to the recitation of the divine Office, that they satisfy this obligation.

The days on which these plenary indulgences may be gained are the Feasts of: Christmas, the Epiphany, Easter, the Ascension, Pentecost, Holy Trinity, Corpus Christi, the Sacred Heart, the Purification, the Annunciation, the Assumption, the Nativity of the Blessed Virgin, the Immaculate Conception, the Nativity of St. John Baptist, both Feasts of St. Joseph, SS. Peter and Paul, St. Andrew, St. James, St. John, St. Thomas, SS. Philip and James, St. Bartholomew, St. Matthew, SS. Simon and Jude, St. Matthias, All Saints.

2. A plenary indulgence *in articulo mortis,* which is gained on these conditions (besides keeping the blessed object): that the person *in articulo mortis* commend his soul to God, confess and receive Holy Communion, or at least have a contrite heart, invoke the Name of Jesus by pronouncing it if he can, otherwise by devoutly invoking it in his heart, and that he accept death from the hand of God as the wages of sin. It may be noted that these conditions are exactly the same as those for gaining a plenary indulgence *in articulo mortis* with a crucifix which has been blessed with the so-called *toties quoties* indulgence, with the single exception that for this latter it is necessary only to kiss or touch the crucifix, not to keep it.[96] There is nothing to prevent both indulgences from being attached (with a single sign of the cross) by a priest having both faculties, to a crucifix which remains in the possession of the dying person.

The Apostolic indulgences can be gained cumulatively with any other indulgences which may at other times have been granted by the Holy Father for the same pious works.[97]

Indulgences for the Dying. The dying may gain a plenary indulgence *in articulo mortis* in many different ways. To avoid repetition, we give here a mere summary with references. The principal ways are:

---

[96] S. Paen., 23 June, 1929; *AAS,* 21–510; *Digest,* I, p. 434 (*toties quoties*); S. Paen., 11 March, 1939; *AAS,* 31–132; *Digest,* II, p. 224 (Apostolic).

[97] S. Paen., 11 March, 1939; *AAS,* 31–132; *Digest,* II, p. 224.

1. With any object blessed with the Apostolic indulgences as above described.

2. With a crucifix blessed with the *toties quoties* indulgence, as above.

3. By receiving the Apostolic blessing, which any priest assisting the dying can and should give (c. 468, § 2).

4. Through a Mass offered for the dying person at a privileged altar.[98]

5. By accepting death with sincere love of God and true contrition. No special formula of words is required, though it would be convenient to have one at hand to express the substance of the act.[99] The following words contain the substance of the act: "O Lord my God, even now I accept from Thy Hand with a calm and willing mind whatever kind and manner of death shall please Thee, with all its anguish, pain, and suffering."[100] This act may be elicited at any time during life; the indulgence is gained once, *in articulo mortis*.

6. Finally, there are a number of ejaculations or prayers to which a plenary indulgence *in articulo mortis* is attached on condition that during life the person frequently made the same ejaculation or prayer. The other conditions are: confession and Communion, or at least a contrite heart, the invocation of the Name of Jesus, *ore, si potuerint, sin minus corde,* and the patient acceptance of death as the wages of sin. Some of these ejaculations or prayers are as follows (the number in parentheses to the left is the number in the *Preces et Pia Opera*):

(26) Acts of faith, hope, charity, and contrition (together), according to any formula in an approved catechism.

(88) Jesus.

(268) Mary.

(301) The Salve Regina . . . (Hail, Holy Queen . . .)

(302) We fly to thy patronage, O Holy Mother of God . . .

(415) The prayer to the Guardian Angel: Angele Dei, qui custos es mei . . .

Indulgences of All Souls' Day. 1. A plenary indulgence applicable only to the Poor Souls, on the usual conditions (but saying *six Paters, Aves, and Glorias* at each visit) can be gained on All Souls' Day or on the following Sunday.[101]

---

[98] Cf. privilege granted by Benedict XV to priest members of the Pious Union of the Death of St. Joseph, *AAS*, 10–317, and interpretation by the Holy Office, 9 Nov., 1922; *Digest*, I, p. 449.

[99] Cf. *Preces et P. O.*, n. 591, which requires merely an act of the will (*propositum emittunt*).

[100] Cf. Anler-Bonzelet, *Pastoral Companion*, ed. 1943, p. 135.

[101] Holy Office, 25 June, 1914; *AAS*, 6–378; S. Paen., 2 Jan., 1939; *AAS*, 31–23; *Digest*, II, p. 230.

2. A plenary indulgence can be gained once a day during the entire Octave of All Souls' Day, on the usual conditions, for visiting a cemetery and praying for the departed.[102]

3. All Masses on All Souls' Day (c. 917, § 1), and during the entire Octave[103] are privileged as if said at a privileged altar.

The Heroic Act of Charity. This is an act by which a person offers to God for the Souls in Purgatory all the satisfactory value of his good works during life, and all the suffrages which may come to him in any way after his death.[104] It includes all indulgences applicable to the living, which a person might otherwise gain for himself, and all indulgences gained for the Souls in Purgatory; but it does not prevent the person from offering suffrages for this or that soul in particular, without intending to revoke the act.[105] The surrender of these acts of satisfaction into the hands of the Blessed Virgin to be applied to the souls as she pleases is a beautiful tribute of love and devotion to her, but is not essential for the indulgences.[106]

Indulgences and privileges. The principal ones are:

1. Priests who have made the Heroic Act enjoy the personal privilege of a privileged altar every day.[107]

2. All the faithful who have made it can gain a plenary indulgence applicable only to the departed on every day on which they receive Holy Communion, with the other usual conditions.[108]

3. They can also every Monday, by hearing Mass and offering it for the Poor Souls, gain for them a plenary indulgence, on the usual conditions.[109]

4. They can gain for the departed all indulgences, even those which are not otherwise applicable to them.[110]

The Portiuncula Indulgence. This is a plenary indulgence to be gained *toties quoties* by visiting a church or chapel enriched with the privilege, on Aug. 2, or on the Sunday following in case that has been legitimately substituted for Aug. 2, and fulfilling the other conditions (*six Paters, Aves, Glorias* according to the intention of the Holy Father at *each* visit, confession and Communion). Originally granted to the Chapel of the Portiuncula, St. Mary of the Angels,

---

[102] S. Paen., 31 Oct., 1934; *AAS,* 26–606; *Preces et P. O.,* n. 546.
[103] *Preces et P. O.,* n. 545.
[104] The Heroic Act was propagated by the Theatines and blessed with indulgences by Benedict XIII. Cf. S. C. Indulg., 20 Nov., 1854, *Urbis et Orbis; Rescripta Auth.,* n. 392; *Preces et P. O.,* n. 547.
[105] Cf. Cappello, *De Poenitentia,* n. 1001.
[106] S. C. Indulg., 18 Dec., 1885, ad 3; *Acta Sanctae Sedis,* Vol. 18, p. 337.
[107] *Preces et P. O.,* n. 547, b.   [108] *Ibid.,* n. 547, a, 1°.   [109] *Ibid.,* n. 547, a, 2°.
[110] S. C. Indulg., 20 Nov., 1854, *Urbis et Orbis, Rescripta Auth.,* n. 392.

at Assisi, it was later extended especially to churches and chapels of the Franciscan order, and finally made even more generally available. The privilege can now be obtained from the Sacred Penitentiary, upon recommendation from the Ordinary of the place, by all cathedral and parochial churches, and moreover by other churches and oratories for which, in the judgment of the Ordinary, the convenience of the faithful seems to demand it.[111] A person may gain the indulgence on the 2nd of August in one church and then gain it again in another church on the following Sunday when that day has been lawfully substituted for the 2nd of August.[112]

Little Treasury of Plenary Indulgences. The following list contains some of the plenary indulgences which can easily be gained daily, weekly, or monthly, especially by priests and religious. Similar lists or treasuries have been published recently with the *Imprimatur* respectively of the Bishops of Melbourne, Australia, and Trent, Italy. It does not purport to be a summary of indulgences, nor a complete list, but merely a selection from the official collection of 1938, *Preces et Pia Opera,* to which reference is made by the number in parentheses at the left of each item.

1. *Daily Plenary Indulgences:*

   a. *Toties quoties:*

   (164) The Way of the Cross (no other conditions required).

   (360) A third part of the rosary before the Blessed Sacrament (confession, Communion, short meditation on the mysteries).

   b. *Once daily:*

   (171) The prayer *En ego,* or Behold, O kind and most sweet Jesus (before a crucifix; confession, Communion, prayers according to the intention of the Pope).

   (254) The prayer to Christ the King (usual conditions).

   (678) Reciting the Breviary before the Blessed Sacrament (usual conditions). This can be gained not only by priests, deacons, subdeacons, but also by all tonsured clerics, and by male novices and scholastics of all religious institutes, even though not obliged to recite the divine Office (n. 674), and by religious women and pious women living in common, who are bound by

---

[111] Cf. *Preces et P. O.,* n. 648, and the *later* document, S. Paen., 1 May, 1939; *AAS,* 31–226; *Digest,* II, p. 230.

[112] Cf. S. Paen., 13 Jan., 1930; *AAS,* 22–43; *Digest,* I, p. 456.

the rules of their institute to the recitation of the divine
Office, excluding in this case novices and students (n.
697). It applies to clerics who recite before the Blessed
Sacrament prayers into which the Office was duly
commuted. (Confession, Communion, prayers according to the intention of the Holy Father: no additional
visits prescribed).

(164) Communion on the same day on which one has made
the Stations of the Cross (this, in addition to the
toties quoties indulgence mentioned on page 354). No
other conditions.

Mass at a privileged altar for a departed soul. (The indulgence applies only to the departed soul.)

(561) Half an hour of prayer before the Blessed Sacrament in
any church or public oratory, for vocations to the
priesthood. (Confession, Communion).

2. Weekly plenary indulgences:

(107) My Lord and my God! (At elevation of Host during
Mass or when Blessed Sacrament is exposed; ejaculation
to be made with faith, piety, and love every day for
a week; other conditions: confession, Communion,
prayers according to the intention of the Holy Father).

(121) Visit to the Blessed Sacrament every day for a week,
saying *six Paters, Aves, Glorias* each time. (Confession,
Communion; no other prayers or visits prescribed).

(122) Spiritual visit to Blessed Sacrament every day for a week,
saying *six Paters, Aves, Glorias* each time. (Spiritual
visit means imaginary visit made at home or elsewhere
in spirit of faith in real presence, by persons prevented
by sickness or other just cause from making actual
visit. The usual conditions).

3. Monthly plenary indulgences: A plenary indulgence can be
gained each month for the recitation, daily during the month,
of each of the prayers or ejaculations listed below. The *usual
conditions* are required; therefore, confession, Communion (cf.
cc. 931, 933), and as many visits and prayers (*one Pater, Ave,
Gloria* each time) according to the intention of the Holy Father
as one wishes to gain plenary indulgences each month:

(88) Jesus!

(268) Mary!

(256) Jesus, Mary, Joseph!

(589) Jesus, Mary, Joseph, I give you my heart and my soul!

(589) Jesus, Mary, Joseph, assist me in my last agony!

(589) Jesus, Mary, Joseph, may I breathe forth my soul in peace with you!

(19) Into Thy hands, O Lord, I commend my spirit!

(21) Deign, O Lord, to keep me from sin this day! (Morning).

(21) Deign, O Lord, to keep me from sin this night! (Evening).

(58) Jesus, Son of David, have mercy on me!

(195) Heart of Jesus, I trust in Thee!

(196) Jesus meek and humble of heart, make my heart like unto Thine!

(211) Most Sacred Heart of Jesus, have mercy on us!

(55) My Jesus, mercy!

(205) Sacred Heart of Jesus, protect our homes!

(28) Lord, increase our faith!

(161) We adore Thee, O Christ, and we bless Thee, because by Thy holy Cross Thou hast redeemed the world! (Together with the Apostles' Creed).

(105) Anima Christi, sanctifica me, . . . etc.

(112) O Salutaris . . . etc. (as at Benediction, but to be gained even outside Benediction, and privately).

(646) The divine praises (as at Benediction, but gained also privately).

(135) Spiritual Communion.

(39) Suscipe, Domine . . . etc. (St. Ignatius Loyola).

(26) Act of faith. (Any formula found in an approved catechism).

(26) Act of hope. (Any formula found in an approved catechism).

(26) Act of charity. (Any formula found in an approved catechism).

(26) Act of contrition. (Any formula found in an approved catechism).

(325) O Mary conceived without sin, pray for us who have recourse to thee!

(302) We fly to thy patronage, O Holy Mother of God, despise not . . . etc.

(352) Sweet Heart of Mary, be my salvation!

(300) The Angelus (or Regina Coeli during paschal time), *morning, noon,* and *evening.*

(301) Salve Regina . . .

(309) Memorare . . .

(283) Maria, Mater gratiae, Mater misericordiae, tu nos ab hoste protege, et mortis hora suscipe!

(134) The prayer for the promotion of daily Communion: O sweet Jesus, who didst come into the world . . . etc.

(34) Three Glorias, morning, noon, and evening (3 each), in thanksgiving to the Holy Trinity for the exalted privileges of the Blessed Virgin.

(431) *Pater, Ave, Gloria,* with the invocation: St. Joseph, pray for me! (Before an image of St. Joseph).

(415) The invocation to the Guardian Angel: Angele Dei, qui custos es mei . . .

(682) The *oratio pro seipso sacerdote* (from the Missal).

(664) The prayer from the Litany of the Saints: Ure igne Sancti Spiritus renes nostros et cor nostrum, Domine, ut Tibi casto corpore serviamus et mundo corde placeamus. Per Christum Dominum nostrum. Amen.

(11) Doce me, Domine, facere voluntatem tuam, quia Deus meus es Tu.

(16) Sanctus Deus, Sanctus fortis, Sanctus immortalis, miserere nobis.

(16) Tibi laus, tibi gloria, tibi gratiarum actio in saecula sempiterna, O beata Trinitas!

(20) Deus, in adiutorium meum intende: Domine ad adiuvandum me festina!

(25) Laudate Dominum omnes gentes; laudate eum omnes populi: quoniam confirmata est super nos misericordia eius et veritas Domini manet in aeternum.

(128) Perceptio Corporis tui, Domine, quod ego indignus sumere praesumo . . . etc. (third prayer before Communion, from the Missal).

(129) Domine, non sum dignus ut intres sub tectum meum, sed tantum dic verbo et sanabitur anima mea (*three times*).

(157) O Crux, ave, spes unica!

CHAPTER XI

THE SACRAMENT OF ORDERS

Section 1. The Minister of Sacred Ordination (cc. 948–967)

PRELIMINARY SURVEY

Definitions (cc. 948–950)
Ordinary and Extraordinary Minister (cc. 951–952)
Episcopal Consecration (cc. 953–954)
Proper Bishop for Ordination (cc. 955–957)
Dimissorial Letters (cc. 958–963)
Ordinations of Religious (cc. 964–967)

We have seen in canon 107 that by divine institution the members of Christ's Church are divided into two classes, the clergy and the laity. Canon 108 informs us that by reason of that same divine institution the clergy are organized into a sacred hierarchy of orders in which there is a subordination of one class to another. In this hierarchy of orders, the episcopate, the priesthood, and the diaconate are of divine origin; the subdiaconate and the minor orders are of ecclesiastical origin. The Code deals with the sacrament of orders from a purely canonical standpoint, leaving it to the theologians to determine the matter and form of the sacrament of orders, as well as all other questions of a dogmatic nature. Space permits only a paraphrase of the canons with an occasional brief commentary. Irregularities and impediments to orders, however, will be given a fuller treatment because of their practical importance for seminarians.

Definitions. By reason of Christ's institution, the sacrament of Orders separates clerics from the laity for the government of the faithful and for the ministry of divine worship (c. 948).

Major or *sacred* orders include the priesthood, the diaconate, and the subdiaconate; *minor* orders comprise the orders of acolyte, exorcist, lector or reader, and porter (c. 949). The term *priesthood* includes the episcopate as well as the simple priesthood.

The terms: *to ordain, order, ordination, sacred ordination,* comprise besides episcopal consecration, all the orders enumerated in canon 949 as well as first tonsure, unless some other meaning is to be taken by reason of the nature of the matter treated or from the context of the wording of the law (c. 950).

Ordinary and Extraordinary Minister of Orders. The ordinary minister of sacred ordination is a consecrated Bishop; the extraordinary minister is a priest who, though lacking episcopal consecration, has received the power of conferring certain orders either by law or by special indult from the Apostolic See (c. 951). Without permission of the Apostolic See nobody may promote to a higher order one who has been ordained personally by the Roman Pontiff (c. 952). The ordinary minister ordains by reason of the power received in episcopal consecration. This power can never be lost; hence he can always ordain validly anywhere, even though not always lawfully. The power of the extraordinary minister is derived from his delegation; hence its valid use is limited by time and by other conditions placed upon the delegated power. (See cc. 239, § 1, 22°; 294, § 2; 323, § 2; 957, § 2; 964, § 1.) The delegated power granted to the extraordinary minister refers only to the orders which are not a sacrament and which have been established by the Church; namely, tonsure, minor orders, and the subdiaconate.

Episcopal Consecration. Episcopal consecration is reserved to the Roman Pontiff; hence, no Bishop is allowed to consecrate another Bishop unless he is certain that he has a papal mandate (c. 953). A Bishop who is to consecrate another Bishop must be assisted in the consecration by two other Bishops unless a dispensation has been obtained from the Apostolic See (c. 954). This requirement is for the licitness of the consecration, not for its validity.

Proper Bishop for Ordination. Each one must be ordained by his proper Bishop or with legitimate dimissorial letters from him (c. 955). Such dimissorial letters are required even for first tonsure in order that a Bishop may licitly advance one who is not his own subject.[1]

In the case of ordination of seculars (as opposed to religious) the proper Bishop is solely the Bishop of the diocese in which the person to be ordained has a domicile together with origin, or has a simple domicile without origin. In the latter case the person to be ordained must confirm by oath his intention to remain in the diocese for life. There are three exceptions, however, to this latter rule. No such oath need be taken: (1) by one who is to be ordained if he already has

---

[1] Code Com., Feb. 17, 1930; *AAS*, 22 (1930), 195; *Digest*, I, p. 91.

been incardinated into a diocese by first tonsure; (2) by one who is to be ordained for the service of another diocese according to the provisions of canon 969, § 2; (3) by a professed religious who is to be ordained according to the provisions of canon 964, n. 4 (c. 956).

It is to be noted that the term *proper Bishop* is used in a restricted sense in this canon as compared with its use in canon 94, § 1 which allows a lay person to get a proper Bishop even by quasi-domicile. Domicile is defined in canon 92; place of origin, in canon 90.

The general rule laid down in this canon is clear enough. The proper Bishop for the ordination of a secular candidate is the Bishop of the diocese in which the candidate has either a domicile together with origin or a simple domicile without origin. In this latter case the candidate must take an oath as to his intention to remain for life in the diocese in which he has his domicile. The rule is absolute in the case of a candidate who is to be promoted to first tonsure.

Another kind of proper Bishop may be found in the case of a cleric who has been ordained by his own Bishop but for another specific diocese in which as yet he has no domicile. By being tonsured for that diocese (with the permission of its Bishop, of course) he is automatically incardinated into that diocese.[2] Furthermore, the Bishop of the second diocese becomes his proper Bishop for all subsequent orders, even though the cleric in question has not yet acquired a domicile in that diocese.[3] This case is not an exception to canon 956, but may be said to be included in it implicitly inasmuch as the canon is a substantial restatement of pre-Code legislation on the subject.[4] Two decrees of the S. Cong. of the Council[5] expressly allowed a Bishop who had incardinated a cleric from another diocese to issue dimissorial letters for subsequent orders without previous actual domicile of the candidate. The mere omission of an explicit mention of this case in canon 956 did not necessarily imply that it had been revoked; hence it was at least doubtful, and canon 6, n. 4, would solve the doubt in favor of the old law.

Certain cases can arise in which a candidate for orders has no proper

---

[2] See answers of Code Commission: Aug. 17, 1919 (private answer given to Cardinal Logue, Archbishop of Armagh); *Digest*, I, p. 89; and July 24, 1939, *ad* I, *AAS*, 31 (1939), 321; *Digest*, II, p. 52.

[3] See answers of Code Commission, Dec. 7, 1931 (private answer given to the bishop of Santa Fe in South America); *Digest*, II, p. 51; July 24, 1939, *ad* II; *AAS*, 31 (1939), 321; *Digest*, II, p. 238.

[4] See comment in *Il Monitore Ecclesiastico* (1920), p. 58; also Bouscaren, *Periodica*, 19 (1940), 141–145.

[5] *A primis* of July 20, 1898, n. 4; *Fontes*, VI, n. 4307, p. 777; and *Vetuit* of Dec. 22, 1905; *Fontes*, VI, n. 4327, p. 831.

Bishop because he has lost his domicile (see cc. 95 and 585). In such a case the candidate can get a proper Bishop only by establishing a domicile in the diocese of a Bishop who is willing to receive him and by taking the oath prescribed. If this is impracticable because of the distance and the expense involved, the only solution left is to obtain an indult from the S. Congregation of the Sacraments which grants the benevolent Bishop the faculty to issue dimissorial letters for the reception of tonsure without domicile (or for subsequent orders in the case of a secularized religious who had received the tonsure before leaving his institute) on condition that the candidate take an oath to go to his new diocese on completion of his studies with the intention of spending his life there.

The proper Bishop for a nonexempt professed religious is the Bishop of the diocese in which the religious house to which the candidate belongs is situated (c. 965).

Vicars and Prefects Apostolic, Abbots and Prelates *nullius,* who are consecrated Bishops, are considered as diocesan Bishops in all things pertaining to ordination **(c. 957, § 1).** If the above mentioned are not consecrated Bishops, they may, nevertheless, in their own territory but only during their tenure of office, confer the first tonsure and minor orders both upon their own subjects according to canon 956 and upon others who present the proper dimissorial letters. Any ordinations held by them beyond these limits are null and void **(c. 957, § 2).**

Dimissorial Letters. As long as they retain jurisdiction in their territory, the following can grant dimissorial letters to secular (as opposed to religious) candidates for orders:

1. Their proper Bishop after he has lawfully taken possession of his diocese in accordance with the prescriptions of canon 334, § 3, even though he has not yet received episcopal consecration;

2. The Vicar General, but only by reason of a special mandate of the Bishop;

3. The Vicar Capitular (administrator of vacant diocese) with the consent of the chapter (diocesan consultors) but only after the diocese has been vacant for a year; or, within the year, but only in the case of those who are obliged (*arctati*) to receive a certain order by reason of a benefice actually received or to be received; or in case the needs of the diocese demand that a certain office be provided for without delay.

4. Vicars and Prefects Apostolic, Abbots and Prelates *nullius,* may grant dimissorial letters even for major orders although they them-

selves are not consecrated Bishops (c. 958, § 1). Pro-vicars Apostolic (see cc. 309, 310) may grant dimissorial letters unreservedly without waiting for a year.[6]

The Vicar Capitular (Administrator) should not grant dimissorial letters to anyone to whom the Bishop had previously refused to grant such letters (c. 958, § 2).

Whoever can grant dimissorial letters for receiving orders can himself confer those orders, provided he has the necessary power of orders (c. 959). Hence not only the Abbot mentioned in canon 964 but every religious superior who is a consecrated Bishop can confer orders on his religious subjects.

Dimissorial letters should not be granted unless all testimonials required by canons 993–1000 be at hand (c. 960, § 1). If, after dimissorial letters have been granted, new testimonials should become necessary according to canon 994, § 3, no Bishop who is not the candidate's proper Bishop should ordain him without them (c. 960, § 2). Should the candidate have spent sufficient time in the territory of the ordaining Bishop to contract an impediment according to canon 994, the latter Bishop will himself collect the testimonials directly (c. 960, § 3).

Dimissorial letters may be sent by the proper Bishop, even though he be a Cardinal Bishop of a suburban see (of the city of Rome), to any Bishop who is in communion with the Apostolic See, with the exception of a Bishop who belongs to a rite different from that of the candidate for orders. In this latter case an apostolic indult is required (c. 961). The dimissorial letters need not be addressed to any particular Bishop; they may be directed "to any Bishop in communion with the Holy See." But for religious, see canon 965 below. A Bishop who has a subject belonging to an Eastern rite may issue dimissorial letters for his subject, but only in favor of a Bishop belonging to the same rite as the subject who is to be ordained.

After receiving legal dimissorial letters, any Bishop may licitly ordain one who is not his own subject, provided there is no reason for him to doubt the authenticity of the letters. The prescription of canon 994, § 3, however, must be observed (c. 962). The person granting dimissorial letters, as well as his successor in office, may limit them or recall them; but once granted they are not annulled by the fact that the person who granted them (grantor) has lost his right to grant them — by death, resignation, or removal from office (c. 963).

---

[6] Code Com., July 20, 1929, ad I; *AAS*, 21 (1929), 573; *Digest*, I, p. 462.

Ordinations of Religious. 1. An Abbot actually holding office with ordinary jurisdiction over his subjects (*abbas regularis de regimine*) — therefore not merely a titular or retired Abbot — even though he be not an Abbot *nullius,* can confer first tonsure and minor orders provided the candidate is his subject by profession of at least simple vows, and provided the Abbot be a priest who has lawfully received the abbatial blessing. Under any other conditions, all orders conferred by him are invalid unless he is a consecrated Bishop. All privileges to the contrary are revoked (**c. 964, 1°**). Hence those Abbots who by reason of their election are considered to be blessed must actually receive the abbatial blessing before they can confer tonsure and minor orders.

2. Exempt religious cannot be licitly ordained by any Bishop without dimissorial letters from their own major superior (**c. 964, 2°**).

3. The religious superiors referred to in canon 574 may grant dimissorial letters for subjects who have temporary vows, but only for tonsure and minor orders (**c. 964, 3°**); for major orders they may grant such letters only for candidates who have made profession of perpetual vows.

These dimissorial letters must contain not only the permission of the major superior for the ordination of the candidate but they must also testify that the candidate has made profession of temporary or perpetual vows (as the case may be), that he is a subject of the superior, that he has the moral qualities required by church law, that he has completed the studies prescribed, that he has made the retreat required (or will make it), and that he has taken the oath required before the subdiaconate.[7] If the ordaining Bishop has a positive doubt as to completion of the studies required on the part of the candidate, he may investigate. However, he is not bound to do so since the presumption favors the correctness of the superior's statement. If, however, the ordaining Bishop is morally certain that the required studies have not been completed, he may not proceed to the ordination of the candidate. As to the ordaining Bishop's right to examine the religious candidate regarding his knowledge of theology, see canon 997, § 1.

4. In all other cases not included in the preceding numbers, the ordination of religious is governed by the law of secular candidates. Any indult granted to superiors to give dimissorial letters for major orders to religious professed of temporary vows is revoked (**c. 964, 4°**).

---

[7] Instruction of the Sacred Congregation of Religious, Dec. 1, 1931; *AAS,* 24 (1932), 74 ad 19; *Digest,* I, p. 482.

The Bishop to whom the religious superior should send dimissorial letters is the Bishop of the diocese in which the religious house to which the candidate for orders belongs is located (c. 965). Some religious orders enjoy a privilege whereby the major superiors may issue dimissorial letters directed to "any Bishop in communion with the Holy See." For such a privilege to be valid, it must have been granted after the Council of Trent and granted directly to the order by name and not by way of communication of privileges.[8]

Only in the following cases may the religious superior, who enjoys no special privilege issue dimissorial letters to another Bishop: (1) when the diocesan Bishop has given him permission to do so; (2) when the diocesan Bishop belongs to a rite different from that of the religious candidate for orders; (3) when the diocesan Bishop is absent; (4) when the diocesan Bishop does not intend to confer orders at the next lawful time in conformity with canon 1006, § 2; (5) finally, when the diocese is vacant and the person governing it is not a consecrated Bishop (c. 966, § 1).

In each of these cases it is necessary that the ordaining Bishop be certain of the exception by reason of an authentic testimonial issued by the episcopal curia (c. 966, § 2). For the penalty imposed for the violation of this canon, see c. 2373, n. 4.

Religious superiors are warned not to use fraudulent means to deprive the diocesan Bishop of his right of ordaining, either by sending their subject who is a candidate for orders to another house, or by intentionally postponing the issuance of dimissorial letters to a time when the Bishop will either be absent or does not intend to confer orders (c. 967). Superiors presuming to violate the prescriptions of canons 965–967 incur *ipso facto* suspension from the celebration of Mass for a month (c. 2410). A candidate who presents himself for ordination without dimissorial letters, or with false ones, is *ipso facto* suspended from the order thus received (c. 2374).

Section 2. The Subject of Sacred Ordination (cc. 968–982)

PRELIMINARY SURVEY

Conditions for Valid Ordination (c. 968)
General Conditions for Licit Ordination (cc. 969–972)
Special Requisites for Candidates to Orders (cc. 973–982)

---

[8] Benedict XIV, *Impositi nobis*, Feb. 27, 1747; *Fontes*, II, n. 376, p. 61, § 13. See also, O'Brien, *Exemption of Religious in Church Law*, p. 190.

Conditions for Valid Ordination. Only a person of the male sex who has been baptized can validly receive the sacrament of orders **(c. 968).** The canon demands two things for the valid ordination of clerics: (1) *the male sex* — the constant practice of the Church from the earliest days as well as the unanimous teaching of the Fathers and Doctors of the Church have excluded women from the reception of orders; (2) *baptism by water* — it is only by baptism that a man can become a member of Christ's Church and thus receive the right to the other sacraments (c. 87). A third requisite is supposed in the case of an adult: *the intention to receive the sacrament* — this is required for validity in adults; an habitual, express intention suffices, that is, a positive act of the will once formed and never retracted before the reception of orders.

General Conditions for Licit Ordination. Supposing the requirements for valid ordination just mentioned, the candidate cannot be ordained licitly unless he has the necessary qualities required by the sacred canons and is free from all irregularities and other impediments. The candidate's own Ordinary is the sole judge in this matter **(c. 968, § 1).** The nature of these qualities and the various kinds of irregularities and impediments to orders will be explained later.

One who possesses these qualities, and has a right intention, and is admitted to orders by his Bishop, may be said to have a *vocation to the priesthood.* An interior desire or sensible attraction of the Holy Spirit is not required. Even though a person were to feel such an attraction, he would have no right to ordination unless freely called by his own Bishop.[9]

A person who is kept back by an irregularity or other impediment is forbidden to exercise the orders already received, even though the irregularity or impediment arose after ordination through no fault of his own **(c. 968, § 2).**

No one may be ordained for the secular clergy who in the judgment of his own Bishop is not necessary or at least useful for the churches of the diocese **(c. 969, § 1).** Bishops are forbidden to confer orders upon more subjects than they can usefully employ in the churches of the diocese. Formerly clerics were attached to a definite church by ordination. This is no longer the case since they are now ordained for the service of the diocese in general. Hence the Bishop is to take into

---

[9] See Letter of Card. Merry de Val, Secretary of State, July 2, 1912; *AAS*, IV, 485. Also Cappello, *De Sacra Ordinatione*, nn. 362–377.

account the general needs of the diocese rather than those of an individual church.

The Bishop, however, is not forbidden to promote one of his subjects to orders who will later be destined for the service of another diocese after proper and lawful excardination and incardination (c. 969, § 2). This is an exception to the general rule laid down in the first paragraph. Even though the Bishop has a sufficient number of clerics for his own diocese he may ordain one of his subjects and thus incardinate him into the diocese but with the understanding that, when called upon, he will join some needy diocese after having been freed from his own diocese by excardination (see c. 112). It may also happen that the Bishop has a particular diocese in mind; and, with the consent of the Bishop of that diocese, he ordains his own subject for that diocese. In this case by the reception of first tonsure the candidate automatically becomes incardinated into the diocese for which he is to be ordained.[10]

The candidate's own Bishop or the major religious superior can refuse his subject advancement to orders for any canonical cause, even for an occult one, and extrajudicially. The candidate has a right to appeal to the Holy See, or to his superior general if the candidate is a religious who has been refused by his provincial superior (c. 970). By canonical cause is meant any kind of irregularity, impediment, or defect which would hinder the candidate from receiving orders according to the sacred canons. The Bishop or religious superior is not obliged to make known to the candidate the reason for his refusal, but in case of recourse he would have to inform the Holy See.[11] The Ordinary may make his refusal known either orally or in writing without any special formalities. Canons 973, § 3 and 2222, § 2 give the Ordinary even greater powers in this matter.

It is a grave wrong to force anyone, in any way or for any reason whatsoever, to embrace the clerical state or to prevent anyone who is canonically qualified from embracing the clerical state (c. 971). Those who force a person to enter the clerical state are punished with excommunication incurred *ipso facto* (c. 2352).

To avoid the danger of such a forced ordination, an Instruction of the S. Congregation of the Sacraments[12] requires the secular candidate

---

[10] See canon 111, § 2 and Cod. Com., Aug. 17, 1919; *Digest*, I, p. 89; and July 24, 1939, ad I; *AAS*, 31 (1939), 321; *Digest*, II, p. 52.

[11] S.C.C., March 21, 1643, ad 4; *Fontes*, V, n. 2642, p. 296.

[12] Dec. 27, 1930; *AAS*, 23 (1931), 120–127; *Digest*, I, pp. 463–473.

for the subdiaconate to "make a statement, written in his own hand and confirmed by oath that he is receiving sacred orders altogether freely, and that he fully understands all the obligations annexed thereto. The same declaration is likewise required of candidates before they are promoted to the other sacred orders, namely the diaconate and the priesthood" (Instr. Sec. 3, 1). An Instruction of the S. Congregation of Religious[13] requires a similar declaration, signed by the religious candidate in his own hand and sworn to before the superior. This declaration must be made before the candidate is presented for the subdiaconate or, in the case of a regular, before the profession of solemn vows.

Care should be taken that aspirants to sacred orders be received in a seminary from their early years; all, however, are obliged to dwell in a seminary at least during the entire period of theological studies unless in special cases the Ordinary for a grave reason shall give a dispensation, for which, however, he shall be responsible in conscience (c. 972, § 1). Aspirants to orders who lawfully live outside a seminary are to be entrusted to the care of a pious and competent priest, who shall watch over them and train them to lead a devout life (c. 972, § 2).

Special Requisites in Candidates for Orders. The first tonsure and orders are to be conferred only upon candidates who intend to go on to the priesthood and of whom it may be reasonably judged that they will one day become worthy priests (c. 973, § 1). Should one who is ordained refuse to receive higher orders, he can neither be forced by the Bishop to receive them nor forbidden the exercise of orders already received, unless he has incurred a canonical impediment or unless in the judgment of the Bishop there exists some other grave reason (c. 973, § 2). A Bishop should not confer sacred orders upon anyone unless he is morally certain by reason of positive proof that the candidate is canonically fit; otherwise he not only sins most grievously but also runs the risk of sharing in the sins of others (c. 973, § 3).[14] The same responsibility rests upon religious superiors in regard to their subjects who are candidates for orders.[15]

Special Requirements for Licit Ordination. (1) The candidate must have received the sacrament of Confirmation. (2) His moral habits

---

[13] See Instruction of the S. Cong. of Religious, Dec. 1, 1931; *AAS,* 24 (1932), 74; *Digest,* I, pp. 473–482.

[14] Read the Instruction of the S. Cong. of the Sacraments, *loc. cit.*

[15] See Instruction of the S. Cong. of Religious, Dec. 1, 1931; *AAS,* 24 (1932), 74; *Digest,* I, pp. 473-482.

should be in agreement with the order to be received.[16] (3) He must have the canonical age, (4) as well as the intellectual training required. (5) He must receive his orders in the proper sequence, (6) and observe the intervals between them. (7) Finally, he must have a canonical title for the reception of major orders (c. 974, § 1).

In regard to episcopal consecration, the provisions of canon 331 should be observed (c. 974, § 2).

Age Required for Major Orders. The subdiaconate shall be conferred only upon one who has completed his twenty-first year, the diaconate upon one who has completed his twenty-second year, and the priesthood upon one who has completed his twenty-fourth year (c. 975). Dispensations are seldom granted for the earlier reception of the subdiaconate or the diaconate; they are granted (for a year or, at most, for a year and a half) for the earlier reception of the priesthood, especially because of a dearth of priests.

Age Required for Minor Orders. While no prescribed age is required for the reception of tonsure and minor orders, still the law limits their reception as follows: No secular or religious candidate shall be promoted to first tonsure before he has begun his course in theology (c. 976, § 1). Though nothing is said about the time when minor orders are to be received, in view of the following paragraphs and of canon 978 they will normally be conferred during the first three years of the theological course.

Besides observing the prescription of canon 975 with regard to age, the subdiaconate shall not be conferred until toward the end of the third year of theology; the diaconate shall be conferred only after the fourth year has begun; and the priesthood, after the middle of the same fourth year (c. 976, § 2). Many religious orders and some congregations enjoy a privilege whereby their members may be promoted to sacred orders at such times as to enable them to be ordained priests at the end of the third year of theology. All such privileges, even though granted personally by the Supreme Pontiff himself either *viva voce* or by rescript signed by his own hand, are subject to the following prescriptions unless exception from them has been expressly made: (1) Such priests who have been ordained early must continue their study of theology until the prescribed four years have been completed;

---

[16] See the excellent recommendations of the Council of Trent, *Sess.* XXII, *de Ref.*, c. 4, 11–14; also the two Instructions quoted in the preceding number, one for secular candidates, the other for religious candidates for orders. As to moral qualifications, see especially Vermeersch, *Periodica*, Vol. XVII, p. 231*.

(2) meanwhile they are forbidden any ministry of souls; that is they should not be *employed* in preaching or hearing confessions or in the exterior works of the institute; (3) these points are a grave responsibility binding the conscience of superiors.[17] Since the declaration of the Sacred Congregation of Religious uses the term "employed" (*destinentur*), some canonists[18] are of the opinion that the prohibition refers to habitual or frequent ministry of souls. They allow an *occasional* exercise of the ministry, preaching and hearing confessions, during the fourth school year and a greater latitude during the vacation period preceding it.

The theological course must not be made privately but in a theological school established for this purpose, and it must be conducted according to the course of studies prescribed in canon 1365 (c. 976, § 3).

Orders are to be conferred in their proper sequence in such wise that it is absolutely forbidden to skip one or more orders (c. 977). This prescription applies to minor orders as well as to major orders. Its violation is punished by *ipso facto* suspension from the order thus received (c. 2374); and the Holy See requires that the order skipped shall be conferred even in the case of one who may have received several higher orders.[19]

Proper Intervals of Time Between Orders (*Interstitia*). Between ordinations the proper time intervals must be observed, and during these intervals those promoted to orders should exercise themselves in their order according to the regulations of the Bishop (c. 978, § 1).

It is left to the prudent judgment of the Bishop to determine what interval of time shall elapse between the tonsure and the order of porter, as well as between the single minor orders. Acolytes must wait at least a year before being promoted to the subdiaconate; subdeacons and deacons at least three months in their respective orders before being promoted to the diaconate and the priesthood respectively, unless in the judgment of the Bishop the need or the advantage of the Church demands otherwise (c. 978, § 2). One may follow either the calendar year or the ecclesiastical year in determining these times. Thus a candidate who was ordained an acolyte on Holy Saturday may receive the subdiaconate on the following Holy Saturday, even though 365 days may not have elapsed. Again, the period between the ember

---

[17] S. Cong. Rel., Oct. 27, 1923; *AAS*, 15 (1923), 549; *Digest,* I, p. 483.
[18] Schaefer, *De Religiosis,* ed. 3, n. 298, p. 647.
[19] Vermeersch-Creusen, *Epitome,* II, n. 248.

seasons may be taken as the equivalent of three months, even though it does not amount to ninety days.

Without a special permission of the Roman Pontiff, however, it is never allowed to confer minor orders with the subdiaconate, or to confer two sacred orders on the same day. All contrary customs are reprobated. Nor is it allowed to confer first tonsure along with one or more of the minor orders, nor may all the minor orders be given on the same day (c. 978, § 3).

Canonical Title. For secular clerics their canonical title is the title of a benefice; or if this be lacking, the title of patrimony or the title of subsidy (*pensio*) (c. 979, § 1). By "title for ordination" is meant a stable source of income sufficient for the support of the cleric who wishes to receive major orders. "Title of benefice" means the assured possession of a benefice whose income is sufficient to support the cleric in his proper order. In practice this title occurs today only in the consecration of a Bishop. "Title of patrimony" means that the candidate has sufficient personal property to support himself. "Title of subsidy" includes any assured income for life arising from a grant made to the candidate for orders either by the state, or by the Church, or by some private person.

The title required for ordination must have two qualities: it must be truly certain that it will last for the entire lifetime of the person ordained, and it must be truly sufficient to support him properly in his clerical order according to the norms established by the Ordinaries with a view to the various needs and circumstances of time and place (c. 979, § 2).

Should a cleric ordained in major orders lose his title, he must provide himself with another unless the Bishop judges that his support can be satisfactorily provided for in some other way (c. 980, § 1).

Ordinaries who without an apostolic indult knowingly ordain a subject who has no canonical title must themselves, if the need arise, supply the subject with the necessary sustenance until his proper support can be provided for in some other way. This provision also binds the successors of such Ordinaries (c. 980, § 2).

Should a Bishop ordain a candidate without a title under an agreement that the ordained cleric will not ask support from him, such an agreement has no validity (c. 980, § 3).

If not even one of the titles enumerated in canon 979, § 1 is at hand, it may be supplied by the title of "service of the diocese" and, in places subject to the Sacred Congregation of the Propagation of the Faith, by the title of "the mission." However, a candidate ordained under either of these titles must take an oath to devote his entire life to the service of the diocese or mission under the authority of the Ordinary of the place at the time (c. 981, § 1). The title "service of the diocese" consists in the personal labors of the ordained cleric in behalf of the diocese on the one hand, and the corresponding obligation of the Bishop to support him on the other.

An Ordinary who has promoted a cleric to the priesthood under the title of service of the church or mission is obliged to confer upon him a benefice, or office, or a subsidy, sufficient to provide for his proper support (c. 981, § 2).

For regulars (see c. 488, 7°) the canonical title for ordination is their solemn religious profession or the "title of poverty," as it is called (c. 982, § 1).

For religious with simple perpetual vows it is the "title of the common table," or the "title of the congregation," or some similar title according to the ruling of the constitutions (c. 982, § 2).

All other religious are governed by the regulations for secular clerics regarding the title for ordination (c. 982, § 3). This same rule holds for members of societies living in common without public vows (c. 678).

Section 3. Irregularities and Simple Impediments (cc. 983–991).

PRELIMINARY SURVEY

Nature of Irregularity and Simple Impediment (c. 983)
Irregularities by Defect (c. 984)
Irregularities by Delict (c. 985)
Simple Impediments (c. 987)
Conditions for Incurring Irregularities (cc. 986; 988)
Multiplication of Irregularities (c. 989)
Dispensations From Irregularities (cc. 990–991)

Nature of Irregularity and Simple Impediment. An irregularity may be defined as a perpetual impediment established by ecclesiastical law forbidding primarily the reception of orders and secondarily the exercise of orders already received (c. 968). A simple impediment differs from an irregularity only in this that it is not perpetual; that is, it is of such a nature that it can cease to exist in the course of time.

Only those irregularities can be contracted which are expressly listed in the following canons (c. 983). Hence there is no such thing as an irregularity *ab homine*. Irregularities and simple impediments forbid the reception of orders, including first tonsure, but do not make their reception null and void. They likewise forbid the exercise of orders already received; but if orders thus received are exercised, the acts performed are valid though gravely illicit.

Irregularities do not partake of the nature of a penalty since they can be incurred because of a defect which is entirely inculpable. Even in the case of impediments arising from a delict, the Church is intent on excluding the unworthy from her divine ministry rather than on punishing the crimes which have made them unworthy.

Irregularities are divided into two classes: those arising from a *defect,* and those arising from a *delict.* Each division contains seven irregularities; and, in addition, there are seven simple impediments. It may be helpful to visualize these before explaining them in detail.

(c. 984) *Irregularities by Defect*	(c. 985) *Irregularities by Delict*	(c. 987) *Simple Impediments*
1. Illegitimacy	1. Apostasy, heresy, schism	1. Son of non-Catholic
2. Physical defects	2. Baptized by non-Catholic	2. Married man
3. Mental defects	3. Orders — vows — marriage	3. Forbidden office
4. Bigamy (canonical)	4. Homicide — abortion	4. Slavery
5. Infamy *at law*	5. Mutilation — suicide	5. Military service
6. Judge — death sentence	6. Doctor — surgeon — death	6. Neophyte
7. Public executioner — assts.	7. Prohibited exercise of orders	7. Infamy *by fact*

Irregularities by Defect. An irregularity by defect is one which arises from a *lack of some quality* required either for the reception of an order or for its proper exercise. Ordinarily these irregularities do not imply culpability, though in the case of illegitimacy there is culpability on the part of the parents; and in the case of infamy at law, on the part of the candidate himself.

1. *Illegitimacy or defect of birth (defectus natalium)*. Illegitimate children are irregular whether their illegitimacy be public or occult unless they have been legitimated or have made profession of solemn vows (c. 984, 1°). Illegitimate children are those who have been born out of true or putative wedlock (c. 1114). They are irregular even though their illegitimacy is occult. Foundlings are not to be considered illegitimate, especially if a written statement regarding their baptism is attached to them. If nothing is known about them, it is customary to obtain a dispensation (see c. 15). Doubtfully illegitimate children are not to be considered irregular.

This irregularity may be removed in two ways: by the profession of solemn vows and by legitimation. Once legitimated by solemn vows, the candidate for orders does not again become irregular if he leaves his institute.

Illegitimate children are automatically legitimated by the subsequent marriage of their parents under the conditions laid down in canons 1051 and 1116. In all other cases a rescript of the Holy See is required to legitimate them.

2. *Physical defects (defectus corporis)*. Those physically defective persons are irregular who by reason of such defects are prevented either from the *safe* performance of the sacred ministries because of physical weakness, or from their *dignified* performance because of some deformity. However, a graver defect is required to impede the exercise of orders already received; nor does a defect prohibit the exercise of acts which can be properly performed in spite of it (c. 984, 2°).

Two points are to be attended to when there is question of a physical defect: *weakness* of a member which would prevent the safe performance of ministerial acts, and such *deformity* as would detract from the fitting or becoming performance of such acts. Becoming performance requires two things: (1) that the faithful are not disgusted or offended by reason of the physical defect of the person performing the sacred act; (2) that by reason of the deformity liturgical laws are not violated in a matter of importance.

The principal physical defects which induce irregularity are the following: weakness of members, mutilation, blindness, deafness, defect of speech, deformity. A word about each:

Weakness of members. Included under this heading are all persons who cannot stand either because of disease or because of general physical weakness; likewise such as are subject to great trembling of hands, legs, or feet. In all these cases the irregularity is incurred only when the condition is permanent.[20]

Mutilation. Those who have lost one or both arms, or one or both hands, are certainly irregular; likewise those who have lost two fingers and half a hand, or the three last fingers of one hand; those who have lost a thumb, especially the thumb of the right hand. Authors dispute about the loss of an index finger. The better opinion, one safe to follow in practice, seems to be that a person who has lost an index finger is not irregular if he can safely hold and break the Sacred Host with his thumb and second finger. The same rule is to be applied in the case of a missing joint of thumb or forefinger. Those who have lost a foot or a leg are not irregular, provided that with the help of an artificial limb they are able to stand securely and perform all the ceremonies prescribed.[21]

Blindness. One totally blind, or one whose eyesight is so weak that he cannot offer the Holy Sacrifice safely or with the proper dignity, is certainly irregular.[22] The myth of the "canonical eye" has been exploded by an answer of the S. Congregation of Religious[23] which stated that the mere privation of the use of the left eye (*defectus oculi sinistri*) if no other deformity or obstacle exists, is not sufficient to constitute an irregularity. The answer supposes, however, that the deformity is concealed by a glass eye (artificial eye) to prevent disgust on the part of the faithful and that the person has such good use of the right eye that he can read the Missal without unbecoming bending or turning of the head.

Caecutientes. A priest who is losing his sight, or whose sight is so weak either accidentally or habitually that he can read only very large type, may obtain a dispensation from the Sacred Congregation of Rites through the Apostolic Delegate (faculty n. 41) which will allow him to celebrate daily either a votive Mass of the Blessed Virgin or the so-called daily Mass of the Dead (*Missa quotidiana defunctorum*).[24]

Deafness. Those who are entirely deaf (in both ears) are certainly irregular for the reception of orders. Those who are only partially

---

[20] For various cases in which the S. Cong. of the Council has granted dispensations from the irregularity, see Cappello, *De Sacramentis,* Vol. II, Pars III, *De Sacra Ordinatione,* pp. 438–439.

[21] For dispensations in these cases, see Cappello, *op. cit.,* 439–444.

[22] For dispensations, see Cappello, *op. cit.,* 445–446.

[23] S. Cong. Rel., Nov. 28, 1924, to Procurator General of the Capuchin Order; *Digest,* I, p. 486.

[24] See Instruction of S. C. Rit., Jan. 21, 1921; *AAS,* 13 (1921), 154; *Digest,* I, p. 370.

deaf, even though completely deaf in one ear, are not irregular. If complete deafness comes after ordination to the priesthood, the afflicted priest may be allowed to celebrate Mass but not to hear confessions.

Defect of speech. A person who cannot speak at all is not only irregular but is forbidden the clerical state by divine law. A person who cannot pronounce words properly, or who pronounces them in unintelligible fashion, or who stutters in such a way as to cause laughter in his hearers is certainly irregular.

Deformity. A person who is so visibly deformed that his appearance causes disgust, or laughter, or great surprise to the faithful is certainly irregular. Under this heading would come hunchbacks, midgets, those who have no nose, or no lips, or who have an ugly cancer on the face. A person who has lost both ears is not irregular if his deformity is hidden by his hair.

In all cases of physical defect the judgment as to whether such defect amounts to an irregularity or not rests with the Ordinary of the candidate who wishes to receive orders or of the cleric who wishes to exercise orders already received. In the case of regulars (religious with solemn vows) the more probable opinion holds that the major superior is to pass judgment in the case of a cleric who has already received orders and wishes to exercise them. When there is question of receiving orders, the more probable opinion favors the religious superiors; but this opinion is of little moment since the Bishop who is to ordain the religious candidate need not accept the decision of the regular superior but may pass his own judgment in the case.

Before passing judgment in these cases, the Ordinary, whether Bishop or regular superior, should consider the report of a master of ceremonies in whose presence the candidate shall have made an experiment of his physical ability to perform the sacred rites.

When there is question of the irregularity of physical defect, one must keep in mind the great progress which has been made during the past few years in the art of making artificial legs, arms, hands, and fingers. Because of these helps and because of the skill in using them which can be acquired by practice, the Holy See is more willing to dispense than was the case years ago. This should be kept in mind when reading older decrees in which a dispensation was refused in certain cases.

3. *Mental defects (defectus animi).* Included under this heading are epilepsy, insanity, and diabolical possession. Once incurred, the

irregularity for the reception of orders remains even though the candidate becomes entirely free from the defect which gave rise to the irregularity. If the irregularity is incurred *after* the reception of orders, and if it is certain that the cleric has been entirely freed from the defect which gave cause to it, Ordinaries may allow their subjects to resume the exercise of the orders already received **(c. 984, 3°)**.

Good authors make an exception in the case of epilepsy with which the candidate was afflicted before the age of puberty and which, in the opinion of a reliable doctor, has entirely disappeared. This opinion may be safely followed in practice.

4. *Canonical bigamy* *(defectus sacramenti)*. Canonical bigamy implies two things: that there were two or more successive marriages, and that all were valid marriages **(c. 984, 4°)**. To incur the irregularity, it is not necessary that the marriages have been consummated. The irregularity is also incurred by a man married twice before baptism, or once before and once after baptism.

5. *Infamy at law (defectus famae)*. Those who have been branded with infamy by the law are irregular **(c. 984, 5°)**. Infamy in general is a lack of good name or reputation, or at least a serious diminution of the same. It is evident how necessary a good reputation is for a cleric. In the present instance only infamy contracted or imposed *by law* constitutes the irregularity. Infamy is sometimes imposed *by law ipso facto* (see cc. 2314, § 1, 3°; 2320; 2328; 2343, § 1, 2°, and § 2, 2°; 2351, § 2; 2356; 2357, § 1); it is to be imposed by declarative sentence in two cases (see cc. 2314, § 1, 2°, and 2359, § 2). It may be well to note here that by its nature infamy by law is perpetual and that only the Holy See can dispense from this penalty (c. 2295). Once the penalty has been removed by dispensation, the irregularity ceases. Infamy *of fact* is a simple impediment to orders.

6. *Judges who have imposed the death sentence (defectus lenitatis)* **(c. 984, 6°)**. By judge is meant not only an individual person but also a collegiate tribunal. What about the twelve tried and true men called "jurors"? If the jurors merely pronounce a person "guilty" and the judge then pronounces the death sentence, the jurors would not incur the irregularity, but if in some particular case the jury actually sentences a person to death, the jurors incur the irregularity.

This irregularity is based on the idea that it is unbecoming for one who by pronouncing sentence of death has shown himself in some sense lacking in mercy should, as a Catholic priest, become the personal representative of the merciful Saviour. Hence the name *defectus lenitatis christianae.* Only *baptized* persons, therefore, incur the irregularity.

7. *Those who have accepted the office of public executioner, as well as their immediate and voluntary assistants in carrying out the death sentence* (c. 984, 7°). A public executioner (headman or hangman) incurs the irregularity by the very act of assuming his office; his immediate and voluntary assistants incur it only after they have actually taken part in an execution. In both cases the person must act voluntarily and without any compulsion. Hence soldiers who are ordered to take their place in a firing squad would not incur the irregularity. Only baptized persons incur the irregularity, not those who have performed such acts before baptism. The witnesses at a trial, attorneys, notaries, those who conduct the condemned person to the scaffold or to the electric chair, the builders of the scaffold, and other similar persons are not included.

Irregularities by Delict. An irregularity *by delict* is one which is incurred by reason of certain specified personal, grievous, external consummated sins committed after baptism, which sins render the person unworthy of the clerical state or of exercising orders already received. The irregularities by delict are seven in number:

1. *Apostates from the faith, heretics, schismatics* (c. 985, 1°). These terms are used in the meaning given to them in canon 1325, § 2. It is required and suffices that the delict be manifested *externally* in any manner whatever, even though the delict remain occult. It must, however, be a formal sin (see c. 986). This is presumed in the external forum (c. 2200, § 2). If one assumed to be a heretic *has never been baptized,* or if it is proved that his baptism was *certainly invalid,* he does not incur the irregularity; if his baptism is doubtfully valid, the irregularity is doubtful; but in practice it is advisable to get a dispensation from the Ordinary *"ad cautelam"* (see c. 15). This is in conformity with the practice of the Holy See. According to the more common opinion, boys under fourteen are presumed to be guiltless of this delict in the external forum; hence they probably are not irregular if they are converted before they have completed their fourteenth year. The Ordinary can certainly dispense in these cases (see c. 15). Finally, the irregularity does not cease with conversion to the Catholic faith since by its nature it is perpetual.[25]

2. *Those who, except in case of extreme necessity, have allowed*

---

[25] See Decree of the Holy Office, Dec. 4, 1890; *Fontes,* IV, n. 1129, p. 456.

themselves to be baptized by non-Catholics in any manner whatsoever (c. 985, 2°). This irregularity can be incurred by adults only, since *consent* and *voluntary* reception of baptism are required as well as knowledge of the status of the non-Catholic minister. Even *impuberes* incur the irregularity provided they have sufficient use of reason to know the meaning of their act. The term "in any manner whatever" includes conditional and absolute, solemn or private baptism in any rite. By "non-Catholic" is meant a heretic or schismatic but not an infidel, since the legislator mentions infidels expressly when he wishes to include them under this term (see c. 1099, § 1, 2°). Strict interpretation of the term is required here since we are dealing with a restriction of rights (see c. 19).

3. *Those already married or in sacred orders or with religious vows who attempt marriage.* This irregularity is incurred in five cases: (1) a married man attempts a second marriage while his wife is still living; (2) a cleric in major orders who attempts marriage; (3) a religious man with solemn or simple, perpetual or temporary vows who attempts marriage; (4) a man who is free to marry attempts marriage with a religious woman who has either solemn or simple, perpetual or temporary vows; (5) a man who is free to marry attempts marriage with a woman who is validly married and whose husband is still alive (c. 985, 3°). According to the present practice of the Holy See, the dispensation from this irregularity is reserved to the Holy Office.[26]

4. *Those who have committed voluntary homicide or procured an abortion (the effect following) as well as their co-operators* (c. 985, 4°). The intention to kill must be present, and death must follow as the direct result of the act. Any willful attempt at homicide or abortion would be gravely sinful, but it would not induce the irregularity unless the effect actually took place. Death resulting from legitimate self-defense would not cause this irregularity. Though one may sin gravely by an action which results in the death of a person or in an abortion, or by failing to take due precautions (*omissio debitae diligentiae*) to prevent such death, the irregularity would not be incurred if the death was not intended. Accidental homicide or abortion which occurs contrary to intention does not induce the irregularity.

All formal, primary co-operators likewise incur the irregularity (see explanation of c. 2209, §§ 1, 2, and 3, p. 798).

5. *Those who have mutilated themselves or others, or who have*

---

[26] Lopez, *Periodica,* 1937, p. 504.

attempted suicide (c. 985, 5°). In order to induce the irregularity, the mutilation must be notable, that is, a part of the body which has its own function distinct from that of other members must be cut off; for instance, a hand, a foot, an eye, complete castration. If the member is not cut off, but merely rendered useless, no irregularity is incurred though the act may be grievously sinful.

Attempted suicide consists in trying to kill oneself by shooting, poison, hanging, or any other method, even though the attempt does not result in a wound of any kind. However, the simple *delicti conatus* (see c. 2212, § 1) is not sufficient to induce the irregularity, but the attempt must amount to a *delictum frustratum* (see c. 2212, § 2).

6. *Clerics who practice medicine or surgery without permission, provided that death results from such practice* (c. 985, 6°). Clerics are forbidden to practice medicine or surgery without an apostolic indult (see c. 139, § 2). Two conditions are required to incur the irregularity: illicit exercise of medicine or surgery, and death resulting directly and immediately from it. Hence, if a cleric has permission or acts without permission in a case of great necessity, he would not become irregular if death followed his ministration. Since religious are bound by the obligations of clerics (c. 592), a religious who is not yet a cleric could incur this irregularity.

7. *Those who perform an act of orders reserved to clerics in sacred orders, either when they lack the order or when they are forbidden to exercise an order already received because of a personal, medicinal, vindictive, or local canonical penalty* (c. 985, 7°). The irregularity arises from a twofold source: (*a*) by exercising the functions of a sacred order not yet received; (*b*) by exercising the functions of a major order actually received but which the cleric is forbidden to exercise by reason of a canonical penalty.

a. Performance of acts reserved to clerics in sacred orders. Under this section any layman or cleric becomes irregular by exercising the function of a sacred order (subdiaconate, diaconate, priesthood, episcopate) which he has not yet received. According to a decree of the Sacred Congregation of Rites[27] the office of subdeacon at a solemn Mass may for a reasonable cause be filled by one in minor orders, or by one who is *at least tonsured*. Hence a layman is never allowed to act as subdeacon. The cleric who acts as subdeacon in this case is not permitted to perform the following actions: (1) he may not wear the

---

[27] May 10, 1906, *Decr. Auth.* I, n. 4181, p. 80.

maniple; (2) he may not wipe the chalice at the Offertory nor pour the water into it; (3) he may never touch the chalice during the canon of the Mass nor remove and replace the pall; (4) after the ablution he may not purify the chalice, but this should be done by the celebrant himself. It is well to note here that Pius X approved this decree in its entirety, revoked all contrary privileges and customs, and declared them abrogated. To incur the irregularity, a cleric in minor orders who acts as subdeacon must *voluntarily* and *consciously* do *all four* things prohibited. If he omits one of them, he does not become irregular though he may sin grievously by performing the other forbidden acts.

No subdeacon, much less a cleric in minor orders, may wear a stole *and* sing the gospel at a solemn Mass or perform any other function of the deacon. If he does so, he becomes irregular.

b. Exercise of orders prohibited by reason of canonical penalty. Since the canon requires that this prohibition be imposed as a *penalty,* a secularized religious who says Mass in violation of the prohibition of canon 641, § 1 does not thereby become irregular. In occult cases, a cleric who has thus become irregular may take advantage of the provisions of canon 2232, § 1 whenever there is danger of losing his good name by the observance of the irregularity.

The usurpation of the power of jurisdiction only, or of orders which are not sacred, does not induce an irregularity.

Simple Impediments to Ordination. An impediment differs from an irregularity only by reason of the fact that it is not of its nature perpetual. It can cease in the course of time.

1. *Sons of non-Catholics as long as their parents remain in error* (c. 987, 1°). In the old law the impediment extended to two generations, but the present law includes only the first generation.[28] The impediment is incurred, however, even though only one parent be a non-Catholic, and also in the case of a mixed marriage contracted with a dispensation for which the promises were made.[29] The term "non-Catholic" is restricted to members of a heretical or schismatical sect; it does not include infidels unless they are members of an atheistic sect.[30] It is a probable opinion, which may be safely followed in practice, that after the death of the non-Catholic parent or parents, the son is no longer impeded from the reception of orders. All sons are included in the impediment, both legitimate and illegitimate.

---

[28] Code Com., July 14, 1922, ad 9; *AAS* 14 (1922), 528; *Digest,* I, p. 487.

[29] Code Com., Oct. 16, 1919, ad 13; *AAS* 11 (1919), 478; *Digest,* I, p. 487.

[30] Code Com., July 30, 1934; *AAS,* 26 (1934), 494; *Digest,* II, p. 286. For the meaning of "atheistic" see *Periodica,* 23, p. 146.

2. *A married man whose wife is still living* (c. 987, 2°). Pre-Code legislation permitted a husband to receive orders provided that his wife freely entered a monastery. The present legislation requires the permission of the Holy See in all cases even though the wife gives her permission and takes a vow of chastity. The permission is granted very rarely. If a married man has received sacred orders in good faith without a dispensation, he is forbidden to exercise the orders received (c. 132, § 3; see also c. 1114).

3. *One holding an office forbidden to clerics* (c. 987, 3°). Such offices are enumerated in canon 139. Once the office is given up, the impediment ceases.

4. *Slaves in the strict sense of the term are impeded until they obtain their liberty* (c. 987, 4°). This case is still a possibility in certain missionary countries, though it occurs rarely.

5. *Those obliged to ordinary military service by civil law until they have fulfilled their obligation* (c. 987, 5°). By *ordinary* military service is meant regular military duty of obligation for a year or more in time of peace. Hence, occasional periods of training (e.g., summer camps) even though of obligation to all would not be included in the impediment; nor would the extraordinary military service induced by actual war. However, a young man who is obliged to ordinary military service is impeded from the reception of orders even though he has not yet reached the age required by law for such training; likewise one, who, having been called, has been declared temporarily unfit.[31] Those exempted from active military service but obliged to serve in hospital units during their period of training are probably not included under the impediment.

6. *Neophytes are impeded from the reception of orders until, in the judgment of their Ordinary, they have been sufficiently tested* (c. 987, 6°). A neophyte is one who has been converted to the faith as an adult and has received baptism unconditionally. Hence, the term does not include a convert who has been baptized only conditionally. The purpose of the impediment is to give the convert sufficient opportunity to grow strong in the faith and in the practice of Christian virtues before promoting him to orders.

7. *Those who as a matter of fact have lost their good name or reputation as long as in the judgment of the Ordinary this condition lasts* (c. 987, 7°). One is said to be infamous in fact (*infamia facti*

---

[31] Code Com., June 3, 1918; *AAS* 10 (1918), 344; *Digest,* I, p. 487.

laborare) or to have lost his good reputation when, because of some crime committed or because of his depraved morals, he has lost the good opinion which upright and serious people had of him. The impediment lasts until the person has regained his good reputation by making amends for his misdeeds and leading a good Christian life. The Ordinary is the judge in each case. If an innocent man has been defamed and thereby lost his good reputation unjustly, he may not be promoted to orders until his innocence has been made known.

Conditions for Incurring Irregularities. First of all the irregularity, whether it be an irregularity by defect or by delict, must be *certain,* that is, the fact on which it is based must certainly exist. Hence, a doubtful irregularity is no irregularity.

Ignorance does not excuse from any irregularity or simple impediment **(c. 988).** This is in accordance with the principle of law laid down in canon 16, § 1. The purpose of irregularities and simple impediments is to safeguard the decorum and dignity of the clerical state by excluding both unworthy persons and those who, through no fault of their own, might make the sacred ministry less acceptable to the faithful.

Irregularities by defect and simple impediments (except the last) do not imply any moral guilt on the part of the candidate who has incurred them. He is simply the victim of circumstances which prevent him from being accorded the favor of ordination.

Irregularities by delict, however, are not incurred unless the delict is a grave external sin, public or occult, committed *after baptism* except the case of c. 985, 2° **(c. 986).** This is in full accord with the definition of a delict as given in canon 2195. The delict must be *external* in order to bring it into the external forum of the Church. It must be both subjectively and objectively grave because the unworthiness for which the irregularity of delict has been established arises only from a grave fault. Only delicts committed after baptism induce the irregularity because the Church does not consider sins which have been completely deleted by baptism. (For the meaning of public and occult, see canon 2197, 1°).

Multiplication of Irregularities. Irregularities and simple impediments are multiplied by reason of their different causes but not by a repetition of the same cause except in the case of voluntary homicide **(c. 989).** This multiplication of irregularities and simple impediments must be taken into account when there is question of dispensation (see c. 991). It occurs only when there are entirely different *causes* for the irregularities. Thus a person who is illegitimate and who mutilates himself is bound by two irregularities. Only in the case of voluntary homicide is the irregularity multiplied by a repetition of the *same* cause. Authors dispute whether this exception includes abortion. Since all laws regarding irregularities are to be interpreted strictly (they deal with restriction of rights — see c. 19 — and of odious matters), the probable opinion that abortion is not included should be followed. In canon 985, 4° and in canon 990, § 1 the lawgiver lists abortion as a special form of homicide, but does not mention it in canon 989. The presumption therefore is that in c. 989 the omission is intentional.

Dispensation From Irregularities.   Once incurred, an irregularity ceases only by dispensation since by its very nature it is perpetual. Simple impediments cease when their cause ceases — for instance, the conversion of a non-Catholic parent, military service performed; otherwise they also must be removed by dispensation.

The Roman Pontiff can dispense from all irregularities and impediments. This power is exercised: through the Sacred Penitentiary for the internal forum in all cases; for the external forum, through the S. Congregation for the Propagation of the Faith and the S. Congregation for Oriental Churches for their respective subjects; through the S. Congregation of the Sacraments, for all seculars, lay and cleric, except in the case of a priest already ordained who has incurred an irregularity *ex delicto*. This latter case is under the jurisdiction of the S. Congregation of the Council.[32] The S. Congregation of Religious has jurisdiction in this matter in favor of religious.

Ordinaries have no jurisdiction to dispense from irregularities *ex defectu* or from simple impediments except that given in canons 15 and 81.

Ordinaries may, however, dispense either personally or through others from all irregularities arising from an *occult delict* excepting, however, the case of voluntary homicide or abortion and all cases which have been brought before a court for formal trial (c. 990, § 1). "Ordinaries" here includes major superiors of exempt clerical institutes for their subjects (see c. 198, § 1). All Ordinaries can dispense their subjects both for the reception of orders and for the exercise of orders already received.

The same faculty is granted to any confessor for all more urgent

---

[32] S. C. Consist., Nov. 28, 1911; *AAS* 3 (1911), 658; *Fontes*, V, n. 2082, p. 51.

occult cases in which the Ordinary cannot be approached without danger of grave harm or loss of reputation; but the confessor can use this faculty only in favor of a penitent already ordained and only for the licit exercise of orders already received, not for the reception of further orders (c. 990, § 2). In these cases it is not necessary to have recourse to the Holy See or to the Bishop after the dispensation has been granted.

Some exempt religious have the privilege of dispensing all penitents in sacramental confession for the internal forum only from all irregularities *ex delicto* without exception. Usually the use of this faculty is confined to the time of missions and retreats.

The *major superiors* of regulars (*Ordinarii regulares*) have the power, either by direct privilege or by communication, to dispense all their subjects from all irregularities. This power is restricted to the internal forum in the case of the irregularity arising from voluntary homicide. Moreover, *local superiors* (of regulars only) have the power to absolve on the Monday after the first Sunday after Lent, either personally or through confessors delegated by them, all *their subjects,* including novices, who live within the cloister under obedience, from all irregularities, no matter on what occasion or for what reason they were contracted. Both of these faculties, namely, that of major superiors and that of local superiors, are sometimes restricted by being reserved in whole or in part to the superior general. Hence, regulars should consult their own legislation before attempting to use such faculties.[33]

No particular form is prescribed for granting a dispensation from an irregularity *ex delicto*. An external manifestation of the will on the part of the person dispensing, given in any form whatever, is required and suffices for the validity of the dispensation. The following or some similar form may be used: "*Auctoritate mihi concessa, dispenso tecum super irregularitate quam incurristi propter talem causam (v.g., propter abortum) in nomine Patris, etc.*" Or one may use one of the forms suggested in the Roman Ritual, III, cap. V, nn. 2–4.

All irregularities and simple impediments by which a person is bound must be mentioned in the petition for dispensation from irregularities and impediments; if this is not done, a general dispensation is nevertheless valid for those omitted in good faith (with the exceptions mentioned in c. 990, § 1), but not for those omitted in bad faith (c. 991, § 1). When there is question of the irregularity arising

---

[33] See Vermeersch-Creusen, *Epitome Iuris Canonici*, II, n. 261, p. 180. They give the Constitution of Pius V, *Dum ad Congregationem,* June 13, 1571, and the Brief of Paul III, *Exponi nobis nuper,* March 12, 1545, as the sources of these faculties.

from voluntary homicide, the number of times the delict was committed must also be given under pain of invalidity of the dispensation granted (c. 991, § 2). This does not hold for cases of abortion, as explained above (see c. 989).

A general dispensation granted for the reception of orders is valid also for the reception of *major* orders; and the candidate who has been dispensed can obtain nonconsistorial benefices (see c. 1411) even those to which the care of souls is attached; but he cannot be made a Cardinal, a Bishop, an Abbot or Prelate *nullius,* or a major superior in an exempt clerical institute without a new and special dispensation (c. 991, § 3). Any dispensation from irregularities or simple impediments granted in the external forum should be in writing. If given in the internal sacramental forum, it may be oral only. If given in the internal but extra-sacramental forum, it should be given in writing and it must be recorded in the secret archives of the curia (c. 991, § 4).

Section 4. Prerequisites to Sacred Ordination (cc. 992–1001)

PRELIMINARY SURVEY

Manifestation of Intention (c. 992)
Various Testimonials Required (c. 993–995)
Examinations Before Ordination (cc. 996–997)
Bans for Ordination (cc. 998–1000)
Spiritual Retreat Before Ordination (c. 1001)

Manifestation of Intention. All candidates for orders, whether they be seculars or religious, must in due time before ordination make their intention known, either personally or through others, to the Bishop or to another who takes the Bishop's place in this matter (c. 992). Besides this manifestation of intention, both secular and religious candidates must make the written declaration required in the respective instructions issued by the S. Congregation of the Sacraments and the S. Congregation of Religious (cf. Sec. 2, pp. 366–367). "The person who takes the Bishop's place" may be the Vicar General, the Vicar Capitular, or the Administrator, and in the case of religious the major superior. "In due time" is generally interpreted to mean at least one month before the ordination is to take place.

Various Testimonials Required. Secular candidates and all religious candidates who are governed by the law of seculars in the matter of ordinations must present the testimonials listed below (c. 993). The obligation contained in this canon is a grave one binding in conscience. The matter is of the utmost importance since it concerns the dignity and the respect of the clerical state. All religious who are not exempt are subject to the canon (see c. 964, 4°). The following documents must be presented by all candidates:

1. *Testimonial of the last order received, or in the case of first tonsure testimony of baptism and confirmation.* The only exception to this rule is that which occurs when the Bishop who conferred the previous order is also to confer the next order. This exception is made because the archives of the ordaining Bishop contain the records of the order previously received (c. 1010, § 1).

2. *Testimonial regarding the studies made as required for each order by canon 976.*

3. *Testimonial of the rector of the seminary, or of the priest under whose guidance the candidate is living outside the seminary (c. 972, § 2), regarding the moral character of the candidate.*

4. *Testimonial letters of any local Ordinary in whose territory the candidate has dwelt for the length of time required to contract a canonical impediment.* These testimonial letters simply testify that the candidate has not incurred any canonical impediment during his sojourn in the territory of the signer. *Canonical impediment* means any irregularity or simple impediment to orders.

5. *In the case of a religious candidate these testimonial letters are to be issued by his own major superior.*

Time required to contract a canonical impediment. As a general rule the time required to contract a canonical impediment is three months for soldiers, six months for others — both after the age of puberty. However, the ordaining Bishop may according to his prudent judgment demand testimonial letters for even a shorter period and for the time before puberty (c. 994, § 1). The period of three or six months is to be considered as a moral unit, not physically.[34]

If the local Ordinary is not acquainted with the candidate, either personally or through others, so that he is unable to testify that the candidate has incurred no canonical impediment, or if the candidate has lived in so many dioceses that it becomes impossible or too difficult to obtain all the testimonial letters required, then the ordaining Bishop shall provide for the case at least by having the candidate take a supplementary oath (c. 994, § 2).

---

[34] S. C. C., June 25, 1904; *Fontes,* VI, n. 4318, p. 811.

If after the testimonial letters have been received and before actual ordination for which they were given, the candidate again dwells in the same territory for the space of time mentioned above, new testimonial letters must be issued by the local Ordinary (c. 994, § 3).

The religious superior who issues dimissorial letters for an exempt religious (see c. 964) must testify not only that the candidate has made his religious profession and is a member of the religious family under his jurisdiction, but he must also testify to the studies made by the religious and to all other points required by law (c. 995, § 1). See the explanation given under c. 964, 2° above.

The Bishop who has received such dimissorial letters needs no further testimonial letters for the ordination of an exempt religious candidate (c. 995, § 2).

Examinations Before Ordination. Every candidate for orders, whether secular or religious, must undergo beforehand a careful examination regarding the order to be received (c. 996, § 1). This examination should deal principally with the matter and form of the order to be received, the minister, the conditions required for its reception, its effects, etc.

Candidates for sacred orders shall also undergo an examination in other treatises of sacred theology (c. 996, § 2). One special examination in sacred theology is sufficient for all three sacred orders. However, the Bishop may allow the ordinary examinations taken in the course of the candidate's theological studies to take the place of the special examination prescribed by this canon.

In these examinations it is the Bishop's right to determine the method to be followed, the examiners, and the treatises to be covered (c. 996, § 3).

This examination, whether of secular or religious candidates, is to be held by the local Ordinary who ordains the candidate in his own right or who issues dimissorial letters for him. For a just reason, however, he may entrust the examination to the Bishop who is to ordain the candidate, provided the latter is willing to undertake the burden (c. 997, § 1). In this canon exempt religious are not included under the term "religious candidate." This would seem to follow from the second paragraph of the canon in which there is question of a religious in whose dimissorial letters (see cc. 965 and 966) his own Ordinary gives testimony that he has been examined in accordance with the requirements of canon 997, § 1. Even in the case of other religious candidates included in the canon, the Bishop may accept as sufficient the examinations passed by the candidate in his own house of studies, provided that the studies have been made in conformity with the prescriptions of canon 589.

The Bishop ordaining a secular or religious candidate who is not his own subject and who presents legitimate dimissorial letters which give testimony that the candidate has been examined in conformity with the requirements of § 1 above and has been found suitable, may rest satisfied with this testimony. However, he is not obliged to do so; and if he thinks the candidate is not suitable, he should not ordain him (c. 997, § 2). The ordaining Bishop may *always* rest satisfied with the testimony given in the dimissorial letters regarding studies. Generally speaking, he should do so unless he has special reasons to the contrary, or at least some positive doubt concerning the fitness of the candidate. In these cases he may and should demand another examination before ordaining or refusing to ordain.

Bans for Ordination. Except in the case of religious with perpetual vows (simple or solemn), the names of all candidates for each sacred order shall be publicly announced in the parish church of each candidate. For a just cause, however, the Ordinary may prudently dispense from such publication, or order that it be made in other churches, or substitute for oral publication by publicly posting the names of the candidates near the entrance to the church for a number of days, including at least one feast day (c. 998, § 1). The purpose of this prescription is to give the faithful the opportunity of making known any canonical impediment of which they may be aware. When the sacred orders are received with the proper time intervals, the publication of the candidate's name must be made before each sacred order is received. If, however, by reason of an apostolic indult, all three sacred orders are to be received within a short space of time (one or two weeks), one publication will suffice for all three orders. Religious with perpetual vows are excepted because by profession of perpetual vows they have lost their diocese (c. 585).

This publication is to be made during Mass on a holyday of obligation (see c. 1247, § 1), or on some other day and hour when a large congregation is present in the church (c. 998, § 2). If the candidate is not ordained within six months after publication, the publication should be repeated unless the Ordinary judges otherwise (c. 998, § 3).

All the faithful are under obligation to make known to the Bishop or to the parish priest before ordination any impediments to sacred orders of which they have knowledge (c. 999). Impediments here include not only irregularities and simple impediments to orders, but also anything which would prohibit the reception of orders, such as a lack of proper moral character, etc.

The Ordinary shall assign to the parish priest who makes the publication, or to another if that seems expedient, the duty of investigating among reliable persons the life and moral character of the candidates and of transmitting to his curia testimonial letters embodying the results of the investigation and of the publication of names (c. 1000). After the investigation and the publications have been made, the parish priest must send his report to the episcopal curia even though nothing detrimental to the character of the candidate has been discovered.

The Ordinary shall likewise make other inquiries, even private ones, if that be judged necessary or opportune (c. 1000, § 2).

Spiritual Retreat Before Ordination. All candidates for orders must make a retreat before receiving them. The retreat before the reception of tonsure and minor orders must be at least three full days; before each sacred order, at least six full days. If the candidate is to receive several major orders within a period of six months, the ordinary may shorten the retreat before the reception of the *diaconate,* but not to less than three full days (c. 1001, § 1). The term "Ordinary" is to be taken in the meaning given it in canon 198, § 1. Only before the reception of the diaconate may the Ordinary shorten the retreat to three full days. However, if by reason of an apostolic indult, sacred orders are conferred upon a candidate on distinct consecutive or proximate days so that there is not time to observe the prescription of this canon, then the first sacred order received shall always be preceded by spiritual exercises for at least six full days; the other orders, by at least one day of spiritual retreat if in the judgment of the Bishop according to c. 1001, § 2, this can be done.[35]

If after having made the prescribed retreat a candidate's ordination is deferred beyond six months for any reason whatsoever, he shall make another retreat; if the ordination is deferred for less than six months, the Ordinary shall decide whether the retreat is to be made again or not (c. 1001, § 2). For a just cause the retreat may be made some time in advance of the day of ordination.

This spiritual retreat is to be made by religious candidates in their own house or in another at the prudent discretion of the superior; by

---

[35] C. S. Sacr., May 1, 1928; *AAS,* 20 (1928), 359; *Digest,* I, p. 489.

secular candidates, either in the seminary or in some other pious or religious house designated by the Bishop (c. 1001, § 3). The Bishop shall be informed regarding the retreat by the superior of the house in which it was made; in the case of religious, by the testimony of their own major superior (c. 1001, § 4).

Note. Concerning the profession of faith and the oath against Modernism to be taken before the reception of the subdiaconate, see canon 1406, § 1, 7°.

Section 5. Rites, Ceremonies, Time, and Place of Sacred Ordination (cc. 1002-1011)

PRELIMINARY SURVEY

Rites and Ceremonies of Sacred Ordination (cc. 1002–1005)
Time of Sacred Ordination (cc. 1006–1007)
Place of Sacred Ordination (cc. 1008–1009)
Record, Certificate, Notification (cc. 1010–1011)

Rites and Ceremonies of Sacred Ordination. In every order to be conferred, the minister shall observe exactly the proper rites as described in the Roman Pontifical or in other books of rites approved by the Church. Any omission or change of any rite is absolutely forbidden (c. 1002). "Other books" includes the rituals of the Eastern Churches and the local diocesan or regional rituals which are in use with the special permission of the Holy See.

The Mass of ordination or of episcopal consecration must always be celebrated by the minister of ordination or consecration (c. 1003). It is never allowed, therefore, for the Vicar General or some other prelate to say the Mass during which the Bishop confers orders. The Holy See rarely grants a dispensation in this matter.

A candidate who has already received some orders in an Eastern rite and who has obtained an indult from the Holy See to receive higher orders in the Latin rite must first receive according to the Latin rite those orders which he did not receive in the Eastern rite (c. 1004). This prescription refers to the usage of some Eastern rites which have only two or three minor orders.

All who have received a major order are obliged to receive Holy Communion in the ordination Mass itself (c. 1005). This precept applies only to major orders, not to tonsure and minor orders. It is very becoming, however, that it should be observed in the reception of these orders also; and it is an almost universal custom to do so.[36]

Newly ordained priests are bound *sub gravi* to receive Holy Communion in the ordination Mass since it is an integral part of the Eucharistic Sacrifice which they have offered with the ordaining Bishop; subdeacons and deacons are said to be bound *sub levi* to receive Holy Communion during the ordination Mass.

Though it is beyond the scope of this book to discuss the rites of ordination in detail, still we cannot refrain from recommending to the reader an extremely valuable article which brings together all the decisions of the Holy See regarding the rite of ordination in two classified summaries. The article was written by the Reverend F. X. Hecht, P.S.M., and published in *Periodica,* Vol. 23, p. 73.

A digest of that part of Father Hecht's summary which deals with the *priesthood only* will be found in Bouscaren, *Digest,* II, pp. 240–247.

Time of Sacred Orders. Episcopal consecration must be conferred during Mass on a Sunday or feast day (*dies natalitius*) of an Apostle (c. 1006, § 1). The feasts of the Apostles are limited to the twelve (including St. Paul but not St. Barnabas); feasts of the Evangelists SS. Luke and Mark are excluded. Nor may episcopal consecration be held on holy days of obligation, whether actual (see c. 1247, § 1) or suppressed, without a special indult from the Holy See.[37]

Sacred or major orders are to be conferred during Mass on Ember Saturdays, on the Saturday before Passion Sunday, and on Holy Saturday (c. 1006, § 2). For a grave reason, however, the Bishop may confer sacred orders on a Sunday or holy day of obligation (c. 1006, § 3). The gravity of the cause is to be interpreted by the Bishop. "Grave reason" here includes: absence of the Bishop from the diocese for some time, poor health of the candidate, the need of priests in the diocese. Suppressed feasts are not included in the term "holy days of obligation."[38] Bishops may, however, confer sacred orders on holy days of obligation for the universal church (see c. 1247, § 1) even though such days are not observed in their territory.[39]

By reason of a special indult granted to the Bishops of the United States by the S. Congregation of the Sacraments, May 8, 1940, and approved by His Holiness, Pius XII on the same day, all Archbishops.

---

[36] S. R. C., *Decreta Authentica,* nn. 2692 *ad* 16; 3012 *ad* 3; 3105 *ad* 2; 3186; 3274 *ad* 2.
[37] S. R. C., Apr. 4, 1913; *AAS* 5 (1913), 186.
[38] Code Com., May 15, 1936; *AAS* 28 (1936), 210; *Digest,* II, p. 248.
[39] See Letter of Apostolic Delegate, May 13, 1938; *Digest,* II, p. 248.

and Bishops of the United States may hold sacred ordinations outside the times fixed by law, to-wit on feasts of the double rite of the first or second class, even though they are not days of obligation, and on some Saturdays at the close of the scholastic year.[40]

The privilege to receive orders *extra tempora* granted to some religious institutes and ecclesiastical colleges is usually understood to permit the conferring of orders on any Sunday or holy day of obligation, including suppressed feasts. Regulars frequently have the privilege of being ordained on three consecutive feast days without any interruption. All such privileges survive after the Code by reason of canon 4. They are to be interpreted according to the wording of the indult or privilege.

The first tonsure may be conferred on any day and at any hour; minor orders, on any Sunday or feast of a double rite (*festum duplex*) but in the morning only (c. 1006, § 4). Both tonsure and minor orders may be conferred outside of Mass.

Any custom contrary to the prescriptions of the preceding paragraphs is reprobated; and these prescriptions are also to be observed when by apostolic indult a Bishop of the Latin rite ordains a cleric of an Eastern rite, and vice versa (c. 1006, § 5). For the effect of a *reprobated* custom, see canon 5.

Whenever an ordination is to be repeated or some ceremony supplied, whether absolutely or conditionally, this may be done outside the prescribed times and secretly (c. 1007). Such a repetition or supplying of ceremonies may be made on any day whatever, even on a ferial day.

Place of Sacred Ordination. No Bishop may confer orders which require the *exercise of pontificals* outside his own territory except with the permission of the local Ordinary. An exception is contained in canon 239, § 1, 15° in favor of Cardinals (c. 1008). For the meaning of "exercise of pontificals" see canon 337, § 2.

General ordinations should be held publicly in the cathedral church in the presence of the canons of that church, who are to be invited to attend. If general ordinations are held in some other place in the diocese, this should be done as far as possible in a church of greater dignity and in the presence of the local clergy (c. 1009, § 1).

General ordinations are those held on the six Saturdays specified in c. 1006, § 2, at which all candidates desiring to be ordained may be present. Ordinations held on other days are called particular ordinations.

---

[40] *Digest*, II, p. 249.

The Bishop is not forbidden, however, to hold particular ordinations for a just reason in other churches of the diocese, or in the chapel of the episcopal residence, or of the seminary, or of a religious house (c. 1009, § 2). Any good reason will suffice.

First tonsure and minor orders may also be conferred in private oratories (c. 1009, § 3). No particular reason is required to do so.

Record, Certificate, Notification of Ordination. After an ordination has been held, the names of the individuals ordained, the name of the minister of ordination, and the place and date of the same shall be entered in a special book which is to be carefully preserved in the curia of the place in which the ordination took place, together with all documents pertaining to the ordination (c. 1010, § 1). Such documents include dimissorial letters, testimonial letters required in accordance with canon 993, indults of dispensation, etc.

To each candidate ordained an authentic testimonial of the order received shall be given; and if a candidate was ordained with dimissorial letters by a Bishop not his own, he shall show his testimonial of ordination to his own Ordinary so that the ordination may be recorded in a special book to be kept in his archives (c. 1010, § 2). This prescription applies not only to secular candidates who are ordained but also to religious who are ordained with dimissorial letters from their major superiors.

Furthermore, the local Ordinary, or the major religious superior in the case of religious ordained with dimissorial letters issued by him, shall send notice of the ordination of each *subdeacon* to the pastor of the church in which he was baptized so that the latter may enter it in the register of baptisms in accordance with the prescription of canon 470, § 2 (c. 1011). By local Ordinary is here understood the proper Ordinary of the cleric who has been ordained, whether he ordained him personally or issued testimonial letters for his ordination by another Bishop.

CASES AND QUESTIONS

1. What is meant by major orders? Sacred orders? Minor orders? Tonsure? (C. 949).

2. Who is the ordinary minister of the sacrament of orders? (C. 951).

3. Who is the extraordinary minister? How are his powers restricted? (Cc. 951; 957, §§ 1 and 2; 964, 1°).

4. What is meant by "proper Bishop for ordination?" (Cc. 955, 956).

5. At the age of 20 Henry moved from Washington, D. C., to St. Paul, Minnesota, with the intention of making his permanent residence there. A year later he entered the seminary. Who is his proper Bishop for ordination? (Cc. 92, 93, 956).

6. John's father is an army officer who has never been stationed in one place for more than seven years. John enters a seminary and is only 20 years old when he is to be tonsured. Who can issue dimissorial letters? (Cc. 93; 956).

7. Titius is studying in the seminary of an Eastern diocese and has been tonsured. The Bishop of Alaska gives the seminarians a talk and appeals for volunteers. Titius offers himself and is accepted. How is the transfer to be made? Who is the proper Bishop for the subsequent ordinations of Titius? (Cc. 956 and 969, § 2).

8. The Bishop of diocese T, while visiting in the diocese of Springfield, contacts Joseph, a likely lad, and accepts him for his diocese. Joseph goes to the Springfield seminary and in due time the Bishop of Springfield confers the tonsure on him for service in the diocese of T. Which Bishop is the proper Bishop for the subsequent ordinations of Joseph? (C. 969, § 2, and Code Commission, June 24, 1939, ad I et II, *AAS*, 31 [1939], 321; *Digest*, II, p. 52 and p. 238).

9. The Bishop of a diocese in the United States makes a trip to Europe to get recruits for his diocese. He succeeds in getting six candidates from various European countries, brings them to Washington, D. C., where he leaves them at the Theological College of the Catholic University to make their theological studies. Who is the proper Bishop of ordination for these young men? (Cc. 90, 93, 956 and explanation in text).

10. What do you mean by dimissorial letters for ordinations? Who can issue them? (Cc. 958-966).

11. What are the three requisites for *valid* ordination? (C. 968).

12. Samuel, the pious son of pious parents, entered the seminary and made his studies with great difficulty. He has passed his examination on the rubrics of the Mass with satisfaction, but knows little of the theology of the Mass. He will probably never be allowed to hear confessions because of his meager understanding of moral theology. His Bishop consults you as to whether he should ordain Samuel or not. What would you advise? (Cc. 968, § 1; 974, § 1, 4°; 969, § 1; 973, § 3).

13. Sylvester, a cleric in minor orders, doubts whether he should receive the subdiaconate or return to the world. He still hesitates on the morning of ordination itself, but finally decides to go ahead, as he will be able to get a dispensation should he desire to return to the world and get married. What would you say to Sylvester? (C. 973, § 1).

14. Does § 2 of c. 976 bind religious as well as § 1 of the same canon? The reason for doubt is contained in the decree, *Auctis modum,* of Novem-

ber 4, 1892, ad 6, in which Pope Leo XIII, through the S. Congregation
of Bishops and Regulars, allowed religious to be ordained to the priesthood at the end of third year of theology. (C. 6, 1°).

15. What is the difference between an irregularity and a simple impediment? (Cc. 983, 987).

16. Are those who have suffered from epilepsy but now are completely
cured irregular so that they require a dispensation to receive orders? To
exercise orders? (C. 984, 3ⁿ).

17. What is the difference between *infamia juris* in c. 984, 5°, and
infamia facti in c. 987, 7°? (Cc. 2293 and 2294).

18. Wilfrid has a glass eye. Is he irregular? (C. 984, 2°, and S. Congregation of Religious, Nov. 28, 1924, *Digest*, I, p. 486).

19. What is meant by "voluntary homicide" in c. 985, 4°? (See explanation of text.)

20. Claude, the son of unbaptized parents who attend no church, is
converted and enters a seminary to prepare for the priesthood. Does he
need a dispensation from the simple impediment listed under c. 987, 1°?
(See explanation of text.)

21. Does ignorance of an irregularity or simple impediment excuse from
it? (C. 988).

22. James, a venerable but infirm Bishop, cannot say the ordination
Mass and confer orders without great difficulty. He is very desirous of
ordaining a class because his nephew is one of the class. So he has his
Vicar General (who is an auxiliary Bishop) say the Mass and perform
all the nonessential rites while he (James) performs only those functions
which are essential to the validity of the orders. What would be your
judgment in regard to the validity and licitness of the actions of the
venerable James? (C. 1003).

Readings:

Augustine, *Commentary*, IV, pp. 409–549; Ayrinhac, *Legislation on the
Sacraments*, pp. 307-397; Browne, *Incardination and Excardination*, I.E.R.,
48 (1936), 531–537; Forrest, *A Much Discussed Sacrament*, A.E.R., 82
(1930), 475–483; Hickey, *Irregularities and Simple Impediments*, C.U.,
1920, (n. 7); Kinane, *Lawful Bishop for Ordinations of Seculars*, I.E.R.,
11 (1918), 62–64; Moeder, *Proper Bishop for Ordination and Dismissorial
Letters*, C.U., 1935 (n. 95); Plassmann: *Entering the Priesthood by the
Door*, A.E.R., 86 (1932), 449–460; Schaaf, *Proper Bishop for Ordination
of Seculars*, A.E.R., 90 (1934), 352–365; *Proper Bishop for Ordination of
Religious*, A.E.R., 90 (1934), 491–509; Woywod, *Commentary*, I, pp.
485–559.

PART FIVE: MARRIAGE

CHAPTER XII

GENERAL PROVISIONS: PRELIMINARIES: IMPEDIMENTS IN GENERAL

Section 1. General Provisions (cc. 1012–1016)

PRELIMINARY SURVEY

Nature of Marriage (c. 1012)
Purpose and Essential Properties (c. 1013)
Favored by the Law (c. 1014)
Legal Terms (c. 1015)
Provinces of Civil and Canon Law (c. 1016)

CANON 1012. § 1. Christ our Lord elevated the very contract of marriage between baptized persons to the dignity of a sacrament.

§ 2. Therefore it is impossible for a valid contract of marriage between baptized persons to exist without being by that very fact a sacrament.

Nature of Marriage. 1. Marriage is *always,* by its very nature, *a contract.* This does not mean that it is merely a civil contract, nor does it in any way justify the absurd contentions of some so-called "Liberal" movements which seek to reduce marriage to the level of a merely civil transaction.

2. Marriage is by nature a *sacred contract.* We do not say, a sacrament; this, it could not be by nature, because the sacraments are all supernatural, having been established by Christ, the God-Man, as the author of a supernatural religious society. But it is a sacred contract, and that by its very nature. God established marriage as the natural means of propagation for his choicest earthly creatures. It is sacred for that reason. It is moreover sacred because it is a means of mutual

help for husband and wife — help, not merely to material or temporal progress, but to their only true destiny, which is God. It is sacred, finally, because it mystically represents the union of the divine and human natures in the Incarnation of the Son of God.[1] This essentially sacred character of the very contract of marriage is recognized by unanimous consent among the more civilized peoples, all of whom have introduced a religious rite in the conjugal union. "Where marriage is destitute of any religious character, we have a sure indication that the condition of a people is barbarous, or that the decay of its civilization has set in."[2] In this as in other respects, some of our ultra-modern "Liberals," while they talk of "progress," are actually harking back with pride to the manners and morals of cave and jungle.

3. When it is *between two baptized persons,* the very contract becomes a *sacrament.* This, because Christ our Lord elevated the natural sacred contract of marriage to that supernatural dignity.[3]

a. For this supernatural elevation to take place in any concrete instance, it is necessary and sufficient that *both parties* be validly baptized and validly married. It is now morally certain that the baptism of only one party does not make the marriage a sacrament even for that party.

b. Even Protestants, therefore, if both are validly baptized, as they may well be even in a Protestant sect, if they marry validly,[4] receive a sacrament of Christ. This fact, though contrary to their dogmatic tenets, is very consoling to Protestants.

c. Marriage has this sacramental character *from the moment of its celebration,* if both parties are then already validly baptized; it acquires it *later* if the baptism of either party or both takes place after the marriage.

4. The *matter and form* of the sacrament have been the subject of much theological discussion. Without going into diversities of opinion, we give briefly the doctrine which has the support of such theologians as St. Robert Bellarmine, Suarez, Sanchez, the Salmanticenses, De Lugo, Schmalzgrueber, Benedict XIV, Gasparri, Cappello, and a host of moderns. According to them the *lawful contract* itself is both the matter and the form of the sacrament. The *matter* is the mutual *offer,* made by words or signs expressing genuine internal consent to the

---

[1] See Leo XIII, *Arcanum.*
[2] Joyce, *Christian Marriage,* p. 37.
[3] Cf. Gasparri, *De Matrimonio,* I, p. 31.
[4] For valid marriage it is necessary that they be free from all invalidating impediments of divine *and ecclesiastical* law.

contract; the *form* is the mutual *acceptance* similarly expressed. In order to constitute a contract, the consent must be both interiorly genuine and mutually expressed externally. Genuine and lawfully manifested consent on both sides thus constitutes the contract; and it at the same time constitutes the sacrament. This doctrine is therefore exactly conformed to the principle expressed in the canon, that the contract itself is the sacrament.[5]

Definition of Marriage. The Code develops the doctrine of marriage gradually in successive canons; we shall follow the same order, but we must have a definition. By anticipating the canons which define the essential object of the marriage contract (c. 1081) and the essential purposes and properties of marriage (c. 1013), we may frame this definition: *Marriage is a lawful and exclusive contract by which a man and a woman mutually give and accept a right over their bodies for the purpose of acts which are in themselves suitable for the generation of children.*[6]

CANON 1013. § 1. The primary end of marriage is the procreation and education of children; its secondary end is mutual help and the allaying of concupiscence.

§ 2. The essential properties of marriage are unity and indissolubility, which acquire a peculiar firmness in Christian marriage by reason of its sacramental character.

Ends or Purposes of Marriage. The first paragraph defines the ends of marriage as an institution, that is, the purposes which the Creator intends in instituting marriage. These are: (1) *primary* end, the procreation and education of children; (2) *secondary* end, mutual help and the allaying of concupiscence. The truth of this statement is proved in the science of ethics and is derived from the consideration, in the

---

[5] For fuller explanation, see Vermeersch, *What Is Marriage,* pp. 28–32.

[6] This definition does not express the secondary end of marriage, which is nevertheless very important and may even be predominant *in the minds of the parties,* namely, mutual love and assistance, and the allaying of concupiscence. **Canonical Readings on Marriage.** *a.* Best historical and theological treatise: Joyce, *Christian Marriage.*

b. Best canonical treatise: Payen, *De Matrimonio* (3 vols.), or Cappello, *De Matrimonio.* Others notably excellent: Gasparri, *De Matrimonio;* Wernz-Vidal, *De Matrimonio.* In English: Nau, *Marriage Laws of the Code;* Ayrinhac-Lydon, *Marriage Legislation in the New Code of Canon Law.*

c. Most authoritative modern pronouncement: *Encyclical on Christian Marriage, Casti connubii,* Pius XI; English text published by the America Press.

d. Most thorough brief explanation of the Encyclical: Vermeersch, *Catechisme de l'encyclique, Casti connubii;* English translation, *What Is Marriage,* America Press.

e. Best manuals for information on state marriage laws: May, *Marriage Laws and Decisions in the United States* (Russell Sage Foundation, 1929); Alford, *Ius Matrimoniale Comparatum* (Kenedy, N. Y.: distributors); Vernier, *American Family Laws* (Stanford University Press).

light of reason, of the existing order of created nature, in which marriage is evidently the only suitable means of providing for these ends. If that is so, it must have been designed by the All-wise Creator for those ends; in other words, these are the ends of marriage *as an institution*.

Are these same ends necessarily *intended by individuals* who contract marriage? We must distinguish. (1) The parties may not positively exclude or hinder the primary end by contracting a so-called marriage with the deliberate intention of perverting it from its primary purpose (cf. c. 1086). (2) But it is not necessary that the primary purpose of marriage as an institution be also first in the minds of the parties, nor even that it be *positively* intended by them. Procreation may be impossible because of sterility (cf. c. 1068), and yet, provided the parties are capable of the act which is the essential object of the contract (cf. c. 1081), their marriage would be valid and licit, though it were contracted with only the secondary end in view, or even for some good purpose which was entirely extrinsic to the contract, for example, the reconciliation of the families.[7]

The Holy Office, in a decree of 1 Apr., 1944, again stressed the primacy of procreation and education. To the question: "Whether the views of certain recent writers can be admitted, who either deny that the primary end of marriage is the procreation and education of children, or teach that the secondary ends are not essentially subordinate to the primary end, but are equally principal and independent," the reply was: "In the negative." Cf. *AAS,* Vol. 36, p. 103.

Essential Properties. The second paragraph deals with the essential properties of marriage.

Unity. 1. This means *exclusiveness* on both sides; that is, it must be between one man and one woman.

2. *Polygamy,* which is the general name of the vice opposed to this unity, has two forms: (*a*) *polygyny,* where one man has several wives; and (*b*) *polyandry,* where one woman has several husbands. Both are contrary to the natural law of marriage, but in different degrees. Polyandry is opposed both to the primary and secondary ends, in as much as it not only interferes with the perfect self-surrender which is love, but also, by throwing doubt on paternity, deprives marriage of one of its resources intended for the education of the child. Polygyny is directly opposed to the secondary end in as much as it hinders

---

[7] Cf. V-C, *Epit.,* II, n. 275; also *Theological Studies,* Vol. 4, p. 477 (Lonergan: *Finality, Love, Marriage*).

domestic peace and reduces each of the wives to a condition of too great inferiority; indirectly, it tends also to prejudice the child's education.

3. Accordingly, *polyandry* is opposed to a *primary precept* of the natural law, whereas *polygyny* is directly opposed only to a *secondary precept*. It is by this fundamental distinction, based on natural reason, that St. Thomas[8] explains how it was possible that God should have permitted a plurality of wives in the Old Testament. The Creator thus dispensed from His own law, but only from one of its secondary precepts, making up for the harm thus permitted by special dispositions of His Providence for higher ends.[9] The same explanation is applicable to the permission of divorce in the Old Law, a permission which involved a similar dispensation from the secondary precept of the natural law concerning the indissolubility of marriage.

Indissolubility. 1. Marriage is by nature indissoluble in the sense that the bond cannot be dissolved by any *merely human authority*.

2. The *proof* of this proposition from natural reason pertains to ethics; it is based on these considerations: (*a*) The harm which the breaking of the union between man and wife necessarily inflicts upon the children; (*b*) the obstacle which the mere possibility of divorce puts in the way of a perfect union; (*c*) the irreparable consequence which the consummation of marriage entails for the bride.[10]

3. It follows that divorce by *human authority,* that is, either by the parties themselves or by the civil law, is dangerous to the primary end of marriage (education), and directly opposed to its secondary end; and that it is therefore forbidden, not by the Church merely, but by the law of God.[11]

4. It also follows that *God alone can make exceptions* to the law of indissolubility. The exceptions which He has in fact made are:

a. In the Old Law, divorce was permitted or tolerated by dispensation from this secondary precept of the natural law, as explained above. But this exception was revoked by our Lord Jesus Christ, who restored marriage to its pristine purity and indissolubility. This restoration, concerned as it is with the order of nature, is effective not only for Christians but for all men.[12]

b. The tradition and practice of the Church going back to the twelfth

---

[8] *Suppl.,* III, q. 65, art. 1 and 2.
[9] Cf. Vermeersch, *What Is Marriage,* p. 10.
[10] Cf. Vermeersch, *What Is Marriage,* p. 11.
[11] Cf. Joyce, *Christian Marriage,* p. 21.
[12] Cf. Vermeersch, *What Is Marriage,* pp. 11, 12.

century[13] make it certain that Christ, in His commission to His Church, gave the Sovereign Pontiff the power to dissolve, for grave reasons, a marriage even between Christians, provided it has *not been consummated* (cf. c. 1119).

c. By the *Pauline Privilege* a marriage between two unbaptized persons, even though consummated, may, after the baptism of one of them and upon proof of the "departure" of the other, be dissolved in favor of the faith (cf. c. 1120).

d. Lastly, "according to an opinion which is enjoying more and more credit, a marriage which has been *consummated while it was not a sacrament* can be dissolved by the Supreme Pontiff for grave reasons."[14]

5. *Absolute* indissolubility, therefore, can be predicated only of Christian marriage after it has been consummated (cf. c. 1118).

CANON 1014. Marriage enjoys the favor of the law; hence, in doubt, the validity of marriage is to be upheld until the contrary is proved, except as provided in canon 1127.

Historical Background. The principle here announced is the result of the practical solution by the Holy Office of difficult cases regarding marriage especially in pagan countries where the Church's missionaries were at work. A group of cases from Central Oceania in 1872 presented facts such as these: one or both parties to a pagan marriage wished to be instructed and baptized in the faith; the fact of the celebration of the marriage was not open to serious doubt, or at least the party now seeking baptism was in good faith regarding the validity of his or her marriage, and the parties were living together without giving rise to any scandal or suspicion; but the missionaries could not be *certain* that the marriage was really valid; in these circumstances, could they conscientiously baptize such parties? In reply the Holy Office laid down substantially the principle which is here incorporated in the Code.[15]

Principle. The principle is broader than the particular cases from which it originated; it is now of general application.

1. It establishes a *presumption in favor of the validity of marriage* in all cases where there is a positive and probable doubt, that is, reasons both for validity and against it. A *doubt of law* exists when the fact

---

[13] Cf. Joyce, *Christian Marriage,* p. 427.
[14] Vermeersch, *What Is Marriage,* p. 26. Cf. c. 1125.
[15] Cf. Holy Office, 18 Dec., 1872, and 24 Jan., 1877, in *Collectanea S. C. Prop. Fid.,* II, nn. 1392, 1465, or in *Fontes,* nn. 1024, 1050, Vol. IV, pp. 327, 366.

of the celebration of the marriage is certain, but its validity is doubtful. A *doubt of fact* exists when the very fact of the marriage is doubtful, but is favored at least by this circumstance, that the parties are in possession of a decent public repute as man and wife. In all cases the presumption, both in the external and internal forum, is in favor of a valid marriage.

2. This is a *praesumptio iuris,* but not *iuris et de iure* (cf. cc. 1825, 1826); hence the canon adds, "until the contrary is proved"; evidence to the contrary is admissible.

3. The constant practice of the Roman Curia in dealing with marriage cases is in strict accord with this principle. Subject to the exception about to be noted, in all cases where the evidence for nullity is not conclusive, the decision is: *non constare de nullitate;* that is, the presumption in favor of validity has not been overcome by contrary evidence.

Exception. The sole exception is the one provided for in canon 1127; namely, "in doubt, the privilege of the faith enjoys the favor of the law." It will be best to reserve the explanation of this principle until that canon is reached.

Before the Code, disparity of cult invalidated a marriage between a validly baptized heretic and an unbaptized person. In case the baptism of the heretic was doubtful the presumption was in favor of valid baptism, and hence against the validity of the marriage. Since the Code, the presumption is in favor of the validity of the marriage until it is proved that one party was baptized in the Catholic Church and that the other was unbaptized (c. 1070, § 2).

CANON 1015. § 1. A valid marriage of baptized persons is called *ratum* if it is not yet completed by consummation; *ratum et consummatum,* if there has taken place between the parties the conjugal act to which the matrimonial contract is by nature ordained and by which husband and wife are made one flesh.

§ 2. After the celebration of marriage, if the parties have cohabited together, the consummation of the marriage is presumed until the contrary is proved.

§ 3. A marriage between unbaptized persons, validly celebrated, is called *legitimum.*

§ 4. An invalid marriage is called *putativum* if it was celebrated in good faith on the part of at least one of the parties, until both parties become certainly informed of its nullity.

Legal Terms.[16] 1. *Ratum:* a marriage which is sacramental (be-

---

[16] For convenience and precision the Latin terms are retained.

tween validly baptized persons, not necessarily Catholic) but which has not been consummated by the conjugal act. Exactly what is required for the consummation of marriage will be explained under canon 1119.

2. *Ratum et consummatum:* a marriage which is both sacramental and consummated. This term is used strictly of marriages which have been consummated *after* they became sacramental by the baptism of both parties. If the consummation took place *only before* this, it is better to call the marriage *consummatum et ratum* (cf. c. 1125).

3. *Legitimum:* a marriage between unbaptized persons. The Code gives no specific term for marriages in which only one of the parties is baptized. Such a marriage is not sacramental, and hence cannot be called *ratum*.

4. *Putativum:* an invalid marriage celebrated in good faith on the part of at least one of the parties, until both parties become certain of its nullity. Note that a putative marriage is *invalid;* all the others here classified are valid marriages.

It will make for clearness to use these terms as much as possible in their strict technical sense. Even the Code, however, does not invariably do so. If the term *legitimum* were so used in canon 331, § 1, 1°, it would mean that, in order to be eligible for a bishopric, one must have been born of infidel parents; the term there means simply any valid marriage.

CANON 1016. **The marriage of baptized persons is governed not only by divine law but also by canon law, without prejudice to the competency of the civil power as regards the merely civil effects of such marriage.**

Laws Governing Marriage. In these simple words the Church of Christ serenely claims for herself as part of her commission from her Divine Founder the entire control of the substance of Christian marriage, leaving to the state the control of its "merely civil effects." To justify this claim would be beyond the scope of this book.[17]

The Divine Law. Marriage as a natural institution is of course subject to the divine *natural law,* whether the parties are Christians or not. Moreover, as we have seen, Christ, with *divine authority,* restored marriage to its pristine purity, as regards unity and indissolubility, not for Christians alone but for all men.[18]

---

[17] See the great Encyclicals on marriage, Leo XIII, *Arcanum,* and Pius XI, *Casti connubii;* also Joyce, *Christian Marriage,* pp. 214–268.

[18] Cf. Vermeersch, *What Is Marriage,* pp. 7–12.

Canon Law. 1. Marriage *as a sacrament* evidently falls under the exclusive control of the Church, subject of course to the divine natural and positive law.[19] But it is not sufficient to claim for canon law the control merely of the *sacrament*. The Church claims control of the *contract,* even when it is not a sacrament, provided one of the parties is baptized. The reason is that the contract is indivisible; and since it affects intimately one party who is a member of the Church, the Church has jurisdiction directly over the entire contract and thus indirectly also over the unbaptized party, although the Church does not legislate directly for unbaptized persons (cf. c. 12). Canon 1016 expresses this truth delicately by declaring the control of canon law, not merely over marriages *between baptized persons,* but over *the marriage of baptized persons.*[20]

2. The control of marriage by canon law is subject to the divine law in the sense that it can ordain nothing which is *contrary* to the divine law; but the Church can and does establish conditions which go *beyond* the requirements of divine law, and which affect not only the licitness but even the validity of marriage. It should be carefully noted that her jurisdiction is not limited to determining the capacity of the parties by establishing *impediments,* but includes also direct control over the contract, for example by imposing requirements as to the *form* of marriage (cf. c. 1094).

3. An objection may be framed against this position, on theological grounds, as follows: the Church has no power to modify the substance of the sacraments, because the matter and form of all the sacraments were determined by Christ. But to require certain formalities, for example the presence of the pastor or Bishop, for the validity of marriage is to modify the very offer and acceptance which constitute the matter and form of the sacrament. Therefore this is beyond the power of the Church.

There are two possible replies. *a.* Joyce expresses a preference for the more radical of the two, which consists in a denial of the major premise. This denial is based on an opinion defended by some theologians that "the Church has authority to determine the sacramental symbols of all the sacraments except baptism and the Holy Eucharist; and that at the Council of Trent she exercised this power as regards matrimony."[21]

b. Without abandoning the opinion which still is more commonly

---

[19] Cf. Conc. Trid., *Sess.* XXIV, *De matr.,* can. 3, 4, 9.
[20] Cf. Augustine, *A Commentary on Canon Law,* V, p. 25.
[21] Cf. Joyce, *Christian Marriage,* p. 129.

held, that the Church has no power directly to modify the matter and form of any sacrament, we may point out that in requiring certain formalities for the valid expression of consent, the Church is exercising control directly over the *contract,* and not over the sacrament as such. It is true that a valid contract between baptized persons becomes by that very fact a sacrament; but it must be a *valid contract first* — not in point of time, of course, but logically. And the conditions imposed by the Church are required directly for the validity of the contract. Hence no change whatever is effected in the institution of Christ, which elevated the *valid and lawful contract,* and none other, to the dignity of a sacrament. Joyce thinks this argument too subtle. It is advanced by Wernz, Vidal, Cappello, Gasparri,[22] and others, and to us seems quite valid.

4. In practice the power of the Church, legislative, judicial, coercive, extends to all marriages in which one of the parties is baptized. It includes: (*a*) the imposition of conditions for the licitness and validity of the contract; (*b*) establishing impedient or diriment impediments; (*c*) judicial jurisdiction over matrimonial cases, even concerning the nullity of the bond; (*d*) enforcing observance of her laws by ecclesiastical penalties. Even heretics are *per se* objectively bound by these laws unless excepted therefrom (cf. cc. 12, 87, 1038, § 2). Exceptions are made for non-Catholics in certain cases only (cf. cc. 1070, 1099).

The Civil Law. 1. As regards *Christian marriage,* that is, any marriage in which at least one party is a Christian, the power of the state is limited to prescribing reasonable *regulations,* and governing the *merely civil effects.*

a. Reasonable regulations are those which, *without infringing on the divine or ecclesiastical law,* are imposed for the protection of the public order, health, and safety; for example, laws requiring license, registration, etc.[23]

---

[22] Wernz, *Ius Decretalium,* IV, part 1, n. 158; Wernz-Vidal, *De Matrimonio,* n. 531; Cappello, *De Matrimonio,* I, n. 57; Gasparri, *De Matrimonio,* I, n. 227.

[23] As regards state laws requiring medical certificate of freedom from disease as a prerequisite either for licitness or validity of marriage, we must hold that, in the case of baptized persons, they exceed the limits of the state's authority. In the recent controversy over this point, we believe that Father Connell remained in possession of the field after a thorough discussion with several able opponents. Cf. *America,* 2 July, 1938, Vol. 59, p. 294 (Blakely); *Ecclesiastical Review,* Vol. 99, pp. 507–518 (Connell); Vol. 100, p. 322 (Moore); Vol. 100, p. 331 (Connell); Vol. 100, p. 445 (Connell); Vol. 101, p. 7 (Donnelly); Vol. 101, pp. 21, 28 (Connell). See also Nau, *Marriage Laws of the Code,* pp. 12–33. The Church, of course, does not object to such legislation as long as it does not contravene the law of God.

b. Civil effects are the consequences of marriage in civil life. These are many and varied, and are mostly inseparable from the substance of marriage; e.g., parental authority, the right of husband and wife to cohabit, etc. These are civil, but not merely civil effects. *Merely civil effects* are those civil consequences of marriage which are separable from its substance; for example, the right of the wife to the husband's name, her right of succession, of dower, etc. Subject always to the divine and ecclesiastical law, these are within the province of the state even in Christian marriage.

2. As regards marriages between unbaptized persons, the state can lawfully: (*a*) establish impediments, even such as affect the validity of the contract;[24] (*b*) prescribe other conditions, even affecting the validity, such as a requisite legal form for valid consent.[25] To dissolve the bond of a valid marriage, even between unbaptized persons, is entirely beyond the power of the state, since it is contrary to the divine law.

Question. Where a Catholic marries an unbaptized person, a dispensation from disparity of cult is required. Let us suppose that this has been obtained, but that the unbaptized person is incapacitated by a diriment impediment established by the civil law, from which no dispensation has been given. Is such a marriage valid? *In favor of validity,* it is argued that the contract, being indivisible, must be governed exclusively by one power or the other, the Church or the state, and that the right of the Church should prevail.[26] *Against validity,* this perfectly logical argument is adduced: the state and not the Church has power to establish diriment impediments for unbaptized persons; the unbaptized party is therefore incapable of valid marriage; moreover, the Church admits that if a diriment impediment affects only one party, it invalidates the entire contract (c. 1036, § 3). Hence the marriage should be considered invalid.[27] The latter opinion seems theoretically preferable; but since there is at least a doubt of law, the presumption of canon 1014 in favor of validity should prevail, so that

---

[24] Cf. Vermeersch, *What Is Marriage,* p. 14.

[25] This may be admitted as *probable.* An argument against its *certainty* is a reply of the Holy Office, 23 June, 1938, where it was held, regarding marriages of Chinese infidels without the formalities required by the civil law: "It is *not certain* that the marriages of Chinese infidels in these circumstances are invalid." See *Sylloge S. C. Prop. Fid.,* n. 206 *quater; Digest,* II, p. 250.

[26] Cf. Cappello, *De Matrimonio,* n. 67; Wernz, *Ius Matrimoniale,* I, n. 60, *Scholion;* Wernz-Vidal, *De Matrimonio,* n. 52; De Smet, *De Matrimonio,* n. 412, note 3, and n. 438.

[27] Cf. Gasparri, *De Matrimonio,* n. 256; D'Annibale, III, n. 294; V-C, *Epit.,* II, n. 278.

if the question arises after an actual marriage, it should be considered valid.

Section 2. Preliminaries (cc. 1017–1034)

PRELIMINARY SURVEY

CANON 1017. § 1. A promise of marriage, whether it is unilateral or bilateral which is called an engagement, is null for both the internal and external forum, unless it is made in writing signed by the parties and by either the pastor or Ordinary of the place or at least two witnesses.

§ 2. In case both parties, or either party have never learned to write, or cannot write, it is required for validity that this fact be noted in the writing itself, and that an additional witness sign the document with the pastor or Ordinary of the place or with the two witnesses mentioned in § 1.

§ 3. From a promise of marriage, even if it be valid and there be no just cause excusing from its fulfillment, there arises no right of action to compel the celebration of the marriage; but there is a right of action for damages, if any are due.

Notes on the Engagement Contract. 1. Without the formalities here required the engagement is void *even in the forum of conscience.*

2. All the persons whose signatures are required must sign *in each other's presence.* This interpretation, made in a reply of the Sacred Congregation of the Council, 27 July, 1908,[28] is carried into this canon in virtue of the rule laid down in canon 6, 2° and 3°.

3. In case a suit is begun for damages for unjust breach of an en-

---

[28] Cf. *Fontes,* n. 4350, Vol. VI, p. 893.

gagement contract, the contemplated marriage of the defendant with a third party is not to be stopped pending the suit.[29]

4. Both marriages and engagements are governed by the law which was in effect when they were contracted, except as provided in canon 1017, § 3.[30]

5. The engagement contract may also be concluded by proxy.

CANON 1018. The pastor must not fail prudently to instruct the people regarding the sacrament of matrimony and its impediments.

Parochial Instructions on Marriage. 1. The *matter* is abundant: the nature of marriage, its beautiful elevation to the dignity of a sacrament, its graces, the jurisdiction of the Church, necessity of observing her laws, the primary purpose of marriage, the sin and social plague of birth prevention, mutual helpfulness of husband and wife, marriage as a state of consecration to duty and to God, Christian example the best antidote for prevalent vices against marriage, Catholic education of children, the impediments, especially that of mixed religion. The Encyclical, *Casti connubii,* will provide inspiration.

For practical features of these instructions, especially as regards mixed marriages, see *Clergy Review,* Vol. 24, p. 355 (Gits: *Instruction to the Faithful on Mixed Marriages*).

2. The *manner* is to be "prudent" — a gentle reminder to avoid alike sensationalism and pale aloofness, but to give the people the instruction they so sorely need and want — clear, earnest, sympathetic, practical.

CANON 1019. § 1. Before a marriage is celebrated it must be certain that nothing stands in the way of its valid and licit celebration.

§ 2. In danger of death, if other proofs cannot be had, and in the absence of indications to the contrary, the sworn statement of the contracting parties that they have been baptized and are under no impediment is sufficient.

Principles. 1. Before a marriage is celebrated it must appear with *moral certainty from a careful investigation,* that there is no obstacle to its valid and licit celebration. This preliminary investigation consists chiefly of two procedures: the personal examination of the parties (c. 1020), and the publication of the banns (cc. 1022–1025).

2. The *danger of death* which is one of the conditions for being content with less rigid proof, means a *probability* of death affecting *either* party, from *any cause,* intrinsic or extrinsic.

---

[29] Cf. Code Com., 3 June, 1918; *AAS,* 10–345; *Digest,* I, p. 495.
[30] Cf. Code Com., 3 June, 1918; *AAS,* 10–346; *Digest,* I, p. 496.

CANON 1020. § 1. The pastor who has the right to assist at the marriage shall, a suitable time beforehand, carefully investigate whether there is any obstacle to the celebration of the marriage.

§ 2. He must ask the man and the woman, even separately and cautiously, whether they are under any impediment, whether they are giving their consent freely, especially the woman, and whether they are sufficiently instructed in Christian doctrine, unless in view of the quality of the persons this last question should seem unnecessary.

§ 3. It is the province of the Ordinary of the place to lay down special rules for this investigation by the pastor.

Notes. 1. This responsibility lies on the *pastor,* even though some one else is to perform the marriage. The pastor who *has the right to assist* at the marriage is determined according to canon 1097.

2. In case one of the parties is living elsewhere and cannot conveniently come for this examination by the proper pastor, the examination may be conducted by the party's own pastor, who will report to the pastor who has the right to assist (cf. c. 1029).

3. The pastor must question the parties *separately* about the freedom of their consent. If this provision were always obeyed we should probably have no nullity trials on the ground of force and fear. No priest should assist at a marriage if there is any reasonable ground of suspicion regarding the freedom of consent on both sides. The conversation should be conducted *cautiously,* that is, with tact and prudence.

4. An Instruction on this subject was issued in 1921 by the Sacred Congregation of the Sacraments. A later instruction, 29 June, 1941, goes into much greater detail, and even adds some new safeguards. This latest instruction deserves careful study.[31]

5. If either or both parties are ignorant of Christian doctrine, the priest should do his best to instruct them at least in the rudiments, but should not refuse to marry them as provided in the case of "public sinners" by canon 1066.[32]

6. The Ordinary may prescribe special rules for this examination. Some chancery offices have carefully prepared formulas containing clear and tactfully worded questions on all the principal impediments. Sometimes the formula includes a question on the intention of the parties regarding the primary purpose of marriage. If prescribed by the Ordinary this question is reasonable, since the exclusion of the primary obligation of marriage renders the contract null and void.

---

[31] S. C. Sacr., 4 July, 1921; *AAS,* 13–348; *Digest,* I, p. 497; 29 July, 1941, *AAS,* 33–297; *Digest,* II, p. 253. A very careful summary of this latest instruction by O. M. Cloran, S.J., is published by the Newman Book Shop.

[32] Code Com., 3 June, 1918; *AAS,* 10–345; *Digest,* I, p. 496.

Needless to say, it requires special tact and prudence on the part of the examining priest. The parties may also be required to swear to the truth of their answers.[33]

CANON 1021. § 1. Unless baptism was conferred in his own territory, the pastor shall require a baptismal certificate of each party, or of the Catholic party only, if the marriage is to be contracted with a dispensation from disparity of cult.

§ 2. Catholics who have not yet received the sacrament of confirmation should receive it before being married, if they can do so without grave inconvenience.

Baptism. 1. As a rule the baptismal certificate is required of both parties if both are baptized. Hence in a mixed marriage between Catholic and Protestant, *per se* the certificate should be required also of the Protestant party. The practice of being content with a bare assurance from the Protestant party that he or she has been baptized is clearly contrary to the text of the Code, and exposes the marriage to the danger of objective nullity unless a dispensation from disparity of cult has been obtained *ad cautelam*.

2. From the Catholic party a *recent* baptismal certificate is required — the latest instruction requires that it be of not more than six months before the date of the marriage — because only a recent inspection of the baptismal record will show what this testimonial is designed to prove, namely, not only the baptism, but also the freedom from certain public impediments (public vows, previous marriage), which are required by law to be recorded there (cf. c. 470 § 2).

3. Only in case an official certificate *cannot be obtained* can it be supplied by other proof.

4. If the baptism of the parties took place *in the very parish* where this examination is being made, no certificate is required, because all the pastor has to do in that case is to inspect the record of baptisms in his own parish, which he is of course obliged to do.

Confirmation. The parties should be asked whether they have been confirmed, and if either of them has not yet received this sacrament they should do so before marriage, unless this would subject them to grave inconvenience. In doubt regarding the sufficiency of the excuse, the Ordinary should be consulted. No certificate is required, since the fact of confirmation is sufficiently proved from the baptismal record (cf. c. 470, § 2).

---

[33] Cf. Donovan, *The Pastor's Obligation in Pre-nuptial Investigations,* 1938, Cath. U. Canon Law Studies, n. 115.

CANON 1022. The pastor must announce publicly who are about to contract marriage.

Banns of Marriage. The necessity of the banns affects, not the validity, but only the licitness of marriage. The Fourth Lateran Council (A.D. 1215) enacted the first general law requiring the publication of banns, which before that had become customary in many places. The law was not well observed; it went into desuetude, but was revived by the Council of Trent.[34] The obligation is grave and remains binding even though the pastor is certain that no impediment exists (cf. c. 21); but it is probable that a pastor sins only venially by omitting two of the three publications, if he is morally certain that there is no impediment.[35]

CANON 1023. § 1. The announcement of the banns of marriage must be made by the parties' own pastor.
§ 2. If since attaining puberty a party has lived in another place for six months, the pastor should take the matter up with the Ordinary, who in his prudent discretion may either require that the banns be published there, or direct that other proofs or presumptive evidence regarding the freedom of the person to marry be gathered.
§ 3. Even in the case of a briefer period of residence, if there is any ground for suspecting that an impediment was incurred, the pastor should consult the Ordinary, who should not permit the marriage until the suspicion has been removed as provided in § 2.

Notes. 1. The banns must be published in the parish where the parties, or either of them, have a domicile or quasi-domicile (c. 94). Since both parties may have separate domiciles, and even quasi-domiciles besides, it is obvious that several pastors may be responsible for this duty. Each makes the publication in his own parish. As regards *dispensation* from the banns, see canon 1028.

2. *Former domiciles* (which have been lost according to canon 95) are not necessarily to be considered; but in case the party lived there *after puberty for as much as six months,* the Ordinary should be consulted; he will require either the banns to be published there or other evidence to be collected to make sure that the party incurred no impediment during that time. If there is positive ground for suspecting that an impediment was incurred, a similar procedure must be followed even in case of a shorter period of residence. The age of puberty is defined in canon 88, § 2: fourteen for boys, twelve for girls.

---

[34] *Sess.* XXIV, *de ref. matr.,* cap. I.
[35] Cf. Roberts, *The Banns of Marriage,* 1931, Cath. U. Canon Law Studies, n. 64.

3. The *evidence* to be collected in such cases must, according to the instruction of 1941, include the oath of the party himself, but is not necessarily limited to that. The matter is left to the discretion of the Ordinary.[36]

CANON 1024. **The publications are to be made for three successive Sundays or other days of obligation, in the church, during the solemnities of the Mass or during other divine services attended by many of the people.**

Time, Place, and Form of Publication. 1. The *time:* three successive Sundays or feast days of obligation, during the Mass or other services attended by many of the people.

a. The *common* feasts of obligation are enumerated in canon 1247. But in view of the purpose of the law the meaning seems clearly to be that the publications be made on Sundays or feasts that are of obligation *in that place.* Hence if the place has particular feasts of obligation these may be included. Conversely, if some of the common feasts are not of obligation there, those days are not proper for the publication of the banns.

b. That the Sundays or feast days be *successive* is not required for *validity.* If the pastor without excuse allows an interruption of the publications so that the days are not successive, the sin is certainly venial if, without sufficient reason for the omission, only one Sunday or feast day intervenes on which there is no publication, and it is probably still only venial if several intervene.

2. The *place* is the "church." It is not strictly required that it be the *parish* church; any church or public oratory (cf. c. 1191, § 1), during services attended by many people of the place, would satisfy the law, provided the publications were made there by authority of the *pastor.*

3. The *form* of the announcement is not prescribed. The formula given in the Roman Ritual[37] is not preceptive. What is required is that it clearly designate and identify the persons who are to be married, and be in accord with the essential purpose of the law. It should therefore state whether the announcement is the first, second, or third, and whether a dispensation from any of the announcements has been obtained; it should also proclaim the obligation of the faithful to reveal any impediments they may know of, since this is the

---

[36] Cf. Code Com., 3 June, 1918; *AAS*, 10–345; *Digest*, I, p. 499.
[37] Tit. VII, cap. 1, n. 8.

very purpose of the law requiring the banns to be published.[38] May the notice be *printed* and distributed with other parish notices instead of being announced *viva voce?* This does not seem to be absolutely excluded by the law. However, the oral announcement should probably be retained as more solemn and more appropriate.[39]

CANON 1025. **The Ordinary of the place may, for his own territory, substitute for the publications the public posting of the names of the contracting parties at the doors of the parochial or other church for the space of at least eight days, provided, however, that two feast days of obligation are included within the period.**

Extraordinary Method of Publication. This may be substituted for the ordinary method at the discretion of the Ordinary, for his own territory only.

CANON 1026. **The publications are not to be made for marriages which are contracted with a dispensation from the impediment of disparity of cult or mixed religion, unless the Ordinary of the place in his prudent discretion, in the absence of all scandal, deem it advisable to permit them, provided that the apostolic dispensation has been obtained beforehand and that the religion of the non-Catholic party be not mentioned.**

Cases in Which the Banns Are Omitted. 1. In *all mixed marriages,* whether the non-Catholic party be baptized (the impediment is then that of mixed religion), or unbaptized (disparity of cult), the banns are *regularly to be omitted.* Their publication may be *permitted* by the Ordinary under the conditions named: (*a*) that there be some prudent reason therefor; (*b*) that there be no danger of scandal; (*c*) that the dispensation from the impediment has been obtained beforehand; (*d*) that the religion of the non-Catholic party be omitted from the announcements.

2. The banns must also be omitted in *marriages of conscience* (cf. c. 1104).

3. The publications *may* be omitted: (*a*) in the *marriage of princes;* (this ancient privilege is still in effect; it would probably apply to a President of the United States or a Governor of a State, and to their sons and daughters); the reason for omitting the banns in marriages of the nobility may be that their genealogy and personal history are better known; (*b*) in *danger of death;* (*c*) in case of *necessity,* where

---

[38] Cf. Cappello, *De Matrimonio,* n. 167.
[39] Cf. also Ayrinhac-Lydon, *Marriage Legislation,* n. 41, § 3; Nau, *Marriage Laws of the Church,* pp. 44, 52; *The Jurist,* Vol. 6, p. 81 (Martin on printed banns).

the marriage cannot be deferred without grave inconvenience, and there is not time to apply for a dispensation from the banns.

4. What if one of the parties is a non-Catholic, but is to be received into the Church on the eve of the wedding? *Per se,* the banns should be published, or a dispensation from them should be asked in advance. If, however, the party's conversion on the eve of the wedding comes as a surprise, the inconvenience of postponing the wedding would excuse from making the publications.[40]

CANON 1027. All the faithful are bound, if they know of any impediment, to make known the same to the pastor or Ordinary of the place before the celebration of the marriage.

The Obligation to Reveal Impediments. 1. This obligation arises from the *natural and divine law,* in as much as all are obliged to the extent of their power to prevent irreverence to the sacrament, sin, and harm to the neighbor, some or all of which evils necessarily result from illicit or invalid marriage. It is also binding as an *ecclesiastical* law according to the terms of this canon, on all persons who *know* (with certainty or at least serious probability) of any impediment. After the celebration of the marriage the *canonical* obligation ceases; the *natural* obligation may persist, if there is hope of validating the marriage.

2. The canonical obligation is a grave one in conscience, to reveal the impediment to the pastor or to the Ordinary of the place, and as soon as possible.

Causes Excusing From the Obligation. 1. If the knowledge of the impediment came through *sacramental confession,* the obligation of the seal absolutely forbids its revelation under any circumstances.

2. If the knowledge came as a strictly *professional secret* (to a priest consulted outside confession, or to a doctor or lawyer professionally) it *may but need not* be revealed. Some authors argue that the secret *should not,* even in these circumstances, be divulged, for the reason that the harm done to professional confidence is a public evil, which outweighs the private evil prevented by the revelation. Others hold that it may be revealed, because the professional secret is subject to the condition that it does not bind if keeping it would involve serious harm to an innocent third party.[41] But a mere *natural* secret or one confided under *promise* of secrecy would not provide a sufficient ex-

---

[40] Cf. also Ayrinhac-Lydon, *Marriage Legislation,* p. 40; Schenk, *Mixed Religion and Disparity of Cult,* 1929, Cath. U. Canon Law Studies, n. 51, p. 282.
[41] Cf. Cappello, *De Matrimonio,* n. 173; Vermeersch, *Theol. Mor.,* II, n. 699; Wernz-Vidal, *De Matrimonio,* n. 131; Ayrinhac-Lydon, *Marriage Legislation,* n. 44; Nau, *Marriage Laws,* n. 17, p. 25; Payen, *De Matrimonio,* I, n. 478; III, *casus* 62; Noldin, *Theol. Mor.,* II, n. 670.

cuse, because usually the harm done by revelation in such a case is a private one and not proportionate to the gravity of the law. The promise of secrecy is subject to this implied condition.

3. In general if the damage prudently anticipated to oneself, or the public, or to a third person other than the parties to the marriage, as a result of the revelation, is greater than the good to be expected from it, there is no obligation. The damage done to the contracting parties themselves by revelation is not considered in this connection unless it is extraordinarily grave, because it is usually outweighed by the advantage resulting to them by being saved from contracting invalidly or sinfully.

4. It is sometimes said that the obligation ceases if the revelation would be *evidently useless*. We hesitate to accept this principle as it stands. To leave canonical obligations to the private judgment of individuals regarding their utility is dangerous (cf. c. 21). But if the person who knows of the impediment takes prompt and efficacious steps to dissuade the parties from the marriage, both the natural and canonical obligations cease, because the marriage is then no longer imminent.[42]

CANON 1028. § 1. The local Ordinary of the parties can in his prudent discretion and for just cause dispense from making the publications, even in another diocese than his own.

§ 2. If there are several Ordinaries of the parties, that one in whose diocese the marriage is celebrated has the right to dispense; in case the marriage is being contracted outside the parties' own dioceses, then any Ordinary of either party can dispense.

Dispensation From the Banns. 1. The dispensation is to be given for just cause, by the *local Ordinary of the parties* (*loci Ordinarius proprius*); that is, the Ordinary of the place where the parties, or either of them, have a domicile or quasi-domicile (c. 94, § 1). He can dispense from the banns *even outside his own diocese*.

2. We know already from canon 1023 that the banns may have to be published in several dioceses. Since each party may have a separate domicile and quasi-domicile, there can be as many as four (possibly more) *local Ordinaries of the parties*. For convenience, the canon provides for this case as follows: (*a*) if the marriage is to be celebrated *in one of the dioceses* where either party has a domicile or quasi-domicile, the Ordinary of that diocese has the *right* to dispense (the canon does not say that he *alone* has the *power*); (*b*) if the marriage

---

[42] Cf. Cappello, *De Matrimonio*, n. 174.

is to be celebrated *outside those dioceses,* any of the proper Ordinaries (local Ordinaries of either party) can dispense.

3. If there are several Ordinaries proper to the parties, and the marriage is to be celebrated in one of the dioceses where either party has a domicile or quasi-domicile, would a dispensation from the banns be *valid* if given by an Ordinary of the parties, other than the Ordinary of the place of the marriage? Yes, because the canon states that the proper Ordinary has the power; and the person dispensing in the case supposed is a proper Ordinary (an Ordinary of the parties). The *right* to dispense in this case belongs only to the Ordinary of the place of the marriage (c. 1028, § 2).[43]

4. The dispensing power here given to the Ordinary is attached to his office by the law itself; hence it is ordinary jurisdiction (cf. c. 197). Diocesan faculties sometimes give *pastors* the power to dispense for just cause from *one publication.* Such a power is delegated *ad universitatem negotiorum,* and hence can be subdelegated in any individual case according to canon 199, § 3.

CANON 1029. If another pastor has conducted the investigation or the publications, he must immediately by an authentic document send information as to the result of the same to the pastor who must assist at the marriage.

State of the Question. The investigation here mentioned begins with the examination of the parties as prescribed in canon 1020 and includes whatever further inquiry may be necessary to establish moral certainty that they are free to marry. Regularly, as we have seen, it is conducted by the pastor who has the right to assist at the wedding; but sometimes one of the parties may have to be examined by another pastor. As regards the publications, it is not at all unusual that they may have to be made in other parishes than the one where the marriage is to take place, namely, when either party has a domicile or quasi-domicile elsewhere. The result of both the investigation and the publications, if they have been made elsewhere, must be made known to the pastor who is to assist at the marriage, immediately, by an authentic document, even if no impediment has been discovered.

An authentic document means a letter signed by the pastor, and sealed with the parish seal. If these conditions are met, the report is *authentic,* and that is all that the Code explicitly requires. If the pastor sending the report belongs to a different diocese than the pastor to

---

[43] Cf. Cappello, *De Matrimonio,* n. 169.

whom the report is sent, it is required that the record be transmitted through the chancery office.[44]

CANON 1030. § 1. After the investigations and publications are finished, the pastor should not assist at the marriage until he has received all the necessary documents, and, unless there is reasonable cause to the contrary, until three days have elapsed since the last publication.

§ 2. If the marriage is not contracted within six months, the publications must be repeated unless the Ordinary of the place judges otherwise.

Notes. 1. The necessary documents which the pastor is to wait for are chiefly: (*a*) *reports* from other pastors on the result of any investigation or publication which they may have conducted (cf. c. 1029); (*b*) rescripts containing any dispensations which may be required.

2. He must moreover *wait three days* from the last publication unless some reasonable cause excuses from this requirement. Serious inconvenience to the parties would certainly be reason enough. The Ordinary need not be consulted about this; it is left to the pastor's discretion.

3. The reason for the *repetition of the banns* is that, if six months have intervened, it is quite possible for some new impediment to have arisen in the meantime. If there is no indication of this the Ordinary will usually permit the marriage without the repetition of the banns.

CANON 1031. § 1. If a doubt has arisen regarding the existence of some impediment:

1° The pastor shall investigate the matter more thoroughly by questioning at least two trustworthy witnesses under oath, unless the impediment is one which if known would injure the good reputation of the parties, and if necessary he shall also question the parties themselves in the same way;

2° He shall make or finish the publications, if the doubt arose before they have been begun or before they are finished;

3° If he prudently judges that the doubt still exists he must not assist at the marriage without consulting the Ordinary.

§ 2. If a certain impediment has been discovered:

1° If the impediment is an occult one, the pastor shall make or finish the publications and report the matter, without mentioning the names, to the Ordinary of the place or to the Sacred Penitentiary;

2° If it is a public impediment, and is discovered before the publi-

---

[44] "In order that the proof of freedom to marry may be obtained with greater security by the pastor of the parties . . . pastors shall ask for and forward these documents through the chancery." S. C. Sacr., 26 June, 1921; *AAS*, 13-348; *Digest*, I, p. 498. The later instruction is even more explicit. Cf. *Digest*, II, p. 255.

cations are begun, the pastor shall go no further until the impediment has been removed, even though he knows that a dispensation has been obtained for the forum of conscience alone; if it is discovered after the first or second publication, the pastor shall finish the publications and report the matter to the Ordinary.

§ 3. Finally, if no impediment either doubtful or certain has been discovered, the pastor shall, after having finished the publications, admit the parties to the celebration of the marriage.

Procedure in Doubt or Certainty Regarding Impediment. It is a comfort to read a canon so carefully drawn to meet every contingency. Without its guidance a pastor would often find himself embarrassed as to further procedure in case a doubtful or certain impediment is discovered either before the banns are begun or before they are finished.

Rules. 1. *In doubt* (a reasonable doubt, of course, is meant; that is, a reasonable probability that an impediment exists):

a. Investigate by questioning witnesses, including the parties if necessary, under oath. But be careful of the reputation of the parties; hence avoid questioning other witnesses if this would injure it.

b. Go on with the *publications,* or even begin them if they have not yet been started.

c. Consult the Ordinary before going on with the marriage, if the doubt still persists after the investigations.

2. If a *certain* impediment is discovered, it will necessarily be either occult or public in the sense of canon 1037:

a. If it is *occult:*

1) Go on with the publications, or begin them as the case may be, notwithstanding this occult impediment. It is not easy to see why the publications should be *begun* in the face of a *certain impediment,* even though it be occult; but that is clearly the rule.

2) In order to get a dispensation, refer the matter, without mentioning names, either to the Ordinary if he has faculties to dispense, or to the Sacred Penitentiary.

b. If it is *public:*

1) If the publications have not been begun, *do not begin* them until the impediment is removed, even though a dispensation has been obtained for the internal forum. The impediment being public, a dispensation for the external forum is needed. The pastor will proceed to obtain it as provided in the next paragraph.

2) If the publications have been begun but not finished, *finish* them notwithstanding the certain and public impediment, and refer the

matter to the Ordinary. This is of course for the purpose of getting
a dispensation if possible. The Ordinary himself may have the faculty
to dispense, either in virtue of his quinquennial faculties, or by canon
1045 if "all is prepared for the wedding"; if he has not the faculty, he
will forward a request for the dispensation to the Holy See. All petitions to the Holy See for dispensations from *public* impediments are
forwarded through the Ordinary.

Summary of Procedure Regarding Publications. 1. *If the publications have been begun,* they are *always to be completed,* regardless
even of a certain and public impediment. (In case of positive and
certain scandal from the continuance of the publications, they should
of course be suspended.)

2. If the publications *have not been begun,* they are *to be deferred*
upon discovery of a *certain and public* impediment, but in *no other case.*

Question. A difficult moral question arises when the pastor or the
Ordinary alone knows of an impediment. Is he then obliged to
prevent the marriage?

1. If he knows it from *sacramental confession only,* he may under
no circumstances use the knowledge to obstruct the marriage. In the
forum of conscience, if the penitent is conscious of the impediment,
the confessor will, of course, warn him of the grave duty to put off
the marriage until the impediment is removed, and will deny him
absolution if he refuses. If the penitent is unaware of the impediment,
the confessor should warn him if there is reasonable hope that he
will be tractable; if not, and the marriage cannot be put off, again the
confessor's hands would be tied as far as the external forum is concerned, and it would be wiser to leave the penitent in good faith.

2. If he knows it *only as a professional secret,* he should not reveal it,
nor use the knowledge to stop the wedding.[45]

3. If he knows it *from other sources,* he is bound to refuse to assist
at the marriage, and to try to stop the marriage by proof of the
impediment in the external forum. Beyond this the pastor could not
go. But the Ordinary could forbid the parties to marry as long as
the impediment lasts, even though it is occult; and as long as they
remained his subjects this prohibition would be binding even outside
the territory (cf. c. 1039); but it might not in every case be effective
to prevent a valid marriage.[46]

---

[45] In this disputed question we adhere to the opinion of several grave authors because
their reasons appear to us convincing. See authorities cited in note 41, this chapter.

[46] Cf. Cappello, *De Matrimonio,* n. 179.

CANON 1032. Except in case of necessity the pastor should never assist at the marriage of persons who are *vagi* as described in canon 91, unless, after referring the matter to the Ordinary of the place or to a priest delegated by him, he has obtained permission to assist.

Marriage of Persons Without Fixed Abode. 1. *Vagi* are defined in canon 91 as persons "who have neither a domicile nor a quasi-domicile anywhere." Since canon 91 is explicitly referred to in our canon, we must plainly take this definition as applicable here. Hence, under this law a person is still a *vagus* as long as he has no domicile or quasi-domicile, even though he have a *menstrua commoratio* or month's residence according to canon 1097, § 1, 2°.[47]

2. It is not immediately clear from the text whether the pastor must consult the Ordinary and obtain his permission to assist at the marriage if *only one* of the parties is a *vagus*. But this is in fact the sense of the law, as may be seen from its purpose, which is to provide for the special difficulties which occur in ascertaining the freedom of persons of this kind from impediments; for an impediment on the side of one party alone is sufficient to render the marriage illicit or null (c. 1036, § 3). It is also clear from the source of this canon, namely the Council of Trent.[48]

3. What would constitute a *case of necessity* such as to excuse from observing this provision? A grave necessity is usually understood as any case where the observance of the law would impose a notable inconvenience either on the pastor or the parties. *Per se,* the law is gravely binding in conscience.

4. Immigrant laborers from Europe may or may not be *vagi*. But an Instruction of the Sacred Congregation of the Sacraments calls attention to the provision of this canon and declares it applicable to them even if they have acquired a domicile or quasi-domicile.[49] Strictly speaking, they would in that case seem to fall more directly under the provisions of canon 1023, § 2.

CANON 1033. The pastor must not fail, with due regard to the condition of the persons concerned, to instruct the parties on the sanctity of the sacrament of matrimony, the mutual obligations of husband and wife, and the duties of parents toward their children; and he must earnestly exhort them to make a careful confession of their sins before the marriage, and to receive with devotion the Most Blessed Eucharist.

[47] Cf. Cappello, *De Matrimonio,* n. 687; *contra,* Augustine, *A Commentary,* Vol. 5, p. 76.

[48] *Sess.* XXIV, *de ref. matr.,* cap. 7; cf. also V-C, *Epit.,* II, n. 293.

[49] Cf. S. C. Sacr., 4 July, 1921, n. 4; *AAS,* 13–348; *Digest,* I, p. 497.

Instruction of the Parties. 1. This is a *personal instruction,* not to be confused with the *general* parochial instructions on marriage (c. 1018), nor with the previous *examination* of the parties (c. 1020).

2. It is the duty of the *pastor of the parties,* or of one of them, preferably of the bride-to-be. Because of the experience, prudence, and tact which it requires, it is recommended that it be performed by the pastor in person.

3. The *subject* of this instruction is the *sanctity of marriage,* the *mutual obligations* of husband and wife, and the *duties of parents* to their children. "The pastor should explain the obligations of married life, mutual love, mutual fidelity, protection on the part of the husband, submission on the part of the wife, the licitness of the conjugal act, the mutual obligation of rendering the debitum, the licitness of all acts which are ordained toward generation, the illicitness of others, that in doubt the parents or confessor should be consulted. He should also explain and seriously inculcate the obligations of parents toward their children, that baptism is to be conferred as soon as possible, Catholic education attended to from the earliest years, moral and physical care to be provided."[50] If the pastor finds the parties, or either of them, utterly ignorant of the conjugal obligation, it would be better to refer them to married relatives, provided these are morally sound and will really give them the needed instruction; otherwise the pastor himself must at least make the parties understand that God has provided for the procreation of children through a physical co-operation of husband and wife, and that the acts ordained to this are not only licit but sacred, always to be done rightly and in God's presence.

4. On the *manner and circumstances* of this instruction, Cappello has these very judicious remarks: "This instruction must be given carefully and with the greatest prudence, so that not a word fall from the lips of the pastor which might give the slightest offense or scandal to the faithful soul. Hence it must be given neither perfunctorily nor apart and as it were in whispers. He may instruct either the man or the girl, but usually it will be best to speak to both together, or, at least as regards the girl, in the presence of other persons. The practice of reserving this instruction for the sacramental confession of the parties is not in harmony with the nature of the judgment which is

---

[50] Cappello, *De Matrimonio,* n. 184. Cf. Kelly, *Modern Youth and Chastity* (Queen's Work); *This is a Great Sacrament* (Correspondence course, Marriage Preparation Service, The Catholic Centre, 125 Willbrod St., Ottawa).

exercised in the tribunal of penance, nor with the words of the canon, and consequently does not commend itself."[51]

5. *Extent of the obligation.* If it is certain that the parties have not the necessary instruction, the obligation to give it is *per se* grave; otherwise, it is slight. In a particular case if the parties are *known to be fully instructed*, it could be omitted altogether without sin; but at least a few words on mutual forbearance, love, patience, and the Catholic education of the children will always be appropriate. The above directions seem quite in accord with the text of the canon which prescribes that the instruction be given "with due regard to the condition of the persons concerned."

Exhortation to Receive the Sacraments. 1. *Baptism* and *confirmation* have been taken care of in canon 1021.

2. The parties are to be earnestly exhorted to make a good *confession* before the marriage. Matrimony is a sacrament of the living; hence must be received in the state of grace. Although sacramental confession is not prescribed as a strict duty, it is the most secure means to insure that the state of grace be present. If a *public sinner* refuses to go to confession before marriage, the pastor should not assist except for a grave reason, usually to be approved by the Ordinary (c. 1066). The confession before marriage enjoys the special privilege that reservations of sins are then not effective (c. 900, 1°).[52]

3. *Holy Communion* too should be received, though there is no strict obligation. The ideal Catholic marriage is performed at the nuptial Mass, with the bride and groom receiving together the Body of Christ, of whose Mystical Body they became members in baptism and are becoming special instruments in marriage.[53] Strictly speaking this Communion comes after the marriage, since that takes place before the Mass; but it ideally satisfies the requirements of the law. The words "before the marriage" apply strictly to confession.

CANON 1034. The pastor must seriously dissuade minor sons and daughters from contracting marriage without the knowledge or against the reasonable wishes of their parents; in case they refuse to obey, he should not assist at their marriage without having first consulted the Ordinary.

Marriages of Minors. 1. The *validity* of the marriage of minors, even against the wishes of their parents, provided they have reached

---

[51] *De Matrimonio,* n. 184.
[52] Cf. Code Com., 10 Nov., 1925; *AAS,* 17–583; *Digest,* I, p. 415.
[53] Cf. Tromp, in *Periodica,* Vol. 25, p. 1*.

the canonical age (cf. c. 1067), is no longer in question, and has not been since the Council of Trent.[54]

2. As regards *licitness,* the following principles of the *natural law* must be presupposed: parents have no right to control absolutely the marriages of their children by imposing or forbidding either marriage in general or a particular marriage, because children are not thus subject to parental authority in the choice of a state of life, and because the right transferred in marriage is intimately personal and outside the scope of parental authority. Yet minor children should, even in this matter, *consult* their parents and follow their *reasonable* wishes. To marry *without the knowledge* of their parents would be a grave sin, unless a reasonable cause justifies it; to marry *against their wishes* would be a grave sin, a venial sin, or no sin at all, according as the opposition of the parents is based on a reasonable and serious cause, merely reasonable causes, or causes which are unreasonable and imaginary. But the gravity and reasonableness of the cause are always to be weighed with due regard to the natural rights and personal needs of the contracting party. *"Suprema lex, salus animarum."*[55]

The Canonical Provisions. 1. *Minor sons and daughters* are boys and girls who have not completed their twenty-first year (c. 88, § 1), and who are not legally emancipated from parental authority.

2. These should be seriously dissuaded from marrying *without the knowledge* or *against the reasonable wishes* of their parents. Parents here normally include both father and mother, but if the father is living and acting as head of the family, it is his knowledge and consent which are paramount; otherwise, those of the mother. Whether the objection of the parents is reasonable or not is a question for prudent moral judgment in each case.[56]

3. The requirements of the *civil law* of the state should be taken into account, but this subject is touched upon under canon 1067.

---

[54] *Sess.* XXIV, *de ref. matr.,* cap. 1. For the history of the development of the law in this regard, see Joyce, *Christian Marriage,* pp. 71, 116, and more briefly, Augustine, *A Commentary,* V, p. 79.

[55] Cf. Gasparri, *De Matrimonio,* I, n. 194.

[56] For a very full and helpful discussion of this point of pastoral theology, see Cappello, *De Matrimonio,* nn. 186-190.

Section 3. Impediments in General (cc. 1035-1057)

PRELIMINARY SURVEY

General Principle of Personal Liberty (c. 1035)
Impedient and Diriment Impediments (c. 1036)
Public and Occult Impediments (c. 1037)
Power to Establish Impediments (c. 1038)
Power of Ordinaries of Places (c. 1039)
Abrogation of and Dispensation From Impediments (c. 1040)
The Effect of Custom (c. 1041)
Major and Minor Impediments (c. 1042)
Danger of Death: Powers of the Ordinary (c. 1043) ; of the
     Pastor, Assisting Priest, and Confessor (c. 1044)
Urgent Case: Powers of the Ordinary, Pastor, Assisting Priest,
     and Confessor (c. 1045)
Notice and Record of the Dispensation: for the External
     Forum (c. 1046); for the Internal Extra-sacramental
     Forum (c. 1047)
Use of Faculties to Dispense (cc. 1048–1050)
Implicit Legitimation of Children (c. 1051)
Implicit Grant of Dispensation Not Asked (c. 1052)
Implicit Dispensation From Impediment of Crime (c. 1053)
Dispensation From Minor Impediment (c. 1054)
Execution of Rescript Containing Dispensation (c. 1055)
Fees, etc. (cc. 1056, 1057)

CANON 1035. All persons who are not prohibited by law can contract marriage.

Principle of Liberty. This principle is founded on the natural liberty of the individual. Marriage is a natural society in the sense that it is founded by God as the Author of nature, who intends that mankind in general shall through it provide for the propagation of the race. The right to marry is a natural right, not to be denied unless a valid prohibition of natural or ecclesiastical law can be proved. The natural law itself forbids marriage to persons who are incapable of the act which is the object of the contract (c. 1068), or who lack the mental capacity to understand in a suitable manner the object of the contract (c. 1082). That the ecclesiastical law can establish conditions requisite to the validity or licitness of marriage has already been stated under canon 1016.

Impediments. 1. An impediment may be *broadly* defined as a circumstance which renders a marriage either illicit or invalid. Before the Code the word had this broad meaning and was applied to three different classes of circumstances which either forbade or invalidated marriage; namely, those affecting matrimonial *consent,* the *form* of marriage, or the *qualities* of the contracting parties. The Code has narrowed the term by applying it only to the last class of circumstances, those affecting the *persons.* Only in canon 1971 does the Code use the term "impediment" in the broader sense, as including circumstances affecting the form of marriage and matrimonial consent.[57]

2. A *strict definition* of impediment under the Code is: a circumstance attaching to the person which according to law renders his marriage illicit or invalid. It will be seen that error, force, and fear (that is, coercion of matrimonial consent), clandestinity (that is, absence of the formalities required by law in the expression of consent), are not impediments in this strict and proper sense. The temporary prohibition which may be imposed by a Bishop on his subjects according to canon 1039, § 1, although it would render a marriage illicit, is not classed as an impediment, because it is not imposed by law but by precept.

Classifications of Impediments. Impediments are:

1. Of *divine law* or of *ecclesiastical law,* according to their origin;

2. *Impedient* (merely prohibitive) or *diriment* (invalidating), according to their effect (c. 1036);

3. *Absolute* or *relative,* according as they affect the person regardless of, or only in relation to certain other persons;

4. *Public* or *occult,* according as they can or cannot be proved in the external forum (c. 1037);

5. *Permanent* or *temporary,* according to their duration;

6. *Certain* or *doubtful;*

7. *Dispensable* or *non-dispensable,* according as they can or cannot be removed by dispensation;

8. *Major* or *minor,* according to their grade (c. 1042).

Number of Impediments. 1. There are two or three *impedient impediments,* according as legal relationship is counted or not, depending on the law of the state. They are: simple vow (c. 1058); mixed religion (c. 1060 sq.); legal relationship through adoption, if according to the civil law it forbids marriage (c. 1059).

2. There are twelve or thirteen *diriment* impediments: want of age

---

[57] See Code Com., 12 March, 1929; *AAS,* 21–171; *Digest,* I, p. 807. Cf. Gasparri, *De Matrimonio,* I, n. 205.

(c. 1067); impotence (c. 1068); existing bond of previous marriage (c. 1069); disparity of cult (c. 1070); sacred orders (c. 1072); solemn religious vow (c. 1073); abduction (c. 1074); crime (c. 1075); consanguinity (c. 1076); affinity (c. 1077); public propriety (c. 1078); spiritual relationship (c. 1079); and legal relationship through adoption, if according to the law of the state it invalidates marriage (c. 1080).

In the United States and its Territories, legal relationship through adoption is not usually an impediment either to the licitness or validity of marriage according to the civil law.[58]

Doubt. Is a *doubtful* impediment binding? We must distinguish impediments of ecclesiastical law from those of divine law, and doubt of law from doubt of fact.

1. In impediments of *merely ecclesiastical law,* whether impedient or diriment:

a. If there is a *doubt of law,* the impediment is not binding (c. 15). This supposes, however, that one consult either the chancery or other canonical authorities to make sure that a doubt of law really exists; because it means an objective doubt, not a merely subjective one, much less mere ignorance of the law.

b. If there is a *doubt of fact,* the law remains effective, but the Ordinary has *power to dispense in accordance with canon 15.* If the doubt of fact is reducible to a doubt of law, probabilism would allow the marriage if after due inquiry it is still positively probable that the impediment does not exist.

2. In impediments of *divine law,* if we are to understand the doctrine, it will be best to consider some of the impediments separately.

a. Mixed religion and *disparity of cult* are *impedient* impediments by *divine law, if there is danger of perversion to the Catholic party or to the children.* Note that in this case the divine law forbids, but does not invalidate the marriage. In doubt, such a marriage is still forbidden. The doubt is one of fact, not reducible to a doubt of law. Hence probabilism has no application.

---

[58] Legal adoption is a diriment impediment in the Territory of Puerto Rico. Alford, *Ius Matrimoniale Comparatum,* p. 112. According to the *Annotated Laws of Massachusetts,* Vol. VI, Chap. 210, Sec. 6, a legal court decree of adoption gives rise to "all the legal consequences of the natural relation of child and parent, between the child and the petitioner." Since one of the legal consequences of the natural relation is a prohibition of marriage, it would seem that legal adoption would make a marriage between the adopted child and the adopting parent voidable according to the laws of Massachusetts. We are informed that the laws of Rhode Island and Connecticut are similar in this respect to those of Massachusetts. The above information was kindly provided by the Reverend Daniel F. Creeden, S.J., of Weston College, Weston, Massachusetts.

b. Vow is an impediment of divine law; but, by that law, it is *only an impedient* one, whether it be a simple private vow (c. 1058), or the public vow involved in sacred orders (c. 1072) or in solemn religious profession (c. 1073). In the first case (private vow), we think that in doubt either of law or fact, the vow would not be binding to prevent a licit marriage, according to the rule of probabilism. In the case of sacred orders or solemn profession, the public nature of the obligation requires that, even in case of doubt, marriage be not permitted until a dispensation has been obtained.[59]

c. Consanguinity is a *diriment impediment of divine law* in the following cases: (1) *certainly,* in the first degree of the direct line; (2) *most probably,* in all degrees of the direct line, and in the first degree of the collateral line.[60] In all these cases, whether the doubt is of fact or even of law, marriage would be positively illicit, and no application of probabilism could render it licit. The reason is that there is not question *merely* of the licitness of an act, but of assuming, perhaps invalidly, a bond which determines the whole state of life. This is confirmed by canon 1076, § 3.

d. With the sole exception of impotence, the same reasoning applies to the remaining diriment impediments of divine law, namely, *ligamen,* or the bond of a pre-existing valid marriage. A second marriage is permitted only upon moral certainty that the previous bond has been released by death.

e. "If the impediment of *impotence* is doubtful, whether in law or in fact, the marriage is not to be prevented" (c. 1068, § 2). This unique exception will be explained in its proper place.

Ignorance. Ignorance may be culpable or inculpable, and it may concern a merely impedient or a diriment impediment.

1. *Inculpable* ignorance excuses from a *merely impedient* impediment on general moral principles; *culpable* ignorance does not entirely excuse.

2. From a *diriment* impediment, even if it be merely ecclesiastical, no ignorance, culpable or inculpable, excuses (c. 16, § 1).

Moral Impossibility. Does the law establishing an impediment remain urgent if its observance involves such extreme difficulty in an individual case that it amounts to moral impossibility? We may

---

[59] In this case the dispensation is not directly from the divine law, but from the effects of an act of the human will which brought the subject within the operation of the divine law. See p. 433.
[60] Cf. Cappello, *De Matrimonio,* nn. 518, 519.

admit, with several very grave authorities, that in such a case even a *diriment* impediment of merely *ecclesiastical law* would cease to be binding. The examples given are in accord with the principles regarding the extraordinary application of *epikeia*.

A man living in concubinage is at the point of death; an impediment of ecclesiastical law prevents licit or even valid marriage; it is impossible to ask for a dispensation; he is in proximate danger of sin and of eternal ruin unless he can validly and licitly marry. Probably the ecclesiastical law in these circumstances would cease to bind.[01]

The same principle is applied to the use of a marriage already invalidly contracted. A woman who married in good faith later becomes conscious that her marriage is invalid because of a diriment ecclesiastical impediment. She cannot refuse conjugal relations without incurring the gravest dangers, such as death or serious bodily harm. She may consider the law relaxed through *epikeia,* and render the marriage debt. Some even hold that the marriage would be validated once for all; but afterward, if an opportunity occurs for seeking a dispensation, it should be asked for, at least *ad cautelam.*[62]

Use of Marriage When It Is of Doubtful Validity. This quite practical question may be thus briefly answered:

1. If the doubt is *merely negative,* no attention is to be paid to it; the use of marriage is perfectly licit.

2. If the doubt is *positive,* it must be investigated.

3. Pending the inquiry; if *both parties are in doubt,* they should abstain; if *only one is in doubt,* he or she may not ask but may render the *debitum,* provided the other party has not lost the right to ask it.

4. If the *doubt persists after the investigation,* the marriage is to be considered as valid in both the internal and external forum (c. 1014); hence its use is licit.[63]

CANON 1036. § 1. An *impedient* impediment contains a grave prohibition against contracting marriage; which, however, is not rendered invalid if it is contracted notwithstanding.

§ 2. A *diriment* impediment both gravely prohibits the marriage and prevents it from being contracted validly.

§ 3. Although an impediment exist on the part of only one party, it nevertheless renders the marriage either illicit or invalid.

---

[61] Cf. Ballerini-Palmieri, I, n. 318; Cappello, *De Matrimonio,* n. 199; Payen, *De Matrimonio,* I, n. 567; Noldin, *Theol. Mor.,* I, n. 199; Gasparri, *De Matrimonio,* n. 711.
[62] Lehmkuhl, *Theol. Mor.,* II, n. 1054; Arregui, *Summarium,* n. 731; St. Alphonsus Liguori, VI, n. 613.
[63] Cf. Cappello, *De Matrimonio,* n. 812.

Notes. 1. An impediment which directly affects only one of the parties nevertheless renders the marriage illicit or invalid as the case may be, because the contract is indivisible; it cannot be invalid or illicit for one party by reason of an impediment, and at the same time valid or licit for the other.

2. Whether this principle is applicable so as to give effect to an impediment of the civil law which directly affects an unbaptized person in a marriage with a Catholic who has been dispensed from disparity of cult, is a disputed question which we have briefly discussed under canon 1016.

3. Formerly it was the rule that in dispensing a Catholic party from disparity of cult, the Church was understood to dispense also from those impediments from which the unbaptized party was exempt, so that the exemption of the unbaptized party was communicated to the Catholic party. This rule is now certainly abrogated.[64]

CANON 1037. An impediment is considered public if it can be proved in the external forum; otherwise it is occult.

Public and Occult Impediments. 1. This distinction is of great practical importance, because the two classes of impediments are handled in an entirely different manner both as regards the obtaining of the dispensation and the procedure afterward.

2. A *public* impediment is one which *can be proved in the external forum*. Among the principal means of proof in the external forum are: two trustworthy witnesses testifying to facts within their personal knowledge (c. 1791, § 2), or one unexceptionable qualified witness upon official acts (c. 1791, § 1), or an authentic public document (cf. c. 1816). Now some impediments are by their very nature such that normally they are capable of proof in one of these ways; for example, sacred orders, solemn religious profession, disparity of cult, consanguinity, affinity, public propriety, spiritual or legal relationship, *usually* can be proved from public records. These are called impediments *public by nature*. Yet they may be in fact occult, and will be so classed according to this canon, if the record which normally should furnish the proof in the external forum happens to be wanting. Conversely, there are impediments which *usually* are neither matters of public record, nor observed by witnesses, nor capable of proof in any legal manner in the external forum, and are consequently not public by

---

[64] Cf. S. C. Prop. Fid., 20 May, 1931; *Sylloge*, n. 157; *Digest*, I, p. 512, and note; Holy Office, 30 June, 1932; *Sylloge*, n. 169; *Digest*, II, p. 291. For a discussion of this former practice, see *Clergy Review for Sept.*, 1939, p. 265.

nature. Yet they may be *public in fact,* inasmuch as it may happen that they are capable of proof owing to exceptional circumstances.

3. An impediment is said to be only *materially public* if the fact from which it arises is known, but is not known to constitute an impediment. It is said to be *formally public* if the impediment is known as such. The Code Commission has declared that, to constitute a public impediment, it is sufficient that the fact from which it arose be public. Hence the distinction between materially and formally public is now of relatively slight consequence.[65]

4. Formerly *occult* impediments were divided into *entirely occult* (known to no one) and *simply occult* (known to few persons). The latter would be classed as public under the Code if capable of proof in the external forum. Yet for one purpose this old classification remains practical; namely, these so-called "simply occult" impediments may still be handled through the Sacred Penitentiary instead of having to be treated as public impediments, in the external forum.

5. The term "impediments by nature public" in canon 1971, was interpreted by the Rota in a sense quite different from that of canon 1037.[66]

CANON 1038. § 1. To declare authoritatively when the divine law forbids or invalidates a marriage belongs solely to the supreme authority of the Church.

§ 2. The same supreme authority has the exclusive right to establish for baptized persons impedient or diriment impediments either by way of general or particular law.

Power to Interpret the Divine Law. 1. The right of the Church to interpret the divine law infallibly in matters of morals is included in her divine commission.

2. This right is exercised in defining impotence (a diriment impediment by the natural law) and the conditions under which disparity of cult and mixed religion make marriage illicit by divine law (cf. cc. 1068, 1060, 1071).

Power to Establish Impediments. 1. The right of the Church in general has been briefly explained under canon 1016. The present canon declares that this right is vested *exclusively in the supreme authority* of the Church, that is, in the Holy See, whether the law be general or particular. Bishops have, in this matter, only the limited

---

[65] Code Com., 25 June, 1932; *AAS,* 24–284; *Digest,* I, p. 501.
[66] Cf. Rota, 11 Aug., 1928; *S. R. Rotae Decisiones seu Sententiae,* Vol. 20, p. 402; *Digest,* II, p. 543.

power of forbidding marriage temporarily in individual cases (c. 1039).

2. This power of the Church is exercised *directly* over *baptized persons only*. This includes heretics and schismatics, unless they are expressly exempted by the terms of the law (cc. 12, 87). Unbaptized persons may be affected *indirectly,* when they contract marriage with a baptized person.

3. If the validity of baptism is doubtful, there is a general presumption, at least in the external forum, in favor of its validity, and hence in favor of the obligation of the person to obey the laws of the Church; but if the doubt persists, after the marriage, the presumption in favor of the marriage would prevail, except where the privilege of the faith is involved (cc. 1014, 1127).[67]

4. As to infidels, the Church has no power directly. They are subject to the natural and divine, but not to the ecclesiastical law. Has the state power to establish impediments for marriages in which both parties are unbaptized? Most probably, yes, though the question is disputed.[68] But the state has of course no power to dissolve a valid marriage once contracted.

CANON 1039. § 1. Ordinaries of places can forbid marriage in a particular case, but only temporarily, for just cause, and as long as such cause continues, to all persons actually stopping in their territory, and to their subjects even outside their territory.

§ 2. Only the Apostolic See has power to add an invalidating clause to the prohibition.

Power of Ordinaries. 1. They can forbid marriage (but not under pain of nullity) to any person actually staying in their territory, and to their own subjects even outside it, but only *in an individual case, for just cause,* and *while it lasts.* Such is the direct power given by this canon.

2. *Indirectly,* they could prevent a valid marriage in the territory by forbidding any pastor to assist. In issuing such a general prohibition a Bishop would be gravely bound to remain within the bounds of justice and the law.

Pastors have no power whatever to "forbid marriage." If the term is used in connection with them, it simply means that they declare to the parties that according to law they have no right to marry.

---

[67] Cf. Payen, *De Matrimonio,* I, n. 538, 4.

[68] Cf. Vermeersch, *What Is Marriage,* p. 14; Wernz, *Ius Decretalium,* IV, part I, n. 75; and an extended, and to us conclusive argument in Gasparri, *De Matrimonio,* I, nn. 240–256.

CANON 1040. No one except the Roman Pontiff can abrogate or derogate from impediments of ecclesiastical law, whether they be impedient or diriment; nor dispense from the same unless this power has been given either by the common law or by a special indult from the Apostolic See.

State of the Question. *Derogation* from a law means a partial abrogation of it. The direct provisions of this canon seem simple enough. But the canon brings under discussion the whole subject of *dispensing from matrimonial impediments,* which is of considerable practical importance and some difficulty.

Dispensation. 1. A dispensation is a *relaxation of the law* in a particular case (c. 80).

2. It is an act of *jurisdiction* (*voluntary;* cf. c. 201 § 3); hence it is invalid if done by one who lacks jurisdiction.

3. A *just cause* is always required for licitness; and if the dispensation is granted by one inferior to the legislator, it is required for validity (c. 84, § 1); but in doubt as to the sufficiency of the cause, a dispensation may be licitly asked, and validly and licitly given (c. 84, § 2).

4. Persons other than the Roman Pontiff must *obtain the necessary jurisdiction* to dispense, either through the common law or through special indult.

5. A dispensation for the *internal* forum is sufficient when the impediment is *occult;* but when it is public a dispensation is *per se* necessary also for the external forum.

6. Since dispensations are frequently granted by *rescripts,* all the provisions of the Code on rescripts (cc. 36–62) here become of immediate practical concern.

7. *Historically,* the practice of granting dispensations from impediments for marriage dates only from the twelfth or thirteenth century.

Power and Practice of the Roman Pontiff. 1. The Roman Pontiff cannot dispense from the *absolute* provisions of the *divine* law, natural or positive; that is, where the divine law is binding on persons independently of any act of their own free will; for example, in impotence, consanguinity in the first degree of the direct line. The same is true of certain "impediments" in the broad pre-Code sense, such as want of consent, ignorance of the substance of the contract.

2. Within certain limits he can dispense from the so-called *conditional* provisions of the divine law; that is, where the divine law is binding only because of some act of the free will of the parties; for

example, a vow, an oath, or a contract. This is not a dispensation in the strict sense, because it is not a relaxation of the law itself directly, but of a human act which brought the subject within the law. It is thus that the Roman Pontiff can dispense from solemn vows in religion, sacred orders, and even from the bond of a former marriage, provided it is not *ratum et consummatum*.[69]

3. From *all impediments of merely ecclesiastical law,* the Holy Father *can* dispense. He *does not* do so, however, in the following cases: (*a*) when there is doubt whether the impediment in question is of divine law; for example, in consanguinity in the first degree of the collateral line; (*b*) sacred order, in a Bishop; (*c*) crime, including murder, which has become public.

4. Impediments of ecclesiastical law which are dispensed only very rarely and for the gravest reasons are sacred order of the priesthood and affinity in the direct line when the marriage was consummated. Those next in order of difficulty as regards dispensation are: crime, including murder, when not public; want of canonical age, solemn religious profession, disparity of cult for marriage with a Mohammedan.

The Roman Curia. In granting dispensations from matrimonial impediments, the Roman Pontiff acts through various departments of the Roman Curia:

1. For dispensations in the *external forum,* he uses:

(*a*) The *Holy Office* for disparity of cult, mixed religion, and any other impediment which exists concurrently with either of these; (*b*) the *Sacred Oriental Congregation* for all impediments where either party is an Oriental, subject however to the prerogatives of the Holy Office; (*c*) the *Sacred Congregation of Religious,* for dispensation from religious vows; (*d*) the *Sacred Congregation of the Sacraments,* for other impediments, if neither party is an Oriental Catholic; (*e*) the *Sacred Congregation for the Propagation of the Faith,* in mission territories which are subject to it.

All applications for dispensations in the external forum must be presented through the diocesan chancery. It is usual to apply through the chancery of the diocese where one of the parties, preferably the bride, has a domicile or quasi-domicile, or is actually staying. The application will be formulated by the chancery upon information supplied by the pastor, and should contain the following data: the full names of both parties; the domicile or quasi-domicile, or place of

---

[69] Cf. Genicot, *Theol. Mor.,* I, n. 138.

actual residence, of the parties; the existing impediment in its exact kind and degree (e.g., consanguinity in the third degree of the collateral line, touching the second); the number of impediments, including multiple consanguinity or affinity; the religion of the parties if either is non-Catholic; the circumstances; whether the marriage is to be contracted or has been already contracted; a canonical cause for the dispensation; and finally, whether the parties are poor or not (so that the tax may be properly assessed or remitted).

2. For dispensations in the *internal* forum, the Roman Pontiff uses the Sacred Penitentiary for all impediments, for all persons including Orientals, but *per se* only for occult impediments, except as noted below.[70] Applications for dispensations in the internal forum may be transmitted through the diocesan chancery, always without prejudice to the seal of confession; but it is always proper and is in fact the regular procedure for the confessor to apply directly to the Sacred Penitentiary.

a. Dispensation for the *internal forum only* is usually not granted when the impediment is by nature public, even though it be occult in fact; nor when it is public in law or in fact and such that it may become actually known to many persons. But such a dispensation may be granted for a public impediment which is neither actually known nor likely to become known to more than a very few.[71]

b. Examples of such *simply occult* impediments in which the Sacred Penitentiary may grant a dispensation for the internal forum notwithstanding the public nature of the impediment are crime, vows, consanguinity resulting from occult copula.

c. If *both a public and occult* impediment occur in the same case, the dispensations must be asked for separately, the one for the public impediment, of the proper department without mentioning the other; the one for the occult impediment, of the Sacred Penitentiary mentioning the existence of the other impediment but omitting the names of the persons.

d. Form of application to the Sacred Penitentiary. This may be in the form of a letter addressed as follows: *All' Eminentissimo Cardinale Penitenziere Maggiore, Palazzo del S. Uffizio, Citta del Vaticano.* If in Latin, the letter begins: *Eminentissime Princeps;* if in English, *Your Eminence.* The Sacred Penitentiary may be addressed in any language. If the application is entrusted to an agent in Rome, it must be enclosed in a special inner envelope securely sealed.[72]

---

[70] See c. 258 and S. C. Or., 10 May, 1930; *AAS,* 22–394; *Digest,* I, p. 174.
[71] Cf. Gasparri, *De Matrimonio,* I, nn. 210, 289; Cappello, *De Matrimonio,* n. 227.
[72] S. Paen., *Monitum,* 1 Feb., 1935; *AAS,* 27–62; *Digest,* II, p. 219.

e. Contents of application to the Sacred Penitentiary. If the dispensation is asked for the *sacramental* forum, fictitious names (Titius, Titia) should be substituted for those of the parties, and all personal circumstances which might betray their identity should be omitted. For the rest, the application should give the same information regarding the impediment, reasons for dispensation, etc., which are required in the application for the external forum. If the application is for a dispensation in the *extra-sacramental forum,* the names and residences of the parties should be given, because the dispensation has to be registered (secretly) according to canon 1047.

3. During the *vacancy of the Apostolic See,* the faculties of the various departments of the Roman Curia are not suspended entirely. The Sacred Congregations retain their *ordinary* jurisdiction, but cannot exercise powers for which they would need the specific approval of the Roman Pontiff.[73] The powers of the Cardinal Major Penitentiary are even enlarged for the forum of conscience, for urgent cases.[74]

Dispensing Powers of Ordinaries. The power of Ordinaries to dispense from matrimonial impediments must be derived from the common law or from special indults of the Holy See (c. 1040).

1. The *common law* gives to Ordinaries the power to dispense: (*a*) from simple non-reserved vows, according to canon 1313; (*b*) from any impediment from which the Holy See usually dispenses, if there is doubt of fact, according to canon 15; (*c*) from any impediment from which the Holy See usually dispenses, if recourse to the Holy See is difficult and the delay occasioned thereby involves danger of grave harm, according to canon 81; (*d*) in danger of death, according to canon 1043; (*e*) when all is prepared for the marriage, according to canon 1045. These provisions have been or will be explained in their proper place.

2. *Special indults* may contain further powers.

3. Jurisdiction over the person is in general required for the validity of the use of dispensing power (c. 201, § 1). The law or indult conferring jurisdiction for dispensing from matrimonial impediments frequently include explicitly the power to dispense *peregrini,* or "all persons actually staying in the territory" (cf. c. 1043). Where such a clause is *not* explicitly in the grant of faculties, it is disputed whether the Ordinary has power to dispense others than his own subjects. The view which affirms this power is not theoretically certain, but was

---

[73] Const. *Vacante Sede* (Doc. I), nn. 23, 24, 25.
[74] Cf. Pius XI, 25 March, 1935; *AAS,* 27–112; *Digest,* II, p. 114, ref.

probable before the Code, and remains probable since the Code (cf. c. 209).[75]

Dispensing Power of Pastors, Confessors, Priests. These are entirely limited to the powers granted them in danger of death (c. 1044), and when all is prepared for the marriage (c. 1045), which will be explained in connection with those canons.

Canonical Causes for Dispensations. An instruction of the Sacred Congregation of Propaganda, 9 May, 1877,[76] names sixteen canonical causes. Two later documents of the Apostolic Datary name twenty-eight, of which some are new, but not all are canonical.[77]

Rules Governing Rescripts Applied to Dispensations. If a dispensation is granted by rescript, the rules of canons 36–62 will be applicable.

1. The form of the rescript (*gratiosa* or *commissoria*) will be of immediate practical consequence. Rescripts for the *internal* forum are usually *in forma commissoria,* as are also those for the *external* forum issued by the Holy See; whereas those for the *external* forum issued by Ordinaries are usually *in forma gratiosa.*

2. If a dispensation is granted by rescript *in forma gratiosa,* it takes

---

[75] Cf. *Irish Eccl. Rec.,* Vol. 64, p. 268 (Conway), citing an earlier article by Kinane, in *Irish Eccl. Rec.,* 1930, p. 295.

[76] Cf. Gasparri-Seredi, *Fontes,* n. 4890, Vol. VII, p. 459.

[77] Cf. Ayrinhac-Lydon, *Marriage Legislation,* p. 378 a; Cappello, *De Matrimonio,* nn. 257–269.

As an example of modern practice, the following list, sanctioned by the Chancery of the Archdiocese of Chicago, may be of interest:

1. Canonical Reasons Sufficient in Themselves:

a. *Promissio amplectendi religionem Catholicam;*
b. *Spes fundata conversionis partis acatholicae;*
c. *Nimia, suspecta, periculosa familiaritas;*
d. *Periculum matrimonii mere civilis vel coram ministello;*
e. *Periculum apostasiae ex negata dispensatione;*
   (Note: In *d* and *e,* if the danger arises from a *threat,* it ceases to be a canonical reason.)
f. *Remotio gravium scandalorum;*
g. *Praegnantia ideoque legitimatio prolis;*
h. *Revalidatio matrimonii invalidi;*
i. *Infamia mulieris ex suspicione orta;*
k. *Grave periculum incontinentiae.*

2. Supplementary, But Not Sufficient in Themselves:

a. *Aetas feminae superadulta* (has completed her 24th year);
b. *Oratrix orbata;*
c. *Oratrix ex natalibus illegitimis;*
e. *Oratrix infirmitate vel deformitate detenta;*
f. *Orator viduus prole oneratus;*
d. *Omnia ad nuptias iam praeparata;*
g. *Propositum contrahendi plane divulgatum;*
h. *Mutuum auxilium in provecta aetate.*

effect, that is the impediment is removed, at the moment when the rescript is dated; if *in forma commissoria,* at the moment of execution (c. 38).

3. It is at the moment when the rescript takes effect that the essential recitals of the petition must be true (c. 41).

4. What this essential truth consists of, that is, what must be stated in order that the rescript be *valid,* depends on the *stylus Curiae,* according to canons 40, 42, and 45; but if the dispensation is granted for a *minor* impediment (c. 1042) no omission or false statement in the petition will invalidate it, even though the sole motivating cause set forth be false (c. 1054).

CANON 1041. Any custom which introduces a new impediment or which is contrary to existing impediments is reprobated.

Effect of Custom. 1. *Historically,* custom has been responsible for some of the impediments, e.g., disparity of cult.

2. *In the future,* the modification of existing impediments or any addition to them by custom is made impossible; for the present canon declares such customs reprobated; a custom which is expressly reprobated is unreasonable (c. 27, § 2); and no unreasonable custom can ever obtain the force of law (c. 27, § 1).

CANON 1042. § 1. Some impediments are of minor, others of major grade.

§ 2. Impediments of minor grade are:
1° Consanguinity in the third degree of the collateral line;
2° Affinity in the second degree of the collateral line;
3° Public propriety in the second degree;
4° Spiritual relationship;
5° Crime resulting from adultery with a promise of or attempt at marriage, even by a merely civil contract.
§ 3. The impediments of major grade are all the others.

State of the Question. This distinction between major and minor impediments relates chiefly to the facility with which they are dispensed. Perhaps the most important practical question is that stated in canon 1054.

Minor Impediments. These five impediments can be rather easily remembered. They include all the impediments based on *relationship* (except legal adoption, where that impediment exists by civil law), but only the least or most remote degree of each of these impediments, and the first or least serious degree of the impediment of crime, namely, that in which no homicide is involved. Since spiritual relationship has no degrees, it is always minor. As all these are diriment impediments, it may be asked whether the distinction in any way affects the impedient impediments. There is no positive indication that it does, and we would say that none of the impedient impediments can be considered of minor grade so as to benefit from canon 1054. Several canonists hold this explicitly as to the impedient impediment of mixed religion.[78]

CANON 1043. In danger of death, the Ordinaries of places, in order to provide for the consciences of the parties, and in a proper case for the legitimation of children, can, both as to the form to be observed in the celebration of marriage and as to all and each of the impediments of ecclesiastical law, public or occult, even multiple, except the impediments arising from the sacred order of priesthood and from affinity in the direct line when the marriage has been consummated, dispense their own subjects anywhere, and all persons who are actually staying in their territory, provided that scandal be removed and that, if the dispensation is granted from disparity of cult or mixed religion, the usual promises be given.

Dispensing Power of Ordinaries of Places in Danger of Death. This complicated canon can be made rather clear if its various elements are studied separately.

1. *Ordinaries of places* are those mentioned in canon 198; Bishop, Vicar General, temporary Administrator during vacancy, etc.

2. The *circumstances* requisite for the use of the powers here granted are: (*a*) danger of death; (*b*) that there exist a need of providing for the conscience of one of the parties or of legitimating children; (*c*) that all scandal be removed; (*d*) that the *cautiones* be given if the dispensation from disparity of cult or mixed religion be granted.

3. *Danger of death* means here, not *in articulo mortis,* or *extreme* danger, but ordinary danger, that is a probability of death. It may affect either the party directly dispensed, or the other party; and it need not be caused by present illness, but may be from any cause, such as impending operation, military action, capital punishment.

4. It is sufficient that the *conscience of either party* is provided for by the dispensation; the reason need not be the present need of sacramental absolution; it may be, for example, to remove some grave cause of contention, such as legal controversy over property, or any other obstacle to peace of mind.

---

[78] Cf. Augustine, *A Commentary,* V, p. 94; Cappello, *De Matrimonio,* n. 206; Payen, *De Matrimonio,* I, n. 601.

5. The *legitimation of children* gives rise to several questions. First, is this required in addition to the provision for the conscience? It is not. Although the canon uses the copulative *et,* it is understood as disjunctive, from the common interpretation before the Code (cf. c. 6). Second, where the reason is legitimation of children, will this be sufficient if the only children to be legitimated are either *adulterine* (conceived while one of the parties was bound by another marriage) or *sacrilegious* (conceived by copula which was illicit because of sacred orders or solemn religious profession of one of the parties). Theoretically we think it clear that the legitimation of such children is not contemplated in this canon. The reason is that such children are legitimated neither by the dispensation (cf. c. 1051) nor, at least ordinarily, by the subsequent marriage of the parties (cf. cc. 1114, 1116); and the present canon must be understood in the light of those provisions of law. Practically, however, since the contrary opinion has some extrinsic probability, we think that in danger of death it would be safe to act on it.

6. *Scandal must be removed.* This affects the *licitness* of the dispensation.[79]

7. If the dispensation is from mixed religion or disparity of cult the *cautiones* must be given. It was formerly disputed whether this was required for the *valid* use of the power; but since the Decree of the Holy Office,[80] it must be admitted that the dispensation would be invalid without it, even in danger of death.[81] If, however, there is real urgency and no time to fulfill this condition, the dispensation would be valid provided all the conditions imposed by divine law were fulfilled; because no purely ecclesiastical law binds in such extreme necessity.

8. The *persons* in whose favor the dispensation may be granted are "their own subjects anywhere, and all persons actually staying in their territory."

9. The power granted is *ordinary,* since it is attached by law to the office of Ordinaries of places (cf. c. 197, § 1). It can be delegated according to canon 199, § 1.

10. *Scope* of the power. It includes dispensation from: (*a*) the *form* of marriage (cf. c. 1094); (*b*) *all impediments of ecclesiastical law with*

---

[79] Cf. Ayrinhac-Lydon, *Marriage Legislation,* p. 69; Chrétien, *De Matrimonio,* p. 172; Augustine, *A Commentary,* V, p. 101; Payen, *De Matrimonio,* I, n. 646.

[80] Holy Office, 14 Jan., 1932; *AAS,* 24–25; *Digest,* I, p. 505.

[81] Cappello, who had been of the contrary opinion, comes to this conclusion in *Periodica,* Vol. 21, p. 100, and in later editions of *De Matrimonio.*

two exceptions, namely the sacred order of the priesthood, and affinity in the direct line when the marriage (from which the affinity arose) was consummated. This affinity would exist, e.g., between a man and his stepdaughter or daughter-in-law.

11. Note that dispensation even from the form of marriage does not dispense from *renewing* consent. No power is granted for a *sanatio in radice.*

CANON 1044. In the same circumstances as those mentioned in canon 1043, and only for cases in which not even the Ordinary of the place can be reached, the same power of dispensing belongs to the pastor, to the priest who assists at the marriage in accordance with canon 1098, n. 2, and to the confessor, but in this last case for the internal forum and in the act of sacramental confession only.

In Danger of Death, Powers of the Pastor. 1. The *power granted* (where the Ordinary cannot be reached) is exactly the same as that given to Ordinaries by canon 1043. It is *ordinary* power, capable of delegation. Its *scope* is the same as to form and impediments.

2. The *persons* in whose favor it may be used are the same, *mutatis mutandis;* i.e., the pastor's own subjects anywhere, and all persons actually staying in his parish.

3. The *circumstances* are the same, with the added requisite that *the Ordinary of the place cannot be reached.* If it is *certain* that the Ordinary can be reached, no power is conferred on the pastor by this canon, hence a dispensation by him would be invalid.[82] The Code Commission has decided that if the Ordinary can be reached *only by telegraph or telephone,* it may be considered that he cannot be reached, and the power may be used.[83] However, there is certainly no harm in using telegraph, telephone, or any other means to obtain the Ordinary's express delegation.

4. A question of *delegation by the pastor* arises. Is this power delegated implicitly whenever the pastor gives a particular delegation to assist at a particular marriage? We would say yes, since under these circumstances the power to assist would be useless without the dispensing power.[84]

5. Could this power be used by an assistant (*vicarius co-operator*) who has general delegation for all marriages in the parish? Though

---

[82] Cf. Cappello, *De Matrimonio,* n. 237.
[83] Code Com., 12 Nov., 1922; *AAS,* 14–662; *Digest,* I, p. 502.
[84] Cf. Payen, *De Matrimonio,* I, n. 667; Cappello, *De Matrimonio,* n. 237; V-C, *Epit.,* II, n. 311.

this case is less strong than the case of a particular delegation, an affirmative answer is still probable (cf. c. 209).

6. Since no limitation is imposed, the pastor's power, like that of the Ordinary, extends to the external as well as to the internal forum (c. 202, § 3).

7. This power may also be used to validate a marriage.

Power of the Assisting Priest. Since his powers are exactly the same as those of the pastor it is only necessary to determine precisely who is here meant by assisting priest. It means any priest who, *together with two witnesses,* assists at a marriage in danger of death, when neither the Ordinary nor the pastor nor an authorized ,delegate can be had, according to canon 1098, 2°. If two witnesses are not present, the priest, in our humble judgment, is not assisting "in accordance with canon 1098, 2°," and hence has not the powers here given to the priest *so* assisting.[85]

Powers of the Confessor. 1. The confessor here means any priest who here and now has faculties to absolve the person whose confession he hears, or any priest who actually hears the confession of a person in danger of death (c. 882).

2. His powers are limited to the *internal forum* and to the *act of sacramental confession;* but it is not necessary that the confession be sacramentally valid, nor that absolution be given.

3. Does the above limitation on the confessor's powers implicitly *exclude* all impediments which are *public* by nature? Some canonists answer affirmatively because a dispensation from a public impediment, given in the internal sacramental forum, is something of an anomaly, and creates a conflict between the internal and external fora.[86] There are, however, solid reasons and respectable authorities on the other side; namely Arendt, Chelodi, Vermeersch, Vromant, Wouters. Since there is here question of danger of death, this probable opinion could certainly be used.[87]

4. It is good to recall that the confessor may acquire faculties for the external forum by acting in the character of assisting priest.

CANON 1045. § 1. Ordinaries of places can, subject to the clauses at the end of canon 1043, grant a dispensation from all the impedi-

---

[85] Payen, *De Matrimonio,* I, n. 668, III, p. 126, and Cappello, *De Matrimonio,* n. 239, do not touch this question explicitly.

[86] Cf. Gasparri, *De Matrimonio,* n. 398. Cappello, who in former editions strenuously urged this argument, modifies his views considerably in the latest edition (1939), *De Matrimonio,* n. 238.

[87] Cf. Payen, *De Matrimonio,* I, n. 673. Cappello, *De Matrimonio,* n. 238, would limit the power to occult impediments or those which are occult in fact, even though public by nature, and which are unlikely to become known.

ments mentioned in the said canon 1043, whenever the impediment is discovered when everything is already prepared for the marriage, and it cannot, without probable danger of grave harm, be deferred until a dispensation is obtained from the Holy See.

§ 2. This faculty is good also for the validation of a marriage already contracted, if there is the same danger in delay and there is not sufficient time for recourse to the Holy See.

§ 3. In the same circumstances, all the persons mentioned in canon 1044 have the same faculty, but only for occult cases in which not even the Ordinary of the place can be reached, or in which he cannot be reached without danger of the violation of a secret.

Powers of the Ordinary When All Is Prepared for the Marriage. 1. "When the impediment is discovered when everything is prepared for the marriage, etc." The Code Commission has decided that this condition is fulfilled even if the impediment was known before, but is reported to the Ordinary or pastor only after everything is prepared.[88] Even the bad faith of the parties (in concealing the impediment until then) would not, according to some authorities, impair the power to dispense.[89] The Rota, in discussing this provision in a recent case, remarked that all the material preparations need not be complete; the condition is verified when the wedding is so imminent that it must be celebrated within a shorter time than that which will be required under the circumstances to obtain a dispensation from the Holy See. The fact that the ring was not engraved nor the invitations issued does not necessarily exclude the condition.[90] But some actual preparation must have been made, not merely by the pastor but by the parties.[91]

2. What is the *scope* of the power granted by this canon? "All the impediments mentioned in the said canon 1043." These words seem very clear, yet they are not. The serious question arises whether the want of *form* is to be considered as one of those impediments. The weight of authority and the better reasons are for the negative, namely, that the power to dispense from the *form* of marriage is not included here.[92] Yet some notable authorities hold that the form is included, and this opinion may be considered at least extrinsically probable.[93]

---

[88] Code Com., 1 March, 1921; *AAS*, 13–177; *Digest*, I, p. 502.

[89] Cf. V-C, *Epit.*, II, n. 308, 2; Payen, *De Matrimonio*, I, n. 650. *Contra*, Wernz-Vidal, *De Matrimonio*, n. 413, note 59.

[90] Cf. Rota, 25 May, 1925; *S. R. Rotae Decisiones*, Vol. 17, p. 195; *Digest*, II, p. 277.

[91] Cf. Rota, 14 March, 1927; *S. R. Rotae Decisiones*, Vol. 19, p. 70; *Digest*, II, p. 278.

[92] Cf. Creusen, Chelodi, Ferreres, Wernz-Vidal, Cappello, De Smet (in later editions), Gasparri, and Payen, *De Matrimonio*, I, n. 648.

[93] It is held by Arendt, Vermeersch, Vromant, De Smet. Cf. *Periodica*, Vol. 16, p. 1. Payen (*De Matrimonio*, I, n. 648, p. 483, note 1) admits this opinion as extrinsically probable. In this we agree.

3. The power is granted "subject to the clauses at the end of canon 1043." Specifically, these clauses (following the word *dispensare* in the Latin text) determine the *persons* to be dispensed, provide for the removal of *scandal,* and require the *cautiones* in case of mixed religion or disparity of cult.

4. It may be used not only for marriages to be contracted, but also for the validation of marriages which have already been contracted invalidly. The same is true of canons 1043, 1044.

Powers of the Pastor and Assisting Priest. These powers are limited by the clause, "only for occult cases in which not even the Ordinary of the place can be reached, or in which he cannot be reached without danger of violation of the secret."

1. As stated above, if the Ordinary can be reached *only by telegraph or telephone,* it is considered that he cannot be reached.

2. The *secret* here means not only the secret of confession but any secret professionally committed to the priest. Hence this condition is fulfilled in every case where the impediment can remain unknown and the parties have a reasonable cause for wishing it to remain so, even to the Ordinary.

3. The clause "only for occult cases" does not limit the power to impediments which are by nature occult, but includes impediments which are by nature public provided they be occult in fact.[94]

Powers of the Confessor. 1. The confessor is grouped in this canon together with the pastor and the assisting priest. Hence it may be asked whether his powers are here limited, as they are in danger of death according to canon 1044, to "the internal forum and the act of sacramental confession." It would seem strange that the confessor should have broader powers here, in a merely urgent case, "when all is prepared for the wedding" than in danger of death. For this reason, and also by general deduction from the nature of the confessor's office, it is more probable that his power is here subject to the same limitation as in danger of death, that is, to the internal forum and the act of sacramental confession.[95]

2. Does the confessor's power here extend to public impediments? On this question there is almost the same division of opinion as upon the power of the confessor in danger of death. Again, the opinion

---

[94] Code Com., 28 Dec., 1927; *AAS,* 20–61; *Digest,* I, p. 503.
[95] Cf. Payen, *De Matrimonio,* I, n. 674; V-C, *Epit.,* II, n. 312; Gasparri, *De Matrimonio,* n. 401.

that public impediments are included is probable,[96] provided of course
that they be occult "cases," i.e., occult in fact.

Casus Perplexus. Before the faculties now contained in canons
1043-1045 were given to Ordinaries, pastors, assisting priests, and confessors, a case could arise where the parties were in extreme necessity,
either in danger of death or when all was ready for the wedding
which could not be postponed without grave danger, and yet, where
not even the Ordinary, and much less the pastor or confessor, had
power to dispense. The term *casus perplexus* was appropriately applied
to such cases, especially where everything was ready for the wedding.
What was the pastor or confessor to do? Various solutions were proposed including the following: in case of an occult impediment the
confessor could declare, without disturbing the good faith of the
parties, that the impediment ceased to be binding because of *epikeia;*
the marriage could then be performed; and to settle all doubt,
a dispensation or *sanatio* was to be obtained later. Before the Code
this solution was called "safe in practice" by as high an authority as
Wernz, who cites for it St. Alphonsus, the Synod of Ostia under
Cardinal Monaco, and a plenary council of Latin America.[97] Since
the Code, many canonists assert that all need of applying such a solution has been done away with. Others hold that in an urgent case
where canon 1045 does not provide the necessary faculties, the *casus
perplexus* could still arise, and could legitimately be solved according
to the old principles.[98] Arendt proposes a case[99] which he solves on
the theory, not commonly admitted, that canon 1045 includes the power
to dispense from the *form* of marriage. If one declined to follow him
in this opinion, the case could still be solved as a *casus perplexus* upon
the principles that were applied before the Code.

CANON 1046. The pastor or the priest mentioned in canon 1044
shall as soon as possible notify the Ordinary of the place regarding
the grant of a dispensation for the external forum; and the dispensation must be recorded in the marriage register.

Recording the Dispensation. 1. The *pastor or the priest* mentioned
in canon 1044 must register the dispensation. Why is nothing said of

---

[96] See text, c. 1044, Powers of the Confessor, 3, and notes 86 and 87, this chapter.
Vermeersch-Creusen, in the late editions of the *Epitome*, I, n. 312, no longer admit the
power of the confessor for impediments public by nature, even if they are occult in fact.
[97] Cf. Wernz, *Ius Decretalium*, IV, n. 619, note 87.
[98] Cf. Vermeersch, in *Periodica*, Vol. 14, p. 122.
[99] Cf. *Periodica*, Vol. 16, p. 1*.

the confessor? Because the dispensation which he may grant will be in the *internal sacramental* forum, and hence is by no means to be recorded.

2. The dispensation for the *external forum* is to be registered in the parish matrimonial register, as is also the validation if it has taken place. In this case the marriage is also to be recorded in the baptismal register, if the parties or either of them were baptized in that parish; otherwise, notice of the marriage must be sent to the pastor of the church where the baptism was conferred (c. 1103, § 2).

3. The *notice to the Ordinary* is merely a disciplinary measure, to help the Ordinary to restrain abuses in so serious a matter. The notice is to be given as soon as possible, that is within three days.

CANON 1047. Unless the rescript of the Sacred Penitentiary provide otherwise, a dispensation from an occult impediment, granted for the internal non-sacramental forum must be registered in a book to be carefully kept in the secret archives of the Curia referred to in canon 379; nor is any other dispensation necessary for the external forum, even if the occult impediment afterward become public; but it is necessary if the dispensation was granted only in the internal sacramental forum.

State of the Question. This canon deals with registering dispensations granted for the *internal non-sacramental* forum. Such dispensations may be granted, not only by the Ordinary, pastor, or priest in virtue of canons 1043, 1044, or 1045, but also (whenever the impediment is occult but not connected with sacramental confession) by any priest acting in pursuance of a rescript from the Sacred Penitentiary. The question is how are such dispensations to be recorded.

Rules. 1. If the dispensation is granted in pursuance of a rescript of the Sacred Penitentiary, and is of such a nature that it must be kept secret even from the Ordinary, then the rescript itself will provide that no record is to be made even in the secret archive of the Curia; instead, a secret record will be kept by the Sacred Penitentiary itself. This is the rather exceptional practice which is referred to in the opening words of the canon.

2. Ordinarily, that is, in all cases where there is no special need of such extraordinary secrecy, although the dispensation, being for the internal forum, must not be recorded in the regular parish registers, it should be recorded in a special book to be kept in the secret archive of the Curia which is referred to in canon 379.

3. A dispensation for the *internal non-sacramental* forum, which has

been secretly recorded in either of these ways, will be good for the external forum in case the impediment afterward become public. This transfer to the external forum is effected by a simple official testimonial from the custodian of the secret register, that the dispensation was obtained and is of record.

4. A dispensation for the internal *sacramental* forum is not recorded anywhere, even secretly; consequently if the impediment afterward become public, a dispensation for the external forum will be required.

CANON 1048. If a petition for a dispensation has been sent to the Holy See, Ordinaries of places must not use their faculties, in case they have any, except as provided in canon 204, § 2.

Use of Faculties. This is a rule of courtesy and common sense. It in no way affects the validity of the dispensation. The rule here given is but an application of canon 204, § 2, which applies expressly to both ordinary and delegated jurisdiction.[100]

CANON 1049. § 1. In the case of marriages already contracted or to be contracted, one who has a general indult to dispense from some particular impediment, can, unless the indult itself expressly provides otherwise, dispense from it even if the same impediment is multiple.

§ 2. One who has a general indult to dispense from several impediments of different kinds, diriment or impedient, can dispense from the same even though they are public, when they occur in one and the same case.

Use of Dispensing Power Delegated by General Indult. An *indult* means an act of the superior granting the power; such power is always *delegated,* since it does not fulfill the definition of ordinary jurisdiction (c. 197). An indult is *particular* if it is granted for one or two cases or for a few determinate persons; otherwise it is *general.* The two rules of this canon declare that a *general* indult is good even when the particular impediment dispensed is multiple (cf. c. 1076, § 2), or when several impediments over which the power to dispense is granted, occur not separately but cumulatively in the same case, and this, even though they are public.

CANON 1050. If it happen that together with a public impediment or public impediments from which a person can dispense by virtue of an indult, there concur another impediment from which he cannot dispense, he must apply to the Apostolic See for all of them; if, however, the impediment or impediments from which he can dispense are

---

[100] Cappello, *De Matrimonio,* n. 247, and Payen, *De Matrimonio,* I, n. 700, limit this canon to delegated jurisdiction. *Contra,* Vermeersch-Creusen, *Epit.,* II, n. 314. All admit that the canon does not affect validity.

discovered after the dispensation has been obtained from the Holy See, he may use his faculties.

Notes. 1. This canon applies whether the indult is *general or particular.*

2. It affects only the *licitness,* not the validity, of the use of power.

3. It applies only to *public* impediments. When a person has power to dispense from an occult impediment, he may always use it notwithstanding the concurrence in the same case of other impediments over which he has no power.

4. But if a *public* impediment for which he has power concurs with another impediment (*public or occult*)[101] for which he has no power, he must apply to the Holy See for dispensation from all the impediments.

5. If he has already obtained from the Holy See the dispensation from the impediment over which he had no power, and then discovers in the same case other impediments, public or occult, over which he has power, he may dispense from them; he is not obliged to send the whole case back to the Holy See.

CANON 1051. By a dispensation from a diriment impediment, granted either in virtue of ordinary power or of power delegated through a general indult, not however by a rescript in particular cases, there is granted also *ipso facto* the legitimation of the children in case any have been already born or conceived by the parties who are being dispensed, with the exception, however, of adulterine and sacrilegious offspring.

Implicit Legitimation of Children. Children who are not born legitimate according to canon 1114 may be legitimated:

1. By an indult of legitimation from the Holy See;

2. By the subsequent marriage, or validation of the marriage, of the parents, according to canon 1116;

3. By the grant of a dispensation from a diriment impediment, as provided in this canon 1051.

Requisites. 1. The dispensation must be granted either in virtue of *ordinary* power (for example, by a Bishop or pastor in virtue of canons 1043–1045), or in virtue of delegated power granted by a *general* indult (for example by a Bishop or Vicar General in virtue of quinquennial faculties). If the dispensation or power to dispense is granted by a rescript in the particular case, it will not implicitly effect the legitimation of children.

---

[101] Cf. Payen, *De Matrimonio,* I, n. 703. *Contra,* V-C, *Epit.,* II, n. 314.

2. A child is called *adulterine* if it was conceived in adultery, that is, while either party was bound by the bond of another valid marriage; it is called *sacrilegious* if it was conceived by copula which was illicit because of the sacred order or solemn religious profession of one of the parties, even though they were validly married. Adulterine and sacrilegious offspring are not legitimated by the dispensation.

3. The legitimation takes place *ipso facto,* that is, upon the granting of the dispensation itself, independently of the subsequent marriage of the parties, even though the failure to follow up the dispensation by actual marriage be due to the fault of the parties.[102]

Questions. 1. Is implicit legitimation effected when a dispensation is given in a particular case by the Holy See? If the dispensation were given, even by a particular rescript, *in forma gratiosa,* the legitimation would follow.[103] The reason is that the Holy See acts in such a case by *ordinary* power, and the words of the canon denying such effect to a dispensation granted by particular rescript apply rather to rescripts from authorities inferior to the Holy See. If, however, the rescript from the Holy See were *in forma commissoria* (the usual case) it would not *implicitly* carry legitimation, though it might expressly grant it even though it were not asked.[104] The reason here is that the dispensation is granted, not by the Holy See, but by an inferior in virtue of a particular rescript.

2. What if the dispensation is granted, for example, by a pastor in virtue of power subdelegated to him by the Ordinary in accordance with the quinquennial faculties? If the subdelegation to the pastor was by a *particular* indult, legitimation would not be implicitly effected; but it would be if the subdelegation were by *general* indult, e.g., by a pagella of faculties which might be issued by a Vicar Apostolic to quasi-pastors in mission countries.

CANON 1052. **A dispensation from an impediment of consanguinity or affinity, granted for a certain degree of the impediment, is valid, even though there is in the petition or in the grant an error regarding the degree, provided the degree which really exists is inferior, or even though another impediment of the same kind, in an equal or inferior degree, has been concealed in the petition.**

Notes. 1. Note that this canon does *not* apply to the impediment of *public propriety.* Only consanguinity and affinity are mentioned.

---

[102] Cf. Payen, *De Matrimonio,* n. 711; Cappello, *De Matrimonio,* n. 291. *Contra,* Gasparri, *De Matrimonio,* n. 358.
[103] Cf. Cappello, *De Matrimonio,* n. 291.
[104] Cf. Payen, *De Matrimonio,* n. 713.

2. The implicit dispensation is good only for an impediment *of the same kind,* and of equal or inferior degree; for example, if the dispensation is asked and granted for consanguinity in the second degree of the collateral line (first cousins), and the actual impediment is consanguinity in the third degree, it is dispensed; or if, in addition to consanguinity in the second degree of the collateral line, for which dispensation is asked for and granted, there exists also consanguinity in the third degree, which is not mentioned, the latter impediment also is dispensed. But a dispensation asked and granted for consanguinity in the second degree is not good for affinity in the third degree, or vice versa.

3. The second degree *touching the first,* although it is classed as second degree (c. 96, § 3), is really not precisely equal to the pure second degree. Consequently it is very doubtful whether this canon would apply to a case where a dispensation from consanguinity in the second degree was asked, whereas the degree which alone existed, or which existed in addition to the one mentioned, was consanguinity in the second degree *touching the first.*[105] The same may be said of affinity in the second degree touching the first.

4. We have noted that, *for the application of this canon,* the dispensation must be asked for and granted for an impediment at least of the same kind as the one which really exists. But if the dispensation is asked for the impediment which really exists, and the grant of the dispensation is made, by mistake, for an impediment even of another kind, canon 47 would apply and the dispensation would be valid, provided that, in the judgment of the Ordinary, there were no doubt that the intention was to dispense from the actually existing impediment.

5. The rule of this canon was not in effect before the Code.[106]

CANON 1053. A dispensation granted by the Holy See from a marriage which was *ratum et non consummatum,* or a grant by the Holy See of permission to contract another marriage because of the presumed death of a former spouse, always carries with it a dispensation from the impediment arising from adultery with the promise of or attempt at marriage, in case such dispensation is needed, but by no means from the impediment mentioned in canon 1075, nn. 2 and 3.

---

[105] Cf. S. C. Sacr., 1 Aug., 1931; *AAS,* 23–413; *Digest,* I, p. 514. Cappello seems to suggest that such a dispensation might be valid: *"Hodie dubitatur num sit invalida,"* De Matrimonio, n. 277, 6.

[106] Cf. Rota, 13 Jan., 1921; *AAS,* 14–472; *Digest,* I, p. 504.

Implicit Dispensation From the Impediment of Crime. 1. The *reason* for this provision is that in both of the circumstances mentioned; first, when a marriage is dissolved by the Holy See as *non consummatum,* and secondly, when, after the long absence of a husband or wife, the other party finally obtains permission (from the Holy See) to contract another marriage on the morally certain presumption that the former partner is dead, *it may happen* that adultery with a promise of or attempt at marriage has intervened. This would create the impediment of crime mentioned in canon 1075, 1°, supposing that the conditions there mentioned were fulfilled; and yet, since such matters usually remain occult, the impediment might not be known, and, through ignorance, no dispensation would be asked. Hence, to prevent invalid marriages in these cases, the law gives an implicit dispensation.

2. It applies only to the *lowest degree* of the impediment of crime; the other degrees, in which homicide is involved, are by no means dispensed implicitly.

3. It applies in two distinct cases: (*a*) where the Holy See grants a dissolution of a non-consummated marriage (cf. c. 1119); and (*b*) where the Holy See, and not merely a Bishop (cf. discussion under canon 1069, question 1) grants permission to contract a new marriage because of the presumed death of the former partner.

CANON 1054. A dispensation granted from a minor impediment is not invalidated by any defect, whether of misstatement (*obreptio*) or of omission (*subreptio*), even though the only final cause stated in the petition is false.

Dispensation From Minor Impediments. 1. Minor impediments are those mentioned in canon 1042, § 2.

2. According to the general rules governing rescripts: *essential truth* of the recitals of the petition is a condition for validity (c. 40); what amounts to *want of essential truth,* either by omission or misstatement, is defined (c. 42); only essential *misstatement* will be fatal if the rescript contains the clause *motu proprio* (c. 45). But the canons cited all provide for the present exception in favor of dispensations from minor impediments.

3. This canon makes the extraordinarily liberal rule that *no omission or misstatement,* however important it may seem to be, invalidates a dispensation granted from a minor impediment.

4. Note that the *dispensation must have been granted from the*

existing impediment. If a dispensation is asked for and granted from a minor impediment of consanguinity, whereas the only existing impediment is a minor one of affinity, this latter impediment remains undispensed, not because the dispensation is invalidated, but because it cannot conceivably be construed so as to touch the case. Even canon 47 would not help here, because the needed dispensation was not even *asked*.

5. Canon 2361 provides that the Ordinary may punish fraud or falsehood committed in asking for any rescript from the Holy See or from the Ordinary of the place, without prejudice to the validity of the rescript.

CANON 1055. Dispensations from public impediments which are committed to the Ordinary of the petitioners are to be executed by the Ordinary who gave the testimonial letter or who forwarded the petition to the Holy See, even though the parties, at the time when the dispensation is to be executed, have left their domicile or quasi-domicile in his diocese and have removed to another diocese, never to return; but notice must be given to the Ordinary of the place where the parties intend to contract the marriage.

State of the Question. Dispensations from the Holy See for the external forum will usually be granted by rescript *in forma commissoria* to be executed by the Ordinary who forwarded the petition. It may happen that the parties in whose favor the dispensation is asked have in the meantime permanently left the diocese. In such a case, who is responsible for the execution of the rescript?

Principle. Such a change of residence does not affect the execution of the rescript. It is to be executed by the same Ordinary who asked for the dispensation notwithstanding the parties' change of residence; and notice is to be given to the Ordinary, not necessarily of their new domicile, but of the place where the marriage is to take place.

CANON 1056. With the exception of a small offering to defray the expenses of the chancery in dispensations for persons who are not poor, Ordinaries of places and their officials are forbidden — and any contrary custom is hereby reprobated — to exact any payment on the occasion of granting a dispensation, unless the faculty to do so has been expressly given them by the Holy See; and if they do exact anything they are bound to restitution.

Taxes and Expenses. 1. The *Holy See,* through the Sacred Penitentiary grants dispensations for the *internal* forum absolutely gratis. Dispensations for the *external* forum are subject to various moderate payments on the score of tax, alms, fees, expenses, etc., except in the case of the poor.[107]

2. *Ordinaries* may demand nothing on the occasion of granting a dispensation, except a moderate tax to defray the expenses of the chancery. In the case of the poor, even this is to be remitted.

CANON 1057. Those who grant a dispensation in virtue of power delegated to them by the Apostolic See must expressly mention the pontifical indult in the dispensation.

Mention of Apostolic Indult. This rule is called to the attention of Ordinaries also in the official notes attached to the formula of their quinquennial faculties.[108]

CASES AND QUESTIONS

1. Is an ordinary mutual engagement to marry valid at least in conscience if it is not executed according to the requirements of canon law? (C. 1017, § 1).

2. X, who intends to marry, knows that he is sterile and cannot have children. Even though sterility is not an *impediment* (cf. c. 1068, § 3), he wonders whether he can validly marry, since he cannot intend the primary end of marriage (c. 1013).

3. John and Mary have had an interview with their pastor preparatory to their marriage. The pastor asked Mary whether she had decided to marry John freely and of her own accord. She thought this a very strange question. John was somewhat put out that the pastor was not satisfied with his baptismal certificate, dated the day of his baptism in infancy. Could you explain the pastor's attitude to Mary and John? (Cf. *Digest,* II, p. 260, n. 7, p. 256, c).

4. A pastor, examining Anthony and Cordelia for a mixed marriage, gets a recent baptismal record from Anthony, but none from Cordelia, who says she was baptized a Methodist. The pastor marries them with a dispensation from mixed religion. Later it turns out that Cordelia was never baptized. Is the marriage valid? (C. 1070, § 1). What should the pastor have done? (C. 1021, § 1).

5. After the banns have been published twice, the pastor discovers that the diriment impediment of affinity (2nd degree, collateral line, cc. 97, 1077, § 1) exists between the parties. Can he get a dispensation from this impediment? (*Digest,* II, p. 33, n. 1). Should he go on with the publication of the banns? (C. 1031, § 2, 2°).

---

[107] Cf. Cappello, *De Matrimonio,* n. 290; Payen, *De Matrimonio,* n. 770.
[108] Cf. *Digest,* II, p. 30.

6. Thomas is only 19, but has finished high school and has a good position. He wants to marry, but his parents think he is too young and that the girl is not socially acceptable. What should the pastor do about this marriage? (C. 1034).

7. Martha's husband was in the tank service on the western front in 1944; he wrote home regularly until December of that year, was reported missing, and has not been heard of since. Some time after the close of the war he is still unaccounted for. Martha believes he is dead, but is not sure. Another man is urging her to marry him. May she do so? What must she do? (Cc. 1035, 1069; *Digest*, I, p. 508).

8. Are non-Catholics in general subject to diriment impediments of the Code? (Cc. 12, 87).

9. Whence do Bishops get their faculties to dispense from matrimonial impediments? (C. 1040).

10. The sole cause assigned in a petition for a dispensation from the Holy See existed at the time of the petition, but ceased to exist between the time when the rescript was given by the Holy See and the time when it was executed by the Ordinary. Is the dispensation valid? (Cc. 38, 41, 1054, 1042).

11. Where should a dispensation from a matrimonial impediment be recorded: (*a*) If given for the external forum? (*b*) For the internal non-sacramental forum? (*c*) For the sacramental forum? (Cc. 1046, 1047).

Readings:

O'Mara, *Canonical Causes for Matrimonial Dispensations*, Catholic University, 1935 (n. 96); Donovan, *The Pastor's Obligation in Pre-nuptial Investigation*, Cath. U., 1938 (n. 115); *Digest*, II, pp. 253–276; Cloran, *A Guide to the Use of the Instruction* (Newman Book Shop); Rice, *Proof of Death in Pre-nuptial Investigation*, Cath. U., 1940 (n. 123); Roberts, *The Banns of Marriage*, Cath. U., 1931 (n. 64); O'Keefe, *Matrimonial Dispensations: Powers of Bishops, Priests, Confessors*, Cath. U., 1927 (n. 45); *Tempus Ageneseos: De Opportunitate Instructionis Populo Tradendae* (Mahoney, in *Clergy Review*, Vol. 17, p. 525); *Ecclesiastical Review*, Vol. 101, pp. 9, 68 (on premarital physical examination); *Periodica*, Vol. 19, p. 90* (Cappello, on consanguinity in third degree collateral line touching the first: major or minor impediment); *Theological Studies*, Vol. 3, p. 333 (Ford: *Marriage: Its Meaning and Purpose*); *The Jurist*, Vol. 4, p. 628 (Decree of Holy Office on primary end of marriage); *Irish Eccl. Rec.*, Vol. 59, p. 270 (Fallon, on meaning of public impediment); Vol. 64, p. 67 (Conway, on causes for dispensation), p. 68 (Conway, on dispensations to *peregrini*).

CHAPTER XIII

PARTICULAR IMPEDIMENTS

Section 1. Impedient Impediments (cc. 1058–1066).

PRELIMINARY SURVEY

Simple Vows (c. 1058)
Legal Adoption (c. 1059)
Mixed Religion:
  Marriage Forbidden (c. 1060)
  Conditions for Dispensation (c. 1061)
  Prudent Effort to Convert Non-Catholic (c. 1062)
  Other Religious Ceremony Forbidden (c. 1063)
  Duties of Pastors (c. 1064)
Undesirable Marriages (cc. 1065, 1066)

CANON 1058. § 1. A marriage is rendered illicit by the following simple vows: of virginity, of perfect chastity, not to marry, to receive sacred orders, and to embrace the religious state.
§ 2. No simple vow renders marriage invalid unless such effect has been decreed for certain persons by special provision of the Apostolic See.

Simple Vows. A *vow* is a deliberate and free promise to God, of something good which is possible and better than its contradictory (c. 1307, § 1). It is *public* if accepted in the name of the Church by a lawful ecclesiastical superior; otherwise it is *private* (c. 1308, § 1). It is *solemn* if it is recognized as such by the Church; otherwise it is *simple* (c. 1308, § 2). All private vows are simple, even though they be *reserved* to the Holy See according to canons 1308 and 1309; but public vows may be simple or solemn. The vows taken in religious *orders* (as distinguished from *congregations*) of men and women, are solemn (c. 488, 2°), as is also the vow of chastity which is implied in the ordination to major orders, beginning with the subdiaconate. These are *diriment* impediments (cc. 1073, 1072). The present canon deals only with simple vows, *impedient* impediments.

Five Simple Vows. A vow, by its very nature, may exclude marriage directly or indirectly, absolutely or conditionally. For example, the vow *not to marry* excludes marriage directly and absolutely. The vows of *virginity* and of *perfect chastity* directly exclude the *use* of marriage, and hence exclude marriage itself conditionally, that is, unless the proximate danger of using it contrary to the vow can be securely removed. The vows *to enter religion* and *to receive major orders* exclude marriage indirectly and conditionally, inasmuch as their object is the assumption of a state of life which makes at least the *use* of marriage illicit. Consequently, *by the divine natural law* itself, these vows are *impedient* impediments to marriage, to the extent that marriage would be a direct violation of the vow, or would induce a proximate danger of its violation.[1] None of these vows is, by the natural law, a diriment impediment. The present canon declares them all, unconditionally, *impedient* impediments *by ecclesiastical law*.

Cessation of Impediment by Circumstances. We must now consider each of these vows separately.

1. The vow of *virginity* has for its object the exclusion of the *first complete act* of carnal pleasure, whether merely internal or also external, and whether otherwise licit, as in lawful wedlock, or otherwise illicit, out of wedlock. Virginity, considered as a virtue, consists of a material and a formal element. The material element is purely physical, and consists of physical integrity; the formal element is mental, and consists of the firm determination never to consent to venereal pleasure. These two elements together constitute formal virginity, which is the object of this vow. Virginity as a virtue is not lost by any violation of physical integrity, provided it be *involuntary,* for example, in a man by involuntary seminal emission, or in a woman by the involuntary destruction of the hymen. Any *voluntary* act of carnal pleasure destroys virginity; but if the act was merely internal, virginity is not irreparably destroyed; it is recovered when the sin is forgiven. If, on the other hand, a voluntary venereal act is consummated externally, virginity is irretrievably lost. The state of grace may be restored, but the flower of virginity is gone forever; the fulfillment of the *vow of virginity* has become impossible, and the obligation of the vow accordingly ceases.

2. The vow of *perfect chastity* excludes, not merely the first, but *every act of venereal pleasure,* internal or external, complete or incomplete, in or out of wedlock. Hence even after virginity has been

---

[1] Cf. Payen, *De Matrimonio,* I, nn. 827–829.

lost, the fulfillment of this vow remains possible for the future, and consequently the vow does not expire. The vow of perfect chastity taken in religion is public, but may be either simple or solemn; taken out of religion it is private and always simple, even when reserved as provided in canon 1309, that is, when taken unconditionally by one who has completed his eighteenth year.

3. The vow *not to marry* excludes directly the celebration of marriage. It does not render the use of marriage illicit, since that is outside the scope of the vow. If it has been violated by celebrating marriage, and that marriage is later dissolved by death, the impediment stands against any future marriage, for its fulfillment is not rendered entirely impossible by a single violation.

4. The vow *to receive a sacred order* has for its object the reception of the subdiaconate, diaconate, or priesthood. It is indirectly violated by marriage, since marriage makes its fulfillment *practically* impossible; but if the marriage is dissolved the vow will remain binding against any future marriage. Probably it does not render the use of marriage illicit after the marriage has been validly contracted.

5. The vow *to enter religion* remains a prohibitive impediment to marriage as long as its fulfillment remains possible. The impediment arises from a vow to enter either a religious order with solemn vows, or a religious congregation with simple vows, perpetual or temporary.

Principles. 1. The five simple vows above named are *prohibitive* impediments of *ecclesiastical* law. How far, and under what conditions they are also impediments by divine law, has been stated above.

2. No simple vow is a *diriment* impediment, unless this has been specially declared by the Holy See. The vows taken by Jesuit scholastics and brothers after the two years of noviceship (perpetual but simple vows), are a diriment impediment to marriage.[2]

Cessation of Vows. Vows cease or expire: by lapse of time, by substantial change in the matter of the vow, by failure of the condition under which the promise was made, by cessation of the final cause, by invalidation, commutation, and dispensation (c. 1311). It will be necessary to say a word on invalidation and dispensation.

Invalidation. A person who lawfully exercises dominative power over the will of one who made a vow can validly, and for just cause even licitly, render the vow null, so that the obligation will in no

---

[2] Cf. c. 1073, and Gregory XIII, *Ascendente Domino*, 25 May, 1584, n. 22; Gasparri-Serédi, *Fontes*, n. 153, Vol. I, p. 269.

case revive (c. 1312, § 1). Since no jurisdiction is required, this may be done by a religious superior, even a woman.

A person who has power, not over the will of the person who made the vow, but over its subject matter, can suspend the obligation for as long a time as its fulfillment involves any detriment to himself (c. 1312, § 2). This suspension of the obligation is sometimes called indirect invalidation; but it is only temporary.

Dispensation. Dispensation is an act of jurisdiction. Since it is done in the name of God, to whom the promise was made, it is always the act of an inferior, and hence a just cause is always required for the *validity* of the dispensation (c. 84). Vows may be dispensed as follows:

1. *Public* vows, temporary or perpetual, by the Holy See or by operation of law. An indult of secularization carries with it a dispensation even from perpetual religious vows as such, not however from the obligation of sacred orders (c. 640). Temporary religious vows are *ipso facto* dispensed upon dismissal from the religious society (c. 648).

2. *Private reserved vows,* by the Holy See (c. 1309).

3. *Private nonreserved* vows, for just cause, and provided the dispensation works no harm to any vested right of third parties, by Ordinaries of places (as to their own subjects anywhere, and as to strangers within their territory), by a superior of an exempt clerical religious society (as to the persons mentioned in canon 514, § 1), and by those to whom the Holy See has delegated the power to dispense (c. 1313).

CANON 1059. In those countries where the legal relationship arising from adoption renders marriage illicit according to the civil law, marriage is illicit also according to canon law.

Legal Adoption. As already stated, this is not usually an impediment to marriage in civil law. In the territory of Puerto Rico it is a *diriment* impediment (cf. c. 1080).[3]

CANON 1060. The Church everywhere most severely forbids the contracting of marriage between two baptized persons of whom one is a Catholic whereas the other is a member of a heretical or schismatical sect; and if there is danger of perversion for the Catholic party and the children, the marriage is forbidden also by the divine law itself.

Mixed Marriages. In common parlance in English any marriage of a Catholic with a non-Catholic is called a mixed marriage. In canonical

---

[3] Cf. Alford, *Ius Matrimoniale Comparatum*, p. 112. As to Massachusetts, Rhode Island, Connecticut, see note 58, preceding chapter.

literature, however, the term is used strictly of marriages between a Catholic and a validly baptized non-Catholic. The impediment which then exists is mixed religion, of which this canon treats. If the non-Catholic party is unbaptized, the impediment is disparity of cult, which is dealt with in canon 1070.

Mixed Religion. This prohibitive impediment exists by ecclesiastical law in every case where one of the parties is a Catholic and the other is validly baptized in a heretical or schismatical sect, even though he has abjured the sect without embracing the Catholic faith. If the baptism of the non-Catholic is doubtful, there certainly exists either the impediment of mixed religion or disparity of cult. The presumption is in favor of the validity of the baptism and of the marriage until the contrary is proved (cc. 1014, 1070); but the marriage is *certainly* forbidden *at least* by the impediment of mixed religion.

Membership in Atheistic Sect: Communism. The Code Commission has declared that "persons who belong or have belonged to an atheistic sect are to be considered, as to all legal effects, even those which concern sacred ordination and marriage, the same as persons who belong or have belonged to a non-Catholic sect."[4] Since Communism is undoubtedly an atheistic sect, this impediment would forbid the marriage of a Catholic with a baptized person who is a full-fledged member of the Communist party.

The Divine Law. The natural law itself renders all mixed marriages gravely illicit if they involve danger of perversion for the Catholic party *or* for the children. The word *et* in the canon must be understood disjunctively, for the principle of the natural law applies equally whether it be the spouse or the children, or both, whose salvation is endangered. Normally, and by the nature of mixed marriages, this danger exists; and as long as it is not removed the Church cannot grant a dispensation. To remove the danger, and to satisfy herself that it is removed, the Church requires certain conditions for the granting of the dispensation.

CANON 1061. § 1. The Church does not dispense from the impediment of mixed religion unless:

1° There are just and grave reasons therefor;

2° The non-Catholic party shall have given a guarantee to remove all danger of perversion from the Catholic party, and both parties shall have given guarantees to baptize and educate all the children in the Catholic faith alone;

---

[4] Code Com., 30 July, 1934; *AAS*, 26–494; *Digest*, II, p. 286.

3° There exists moral certainty that the guarantees will be fulfilled.
§ 2. The guarantees are as a rule to be required in writing.

Conditions for the Dispensation. Three conditions are named: just and grave reason; adequate guarantees; moral certainty that the guarantees will be fulfilled.

The *Cautiones* or Guarantees. 1. The promises or guarantees required by the Code are: on the part of the non-Catholic party the promise to remove all danger of perversion from the Catholic party; and on the part of both the promise to baptize and educate all the children in the Catholic faith and in no other. Some of the diocesan formulas are so worded that "all the children" means "all the children *hereafter* to be born of this union." Yet it may happen that minor children are living who were born either to these parties from a putative or invalid marriage, or to one of them from a former marriage with a different party now deceased. Should the *cautiones* include the promise to have these children also baptized and educated as Catholics? This question had been much discussed and had led to various opinions before the recent decision of the Holy Office which we shall cite presently. Gasparri held unhesitatingly that the promises extend to all children already born who are under the age of reason.[5] Vromant seems to have been alone in holding clearly the contrary view.[6] Others made various distinctions; several exempted from the scope of the promises at least the children already born to the non-Catholic party by a former marriage with a non-Catholic.[7] We have now an authentic reply from the Holy Office. The question was asked: "Whether the promises which must be given according to canon 1061, to have all children baptized and educated only in the Catholic Church, include only children to be born, or also children already born before the marriage." The reply was: "In the affirmative to the first part, in the negative to the second. *Et ad mentem:* the mind of the Sacred Congregation is this: although *per se* according to the canon cited, promises are not required as regards children already born before the celebration of the marriage, yet the parties to the marriage are by all means to be warned of their grave obligation under the divine law to see to the Catholic education also of children who are already born."[8]

2. Diocesan practice sometimes requires promises beyond those re-

---

[5] Gasparri, *De Matrimonio*, n. 451.
[6] Vromant, *De Matrimonio*, p. 134.
[7] Cf. Payen, *De Matrimonio*, I, n. 1126; *Ecclesiastical Review*, Vol. 90, p. 534; *Clergy Review*, 1934, p. 158; 1937, p. 465; *Ius Pontificium*, 1934, p. 232.
[8] Holy Office, 16 Jan., 1942, *AAS*, Vol. 34, p. 22; *Digest*, II, p. 286.

quired by the Code; for example, on the part of the Catholic party, to practice his religion faithfully and strive prudently to effect the conversion of his consort; on the part of the non-Catholic, the promise to adhere to the doctrine of indissolubility and the promise that in case of dispute the custody of the children shall be given to such guardians as to assure the fulfillment of the guarantees regarding their Catholic education; on the part of both, the promise that no other marriage ceremony shall take place, and that the parties will lead a married life in conformity with the teaching of the Church against birth prevention. Such requirements may serve a useful purpose, especially in exceptional cases, where they are regarded as necessary to establish the moral certitude as to the fulfillment of the promises required by the Code; but the validity of the dispensation could scarcely be made to depend upon them provided such moral certitude exists. Diocesan regulations requiring a number of instructions to be given to the non-Catholic party before a mixed marriage are quite common. It would seem advisable to put the guarantees in the form of a contract such as might favor their recognition and enforcement by civil law (see n. 5 *infra*).

3. The *cautiones* are *usually* required *in writing*. While this requirement is not absolute, it should always be met unless solid reasons approved by the Ordinary permit the acceptance of merely verbal promises.

4. The *cautiones* are necessary to the *validity* of the dispensation, *even in danger of death*. But the Holy Office has declared that promises given *implicitly* are sufficient for *validity*. "Although the Holy See has from time immemorial required, and now strictly requires that in all mixed marriages the fulfillment of the conditions be safeguarded by a formal promise *explicitly* demanded and given by both parties (cc. 1061, 1071), still the use of the faculty to dispense, whether it be ordinary or delegated, cannot be called invalid if both parties *at least implicitly gave the cautiones,* that is, if they placed acts from which it must be concluded and can be proved in the external forum that they were conscious of their duty to fulfill the conditions and that they manifested a firm purpose to perform that duty."[9]

5. It is often stated that these promises "do not hold in the civil courts." While it is true that the enforcement has been unsuccessfully

---

[9] The dispensation is invalid if given without any *cautiones;* Holy Office, 14 Jan., 1932, *AAS*, Vol. 24, p. 25; *Digest I*, p. 505; 8 June, 1932; *Digest*, II, p. 291. *Cautiones* given *implicitly* are sufficient for the validity of the dispensation; Holy Office, 10 May, 1941, *AAS*, Vol. 33, p. 294; *Digest*, II, p. 292.

sought in several cases, and that the courts are generally "neutral" where religion is concerned, yet these promises guarantee a right which, on the strength of legal precedents, should be recognized and which may yet be recognized even by the higher courts if properly presented in a strong case, especially if they are made in the form of a contract. A recent decision of the Domestic Relations Court of the City of New York declared it to be a clearly established rule of law that "an ante-nuptial agreement providing for the Catholic faith and education of the children of the parties, in reliance upon which a Catholic has thereby irrevocably changed the status of the Catholic party, is an enforceable contract having a valid consideration."[10]

6. Does the fact that the promises are *insincere when given* render the dispensation invalid? This question has been extensively debated. In our judgment the validity of the dispensation depends on the *moral certainty* of their fulfillment (in the mind of the Ordinary or pastor) rather than on their sincerity, an interior fact which *per se* does not register in the external forum.[11]

CANON 1062. The Catholic party is obliged to strive prudently for the conversion of the non-Catholic party.

This is an obligation of charity by the natural law, independently of the promises and of any canonical obligation.

CANON 1063. § 1. Even though a dispensation from the impediment of mixed religion has been obtained from the Church, the parties may not, either before or after the celebration of the marriage before the Church, apply also, either in person or by proxy, to a non-Catholic minister in his religious capacity, in order to express or renew matrimonial consent.

§ 2. If the pastor knows for certain that the parties intend to violate or that they have violated this law, he must not assist at their marriage except for the gravest reasons, on condition that scandal be removed, and after consulting the Ordinary.

§ 3. It is not forbidden, however, in case the civil law requires it, that the parties present themselves before a non-Catholic minister

---

[10] This noteworthy case is Ramon vs. Ramon, 34 N. Y. Suppl., 2nd series, p. 100, commented on in *The Jurist*, Vol. 3, p. 158. On the civil law aspects of the question we warmly recommend the thorough study by Rev. Robert J. White, *Canonical Antenuptial Promises and the Civil Law*, Catholic University, 1934, published also by the Dolphin Press, Philadelphia. See also O'Brien and O'Brien, *Antenuptial Promises in Restatement of Inter-Church-and-State Common Law*, in *The Jurist*, Vol. 6, p. 50.

[11] Cf. Nau, *Marriage Laws of the Code*, n. 71; Schenk, *Mixed Religion and Disparity of Cult*, 1929; Cath. U. Canon Law Studies, n. 51; *Ecclesiastical Review*, Vol. 91, p. 446; *Homiletic and Pastoral Review*, 1933, p. 742; *Irish Eccl. Record*, Vol. 69, p. 630; *Ius Pontificum*, 1933, p. 207; 1934, p. 270; 1935, p. 64, 191, 196. This entire question is well summarized by Boyle, *Juridical Effects of Moral Certitude in Prenuptial Guarantees*, C. U., 1942 (n. 150), p. 90 sq.

acting only as a civil officer, merely for the purpose of performing the civil act of marriage for the sake of the civil effects.

Civil Effects. In the United States the civil law everywhere recognizes pastors as empowered to officiate at marriages.[12] Consequently it is never necessary to go before a civil officer, and still less before a non-Catholic minister, to secure the civil effects of marriage.

Penalties. The Code itself provides no penalty for contracting marriage before a *merely civil officer* (judge, mayor, justice of the peace), though such a marriage would be invalid for want of form (c. 1094). But a Catholic marrying before a *non-Catholic minister* incurs excommunication (c. 2319). Whether and to what extent the provision of excommunication for this same case by the Third Council of Baltimore (n. 127) remains in effect, we shall discuss under censures.[13]

CANON 1064. Ordinaries and other pastors of souls:
1° Must deter the faithful from mixed marriages to the best of their power;
2° If they are unable to prevent them, must strive by all means to prevent their being contracted in violation of the laws of God and the Church;
3° After mixed marriages have been celebrated either in their own territory or elsewhere, must watch diligently to see that the parties faithfully discharge the promises which they have made;
4° In assisting at such marriages, must observe the prescriptions of canon 1102.

Duties of Ordinaries and Pastors. To deter the faithful from mixed marriages, it is necessary to make parents as well as young people understand the importance of unity of faith in the family. Judicious preaching on the subject is necessary and worth while; but thoroughgoing Catholic education and deep Catholic culture will be necessary to impart this conviction. A Catholic girl gaily announces her engagement to a non-Catholic, and *then* begins to think about his conversion. It is usually too late; she has already betrayed the fact that she does not regard it as of paramount importance.

The vigilance of pastors must include not only mixed marriages which have been celebrated in their own parish, but also those that

---

[12] Authorization is also required from the civil authority for a priest to assist at a marriage, in Hawaii, District of Columbia, Arkansas, Delaware, Kentucky, Maine, Massachusetts, Minnesota, Nevada, New Hampshire, Ohio, Oklahoma, Oregon, Rhode Island, Virginia, and Wisconsin; also in the *cities* of New York and Philadelphia. Cf. Alford, *Ius Matrimoniale Comparatum*, p. 247.
[13] See p. 880.

were celebrated elsewhere, as to the fulfillment of the promises by the parties who are now their parishioners.

In the celebration of mixed marriages, the priest wears no sacred vestments of any kind, such as surplice or stole, but may wear a cassock; all sacred rites are forbidden (c. 1102, § 2), but it is not forbidden to say the Our Father; the priest must ask and receive the parties' expressions of mutual consent according to canon 1095, § 1, 3° (c. 1102, § 1); such marriages may not without special permission of the Bishop be celebrated in the church (c. 1109, § 3), nor in a private house (c. 1109, § 2). Hence, *per se,* the proper place is the parish rectory.

CANON 1065. § 1. The faithful must also be deterred from contracting marriage with persons who have either notoriously abandoned the Catholic faith, even without having gone over to a non-Catholic sect, or have notoriously become members of societies which are condemned by the Church.

§ 2. The pastor must not assist at the above-mentioned marriages without having consulted the Ordinary, who may in view of all the circumstances of the case permit him to assist at the marriage, provided there be a grave reason and the Ordinary in his prudent discretion judge that adequate measures have been taken to insure the Catholic education of all the children and the removal of danger of perversion from the other party.

Undesirable Marriages. This canon and the next enumerate certain marriages at which a pastor should not assist without grave reason and the permission of the Ordinary.

Notorious Abandonment of the Faith. This means more than mere neglect of religious duties. It designates one who professes that he is no longer a Catholic, or openly refuses obedience, not merely to some particular law or decree, but to the Church in general, or habitually sneers at or rejects Catholic doctrine, etc. What happiness can a Catholic expect from marriage with such a person? Grave reasons are indeed required to permit it; but they are not sufficient. It must moreover appear to the satisfaction of the Ordinary that *adequate* measures have been taken to insure the Catholic education of the children and the removal of the danger of perversion. Otherwise the marriage is forbidden by the *divine* law.

Condemned Societies. Notorious membership in condemned societies has the same effect. These societies are in general those which either openly or secretly undermine civil or ecclesiastical authority as such. They include all degrees and forms of masonry and all secret revolutionary societies. The Knights of Pythias, Odd Fellows, and

Sons of Temperance have been condemned as intrinsically evil, though not under censure.[14] In case of doubt whether a society is condemned or not, the criterion proposed by the Third Council of Baltimore (n. 247) may be applied, namely, if the society requires secrecy to be kept even from ecclesiastical authority, or if it exacts a promise or oath of blind obedience, it is to be considered as condemned. If the doubt persists after investigation, we are of opinion that the principle of probabilism would have no application to permit embracing a state of life which *probably* involves grave danger of perversion.

CANON 1066. **If a public sinner or one who is notoriously under censure refuses to go to sacramental confession or to be reconciled to the Church before marriage, the pastor must not assist at his marriage unless there be a grave reason, regarding which he should if possible consult the Ordinary.**

Public Sinners and Persons Notoriously Under Censure. A public sinner is a sinner publicly known to be such, e.g., one whose life is a public scandal, or who is *publicly known* to have been away from the sacraments for years. Persons notoriously under censure are, in this connection, those who are publicly known to be excommunicated or under an interdict. Since marriage is a sacrament, an excommunicated person is forbidden to receive it (c. 2260, § 1); and since it is a sacrament of the living, it should be received in the state of grace. Hence a public sinner should receive sacramental absolution, and an excommunicated person should be reconciled to the Church by absolution from the censure before contracting marriage. Yet, since the danger of perversion in these cases is less acute than in marriages with apostates or members of condemned societies, the prohibition is less severe. The pastor may assist if there is a grave reason, and should "if possible" consult the Ordinary. The priest is neither the recipient nor the minister of the sacrament; hence there is no question of direct sacrilege on his part.

Section 2. Diriment Impediments (cc. 1067-1080)

PRELIMINARY SURVEY

Want of Age (c. 1067)
Impotence (c. 1068)

---

[14] Cf. Sabetti-Barrett, *Theol. Mor.*, p. 1031.

Bond of Prior Marriage (c. 1069)
Disparity of Cult (cc. 1070, 1071)
Sacred Order (c. 1072)
Solemn Religious Vows (c. 1073)
Abduction (c. 1074)
Crime (c. 1075)
Consanguinity (c. 1076)
Affinity (c. 1077)
Public Propriety (c. 1078)
Spiritual Relationship (c. 1079)
Legal Relationship (c. 1080)

CANON 1067. § 1. A man before completing his sixteenth year, and a woman before completing her fourteenth, cannot contract a valid marriage.

§ 2. Although a marriage contracted after the aforesaid age is valid, yet pastors of souls should try to deter young people from marrying before the age at which, according to the received customs of the country, marriage is usually contracted.

Age of Capacity. 1. By the *natural law,* there is no direct requirement as to age; what is required is *mental capacity for matrimonial consent* (cf. cc. 1081, 1082).

2. The *civil law* of our states is extremely diversified. Not only the minimum age for marriage, but the effect of marriage under that age, varies. Hence the laws of the various states must be consulted.[15]

3. The *Code* fixes, for baptized persons, the age of sixteen and fourteen years (complete according to c. 34, § 3, 3°) for males and females respectively. This is irrespective of puberty; hence even before puberty, if these ages were attained, marriage would be valid, though cohabitation would be forbidden. As to parental consent see canon 1034.

4. *Before the Code* (May 19, 1918) the age of capacity was fourteen for males, twelve for females, *nisi malitia suppleat aetatem.* The meaning of this clause was that if a girl attained puberty before completing her twelfth year, or a boy before completing his fourteenth, matrimonial capacity was also acquired. *Malitia* simply meant physical capacity or puberty, together with sufficient knowledge of the object of the contract.

Question. In a marriage between a Catholic and an unbaptized person (with a dispensation from disparity of cult), both are of canonical age, but the unbaptized party is under the minimum age according to state law. Is such a marriage valid? This question is answered in our discussion of canon 1016.[16]

---

[15] A very good summary, of course subject to change, is given by Alford, *Ius Matrimoniale,* n. 89.

[16] See p. 407.

CANON 1068. § 1. Impotence, antecedent and perpetual, whether on the part of the man or the woman, whether known to the other party or not, whether absolute or relative, invalidates marriage by the law of nature itself.

§ 2. If the impediment of impotence is doubtful either in law or in fact, the marriage is not to be hindered.

§ 3. Sterility neither invalidates marriage nor renders it illicit.

Impotence and Sterility. In general *impotence* may be defined as *incapacity for the marital act, sterility,* as *incapacity for generation.* Even though persons be perfectly capable of normal copula, generation may be impossible because of some condition adverse to it in one or both parties. In such a case one or both are *sterile;* but sterility neither invalidates the marriage nor renders it illicit. On the other hand, if they are incapable of the marital act itself, they are *impotent.*

In practice the distinction is not always easy to make. The matter remains difficult even after the explanation which we intend to give; but if the subject is left shrouded in obscurity and sheathed in vague general terms it is unintelligible. To understand this matter a brief explanation of the process of generation is indispensable.

1. *Generation* consists of two series of events which must be distinguished one from the other: the *human act* of generation, and the *natural process* of generation. The former is a human act, capable of being controlled by the will at least in its beginning; the other is a physiological process which cannot be directly controlled by the will.

a. The *human action* of generation consists in copula, which is best defined according to its physiological elements: the penetration of the vagina by the male organ and the emission of true semen within it.

b. The *natural process* of generation includes the whole series of co-ordinated natural functions which take place within the organism of man and woman, and which are designed by God for the procreation of offspring. There is the preparatory physiological process, the development of the germ cells, the *ova* in the ovaries of the female, the sperm in the testicles of the male. Supposing copula to have taken place during a period of fertility, the sperm migrates from the vagina through the uterus and on through the fallopian tubes of the female. In the meantime a female germ cell or *ovum* has been released from the ovary and is destined to pass down the tube in the opposite direction. Under the proper conditions a sperm cell meeting

an *ovum* somewhere en route will penetrate it and unite itself to it
to the exclusion of all other sperms. This union of the two germ cells
is called fecundation. A human body in embryo has been produced;
the soul, immediately created by God, has been united to it; a new
living human being has been generated and is in process of development. The embryo will descend the fallopian tube and attach itself
to the inner surface of the uterus where it develops to maturity and
from which the human child is delivered, normally through the vagina,
at birth.[17]

Without going into minute detail it is evident that throughout this
beautifully co-ordinated process, almost at every stage and in every
part of it, there may occur an accident or a defect which will prevent
generation. The sperm may not encounter a ripe ovum, either because
the woman is permanently sterile or because copula has taken place
during a sterile period when no ova are being released by the ovaries.
Pus germs resulting from infection may attack and kill the sperm or
the ovum before fecundation can take place. The organs which are
essential to generation in the woman may be diseased, useless, or
entirely lacking through deformity or as a result of surgery. In all
these cases generation will fail, and if the condition is permanent,
generation is impossible. Sterility certainly exists.

Is there also impotence? The classical definition as incapacity for the
marital act has always been understood and explained by a formula
which we must confess fails to provide a ready practical solution for
all doubtful cases. That formula was that impotence exists only when
the parties are incapable of "copula which is in itself suitable for
generation." The difficulty is to determine when copula is *in itself*
suitable. For example, can it be called "in itself suitable for generation"
when the woman is incapable of producing ova? When she lacks
ovaries entirely? When even the fallopian tubes and the uterus have
been removed by the so-called "Porro operation"? In view of the
development of the doctrine on impotence and the decisions thereon,
we may *now* say that in all these cases the marital act is *in itself*
suitable for generation, and that the failure of generation is due to
defects not intrinsic to the marital intercourse itself. Hence these are
at least probably cases of sterility and not of impotence. But let us
admit that it would not be easy to come to this conclusion confidently
by the bare application of the classical formula.

A practical criterion, not substantially different from the above, is
this: whatever hinders *only the natural process* of generation constitutes

---

[17] For a good, brief summary, see Nau, *Marriage Laws,* pp. 81–85.

sterility only; whatever hinders the *human action* of generation, that is marital copula, constitutes impotence. Even this criterion will leave some cases difficult and doubtful; but in view of the fuller knowledge of physiological processes which we now have as compared with earlier authors, this formula seems more helpful than any other at the present time. It is stated and explained by several modern authorities,[18] and has been applied in recent decisions of the Rota.[19]

Divisions of Impotence. 1. Impotence may be *certain* (both in law and in fact), or *doubtful* (either in law or in fact).

2. It is *antecedent* if it existed before the marriage; *subsequent* if it arose after it.

3. It is *perpetual* if it cannot be cured by means which are licit and not dangerous to life; otherwise it is *temporary*. Note that impotence may be *perpetual,* and yet may be cured by a dangerous operation and so actually cease; so too, it may be *temporary* in the canonical sense and yet actually persist for a lifetime.

4. It may be *natural* or *accidental; congenital* or *acquired.*

5. It is *absolute* if it prevents marital intercourse of the person with *all* others; it is *relative* if it prevents it with a *certain* person or persons.

6. It is *organic* if due to an organic or physical defect; *functional* if due to defective co-ordination or functioning. *Functional* impotence will usually not be permanent.

Cases and Questions. 1. A man who is *deprived of both testicles* is impotent. This is admitted by all. The reason is not merely that true semen is wanting, but that copula, for such a person, can satisfy neither the primary nor the secondary ends of marriage, and hence cannot be considered true marital intercourse.[20]

2. The *absence of both ovaries* in a woman is sterility, not impotence. The reason for the difference in these two cases is that the product of the testicles, semen, is an essential element in the *human action* of generation, whereas the formation of the ova pertains entirely to the *natural process.* Some theologians however, following Antonelli, would call the woman impotent in this case.[21]

3. *Double vasectomy* (or *fallectomy* in the case of a woman) means the cutting or ligation of both *canales deferentes* in a man, or of both fallopian tubes in a woman. In the former case it prevents the emission

---

[18] Cf. Cappello, *De Matrimonio,* nn. 341–343.

[19] Cf. cases briefly reported in *Digest,* II, pp. 287–289.

[20] Cf. Vermeersch, *De Castitate,* n. 46, near end.

[21] Nau, *Marriage Laws,* p. 86, calls this opinion of Antonelli obsolete. We think it certainly is so. Cf. Ayrinhac-Lydon, *Marriage Legislation,* n. 120.

of semen in the *act of copula;* in the latter case it merely prevents any passage of the ovum or of the sperm through the fallopian tubes, and thus interferes only with the *natural process of generation.* Accordingly it renders a woman sterile only, not impotent. The case of a man is more difficult to solve. If the vessels were merely ligated and so closed without being severed, the condition would not be "perpetual" in the canonical sense, because it could be remedied surgically without danger to life. But the practice now is to cut them and bury the ends in other tissues; and after such an operation, the restoration of male fertility by remedial surgery, according to recent studies of the question, offers slight hope of success.[22] The condition must therefore in that case be regarded as "perpetual." But does it constitute impotence? It must be admitted that there is very weighty authority in favor of an affirmative answer. Among the first to contest this conclusion was Vermeersch, who does not admit that impotence certainly exists in this case. He contends that the *act of copula* can be considered as *in itself* substantially complete *even without true semen,* since the secretion of Cowper's glands and other fluids takes its place to the extent of fulfilling the secondary though not the primary end of marital intercourse. An increasing number of authorities may now be cited for this view, and hence, both on reason and authority, the impotence of the permanently vasectomized male must be considered as seriously doubtful.[23]

4. If the *vagina is so small* that *no penetration* whatever is possible (absolutely or relatively), it is a case of impotence absolute or relative.[24]

---

[22] Cf. Clifford, *Marital Rights of the Sinfully Sterilized,* in *Theological Studies,* Vol. 5 (1944), p. 157.

[23] There is great variance both of opinion and expression on this question.

a. For certain impotence may be cited: Gasparri (*De Matrimonio,* I, p. 470), Cappello (*De Matr.,* nn. 375, 377 "impotentia videtur certa"), Merkelbach (*De Castitate,* p. 16), Wouters (*Manuale Theol. Mor.,* II, n. 774), et al., besides several decisions of the Rota (summarily reported in *Digest,* II, p. 287, n. 5). A *very recent* decision of the Rota (25 Oct., 1945) confirms this view. It is reported in full in *Periodica,* Vol. 35 (1946), p. 5.

b. Against certain impotence: Vermeersch (*Theol. Mor.,* IV, n. 41, and *Periodica,* Vol. 24, p. 43*), Jorio (*Theol. Mor.,* III, 2, n. 1178), Gemelli (in *Scuola Cattolica,* Nov. 1911), Arendt (in *Ephem. Theol. Lov.,* Vol. 9, p. 63), Gennaro (*Theol. Mor.,* Vol. 7, p. 53, note 1), Creusen (*Epit. I. C.,* II, n. 339), Payen (*De Matr.,* I, n. 988 "longe *probabilius* est impotens"), et al.

The entire question is the subject of a doctoral dissertation by Rev. Edward H. Nowlan, S.J., which appeared in *Theological Studies,* Vol. 6 (1945), pp. 392–427.

[24] But cf. Genicot, *Theol. Mor.,* II, n. 484, 3, as to the use of marriage if this condition is discovered only after the marriage. Genicot holds that impotence in this case is only "more probable."

5. Various causes may produce the *entire occlusion of the opening between the vagina and the uterus.* Among these causes, though not all operating in the same way, are complete retroversion or retroflexion of the uterus, deformities, abnormalities, or defects which close the passage, and finally the excision of the uterus itself, leaving the vagina intact but closed at the upper end. These conditions give rise to very difficult cases and it would be dangerous to state a rule of thumb by which all could be solved. Reserving the case of the excised uterus for later discussion and applying to all the others the criterion stated above, we should say that they are cases of sterility rather than impotence, because the defects in question hinder the *natural process* of generation but not the *human action* of intercourse. This is in fact the prevailing opinion.[25] Two competent specialists, however, have taken a contrary view.[26]

6. The *excision of the uterus* together with the ovaries and the fallopian tubes was first done by Doctor Edward Porro of Pavia, in 1876, and is sometimes called the Porro operation. Does the absence of the ovaries or of the uterus, or both, amount to impotence or only to sterility? This is disputed both on authority and intrinsic reasons. Several very respectable authorities hold that these are all cases of impotence;[27] probably a greater number, equally important, deny that any of them are.[28] Four decisions of the Sacred Congregation of the Council are cited in favor of the former opinion, that impotence exists; three decisions of the Holy Office and one of the Sacred Congregation of the Sacraments, to the contrary. A brief analysis of these eight official declarations will clarify the discussion.

a. *For impotence,* four decisions are cited, but in all four of the cases decided by the S. C. Conc.,[29] not only the ovaries and uterus, but *also the vagina* was affected. In the first case the vagina was missing, in the second it was shortened and impenetrable, in the third it was

---

[25] Cf. Gasparri, *De Matrimonio,* citing a decision of the Supreme Signatura, of 27 June, 1931, which confirmed two concordant decisions of the Rota, reported in *Digest,* II, p. 288, n. 4.
[26] Vermeersch, in *Periodica,* Vol. 14, p. (54), contended that it is a case of impotence; but this opinion does not appear in the later editions of his works; cf. *De Castitate,* nn. 46–49. Arendt, in *Periodica,* Vol. 16, p. 70*, evidently approves the former opinion.
[27] Antonelli, Bucceroni, Noldin, Wernz, et al.
[28] Gasparri, D'Annibale, Aertnys, Genicot, Ballerini, De Smet, Tanquerey, Vermeersch, Cappello, Payen, et al.
[29] *In Salernitana,* 9 Aug., 21 March, 27 June, 1863; *In Verulana,* 24 Jan., 22 June, 1871; *In Albinganen.,* 17 Aug., 7 Sept., 1895; *In Monasterien.,* 18 March, 16 Dec., 1899.

partly missing, in the fourth it was so abnormal as to interfere with intercourse itself. Hence these decisions do not prove impotence even where both the uterus and the ovaries are missing, *provided the vagina is intact.*[30]

b. *Against impotence* the four decisions are as follows: (1) The Holy Office (3 Feb., 1887), in the case of a woman who had lost both ovaries, replied after mature and long consideration that the marriage was not to be hindered; (2) in the case of a woman who had lost both ovaries and the uterus, the Holy Office (23 July, 1890) gave the same decision; (3) the same decision was reached (31 July, 1895) in the case of a girl who had lost both ovaries; (4) the S. C. Sacr., in a case similar to the last, gave the same answer (2 Apr., 1909).

We must conclude that, where either the uterus or the ovaries, or both, are missing, provided the vagina is intact, impotence is at least very seriously doubtful, hence practically nonexistent as an impediment.

7. What is the effect of *subsequent* impotence? It cannot, of course, impair the validity of the marriage after the event. As to the use of marriage: (*a*) As long as there is any reasonable hope of a substantial fulfillment of the marital act, it may be attempted. (*b*) If there is no hope, the parties must abstain from acts which would expose either to the proximate danger of pollution. (*c*) If perfect copula is impossible, it is probably licit though true semen be wanting, or though the semen can be deposited only *ad os vaginae,* without penetration. These acts must be carefully distinguished from the same acts in a marriage where the impotence was antecedent and perpetual.

8. What if impotence which was canonically antecedent and perpetual is cured by a dangerous operation after the marriage? The impediment disappears, but the marriage remains invalid until validated according to law.

9. What is to be said of the "triennial experiment" allowed by the old canon law to determine the fact of impotence? This had grown obsolete even before the Code; since it is not mentioned in the Code, it must be considered as suppressed according to canon 6.[31]

Doubtful Impotence. If the impediment of impotence is doubtful either in law or in fact, the marriage is not to be hindered.

1. The *reason* probably is the extreme difficulty of directly solving doubts of law or fact regarding this impediment. To settle the con-

---

[30] The same distinction is supported by recent Rota decisions. Cf. *Digest,* II, p. 288.
[31] Cf. Cappello, *De Matrimonio,* n. 373.

sciences of her children in these obscure and difficult cases, the Church declares that in *all* doubt (probable and prudent, of course) the natural right to marry shall prevail, even though this impediment is of divine law. This rule is not the same as that which is applied to other impediments of the natural law.[32]

2. This rule has some *limitations*. (*a*) Before marriage, the doubt of law or fact should be carefully investigated in the *effort* to reach a theoretically certain conclusion. (*b*) If the doubt persists, the *other party* to the proposed marriage *should be informed* of the doubt.[33]

Is Venereal Disease an Impediment to Marriage? This is a moral rather than a canonical question. The Code says nothing about it, but the natural law does. We must admit that, unless disease results in impotence, it does not render marriage *invalid;* but a person who is afflicted with a terrible and highly contagious disease, such as syphilis, is *forbidden by the natural law* of charity to marry *without informing the other party* of his condition. The prohibition is grave because of the proximate danger, not to say the moral certainty, of grave harm to the other party. The same reason applies to the use of marriage.[34] This prohibition of the natural law is not based on eugenic reasons but on the law of charity. It proves that the Church does not encourage the marriage of diseased persons promiscuously. The Encyclical, *Casti connubii,* condemns the extreme proposals of eugenics, especially sterilization of persons who are naturally fit for marriage upon the suspicion that they would bring forth defective offspring; but it also teaches that even such persons are sometimes to be dissuaded from entering marriage. Nowhere does it defend the right of a person to marry while afflicted with contagious disease, nor deny the right of the state to enact reasonable health regulations, so long as the natural right to marry is not impaired. Vermeersch, in his catechetical analysis of the Encyclical, puts the question: "Admitting that the state has no right to forbid marriage *permanently,* can it forbid it *temporarily* to persons who, for a certain period, would be sources of infection to the persons they might marry?" And he answers: "The state could exercise such power, at least by putting itself in agreement with the competent

[32] We confess something less than complete satisfaction with the reasons assigned by some learned authors who seem to put this impediment on the same footing with other impediments of divine law. Cf. Payen, *De Matrimonio,* I, n. 1012; Aertnys-Damen, *Theol. Mor.,* II, n. 715. Implicitly confirming our view, cf. Cappello, *De Matrimonio,* n. 202. See also discussion under c. 1035, p. 427.

[33] Cf. Genicot, *Theol. Mor.,* II, n. 487.

[34] Cf. Arregui, *Summarium,* n. 243.

authority, which, in the case of baptized persons, is the Church."[35] Unfortunately the laws recently enacted in several states[36] requiring health certification as a condition for the issuance of the marriage license, do not recognize this limitation upon the power of the state. We have therefore felt obliged to condemn them on principle.[37] Such laws are moreover open to several grave practical objections.[38]

CANON 1069. § 1. One who is bound by the bond of a prior marriage, even though it was not consummated, invalidly attempts marriage, without prejudice however to the privilege of the faith.

§ 2. Even though the former marriage be invalid or dissolved for any reason, it is not therefore allowed to contract another until the nullity or dissolution of the former shall have been established according to law and with certainty.

The Bond of a Former Valid Marriage. This, of course, is a diriment impediment by the natural and positive divine law. It makes no difference whether the prior marriage was consummated or not. There is one exception, the privilege of the faith, which will be dealt with under canons 1120–1127.

Presumed Death of Former Spouse. Dissolution of the prior marriage by death leaves the surviving partner free to contract another marriage; but there is often difficulty as to the *proof of death*. In some cases strict proof is impossible, and yet the circumstances may be such that ecclesiastical authority can conclude with moral certainty on the basis of presumptions that the party is really dead. The practice in these cases (both as to proof and presumptions) is governed by an Instruction of the Holy Office of 13 May, 1868, which has since been repeated and applied in a number of cases. For the direction of Ordinaries who may have such cases, it lays down the following rules:

1. *Mere lapse of time,* or a presumption of death according to the civil law, is insufficient.[39]

2. *Official documentary proof* of death should be sought.

3. If this is not available, the testimony of *two witnesses* who knew the deceased, who know the fact of his death, and agree as to its circumstances, should be obtained.

4. In default of these, *one first class* witness may suffice.

---

[35] Cf. Vermeersch, *What Is Marriage,* p. 55, n. 126.
[36] Illinois, New York, New Jersey, etc.
[37] Cf. discussion under c. 1016, p. 406, note 23.
[38] Cf. Nau, *Marriage Laws,* n. 19.
[39] According to the old English common law a man *absent and unheard of for seven years* was presumed to be dead.

5. *Hearsay evidence,* that is, evidence of statements made by persons not now present, may suffice, provided the statements were made *tempore non suspecto* at a time when they would have had no apparent motive for making the statement unless it were true.

6. Next, *presumptions* may suffice to produce moral certainty of death. Here all the circumstances must be carefully weighed; not merely the duration of the absence, but the personal circumstances of the parties, their relations before and during the absence, possible reasons other than death, which might explain the disappearance, etc.

7. *Rumors* of the person's death, if proved to have been current and to have no other reasonable cause, may produce moral certainty.

8. Finally, *notices in the papers,* with all the circumstances considered, should be looked for as furnishing their share of evidence.[40]

Questions. 1. Who has the right to decide these cases?

a. The *pastor* who is to assist at the second marriage can do so, even without consulting the Ordinary, if the death of the former spouse is *proved* by the evidence mentioned in numbers 2, 3, or 4, above.

b. The *Ordinary,* without the intervention of the defender of the bond, may decide the matter if on prudent consideration of all the evidence according to the remaining paragraphs of the Instruction he is *morally certain* of the party's death. This is explicitly stated in paragraph 11 of the Instruction.

c. If the Ordinary cannot, even by the application of these rules, arrive at moral certainty, the matter must be referred, with all the available evidence, or at least a careful summary thereof, to the *Sacred Congregation of the Sacraments.*

2. What is the canonical effect of permission by the Holy See to contract the second marriage? It has two effects: it carries with it an implicit dispensation from the impediment of crime in the lowest degree, should that impediment happen to exist (ç. 1053); and it renders the second marriage *licit.* The validity of the second marriage depends entirely on the question of fact whether the former spouse was actually dead at that time. The decision even of the Holy See in this matter is merely a fallible decision on a concrete question of fact. If it should turn out to have been mistaken, the second marriage is and remains invalid. The permission to marry again is in no sense a dispensation.

---

[40] A number of recent cases are reported in *Digest,* I, pp. 508–511, and II, p. 289. The text of the Instruction of the Holy Office is in Gasparri-Serédi, *Fontes,* n. 1002, IV, p. 306. Cf. Rice, *Proof of Death in Pre-Nuptial Investigation,* Cath. U., 1940.

Declaration of Nullity of Former Marriage. If the former marriage was for any reason *null,* it should not stand as an obstacle to a new union; but its nullity must be proved and a declaration of nullity obtained. In this respect the former marriage will fall into one of three distinct classes.

1. If it was null for *want of form* (cf. c. 1094) no judicial procedure whatever is required, nor even the intervention of the defender of the bond. The whole thing is settled by the Ordinary himself or by the pastor after consulting the Ordinary, in the preliminary investigation prior to the celebration of the marriage.[41]

2. If the prior marriage was null because of one of the *impediments mentioned in canon* 1990 (namely, disparity of cult, sacred order, solemn vow, existing bond, consanguinity, affinity, or spiritual relationship), and if the impediment is proved from certain, authentic, and unexceptionable documents, whereas the want of a dispensation appears with equal certainty from any source, then the declaration of nullity can be given by the Ordinary without the formalities of a trial, but with summons to the parties and with the intervention of the defender of the bond.[42]

3. In *all other cases* the formalities of a trial are required: two concordant decisions for nullity, not necessarily consecutive; and the marriage is permitted after the lapse of ten days from the announcement of the second judgment if no further appeal has been taken.[43]

CANON 1070. § 1. A marriage contracted by a nonbaptized person with a person who was baptized in the Catholic Church or who has been converted to it from heresy or schism, is null.

§ 2. If a party at the time of the marriage was commonly regarded as baptized, or if his or her baptism was doubtful, the marriage must be regarded as valid according to canon 1014, until it is certainly established that one of the parties was baptized and that the other was not.

Disparity of Cult. 1. If there is danger of perversion either to the Catholic party or to the children, this impediment is of *divine law,* and cannot be dispensed from until the danger is removed. But in

---

[41] Cf. Code Com., 16 Oct., 1919; *AAS,* 11–479; *Digest,* I, p. 810.

[42] See c. 1990; the *Instruction on Matrimonial Procedure,* S. C. Sacr., 15 Aug., 1936, Art. 226; *AAS,* 28–313; *Digest,* II, p. 526; Code Com., 16 June, 1931; *AAS,* 23–353; *Digest,* I, p. 811; and Letter of Ap. Del. U. S., 23 Sept., 1938; *Digest,* II, p. 531. The Code Com. has declared that the process under c. 1990 is judicial, and that it applies only to the cases there mentioned; *AAS,* 36–94; *The Jurist,* Vol. 4, p. 627.

[43] See c. 1987, and the same Instruction, Art. 220; *Digest,* II, p. 524.

this aspect it is a *prohibitive* impediment only, since it cannot be shown that such a marriage is invalid by divine law.

2. It is a *diriment impediment of ecclesiastical law*, whether the danger exists or not (cf. c. 21).

3. The removal of the danger is a *condition for the dispensation* from the ecclesiastical law. The means of removing the danger are the same as those prescribed for mixed religion (c. 1071).

Scope of Impediment. 1. *Before the Code* this diriment impediment existed in all marriages where one party was validly baptized (even in heresy or schism) and the other not.

2. *Since the Code* it exists only in marriages where one party is unbaptized and the other is "baptized in the Catholic Church, or converted to it from heresy or schism." The clause "baptized in the Catholic Church" designates a baptism which formally commits the person baptized to the external communion of the Catholic Church. It is the *finis operantis* which must be considered. This will usually be determined by the intention of the minister of the sacrament, unless it is certain either from the intention of an adult subject or of the parents of an infant. The case is obvious where a child is presented to a Catholic priest to be baptized, or where an adult receives formal baptism in the Catholic Church. A doubtful case arises where an infant of non-Catholic parents is baptized by a Catholic priest or layman *contrary to law;* (canons 750–751 outside danger of death, permit such baptism only on certain conditions: the consent of at least one of the parents, provision for the Catholic education of the child, etc.). If a child has been so baptized and has been educated outside the Catholic faith, he is not bound by this law. At least the impediment is doubtful. In practice, recourse should be had to the Holy See.[44] But where a child of non-Catholic parents was baptized *in danger of death* (therefore, quite *according to law*) by a Catholic doctor, but was raised in infidelity and then, after the Code became effective, married an unbaptized person, the marriage was declared invalid because of the impediment.[45] The Code Commission has decided that the impediment applies to persons who were baptized in the Catholic Church, even though they were born of non-Catholic parents and were educated outside the Church.[46] The fact that a person baptized in the Catholic Church afterward abandoned it would not exempt him

---

[44] Cf. Cappello, *De Matrimonio,* n. 412.
[45] Cf. S. C. Prop. Fid., 1 Apr., 1922; *Digest,* I, p. 511.
[46] Code Com., 29 Apr., 1940; *AAS,* 32–212; *Digest,* II, p. 290.

from this law. Canon 1099, § 1, 1°, regarding the form of marriage, explicitly states that members of the Latin Church are bound by the form "even though they afterward abandoned the faith." Although that explicit declaration is wanting in the present canon, it must be implied on the general principle that heresy or schism does not exempt a Catholic from his obligations (c. 87).

Doubtful Baptism. 1. *Before the Code* if a person whose baptism was doubtful (and remained doubtful after investigation) married a person, who was certainly unbaptized, the marriage was regarded as invalid. For at that time the impediment applied to validly baptized heretics, and the presumption *in favor of the validity of baptism* was controlling.[47]

2. *Since the Code,* the presumption *in favor of the validity of marriage* is controlling in all doubtful cases. Hence in all the following cases the marriage is presumptively valid: (*a*) the marriage of *two Catholics,* even though doubt exists as to the validity of the baptism of one of them; here the presumption in favor of baptism agrees with that in favor of marriage; (*b*) the marriage of *a Catholic with a heretic* whose baptism is doubtful; here again both presumptions weigh on the same side; (*c*) the marriage of *two doubtfully baptized persons;* here again the two presumptions support each other; (*d*) the marriage of a *doubtfully baptized Catholic* with a person who is *certainly unbaptized;* here the presumption in favor of valid marriage overrides the presumption in favor of baptism; the result in this case would have been different before the Code.

3. Where *the marriage occurred before the Code and the question of its validity arises after the Code,* which rule is to be followed? The Holy Office, in 1936, applied the pre-Code presumption in favor of the validity of baptism to a marriage which had taken place before the Code, and declared it invalid for disparity of cult.[48]

The rule of canon 1070, § 2 is a *mere presumption* which yields to contrary proof. It suffices in marriages which have been *already contracted* as long as there is no certain proof to the contrary, but it does not insure the objective validity of the marriage. Hence if there is question of a marriage *to be contracted,* and there is doubt as to the baptism of the non-Catholic party, a dispensation from disparity of cult should be obtained *ad cautelam.*

4. The dispensation from disparity of cult no longer carries with it

---

[47] Cf. *Collectanea S. C. Prop. Fid.,* II, n. 1536.
[48] Holy Office, 15 May, 1936; *Digest,* II, p. 290.

implicitly (as it formerly did) dispensation from other impediments. (See *Digest,* I, p. 512; II, p. 291.)

5. For determining the validity of baptism in non-Catholic sects, much useful information is given by Goodwine, *Statistics on Baptism as Observed by Religious Bodies in the United States of America,* in *The Jurist,* Vol. 5, p. 285.

CANON 1071. The prescriptions laid down in canons 1060–1064 regarding mixed marriages must be applied also to marriages against which the impediment of disparity of cult exists.

Dispensation Affects Validity of Marriage. Note that in the case of disparity of cult, if the dispensation is for any reason invalid (for instance, if the *cautiones* are not given, or are given without the moral certainty of their fulfillment) the marriage itself is invalid. It is different, of course, in mixed religion, which is merely a prohibitive impediment.

Question. Among the canons here included by reference is canon 1063, forbidding a non-Catholic *religious* ceremony. The penalty for the violation of *that* canon is excommunication (c. 2319, § 1, 1°). But that canon itself deals with marriages where the dispensation from mixed religion, not disparity of cult, was obtained. Does the same penalty apply where the dispensation was from disparity of cult? This is disputed; while the affirmative opinion is far more probable, the contrary is extrinsically probable also, and hence the parties would probably not incur the excommunication in this case.[49]

CANON 1072. Clerics who are in sacred orders attempt marriage invalidly.

Sacred Order. 1. *Sacred orders* are the subdiaconate and higher orders (c. 949).

2. The diriment impediment is of *ecclesiastical law* only. In its present form it dates from the Second Council of the Lateran, A.D. 1139; it was confirmed by the dogmatic definition of the Council of Trent.[50]

3. The *reasons* for thus safeguarding the celibacy of the higher clergy are the same as for celibacy itself, namely: the state of virginity is in itself more perfect, a celibate clergy is more effective, enjoys greater respect and authority, and follows the example of Christ and the Apostles, and the teaching of the Fathers of the Church.

4. The *condition* for this impediment is the prior valid and free reception of a sacred order, with knowledge of the obligation of celibacy. Freedom in receiving orders is presumed until the contrary is juridically proved (cf. cc. 132, 214). The order must also have been

---

[49] Cf. Cappello, *De Censuris,* n. 369, 4.   [50] *Sess.* XXIV, *de sacr. matr.,* can. 9.

received with *knowledge* that it entails the obligation of celibacy; for the Church would not, indeed could not, impose such an obligation on one who is ignorant of it. It would be incorrect to say that ignorance *excuses* from this law (cf. c. 16); but it undermines one of the essential conditions of the impediment. Knowledge is presumed to have existed. Today it would be practically impossible to prove ignorance.

Questions. 1. Can a *minor* cleric marry? Yes, validly and licitly; but he thereby falls *ipso facto* from the clerical state (c. 132, § 2).

2. What happens if a *sacred* order is received *after* a valid marriage? Under the present discipline this is an extremely unlikely case. A married man may not receive any order (c. 987, 2°). It is true that this is merely a prohibition which might be dispensed from and which, even if disobeyed, would leave the order *valid*. A dispensation would not be given without the consent of the wife and other suitable conditions. If a sacred order were received validly by a married man, without a dispensation, even though it were done in good faith, he could not exercise his order (c. 132, § 3). On the other hand, if it were done validly and licitly, with the consent of the wife, the man would thereby give up his right to the use of marriage. A famous case may serve to illustrate this question. Cornelia Peacock, a non-Catholic American girl born in Philadelphia, married Pierce Connelly, an Episcopalian minister. After the marriage both parties became converts to the Catholic faith, and although the marriage had been blessed with children, she became conscious of a vocation to the religious life, and he, as he thought, of one to the priesthood. By mutual consent, provision being made for the children, each followed the new vocation. Connelly was ordained a priest, but later apostatized and appealed to the English courts for the custody of the children. Mrs. Connelly, who had embraced her new and higher vocation with his full consent, remained faithful to it. She had no obligation to return to him because by the voluntary and deliberate reception of sacred orders he had given up his right to the *use* of marriage, though the marriage, of course, remained valid.[51]

3. In general what is the discipline of the *Oriental* Church? Clerics may marry before receiving the diaconate, and thus men already married may go on to the higher orders while continuing their married life. Bishops, however, must be celibates, and celibate priests are preferred for certain missions, for example, among the Greek Ruthenians in the United States and Canada.[52]

---

[51] Cf. St. Thom., 2ª 2ᵃᵉ, q. 88, art. 7, 11.   [52] See *Digest,* I, pp. 10, 33.

4. What is the practice as to *dispensation* from the impediment of sacred order? *"Raro, rarius, rarissime, numquam."* That is, it is *rarely* given from the subdeaconship, *more rarely* from the deaconship, *most rarely* from the priesthood, *never* from the episcopacy. Yet from the deaconship and subdeaconship it can be given even by a pastor in virtue of canons 1044 and 1045. It is not included without explicit mention in the sentence of deposition, degradation, or reduction to the lay state. Great national catastrophes have at times made general dispensations necessary, such as those given in England by Julius III in 1554, and in France by Pius VII in 1801. But Benedict XV and Pius XI expressed very unyielding views on this matter. (See *Digest,* I, p. 120; II, p. 579.)

5. The *penalty* for a major cleric attempting marriage is excommunication simply reserved to the Holy See, which is incurred equally by the guilty partner (c. 2388, § 1); and degradation for the cleric if, after warning, he fails to amend. Offices held by clerics guilty of this crime are vacated by tacit resignation, that is, by operation of law (c. 188, 5°).

CANON 1073. Likewise marriage is invalidly attempted by religious who have pronounced either solemn vows or vows which by special provision of the Holy See are endowed with the power of invalidating marriage.

Solemn Religious Profession. 1. Religious vows are *solemn* if they are so recognized by the Church (c. 1308, § 2). These are usual in religious orders as distinguished from congregations (c. 488, 2°).

2. The effect of solemn religious profession on a valid marriage already *contracted but not consummated,* is to dissolve the bond of the marriage (c. 1119). But a married person is not admitted to religion without very special provision (c. 542, 1°).

3. Its effect on a *subsequent* attempt at marriage is to make it invalid.

4. *Simple* religious profession does not have this effect, except by special privilege of the Holy See, which has been conferred on the simple profession in the Society of Jesus.[53] Never does simple profession dissolve a previous non-consummated marriage.

5. This impediment is now recognized by the almost unanimous consensus of the authorities as of ecclesiastical law only, though St. Thomas thought differently.[54]

---

[53] E.g., for the Society of Jesus, Const. of Gregory XIII, *Ascendente Domino,* 25 May, 1584; *Fontes,* n. 153, Vol. I, p. 269.

[54] Cf. Cappello, *De Matrimonio,* n. 449; St. Thom., *Suppl.,* q. 53, a. 2; *in IV,* D. 38, q. 1, a. 3, sol. 3.

Constituent Elements. The solemn religious profession must be a *valid* one.

1. The elements of valid religious profession are named in canon 572. It must have been preceded by a *valid novitiate*.

2. The conditions for a valid novitiate are enumerated in canons 542 and 555, in addition to those required by the approved constitutions.

Dispensation. 1. That the Holy See *can dispense* from this impediment is now beyond doubt. The dispensation from the obligation of the vow as such is a dispensation only in the wide sense, as explained under canon 1040, since this obligation arises from divine law and is nondispensable as long as the vow remains in effect. But the Roman Pontiff can relax the vow and so *indirectly* relax the obligation. As for the impediment as such, namely, the invalidating effect attached to the vow, the dispensation is direct and is an exercise of jurisdiction.

2. Because of this distinction, a grave cause is required for the validity of the dispensation from the obligation of the vow; whereas a dispensation from the impediment as such, if given by the Holy See, requires a grave cause for licitness but not for validity.[55]

3. The effect of a dispensation granted by indult depends entirely on the terms of the rescript. It may include a dispensation also from the other two religious vows, poverty and obedience, or it may not. It may be limited to the particular marriage in question, or be so general as to be good also for a different marriage, or even a second one.[56] A dispensation from solemn vows, given in virtue of canons 1043–1045, would in our judgment be limited in its effect to the particular marriage in question. This follows, we think, from the purpose of these canons, which is to provide faculties for use in a particular emergency.

Solemn Profession After Valid Marriage. 1. If the marriage has been consummated, it remains unaffected by the religious profession, except that the use of marriage will have been voluntarily and finally relinquished.

2. If the marriage was not consummated, it is dissolved by solemn profession (c. 1119).

3. No married person, man or woman, can *validly* enter the novitiate (c. 542, § 1); hence for a valid religious profession a papal dispensation from this law would have to be obtained; it is not granted without the consent of the other party.

---

[55] Cf. Cappello, *De Matrimonio*, n. 453.
[56] Cf. Cappello, *De Matrimonio*, n. 454.

Penalty. The penalty for marriage after solemn profession is excommunication simply reserved to the Holy See; it is incurred also by the guilty partner (c. 2388, § 1).

CANON 1074. § 1. Between the abductor and the woman who has been abducted with a view to marriage, there can be no marriage as long as she remains in his power.

§ 2. If the woman, upon being separated from the abductor and placed in a safe and free place, consents to have him for her husband, the impediment ceases.

§ 3. As regards the nullity of marriage, the violent detention of a woman is regarded as equivalent to abduction; that is, when a man, with a view to marriage, violently detains a woman in the place where she is staying or to which she has freely come.

Violent Abduction or Detention. 1. The elements of this impediment are: *either* violent *abduction* from a safe to an unsafe place, or violent *detention* in an unsafe place; violent, in the sense that the woman is unwilling to go or to remain, at least for the purpose of marriage; and the abduction or detention must be with a view to marriage. The impediment exists against the man who is trying to force the marriage, whether the abduction or detention be done by him in person or by his servants or agents.

2. This impediment is of ecclesiastical law only. Before the Council of Trent it did not exist as such, but the elements which now constitute it were then considered as evidence of force and fear invalidating marriage (cf. c. 1087). From the Council of Trent to the Code, the impediment existed as regards abduction only; the inclusion of detention dates from the Code.[57]

3. The impediment does not cease by the mere fact that the woman freely consents to the marriage. Her consent may be entirely free, yet the marriage will be null, not for want of consent but because of the impediment. The impediment ceases without a dispensation only when the woman consents, after having been brought to a safe place apart from the abductor. When such an impediment has existed it will be prudent, even after it has ceased, not to assist at the marriage without consulting the Ordinary.

4. Dispensation is included in the faculties of canons 1043–1045. However, circumstances such as to justify this dispensation would be *extremely* rare.

CANON 1075. The following persons cannot validly contract marriage:

---

[57] Cf. Conc. Trid., *Sess.* XXIV, *de ref. matr.*, cap. 6.

1° Persons who, during the existence of the same lawful marriage, have consummated adultery together and have mutually promised each other to marry, or have attempted marriage even by a mere civil act;

2° Those who, likewise during the existence of the same lawful marriage, have consummated adultery together, and one of whom has killed the lawful spouse;

3° Those who, even without committing adultery, have by mutual co-operation, physical or moral, killed the lawful spouse.

The Impediment of Crime. This unsavory subject has the additional merit of being quite complicated. A summary outline of the three degrees must suffice.

First Degree: Adultery With Promise of or Attempt at Marriage.

1. Adultery here means *consummated* adultery, and *formal on both sides,* that is, with knowledge on the part of both parties of the same existing valid bond of marriage. Since guilty knowledge is an element of the crime, it is probable that even crass ignorance would excuse from it (cf. c. 2229).

2. There is moreover required either a *promise of marriage* or an *attempt at marriage* during the existence of the same bond which is violated by the adultery.

3. The *promise* may be before or after the adultery, but if before, it is essential that it be unrevoked by either party at the time the adultery takes place. It must be sincere, mutual, exteriorly manifested and accepted during the existence of the bond of matrimony. It must be absolute, to the exclusion probably even of a condition which has been verified during the existence of the bond. Its object must be to marry validly after the death of the lawful spouse. It is disputed whether the impediment exists if the promise was made at a time when at least one of the parties was ignorant of the existence of the bond which was later violated by the adultery. As long as the negative opinion is probable, it may be followed in practice (c. 15).

4. The *attempt* at marriage must be a sincere mutual expression of matrimonial consent *de praesenti,* with knowledge on the part of both parties of the existing bond. But if one party was ignorant of the bond at the time of the attempt, but learned of it afterward and continued the adulterous union, the impediment is incurred. The attempt and the adultery must both take place during the existence of the bond. Persons divorced from a valid marriage, who marry again during the life of their former partner, and consummate the second so-called marriage, incur this form and degree of the impediment of crime;

(we are supposing *formal adultery on both sides,* the partner in the second marriage knowing that the former husband or wife is still alive). However, if one of the parties, in good faith, holds the heretical opinion that a civil divorce gives the right to remarry, the adultery would not be formal, and the impediment would not be incurred. Cf. Nau, *Marriage Laws,* n. 79, note 12, citing Chelodi, *Ius Matrimoniale,* n. 93, 2.

Second Degree: Adultery and Murder Without Conspiracy. 1. *Adultery* must be *consummated* and *formal* on both sides with regard precisely to the same existing bond of marriage which is violated by the murder.

2. The *murder* is here supposed to be effected by only one of the parties; (if both parties co-operate in this, you have the third degree). It makes no difference whether the murderer be the physical or moral cause of death, provided he is the efficacious cause (for example, morally, by command, advice, or persuasion which is proved to have been really efficacious), nor whether it be his own or the other party's lawful partner who is killed. The killing must not only be intentional but done *with the intention of contracting marriage* with the other party afterward. This will be presumed in the external forum if adultery and murder are proved. It is commonly held that this intention (to marry the other party) must be *manifested exteriorly;* but it is disputed whether it must be manifested *to that party.* As long as this requisite is solidly probable, it may be held that the impediment does not exist without it. A special question arises where an interval of time elapses between the placing of the efficacious cause of death, whether physical or moral, and the death itself, if the adultery takes place during that interval. Of course, the adultery must take place before the actual death, for after that it is not adultery, the bond having been dissolved. But the question is, is it necessary that the adultery take place before the cause of death has been placed (for it is at that moment that the guilt of murder is incurred). The common opinion is that this is not necessary; but there are both reason and authority on the other side, hence a *dubium iuris;* practically, therefore (c. 15), the impediment is not incurred if the adultery takes place only after the efficacious cause of death has been placed.

Third Degree: Murder by Conspiracy: 1. In this degree, adultery is not required.

2. The *murder* of the lawful spouse (of either party) must have been done by the mutual efficacious co-operation, physical or moral, of both parties, with the intention not only of killing the lawful spouse, but

of afterward marrying each other. It is held by some, against the almost common opinion, that this intention to marry must be entertained by both parties, and that it must moreover be manifested exteriorly and mutually, though not necessarily in explicit written or spoken terms. Because of this *dubium iuris* the impediment practically does not exist without this mutual manifestation. But in the external forum such manifestation will be presumed from the circumstances of the killing, unless the contrary is proved.

Multiplicity of the Impediment of Crime. It is multiplied *ratione delicti* if two lawful spouses are murdered; it is multiplied *ratione matrimonii* if adultery formally violates two existing bonds of marriage, both parties to the crime being lawfully married to third parties and mutually known to be so. The extent of the multiplicity is difficult to determine, but need not be stated provided the essential circumstances are expressed in the petition for the dispensation.

Does This Impediment Affect Unbaptized Persons? We must distinguish times and persons.

1. If one party is baptized and is guilty of adultery with a promise of or attempt at marriage with an unbaptized person, the impediment is incurred directly by the baptized person and is binding on both when they later wish to marry (c. 1036, § 3).

2. If both are unbaptized and complete all the elements which constitute any degree or form of the impediment before their conversion, and then one or both are baptized, no impediment is incurred.

3. The same is probably true in a similar case where some of the elements are done before and others after the conversion of the party or parties.

4. If one party is baptized and is guilty (either alone or in complicity with the other party) of murder of the lawful spouse, the impediment is incurred, though the other party was unbaptized. But if the baptized party is guiltless of the murder, no impediment is incurred by either party — not by the baptized party because he or she was not guilty, nor by the other because he or she is not directly subject to the ecclesiastical law.

It comes to this: Unless at least one of the parties was baptized at the time when he or she was guilty of *all the constituent elements* of some form or degree of the impediment, it is not incurred.

Dispensation. 1. The *first degree* is *implicitly* dispensed whenever the Holy See dissolves a sacramental non-consummated marriage or grants permission to marry again because of the presumed death of a former spouse (c. 1053).

2. *Explicit* dispensation *can be given* for all degrees; it is more easily given for the first degree, particularly if there has been no scandal; in the second or third degree, where the murder is publicly known, there is no recorded case of a dispensation having been granted.[58]

CANON 1076. § 1. In the direct line of consanguinity, marriage is invalid between all the ancestors and descendants, legitimate or natural.

§ 2. In the collateral line, it is invalid up to the third degree inclusive, but with the understanding that the matrimonial impediment is multiplied only as often as the common ancestor is multiplied.

§ 3. Marriage must never be allowed if there exists any doubt that the parties may be related by consanguinity in any degree of the direct line or in the first degree of the collateral line.

Consanguinity. 1. The *relationship* and its two *lines* and various *degrees* have been explained under canon 96.

2. It constitutes a *diriment impediment* in all degrees in the direct line, and up to the third degree inclusive in the collateral line. Before the Code, the diriment impediment included the fourth degree of the collateral line.

3. The impediment is *certainly of divine law* as to the first degree of the direct line, *probably* also as to the other degrees. In the collateral line, it is *probably* of divine law as to the first degree, certainly of ecclesiastical law as to the others.

Multiplicity. 1. *Before the Code,* this impediment was multiplied not only when the persons were descended from more than one independent common ancestor, but also when they were descended from the same common ancestor by distinct lines of descent.

2. *Under the Code,* consanguinity is multiplied *only when the common ancestor is multiplied.* For this purpose, in the usual case, only the *first* or *proximate* common ancestor is considered. For example, the father and mother (both considered as one) are one proximate ancestor common to a brother and sister of the full blood; in this case the grandparents are not considered as additional common ancestors. If they were, all consanguinity would be multiplied indefinitely. Remote common ancestors are considered as multiplying consanguinity, only if they are reached by the two parties by distinct lines, and not by both parties by the same line through the first common ancestor. (See illustration *a, infra.*)

---

[58] Cf. Donohue, *The Impediment of Crime,* Cath. U., 1931; cases in *Digest,* II, pp. 293–295.

3. It will be seen that multiple consanguinity under the rule of the Code *can happen* in several ways: (*a*) when a man marries a woman who is related to him; (*b*) when two persons related to each other (for example, two brothers) marry two other persons who are related to each other (for example, two sisters); (*c*) when a man marries successively two sisters (or a woman marries two brothers) and has issue by each.

ILLUSTRATIONS

a. John and Mary, first cousins, marry. Their daughter Anne is related by multiple consanguinity (in the second and third degrees of the collateral line) to her cousin Thomas. Thomas and Anne have as common ancestors, Titus and Luke.

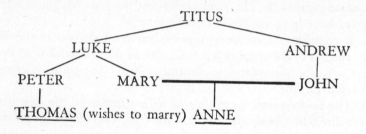

b. Francis and Charles, brothers, respectively wed Florence and Cecile, sisters. The descendants of one couple will be related by multiple consanguinity to those of the other. Martha and George have as common ancestors, Lucius and Caius.

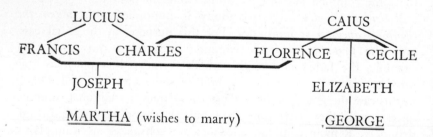

c. Brutus successively married two sisters, Cleo and Andromeda, and had issue by each. The descendants of the first marriage will be related by multiple consanguinity to those of the second. Mark and Caroline have as common ancestors, Brutus and Edward.

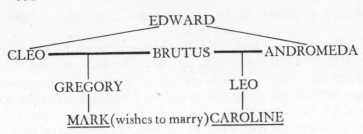

Dispensation. 1. A dispensation is *never* granted when the impediment is *probably of divine law,* for example, the first degree of the collateral line (brother and sister) or remoter degrees of the direct line.[59]

2. Very special reasons and a personal recommendation by the Ordinary are required in the case of uncle and niece, aunt and nephew, that is, the second degree of the collateral line touching the first.[60]

3. The third degree of the collateral line, even when mixed with the second, is a minor impediment (c. 1042, § 2, 1°), and as such rather easily dispensed.

Unbaptized persons are bound by those degrees of the impediment which are of divine law. But if the marriage has already been performed, and there is no grave scandal, the parties upon conversion need not be separated unless the impediment of divine law is *certain. In dubio standum est pro valore matrimonii* (c. 1014).[61]

CANON 1077. § 1. Affinity in the direct line in any degree invalidates marriage; in the collateral line it invalidates it up to the second degree inclusive.

§ 2. The impediment of affinity is multiplied:
1° As often as the impediment of consanguinity from which it arises is multiplied;
2° When marriage is successively repeated with a blood relative of a deceased spouse.

Affinity. 1. The nature of this relationship has been explained under canon 97; its lines and degrees are exactly the same as those of the consanguinity on which it is based.

2. As a diriment impediment it is entirely of ecclesiastical law, ex-

[59] Cf. Code Com., 3 June, 1918; *AAS,* 10–346; *Digest,* I, p. 513.
[60] Cf. S. C. Sacr., 1 Aug., 1931; *AAS,* 23–413; *Digest,* I, p. 514.
[61] Cf. Gasparri, *De Matrimonio,* n. 708; Wahl, *The Matrimonial Impediments of Consanguinity and Affinity,* Cath. U., 1934.

tending to all degrees of the direct line and to the second degree inclusive of the collateral line.

3. *Before the Code* both the *basis* and the *scope* of this impediment were different from what they now are. The *basis* was not a valid marriage but carnal copula in or out of wedlock, which produced affinity between one of the parties and the blood relatives of the other. The scope was different, for, besides all degrees of the direct line, it extended also to the fourth degree inclusive of the collateral line, if its basis was licit intercourse, and to the second degree of the same line if its basis was illicit intercourse.

Multiplicity. As we saw under canon 97, this impediment is based on two concurrent elements, a valid sacramental marriage, and a blood relationship between one party to the marriage and other persons. The multiplication of either element multiplies the impediment. If the consanguinity from which the affinity arises is multiple, the affinity will be multiple to exactly the same extent on that ground. If, on the other hand, the consanguinity is simple and has already furnished the basis for simple affinity resulting from one marriage, and now the surviving partner of that marriage marries a relative of the deceased spouse, the affinity is multiplied. *Before the Code* the impediment of affinity became multiple from four sources; but that matter is not only complex but obsolete.[62]

Dispensation. Since this impediment is of ecclesiastical law it can be dispensed in any degree even in the direct line. However, *in the direct line, when the marriage from which the affinity arose had been consummated,* the dispensation is rare. Formerly it was never given, and it is still one of the most difficult of ecclesiastical impediments to dispense from, being among the two exceptions to canons 1043–1045. But there are modern instances in which this dispensation was given. In the *collateral line,* affinity is rather easily dispensed from. In the second degree of the collateral line it is a minor impediment (c. 1042, § 2, 2°).

The case of Henry VIII is interesting in this connection. His first wife, Catherine of Aragon, was the widow of his deceased brother Arthur, so that a dispensation from affinity in the first degree of the collateral line was necessary for the marriage (supposing Catherine's first marriage to have been consummated), and had been obtained. When Henry later wished to marry Anne Boleyn, he contended

---

[62] Cf. Cappello, *De Matrimonio,* n. 532.

among other things that his marriage to Catherine was invalid on the ground that the impediment of affinity was of divine law and that therefore dispensation from it was beyond the power of the Pope. Joyce, however, writes: "Though it was notorious that the union (between Arthur and Catherine) had never been consummated, the King had perjured himself on the subject, and his testimony had been accepted as basis for the divorce."[63]

Questions. 1. Does affinity arise from a so-called legitimate marriage between unbaptized persons? Although the Church does not legislate for infidels she could easily make the impediment applicable to them should either party afterward receive baptism; and the question is, has she done so? We discussed it under canon 97, and found some difference of opinion among canonists, and a *dubium iuris;* hence the impediment does not apply.

2. John, a widower who has a daughter by his first marriage, marries Mary, a widow who has a son by her first marriage. Later Mary's son wishes to marry John's daughter. Is there affinity here? No. Affinity exists *"only* between the man and the blood relatives of the woman, and between the woman and the blood relatives of the man" (c. 97, § 2).

CANON 1078. The impediment of public propriety arises from an invalid marriage, whether consummated or not, and from public and notorious concubinage; and it invalidates marriage in the first and second degree of the direct line, between the man and the blood relatives of the woman, and *vice versa.*

Public Propriety. The relationship between a man and a woman which creates this impediment between one of them and the relatives of the other, is twofold, or rather alternative: *either* an *invalid marriage,* consummated or not, *or public and notorious concubinage.*

1. *Invalid marriage* means an apparent contract between man and woman which has at least the appearance of marriage, but is invalid. A so-called civil marriage, where a Catholic is concerned, is held not to have even the appearance of marriage, and hence does not create this impediment, in the absence of actual cohabitation.[64]

2. *Public and notorious concubinage* must be defined. Concubinage means a cohabitation between a man and a woman, established on a more or less durable basis without marriage. Since there is question of misconduct (a crime in the canonical sense), the terms must be defined according to canon 2197. A crime is public when it is either

---

[63] Cf. Joyce, *Christian Marriage,* p. 544.
[64] Cf. Code Com., 12 March, 1929; *AAS,* 21–170; *Digest,* I, p. 516.

already generally known or is committed under such circumstances that one must conclude it will easily become generally known (c. 2197, 1°). It is notorious, either in law or in fact. It is notorious in law after a judgment of a competent court which has become *res iudicata,* or after a confession in open court according to canon 1750 (c. 2197, 2°). It is notorious in fact when it is publicly known and was committed in such circumstances that no maneuver can keep it secret and no legal defense can excuse it (c. 2197, 3°). Such then must be the concubinage which gives rise to this impediment.

Extent of the Impediment. 1. It invalidates marriage *in the direct line only,* to the second degree inclusive. For example, a man cannot validly marry the mother or grandmother, nor the daughter or granddaughter, of a woman who was his mistress or pseudo-wife.

2. *Before the Code,* both the basis and the scope were different. It then arose from an engagement contract, and in this form invalidated marriage to the first degree of the direct or of the collateral line; and it also arose from a marriage which had not been consummated, and in this form it extended to the fourth degree of either line, inclusive.

Questions. 1. Is this impediment ever multiple? Practically, no, since the Code says nothing about it, and thus creates at least a *dubium iuris.* Theoretically it would seem to be multiple in the extraordinary supposition that a man, having first invalidly married or practiced public and notorious concubinage with the grandmother, afterward did the same with the mother, and finally proposed to marry the daughter!

2. If the parties concerned were unbaptized at the time of the relations but are afterward converted, does the impediment exist? It is certain that it did not before the Code, but this is a very weak argument. A better one is that there exists at least a *dubium iuris;* hence practically no impediment.

3. If the *invalid marriage* which bases the impediment is later validated, affinity arises (because of the valid marriage) between the man and the blood relatives of the woman. Does the impediment of public propriety, between the same persons, therefore cease *ipso facto?* We see no really cogent reason, theoretically, for affirming that it does; the impediment is of its nature permanent. Yet, since it is at least probable that the Church wishes the later impediment (affinity) to be substituted for the earlier one (public propriety), there is a *dubium iuris,* and again no impediment of public propriety, practically.

Dispensation. Public propriety in the more remote degree (second of the direct line) is a minor impediment (c. 1042, § 2, 3°). Even the first degree offers no great difficulty so long as there is no danger that the second partner may be the man's daughter, a possibility if he had relations with her mother before her birth (cf. c. 1076, § 3).

CANON 1079. The only spiritual relationship which invalidates marriage is that mentioned in canon 768.

Spiritual Relationship. 1. By *baptism* "the person baptizing and the sponsor contract a spiritual relationship only with the person baptized" (c. 768). Hence this impediment exists only between the person baptized on the one hand and the minister or sponsor on the other. *Confirmation* also gives rise to a spiritual relationship (c. 797); but this is not an impediment to marriage.

2. *Before the Code,* the impediment of spiritual relationship arose from both baptism and confirmation, and in each case not only between the person baptized and the minister, and between the person baptized and the sponsor, but also between the parents of the person baptized and the minister and sponsor.

3. In baptisms and confirmations conferred before the Code, the spiritual relationship then contracted remains after the Code, but it is no longer an impediment except as provided in canon 1079.[65]

Questions. 1. Does the impediment arise in *conditional* baptism? As regards the sponsor it does not unless the same sponsor acted both in the first and in the conditionally repeated baptism (c. 763, § 2). As to the minister, though there is no express provision, the same answer should be given.

2. Does the impediment exist if the minister of the baptism was at that time an infidel, is later converted and wishes to marry the person he baptized? No. At the time of the baptism the infidel was incapable of spiritual relationship; at the time of his conversion, the baptism was past. Neither relationship nor impediment exists.

3. The relationship and impediment result from *private baptism,*[66] but not from the mere supplying of the ceremonies, since that is not baptism (cf. c. 762, § 2).

---

[65] Cf. Code Com., 3 June, 1918; *AAS*, 10–346; *Digest*, I, p. 344.

[66] This is the general rule. We see no reason for a different view even when the baptism is one of urgent necessity, conferred in danger of death. Nau, in *Marriage Laws of the Code*, p. 116, note 20, cites Wernz-Vidal in favor of this exception, but we have found no support for it there. See Wernz-Vidal, *De Matrimonio*, n. 393, p. 470, note 42.

4. Who contracts the relationship and impediment with the person baptized when the sponsor acts by proxy, being physically absent from the baptism? The principal, not the proxy, contracts it.[67]

5. If the sponsor in baptism has not the qualities required for validity by canon 765, does he contract the impediment? No (cc. 765, 768, 1079).

6. If there are several sponsors, do they all contract it? Yes, if they fulfill the conditions of canon 765 for valid sponsorship.

7. Is this impediment ever multiple? It would be so in the extraordinary supposition that someone acted as both minister and sponsor of baptism, and later wished to marry the person so baptized.

CANON 1080. Persons who according to the civil law are regarded as incapable of marrying each other because of a legal relationship arising from adoption, cannot validly contract marriage together according to canon law.

Legal Relationship. This diriment impediment of civil law exists in the Colony of Puerto Rico, and in some States.[68]

CASES AND QUESTIONS

1. Does a simple vow of chastity in a religious institute ever constitute a diriment impediment to marriage? (Cc. 1058, 1073).

2. Is the impediment of mixed religion diriment or merely impedient? Of divine or merely ecclesiastical law? (C. 1060).

3. Do the guarantees in a mixed marriage include the children already born? Is there any obligation to see to their Catholic education? Are both your answers true also when the non-Catholic party to the marriage is unbaptized? (*Digest*, II, p. 286; c. 1071).

4. Are the guarantees alone sufficient to produce moral certainty of their fulfillment? (C. 1061, § 1, 2° and 3°).

5. Are the parties in a mixed marriage ever permitted to repeat the ceremony before a non-Catholic minister as such? Before a justice of the peace? (Cc. 1258, 1063, §§ 1 and 3).

6. Would guarantees in a mixed marriage given implicitly be sufficient for the validity of the dispensation? What would amount to implicit guarantees? (*Digest*, II, p. 292).

7. A Catholic girl married an infidel with dispensation from disparity of cult. In a suit for declaration of nullity of this marriage, she is able to prove that the man's promises were insincere and that he never had any

---

[67] Cf. S. C. Sacr., 25 Nov., 1925; *AAS*, 18–43; *Digest*, I, p. 338.
[68] Cf. Alford, *Ius Matrimoniale Comparatum*, n. 163. See also note 58, Chapter XII.

intention of living up to them. Will the court declare the marriage invalid?

8. What is the general notion of impotence as distinguished from sterility? When is it an impediment to marriage? (C. 1068, § 1). Does double fallectomy in a woman certainly result in impotence? What do you say of double vasectomy in a man? Explain the meaning of *impotentia perpetua*.

9. Angelina's husband deserted her soon after the marriage. Nine years have passed without news of him. She has been living with another man under promise of marriage, and now desires to marry him. Should the pastor assist in this second marriage? Can the Ordinary permit it? Could the Holy See permit it? What would be the effect of permission from the Holy See: (*a*) As to the bond of the first marriage? (C. 1069); (*b*) As to the impediment of crime in the second marriage? (C. 1053; cf. *Digest*, I, p. 508).

10. Is affinity in the second degree of the collateral line, touching the first, a major or minor impediment? (Disputed question; cf. *Irish Ecclesiastical Record*, Vol. 64, p. 267). What causes would be sufficient for a dispensation from it by the Ordinary? (*Digest*, II, p. 33, n. 2).

11. How is the lawful age for marriage under canon 1067 to be computed? (C. 34, § 3, 3°).

12. James, a Presbyterian validly baptized, married Vera, unbaptized, in 1917. Was the marriage valid? What if the marriage had been celebrated in 1919? (C. 1070).

13. Martin's parents were both non-Catholics, and he never received any religious education whatever, though he knows that he was baptized in infancy by a Catholic nurse during a serious illness. He marries Amelia, unbaptized, before a justice of the peace. (*a*) Is Martin "baptized in the Catholic Church"? (*b*) Is his marriage invalid for disparity of cult? (*Digest*, II, p. 290); (*c*) Is it invalid for want of the canonical form? (C. 1099, § 2).

14. What is the effect on marriage, of solemn religious profession: (*a*) Before the marriage? (C. 1073); (*b*) After a non-consummated marriage? (C. 1119); (*c*) After a marriage which has been consummated?

15. Explain summarily the three degrees of the impediment of crime (c 1075). Which degree is a minor impediment? (C. 1042).

Readings:

White, *Canonical Ante-nuptial Promises and the Civil Law*, Catholic University, 1934 (n. 91), published also by the Dolphin Press, Philadelphia; Boyle, *The Juridic Effects of Moral Certitude on Pre-nuptial Guarantees*, Cath. U., 1942 (n. 150); Heneghan, *The Marriages of Unworthy Catholics*, Cath. U., n. 188; Rice, *Proof of Death in Pre-nuptial Investigation*, Cath. U., 1940 (n. 123); Schenk, *The Matrimonial Impediments of Mixed Religion and Disparity of Cult*, Cath. U., 1929 (n. 51); Donohue, *The*

Impediment of Crime, Cath. U., 1931 (n. 69); Wahl, *The Matrimonial Impediments of Consanguinity and Affinity,* Cath. U., 1934 (n. 90); Ter Haar, *De Matrimoniis Mixtis Eorumque Remediis; The Australasian Catholic Record,* 1932, p. 154 (Nevin, on sufficient cause for dispensation from mixed religion); *Irish Ecclesiastical Record,* Vol. 59, p. 543 (Fallon, on the guarantees in validation of a mixed marriage); *The Jurist,* Vol. 3, p. 475 (Hammill, on the impediment of nonage), Vol. 4, p. 158 (Hannan, on dispensations by a Chancellor).

CHAPTER XIV

MATRIMONIAL CONSENT: THE FORM OF MARRIAGE: OTHER PROVISIONS

Section 1. Matrimonial Consent (cc. 1081-1093)

PRELIMINARY SURVEY

CANON 1081. § 1. Marriage is effected by the consent of the parties lawfully expressed between persons who are capable according to law; and this consent no human power can supply.

§ 2. Matrimonial consent is an act of the will by which each party gives and accepts a perpetual and exclusive right over the body, for acts which are of themselves suitable for the generation of children.

Matrimonial Consent. 1. *Necessity.* Marriage is always by its very nature a contract, even when it is not a sacrament. Now, a contract can be effected in no other way than by the consent of the parties, or, as the English law is fond of saying, by "the meeting of the minds." Consent is thus necessary to marriage according to its very nature, and it follows that neither the state nor the Church, nor any human power, can supply it. When a marriage is validated by a *sanatio in radice* (cf. c. 1138), the Church dispenses from the *renewal* of consent, but never from consent itself.

2. *Definition.* The second paragraph of the canon defines matrimonial consent by its object. Every contract transfers some right, and

the right which it transfers is called the *object* of the contract (not the *purpose,* but the *matter*). Matrimonial consent is an act of the will by which each party gives and accepts a perpetual and exclusive right over the body, for acts which are of themselves suitable for the generation of children. Without the mutual transfer of this right there can be no marriage, because this right is the essential object of the marriage contract by the law of nature and the divine positive law. Neither human evolution, nor custom, nor the law of the state, nor the law of the Church can change this. The right is by its nature perpetual and exclusive in the sense explained under canon 1013. Each party "gives and accepts" this right; but two distinct acts are not required of each party. The *mutual* acceptance includes a mutual offer.

3. *Conditions of consent.* We have spoken of consent in itself: its nature (an act of the will), and its object (the conjugal right). These constitute the consent in itself; but in order that it be juridically effective to produce the bond of marriage, other conditions may be necessary. Some mutual expression of this consent is required by the very nature of marriage as a contract. Hence the canon speaks of consent *lawfully expressed.* The conditions of such lawful expression are treated under the canons regarding the form of marriage (c. 1094 seq.). Moreover the *parties* must be *capable according to law.* The capacity of persons is determined by the natural law, and moreover by the state law for unbaptized persons, by the canon law for those who are baptized.[1]

Cases. There is scarcely any subject in which the study of cases will be so well repaid as in matrimonial consent; but merely to outline one or two cases in this text would mean nothing. Many cases must be studied in some detail and with particular reference to various grounds of nullity.[2]

CANON 1082. § 1. In order that matrimonial consent may be possible it is necessary that the contracting parties be at least not ig-

---

[1] See c. 1016, p. 404.
[2] Cases on matrimonial consent (references are to volume and page of the *Canon Law Digest*):
    a. Ignorance of the essence of marriage, Vol. II, pp. 296–299.
    b. Insanity, I, p. 518; II, p. 299.
    c. Civil marriage, I, p. 518; II, p. 302.
    d. Simulated consent, I, p. 521; II, pp. 301, 304 sq.
    e. Error, I, p. 520.
    f. Force and fear, I, pp. 523–530; II, pp. 320–325.
    g. Conditions contrary to substance, I, pp. 532–537; II, pp. 307–320.
    h. Conditions in general, I, p. 537; II, pp. 325–331.

norant that marriage is a permanent society between man and woman for the procreation of children.

§ 2. This ignorance is not presumed after puberty.

Knowledge of the Nature of Marriage. 1. Since marriage is a contract whose essential object (matter) is the conjugal right, it seems evident that matrimonial consent is impossible without *some knowledge* concerning the right which the contract purports to transfer. *Nil volitum nisi cognitum.*

2. *Before the age of reason* persons have not sufficient discretion to make any contract. But marriage is peculiar in this, that its essential object is commonly hidden by nature itself from young people even after the age of reason, until *about the time of puberty.* Hence, for marriage, the mere age of reason does not usually give sufficient knowledge. The opinion attributed to Sanchez, that the degree of discretion requisite for responsibility for mortal sin suffices also for marriage, although it has been gravely quoted in some modern decisions, is quite discredited and need not be discussed. It is certain that more than that is required.

3. Let us try to understand the formula which the Code uses. It seems to require *as a minimum:*

a. Knowledge that marriage is a *permanent* society between man and woman. Permanent here does not mean indissoluble; for it is certain that knowledge of the indissolubility of marriage is not required (cf. c. 1084). What is required is the knowledge that marriage is a more or less stable, permanent arrangement, not a mere transient companionship. This, *at least.* For this alone is not enough. This knowledge is commonly had before the age of puberty. Many little children know that their fathers and mothers are married, that marriage is more or less permanent. This knowledge has nothing to do with puberty.

b. But the canon moreover requires the knowledge that marriage is a society *for the procreation* of children. One cannot but regret the reticence with which some authors and even some decisions shroud this precise provision of the Code in glittering generalities. Little light is thrown on it by saying that insane persons and those who "lack the necessary discretion" are incapable of matrimonial consent. The Code is not concerned only about the insane; it deals with normal people also, and undertakes to state as accurately as possible what knowledge is required. Some, in citing this provision, change it, and say that what is required is knowledge that marriage is a permanent society for *having* children. If that were true, there is scarcely a child of seven or eight years who would not have sufficient knowledge for the marriage contract. Children quite commonly know that father and mother are married, and that only married people have children. This knowledge has nothing to do with puberty; yet the canon in the second paragraph fixes the age of puberty as the time when essential knowledge is presumed to be acquired. The mere knowledge that marriage is for the purpose of *having children* might be quite consistent with entire ignorance regarding the conjugal right which is the essential matter of the contract (c. 1081). Can a person transfer a right of whose existence he has not the slightest knowledge? Evidently not. We think the Code advisedly uses the words *for procreating children* instead of for *having* children. And we are trying to explain the words of the Code.

What Degree of Knowledge Is Required. A recent decision of the Rota expressed this rather succinctly as follows: "It is not necessary that the parties explicitly intend to assume all the rights and duties which derive from the nature of marriage; but it is sufficient that they in a general way intend to contract marriage as others do, or as it was instituted by God. Nor is it necessary that they know the way in which children are procreated, provided they do know that it is done by their own mutual co-operation."[3] It will be noted that the first part of this passage refers to the intention of the will, the second to the knowledge requisite for consent. It is this second part which concerns us. We may conclude:

1. Some knowledge of *procreation* is necessary; that is, that children are procreated by the mutual co-operation of husband and wife. It seems certain that this must be known to be a *bodily co-operation,* not a merely mental one.[4]

2. Explicit *knowledge of the act of copula* is certainly not required. "Distinct and explicit knowledge, either of the acts themselves, or of the way in which, or the organs by which they are exercised, or of their juridical importance for the marriage contract, is not required."[5]

Presumption of Knowledge or Ignorance. 1. A presumption is defined as a probable conjecture of something which is uncertain (c. 1825). It may take the place of proof when proof is wanting. A presumption *iuris simpliciter* yields to contradictory proof; a presumption

---

[3] Rota, 20 Jan., 1926; *S. R. Rotae Decisiones,* Vol. 18, p. 4; *Digest,* II, p. 296.
[4] Cappello treats this matter with the courage which is required to say things clearly. Cf. *De Matrimonio,* n. 582.
[5] Cf. Rota, 30 July, 1927; *S. R. Rotae Decisiones,* Vol. 19, p. 351; *Digest,* II, p. 298.

iuris et de iure excludes contrary proof (c. 1826). The presumption established by the present canon is *iuris simpliciter*.

2. *Before puberty* (c. 88, § 2) ignorance is presumed, and knowledge must be proved. After puberty, knowledge is presumed, ignorance must be proved.

Cases. Published reports of cases adjudicated by the Rota on want of mental capacity due to insanity are rather plentiful; but cases on want of knowledge sufficient to support the contract in persons not insane are rather rare.[6]

CANON 1083. § 1. Error regarding the person makes marriage invalid.

§ 2. Error regarding a quality of the person, even though it is the cause of the contract, invalidates marriage in the following cases only:

1° If the error regarding the quality amounts to an error regarding the person;

2° If a free person contracts marriage with a person whom he or she believes to be free, but who is on the contrary in a condition of slavery in the proper sense.

Error of Fact. These are of two classes: error regarding the *identity* of the person with whom marriage is contracted; and error regarding some *quality* of the person. The former makes marriage invalid; the latter, with two exceptions (of which one is merely apparent) does not.

Error Regarding the Person. In marriage the identity of the person is by the nature of things an essential element; consequently an error here is substantial and invalidates the contract (cf. c. 104). Cases of this sort are naturally rare.[7]

Error Regarding a Quality of the Person. The qualities of the person with whom one contracts marriage are not of their nature substantial elements. This is true even though the error is the cause of the contract (*etsi det causam contractui*), that is, even though, *but for the error, the contract would not have been made.* For example, a man wishes to marry a wealthy girl; he would knowingly marry none other; he thinks that Jane is wealthy and marries her for that reason. Jane turns out to be penniless. The marriage is not for that reason invalid.

---

[6] Cf. *Digest*, II, p. 296 sq. One of the most consummate jurists we know of, R. Bidagor, S.J., of the Gregorian University, has two scholarly articles on this subject in *Periodica*, Vol. 29, p. 269, and Vol. 30, p. 5.

[7] Cf. Rota, 16 Apr., 1913; *AAS*, 5–372; *Digest*, I, p. 520.

Exceptions. Two exceptions are mentioned. *First:* error regarding a quality of the person invalidates marriage if it *amounts to an error regarding the person.* This exception is only apparent; the error in reality is as to the person, who is identified in the mind of the other party by a certain personal quality. For example, two sisters look almost exactly alike; John is in love with one of them whom he distinguishes from her sister chiefly by her blonde hair; on the day of the wedding the other sister, having dyed her hair, is substituted for the chosen one, and matrimonial consent is mutually expressed. This error may be called one regarding a quality of the person (blonde hair) but under the circumstances it was much deeper than that; it concerned the person's identity. Hence the marriage is invalid.

Second, marriage is invalid if a person who is free marries one whom he believes to be free but who is a slave in the full sense of the word. This could still happen perhaps in some mission countries.

Condition as to Quality of Person. Even a quality of the person, however unimportant in itself, may be made a condition *sine qua non* to matrimonial consent. In such case the marriage will be invalid if the condition is not fulfilled, that is, if the quality does not really exist. These are cases, not of error, but of conditioned consent; they will be treated under canon 1092.

CANON 1084. Simple error regarding the unity, or indissolubility, or sacramental dignity of marriage, even though it is the cause of the contract, does not vitiate matrimonial consent.

State of the Question. Marriage is essentially one and indissoluble, and if both parties are baptized it is moreover a sacrament (c. 1013, § 2). An error upon any of these points is an error of law, and a very serious one, which might seem at first sight to invalidate the contract. Yet the canon declares that mere error, even on so fundamental a point, and even if the error is the cause of the contract, does not vitiate the consent. This is by no means an easy matter to grasp; a concrete illustration may be of service. Anna, a Protestant, married Boni, a Catholic, with a dispensation from mixed religion. Anna, before and at the time of the marriage, entertained false notions about marriage; in particular she shared the common Protestant view that marriage is dissoluble by a civil divorce. She was in error regarding the essential indissolubility of marriage. Yet the final decision in this case was that the error did not vitiate the consent.[8]

[8] An actual case (De Castellane-Gould), Rota, 8 Feb., 1915; *AAS,* 7–292; *Digest,* I, p. 535.

Simple Error. The application of the principle will be difficult because of obscure or conflicting evidence in particular cases; but the principle itself must be clearly understood to begin with. The key to it is in the term *simple* error, which we must clearly define. Error is a false judgment of the mind, in this case concerning an essential property of marriage, indissolubility. The error is *simple* if it remains in the mind without passing over into the will, and so without modifying the act which the will elicits, that is, the act of consent. On the other hand, if the error modifies the act of the will, so that the consent of the will is explicitly directed to a dissoluble marriage, it is no longer simple error; it is then an error explicitly incorporated as a condition in the contract, and inevitably vitiates the matrimonial consent. But the difficulty is to understand how an error so fundamental about the nature of marriage can remain fixed in the mind and at the same time leave unimpaired the act of the will, matrimonial consent. Let us for the sake of clearness put this objection in quasi-scholastic form.

Objection. Simple error in the sense explained seems to be psychologically impossible; hence every error must affect and vitiate the consent. Proof:

The will embraces its object *as represented by the mind*.

But by supposition the mind *represents marriage as dissoluble*.

Therefore the will embraces marriage as dissoluble.

Reply. Distinguish the major premise: the will embraces its object as represented by the mind; that is, the will cannot embrace an object which is *in no way represented,* I grant; the will embraces the object *under every aspect* in which the mind represents it, I subdistinguish: it does so *explicitly,* I deny; *implicitly,* I subdistinguish again: it does so implicitly *if there is no actual prevailing intention to the contrary,* I grant; it does so implicitly *even in the face of an actual prevailing intention to the contrary,* I deny.

Explanation. We do not say that simple error will be verified in every case; on the contrary, there will be cases where the will explicitly and positively chooses a vitiated form of marriage, for example a trial marriage, from which indissolubility is positively excluded. In such cases the consent is vitiated, and the marriage is null (c. 1092, 2°). But simple error is also possible. It exists when the error in the mind remains speculative and is not actually incorporated in the choice made by the will. In these cases there is a so-called conflict of intentions and the problem is to determine the prevailing intention.

By supposition, there is no explicit choice of a dissoluble marriage; there tends to be an implicit one, but this implicit choice is outweighed or overcome by the actual choice of marriage such as it is, that is, including all the essential properties which belong to it by the natural law.

Objection Pressed. The canon states that simple error does not vitiate consent even when it is the cause of the contract. Surely this is an impossible case. If the error is the *cause of the contract, it must influence the will,* and so it is no longer simple error in the sense explained.

Reply. Error is the cause of the contract when, but for the error, the contract would not have been made. We have admitted that such error *tends to influence the will,* tends to be implicitly included in the choice made by the will. But this tendency toward an implicit choice is contradicted by the explicit choice of marriage which the will actually makes. After all, we are speaking of persons who have actually elicited and expressed consent to marriage. In the conflict of intentions, the actual and explicit intention prevails, and so the error remains actually without influence on the choice of the will; that is, it is simple error. The fact that the will *would not have* chosen marriage in the absence of the error is a hypothetical fact; the actual fact is that the will has chosen marriage, without making any explicit modification. The actual intention prevails over the hypothetical one.

Cases. It cannot be too carefully noted that the application of this principle to concrete cases is always extremely difficult. Cases do not come into the matrimonial court neatly labeled "simple error," or "condition contrary to the substance of marriage." They come in a jumble of confused and conflicting testimony, and the problem of the court is to determine to which class they belong. If they turn out to be of the first class, the marriage is valid so far as consent is concerned (c. 1084); if they are of the second class, the marriage is null (c. 1092, 2°). The case which we chose for illustration was classed in opposite categories by successive decisions of the Rota, and finally the marriage was upheld as a case of simple error.[9]

CANON 1085. The knowledge or belief that the marriage is null does not necessarily exclude matrimonial consent.

State of the Question. It may happen that one or both parties con-

---

[9] Cf. note 8, this chapter. See also Rimlinger, *Error Invalidating Matrimonial Consent.* Cath. U., 1932.

tract marriage in the belief or with the certain knowledge that the marriage will be invalid. The question is whether such knowledge or belief impairs matrimonial consent. It does not. The marriage may be invalid for some other reason, but it will not necessarily be invalid for want of consent.

Examples. 1. A person contracts marriage with knowledge of the existence of a diriment impediment. He knows the marriage will be invalid for that reason; yet he wishes to contract marriage in as far as he can. Matrimonial consent exists; and though the marriage is invalid because of the impediment, yet it may afterward be validated even without renewal of consent (cf. cc. 1138, § 1, 1139, § 1).

2. A person contracts marriage in the erroneous belief that a diriment impediment exists. He expects the marriage to be invalid because of the impediment, but he wishes to contract marriage in as far as he can. The marriage is valid.

CANON 1086. § 1. The internal consent of the mind is always presumed to be in agreement with the words or signs which are used in the celebration of the marriage.

§ 2. But if either party or both parties by a positive act of the will exclude marriage itself, or all right to the conjugal act, or any essential property of marriage, the marriage contract is invalid.

State of the Question. The first paragraph expresses a mere presumption of law as to the existence of internal consent; the second declares that internal consent must actually exist on both sides.

Presumption of Internal Consent. 1. Consent, being an act of the will, is by its nature an internal act which cannot be directly perceived by the senses. Yet marriage, being a contract, requires for validity exterior expression of consent by word or sign (c. 1088, § 2), and as a sacrament it also requires a sensible sign. Obviously there is a general presumption that such expression is sincere, and no further proof of consent is required.

2. This presumption is a very strong one because of the large human experience on which it is based. Yet it is but a presumption of law; it may be overcome by contrary proof (cc. 1825, 1826).

Necessity of Internal Consent. 1. Mere external expression of consent cannot constitute marriage; *genuine internal consent on both sides* is so necessary that no human power can supply it, and much less can the Church presume it in a case where it is known not to exist (c. 1081, § 1).

2. Hence if *either party by a positive act of the will excludes any*

essential element of true matrimonial consent, the marriage is invalid. The canon names the elements which cannot be excluded; they are "marriage itself, or all right to the conjugal act, or any essential property of marriage." Let us take them in order:

a. Marriage itself cannot be excluded. Externally the man says, "I take N.N. for my wife"; interiorly, by a positive act of the will, he says, "I do not." It is certain that this marriage is invalid in the internal forum.

b. All right to the conjugal act cannot be excluded without destroying matrimonial consent. This right is the essential object of the contract (c. 1081, § 2); and it is of its very nature perpetual and exclusive. Hence we must not lay undue stress on the word *all,* as if *part* of the right could be excluded without impairing matrimonial consent. It cannot. For example, if the very right to the conjugal act (and not merely its exercise) is excluded, even for only a prescribed time, the marriage is null (cf. c. 1092, 2°).

c. No *essential property* of marriage can be excluded; these are *unity* and *indissolubility* (c. 1013, § 2).

d. If any of the above are excluded by *either party by a positive act of the will,* the marriage is invalid. This is true *in the internal forum,* even if the exclusion was in no way manifested externally. To hold otherwise would be to hold that you can have valid marriage without consent, which is a manifest contradiction of common sense and of canon 1081, § 1.[10] But the act of the will excluding an essential element of consent must be a *positive act.* This means an act, not externally declared, but *explicitly made* at least internally. It is opposed both to simple error, which is entirely in the mind, and to a mere habitual inclination of the will, which is not an explicit act at all (cf. c. 1084).

Proof of Simulation. When consent is externally expressed but internally wanting or deficient, the marriage is invalid *in foro interno,* that is in reality before God, but valid *in foro externo,* that is before the Church, by reason of the presumption (which is then contrary to the truth). To remove this regrettable conflict between the internal and external fora, two alternative courses are *per se* possible: first, the validation of the marriage *in foro interno* by true consent (c. 1136, § 2), or second, proof of want of consent *in foro externo.* This latter course may be impossible; always it will be difficult. The elements to be proved are the following: (*a*) the existence of a cause sufficient

---

[10] Cf. apparently *contra,* Augustine, *A Commentary,* V, p. 240.

to explain the simulation; (*b*) circumstances existing before, at the time of, and after the marriage which prove to a moral certainty that the external expression of consent was not genuine. Testimony of the guilty party admitting simulation of consent is admissible, but is not in itself sufficient to prove it.[11]

Note on Declaration of Nullity in Such Cases. Although the *procedure* in matrimonial cases is not our concern, yet it must not be supposed that in all these cases a declaration of the nullity of the marriage can be obtained. Even though a marriage be certainly invalid, it may be practically impossible to have it so adjudicated. The reason for this is not only the possible lack of sufficient proof, but also the established rule of procedure that a party to a marriage, who was the *guilty cause* of the nullity of the marriage, is deprived of the right to impugn it. He has no standing in court (cf. c. 1971, § 1, 1°).[12]

CANON 1087. § 1. Likewise invalid is a marriage entered into through force or grave fear unjustly inspired from without, such that in order to escape from it a party is compelled to choose marriage.

§ 2. No other fear, even if it furnish the cause for the contract, entails the nullity of marriage.

Force and Fear. This obstacle to consent is called force and fear; yet the text of the canon names the two disjunctively, and the decisions show clearly that the two need not exist together. *Force* means a physical impulse from without which cannot be resisted. Such force cannot compel the interior assent of the will (*actus elicitus*), but it can compel the *actus imperatus,* so that the person is said to act against his will. There being no true interior consent, such a marriage is null by the natural law. *Fear* means trepidation of mind because of an impending evil. In the present connection it is the result of either physical or moral violence, and that is why it is joined to force. It may be so extreme as to deprive a person of the use of reason, and in such case the marriage would be invalid by the natural law. But usually fear, though grave, does not compel the will even as to its *actus imperatus;* it merely puts strong pressure on the will inducing it to *choose marriage* as the only means of escaping the threatened evil. Such a choice is a human act; it is *voluntarium simpliciter,* though *involuntarium secundum quid,* like the choice made by the mariner

---

[11] Cases on simulation of consent, see *Digest,* I, pp. 521, 522; II, pp. 301, 304.

[12] Cf. Code Com., 12 March, 1929, *AAS,* 21–171, *Digest,* I, p. 807; Code Com., 17 July, 1933, *ad* II, *AAS,* 25–345, *Digest,* I, p. 808; Code Com., 27 July, 1942, *AAS,* 34–241, *Digest,* II, p. 548; Instruction on Matrimonial Procedure, Art. 37, § 1, *Digest,* II, p. 481; Letter of Apostolic Delegate, 23 Sept., 1938, *Digest,* II, p. 531.

who voluntarily jettisons valuable cargo to save the ship. *In general* such acts are valid but may be rescinded (c. 103, § 2). Why is marriage made an exception to this rule? For two reasons: first, by its very nature the marriage relationship should be based on a perfectly free choice; second, marriage, if valid, is permanent and indissoluble; rescission is not to be contemplated. Authors dispute whether marriage contracted through grave fear is invalid solely because of ecclesiastical law, or also by the natural law.[13]

Fear. To render marriage invalid, fear must have *all* the following qualities and adjuncts: it must be grave, inspired from without, unjustly, and such that in order to escape it the person is compelled to choose marriage.

1. It must be *grave,* absolutely or relatively. Fear is absolutely grave if the evil in question is grave for any person; relatively grave if the evil feared is grave for the particular person in question, considering age, sex, other circumstances. In both cases the evil must be imminent, or at least must be believed to be imminent. Death, mutilation, loss of fortune, loss of reputation, are considered evils absolutely grave; others may be relatively grave considering the circumstances of the person.

Reverential fear deserves special mention because of its frequent occurrence in the decisions. It means the expectation of future harm as a result of displeasure on the part of a parent, superior, or other person under whose authority one is and to whom one owes reverence. In itself, reverential fear is slight, but it may be grave from its circumstances. It becomes grave when "to this reverence are added importunate and insistent entreaties, long and strenuous persuasion, constant nagging, imperious words, and similar circumstances. Then reverential fear becomes *qualificatus* and truly grave in itself; consequently it invalidates marriage."[14] Under these circumstances reverential fear can be grave even without threats. It may also be grave if the indignation of the parent is likely to be permanent.[15]

2. Fear must be *inspired from without,* that is, by another person, a free agent. Literally, fear may come from without if it comes from an external necessary cause, for example, a stroke of lightning; but such fear is outside the scope of this canon. Before the Code, a classical dispute existed as to whether it was also required that the fear be

---

[13] See Vermeersch, *What Is Marriage,* nn. 20–22; Cappello, *De Matrimonio,* n. 609, prefers the latter opinion; Gasparri, *De Matrimonio,* nn. 840, 841, the former.

[14] Rota, 11 Aug., 1927; *Decisiones,* Vol. 16, p. 426; *Digest,* II, p. 321.

[15] Cf. Rota, 24 March, 1926; *Decisiones,* Vol. 18, p. 93; *Digest,* II, p. 323, n. 13.

applied precisely with the purpose of compelling assent to marriage. Cardinal Gasparri relates that the Commission which framed the Code rejected a draft of a canon incorporating that requirement. He holds that, in adopting the canon in its present form, the Commission settled the question, so that it is not required that fear be injected for the direct purpose of compelling assent.[16] This opinion seems certainly correct. We cannot read into the canon words which are not there, especially when we know that they were explicitly rejected.

3. Fear must be *inspired unjustly*. This again requires a *free* external agent, since the criterion of justice is inapplicable to any other. This condition is fulfilled when the evil threatened is unjust either *in itself* or in the *manner in which it is applied*. The threat of a prison sentence for a seducer, as an absolute alternative to marriage, is unjust in substance, because the payment of compensatory or punitive damages is a choice to which the culprit is justly entitled. A threat of imprisonment or other violence without due process of law, or made by persons not vested with legal authority, is *unjustly applied,* even though the punishment be justly merited. In a recent case, a young woman's grandmother (who was in fact supporting her though not obliged to do so) threatened to withdraw financial support from the girl unless she married according to her dictation. The girl chose the prescribed marriage as the only alternative to suffering this grave loss. Was this fear *unjustly inspired?* The Rota held that it was, because, though the person making the threat had the right to carry it out (being under no obligation to provide support for the girl), yet she had no right to exact marriage by means of the threat.[17]

4. Fear must be such that *in order to escape it the person is compelled to choose marriage*. The circumstances must be such that, in the mind of the victim of the fear, there is no alternative.

Question. Does this obstacle to consent apply to the marriage of infidels? If either party was baptized at the time of the marriage, the fear above described invalidates the marriage regardless of the question which party suffered the fear; if neither party was baptized, the answer depends on whether this law is merely ecclesiastical or also divine. Since that is a real *dubium iuris,* such a marriage is probably invalid and probably valid; hence the general presumption in favor of validity should prevail.[18]

---

[16] Cf. Gasparri, *De Matrimonio,* n. 856.
[17] Rota, 13 Aug., 1924; *Decisiones,* Vol. 16, p. 365; *Digest,* II, p. 320.
[18] Cases, see *Digest,* I, pp. 523–530; II, pp. 320–325.

CANON 1088. § 1. In order that marriage be contracted validly it is necessary that the contracting parties be present either in person or by proxy.

§ 2. The parties must express matrimonial consent in words; and they may not use equivalent signs if they are able to speak.

Requisite Manner of Expressing Consent. 1. For *validity* it is required that the parties be present, either in person or by proxy. Marriage by proxy is governed by canons 1089 and 1091.

2. For *licitness,* it is necessary that consent be expressed in words if the parties are able to speak. Expression of consent by intelligible signs would be valid, and if the parties cannot speak, also licit. Where words are used in a language which cannot be directly mutually understood, the services of an interpreter are needed (cc. 1090, 1091).

CANON 1089. § 1. Without prejudice to diocesan statutes which may be imposed in addition hereto, in order that marriage be validly contracted by proxy, there is required a special mandate to contract it with a certain person, which must be subscribed by the principal and by either the pastor or the Ordinary of the place where the mandate is given, or by a priest delegated by either of these, or by at least two witnesses.

§ 2. If the principal cannot write, this fact must be noted in the mandate itself and another witness must be added who shall himself also sign the document; otherwise the mandate is invalid.

§ 3. If, before the proxy has contracted in the name of the principal, the latter has revoked the mandate or become insane, the marriage is invalid, even though these facts were unknown to the proxy or to the other contracting party.

§ 4. In order that the marriage be valid, the proxy must perform his office in person.

CANON 1090. Marriage can also be contracted through an interpreter.

CANON 1091. The pastor must not assist at a marriage which is to be contracted by proxy or through an interpreter, unless there be a just cause of doing so, and the authenticity of the mandate and the veracity of the interpreter be beyond all doubt, and if there is time he must moreover have the permission of the Ordinary.

CANON 1092. A condition once placed and not revoked:

1° If it is a condition regarding a future event which is necessary, or impossible, or immoral but not contrary to the substance of marriage, is to be considered as not having been made;

2° If it concerns the future and is contrary to the substance of marriage, it makes the marriage invalid;

3° If it concerns the future and is licit, it suspends the validity of the marriage;

4° If it concerns the past or the present, the marriage will be valid or not according as the matter concerning which the condition is made, exists or not.

Conditional Consent. Just as in any other contract, so, too, in the contract of marriage, it is possible to make one's consent conditional. This is by no means licit without a grave reason, because of the grave difficulties to which it may lead. This canon is concerned not with the licitness of conditional consent but solely with its effect upon the validity of the marriage.

Necessary or Impossible Future Condition. This cannot but strike one as a very impractical subject. What person in possession of his senses would condition his matrimonial consent upon a future condition whose realization was either *necessary* or *impossible?* The classical examples are: "I take you for my wife if the sun rises tomorrow" (necessary future condition); "I take you for my wife if the sun fails to rise tomorrow" (impossible future condition). Absurd as the case seems to be, yet it is possible, and so the law provides for it. Such a condition will be disregarded, counted for nothing. Here we encounter a serious difficulty. How can the Church so provide? In the case of an impossible condition, to disregard it amounts to supplying consent; and we have seen that this no human power can do (c. 1081, § 1). The answer to the objection is to grant it and then to revise our understanding of the meaning of this provision. The Church does not pretend to supply consent; but she does indulge the very reasonable presumption that future necessary or impossible conditions, even if expressed, are not seriously intended. This is what the provision means. It establishes a mere presumption of law, which yields to contrary evidence. Hence if conclusive proof is adduced showing that the condition was seriously intended, it must be given effect according to the mind of the parties. A necessary condition suspends the marriage until the event actually occurs; an impossible condition makes the marriage invalid.[19]

Immoral Future Condition Not Contrary to Substance of Marriage. The provision here is the same and has exactly the same force. It is reasonable to presume such a condition is not intended; but the presumption yields to proof. If the condition is seriously meant the marriage will be suspended until the condition is fulfilled, and thereupon it will become valid.

---

[19] Cf. Gasparri, *De Matrimonio*, nn. 881–887; Cappello, *De Matrimonio*, n. 629.

Future Condition Contrary to the Substance of Marriage. 1. A future condition may be contrary to the substance of marriage in three ways, namely by excluding the essential object of the contract (c. 1081, § 2) or either of its essential properties, unity or indissolubility (c. 1013, § 2). These conditions are *contra bonum prolis* (exclusion of the right, or exclusion of children), *contra bonum fidei* (exclusion of marital fidelity, or unity), and *contra bonum sacramenti* (exclusion of indissolubility).[20]

2. It is necessary to explain the distinction between a true *condition* and a *mode* in a contract. A *condition* strictly means a condition *precedent,* that is a circumstance which is made a prerequisite to consent, and upon which the validity of the contract depends. A *mode* on the other hand is a circumstance which is incorporated into the contract but which is not intended to affect in any way the main clauses of the contract. A stipulation affecting the same general subject might be interpreted as a mode or as a condition depending on the intention of the parties as expressed in the agreement. The point is that if it is found to be a mode it is outside the provisions of the present canon because a mode is essentially different from a condition.[21]

3. In the conditions *contra bonum prolis* and *contra bonum fidei,* it is necessary to distinguish between the exclusion of the *right itself,* with the corresponding *obligation,* and the exclusion merely of the *fulfillment of the obligation.* Only the radical exclusion of the *right and obligation itself* impairs matrimonial consent; if the condition affects only the *fulfillment of the obligation,* the contractual consent is not impaired and the marriage is valid. This distinction is constantly insisted on in the decisions of the Rota; only the careful study of many cases can make its application thoroughly understood. In the absence of full proof that the intention was to exclude the obligation itself, the presumption (cf. c. 1014) will be that only its fulfillment was excluded, and the decision will be *non constat de nullitate.*

4. This distinction between exclusion of the obligation itself and exclusion of its fulfillment has no place in the condition *contra bonum sacramenti* (against indissolubility). There, the consent is necessarily impaired at its source; the bond itself is assumed without indissolubility, and therefore invalidly. But in these cases the very serious question, a question of fact, is this: was there really a condition, or at least

---

[20] On the three blessings of marriage, cf. Pius XI, Encyclical, *Casti connubii;* Vermeersch, *What Is Marriage.*

[21] Cf. Rota, 28 Nov., 1914; *Decisiones,* Vol. 6, p. 323; *Digest,* I, p. 531.

a *positive act of the will* excluding indissolubility, or only an act of the mind (simple error) falsely supposing that indissolubility is not a necessary element of true marriage.[22]

Examples. a. One party to the marriage declared beforehand that he would never consent to have any children. If his intention (to be judged by the court from all the evidence and circumstances) was to exclude the obligation itself, this amounted to a condition contrary to the substance of marriage, that is, *contra bonum prolis,* and the marriage would be declared null. See cases reported in *Digest,* II, pp. 307–313.

b. A man who had regular illicit relations with other women before his marriage, continued them afterward, showing no consideration for his wife. It was proved that he intended to violate the obligation of marital fidelity, but the proof was insufficient to show that he excluded the obligation itself. Hence the decision was *non constare de nullitate. Digest,* II, p. 314. But in another case the man, before the marriage, had the effrontery to present for his bride's signature and acceptance a declaration that he "was to have his own way in everything." The evidence showed that he actually intended to reserve to himself the right to indulge illicit relations with other women after his marriage. This marriage was declared null because of this condition *contra bonum fidei. Digest,* II, p. 313.

c. Where the parties agreed beforehand that, in case their marriage proved unsatisfactory, they would dissolve it by divorce, the consent was vitiated by this condition *contra bonum sacramenti. Digest,* II, p. 316; I, p. 536 (Marconi-O'Brien). But a mere simple error by which a person is convinced that marriage is dissoluble by divorce does not vitiate consent. Cf. De Castellane-Gould, *Digest,* I, p. 535 and cases reported in *Digest,* II, pp. 314–320.

Future Licit Condition. If the intention is to condition the validity of the marriage upon a future event which involves no moral turpitude, that intention is given effect, that is, the validity of the marriage is held in suspense until the condition is fulfilled. This must not be confused with a mere conditional *promise* of marriage. There is question here of a present expression of matrimonial consent: "I take you for my wife here and now, but on condition that my father, tomorrow, expresses his consent to our union."

1. If the consent, given conditionally, is revoked before the fulfillment of the condition, the marriage never takes effect.

---

[22] Cases, *Digest,* I, pp. 532–537; II, pp. 307–320.

2. On the other hand if the *condition is revoked* and the parties wish to make their consent absolute, the marriage becomes effective at once. The exercise of the marital right after conditional consent and before the condition is verified is presumed to be a revocation of the condition and an expression of absolute consent.[23] This presumption is *iuris et de iure* (cf. c. 1826), at least in the old law.

Condition Concerning Present or Past. *Theoretically* these cases involve no difficulty. If the present or past condition exists as a fact at the time of the marriage, the marriage is valid; otherwise it is null. *Practically* of course it is no easy matter to determine, first whether a certain condition regarding a present or past fact was really made, and secondly whether it was verified. This is a matter of sifting and weighing evidence in actual cases.[24]

Examples. a. Where a man conditioned his matrimonial consent upon the existence of physical integrity (virginity) on the part of the woman at the time of the marriage, and it was proved that she was not a virgin, the marriage was declared null. *Digest,* II, p. 330, n. 14. But in another case the evidence proved only that the man had a general intention to marry a virgin; he believed that the woman was a virgin, would not have married her had he known that she was not. The court held that it was a case of simple error regarding a quality of the person; and a simple error, even if it is the cause of the contract, does not invalidate matrimonial consent. Hence the decision was *non consare de nullitate. Digest,* II, p. 330, n. 11.

b. A girl about to marry was warned by friends that the man had led a dissolute life and would probably continue to do so after marriage. She told him explicitly before the marriage that she did not intend to marry him if the charges were true. They were true in fact, but she allowed herself to be persuaded that they were false, and so married him. Upon proof that the condition (as to a past fact) was made and was not verified, the Rota declared the marriage null. The false subjective assurance on the part of the girl that the condition was verified, did not necessarily imply a revocation of the condition. *Digest,* II, p. 330, n. 13. But in another case, where the man claimed to have conditioned his consent upon the fact that the woman had had no previous relations with other men, the evidence failed to show that he actually made this condition; hence it was rather a case of

---

[23] Cf. Wernz, *Ius Decretalium,* IV, part 2, n. 298, note 28, cited by Rota, 18 May, 1922; *Decisiones,* Vol. 14, p. 155; *Digest,* II, p. 325.

[24] Cases in *Digest,* I, pp. 537–539; II, pp. 325–331. See also Timlin, *Conditional Matrimonial Consent,* Cath. U., 1934.

simple error regarding a quality of the person. The decision was *non constare de nullitate. Digest,* II, p. 329, n. 6.

c. The *present fact* upon which consent is conditioned may be a state of mind or present intention on the part of the other party. Such a condition must be clearly distinguished from a mere promise, and also from a condition regarding the future. A girl seriously limited her matrimonial consent by the condition that the man sincerely undertake to help her father in his shop with a view to succeeding to the business. The evidence showed that it was a condition *de praesenti* (present sincere intention on the part of the man), and not merely the exaction of a promise from him. Upon proof that this condition was made and that it was not verified, the marriage was declared null. *Digest,* II, p. 327, n. 1. In another case a girl, about to marry a nominal Catholic, seriously warned him beforehand that he must practice his religion. Later, the marriage having proved unhappy, she claimed that she had made his *present sincere intention* to practice his religion a condition to her consent. But the evidence failed to prove this. Rather, it tended to show that she had merely relied upon his *promise* to practice his religion. This would not impair matrimonial consent, even though the promise were not fulfilled, or even though it were insincerely made. *Non constat de nullitate. Digest,* II, p. 331, n. 16.

These examples and many others should teach us not to form confident judgments upon the invalidity of a specific marriage for want of consent upon the bare statement of a summary of facts. The principles are fairly clear, but the facts and circumstances of various cases are almost infinitely variable. Each case will depend upon the evidence actually adduced to prove that the marriage was invalid.

CANON 1093. Even though a marriage has been contracted invalidly because of an impediment, the consent which has been given is presumed to persevere until its revocation shall have been proved.

State of the Question. It is supposed that in a given case matrimonial consent has been duly expressed. The consent so given is presumed to continue in existence until it is proved to have been revoked; and this is true even though the marriage was invalid for some other cause, for example, because of an impediment. As to the proof for revocation of consent, see discussion under canon 1138.

The chief application of this rule is to a *sanatio in radice,* where an invalid marriage is validated without the *renewal of consent.* Consent must *exist* at the time of the *sanatio;* but the presumption of canon

1093 is sufficient to show that it does exist, provided it was once expressed, even in an invalid marriage, and not revoked.

Section 2. The Form of Marriage, etc. (cc. 1094–1107)

PRELIMINARY SURVEY

The General Requisite as to Form (c. 1094)
The Pastor or Ordinary Who Can Assist or Delegate (c. 1095)
Requisites of Delegation (c. 1096)
Requisites for Licit Assistance (c. 1097)
Form in Extraordinary Cases (c. 1098)
Persons Bound by the Law (c. 1099)
The Rite (c. 1100)
The Solemn Nuptial Blessing (c. 1101)
Mixed Marriages (c. 1102)
Registering the Marriage (c. 1103)
Marriages of Conscience (cc. 1104–1107)

CANON 1094. Only those marriages are valid which are contracted before the pastor or the Ordinary of the place, or a priest delegated by either of these, and at least two witnesses, but in accordance with the rules laid down in the canons which follow, and with the exceptions mentioned in canons 1098 and 1099.

Terms Explained. The *form* of marriage in general means the formalities which are required in the expression of consent. The liturgical requisites (*liturgical form*) are dealt with in canons 1100–1102. Of the juridical requisites, some concern only the licitness (*accidental juridical form*), others the validity (*substantial juridical form*) of marriage.

Historical Notes. 1. Before the Council of Trent, there was *no legislation* on the form of marriage as affecting its *validity.*[25]

2. The first invalidating law was the *Tametsi,* so called from its initial word, or Cap. 1 of Session XXIV of the Council of Trent, *De Reformatione Matrimonii,* enacted in 1563. It required for the validity of marriage the presence of the pastor or Ordinary of one of the parties according to domicile or quasi-domicile. There were two radical difficulties in the application of this law, first the difficulty of determining domicile, and secondly the fact that the law was not

---

[25] Cf. Joyce, *Christian Marriage,* pp. 102–115; Cappello, *De Matrimonio,* n. 658.

promulgated everywhere. Thus the validity of marriages depended on a complicated legal question (domicile or quasi-domicile at time of marriage) and on a complicated historical question (whether or not the law had been promulgated in the place of the marriage).

3. The *Tametsi* was modified to some extent by the *Benedictine privilege,* a declaration of Pope Benedict XIV, 4 Nov., 1741, which *exempted heretics* from the law when they married among themselves or with Catholic parties.[26]

4. *Common law marriage.* In places where the *Tametsi* had not been promulgated, the expression of consent was subject only to the natural law. But the question arose whether mere cohabitation as man and wife, after an engagement to marry, should be construed as sufficient expression of matrimonial consent. Successive Popes had held that it should be so construed, and hence such marriages (roughly equivalent to what are called in American law "common law marriages") had been consistently regarded as valid. But Leo XIII, by a decree of 15 Feb., 1892, entitled *Consensus mutuus,* revoked this presumption on the ground that such cohabitation is no longer regarded as an expression of matrimonial consent.[27] From that time, therefore, until the *Ne temere,* although no ecclesiastical law regarding form existed in those places, cohabitation after an engagement can no longer be considered as an expression of matrimonial consent.

5. *Ne temere* is the title (taken from its initial words) of a decree of the Sacred Congregation of the Council, effective April 19, 1908. Substantially its provisions are the same as those of the Code, with these differences:

a. For the use of the *extraordinary* form, it was required that the marriage be in the interest of conscience or for the legitimation of children.

b. In danger of death the presence of a priest with the two witnesses was required, though not outside danger of death when the difficulty of obtaining the assistance of the pastor, Ordinary, etc., was likely to last a month.

---

[26] The *Tametsi* was binding on all validly baptized persons including heretics. The *Benedictine Declaration* failed to exempt heretics from the law, when they married unbaptized persons. For text, see *Fontes,* n. 3527, Vol. V, p. 967. For a summary of the places in the United States where the *Tametsi* and the Benedictine Declaration were promulgated, see Conc. Balt. III, p. cvii; also Bonzelet, *Pastoral Companion,* ed. 1943, p. 113; Sabetti-Barrett, *Theol. Mor.,* n. 903, p. 907; Heneghan, *The Decree Tametsi in the U. S.,* in *The Jurist,* Vol. 3, p. 318.

[27] Cf. *Fontes,* n. 613, Vol. III, p. 381. See also Dillon, *Common Law Marriage,* Cath. U., 1942, n. 153; Alford, *Common Law Marriage in Relation to the Code,* in *The Jurist,* Vol. 2, p. 248.

c. There was no provision in the *Ne temere* exempting the children of non-Catholics, even though they were educated from infancy outside the Church.

The *Ne temere* remedied the two greatest drawbacks of the *Tametsi;* for, first, it was *promulgated everywhere;* secondly, it required for validity the assistance of the Ordinary or pastor *of the place* where the marriage was celebrated, and not *of the parties,* if one or both contracted the marriage outside the limits of their own parish.[28]

6. The Code, effective May 19, 1918, adopted, with these few minor modifications, the law already enacted by the *Ne temere.*

Right of the Church to Prescribe Form. 1. The fact that the Church has for centuries claimed this right is conclusive proof that she possesses the power. It is therefore certainly erroneous to limit the power of the Church to impediments affecting the personal capacity of the parties. Her power certainly extends to the entire contract, subject to the natural and divine law, and leaving to the state the control of merely civil effects (cf. c. 1016).

2. Though some theologians hold that in prescribing the form of marriage the Church has exercised direct control over the form of the sacrament, we may also hold that the legislation on form affects directly only the juridical expression of consent, and only indirectly the form of the sacrament.

General Principle. Church law requires for the validity of marriage that it be celebrated in the presence of the pastor or Ordinary of the place, or of a priest delegated by either of these, and at least two witnesses.

Notes. 1. *Pastor* includes: (*a*) One who has the *title* to the parish —a pastor in the strict sense (c. 451, § 1); (*b*) *quasi-pastors* in mission countries (cc. 216, § 3; 451, § 2, 1°); (*c*) those parochial *vicars who have full parochial powers* (c. 451, § 2, 2°) as enumerated in the explanation of canon 451. An assistant or curate (*vicarius co-operator*) does not receive this power as ordinary jurisdiction, but may receive general delegation.[29]

2. *Canonical possession* of the parish or benefice is required for validity (c. 1095, § 1, 1°).

3. *Territorial limits* must be attended to (cf. c. 1095).

4. *Witnesses* must be two, physically and morally present simultane-

---

[28] Cf. *Fontes,* n. 4340, Vol. VI, p. 867.
[29] Cf. Code Com., 13 Sept., 1933; *Digest,* II, pp. 332, 333; I, p. 541. Some diocesan pagellas give general delegation to all assistants for marriages within the parish.

ously with the pastor or Ordinary and capable of testifying to the fact of the marriage. There are no other requisites for the validity of the attendance of the witnesses.

CANON 1095. § 1. The pastor and the Ordinary of the place validly assist at marriage:

1° Only from the day upon which they took canonical possession of their benefice according to canons 334, § 3, 1444, § 1, or entered upon their office, and provided they have not been excommunicated or placed under an interdict or suspended from office by a condemnatory sentence, or been so declared by a declaratory sentence;

2° Only within the limits of their own territory; in which they can validly assist at marriages not only of their own subjects but also of persons who are not their subjects;

3° Provided that they ask and receive the consent of the contracting parties without being coerced either by force or by grave fear.

§ 2. The pastor and the Ordinary of the place who can validly assist at a marriage can also grant to another priest the permission to assist at a marriage within the limits of their respective territories.

Time When Power to Assist at Marriages Begins. 1. The very definite provisions of this canon exclude all moral computation; the authority begins on the day stated and not before. Bishops and titular pastors have *benefices,* but some others with power to assist at marriages have simple *offices;* hence the canon provides for both.

2. If there is question of a *benefice* (c. 1409), the authority of the pastor or Ordinary begins from the day when he takes canonical possession. The manner of taking possession is prescribed for resident Bishops by canon 334, § 3. For pastors, canon 1444, § 1 merely provides that they must take possession of their benefice as provided by particular law or local custom, unless the Bishop for just cause dispense expressly and in writing from that method; in which case the dispensation itself amounts to a taking of possession.

3. In the case of an *office* only, the titular must have possession of the office.

4. Excommunication, interdict, and suspension are three species of censures or medicinal penalties (cf. c. 2255, § 1). If the penalty is *latae sententiae* (cf. c. 2217, § 1, 2°), it is incurred at once and may or may not afterward be declared by a sentence or judgment (*declaratory* sentence); if it is *ferendae sententiae,* it is incurred only when the sentence or judgment imposes it (*condemnatory* sentence). Note that these penalties deprive one of authority in regard to marriage, only when they are *declared or imposed by judgment.* Also, not every

suspension is a suspension *from office* (cf. c. 2279). Suspension *from jurisdiction,* even after judgment, does not incapacitate the pastor or Ordinary from assisting at marriages, because such assistance is *not strictly* an act of jurisdiction. The same is true of suspension from orders, from divine services, or from a benefice, even after a declaratory or condemnatory sentence.[30]

Territorial Limits. 1. The principle of *pure territorial jurisdiction* (in the broad sense) is adopted from the *Ne temere:* the pastor and Ordinary assist validly, only within their territory, at marriages of all parties, whether they be their own subjects or not. As to purely personal pastors, although they have no territorial jurisdiction, the power which they had under the *Ne temere* to assist at the marriages of their own subjects anywhere is retained under the Code (cf. c. 216, § 4).

2. A *church belonging to exempt religious* is considered within the territory of the parish for this purpose.[31]

3. *National pastors* in the United States seem to come within the reply of the Sacred Congregation of the Council, 1 Feb., 1908, ad VIII, which declared that where a pastor has no territory exclusively his own, but has territory cumulatively with other pastors, all the pastors can assist at marriages anywhere in their territory, even if it be shared cumulatively with another pastor.[32]

4. *Personal pastors in the broad sense,* who have merely certain persons or families within a definite territory as their subjects, seem to be covered by the reply to question IX in the same document. These can assist, anywhere in the territory, at the marriages of their own subjects only.

5. *Chaplains of hospitals* or other institutions which are withdrawn from parochial jurisdiction according to canon 464, § 2, can assist at marriages of their subjects in that place, provided they have full parochial powers there.[33]

6. *Military chaplains* and other *purely personal pastors,* that is, those whose jurisdiction is entirely and exclusively over persons without regard to territory, can assist at the marriages of those persons only, anywhere. This was true before the *Ne temere,* and no change in this respect was made by it or by the Code (cf. cc. 216, § 4; 451, § 3). Under

---

[30] Cf. Cappello, *De Matrimonio,* n. 662.

[31] Cf. S. C. Sacr., 13 March, 1910, ad VIII; *AAS,* 2–193; *Fontes,* n. 2101, Vol. V, p. 77.

[32] Cf. *Fontes,* n. 4344, Vol. VI, p. 881.

[33] S. C. Conc., 1 Feb., 1908, ad X; *Fontes,* n. 4344, Vol. VI, p. 881.

the Code, however, their jurisdiction is no longer *exclusive,* but is cumulative with that of the pastor of the place (c. 1095, § 1, 2°) within his own territory. For the faculties of military chaplains of the armed forces of the United States regarding marriage, see *Digest,* II, p. 597. The unique exception for the East Indies, making the jurisdiction of personal pastors exclusive,[34] was based on provisions of a concordat, but this has been changed by later concordats.

Delegation of the Power. This is subject to the limitations of canon 1096.

CANON 1096. § 1. The permission to assist at a marriage, granted in accordance with canon 1095, § 2, must be given expressly to a certain priest for a certain determinate marriage, all general delegations being excluded except in the case of parochial assistants for the parish to which they are attached; otherwise it is invalid.

§ 2. The pastor or Ordinary of the place must not grant permission unless all the requirements established by law for proving the freedom of the parties to marry have been fulfilled.

Requisites of Delegation. 1. What is called here a "permission" is really a *delegation of power,* necessary for the validity of the marriage. Though the power delegated is not strictly jurisdiction, it follows the same general rules, except where penalties are concerned.

2. This delegation must be *express,* and must be given to a particular priest, for a particular marriage. General delegation can be given only to parochial assistants or curates (*vicarii co-operatores*) for the parish to which they are assigned. Some diocesan faculties grant this general delegation to all assistants. It may also be given them by the pastor (c. 199, § 1). General delegation for marriages cannot be given even to an episcopal delegate. The Code Commission was asked: "Whether an episcopal delegate to whom is granted the delegated faculty *ad universitatem negotiorum* according to canon 199, § 1, is thereby understood to receive, or at least can receive, general delegation to assist at marriages, in view of canon 1096, § 1." The reply was: "In the negative." (Code Com., 25 Jan., 1943; *AAS,* 35–58; *The Jurist,* Vol. 3, p. 502.)

3. Particular delegation may be made by a temporary administrator (*vicarius oeconomus*), by the vicar substitute (*vicarius substitutus*) after he has been approved by the Ordinary, by the supplying priest appointed by the pastor for a sudden absence, even without the approval of the Ordinary provided the latter has been notified of the

---

[34] Cf. S. C. Sacr., 2 June, 1910; *AAS,* 2–447.

designation of the supplying priest and has not provided otherwise.[35] Where a pastor notifies the superior of a monastery that he designates to assist at a particular marriage to take place the following Sunday at the filial church, whatever religious priest the superior shall select to say Mass there on that Sunday, the delegation is insufficient.[36]

4. Delegation may be made *with power to subdelegate;* and an assistant in a parish, who has received general delegation, may subdelegate a particular priest for a particular marriage.[37] He could not, however grant his subdelegate the power to subdelegate again, unless this power was granted to him by one having ordinary power in this matter, that is, by the pastor or the Ordinary.[38]

5. Delegation should not be made until the requirements of law regarding the proof of freedom to marry (cf. cc. 1019, 1020) have been fulfilled.

6. The recipient of express delegated power must be a *priest;* and this, *ad validitatem* (c. 1095, § 2), but if the delegation is made to one who is commonly believed to be a pastor (hence also a priest), though he lacks valid priestly orders, and he assists at a marriage in his putative parish, common error would supply power in him and the marriage would be valid, since it is quasi-jurisdiction and not the power of order that is required.[39] It is not required that the person delegated be approved for confessions.

7. Delegation to the same person for several determinate marriages, or to several determinate persons for the same marriage, would be valid.[40]

8. The case of *common error* supplying jurisdiction (or quasi-jurisdiction, i.e., the power to assist at a marriage), is a rather remote possibility. Mere common ignorance of the law requiring particular delegation certainly does not supply jurisdiction.

CANON 1097. § 1. The pastor or Ordinary of the place may licitly assist:

1° After they have satisfied themselves according to law regarding the freedom of the parties to marry;

2° After they have moreover satisfied themselves that one of the contracting parties has a domicile or quasi-domicile or a month's

---

[35] Code Com., 20 May, 1923; *AAS,* 16–114; *Digest,* I, p. 540.
[36] Code Com., 20 May, 1923; *AAS,* 16–115; *Digest,* I, p. 540.
[37] Code Com., 28 Dec., 1927; *AAS,* 20–61; *Digest,* I, p. 541.
[38] Cf. Ayrinhac-Lydon, *Marriage Legislation,* p. 250.
[39] Cf. Wernz, *Ius Decretalium,* IV, part 1, n. 180, note 213.
[40] Cappello, *De Matrimonio,* n. 674.

residence, or, in the case of a *vagus,* that he or she is actually stopping in the place of the marriage;

3° Provided that, if the conditions mentioned in n. 2 are wanting, they have the permission of the pastor or Ordinary of the domicile or quasi-domicile or place of a month's residence of one of the parties, unless the parties are *vagi* who are actually traveling and have no place of sojourn anywhere, or unless some grave necessity occur which excuses from asking the permission.

§ 2. In every case let it be taken as the rule that the marriage should be celebrated before the pastor of the bride-to-be, unless a just reason excuses therefrom; marriages, however, between Catholics of different rites, unless there be some special provision of law to the contrary, are to be celebrated in the rite of the groom and before his pastor.

§ 3. A pastor who assists at a marriage without the permission required by law, may not take the stole fees for himself, but must remit them to the proper pastor of the parties.

State of the Question. This entire canon refers to licitness and in no way affects the validity of the marriage. The *permission* of the pastor or Ordinary of one of the parties is now required for licit assistance, whereas before the *Ne temere* delegation from said pastor or Ordinary was required for validity.

Conditions of Licit Assistance. 1. The pastor or Ordinary of the place must first ascertain the freedom of the parties to marry, as provided in canons 1019, 1020. The proper pastor for this investigation is usually the pastor of the bride, but may be the pastor of the groom.[41]

2. Moreover, unless he is also in some sense the proper Ordinary or pastor of at least one of the parties, he must have the permission of the proper Ordinary or pastor, according to the following rules:

a. The proper pastor and Ordinary are those of the person's domicile or quasi-domicile. In the case of a *vagus* the pastor and Ordinary of the place where he is stopping are his proper pastor and Ordinary. A person who has only a diocesan domicile or quasi-domicile has as his proper Ordinary the Ordinary of the diocese where his domicile is, and as his proper pastor the pastor of the parish where he is actually stopping.

b. Month's residence is, for this purpose only, equivalent to domicile or quasi-domicile. A person's proper pastor or Ordinary according to month's residence is the pastor of the parish or the Ordinary of the diocese in which, for a morally continuous month before the marriage, the person has resided.

---

[41] S. C. Sacr., 29 June, 1941; *AAS,* 33–297; *Digest,* II, p. 255. Cf. also Cloran, *A Guide to the Use of the Instruction* (Newman Book Shop).

c. Two exceptions are mentioned, in which no permission need be asked: first, if the parties are *vagi* who are actually traveling and have no place of sojourn anywhere; second, if there occur a grave necessity. The first case is one of impossibility to ask permission because there is no one of whom it could reasonably be asked, the parties being not only both *vagi,* but also without any actual place of sojourn (*commoratio*), and hence having no proper pastor even in the place where they happen to be in transit (cf. c. 94, § 2). Permission of the Ordinary should, however, be obtained according to canon 1032, to assist at the marriage of a *vagus,* except in case of necessity. The second exception is where grave necessity excuses from asking permission of the proper pastor. A girl from New York is engaged to a naval officer who is momentarily pausing in San Francisco. While she is visiting in that city, he receives sailing orders; they wish to marry before his departure, and there is no time to receive an answer from New York by mail. It would seem to be a case of necessity excusing from the asking of this permission. But the freedom of the parties to marry would have to be established according to law (cf. c. 1020).

3. Where the permission is to be obtained, it should as a rule be obtained from the pastor of the bride-to-be; that is, the pastor either of her domicile or quasi-domicile or month's residence; but any reasonable cause is sufficient for asking it rather of the pastor of the groom. In the case of Catholics of different rites, where, for example, the man belongs to an Oriental Catholic rite and the woman to the Latin rite, the marriage should be performed before the pastor of the man and according to his rite; and permission if it is needed must be obtained from the man's pastor, unless there is special provision to the contrary. Greek Ruthenians, both in the United States and in Canada are under a special provision to the contrary; their marriages with Catholics of the Latin rite are to be before the pastor of the bride.[42] The *rite* of the marriage means the complexus of ceremonies in its celebration, whereas the juridical *form* means the required assistance of the designated official witness, with two other witnesses. These two terms must not be confused.

Fees Received in Connection With Assistance at Marriage. 1. If the permission of the proper pastor (domicile, quasi-domicile, or month's residence) of either of the parties was *required by law and was not obtained,* the offering received by the officiating priest, even if he be

---

[42] Cf. *Digest,* I, pp. 15 and 38; *AAS,* 21–152, Art. 39; *AAS,* 22–346, Art. 45. Also *Digest,* II, p. 6.

the pastor of the place or have delegation from him, must be sent to the proper pastor (c. 1097, § 3). This applies to the stole fee as such, not to any excess which was intended as a personal gift.[43] In remitting the fee, preference should be given, *ceteris paribus,* to the pastor of the bride; if there are several of these, it should, in the absence of diocesan regulations assigning the fee, be divided among them, including probably the pastor of month's residence if any.[44] The Bishop of the place may and should make regulations assigning the fee in such cases.

2. If the *permission was obtained and there is no diocesan regulation* assigning the fee even in that case to the proper pastor of the parties, then the pastor of the place is entitled to the fee (cc. 462, 463) and the officiating priest to any excess which was intended as a personal gift to him.[45]

3. If *permission was obtained but diocesan regulations assign the fee* even in that case to the proper pastor of the parties, these must be observed. The proper pastor receives the stole fee and the officiating priest the excess intended as a personal gift.[46]

4. If permission was obtained of the pastor of the groom, the fee may be retained, as permission of the bride's pastor is not strictly required.[47]

CANON 1098. In case it is impossible without grave inconvenience to have or to reach a pastor or Ordinary or delegated priest who can assist at the marriage in accordance with canons 1095, 1096:

1° In danger of death, marriage is valid and licit when celebrated before the witnesses alone; and even outside danger of death, provided it is prudently foreseen that the aforesaid condition of affairs will last for a month;

2° In both cases, if any other priest who can be present is available, he must be called and must assist at the marriage together with the witnesses, without prejudice to the validity of marriage before the witnesses alone.

State of Question. This canon provides for an *extraordinary form* of marriage, that is, before two competent witnesses only. Marriage

---

[43] Cf. Cappello, *De Matrimonio,* n. 689, 2.

[44] Cappello, *De Matrimonio,* n. 689, 5, would exclude the latter; but we think he must be considered one of the proper pastors *in this connection.*

[45] Cf. Anler-Bonzelet, *Pastoral Companion,* ed. 1943, n. 236; Augustine, *The Pastor According to the New Code,* p. 155.

[46] Cf. Vermeersch-Creusen, *Epitome,* II, n. 402.

[47] Cf. Carberry, *The Juridical Form of Marriage,* 1934, Cath. U. Canon Law Studies, n. 84, p. 113; *Australasian Catholic Record,* Jan., 1940, p. 66; Clifford, "The Interpretation of Canon 1097," in *Ecclesiastical Review,* Vol. 108, p. 116.

so celebrated is valid in two distinct cases: in danger of death, and outside danger of death, but in both cases, under certain prescribed conditions.

Extraordinary Form in Danger of Death. The following conditions are required for *validity:*

1. Danger of death of either party must exist according to prudent moral estimation (from any cause).

2. It must be impossible to have or to reach the Ordinary or pastor who should normally assist, or a delegate of either. Moral impossibility, that is, grave inconvenience is sufficient. Such impossibility exists when the pastor or Ordinary, though materially present in the place, is unable by reason of grave inconvenience to assist at the marriage.[48] If the pastor or Ordinary can be reached only by telegraph or telephone, it may be considered that he cannot be reached.[49] The grave inconvenience may consist in the disclosure of former hidden misconduct of the parties, which would be revealed by asking the pastor or Ordinary to assist.[50] When the pastor cannot assist at the marriage because of a prohibition of the civil law, it is considered that he cannot be had without grave inconvenience (S. C. Sacr., 24 Apr., 1935; *Digest,* II, p. 236). Grave inconvenience for the parties themselves, or for either of them, is sufficient (Code Commission, 3 May, 1945; *AAS,* Vol. 37, p. 149).

3. The presence of two competent witnesses is required for validity.

It is not required that the marriage be for the purpose of peace of conscience or the legitimation of children.

Licitness. If *any priest* (except, probably, a *vitandus* or one who is *under sentence* of censure) can be *easily had (si praesto sit)*, he must be called and must assist; if he assists, he has the faculties mentioned in canons 1044, 1045.

Extraordinary Form Outside Danger of Death. The conditions are exactly the same except that the danger of death is absent and the moral impossibility of reaching the pastor or Ordinary or a delegate of either must not only exist at the time of the marriage but must be prudently foreseen as likely to last for a month. If a nondelegated priest assists with the witnesses, he has the faculties mentioned in canon 1044.

---

[48] Code Com., 25 July, 1931; *AAS,* 23–388; *Digest,* I, p. 542.
[49] Cf. Code Com., 12 Nov., 1922; *AAS,* 14–662; *Digest,* I, p. 502.
[50] Cf. Cappello, *De Matrimonio,* n. 691.

CANON 1099. § 1. The following persons are obliged to observe the form above prescribed:

1° All who are baptized in the Catholic Church or who have been converted to it from heresy or schism, even though the former or the latter may later have left the Church, whenever they contract marriage among themselves;

2° The same persons above mentioned, if they contract marriage with non-Catholics, either baptized or not baptized, even after obtaining a dispensation from the impediment of mixed religion or disparity of cult;

3° Orientals, if they contract with Latins who are bound by this form.

§ 2. But, without prejudice to the provisions of § 1, n. 1, non-Catholics, whether baptized or not baptized, if they contract among themselves, are nowhere bound to observe the Catholic form of marriage; likewise exempt are persons born of non-Catholic parents, even though they have been baptized in the Catholic Church, who have grown up from infancy in heresy or schism or infidelity, when they contract with a non-Catholic party.

Who Are Bound to Observe the Form? 1. *Latin Catholics* are always bound, whether they marry among themselves, or marry non-Catholics, or marry Oriental Catholics, subject to the single exception stated in § 2. A woman of the Latin rite who transfers to the Oriental rite of the man *in matrimonio ineundo* according to canon 98 is not exempt from the Latin form (Code Commission, 29 Apr., 1940; *AAS,* 32-212; *Digest,* II, p. 49).

2. *Oriental Catholics* are bound by *this* form only when they contract with Latin Catholics who are so bound. The question whether Oriental Catholics marrying among themselves are bound by *their own law* of form will vary with the different rites.[51] The Greek Ruthenians in the United States and Canada are bound by the *Ne temere* in this matter.[52]

3. *Non-Catholics* are not bound by this form when they marry among themselves; but they are when they marry Latin Catholics, except as provided in the exception stated in § 2.

Exception. According to the text of § 2, persons born of non-Catholic parents, even though they have been baptized in the Catholic Church, who have grown up from infancy in heresy or schism or

---

[51] Cf. Cappello, *De Matrimonio,* n. 968. The best available summary of the laws of the various Oriental Catholic churches regarding the form of marriage is Gulovich, *Matrimonial Laws of the Catholic Eastern Churches,* in *The Jurist,* Vol. 4, p. 200. A full dissertation by Marback, *Marriage Legislation for the Catholics of the Oriental Rites in the U. S.,* appeared in 1946.

[52] Cf. *Digest,* I, pp. 15, 38; *AAS,* 21-152, Art. 39; *AAS,* 22-346, Art. 45.

infidelity, are exempt from this law when they contract with a non-Catholic party. On the application of this exemption, cf. Allen, *The Test of Catholicity under Canon* 1099, in the *Jurist,* Vol. 3, p. 595, and Vol. 4, p. 124. Does this exemption apply to these same persons (*ab acatholicis nati,* etc.) when they contract marriage with an *Oriental Catholic who is not bound to any form* for contracting a valid marriage? Yes (S. C. Or., 9 July, 1942; *Digest,* II, p. 338).

The Code Commission has held: (*a*) that the term "born of non-Catholic parents" includes persons born of a mixed marriage, one parent being a non-Catholic, the other a Catholic;[53] (*b*) that the same term includes children of apostates;[54] (*c*) that the reply reported above under (*a*) was declarative, not extensive.[55]

Though children of non-Catholic parents are exempt from the law of form according to this canon and its interpretations, yet they are bound by the impediment of disparity of cult when they marry an unbaptized person.[56]

The Holy Office held valid a marriage contracted in 1922, after the Code but *before the decision* of the Code Commission cited above under (*a*), with a non-Catholic by a girl who had been born of a mixed marriage, baptized in the Catholic Church, but brought up from infancy without any Catholic training.[57] What is the reason underlying this decision? Is it that the reply of the Code Commission was retroactive (cf. c. 17, § 2), or rather that the application of the law of the Code to this party in 1922 was *legally doubtful* and hence not binding (c. 15)?

CANON 1100. Except in case of necessity, in the celebration of marriage the rites which are either prescribed in ritual books approved by the Church or sanctioned by praisewothy customs must be observed.

The Rite. A brief summary of the rite:

1. Vested in surplice and white stole (or if Mass is to follow, in all vestments except the maniple), the priest says a few words.

2. He then asks and receives the consent of the parties according to the formula.

3. He then joins their right hands and each repeats after him the

---

[53] Code Com., 10 July, 1929; *AAS,* 21–573; *Digest,* I, p. 543.
[54] Code Com., 17 Feb., 1930; *AAS,* 22–195; *Digest,* I, p. 544.
[55] Code Com., 25 July, 1931; *AAS,* 23–388; *Digest,* I, p. 544.
[56] Code Com., 29 Apr., 1940; *AAS,* 32–212; *Digest,* II, p. 290.
[57] See *Digest,* I, p. 544, private reply of Holy Office, 9 June, 1931.

formula expressing present acceptance of the other as a life partner; after which the priest pronounces them man and wife, sprinkles them with holy water, blesses the ring and repeats the formula for the groom who places it on the bride's finger.

4. Some prayers follow.

5. Then the Mass, with solemn nuptial blessing (see c. 1101).

6. At the end of the Mass, after the third special prayer of the blessing, the priest again says a few words.

This function is reserved to the pastor according to canon 462.

CANON 1101. § 1. The pastor should see to it that the parties receive the solemn blessing, which may be given them even after they have lived a long time in the married state, but only at Mass, with the observance of the special rubric, and except during the forbidden time.

§ 2. The solemn blessing can be given either in person or through a representative, by that priest alone who can validly and licitly assist at the marriage.

The Solemn Nuptial Blessing. This has various forms:

1. Primarily it occurs in the votive Mass *pro sponso et sponsa,* and consists of three additional special prayers, of which two are said by the priest standing at the Epistle side of the altar, facing the bride and groom, immediately after the *Pater Noster;* and the third at the center of the altar, facing the bride and groom, after the *Bendicamus Domino.*

2. In case another Mass than the votive Mass *pro sponsis* must be said according to the rubrics, the solemn blessing consists of exactly the same prayers, the oration, secret, and postcommunion of the Mass *pro sponso et sponsa* being added to those of the day *sub unica conclusione,* and the three special prayers being said in the same way as above described, except that the last one follows the *Ite, Missa est.*

3. *Outside of Mass* the solemn blessing may not be given without an apostolic indult (c. 1101, § 1). This indult, however, is contained in the quinquennial faculties of Ordinaries, and is commonly subdelegated by them.[58] But when given outside of Mass in virtue of such an indult the blessing has, of course, an entirely different form, which is given in the Roman Ritual.[59]

4. There are certain cases in which the solemn nuptial blessing itself *cannot be given* in any form, for example, if the bride is a widow

---

[58] See Quinquennial Faculties, Faculties from the S. C. Rit., n. 5, *Digest,* II, p. 37.

[59] *Rituale Romanum,* Appendix, *De Matrimonio,* I.

who received it in her former marriage (c. 1143). In such cases, but only by apostolic indult *a substitute for the solemn blessing* may be used. This indult, too, is included in the quinquennial faculties,[60] and is commonly delegated. The form is given in the Roman Ritual.[61]

Except During the Forbidden Time. 1. The forbidden time here referred to is accurately stated in canon 1108, § 2; namely, from the first Sunday of Advent to Christmas, inclusive, and from Ash Wednesday to Easter, inclusive.

2. During this time, though marriage is permitted, the solemn blessing is forbidden, but the Ordinary can give permission for it, subject to liturgical laws (cf. c. 1108, § 3).

With the Observance of the Special Rubric. 1. The votive Mass *pro sponso et sponsa* may be said, outside the forbidden time (or, with the permission of the Ordinary, even during the forbidden time) with the following *exceptions:* Sundays, feasts of obligation though suppressed, doubles of the first or second class, privileged octaves of the first or second order (namely, the octaves of Epiphany, Easter, Pentecost, Corpus Christi), privileged *ferias* (namely, Ash Wednesday and the first three days of Holy Week), privileged vigils (namely, those of Pentecost, Christmas, and Epiphany), and All Souls' Day.[62] It is also excluded when a conventual Mass must be said, or a single Mass during the Major or Minor Litanies, with procession.

2. On the days when this Mass cannot be said (except on Good Friday and All Souls' Day), even during the forbidden time if the Ordinary has given permission for the solemn blessing, the oration, secret, and postcommunion of this Mass are added to those of the Mass of the day, *sub unica conclusione,* and the three special prayers of the blessing are given as in the Mass *pro sponsis*. It is done in this way even on Christmas and Easter, if the Ordinary has given permission for the blessing.[63]

By canon law itself, all forms of the nuptial blessing are forbidden:

1. If the bride has already received it in a former marriage (c. 1143);

2. Outside of Mass, without an apostolic indult (c. 1101);

3. During the forbidden time, unless permitted by the Ordinary (cc. 1101, § 1; 1108, §§ 2 and 3);

---

[60] See *Digest*, II, p. 37, n. 5.

[61] *Rituale Romanum*, Appendix, De Matrimonio, II.

[62] Cf. O'Connell, *The Celebration of Mass*, I, p. 94; Moretti, *Caeremoniale*, II, p. 548; *Roman Missal, Rubrica ante Missam pro sponso et sponsa; Additiones et Variationes,* II, 2.

[63] S. C. Rit., 14 June, 1918; *AAS*, 10–332; *Digest*, I, p. 547.

4. In mixed marriages (c. 1102, § 2).

In the first three cases, the substitute formula of the Roman Ritual (Appendix, *De Matrimonio,* II) may be used with the apostolic indult. In the case of mixed marriage, even this is excluded, without special permission (c. 1102, § 2).

We think it necessary to sum up this rather complicated matter in a condensed outline.

A SUMMARY OF CANONICAL AND LITURGICAL LAWS ON THE NUPTIAL BLESSING

The Nuptial Blessing Has Different Forms and One Substitute:

It is given:

1. In the Mass *pro sponso et sponsa* whenever that is permitted.
2. Otherwise, in the Mass of the day, with commemorations and special prayers.
3. Outside of Mass, with an apostolic indult (*Rit. Rom.,* Appendix, *De Matrimonio,* I).
4. As a substitute, when the blessing itself cannot be given, certain prayers can be used, with an apostolic indult (*Rit. Rom.,* Appendix, *De Matrimonio,* II).

The Nuptial Blessing May Not Be Given:

1. During the *closed time* (see below) without the permission of the Ordinary (c. 1108). With this permission the blessing may be given even during the closed time, and even then in the special votive Mass *pro sponso et sponsa,* if that is permitted according to the rubrics (S. C. Rit., 14 June, 1918; *AAS,* 10–332; *Digest,* I, p. 547).
2. Nor *outside of Mass,* without an apostolic indult (c. 1101, § 1). Bishops have this indult, with power to subdelegate (see Quinquennial Faculties, *Digest,* II, p. 37). The form of this blessing is n. 3 above.
3. Nor *if the bride has already received it* in a former marriage (c. 1143).
4. Nor in a *black Mass,* nor on *All Souls' Day.*
5. Nor in a *mixed marriage* (c. 1102, § 2).
   (If the nuptial blessing cannot be given because of any of the reasons mentioned in 1–3, the substitute blessing may be used, with an apostolic indult. This indult is also in the Quinquennial Faculties, with power to subdelegate.)

The Closed Time: From the First Sunday of Advent to Christmas, inclusive, and from Ash Wednesday to Easter, inclusive — marriage

permitted, but not the solemn nuptial blessing; the Ordinary may, however, permit this, except as noted above (c. 1108, § 3).

The Special Votive Mass Pro Sponso et Sponsa:

1. *When Is It Permitted?* At all times *except:*
   a. During the *closed time,* unless the Ordinary permits it;
   b. When the *rubrics forbid it.* It is so forbidden (in or out of the closed time):
      1) On Sundays and feasts of obligation, even suppressed (for list of these, see *Digest* I, p. 254, or *AAS,* 12–42).
      2) On doubles of I or II class.
      3) On privileged vigils; i.e., the vigils of Christmas, Epiphany, Pentecost (cf. *Digest,* I, p. 547).
      4) Within privileged octaves of I or II order; i.e., during the octaves of Epiphany, Easter, Pentecost, Corpus Christi.
      5) On privileged ferias; i.e., Ash Wednesday and the first three days of Holy Week.
      6) If an obligatory conventual Mass could not otherwise be said.
      7) On the Major or Minor Litanies, when only one Mass is said, with procession.
2. *How Is the Blessing Given in This Mass?* It consists of three special prayers, two after the *Pater Noster,* said at the Epistle side, facing the bride and groom, the third after the *Benedicamus Domino,* said at the center of the altar, and followed by an aspersion with holy water (cf. O'Connell, *The Celebration of Mass,* I, p. 92).

The Nuptial Blessing in Another Mass Than the Special Votive Mass:

When the Mass *pro sponso et sponsa* is not permitted (see above), the Mass of the day is said, with the commemoration from the Mass *pro sponso et sponsa* in the first place, *sub unica conclusione,* other commemorations according to the rubrics, and the three prayers of the blessing said in the same way as in the Mass *pro sponso et sponsa.*

CANON 1102. § 1. In marriages between a Catholic and a non-Catholic party, the questions regarding consent must be put according to canon 1095, § 1, n. 3.

§ 2. But all sacred rites are forbidden; in case it is foreseen that graver evils will result from this prohibition, the Ordinary may permit some of the usual ecclesiastical ceremonies, excluding always the celebration of Mass.

Mixed Marriages: The Questions Regarding Consent Must Be Put.

This provision revokes the permission given by the Holy Office allowing "passive assistance" in certain places.[64]

But All Sacred Rites Are Forbidden. 1. Not merely the nuptial
Mass, but any Mass which from the circumstances might be taken as
an adjunct to the ceremony, is forbidden.[65]

2. Other sacred rites are equally forbidden, but the Ordinary may
permit some of the usual ceremonies, except the Mass.

3. The place for the ceremony is *outside the church,* unless the
Ordinary, to prevent more serious evils, permits it to be held in
the church (c. 1109, § 3).

4. The usual practice is as follows: the priest wears street clothes or
a cassock; gives a short talk (an excellent one is that given in the
priests' small ritual). If a dignitary is present it is proper to ask him
to give the talk, and a priestly blessing. Although mixed marriages in
general are forbidden for good and serious reasons, yet when one is
actually taking place with the Church's permission, there is no need
of being more severe than the Church herself. A little sentiment is
proper, reasonable, and beautiful. Let the parties feel the joy and
sacredness of marriage. If the non-Catholic party is baptized, they
may be told that their union is a sacrament; that by administering it
to each other they have already begun to be to each other what their
holy state calls upon them to be through life — mutual helpmates in
the supernatural life, companions on the road to heaven.

CANON 1103. § 1. After the marriage, the pastor or the one who
is taking his place must as soon as possible enter in the marriage
record the names of the contracting parties and witnesses, the place
and date of the celebration of the marriage and other entries according to the method prescribed in ritual books and by his Ordinary;
and this, even though another priest delegated by himself or by the
Ordinary assisted at the marriage.

§ 2. Moreover, according to canon 470, § 2, the pastor shall note
also in the baptismal register that the party has contracted marriage
on a certain day in his parish. In case the party was baptized elsewhere, the pastor of the marriage shall, either personally or through
the episcopal Curia, send notice of the marriage to the pastor of
baptism, so that the marriage may be recorded in the baptismal
register.

§ 3. When marriage is contracted according to canon 1098, the
priest, if he assisted at it, otherwise the witnesses are bound *in solidum*

---

[64] Code Com., 10 March, 1928; *AAS*, 20–120; *Digest*, I, p. 546. The permission,
which is revoked by the Code, was given by the Holy Office for Germany and other
places, 21 June, 1912. Cf. *AAS*, 8–316.
[65] Code Com., 10 Nov., 1925; *AAS*, 17–583; *Digest*, I, p. 546.

with the contracting parties to see to it that the marriage be recorded as soon as possible in the prescribed books.

Registration of the Marriage. This matter is again insisted on and the manner of doing it is described in detail in the recent Instruction on Investigation of the Parties' Freedom to Marry.[66] If the place of baptism was Russia, it is sufficient to send notice of the marriage to the Commission for Russia.[67]

CANON 1104. Only for the gravest and most urgent reasons, and by the Ordinary of the place in person, not by the Vicar General without a special mandate, can it be permitted that a *marriage of conscience* be contracted; that is, that a marriage be celebrated without the banns and in secret, according to the canons which follow.

Marriage of Conscience. This means not any marriage contracted through motives of conscience, but a secret marriage permitted by the Ordinary for grave reasons and whose secrecy is protected by law according to the following canons. For example, it might happen in certain countries that a military officer or a special employee in certain services would lose his position or his chance of promotion if known to be married; or that a man and woman publicly living together and passing, without scandal, for man and wife, would suffer loss of reputation by a public ceremony.

CANON 1105. The permission to celebrate a marriage of conscience carries with it the promise and the grave obligation of keeping secrecy on the part of the priest who assists at the marriage, the witnesses, the Ordinary and his successors, and even the other contracting party as long as the first does not consent to the divulgation of the marriage.

CANON 1106. The obligation of this promise on the part of the Ordinary does not extend to a case in which any scandal or serious harm to the sanctity of marriage is imminent as a result of the observance of secrecy, or in which the parents fail to see to the baptism of the children born of such a marriage, or have them baptized under false names, unless in the meantime within thirty days they give notice to the Ordinary of the birth and baptism of the child, with the true indication of the parents, nor to a case in which they neglect the Christian education of the children.

CANON 1107. A marriage of conscience is not to be recorded in the usual matrimonial and baptismal registers, but in the special book

---

[66] S. C. Sacr., 29 June, 1941, *AAS*, 33–297, *Digest*, II, p. 253. Cf. Cloran, *A Guide to the Use of the Instruction* (Newman Book Shop).

[67] Commission for Russia, 13 July, 1928; *AAS*, 20–260; *Digest*, I, p. 259.

mentioned in canon 379, which is to be kept in the secret archives of the Curia.

Section 3. Other Provisions (cc. 1108–1117)

PRELIMINARY SURVEY

Time of Marriage (c. 1108)
Place of Marriage (c. 1109)
Primary Effect: the Bond (c. 1110)
Mutual Rights Begin Immediately (c. 1111)
Wife Shares Canonically in State of Husband (c. 1112)
Duties of Parents Toward Their Children (c. 1113)
Legitimacy (c. 1114)
Presumptions of Fatherhood and Legitimacy (c. 1115)
Legitimation by Subsequent Marriage (cc. 1116, 1117)

CANON 1108. § 1. Marriage may be contracted at any time of the year.

§ 2. Only the solemn blessing of marriage is forbidden from the first Sunday of Advent until the day of the Nativity of Our Lord inclusive, and from Ash Wednesday, until Easter Sunday inclusive.

§ 3. But Ordinaries of places can, subject to liturgical laws, permit the blessing even during the aforesaid time, for just cause, notifying the parties that they should abstain from excessive festivity.

Time of Marriage. 1. It may be celebrated at any time of the year. May it be celebrated at any time of the day? In the absence of special diocesan regulations, yes; though the Ordinary can regulate the hours of sacred rites in churches (c. 1171), and could probably forbid evening weddings.[68]

2. The forbidden time excludes only the solemn blessing, and even this may be permitted by the Ordinary for just cause, subject to liturgical laws. See summary under canon 1101.

3. This discipline is far more lenient than it once was. Formerly even a wedding breakfast was forbidden, and the closed time was longer.

CANON 1109. § 1. Marriage between Catholics should be celebrated in the parish church; it may however be celebrated in another church or oratory, whether public or semi-public, only with the consent of the Ordinary of the place or the pastor.

§ 2. Ordinaries of places can permit that marriage be celebrated in

---

[68] Cf. Ayrinhac-Lydon, *Marriage Legislation*, p. 286; Dodwell, *The Time and Place for the Celebration of Marriage*, Cath. U., 1942, p. 88.

a private house only in an extraordinary case and always on condition
that there be a just and reasonable cause; but Ordinaries must not
permit it in churches or oratories of a seminary or of religious
women, unless in case of necessity and with suitable safeguards.

§ 3. But marriages between a Catholic and a non-Catholic party
are to be celebrated outside the church; in case the Ordinary
prudently judges that this cannot be observed without giving occasion to greater evils, it is left to his prudent discretion to dispense
from this requirement, without prejudice however to the provision of
canon 1102, § 2.

Place of Marriage. 1. Marriages *between Catholics* should be in the
parish church; but this is not an inflexible rule. With the consent of
the Ordinary or of the pastor they may be celebrated in any public or
semi-public oratory, except one connected with a seminary or a house
of religious women. For a marriage in these places the permission of
the Ordinary is needed, and he should grant it only in case of
necessity and with suitable safeguards.

2. *Mixed marriages,* whether the non-Catholic party is baptized or
not, should be celebrated outside the church unless the Ordinary
dispenses from this regulation. Probably such marriages are not forbidden in the sacristy.[69]

3. *Private houses* are not the normal place for marriage. It is not
clear whether this prohibition applies only to Catholic marriages,
mentioned in the preceding paragraph of the canon, or also to mixed
marriages, mentioned in the succeeding paragraph. Probably, to both,
since the canon makes no distinction and it seems unbecoming to
introduce one in favor of mixed marriages. (Cf. Dodwell, *The Time
and Place for the Celebration of Marriage,* pp. 108, 127.) Ordinaries
may prudently use their power to dispense in this matter.

Corollary: The Churching of Women After Childbirth. 1. This is a
pious custom of great antiquity in the Latin Church, which perhaps
owes its origin to the example given by the Blessed Virgin in the
mystery of the Presentation.

2. It is not obligatory as far as the mother is concerned, but a pastor
is bound to perform it if reasonably asked to do so (cf. c. 464, § 1).
Catholic mothers are entitled to it after the birth of a legitimate
child, even though the child was born of a mixed marriage or died
without baptism.

3. It is not a reserved parochial function (c. 462).

---

[69] Wernz-Vidal, *De Matrimonio,* n. 579, note 29.

CANON 1110. By a valid marriage there is produced between the parties a bond which is by nature perpetual and exclusive; moreover Christian marriage confers grace upon the parties if they place no obstacle to it.

Primary Effect of Marriage. The matrimonial bond, primary effect of every valid marriage, is by nature perpetual and exclusive.

Graces of Christian Marriage. Christian marriage here means a sacrament. Such is a marriage between two Catholics, between a Catholic and a validly baptized Protestant or schismatic, or between two validly baptized Protestants or schismatics; not, however, between a Catholic and an unbaptized person, even if performed in the church and with a dispensation. The form of the sacrament is the mutual acceptance expressed in the valid contract. The sacramental graces include an increase of sanctifying grace and actual graces. "This sacrament not only increases sanctifying grace, the permanent principle of the supernatural life, in those who . . . place no obstacle in its way, but also adds particular gifts, dispositions, seeds of grace, by elevating and perfecting the natural powers in such a way that the parties are assisted not only in understanding but in knowing intimately, in adhering to firmly, in willing effectively, and in putting into practice those things which pertain to the marriage state, its aims and duties. In fine, it gives them the right to the actual assistance of grace, whensoever they need it for fulfilling the duties of their state."[70]

Obstacles to Grace. Recall the following from sacramental theology:

1. *Obex sacramenti,* or an obstacle to the sacrament, is want of intention, rendering the sacrament invalid. This is not the question here.

2. *Obex gratiae,* or an obstacle to grace, is want of faith, or absence of the required state of sanctifying grace; it leaves the sacrament valid but renders it sterile, void of grace (*informe, infructuosum*). It is of this that the canon speaks.

3. When an *obstacle to grace is removed,* sacraments which are validly conferred are said to *revive,* that is, to become fruitful, with the exception of the Holy Eucharist, and probably also of penance. Hence sacramental marriage validly received by parties who were not at the time in the state of grace, would confer the sacramental graces if and when the parties afterward recovered sanctifying grace.

CANON 1111. From the very beginning of the marriage both

---

[70] Pius XI, Encyclical, *Casti connubii.* Cf. Vermeersch, *What Is Marriage,* p. 29, n. 76.

parties have the same right and duty as regards the acts peculiar to the conjugal life.

Conjugal Rights. 1. The right which is the *essential object* of the marriage contract has been sufficiently discussed under canons 1081 and 1082. This right remains radically as long as the marriage bond lasts, though its exercise may have been forfeited or suspended (cc. 1129, 1131).

2. Other rights pertain to the *integrity of conjugal life;* such are the right to cohabitation of bed and board. This community of life may in exceptional cases be suspended, as in marriages of conscience.

3. Both parties have these rights *from the beginning of the marriage.* This is a change from the old law, which allowed either party during the first two months to refuse the marriage debt if either wished to consider entering a religious institute of solemn vows. Now, such deliberations must precede the marriage. Married persons cannot validly enter the novitiate while the marriage lasts (c. 542, 1°).

4. The right of *both parties* is *equal* in this respect; the authority of the husband as head of the family is by no means absolute, and does not extend to depriving the wife of her personal rights.[71]

CANON 1112. Unless the contrary is provided by special law, the wife shares in the status of her husband as regards canonical effects.

Canonical Effects are effects of the marriage in canon law; for example, the wife's participation in the husband's *status* (privileges, etc.) according to this canon; in his *domicile* (c. 93); *capacity to be sued* in a certain jurisdiction (c. 1561); *right of burial* in a certain place (c. 1229, § 2), etc.

Merely Civil Effects (cf. c. 1016) are regulated by civil law, subject always to the natural law. Such are, for example, rights of succession to property, the use of the husband's family name, etc.[72]

CANON 1113. Parents are bound by a most serious obligation to provide to the best of their power for the religious and moral as well as for the physical and civil education of their children, and also to provide for their temporal welfare.

Duties of Parents. *Education* may be defined as the progressive and harmonious development of the faculties by which children are gradually and properly formed into perfect men and women. This is the

---

[71] Cf. Vermeersch, *What Is Marriage,* nn. 53–58, pp. 23–24.
[72] Cf. V-C, *Epit.,* II, n. 416.

primary duty of parents to their children. It includes physical education, that is, the development of proper physiological habits, the providing of proper food and living conditions, and training in some occupation which will provide a livelihood; and spiritual education, that is, moral and religious training. In order to fulfill these duties, parents have by the law of nature parental authority. The natural right of parents to control the education of their children, subject, of course, to the natural law and free from unreasonable state control, has been recognized and stanchly defended by the Supreme Court of the United States,[73] and this decision of the U. S. Supreme Court was explicitly commended by Pope Pius XI.[74] The choice of a state of life is not part of the child's education; it is a purely personal matter in which the child must make the choice, under wise guidance, having in view the true purpose of life, which education must reveal. Here the parents' duty and right are limited to guidance, aid, advice. "Education" which fails to reveal to the child the only true purpose of life, that is, the attainment of his supernatural destiny, is not education.

Some Duties Mentioned Elsewhere in the Code. 1. To see that their children receive *baptism* as soon as possible (c. 770).

2. To see that they receive *catechetical instruction* (c. 1335). This duty is emphasized in the Decree on Catechetical Instruction.[75]

3. To see that they receive *Holy Communion* at Easter time (c. 860).

4. To see that they *attend Catholic schools* (c. 1374).

5. *Negative* duties regarding a *state of life* are: they must not deter children from the choice of a higher life (cc. 538, 971), nor coerce them to adopt such a life (cc. 971, 2352); nor coerce them to marry (c. 1087).

CANON 1114. Children who are conceived or born of a valid or putative marriage are legitimate, unless at the time of conception the use of the marriage theretofore contracted was forbidden to the parents because of solemn religious profession or the reception of a sacred order.

The Principle of Legitimacy. Putative marriage is defined in canon 1015, § 4. However, a marriage is usually not regarded as putative if it is invalid for want of form. This apparent limitation on the definition

---

[73] Pierce vs. Society of the Holy Names of Jesus and Mary; 268 U. S. 510 (the "Oregon School Case").

[74] *Encyclical on Christian Education*, America Press edition, p. 11.

[75] Cf. S. C. Conc., 12 Jan., 1935; *AAS*, 27–145; *Digest*, II, p. 412.

as given in the Code is implied in the older law. But it remains true that in special circumstances such a marriage may be putative.[76] If a marriage is either valid or putative, either at the time of conception or at the time of birth, the children are born legitimate, subject to the exception to be stated.

Exception. Though a marriage be putative, or even valid, its use may afterward become illicit because of the reception of sacred orders by the man, or the solemn religious profession of either the man or the woman (cf. cc. 1072, 1073). A child conceived at such a time is not born legitimate, though the marriage be putative or valid.

Classifications of Illegitimacy. Illegitimate children may be either *natural* or *spurious;* they are *natural* if no impediment existed which would have prevented the parents from contracting validly; otherwise they are *spurious.* These are further classified as: *sacrilegious,* if solemn religious profession or sacred order existed either as an impediment or as an obstacle to the licit use even of a valid marriage; *adulterine,* if the impediment of *ligamen* existed; *incestuous* if conceived in incest outside the direct line; *nefarious* if conceived in incest in the direct line; *simply spurious* if some other diriment impediment existed. These distinctions are not all of equal canonical importance.[77]

CANON 1115. § 1. The father is he who is indicated by a lawful marriage, unless the contrary is demonstrated by evident proofs.

§ 2. Children born at least six months later than the date of the marriage or within ten months after the date when conjugal relations ceased, are presumed to be legitimate.

Presumption of Fatherhood. This presumption of the Roman law has passed into the jurisprudence of nearly all civilized countries as well as into the Code. A child born of a married woman is presumed to be the child of her lawful husband. This is a *praesumptio iuris simpliciter* (cf. cc. 1825, 1826), admitting of contrary proof; but it is overcome only by *evident* proofs. To overcome it, it must be proved that during the entire time when conception might have occurred intercourse was impossible by reason of absence, impotence, or separation. Confession of adultery on the part of the woman, even confirmed by the testimony of her supposed partner in crime, is not sufficient.

Presumption of Legitimacy. This is not a different presumption from the one already explained, but a further specification of the same;

---

[76] Cf. Cappello, *De Matrimonio,* n. 746; Wernz, *Ius Decretalium,* IV, n. 682.
[77] Cf. Payen, *De Matrimonio,* II, n. 2162.

that is, it specifies the time when the child must be born in order that the above presumption shall be operative. We have seen (c. 1114) that a child born of persons who are married is simply legitimate; and this would be true according to that canon even if the child were born the day after the marriage. But in that case it might *have to be proved* that the child was really the child of the lawful husband. There would indeed exist a *general presumption* of legitimacy unless the husband immediately repudiated the child; but the *strict presumption* mentioned in c. 1115, § 1, would not exist; that presumption arises only when the child is born either *six months or more after the date of the marriage,* or *ten months or less after the ceasing of conjugal relations.*

These are the approximate limits of the period of gestation. A child born *less than six months after the marriage* cannot have been *conceived* in wedlock; and the same is true of a child born *more than ten months after the latest possibility of marital intercourse.* In the latter case, supposing that the impossibility of intercourse were proved, the child would be evidently illegitimate; in the former case he would be legitimate if the husband were his father, but this conclusion would not be favored by the very special presumption of this canon.

These periods of time are to be computed according to canon 34, § 3; that is, according to the calendar, excluding the fractional first day and including all of the corresponding day in the sixth or tenth month. It may be objected that the period of gestation is not affected by accidental calendar variations. Perfectly true; but there is nothing to prevent the Code from adopting a slightly variable standard, provided it is definite and determinable according to law in any individual case. It has done so here (cf. c. 34, § 3). Cappello substitutes 180 days for six months, and 300 days for ten months (*De Matrimonio,* n. 748).

Foundlings are presumed to be legitimate until the contrary is proved.

CANON 1116. By the subsequent marriage of the parents, whether true or putative, whether newly contracted or validated, even though it was not consummated, the children are made legitimate, provided the parents were legally capable of contracting marriage together at the time of conception, or of pregnancy, or of birth.

Legitimation by Subsequent Marriage. 1. There is question here of *legitimation;* the child is supposed to have been born illegitimate, and is legitimated by the subsequent marriage of his parents.

2. The marriage is *subsequent to the child's birth;* if it took place before his birth though subsequent to his conception, he would be born legitimate and would not need legitimation (c. 1114).

3. But *not every subsequent marriage* has this effect; it is necessary that at the time of conception, or of birth, or at some time between the two, the parties be capable according to law of contracting a valid marriage.

Notes. 1. Is a child who was conceived while the parents were under the impediment of age or disparity of cult legitimated by the marriage of his parents after his birth, provided the impediment has ceased at the time of the marriage? This question was asked of the Code Commission, and the reply was, no; which is in strict accord with the text of the canon.[78]

2. By canon 1051, the *dispensation from an impediment* may under certain conditions carry with it an implied legitimation of children already conceived or born.

CASES ON LEGITIMACY AND LEGITIMATION

1. Sempronius, a married man, begot a child of Bertha, an unmarried woman. After the child's birth Sempronius' wife dies, and soon afterward he marries Bertha without a dispensation. Was the child legitimate at birth? Is he legitimated?

2. Titus and Anita after being engaged for some time yield to temptation and a child is conceived. Knowing her pregnancy, Anita hastens the marriage, and the child is born three months after the wedding. Is he legitimate? Legitimated?

3. Andrew, soon after his marriage to Andromeda, is sent to South America on business and is away for one year. On his return he finds that a child was born to his wife just one month before his arrival. Legitimate or not?

4. Cleopatra, unmarried, conceives of Timon, also unmarried, and has a child. Later, Timon is rather urgently persuaded to marry Cleopatra, but he departs immediately thereafter, never consummating the marriage. Is the child legitimated?

5. Cassandra, who has conceived of Alexander, soon afterward marries Anthony. Her child is born seven months after the wedding. What is the presumption and what is the fact regarding his legitimacy?

6. Antonio, not quite sixteen, marries Marinella, just sixteen, before the pastor and two witnesses but without any dispensation. The marriage is

---

[78] Code Com., 6 Dec., 1930; *AAS*, 23–25; *Digest*, I, p. 550.

kept secret for some time, and is not consummated until two years later. When the first child is born Antonio is nineteen. Knowing their marriage was invalid, both parties go through a public ceremony to validate it. Was the child legitimate? Is he legitimated?

7. Caesarius, unbaptized, married Clementine, a Catholic. After the birth of two children, Clementine discovers to her horror that no dispensation from disparity of cult had been obtained. Her grief so moves Caesarius that he becomes a Catholic and receives baptism. Is the marriage validated? Are the children legitimate?

8. Ariadne and Seneca, second cousins (third degree of the collateral line) lived together in public and notorious concubinage for five years and had three children. Now they obtain a dispensation from the Ordinary[79] and are duly married. Are the children legitimated?

9. Brutus was born of a Catholic mother and an infidel father, both parties having at their marriage deceived the pastor by a false certificate of baptism. Later both repent, a dispensation is obtained from the Holy Office, but before the renewal of consent the man dies suddenly. Is the son Brutus legitimate or legitimated?

10. Bertha, wife to Titus, commits adultery with Sempronius and conceives a child of him. Before the birth of the child, Titus dies, and Bertha marries Caesar. The child is born during this marriage. After a few years Caesar dies and Bertha finally marries Sempronius, the father of her child. Give a reasoned answer on the status of the child.

CANON 1117. Children legitimated by a subsequent marriage are regarded as in all respects equivalent to legitimate children as regards canonical effects, unless the contrary is expressly provided.

Principle. As regards canonical effects, legitimation by subsequent marriage is equivalent to legitimacy, unless the contrary is expressly provided by law.

Notes. 1. The Code Commission declared that this is true regarding the effect of legitimacy which is mentioned in canon 1363, § 1, namely, fitness for licit admission to the seminary.[80] This reply confirms the literal interpretation of this canon, although canon 1363, § 1, does not expressly mention it (cf. c. 984, 1°).

2. Cases where the contrary is expressly provided by law are: e.g.: canon 232, § 2, 1° (Cardinal); canon 331, § 1, 1° (Bishop); canon 320, § 2 (Abbot and Prelate *nullius*).

3. Where the subsequent marriage is a validation by way of *sanatio in radice* (cf. c. 1138) it has certain special consequences.

---

[79] Cf. Quinquennial Faculties, S. C. Sacr., n. 1; *Digest*, II, p. 33.
[80] Code Com., 13 July, 1930; *AAS*, 22–365; *Digest*, I, p. 661.

CASES AND QUESTIONS

1. In a forum discussion, one of the speakers states that the Catholic Church regards all Protestant marriages as mere concubinage, because she recognizes only indissoluble marriages, whereas Protestants believe in divorce. Can you answer this charge in a way that will be clear and acceptable to the mixed audience? (Cc. 1084, 1012, § 2, 1110).

2. X contends that the ordinary non-Catholic marriage can usually be declared null for want of consent, because "indissolubility is excluded." What do you say? (Cc. 1084, 1086, § 1).

3. John, a Catholic, is so desirous to marry Caroline, an Episcopalian, that he conceals the fact that they are second cousins. They are married with a dispensation from mixed religion, but not from consanguinity (3rd degree collateral line, cc. 96, § 3, 1076, § 2). The marriage is invalid for consanguinity. Is it also invalid for want of consent, inasmuch as John knew he was contracting invalidly? (C. 1085).

4. In a seminarians' discussion group, X, who has read a standard author on matrimonial consent, contends that if one party alone positively excludes the primary purpose of marriage, without any manifestation of this intention to the other party, the marriage is valid: "*tantum conditio in pactum deducta matrimonium irritat.*" Y, who has read carefully a few cases, contends that in such a case the marriage is invalid. Who is right? (C. 1086, § 2).

5. A man of 25, but of weak and flexible character, was forced by his father, a violent man, to marry a girl he had seduced. Could the fear thus produced by the father be considered unjust? On what would the court's decision regarding the nullity of the marriage chiefly depend? (C. 1087; *Digest,* II, p. 323, n. 12).

6. What conditions are required by law for the validity of a marriage by proxy? (C. 1089). Cf. *Conference Bulletin of the Archdiocese of New York,* Vol. 20, pp. 1–18 (March, 1943), *Instructions for Priests Arranging Proxy Marriages for Military Personnel* (Monsignor McCormick).

7. How can the Church consider a future condition whose fulfillment is impossible, as though it had not been made? Does the Church supply matrimonial consent in this case? (Cc. 1092, 1°, 1081, § 1).

8. Can the administrator of a vacant parish validly assist at marriages in the parish? (Cc. 1095, § 1, 1°, 451, § 2, 2°, 473, § 1).

9. A religious priest is asked by a neighboring pastor to "take charge of the parish for a few days." While he is thus in charge, he assists at a marriage in which all the preliminaries had been taken care of by the pastor. Is it valid? (Cf. c. 1096, § 1; A Coronata, *Institutiones,* Vol. I, n. 490, p. 593, note 7, but see reply of Code Com., 25 Jan., 1943, cited in text under c. 1096, *AAS,* 35–58). What should the religious substitute have done? (C. 1095, § 2).

10. St. Conrad's is a "national" parish for all German-speaking Cath-

olics in the city. Can the pastor *validly* assist, anywhere in the city, at the marriage of two non-German-speaking Catholics, who belong to one of the other parishes in the city? (C. 1095, § 1, 2°, S. C. Conc., 1 Feb., 1908, ad VIII, *Fontes*, n. 4344, Vol. VI, p. 882). Could the pastor of one of the regular territorial parishes *validly* assist, in his own parish, at the marriage of two German-speaking Catholics who belong to St. Conrad's? Could he do the same in any other parish of the city?

11. Can the pastor of a parish in which there is a military camp validly assist at the marriage of a soldier in the camp? (*Digest*, II, p. 589, p. 597, n. 17).

12. In a certain marriage, the groom resides in New York; the bride, though a respectable person, has no permanent residence; she is a *vaga*, and is staying in St. Charles's parish in Cincinnati, where the marriage is to take place. Can the pastor of St. Charles validly and licitly assist? (Cc. 1095, § 1, 2°, 1097, § 1, 2°). Should he obtain any permission from the Ordinary? (C. 1032).

13. The usual fee for marriages in a certain ecclesiastical province is $25. X, a religious priest not connected with the parish, obtains delegation and permission from the pastor and so assists at the marriage of a near relative. The groom makes an offering of $50. Is X entitled to keep the entire offering (for his religious institute)? Under what conditions may he keep the surplus over the regular fee? (Cc. 462, 4°, 463, § 3).

14. A hospital chaplain who has no faculties for marriage finds a Catholic man in danger of death. His "wife" is at his bedside. He talks to both of them, learns that she is a non-Catholic and that their marriage was celebrated only before a justice of the peace. Both are anxious to validate the marriage. The hospital is in a small place far from the seat of the diocese, and the pastor is away for several days. The man's condition is critical; he may not live that long. The chaplain declares a dispensation from disparity of cult, obtains from both parties verbally the promises required by canon 1061, calls two nurses to act as witnesses, and receives from both parties the expression of present mutual matrimonial consent. The man goes to confession, receives the last sacraments, and dies in peace the next day. Discuss the case (cc. 1137, 1098, 1°, 1044). What registrations will have to be taken care of? (Cc. 1046, 1103).

15. Can a pastor validly assist at a marriage in a pious or religious house which has been withdrawn from his jurisdiction according to canon 464, § 2? (Cf. Cappello, in *Periodica*, Vol. 18, p. 150*).

Readings:

Rimlinger, *Error Invalidating Matrimonial Consent*, Cath. U., 1932; Sangmeister, *Force and Fear as Precluding Matrimonial Consent*, Cath. U., 1932; Timlin, *Conditional Matrimonial Consent*, Cath. U., 1934; Carberry, *The Juridical Form of Marriage*, Cath. U., 1934; Dillon, *Common Law*

Marriage, Cath. U., 1942; Dodwell, *The Time and Place for the Celebration of Marriage,* Cath. U., 1942; McDevitt, *Legitimacy and Legitimation,* Cath. U., 1941; Gulovich, *Matrimonial Laws of the Catholic Eastern Churches,* in *The Jurist,* Vol. 4, p. 200; *Irish Ecclesiastical Record,* Vol. 39, p. 410 (a case on conflict between internal and external forum); Vol. 38, p. 411 (case on conditional consent); Vol. 49, p. 85 (case on restriction of *debitum* to safe period); *Periodica,* Vol. 23, p. 201* (Vermeersch, two cases on assistance by pastor); *Irish Eccl. Rec.,* Vol. 38, p. 520 (on legitimacy and legitimation); *Ecclesiastical Review,* Vol. 108, p. 116 (Clifford, on interpretation of canon 1097); *Clergy Review,* Vol. 21, p. 358 (Mahoney, nuptial blessing on All Souls' day); *The Jurist,* Vol. 2, p. 248 (Alford, on common law marriage); Vol. 3, p. 595 and Vol. 4, p. 124 (Allen, on the test of Catholicity under canon 1099); Vol. 3, p. 612 (Hannan, on the presumption of legitimacy, canon 1115).

CHAPTER XV

DISSOLUTION, SEPARATION, CONVALIDATION

Section 1. Dissolution of the Bond (cc. 1118–1127)

PRELIMINARY SURVEY

Absolute Indissolubility (c. 1118)
Dissolution of Non-consummated Marriage (c. 1119)
The Pauline Privilege (c. 1120)
The Interpellations (c. 1121)
Form and Procedure of Interpellations (c. 1122)
The Right to Marry Again (c. 1123)
The Right Not Lost by Cohabitation (c. 1124)
Dissolution of Natural Bond (c. 1125)
Time When Dissolution Effective (c. 1126)
The Privilege of the Faith in Doubtful Cases (c. 1127)

CANON 1118. Marriage which is *ratum et consummatum* cannot be dissolved by any human power, nor by any cause save death.

Absolute Indissolubility. Indissolubility is an essential property of marriage by the natural law; hence every valid marriage is indissoluble in some sense, but not absolutely. It is indissoluble by the parties or by any human power. Both of the essential properties of marriage "acquire a peculiar firmness in Christian marriage by reason of its sacramental character" (c. 1013). In the present canon, the term *ratum* means Christian marriage, that is, one in which both parties are validly baptized, and which is therefore a sacrament. *Consummatum* means that the marriage is moreover (*after* becoming a sacrament by the baptism of both parties) consummated by the exercise of the conjugal right. Such a marriage alone is absolutely indissoluble until death.

The *fact* of this indissolubility is proved from the dogmatic definition of the Council of Trent.[1]

As to the *reason:* "The ultimate reason for this inflexibility may be found in the mystical signification of Christian marriage. According

[1] *Sess.* XXIV, *de sacr. matr.*, canons 5, 7.

547

to St. Paul (Ephesians 5:32), marriage between Christians reproduces the perfect union which exists forever between Christ and His Church. Now this reproduction is achieved in its perfection in marriage between baptized persons which has been consummated. Common sense teaches us that by the use of the conjugal right marriage receives a sort of completion; something irreparable has taken place; the affective and verbal self-surrender has been supplemented by an actual physical one which justifies the expression, very significant in itself, of *consummated marriage*. It is consummated in the physical order, and it is also consummated in the symbolical and mystical order, in which it represents the indefectible union between Christ and His Church."[2]

CANON 1119. Non-consummated marriage between baptized persons or between a baptized and a non-baptized person, is dissolved both *ipso iure* by solemn religious profession, and through a dispensation granted for just cause by the Apostolic See, at the request of both parties or of either party, even though the other be unwilling.

Non-consummated Marriage. 1. The consummation of marriage is effected by conjugal copula, which has been defined according to its physiological elements as the penetration of the vagina by the male organ and the emission of true semen within it. If any of these elements is wanting there is no consummation.

2. If conjugal intercourse has been had only with the use of contraceptive instruments several cases may be distinguished: if the instrument was used by the man, there is no consummation; if it was used by the woman the case would be doubtful.

3. If birth prevention has taken the form of onanism in the strict sense, it may be admitted that the act is not a consummation of the marriage; but if this fact appears in the course of proceedings for a dispensation from the bond, the dispensation will not be granted, even though it be proved that the marriage was not consummated.[3]

4. Intercourse before marriage is not a consummation of the marriage.

Dissolution of Non-consummated Marriage. 1. Such a marriage has its natural indissolubility; it is indissoluble by the parties themselves or by any merely human power. It can be dissolved extrinsically by the Church using the divine authority entrusted to it by Christ.

---

[2] Vermeersch, *What Is Marriage*, n. 68, p. 26.
[3] S. C. Sacr., Instruction, 7 May, 1923, n. 11; *AAS*, 15–389; *Digest*, I, p. 768.

2. From what source do we know that the Church has this power? We know it from the practice of the Church. Beginning with the fifteenth century (Martin V and Eugene IV) we have a long and increasing line of papal dispensations from the bond of non-consummated marriage. Now this universal practice and teaching, even for a few centuries only, is infallibly correct, because the Church herself is infallible in faith and morals.

3. In what sense the Church here dispenses from a divine law has been briefly explained in connection with canon 1040.[4]

4. The Church exercises her power only in cases where at least one of the parties is baptized. If both are baptized, the marriage is called *ratum et non consummatum;* if only one is baptized, it is merely *non consummatum.*

Dissolution by Solemn Religious Profession. 1. The profession must be valid, and this requires that it be preceded by a valid noviceship (c. 572). A married man or woman cannot be validly admitted to the noviceship (c. 542). Hence dissolution of the bond by solemn profession cannot occur unless the Holy See has already dispensed from this law. In practice, either the other party also voluntarily embraces a life of chastity or the party entering religion is permitted to make the solemn profession immediately after the noviceship, so that the other will not have so long to wait in case he or she decides to marry again.

2. The solemn profession is that which is recognized as such by the Church (c. 1308); normally, it is pronounced only after at least three years of temporary profession (c. 574, § 1).

3. The record of the profession of solemn vows must be inscribed in the marriage record and in the baptismal record of the parties.

Dissolution by Papal Dispensation. 1. The dispensation from the bond of non-consummated marriage may be given by the Holy Father in individual cases upon proof of two things: first, the existence of a just cause for it; second, the fact that the marriage has not been consummated. A just cause is here required for validity of the dispensation (c. 84).

2. Among the causes that are recognized as sufficient are: irreconcilable discord; probable danger of grave scandal from this or other causes; probable existence of impotence with danger of incontinence; civil divorce obtained by one party with danger of incontinence; partial proof that the marriage was invalid for want of consent or for

---

[4] Cf. Joyce, *Christian Marriage,* pp. 427–466.

some diriment impediment; contagious disease contracted after the marriage; danger of perversion, etc.

3. The procedure is regulated in detail by a decree of the Sacred Congregation of the Sacraments, 7 May, 1923. It may be briefly summarized as follows: first, a petition is drawn up asking for the dispensation, and is transmitted through the Ordinary to the Sacred Congregation of the Sacraments in Rome; the Sacred Congregation, if it approves the petition, will delegate the Ordinary to conduct the hearings in the case (in exceptional cases, it may instead commit the case to the Rota); if the Ordinary is so authorized, he must appoint a judge, a defender of the bond, etc., and proceed to take testimony; the evidence consists of legitimate inferences and presumptions, a physical examination by experts, the testimony of direct witnesses on the opportunity for consummation (on this fact the parties themselves are competent witnesses, but their testimony is not itself sufficient to prove it), and witnesses "of the seventh hand," that is, a number of character witnesses, usually seven; at the conclusion of the trial the judge does not pronounce judgment, but sends the entire record to Rome; the Sacred Congregation decides the case on the record; if the decision is favorable, it recommends the dispensation, the Holy Father then usually grants it, and the rescript containing it is sent to the party *in forma gratiosa* (cf. c. 38), but must be shown to the Ordinary (cf. c. 51). It must then be registered in the marriage and baptismal records of the parties. It carries with it implicitly a dispensation from the impediment of crime in the lowest degree should that be necessary (cf. c. 1053).[5]

4. Two interesting questions arise, quite apart from the regular procedure. First, in a case which is altogether occult, might recourse be had to the Sacred Penitentiary? Most authorities say no. There are, however, some reasons for an affirmative answer.[6] Second, can the Holy See grant the dispensation if both parties oppose it? This is an extraordinary case, and the law makes no provision for it (cf. c. 1973). Probably it could be done.[7]

---

[5] The Instruction of the S. C. Sacr., 7 May, 1923, is in *AAS*, 15–389, *Digest*, I, p. 764. Special faculties for the duration of the war were given to the Apostolic Delegate to the United States, to permit the canonical procedure in non-consummated marriage, without recourse to the Holy See: S. C. Sacr., 17 July, 1942, *Digest*, II, p. 462. There is an instruction of the Holy Office, 12 June, 1942, urging due precautions in cases of impotence and non-consummation; *AAS*, 34–200, *Digest*, II, p. 549. A summary of some decisions of the Rota on non-consummation, *Digest*, II, p. 339. There is also a special instruction on precautions to prevent fraudulent substitution of persons; S. C. Sacr., 27 March, 1929; *AAS*, 21–490; *Digest*, I, p. 792.

[6] Cf. Cappello, *De Matrimonio*, n. 765.   [7] Cf. Cappello, *De Matrimonio*, n. 757, 2.

CANON 1120. § 1. Legitimate marriage between non-baptized persons, even though it has been consummated, is dissolved in favor of the Faith by virtue of the Pauline privilege.

§ 2. This privilege does not apply in the case of a marriage between a baptized and an unbaptized person which was entered into with a dispensation from the impediment of disparity of cult.

General Scope of Canons on Dissolution. The last of this group of canons, canon 1127, deals with the privilege of the Faith in doubtful cases; that is, where there is doubt about some element which would be required to bring the case strictly within the Pauline privilege. Hence, the terms "Pauline privilege" and "privilege of the Faith" are not perfectly co-extensive. Canon 1125 deals with the dissolution of the natural bond of marriage even where it is certain that the requisites for the Pauline privilege are wanting. The other canons, 1120, 1124, and 1126 deal with the Pauline privilege.

The Pauline Privilege. 1. It may be briefly defined as a privilege by which a lawful marriage between non-baptized persons, even if consummated, is dissolved in favor of the Faith, according to canon law. The doctrine is founded on Holy Scripture.[8] An excellent textual analysis, together with the theological development of the doctrine, is given by Joyce, *Christian Marriage*, pp. 467–487.

2. It is disputed whether the doctrine here announced is immediately of divine or of apostolic origin. The latter would mean that it was announced by St. Paul by divine authority and then extended to the whole Church under the authority of St. Peter. Certain pontifical documents contain language favoring the immediate divine origin of the privilege, while the Pauline text itself seems rather to place the immediate authority for the doctrine in the Apostle himself. The question is not of great practical consequence; either opinion is probable, and is sufficient for practical purposes. Ultimately the doctrine is of divine origin, beyond any doubt.

Conditions. 1. Strictly speaking the Pauline privilege allows the dissolution only of "legitimate marriage between non-baptized persons." The first condition is that the marriage be between two non-baptized persons.

2. Yet, as long as both remain infidels, the Church will take no jurisdiction over the marriage. The use of the privilege supposes that one of the parties, and only one, after the marriage receives valid baptism (cf. c. 1121, § 1). Since heretical baptism may be valid, it is

---

[8] 1 Cor. 7:12–15.

now morally certain that valid baptism even in a heretical sect is a sufficient foundation for the use of the privilege. But there would be practical difficulties in the procedure unless the person became a Catholic.

3. The departure of the infidel party must be proved either by the interpellations duly made or under circumstances in which there has been a lawful dispensation from making them (cf. cc. 1122, 1123). This "departure" of the infidel is not a sufficient foundation for the use of the privilege if the departing infidel had just cause for it, given by the converted party since baptism (c. 1123).

4. The use of the privilege consists in contracting a new marriage with a *Catholic* party (c. 1124). As far as divine law is concerned, it is probable that marriage even with a validly baptized heretic, validly contracted, would satisfy the conditions of the privilege. If the second marriage were with an infidel it would be invalid because of disparity of cult unless a dispensation were obtained; and under these circumstances a dispensation would scarcely be granted. However, the Holy See has occasionally granted such a dispensation, and thus permitted the marriage with an infidel to dissolve the former bond. In such a case recourse must be had to the Holy See; the Ordinaries cannot use their habitual faculties to dispense from disparity of cult. Cf. Holy Office, 22 Nov., 1871; *Fontes,* n. 1019, IV, p. 323; Léry, *Le Privilège de la Foi,* n. 102, p. 132.

Legitimate Marriage Between Non-baptized Persons. 1. The canon specifies that the privilege does not apply in a marriage between a baptized and a non-baptized person, contracted *with a dispensation* from disparity of cult.

2. What if such a marriage were contracted *without a dispensation,* e.g., by a validly baptized heretic with an infidel since the Code? It is morally certain both on reason and authority that the privilege does not apply in such a case.[9] It is true that the Holy Office in 1924 decided a case of this kind favorably by allowing the woman, after her conversion to the Catholic Faith, to contract a new marriage with a Catholic. But this seems to be rather a dissolution of the natural bond of marriage than an application of the Pauline privilege.[10]

3. Finally, what of a marriage contracted since the Code by a heretic whose baptism is positively doubtful, with an infidel? At least one writer[11] contends that the Pauline privilege could be applied in

---

[9] V-C, *Epit.,* II, n. 428.   [10] Cf. *Digest,* I, p. 551.
[11] Santini, in *Periodica,* Vol. 21, p. 172*.

such a case, even without having recourse to the privilege of the Faith *in re dubia* (c. 1127). He cites in support of his contention a private reply of the Sacred Congregation for the Propagation of the Faith. His principle is that where there is a positive probability of the existence of the conditions requisite for the Pauline privilege, the privilege may simply be used, and that the privilege of the Faith *in re dubia* is for cases where such positive probability is wanting. A later decision of the Holy Office contradicts this conclusion, at least for the case proposed. The Holy Office, asked, whether in such a case the Ordinaries of either party, later converted to the Catholic Faith, can permit them to use the Pauline privilege in virtue of canon 1127, replied: "Recourse must be had to the Holy Office in each case."[12]

CANON 1121. § 1. Before the party who has been converted and baptized can validly contract a new marriage, he or she must, except as provided in canon 1125, interpellate the non-baptized party:
1° Whether he or she is also willing to be converted and to receive baptism;
2° Or at least to cohabit peacefully with the other party without offense to the Creator.
§ 2. These interpellations must always be made unless the Holy See shall have declared otherwise.

The Interpellations. 1. Among the requisite conditions is the "departure" of the infidel party. For proving this condition, the normal means are the interpellations, that is, questions put by the converted party to the other: first, whether he or she is willing to be converted and receive baptism; second, whether he or she is at least willing to cohabit peacefully with the other party, without offense to the Creator. A negative answer, either express or tacit, to both questions, amounts to departure.

2. If the infidel party is willing to be converted, but unwilling to cohabit with the converted party, this would seem evidently to amount to departure; and several replies of the Holy Office confirm this view.[13] The departure need not be caused by the conversion of the Catholic party. The motive is immaterial.

3. If the party, though unwilling to be converted, is willing to cohabit *peacefully and without offense to the Creator,* there is no departure, and the privilege cannot be used. This phrase means that if

[12] Holy Office, 10 June, 1937, ad 2; *AAS,* 29–305; *Digest,* II, p. 343.
[13] Holy Office, 8 July, 1891; *Collectanea,* II, n. 1760; Holy Office, 26 Apr., 1899; *ibid.,* n. 2044.

cohabitation with the infidel would place the Catholic party in danger of perversion, that is, in danger either of losing the faith or of committing any grave sin, such willingness to cohabit is not considered, and the privilege may be used as for "departure." The Holy Office has held this where the infidel refused to permit the Catholic education of the children.[14] If the danger of perversion is not certain but probable, a distinction is in order: in the absence of interpellations or a dispensation from them, the case should be referred to the Holy Office; but if the uncertainty results from a doubt regarding the sincerity or import of the replies to the interpellations, resort may be had to canon 1127, and the Ordinary can decide in favor of the faith.

4. To satisfy the conditions, the "departure" must not be justified by a cause given by the Catholic party *since baptism* (c. 1123).

5. A negative reply to the interpellations may be either express or tacit (see c. 1123).

6. The interpellations are regularly made *after the conversion* of the Catholic party, and before that of the other.

Necessity of the Interpellations. 1. If the departure is not proved from other sources, then the interpellations are required for the *validity* of the second marriage. This is illustrated by a recent decision of the Rota.[15]

2. If the departure is certain from other sources, canon law still requires the interpellations or a lawful dispensation from them. Is this required for the *validity* of the second marriage or only for licitness? The text, *antequam coniux novum matrimonium valide contrahat,* seems to make it a requisite for validity, though it does not refer specifically to cases in which the departure is already certain. Accordingly some contend that the interpellations are necessary for validity even where departure is already certain from other sources.[16] But the contrary is probable and is defended by several authors.[17] Consequently, *after the fact* of a second marriage under these conditions, it should be considered valid until a definite reply could be had from the Holy Office to whom the matter should be referred. *Before the fact,* recourse should be had to the Holy Office.

Exceptions. Two exceptions are mentioned: first, the cases provided for in canon 1125; second, those in which the Holy See shall have "declared otherwise"; that is, where the Holy See has dispensed from

---

[14] Holy Office, 14 Dec., 1848; *Collectanea,* I, n. 1036.
[15] Rota, 5 Dec., 1925; *Decisiones,* Vol. 17, p. 396; *Digest,* II, p. 341.
[16] Cf. Cappello, *De Matrimonio,* n. 776.
[17] Cf. Wernz-Vidal, *De Matrimonio,* n. 632, note 68.

the interpellations. Though the Code nowhere uses the term "dispensation" in connection with the interpellations (cf. cc. 1121, § 2, 1123), we follow the common usage in calling such a declaration a dispensation.

Remaining Questions. Two important matters must be kept in mind though their treatment is deferred: first, the extent of the power of Ordinaries to dispense from the interpellations; second, a peculiar and grave consequence which follows from such dispensation (cf. c. 1125).

CANON 1122. § 1. The interpellations are to be made regularly, at least in summary and extrajudicial form, by authority of the Ordinary of the converted party, and the same Ordinary shall also grant to the infidel party, if he or she ask for it, an extension of time in which to deliberate, warning the said party however that in case the time so extended elapses without a reply, a negative reply will be presumed.

§ 2. Interpellations, even when made privately by the converted party himself, are valid, and indeed even licit in case the form above prescribed cannot be observed; but in this case they must be proved for the external forum by at least two witnesses or by some other lawful manner of proof.

Form of the Interpellations. 1. The *quasi-judicial* form would mean that the parties and witnesses personally appeared before the Ordinary or his delegate, and had their answers to the questions certified before him, together with the supporting documents. This is not required and is seldom done.[18]

2. The *epistolary juridical* form is the usual method: juridical, because done by authority of the Ordinary, epistolary because in the form of a letter. Upon satisfactory proof informally presented to the diocesan authorities, the marriage is shown to have taken place while both parties were unbaptized; one party has been directed to take instructions and receive baptism before the interpellations are made; then the interpellations are sent by registered mail, including notice that if no answer is received within a stated time the other party intends to marry again, and that this second marriage will effect the dissolution of the former one. Upon receipt of a negative answer or the lapse of the time without reply, the Ordinary issues a decree certifying to that fact and authorizing the party to proceed to the second marriage. One

---

[18] The procedure is described in detail by Woeber, *The Interpellations,* Cath. U., 1942, p. 75.

should make himself familiar with the formulas used by the diocesan chancery.

3. The *private* form of interpellations would be a letter sent by the party on his own authority. This is *always valid,* but provision must be made for proof in the external forum. Two witnesses should be present at the signing and mailing of the letter, and should also inspect the reply, and then take oath to the facts. It is safer to use the juridical epistolary form, which automatically takes care of the matter of proof. The private form is *licit* only when the juridical form cannot be used.[19]

CANON 1123. If the interpellations have been omitted in pursuance of a declaration made by the Holy See, or if the infidel party has replied to them in the negative, expressly or tacitly, the baptized party has the right to contract a new marriage with a Catholic person, unless since baptism he or she has given the non-baptized party a just cause for departing.

The Right to Contract a New Marriage. 1. This right arises when the interpellations have been "omitted in pursuance of a declaration by the Holy See," or when a negative answer, express or tacit, has been received. Failure to answer within the time is a tacit negative answer.

2. The right is lost if the departure of the infidel party is justified by a cause given by the converted party since baptism. Any cause given before baptism is not sufficient; it is as though baptism wiped out all traces of past misconduct. However, a cause for departure given by the converted party even after baptism does not deprive him of the Pauline Privilege unless the infidel party knows of it. Cf. Holy Office, 19 Apr., 1899; *Fontes,* n. 1220, ad 1, IV, p. 513; Léry, *Le Privilège de la Foi,* n. 114, p. 150.

3. The new marriage must normally be with a Catholic party, though it is probable that marriage with a heretic after the interpellations would be valid. The Holy See could even, but most probably would not, dispense from disparity of cult and so permit a second marriage with an infidel.

CANON 1124. The baptized party, even though since receiving baptism he or she may have again lived in matrimonial relations with the infidel party, does not thereby lose the right to contract a new marriage with a Catholic, and can therefore make use of this right in case the infidel party later changes his or her mind and departs with-

---

[19] Cf. Gregory, *The Pauline Privilege,* 1931, Cath. U. Canon Law Studies, n. 68; Vermeersch, *Casus Apostoli;* Ramstein, *The Pastor and Marriage Cases,* 1936, pp. 185–195; Wanenmacher, *Canonical Evidence in Marriage Cases,* nn. 94–96, 115, 372, 375.

out just cause or ceases to cohabit peacefully without offense to the Creator.

State of the Question. This canon answers one very important question, a practical one: What if, after the baptism of the converted party, or even after the interpellations, a reconciliation is effected and the parties live together matrimonially, consummating the marriage anew? Does this deprive the Catholic party of the use of the Pauline privilege? It does, as long as this condition continues; but should the infidel party once more "depart" without a new justifying cause, new interpellations could be made and the converted party could use the privilege. The necessity of new interpellations is usually not mentioned by authors who treat of this canon. Probably they are not strictly necessary, since the canon does not mention them. But evidently the new "departure" must be proved. Some authors hold that a repetition of the interpellations is not required.[20]

CANON 1125. Those provisions which concern marriage in the Constitutions, *Altitudo,* of Paul III, 1 June, 1537, *Romani Pontificis,* of St. Pius V, 2 Aug., 1571, and *Populis,* of Gregory XIII, 25 Jan., 1585, and which were written for particular places, are extended to other regions also in the same circumstances.

The Constitutions of Canon 1125. These three Constitutions were enacted in the sixteenth century for use in certain designated missionary countries. A careful study of the text of each is necessary in order to understand this canon (Code, Documents VI, VII, VIII). The following is a brief analysis.

The Constitution, *Altitudo.* 1. It deals with *polygamists* who do not remember which of their wives they married first.

2. It provides that such a man after conversion to the faith, if he still does not remember which of his wives was first, may choose any of them, marry her by present expression of consent, and keep her to the exclusion of all the others. No interpellations are necessary, since they are not mentioned.

3. If, however, he remembers which wife he first married lawfully, he must keep her and may not choose another.

4. If the wife chosen is unbaptized, disparity of cult exists. Is a dispensation necessary? Burton (*op. cit.,* p. 147) holds that it is not required. We think this is at least probable. Others (Vromant, *De*

---

[20] Woeber, *The Interpellations,* p. 71, citing Payen, *De Matrimonio,* n. 2344. Cf. Holy Office, 11 July, 1866, ad 3; *Collectanea,* I, n. 1295. Also, without qualification, Léry, *Le Privilège de la Foi,* n. 56

Matrimonio, n. 357; Léry, *Le Privilège de la Foi,* p. 102) recommend that a dispensation be given by the Ordinary. In this case the *cautiones* probably are not strictly required; but the divine law itself requires, for licitness, moral certainty that there will be no danger of perversion.

The Constitution, *Romani Pontificis.* 1. It deals with *polygamists* who in infidelity had more than one wife, and permits them upon their conversion to choose any of their wives who is willing to receive baptism with them, and to keep her to the exclusion of the others even though she was not the first one whom they lawfully married.

2. It says nothing about interpellations and declares that the marriage with the wife so chosen is licit and valid.

3. Although the renewal of consent is not explicitly mentioned in the Constitution, it must be made (Burton, p. 163; Léry, n. 83, p. 109).

The Constitution, *Populis.* 1. It deals with marriages contracted between two non-baptized persons.

2. It grants to certain persons the faculty to *dispense from the interpellations* under certain conditions, and permits the party separated from his or her former spouse, to remarry.

3. It declares that these new marriages are to be considered valid and firm even though it afterward become known that the former infidel spouse was prevented from declaring his or her will, or even was converted and baptized before the second marriage took place.

4. The *conditions* under which the power to dispense is given are: that the first marriage was contracted in infidelity, and that it appear from a summary extrajudicial inquiry either that the absent spouse cannot be interpellated according to law, or has failed to reply within the stated time.

5. The persons to whom the power is granted are Ordinaries, pastors, and approved confessors of the Society of Jesus.

Extension of These Constitutions. In the words of the Code, these Constitutions "which were written for particular places, are extended to other regions also *in the same circumstances.*" At first sight two widely different interpretations of these words are possible, and there are consequently two opinions. The first holds that the Constitutions are extended only to other *regions where the same circumstances* now exist. Those circumstances were those of the sixteenth-century African slave trade, the forcible separation of husband and wife by slave raiders. This opinion is advanced by some of the earlier writers after the Code.[21] It would deprive this canon of any wide application in civil-

---

[21] Cf. Augustine, *A Commentary,* V, p. 364; Gregory, *The Pauline Privilege.*

ized countries. The second opinion holds that the words *in the same circumstances* refer to individual cases. This would make the Constitutions applicable *in any case where the required circumstances are realized.*[22] In our judgment the second opinion is certainly true and should be followed.[23] The forcible separation of husband and wife is not a condition required for the use of the power granted, even in an individual case. That was merely a circumstance which occasioned the original grant of the power.[24]

Application of the Constitutions. 1. All these Constitutions apply as well to women as to men.

2. The Constitution *Altitudo* will be of rare application, since it applies only to *polygamists who do not know which consort was the first.*

3. The Constitution, *Romani Pontificis* includes *successive polygamists,* and would apply to any man or woman who, after a presumably valid marriage contracted in infidelity with an unbaptized person, obtains a divorce and contracts another marriage with an unbaptized person.[25] Hence any such person, if sincerely converted to the Catholic faith, may choose either his present partner or any of his former partners, provided the one so chosen is willing to become a Catholic with him; and these two may then proceed to a new expression of marital consent, which will be a licit and valid marriage and will have the effect of dissolving the natural bond of the previous valid marriage. Interpellations are not required.[26] Woods seems to require either that there be some doubt about the validity of the former marriage, or that the first wife cannot be interpellated. These conditions do not seem to be required because they are not mentioned in the Constitution. The preamble does observe that in many cases the first wife would be hard to find, but it does not make this a condition to the use of the power granted. The omission of the interpellations in virtue of this Constitution is the only thing that differentiates such a case from an ordinary application of the Pauline privilege. It is handled, in other respects like a case of the Pauline privilege, by

[22] Cf. Wernz-Vidal, *De Matrimonio,* n. 633; Cappello, *De Matrimonio,* n. 787; V-C, *Epit.,* II, n. 436; Vermeersch, in *Periodica,* Vol. 20, p. 1*; Woods, *The Constitutions of Canon 1125,* pp. 73–82; Schaaf, in *Eccl. Rev.,* Vol. 86, p. 537; Wanenmacher, *Canonical Evidence in Marriage Cases,* n. 97.

[23] Cf. Bouscaren, *An Inquiry into the Practical Application of Canon 1125 Outside Mission Countries,* in *Analecta Gregoriana,* IX, p. 279.

[24] Cf. Vermeersch, in *Periodica,* Vol. 20, p. 4*.

[25] Cf. Woods, *The Constitutions of Canon 1125,* p. 93; Burton, *A Commentary on Canon 1125,* Cath. U., 1940.

[26] Cf. Payen, *De Matrimonio,* II, n. 2406; Burton, *op. cit.,* p. 156.

presenting to the Ordinary, in a summary extrajudicial hearing, documentary evidence of the marriages and non-baptism of all the parties concerned, of the subsequent baptism of the party seeking the privilege and of the one among his spouses whom he has chosen. The Ordinary should declare that these conditions exist and that the interpellations are not necessary. The results of the summary hearing should be preserved at the Chancery, and the parties authorized by informal decree to proceed to celebrate their marriage.

4. The Constitution *Populis* is more widely applicable, dealing as it does with *ordinary infidel marriages*. It gives Ordinaries power to *dispense from the interpellations* in cases where, after a presumably valid marriage between infidels, one party embraces the faith and the other "either cannot be interpellated according to law or has failed to reply within the stated time."

Faculty of Ordinaries to Dispense From the Interpellations. 1. The power to dispense from the interpellations is reserved to the Holy See by canons 247, 1121, and 1123. But these canons must be construed in conformity with other provisions of law; they are expressly modified by canon 1125.

2. The faculty is not contained in the Quinquennial Faculties for Bishops of the United States, but is regularly granted to Ordinaries of places in certain mission countries.[27]

3. As to canon 1125: if a case comes within the provisions of either the first or the second of the Constitutions mentioned in that canon (either the Constitution of Paul III, *Altitudo,* or that of St. Pius V, *Romani Pontificis*), the dispensation from the interpellations is *contained in the law itself.* If the case comes within the provisions of the Constitution of Gregory XIII, *Populis,* the interpellations are required, but *power is given to Ordinaries of places* (and to the other persons mentioned) *to dispense* from them. The extent of this power is somewhat difficult to determine with certainty, as authors are not entirely in accord.

a. Vermeersch, in a valuable commentary of the faculties granted in mission lands by the Sacred Congregation for the Propagation of the Faith, which he contributed to *Periodica* in 1923, interpreting nn. 24 and 25 of those faculties (Formula III Minor et Maior),[28] expressed the view that the faculty to dispense from the interpellations

---

[27] Cf. Vermeersch-Creusen, *Epitome,* I, Appendix II.

[28] Cf. Burton, *A Commentary on Canon 1125,* p. 108; Woods, *The Constitutions of Canon 1125* (Milwaukee: Bruce).

which is given in those formulae is the same as that which is given
to all Ordinaries of places by canon 1125, and that consequently the
interpretations of the formulae by the Sacred Congregations may
serve as a safe norm by which to measure the extent of the power
now granted to all Ordinaries of places by canon 1125. He gives as
examples the following cases as within the power of Ordinaries to
dispense from the interpellations: when the place of residence of the
former spouse is entirely unknown or inaccessible; when the distance
is too great an obstacle (the distance which is *per se* sufficient for this
has never been authentically defined); when the former spouse has
failed to reply within the time; when *for any reason* it is certain that
the interpellations would be *utterly useless;* when, though the party
could be reached, the interpellations would involve manifest danger
of grave harm to the innocent party or to other Christians.[29]

b. In an article which we contributed to *Miscellanea Vermeersch* in
1935, we took the same view of the power of Ordinaries to dispense
from the interpellations.[30] Although that view seems to us still to be
not entirely devoid of probability, yet, upon a re-examination of the
question, it seems better to keep the faculties granted to Ordinaries
by special indults distinct from those which are given by canon 1125.
Burton has pointed out that, even in interpreting the faculties of the
mission formulae, the Sacred Congregations have not been entirely
consistent, as some of their replies have interpreted the faculties as
applying to cases where the interpellations would be useless or harmful,
but not impossible, whereas other replies have limited them to cases
of very great difficulty amounting to moral impossibility.[31] The more
common opinion of authors accordingly now is that a moral impossibility of making the interpellations is sufficient, but that their evident
inutility or the danger of harm connected with making them is
not sufficient.[32]

c. This latter view, which we accept for practical purposes, is
evidently more in accord with the text of the Constitution, *Populis,*

---

[29] Cf. Vermeersch, *Commentaria de Formulis Facultatum Quas S. C. Prop. Fid. Con-
cedere Solet,* in *Periodica,* Vol. II, pp. 33–144, nn. 120, 121, and especially p. 139, note.
[30] Cf. Bouscaren, *An Inquiry into the Practical Application of Canon 1125 Outside
Mission Territories,* in *Miscellanea Vermeersch,* Vol. I (*Analecta Gregoriana,* Vol. IX), p.
279; also Wanenmacher, *The Evidence in Ecclesiastical Procedure Affecting the Marriage
Bond,* nn. 97–99.
[31] Burton, *A Commentary on Canon 1125,* Cath. U., 1940, pp. 169, 170.
[32] Burton, *loc. cit.* Cf. also Léry, *Le Privilège de la Foi,* n. 89; Vromant, *De Matrimonio,* n. 348; Payen, *De Matrimonio,* II, n. 2409, § 3; Cappello, *De Matrimonio,* n.
787, § 6.

and provides a safe norm according to which Ordinaries of places may act in dispensing from the interpellations in cases which come within the terms of the Constitution. Woeber, at the close of a dissertation on the interpellations, remarks: "It appears to the writer that Ordinaries of the United States are either unaware of their power or are loath to use the extraordinary faculty to dispense (from interpellations) given them in the common law by canon 1125."[33]

4. It cannot be objected that this interpretation destroys the reservation to the Holy See which is expressed in canons 247, 1121, and 1123; for these canons reserve the power to the Holy See, "except as provided in canon 1125" (c. 1121, § 1) and "unless the Holy See has declared otherwise" (c. 1121, § 2). Our interpretation therefore gives effect to all the provisions of the Code on the subject. Ordinaries will, of course, use prudence and caution in the exercise of this very grave power; but it is in their hands for prudent administration in favor of the faith.

5. If there is danger of grave harm in delay until a dispensation from the interpellations could be obtained from the Holy See, canon 81 may be invoked, and the Ordinary could grant the dispensation.[34]

Dispensing Power of Pastors and Others. Pastors and priests of the Society of Jesus approved for confessions (by the Ordinary of the place according to canon 874) have, under the Constitution *Populis,* the same power to dispense from the interpellations as Ordinaries. Their power is not limited to the internal forum. But they should not use this power in the external forum against the wishes of the Ordinary, as this would cause endless confusion. The Ordinary could make reasonable regulations governing the matter, without prejudice however to the validity of their use of the power granted by the Code.

Effect of Dispensing From the Interpellations. The following is from the Constitution, *Populis:* "And We decree that these marriages are never to be rescinded, but will be valid and firm, and the children born from them will be legitimate, even though it *afterward become known* that the former infidel partners were prevented by some just cause from declaring their will, and even that *at the time of the second marriage they had already been converted to the Faith."* It is certain that if the conversion of the infidel partner were known beforehand the simple Pauline privilege could not be used. This clause, therefore,

---

[33] Woeber, *The Interpellations,* Cath. U., 1942, p. 137.
[34] Cf. Wanenmacher, *op. cit.,* n. 97; Schaaf, in *Eccl. Rev.,* Vol. 86, p. 533; Foley, in *Eccl. Rev.,* Vol. 91, p. 503; Woeber, *The Interpellations,* p. 129.

is one proof that the Holy See has a power exceeding that of the Pauline privilege, namely, the power to dissolve a marriage contracted in infidelity even after both parties are baptized, provided the marriage has not thereafter been consummated.[35] In several replies the Holy Office refers to this result as a peculiar effect of dispensation from the interpellations; and canonical writers commonly use the same language. This can only mean that a case which appeared to be an ordinary application of the Pauline privilege, and in which the normal procedure of the Pauline privilege with a dispensation from the interpellations has been employed, may *afterward* turn out to be an instance in which the Supreme Apostolic authority has acted to dissolve the natural bond of marriage beyond the limits of the privilege. In such a case the Supreme Authority has acted through the dispensation from the interpellations; and it makes no difference who granted the dispensation provided it was granted validly according to law. In cases where the baptism of both parties is known *beforehand,* the Holy See can and sometimes does grant directly a dispensation from the natural bond of marriage in favor of the faith.

Direct Dissolution of the Natural Bond by the Holy See. The only marriage which is absolutely indissoluble is one which is *ratum et consummatum* (c. 1118); that is, which has been consummated *after* the valid baptism of both parties. Now, in the last paragraph we have considered the dissolution of a marriage which is *consummatum et ratum;* that is, which was presumably consummated before, but certainly not after the baptism of both parties. Hitherto, however, we have spoken only of marriages which were *contracted in infidelity.* Does the power of the Supreme Pontiff extend to the dissolution of a marriage between a validly baptized heretic and an infidel, provided it was not consummated after the baptism of both parties? Recent practice of the Holy See makes an affirmative answer certain. In one case, decided on 5 Nov., 1924, on a petition from the Bishop of Helena, the facts were these. A man, unbaptized, married a baptized Anglican (after the Code, no dispensation being required). Divorce followed, and the woman married again. The man, wishing to receive Catholic baptism and to marry a Catholic girl, was permitted to do so.[36] Cases of this kind are reserved to the Holy Office exclusively

---

[35] Cf. Kieda, *Direct Dissolution of a Legitimate Marriage,* in *The Jurist,* Vol. 2, 1942, p. 134; Rayanna, *De Const. S. Pii V, Romani Pontificis,* in *Periodica,* Vol. 27, pp. 295–331; Vol. 28, pp. 24–52; 112–134; 190–209; Burton, *A Commentary on Canon 1125,* 1940, Cath. U. Canon Law Studies, n. 121.

[36] See *Digest,* I, p. 553.

(c. 247). They may be presented, however, through a petition drawn up by the pastor and addressed to the Holy Office but sent to the Ordinary, either of the place where the marriage occurred or of the place where the Catholic party has a domicile or quasi-domicile (c. 1964). The Ordinary, after having obtained permission from the Holy Office to do so, conducts the investigation and sends the case to the Holy Office.[37]

CANON 1126. The bond of the former marriage which was contracted in infidelity is dissolved only at the time when the baptized party contracts a new marriage validly.

The Time When the Former Marriage Is Dissolved. 1. Primarily this canon applies to the Pauline privilege, declaring that the former valid marriage subsists until the moment when a second marriage, valid by reason of the Pauline privilege, takes place.

2. What of those cases where the marriage took place in infidelity but has become *ratum* by the baptism of both parties before the second marriage takes place? We have seen that the dissolution of such marriages is effected by positive action of the Supreme Pontiff which transcends the Pauline privilege, rather than by the privilege itself. Gasparri thinks nevertheless that canon 1126 applies to such cases also. He bases his opinion upon a certain analogy with the Pauline privilege and also upon the position of canon 1126, which comes after the canon in which those cases are dealt with.[38] The question is practical. Suppose, for example, that *after* the rescript granting the dissolution of the marriage, and *before* the party who asked for it marries again, the *other party* marries. If Gasparri's opinion is correct (and we think it is), that marriage is invalid because of the impediment of *ligamen,* though it is certain that, upon the second marriage of the Catholic party, the impediment would disappear. However, cases in which this question is involved should be referred to the Holy Office.

3. Does canon 1126 apply also to cases like the Helena case, where the marriage was between a baptized and a non-baptized person? We think not, for two reasons: first, those cases have no real analogy with the Pauline privilege; it is certain that they are beyond its scope; second, the text of the canon seems conclusive; it speaks only of the "bond of the former marriage contracted in infidelity." Consequently

---

[37] Cf. Ramstein, *The Pastor and Marriage Cases,* p. 202.
[38] Cf. Gasparri, *De Matrimonio,* n. 1167.

in cases of this type the dissolution is effected by the Pontifical re-script itself independently of the subsequent marriage.

CANON 1127. In doubt, the privilege of the faith enjoys the favor of the law.

State of the Question. One of the first canons on marriage declared that marriage enjoys the favor of the law, so that "in doubt the validity of the marriage is to be upheld until the contrary is proved, *except as provided in canon* 1127." We have now to consider this exception.

Doubt. 1. A *practically insoluble* doubt is meant. Every effort must have been made to ascertain the truth, without resulting in certitude.

2. This doubt is not the same as the positive and probable doubt of canon 209. It may be considered to exist whenever certainty cannot be reached from the facts or legitimate presumptions, even though no really solid reasons can be adduced for either side.[39]

3. The doubt *may concern:* the validity of a former marriage con-tracted in infidelity; the identity of the former spouse; the validity of the baptism of either party; the sincerity of the reply to the inter-pellations; the sufficiency of reasons for dispensing from the inter-pellations; the existence of the former marriage; or the existence of any condition requisite for the use of the Pauline privilege.

4. The *effect of the doubt* is not to change the objective fact which is in question, but merely to legitimize the new marriage and permit the dissolution of the earlier one *even in case that is valid.* Hence the earlier marriage *must be such that,* in any event *it can be dissolved* at least by Pontifical authority. Hence this canon does not apply where the *baptisms of both parties to a consummated marriage* are in doubt. For if both baptisms are objectively valid — a question of fact which is in no way affected by a subjective doubt upon it — then the marriage is *ratum et consummatum,* and such a marriage is indissoluble even by papal authority. This conclusion, commonly held even before, has been placed beyond dispute by a reply of the Holy Office.[40]

The Privilege of the Faith. The term evidently has a wider meaning than the Pauline privilege. It may be defined as the right to contract a

---

[39] Cf. Léry, *Le Privilège de la Foi,* n. 110, note 2; Kearney, *The Principles of Canon 1127,* p. 50; Payen, *De Matrimonio,* II, n. 2415 *bis,* p. 757; Cappello, *De Matrimonio,* n. 788; Wolf, *Aut-Aut Causae,* in *The Jurist,* Vol. 6, p. 344. Léry wisely observes that some authors, while they require a positive doubt, do not say that it must exist for both opposite probabilities. In point of fact, doubts in practice remain insoluble precisely because of *lack of positive evidence.*

[40] Reported in text a few lines farther on.

new marriage with a Catholic in every case where such a marriage would result in favor of the faith, and where, notwithstanding insoluble doubts, it is at least certain that the former marriage can be dissolved by Pontifical authority.

Can the Ordinary Act in These Cases? Until recently it was generally held that the Ordinary could act in all cases of this kind. The theory was that this canon included an implicit grant to the Ordinary of the papal power to dissolve the former marriage in case such power was actually necessary. A recent reply of the Holy Office, however, compels a modification of this view. Two questions were asked:

1. Whether, in a marriage contracted by two non-Catholics whose baptisms are doubtful, where the doubt regarding baptism is insoluble, the use of the Pauline privilege can be permitted to either of the parties upon his or her conversion to the faith, in virtue of canon 1127?

Reply: *In the negative.*

2. Whether, in a marriage contracted between a non-baptized person and a non-Catholic whose baptism is doubtful, where the doubt regarding baptism is insoluble, Ordinaries can permit to either party upon his or her conversion to the faith the use of the Pauline privilege in virtue of canon 1127?

Reply: *Recourse must be had to the Holy Office in each case.*[41]

The Ordinary May Resolve the Doubt in favor of the faith, where the doubt concerns:

1. The *fact or the validity of a marriage* contracted in infidelity.

2. The *identity of the first husband* or wife in a case arising under the Constitution, *Altitudo,* of Paul III (c. 1125).

3. The *sufficiency of the reason* for granting a dispensation from the interpellations, where the Ordinary has the power to dispense from them either under the Constitution, *Populis,* of Gregory XIII (c. 1125) or by special faculties in mission countries.

4. The *meaning or the sincerity of the replies* of the infidel party to the interpellations.

5. The *legitimacy or non-legitimacy of the departure* of the infidel party; for example, if the converted party has indeed, after baptism, given cause for such departure, but the infidel in his reply to the interpellations shows that he is either ignorant of that fact or cares nothing about it. On this case, cf. Léry, *Le Privilège de la Foi,* p. 150; Payen, *De Matrimonio,* II, nn. 2262, 2279; Cappello, *De Matrimonio,* n. 770, 7.

---

[41] *AAS,* 29–305; *Digest,* II, p. 343.

6. The *length of time to be allowed for a reply* to the interpellations. For example, the time allowed for a reply had not yet expired, but no reply has yet been received, and the need for the new marriage is urgent. Cf. Léry, p. 151; Vermeersch, in *Periodica,* Vol. 10, p. (27).

7. Finally, the doubt may concern the *verification of any of the conditions requisite for the use of the Pauline Privilege,* except, as stated above, the baptism of one or both parties.

Purposes for Which Such Doubts May Be Resolved in Favor of the Faith. In all the above cases, the Ordinary may resolve the doubt in favor of the faith, that is, in favor of the liberty of the converted party. Hence the latter may:

1. Contract a new marriage with a Catholic.

2. Validate a marriage previously contracted with a Catholic, which marriage was null or of doubtful validity.

3. Renew matrimonial consent and continue to live with the infidel party. In this case, it seems that no dispensation from disparity of cult is strictly necessary. As to the *cautiones,* Léry, p. 152, holds that they are not to be demanded, but the conditions of the divine law regarding absence of danger of perversion must be assured.

4. Receive baptism and continue to cohabit with the infidel party, even though the marriage is of doubtful validity and cannot be validated.

5. Remain in possession of a marriage already contracted but of doubtful validity because of a prior marriage whose validity is doubtful. Cf. Léry, p. 152; Kearney, *The Principles of Canon 1127,* p. 136.

Note on So-called "Aut-Aut" Cases. Marriage cases submitted to the Ordinary may present a dilemma resulting from an insoluble doubt, and yet it may be certain that the prior marriage is either invalid or at least soluble, and the party consequently free to marry, although the precise status of the former marriage may be impossible to determine. These *"aut-aut"* cases may or may not involve the Pauline Privilege and the privilege of the faith.

1. An *aut-aut* case in which the *privilege of the faith is not involved* would be the following: John married Susan in 1917 before a Justice of the Peace. Susan was validly baptized in infancy in a heretical sect. John's baptism is veiled in insoluble doubt. These are the circumstances: he was instructed in the Catholic faith at the age of ten at the instance of Catholic friends. Since then he has received the sacraments frequently, has always regarded himself as a Catholic, and at the time of the marriage tried in vain to persuade Susan to consent to

the celebration of the marriage according to the Catholic form. All that can be learned about his infancy is that his parents were Latin Catholics who had ceased long ago to practice their religion. No record of John's baptism can be found. The dilemma is this: if John was not baptized, his marriage to Susan (validly baptized) is invalid because of disparity of cult (before the Code); if John was validly baptized (either as a Latin Catholic or in a heretical or schismatical sect before his conversion to the Catholic faith) his marriage is invalid for want of the juridical form. To make the dilemma perfect, it is necessary that the investigation certainly exclude any affiliation of John to the Oriental Catholic rite, because some Catholic Orientals are not bound to any juridical form of marriage. In this dilemma, then, it is impossible to determine which horn is true, but it is certain that one or the other is true, and hence that the marriage is invalid. The Ordinary can so declare, and John will be free to contract another marriage.

2. A case *involving the Pauline Privilege* is this: John, certainly unbaptized and single, married Susan, unbaptized, in 1928. Susan had been previously married in 1920; her first husband is still living, but refuses to co-operate in any investigation of that first marriage or of his status regarding freedom to marry at that time. Susan, still unbaptized, has separated from John; John now receives Catholic baptism; Susan is interpellated and replies negatively to both questions. The dilemma is this: the first marriage of Susan is either valid or invalid. If it is valid, it invalidated Susan's marriage to John (*ligamen*); if it is invalid, her marriage to John is valid but *legitimum inter non baptizatos,* and hence subject to the Pauline Privilege. It is therefore certain that John can at least use the Pauline Privilege; and the conditions of the interpellations have been fulfilled. Hence, the Ordinary, without determining the status of Susan's first marriage, declares the free status of John to marry a Catholic.

A case *involving the Pauline Privilege and a doubt as to the baptism of one of the parties:* John married Susan in 1917 before a heretical minister. John was certainly unbaptized; the baptism or non-baptism of Susan prior to the marriage remains in insoluble doubt, but it is certain that she has not been baptized since the marriage. Susan has separated from John; John now receives Catholic baptism, interpellates Susan through the Chancery, and receives negative replies to both questions. The dilemma is this: if Susan was validly baptized before the marriage, the marriage was invalid because of disparity of cult (before the Code); if Susan was not validly baptized at that time, the

marriage was valid but *legitimum inter non baptizatos,* and hence
subject to the Pauline Privilege.

Can the Ordinary Act in Cases of This Last Class? Wolf, in an
excellent article from which we have adapted these cases (*"Aut-Aut"
Causae,* in *The Jurist,* Vol. 6, pp. 344–377) holds that he can. "The
solution reached here," he writes, "is no violation of the restriction of
the Holy Office, since the Ordinary is not declaring that the Pauline
Privilege is applicable, but is applying canon 1127 to decree the party's
free state in favor of the faith." We believe that this conclusion is
correct. It may be objected that, even in declaring the free state of
the party to marry, the Ordinary is implicitly declaring that the Pauline Privilege may be used, and, since the case involves a doubt as to
the valid baptism of one of the parties, it should, according to the reply
cited above, be submitted to the Holy Office.

Since this is a very practical matter, let us examine this objection.
The reply of the Holy Office was evidently intended, not to restrict
the use of the Pauline Privilege in cases where it is certainly allowed
by law, but rather to safeguard the marriage bond in cases where the
Pauline Privilege is really doubtful because of an insoluble doubt regarding the baptism of one of the parties. The decision of the Ordinary in no sense resolves any doubt concerning the fact of the baptism
or non-baptism of the party, nor does it rely on any such doubt in declaring the party's freedom to marry. The Ordinary considers both
horns of the dilemma, and reaches a conclusion which is not doubtful
but certain. Susan's baptism is doubtful; therefore, it may have been
valid and it may have been invalid. In the first horn of the dilemma,
her baptism is assumed to have been valid, and it is seen with certainty
that, in that event, the marriage is invalid. In the second horn of the
dilemma, the baptism is assumed to have been invalid, and it is seen
with certainty that, in that event, the Pauline Privilege may be used.
There is no extension of the Pauline Privilege, no application of it to
a doubtful case. The reply of the Holy Office is not contravened, because that reply remains in full force for the cases which it intends to
safeguard, namely, cases in which a valid legitimate marriage is to be
dissolved by the Pauline Privilege *through a decision of the Ordinary
which resolves the doubt concerning baptism.* The Holy Office reserved to itself the resolution of doubts concerning baptism in Pauline
Privilege cases. Here, the Ordinary's decision does not purport to
resolve any such doubt. It leaves that doubt unsolved, and acts upon
a certainty which is independent of the doubt.

Section 2. Separation (cc. 1128–1132)

PRELIMINARY SURVEY

CANON 1128. Husband and wife are obliged to observe community of conjugal life unless a just reason excuses them.

Community of Conjugal Life. This includes normally the habitual sharing of bed, board, and home; it is in general obligatory as a necessary means to the full attainment of the primary and secondary ends of marriage. As to conjugal intercourse in the strict sense, mutual consent for a just cause is sufficient reason for abstinence, provided there is no danger of incontinence. This is not called separation, and does not necessarily prejudice the other elements of conjugal life. Complete and perpetual separation, even by mutual consent, will scarcely ever be licit, because of the danger of incontinence and of scandal. It may, however, be permitted by the Holy See if both parties wish to enter religion, or if the woman wishes to enter religion and the man to be ordained to the priesthood, due provision being made for the children, if any. Even without mutual consent either party may be entitled to separation, either temporarily or permanently, for grave reasons according to the two following canons.

CANON 1129. § 1. Either party to the marriage, by reason of adultery on the part of the other, has the right, though the marriage bond remains intact, to terminate the community of life even permanently, unless he consented to the crime, or was the cause of it, or condoned it expressly or tacitly, or himself committed the same crime.

§ 2. There is a tacit condonation if the innocent party, after learning of the adultery, of his own accord receives the other with conjugal affection; condonation is presumed, unless the injured party within six months expels or deserts the adulterer, or brings a legal accusation against him.

Adultery. This is the *only cause* for permanent separation without mutual consent. It means formal and consummated adultery. The right to separation on this ground is lost:

1. If the other party *consented* to the crime;

2. Or *was the cause* of it, that is, proximately and directly; for example, by frequently unjustly refusing the marriage debt, failing to provide under circumstances which made such failure a proximate cause of infidelity on the part of the other, desertion, etc.;

3. Or if the innocent party *condoned* the crime expressly or tacitly;

4. Or himself *committed the same crime;*

5. Or if the crime was committed *only before baptism*. This is not mentioned in the canon, but is derived from the very firm doctrine of the Church that baptism entirely obliterates crimes committed in the past.

Tacit Condonation. If the injured party after certain knowledge of the crime, *of his own accord* receives the other party with conjugal affection, this amounts to tacit condonation; not, however, if the conjugal treatment results from fear or the danger of grave inconvenience, for then it is not spontaneous; nor if the conjugal treatment is accorded before the crime has been learned with certainty.

After six months, if the injured party neither expels nor abandons the guilty partner, condonation is *presumed;* this presumption yields to contrary proof.

CANON 1130. The innocent party who has departed legally, whether in pursuance of a judicial decree or on his own authority, is never bound to admit the adulterous partner again to conjugal life; but he may either receive or recall the party, unless the latter has in the meantime with his consent embraced a state of life inconsistent with marriage.

Manner of Separation for Adultery. The innocent party may terminate the conjugal life either in pursuance of a decree of an ecclesiastical court upon proof of the fact, or on his own authority provided the crime of adultery is *certain* and *public* in the sense of canon 2197, that is, either commonly known or committed under such circumstances that it must easily become common knowledge. Hence as long as the crime is doubtful or not commonly known, the injured party could not legally depart on his own authority.

Effect of Such Separation. In either case the separation is permanent unless the injured party readmits or recalls the other to conjugal life. The only case in which this may not be done is when the other party has, by mutual consent, embraced a state of life contrary to marriage, that is, either the religious life or sacred orders.

CANON 1131. § 1. If one of the parties has joined a non-Catholic sect; or educated the children as non-Catholics; or is living a criminal and ignominious life; or is causing grave spiritual or corporal danger to the other; or makes the common life too hard by cruelty — these and other things of the kind are so many lawful reasons for the other party to depart, on the authority of the Ordinary of the place, and even on his own authority if the grievances are certain and there is danger in delay.

§ 2. In all these cases, when the cause of the separation has ceased to exist, the common life is to be restored; but if the separation was decreed by the Ordinary for a definite or indefinite time, the innocent party is not bound to the common life unless by decree of the Ordinary or upon expiration of the time.

Causes for Temporary Separation. The causes stated are not exclusive, since *other things of the kind* may also be lawful reasons.

Manner of Separation. 1. It is usually by authority of the Ordinary of the place. Should this authority be exercised by administrative decree or strict judicial procedure? By administrative decree unless the Ordinary determines otherwise either *ex officio* or at the instance of the parties.[42] Whichever form of authority is exercised in the first instance, the same should be used in the second instance.[43] Several cases where judicial procedure was resorted to, and which were appealed to the Rota, are reported in *Canon Law Digest*.[44]

2. By way of exception the separation may be made on private authority, that is, if the legal cause is certain and there is danger in delay.

Duration of Separation. 1. If the injured party departed on his own authority he is bound to restore the common life as soon as it is certain that the legal reason has entirely ceased.

2. If the separation was by decree of the Ordinary for a definite time, the common life is to be restored at the expiration of that time.

3. If the decree was for an indefinite time, the injured party is not bound to return until ordered to do so by a new decree of the Ordinary.

Notes for the Sacramental Forum. 1. A party seeking separation should normally be referred to the Ordinary.

2. However, since people usually hesitate to enter into direct communication with diocesan officials in these matters, it will usually be

---

[42] *AAS*, 24–284; *Digest*, I, p. 554.
[43] *Ibid.*
[44] *Digest*, II, p. 344.

well not to insist on this obligation if the parties are unaware of it, especially if the separation is already in effect and there is no great scandal connected with it.

3. Obviously the confessor should not readily advise nor easily permit separation for any but the gravest causes. For disagreements, quarrels, etc., he should counsel mutual patience and forbearance.

The Question of Co-operation in Civil Divorce: Judge: Lawyer. 1. If the marriage in question is invalid, and has been so declared by ecclesiastical authority, or if at least the permission of the Ordinary has been given to obtain a civil divorce, the divorce, in the absence of scandal, is simply licit; and co-operation is licit.

2. Even though the marriage is valid, civil divorce as a mere means of settling civil matters may sometimes be allowed to the parties, in the absence of scandal and provided they have no intention of contracting another marriage. In this case also co-operation will be licit.

3. In other cases, where it is wrong for the parties to seek a civil divorce, may a judge decree a civil divorce according to law, or may a lawyer represent the plaintiff in obtaining it? Respectable moral authorities hold that the legal proceedings of divorce cases, prescinding from the intention of the parties to marry again, are *not malum in se;* and hence that the co-operation of judge or lawyer, *for a proportionate reason* may be permitted on the principle of the double effect. The application of the principle differs for the judge and for the lawyer. If Catholic judges were absolutely to decline all such cases, well-qualified candidates for the bench would be excluded from this career of public service, and not merely their private fortunes but the public good would thereby be compromised. This is a proportionate reason for allowing judges generally, in the absence of scandal and within the limits of reasonable necessity, to act in divorce cases. It is more difficult to find a proportionate cause to excuse the plaintiff's lawyer. The mere private advantage (the fee, even a substantial one, which he would lose by declining the case) does not seem to be a cause sufficient to compensate for the very great public evil which results from divorce. Consequently we think a lawyer may not do this except in an extraordinary case where either a public good or a *paramount* private advantage is at stake.[45]

---

[45] Cf. Arregui, *Summarium Theol. Mor.,* Ed. 12, n. 461; Genicot-Salsmans, *Theol. Mor.,* II, nn. 561, 562; Lehmkuhl, *Theol. Mor.,* II, n. 921, note; Cappello, *De Matrimonio,* nn. 833–840; *Eccl. Rev.,* 1932, p. 73.

CANON 1132. When a separation has been effected, the children are to be educated under the care of the innocent party, or, if one of the parties is a non-Catholic, under the care of the Catholic party, unless in either case the Ordinary decrees otherwise for the good of the children themselves, always without prejudice to their Catholic education.

Custody and Education of the Children. 1. If both parties are Catholics, the custody and education of the children should usually be entrusted to the innocent party.

2. If only one is a Catholic, to the Catholic party.

3. In either case the Ordinary may make a different provision, for the welfare of the children, always safeguarding their Catholic education.

State laws which result directly or indirectly in depriving Catholic children of Catholic education are against the natural law. Catholics should be so instructed in this matter that they will exercise all legal means to remedy this grave injustice. The system of taxation which burdens Catholic citizens with the support of so-called "public" schools which Catholics may not in conscience attend, is an evident violation of fundamental justice. Efforts to remedy these grave abuses have been consistently opposed by Masonic and so-called "Liberal" elements.

Ante-nuptial promises, guaranteeing the Catholic education of children, have been ably presented, from the standpoint of the laws of the States, as proper foundation for a suit in equity. Though this right has not yet been fully recognized by higher American courts, its study is recommended to Catholic lawyers.[46]

---

[46] Cf. White, *Canonical Ante-nuptial Promises and the Civil Law,* 1934, Cath. U. Canon Law Studies, n. 91 (Dolphin Press). See also O'Brien and O'Brien, *Antenuptial Promises in Restatement of Inter-Church-and-State Common Law,* in *The Jurist,* Vol. 6, p. 50.

Section 3. Simple Convalidation (cc. 1133–1137)

PRELIMINARY SURVEY

Simple Validation of Marriage Invalid by Reason of
Impediment (c. 1133)
The Renewal of Consent (c. 1134)
Manner of Renewal of Consent (c. 1135)
Simple Validation of Marriage Invalid for Want of Consent
(c. 1136)
Simple Validation of Marriage Invalid for Want of Form
(c. 1137)

CANON 1133. § 1. In order to validate a marriage which is invalid because of a diriment impediment, it is required that the impediment cease or be dispensed, and that consent be renewed at least by the party who is aware of the impediment.

§ 2. This renewal of consent is required by ecclesiastical law for the validity of the marriage, even though both parties gave their consent in the beginning and have not revoked it.

Validation of Marriage Not a Hasty Procedure. When an existing marriage is found to be invalid, various courses of action are available according to circumstances, and all should be carefully considered before compromising the matter in any way. *Never be hasty to validate a marriage,* is in general good advice. Above all, never be hasty in *informing the party* that his or her marriage is invalid.

1. In some cases of invalid marriage, *separation,* followed by a declaration of nullity, may be the best or the only course; for example, if the parties are certainly unsuited to each other, or if the Catholic party does not wish to validate the marriage, or if it cannot be validated.

2. In some extraordinary cases *cohabitation as man and wife* must be permitted by leaving the parties in good faith; for example, the marriage is absolutely incapable of validation; the parties are in good faith but would probably not have the courage to make the heroic sacrifice of separation.

3. *Cohabitation as brother and sister* is very rarely to be permitted, because of the normal danger of incontinence. In a proper case, however, and in the absence of scandal, it may be permitted by the confessor without recourse to diocesan authorities, since in such a case it concerns only the internal forum.

4. *Validation* of the marriage may be the proper course *after due consideration*.

State of the Question. 1. *Simple convalidation* means the validation of a marriage with renewal of consent on the part of one or both parties.

2. *Sanatio in radice* means the validation of marriage without any renewal of consent.

3. This canon and all those of this section deal exclusively with the first method, *simple validation*. *Sanatio in radice* is dealt with in the next section.

4. A marriage may be invalid for any of the following reasons: a diriment impediment, want of consent, or want of form. Canon 1133, § 1, applies to simple validation where the marriage is invalid because of an impediment; § 2 applies to all cases of simple validation.

Requisites for Simple Convalidation. 1. The impediment must either cease or be dispensed. Some impediments may cease through lapse of time or change of circumstances, as want of canonical age, a prior bond of marriage, disparity of cult, impotence, abduction. Some which were in effect before the Code ceased on May 19, 1918; e.g., the obsolete forms of affinity, public propriety, and spiritual relationship; consanguinity in the fourth degree of the collateral line. If the impediment which rendered the marriage null has not *ceased* in any of these ways, it must be *dispensed*.

2. There must be a *renewal of consent* at least by the party who is aware of the impediment. It is not sufficient that matrimonial consent exist on both sides. It exists if it was once lawfully expressed and has not been revoked (c. 1093); but a *renewal of consent* is nevertheless *required for validity* by ecclesiastical law.[47]

a. As a rule *only the party who is aware* of the impediment need renew consent. Hence the subterfuges which were formerly employed to get an expression of consent from the other party without disclosing the invalidity of the marriage are now entirely unnecessary.

b. If, however, the impediment is public, both parties must renew consent (c. 1135, § 1); and in that case if one party did not know of the invalidity he would have to be informed of it and to renew consent.

---

[47] Cappello, in *Ius Pontificium*, Vol. 20, p. 25, proposes the opinion that baptized non-Catholics should not be subject to this norm requiring renewal of consent in simple convalidation. Donnelly examines and rejects this opinion in *Theological Studies*, Vol. 3, p. 189.

c. Pre-Code marriages which were invalid because of some impediment which has been removed by the Code for the future, are not *ipso facto* validated. The reason is that the law of the Code is not retroactive (c. 10); hence these marriages must be validated as provided in the Code.

CANON 1134. The renewal of consent must be a new act of the will having for its object the marriage which is known to have been invalid from the beginning.

Renewal of Consent. 1. A *new act of the will* is required because consent is an act of the will; hence *consent* is not *renewed* unless a new act of the will is elicited.

2. This act must have *marriage for its object,* because it is matrimonial consent which is required.

3. The marriage must be *known to have been invalid* from the beginning, because otherwise the party cannot now intend to transfer the essential right of marriage. One does not transfer a right which he believes to be already vested in the other party. Yet, without this present intention to transfer the right, the substance of matrimonial consent is lacking. After the declaration of nullity of the Vanderbilt-Marlborough marriage by the Rota in 1926, many people were surprised that, even though the marriage may have been null in the beginning, it should not have been validated by ten years of cohabitation. One sufficient reason why it was not so validated was that the woman whose free renewal of consent was required never suspected that the marriage was legally null, though she knew well enough that she had been the victim of coercion.[48]

4. The renewal of consent must be *absolute.* Certainly a merely hypothetical renewal is insufficient; for example, "If we were not married I should now wish to take you for my wife." This is insufficient because it is not an act of the will at all, but merely a reflection about an act which might be elicited under other circumstances. A more difficult case is presented if a person who reasonably suspects that his marriage is invalid, without being absolutely certain of the fact, should say: "If our marriage is invalid I here and now renew my matrimonial consent with the intention of validating it." Practically such a renewal is unnecessary because in doubt the marriage is presumed to be valid both in the internal and external forum (c. 1014).

---

[48] Cf. *AAS*, 18–501; *Digest*, I, p. 523.

CANON 1135. § 1. If the impediment is public, consent must be renewed by both parties in the form prescribed by law.

§ 2. If it is occult and known to both parties, it is sufficient that consent be renewed by both parties privately and secretly.

§ 3. If it is occult and unknown to one of the parties, it is sufficient that only the party who is aware of the impediment renew his consent privately and secretly, provided the other party perseveres in the consent once given.

Manner of Renewing Consent. In the validation of a marriage which was void *because of an impediment,* the manner of renewing consent varies according to the circumstances.

1. If the impediment is *public* (in the sense of canon 1037), consent must be renewed by *both parties,* and in the form prescribed by law, that is, according to canons 1094–1099. Normally both parties will already be aware of the impediment since it is a public one. In the extraordinary case where one party had remained ignorant of the impediment, he or she would have to be informed of the invalidity of the marriage and then join in the formal renewal of consent.

2. If the impediment is *occult and known to both parties,* consent must be renewed by both parties privately and secretly, that is without the form prescribed by canons 1094–1099. Even in this case, however, the renewal must be an explicit, external, mutual act, though not necessarily simultaneous; in other words, it must meet all the requirements of a consent sufficient to establish a contract. Marital intercourse in itself is not sufficient for this; but it might be so through circumstances, for example, if both parties knew their marriage had been invalid, and if this act were mutually understood as an expression of marital consent.[49]

3. If the impediment is occult and *unknown to one of the parties,* it is sufficient that only the party who is aware of the impediment renew consent, privately and in secret, that is, without the form. But the consent of the other must continue to exist. It will be presumed to continue until its revocation is proved (c. 1093). In this case the party who renews consent need only make an internal act of the will to that effect; no mutual, external act is required.[50] In practice it is recommended that the confessor elicit from the party an explicit expression of consent.

4. What if the impediment is occult and *unknown to both parties?* The law makes no provision for validating such a marriage, at least

[49] Cf. Gasparri, *De Matrimonio,* II, n. 1192.
[50] Cf. Cappello, *De Matrimonio,* n. 845, 3, b.

by renewal of consent. One party would have to be told of the impediment and then renew consent as in the case last mentioned. Otherwise a *sanatio* would have to be obtained.

CANON 1136. § 1. A marriage which is invalid for want of consent is validated if the party who had not consented, now consents, provided the consent given by the other party continues to exist.

§ 2. If the want of consent was merely internal, it is sufficient that the party who had not consented, give his consent interiorly.

§ 3. If it was also external, it is necessary to manifest consent also externally, either according to the form prescribed by law, if the want of consent was public, or in some other way privately and in secret, if it was occult.

Marriage Null for Want of Consent. In this case the want of consent which made the marriage null must fall under one of three different categories: it was merely internal, or external but occult, or external and public.

1. If, for example, a person while externally expressing matrimonial consent, withheld it interiorly by a positive act of the will excluding marriage, or the conjugal right, or one of the essential properties of marriage, that marriage would be null (c. 1086, § 2). All that is needed to validate it is what was wanting in the original contract, namely, interior consent on the part of that person.

2. If a person placed some invalidating condition to his consent (cf. c. 1092) and did so by an external act, but one which cannot now be proved in the external forum, the want of consent is external but occult. To validate such a marriage, an external expression of consent is required, but not a strictly public one; that is, the form of law is not required.

3. Finally the want of consent may have been both external and public, that is, capable of proof in the external forum; for example, where circumstances sufficient to establish grave invalidating fear according to canon 1087 can be proved by adequate evidence. In this case the consent must be expressed by both parties not only externally but publicly according to the form of law. For this reason, in the Vanderbilt-Marlborough case and in countless others where the marriage was invalid for public coercion, the marriage could not be validated by cohabitation.

CANON 1137. In order that a marriage which is invalid for want of form be made valid, it must be contracted anew in the form prescribed by law.

Marriage Null for Want of Form. This canon taken alone would seem to contradict canon 1139, § 1, where it is clearly stated that a marriage which is invalid for want of form can be made valid, not only without the form, but without even a renewal of consent. We must take the two canons together: canon 1137 is of *simple validation* by renewal of consent in the form prescribed by law; canon 1139 is of *sanatio in radice,* without even a renewal of consent.

Section 4. *Sanatio in Radice,* etc. (cc. 1138–1143)

PRELIMINARY SURVEY

General Features of a *Sanatio* (c. 1138)
Marriages Which Can Be So Validated (c. 1139)
Marriages Null for Want of Consent (c. 1140)
The Power to Heal *in Radice* (c. 1141)
Licitness of Second Marriage (c. 1142)
Repetition of Nuptial Blessing (c. 1143)

CANON 1138. § 1. The healing of a marriage *in radice* is its validation, involving, besides the dispensation or cessation of the impediment, a dispensation from the law requiring renewal of consent, and retroaction by fiction of law, as regards canonical effects, to the past.

§ 2. The validation takes place at the moment when the favor is granted; but the retroaction is understood as going back to the beginning of the marriage, unless express provision is made to the contrary.

§ 3. The dispensation from the law requiring renewal of consent can be granted even without the knowledge of one or both of the parties.

Sanatio in Radice. Two distinctive features, besides the dispensation or cessation of the impediment, mark a *sanatio:* (1) dispensation from the law requiring renewal of consent; and (2) retroactivity.

1. *Renewal* of consent is not required of either party. But matrimonial consent must *exist on both sides* at the time of the *sanatio.* That is required by the natural law, and no human power can dispense from it (c. 1081, § 1). Matrimonial consent as such may exist even though the marriage be known or believed to be invalid for some other cause (c. 1085); and once given it is presumed to continue until its revocation is proved (c. 1093). It is not revoked by a merely hypothetical act of the will, as, for example, if the party *would* wish to be

free of the bond if he suspected that he could. Refusal to renew consent
is not equivalent to a revocation of consent. Even a petition for
separation or for a declaration of nullity is not in itself a revocation
of consent. Hence, though the *sanatio* will not be granted while the
case is pending, after a decision *non constare de nullitate,* a *sanatio*
could be given, the matrimonial consent once given not being necessarily revoked by the petition for nullity.

2. Retroaction by fiction of law means that *from the time of the
sanatio* the law regards the marriage as though it had been valid
from the beginning. As to the legitimation of children the effect is
that from that time they are regarded as if they had been born legitimate. This legitimation extends to *all canonical effects.* It is therefore
fuller than the legitimation effected by the subsequent marriage of
the parents or the simple validation of their marriage (c. 1116).

Perfect and Imperfect *Sanatio*. A *sanatio* is called *perfect* if there is
a dispensation of both parties from renewal of consent and the retroaction is effective in all respects back to the time of the marriage. If
any of these elements is lacking the *sanatio* is *imperfect.* It is such
for example:

1. If only one party is dispensed from renewal of consent, while
the other party renews consent;

2. If the *sanatio* is given after the death of one of the parties, since
in that case the bond of marriage cannot be brought into being,
though the other effects be produced by fiction of law. The bond
cannot be effected because mutual consent does not exist at the time
of the *sanatio.*

3. If the retroaction does not extend so far back as the marriage
itself. This would be true, for example, if mutual matrimonial consent had not existed at the time of the marriage, but only at some
later date. A *sanatio* subsequently given could be retroactive only to
the time when matrimonial consent existed (cf. c. 1140, § 2).

Historical Notes. 1. The earliest certain instances of *sanatio in
radice* were in 1301, when Boniface VIII thus validated marriages
between the King and Queen of Castile after the King's death (an
imperfect *sanatio*), and between King Ildephonse of Portugal and the
Countess of Poland during their lives (a perfect *sanatio*).

2. About the middle of the fourteenth century, John of Andrea
explained and defended the theory of such validations, but they were
extremely rare in practice.

3. In the seventeenth century, they became more frequent. In the

next century Benedict XIV (1740–1785) explained the doctrine at length, and they came into general use.

4. Some general *sanationes in radice* have been given: by Julius III in England in 1554; by Clement VIII for Greek Orientals in 1595; by Pius VII for France in 1801 and 1809; by Pius X for Germany in 1906, and for Hungary in 1909; finally for the universal Church in 1912.[51]

CANON 1139. § 1. Any marriage which was contracted with the consent of both parties which was naturally sufficient but juridically ineffective because of a diriment impediment of ecclesiastical law or because of defect of the form required by law, can be healed *in radice,* provided the consent continues to exist.

§ 2. But a marriage which was contracted with an impediment of the natural or divine law, even though the impediment has since ceased to exist, is not healed *in radice* by the Church, even from the time when the impediment ceased.

Marriages Which Can Be Healed *in Radice*. Marriages can be invalid for defect of consent, defect of form, or a diriment impediment. This canon 1139 deals with the last two causes, canon 1140 with the first.

1. Marriages invalid for defect of form can be healed *in radice.* This explicit statement forms a contrast with the rule of canon 1137, which requires the legal form when such a marriage is validated with renewal of consent. The conditions under which this power is exercised will be considered under canon 1141.

2. Marriages invalid because of a diriment impediment of ecclesiastical law can be healed *in radice.*

3. If a marriage is invalid because of a diriment impediment of natural or divine law, the Church *does not* grant a *sanatio.* This is a mere statement of fact. Some authors hold that a *sanatio* under such circumstances is beyond the power of the Church; but the canon does not say this. Gasparri relates that the statement that the Church *cannot* heal such marriages *in radice,* which was contained in an earlier reply of the Holy Office, was purposely changed when the Code was framed, to read "the Church *does not.*"[52] To heal such a marriage *perfectly,* that is, with retroactive effect back to the time of the marriage, so as to consider the bond valid in spite of such an

---

[51] Cf. *AAS*, 9–13; Digest, I, p. 556.
[52] Gasparri, *De Matrimonio*, II, nn. 1215–1219.

impediment, is evidently beyond the power of the Church, which claims no authority to dispense from divine law directly. But if there is question of an *imperfect sanatio,* effective only back to the time when the impediment ceased, this argument has no force. Nor is it convincing to state that in the face of such an impediment matrimonial consent is impossible. The consent will be juridically ineffective without a *sanatio,* but it is naturally sufficient (c. 1085) and the *sanatio* can give it juridical effect. As a matter of fact there are recorded cases where the Church granted a *sanatio* (imperfect) back to the time when the impediment ceased.[53]

CANON 1140. § 1. If the consent is wanting in both parties or in either party, the marriage cannot be healed *in radice,* whether the consent was wanting from the beginning or was originally given and later revoked.

§ 2. If consent was wanting in the beginning but was afterward given, a *sanatio* can be granted from the moment when consent was given.

Consent Must Exist. The absolute necessity of the existence of consent at the time of the *sanatio* has been sufficiently insisted on. But the further question answered by this canon is: can a marriage which was invalid for want of consent be healed *in radice,* at least after the consent has been supplied? The answer is yes, but it will be an *imperfect sanatio,* since it does not go back to the time of the marriage. To consider the marriage valid before consent would be an absurdity exceeding the limits of a fiction of law; for a fiction of law is but a disposition of law contrary to fact, made for just cause in a matter which is *possible.*[54] A valid marriage without consent is an impossibility. No fiction of law can conjure up such a chimera.

CANON 1141. A *sanatio in radice* can be granted only by the Apostolic See.

Power to Heal *in Radice.* This power resides in the Holy See. The competent agency is: (1) for the internal forum, the Sacred Penitentiary; (2) for the external forum in marriages other than mixed, the Sacred Congregation of the Sacraments; (3) for the external forum in mixed marriages, the Holy Office.

Delegated Faculties. 1. *Apostolic Delegates* are given certain faculties to heal marriages *in radice.*[55] The use of the faculty is in general

---

[53] Cf. S. Poen., 25 Apr., 1890; Cappello, *De Matrimonio,* n. 854.
[54] Cf. V-C, *Epit.,* I, n. 101.
[55] Cf. *Digest,* I, p. 181.

limited to cases where the renewal of consent is morally impossible.

2. *Quinquennial Faculties of Ordinaries* also include the faculty to heal marriages *in radice* in certain cases and under stated conditions.[56]

Reasons for *Sanatio in Radice*. 1. In general a grave reason is required *for validity*. If the *sanatio* is granted by anyone inferior to the Holy See, this follows directly from canon 84, § 1; if granted by the Holy See itself, the dispensation would be valid but illicit if given without cause; and, since there is a general presumption that the Holy See does not wish to act illicitly, the certain absence of cause for the dispensation would create a presumption of invalidity (cf. cc. 40, 42).

2. The sufficient reason generally is that renewal of consent cannot be obtained, either because one of the parties cannot be induced to renew consent or because such renewal would involve grave damage or inconvenience, or would occasion scandal. The last case would be verified if, for example, the marriage were originally invalid through the fault or negligence of the pastor or Ordinary, which would become known if renewal of consent were asked.

Practical Notes. 1. The petition should state exactly the reason why the marriage is null and the facts showing that there is proper cause for a *sanatio*. If the matter concerns only the internal sacramental forum, fictitious names are given.

2. The petition may be made by either party to the marriage, or by a third party even without their knowledge (cf. c. 1138, § 3).

3. The rescript granting the *sanatio* may be *in forma gratiosa* or *in forma commissoria:*

a. If it is *in forma gratiosa* it will be effective from the moment when it was given (c. 38); the pastor or confessor who receives it for the parties will be instructed to notify them (or the party at least who knows of the invalidity of the marriage) that the marriage is now validated.

b. If it is *in forma commissoria* it will name the person who is to execute it. This will be, for the internal forum the confessor himself, for the external forum the Ordinary, who may act through a pastor. The executor named must carry out the instructions given him in the rescript. The marriage is validated only at the moment when he executes the rescript (c. 38). For the internal sacramental forum, the confessor may do this in the confessional itself by merely declaring to the party that the marriage is healed by grant of the Holy See.

---

[56] Cf. Quinquennial Faculties, *Digest,* II, p. 30.

4. The *sanatio* must be recorded in the baptismal and matrimonial registers or in the special record as provided in canons 1046, 1047, unless it concerns only the sacramental forum, in which case it is not recorded at all.

CANON 1142. Although chaste widowhood is more honorable, yet second and further marriages are valid and licit, without prejudice to the provision of canon 1069, § 2.

Second and Further Marriages Valid and Licit. It is here assumed that the former marriage has been dissolved by death or in some other lawful way, or has been legally declared to have been null from the beginning. Canon 1069, § 2 requires for the *licitness* of the second marriage due proof of the dissolution or nullity of the former one.

Historical Notes. 1. St. Paul says: "But I say to the unmarried and to the widows: it is good for them if they so continue. . . . A woman is bound by the law as long as her husband liveth; but if her husband die she is at liberty: let her marry to whom she will, only in the Lord."[57]

2. Among the Fathers, SS. Ambrose, Jerome, Basil, Augustine, and others declared the licitness of second marriages, though they esteemed widowhood as preferable.

3. The Church defended such marriages as both valid and licit against the Montanists, Novatians, Waldensians, and other heretics. It is true that in the Oriental Church in the fourth century, third and fourth marriages were forbidden under pain of nullity, owing to abuses peculiar to the time.

4. In the early Church a penance was imposed on the faithful contracting a second marriage. The irregularity declared by canon 984, 4° is probably a remnant of this ancient discipline.

CANON 1143. A woman to whom the solemn nuptial blessing has once been given cannot receive it again in a subsequent marriage.

Notes. 1. If the bride has been married before and received the solemn nuptial blessing on the former occasion, she cannot receive it again; but in lieu of the blessing the prayers of the Ritual[58] may be used by Apostolic indult, which can usually be obtained by subdelegation from the Ordinary (see c. 1101).

2. There is no objection to blessing the ring or giving a simple

---

[57] 1 Cor. 7:8, 39.
[58] *Rit. Rom.*, Appendix, *De Matrimonio*, II.

blessing to the bridal couple; it is only the solemn nuptial blessing which is forbidden.

3. If only the groom was married before, or if the bride was formerly married but never before received the solemn nuptial blessing, she may receive it at the second marriage.

4. The reason for the prohibition is purely liturgical; to emphasize the importance and beauty of this unique blessing.

CASES AND QUESTIONS

1. Two non-Catholics who are validly baptized in heretical churches marry and live together for a short time. Can this marriage be dissolved: (a) by civil divorce; (b) by solemn religious profession or sacred orders; (c) by the Pauline Privilege; (d) by papal dispensation; (e) by permission of the Holy See to marry again because of the presumed death of the former spouse? (C. 1118).

2. What two questions must regularly be asked of the other party before the use of the Pauline Privilege? (C. 1121, § 1). What is the effect of a negative answer to the first question, if the second is answered affirmatively? Of a negative answer to the second? What amounts to a tacit negative answer to both? What is the meaning of the phrase, *pacifice sine contumelia Creatoris,* in the second question?

3. Can the Ordinary, on application by one of the parties for the Pauline Privilege, proceed to make the interpellations without referring the matter to the Holy See? (C. 1122, § 1). Can the Ordinary dispense from the interpellations in the ordinary case of the Pauline Privilege? (Cc. 1121, § 2, 1125).

4. Explain briefly three ways of making the interpellations: judicial, epistolary, private. Are interpellations made privately by the party himself valid? Licit? (C. 1122, § 2).

5. Can you give a brief summary of the Constitutions mentioned in canon 1125? What is the effect *on the interpellations,* of the first two of those Constitutions? Of the third?

6. Does canon 1125 apply to all countries or only to those where the conditions described in the Constitutions are fairly general? Do they apply also to wives, or only to husbands?

7. State the essential facts of the so-called "Helena case." Are there other similar cases on record? (*Digest,* I, pp. 551–554; II, pp. 341–343).

8. To whom are these cases reserved? What are the essential conditions? The procedure? (Cf. Ramstein, *The Pastor and Marriage Cases,* p. 202.)

9. In the use of the Pauline Privilege, at what moment is the bond of the valid infidel marriage dissolved? (C. 1126). Does this apply also to cases coming under canon 1125? To cases like the Helena case?

10. Nathan, unbaptized, married Cymbeline, also unbaptized. The marriage was unhappy, resulted in divorce. Some years later, Cymbeline is courted by John, a Catholic; she wants to marry him and is willing to embrace the Catholic faith: Is this a case where the Pauline Privilege could be used? (C. 1120, § 1). Cymbeline now receives baptism; the interpellations are sent to Nathan by the Ordinary; no reply within the time. Cymbeline marries John. Later it is learned that before this marriage Nathan had been converted and baptized a Catholic. Is Cymbeline's second marriage valid? Can Nathan now marry again?

11. Frank and Matilda, Catholics, were duly married. Frank became addicted to drink; family life, especially in view of several small children, became impossible; Matilda obtained from the Ordinary an indefinite decree of separation. After several years, Frank is entirely reformed; the cause for separation has entirely ceased. Is Matilda obliged to return to him? What if he obtains a decree from the Ordinary requiring her to do so? (C. 1131, § 2).

12. What would be your advice to a young lawyer who consults you about accepting his first divorce case? To a Catholic judge who finds that his office necessarily involves him in divorce proceedings?

13. What is required for the simple convalidation of a marriage which was invalid because of a public diriment impediment? An occult diriment impediment? (C. 1133). What if the marriage was invalid for want of form? (C. 1137).

14. In a marriage which is invalid for want of consent, explain the distinction between a defect of consent which is public, one which is occult but external, and one which is merely internal. How must consent be renewed in each of these cases? (C. 1136).

15. Consuela married Duke under unjust compulsion from her mother; was unhappy but made the best of it, lived with him for ten years and had several children by him. In a trial to have the marriage declared null for force and fear, the unjust compulsion was fully proved, but it is objected that the marriage was validated by her consent to conjugal relations. Discuss the merits of this argument (c. 1136, § 3).

16. In granting a *sanatio in radice,* does the Church dispense from matrimonial consent? (Cc. 1138, § 1; 1081, § 1). What would you say is the root (*radix*) in which the *sanatio* is operative?

17. X and Y were married without a dispensation from a diriment impediment of ecclesiastical law which was known to both parties. Can this marriage be validated by a *sanatio in radice?* Was true matrimonial consent originally given? (C. 1085). Does it still exist? (C. 1093).

18. In a discussion group, S states that a *sanatio* is *impossible:* (*a*) when the marriage is null for want or form, citing canon 1137; (*b*) when it is invalid for a diriment impediment of divine law which has ceased, citing canon 1139, § 2. Your opinion?

19. Have the Ordinaries of the United States any faculties for *sanatio in radice?* Ordinary or delegated? (C. 1141; *Digest,* II, p. 30 sq.).

Readings:

Gregory, *The Pauline Privilege,* Cath. U., 1931; Woeber, *The Interpellations,* Cath. U., 1942; Burton, *A Commentary on Canon 1125,* Cath. U., 1940; Woods, *The Constitutions of Canon 1125* (Milwaukee: Bruce); Kearney, *The Principles of Canon 1127,* Cath. U.; Brennan, *The Simple Convalidation of Marriage,* Cath. U., 1937; Harrigan, *The Radical Sanation of Invalid Marriages,* Cath. U., 1938; *Periodica,* Vol. 19, p. 87* (Cappello, on dissolution of natural bond); Vol. 17, p. 241* (Vermeersch, on private interpellations); Vol. 20, p. 108* (Vromant, on application of the Constitution, *Populis*); *Irish Ecclesiastical Record,* Vol. 41, pp. 302, 530 (*sanatio in radice*); *Australasian Catholic Record,* 1932, p. 12 (Nevin, on *cautiones* in mixed marriage healed *in radice*); 1937, p. 234 (Nevin, case where non-Catholic party refuses to allow Catholic education of children); *Theological Studies,* Vol. 3, p. 189 (Donnelly, on renewal of consent by non-Catholics in simple convalidation); *The Jurist,* Vol. 2, p. 134 (Kieda, on papal dissolution of legitimate marriage); Léry, *Le Privilège de la Foi;* Wolf, *Aut-Aut Causae,* in *The Jurist,* Vol. 6, p. 344.

PART SIX: SACRED PLACES AND TIMES: DIVINE WORSHIP: THE TEACHING OFFICE OF THE CHURCH: CHURCH PROPERTY

CHAPTER XVI

SACRED PLACES AND TIMES

Plan of This and Following Chapter. Sacred places are dealt with in the Code under four titles, namely, churches, oratories, altars, and ecclesiastical burial; sacred times are feast days of obligation, and days of fast or abstinence or both. Divine worship includes canons on the custody of the Most Blessed Sacrament, the worship of saints, images and relics, sacred processions, sacred furnishings, and vows and oaths. Limitations of space dictate a rather summary treatment of most of this matter. We will give the substance of nearly all the canons, with little commentary except where it is called for in those parts of the subject which are most important in a seminary course.

Section 1. Sacred Places in General: Churches: Oratories: Altars (cc. 1154–1202)

Article 1. Sacred Places in General (cc. 1154–1160)

PRELIMINARY SURVEY

Sacred Places Defined (c. 1154)
Consecration of a Sacred Place (c. 1155)
Blessing of a Sacred Place (c. 1156)
Consent of the Ordinary (c. 1157)
Recording the Consecration or Blessing (c. 1158)
Proof (c. 1159)
Exemption of Sacred Places From Civil Authority (c. 1160)

Sacred Places. Sacred places are those which are destined for divine worship or for the burial of the faithful, by a consecration or blessing prescribed for this purpose by approved liturgical books (c. 1154). Such a blessing (or consecration) is called a *constitutive,* as opposed to a merely *invocative* one, because it constitutes the place a sacred place. If a special formula is prescribed, it is required for validity (c. 1148, § 2).

Consecration. The consecration of a place, even of one which belongs to regulars, pertains to the Ordinary of the territory in which the place is, provided the Ordinary has the episcopal character, not however to the Vicar General without special authority, without prejudice to the right of Cardinals to consecrate the church and altars of their titular place (c. 1155, § 1). This provision deals with licitness of consecration; a consecration is *valid* provided it is done by one having the episcopal character or the power to do so from the law or an apostolic indult (c. 1147, § 1). But licit consecration requires moreover the consent of the Ordinary according to canon 1157, below.

The Ordinary of the territory, even though he lack the episcopal character, can give to any Bishop of the same rite permission to perform consecrations in his territory (c. 1155, § 2). An Abbot or Prelate *nullius,* if he is not a consecrated Bishop, is not included in this provision as one who can actually perform the consecration, notwithstanding cc. 215, § 2, and 323, § 2.[1] But he could give the permission to do so to one who is a Bishop.

Blessing. The right to bless a sacred place, if the place belongs to the secular clergy or to a nonexempt or lay religious institute, pertains to the Ordinary of the territory in which the place is; if it belongs to an exempt clerical religious institute, the right pertains to the major superior; either of these can delegate another priest to perform the blessing (c. 1156). Again there is question here merely of licitness; the *validity* of a blessing is governed by canon 1147, §§ 2 and 3 (any priest *can* do it if the blessing is not specially reserved).

Consent of the Ordinary. Any privilege to the contrary notwithstanding, no one may consecrate or bless a sacred place without the consent of the Ordinary (c. 1157). The Ordinary here includes the major superior of a clerical exempt institute (c. 198).

Recording the Consecration or Blessing. A testimonial of the consecration or blessing must be drawn up, and one copy thereof is to be kept in the episcopal Curia, the other in the archives of the church

---

[1] Code Com., 29 Jan., 1931; *AAS,* 23–110; *Digest,* I, p. 194.

(c. 1158). However, in the case of a blessing (but not a consecration) of a place belonging to regulars, the first-mentioned copy of the record is kept in the archives of the Ordinary (major superior) of the religious to whom the place belongs.[2]

Proof. The consecration or blessing of a place, provided no harm is done to anyone, is sufficiently proved by even one unexceptionable witness (c. 1159, § 1). If it is legitimately proved, neither the consecration nor blessing can be repeated; but in doubt, it may be done *ad cautelam* (c. 1159, § 2).

Exemption From Civil Authority. Sacred places are exempt from the jurisdiction of the civil authority, and in them the lawful authority of the Church freely exercises its jurisdiction (c. 1160).

Article 2. Churches (cc. 1161–1187)

PRELIMINARY SURVEY

---

[2] A Coronata, II, n. 727; Vermeersch-Creusen, *Epit.*, II, n. 472; De Meester, *Compendium*, III, n. 1116, p. 19, note 4.

Church Defined. By the term "church" is understood a sacred structure devoted to divine worship for the principal purpose of being used by all the faithful for public divine worship (c. 1161). An oratory (cf. c. 1188, § 1) is distinguished from a church in that it is not *principally destined for public worship by all the faithful,* even though, in the case of a public oratory, they have the right to go there. So too, a special shrine, if principally destined to do honor to a particular saint or locality, is not a church.

Consent of the Ordinary of the Place. No church shall be built without the express consent in writing of the Ordinary of the place, which cannot be given by the Vicar General without a special mandate (c. 1162, § 1). In the case of a cathedral or collegiate church, the consent of the Holy See is required.[3] The Ordinary shall not give his consent unless he prudently foresees that the necessary funds for the building and upkeep of the new church, for the support of its personnel, and for the other expenses of worship will be forthcoming (c. 1162, § 2).

Lest the new church might cause harm to those already established, without proportionate compensating advantage to the faithful, the Ordinary, before giving his consent, should consult the rectors of neighboring churches who have an interest in the matter, without prejudice to the provision of canon 1676 (c. 1162, § 3). The canon cited provides for legal action by the injured parties, if any.

Even members of a religious institute, although they may have obtained the consent of the Ordinary of the place to establish a new house in the diocese or town, before they build a church or public oratory in a definite and determined place, must obtain the permission of the Ordinary of the place (c. 1162, § 4). This provision must be taken in connection with canon 497, § 2. The permission to establish a new house carries with it, in the case of clerical religious, that of having a church or public oratory annexed to it; but permission must be obtained for the erection of the church or oratory on the particular site chosen for it.

Blessing and Laying of the Cornerstone. The blessing and laying of the cornerstone of a church pertains to the persons mentioned in canon 1156 (c. 1163); that is, to the Ordinary of the territory, or, for a church belonging to clerical exempt religious, the major superior.

Form of the Structure. Ordinaries shall see to it, taking counsel of experts if need be, that in the construction and remodeling of churches traditional Christian styles of architecture and the standards of sacred

---

[3] A Coronata, II, n. 732.

art be observed **(c. 1164, § 1)**. No door or window of a church should open upon lay residences; and the spaces, if any, under the pavement or above the church should not be put to merely profane uses **(c. 1164, § 2)**. *Merely* profane uses are such as are *in no way* connected with the sacred and religious purpose of the church; hence parish libraries, meeting rooms, and the like, would be permitted.

Consecration of Church, or Altar. Divine services cannot be held in a new church before it has been devoted to divine worship by solemn consecration or at least by blessing **(c. 1165, § 1)**. Yet it is commonly admitted that Ordinaries can permit services to be held regularly in a "provisional" church, not blessed, while the permanent church is awaiting construction.[4]

If it is prudently foreseen that a church will be converted to profane uses, the Ordinary shall not give his consent for its erection, or at least, if it is already erected, shall not consecrate or bless it **(c. 1165, § 2)**. Cathedral churches, and if possible also collegiate, conventual, and parochial churches, should be solemnly consecrated **(c. 1165, § 3)**. A church built of wood, or of steel or other metal, may be blessed but not consecrated **(c. 1165, § 4)**. An altar may be consecrated though the church be not; but at least the main altar, or if that is already consecrated, a secondary altar should be consecrated with the church **(c. 1165, § 5)**. A church built of reinforced concrete can be consecrated provided the twelve positions for the crosses, and the posts of the principal entrance be of stone.[5]

Norms Governing Consecration. The consecration of churches, though it can be done on any day, is more appropriately done on a Sunday or other feast day of obligation **(c. 1166, § 1)**. The consecrating Bishop and the persons who ask for the consecration of the church shall observe a fast on the day preceding the consecration **(c. 1166, § 2)**. If several Bishops take part, all are obliged. The persons asking for the consecration would be, for example, a religious superior or the members of a chapter.

On the occasion of consecrating a church or altar, the consecrating Bishop, even though he have no jurisdiction in the territory, grants an indulgence of one year to persons who shall visit the church or altar on the day of consecration itself, and on the anniversary an indulgence of fifty days if he is a Bishop, one hundred if he is an Archbishop, two hundred if a Cardinal **(c. 1166, § 3)**. Since the gen-

---

[4] Cf. De Meester, *Compend.*, III, n. 1125, p. 27, note 2, citing Gasparri, Many.
[5] S. C. Rit., *Decr. Auth.*, n. 4240.

eral power of Bishops, Archbishops, and Cardinals to grant indulgences has been enlarged after the Code to one hundred, two hundred, and three hundred days respectively,[6] we think that this particular power is also implicitly enlarged to one hundred days for a Bishop, two hundred for an Archbishop, and three hundred for a Cardinal. The *rite* for a consecration is given in the *Pontificale Romanum,* for a blessing, in the *Rituale Romanum.*

Liturgical Observance of the Anniversary of Consecration. The feast of the consecration of a church shall be celebrated every year according to liturgical laws (c. 1167).

Liturgical Title. Every church which is consecrated or blessed shall have its proper title, which may not be changed after the church has been dedicated (c. 1168, § 1). The titular feast also shall be celebrated yearly according to liturgical laws (c. 1168, § 2). Churches cannot be dedicated to the Blessed without an indult from the Holy See (c. 1168, § 3).

Church Bells. It is proper that every church should have bells with which to call the faithful to divine services and other acts of religion (c. 1169, § 1). Church bells, too, should be consecrated (if the church is consecrated) or (otherwise) blessed according to the rites prescribed in liturgical books (c. 1169, § 2). The use of church bells is subject exclusively to ecclesiastical authority (c. 1169, § 3). Without prejudice to conditions which have been laid down, with the approval of the Ordinary, by persons who may have donated the bells for a church, a bell which is blessed may not be put to merely profane uses, except in case of necessity, or with the permission of the Ordinary, or finally if such use is allowed by legitimate custom (c. 1169, § 4). As regards the consecration or blessing of bells, the provisions of canons 1155 and 1156 are to be observed (c. 1169, § 5).

Loss of Consecration. A church does not lose its consecration or blessing unless it is entirely destroyed, or most of its walls collapse, or the church is converted to profane uses by the Ordinary of the place according to canon 1187 (c. 1170). Recall that "profane" here means merely nonsacred.

Sacred Functions. In a sacred edifice which has been legitimately dedicated, all ecclesiastical rites can be performed, without prejudice to parochial rights, privileges, or legitimate customs; but the Ordinary for just cause can prescribe especially the hours of sacred rites, except for a church which belongs to an exempt religious institute, and with-

---

[6] S. Paen., 20 July, 1942; *AAS,* 34–240; *Digest,* II, p. 221.

out prejudice to the provision of canon 609, § 3 **(c. 1171)**. The canon cited cautions religious superiors not to allow divine services in their own churches to do harm to the catechetical instructions or explanations of the Gospel in the parish church. The judgment as to whether such harm would be done pertains to the Ordinary; the harm, if it is judged to exist, could be remedied in two ways: by changing the hours of services in the religious church, or by giving equivalent catechetical instructions and explanations of the Gospel there.[7]

Violation of a Church. A church is violated only by the following acts, provided they are certain, notorious, and done in the church:

1. The crime of homicide;
2. An injurious and grave shedding of human blood;
3. Impious and sordid uses to which the church has been put;
4. The burial of an infidel or of an excommunicated person after a declaratory or condemnatory sentence **(c. 1172, § 1)**.

By *violation* a church does not lose its consecration; it remains a sacred place, but is regarded as so affected by the crime that it is unfit for divine services until due expiation has been made by *reconciliation*. The acts which violate a church must be *notorious* (in law or in fact, according to c. 2197, 2°, 3°). They must be done *in the church;* the interior chapels, choir, organ loft, confessionals are parts of the church; the sacristy, the outside stairs and portico, the bell tower, are not. A crypt is part of the church if it contains chapels and has an inside connection with the church, otherwise not.

The crime of *homicide* here includes suicide because it was so considered before the Code (cf. c. 6). If the person was in the church when he received the mortal attack (of whatever kind, wounding, poison, etc.) the act is considered to have been done in the church, though the assailant were outside and the victim died outside. The *effusion of human blood* must be *grave* (resulting from a theologically grave sin), *injurious* (in violation of a strict right); if it results from attempted suicide it is not injurious in this sense; moreover the effusion of blood must be physically grave in quantity, though only a small quantity of blood need be actually shed in the church. *Impious or sordid use* supposes that such use be continued for some time and be not an isolated act. *Burial* here means actual entombment, not the funeral services (cf. c. 1175).

By the violation of a church, the cemetery, even though it be con-

---

[7] Vermeersch-Creusen, *Epit.*, II, ed. 5, n. 488.

tiguous, is not regarded as violated, nor is the church violated by the violation of the cemetery (c. 1172, § 2). But the same acts which violate a church violate a cemetery if done there (cf. c. 1207).

Consequences of Violation. In a church which has been violated, and before its reconciliation, it is forbidden to celebrate divine services, administer the sacraments, or conduct funeral services (c. 1173, § 1). In this provision, *"sepelire"* includes not only the burial (which is permitted only exceptionally in any church — c. 1205, § 2), but any part of the funeral services (cf. c. 1204). In urgent necessity, for example, if a great feast is at hand and there is not time for the reconciliation, services could be held, consulting the Ordinary in advance if possible (St. Alphonsus, VI, n. 361). If the violation occurs during divine services, these should be immediately discontinued; if before the canon or after the Communion at Mass, the Mass should be stopped; otherwise, the priest should continue the Mass up to the Communion (c. 1173, § 2).

Reconciliation of a Violated Church. A church which has been violated should as soon as possible be reconciled according to the rites prescribed in approved liturgical books (c. 1174, § 1). If there is doubt whether the church has been violated, it can be reconciled *ad cautelam* (c. 1174, § 2). A church which has been violated by the burial of an excommunicated person or infidel shall not be reconciled until the remains have been removed from it, if that can be done without grave inconvenience (c. 1175).

Who Can Reconcile a Church. A blessed church can be reconciled by its rector or by any priest with at least the presumed consent of the rector (c. 1176, § 1). The valid reconciliation of a consecrated church pertains to the persons mentioned in canon 1156 (c. 1176, § 2). But in case of grave and urgent necessity, if the Ordinary cannot be reached, the rector of a consecrated church may reconcile it, giving notice to the Ordinary afterward (c. 1176, § 3).

The Water to Be Used in the Reconciliation of a Church. The reconciliation of a blessed church can be done with common holy water; but that of a consecrated church must be done with water blessed for that purpose according to liturgical laws; this water, however, may be blessed not only by a Bishop but as well by the priest who performs the reconciliation (c. 1177).

Care and Use of Church. All persons to whom this charge belongs should see to it that in churches the cleanliness which befits the house of God be preserved; business and trafficking, even for pious purposes, and in general whatever is out of harmony with the holiness of the place, should be excluded (c. 1178). The persons responsible are the rector and local Ordinary for a secular or nonexempt church, and for an exempt church the rector and the major superior. Nonreligious banners may be admitted to the church, provided they do not belong to forbidden societies or contain forbidden symbols (*Digest*, I, p. 581).

The Right of Asylum. A church enjoys the right of asylum, so that guilty persons who take refuge in it must not be taken from it, except in case of necessity, without the consent of the Ordinary, or at least of the rector of the church (c. 1179).

Privileges of a Basilica. No church can be honored with the title of a basilica except by apostolic grant or immemorial custom; in either case its privileges are to be determined from the terms of the grant or the tenor of the custom (c. 1180). Major basilicas are the churches of St. John Lateran, St. Mary Major, St. Peter's, St. Paul's Outside the Walls (in Rome), and those of St. Francis of Assisi and of St. Mary of the Angels (in Assisi). Minor basilicas are a number of other churches which have received this special status by apostolic grant or by custom immemorial.

Free Admittance. Admission to the Church for sacred rites must be entirely free, and every custom to the contrary is reprobated (c. 1181). One of the sources of this canon is a Letter of the Sacred Congregation for the Propagation of the Faith to the Bishops of the United States (15 Aug., 1869; *Fontes*, n. 4875, VII, p. 415), which states that there is no intention to forbid the taking up of collections at the Offertory. Neither is it forbidden to charge for pews or seats. However, the forbidden practice of making forced collections at the church door continued after the prohibition of 1869, and was again gravely censured in 1911 by the then Apostolic Delegate to the United States (see *Ecclesiastical Review,* Vol. 45, 1911, p. 594).

Administration of Maintenance Fund. With due regard to the provisions of canons 1519–1528, the administration of funds which are destined for the repairs and decoration of the church and for the maintenance of divine worship in it belongs, in the absence of some special title or legitimate custom to the contrary, to the Bishop with his chapter in the case of a cathedral church, to the chapter in the case of a collegiate church, to the rector in the case of other churches (c. 1182, § 1). Also offerings made for the benefit of a parish or mission, or of a church situated within the limits of a parish or mission, are administered by the pastor or mission priest, unless the church is one which has its own administration distinct from that of the parish or mission, or unless there is a special law or legitimate custom to the contrary (c. 1182, § 2). The pastor, the mission priest, and the rector of a secular church whether he himself be a secular or a religious, must administer these offerings according to the sacred canons, and give an account of them to the Ordinary of the place according to canon 1525 (c. 1182, § 3).

Practical Notes. 1. The first practical question is, who is the owner of these funds. A church is a moral person in its own right; a parish or mission (quasi-parish — c. 216, § 3) is a moral person which may be distinct even from its parish or mission church. Funds destined for the maintenance of the church belong to the church; offerings made for the benefit of a parish or mission belong to the parish or mission. Hence we are dealing in this canon with two different funds belonging to two different moral persons. Each must be distinguished also from funds which belong to other persons, moral or physical; e.g., stole fees (which belong to the pastor as a physical or moral person — c. 463, § 1); the capital funds of a parochial benefice as such (a moral person), which belongs to the benefice, subject to the right of the beneficiary to take his living from the income (c. 1473).

2. This canon says nothing about the ownership, but determines who is the lawful *administrator* of the funds mentioned. Such administration is subject also to the general laws governing all administration of church property (cc. 1519–1528). The administrator is the rector, for the funds which belong to the church, "unless the church is one which has its own administration"; a church which is in the care of a religious pastor, but which does not belong to religious, has for its administrator the Ordinary of the place (who may, however, delegate the administration to the pastor); a church which belongs to religious has for its administrator the religious superior (c. 630, § 4); but if it is a parish church an account must be rendered to the Ordinary of the place.[8]

Council of Maintenance. If other persons also, clerical or lay, are admitted to the administration of the property of a church, all of them, together with the ecclesiastical administrator mentioned in canon 1182 or the person taking his place, who shall act as chairman, constitute the council of the church (c. 1183, § 1). The members of this

---

[8] Cf. Code Com., 25 July, 1926, ad IV; *AAS*, 18–393; *Digest*, I, p. 699. Best commentary on this canon, Vromant, *De Bonis Ecclesiae Temporalibus*, nn. 193 sq., p. 211 sq.

council, unless there is lawful provision to the contrary, are appointed by the Ordinary or his delegate and can for grave cause be removed by him (c. 1183, § 2). The Code here uses the term "*consilium fabricae ecclesiae*," which we call the council of maintenance to distinguish it from the Council of Administration mentioned in canon 1520, where there is question of the administration of *diocesan* funds. The council of maintenance is commonly called the Board of Trustees, or Council-men. The legislation of the Third Council of Baltimore on this matter (nn. 284–287) is still in effect. The chief point is that this council or its members are in no sense the owners of church property; even in its administration their power is merely advisory; their employment even in this capacity is not prescribed but merely permitted or recommended.

Limitations on the Authority of the Council. The council of maintenance must attend to the proper administration of the property of the church, observing the provisions of canons 1522 and 1523; but it must not interfere in any way in matters which pertain to spiritual government, especially:

1. In the practice of worship in the church;

2. In the manner and time of ringing the bells, and in the charge of maintaining order in the church and cemetery;

3. In prescribing the manner in which the taking up of collections, the making of announcements, and other acts pertaining in any way to divine worship and the interior arrangements of the church, shall be done;

4. In the material arrangement of the altars, the communion rail, the pulpit, the organ, the choir loft, the *sedilia,* the pews, the collection boxes, or other things which pertain to the exercise of divine worship;

5. In admitting or discarding sacred vessels or other objects which are destined either for use or as articles of worship or as ornaments in the church or sacristy;

6. In the inscription, arrangement, or custody of the parish books or other documents pertaining to the parish archives (c. 1184).

Appointment of Personnel. The sacristan, singers, organist, altar boys, sexton, grave diggers, and other subordinates, with due regard to lawful customs and agreements and to the authority of the Ordinary, are appointed, controlled, and dismissed exclusively by the rector of the church (c. 1185).

Responsibility for Maintenance. Without prejudice to peculiar lawful customs and agreements, or to the obligation which may rest on any person even in virtue of a provision of civil law:

1. The obligation of making repairs to a *cathedral* church rests upon the following, in the order named:

On the maintenance fund, excepting that part of it which is needed for the celebration of divine worship and for the ordinary administration of the church;

On the Bishop and canons in proportion to their surplus income after deducting what is necessary for their reasonable support;

On the faithful of the diocese, who however should be induced rather by persuasion on the part of the Ordinary than by coercion, to bear the necessary expenses according to their means.

2. The obligation of making repairs to a *parish* church rests upon the following in the order named:

On the maintenance fund, as in the case of a cathedral church;

On the patron (cf. cc. 1448–1471);

On persons who derive any profit from the church, in a proportion to be determined by the Bishop on the basis of the profit received by the respective persons;

On the faithful of the parish, who however, as above stated, should rather be exhorted than compelled by the Ordinary to make the necessary sacrifice.

3. As regards *other churches,* the same provisions hold good, with due proportion **(c. 1186).**

On the financial support of *parish schools* in the United States, see Third Council of Baltimore, nn. 200–207.

Withdrawal of a Church From Sacred Use. If a church can in no way be used for divine worship and if there is no means to restore it, the Ordinary of the place can convert it to profane but not to sordid use; in which case the obligations and income, together with the title of the parish if it is a parish church, shall be transferred by the same Ordinary to another church **(c. 1187).**

Article 3. Oratories (cc. 1188-1196)

PRELIMINARY SURVEY

Definition and Classification (c. 1188)
Oratories of Cardinals and Bishops (c. 1189)
Private Cemetery Chapels (c. 1190)
Services in Public Oratories (c. 1191)
Semipublic Oratories: Authority to Erect (c. 1192)
Services in Semipublic Oratories (c. 1193)
Mass in Private Oratories (cc. 1194, 1195)
Blessing of Oratories (c. 1196)

Definition and Classification. An oratory is a place devoted to divine worship, not however principally for the purpose of serving the faithful in general for public religious worship **(c. 1188, § 1).**

An oratory is:

1. *Public,* if it is erected chiefly for the use of some college or even of private individuals, but on such terms that all the faithful have the right, legitimately proved, of having access to it at least at the time of divine services;

2. *Semipublic,* if it is erected chiefly for the convenience of some community or group of the faithful who use it, but is not freely available to everyone;

3. *Private* or *domestic,* if it is erected in a private house only for the benefit of some family or private person **(c. 1188, § 2).**

Chapels in convents and religious houses are classed as semipublic oratories, but there is a distinction to be made between the principal oratory and secondary ones (cf. c. 1192, § 4). A fixed and permanent chapel on board a ship is a public oratory.[9] Oratories erected in the room of a saint, where he was born or died, and to which the public is regularly admitted, are regarded as public oratories.[10] The requirement that a semipublic oratory be "erected" for the convenience of a community seems to be equivalently fulfilled if it is *used* for their convenience.[11]

Oratories of Cardinals and Bishops. The oratories of Cardinals of the Holy Roman Church and of Bishops, whether residential or titular, although they are private, yet enjoy all the rights and priv-

---

[9] S. C. Rit., 4 March, 1901; *Decr. Auth.,* n. 4069, ad V; *Fontes,* n. 6309, Vol. VIII, p. 358.

[10] Vermeersch-Creusen, *Epit.,* II, ed. 5, n. 498.

[11] S. C. Rit., 23 Jan., 1899; *Decr. Auth.,* n. 4007; *Fontes,* n. 6288, VIII, p. 343.

ileges of semipublic oratories (c. 1189). Apostolic Nuncios, Internuncios, and Delegates can have a chapel which by the indulgence of the Holy See is regarded as a public one.[12]

Private Cemetery Chapels. Chapels erected by families or private persons in cemeteries for the burial of their own people are private oratories (c. 1190). These differ, however, from other private oratories in two respects: the faithful can satisfy the Sunday precept by hearing Mass there (c. 1249); and the Ordinary of the place can permit several Masses there regularly (c. 1194). A cemetery chapel erected by a religious community for its use would be semipublic.[13]

Services in Public Oratories. Public oratories are governed by the same rules of law as churches (c. 1191, § 1). Hence in a public oratory, provided it has been perpetually dedicated to the public worship of God by blessing or consecration according to canons 1155 and 1156, all sacred functions can be celebrated, unless there is some prescription of the rubrics to the contrary (c. 1191, § 2). Strictly parochial functions are indirectly excluded by canon 462. The rubrics might forbid certain functions there because of the lack of facilities, e.g., in certain functions of Holy Week. The reservation of the Blessed Sacrament is governed by canon 1265.

Authority to Erect Semipublic Oratories. A semipublic oratory may not be erected without the permission of the Ordinary (c. 1192, § 1). The Ordinary shall not give this permission without having visited the oratory beforehand, either in person or through some other ecclesiastic, and found it properly appointed (c. 1192, § 2). Once the permission has been given, the oratory cannot be converted to profane uses without the authority of the same Ordinary (c. 1192, § 3). In colleges or common residences for young students, and in high schools, academies, forts, barracks, prisons, hospitals, etc., besides the principal oratory, other minor ones are not to be erected unless, in the judgment of the Ordinary, necessity or notable advantage require it (c. 1192, § 4).

Throughout this canon the term "Ordinary" includes the major superior of clerical exempt religious, for oratories in exempt places which are under his jurisdiction. The fourth paragraph of the canon, requiring a *special judgment* of the Ordinary as to the need or advantage of *secondary oratories* besides the principal one, does not

---

[12] See Faculties of Apostolic Delegate, n. 52; *Digest*, I, p. 185.

[13] Cf. c. 1188, § 2, 2°; Vermeersch-Creusen, *Epit.*, II, n. 499; De Meester, *Compendium*, III, n. 1150, p. 57, note 1.

apply to religious houses, since they are not enumerated among the places where the provision applies; but religious houses are nowhere excepted from the provision of paragraph 1, which requires the permission of the Ordinary for the erection of any semipublic oratory. Hence, for the erection of a secondary oratory in a nonexempt convent of sisters, the permission of the Ordinary of the place is required, but this permission may be given without the *special* judgment of the Ordinary as to the need or advantage.

Services in Semipublic Oratories. In semipublic oratories which have been legitimately erected, all divine services and liturgical functions can be celebrated, unless the rubrics provide otherwise or the Ordinary has made some exceptions **(c. 1193)**. Parochial functions are excluded **(c. 462)**; the Sunday precept is fulfilled by hearing Mass **(c. 1249)**; the reservation of the Blessed Sacrament is governed by canon 1265.

Mass in Private Oratories. In the private chapels of cemeteries, which are mentioned in canon 1190, the Ordinary of the place can permit regularly the celebration of even several Masses; in other private oratories, he can permit only one Mass, and *per modum actus,* in an extraordinary case, for just and reasonable cause; the Ordinary, however, should grant these permissions only in accordance with canon 1192, § 2 **(c. 1194)**.

In private oratories which have an indult from the Holy See, unless the indult provides otherwise, after the Ordinary has visited and approved the oratory as provided in canon 1192, § 2, one low Mass may be celebrated on every day except the more solemn feast days; but other ecclesiastical functions should not be held there **(c. 1195, § 1)**. But the Ordinary, provided there is a just and reasonable cause distinct from the reasons for the granting of the indult, can permit *per modum actus* the celebration of Mass also on the more solemn feast days **(c. 1195, § 2)**.

Blessing of Oratories. Private oratories can neither be consecrated nor blessed as churches are **(c. 1196, § 1)**. Although private and semipublic oratories receive only the common blessing of places and houses, or none at all, yet they must be reserved exclusively for divine worship and free from all domestic use **(c. 1196, § 2)**.

Article 4. Altars (cc. 1197–1202)

PRELIMINARY SURVEY

Definition: Classification (c. 1197)
Structure of Altars (c. 1198)
Consecration (c. 1199)
Loss of Consecration (c. 1200)
Liturgical Title (c. 1201)
Use and Position (c. 1202)

Altars. An altar in general means a structure upon which sacrifice is offered to God. Many historical documents attest that altars were used for this purpose from the earliest times. "And Jacob, arising in the morning, took the stone, which he had laid under his head, and set it up for a title, pouring oil upon the top of it. . . . And he made a vow, saying: . . . And this stone, which I have set up for a title, shall be called the house of God" (Gen. 28:18–22). In the early Church the Holy Sacrifice of the New Law was offered upon wooden altars at the tombs of the martyrs, and those early altars were not consecrated. Later, as stone altars came into use, a rite for their consecration was introduced by Pope St. Sylvester, who had baptized the Emperor Constantine. The present liturgical immovable altar corresponds to those of the early centuries in that it has a table, a support, and a "sepulcher."

Definition and Classification of Altars. In a liturgical sense:

1. The term *immovable* or *fixed* altar means an altar table together with its supports which are consecrated with it *per modum unius;*

2. The term *movable* or *portable* altar means a stone, usually small, which is consecrated alone and is called a *portable altar* or a *sacred stone;* or such a stone together with its support, which, however, was not consecrated with it (c. 1197, §1).

In a consecrated church at least one altar, preferably the main altar, should be immovable; but in a blessed church all the altars may be movable ones (c. 1197, §2).

Structure of Altars. Both the table of an immovable altar and the altar stone (of a portable altar) must consist of a single natural stone, which is of one piece, and not friable (c. 1198, §1). In an immovable altar the stone table or top must extend the entire length of the altar and must be suitably joined to its support; the lower part of the altar also, or at least the sides or columns which support the table, must be of stone (c. 1198, § 2). An altar stone must be large enough so that at least the host and the greater part of the base of the chalice may rest on it (c. 1198, § 3). Both an immovable altar and altar stone should, according to liturgical laws, have a *sepulcrum* or cavity containing relics of the saints, and having a stone cover (c. 1198, § 4).

The stone must be *natural* (neither cement nor composition), *of one piece* (the consecration would be doubtful if it consisted of two or more stones joined together), *not friable* (gypsum, pumice are excluded; slate, schist are admitted). "Must extend the entire length of the altar." The S. C. of Rites reprobated an altar table surrounded by a frame of wood, or even of marble.[14] It does not follow that the consecration would be invalid. "Suitably joined to its support." Stone resting on stone, without cement, is sufficient, but a firm junction with cement is safer (cf. c. 1200, § 1). An altar is "fixed" or "immovable" though it be not firmly fixed to the floor. The *sepulcrum,* a small cavity containing a sealed vessel with relics of the saints, may be in the stone support of a fixed altar, or in the top.

Consecration. In order that the Holy Sacrifice of the Mass may be celebrated on it, an altar must be consecrated according to liturgical laws; that is, the entire altar if it is an immovable one, or if movable, the altar stone alone, must be so consecrated (c. 1199, § 1). All Bishops, without prejudice to special privileges, can consecrate portable altars; as regards immovable altars the provision of canon 1155 is to be observed (c. 1199, § 2). The consecration of an immovable altar, if it is done apart from the dedication of the church, although it can be done on any day, is more appropriately performed on a Sunday or other feast day of obligation (c. 1199, § 3).

Valid Consecration. The following have the power:

1. For *portable* altars: all Bishops (cc. 1147, § 1; 1199, § 2); Cardinals, without limitation as to territory (c. 239, § 1, 20°); Vicars and Prefects Apostolic in their own territory only (c. 294, § 2); Abbots and Prelates *nullius* in their own territory only (c. 323, § 2); priests who have received the power by subdelegation from the Ordinary of the place according to the Quinquennial Faculties (*Digest,* II, p. 37).

2. For *immovable* altars: all those mentioned in n. 1, except Vicars and Prefects Apostolic. These could, of course, receive the power by *special* delegation from the Holy See, but they do not have it by law (c. 294, § 2).

---

[14] *Decr. Auth.*, nn. 3640, 3797.

Licit Consecration. The consent of the Ordinary (local or religious as the case may be) is always required (c. 1157). Indulgences should be granted by the consecrator according to canon 1166, § 3.

Loss of Consecration. An immovable altar loses its consecration if the table or top is separated even for a moment from its base; in which case the Ordinary can permit that a priest consecrate it again with the short rite and formula **(c. 1200, § 1).**

Both an immovable altar and an altar stone lose their consecration:

1. If they are broken in a manner which is notable either by reason of the size of the fracture or because it affects the part where the stone was anointed;

2. If the relics are removed or broken, or the cover of the *sepulcrum* is removed, except the case where the Bishop himself or his delegate removes the cover in order to set it more securely or to repair or replace it with another cover, or in order to examine the relics **(c. 1200, § 2).**

A slight fracture of the cover does not cause execration, and any priest can repair it with cement **(c. 1200, § 3).**

The execration of a church does not entail the execration of the altars in it, whether they be immovable or movable; and the converse is also true **(c. 1200, § 4).**

Faculties to reconsecrate both immovable and portable altars which have lost their consecration may be subdelegated according to the Quinquennial faculties (*Digest,* II, p. 37). The rite and formula for the various cases are in the Roman Ritual.

Liturgical Title. As in the case of a church, so, too, every altar, at least every immovable altar, of a church must have its proper title **(c. 1201, § 1).** The primary title of the main altar must be the same as the title of the church **(c. 1201, § 2).** The title of a portable altar can be changed with the permission of the Ordinary; not, however, that of an immovable altar **(c. 1201, § 3).** Without an apostolic indult, altars cannot be dedicated to the Blessed, even in churches and oratories to which an office and Mass in their honor have been granted **(c. 1201, § 4).**[15]

Use and Position. Both an immovable and a movable altar must be reserved exclusively for divine services and especially for the celebration of Mass, and entirely exempt from profane uses **(c. 1202, § 1).** No corpse may be buried beneath the altar; and if any are buried near it they must be at least one meter away from it; otherwise Mass may not

---

[15] On these various provisions, see S. C. Rit., *Decr. Auth.,* nn. 1156, 1162, 2752.

be celebrated at that altar until the corpse has been removed (c. 1202, § 2).

The distance of a corpse from the altar must be *at least* one meter, notwithstanding an earlier decree of the S. C. Rites (n. 3944); the distance is to be measured from the altar itself, not from the *predella* (*ibid., Decr. Auth.,* n. 3944); the presence of a body in a crypt directly beneath the altar but entirely separated from it was permitted by the S. C. Rit. (n. 3460, ad 2); as to the removal of corpses already buried, proportionate inconvenience was admitted as excusing from this prescription (*Decr. Auth.,* n. 3339).

Section 2. Ecclesiastical Burial (cc. 1203–1242)

Article 1. General Provisions: Cemeteries (cc. 1203–1214)

PRELIMINARY SURVEY

Burial Obligatory: Cremation Forbidden (c. 1203)
Elements of Ecclesiastical Burial (c. 1204)
Cemeteries to Be Blessed: Burial in Church Exceptional (c. 1205)
Catholic Burial Grounds (c. 1206)
Interdict, Violation, Reconciliation of Cemeteries (c. 1207)
Parish, Religious, Particular Cemeteries (c. 1208)
Cemetery Lots (c. 1209)
Care of Cemeteries (c. 1210)
Cemetery Monuments (c. 1211)
Place for Nonecclesiastical Burial (c. 1212)
Decent Period Must Elapse Before Burial (c. 1213)
Exhumation of Remains (c. 1214)

Burial Obligatory: Cremation Forbidden. The bodies of the faithful deceased must be buried; and their cremation is reprobated (c. 1203, § 1). If a person has in any way ordered that his body be cremated, it is illicit to obey such instructions; and if such a provision occur in a contract, last testament, or in any document whatsoever, it is to be disregarded (c. 1203, § 2).

Notes. 1. Nearly all peoples have regarded the disposal of bodies of the dead as a religious act, but not all disposed of them in the same way. Both burial, and cremation were in use among the ancient Greeks and Romans; cremation was also practiced among the Germans, Celts, Hindus, and Japanese. The Egyptians and the Jews buried their dead. Christians followed this practice for two very weighty reasons: because of their faith in the resurrection of the body, and out of respect for the body as a member of Christ. Of course, cremation can in no way impair the hope of resurrection; yet it was supposed to do so by some of the early persecutors of the martyrs.

2. After the pagans themselves, following the example of the Christians, had for the most part abandoned cremation, certain pseudo-scientific societies, about the middle of the nineteenth century, became active in trying to restore the practice of cremation; since which time it has been several times condemned by the Holy Office.

3. Cremation was again severely condemned by the Holy Office in 1926.[16]

4. Yet it is not intrinsically wrong, and is therefore permitted in grave public necessity, for example, in a pestilence when public safety requires the quick disposal of corpses and there is not time for burial.

5. Ecclesiastical burial is denied to anyone who before death gave orders that his body be cremated, even though the instructions were not carried out, unless he repented before death (c. 1240, § 1, 5°). And "in all these cases in which it is forbidden to hold the ecclesiastical funeral rites for the deceased, it is not even permitted to honor his ashes with ecclesiastical burial, nor in any way to preserve them in a blessed cemetery; but they are to be kept in a separate place according to canon 1212. And if the civil authorities of the place . . . require the contrary course, let the priests who are concerned in the case . . . abstain from all co-operation."[17]

6. A dead fetus, if it was baptized, is also to be buried in a place which is blessed, preferably in a cemetery rather than on the hospital grounds. There are many funeral directors who will gladly discharge this duty for a hospital. If a fetus that has been taken from a dead mother dies, the proper procedure is to replace it in the uterus, when this can be done conveniently, and to bury it with the mother. It should never be burned unless such action is necessary to prevent contagion.[18]

7. As to the amputated limbs of baptized persons (here only Catholics are strictly included), the Holy Office declared that these parts

---

[16] Holy Office, 19 June, 1926; *AAS*, 18–282; *Digest*, I, p. 564. Cf. *Periodica*, Vol. 18, p. 62*.
[17] Holy Office, 19 June, 1926; *AAS*, 18–282; *Digest*, I, p. 564, and Code Com., 10 Nov., 1925; *AAS*, 17–583; *Digest*, I, p. 583.
[18] See Bowen, *The Baptism of the Infant and the Fetus* (St. Joseph Mercy Hospital, Dubuque, Iowa). This little pamphlet, accurate and practical, is highly recommended.

of the body should be buried in a blessed place, if that can be done conveniently. The place need not be a cemetery.[19]

Elements of Ecclesiastical Burial. Ecclesiastical burial consists in the transfer of the remains to the church, the celebration of funeral services over them at the church, and their deposition in a place legitimately destined for the burial of the faithful (c. 1204).

Cemeteries to Be Blessed: Burial in Churches Exceptional. The remains of the faithful are to be buried in a cemetery which is blessed according to the rites prescribed in approved liturgical books, either by a solemn or simple blessing performed by the persons mentioned in canons 1155 and 1156 (c. 1205, § 1). Bodies shall not be buried in churches, except that residential Bishops, and Abbots and Prelates *nullius* may be buried in their own church, and excepting also the Roman Pontiffs, royal personages, and Cardinals of the Holy Roman Church (c. 1205, § 2).

Notes. 1. A different rite and formula is used in three different cases: first, for the solemn blessing (consecration) of a cemetery (Roman Pontifical); second, for the simple blessing of a cemetery (Roman Ritual); third, for the simple blessing of a grave (Roman Ritual, Tit. VI, cap. 3, n. 12).

2. Burial in a crypt or subterranean church is forbidden, if it is properly a church, devoted to divine worship.[20]

3. In a particular case, the S. C. of the Council disapproved the custom of transferring the bodies some years after burial, for deposition in the church, or of preserving the heart in a sealed urn in the church.[21]

4. Only deceased Supreme Pontiffs may be buried *in an elevated place* in churches. Even Bishops may not be buried under the altar or nearer than one meter to it.

Catholic Burial Grounds. The Catholic Church has the right to have its own cemeteries (c. 1206, § 1). If in any place this right of the Church is violated and there is no prospect of repairing the wrong, Ordinaries of places must see to it that the public cemeteries be blessed, if those who are buried there are mostly Catholics, or at least that there be a place in them, properly blessed, which is reserved for Catholics (c. 1206, § 2). If even this much cannot be secured, the individual graves are to be blessed singly according to the rites

---

[19] Holy Office, 3 Aug., 1897; *Fontes*, n. 1189, IV, p. 494.
[20] Code Com., 16 Oct., 1919; *AAS*, 11–478; *Digest*, I, p. 566.
[21] S. C. Conc., 10 Dec., 1927; *AAS*, 20–261; *Digest*, I, p. 566.

prescribed in liturgical books (c. 1206, § 3). Strictly Catholic cemeteries are either: parochial (for one or several parishes — c. 1208, § 1); exempt (for exempt religious — c. 1208, § 2); or particular (for families or moral persons, including nonexempt religious, with the permission of the Ordinary — c. 1208, § 3).

The rite for the blessing of a single grave (Roman Ritual, Tit. VI, cap. 3, n. 12) supposes that the cemetery is not blessed. If the cemetery is already blessed, this part of the rite is omitted in the case of a simple grave, but if the grave is a monument, or is lined with brick or stone, it should be blessed.[22] Any priest conducting the funeral services can do it.

Interdict, Violation, Reconciliation of Cemeteries. The provisions of the canons on interdict, violation, and reconciliation of churches apply also to cemeteries (c. 1207).

Parish, Religious, Particular Cemeteries. Every parish should have its own cemetery, unless one which is common to several parishes be legitimately established by the Ordinary of the place (c. 1208, § 1). Exempt religious can have their own cemetery distinct from the common one (c. 1208, § 2). The Ordinary of the place can permit also that other moral persons or private families have a special burying ground outside the common cemetery and blessed as a cemetery (c. 1208, § 3).

Cemetery Lots. In parochial cemeteries, with the written permission of the Ordinary of the place or his delegate, and in the special cemetery of another moral person, with the written permission of the superior, the faithful can have their own particular burial plots; and these may also be alienated with the permission of the same Ordinary or superior (c. 1209, § 1). The graves of priests and clerics should if possible be apart from those of the laity and in a place more suited to their state; and where it can conveniently be done separate places should be assigned to priests and to clerics of lower grades (c. 1209, § 2). The bodies of infants too, as far as it can conveniently be done, should be buried in a special place separate from those of other persons (c. 1209, § 3).

Care of Cemeteries. Every cemetery should be properly enclosed on all sides and carefully guarded (c. 1210).

Cemetery Monuments. Ordinaries of places, pastors, and superiors whose responsibility it is, should see to it that in cemeteries the

---

[22] S. C. Rit., *Decr. Auth.*, nn. 3400, 3524.

epitaphs, memorial tablets, and monuments contain nothing which is out of harmony with Catholic truth and sentiment (c. 1211). Whatever suggests mere inconsolable grief, perpetual separation, or on the other hand eulogies so excessive as to transgress the bounds of Christian humility, would seem to be out of place. There is a notable contrast between Catholic cemeteries with such monuments as the Cross of Christ, symbol of victory and resurrection, and certain others whose monuments carry no suggestion of faith or hope in a future life.

Place for Nonecclesiastical Burial. Besides the blessed cemetery there should if possible be another place, likewise enclosed and protected, for the entombment of those who are not entitled to ecclesiastical burial (c. 1212).

Decent Period Must Elapse Before Burial. No corpse shall be buried, especially if death was sudden, until a proper period of time has elapsed which shall be sufficient to remove all doubt as to actual death (c. 1213). To safeguard the temporal welfare of the community the state can, without interfering with the authority of the Church, determine: what this reasonable period of time should be in ordinary cases; the depth of the grave; the distance between graves; even the burning of bodies in time of pestilence or in other grave public necessity; the *post mortem* examination of corpses to determine the cause of death if the public welfare requires it.

Exhumation of Remains. Without the permission of the Ordinary, it is unlawful to exhume a body which has received permanent ecclesiastical burial anywhere (c. 1214, § 1). The Ordinary shall never give this permission if the corpse to be exhumed cannot with certainty be distinguished from others (c. 1214, § 2).

Exhumation may become necessary for various reasons, e.g., by the state law, to investigate a suspected crime, or even by ecclesiastical law, to honor the relics, or as a condition for the reconciliation of a violated church or cemetery (c. 1175). Ecclesiastical burial is *de se* perpetual; it may be provisional in special circumstances, for instance, if, in time of war, fallen soldiers are buried, even in a cemetery, with the understanding that relatives may later reclaim the remains for permanent burial elsewhere.[23] The Ordinary whose permission is required is the Ordinary of the place, except where the cemetery belongs to clerical exempt religious, in which case it is the major superior.

---

[23] Cf. Vermeersch-Creusen, *Epit.*, II, n. 524.

Article 2. Funeral Services and Burial (cc. 1215–1238)

PRELIMINARY SURVEY

Obligation to Hold Church Services (c. 1215)
The Proper Church for the Services (cc. 1216–1218)
Exceptional Cases: Cardinals, Bishops, Prelates (c. 1219)
Beneficiaries (c. 1220)
Religious (c. 1221)
Other Cases (c. 1222)
Choice by the Deceased of a Church or Cemetery
(cc. 1223–1229)
Various Provisions as to Proper Church and Pastor (c. 1230)
Burial (c. 1231)
Right to Accompany the Remains (c. 1232)
External Arrangements of Funeral Services (c. 1233)
Funeral Fees (cc. 1234, 1235)
The Pastor's Portion (cc. 1236, 1237)
Record of Death (c. 1238)

Obligation to Hold Church Services. Unless some grave reason prevents it, the bodies of the faithful, before being buried, must be transferred from the place where they are to the church, where the funeral, that is, the entire sequence of funeral services which are described in approved liturgical books, shall be performed (c. 1215). A grave cause is required to excuse from this precept; danger of offense on the part of the faithful and clergy because of a contrary custom does not excuse from bringing the body to the church.[24] But difficulties occasioned by state laws were held to excuse from it in a particular case.[25]

The Proper Church for the Services. The church to which the remains should be transferred for the funeral is, according to the common law, the church of the deceased's own parish, unless the deceased legitimately chose some other church (c. 1216, § 1). If the deceased had more than one proper parish, the church for the funeral is that one among his proper parishes in which he died (c. 1216, § 2).

The proper parish of a deceased is determined according to canons 93–95. If at the time of death he had more than one domicile or quasi-domicile, he had more than one proper parish. Three cases may be

---

[24] Code Com., 16 Oct., 1919; *AAS*, 11–479; *Digest*, I, p. 569.
[25] S. C. Rit., 28 Feb., 1920; *AAS*, 12–128; *Digest*, I, p. 569.

suggested here: (1) if the deceased legitimately chose a church for his funeral, that is the proper church though it be not his parish church and though he did not die in that parish (c. 1223); (2) if he made no choice, the proper church is his parish church, and if he had several parishes it is the church of the one *of those parishes* in which he died; (3) if he died outside his proper parish or parishes, the case is governed by canon 1218.

In Doubt. In doubt as to the right of some other church, the right of the proper parish church of the deceased shall always prevail (c. 1217).

The Proper Church in Case the Deceased Died Outside His Proper Parish. Although death occurred outside the proper parish of the deceased, the remains are nevertheless to be brought to the church of that one of his proper parishes which is nearest (to the place of death), if they can be brought there conveniently by carrying them on foot; otherwise, they are to be brought to the church of the parish in which the death occurred **(c. 1218, § 1).** The canon here uses the expression *"pedestri itinere asportari,"* which literally means transferring the remains by carrying them on foot. Since in our country, at least in the cities, this is seldom done, the whole question of the convenience of transporting the remains to the proper parish church is left to the Ordinary (cf. paragraph 2).

It pertains to the Ordinary to determine for his territory, in view of the circumstances, the distance and other conditions which would make it inconvenient to transfer the remains to the church of the funeral or to the place of burial; in case the parishes concerned (that is, the nearest proper parish and the parish where the death occurred) are in different dioceses, this decision shall be made by the Ordinary of the diocese in which the death occurred **(c. 1218, § 2).**

Even though the transfer of the remains to the church of the funeral or to the place of burial is actually inconvenient, nevertheless the family, the heirs, or other interested persons always have the right to make such transfer, provided they pay the expenses thereof **(c. 1218, § 3).** "Other interested persons" would be, for example, a religious superior (cf. c. 1221, § 2). Interested parties "always" have this right, therefore even in case the deceased had several proper parishes, and they undertake the expenses of transporting the remains to one of these in preference even to one of the others which could more easily be reached.[26]

---

[26] Cf. A Coronata, II, n. 799, p. 99, note 1.

Cardinals: Bishops: Prelates. If a Cardinal of the Holy Roman Church died in Rome, the body is to be transferred for the funeral, unless he chose some other church, to the church designated by the Roman Pontiff; if he died outside of Rome and did not choose any other church, it is to be transferred to the church of the highest dignity in the city or place where he died **(c. 1219, § 1).** We understand the clause *"nisi Cardinalis aliam elegerit"* as modifying the entire paragraph, in accordance with authority and the text of canon 1223, § 1. "Funeral" here does not necessarily include the burial; the latter is to be in the place of his choice if any, or in his family vault if he has one, or in default of these in his titular church. The dignity of churches is in the following order: major basilicas, cathedral churches, quasi-cathedral churches, abbatial churches, collegiate churches, parish churches to which a deanery is attached, other parish churches, churches of regulars. If a Cardinal is also a residential Bishop, the next paragraph applies.

In the case of a deceased residential Bishop, even if he be a Cardinal, or of an Abbot or Prelate *nullius,* the body is to be brought for the funeral to the cathedral, abbatial, or prelatial church as the case may be, if that can conveniently be done; otherwise to the church of highest dignity in the city or place, unless in either case the deceased chose some other church **(c. 1219, § 2).** As to the burial, it may be in their own church **(c. 1205, § 2),** and this is to be preferred even to the family vault, but not, of course, to any place chosen by the deceased. Titular Bishops follow the common law as to funeral and burial. In the case of the Roman Pontiffs, both funeral and burial are to be in the Vatican Basilica unless they chose another church or place of burial.

Beneficiaries. Residential beneficiaries are to be transferred to the church of their benefice, unless they chose some other church for their funeral **(c. 1220).** Pastors in the United States are residential beneficiaries,[27] but it is probable that the canon would be obligatory only in the case of irremovable pastors; it does not apply to parochial vicars. For the *burial* of residential beneficiaries, the order of choice is as follows: first, the place chosen by the deceased; in default of a choice, a cemetery reserved for beneficiaries, or a family vault, or the parish cemetery, in that order.

Religious, Novices, and Servants in a Religious House. The

---

[27] Cf. c. 1411, 3°, 465, § 1, and Letter of Apostolic Delegate, 10 Nov., 1922; *Digest,* I, p. 149.

remains of deceased professed religious and novices are to be transferred for the funeral to the church or oratory of their house or at
least of their institute, unless in the case of novices they chose another
church for their funeral; but the right to take charge of the remains
and transport them to the funeral church always belongs to the
religious superior (c. 1221, § 1). *This paragraph* applies only to *male*
religious and *male* novices, because a special provision is made for
females in canon 1230. Novices have, but professed religious have not,
the right to choose the church for their funeral and the place for
their burial (cf. cc. 1223, § 1, 1224, 2°).

If the persons mentioned in paragraph 1 die in a place remote
from their house, so that they cannot conveniently be transported to
the church of their house or at least of their institute, the funeral is
to be held in the church of the parish in which they died, unless in
the case of a novice he chose another church, and without prejudice
to the right of superiors mentioned in canon 1218, § 3 (c. 1221, § 2).
The above provisions refer to the *funeral;* the *burial* is governed
by canon 1231.

What is said of novices in paragraphs 1 and 2 applies also to
servants actually in service and residing permanently within the
house or its annexes; but if these persons die outside the house their
funeral is governed by canons 1216–1218 (c. 1221, § 3). This rule
applies equally to female servants in a convent of religious women.
The reason is that the terms used throughout this canon are general,
and in the case of servants no separate provision is made for females,
such as is made in canon 1230 for religious women and novices.[28]
No part of this canon applies to *postulants.*[29]

Other Cases. As regards deceased persons who were living in a religious house, even of regulars, or in a college (in the Roman sense,
that is, a residence for clerics or students) as guests, students, or
patients, and as regards persons who die in a hospital, the provisions
of canons 1216–1218 are to be observed, unless it is clear that some
particular law or privilege applies to them; as to those who die in
a seminary, let canon 1368 be observed (c. 1222). The canon last
cited gives to the rector of a seminary the rights of a pastor in certain
matters, for persons who live there permanently; hence their funeral
should be in the church or oratory of the seminary.

Choice of Funeral Church or Cemetery. All persons have the right

---

[28] Cf. Vermeersch-Creusen, *Epit.,* II, ed. 5, n. 530, p. 372.
[29] Cf. Code Com., 20 July, 1929; *AAS,* 21–573; *Digest,* I, p. 572.

to choose the church for their funeral or the cemetery for their burial, unless they are expressly forbidden this choice by law (c. 1223, § 1). A wife, and children who have attained puberty, are in making this choice entirely free from marital or parental authority (c. 1223, § 2). Note that the choice is twofold: either of a church for the funeral or of a place of burial, or of both. If only a church is chosen, the burial is to be in the cemetery of that church (c. 1231, § 1); if only a cemetery is chosen, the converse does not necessarily follow. Vermeersch has shown that the so-called axiom *"ubi tumulus, ibi funus"* is not only no axiom but does not even express a general presumption under the present law.[30] The choice of a place of burial may indeed indicate a choice of the church for the funeral; but whether it is to be so understood or not depends on all the circumstances; if, after considering everything this implicit choice remains doubtful, the presumption is in favor of the church of the deceased's own parish according to canon 1217. An interesting recent case illustrates this point.[31] Having a family vault in a church does not amount to choice of the church for the funeral (Code Commission, 4 Jan., 1946; *AAS*, 38–162).

Certain Persons Excluded From This Choice. The following persons are forbidden to choose the church for their funeral or the cemetery for their burial:

1. Those who have not reached puberty; but the parents or guardian can make this choice for a boy or girl even after their death;

2. Professed religious of whatever grade or dignity, unless they are Bishops (c. 1224).

If such a choice was made before religious profession it is regarded as canceled upon profession. Novices, and, *a fortiori,* postulants, are not excluded from this choice. Superiors can permit (e.g., at the request of the family) that a deceased religious be buried elsewhere than in the cemetery of the community.

Limitations Upon Choice of Church. In order that the choice of a church for the funeral be valid, it must be a choice of a parish church, or of a church of regulars, not however of monastic nuns (except in the case of women who were living permanently within the cloister of that monastery as servants, students, patients, or guests), or of a church which is subject to the right of patronage (*ius patronatus* —cf. cc. 1448–1471), or of some other church which has the right to

---

[30] Cf. *Periodica*, Vol. 16, p. 157*.
[31] Cf. S. C. Conc., 11 July, 1931; *AAS*, 25–373; *Digest*, I, p. 574.

conduct funeral services **(c. 1225).** A church other than those mentioned might have such right by apostolic privilege, by grant of the Bishop, by custom, or by agreement between pastors. Although canon 600 forbids entrance into a monastery of nuns to *all persons* except those mentioned there, yet special permission may be obtained for the presence of female servants or students. (See Schaefer, *De Religiosis,* ed. 3, n. 353.) According to the present canon, only these can choose the monastery church for their funeral.

How the Choice Is to Be Made. One can choose a church for his funeral or a cemetery for his burial either personally or through another person lawfully authorized to make the choice for him; and the fact of the choice or of the authority to make it can be proved in any legitimate way **(c. 1226, § 1).** If the choice is left to another, the latter may fulfill his charge after the death of the principal **(c. 1226, § 2).** But relatives cannot make the choice without any commission to do so from the deceased.[32]

Freedom of Choice. Religious and all clerics are strictly forbidden to induce anyone to make a vow, oath, or solemn or other promise to choose their church or cemetery for his funeral or burial, or not to change a choice of such church or cemetery already made; and if they violate this provision the choice is invalid **(c. 1227).**

Further Requisites for Burial Elsewhere Than in Proper Parish Cemetery. If choice was made of a cemetery for burial other than the cemetery of the proper parish of the deceased, the body should be buried there, provided there is no objection on the part of those who have control of that cemetery **(c. 1228, § 1).**

If choice has been made of a cemetery of religious for burial, the consent of the religious superior, according to the constitutions of the institute, is required and is sufficient in order that the body may be buried there **(c. 1228, § 2).**

As to burial in a cemetery of *religious:*

1. All *exempt* religious can have their own cemetery (c. 1208, § 2);

2. *Nonexempt* religious can have their own cemetery, with the permission of the Ordinary of the place (c. 1208, § 3);

3. Supposing that in either case the cemetery is lawfully established, nothing further is required for burial there than that the deceased chose it, and that the religious superiors permit it (cf. c. 1209, § 1).

Family Vaults. If a person who has a family vault in some cemetery

---

[32] Cf. S. C. Conc., 9 July, 1921; *AAS,* 13–534; *Digest,* I, p. 573; also S. C. Conc., 15 Nov., 1930; *AAS,* 25–155; *Digest,* I, p. 576.

dies without having chosen a burial place elsewhere, he is to be buried in his family vault if the body can be conveniently brought there, without prejudice to the provision of canon 1218, § 3 (c. 1229, § 1). The family vault of a wife is that of her husband, and if she had several husbands that of her latest one (c. 1229, § 2). If a person has more than one family vault, or in the case of a wife if her husband has more than one vault, the family or heirs of the deceased shall make the choice among them (c. 1229, § 3).

Notes. 1. A family vault (*sepulcrum maiorum*) means a burial ground in which one's ancestors are buried, with provision for the burial of the present deceased. It supposes that some earlier member of a family acquired a place of burial for himself and his family, or for himself and his heirs, or for himself, his family, and his heirs. Whether a deceased person has or has not a family vault will depend on the question of fact whether he does or does not come within the terms of the provisions made by the person who established the family vault.

2. If a deceased person has a family vault, that place is to be preferred for his burial, provided he did not choose some other place, and provided also that the body can conveniently be brought to the family vault *or* that the "interested persons" mentioned in canon 1218, § 3 bear the expenses of transporting it there.

3. A wife is not forbidden to choose her place of burial (cf. c. 1223, § 1), nor to have a family vault of her own; but in this latter case, if the husband also has a family vault, it is to be preferred to the family vault of the wife. This provision of canon 1229, § 2 applies even though the wife, after the death of her husband, has changed her domicile. But it does not apply to a wife who is legitimately separated from her husband.[33]

4. An illegitimate child is to be buried in the family vault of the father if the latter's paternity was notorious or if he acknowledged the child; otherwise in the vault of the mother.

Various Provisions as to Proper Church and Pastor. Canon 1230 includes a variety of provisions. All the paragraphs (1–7) deal with the right to take charge of the remains, accompany them to the church, and perform the funeral services there; paragraph 7 deals

---

[33] Cf. A Coronata, II, n. 802; Many, *De Locis Sacris*, n. 168. In some of the details, many distinctions and divergences of opinion will be found, especially among pre-Code authorities. The brief outline given in the text seems to us to be supported by good authority, and to conform to the provisions of the Code as applied to conditions in our country.

moreover with the right to accompany the remains to the cemetery; two paragraphs refer to the proper church for the funeral services, namely, paragraph 5 in the case of religious women, and paragraph 7 in a special case.

The proper pastor of the deceased has not only the right but also the duty, except in a case of grave necessity, to take charge of the remains personally or through another, to accompany them to his parish church, and there to perform the funeral services, without prejudice to canon 1216, § 2 (c. 1230, § 1). This is the ordinary case where the deceased died and is buried in his own parish. If he had several proper parishes and died in one of them the pastor of that parish has the right and duty to the exclusion of the other pastors (c. 1216, § 2).

If the death occurred in the territory of a parish to which the deceased did not belong, and the body can conveniently be brought to the church of his proper parish, the proper pastor of the deceased has the right, upon giving previous notice to the pastor of the place, to take charge of the body, accompany it to his church, and hold the funeral services there (c. 1230, § 2).

If the church of the funeral is a church of regulars or any church which is exempt from the jurisdiction of the pastor, the pastor, under the cross of the church of the funeral, takes charge of the body and accompanies it to the church; but the rector of the church performs the services (c. 1230, § 3).

But if the church of the funeral is not exempt from the jurisdiction of the pastor, the celebration of the services, in the absence of a peculiar privilege, pertains not to the rector of the church where the services are held but to the pastor in whose territory the church is situated, provided the deceased was a subject of the pastor (c. 1230, § 4).

Religious women and novices who die in the religious house are to be brought by the other religious women to the limits of their cloister; from that point, if the religious are not subject to the jurisdiction of the pastor, the chaplain conducts the remains to the church or oratory of the house to which the deceased belonged, and there conducts the services; if the religious are subject to the jurisdiction of the pastor, paragraph 1 applies (that is, the pastor takes charge and accompanies the body to the church or oratory and performs the services); finally, as regards religious women who die outside the religious house, the general provisions of the canons are to be observed

(c. 1230, § 5). This provision applies neither to postulants nor to servants in a convent. The former are governed by the general law; the latter follow the rule stated generally for servants in religious houses in canon 1221, § 3. The provision that the religious sisters of the deceased shall bring the body to the limits of the cloister applies strictly only to the papal cloister.[34]

In the case of a Cardinal or Bishop who dies outside Rome in his episcopal city, the provision of canon 397, 3° is to be observed (that is, the right and duty of conducting the services belong to the dignitaries and canons of the cathedral church in the order of precedence among them) **(c. 1230, § 6).**

If the body is sent to a place where the deceased neither had his proper parish nor chose according to law the church for his funeral, the right to take charge of the body, to perform the services if they are to be performed, and to accompany the body to the place of burial, pertains to the cathedral church of the place; and if there is no cathedral church, to the church of the parish in which the cemetery is located, unless local custom or diocesan statutes provide otherwise **(c. 1230, § 7).** This provision gives a supplementary norm to cover cases where there can be no question of the proper pastor of the deceased; as, for example, in the case of a body washed ashore in a foreign land, or sent for funeral and burial to a distant place where the deceased has neither a proper pastor nor a church legitimately chosen for his funeral.[35] In the latter case funeral services might already have been held, and would not be repeated; therefore the canon speaks of "the right to perform the services if they are to be performed." In a case involving the right to conduct services over a body which had been exhumed and transported to another place, the S. C. of the Council stated this rule: "In the transfer of a body for reburial after exhumation, if the funeral services were performed in the first burial, none are prescribed in the second; and if they are held they are not reserved to any particular pastor. If the due ceremonies were not observed in the first burial, they are to be performed in the second by the pastor of the deceased's domicile according to canon 1216."[36]

Burial. After the funeral services have been performed in the church the body is to be buried according to liturgical books in the

---

[34] A Coronata, II, n. 805.
[35] Cf. S. C. Conc., 12 Nov., 1927; *AAS*, 20–142; *Digest*, I, p. 580, n. 6.
[36] Cf. S. C. Conc., 12 Jan., 1924; *AAS*, 16–188; *Digest*, I, p. 571.

cemetery of the church where the funeral services were held, without
prejudice to canons 1228 and 1229 (c. 1231, § 1). Hence if the deceased
made no choice of a place of burial, and has no family vault, the
place of burial is the cemetery of the church where the funeral
services were held.

The priest who performed the services in the church has not only
the right but also the duty, except in a case of grave necessity, to
accompany the remains, either personally or through another, to the
place of burial (c. 1231, § 2).

Right to Accompany the Remains. The priest who accompanies the
remains to the church of the funeral or to the place of burial can
freely pass, even wearing the stole and accompanied by the cross,
through the territory of another parish or diocese, even without the
permission of the pastor or Ordinary (c. 1232, § 1).

If the body is to be buried in a cemetery to which it cannot
conveniently be brought, the pastor or rector of the church of the
funeral cannot claim the right to accompany it beyond the confines
of the city or place (c. 1232, § 2).

External Arrangements of Funeral Services. The pastor may not,
without a just and grave reason approved by the Ordinary, exclude
secular clerics, religious, and pious societies which the family or the
heirs may wish to invite to conduct the body to the church of the
funeral or to the place of burial, and to assist at the funeral; however,
the clerics who are attached to the church itself should, in preference
to all others, be invited by the family and the heirs (c. 1233, § 1). This
last provision does not include the members of the chapter of a
cathedral or collegiate church as such.[37]

Societies or emblems manifestly hostile to the Catholic religion
should never be admitted (c. 1233, § 2).[38]

Those who accompany the remains must comply with the wishes
of the pastor as to the conduct of the funeral, without prejudice to
their respective rights of precedence (c. 1233, § 3).

Clerics shall not carry the body of a layman, whatever may have
been his condition or dignity (c. 1233, § 4). This provision is not
intended to forbid such service in case of necessity.

Funeral Taxes and Fees. If there is no existing schedule of funeral
taxes or offerings, Ordinaries of places shall establish one for their
respective territories, taking counsel of the cathedral chapter and, if

[37] Code Com., 8 Apr., 1941; *AAS*, 33–173; *Digest*, II, p. 354.
[38] See Instruction, S. C. Rit., 15 Dec., 1922; *AAS*, 16–171; *Digest*, I, 581.

they think fit, also of the rural deans of the diocese and the pastors
of the episcopal city; in doing so they shall take into account legitimate
particular customs and all the circumstances of persons and places;
in this schedule they shall moderately determine the rights of all
concerned, so that all occasion of contention and scandal be avoided
(c. 1234, § 1). This is one of the exceptions to the rule of canon 1507,
§ 1, which requires taxes in general to be uniform throughout an
ecclesiastical Province according to a schedule to be adopted by a
Provincial Council or meeting of Bishops. This schedule of funeral
offerings is binding also on exempt religious.[39]

If the schedule provides for different classes, the persons interested
have the right to choose the class which they prefer (c. 1234, § 2).

Justice in Demanding Offerings: Free Service to the Poor. All are
strictly forbidden to demand as an offering for the burial or funeral
or for the celebration of the anniversary of the deceased, anything
beyond the amount fixed in the diocesan schedule of taxes (c. 1235).
The poor are to have a decent funeral and burial entirely gratis, with
funeral services as prescribed by liturgical laws and the diocesan
statutes (c. 1235, § 2). To make it easier for the poor to have a funeral
Mass, it is allowed to have a low Mass instead of the *Missa cantata*.[40]

The Pastor's Portion. Without prejudice to particular laws, whenever one of the faithful has his funeral elsewhere than in his proper
parish church, the proper pastor of the deceased is entitled to his
canonical portion (of the fees), except in a case where the body cannot
be conveniently transported to the proper parish church (c. 1236, § 1).
This provision contemplates cases where *according to law* the funeral
is held elsewhere (e.g., under canon 1230, § 7 or where the deceased
chose another church); if the holding of the funeral elsewhere was
contrary to the right of the pastor, the latter is entitled, not merely
to a canonical portion but to the entire offerings (c. 463, § 3). Particular
laws (and privileges — c. 4) may modify the right of the pastor to
the canonical portion.

If the deceased has more than one proper parish to which the
body can conveniently be brought, and the funeral is held elsewhere,
the pastor's canonical portion is to be divided among all the proper
pastors of the deceased (c. 1236, § 2). This does not apply to a case
where the deceased had more than one proper parish, but only one

---

[39] Code Com., 6 March, 1927; *AAS*, 19–161; *Digest*, I, p. 582.
[40] S. C. Rit., 9 May, 1899; *Decr. Auth.*, n. 4024.

to which the body could conveniently be brought; in that case the pastor who performs the services (being one of the proper pastors of the deceased) receives the entire offerings.

Source and Amount of the Pastor's Portion. 1. *Source.* The pastor's portion is to be drawn from all the emoluments which are established for the funeral and burial in the diocesan schedule, and from no other source **(c. 1237, § 1).**

2. *A special case.* If for any reason the first solemn funeral service is held, not immediately, but within a full month from the day of burial, even if on that day (the day of burial) some minor public services were held, the pastor's portion is nevertheless to be paid out of the emoluments of the latter funeral services also (that is, the solemn services) **(c. 1237, § 2).** The point here is in the distinction between *solemn* and *minor* services; the recital of the Office of the Dead, the services at the grave, are minor services; the solemn services include the funeral Mass. The month is computed from midnight following the day of burial.

3. *Amount.* The amount of the pastor's portion is to be determined in the diocesan schedule; and if the parish church and the church of the funeral belong to different dioceses the amount is determined according to the schedule of the church of the funeral **(c. 1237, § 3).**

The Record of Death. After the burial, the minister shall inscribe in the register of deaths the name and age of the deceased, the name of his parents or spouse, the date of death, the sacraments which he had received, and the place and time of the burial **(c. 1238).** The register of deaths is one of the parish registers which all pastors are bound to keep **(c. 470, § 1).** If the minister of the burial is the proper pastor of the deceased, this record is sufficient; otherwise the minister would do well to send a copy of the record to the proper pastor, though the law does not explicitly require this.

Article 3. The Right of Ecclesiastical Burial (cc. 1239–1242)

PRELIMINARY SURVEY

General Principles (c. 1239)
Persons Excluded From Ecclesiastical Burial (c. 1240)
Effect of This Exclusion (c. 1241)
Removal of the Body of a *Vitandus* (c. 1242)

General Principles. Persons who die without baptism are not to be admitted to ecclesiastical burial **(c. 1239, § 1).** Catechumens who through no fault of their own die without baptism are to be considered (in this connection) as baptized **(c. 1239, § 2).** All baptized persons are to receive ecclesiastical burial unless they are expressly excluded from it by law **(c. 1239, § 3).**

Ecclesiastical burial is to be taken as defined in canon 1204. Infants who die without baptism are not entitled to the full rites of ecclesiastical burial; but they may be buried in an unblessed portion of a cemetery (c. 1212). Their burial even in consecrated ground would not violate the cemetery, notwithstanding cc. 1172, § 1, 4°, and 1207; nor would the penalty of canon 2339 be incurred by ordering their burial there.[41] An unborn and unbaptized fetus of a Catholic mother may be buried with the mother, and even an infant already born of a Catholic mother, if he dies with her, may probably be treated in the same way although he did not receive baptism.[42] If Catholic baptism is even probable, ecclesiastical burial should be granted.

Catechumens are treated as if baptized, if they remained unbaptized through no fault of their own. This does not include infants, but refers rather to would-be converts, persons under instruction or who had indicated a positive desire to begin instruction for reception into the Church.

All baptized persons here include only Catholics. The reasons for this interpretation are: the whole tradition of the Church; the fact that in this part of the Code the law seems to concern itself only with the funeral and burial of Catholics (cf. the expression *"fidelium"* in cc. 1203, 1205, 1215, etc.); the provision of canon 87 which excludes from the rights of Christians, even baptized persons where there exists an "obstacle to the bond of ecclesiastical communion." Failure to adhere visibly to the external worship and discipline of the Church is such an obstacle. Hence in general non-Catholics even though baptized and in good faith are not really entitled to Catholic ecclesiastical burial, and this, independently of any crime on their part.[43] As to their burial in a Catholic cemetery, see end of this Article.

Persons Excluded From Ecclesiastical Burial. The following are deprived of ecclesiastical burial, unless before death they gave some sign of repentance:

---

[41] Cappello, *De Censuris*, n. 402, 3.
[42] Cf. Arregui, *Theol. Mor.*, n. 913, note 1; *contra*, Beste, *Introductio in Codicem*, p. 603.
[43] Cf. Kerin, *Privation of Christian Burial*, Cath. U., 1941, p. 187.

1. Notorious apostates from the Christian faith, or persons who notoriously belong to a heretical or schismatical sect or to a Masonic sect or other society of the same sort;

2. Persons who are excommunicated or interdicted, after a condemnatory or declaratory sentence;

3. Those who killed themselves of deliberate purpose;

4. Those who die in a duel, or from a wound received in a duel;

5. Those who gave orders that their body be cremated;

6. Other public and manifest sinners (c. 1240, § 1).

In any of the above cases, if a doubt arises, the Ordinary should be consulted if time permits; if the doubt persists, the body should receive ecclesiastical burial, but in such a way that scandal be avoided (c. 1240, § 2).

Notes. 1. The privation of ecclesiastical burial by this canon has the nature of a *penalty,* and hence is to be strictly interpreted; moreover *any sign* of repentance before death excuses from the penalty; this means some positive sign, such as calling for a priest, kissing a crucifix, an expressed desire not to die without the sacraments. In doubt the Ordinary is to be consulted, but if the doubt in favor of the deceased remains, the decision should be in his favor.

2. Apostasy must be from the *Christian* faith (apostasy from Catholicism would not be enough), and must be *notorious,* as a delict or crime according to canon 2197. True *membership* is required in a sect or Masonic society; general sympathies with such sect or society would not suffice. The membership must be *notorious.* An atheistic sect is included here.[44] Masonic sects and similar societies include the Knights Templars, but probably not the Knights of Pythias, Odd Fellows, though these also are forbidden.[45]

3. Suicides are included in this privation only if their act was deliberate, and *notoriously* so; though the word "notorious" does not occur in this place in the text, it is correctly inferred from the fact that suicides are classed with "other public and manifest sinners" of n. 6.[46] Such notoriety will be rare, and scandal unlikely, where the more or less common opinion prevails that suicide usually results from nervous or mental derangement.

4. The penalty is incurred by those who *ordered* their bodies to be

---

[44] Code Com., 30 July, 1934; *AAS,* 26–494; *Digest,* II, p. 286.

[45] Ayrinhac-Lydon, *Penal Legislation,* n. 258; Quigley, *Condemned Societies,* Cath. U., 1927.

[46] Kerin, *Privation of Christian Burial,* p. 202.

cremated, even though the orders were not obeyed.[47] If, without such orders, the body has been actually cremated, ecclesiastical burial is still prohibited except in as far as scandal can be efficaciously prevented.[48]

5. The words "public and manifest sinners" are in themselves clear, but their application is difficult. Any notorious crime (c. 2197) would make the perpetrator a public sinner; but it must be admitted that the term applies also to one against whom no notorious crime in the canonical sense can be proved, because if the sinful life of the deceased is public and manifest, inevitable scandal would attach to granting him ecclesiastical burial. In doubtful cases the decision must be left to the Ordinary.

6. Finally it should be noted that privation of ecclesiastical burial does not necessarily forbid a priest to visit the home of the deceased and to say some private nonliturgical prayers for his soul. Even private Masses for him are not forbidden.

Effect of Privation of Ecclesiastical Burial. When ecclesiastical burial is excluded, any funeral Mass, even an anniversary one, and all other public funeral services must also be denied (c. 1241).

The penalties connected with this subject are: (1) those who *dare to command or compel* ecclesiastical burial contrary to canon 1240 incur an excommunication reserved to no one; (2) those who *freely grant* it contrary to the same canon incur an interdict from entrance into the church, reserved to the Ordinary (c. 2339).

Removal of the Body of a *Vitandus.* If it can be done without grave inconvenience, the body of an excommunicated *vitandus* which has been buried contrary to law in a sacred place, must be exhumed, observing the prescription of canon 1214, § 1 (that is, with the permission of the Ordinary), and interred in the nonsacred place mentioned in canon 1212 (c. 1242).

Special Questions. 1. *May baptized non-Catholics receive ecclesiastical burial?* We have seen that non-Catholics, though baptized and in good faith, are usually excluded from ecclesiastical burial, not because of any crime on their part, but simply because of the absence of a strict right to it. Evidently also it would be rare for a non-Catholic to desire Catholic burial. Yet the case might arise, for example, where a non-Catholic husband of a Catholic woman had lived a sincere and good life, kept the antenuptial promises, showed sympathy with

---

[47] Code Com., 10 Nov., 1925; *AAS,* 17–583; *Digest,* I, p. 583.
[48] Holy Office, Instruction, 19 June, 1926; *AAS,* 18–282; *Digest,* I, p. 564.

Catholic doctrine, and even perhaps expressed a desire to become a Catholic when fully convinced. The Catholic widow might ask for it; and there might be reasons of general policy in favor of the request, for example, "to prevent a non-Catholic minister from claiming the funeral to the sorrow and scandal of the Catholic family; to prevent an entirely irreligious funeral; to avoid scandal among the faithful, who cannot understand the legal provisions by which the worst sinners may receive Christian burial by last-minute repentance, while good men who have been friendly to the Church . . . are denied it."[49] Would it, in such a case, be absolutely forbidden? Such a person is not excluded by canon 1240, § 1, 1°, because there can be no question of a *notorious delict*. For such a case, admittedly exceptional, it seems that the Bishop could grant Christian burial to a baptized non-Catholic "who is publicly known, or can be publicly known by the announcement of his wish, to have desired, in so far as he was able under the circumstances, to be united to the Church of Christ."[50] The decision would pertain to the Bishop in view of all the circumstances of each case.

2. *May unbaptized non-Catholics be buried in Catholic cemeteries?* Here there is no question of ecclesiastical burial in the full sense; that is definitely excluded by canon 1239, § 1. But the question is, could burial in blessed ground be permitted in an individual case, to prevent greater evil. The question was presented to the Holy Office in 1859 in this form: "Whether in consideration of a bond of consanguinity or of marriage, non-Catholics may licitly be buried in the family vault of Catholic families." The reply was: "The Bishops should make every effort to see that everything is done according to law; but in cases where this cannot be effected without scandal and danger, the practice may be tolerated."[51] The Holy Office later declared that the provision of the Second Council of Baltimore (n. 389) was to be understood in the light of this reply, namely, as merely passive toleration, in particular cases, to avoid greater evil.[52] Consequently, whatever may be the interpretation of the provision of the Council of Baltimore (some authors contend that it can strictly be applied only in case the burial is in a family mausoleum as opposed to a simple family plot), it is permitted to rely on the reply of the

[49] Kerin, *Privation of Christian Burial*, p. 239.
[50] Kerin, *loc. cit.*
[51] Holy Office, 30 March, 1859; *Fontes*, n. 949, IV, p. 223.
[52] Holy Office, 4 Jan., 1888; *Fontes*, n. 1107, IV, p. 433; cf. also note to the reply last cited, *Fontes*, IV, p. 224.

Holy Office, in which no distinction was made between a mausoleum and a family plot. The term there used, *"sepulcrum gentilitium"* is not limited to a constructed monument or mausoleum; it means a family vault or family burial plot. There is, therefore, good reason as well as authority for the conclusion that the burial of a non-Catholic, even though he be unbaptized, in a blessed Catholic family vault or plot, might be passively tolerated (not positively approved as a privilege) by the Bishop in a particular case, where such action seemed necessary to avoid greater evil.[53]

3. *The burial of Catholics in non-Catholic cemeteries.* The First Council of Baltimore (n. 80) forbade ecclesiastical rites in the funerals of the faithful in cases where the body is buried in *sectarian* cemeteries, or even in *nonsacred* cemeteries if Catholic cemeteries are available. The Second Council of Baltimore, after commemorating this earlier provision, proceeded to modify it (n. 392). Finally, the Third Council of Baltimore approved the more lenient provisions of the Second Council, and modified them still further in these terms: "When there is question of the burial of converts whose surviving non-Catholic relatives have a private vault in a non-Catholic cemetery, or even in the case of the burial of Catholics who, before the law of the First Council (1853), had their own burial plots, or afterward acquired such lots in good faith (*certe sine fraude post legem acquisierunt*), we declare that in these cases it is permitted to perform ecclesiastical rites either at the home or at the church whenever the Bishop has not for grave reasons forbidden it. . . . With the exception of the above cases, pastors may never perform the aforesaid rites in the burial of the faithful in a non-Catholic cemetery, unless with the express permission of the Ordinary" (n. 318).

These provisions, however, have been repealed by the law of the Code (c. 1205),[54] which requires Catholics to be buried in consecrated or blessed ground, but does not, be it noted, *expressly* forbid all ecclesiastical rites if that is not done. Without relying on the lenient provisions of the two later Baltimore Councils *as law*, several writers who have considered carefully the question as applied to the United States conclude that "the granting or the refusing of Christian burial, in so far as such action would be the result of the choice of a place of burial, depends, by force of circumstances in this country, wherever

---

[53] Cf. Donnelly, *Certain Problems of Ecclesiastical Burial*, in *Ecclesiastical Review*, Vol. 103, pp. 1–5; Kerin, *Privation of Christian Burial*, p. 240.

[54] Cf. Barrett, *A Comparative Study of the Councils of Baltimore and the Code of Canon Law*; Kerin, *Privation of Christian Burial*, p. 249.

no diocesan statutes have regulated it, upon the discretion of the Ordinary, who is to be governed by the exigencies of places and persons so that he may decide what will be to the best interest of souls in his diocese."[55] The reasons justifying this conclusion are briefly these: (1) the practice of Bishops in the United States in this matter, following the lenient provisions of the Second and Third Councils of Baltimore, and presumably going back indefinitely in the period before the strict provisions of the First Baltimore Council, amount to an immemorial custom, which, according to canon 5, may still be tolerated if the Bishops find it cannot be prudently eradicated; (2) in the absence of absolute prohibition by the Holy See of ecclesiastical rites for Catholics who are buried in non-Catholic cemeteries, the conditions required by canon 81 for dispensation by Ordinaries from the law requiring burial in blessed cemeteries, are verified; (3) the recent reply of the Holy Office,[56] in view of its terms, is not an *absolute* prohibition.

Days When Funeral Mass Permitted in the United States. In this connection the terms of the new indult should be consulted.[57]

CASES AND QUESTIONS

1. Can an exempt church belonging to regulars in diocese A be *validly* consecrated by the Bishop of diocese B? (C. 1147, § 1). May it be consecrated *licitly* by the same Bishop with *only* the permission of the Bishop of diocese A? (Cc. 1155, §§ 1, 2; 1157). Or with *only* the permission of the major superior? (C. 1155, §§ 1, 2). Can it be consecrated validly by the major superior (Ordinary) of the exempt order if he is not a Bishop? (C. 1147, § 1).

2. Funeral services were held in a church for a person who had been excommunicated by a declaratory sentence. Was the church violated thereby? (C. 1172, § 1). Was the Catholic cemetery in which the deceased was buried violated? (Cc. 1207, 1172, §§ 1, 2). What penalty if any was incurred? (Cc. 1240, § 1, 2°, 2339). Would the church or the cemetery need to be consecrated anew? (Cc. 1174, § 1, 1170).

3. The superioress of a congregation of sisters, who wishes to establish a secondary chapel in the convent, asks what permission is needed, and whether it would be difficult to obtain. What would you say? (C. 1192, §§ 1-4).

[55] Kerin, *op. cit.*, p. 254; Donnelly, in *Ecclesiastical Review*, Vol. 103, p. 5.
[56] Holy Office, 13 Feb., 1936; *Digest*, II, p. 348.
[57] Indult, S. C. Rit., 16 Oct., 1940; *Digest*, II, p. 200.

4. Must the top of a fixed altar be cemented to its stone support? (C. 1198, § 2). Would you recommend this? Why? (C. 1200, § 1). May an altar be consecrated alone, without consecrating at the same time also the church? May a church be consecrated without consecrating an altar at the same time? (C. 1165, § 5).

5. Can a Prefect Apostolic who is not a Bishop consecrate an immovable altar in his territory? (C. 294, § 2). How should such an altar be consecrated? (Cc. 1147, § 1, 1199, § 2, 1155, §§ 1, 2).

6. Mother Symphorosa, Superior General of a papal congregation of hospital sisters, writes that in many of the hospitals conducted by her sisters, amputations of arms or legs are of frequent occurrence. The practice has been to bury these amputated members in a corner of the hospital grounds which is not blessed, or sometimes on the advice of the doctors, to burn them in a special incinerator. Some of the persons who undergo these amputations are Catholics, others baptized non-Catholics, others unbaptized. What should be done in the future? (Holy Office, *Fontes*, n. 1189, Vol. IV, p. 494).

7. A congregation of religious women approved by the Holy See wishes to have a cemetery on the convent grounds. Whose permission is required? (C. 1208, § 3). Who may bless this cemetery? (Cc. 1147, § 2, 1156).

8. An exempt religious order, in moving one of its houses to a new location, wishes to move also some of the bodies buried in their cemetery. What permission is required? (C. 1214). What if there were question of moving a convent of a non-exempt papal congregation with its cemetery?

9. X, a member of St. John's parish, Springfield, before his death expressed the wish to be buried in the cemetery of an exempt religious order in St. Louis. What is the proper church for his funeral? Where should he be interred? (Cc. 1216, § 1, 1231, § 1, 1228, § 1).

10. F has a domicile in Cincinnati, St. Joseph's parish, and a quasi-domicile in New York, St. Athanasia's parish. He dies in Covington, Kentucky, having made no choice of any church for his funeral. Where should the funeral be conducted? (Cc. 1216, § 1, 1218, § 1). What if he had died in New Rochelle, just outside New York? In the latter case, could the relatives move the body to Cincinnati? (C. 1218, § 3).

11. Mary, a girl of 18 whose home is in St. Thomas' parish, Buffalo, is a postulant in a diocesan convent in Toronto. Taken seriously ill and facing death, she expresses a wish to be buried from the convent chapel and interred in the community cemetery. Her parents would like to bring her back to Buffalo to be buried from their parish church. Discuss the case (cc. 1223, § 1, 1224, 2°, 1228, §§ 1, 2, 1216, § 1).

12. Anthony, of St. Ignatius' parish, Chicago, died at his home in that parish. His widow chooses Holy Family church in Chicago for the funeral, saying that she is sure Anthony would have wished it. Where should the funeral be held? (Cc. 1223, § 1, 1226, 1216, § 1).

13. Martha, a Catholic, had married outside the Church and ceased practicing her religion for seventeen years. On her deathbed she called for a priest and expressed a desire to be reconciled to the Church and receive the Sacraments; but the priest arrived too late. Is she entitled to Christian burial? (Cc. 1239, § 3, 1240, § 1).

14. Charles, student of canon law, decides that there is nothing in the Code to prevent the average baptized non-Catholic from receiving Catholic burial (c. 1239, § 3). William, a fellow seminarian, contends that they are excluded by canon 1240, § 1, 1°. How would you decide the argument? (Cf. text).

15. Estelle was born a Catholic, but her family burial plot (established by her non-Catholic father) is in a private non-Catholic cemetery. She lived and died a good Catholic. The relatives arrange for her burial in the family plot, but the pastor tells them that it will be impossible to have Catholic funeral services if she is to be buried there. Much disturbed, the relatives appeal to the Bishop. What is the law on this case? What *may* the Bishop do? (Text, special questions, n. 3). Should the grave in any event be blessed? (C. 1206, § 3).

Readings:

Ziolkowski, *The Consecration and Blessing of Churches,* Cath. U., 1943; Gulczynski, *The Desecration and Violation of Churches,* Cath. U., 1942; Feldhaus, *Oratories,* Cath. U., 1927; Bliley, *Altars According to the Code of Canon Law,* Cath. U., 1927; Power, *The Blessing of Cemeteries,* Cath. U., n. 185; O'Reilly, *Ecclesiastical Sepulture in the New Code of Canon Law,* Cath. U., 1923; Kerin, *The Privation of Christian Burial,* Cath. U., 1941; *Clergy Review:* Vol. 11, p. 416 (case on public sinners and Christian burial); Vol. 21, p. 116 (Mahoney, on reconciliation of bombed churches); *Australasian Catholic Record* (1934), p. 54 (Nevin, the law regarding burial); *Ecclesiastical Review:* Vol. 83, p. 535 (may non-Catholic husband be buried in the family lot in a Catholic cemetery?); Vol. 84, p. 629 (right to choose church of funeral or place of burial); Vol. 86, p. 192 (burial of non-Catholic member of family in Catholic cemetery); Vol. 103, p. 5 (Donnelly, questions on Catholic burial); *Irish Ecclesiastical Record* (1931), p. 536 (Fallon, on reconsecration of portable altar); *Periodica:* Vol. 16, p. 57* (Vermeersch, against axiom *"ubi tumulus, ibi funus"*); Vol. 16, p. 67* (Vermeersch, questions on c. 1230, § 7); Vol. 18, p. 62* (C.S., article on cremation); Vol. 20, p. 146* (Vermeersch on pastor's right to accompany funeral).

Section 3. Sacred Times (cc. 1243–1254)

PRELIMINARY SURVEY

What Are Sacred Times (c. 1243)
Power to Establish Them (c. 1244)
Power to Dispense From Their Observance (c. 1245)
How the Day Is Measured (c. 1246)
Feast Days of Obligation for the Universal Church (c. 1247)
The Observance of Feast Days of Obligation (c. 1248)
Place for Fulfilling the Precept of Hearing Mass (c. 1249)
The Law of Abstinence (c. 1250)
The Law of Fast (c. 1251)
Days of Fast or Abstinence or Both (c. 1252)
Indults, Vows, Religious Constitutions, Unaffected (c. 1253)
Subjects of the Law of Fast and Abstinence (c. 1254)

Sacred Times. Sacred times in general are times set aside for the special worship of God by positive religious worship, by resting from certain occupations, by acts of penance and self-denial consisting in fast, or abstinence, or both. The Code expresses this principle in terse juridical language:

Sacred times are feast days; to which are added days of abstinence and fast **(c. 1243)**.

Power to Establish Sacred Times. The power to establish, transfer, or abolish feast days and days of abstinence and fast common to the universal Church belongs exclusively to the supreme ecclesiastical authority **(c. 1244, § 1)**, that is, to the Holy See. Ordinaries of places can establish special feast days or days of abstinence and fast for their dioceses or territories, only *per modum actus* **(c. 1244, § 2)**.

In the early centuries the Holy See did not exercise its power to establish sacred times, and hence Bishops did so for their respective dioceses. Pope Urban VIII urged the Bishops to desist from this practice, and it had practically ceased several centuries before the Code. The S. C. of Rites in 1703 denied this power to the Bishops (*Decr. Auth.* n. 2113), but this decree did not have the force of general law. Hence, until the Code, most authors agree that the Bishops had the power, at least in theory. It is now definitely limited to establishing feast days or days of fast and abstinence *per modum actus;* that is, to affix the obligation to certain days in a single year, or at most for two or three years. Ordinaries cannot transfer nor abolish any of the days fixed by the Code. The limited power to establish days *per modum actus* is given only to Ordinaries of places, not to religious Ordinaries.

Power to Dispense. Not only Ordinaries of places but also pastors, in single cases and for a just cause, can dispense individual persons and families subject to them, even outside their territory, and in their territory also those domiciled elsewhere (*peregrinos*), from the common law of the observance of feast days, and likewise of the observance of abstinence or fast, or of both (c. 1245, § 1).

Ordinaries, because of a special large concourse of people or for reasons of public health, can also dispense their whole diocese or territory from the law of fast or abstinence or both (c. 1245, § 2).

In a clerical exempt religious institute the same dispensing power is enjoyed by superiors, to be exercised by them after the manner of pastors, in regard to the persons mentioned in canon 514, § 1 (c. 1245, § 3).

Notes. 1. All these persons, that is, Ordinaries of places, pastors, and superiors in clerical exempt institutes, have ecclesiastical offices in the strict sense; consequently the dispensing power here given them by the Code is *ordinary* jurisdiction (c. 197, § 1) and can be delegated to others (c. 199, § 1).

2. The power of Ordinaries and pastors to dispense from the observance of *feast* days is limited to individual cases (persons or families); Ordinaries can dispense their whole territory only from fast or abstinence or both, and only for reasons of public health or because of a great special concourse of people; this last circumstance is verified in the case of an extraordinary attendance of the people of a single parish at a feast celebrated in the church.[58] The concourse need not be for a religious purpose.

3. Pastors can never dispense their whole parish either from the observance of feast days or of fast and abstinence.

4. Superiors (not only major superiors) in clerical exempt institutes can dispense from the observance of feasts or fast and abstinence "after the manner of pastors," therefore only in individual cases, the following persons: (1) their habitual subjects, that is, religious living permanently in the house; (2) religious of their institute from other houses, staying temporarily in the house; (3) persons mentioned in canon 514, § 1, that is, persons living night and day in the house as servants, pupils, guests, or patients. "Individual cases" might here

---

[58] Code Com., 12 March, 1929; *AAS*, 21–170; *Digest*, I, p. 584.

include a group of persons, part of their community, which could be compared to a family in a parish.

5. *Legal holidays.* Ordinaries of the United States who have obtained the renewal of the indult first granted *ad quinquennium* in 1931 may dispense their subjects (without restriction, therefore the whole territory) from fast or abstinence, or both, on *civil holidays.*[59]

6. *War indult.* All Ordinaries of places received by indult in 1941, "in view of the peculiar circumstances of the present time" the power to give a general dispensation within their territory from the law of fast and abstinence, in favor also of exempt religious. Two days, however, are excepted: for the faithful of the Latin rite, Ash Wednesday and Good Friday (as to both fast and abstinence); for the faithful of other rites, two days to be determined by their Ordinaries.[60]

7. The *Workingmen's* indult, the *Saturday–Wednesday* indult and the *Military Faculties,* will be considered later.

Manner of Computing the Day. The reckoning of a feast day and likewise of a day of abstinence and fast is to be from midnight to midnight, except as provided in canon 923 **(c. 1246).** The canon cited provides for the gaining of an indulgence which is attached to a certain day. In reckoning a day from midnight to midnight, it is evident that the same time (any of those mentioned in canon 33, § 1) must be used in determining the beginning and the end of the day. This results not from any mythical obligation of "consistency," but from the definite provision of canon 32, § 1: "a day consists of twenty-four hours." In traveling eastward one will necessarily shorten the day *per accidens* by reckoning the successive midnights according to the usual time of the place where he is. This is, of course, licit. It is disputed whether the option allowed by canon 33 applies to the observance of the Sunday rest from servile work (it is not mentioned). The affirmative opinion is probable.[61]

Feast Days of Obligation. Feast days of obligation in the universal Church are only the following: all Sundays, the feasts of the Nativity, the Circumcision, Epiphany, the Ascension, Corpus Christi, the Immaculate Conception, the Assumption, St. Joseph (March 19), SS. Peter and Paul, All Saints (c. 1247, § 1) — five for our Lord, two for the Blessed Virgin, three for the saints. By indult of 25 Nov., 1885, the days of obligation, except Sundays, are reduced to six, for all

---

[59] See *Digest,* I, p. 584.

[60] S. C. for Extraordinary Ecclesiastical Affairs, 19 Dec., 1941; *AAS,* 33–516; *Digest,* II, p. 363.

[61] Cf. Vermeersch-Creusen, *Epit.,* I, n. 148.

dioceses of the United States, namely: the feasts of the Immaculate Conception, the Nativity, the Circumcision, the Ascension, the Assumption, All Saints.[62]

The feast days of patrons are not days of ecclesiastical precept; but Ordinaries of places may transfer the external solemnity of the feast to the following Sunday (c. 1247, § 2). The patron of a place (city, diocese, country) is the saint chosen in accordance with the decree of the Sacred Congregation of Rites (*Decr. Auth.*, n. 526), or conferred directly by Apostolic Letter as a special advocate and protector. Thus the Patroness of the United States is the Immaculate Conception.

If in any place any of the feasts above mentioned has been legitimately suppressed or transferred, no change is to be made without consulting the Holy See (c. 1247, § 3).

The Observance of Feast Days of Obligation. On feast days of obligation Mass must be heard; and one must abstain from servile work, from judicial proceedings, and also, unless legitimate custom or special indults permit them, from public trafficking, public gatherings of buyers and sellers, and all other public buying and selling (c. 1248). The details of these obligations and the causes which excuse from them pertain to moral theology.

Place for Fulfilling the Precept of Hearing Mass. The precept of hearing Mass is fulfilled by being present at Mass celebrated in any Catholic rite, either in the open (*sub dio*) or in any church or public or semipublic oratory, or in the private cemetery chapels mentioned in canon 1190, but not in other private oratories unless this privilege was granted by the Holy See (c. 1249).

1. The Mass may be celebrated in *any Catholic rite;* therefore an Oriental may satisfy the precept by hearing Mass according to the Latin rite, and a Latin by hearing it according to any of the Catholic Oriental rites.

2. The place may be *in the open,* the Mass being celebrated at a portable altar. A portable altar on board a ship, in an accessible place (not, for example, in a private cabin) is considered as morally equivalent to an altar in the open.[63]

3. The Mass may be in a *public or semipublic oratory.* Even secondary chapels in convents, hospitals, religious houses, etc., are semipublic. A permanent chapel on board a ship is a public oratory.[64]

---

[62] Cf. *Conc. Balt. III*, pp. cv–cix.
[63] A Coronata, II, n. 824. We do not, however, agree with this author that attendance at Mass said *anywhere* on a portable altar would satisfy the precept.
[64] S. C. Rit., *Decr. Auth.*, n. 4069, ad V.

Private chapels of Cardinals and Bishops are considered semipublic (c. 1189); those of Apostolic Nuncios, Internuncios, and Delegates, public, by special privilege.

4. The precept is satisfied by hearing Mass in a *private cemetery chapel,* but not in other private oratories unless the Holy See has granted that privilege. In granting the privilege of having a domestic or private oratory, the Holy See usually limits the persons who can satisfy the precept by hearing Mass there to the relatives by blood or marriage of the person in whose favor the privilege of having the oratory is granted; other persons, therefore, do not satisfy the precept.

5. Cardinals (c. 239, § 1, 7°) and Bishops (c. 349, § 1, 1°) have the privilege of celebrating Mass on a portable altar or of having such a Mass celebrated by a priest and assisting at it. Anyone who assists at such a Mass anywhere would seem to satisfy the precept.[65]

The Law of Abstinence. The law of abstinence forbids taking as nourishment meat, meat juices, but not eggs, milk products, nor condiments of any kind though made from animal fats **(c. 1250).**

1. The Code does not define *flesh meat;* it is to be defined according to common estimation and custom (even local custom) rather than in scientific biological terms. The general rule is that animals which live on land and have warm blood are considered meat; others, not. Thus fish, frogs, turtles, snakes, snails, oysters, clams, crabs, lobsters are not meat. Some authors seem to suggest that there is doubt as to certain animals which live partly in the water, for example, muskrats, beavers, otters, and even ducks. There would seem to be no doubt that these are meat, unless according to local custom or local common estimation they are considered not to be meat. In this case they could be eaten without violating the law of abstinence.

2. *Meat juices* include beef tea, bouillon, any soup made from meat. Jello, or "calf's foot jelly," even though made from meat, is by common estimation and custom considered not meat; but jellied bouillon is meat.

3. *Condiments* are allowed even if made from meat, provided they are used as condiments, as suet, oleomargarine, lard sometimes are.

4. *Diocesan lenten regulations,* and also notations in diocesan *ordos,* furnish valuable norms which may be relied upon as interpretations of custom and common estimation in various localities.

The Law of Fast. The law of fast prescribes that not more than one

---

[65] Cf. Vermeersch-Creusen, *Epit.,* II, n. 563.

full meal be taken per day; but it does not forbid that some food be taken in the morning and evening, observing the approved custom of the place as regards the quantity and kind of food (c. 1251, § 1). It is not forbidden to eat meat and fish at the same meal, nor to interchange the evening collation with dinner (c. 1251, § 2).

1. *The principal meal.* Neither the quantity nor the kind of food is limited; meat and fish may be taken at the same meal. An interruption of half an hour, for any reason, or of even an hour by reason of necessity or work, is permitted. The time of the principal meal may be anticipated by one hour, that is, it may be taken at 11 o'clock. (Cf. Genicot-Salsmans, *Theol. Mor.,* Vol. I, n. 438.)

2. *Breakfast (frustulum matutinum).* Primarily, not much more than two ounces; yet a probable opinion holds that the quantity may be what is needed to enable one to do one's work without inconvenience.[66] As to quality, meat is definitely excluded;[67] aside from this, custom governs. The custom in the United States limiting the frustulum to bread and coffee (or tea, chocolate) has some sanction in a document of the Holy Office (8 Aug., 1887; cf. Putzer, *Commentarius in Facultates Apostolicas,* n. 169), but diocesan lenten regulations will be the best guide.

3. *The collation (refectio serotina).* As to *quantity,* the common norm is eight ounces of solid food, *or* the fourth part of a full meal. The latter norm is called "relative" and is favored by many authors especially for northern climates and places where wine is not common and where the principal meal is an ordinary one. Even the absolute norm of eight ounces is not mathematically rigid. If one can observe the substance of the law by taking a little more, and not otherwise, Vermeersch thinks he should be encouraged to do this rather than to ask for a dispensation. Many admit this would be licit. Liquids that are not primarily food (beer, wine, coffee) are not counted as food, nor, probably, the water in soup or porridge. As to *quality,* meat is excluded; the rest depends on custom. Many authors exclude eggs and milk products, but these opinions are based on European customs; these are commonly allowed in the United States. Several authors allow the interchange of the collation with breakfast, for a reasonable cause. Questions regarding grave matter, excusing causes, etc., are treated in moral theology.

---

[66] Cf. Vermeersch, in *Periodica,* Vol. 22, p. 60*; Twomey, *The Lenten Fast,* in *Ecclesiastical Review,* Vol. 98, pp. 97–110.

[67] Code Com., 29 Oct., 1919; *AAS,* 11–480; *Digest,* I, p. 586.

4. There is no change in the fast or abstinence for Christmas eve.[68] The obligation of a vow (by members of a community or residents of a place) is binding only on those individuals who made the vow.[69]

Days of Fast or Abstinence or Both. The law of abstinence alone is to be observed on all Fridays (c. 1252, § 1). The law of abstinence and fast together is to be observed on Ash Wednesday, the Fridays and Saturdays of Lent, the Ember Days, and on the vigils of Pentecost, the Assumption, All Saints, and the Nativity (c. 1252, § 2). The law of fast alone is to be observed on the other days of Lent (c. 1252, § 3). On Sundays or holydays of obligation the law of abstinence, or of abstinence and fast, or of fast alone, ceases, except on a feast of obligation during Lent; and the vigils are not anticipated; likewise the law ceases on Holy Saturday at noon (c. 1252, § 4).

1. The law ceases on all Sundays and feast days of obligation, except feast days of obligation during Lent. Sundays during Lent are not days of fast nor abstinence, but feast days of obligation during Lent are days of fast, and if they fall on an abstinence day, also days of abstinence. This includes the feast of St. Joseph.[70]

2. The new rule regarding nonanticipation of vigils applies throughout the year; that is, if the vigil of a feast is by law a day of fast and abstinence but happens to fall on a Sunday, neither the Sunday nor the day preceding are to be observed as a day of fast and abstinence.

Indults, Vows, Religious Constitutions Unaffected. By these canons no change is made in particular indults, vows of any physical or moral person, nor in the constitutions and rules of any approved religious society or institute of men or women living in common even without vows (c. 1253).

1. *The Workingmen's Indult.* This indult was originally granted by the S. C. for the Propagation of the Faith, to Cardinal Gibbons for all the Ordinaries of the United States, 15 March, 1895, and has since been periodically renewed.[71] However, in 1932, the Apostolic Delegation advised the Ordinaries that it is the desire of the Holy See that in future the Ordinaries apply individually and directly to the Holy See for each renewal.[72] Consequently it is now subject to some variation according to the terms of the petition or of the

---

[68] S. C. Conc., 13 Nov., 1937; *AAS*, 30–160; *Digest*, II, p. 362.

[69] S. C. Conc., 18 Jan., 1936; *AAS*, 29–343; *Digest*, II, p. 391.

[70] Code Com., 24 Nov., 1920; *AAS*, 12–576; *Digest*, I, p. 588.

[71] For the text as originally granted, see *Digest*, I, p. 591, or *Ecclesiastical Review*, Vol. 12, p. 425.

[72] See *Digest*, II, p. 364.

indult granted to various Ordinaries. The following notes refer to
the original text.

a. It applies to *abstinence* only, and gives to each Ordinary the
faculty to permit to workingmen and their families the use of flesh
meat on days of abstinence, with the exception of Fridays, Ash
Wednesday, the entire time of Holy Week, and the Vigil of
Christmas.

b. There has been considerable discussion as to whether workingmen (*operarii*) include professional men, priests, office workers, etc.
From the meaning of the term itself and from interpretations given
to it by the Holy See in other connections, we think it applies only
to manual workers.[73] This interpretation is confirmed at least by certain
diocesan *ordos* which we know of.

c. The families of workingmen are explicitly included. Hence if
the breadwinner of the family (husband, wife, son, daughter) is a
working person, the whole family enjoys the indult.

d. Do members of the family profit from the indult when they
eat away from home? Some deny this, but we have seen no argument in support of the negative opinion. The language of the indult
is explicit: *"non tantum operariis sed etiam eorum familiis, ita ut
omnia eorundem membra de indulto participent."* However, if a
member of the family other than the breadwinner is living permanently apart from the family, the reason for including such member
in the benefit of the indult would disappear.

e. The exemption from abstinence under this indult applies to all
meals, so that a person *who is not bound by the law of fast* could
eat meat at all meals.

2. *The Saturday-Wednesday Indult.* Bishops of the United States
have for some time enjoyed also an indult empowering them to
transfer the Lenten abstinence from Saturdays to Wednesdays during
Lent. This indult is now to be applied for by the individual Ordinaries
for their respective dioceses. Consequently it also is subject to change
according to the terms of the grant in each case. If, as is the case
in certain dioceses, the Ordinary does not ask for the power to
transfer the obligation of abstinence from Saturday to Wednesday in
Holy Week, or does not actually make that transfer, then Wednesday
of Holy Week is not a day of fast or abstinence, and Holy Saturday
is such a day until after noon only. If the transfer is made for all

---

[73] Cf. S. Paen., 9 March, 1925, *AAS*, 17–327; *Digest*, II, p. 225.

Wednesdays of Lent, the Wednesday of Holy Week becomes a day of fast and abstinence.[74]

3. *The War Indult.* An indult during the war empowers all Ordinaries of places, of whatever rite, to give a general dispensation in their respective territories from the law of fast and abstinence. Two days are, however, excepted: for the faithful of the Latin rite, Ash Wednesday and Good Friday; for the faithful of other rites, two days to be determined by their Ordinaries. Cf. S. C. for Extraordinary Ecclesiastical Affairs, 19 Dec., 1941; *AAS,* 33–516; *Digest,* II, p. 363. The duration of this indult has since been extended indefinitely by the Holy See (*donec aliter provideatur*) by an indult of the S. C. Conc., 22 Jan., 1946; *AAS,* 37, p. 173.

4. *Military Faculties.* The Military Faculties for the United States provide: "You and your subjects *are dispensed by the Holy See* from the law of fast and abstinence on all days of the year, except the Vigil of Christmas, Ash Wednesday, Good Friday, and Holy Saturday until noon." The subjects referred to include: men in active military service either of the Federal Government or of particular states; the wives, children, relatives and servants of the men of the armed forces who reside in the same house with them; all civilians staying within the limits of the military reservation; all religious — both men and sisters — also others, even lay persons, who are attached to military hospitals; all priests who are subjects of the Military Vicar by reason of service with the armed forces. This dispensation is not limited to the duration of the war.[75]

Subjects of the Law of Fast and Abstinence. All persons who have completed their seventh year are bound by the law of abstinence (c. 1254, § 1). All persons from the completion of their twenty-first to the beginning of their sixtieth year are bound by the law of fast (c. 1254, § 2). The law of fast is the same for women as for men.[76]

CASES AND QUESTIONS

1. An international diplomatic conference is in session in San Francisco; the city is crowded to capacity with delegates and visitors. Can the Bishop dispense the whole diocese from fast and abstinence during the conference?

---

[74] See *Digest,* II, p. 361.
[75] See Military Faculties, first paragraph, *Digest,* II, p. 587, and Part I, n. 25, *Digest,* II, p. 603.
[76] Code Com., 13 Jan., 1918; *Digest,* I, p. 593.

(C. 1245, § 2). Can the Vicar General do the same? (Cc. 198, § 1, 368, § 1). Would a clerical exempt religious house in the diocese benefit from such a dispensation given by the Bishop? (C. 620). Could the local superior of such a house give the dispensation for his entire community? (C. 1245, § 3).

2. A visitor from a European country where the common law is in force is in the United States on the Feast of Corpus Christi. Is he obliged to attend Mass? (C. 14, § 1, 3°). Would a resident of the United States, while in the same European country, be obliged on that day? (C. 14, § 1, 3°).

3. In the parish of St. Mechtilde a new church is under construction, and the school basement is being used as a provisional church; it has not been blessed as a church or oratory. Do the people satisfy the precept by hearing Mass there? (C. 1249 and text, c. 1171).

4. John, twelve years old, son of a machinist, attends a Catholic high school and carries his lunch from home. The Workingmen's Indult has been applied in the diocese by the Bishop. John's mother wonders whether she can put in a meat sandwich for John's lunch on the Wednesdays of Lent.

5. In a city where the Workingmen's Indult is in effect, a Catholic high school, which conducts a cafeteria for the students, serves, at one price, only a regular meal which includes meat. No change is made for Wednesdays of Lent. "These days," says the principal, "everybody is working at something; our boys are practically all from workingmen's families."

6. Michael, a pilot in the air force, is on furlough for two weeks at home with his wife and baby. Is he dispensed from abstinence on Friday? Is his wife dispensed while he is at home? (Military Faculties, Digest, II, pp. 587, 603).

7. A priest of a regular order is "on supply" for a week only at a military camp; he has obtained no special delegation of faculties from the military chaplain. Is he dispensed from Friday abstinence while in camp? (Military Faculties, first paragraph, n. 2; Digest, II, p. 587, and Part I, n. 25; Digest, II, p. 603).

8. You have as traveling companions on a Pullman two Catholic laymen who happen to be lawyers. They get into a discussion as to the observance of abstinence on Wednesday of Holy Week. One says: "I think it is a day of abstinence." The other says: "I don't think so, at least in our diocese." They refer the issue to you. Would you settle it by a categorical "answer"? Could you perhaps clarify the discussion by pointing out its juridical basis?

Readings:

Guiniven, *The Precept of Hearing Mass*, Cath. U., 1942; *Clergy Review*, Vol. 10, p. 229 (on dispensing power of parish priest); *Ecclesiastical Review*: Vol. 13, p. 295; Vol. 14, p. 474; Vol. 16, p. 432; Vol. 29, p. 61; Vol.

36, p. 304; Vol. 53, p. 329; Vol. 54, pp. 209, 211; Vol. 62, p. 309; Vol. 80, p. 187; Vol. 82, p. 295 (on Workingmen's Indult); Vol. 86, p. 426; Vol. 89, p. 286 (on pastor's power to dispense from fast, abstinence); Vol. 83, p. 539 (reasons excusing from fast); *Irish Ecclesiastical Record,* Vol. 41, p. 534 (meaning of *operarii*); *Periodica,* Vol. 16, p. 271* (Vermeersch) and Vol. 19, p. 124* (Jombart and Vermeersch), on hearing Mass on board ship; Vol. 22, p. 60* (Vermeersch, *de frustulo et coenula quadragesimali*); Vol. 22, p. 141* (Mostaza, can Bishop forbid hearing Mass in semipublic oratory?); Vol. 28, p. 52 (*de satisfactione praecepti ab audientibus Missam ex licentia Ordinarii extra oratorium celebratam*).

CHAPTER XVII

DIVINE WORSHIP

Section 1. General Principles (cc. 1255-1264)

PRELIMINARY SURVEY

Degrees and Kinds of Worship (c. 1255)
Public and Private Worship (c. 1256)
Exclusive Authority of Holy See Over Liturgical Worship
(c. 1257)
Co-operation in Worship With Non-Catholics (c. 1258)
Authority of the Ordinary (c. 1259)
Ministers of Worship Subject to Ecclesiastical Authority
(c. 1260)
Vigilance of Ordinaries Regarding Worship (c. 1261)
Norms for Persons Assisting at Worship (cc. 1262, 1263)
Sacred Music and Singing (c. 1264)

Degrees and Kinds of Worship. The worship which is due to the Most Holy Trinity, to each of the Divine Persons, to our Lord Jesus Christ, even under the Sacramental Species, is *cultus latriae;* that which is due to the Blessed Virgin Mary is *cultus hyperduliae;* that which is due to others who reign with Christ in heaven is *cultus duliae* (c. 1255, § 1). To sacred relics and images also there is due a veneration and worship which is relative to the person to whom the relics and images refer (c. 1255, § 2).

1. Worship (*cultus*) in general means the manifestation of submission toward another in recognition of his excellence. It contains three acts: an act of the intellect recognizing the worthiness of the object of worship; an act of the will commanding submission because of that excellence; and an external act expressing the submission. If the excellence of the person to whom the worship is given is uncreated, you have the highest kind of worship, adoration in the strict sense, *cultus latriae,* which is due to God alone; if the excellence of the person is a created but altogether singular excellence, the worship is *cultus hyperduliae,* which in Catholic practice is given to the Blessed

643

Virgin because of her singular privileges especially as Mother of God; if the excellence of the person is of a lesser degree than this, the worship is *cultus duliae,* which is due to the saints and angels.

2. If an object is worshiped because of an excellence which is its own, the worship is called *absolute;* if on the other hand an object is worshiped because of the excellence of some other object with which the first object has a moral connection, the worship is *relative.* The excellence of an object of worship can be *its own* in two senses: by identity, that is, by the very inherent form (essence) of the object itself; or by a substantial union with another object.

3. The extended discussion of these fundamental distinctions pertains to dogmatic theology; but a few examples may illustrate them briefly:

a. Cultus latriae: absolute — to the Most Holy Trinity, to each of the Divine Persons, to Christ our Lord, to Christ under the Sacramental Species, to the Sacred Humanity of Christ or to any part of it, for example, the Sacred Heart (because of its *own* excellence in the second sense mentioned above, by *substantial union* with the Word of God); *relative* — to an image or relic of Christ, for example, a picture of the Sacred Heart, a relic of the true Cross, any crucifix representing Christ.

b. Cultus hyperduliae: absolute — to the Blessed Virgin herself; *relative* — to an image, statue, shrine of the Blessed Virgin.

c. Cultus duliae: absolute — to any of the saints or angels in heaven; *relative* — to any image, relic, or shrine of a saint.

Public and Private Worship. If worship is offered in the name of the Church by persons lawfully deputed for this function and through acts which, by institution of the Church are to be offered only to God, and the saints and blessed, the worship is *public;* otherwise, it is *private* (c. 1256).

There is a latent difficulty in this canon. According to the literal text it would seem to lay down *three* conditions which must be verified *together* in order that worship be public; and the canon is understood in this sense by several authors.[1] Yet, if it is understood in this sense, this canon is very difficult to reconcile with certain other canons which treat of public worship, notably canons 2057 and 1283, § 1. Moreover, the document cited as a footnote to canon 1256 suggests a different interpretation which is reasonable and also consistent with

[1] Cf. A Coronata, II, n. 831.

the term "public worship" as used in other parts of the Code. In that document, Benedict XIV says: "It is beyond doubt that those acts partake also of the nature of public worship, which are done privately, if they are of the kind which have been instituted by the Church for showing solemn veneration toward the Blessed or the Saints; and the acts above mentioned were of this kind."[2] Now, the acts of which there was question, were done by private persons who were in no way "deputed by the Church"; and the same is true of acts of public worship which are forbidden by canon 1283, § 1, and of those which are to be investigated according to canon 2057. Consequently, we think the true meaning of canon 1256, in the light of its sources and of other parts of the Code, is as follows. Public worship has two forms. It is public: (1) if it is offered in the name of the Church by persons lawfully deputed for that function; and (2) if it is offered by anyone (even by private persons in no way deputed for it) through acts which, by institution of the Church, are to be offered only to God, and the saints and blessed.[3] Such acts are: placing on the altar an image of the person to be venerated; depicting a person with an aureola or halo; placing a votive offering at their grave; keeping a lighted candle before their relics or exposing the same for public veneration, etc.

Exclusive Authority of the Holy See Over Liturgical Worship. It pertains exclusively to the Holy See to control the sacred liturgy and to approve liturgical books (c. 1257). Various definitions are given of *liturgy:* the order of worshiping God by public action of the Church (Vermeersch-Creusen); the public and ritual worship of God (Hanssens); the ecclesiastical ordination of public worship (Callewaert).[4] It may be divided into *latreutical* liturgy (concerning the Holy Sacrifice of the Mass and sacred functions), and *sacramental* liturgy (concerning the sacraments). A distinction may also be made between the *liturgy* itself, of which the Code does not treat as a whole (cf. c. 2), and the *law of liturgy,* which is to some extent included in the very canons which we are considering. The principal liturgical books are: *The Roman Missal, The Roman Breviary, The Roman Martyrology, The Roman Pontifical, The Bishop's Ceremonial* (for Bishop's functions), *The Roman Ceremonial* (for functions of the Papal Chapel),

---

[2] Benedict XIV, Const., *Quamvis iusto,* 30 Apr., 1749, § 12; *Fontes,* n. 398, II, p. 230.
[3] Cf. Vermeersch-Creusen, *Epit.,* II, n. 574; Claeys-Bouuaert-Simenon, *Manuale,* III, n. 69, p. 60; De Meester, *Compendium,* III, n. 1248, p. 147, note 4; Beste, *Introductio in Codicem,* p. 612.
[4] Cf. Hanssens, in *Gregorianum* (1927), p. 204.

The Roman Ritual, The Memoriale Rituum (Benedict XIII, 1725, promulgated for the Universal Church by Pius VII, 1825), *The Propria Officiorum et Missarum* (the *"ordo"* for a diocese, or religious order or congregation), *The Instructio Clementina* (regulating the Forty Hours' devotion), and the officially published *Collection of Decrees of the S. C. of Rites.*

Co-operation in Worship With Non-Catholics. It is illicit for Catholics in any way to assist actively or take part in sacred worship of non-Catholics (c. 1258, § 1). Passive or merely material presence, for the sake of civil courtesy, duty, or respect, for a grave reason which in case of doubt should have the approval of the Bishop may be tolerated, at the funerals, weddings, and other such celebrations of non-Catholics, provided there is no danger of perversion or of scandal (c. 1258, § 2).

1. *Active participation.* A person would participate actively in the worship of non-Catholics if, besides being physically present in the place where such worship was being conducted, he placed some positive act of worship in common with the non-Catholic worshipers. Such co-operation would be *formal* if it were done with the intention of really taking part in the worship; it would be merely *material* if done without that intention but for some other reason, for example, mere civility or friendship. *All active participation* is forbidden by the first paragraph of this canon, whether it be formal or merely material.

2. *Passive presence.* The second paragraph speaks of "merely passive or material presence." A person is passively present if he is present without joining in any positive act of worship; his presence is voluntary, but he abstains from any positive action. It is conceivable that even merely passive presence might be accompanied by an internal intention to approve, assent to, or encourage the non-Catholic worship; if that were true it would be formal co-operation in an evil act, and forbidden by the natural law. The canon supposes that this is not the case, and consequently that the passive presence is merely material. Even then such presence is not simply permitted because, though not intrinsically wrong by reason of its object (the thing done) it is likely to be wrong by reason of its circumstances or consequences. Hence three conditions are laid down for its licitness: (1) that there be a grave reason based on considerations of civil courtesy, duty, or respect; (2) that in case of doubt the sufficiency of the reason be approved by the Bishop; (3) that there be no danger either of perversion or

scandal. The functions at which such presence is then permitted are given by way of example, "funerals, weddings, and other similar celebrations." Applications of this canon are very numerous and varied; their discussion pertains rather to moral theology.[5]

Authority of the Ordinary. Prayers and exercises of piety are not to be permitted in churches or oratories without the revision and express permission of the Ordinary of the place, who in difficult cases shall refer the whole matter to the Holy See (c. 1259, § 1).

1. Since, as we have seen, all sacred rites and sacred worship in general are permitted by the common law in churches (c. 1171) and even in semipublic oratories (c. 1193) the present canon refers only to prayers which are not yet approved, and to exercises of piety which are not yet in common use.

2. If there is question of a semipublic oratory of a clerical exempt religious institute, the revision of the prayers and the permission for the exercises of piety would seem to pertain to the religious Ordinary (major superior). For such prayers and exercises are not in the fullest sense "public"; and the present canon does not expressly derogate from the general rule of exemption stated in canon 615.[6]

The Ordinary of the place cannot approve new litanies for public recitation (c. 1259, § 2). This refers to public recitation only; but the recitation of a litany is public, even without the intervention of a priest or ecclesiastical minister, if it is done "by a number of persons together in a church or public oratory."[7] New litanies are any not yet approved for public recitation. Those approved are the litanies: of the Saints, of the Holy Name, of Loretto, of the Sacred Heart, of St. Joseph, for the dying (Roman Ritual, *Ordo commendationis animae*).

Ministers of Worship Subject to Ecclesiastical Authority. In the exercise of worship the ministers of the Church must depend exclusively on ecclesiastical superiors (c. 1260). One of the documents cited in the footnotes to this canon is the Encyclical *Iamdudum,* of Pius X, in which the Holy Father exposes and protests against the iniquitous anticlerical laws of Portugal during the years immediately preceding (1906-1910).[8] It is a useful study of the methods and incredible

---

[5] For a fuller explanation of this canon and a study of its sources, see Bouscaren, in *Theological Studies*, Vol. 3, pp. 475-512.
[6] Cf. Vermeersch-Creusen, *Epit.*, II, n. 579.
[7] Cf. S. C. Rit., *Decr. Auth.*, nn. 3555, 3820, 3916, 3981.
[8] Pius X, 24 May, 1911; *Fontes*, n. 692, III, p. 794.

effrontery of the attacks against the Church which have been set in motion more than once under the guise of a false liberalism. The present canon is a declaration of independence on behalf of the Church, which will never be retracted.

Vigilance of Ordinaries Regarding Worship. Ordinaries of places must be watchful that the provisions of the sacred canons regarding divine worship be sedulously observed, and especially that, in divine worship whether public or private or in the daily life of the faithful, no superstitious practice be introduced, and that nothing be admitted which is foreign to the faith, or out of harmony with ecclesiastical tradition, or has the appearance of base profit seeking **(c. 1261, § 1).** If the Ordinary of the place makes any laws for his territory in this matter, all religious including those who are exempt are obliged to observe them; and the Ordinary can visit their churches or public oratories for this purpose **(c. 1261, § 2).**

1. The object of this vigilance and visitation of the Ordinary of the place is threefold; he is to see to it: (*a*) that the canons on divine worship be observed; (*b*) that no superstitious practice be introduced; (*c*) that nothing be admitted which is foreign to faith, or inconsistent with tradition, or which savors of profit seeking. The Holy Office in 1937 appealed to the Bishops to be very vigilant against certain unworthy new forms of devotion; particular mention was made of "images which are theologically false . . . superstition in the invocation of Saints and in the use of sacred images . . . and new forms of worship and devotion, often enough ridiculous, usually useless imitations or corruptions of similar ones which are already legitimately established."[9] The Holy Office has also decided that a special devotion to the Sacred Head of our Lord is not to be introduced;[10] and also that it is not allowed to encourage among the faithful the forms of devotion commonly called the *devotion to the annihilated love of Jesus,* and the *Rosary of the Most Sacred Wounds of Our Lord Jesus Christ.*[11] A decree of the S. C. of the Council on the publication of favors and offerings in certain pious papers stated that "the way in which these heavenly favors are reported, namely, in ill-considered words and without the slightest proof of their authenticity, cannot be approved, especially since the favor received is often reported

---

[9] Holy Office, 26 May, 1937; *AAS*, 29–304; *Digest*, II, p. 372.
[10] Holy Office, 18 June, 1938; *AAS*, 30–226; *Digest*, II, p. 397.
[11] Holy Office, 12 Dec., 1939; *AAS*, 32–24; *Digest*, II, p. 400.

as being connected with the money offering, as if one depended upon the other." Ordinaries were urged to be strict in the censorship of such papers.[12]

2. As to the visitation of the churches of regulars by the Ordinary of the place, the Code Commission declared: (a) that where the diocesan laws do not contain new matter as contemplated by canon 1261, but merely urge existing ecclesiastical laws, the Ordinary cannot make a visitation; and (b) that, generally speaking, the Ordinary may use his right of visitation only in as far as he has positive information that the particular laws enacted by him are not being observed in the churches of exempt regulars.[13]

Norms for Persons Assisting at Worship. *Men and women.* It is to be desired that, in accordance with the ancient practice, women in church should be separated from men (c. 1262, § 1). Men while assisting at sacred rites whether in the church or outside should have their heads uncovered, unless the approved practice among the people or special circumstances demand the contrary; women should have their heads covered and should be modestly dressed, especially when they approach the Holy Table (c. 1262, § 2).

Popular customs may modify this provision as the text indicates. In China the custom among men of keeping the head covered in sign of respect was so general that in 1883 the Sacred Congregation of Propaganda even tolerated the practice of allowing a priest to wear a cap while celebrating Mass.[14] As to the modesty in women's dress, the S. C. of the Council issued an instruction in 1930.[15]

Special places in church. A separate place in church may be reserved for public officials according to their dignity and station, and in accordance with liturgical laws (c. 1263, § 1). Without the express consent of the Ordinary of the place, none of the faithful may have a special place in church reserved for himself and his family; and the Ordinary should not give his consent unless sufficient provision is made for the convenience of the rest of the faithful (c. 1263, § 2). Concessions of this kind are always subject to the tacit condition that the Ordinary can, for just cause, revoke the concession no matter how long it has been in effect (c. 1263, § 3). Paragraph 2 does not forbid the use of pews, to be rented and reserved for the pewholders. It refers

---

[12] S. C. Conc., 7 June, 1932; *AAS*, 24–240; *Digest*, I, p. 596.
[13] Code Com., 8 Apr., 1924; *Digest*, II, p. 374.
[14] S. C. Prop. Fid., 18 Oct., 1883; *Collectanea*, n. 1606, ad XVI.
[15] S. C. Conc., 12 Jan., 1930; *AAS*, 22–26; *Digest*, I, p. 212.

rather to a fixed place in the church, for example, the Lady Chapel, which a person or family might wish to occupy regularly as of right.

Sacred Music and Singing. Music, whether instrumental, from the organ or other instruments, or vocal, in which there is any tinge of the lascivious or impure, must be entirely excluded from churches; and the liturgical laws regarding sacred music must be observed (**c. 1264, § 1).** Religious women, if they are permitted by their own constitutions or the liturgical laws, with the permission of the Ordinary of the place, to sing in their own church or oratory, are to do so from a place where they cannot be viewed by the people (**c. 1264, § 2).**

1. All that is lascivious or impure must be excluded. To judge of such a defect in instrumental music requires some discernment. Anything suggestive of a dancing measure is not necessarily lascivious, though the documents would seem to disfavor such music also as profane and little suited to express the beauty of the liturgy.

2. Liturgical laws regarding sacred music are to be observed. The most fundamental modern document on the subject is the *Motu proprio* of Pius X, which demands especially three qualities in sacred music: it must be *sacred,* it must be *artistic,* and it must be *universal.* It must be sacred because it is designed to express realities whose sacredness is supreme; and it must be a true specimen of sacred art. Every art is designed to express beauty in some form; the beauty which the liturgy must strive to express with the aid of all the arts is God Himself, who is Beauty Substantial, Eternal, Infinite.[16] Pius XI reaffirmed the provisions of this *Motu proprio,* and made further recommendations to the Bishops for the cultivation of both Gregorian chant and polyphonic music.[17]

3. The *Motu proprio* of Pius X was quite severe in excluding women from all part in liturgical singing (n. 13). However, the S. C. of Rites has since shown the mind of the Holy See to be rather lenient in yielding partly to local customs in this matter. A decree addressed to the Archbishop of New York in 1908 permits women to sing in church choirs, but requires that women and girl choristers occupy a separate place from the men and boys.[18]

---

[16] Cf. Pius X, *Motu proprio,* 22 Nov., 1903; *Fontes,* n. 654, III, p. 608.
[17] Pius XI, 20 Dec., 1928; *AAS,* 21–33; summary in *Digest,* I, p. 598.
[18] S. C. Rit., 18 Dec., 1908; *Decr. Auth.,* n. 4231.

Section 2. Custody and Worship of the Most Blessed Sacrament (cc. 1265–1275)

PRELIMINARY SURVEY

Places Where the Most Blessed Sacrament Is to Be Kept
(cc. 1265–1269)
Manner of Keeping the Most Blessed Sacrament
(cc. 1270–1272)
Eucharistic Worship (cc. 1273 1275)

Places Where the Blessed Sacrament Must or May Be Kept. The Most Blessed Eucharist, provided there is someone to take care of it, and provided that a priest regularly says Mass in the sacred place at least once a week:

1. *Must* be kept in the cathedral church, in the principal church of an Abbacy or Prelacy *nullius,* and of a Vicariate or Prefecture Apostolic, in every parochial or quasi-parochial church, and in a church attached to a house of exempt religious whether of men or of women.

2. It *may* be kept, with the permission of the Ordinary of the place, in a collegiate church, and in the principal oratory, whether it be public or semipublic, of a pious or religious house and of an ecclesiastical college conducted by secular clerics or religious (c. 1265, § 1).

In order that the Blessed Eucharist may be kept in other churches or oratories, an Apostolic indult is required; the Ordinary of the place can grant this permission only for a church or public oratory for a just cause and *per modum actus* (c. 1265, § 2).

No one is permitted to keep the Most Blessed Eucharist in his possession or to carry it with him on a journey (c. 1265, § 3).

Notes. 1. The first paragraph speaks of the condition that the priest must say Mass at least once a week "in the sacred place"; yet the place need not be sacred in the strict sense, since a semipublic oratory need not necessarily be blessed (c. 1196, § 2).

2. The one who takes care of the Blessed Sacrament may be a lay person, provided a priest be responsible for the key.[19]

3. A collegiate church is one which has a canonically erected college or chapter of clerics; but an ecclesiastical "college" means simply a house of residence under the control of the Church, for young men

---

[19] S. C. Sacr., 26 May, 1938; *AAS*, 30–198; *Digest*, II, p. 377.

who are being educated for the clerical or religious life. (See Vermeersch-Creusen, *Epit.*, Vol. II, n. 589, p. 412.)

4. The Blessed Sacrament *need* not be kept in an *oratory* attached to a house of exempt religious; the canon mentions only churches.

5. It would seem that Bishops need an Apostolic indult to keep the Blessed Sacrament in their chapels; but the Apostolic Delegates have this privilege in their faculties.[20]

6. The power of Ordinaries to permit keeping the Blessed Sacrament might *per accidens* be extended to a semipublic oratory, e.g., in an urgent case (c. 81), or where the permission is granted temporarily, with due precautions, for a semipublic oratory which is being used provisionally in place of a church.

Churches to Be Open. Churches in which the Most Blessed Eucharist is kept, especially parish churches, must be open to the people every day at least for some hours (c. 1266).

Only in the Principal Oratory: Never in a Monastery of Nuns. Every privilege to the contrary being revoked, the Most Blessed Eucharist may not be kept in a religious or pious house, except either in the church or in the principal oratory; nor in the case of nuns can it be kept in the choir or within the walls of the monastery (c. 1267). The last provision refers only to a monastery of nuns who are under strict papal cloister; the reason is that in such case a priest would not have access to the place where the Blessed Sacrament is kept.

Interpretation. The Code Commission gave the following interpretation: "The meaning of canon 1267 is this: if a house of religion or piety is connected with a public church and makes use of it for its ordinary daily exercises of piety, the Blessed Sacrament may be kept there only; otherwise it may be kept in the principal oratory of the said house of religion or piety (without prejudice to the right of the church if there is one), and nowhere else, unless in the same material building there are distinct and separate families, so that formally they constitute distinct houses of religion or piety."[21] Thus, if a novitiate is under the same roof with other departments of a religious house, and has a secondary chapel, it is not forbidden that the Blessed Sacrament be kept there as well as in the principal chapel of the house.

Place for the Blessed Sacrament in the Church. The Most Blessed Eucharist may not be kept constantly or habitually in more than one altar of the same church (c. 1268, § 1). It should be kept in the most

---

[20] Cf. Vermeersch-Creusen, *Epit.*, II, n. 589.
[21] Code Com., 3 June, 1918; *AAS*, 10–346; *Digest*, I, p. 600.

distinguished and honorable place in the church, and hence as a rule at the main altar unless some other be considered more convenient and suitable for the veneration and worship due to so great a Sacrament, observing the provisions of liturgical laws as to the three last days of Holy Week (c. 1268, § 2). But in cathedral, collegiate, or conventual churches, in which choral services are to be celebrated at the main altar, in order that ecclesiastical offices may not be interfered with, it is advisable that the Most Blessed Eucharist be not kept at the main altar, but in another chapel or altar (c. 1268, § 3). Rectors of churches should see to it that the altar at which the Most Blessed Sacrament is kept be more beautifully adorned than any other, so that by its very appointments it may the more effectively move the faithful to piety and devotion (c. 1268, § 4).

If the Blessed Sacrament is exposed for perpetual adoration at the main altar, it is to be kept in a tabernacle at another altar for the Communion of the faithful.[22] The prohibition against keeping the Blessed Sacrament at more than one altar in the same church is modified by the words "continuo seu habitualiter"; it is not forbidden to do this temporarily for some transient reason, in order to give Communion to the faithful more conveniently. After the Mass of Holy Thursday, one Host is kept in the repository, which is apart from the main altar. At that time also, until the Mass of Holy Saturday, the Blessed Sacrament should be kept also in some other place for the Communion of the faithful. This matter is regulated in detail by an instruction of the S. C. of the Sacraments.[23]

Structure and Custody of the Tabernacle. The Most Blessed Sacrament must be kept in an immovable tabernacle set in the middle of the altar (c. 1269, § 1). The tabernacle must be well constructed, solidly enclosed on all sides, properly adorned according to liturgical laws, empty of all other objects, and must be so carefully guarded that all danger of sacrilegious profanation shall be precluded (c. 1269, § 2). For a grave reason approved by the Ordinary of the place, it is not forbidden to keep the Blessed Sacrament during the night outside the altar, but on a corporal, and in a safe and suitable place, observing the provision of canon 1271 (regarding the tabernacle lamp) (c. 1269, § 3). The key of the tabernacle in which the Most Blessed Sacrament is kept must be most carefully guarded, and this is a grave

---

[22] S. C. Rit., 18 May, 1878; *Decr. Auth.*, n. 3449.
[23] S. C. Sacr., 26 March, 1929; *AAS*, 21–631; *Digest*, I, p. 353.

obligation in conscience upon the priest who has charge of the church or oratory **(c. 1269, § 4).**

The best commentary both on the meaning and importance of these provisions is the recent instruction of the S. C. of the Sacraments. Without adding anything really new to the law, it lays down practical norms of great value regarding the structure of the tabernacle, the custody of the key, the precautions (including the installation of burglar alarms) to be taken against theft; and concludes by urging four *precepts* upon the Ordinaries of places, as follows: (1) in their visitation, they are to investigate this matter and order obedience to the law, under penalty; (2) in case of sacrilege, an informative process is to be instituted against the pastor or priest, whether secular or religious (even exempt) who was nominally responsible; the record is to be sent to the S. C. of the Sacraments with the recommendation of the Ordinary; (3) they are to consider the gravity of the penalty provided by canon 2382 against a pastor who is gravely negligent in this matter; and they are given the necessary faculties to inflict these penalties cumulatively with religious superiors even upon exempt religious; but the informative process is always reserved to the Bishop; (4) finally, they are to inquire into any privileges of keeping the Blessed Sacrament, which may be claimed by Apostolic grant, and Bishops can in a proper case revoke such privileges, where they find either that grave abuses have occurred or that all the requisite conditions for the safe custody of the Blessed Sacrament are not being observed.[24] A recent decree of the S. C. of the Sacraments makes special provisions for the custody of the Blessed Sacrament in air-raid shelters or in a protected basement of the Church, when there is danger of bombardment.[25]

The Ciborium for the Consecrated Hosts. The consecrated Particles, sufficient in number to provide for Communion for the sick and the rest of the faithful, shall always be kept in a ciborium made of solid and suitable material, which shall be clean and well closed with a cover, and draped with a veil of white silk, which may be ornamented **(c. 1270).** A ciborium is not to be consecrated; it should, however, be blessed, though because of a *dubium iuris* not even this seems to be required of strict obligation. The formula is in the Roman Ritual. Glass, wood, are not sufficiently solid materials; iron, lead, brass, stone are commonly considered unsuitable. Copper, gilded on the inside,

---

[24] S. C. Sacr., 26 May, 1938; *AAS*, 30–198; *Digest*, II, p. 377.
[25] S. C. Sacr., 15 Sept., 1943; *AAS*, 35–282; *The Jurist*, Vol. 4, p. 318.

is admitted, and even the gilding is not strictly required. Silver and gold are, of course, appropriate. It is a laudable practice, not of strict obligation, that the ciborium containing the Sacred Hosts should rest on a corporal inside the tabernacle.

The Tabernacle Lamp. Before the tabernacle in which the Most Blessed Sacrament is kept, at least one lamp is to be kept burning constantly day and night from olive oil or beeswax; where olive oil cannot be had, it is within the prudent discretion of the Ordinary of the place to allow as substitutes for it other oils, of vegetable origin if possible (c. 1271).

1. "Before the altar," that is, near it, and either in front or to the side, not on the altar nor behind it. It is tolerated that the lamp be of colored glass (red or green). It may be on a stand, or hung from the ceiling, or held on a bracket from the wall.

2. Electric light instead of an oil lamp has never been permitted permanently, but only as a last resort for lack of oil or beeswax. In 1942 the S. C. of Rites reviewed the earlier decrees on this matter, and again committed it to the prudence of Ordinaries, "so that, while the peculiar ordinary or extraordinary circumstances of the present war continue, wherever olive oil or beeswax are either entirely lacking or cannot be obtained without grave inconvenience and expense, the lamp before the Blessed Sacrament may be maintained with other oils, vegetable if possible, and in the last resort even electric light may be used."[26] The Archbishops and Bishops of Quebec authorized the use of mineral oils or their extracts, such as paraffin.[27]

Hosts to Be Fresh and Frequently Renewed. The consecrated Hosts, both for the Communion of the faithful and for the exposition of the Most Blessed Sacrament, shall be fresh and shall be frequently renewed, the old ones being properly consumed, so that there be no danger of corruption; and the instructions which the Ordinary of the place may make in this regard shall be faithfully observed (c. 1272). The S. C. of the Sacraments condemned the practice of using hosts which are two or three months old.[28] The S. C. of Rites refused to approve the practice of renewing the hosts only once or twice a month, and referred to the Bishops' Ceremonial, which requires renovation once a week.[29] However, it is generally admitted that, in the absence of any danger of corruption, to renew them every two

[26] S. C. Rit., 13 March, 1942; *AAS*, 34–112; *Digest*, II, p. 390.
[27] Cf. *The Jurist*, Vol. 3, p. 158.
[28] S. C. Sacr., 7 Dec., 1918; *AAS*, 11–8; *Digest*, I, p. 352.
[29] S. C. Rit., *Decr. Auth.*, n. 3621.

weeks is sufficient. The latest instruction on the subject by the S. C. of the Sacraments merely cites the canon, without determining the time more precisely.[30]

Promotion of Eucharistic Devotion. Those who are engaged in the religious training of the faithful should make every effort to encourage in them devotion to the Most Blessed Eucharist, and should especially exhort them to assist at the Holy Sacrifice of the Mass and to visit the Most Blessed Sacrament not only on Sundays and holy-days of obligation, but also frequently during the week (c. 1273).

Exposition of the Blessed Sacrament. In churches or oratories which have the right to keep the Most Blessed Sacrament, private exposition, that is with the ciborium, may be had for any just cause without permission from the Ordinary; and public exposition, that is, with the *ostensorium,* can be had in all churches during Mass and at Vespers on the Feast of Corpus Christi and during its octave, but not at other times except for a just and grave cause, especially a public one, and with the permission of the Ordinary of the place, even though the church belong to an exempt religious institute (c. 1274, § 1). The minister of exposition and reposition of the Most Blessed Sacrament is a priest or deacon; but the minister of Eucharistic Benediction is only a priest; a deacon cannot give it except where, in accordance with canon 845, § 2, he has brought Viaticum to the sick (c. 1274, § 2).

Notes. 1. Exposition is *public* when the Blessed Sacrament is exposed in the *ostensorium; private,* when in the ciborium (and in this case the ciborium must not be withdrawn from the tabernacle and must remain covered with its veil). Public exposition includes Eucharistic benediction.[31]

2. Public exposition during Mass and Vespers on the Feast of Corpus Christi and during the octave (without any permission) is allowed only in *churches,* not in oratories, even public ones; and only in those churches which can keep the Blessed Sacrament.[32]

3. But at other times (for a just and grave cause and with the permission of the Ordinary of the place), public exposition may be had not only in churches but also in public and even semipublic oratories. The reason is that this was expressly permitted in the pre-Code law,[33] and the Code does not expressly derogate from the old rule.

---

[30] S. C. Sacr., 26 March, 1929; *AAS,* 21–631; *Digest,* I, p. 353.
[31] Code Com., 6 March, 1927; *AAS,* 19–161; *Digest,* I, p. 602.
[32] Code Com., 14 July, 1922; *AAS,* 14–529; *Digest,* I, p. 602.
[33] Cf. S. C. Rit., *Decr. Auth.,* nn. 1090, 3703.

4. May exempt regulars have benediction with the ostensorium in their own churches or oratories, but *with the doors closed,* without the permission of the Ordinary of the place, but with that of their own religious Ordinary? This is a disputed question. Before the Code, Cavalerius, Bouix, and Wernz[34] held the affirmative as at least probable. Several authors admit the probability of this opinion even since the Code,[35] on the ground that such exposition may still be considered private.

5. During the *month of October,* Leo XIII in 1885, ordered public exposition to be held every day with the recital of the Litanies and Rosary, in all *parish* churches. This decree remains in effect, since it is not expressly revoked. For this, therefore, no permission of the Ordinary of the place is needed.[36]

The Forty Hours' Devotion. The devotion of the Forty Hours must be held every year with as much solemnity as possible, on days to be determined with the consent of the Ordinary of the place, in all parish churches and in other churches in which the Blessed Sacrament is habitually kept; and if in any place, owing to peculiar circumstances, it cannot without grave inconvenience be held with the reverence due to so great a Sacrament, the Ordinary of the place shall see to it that on determined days the Most Blessed Sacrament be exposed in a solemn manner (c. 1275). For the study of ritual matters concerning the Forty Hours' devotion, several decrees must be consulted.[37]

Section 3. Worship of Saints, Images, Relics (cc. 1276–1289)

PRELIMINARY SURVEY

The Worship of Saints (cc. 1276–1278)
The Worship of Sacred Images (cc. 1279–1280)
The Worship of Sacred Relics (cc. 1281–1289)

General Principle: This Worship Is Good and Useful. It is a good and useful thing prayerfully to invoke the Servants of God who are

---

[34] *Ius Decretalium,* III, n. 553, note 235.
[35] Cf. Vermeersch-Creusen, *Epit.,* II, n. 599; Cappello, *De Sacramentis,* I, nn. 416, 417, VII; A Coronata, II, n. 853.
[36] Cf. Cappello, *De Sacramentis,* I, n. 417, V.
[37] Cf. *Instructio Clementina* (Clement XII, 1 Sept., 1731) in Appendix of *Decr. Auth.* S. C. Rit., Vol. III, p. 376, and commentary by Gardellini, *Decr. Auth.,* Vol. IV, pp. 3–138; S. C. Rit., 26 Feb., 1919; *AAS,* 11–142; *Digest,* I, p. 367; S. C. Rit., 27 Apr., 1927; *AAS,* 19–192; *Digest,* I, p. 375.

reigning with Christ, and to venerate their relics and images; but all the faithful should with filial devotion honor above all others the Blessed Virgin (c. 1276). This canon needs no commentary. There is scarcely any trait so universal and so deeply seated in human nature as the inclination to honor, not only persons who are powerful and loved and who are united to us by any genuine bond, but also their images and relics. To object to this practice in the supernatural order amounts practically to ignoring or denying the fact that there is a supernatural order. To invoke any particular one of the saints is here declared merely "good and useful"; but filial devotion to the Blessed Virgin is presented as *almost a precept,* and that for *all the faithful.*

Public Worship of Saints and Blessed. Only those servants of God may be honored with public worship, who are by authority of the Church numbered among the saints or blessed (c. 1277, § 1). The worship of *duliae* is due to those who are canonically recorded in the catalogue of the saints; saints may be honored in all places and by any acts which belong to that kind of worship; but the blessed may be honored only in the place and manner which the Roman Pontiff may have allowed (c. 1277, § 2).

1. The authority of the Church for canonization and also, under the present law, for beatification, is solely that of the Holy See.

2. The procedure for canonization and beatification is outlined in canons 1999–2141.

3. Canonized saints:

a. Are entitled to the worship of *duliae* (c. 1277, § 2);

b. May be invoked in public prayers of the Church; whereas it is not allowed to pray *for* them;

c. May have churches and altars erected in their honor (not so the blessed, without an Apostolic indult — cc. 1168, § 3, 1201, § 4);

d. May have the Holy Sacrifice of the Mass and the divine Office offered in their honor (as may also the blessed according to c. 1201, § 4);

e. May have a feast day in their honor;

f. May be represented with an aureola or halo as a token of glory;

g. May have their relics publicly exposed and honored in churches (which practice in the case of the blessed is limited by canon 1287, § 3);

h. May be chosen as heavenly patrons (not so the blessed without an Apostolic indult — c. 1278).[38]

Patron Saints. It is praiseworthy also, observing the norms that

---

[38] Cf. Wernz, *Ius Decretalium,* III, n. 367.

govern the matter, that patron saints of nations, dioceses, provinces, confraternities, religious institutes, and other localities and moral persons be chosen, and, upon confirmation by the Holy See, be constituted patrons; the blessed, however, cannot be so constituted without a special indult of the Holy See (c. 1278). The manner of choosing a patron saint has been briefly referred to in connection with canon 1247, § 2 (S.C.R., n. 526). Patron saints have also been constituted by the Holy See for various forms of apostolic work: St. Thomas Aquinas, patron of all Catholic schools; St. Camillus de Lellis, patron of hospitals; St. Vincent de Paul, patron of all charitable societies which owe their origin in any way to his influence; St. Peter Claver, patron of apostolic work for the Negroes; St. Francis Xavier and St. Theresa of the Infant Jesus, patrons of missionaries and missions; St. Ignatius of Loyola, patron of spiritual exercises.

Sacred Images. No one may place or cause to be placed in churches, even though they be exempt, or in other sacred places, any unusual image, unless it has been approved by the Ordinary of the place (c. 1279, § 1). And the Ordinary shall not approve of images to be exposed publicly for the veneration of the faithful, if they are not in conformity with the approved usage of the Church (c. 1279, § 2). The Ordinary shall never permit to be shown in churches or other sacred places, images which represent a false dogma, or which are not sufficiently decent and moral, or which would be an occasion of dangerous error to the unlearned (c. 1279, § 3). If images which are exposed for public veneration are solemnly blessed, this blessing is reserved to the Ordinary, who can, however, delegate it to any priest (c. 1279, § 4).

The Holy Office has declared that the Blessed Virgin may not be represented in priestly vestments, nor the Holy Spirit in human form, either with the Father and the Son or separately.[39] Sacred images need not be solemnly blessed; if they are so blessed, the blessing is reserved to the Ordinary, which means the religious Ordinary if the place where the picture is to be exposed belongs to clerical exempt religious (by analogy with canon 1156). The formula is in the Roman Ritual.

Precious Images. Images which are precious, that is, remarkable for antiquity, artistic value, or for the devotion toward them, and which are exposed for the veneration of the faithful in churches or public

---

[39] Holy Office, 8 Apr., 1916; *AAS*, 8–146, and 16 March, 1928; *AAS*, 20–103; *Digest*, I, p. 617.

oratories, if they need to be repaired, are never to be restored without the written consent of the Ordinary, who, before giving the permission, should consult prudent and competent experts **(c. 1280)**. Again, the Ordinary means the religious Ordinary if the place belongs to clerical exempt religious.

Alienation or Transfer of Distinguished Relics, Precious Images. Distinguished relics or precious images, and likewise all relics or images which are honored in any church with great devotion on the part of the people, cannot be validly alienated nor permanently transferred to another church without the permission of the Holy See **(c. 1281, § 1)**. Distinguished relics of the saints or blessed are the body, the head, the arm, the forearm, the heart, the tongue, the hand, the lower part of the leg (knee to ankle), or that part of the body in which a martyr suffered, provided it be entire and not small **(c. 1281, § 2)**.

Keeping Relics. Distinguished relics of the saints or blessed may not be kept in private houses or private oratories without the express permission of the Ordinary of the place **(c. 1282, § 1)**. Relics which are not distinguished may with due respect be kept also in private houses and may be piously worn by the faithful **(c. 1282, § 2)**. A complete summary classification of relics in point of dignity is the following: (*a*) relics *sui generis,* e.g., a relic of the True Cross, the Sacred Shroud (at Turin); (*b*) distinguished relics as defined above; (*c*) first-class relics, not distinguished, but pertaining to the body of the saint; (*d*) "relics" in the broad sense, an article which the saint used, or which has touched his body. We shall find special provisions regarding relics of the True Cross in canons 1287 and 1288.

Authentication of Relics. Only those relics may be honored with public worship in churches, even in the churches of exempt religious, which are certified as genuine by an authentic document from some Cardinal of the Holy Roman Church, or local Ordinary, or other ecclesiastic who has received the faculty to authenticate relics by Apostolic indult **(c. 1283, § 1)**. The Vicar General cannot, without a special mandate, declare the authenticity of relics **(c. 1283, § 2)**. The Code Commission has declared that the limitation upon the powers of the Vicar General applies: (1) to a relic which has been taken from one which was already authenticated; (2) to the giving of a new certificate of authenticity, or to the placing of a seal upon a relic.[40]

---

[40] Code Com., 17 July, 1933; *AAS*, 25–345; *Digest,* I, p. 603.

Ordinaries of places, if they know for certain that a relic is not authentic, shall prudently withdraw it from the devotion of the faithful. **(c. 1284).**

Renewal of Lost Certificate, Etc. Sacred relics whose certificate of authenticity has been lost through civil disturbances or by any other accident, are not to be exposed for public veneration without a previous decision by the Ordinary of the place; the Vicar General cannot make this decision without a special mandate **(c. 1285, § 1).** Ancient relics nevertheless are to be retained in that veneration which they theretofore received, unless it is clear from certain proof that they are false or supposititious **(c. 1285, § 2).**

Considering the historical fact of the plundering of churches and monasteries, it is not surprising that there has existed at certain times a traffic in false relics, and even in genuine ones. In 1892 the S. C. of Rites refused to permit relics to be exposed for public veneration without a document of authenticity, even though they were enclosed in their ancient reliquaries which might be identified as having belonged to the plundered monasteries.[41] Leo XIII complained of the traffic in relics which was going on in Rome itself.[42] A practical difficulty is that of distinguishing clearly between the relics mentioned in paragraph 1 and those mentioned in paragraph 2. Relics which have lost their authentication may be ancient; they are not to be exposed without a previous decision by the Ordinary (§ 1), and yet, if they are ancient they are to receive the same veneration which they received before (§ 2). The point is this: in paragraph 2 there is question of relics which are ancient, and which have been held in veneration for centuries without interruption; these are to continue to receive veneration; in paragraph 1, there is question of relics, which may be represented as ancient, and *may* even be so in fact, but which *have not been in continuous veneration;* they have passed through other hands, and are therefore suspect without their certificate of authenticity.

Ill-advised Attacks on Authenticity to Be Curbed. Ordinaries of places shall not permit, especially in sermons and in books, papers, or reviews which are designed to promote piety, that questions regarding the authenticity of sacred relics be agitated, when they rest on bare conjectures, merely probable arguments or prejudiced opinions, espe-

---

[41] S. C. Rit., *Decr. Auth.*, n. 3779, ad V.
[42] S. C. Ind. et Reliq., *Collectanea*, II, n. 1506.

cially if expressed in language which smacks of mockery and disrespect (c. 1286).

True historical criticism is characterized by learning, prudence, and precaution against giving scandal to the common people; such genuine research serves both truth and devotion, gradually corrects errors, and paves the way for the conversion of intellectual persons. Such criticism is, of course, allowed and encouraged by the Church; but its usual medium is not "sermons, and books, papers or reviews designed to promote piety." The canon is aimed at a false and shallow criticism, into which even Catholics might be betrayed especially through vanity. Mockery and disrespect against reputed sacred relics would be forbidden by the natural law itself. The further provisions of the canon law are stated in careful terms; the Ordinary of the place has certain powers to control what is said in sermons (cf. cc. 1337 sq.) and published in books, papers, and reviews (cf. c. 1385, § 1, 2°).

Norms for the Veneration of Relics. Relics, when exposed for veneration, should be enclosed and sealed in their containers or reliquaries (c. 1287, § 1). Relics of the Holy Cross must never be exposed for public veneration in the same reliquary with relics of the saints, but must have their own separate reliquary (c. 1287, § 2). Without a special indult, relics of the blessed are not to be carried in processions or exposed in churches, except where an Office and Mass in their honor are celebrated by concession of the Holy See (c. 1287, § 3). In the same places mentioned in paragraph 3, images of the blessed may be exposed for public veneration.[43] Note that the worship due to relics of the True Cross is a *relative* worship of *latriae*.

Relics of the Holy Cross. The relics of the True Cross, which a Bishop may wear in his pectoral cross, pass, on his death, to the cathedral church, and are to be transmitted to his Episcopal successor; in case the deceased was the Bishop of more than one diocese, it passes to the cathedral church of one of his dioceses in whose territory he died, or if he died outside his diocese, in that one from which he last departed (c. 1288). The last part of this canon refers to a Bishop who had several dioceses, not successively but at the same time, when he died. This is a possible case; for example, a Bishop may become Apostolic Administrator of another diocese without relinquishing his own. The entire canon concerns only the relics of the True Cross; the reliquary (pectoral cross) and other relics can be freely disposed of (cf. c. 1299); but relics can never be *sold*.

---

[43] S. C. Rit., 24 July, 1915; *Decr. Auth.*, n. 4330; *AAS*, 7-389.

Care of Sacred Relics. It is an act of impiety to sell sacred relics; hence Ordinaries of places, rural deans, pastors, and others who have the care of souls, must carefully see to it that sacred relics, especially those of the Holy Cross, be not offered for sale, especially on the occasion of the settlement of estates or of promiscuous sales, and that they do not pass into the hands of non-Catholics **(c. 1289, § 1).** Rectors of churches, and other persons who are responsible for sacred relics must be vigilantly careful that they be not in any way profaned, nor lost through negligence, nor improperly cared for **(c. 1289, § 2).**

Section 4. Sacred Processions (cc. 1290–1295)

PRELIMINARY SURVEY

Definition, Classification of Sacred Processions (c. 1290)
Corpus Christi Processions (c. 1291)
Extraordinary Processions (c. 1292)
Processions of Religious Outside Their Churches (c. 1293)
Permission to Introduce, Transfer, or Abolish Processions
    (c. 1294)
Manner of Conducting Processions (c. 1295)

Definition: Classification. The term "sacred processions" signifies solemn supplications performed by the people under the leadership of the clergy by proceeding in order from one sacred place to another, for the purpose of fostering piety, commemorating and giving thanks for God's blessings, or imploring His help **(c. 1290, § 1).** *Ordinary* processions are those which are held on certain days of the year according to liturgical laws or the customs of the various churches; *extraordinary,* are those which are held on other days for some public cause **(c. 1290, § 2).** The Roman Ritual mentions the following ordinary processions: for the Feast of the Purification; for Palm Sunday; for the Major and Minor Litanies (Feast of St. Mark and Rogation Days); *Corpus Christi* processions. The first paragraph of the canon defines *public* processions. A procession is *private* if it remains within a church or monastery, or (though it proceed through the streets) does not go from one sacred place to another, or is limited to the people and clergy of one parish or confraternity, or is not held for one of the purposes mentioned.

Corpus Christi **Processions.** Unless an immemorial custom provides otherwise, or local circumstances in the prudent judgment of the Bishop require otherwise, on the Feast of *Corpus Christi* only one procession in each place, and that a solemn one through the streets shall be held, by the church of the highest dignity in the place; and all clerics, all religious communities of men, and all lay confraternities shall take part in it, with the exception of regulars who live perpetually within a strict cloister or who live more than three miles from the city (c. 1291, § 1). Within the octave of the Feast, the other parishes and churches, including those of regulars, may have their own processions outside the bounds of the church; but in places where there are several churches it pertains to the Ordinary of the place to determine the days, hours, and routes for the respective processions (c. 1291, § 2).

Some regulars have a special privilege exempting their communities from the obligation of taking part in the procession on the Feast; e.g., the Theatines, Barnabites, Society of Jesus, Discalced Carmelites. The Carthusians and Camaldolese are excused by their strict cloister. The right of the pastor to lead processions outside his church (but within his parish — c. 462, 7°) applies though the procession starts from a church which is not a filial church and has its own rector,[44] and applies also to the processions of exempt religious outside their churches and cloisters.[45] But these interpretations *do not apply to the Corpus Christi processions,*[46] that is, a *Corpus Christi* procession held in accordance with canon 1291, § 2, by a nonparochial church or by exempt religious, is not led by the pastor, but by the rector of the church.

Extraordinary Processions. The Ordinary of the place, upon consultation with the cathedral chapter, can, for a public and extraordinary cause, decree extraordinary processions; and in these, as well as in the ordinary and customary ones, the persons mentioned in canon 1291, § 1, must participate (c. 1292).

Processions of Religious Outside Their Churches. Religious, even exempt, may not lead public processions outside their churches and cloisters without the permission of the Ordinary of the place, except as provided in canon 1291, § 2 (c. 1293). The right of the pastor to lead public processions (c. 462, 7°) does not apply to processions of exempt religious within the octave of *Corpus Christi,* nor at other

---

[44] Code Com., 12 Nov., 1922; *AAS,* 14–661; *Digest,* I, p. 251.
[45] Code Com., 10 Nov., 1925; *AAS,* 17–582; *Digest,* I, p. 252.
[46] Cf. Beste, *Introductio in Codicem,* p. 290.

times if the permission of the local Ordinary has been obtained.[47]
The Order of Preachers has a special privilege of holding public
processions outside its churches on the first Sunday of October.[48]

Permission to Introduce, Transfer, or Abolish Processions. Neither
a pastor nor anyone else can introduce new processions, nor transfer
or abolish customary ones, without the permission of the Ordinary
of the place **(c. 1294, § 1).** All clerics who are attached to a certain
church must take part in the processions which are proper to that
church **(c. 1294, § 2).**

Manner of Conducting Sacred Processions. Ordinaries should see
to it that all improper practices, if any exist, be removed from sacred
processions, and that they be conducted in proper order and with that
modesty and reverence on the part of all, which are decidedly called
for in pious and religious acts of this kind **(c. 1295).**

Section 5. Sacred Furnishings (cc. 1296–1306)

PRELIMINARY SURVEY

Custody and Style of Sacred Furnishings (c. 1296)
Who Must Provide Sacred Furnishings (c. 1297)
Disposal of Furnishings of a Deceased Cardinal (c. 1298)
Of a Deceased Residential Bishop (c. 1299)
Of a Deceased Beneficiary (c. 1300)
Disposal by Last Testament (c. 1301)
The Duty of Caring for Sacred Furnishings (c. 1302)
Moderate Charge for Use of Sacred Furnishings (c. 1303)
Power to Bless Sacred Furnishings (c. 1304)
Loss of Blessing or Consecration (c. 1305)
Touching of Sacred Vessels: Washing of Sacred Linen
    (c. 1306)

General Notions. *Supellex* is a difficult word to translate; in its
general and literal sense it means household furniture. *Sacra supellex*
includes in a general way all the movable property with which the
house of God is furnished, or "all the things, especially those that
are consecrated or blessed, which are used for the exercise and
embellishment of divine worship, and most particularly for the celebration of Mass and the administration of the sacraments." Not all

---

[47] Cf. Beste, *op. cit.,* p. 291.
[48] Cf. Prümmer, *Manuale Iuris Ecclesiastici,* n. 395.

articles connected with worship are equally sacred; for example, a chair might be used in the sanctuary for sacred functions, and still occasionally be put to profane use. Even the articles used exclusively for worship need not necessarily in every case receive a constitutive blessing. Sacred furnishings in a rather strict sense include (*a*) sacred vessels: chalice, paten, pyx, ciborium, ostensorium, lunula, custodia, cruets, oil stock; (*b*) the ornaments of the chalice and altar: corporal, pall, altar cloths, purificator, tabernacle cover, antependium, veil, burse, communion paten; (*c*) the priestly vestments: amice, alb, cincture, maniple, stole, chasuble, dalmatic, cope, humeral veil, and certain other vestments peculiar to Bishops; (*d*) symbols and utensils of the altar: missal, crucifix, thurible, boat, spoon, bells, candelabra. Only the chalice and paten must be consecrated; of the others some must, others may be blessed; many are governed as to form, material, etc., by minute prescriptions of the S. C. of Rites.

Custody and Style of Sacred Furnishings. Sacred furnishings, especially those which according to liturgical laws must be blessed or consecrated and which are used for public worship, must be carefully kept in the sacristy of the church or in some other safe and suitable place, and must not be put to profane use (c. 1296, § 1). An inventory of all sacred furnishings must be made and accurately kept according to canon 1522, nn. 2 and 3 (c. 1296, § 2). As to the material and style of sacred furnishings, liturgical prescriptions, ecclesiastical tradition, and as far as possible also the norms of sacred art are to be observed (c. 1296, § 3).

No article destined for worship and made sacred by a constitutive blessing should ever be put to profane use; such use would be rather easily excused in other cases, for example, a chair or carpet used in the sanctuary.

Who Must Provide Sacred Furnishings. In the absence of other provision, the persons who are bound, according to canon 1186, to provide for the maintenance of the church, must also supply it with the sacred furnishings which are needed for worship (c. 1297).

Disposal of Furnishings of a Deceased Cardinal. All sacred furnishings which belonged to a deceased Cardinal of the Holy Roman Church who was domiciled in Rome, even though he were Bishop of one of the Suburban Sees or an Abbot *nullius,* except his rings and pectoral crosses, with their sacred relics, and also all other articles which were permanently destined for divine worship, without regard to the quality and nature of the income from which they were purchased, go to the Pontifical sacristy, unless the Cardinal gave them or left them by will to some church or public oratory or pious place or to some ecclesiastical or religious person **(c. 1298, § 1)**. It is to be desired that a Cardinal who wishes to make use of this power of disposal should give the preference at least in part to those churches which he has as his title, or for administration, or *in commendam* **(c. 1298, § 2)**.

Notes. 1. This canon deals only with sacred furnishings which *belonged to* the deceased Cardinal; articles which *belong to the church* cannot be disposed of by any person other than their owner. It applies to all articles which were *permanently destined for worship,* even though by nature capable also of profane use.

2. These articles can be disposed of by the Cardinal, either by gift or by will, but only to the persons mentioned; and this, "without regard to the quality or nature of the income from which they were purchased," that is, even though they were purchased from the income of the Cardinal's benefices (cf. c. 239, § 1, 19°).

3. Certain articles are *excepted,* namely, "his rings and pectoral crosses with their sacred relics." The ring and pectoral cross can even be sold. This is explicitly permitted as to the pectoral cross in an Encyclical of the *Vicariatus Urbis* of 25 March, 1899.[49] Relics of the Holy Cross are governed by canon 1288; other relics, if not distinguished may, it seems, be given or willed even to private persons (cf. c. 1282, § 2) but never sold (c. 1289, § 1).

4. If the Cardinal has not disposed of the articles which he can dispose of and which are not excepted, they go to the Papal sacristy.

5. The preference to be given to his own churches is not preceptive. A *commenda* is an arrangement by which the custody of a church, together with part of its revenues, are given to an ecclesiastic either permanently or temporarily (cf. c. 1412, 5°).

6. A Cardinal who is also a residential Bishop (and hence domiciled outside Rome) is governed by canon 1299.

Furnishings of a Deceased Bishop. Sacred furnishings which belonged to a deceased residential Bishop, even though he were also a Cardinal, go to his cathedral church, except his rings and pectoral crosses with their sacred relics, observing the provision of canon 1288 (regarding the relics of the Holy Cross), and excepting also all furnishings of whatever kind which are legitimately proved to have

---

[49] *Collectanea,* II, n. 1699.

been acquired by the deceased Bishop from funds which did not belong to the church itself, and which are not shown to have passed into the ownership of the church (c. 1299, § 1). If the Bishop has governed two or more dioceses successively, or has governed at the same time two or more dioceses that were united or given to him for perpetual administration and each of which had its own proper and separate cathedral church, then such sacred articles as are proved to have been acquired from the income of only one diocese go to the cathedral church of that diocese; otherwise, the articles are to be divided equally between the various cathedral churches, provided the income of the dioceses was not divided but constituted permanently one episcopal benefice (*mensa episcopalis*); but if the incomes were divided and separate, the division of the furnishings is to be made among the various cathedral churches in proportion to the revenue which the Bishop received in each of the dioceses and the time during which he governed each diocese (c. 1299, § 2). A Bishop is obliged to draw up in authentic form an inventory of sacred articles, in which he must state truthfully when each article was acquired, and must distinctly designate any articles which he acquired, not from the income and revenues of the church, but either with his own funds or by gift made to him; otherwise, all are presumed to have been acquired from the revenues of the church (c. 1299, § 3).

Notes. 1. A beneficiary in general cannot *freely dispose* of the revenues of his benefice; he can *use them freely for his necessary support,* but is obliged to devote the surplus to the poor or to pious causes (c. 1473). An exception is made for Cardinals (c. 239, § 1, 19°); but if a Cardinal is also a residential Bishop, the present canon derogates from that privilege as regards the disposal of his sacred furnishings, unless it is legitimately proved that they were acquired from funds which did not belong to the church; the surplus revenue of the episcopal benefice is here included among funds which "belonged to the church."

2. If it is legitimately proved that articles were acquired with funds which did not belong to the church, in this sense, then those articles are excepted from the general provision of this canon (requiring that the articles go to the cathedral church), *unless it is proved* that the articles afterward passed to the ownership of the church.

3. The proportionate division among two or more cathedral churches is based on the *time* during which the Bishop governed each diocese *and the revenues* which he personally received from each; therefore

the problem is solved by multiplying the time by the yearly (or monthly) personal revenue for each diocese, and making the division in proportion to the totals so obtained.

4. The principal source for the fuller understanding of this and the preceding canon is an Apostolic Letter of Pius IX, *Quum illud,* 1 June, 1847.[50]

Disposal of Furnishings of a Deceased Beneficiary. The provisions of canon 1299 apply also to a cleric who has obtained a secular or religious benefice in any church (c. 1300).

Legal Formalities Are to Be Observed. Cardinals, residential Bishops, and other clerical beneficiaries are obliged to see to it that the canonical provisions of canons 1298–1300 are made duly effective also in the forum of civil law, by drawing up the will or other instrument in a form which is valid in civil law (c. 1301, § 1). Hence they must in due time and in a form which is valid in civil law designate some person of good reputation in accordance with canon 380, who, in the event of their death, shall take possession, not only of the furnishings, but also of the books, documents, and other things which pertain to the church and which are found in the houses of the deceased persons above mentioned, and transmit them to the persons entitled to receive them (c. 1301, § 2).

Due Care of Sacred Furnishings. Rectors of churches and other persons charged with the care of sacred furnishings must sedulously provide for their conservation and elegance (c. 1302).

Moderate Charge for Use of Sacred Furnishings. The cathedral church must freely supply sacred furnishings and other things which are necessary for the Sacrifice of the Mass or for other pontifical functions, to the Bishop when he celebrates even privately, not only in the cathedral church but also in other churches of the city or suburb (c. 1303, § 1). If a church is poor, the Ordinary can permit that a moderate charge be made for the use of the furnishings and other things necessary for the Sacrifice of the Mass, to be paid by priests who celebrate in that church for their own convenience (c. 1303, § 2). It pertains to the Bishop, but not to the Vicar Capitular or Vicar General without a special mandate, to fix this charge, and none, even exempt religious, are allowed to demand more (c. 1303, § 3). The Bishop shall determine this charge for the entire diocese, if possible in the diocesan Synod, or out of the Synod after consulting his chapter (c. 1303, § 4).

[50] *Fontes,* n. 505, II, p. 817.

Power to Bless Sacred Furnishings. The blessing of those articles of sacred equipment, which according to liturgical laws ought to be blessed before being put to their proper use, can be given by the following persons:

1. Cardinals of the Holy Roman Church and all Bishops;

2. Ordinaries of places who lack the episcopal character, for churches and oratories of their own territory;

3. A pastor for the churches and oratories which are within the limits of his parish, and rectors of churches for their own churches;

4. Priests delegated by the Ordinary of the place, according to the terms of the delegation and within the jurisdiction of the person delegating;

5. Religious superiors, and priests of their institute delegated by them, for their own churches and oratories and for the churches of monastic nuns who are subject to them (c. 1304).

Blessings given by any priest are valid (c. 1147, § 3), provided he uses the proper formula, if one is prescribed (c. 1148, § 2); but in the case of reserved blessings a blessing by a priest would be illicit unless he is duly delegated. Since the power here concerned is a power of order, not of jurisdiction, its delegation is governed by canon 210.

Loss of Blessing or Consecration. An article of sacred equipment which is blessed or consecrated loses its blessing or consecration:

1. If it has suffered such lesions or transformations that it has lost its original form and is considered no longer fit for use;

2. If it has been put to degrading uses or has been exposed for public sale (c. 1305, § 1).

A chalice and paten do not lose their consecration because the gold plating is worn off or because they have been regilded; but in the first instance there is a grave obligation to have them gold-plated again (c. 1305, § 2).

Touching of Sacred Vessels: Washing of Sacred Linens. Care must be taken that the chalice and paten, and, until they are washed, the purificators, palls, and corporals, which were used in the Sacrifice of the Mass, be not touched except by clerics or the persons who have the custody of these articles (c. 1306, § 1). Purificators, palls, and corporals, which have been used in the Sacrifice of the Mass, are not to be washed by lay persons, even religious, until they have first been washed by a cleric in major orders; and the water of the first washing is to be poured into the sacrarium, or if there is none, into the fire (c. 1306, § 2).

Section 6. Vows and Oaths (cc. 1307–1321)

PRELIMINARY SURVEY

Vow: Definition, Etc. A vow, that is, a deliberate and free promise made to God of a good which is possible and better, must be fulfilled, the obligation being based on the virtue of religion (c. 1307, § 1). All persons who have a sufficient use of reason are capable of making a vow, unless they are forbidden to do so by law (c. 1307, § 2). A vow which is made as the result of grave and unjust fear is null by law (c. 1307, § 3).

Notes. 1. A *promise* is different from a mere *resolve;* moreover the promise must be deliberate and free, and made *to God.* A promise can be made to God in honor of a saint, but a promise made to a saint, though in a way sacred, is not a vow.

2. Obstacles to *freedom* in this matter are *fear* and *error.* Fear, in order to invalidate a vow, must be grave and unjust. These qualities of fear have been explained in connection with marriage (c. 1087) and may here be taken in the same sense. To be unjust, the fear must come from a free external cause, and must be the cause, not merely the occasion of the vow; but it need not have been produced for the purpose of eliciting the vow. *Error* always invalidates a vow if it is *substantial* error; that is, if it concerns the substance of the matter (object) of the vow, or the existence of a condition which was implicitly supposed, or the final cause of the vow, as in the case of a vow made for the recovery of a person thought to be ill, but who in fact is already either recovered or dead. In the vows of religious profession and sacred orders, substantial error is required in order to

invalidate the vow. But in other cases an error which *gives cause to the vow,* even though it be not substantial, invalidates it. An error *gives cause to the vow* if it is such that, had the one vowing known the truth, he would not have made the vow. Note that a different rule applies to marriage (c. 1084): *"simplex error, etsi det causam contractui, non vitiat consensum matrimonialem."*

3. The object of the vow must be a good, which is possible and better. A vow to commit an evil act would be no vow. Physical impossibility, if it existed at the time of the vow, makes it null; if it comes afterward, it excuses from the vow. The same is to be said of moral impossibility, provided it affects the substance of the vow. The object of the vow must be "better"; that is, an act of virtue which is better than its voluntary omission, and which does not constitute an obstacle to a better act. Thus to marry may *in an individual case* be better than not to marry, provided such a vow does not constitute an obstacle to embracing a higher state.

4. Capacity requires a *sufficient* use of reason; sufficient, that is, in consideration of the object of the vow. Thus a boy or girl of 11 would scarcely have a *sufficient* use of reason to make a vow of perpetual chastity, at least without special supernatural enlightenment.

Classifications. A vow is *public* if it is accepted by the legitimate ecclesiastical superior in the name of the Church; otherwise it is *private* (c. 1308, § 1). It is *solemn* if it has been acknowledged as such by the Church; otherwise it is *simple* (c. 1308, § 2). It is *reserved* if only the Holy See can grant a dispensation from it (c. 1308, § 3). It is *personal* if an action of the person vowing is promised; *real* if a thing is promised; *mixed,* if it partakes of the nature of both a personal and a real vow (c. 1308, § 4). A further classification is that of *absolute* and *conditional* vows. A special form of the latter is a *penal* vow; e.g., "If I commit an act of impatience today, I vow to do a certain act of penance in reparation."

Private Reserved Vows. Private vows reserved to the Holy See are only the vow of perfect and perpetual chastity and the vow to enter a religious institute of solemn vows, made absolutely and after the completion of the eighteenth year (c. 1309).

1. The two requisite conditions apply cumulatively to both vows; in both cases the vow, in order to be reserved, must be absolute, not conditional, and must be made after the completion of eighteen years of age (after midnight following the eighteenth birthday — c. 34, § 3, 3°).

2. The vow of perfect and perpetual chastity must be distinguished from other vows relating to chastity (marital chastity, virginity, celibacy).[51] This vow is supposed to be taken with the intention of assuming a *grave* obligation, since its object is *per se* capable of obliging *sub gravi*. If the vow were taken only with the intention of binding *sub levi,* it would not be reserved.

3. The vow to *enter a religious institute of solemn vows* is reserved even though the person has no intention of taking solemn vows; for in such institutes simple vows are taken by some members. But the institute must be one of solemn vows *de facto* and not merely *de iure remoto;* that is, solemn vows must not merely be provided for in the original constitutions but must be actually in practice in the place where the institute which the vow contemplates exists.

4. Before the Code, three special pilgrimages were also the object of reserved vows: to Jerusalem, to Rome, to Compostella.

5. *Public* vows are *all reserved,* except as provided by special canons (e.g., for sacred orders, c. 214, for religious profession, cc. 633–636, 640, 648, 669).

Obligation of Vow. Of itself a vow obliges only the person who made it **(c. 1310, § 1).** The obligation of a real vow passes to the heirs; as does also that of a mixed vow as to that part of it which is real **(c. 1310, § 2).**

Notes. 1. An interesting case on the obligation of a vow made by a community was decided by the S. C. of the Council in 1936.[52]

2. Is the obligation of a real vow, which passes to the heirs, one of justice or of religion? A disputed question, with sponsors and difficulties on both sides. Many authors follow Suarez, who held the obligation to be one of justice.[53] Vermeersch points out the objection to this conclusion with the following illustration: Titius vows a sum of money for the building of a church; dies without fulfilling his vow, and his property passes to his heir. The obligation to fulfill the vow passes to the heir; but is it an obligation of justice? In Titius himself, it was an obligation of religion; by what sort of magic has the nature of the obligation been changed? Vermeersch admits that this would be true if Titius in his will had expressly imposed upon his heir the obligation of fulfilling the vow; but he denies that a tacit intention to impose such obligation suffices. Against Vermeersch's

---

[51] Cf. Genicot, *Theol. Mor.,* I, n. 252.
[52] S. C. Conc., 18 Jan., 1936; *AAS,* 29–343; *Digest,* II, p. 391.
[53] Suarez, *De Religione,* Tit. VI, L. 14, c. 11, n. 7.

opinion (that the obligation of the heir is one of religion only), it may be objected, in the words of the canon, that "a vow obliges only the one who made it"; but this objection loses sight of the qualification *"ratione sui."* *Of itself,* the vow obliges only the one who made it; but by positive law (c. 1310, § 2) this obligation, in the case of a real vow, passes to the heirs — and it remains "the obligation of the vow," that is, an obligation of religion, and not of justice.[54] This dispute has practical consequences: if the obligation of the heir is one of justice, only the Holy See can remit it; if it is one of religion, the rules for the dispensation from a private nonreserved vow would apply.

Cessation of Obligation. A vow ceases by expiration of the time specified for fulfilling the obligation, by a substantial change in the matter promised, on failure of the condition upon which it was made to depend or on cessation of its final cause, and by annulment, dispensation, or commutation **(c. 1311).**

If the matter which is the object of the vow is affected only partially by the change, the vow remains in effect as to the part of the matter not changed. So, too, if the final cause ceases only temporarily, the obligation is suspended but revives when the final cause again exists.

Annulment: Suspension. One who legitimately exercises dominative power over the will of the person who made a vow, can validly, and for a just cause also licitly, invalidate his vows so that the obligation in no case revives **(c. 1312, § 1).** One who has power, not over the will of the person who made a vow, but over the matter of the vow, can suspend the obligation of the vow for such time as its fulfillment would be to his disadvantage **(c. 1312, § 2).**

1. Annulment (*irritatio directa*) is permanent; suspension (*irritatio indirecta*), *per se* temporary.

2. Direct annulment can be exercised only by a person who had dominative power over the will of the person who made the vow, at the time when the vow was made. It is disputed whether this power is from the natural or only from the positive law; the latter opinion is probable.

3. The power of annulment belongs: (*a*) to parents (father, guardian, mother) as to minor children not yet emancipated from parental control (c. 8); some hold, following the pre-Code law, that it applies only to children who have not attained puberty;[55] (*b*) to religious

---

[54] Cf. St. Thomas, 2ª, 2ae, q. 88, a. 3; Vermeersch, *Quaestiones de Religione,* n. 138, Vermeersch-Creusen, *Epit.,* Ed. 5, Vol. II, n. 641.

[55] Cf. Damen, in *Apollinaris* (1929), p. 306.

superiors (even women, since there is no exercise of *jurisdiction*) as to the vows made by their subjects after religious profession, except the vow to transfer to a stricter institute. It does not belong to religious superiors as to the vows of novices, nor to a husband[56] or wife as to the vows of the other spouse. The private vows made before religious profession, however, are suspended *ipso iure* upon profession (c. 1315); and both religious superiors (as to their novice subjects) and husband or wife (as to the other spouse) have, in a proper case, the power of *suspension* of vows.

4. The power of suspension arises from the right which the party exercising it has over the *matter of the vow*. Thus a superior (or novice master — c. 561, § 2) can suspend the vows of a novice which interfere with the discipline of the novitiate; a husband or wife can suspend the vows of the other party which interfere with the full and proper use of the marital right.

Dispensation of Nonreserved Vows. The following persons can for just cause dispense from nonreserved vows, provided the dispensation does not injure vested rights of other parties:

1. The Ordinary of the place as regards all his subjects (anywhere) and also *peregrini* (in his territory);

2. The superior of a clerical exempt institute as regards the persons mentioned in canon 514, § 1;

3. Those to whom the dispensing power has been delegated by the Holy See (c. 1313).

Dispensation is an act of voluntary jurisdiction (c. 201, § 2); superiors of *only* clerical exempt institutes have jurisdiction (c. 501, § 1). The power given by this canon in nn. 1 and 2 is *ordinary* (c. 197, § 1) and hence can be delegated according to canon 199. By privilege, regulars who have jurisdiction for confessions of externs can dispense the faithful from nonreserved vows, even out of confession.

Commutation. A work promised by a nonreserved vow can be commuted by the person who made the vow into a better or equally good work; and can be commuted into a less good work by one who has the power to dispense according to canon 1313 (c. 1314).

1. It is probable (from the old law not expressly revoked) that even a reserved vow can be commuted by the person who made it, to a

---

[56] We are aware that many older authors can be cited for the dominative power of a husband to annul directly the vows of his wife made during marriage; but this opinion was always disputed, and we frankly believe that it is now antiquated. Cf. Pius XI, *Christian Marriage, Catholic Mind*, Vol. 29 (1931), p. 29, and Vermeersch-Bouscaren, *What Is Marriage*, n. 55.

work which is *certainly* better than the one promised by the original vow.

2. If a reserved vow is legitimately commuted (by one who has power, even of dispensation, over reserved vows), the new work substituted for the original one is obligatory, of course, but the vow regarding it is no longer reserved; but if the commutation to a better or equally good work is made by the person who made the vow, the vow remains reserved even as to the new work, but the person has always the right to go back to the work which was originally vowed.

3. Requisite cause for commutation: (*a*) for commutation to a better work, no cause is required (the greater excellence of the new work is itself sufficient cause); (*b*) for commutation to an equally good work, a reasonable (slight) cause is required for licitness only; (*c*) for commutation to a less good work, a proportionate cause is required, *ad validitatem* (by analogy with canon 84, § 2, because here commutation includes the dispensing power).

Suspension of Vows by Religious Profession. Vows made before religious profession are suspended as long as the person who made them remains in religion **(c. 1315).**

Before the Code the obligation of such vows ceased only upon *solemn* profession; now their obligation is merely suspended, but this effect attaches to simple and even temporary profession. Upon perpetual profession (even simple) the religious could commute all former vows in the perpetual profession.

Oaths: Definition, Licitness, Validity. An oath, that is, the invocation of the name of God in witness to the truth, may be made only in truth, in judgment, and in justice **(c. 1316, § 1).** An oath which is prescribed or admitted by canon law cannot validly be made by proxy **(c. 1316, § 2).**

1. No specific formula of words is required; the essential thing is the expressed intention to call God to witness to the truth of a statement or promise; in the former case we have *iuramentum assertorium,* in the latter *iuramentum promissorium.* The expression of the intention can be in words or in unmistakable signs. A priest takes an oath (in a matrimonial court) by placing his hand upon his breast.[57]

2. Conditions for licitness: (*a*) *in truth,* that is, the person must be morally certain of the truth of his statement (in court, personal, first-

---

[57] S. C. Sacr., Instruction, 15 Aug., 1936, Art. 96, § 1; *AAS,* 28–313; *Digest,* II, p. 495.

hand knowledge may be required); (*b*) *in judgment,* that is, with discretion, prudence, consideration, not without some utility; (*c*) *in justice,* a condition which would be violated if one confirmed a calumny or detraction by oath, or promised under oath to do an illicit act.

3. *Per se* nothing prevents one from making an oath by a proxy authorized to do so; but by positive law such an oath is invalid if it is one which is made in pursuance of canonical provisions, either mandatory or permissive.

Obligation. One who freely swears to do something is bound by a special obligation of religion to do what he so promised **(c. 1317, § 1).** An oath which is extorted through force or fear is valid, but may be relaxed by the ecclesiastical superior **(c. 1317, § 2).** An oath which is made without force or fraud and by which a person renounces some private good or advantage which is granted him by law, is to be kept unless it tends toward the loss of eternal salvation **(c. 1317, § 3).**

1. The canon deals principally with promissory oaths, though paragraph 2 applies equally to all oaths. The obligation of an oath is altogether personal; it never passes as such to the person's heirs, though they may be bound on some other title.

2. Force *or* fear is practically equivalent to force *and* fear, fear as a result of force; an oath extorted literally by force would be involuntary and null. The rule here stated follows the general norm of canon 103, § 2; the act is valid, but can be rescinded according to canons 1684–1689. This supposes that the external expression was at least accompanied by a genuine intention to make the oath; an external expression which was a mere pretense might be a sinful deception, but it would not be binding as an oath.

3. If a person freely and without being deceived makes an oath by which he gives up an advantage which he has according to law, his oath is binding on two conditions: that the advantage he gives up is merely a private one (and not a privilege which concerns the public good, as, for example, the privileges of clerics or religious — c. 72, § 3); and second, that the renunciation does not tend toward the loss of eternal salvation. This last condition would fail if the oath did spiritual harm, or an injustice even in the temporal order, to another person; or injured the public spiritual welfare, or was wrong in itself and hence harmful to the soul of the person making the renunciation.

Oaths Accessory to Other Acts. A promissory oath follows the nature and conditions of the act to which it is accessory **(c. 1318, § 1).**

If such an oath is made accessory to an act which tends directly to the harm of other persons or to the detriment of the public welfare or of eternal salvation, the act gains no confirmation from it (c. 1318, § 2).

A promissory oath is not necessarily, but may be, accessory to another act. It will be accessory to another act if that is the intention of the person who makes the oath. The canon supposes that this is the fact; but whether it is so or not in a concrete case will depend upon the interpretation of the will of the person who makes the oath; hence it may not be easy to determine. If a person makes a promise to another and then confirms that promise by oath, the oath "follows the nature and conditions of the promise." The *nature* of a promise is that it can be retracted at any time before it has been accepted by the party to whom it was made; hence the oath, too, can be retracted. The oath also follows the *conditions* of the promise; hence if the promise is to observe a certain set of regulations or constitutions, the obligation of the oath will be governed, both as to its extent and its gravity, by the obligation of the regulations or constitutions to which it is accessory.

If an oath is accessory to a contract, it follows the nature and conditions of the contract. Suppose the contract is subject only to the civil law, and is void according to that law; the oath, too, is null and void. This conclusion may at first sight seem to contradict canon 1317, § 3; cannot a person by oath give up a private advantage which he has under the law, and is not an oath to that effect binding? The answer is *yes,* provided he really intends to give up that advantage; but in that case the oath is not accessory to the contract. A case may illustrate the point. Titius contracts with Caius to sell him a piece of land; for some reason the contract is void according to law. Titius knows or suspects this, and so makes an oath to fulfill the contract notwithstanding this defect. Canon 1317, § 3 applies to this case; Titius is bound by his oath. But in the same case, if the intention of Titius is merely to confirm the contract as it stands, and the contract turns out to be void, Titius is not bound by his oath, because it was merely accessory to the contract; the case is then governed by canon 1318, § 1.

Cessation of Obligation of Promissory Oath. The obligation arising from a promissory oath ceases:

1. If it is remitted by the person in whose favor the oath was made;
2. If the thing promised be substantially changed, or on account of

changed circumstances becomes morally wrong or entirely indifferent, or is an obstacle to a greater good;

3. On default of the final cause or of a condition under which the oath was made;

4. By annulment, dispensation, or commutation according to canon 1320 (c. 1319).

Power to Annul, Dispense, Commute. Those who have power to annul, dispense, or commute a vow, have the same power and in the same way regarding a promissory oath; but if the dispensation from an oath works to the prejudice of other persons who refuse to remit the obligation, the Holy See alone can dispense from it, for the necessity or advantage of the Church (c. 1320).

1. No oath is reserved *as such;* consequently even an oath to observe perfect and perpetual chastity or to enter an institute of solemn vows, made after eighteen years of age and without condition, may be commuted by the person himself to a greater or equal good.

2. But if the oath was accessory to a vow, it follows the nature and conditions of the vow (c. 1318, § 1); hence in the case of a reserved vow the oath also is reserved in the same way.

3. Moreover, if the rights of other persons are involved and they refuse to remit the obligation, all powers to annul, dispense, or commute, cease, and only the Holy See can dispense.

Interpretation. An oath is to be interpreted strictly according to law and the intention of the person who made it, or, if he acted fraudulently, according to the intention of the person to whom he made the oath (c. 1321).

Three principles: 1. An oath is to be interpreted strictly, that is, so as to favor the lesser obligation. No one is to be bound by interpretation to more than he strictly promised.

2. According to law and the intention of the person. The intention is the fundamental norm. A person is presumed to use words in a juridical sense; but a contrary intention, if proved, would prevail.

3. If the person who made the oath acted fraudulently, the oath is to be interpreted according to the intention of the person to whom it was made. This norm applies only in the *external forum;* in the forum of conscience no one can be bound *by an oath* beyond his real intention; but a person who deceived another by oath would be bound in conscience to make good the damage done by his deceit. In the external forum, the above rule is reasonable; for a person to whom an oath is made has a right to accept it as sincere. Hence in

the external forum the intention of the person who accepts the oath (so far as that intention appears from his acceptance of the terms of the oath under all its circumstances) is the norm, if the oath was fraudulent.

4. For interpretation of oaths, it is well to remember that implicit conditions are often to be reasonably presumed; e.g., "in as far as I can," or "subject to the disposition of my superiors," or "provided the circumstances remain the same." Whether such conditions are to be implied or not depends on all the circumstances.

CASES AND QUESTIONS

1. What do you understand by worship? Absolute and relative worship? *Latriae, hyperduliae, duliae?* Classify according to both divisions the worship: of the Blessed Sacrament, of the Sacred Heart of Christ, of the Holy Trinity, of the Holy Spirit, of the Blessed Virgin, of your Guardian Angel, of a crucifix, an image of the Crown of Thorns, the Sacred Shroud (at Turin), a relic of the True Cross, a statue of Our Lady of Lourdes, an altar dedicated to St. Paul, the body of St. Cecilia (c. 1255).

2. Give the true concept of public worship and your reasons for your opinion (c. 1256 and text).

3. May a Catholic invite a non-Catholic to Mass? May he attend a Sunday service of a non-Catholic sect? Can you explain the principles underlying your answers?

4. On what conditions could a Catholic attend a wedding or funeral in a non-Catholic church? (C. 1258).

5. A community of diocesan sisters recites prayers in honor of their blessed foundress as part of their morning prayers in their community chapel. Is the permission of the Ordinary necessary? (C. 1259, § 1, and text).

6. A new Bishop proposes to visit a public oratory of an exempt clerical institute to see whether any superstitious practices are being conducted there. As one of his consultors, what would you advise him? (C. 1261, § 2, and text).

7. Is the custom which is prevalent in the United States, of seating men and women promiscuously in church, contrary to canon law? (C. 1262, § 1). What about the practice of reserving pews and charging rent for them? (Cc. 1263, § 2, 1181).

8. John, newly appointed assistant, tells his pastor that the practice of allowing women to sing in the church choir was expressly prohibited by Pius X. Your comment.

9. A community of religious women approved by the Holy See wishes

to have a secondary oratory for their novitiate which occupies one wing of the mother house. Is the permission of the Ordinary needed? (C. 1192, § 1). Will his permission be needed in order to keep the Blessed Sacrament in the new oratory? (C. 1267, and text; c. 1265, § 1, 2°).

10. Father Pius, a pastor, believes that it is forbidden to leave the tabernacle key on the altar while giving Communion at the Sunday Mass; so he carries it in his sleeve, or hooked to his cincture (cf. Instruction on Custody of the Blessed Sacrament, n. 6, *Digest*, II, p. 383).

11. A Protestant acquaintance remarks to a Catholic woman that she likes some things about the Catholic Church but thinks the worship of relics is "repulsive and ridiculous." Might it be possible for the Catholic to continue the conversation on a friendly basis by asking a few eye-opening questions? (Cf. text on c. 1276).

12. Alexander, a freshman at a secular university, never prays to the Blessed Virgin. "The worship of the Saints," he says, "is a matter of choice" (cf. c. 1276).

13. A community of religious women approved by the Holy See has the arm of their canonized foundress continually exposed in their community chapel. One of the sisters keeps an authenticated relic of the True Cross in her room. Are these practices proper? (C. 1282, §§ 1, 2).

14. Can you suggest a reason for the rule of canon 1287, § 2, that relics of the Holy Cross must not be exposed in the same reliquary with those of the saints? (Cf. c. 1255, §§ 1, 2).

15. Could a priest of an exempt order, giving a retreat to a religious community of women not connected with his order, bless altar linens for the community chapel validly and licitly? (Cc. 1147, § 3, 1304). Can a pastor bless vestments for his church? (C. 1304, 3°). Can he delegate another priest to do it? (C. 210).

16. What is the canonical foundation, if any, for the practice in some countries of accepting a small offering from transient priests who say Mass for their own convenience in a church? (C. 1303, § 2).

17. A student in the American College in Rome wonders whether he is obliged to observe the fast on the eve of the Feast of the Purification of Our Lady (Feb. 1). He learns that the practice owes its origin to a vow made by the people of Rome, but that it now has the force of a local law. Is he bound by the vow? (C. 1310). By the local law? (C. 92, § 2). Would the same be true of a transient visitor in Rome? (C. 14, § 1, 2°).

18. A local superior of a clerical exempt institute in the United States writes to one of his subjects studying in Rome, that he dispenses him from a private nonreserved vow of abstinence. Is this dispensation valid? (Cc. 1313, 2°, 201, § 3).

19. A promised B under oath to pay him a sum of money which was due to B only in virtue of a contract. The contract is void in law; but A wonders whether he is bound by his oath. Can you answer "Yes" or "No"

to this question? Upon what difficult question of fact will the answer depend? (Cc. 1317, § 3, 1318, § 1).

Readings:

Kelleher, *Discussions with Non-Catholics,* Cath. U., 1943; Dooley, *Church Law on Sacred Relics,* Cath. U., 1931; *The Jurist,* Vol. 3, p. 616 (Form of Inventory to Be Filed by a Bishop With His Metropolitan — cf. c. 1299, § 3); *Theological Studies,* Vol. 3, p. 475 (Bouscaren, on co-operation with non-Catholics); *Ecclesiastical Review,* Vol. 82, p. 637 (Catholic pallbearer at non-Catholic funeral); Vol. 85, p. 312 (Catholic girl, bridesmaid at Protestant church wedding); *Irish Ecclesiastical Record,* Vol. 36, p. 641, Vol. 37, p. 76 (questions on co-operation with non-Catholics); *Periodica,* Vol. 19, p. 43* (Vermeersch, on loss of consecration of chalice, alb); Vol. 21, p. 226* (can Bishop order all processions to start from principal church?); Vol. 23, p. 175* (can husband annul vows of wife?); Vol. 23, p. 133* (cases on vows); Vol. 24, p. 189* (Vermeersch, on faculty to authenticate relics — cf. c. 1283); *Ephem. Theol. Lovan.* (1934), p. 774 (Vermeersch, on dispensation, commutation).

CHAPTER XVIII

THE TEACHING OFFICE OF THE CHURCH

Section 1. The Teaching Office in General: Catechetics and
Preaching: Seminaries and Schools (cc. 1322–1383)

Art. 1. The Teaching Office in General (cc. 1322–1326)

PRELIMINARY SURVEY

The Power to Teach (c. 1322)
Definitions of Doctrine (c. 1323)
Conformity to the Mind of the Church (c. 1324)
Professing and Keeping the Faith (c. 1325)
Doctrinal Authority of Bishops (c. 1326)

The Power to Teach. Our Lord Jesus Christ entrusted the deposit
of faith to the Church, that under the constant guidance and assistance
of the Holy Spirit, she might sacredly guard and faithfully explain
this divine revelation. The Church has therefore the right and the
duty, independently of any civil power, to teach all nations the full
evangelical doctrine; and all men are bound by the law of God to
learn this doctrine properly and to embrace the true Church of God
(c. 1322).

This power of teaching pertains in a general way to *jurisdiction* or
government; it is acquired in the same way, that is, by canonical
mission (cf. cc. 109, 1328); it may be withdrawn in the same way;
and it binds the free will of men by precept just as do other exercises
of lawful jurisdiction. Yet it is not strictly jurisdiction in the
evangelization of infidels, for it is certain that the Church claims no
jurisdiction over the unbaptized. She has a mission and obligation to
teach them, and they have an obligation to examine and accept
her doctrine.

The Church *guards* and *explains* this deposit of faith. She does not
add to it, for it was completed and closed with the death of the last
Apostle, St. John. To *guard* means to keep and defend; in doing this

the Church must sometimes declare truths which are not contained in revelation but which are necessary to keep revealed truth. To *explain* means to make clear what is obscure. The so-called development of doctrine through dogmatic definitions may be compared to the sharpening of the focus on a film which is projected on a screen. The details which become discernible with a clear focus are not new; they were all in the original picture, but they are now brought out more clearly.

Definitions of Doctrine. All those truths must be believed *fide divina et catholica,* which are contained in the written word of God or in tradition and which the Church proposes for acceptance as revealed by God, either by solemn definition or through her ordinary and universal teaching. To pronounce a solemn definition is the part of an Ecumenical Council or of the Roman Pontiff speaking *ex cathedra.* No doctrine is to be considered as dogmatically defined unless this is evidently proved (c. 1323).

A doctrine is *de fide divina et catholica* only when it has been *infallibly declared by the Church to be revealed by God.* Hence this term does not apply to doctrines which one knows to have been revealed by God, but which have not been declared by the Church to have been so revealed (*de fide divina*); nor to those which the Church has infallibly declared, but which she does not present formally as having been revealed (*de fide ecclesiastica*); nor to those which the Church teaches without exercising her infallible authority upon them. If a doctrine is not *de fide divina et catholica,* a person is not a heretic for denying or doubting it, though such denial or doubt may be a grave sin (cf. c. 1325, § 2).

Conformity to the Mind of the Church. It is not enough to avoid heresy, but one must also carefully shun all errors which more or less approach it; hence all must observe the constitutions and decrees by which the Holy See has proscribed and forbidden opinions of that sort (c. 1324). Such are all doctrinal decrees of the Holy See, even though they be not infallibly proposed, and even though they come from the Sacred Congregations with the approval of the Holy Father, or from the Biblical Commission.[1] Examples: the Decree of the Holy Office condemning Theosophy;[2] the replies of the Biblical Commission condemning false interpretations of biblical texts.[3] Such decrees do not

---

[1] Cf. Pius X, *Motu proprio,* 18 Nov., 1907; *Fontes,* n. 681, Vol. III, p. 724.
[2] Holy Office, 18 July, 1919; *AAS,* 11–317; *Digest,* I, p. 620.
[3] Bibl. Com., 1 July, 1933; *AAS,* 25–344; *Digest,* I, p. 618.

receive the assent of faith; they are not *de fide catholica*. But they merit genuine internal intellectual assent and loyal obedience.[4]

Obligation to Profess the Faith. The faithful are bound to profess their faith openly whenever under the circumstances silence, evasion, or their manner of acting would otherwise implicitly amount to a denial of the faith, or would involve contempt of religion, an offense to God, or scandal to the neighbor (**c. 1325, § 1**).[5]

Heresy, Apostasy, Schism. One who after baptism, while remaining nominally a Christian, *pertinaciously* (that is, with conscious and intentional resistance to the authority of God and the Church) denies or doubts any one of the truths which must be believed *de fide divina et catholica*, is a heretic; if he falls away entirely from the Christian faith, he is an apostate; finally if he rejects the authority of the Supreme Pontiff or refuses communion with the members of the Church who are subject to him, he is a schismatic (**c. 1325, § 2**).

Discussions on the Faith With Non-Catholics. Catholics are to avoid disputations or conferences about matters of faith with non-Catholics, especially in public, unless the Holy See, or in case of emergency the Ordinary of the place, has given permission (**c. 1325, § 3**). This prohibition applies only to matters of faith and to public discussions *viva voce;* printed debates or conferences are subject only to the rules regarding books.[6]

Doctrinal Authority of Bishops. Individual Bishops, or even groups of Bishops in a particular Council, are not infallible in doctrine; yet the Bishops, under the authority of the Roman Pontiff, are true teachers of doctrine for the faithful under their charge (**c. 1326**). Bishops, singly or in groups, cannot authoritatively decide dogmatic controversies, even in their own territory, since this involves the *supreme* power of the Church's *magisterium*.[7]

---

[4] Cf. Choupin, *Valeur des décisions doctrinales et disciplinaires du S. Siège.*

[5] Cf. Genicot, *Theol. Mor.*, I, n. 196.

[6] Cf. A Coronata, *Institutiones*, II, n. 912; Bouscaren, *Cooperation with Non-Catholics*, in *Theological Studies*, Vol. 3, p. 475; Kelleher, *Discussion with Non-Catholics*, Cath. U., 1943.

[7] Cf. Wernz, *Ius Decretalium*, II, n. 762.

Art. 2. Catechetics and Preaching (cc. 1327–1351)

PRELIMINARY SURVEY

General Norm on Preaching (cc. 1327, 1328)
Catechetical Instruction in General (c. 1329)
Duty of Pastors (cc. 1330–1332)
Clerical and Lay Catechists (c. 1333)
Duty of Religious (c. 1334)
Duty of Parents (c. 1335)
Authority of the Ordinary of the Place (c. 1336)
Canonical Mission and Permission to Preach (cc. 1337–1341)
Orders Required for Preaching (c. 1342)
Preaching by the Ordinary Himself (c. 1343)
Duty of Pastors (cc. 1344–1346)
Matter and Manner of Sermons (c. 1347)
Attendance (c. 1348)
Parish Missions and Work for Non-Catholics
(cc. 1349–1351)

General Norm on Preaching. The office of preaching the Catholic faith is entrusted chiefly to the Roman Pontiff for the universal Church, and to Bishops for their respective dioceses. Bishops are bound to preach the Gospel personally unless excused by some legitimate reason; and they should moreover employ for the proper fulfillment of this office, not only pastors, but other capable preachers as well **(c. 1327).** Since preaching pertains to the power of jurisdiction, not to that of order, and is conferred by canonical mission, not by ordination, this duty rests fully upon a *residential* Bishop when he receives his appointment. The same is true of Abbots and Prelates *nullius,* Apostolic Administrators, Vicars and Prefects Apostolic.

No one may exercise the ministry of preaching unless he has received a mission from his lawful superior, either by special grant of the faculty to preach, or by receiving an office to which the function of preaching is attached according to canon law **(c. 1328).** Fitness to preach is, of course, required, but it is not sufficient. The Council of Trent condemned the error that preachers might preach without being duly ordained and sent.[8]

Catechetical Instruction in General. This means simple instruction on the chief articles of faith, moral duties, and means of salvation. It will vary somewhat according to the persons to whom it is given,

---

[8] *Sess.* XXIII, *de sacr. ordinis,* can. 7.

children, college students, or the faithful in general; and it may be general or adapted to some special purpose, such as First Communion or marriage. In the early Church instruction was gradual: the *proselyte,* having indicated a desire to belong to the Church, was instructed in the principal truths of faith; this done, he was inscribed as a *catechumen;* he then received baptism, became a *neophyte,* and received fuller instruction. In the fifth and sixth centuries adult baptisms, and consequently also adult instruction, were rare, but the instruction of children grew in importance. In the middle ages there was far from total neglect of catechetical instruction;[9] and even before the Reformation the Church was constantly insisting on it. Some famous catechisms of the post-Reformation period are those of St. Peter Canisius (1555–1558), the Roman Catechism, composed in pursuance of the decree of the Council of Trent and published by Pope Saint Pius V (1566), and that of St. Robert Bellarmine (1597–1598). Modern papal documents both before and after the Code form the background and interpretation for these canons.[10]

Duty of Pastors. Especially all pastors of souls have a peculiar and very grave obligation to take care of the catechetical instruction of the Catholic people **(c. 1329).** This applies to residential Bishops, parish priests, and to all who have the care of souls.

1. *Confession, Confirmation, First Communion.* The pastor must: (*a*) at stated times every year, by continuous instruction over a period of many days, prepare the children for the proper reception of the sacraments of penance and confirmation (c. 1330, 1°); (*b*) with very special diligence, especially if possible during Lent, prepare the children for a holy First Communion (c. 1330, 2°). The Third Council of Baltimore (nn. 217, 218) urged that this duty be performed by the pastor or his assistants in person, and moreover that they frequently

---

[9] Cf. Gasquet, *The Old English Bible and Other Essays.*
[10] Cf. Benedict XIV, *Etsi minime,* 7 Feb., 1741; Pius IX, Encyclical, *Nostis,* 8 Dec., 1849; *Fontes,* n. 508, Vol. II, p. 837; Leo XIII, *In mezzo,* 26 June, 1878; *Fontes,* n. 574, Vol. III, p. 116; Conc. Balt. III, nn. 217–219; Pius X, *Acerbo nimis,* 15 Apr., 1905; *Fontes,* n. 666, Vol. III, p. 647; S. C. Conc., 31 May, 1920, demanding a report from the Ordinaries of Italy; *AAS,* 12–229; *Digest,* I, p. 631; Pius XI, *Motu proprio,* 20 June, 1923, creating special Office in the Sacred Congregation of the Council; *AAS,* 15–327; *Digest,* I, p. 632; S. C. Conc. to the Ordinaries of Italy, 23 Apr., 1924; *AAS,* 16–287; *Digest,* I, p. 633; S. C. Conc., Catechetical Office, 24 June, 1924, sends all Ordinaries formula for triennial (later changed to quinquennial) report on catechetical instruction; *AAS,* 16–332; *Digest,* I, p. 634; S. C. Conc., 16 Apr., 1934, issued rules for catechetical meetings; *AAS,* 16–431; *Digest,* I, p. 634; Pius XI, 12 March, 1930, granted a plenary indulgence twice a month to those teaching or learning Christian doctrine; *AAS,* 22–343; *Digest,* I, p. 635; S. C. Conc., 12 Jan., 1935, issued a new Decree on Catechetical Instruction; *AAS,* 27–145; *Digest,* II, p. 412.

visit both the parochial school classes in catechism and Sunday school classes which are not being taught by priests.

2. *Continuation of children's instructions.* Moreover, the pastor must give a fuller and more complete training in the catechism to those children who have recently made their First Communion (c. 1331). The notion that religious instruction should end with First Communion is entirely contrary to the mind of the Church.

3. *Parish instructions to the people.* On Sundays and feast days of obligation, at an hour which he judges best for good attendance, the pastor must also explain the catechism to the grown people in language which they can understand (c. 1332). The Council of Trent had already prescribed catechetical instruction for both children and adults; but the immediate source of this provision is an Encyclical of Pius X.[11]

Clerical and Lay Catechists. In the religious instruction of children the pastor may, and if he is unable to do the work personally he should, make use of the services of other clerics living in the parish, and even if need be of pious lay persons, especially those who are enrolled in the pious sodality of Christian doctrine or in some other similar society which exists in the parish (c. 1333, § 1). Priests and other clerics who are not prevented from doing so by some lawful excuse must help the pastor in this holy work, even under penalties to be inflicted by the Ordinary for refusal (c. 1333, § 2). The sodality which is especially designated here is the Confraternity of Christian Doctrine, founded in Rome in 1560 and approved by Pope St. Pius V in 1571. Its designation is not exclusive, since any other similar society in the parish can take its place. Though canon 711 directs Ordinaries to see that confraternities of the Blessed Sacrament and of Christian doctrine be erected in every parish, the Code Commission declared, as regards the confraternity of the Blessed Sacrament, that pious unions or other sodalities of the Blessed Sacrament might take its place.[12] The same principle evidently applies to the Confraternity of Christian Doctrine. There is a *theoretical* difficulty about lay people teaching the catechism publicly, because such teaching might seem to require a canonical mission, and that would imply jurisdiction. On the other hand lay persons are incapable of ecclesiastical jurisdiction (cf. c. 118). Practically it is certain both from this canon and from many other sources that the help of lay persons of both sexes in teaching catechism even publicly is not only welcomed but earnestly solicited. For centuries

---

[11] Pius X, *Acerbo nimis,* 15 Apr., 1905; *Fontes,* n. 666, Vol. III, p. 647.
[12] Code Com., 6 March, 1927; *AAS,* 19–161; *Digest,* I, p. 334.

lay catechists have been employed in the mission fields. Recent documents on Catholic Action invite the laity to co-operate with the hierarchy very especially in this work. Perhaps the answer to the theoretical difficulty is this. Lay persons thus working with the approval of the hierarchy have a canonical mission only in a broad sense; a mandate, without jurisdiction. They work *ex iurisdictione,* though not *cum iurisdictione.* (Cf. A Coronata, II, n. 914.)

Duty of Religious. If in the judgment of the Ordinary of the place the aid of religious is needed in the catechetical instruction of the people, religious superiors, even exempt, if requested to do so by the local Ordinary, are bound to give such instruction to the faithful, either in person or through their subjects, especially in their own churches, but without interfering with religious discipline **(c. 1334).** This provision applies only to the instruction of adults. The words *especially in their own churches* leave the question open whether the local Ordinary could command the services of *exempt* religious for this instruction outside their own churches. Some hold that he could; others deny it.[13] It seems certain that they should willingly assist in this work if the request is made through their superior and if the work does not interfere with religious discipline (cf. c. 608). If exempt religious have the care of souls, they have the duty and right of instruction as regards both children and adults (cc. 1330–1332). Even though not charged with the care of souls they need no special authorization of the local Ordinary to teach catechism; for this is not preaching in the strict sense, and their canonical mission is contained in the approval of their institute for this work. They must, however, conform to general regulations made by the local Ordinary (cf. c. 1336).

Duty of Parents, Employers. Not only parents and others exercising parental authority, but also masters and employers are bound to see to it that all who are under their authority or in their charge receive catechetical instruction **(c. 1335).**

Authority of the Ordinary of the Place. It pertains to the Ordinary of the place to make regulations regarding the instruction of the people in Christian doctrine; and even exempt religious, whenever they teach nonexempt persons, are bound to observe them **(c. 1336).**

Sacred Preaching. A sermon (*concio*) is a sacred public address, given by one duly empowered by the Church, in order to instruct

---

[13] Prümmer, *Manuale,* n. 404, 2.

the hearers in the Christian faith and to move them to practice it.[14]
The canons of the Code on preaching have for their background
the whole history of the ministry of the word in the Church, especially
the provisions of the Council of Trent and of more recent papal
documents.[15] Among these the provisions of the Third Council of
Baltimore (nn. 214–216), the Encyclical of Benedict XV on Preaching,[16] and the Norms for Sacred Preaching issued in pursuance of it
and with papal approval by the Sacred Consistorial Congregation in
1917[17] deserve special attention. These Norms still remain in effect,
except in the few minor details where they differ from the Code.
Besides the moral earnestness of the Church's solicitude for good
and adequate preaching of the word of God, the point which is noteworthy in these canons is the question of canonical mission: what
authority is required for the faculty to preach. The Code makes very
little change in pre-existing legislation. The chief innovation is in
regard to regulars preaching to the people in or out of their own
churches. For preaching to *the people* (but not to clerical exempt religious) *in their own churches,* regulars formerly needed only the
"blessing" of the Ordinary of the place; now they need from him
the faculty to preach (c. 1338, § 2). For the same kind of preaching
outside their own churches, they formerly needed the Ordinary's
permission in writing; now they must have from him the faculty to
preach, but not necessarily in writing, unless they are from outside
the diocese.[18] We must carefully distinguish between three words
used in these canons: *facultas* (faculty), *licentia* (permission), and
assensus (consent). *Facultas* is the grant of the right to preach; *licentia*
is the permission from some other person, which may also be required
for the licit exercise of the right; finally, *assensus* is the consent of
still another person, which may be needed to exercise the right in
regard to certain persons who are his subjects. For example, a regular
priest from outside the diocese, in preaching to lay religious, needs
faculties from the Ordinary of the place (c. 1338, § 3), the *permission*
of his own religious superior (c. 1339, § 2), and the *consent* of the
religious superior of his hearers (c. 1338, § 3).

Canonical Mission for Seculars and Nonexempt Religious. The
Ordinary of the place alone grants the faculty to preach in his

---

[14] McVann, *The Canon Law on Preaching,* p. 1.
[15] Cf. McVann, *op. cit.,* pp. 7–57.
[16] Benedict XV, *Humani generis,* 15 June, 1917; *AAS,* 9–305.
[17] S. C. Consist., 28 June, 1917; *AAS,* 9–328; *Digest,* I, p. 622.
[18] Cf. Norms, n. 9; *Digest,* I, p. 625.

territory to clerics of the secular clergy and to nonexempt religious (c. 1337).

For Exempt Religious. 1. In a clerical religious institute, if a sermon is to be given *only to the exempt religious or to the persons mentioned in canon 514, § 1* (namely, those who live night and day in the religious house as servants, pupils, guests, or patients) the *faculty* to preach is granted by *their superior* according to the constitutions; and he can grant it also to members of the secular clergy or of some other institute, provided they have been declared qualified by their own Ordinary or superior (c. 1338, § 1).

2. If the sermon is to *other persons or even to nuns who are subject to regular superiors,* exempt religious also must obtain the *faculty* from the *Ordinary of the place* where they are to preach; but if a preacher is to speak to exempt nuns he needs also the *permission* of the *regular superior* (c. 1338, § 2).

3. The *faculty* to preach to members of a *lay religious institute,* even though it be exempt, is obtained from the *local Ordinary;* but the preacher may not use it without the *consent* of the *religious superior* (c. 1338, § 3).

Catechetical instructions are not sermons, and are not included in these canons; neither are lectures or talks at conventions, or occasional talks in a school, even on religious subjects.

Grant of Faculty and Permission to Preach. 1. Ordinaries of places should not without grave cause refuse the faculty to religious preachers who are presented by their own superior; nor should they revoke the faculty once granted, especially in the case of all the priests of a religious house at the same time, except as provided in canon 1340 (c. 1339, § 1). Religious preachers, in order to use licitly the *faculty* they may have received, must have moreover the *permission* of their own superior (c. 1339, § 2).

2. The local Ordinary and the religious superior are bound by a grave obligation in conscience not to grant the *faculty* or the *permission* to preach, without having previously satisfied themselves of the candidate's moral character and also, by examination according to canon 877, § 1, of his sufficient training (c. 1340, § 1). The examination as to qualifications for preaching is mentioned in the Instruction or Norms (n. 14), which speaks not only of learning but also of action or delivery. The examination is not absolutely prescribed, since the Ordinary or superior may know the preacher's qualifications from other sources (n. 16). The reference to canon 877, § 1, which requires

an examination *ad confessiones audiendas,* shows that there would be no objection to having the two together, that is, the examination for preaching together with that for confessions.[19]

Revocation of Faculty or Permission. If, after the faculty or permission has been granted, the Ordinary or superior learn that the preacher has not the needed qualification, they must revoke it; in case of doubt they must settle the matter by certain proof, even if necessary by a new examination (c. 1340, § 2). Upon revocation of the faculty or permission to preach, there is a right of recourse, but without suspensive effect (c. 1340, § 3). One reason for this right of recourse is that the *revocation* affects the reputation of the preacher, which deserves this protection. In case of refusal of the faculty or permission in the first place, there is no explicit provision for recourse; but it does not follow that they can be refused indiscriminately or without solid reason. The Instruction states (n. 11) that an Ordinary who asks for and receives information regarding the qualifications of a preacher is bound to act in accordance with it. Recourse can always be taken to the Holy See even if it is not expressly provided for.[20]

Extradiocesan Preachers, Secular and Religious. These, of course, need the faculty from the Ordinary of the place where they are to preach. The Instruction requires that it be in writing (n. 9). Whoever invites an extradiocesan preacher should notify the Ordinary of the place some time beforehand and obtain his permission. The Ordinary will then have time to ascertain, as he must do before granting the permission unless he is already informed, by inquiry of the proposed preacher's own Ordinary, his qualifications, that is, his learning, piety, and moral character. The Ordinary of whom such inquiry is made is gravely bound in conscience to answer truthfully (c. 1341, § 1). This permission is to be asked in due time: by the pastor if there is question of a parish church; by the rector if the church is not subject to the pastor; by the first dignitary with the consent of the chapter, if it is a capitular church;[21] and by the director or chaplain of the confraternity if the church belongs to a confraternity (c. 1341, § 2). Finally, if the parish church belongs also to a chapter or confraternity (cf. c. 415) the priest who has the right to perform the sacred functions is to ask for the permission (c. 1341, § 3). The Ordinary of the place

---

[19] Cf. McCarthy, *The New Regulations on Preaching,* in *Eccl. Review,* Vol. 57, p. 385.
[20] Cf. McVann, *The Canon Law on Preaching,* p. 71.
[21] The Code requires for this the *consent* of the chapter, though the Instruction (n. 5, a) speaks only of *consulting* the chapter. The Code prevails.

may prudently give pastors general *permission to invite* extradiocesan priests, secular or religious, to preach in their churches; the pastor then has the responsibility of ascertaining the qualifications of the preacher.[22] In practice, the preacher in such cases would be considered to have received implicitly the faculty to preach.

Orders Required for Preaching. The faculty to preach is to be granted only to priests and deacons, not to other clerics, except for reasonable cause according to the discretion of the Ordinary in particular cases (c. 1342, § 1). All laymen, even though they be religious, are forbidden to preach in the church (c. 1342, § 2).[23]

Preaching by the Ordinary Himself. Cardinals have by privilege (c. 239, § 1, 3°) the right to preach the word of God anywhere; and the same privilege is extended to Bishops both residential and titular, with at least the presumed permission of the Ordinary of the place (c. 349, § 1). Local Ordinaries have the right to preach in any church, even though it be exempt, in their territory (c. 1343, § 1). Except in large cities, the Bishop can also forbid the preaching of sermons to the people in other churches of the same place at the hour when he is either speaking himself or having a sermon preached in his presence to the people assembled because of some public and extraordinary reason (c. 1343, § 2). The words *except in large cities* call for a moral estimate; there is excellent authority as well as good reason for considering a city of 100,000 population, including non-Catholics, as "large." If the Ordinary is speaking in person, the rule given applies even *without a public and extraordinary reason,* since these words refer only to the other case, where the sermon is preached by someone else in the Bishop's presence. This is clear from the sources of the canon, if not from the text itself.[24]

Duty of the Pastor. In addition to the duty of explaining the catechism to the people on Sundays and holydays of obligation (c. 1332), the Code places upon all pastors rather explicit obligations as regards preaching. Pastors here include quasi-pastors in mission territories, and all parochial vicars who have full parochial powers (c. 451, § 2).

1. *The Sunday homily.* On Sundays and other days of obligation throughout the year it is the duty of every pastor to preach the

---

[22] Cf. Vermeersch-Creusen, *Epitome,* II, n. 676.

[23] See *America,* March 11, 1939, article by J. M. Kerrish telling of his own preaching, as a Catholic layman and convert, in *Protestant* churches, with the permission of the Catholic hierarchy.

[24] Cf. Benedict XIV, *De Synodo,* Lib. IX, c. 17, n. 7; Vermeersch-Creusen, *Epit.,* II, n. 678, *contra* Prümmer and Augustine.

customary homily to the people, especially at the Mass at which there is usually the best attendance (c. 1344, § 1). The pastor may not habitually satisfy this obligation by proxy, except for a just cause approved by the Ordinary (c. 1344, § 2). The Ordinary may permit that the homily be omitted on certain solemn feasts, or even, for just cause, on certain Sundays (c. 1344, § 3). Strictly speaking, a homily means a familiar explanation of the Scriptures, ending with a moral exhortation; but here the term is used generally, so that any form of development will do for the Sunday sermon, provided it carry a supernatural message in language which the people can understand.[25] According to the text of the Code it should habitually be preached by the pastor in person, and only occasionally by another unless the Ordinary has given permission. But if the pastor is unable to do it himself because of legitimate absence or other relatively grave cause, he must have it done by a substitute, for the duty is both personal and real. The precise amount of negligence which would constitute a grave sin is difficult to determine. Most authorities admit that it is grave to neglect this duty for three months.[26] Canon 2382 provides penalties even to the privation of office, which evidently supposes a grave sin.

2. *Explanations of the Gospel or of doctrine.* These differ from the homily chiefly in their purpose, which is instruction rather than moral exhortation. It is recommended that at the Masses which are attended by the faithful on feast days of obligation in all churches and public oratories, a short explanation of the Gospel or of some part of Christian doctrine be given; and if the Ordinary of the place has prescribed this and given suitable directions for it, all are bound to do it, not only priests of the secular clergy, but religious also, even exempt, in their own churches (c. 1345). By the general law this is merely recommended; it becomes obligatory only if the Ordinary has given directions prescribing it. He may prescribe it at all the Sunday and holyday Masses, or at some of them. In the United States, however, the Third Council of Baltimore (n. 216) prescribed a five-minute explanation of the Gospel at all Sunday and holyday Masses, even during the summer, and that a sermon be preached at the parochial or principal Mass.

3. *Lent and Advent sermons.* Ordinaries of places should see to it that in Lent, and if they see fit also in Advent, in cathedral and

---

[25] Cf. McVann, *The Canon Law on Preaching,* p. 110.
[26] Cf. McVann, *op. cit.,* pp. 106–110.

parish churches, sermons be given more frequently (c. 1346, § 1). Canons and others belonging to the chapter are bound to attend this sermon if it is given in their church immediately after the choir service, unless they are lawfully excused; and the Ordinary may compel them, even under penalty, to do so (c. 1346, § 2). These special sermons need not be preached by the pastor himself.

Matter and Manner of the Sermon. 1. The matter of sermons should be especially the things which the faithful must believe and do in order to be saved (c. 1347, § 1). The Third Council of Baltimore (n. 215) especially urges preachers to speak the word of God with authority, to fortify the faithful against the religious indifferentism and heresies amid which they live, but without offense to non-Catholics who may be present; in moral precepts to be neither overrigid nor lax; to avoid novelties, strange tales, politics, personalities.

2. Preachers should abstain from profane and abstruse subjects which are beyond the grasp of the audience; let them exercise the ministry of the Gospel, not in the "persuasive words of human wisdom," nor with profane display and parade of useless and vain eloquence, but "in the demonstration of the Spirit and of power," ever preaching not themselves but Christ crucified (c. 1347, § 2). If a preacher spreads errors and scandals he is subject to the penalties of canon 2317 (exclusion from the ministry of preaching and hearing confessions, etc.); if he preaches heresy he should be dealt with according to law (c. 1347, § 3). As to language, the Third Council of Baltimore (n. 216) earnestly urges that it be simple, without being crude and flat; as to duration, the sermon at Mass should be short; all preaching requires careful preparation, which consists especially in the study of Sacred Scripture, theology, church history, and in pious meditation.

Attendance at Sermons. The faithful should be admonished and exhorted to attend sermons frequently (c. 1348).

Parish Missions. Ordinaries should see to it that pastors have what is called a mission preached to their people at least every ten years (c. 1349, § 1). Even a religious pastor, in arranging these missions, must abide by the instructions of the local Ordinary (c. 1349, § 2).

Work for Non-Catholics. Local Ordinaries and pastors must look upon the non-Catholics in their dioceses and parishes as commended to them by Almighty God (c. 1350, § 1). In other territories the universal care of missions among non-Catholics is reserved solely to the Holy See (c. 1350, § 2). No one is to be forced against his will to embrace the Catholic faith (c. 1351). Infant children of non-Catholics are not to be baptized without the consent of the parents except in danger of death, or with proper guarantees of a Catholic education and the consent of at least one parent (cf. cc. 750, 751).

Art. 3. Seminaries and Schools (cc. 1352–1383)

PRELIMINARY SURVEY (SEMINARIES)

Right of the Church to Educate Her Clergy (c. 1352)
Priests Should Foster Vocations (c. 1353)
Seminaries: Diocesan, Major and Minor, Interdiocesan (c. 1354)
Means of Financial Support (c. 1355)
The Seminary Tax (c. 1356)
Management and Supervision (c. 1357)
Officials (c. 1358)
Two Boards: Discipline and Management (c. 1359)
Qualifications of Officials (c. 1360)
Confessors (c. 1361)
Scholarships (c. 1362)
Admission (c. 1363)
Studies: in Lower Classes (c. 1364)
        in Philosophy and Theology (c. 1365)
Qualifications of Professors: Method, Etc. (c. 1366)
Exercises of Piety (c. 1367)
Exemption of Seminary (c. 1368)
Supervision and General Training (c. 1369)
Absence From Seminary (c. 1370)
Dismissal (c. 1371)

This preliminary survey is the more necessary as our treatment must be very brief. In the Middle Ages the clergy were educated either privately or in the universities; the history of seminaries in the strict sense dates from the Council of Trent, in which we find in outline the provisions of the Code. To put these provisions into actual practice has been a long, hard battle against many difficulties. The Third Council of Baltimore took up the matter in considerable detail (nn. 135–185), outlining the studies for both major and minor seminaries. The first ecclesiastical seminary in the United States according to the mind of the Council of Trent was St. Mary's Seminary in Baltimore, established in 1791.

Right of the Church. The Church has of its very nature the exclusive right to educate those who wish to devote themselves to the ecclesiastical ministry (c. 1352). This follows necessarily from the nature of the Church as a perfect society; yet even so-called Catholics have claimed for the State the right of supervision over ecclesiastical studies.[27]

Vocations to the Priesthood. A vocation to the priesthood is a call from God, which, however, is usually indicated not by an extraordinary internal inspiration, but by a right intention together with fitness for the life and work so chosen. This fitness is the result of various gifts in the natural and supernatural order, and is proved by probity of life and sufficient learning to give ground for the expectation that the person will sacredly fulfill the functions and keep the obligations of the priesthood.[28] Experience amply proves that the germ of a vocation needs to be fostered, especially by protecting the young soul in whom it is planted from the contamination of vice. Priests and especially pastors must take care especially to protect from the contagion of the world boys who show signs of an ecclesiastical vocation, to train them to piety, instruct them in the rudimentary branches, and foster in them the seed of the divine vocation (c. 1353).

Diocesan and Regional Seminaries. Every diocese should have, in a suitable place chosen by the Bishop, a seminary, that is, a college where, according to the resources and extent of the diocese, a certain number of young men are trained for the clerical state (c. 1354, § 1). Here we have a material description, not a juridical definition of a seminary. Juridically a seminary is an ecclesiastical corporation, a noncollegiate moral person, with the right to own and administer property for the purpose of training young men for the priesthood (cf. c. 99). In the larger dioceses there should be two seminaries: a minor one, where boys are trained in literary studies, and a major one for those who are studying philosophy and theology (c. 1354, § 2). If it is impossible to establish a diocesan seminary, or to get adequate training, especially in philosophy and theology, in the one which is established, the Bishop should send his students to the seminary of some other diocese, unless an interdiocesan or regional seminary has been established by papal authority (c. 1354, § 3).[29]

---

[27] Cf. condemned propositions 33 and 46, Syllabus of Pius IX; Denzinger-Bannwart, nn. 1733, 1746.

[28] Cf. Lahitton, *La vocation sacerdotale,* specifically approved, 2 July, 1912, by a special Commission of Cardinals appointed to examine it by Pope Pius X; also Vermeersch, *De Vocatione Religiosa et Sacerdotali,* Bruges, 1914; Cappello, *De Sacra Ordinatione,* nn. 362–377. These studies of Lahitton and Vermeersch are published in English by Herder.

[29] An important document on seminaries is the Apostolic Letter of Pius XI, 1 Aug., 1922; *AAS,* 14–449; *Digest,* I, p. 643. See also recommendations made by the S. C. of Seminaries, 25 Jan., 1928, for seminaries in the United States; *Digest,* I, p. 647. Many valuable documents will also be found in *Enchiridion Clericorum.*

Financial Support of the Seminary. For the establishment and maintenance of a seminary if it has no sufficient endowment, the Bishop can: (1) require pastors and other rectors even of exempt churches to take up a collection for this purpose in their churches at stated times; (2) impose a tribute or tax in his diocese; (3) if these measures are not enough, he can attribute to the seminary certain simple or nonresidential benefices (c. 1355). The explanation of these financial measures is beyond our scope, as is also that of canon 1356, which defines in detail the administration of the seminary tax.

Government of the Seminary. The Bishop is to make all proper regulations for the administration, government, and advancement of the diocesan seminary, and to see that they are observed, subject to any special prescriptions which may be made by the Holy See (c. 1357, § 1). He should especially visit the seminary frequently in person, watch carefully over the training of the students, and acquire fuller knowledge of their dispositions, piety, vocation, and progress, especially on the occasion of sacred ordinations (c. 1357, § 2). Each seminary should have its rules, approved by the Bishop, for the government both of the students and of those who are engaged in their training (c. 1357, § 3). The entire management and administration of an interdiocesan or regional seminary is governed by the rules established by the Holy See (c. 1357, § 4).

There should be in every seminary a rector for discipline, teachers for instruction, a procurator, distinct from the rector, for financial administration, at least two ordinary confessors, and a spiritual father (c. 1358).

In a diocesan seminary there should be two boards of governors, one in charge of discipline, the other of temporal administration (c. 1359, § 1). Each board shall consist of two priests appointed by the Bishop after consulting the chapter; but the Vicar General, priests who live with the Bishop, the rector and procurator of the seminary, and the ordinary confessors, are excluded from both these boards (c. 1359, § 2). The members are appointed for six years, are not to be removed without grave reason, but can be reappointed (c. 1359, § 3). In matters of importance the Bishop must ask the advice of the members of both these boards (c. 1359, § 4).

It is understood that the rector is not to hear the confessions of the students who live in the same house with him, unless they of their own accord come to him in particular cases for a grave and urgent reason (c. 891). As regards qualifications, the rector, spiritual father, confessors, and teachers should be priests who are outstanding not only for learning but also for virtue and prudence, so that they may be able to help the students by word and example (c. 1360, § 1). All must obey the rector of the seminary in the fulfillment of their respective functions (c. 1360, § 2).

Confessors. In addition to the ordinary confessors, others are to be designated to whom the students can freely go (c. 1361, § 1). If these confessors live outside the seminary, and a student asks that one of them be called, the rector must call him without inquiring in any way into the reason for the request, or showing any displeasure; if the confessors live in the seminary, any student may freely go to them, without prejudice to the discipline of the house (c. 1361, § 2). When there is question of admitting any student to orders, or of expelling him from the seminary, the advice of the confessors is never to be asked (c. 1361, § 3).

Scholarships. One difficulty which could arise regarding scholarships is this. Funds might be left "for the education of clerics," the general intention being that the money should be used for any student in the seminary. The difficulty is that many of them are not yet clerics, since according to canon 976, § 1, first tonsure is to be given only at the beginning of theology. To obviate this difficulty the Code provides that the revenue of endowments given for the education of clerics may be used for any students who have been lawfully received into either a minor or major seminary, even though they have not yet become clerics by receiving the tonsure (cf. c. 108), unless it is expressly provided in the gift that it is for the benefit of clerics only (c. 1362).

Admission. Those admitted to the seminary must be legitimate sons, and have such dispositions and good will as to give hope that they will serve permanently in the ministry (c. 1363, § 1). They must, before being admitted, show testimonials of legitimate birth, of baptism and confirmation, and of good moral character (c. 1363, § 2). Those who have been dismissed from other seminaries or from some religious institute are not to be admitted until the Bishop has asked of their superiors or other persons information regarding the dismissal, and about their character, disposition, and talents, and knows for certain that there is nothing about them which is unbecoming to the priestly state; superiors are gravely bound in conscience to supply this information truthfully (c. 1363, § 3). According to a recent joint decree of the S. C. of Religious and the S. C. of Seminaries and Universities, before receiving into the seminary one who has been a member of a religious family, the Bishop must, moreover, consult the S. C. of Seminaries.[30] This decree does not apply to seminarians who pass from a seminary to a religous institute (S. C. Rel., 11 May, 1942; *Digest,* II, p. 166). According to canon 1117 and a reply of the Code Commission, sons who have been legitimated by the subsequent marriage of their parents may be admitted.[31] In 1918 special provisions were made for readmitting at the conclusion of their military service, boys who had formerly been in the seminary.[32]

Studies. *Lower classes.* In the lower classes of the seminary: (1) the study of religion has the first place, and it should be explained in a manner accommodated to the talents and age of the students; (2) they should learn well especially the Latin language and their own; (3) in other branches they should receive an education which is on a par with the prevailing degree of culture and suitable to the state of clerics in the country where the students are destined to exercise their ministry **(c. 1364).** An instruction of the S. C. of Seminaries for the United States recommends special means to train the students sufficiently in Latin before they begin the study of philosophy and theology.[33]

Philosophy and theology. They must spend at least two years in the study of rational philosophy and kindred branches (that is, their native tongue, Latin, Greek, profane history, mathematics, natural sciences) **(c. 1365, § 1).** The theology course should be at least four years including besides dogmatic and moral theology also Sacred Scripture, ecclesiastical history, canon law, liturgy, sacred eloquence, and ecclesiastical chant **(c. 1365, § 2).** Moreover there should be lectures in pastoral theology, and practical exercises especially on teaching catechism to children, hearing confessions, visiting the sick, assisting the dying **(c. 1365, § 3).** A letter of the S. C. urges that special attention be given to Oriental theology and catechetics.[34] A course in pedagogy is prescribed (S. C. Sem. et Univ., 21 Dec., 1944; *AAS,* 37–173).

Qualifications of Professors, Etc. For teaching philosophy, theology, and canon law, other things being equal in the judgment of the Bishop and boards of governors, those professors should be preferred

---

[30] S. C. Rel. and S. C. Stud., 25 July, 1941; *AAS,* 33–371; *Digest,* II, p. 426; cf. annotations by Cardinal La Puma in *Commentarium pro Religiosis,* 1942, p. 226.
[31] Code Com., 13 July, 1930; *AAS,* 22–365; *Digest,* I, p. 661.
[32] S. C. Consist., 25 Oct., 1918; *AAS,* 10–481; *Digest,* I, p. 99.
[33] Cf. S. C. Stud., 25 Jan., 1928; *Digest,* I, p. 647.
[34] Cf. S. C. Stud., 28 Aug., 1929; *AAS,* 22–146; *Digest,* I, p. 666.

who have obtained a doctorate in some university or faculty recognized by the Holy See, or, in the case of religious, those who have a corresponding testimonial from their major superiors (c. 1366, § 1). The professors should by all means treat the studies of rational philosophy and theology, and the training of the students in these subjects, according to the method, doctrine, and principles of the Angelic Doctor, and should hold these as sacred (c. 1366, § 2). There should if possible be distinct professors at least in Sacred Scripture, dogma, moral theology, and church history (c. 1366, § 3). As to the following of St. Thomas, several recent documents throw light on the meaning of this provision.[35] The requirement of a degree is more strict for Scripture than for the other branches.[36]

Exercises of Piety. The Bishop is to see to it that the students: (1) every day, say morning and evening prayers in common, spend some time in mental prayer, attend Mass; (2) confess at least once a week; receive Communion frequently, with due devotion; (3) on Sundays and feast days, attend solemn Mass and Vespers, serve at the altar and practice sacred ceremonies, especially in the cathedral if in the judgment of the Bishop this can be done without harm to discipline and studies; (4) every year, make the spiritual exercises for several days continuously; (5) at least once a week, hear a spiritual instruction closing with a pious exhortation (c. 1367).

Exemption of the Seminary. Unless in certain seminaries different provisions have been made by the Holy See, the seminary is to be exempt from the jurisdiction of the pastor; and, except as regards marriage and except as provided in canon 891 regarding confessions, the parochial office shall be performed for all persons in the seminary by the rector of the seminary or his delegate (c. 1368). This exemption begins as soon as the seminary exists *de facto* and people are living in it. Marriage is an exception; hence a marriage in the seminary chapel (cf. c. 1109, § 2) would pertain to the pastor. No exception is made for funerals; hence, *per se* it would seem proper that the funeral be attended to by the rector at the seminary, provided the deceased lived there and was not merely a transient. In this matter various considerations might make it advisable for the rector of the seminary to yield his right in favor of the pastor, particularly if the parents and relatives seem to prefer a funeral from the parish

---

[35] Cf. Pius XI, Encyclical, 29 June, 1923; *AAS*, 15–309; *Digest*, I, p. 669; Pius XII, address to clerical students in Rome, 24 June, 1939; *AAS*, 31–245; *Digest*, II, p. 427.

[36] Cf. Pius XI, *Motu proprio*, 27 Apr., 1924; *AAS*, 16–180, which requires at least a baccalaureate.

church. The exemption in general applies to major and minor seminaries, even though other than clerical students also attend it, and also to the seminary villa, even though this be in another diocese,[37] but not to a seminary for the training of religious, unless it has a special privilege or comes within the law regarding exemption of religious.[38] Sisters serving the seminary and living there come within the exemption, and are therefore under the jurisdiction of the rector, except as regards confessions.[39]

Supervision: General Training. The rector of the seminary and others in charge there under his authority should see that the students exactly observe the rules approved by the Bishop, that they follow the course of studies and imbibe the true spirit of the Church (c. 1369, § 1). They should frequently instruct them in the rules of true Christian urbanity, and inspire them to their observance by example; they should also exhort them always to take a reasonable care of their health, to attend to cleanliness of apparel and person, and in their relations with others to cultivate a certain affability together with modesty and gravity (c. 1369, § 2). They should carefully watch that the professors do their work well (c. 1369, § 3). An instruction of the S. C. Sacr. contains very serious prescriptions for testing the character and intention of candidates for sacred orders. This instruction must be read to students in seminaries at the beginning of every scholastic year (S. C. Sacr., 27 Dec., 1930; *AAS*, 23–120; *Digest*, I, p. 463. Similar provisions are made for religious seminaries; cf. *Digest*, I, p. 473).

Absence From the Seminary: Dismissal. Whenever the students remain for any reason away from the seminary, canon 972, § 2 is to be observed, that is, they must be under the care of some suitable pious priest who must watch over them and train them to piety (c. 1370). Troublemakers, incorrigible youths, those who show a rebellious spirit, and those who do not seem morally and psychologically suited to the ecclesiastical state, should be dismissed from the seminary; as should also those who make so little progress in studies that there is no hope that they will ever acquire sufficient learning; especially any should be immediately dismissed who have committed a fault against morals or against the faith (c. 1371).

---

[37] Cf. S. C. Stud., 26 July, 1934; *Digest*, II, p. 425.
[38] Cf. A Coronata, *Institutiones*, II, n. 944; Augustine, *A Commentary*, VI, p. 407.
[39] A Coronata, *op. cit.*, II, n. 944.

PRELIMINARY SURVEY (SCHOOLS)

Religious and Moral Training (c. 1372)
Religious Instruction in Elementary and Secondary Schools
(c. 1373)
Neutral and Mixed Schools (c. 1374)
Right of Church to Establish Schools (c. 1375)
Canonical Erection of Faculty or University (c. 1376)
Academic Degrees (c. 1377)
Privileges Attending Degree of Doctorate, Etc. (c. 1378)
Establishment and Support of Catholic Schools (c. 1379)
Special Studies for Promising Priests (c. 1380)
Ecclesiastical Supervision of Religious Education (c. 1381)
Right of Visitation of Catholic Schools (c. 1382)
Confessors in College Residences (c. 1383)

The general doctrine regarding Catholic education is in part pre-supposed, in part very concisely stated in these canons; it is contained more fully in the Encyclical of Pope Pius XI,[40] which deserves careful study and analysis. Space permits us, however, only to touch upon two strictly canonical aspects of the subject; namely, first, the duty of parents and others regarding Catholic schools; second, the degree of control over Catholic schools which belongs by law to Ordinaries of places.

Necessity of Catholic Schools, Colleges, and Universities. Since education consists essentially in preparing man to attain his last end, "there can be no ideally perfect education which is not Christian education."[41] Hence, the Church has the right to establish for every branch of training, not only elementary but also intermediate and higher schools (c. 1375). If truly Catholic schools are wanting in the elementary and intermediate grades they must be established, and it is desirable also that truly Catholic colleges and universities be established (cf. c. 1379).

In the United States the necessity of Catholic education was emphasized by the three Plenary Councils of Baltimore.[42] The third of these Councils cited on the subject an Instruction of the Holy Office to the Bishops of the United States,[43] and an Encyclical of Leo XIII to the Bishops of France.[44] The need of Catholic schools is the more

---

[40] *On the Christian Education of Youth*, Pius XI, 31 Dec., 1929; *AAS*, 22–49. English copies of the Encyclical may be obtained from the America Press, the Paulist Press, and the N. C. W. C.

[41] Pius XI, *Encyclical on Education*, America Press edition, p. 3.

[42] Cf. *Conc. Balt. I*, n. XIII; *Conc. Balt. II*, n. 430; *Conc. Balt. III*, nn. 194–199.

[43] Holy Office, 24 Nov., 1875; *Fontes*, n. 1046, Vol. IV, p. 362.

[44] Leo XIII, *Nobilissima Gallorum gens*, 8 Feb., 1884; *Fontes*, n. 590, Vol. III, p. 216.

acute as the so-called public schools in the United States, because of their "neutral" character, are of the kind which Catholics are forbidden to attend (c. 1374). Hence the Third Plenary Council provided that within two years after its promulgation a parochial school be established and maintained in every parish.[45]

Support of Catholic Schools and Colleges. The support of Catholic schools and colleges according to their means is a duty of the faithful (c. 1379, § 3). "Whatever Catholics do in promoting and defending the Catholic school for their children is a genuinely religious work and therefore an important task of Catholic Action."[46] This duty of support is insisted on for the United States by the Instruction of the Holy Office already cited, and by the Third Council of Baltimore (n. 202). The same Council also commends and encourages the endowment of Catholic higher schools, colleges, and universities already existing at that time as well as those to be thereafter established (nn. 209, 210, 211).

Duty of Attending Only Catholic Schools. Catholic children may not attend non-Catholic, neutral, or mixed schools, that is, those which are open also to non-Catholics, and it pertains exclusively to the Ordinary of the place to decide, in accordance with instructions of the Holy See, under what circumstances and with what precautions against the danger of perversion, attendance at such schools may be tolerated **(c. 1374).**

1. *Neutral* schools are those which exclude religion by prescinding from it, such as the public schools in the United States. *Mixed* schools are those which admit pupils of any or no religion. Catholic schools, however, even though they admit some non-Catholic pupils, do not come under this classification.

2. Does the provision of canon 1374 apply only to elementary and high schools, or *also the colleges and universities?*

a. The natural law itself forbids Catholics to attend schools, whatever their grade, if they are dangerous to faith or morals. Both common experience and many documents of the Holy See prove that this danger may exist not only in the elementary and high school but in college and university as well.[47] "It is almost if not quite im-

---

[45] *Conc. Balt. III*, n. 199.

[46] Pius XI, *Encyclical on Christian Education* (*AAS*, 22–49), America Press ed., p. 28.

[47] As to elementary and high schools, especially the public schools in the U. S., see Instruction of the Holy Office, 24 Nov., 1875. As to colleges and universities, see S. C. Prop. Fid., 7 Apr., 1860; *Fontes*, n. 4649, Vol. VII, p. 381, and earlier documents there cited; also S. C. Prop. Fid., 6 Aug., 1867; *Fontes*, n. 4868, Vol. VII, p. 405.

possible for those circumstances to exist which would render attendance at non-Catholic universities free from sin."[48] It was in regard
to universities that the Holy See declared: "The unformed and un-
stable characters of young people, the erroneous teaching which is
inhaled as it were with the very atmosphere in those institutions
without being offset by the antidote of solid doctrine, the great power
exerted over the young by human respect and the fear of ridicule on
the part of their fellows — all these things produce such a present and
proximate danger of falling away, that in general no sufficient reason
can be conceived for entrusting Catholic young people to non-Catholic universities."[49]

b. The only thing which this canon adds to the obligation of the
natural law is the provision that it is for the Ordinary of the place
to decide in accordance with the instructions of the Holy See, under
what circumstances and with what precautions against the danger of
perversion, such attendance may be permitted. This is a strict canonical
requirement for elementary and high schools, and applies to them
particularly in the United States.[50] Does it apply equally to colleges
and universities? That is, is it a strict canonical requirement that the
Ordinary of the place be the sole judge as to the circumstances and
safeguards which would make it licit to attend a non-Catholic university? We think that no such strict canonical requirement can be
proved. The Holy See, or individual Bishops for their respective
dioceses, could enact such a requirement. In the absence of such legislation, parents and young people are bound by the natural law to
remove effectively the danger of perversion by employing safeguards
which are really sufficient. It is prudent and advisable, not strictly
obligatory, to consult the Ordinary on the sufficiency of these
precautions.

3. *Exceptions.* Canon 1374 itself plainly intimates that in exceptional
cases attendance at other than Catholic schools may be permitted. The
conditions for such permission are stated in the Instruction of the
Holy Office as follows: "It will usually be a sufficient reason if there
is either no Catholic school at all available, or only one which is
inadequate for the suitable education of the children according to
their condition. In that case, in order that the public school may be

---

[48] S. C. Prop. Fid., 6 Aug., 1867; *Fontes,* n. 4868, Vol. VII, p. 405.
[49] Encyclical of the S. C. Prop. Fid. to the Bishops of England, 6 Aug., 1867; *Fontes,*
n. 4868, Vol. VII, p. 405.
[50] Cf. Holy Office, 24 Nov., 1875; *Conc. Balt. III,* n. 199.

attended with a safe conscience, the danger of perversion which is always more or less connected with its very nature must, by appropriate remedies and safeguards, be rendered remote."[51] The Council of Baltimore itself is rather emphatic in insisting that the rule forbidding attendance at public schools is not absolutely ironclad. "If therefore, for a sufficient reason approved by the Ordinary, Catholics wish to send their children to the public schools, provided the proximate danger be made remote by taking the necessary precautions, we strictly forbid, as the Supreme Pontiff through the Sacred Congregation has expressly forbidden, that any Bishop or priest either threaten to exclude such parents from the reception of the Sacraments, or actually so exclude them. And much more is this to be understood of the children themselves. Hence the pastors of souls, while they are to warn their faithful of the dangers of these schools, must not permit themselves to be led by immoderate zeal to violate either in word or in deed the most wise precepts and counsels of the Holy See."[52]

4. *Particular disciplinary legislation.* The same Instruction of the Holy Office already cited closes with these words: "Parents who neglect to give this necessary Christian training and education to their children, or who permit them to attend schools where spiritual ruin is inevitable, or finally who, although there is a suitable Catholic school properly equipped and ready in the locality, or, although they have means of sending their children elsewhere to receive a Catholic education, nevertheless without sufficient reason and without the necessary safeguards to make the proximate danger remote send them to the public schools — such parents, if they are contumacious, obviously according to Catholic moral doctrine cannot be absolved in the Sacrament of Penance."[53] It must be noted that this provision does not create an excommunication nor reserved case of any kind; it is merely the expression of common Catholic doctrine regarding penitents who have sinned gravely and who are not properly disposed for absolution. Such parents may not be absolved as long as they are contumacious; but they may and should be absolved as soon as they are repentant and seriously promise amendment. In some dioceses, however, Bishops have found it necessary to make a reserved case in this matter, either *ratione censurae* (excommunication *latae sententiae* reserved to the Bishop) or *ratione peccati* (absolution from the sin reserved to the Bishop).

---

[51] Quoted in *Conc. Balt. III*, n. 198.
[52] *Conc. Balt. III*, n. 198.
[53] Holy Office, 24 Nov., 1875; *Fontes*, n. 1046, Vol. IV, p. 362.

In either case the general doctrine of the Code regarding absolution from reserved cases is applicable, even though it be not expressly mentioned in the pagella of the diocese.

Control of the Ordinary Over Catholic Schools. The control of the Ordinary of the place over Catholic schools in his diocese is by no means absolute; it depends on the nature of the school. Parish schools and diocesan high schools are completely subject to his authority, since they are established by the parish and the diocese respectively and are purely parochial or diocesan institutions. Other Catholic schools of whatever grade are subject to his authority only in the particular matters mentioned in the law, that is, especially as regards religious and moral training; and in this matter it is moreover necessary to distinguish three kinds or degrees of control by the Ordinary, namely, first, the *general right of vigilance as to faith and morals,* second, *direct authority as regards religious instruction,* third, the *right of canonical visitation.*[54]

1. General Vigilance as to Faith and Morals. Ordinaries of places have the right and duty to watch that in any schools within their territory nothing is taught and nothing done which is contrary to faith or good morals **(c. 1381, § 2).** This general right and duty of vigilance must be distinguished from the right to make a canonical visitation. This distinction is notable throughout the Code, and particularly in the present instance where the right of vigilance is dealt with in canon 1381, and the right of visitation in canon 1382, which would be superfluous if canonical visitation were included under vigilance. The right and duty of vigilance as regards faith and morals applies to all schools of whatever grade within the diocese; not so, the right of canonical visitation. There are many ways in which vigilance can be exercised without visitation.

2. Direct Authority of the Ordinary as Regards Religious Instruction. We have seen that catechetical instruction *to the people,* is completely under the authority of the Ordinary as to the manner in which it is to be done, etc. (c. 1336). Moreover the religious instruction of youth *in schools* of whatever kind is subject to the authority and inspection of the Church **(c. 1381, § 1).** Inspection implies canonical visitation; and in the absence of a special privilege inspection by the Church means inspection by the Ordinary of the place; but this matter will be more fully explained under canon 1382 which deals expressly with canonical visitation. Ordinaries of places have also the right to approve

---

[54] Cf. Creusen, *L'école Catholique,* in *Nouvelle Revue Théologique,* 1926.

teachers and textbooks of religion; and also to demand in the interest of religion and morality that either teachers or books be removed (c. 1381, § 3).

3. **The Right of Canonical Visitation of Schools, Etc.** Ordinaries of places can also, either in person or through others, visit all schools, oratories, playgrounds, social centers, etc., in matters which concern religion and moral training; and from this visitation the schools conducted by religious of whatever kind are not exempt, with the exception of intern schools for the professed of an exempt religious institute (c. 1382). This canon clearly confers upon the Ordinary of the place the right of canonical visitation not only of schools but of the other institutions mentioned, within his diocese, as regards religious and moral training. In the case of schools, however, notwithstanding the apparently sweeping scope of this canon, there is an exception to its provisions, based on a privilege *contra ius.* As it is a matter of considerable importance this exception and the privilege on which it rests must be examined.

Exemption of Schools of Regulars From Canonical Visitation by the Ordinary. The Code (c. 4) provides that privileges which were in existence at the time of its enactment, though contrary to its provisions, remain in effect unless they are expressly revoked. According to the Commission of Interpretation this is true even though the privileges were acquired by communication.[55] The question is therefore whether at the time when the Code was adopted regulars who conduct schools were in peaceful possession of a privilege contrary to this law; if they were, the privilege remains intact after the Code. The argument for the affirmative is given in detail by Vermeersch.[56] Step by step, the reasoning is as follows:

a. The Constitution of Leo XIII, *Romanos Pontifices,*[57] had for its purpose to settle certain points regarding the exemption of regulars in England. On this matter of the visitation of schools by the Ordinary it declares (n. 19) that elementary parochial schools may be so visited; but the next paragraph (n. 20) states the contrary regarding other schools and colleges in the care of the regulars. "For in these schools right reason demands and We ourselves desire that the privileges granted to them by the Holy See, as was declared in the year 1874, remain firm and intact."

---

[55] Code Com., 30 Dec., 1937; *AAS,* 30–73; *Digest,* II, p. 172.
[56] *Periodica,* Vol. 15, p. (57).
[57] 8 May, 1881; *Fontes,* n. 582, Vol. III, p. 171.

b. This same privilege of exemption of the schools of regulars from the jurisdiction of the Ordinary was again declared and recognized by the S. C. of Propaganda in 1886.[58]

c. It follows that the privilege was in existence and peacefully enjoyed before the Code, and as it is nowhere expressly revoked it remains in effect. Several authors express their agreement with this conclusion.[59]

CASES AND QUESTIONS

1. John, senior in a Catholic college, explains to a group of friends why he has serious doubts about the Assumption of the Blessed Virgin. Is he a heretic? What about his action? (Cc. 1324, 1325, § 2).

2. Andrew, an exempt religious priest, attends an economic conference at which the principal speaker, a nationally known Communist, makes an eloquent plea for atheistic Communism, stressing both its economic and cultural sides. Andrew, who has prepared carefully, takes the floor and refutes the atheistic implications in a thirty-minute talk which has a very good effect on the mixed audience. Should he have had the permission of his superior? Of the Bishop? Of the Holy See? (C. 1325, § 3).

3. May regulars teach catechism to children outside their own churches without special permission from the Bishop? (Cc. 1334, 1336).

4. Do regulars need faculties from the Bishop to preach in their own churches? (C. 1338, § 2). Does a priest religious, with this faculty, need any other permission? (C. 1339, § 2).

5. Francis, young diocesan priest, is refused permission to preach. Has he any recourse? What is your advice? (C. 1340, §§ 1, 3).

6. A pastor of a small country parish says he cannot afford to have special Lenten sermons (c. 1346, § 1).

7. At the diocesan synod one of the members proposes that a statute be passed forbidding pastors to invite extradiocesan priests to preach without previous permission of the Bishop in each case. Comment on validity, necessity, advisability of such a statute (c. 1341).

8. A teaching Jesuit scholastic gives a talk to high school students in the chapel; it turns out to be a sort of sermon. Did he violate the law? (C. 1342).

9. A pastor leaves all the preaching on Sundays to his three assistants (c. 1344, § 1).

10. First Assistant, John, contends that a Sunday sermon should be

---

[58] S. C. Prop. Fid., 18 Jan., 1886, ad 4; *Fontes,* n. 4913, Vol. VII, p. 514.
[59] Cf. Vermeersch-Creusen, *Epit.,* II, n. 718; A Coronata, *Institutiones,* II, n. 950, p. 312, note 6; De Meester, *Compendium,* III, p. 241, note 4; Blat, *De Rebus,* n. 267; Fanfani, *De Iure Religiosorum,* n. 342; O'Brien, *Exemption of Religious in Church Law,* p. 225.

preached at one of the Masses even during the summer. Second Assistant, Harry, agrees with the pastor that this is unnecessary and impractical (*Conc. Balt. III,* n. 216).

11. X, pastor of a large but strictly exempt nonparochial church does not follow the diocesan prescriptions of a definite course of Sunday instructions. "We are exempt," says he, "and besides the law is only directive in this matter" (c. 1345).

12. Is it necessary to have designated confessors in a minor seminary? (C. 1358).

13. The Bishop of a small diocese has as yet no seminary, but there is an interdiocesan seminary for the whole region. Is the Bishop bound to contribute to its support? May he if he prefers send his students to another diocesan seminary? (C. 1354, § 3).

14. How often should a seminarian go to confession? How is this provision binding in conscience? (C. 1367, 2°).

15. While visiting on the grounds of the seminary villa outside the diocese a sister of one of the seminarians dies suddenly. Who has the right to attend to the funeral? (C. 1368; cf. cc. 1216, 1230).

16. A Catholic mother in confession says she is excommunicated because her children are in the public school. What should the confessor do? (C. 1374; *Conc. Balt. III,* n. 198; cf. c. 893, § 1).

17. A Catholic father, after son has been graduated from a Catholic high school, sends him to a secular university, without consulting the Bishop. Discuss the case from the standpoint of obligation and counsel (c. 1374).

18. Could diocesan authorities: specify the tuition fee in a diocesan high school? In a high school belonging to and conducted by regulars in the diocese? Could they, in the two respective institutions: (*a*) control the curriculum? (*b*) Regulate athletics and other extracurricular activities within the school? (*c*) Insist on the removal of a teacher of history or of religion? (*d*) Specify the text and method of teaching religion? (*e*) Make a canonical visitation? (Cc. 1381, 1382).

Readings:

Jansen, *Canonical Provisions for Catechetical Instruction,* Cath. U., 1937; Cox, *The Administration of Seminaries,* Cath. U., 1931; Boffa, *Canonical Provisions for Catholic Schools,* Cath. U., 1939; *Irish Ecclesiastical Record,* Vol. 47, p. 561 (Brenan, on catechetical instruction); Vol. 48, p. 539 (Catholics and State University); *The Acolyte,* 1929, p. 4 (Schaaf, on Catholics in non-Catholic schools); *Ecclesiastical Review,* Vol. 82, p. 388 (Canning, on religious instruction for public school children); Vol. 84, p. 449 (Mons. McCarthy, on obligation of priests to foster vocations); *Periodica,* Vol. 20, p. 16* (Jombart, on hours of study in theological course); *The Jurist,* Vol. 2, p. 380 (Hannan, on ex-seminarian and novice).

Section 2. Previous Censure of Books: Prohibition of Books: Profession of Faith (cc. 1384–1408)

Art. 1. Previous Censure of Books (cc. 1384–1394)

PRELIMINARY SURVEY

Right of the Church: General Scope of the Law on Books (c. 1384)

Religious Writings and Pictures: Permission to Publish (c. 1385)

Clerics and Religious: Personal Permission to Publish Non-religious Books or to Contribute to or Edit Papers and Magazines (c. 1386)

Causes of Beatification (c. 1387)

Indulgences (c. 1388)

Decrees of Roman Congregations (c. 1389)

Liturgical Books (c. 1390)

Translations of Scripture in the Vernacular (c. 1391)

Translations and New Editions of Books: Excerpts From Periodicals (c. 1392)

Rules Regarding Censors (c. 1393)

The *Imprimatur* (c. 1394)

General Principles. Many people today do not know what bad literature is, or believe that there exists a sort of right to publish anything whatever in virtue of what is called the freedom of the press. Literature is morally bad if it endangers faith or morals, and no one has a "right" to publish such literature any more than one has a right to poison wells or sell tainted food. The freedom of speech and of the press which we cherish as part of our free system of government is a valuable compromise, but only a compromise. It does not mean that we imagine all opinions to be equally true or all moral diet equally healthy, for that would be absurd. It means that we do not wish the State to have power to suppress expressions of opinion, because we fear it might abuse that power by suppressing the true and the good along with the false and the bad. In a State which is not constitutionally bound to follow the moral and religious teaching of Christ as infallibly transmitted by His Church, this fear has some foundation; and consequently under our system of government or under any purely political system, Catholics in the same way as other citizens cherish and defend the freedom of the press as a safeguard of essential rights. But in the government of the Church of Christ there are sufficient safeguards against the abuse of the power to control, among her own members, the publication and even the reading of books which might be harmful to faith or morals; and on the other hand, such control is evidently within the scope of the Church's authority, which was given her by Christ in order to help Christians to save their souls. The Church exercises this control in two ways: first, by requiring that certain books be submitted for her official examination and approval before publication (previous censure); second, by prohibiting the publication, reading, retention, sale, or communication of bad books (prohibition of books).

Natural, Divine, Ecclesiastical Law. The *natural* law forbids directly the reading of bad books, and indirectly also their publication, retention, sale, etc. There are in Holy Scripture signs indicating prohibitions of the same general nature also in the *divine positive* law.[60] The *ecclesiastical* law on the subject dates from the early ages of the Church when writings of various heretics were proscribed. The invention of the art of printing by the Catholic Gutenberg was an immense benefit to mankind, but brought with it also the danger of abuse. Successive Popes in the sixteenth century were obliged to enact laws regarding the previous censure and prohibition of books. The Council of Trent (*Sess. XVIII*, 1562) appointed a commission to frame general rules and a specific list of forbidden books; and these were afterward published by Pope Paul IV (1564). Afterward various Popes developed or modified these laws, until Leo XIII in 1897 drew up a Brief containing complete legislation on the subject.[61] The Code substantially adopted these provisions and those of the two great documents of Pius X against Modernism;[62] but revised them completely — *totam de integro ordinavit legis prioris materiam* (c. 22) — so that all previous general laws on this subject, except as contained in the Code, are revoked.[63]

Right and Practice of the Church. The Church has the right to forbid the publication of books by the faithful unless she has officially examined them in advance, and for just cause to prohibit books, by whomsoever they may have been published (c. 1384, § 1). The provisions of canons 1384–1405 inclusive, regarding books, are to be ap-

---

[60] Cf. Matt. 18:7; Matt. 5:29 (condemnation of scandal); Matt. 7:15 (condemnation of false prophets); Rom. 16:17; 1 Tim. 6:20; Acts 19:19 (public burning of magical books).

[61] Leo XIII, *Officiorum ac munerum*, 25 Jan., 1897; *Fontes*, n. 632, Vol. III, p. 502.

[62] Pius X, Encyc., *Pascendi*, 8 Sept., 1907; *Fontes*, n. 680, Vol. III, p. 690; *Motu proprio, Sacrorum Antistitum*, 1 Sept., 1910; *Fontes*, n. 689, Vol. III, p. 774.

[63] Cf. c. 6, 6°.

plied also to daily publications, periodicals, and other published writings of whatever kind, unless the contrary appear (c. 1384, § 2).

1. What is a "book"? Common consent bases the answer on two elements, the *size* of the publication, and its *unity.* As to size or volume, 8 or 10 folia (160 pages in *octavo,* 320 in *sexto decimo,* etc.) are commonly held sufficient to constitute a book. But there must also be a certain unity, either in matter or in purpose. A single copy of a magazine is not commonly called a book because it usually lacks both requisites; a pamphlet lacks the requisite volume or size. Bound volumes of a periodical are considered books *if* they have *certainly* both the required size and the required unity.

2. The canons in which the term "book" includes other published writings of whatever kind, even though they be not strictly books, are canons 1384–1405 inclusive, and those *only.* Hence in penal canons (e.g., c. 2318) the term is taken in its strict sense.

3. Moreover, even in our present canons (1384–1405) the wide interpretation of "books" has exceptions. If any particular canon can reasonably be interpreted as applying only to books in the strict sense, it should be so interpreted (cf. c. 1384, § 2, *nisi aliud constet;* cc. 15, 19).

4. A book or other writing is not regarded as *published* if it is destined only for a designated group, e.g., members of a class in school or college.

Religious Works Require Previous Censure (c. 1385). 1. Even though published by laymen, the following require previous approval:

a. Books of the Sacred Scriptures, or annotations and commentaries of the same. This refers either to the original text or to *ancient* translations; modern translations are specially dealt with (and more severely) in canon 1391.

b. Books which treat of Holy Scripture, theology, church history, canon law, natural theology, ethics, or other such religious and moral branches; also books and booklets of prayers or devotions, or of instruction and training in religion, morals, asceticism, mysticism, and the like, even though they seem to favor piety; and in general all writings which contain anything of special importance to religion and good morals. Since in this paragraph the Code used the terms "books" in the first part, "books and booklets" in the second part, and "writings" in the last part, some authors[64] reasonably hold that *books* here may be taken in the strict sense as opposed to *booklets,* and other *writings.* A matter may be of special importance to religion even •

---

[64] Vermeersch-Creusen, *Epit.,* II, n. 725; A Coronata, II, n. 954.

though it be not essentially religious, e.g., a school tax law. It is for the Ordinary of the place to judge of this.

c. Sacred pictures, no matter by what process they are to be printed, and whether to be published with prayers or without them. This applies whether the picture be new or not. The *imprimatur* should be printed with the picture (c. 1394). The use of the picture is not forbidden merely because it was illegally published without the requisite approval **(c. 1385, § 1).**

2. The permission to publish the books and pictures mentioned in paragraph 1 can be given either by the Ordinary of the place of the author's domicile (or quasi-domicile), or by the Ordinary of the place where the books or pictures are published, or by the Ordinary of the place where they are printed; but if one of these Ordinaries has refused the permission, the author may not ask it of any of the others without informing him that it has been so refused by the former. This applies to all the writings mentioned and to all classes of authors, even those living in Rome, including exempt religious, whose proper *local* Ordinary is the Ordinary of the place where the house to which they are attached is located **(c. 1385, § 2).**

3. Religious must moreover obtain in advance the permission of their major superior **(c. 1385, § 3).**

Special Personal Permission for Clerics or Religious Who Publish, Contribute, or Edit. Secular clerics are forbidden without the consent of their Ordinaries, and religious without the permission of their major superiors and of the Ordinary of the place, to publish books even treating of profane subjects, and to contribute to or edit papers, magazines, or reviews **(c. 1386, § 1).** Note that this is a special personal permission which may be distinct (in scope or as regards the person from whom obtained) from that mentioned in canon 1385. Here "books" has the comprehensive meaning, there being no indication to the contrary (cf. c. 1384, § 2). To "contribute to" designates a *habitual or notable* contribution, because the Code uses a severer term when it wishes to proscribe *all* contribution (cf. c. 1386, § 2). For seculars, "their Ordinaries" are the Ordinary of the place of their incardination, or of their residence if they have a domicile or quasi-domicile elsewhere. For religious (and even exempt religious are included) the Ordinary of the place, according to the more common opinion, designates only the Ordinary of the place where their religious house is. Vermeersch, however, proposes a broader opinion as at least probable; namely, that this permission may be obtained by religious of any of the three Ordinaries mentioned in canon 1385, § 2 (author's residence, place of publication, or place where printed).[65]

Contribution of Any Kind to Anti-Catholic or Bad Periodical: Special Reason and Permission Required, Even for Layman. In newspapers, magazines, and reviews which habitually attack the Catholic religion or good morals, even Catholic laymen must write nothing whatever, unless there is a just and reasonable cause, approved by the Ordinary of the place, for doing so **(c. 1386, § 2)**. The proper local Ordinary of the person is the one most obviously intended here. But a soundly probable (minority) opinion gives the option of obtaining this permission from any of the three Ordinaries mentioned in canon 1385, § 2.

Various Very Special Publications for Which Very Special Permission Is Required. 1. Anything which in any way concerns (pending) causes of beatification and canonization of the Servants of God may not be published without the permission of the Sacred Congregation of Rites **(c. 1387)**. It is a well-supported opinion that only pending cases are meant here; after the case is finished, the permission of the Ordinary is sufficient.

2. The express permission of the Holy See is required in order to publish in any language either an authentic collection of prayers and pious works to which the Holy See has attached indulgences, or a schedule of the Apostolic indulgences, or a summary of indulgences, whether this was already arranged but not yet approved or is now for the first time to be compiled from various sources **(c. 1388, § 2)**.

a. The Apostolic indulgences are those which the Supreme Pontiff announces at the beginning of his reign.[66]

b. A summary of indulgences is a list or group of indulgences; the special permission here mentioned is required only if the list is new, not if it has already been approved.

c. All books of indulgences, summaries, booklets, leaflets, etc., in which the grants of indulgences are contained, may not be published without the permission of the Ordinary of the place **(c. 1388, § 1)**. Several authors hold that the option of canon 1385, § 2, giving a choice of various Ordinaries, applies here. This may be followed in practice. "Books" here has the comprehensive meaning (c. 1384, § 2). Note that books of indulgences in general do not require the permission of the Holy See.

---

[65] Cf. Vermeersch-Creusen, *Epit.*, II, n. 728.
[66] Cf. for Pius XI, *AAS*, 14–143; for Pius XII, *AAS*, 31–132.

3. Collections of the decrees of the Roman Congregations may not be republished without having previously obtained the permission and observing the conditions laid down by the Prefects of the respective Congregations (c. 1389).

4. In publishing liturgical books or parts thereof, as well as litanies approved by the Holy See, the agreement of the text with approved editions must be proved by the attestation of the Ordinary of the place in which they are published or in which they are printed (c. 1390). Approved editions are: first, what is called the *editio typica,* examined by the S. C. of Rites itself and bearing the attestation that it is the model edition; and second, *editiones iuxta typicam,* that is, editions which bear the attestation of the Ordinary that they conform to the original. Litanies approved by the Holy See are those of the Saints, of the dying, of Loretto, of the Holy Name, of the Sacred Heart, and of St. Joseph.

5. Translations of the Sacred Scriptures into the vernacular may not be printed unless they have been approved by the Holy See, or unless they are published under the vigilance of the Bishops and with annotations, especially such as are taken from the Fathers of the Church and from learned Catholic writers (c. 1391).

a. There is question here of new translations into the vernacular, which have not yet been approved by the Holy See. Ancient versions come under canon 1385, § 1, 1°, and require only the permission of the Ordinary (c. 1385, § 2). Likewise a modern version which has already been approved by the Holy See would require, for republication, the permission of the Ordinary only (cc. 1385, § 1, 2°, and 1385, § 2).

b. The vigilance of the Bishops (any of the three mentioned in c. 1385, § 2) means special care on their part in approving the work, not actual supervision.

c. Moreover, annotations are required; otherwise Bishops may not approve the version.[67] Though the annotations must be principally from the sources named, others may be added, such as historical, geographical, and archaeological notes even from sound non-Catholic authorities. If the version is of only parts of Scripture, such as Sunday Epistles and Gospels, the Psalter, etc., custom may permit omitting the annotations. In versions of the Vulgate, variant readings may be given in the footnotes.[68]

---

[67] Cf. Code Com., 20 May, 1923; *AAS,* 16–115; *Digest,* I, p. 684.
[68] Cf. Bibl. Com., 17 Nov., 1921; *AAS,* 14–27; *Digest,* I, p. 684.

d. Mere selections from already approved versions follow the rule given above in *a*.

e. The use of versions published without the required conditions is forbidden (c. 1399, 5°).

Translations and New Editions: Reprints of Articles From Magazines. The approval of the original text of a work does not extend to translations of that work into another language nor to new editions of the work; consequently both translations and new editions of an approved work must be again approved (c. 1392, § 1). Several authors, with Λ Coronata (II, n. 956), hold that this does not apply if the new edition is unchanged from the old. There is now no special provision, as there was under the former law, for authors living in Rome.[69] Excerpts taken from periodicals and published separately are not considered new editions and hence do not need new approval (c. 1392, § 2).[70] But if a work was published serially and the chapters are later assembled and reprinted together, this is a new edition and needs new approval.[71]

Rules Regarding Diocesan Censors. 1. In every episcopal Curia there shall be censors *ex officio* to examine works that are to be published (c. 1393, § 1). The Holy Office recently insisted with all diocesan Curias that their censors should be really capable and should take their charge more seriously.[72] The censors are obliged to make the profession of faith according to canon 1406, § 1, 7°.

2. In performing their office the censors must put aside all undue influence that might arise from the consideration of persons and attend only to the dogmas of the Church and to common Catholic doctrine which is contained in the decrees of the General Councils or in the Constitutions or prescriptions of the Holy See, or in the common opinion of approved authors (c. 1393, § 2). It is clear from this that censors are not to judge according to their private opinions or the tenets of a favorite school, but according to *common* Catholic doctrine. What if they judge the doctrine of a book sound but believe its publication inopportune? They may give their opinion that it is inopportune, but must at the same time clearly approve the publication as regards soundness of doctrine. The Bishop may then use his discretion as to allowing the publication.

---

[69] Cf. Leo XIII, *Officiorum ac munerum*, n. 37.

[70] Cf. S. C. Indic., 23 May, 1898, ad 3; *Fontes*, n. 5152, Vol. VII, p. 728.

[71] Vermeersch, *De Prohibitione ac Censura Librorum*, p. 148.

[72] Holy Office, 29 March, 1941, *AAS*, 33–121, *Digest*, II, p. 436.

3. Censors are to be chosen from both the secular and religious clergy (in the latter case usually upon recommendation from their major superiors), and should be men of mature age, sound erudition, and prudence, who in approving or disapproving of doctrine will follow a safe middle course (c. 1393, § 3). A safe middle course will neither approve temerity nor obstruct progress.

4. The censor must give his judgment in writing. If it is favorable, the Ordinary shall grant permission for the publication, prefixing to it the judgment and the name of the censor. Only in extraordinary circumstances and very rarely may the name of the censor be omitted (c. 1393, § 4). Notwithstanding this provision, some authors hold that even if the censors' judgment is favorable the Ordinary may withhold permission for a really grave cause, such as inopportuneness of the publication at the moment, saving recourse to the Holy See *in devolutivo*.[73] This seems to be correct; it agrees with common sense and satisfies justice; and after all the words of this canon, *potestatem edendi faciat,* do not necessarily imply an absolute precept. It might seem from the text that the censor's name should be printed with the *imprimatur,* since it is supposed to be prefixed to it, and the *imprimatur* itself must be printed (c. 1394). However, neither canon expressly says so, and no good reason seems to require it; neither is it the universal practice. Hence it need not be printed in the book.[74]

5. The censor's name must never be divulged to the authors until he has given a favorable judgment (c. 1393, § 5).

The *Imprimatur*. The permission by which the Ordinary allows the publication is to be given in writing, and must be printed at the beginning or end of the book, paper, or picture, giving the name of the one granting the permission, and also its place and date (c. 1394, § 1). This provision applies to the permission requisite for publication, not to the other personal permissions which may be required by canon 1386. The usual formula, "with ecclesiastical permission," though not in strict conformity with the text of the Code, is regarded as sufficient for books and booklets of minor importance (A Coronata, II, n. 958). This no doubt applies to most reviews and magazines. May the *imprimatur* be omitted from the book for special reasons, e.g., if it is destined for non-Catholics, who would close the book on seeing the Catholic *imprimatur?* Undoubtedly special permission from the Holy

---

[73] Cf. A Coronata, *Institutiones,* II, n. 957, p. 328, note 5.
[74] Cf. Vermeersch-Creusen, *Epit.,* II, n. 727.

SYNOPTICAL OUTLINE: PREVIOUS CENSURE OF BOOKS

Canon	Matter	Note on c. 1399	Divisions of Matter	Approval of Holy See	Approval of Ordinaries
1385	Religious Works	(*)	Scripture: text, *ancient* versions, commentaries.		Approval of Ordinary (one of three) required even for laymen. Religious need, moreover, permission of major superior.
		(†)	Doctrinal *books* on religion, morals, etc. *Books, booklets* of prayer, devotion, etc. *Writings* in which anything of special importance to religion or morals. Sacred pictures.		
1386			(This canon does not deal with *previous censure, but with special permissions*)		
1387	Beatification, canonization		Documents of *pending* cases.	S. C. Rit.	
1388, § 1	Indulgences		a. In general.	Holy See	Approval of Ordinary (probably one of three)
1388, § 2			b. Authentic collection; Apostolic indulgences; Summaries not yet approved.	Prefect of S. C. concerned*	
1389	Decrees of Sacred Congregations		Collections of	Holy See (*Editio typica*)	Ordinary (one of two): certificate of concordance (*Ediziones iuxta typicam*)
1390	Liturgy, etc.		Liturgical books or parts thereof; Litanies approved by the Holy See	Holy See or	
1391	Sacred Scripture	(*)	*Modern versions* in the *vernacular*	Holy See or	Made under vigilance of Ordinary (one of three) *and* with annotations

Notes on application of canon 1399:

(*) Forbidden by c. 1399, 5°, if published without observing the requirements of law.

(†) Forbidden by c. 1399, 5°, if published without observing the requirements of law, and if moreover the book or booklet tells of new apparitions, revelations, visions, prophecies, miracles, or introduces new devotions.

See could be obtained for such a practice. Even without special permission, Vermeersch, by a sort of *epikeia,* allowed this.[75]

If the permission to publish is denied, the reasons for refusing it should be indicated to the author at his request, unless there is a grave reason to the contrary (c. 1394, § 2). Otherwise the author might be at a loss as to what part of the book required amendment.

Art. 2. The Prohibition of Books (cc. 1395–1405)

PRELIMINARY SURVEY

Prohibition of Books, by What Authority? (c. 1395)
Extent of Prohibition (c. 1396)
Denunciation of Bad Books (c. 1397)
Effect of Prohibition (c. 1398)
Books Forbidden by the Law Itself (c. 1399)
Certain Books of Scripture: Conditions for Licit Use (c. 1400)
Cardinals, Bishops, *et al.* Not Bound by Prohibition (c. 1401)
Faculties of Ordinaries (c. 1402)
Permission of the Holy See (c. 1403)
Permission Does Not Exempt From Natural Law (c. 1405)

Who Can Forbid Books? 1. The supreme ecclesiastical authority can, of course, forbid books for the universal Church. The Holy See exercises this power through the Holy Office (cf. c. 247), whose decrees in this matter are binding also on Orientals.[76] Occasionally, for special reasons affecting the matter contained in the book, the prohibition may issue from some other department of the Roman Curia.[77]

2. For all except exempt religious, the right and duty of forbidding books pertains also to particular Councils and Ordinaries of places, for their respective subjects (c. 1395, § 1). Within his own territory a Bishop can forbid a book which was approved by some other Ordinary. *Peregrini* would not be bound by such a local prohibition unless its violation would cause scandal or disturb discipline in the diocese (cf. c. 14). Against a decree forbidding a book there is a right of recourse to the Holy See, but without suspensive effect (c. 1395, § 2).

---

[75] Cf. Vermeersch, *De Prohibitione ac Censura Librorum,* and in *Periodica,* Vol. 14, p. (96); Jombart in *Periodica,* Vol. 21, p. 189.* Vermeersch-Creusen, in *Epit.,* II, n. 729 do not mention this opinion.

[76] Cf. S. C. Or., 26 May, 1928; *AAS,* 20–195; *Digest,* I, p. 685.

[77] Cf. Vermeersch-Creusen, *Epit.,* II, n. 734.

3. In the case of exempt religious, the abbot of an independent monastery and the superior general of a clerical exempt religious institute, with his chapter or council, can forbid books to his subjects for just cause; and if there is danger in delay, the same power belongs also to other major superiors with their council, but they must as soon as possible afterward refer the matter to the superior general (c. 1395, § 3). The *consent* of the chapter or council seems here to be required for *validity;* for without their consent the superior would scarcely be acting with them, and when consent is required it is required for validity (c. 105, 1°).

Extent of Prohibition by the Holy See. Books condemned by the Holy See are to be considered as forbidden everywhere and in whatever language they may be translated (**c. 1396**). This principle, taken from the Constitution of Leo XIII (n. 45), applies to all books condemned by the Holy See by special decree and to all those forbidden by the law itself (cf. c. 1399). In practice, several rules of interpretation must be attended to:

1. *Previous translation or edition.* *a.* Books *particularly condemned or prohibited* are forbidden in all translations or editions which appeared previously, unless the contrary is expressly declared. This rule, taken from the preface to the Index of Leo XIII, was retained in editions of the Index after the Code, and even though it is omitted from some later editions of the Index, this of itself is no sufficient indication of a change in the intention of the legislator.

b. In the case of books *published before the Code and now ipso iure forbidden* (by c. 1399), a distinction is made:

1) If the reason for the condemnation is *intrinsic* (something in the book itself) the future reading, retention, sale, etc., of the previously published edition is forbidden.

2) If the reason is *extrinsic* (e.g., want of the previous approval which is required by law), many authors[78] hold that the previous edition is not forbidden as to future reading, keeping, sale, etc. Though the reasons for this opinion are not entirely convincing to us, it is probable and may be followed in practice.

2. *Future translations and editions.* These are forbidden (cf. c. 1398). But future *volumes* of a work whose first volume has been condemned or prohibited, are merely suspect, not forbidden.

3. *Editions in serial form.* If, either before or after its prohibi-

---

[78] Vermeersch, Hollweck, Pennacchi, Boudinhon, Genicot-Salsmans, Claeys-Bouuaert.

tion, the book appears as a serial in a magazine, it is forbidden also in that form as far as *publication* and *reading* are concerned (cf. c. 1398, § 1). As to *keeping* it, since it would be a grave inconvenience to have to mutilate a complete set of a periodical which is otherwise good and useful, authors commonly hold that the prohibition in this case does not apply to the retention of the book.

4. *Parts of a condemned or forbidden book.* In *general* all authorities hold that the entire book, even as to parts which are not in themselves objectionable, is forbidden. When it comes to applications, however, many distinctions arise. The following may be considered safe practice:

a. If the book is forbidden because of lack of the required previous approval (a defect extrinsic to the book and hence not inhering in any particular part of it), all parts of the book are equally forbidden, even though they be all equally harmless in themselves.

b. If the book is condemned or forbidden for an intrinsic defect:

1) The parts of the book in which the fault is, are forbidden, of course.

2) Other parts, however, are not *per se* forbidden; hence if the bad parts can be either deleted, torn out, or sealed, the book may be kept and the harmless parts read. We need not follow the severe opinion of De Lugo that the parts so exempted from the condemnation must constitute a formally distinct work. It is sufficient that the objectionable parts be effectively segregated or excluded from the book.

3) As to books such as anthologies, miscellanies, *melanges,* which consist of selections from various works some of which are forbidden: if only harmless parts of the condemned works are included in the collection, there is no prohibition; if the collection includes practically the entire forbidden work or its objectionable parts, the entire collection is forbidden; but we think there would still be room for the application of the rule given above, namely, that if the objectionable parts could be effectively segregated or excluded, the prohibition would cease. Moreover, one exception has been introduced by the common practice whereby Catholic authors sometimes quote passages from adversaries for the purpose of refutation.

5. A *play or film based on a forbidden book* is not *for that reason* forbidden.[79]

Force of Certain Clauses. Certain clauses which occur in the Index

---

[79] Cf. Lopez, in *Periodica,* Vol. 24, p. 49*.

and in the Code where it declares books *ipso iure* forbidden (c. 1399) have technical meanings which need explanation.

1. *Opera omnia.* This expression *formerly* implied prohibition of all works of the author named, even future ones; it constituted the first clause in the Tridentine Index, where the prohibition was regarded as made *in odium auctoris.* Now, however, the effect of this clause is as follows:

a. Future works of the named author are merely suspect, *not forbidden.* The clause is a warning that some of the author's works have been condemned and that one should be on one's guard as to all his works.

b. As to *existing* works, if the author is a non-Catholic, this clause forbids all his existing works which treat expressly of religion. If the author is a Catholic, all his works are suspect, but none forbidden by this clause. It amounts to a warning that some of the author's works are forbidden either *ipso iure* or by special decree.

c. Probably (therefore safely in practice) this prohibition applies only to *books* in the strict sense.

2. *Omnes fabulae amatoriae.* We must distinguish the actual meaning of this clause from its practical application. It means all novels or romances, whether strictly love stories or not. Its practical application, however, is this: all novels of the named author are *presumed* to be forbidden unless it is proved that some one of them is not forbidden either by special decree or by the general law. Hence, in the absence of definite information the book is forbidden in virtue of the presumption; but once it is proved that the book is not condemned by particular decree nor by the general law, it is not forbidden by this clause.

3. *Data opera: ex professo.* These expressions occur in canon 1399, 3°, 4°, 6°, 9°. They indicate the principal purpose of the author, or the principal scope of the work, or of a notable part of it (cf. A Coronata, II, n. 963). *Data opera* would apply to one who, in pursuance of his chief purpose, devotes a notable part of his work (one chapter) to expounding and defending heresy. *Ex professo* would apply to a work in which (or in a notable part of which, one chapter) the purpose of defending heresy is frankly apparent.

4. *Donec corrigatur,* means that the work is forbidden until corrections have been made and accepted as satisfactory by the Holy See or other author of the prohibition.

Denunciation of Bad Books. It is the part of all the faithful, and especially of clerics, ecclesiastical dignitaries, and learned men to denounce to the Ordinaries of places or to the Holy See books which they consider pernicious; this service pertains by a particular title to Legates of the Holy See, Ordinaries of places, and rectors of Catholic universities. It is advisable that in the denunciation of bad books not only the title of the book be indicated but also as far as possible that the reasons be given why it is considered that the book should be condemned. Those to whom the denunciation is made must sacredly keep secret the names of those who gave them the information. Ordinaries of places, either personally or through capable priests, must be vigilant as to books which are published or sold in their territory. Books which require a more expert examination, or in regard to which the judgment of the supreme authority seems to be necessary in order to secure the desired results, should be referred by the Ordinaries to the judgment of the Holy See (c. 1397). Ordinaries were especially urged to use their power under this canon in the case of pernicious sensual-mystical literature.[80] A notable example of extracanonical vigilance and activity against bad literature is the long and vigorous campaign organized by Bishop Noll in the diocese of Fort Wayne in which the Bishop enlisted the aid of all decent citizens, Catholic or non-Catholic, against pornographic magazines.

Effect of Prohibition. Canon 1396, treated above, answered questions as to the *extent* of a prohibition, namely, whether certain books, editions, translations, etc., fall under the prohibition. When it is once determined that a certain book is included in the prohibition, a further question arises, namely, what is the *effect,* or in other words what acts in regard to that book are forbidden. This question is answered by canon 1398. The prohibition of books has the effect that, unless due permission is obtained, the forbidden book may not be published, nor read, nor retained, nor sold, nor translated into another language, nor communicated in any way to other persons (c. 1398, § 1). A book which has been in any way forbidden may not again be published unless, after it has been corrected, permission is given by the one who forbade the book, or his superior or successor (c. 1398, § 2).

1. *Publication* means the issuing of books to the public for circulation; it is an act distinct from authorship, and usually of a distinct

---

[80] Cf. Holy Office, 3 May, 1927; *AAS*, 19–186; *Digest*, I, p. 687.

person from the author. The author, however, will always be a guilty co-operator (*mandans*) in the publication, according to canon 2209, § 3. Sometimes the author is named as one of the principal delinquents in penal laws, as, for example, in canon 2318, § 2. Publishing means more than printing; hence when publishing is directly punished by a penal statute, the printer (proprietor of the printing establishment) will not be guilty as a principal; but he will often be guilty of formal co-operation, and always at least of proximate material co-operation, which, in the case of *bad books,* is excused only by the gravest necessity. If his co-operation was necessary to the publishing, he is subject to the penalties of canon 2318, under the rule of canon 2231. Workers in the printing shop are remote material co-operators, and are excused from guilt by grave inconvenience.

2. *Reading* means directly to recognize the type signs and understand their meaning in words. One who pronounces words from a printed page without understanding them is not reading, nor one who listens to another read aloud, nor one who recites from memory what he has read before. Reading braille is reading, but only in a somewhat extended sense. Some authors would exclude it by defining reading as perception of written matter by the sense of sight. Probably such reading would escape a merely ecclesiastical prohibition.

3. *Keeping* or *retaining* is forbidden, whether in one's own custody or in the custody of another as agent; whether the book is one's own property or not; and regardless of the intention to read it or not. Some applications:

a. A *librarian* is not guilty of keeping or retaining books as long as he leaves them in the library. He is bound by the natural law to keep bad books from falling into the hands of others (cf. c. 1403, § 2).

b. A *book-binder* is commonly held not guilty of keeping or retaining a forbidden book; strictly speaking he would seem to come within the terms of the law, but in practice is excused either by ignorance or by the grave inconvenience which refusal to handle the book would entail. The same is true of a servant who keeps a book for his master.

c. What if the book is rare and forms part of a *collection?* It is not kept with a view to reading it, but as we have seen that makes no difference; *finis non cadit sub lege.* Hence, *per se* permission should be asked. However, if from the very way in which it is kept it is obvious that it is not intended to be read, it in a sense loses the character of a book and becomes a mere curio, and hence there is then no strict obligation to ask permission, especially if this would involve some inconvenience.[81]

d. *What is one bound to do* when he has been keeping forbidden books? Either to destroy them or turn them over to someone who has permission to read them — not necessarily, as formerly, to the Bishop. To return them to their owner, if the latter has not permission to keep them, is *per se* a forbidden communication; but in practice it is permitted if necessary to avoid animosity or offense.

4. *Selling* is directly forbidden by the present law; formerly a seller was guilty only as a co-operator with the reader. Even now, selling to one who has permission to keep or read is not forbidden. Those engaged regularly in selling books must moreover observe canon 1404.

5. *Translating* is forbidden.

6. To *communicate* includes giving, lending, restoring. It is now forbidden directly, but only as to the published book or writing. Hence if a book is published as a novel, one telling the story or representing it dramatically on stage or screen is not communicating the book as such.

7. *Defending* a forbidden book physically (e.g., by hiding it from search), or morally (e.g., by argument against the prohibition) was formerly directly forbidden, but is so no longer, except as regards the books specially designated in canon 2318, namely, any books by apostates, heretics, or schismatics, which advocate apostasy, heresy, or schism, or any other books which have been prohibited by name by Apostolic Letter. Other cases of defending forbidden books fall only under the natural law regarding co-operation. The Holy Office, however, has issued a warning to Ordinaries against allowing Catholics to praise works which have been condemned.[82]

Books Forbidden *Ipso Iure*. In the following twelve paragraphs are enumerated the classes of books which canon 1399 declares forbidden by the law itself. In all of them except as noted below in paragraph 5, the term "books" has the comprehensive meaning (c. 1384, § 2), that is, anything in writing, provided it has been published.

1. **Scripture.** Editions of the original text and of ancient Catholic versions of Sacred Scripture even in the Oriental Church, published by non-Catholics; also all translations of Sacred Scripture into any language, made or published by non-Catholics (**c. 1399, 1°**).

---

[81] Cf. Vermeersch, *De Prohibitione ac Censura Librorum,* p. 40.
[82] Cf. Holy Office, 15 March, 1923; *AAS,* 15–152; *Digest,* I, p. 686.

a. The use of all the books mentioned here is *permitted under certain conditions* to those who are studying theology or Sacred Scripture (cf. c. 1400).

b. There is question here only of works published or written by non-Catholics. A recent example is the Italian translation of Scripture by a Waldensian pastor, which the Holy Office in 1925 declared to be forbidden *ipso iure.*[83]

c. What of books of the same kind written or published by Catholics? Editions of the text or of ancient versions by Catholics require previous approval of the Ordinary (c. 1385, § 1, 1°); without this they are forbidden by canon 1399, 5°. *Modern translations into the vernacular* by Catholics require special conditions (c. 1391); if these conditions are not fulfilled, the books are forbidden by canon 1399, 5°.

2. Heresy, Schism, Subversion of Foundations of Religion. Books, no matter who the authors are, which propound heresy or schism, or which in any way attempt to subvert the very foundations of religion (c. 1399, 2°).

a. Heresy, schism are defined in canon 1325, § 2.

b. To propound (*propugnare*) means to promote or defend by argument. A book might so promote or defend heresy or schism without being essentially religious, if that were its purpose and tendency.

c. As to *ancient or obsolete heresies,* several interpretations must be noted:

1) Heretical books which were condemned only before the year 1600 are not now condemned unless they fall within the provisions of this canon. This rule, announced in the Constitution of Leo XIII (n. 1) is retained since the Code. Hence heretical books of Luther, Calvin, Jansenius, if they are not on the Index nor included in any of the divisions of canon 1399, are not forbidden. They are forbidden, if they *propound* heresy.

2) As to books of heretics who wrote before the Reformation and whose errors are entirely obsolete, even though they seem to propound heresies and thus to fall under the terms of this provision, still they may be read, especially by students of theology and learned persons. This benign interpretation comes from the former law and may be retained. Thus the collections of Labbe and Migne are not forbidden.

---

[83] Cf. Holy Office, 1925; *AAS,* 17–137; *Digest,* I, p. 687.

d. Attempting to *subvert the foundations of religion* needs explanation.

1) The foundations of religion are the natural truths which underlie the very idea of divine worship; for example, the existence of God, the spirituality of the soul, the freedom of the will; and those which are necessary before an adult infidel can be brought to embrace the faith; e.g., the probative force of miracles, the motives of credibility in general, the fact of divine revelation, the divine mission of Christ, though not his personal divinity. Some include also those supernatural truths which are the principal dogmas of the Catholic faith. It seems more correct not to include these among the *foundations* of religion; but books which attack them are propounding heresy.

2) Striving in any way to subvert; the emphasis is on the words "in any way"; that is, by argument, ridicule, opprobrium, directly or indirectly. This includes most philosophical works of the Materialist, Positivist, Rationalist schools, books of Theosophy,[84] and all forms of Pantheism.

3. Attacks Against Religion or Morality. Books which have for their principal or one of their notable purposes to attack religion or right morals are also *ipso iure* forbidden (c. 1399, 3°).

a. The words are *qui data opera impetunt.*

b. Morals are thus purposely attacked in two ways: by pornographic works (these are covered also explicitly by n. 9 of this canon), and by pseudo-scientific argument, e.g., as in many books advocating birth prevention.

c. The term *to attack religion* raises a doubt of law. Most authors hold that it means to attack the Catholic religion; others maintain that the attack must be against all religion in order to be condemned. The latter is the less severe opinion, and may be followed.[85]

4. Books of Non-Catholics Treating Professedly of Religion. Books by any non-Catholics which treat professedly of religion are *ipso iure* forbidden unless it is certain that they contain nothing against the Catholic faith (c. 1399, 4°).

a. Here again religion is taken in the broad, general sense. Non-Catholics include infidels.

b. Moral certainty that the books contain nothing against the

---

[84] Cf. Holy Office, 18 July, 1919; *AAS*, 11–317; *Digest*, I, p. 620.
[85] Cf. Vermeersch, *De Prohibitione ac Censura Librorum*, p. 108.

Catholic religion must be had at least from the report of some trustworthy person.

5. Certain Books Published Illegally. The books mentioned in canon
1385, § 1, 1° (namely, books of Sacred Scripture, or annotations and
commentaries on the same), and canon 1391 (namely, translations of
Scripture into the vernacular), and also, of those mentioned in canon
1385, § 1, 2°, books and booklets (of prayer, devotion, or instruction)
which tell of new apparitions, revelations, visions, prophecies, miracles,
or which introduce new devotions, even on the plea that they are
private, if they were published without observing the requirements of
the canons, are *ipso iure* forbidden (c. 1399, 5°). Since in the latter
part of this paragraph the Code itself mentions books and booklets,
it seems that books are to be taken here in the narrow sense, as
not including, for example, periodicals, which are neither books, nor
booklets (A Coronata, II, n. 963).

6. Various Books Against the Catholic Religion. Books which
attack or ridicule any of the Catholic dogmas, which defend errors
proscribed by the Holy See, which disparage divine worship, which
strive to overthrow ecclesiastical discipline, and which purposely (*data
opera*) insult the ecclesiastical hierarchy or the clerical or religious
state, are *ipso iure* forbidden (c. 1399, 6°).

7. Books Favoring Superstition, Etc. Books which teach or approve
of any sort of superstition, fortune telling, divination, magic, spiritism,[86]
or other such practices are *ipso iure* forbidden (c. 1399, 7°).

8. Books Favoring Dueling, Suicide, Divorce, Masonry. Books
which hold dueling, suicide, or divorce licit, or which, treating of
Masonic sects and other such societies, contend that they are useful
and not harmful to the Church and civil society are *ipso iure* forbidden (c. 1399, 8°).

9. Professedly Obscene. Books which purposely treat of, narrate, or
teach lascivious or obscene matter, are *ipso iure* forbidden (c. 1399, 9°).

10. Liturgical Books Altered or Inaccurate. Editions of liturgical
books approved by the Holy See, in which anything has been changed
so that they do not agree with the authentic editions approved by the
Holy See, are *ipso iure* forbidden (c. 1399, 10°). Note that it is not
merely the lack of the required approval which causes these books to
be forbidden, but the lack of concordance with the original. Repetition
of certain parts for greater convenience is not regarded as an alteration.

11. Apocryphal Indulgences, Etc. Books containing indulgences

---

[86] Cf. Holy Office, 27 Apr., 1917; *AAS*, 9–268; *Digest*, I, p. 155.

which are apocryphal or which have been proscribed or revoked by
the Holy See are *ipso iure* forbidden (c. 1399, 11°). Books of indulgences published without the required approval (cf. c. 1388) are
not for that reason forbidden. But if they contain false indulgences
they are forbidden whether published before or after the Code. What
if they contain indulgences which were quite authentic when published but are revoked by omission from the latest collection?[87]
Literally the text seems to declare such books forbidden, but it seems
reasonable to understand the provision as referring only to indulgences
which were apocryphal or already revoked at the time they were
published. Thus *raccoltas* which are out of date, though certainly un-
reliable for present use, are not forbidden.

12. **Pictures Foreign to the Mind of the Church.** Pictures, no matter
how printed, of our Lord Jesus Christ, the Blessed Virgin Mary, the
Angels and Saints, or other Servants of God, which are foreign to
the mind and decrees of the Church are *ipso iure* forbidden (c. 1399,
12°). This provision covers only printed *pictures,* but regardless of
the process. It therefore includes lithographs, rotogravures, and the
like. Note, however, that canon 1279 (regarding the placing of
pictures *in a church,* their public veneration, etc.) is not limited to
printed pictures. The *mind* of the Church is coupled with her *decrees*
because the latter may give certainty which might otherwise be
wanting. An example is a recent decree of the Holy Office regarding
certain pictures of the Sacred Passion.[88]

Exception in Favor of Students. The use of the books mentioned in
canon 1399, 1° (namely, editions by non-Catholics of the text or of
ancient Catholic translations of the Scriptures, and all translations of
Scripture made by non-Catholics), and of books published contrary
to the prescription of canon 1391 (requiring, for translations of Scripture into the vernacular, even by Catholics, either approval of the Holy
See or vigilance of the Ordinary plus annotations) is permitted only
to persons who are in any way engaged in the study of theology or
Scripture, provided the books are faithfully and completely reproduced
and that their introductions or annotations do not attack Catholic
dogmas (c. 1400).

---

[87] *Preces et Pia Opera Indulgentiis Ditata,* published by the Sacred Penitentiary in
1938, abrogated all general grants of indulgences which are not contained therein. Cf. S.
Paen., 31 Dec., 1937; *AAS,* 30–110; *Digest,* II, p. 228.
[88] Holy Office, 30 March, 1921; *AAS,* 13–197; *Digest,* I, p. 686.

a. Those *in any way* engaged in the study of theology or Scripture include all seminary students of theology, all priests unless they have quite abandoned the sacred studies which they are bound to continue (cf. c. 129), and even lay persons who are studying these subjects.

b. When there is question of ancient versions, the proviso regarding faithful reproduction may be taken relatively; that is, it is sufficient that the book be reproduced as it is, even though it contain some errors.

Exemption of Cardinals, Bishops, Ordinaries. Cardinals of the Holy Roman Church, Bishops, even titular ones, and other Ordinaries, using the necessary precautions, are not bound by the ecclesiastical prohibition of books (c. 1401).

General Rules Regarding Permission. 1. If the law applies, permission is necessary, even though the general danger against which the law provides does not exist in the particular case (c. 21).

2. May permission be presumed? Generally not; but in a case of real and urgent necessity it might be; for example, if a judge, professor, or writer has urgent need for good cause to inspect a certain book and there is no time to ask for permission.

3. Once given, the permission is to be interpreted broadly. The reason is that it is not properly a dispensation (which according to canon 85 calls for a strict interpretation); it does not "relax the law" (cf. c. 80), because the law itself provides for permissions; it is rather a personal privilege (cf. cc. 67, 50).

4. Permission, from whomsoever obtained, exempts no one from the natural law against reading books which place the reader in proximate spiritual danger (c. 1405, § 1).

Permission by the Holy See. Permission is granted by the Holy See through the Holy Office (c. 247, § 4). The procedure is simple: a petition is sent, which must be accompanied by the recommendation of the petitioner's Ordinary if he is a secular cleric, of his superior if he is a religious, or of his confessor if he is a layman; the purpose for which the permission is desired and the quality of the person (orders, office, etc.) should be stated in the petition.

Extent of Permission Obtained From the Holy See. Those who have obtained Apostolic permission to read and keep forbidden books are not thereby permitted to read and keep any books forbidden by their Ordinaries, unless the Apostolic indult expressly gave them the faculty to read and keep books no matter by whom forbidden (c. 1403, § 1).

Moreover they are bound by a grave precept so to guard forbidden books that they may not fall into the hands of other persons **(c. 1403, § 2).**

Faculty of Ordinaries to Grant Permission. 1. As regards books prohibited by themselves, Ordinaries have, of course, full power and discretion as to granting permission.

2. As to books forbidden *ipso iure* (c. 1399) or by decree of the Holy See, Ordinaries can grant to their own subjects permission only for particular books and only in urgent cases **(c. 1402, § 1).**

a. Ordinaries here include major superiors in clerical exempt religious institutes (c. 198). The power of all Ordinaries under the Code is ordinary and hence can be delegated.

b. Ordinaries of places have, moreover, a delegated faculty by quinquennial grant to give general permission to individual subjects for not more than three years and with certain exceptions and precautions. This faculty must be exercised by the Ordinary personally.[89]

c. In the use of this or of any other general faculty obtained from the Holy See they must grant the permission only with discretion and for just and reasonable cause **(c. 1402, § 2).**

Rules for Vendors of Forbidden Books. Vendors of books must not sell, lend, or keep those which treat professedly of obscene matters; as to other forbidden books, they must not have them for sale without having obtained due permission from the Holy See, nor sell them to anyone unless they can prudently judge that the buyer is asking for them legitimately (that is, that he himself has permission to read or keep them) **(c. 1404).**

Duty of Ordinaries. Ordinaries of places and others who have the care of souls must judiciously warn the faithful of the danger and harm of reading bad books, especially those that are forbidden **(c. 1405, § 2).**

Penalties. Two distinct penalties relating to forbidden books are provided by canon 2318, as follows:

1. Against the publishers (upon publication) of books of apostates, heretics, and schismatics, which advocate apostasy, heresy, or schism; and against those who defend or *knowingly* read or keep without permission, either the books just mentioned or any others which have been forbidden by name by Apostolic letter. In both these cases the penalty is excommunication *ipso facto* incurred and specially reserved to the Holy See.

---

[89] See *Quinquennial Faculties,* Holy Office, n. 1; *Digest,* II, p. 30.

2. Against authors and publishers who without due permission cause to be printed books of Sacred Scripture or annotations or commentaries of the same. The penalty is excommunication *ipso facto* incurred, and reserved *nemini*.

Article 3. The Profession of Faith (cc. 1406–1408)

Various Professions of Faith. Positive profession of faith may be at times required by the divine law (cf. c. 1325, § 1). It is also required by ecclesiastical law under various circumstances: at baptism the subject or the sponsor for him is required to recite the Apostles' Creed; one converted from heresy makes an abjuration or profession of faith according to a formula prescribed by the Holy Office;[90] finally, the longer formula, with which we are now concerned, is prescribed upon the assumption of certain offices in the Church. This formula, which dates from Pius IV (1564) is printed at the beginning of the Code and forms part of it. In many cases the Oath against Modernism must be taken at the same time.

Who Must Make the Profession of Faith? The following are bound (c. 1406, § 1) to make this profession of faith:

1. All *members of a General or Particular Council or Diocesan Synod,* who have a consultative or deliberate vote; (the president makes the profession before the Council or Synod, all others before the president or his delegate).

2. Persons *promoted to the Cardinalate* (before the Dean of the Sacred College, the *Camerarius* of the Holy Roman Church, and the First Cardinal Priest and First Cardinal Deacon).

3. Persons *appointed Bishops,* even of titular Sees, or *Abbots or Prelates nullius, Vicars or Prefects Apostolic* (before someone delegated by the Holy See).

4. A *Vicar Capitular* (before the cathedral chapter).

5. One *appointed to a dignity or canonry* (before the Ordinary of the place or his delegate and before the chapter; if the Ordinary or delegate is present in the chapter, one profession is sufficient).

6. *Diocesan consultors* (before the Ordinary of the place or his delegate and before the other consultors; if the Ordinary or delegate is present together with the other consultors, one profession is sufficient).

7. The *Vicar General, pastors,* and all who have *received a benefice,* even a manual one (of temporary tenure) *which involves the care*

---

[90] Cf. *Digest,* II, p. 182.

of souls; the *rector and professors* of theology, canon law, and philosophy in seminaries, at the beginning of each scholastic year or at least when they first take up their duties; all who are to be *ordained to the subdiaconate; diocesan censors* mentioned in canon 1393; priests *destined to hear confessions,* and *sacred preachers* before they receive their faculties. (All these make the profession before the Ordinary of the place or his delegate.)

8. The *Rector of a University or Faculty* (before the Ordinary or his delegate); *all professors* in a University or Faculty which has been canonically erected, at the beginning of the scholastic year or at least when they first take up their duties; and also *all who upon examination receive academic degrees* (before the Rector or his delegate).

9. *Superiors in clerical religious institutes* (before the chapter or superior who appointed them, or before their delegate).

Further Provisions and Practical Applications. 1. Those who lay aside one office, benefice, or dignity and assume another even of the same kind, must again make the profession of faith according to this canon **(c. 1406, § 2).**

2. The profession cannot be made validly by proxy nor before a layman **(c. 1407).**

3. All customs contrary to the canons on this profession of faith (cc. 1406–1408) are reprobated **(c. 1408).**

The Oath Against Modernism. The precept and formula for this oath were given by Pius X in the *Motu proprio, Sacrorum Antistitum;*[91] and the Holy Office declared that they remain in effect after the Code.[92] The following are bound to take this oath:[93]

1. Those *to be ordained* to the subdiaconate (before the ordaining Bishop).

2. *Confessors and preachers* before they receive their faculties, but not upon renewal of the same (before the Ordinary who approves them).

3. *Pastors, canons, beneficiaries* before taking possession, hence also before taking a new benefice (before the Ordinary who appoints them).

---

[91] 1 Sept., 1910; *AAS,* 2–655; *Fontes,* n. 689, Vol. III, p. 774.
[92] Holy Office, 22 March, 1918; *AAS,* 10–136; *Digest,* I, p. 50.
[93] Cf. Vermeersch-Creusen, *Epit.,* II, n. 740, where much is condensed in a small space. This summary is based on the *Motu proprio, Sacrorum Antistitum,* 1 Sept., 1910; *Fontes,* n. 689, Vol. III, p. 774 and the various interpretations reported above in the text and the preceding notes.

4. *Officials of the episcopal Curia* including the Vicar General, *officials of ecclesiastical tribunals* including the judges (before the Ordinary of the place); *officials of the Roman Congregations and Tribunals* (before the Cardinal Prefect or Secretary).

5. *Lenten preachers* (that is, those specially appointed, as in European countries, to give a sermon *every day* during Lent). This obligation is *in addition* to that mentioned in n. 2.

6. *Superiors of religious* families or congregations before taking office (before the superior or chapter who appointed them).

7. *Professors or lecturers in seminaries and religious scholasticates,* every year before beginning their work (before their respective superiors).

Applications. 1. How are the profession and oath to be taken when many together are concerned? It is sufficient that the formula (either or both as the case may be) be recited by one, and that each one separately signify his assent under oath by a shorter formula, and sign the formula.[94]

2. Parochial vicars, confessors, preachers, whose faculties are renewed from year to year, need not take the oath (and make the profession) each time.[95]

3. The oath (and similarly the profession of faith) must be taken by pastors and beneficiaries with the care of souls (cf. c. 1406, § 1, 7°) *before taking possession,* and not (as formerly under the provisions of the Council of Trent) within two months after taking possession.[96]

4. Religious are to take the oath (and similarly make the profession) upon receiving sacred orders, before the ordaining Bishop or his delegate; upon receiving faculties for confessions or preaching, before the one from whom these faculties are obtained[97] (or his delegate).

5. The oath (and similarly the profession) if duly taken before the subdiaconate need not be repeated before the other sacred orders; but the Bishop may for just cause require that it be repeated.[98]

6. The oath (and the profession) need not be required in granting, even for a more or less extended time, faculties for confessions to an extradiocesan priest who is approved in his own diocese and has taken the oath there.[99]

---

[94] S. C. Consist., 25 Oct., 1910; *AAS*, 2–856, ad IV.
[95] *Ibid.*, ad V.
[96] S. C. Consist., 1 March, 1911; *AAS*, 3–134.
[97] S. C. Consist., 17 Dec., 1910; *AAS*, 3–25.
[98] S. C. Consist., 28 Apr., 1911; *AAS*, 3–181, ad II.
[99] S. C. Consist., 20 June, 1913; *AAS*, 5–272.

7. Must the oath (and, or, profession) be repeated when required by various titles, e.g., when a person holds several offices or receives the subdiaconate and very shortly afterward (by privilege) the other major orders, and then faculties for confession? No. It is sufficient that it be taken once, but a testimonial proving that is was so taken must be shown to the person who otherwise would have the right to demand that it be taken again.[100]

8. The penalty for contumacious failure to make the profession of faith when required is ultimately privation of the office or benefice (c. 2403).

9. The provisions of canon 1406, 7° and 8°, allowing professors in seminaries and in Universities and Faculties to make the profession once upon taking up their duties, is not duplicated in the provisions regarding the Oath against Modernism; this must be taken *every year*.

CASES AND QUESTIONS

1. Does the Code require new approval for the reprinting of holy pictures which have once been approved by the Ordinary? May prayers destined for private use, *e.g.*, among a community of nuns, be printed without approbation? (C. 1385; cf. *Ecclesiastical Review*, 89–190).

2. Does an unchanged second edition of a book require a new *imprimatur*? (C. 1392; cf. *Periodica*, 24–36*).

3. A priest buys a motion picture film of the Holy Land, with a lecture to accompany it. Does he need ecclesiastical approval for the lecture before speaking it? Did the publisher of the lecture need such approval? Is the showing of the film a publication? Did the Company need approval for the publication of the film itself? (C. 1385; cf. *Periodica*, 26–543).

4. A pious nun, after a series of rather extraordinary spiritual experiences, upon the advice of her confessor writes a pamphlet describing her experiences and outlining practices of devotion toward the Sacred Hands of Our Lord. Do the nun or the confessor deserve censure? What about the previous censorship of the pamphlet? (Cc. 1385, § 1, 2°, 1386, 1399, 5°; Holy Office, 26 May, 1937; 17 Apr., 1942; *Digest*, II, p. 438).

5. A priest writes a textbook of elementary biology. Does the book require ecclesiastical approval? Does the priest need any permission to publish it? Explain the difference between the two parts of this question. (Cc. 1385, 1386).

---

[100] S. C. Consist., 25 Oct., 1910; *AAS*, 2–740, ad I. Writing *before this document appeared,* Vermeersch says the oath must be repeated if the person who should receive it is different for the two titles. Cf. *Periodica*, Vol. 5, pp. 210, 232. That would be theoretically correct, but this later authentic interpretation explicitly makes a more liberal provision.

6. An exempt religious priest is placed by his Provincial in charge of a Sodality magazine. Is previous approval required for the matter so published? (C. 1385).

7. A textbook of canon law contains a section on indulgences. Whose previous approval does it require? (C. 1388, § 1). What of a "Pastor's Guide" containing a section on Liturgy? (Cc. 1385, §§ 1, 2, 1390).

8. A secular priest writes a letter about migratory birds for publication in a "popular" column of the daily paper. Is any *imprimatur* or permission required? (Cc. 1385, 1386).

9. A Catholic girl receives as a gift from a friend a nice copy of the King James version of the New Testament. May she keep and read it? (C. 1399, 1°).

10. Is the use of a Catholic prayer book with no *imprimatur* forbidden? (C. 1399, 5°).

11. A priest librarian of a college library is asked over the telephone whether the following works are on the Index: (1) *Les Miserables*, by Hugo; (2) *Ulysses*, by Joyce; (3) *The Love Life of Abdul Karan*, Anonymous; (4) *Jesus Christ*, by Renan. What should be his general answer? His reply as to each book? (Cf. c. 1399).

12. A certain Encyclopedia is very valuable but contains many articles on religious and historical subjects which betray a strong anti-Catholic bias. The article on Agnosticism presents it as a reasonable and tenable position. May the whole set be kept on the open shelves of a Catholic college library? Must the whole set be disposed of? (C. 1399; cf. *Irish Eccl. Rec.*, 43–80).

13. Could you support by argument the proposition that reading a forbidden book in braille is not forbidden?

14. A collector purchases at an auction a book of original sketches of a modern artist. A few of the pictures are obscene; of the others, some are very beautiful; among the religious drawings many are too realistic to conform to Catholic taste and tradition. May he keep the book? What is to be said of the law as applying to each class of pictures? (Cc. 1405, 1399, 12°).

15. A diocesan censor makes the following report: "The moral doctrine of this book, while it is held by a substantial minority of Catholic moralists, is in my opinion entirely wrong and pernicious. I cannot in conscience approve its publication." The Bishop, though he knows the doctrine is sound, thinks its publication inopportune, and so refuses the *imprimatur*. Comment on both actions.

16. It is customary in a diocesan seminary to make the profession of faith and take the Oath against Modernism every other year. May this be continued?

17. The rector of a seminary asks: "Our *ordinandi* made the profession of faith before receiving the subdiaconate, but did not at that time

take the oath against Modernism. Were they obliged to do so? Must they make the profession and oath before each of the two remaining major ordinations? And again when they receive their faculties?"

18. One of the professors in a religious scholasticate returned a few days late from his vacation; his absence from the profession of faith was not noticed. Is he or the superior subject to the penalties of canon 2403? What should have been done? What is to be done?

Readings:

Pernicone, *The Ecclesiastical Prohibition of Books,* Cath. U., 1932; Canavan, *The Profession of Faith,* Cath. U., 1942; *Periodica,* Vol. 21, p. 189* (Jombart, on omission of *imprimatur*); Vol. 24, p. 49* (Lopez, on film story based on forbidden book); Vol. 26, p. 543 (Creyghton, on *imprimatur* for films, slides, explanatory texts of lectures, etc.); *Ecclesiastical Review,* Vol. 87, p. 313 (can a periodical be placed on the Index?); Vol. 88, p. 628 (Walsh, on refusal of *imprimatur*); *Irish Ecclesiastical Record,* Vol. 37, p. 525 (on meaning of *"libri haereticorum"*); Vol. 43, p. 80 (on use of non-Catholic encyclopedias).

CHAPTER XIX

CHURCH PROPERTY

Section 1. Introductory (cc. 1495–1498)

PRELIMINARY SURVEY

Right of the Church to Own Property (c. 1495)
Right of the Church to Demand Support From the Faithful (c. 1496)
Definition of Terms (cc. 1497–1498)
    Ecclesiastical Things (c. 1497, § 1)
    Sacred Things (c. 1497, § 2)
    Precious Things (c. 1497, § 2)
    Meaning of Term "Church" (c. 1498)

Right of the Church to Own Property. The Catholic Church as a divine institution received its legal personality from God Himself (c. 100, § 1); hence it is independent of any human power both in its origin and in the exercise of its prerogatives. Since the Church is a visible society composed of human beings with bodies as well as souls, it is evident that the Church must have temporal possessions for the fulfillment of her mission. The exercise of external worship, the support of her ministers, as well as the care of orphans, the sick, and the aged, the education of youth — all involve the need of temporal things. Hence the Church asserts her native right to acquire, hold, and administer temporal things for the attainment of the purposes for which she was founded, and that freely and independently of the civil authority (c. 1495, § 1).

This same right to acquire, to hold, and to administer property is extended by the law of the Church to individual churches and other moral persons which have been duly established by church authority as juridical persons according to the norms established by the sacred canons (c. 1495, § 2; cf. also cc. 100, 531, 676).

By *individual churches* we mean groups of the faithful determined by territorial limits under the government of an ecclesiastical superior; such as, dioceses, prelatures and abbacies *nullius,* prefectures and vicariates apostolic (cf. c. 215).

All other moral persons (see canon 100) enjoy the right to acquire, retain, and administer property only by reason of their having been given juridical (legal) personality by the proper ecclesiastical authority through a formal decree of erection (cf. c. 100, § 1). Since this right is given to them by the Church, it is subject to the laws of the Church (*ad normam sacrorum canonum*) and may not be exercised independently of them.

Although a *parish* canonically erected (not the parochial community) has the right to hold and administer church property (see c. 1499, § 2), the mode of tenure will depend upon the organization adopted by the diocese in order to comply with the requirements of the civil law (see Section 2, below, Tenure of Church Property in the United States).

Moral ecclesiastical persons retain their right to own and administer church property inasmuch as, and only so long as they remain in union with the Church which gave them existence. The moment they separate from the unity of the Church, they lose all the rights which they possessed. This principle is acknowledged by the civil law.[1]

The Right of the Church to Demand Support From the Faithful. While the Church has from God all the supernatural means necessary for her sacred mission (jurisdiction, teaching power, sacraments) the purely material goods required for that same end must come from the faithful themselves. In practice the faithful supply these temporal goods voluntarily by the foundation of benefices, schools, hospitals, and other charitable institutions. If these be sufficient for the needs of the Church, such benefactions exonerate the rest of the faithful from the duty of supporting the Church.

If there are no such foundations, then the present generation of the faithful has the obligation of supporting the Church. If this is done voluntarily and with sufficient liberality, there will be no need of imposing positive obligations on individual members. If these free-will offerings are not sufficient for the needs of divine worship, for the decent support of the Church's ministers, and for the necessary upkeep of charitable and educational works which are proper to the Church, then the Church has the right to demand such support from the faithful (c. 1496). Money for this purpose may be raised either by a general tax proportioned to the income of the individual, or by a special tax levied on the occasion of special services on the community as a whole (such as collections taken up during divine services), or on indi-

---

[1] Zollman, *American Church Law* (1933), § 274, p. 260.

viduals on the occasion of some special spiritual administration (such as baptism, marriage, and burial).

Definition of Terms. The term *ecclesiastical goods (bona ecclesiastica)* or *church property,* as we shall henceforth designate it, occurs throughout this chapter. The lawgiver himself has defined it for us as: All temporal goods (whether corporeal or incorporeal, movable or immovable) which belong either to the Church Universal and the Apostolic See, or to some other moral person in the Church (c. 1497, § 1).

Corporeal property is that which is palpable or that which may be perceived by the senses; such as, a field, a house, money.

Incorporeal property is that which is not palpable, not perceivable by the senses, but by the mind only; such as, legal rights and obligations regarding property. Stocks and bonds are sometimes classed as incorporeal. In civil law "incorporeal chattels" include such things as copyrights and patent rights, stocks and personal annuities; "incorporeal hereditaments" include all rights issuing out of corporeal property, or concerning or annexed to the same, such as tithes, offices, franchises, annuities, rents, and easements (the latter including rights of way and rights of pasture, of fishing, of taking game, and the like).

Immovable property is that which cannot be moved from place to place either naturally (as a field or a building) or legally (as windows, doors, fixtures, lights, plumbing, and the like).

Movable property is that which can be transferred from place to place; as livestock, grain, merchandise, money.

Movable property is either *fungible,* i.e., property which may be replaced in kind and which is consumed by the use of it (as grain, fruit, vegetables); or *nonfungible,* i.e., property which is not consumed by the first use of it (as a wagon, a lawn mower).

Sacred things are those which are destined for divine worship by reason of their consecration or blessing (c. 1497, § 2); as a church, a chalice, and the like. These remain *sacred* even though they pass into the possession of private persons.

Precious property includes all church property which has a *special value* by reason of *artistic, historical,* or *material* content (c. 1497, § 2). Church property is said to be precious, not by reason of its quantity nor by reason of the large income it produces, but only by reason of one or more of the three titles mentioned: *art,* such as a painting, a piece of sculpture, or a tapestry; *history,* such as ancient codices, coins, public and private documents, or anything that has special value by reason of its antiquity or because it once belonged to a celebrated personage; *material,* because it is made of precious metal, or adorned with gems and precious stones.

Property which is precious by reason of its *material* content may be evaluated easily enough (see explanation of c. 1532, § 1). The same is not true of things which are precious by reason of *art* or *history* (such as historical documents), since these things may not have much intrinsic value but may be of great importance to a church or pious place. Hence the judgment of experts will have to be obtained in order to determine their *special* value.

Meaning of the term "church." Since the term "church" will recur with great frequency in the canons which follow, the legislator has given us a definition and determined its extension for us. It includes not only the Church Universal and the Apostolic See, but also all moral persons in the Church (as defined in canon 1495, § 2) unless the contrary is evident from the context or from the nature of the matter treated (c. 1498). The term "church" is taken in a broad sense to mean not only a place in which divine worship is held, but also every ecclesiastical moral person constituted as such by church authority for the purpose of religious or charitable activity; e.g., hospitals, schools, religious houses and institutes, as well as chapters of religious persons.

The term "church," therefore, does not include any ecclesiastical associations which are *merely approved* by the Church, such as pious and charitable societies; nor does it include pious and social works established by private persons which do not require ecclesiastical approval and which are not subject to the Ordinaries, such as the Society of St. Vincent de Paul,[2] or the various fraternal organizations of the Catholic laity, e.g., the Knights of Columbus, the Catholic Foresters, Catholic Men's Benefit Association, Ladies' Catholic Benefit Association, and the like. These organizations may be incorporated by the civil law and may be entitled to hold and administer their own property, but such property is in no sense *church property* within the meaning of the canons of this chapter.

---

[2] S. C. Conc., Nov. 14, 1920; *AAS,* 13 (1921), 135; *Digest,* I, p. 714.

Section 2. Acquirement of Ecclesiastical Property (cc. 1499–1512)

PRELIMINARY SURVEY

Acquirement and Ownership (c. 1499)
Property of Moral Persons (cc. 1500–1501)
Tithes and First Fruits (c. 1502)
Begging or Collecting Alms (c. 1503)
Cathedraticum (c. 1504)
Contributions of Various Kinds (cc. 1505–1506)
Stole Fees and Other Taxes (c. 1507)
Prescription (cc. 1508–1512)

Acquirement and Ownership of Church Property. Like all other physical or moral persons, the Church can acquire temporal property by every just means allowed by the natural or the positive law (c. 1499, § 1). In this canon the Code is not speaking of means of acquiring property (such as tithes and first fruits) which are peculiarly and exclusively her own; but it is dealing with means of acquiring property which are common to all. The Code here rejects all unjust limitations which are sometimes imposed on the Church by civil laws, such as limitations regarding the *object* (as when the state denies to the Church the right to receive inheritances or bequests); or limitations regarding the *form* in which property may be held (as when the state imposes its so-called "protective authority" on church property). In this canon, then, the words *positive law* refer to the civil law.

By every just means — the following are just means of acquiring property:

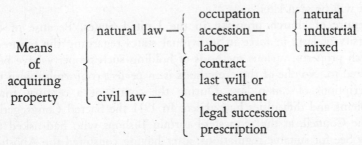

All other forms of acquiring property may be reduced to one or another of the above.

The dominion or ownership of church property belongs to the moral person that has acquired it lawfully; but it remains subject to the supreme authority of the Apostolic See (c. 1499, § 2). Only a moral person can be the subject of ownership of church property; as, a diocese, a parish, religious institutes and their houses, societies of the faithful, pious causes, and the like. Physical persons are never the subjects of ownership of church property, but only the *administrators* of it. Hence it follows that no individual person in the Church, not even an ecclesiastical or religious superior, can dispose of church property freely and independently of church law without violating justice in the strict sense of the word. Church property, therefore, belongs not to the individual persons who make up a moral person, but to the moral personality whose existence and property are distinct and independent of the life and property of the individual persons. Thus the members of a parish which has been incorporated by the Church may not claim the ownership of parish property.

Subject to the Supreme Authority of the Apostolic See. The Apostolic See does not enjoy the ownership properly so called of the property belonging to its subordinate moral persons. However, because of its universal jurisdiction to which these bodies are subject, it does enjoy the *right of eminent domain.* Therefore, it may transfer or alienate such property, not arbitrarily, but when some necessity or some great utility of these bodies requires that it do so. When the Supreme Pontiff uses his power of eminent domain, he does so as the supreme administrator and dispenser of church property. More will be said about this in canon 1518.

In a similar way and with certain exceptions, church property which is located in a diocese is subject to the authority of the Bishop of the diocese. He is not the owner of this property, but the administrator of it, as will be seen later on.

Tenure of church property in the United States. Because of the diversity of laws in force in individual states regarding the tenure of church property, various methods of holding such property have been resorted to. No one of these methods is in perfect conformity with the prescriptions of canon law. During the course of a century, many problems and difficulties had arisen. In 1911 the Sacred Congregation of the Council, at the request of certain Bishops who had asked the Holy See for suitable regulations, after having consulted the Apostolic Delegate and the Most Reverend Archbishops, issued the following norms:

1. Among the methods which are now in use in the United States for holding and administering church property, the one known as

Parish Corporation is preferable to the others, but with the conditions and safeguards which are now in use in the state of New York. The Bishops, therefore, should immediately take steps to introduce this method for handling property in their dioceses, if the civil law allows it. If the civil law does not allow it, they should exert their influence with the civil authorities that it may be made legal as soon as possible.

2. Only in those places where the civil law does not recognize *Parish Corporations* and only until such recognition is obtained, the method commonly called *Corporation Sole* is allowed with the understanding that in the administration of ecclesiastical property the Bishop is to act with the advice, and in more important matters with the consent, of those who have an interest in the premises and of the diocesan consultors, this being a conscientious obligation for the Bishop in person.

3. The method called *in fee simple* is to be entirely abandoned.[3]

No matter what method of tenure be followed, ownership of the property is vested in the moral person (c. 1499, § 2). The Bishop is merely the administrator of such property, even though according to civil law the property is owned by him. All the regulations of canon law must be carried out.

Division of Property of Moral Persons. The territory of an ecclesiastical moral person may be divided in either of two ways: a part may be cut off and united with some other moral personality, or a part may be cut off and itself constituted a new moral person. In either case property which had been intended for the benefit of the whole territory, and all debts which had been contracted for the whole territory, are to be divided with due regard for what is right and just by that ecclesiastical authority which is competent to make the division of the territory. The wills of pious founders and donors, rights lawfully acquired, and particular laws by which the moral person is ruled, must all be safeguarded (**c. 1500**).

A moral person cannot be divided; but its territory or its property, as well as its duties and obligations, may be divided. The canon supposes that the territory has already been divided by competent ecclesiastical authority (cf. cc. 215, 248, § 2, 252, 255, 260, 494, 1422, 1427, § 1). That same authority is to divide the funds (as well as the debts) which are common to the whole territory. This division is to be made according to the principles of equity since a precise mathematical

---

[3] *Ecclesiastical Review*, XLV (1911), 585, 596; *Digest*, II, p. 443. Both these sources describe the "New York System" referred to in Norm n. 1.

division is not always possible. The Church is meticulous in regard to carrying out the intentions of founders and donors of pious causes. Time and again this obligation is repeated in the Code. Similarly, acquired rights are respected. Thus if a parcel of land or a building, which is common property of the territory to be divided, has been leased for a period of years, that lease must be respected in the division of the property. Finally, any particular laws which govern the moral person in this respect must be observed. Thus canon 494 prescribes that when a province of a religious institute is divided or dismembered, the constitutions are to be observed in the distribution of the goods of the province.

Property of an extinct moral person. A moral person may cease to exist either by reason of formal suppression on the part of the authority which created it, or by reason of its own virtual nonexistence for a hundred years (c. 102). In either case, what is to become of its property? Ownership is not transferred to the authority which suppressed it but to the moral person which is the immediate superior of the extinct moral person. However, the interests of founders and others mentioned in canon 1500 must be safeguarded (c. 1501). In the case of a moral personality which is part of an organized hierarchy, there is no difficulty in determining the immediate superior moral person. Thus, in the case of a parish, it is the diocese; in the case of a diocese, the province; in the case of a province, the Holy See. Similarly, the property of an extinct religious house goes to the province; the property of the province, to the general institute.

In the case of *absolutely autonomous* moral persons, such as a confraternity or an entirely independent monastery, the immediate superior moral person will be either the diocese or the Holy See, depending upon whether the confraternity or monastery was in any way subject to the local Ordinary or immediately subject to the Holy See. A pious association may or may not be a moral person. If it has been legitimately established as a moral person, it may have its own administrator but is subject to the Bishop of the diocese in financial matters, not to the pastor in whose parish it holds its meetings (c. 691, § 1).

Tithes and First Fruits. The giving of tithes or the tenth part of the produce of the land as an offering to God and His ministers derives from the Mosaic Law.[4] By custom and particular law it became obligatory in the Middle Ages, especially in the East; but it has long since

---

[4] Deut. 14:22.

become obsolete except in a few churches which have kept the ancient custom by reason of local statutes.

First fruits. The custom of giving the first fruits of the soil, as well as of animals, to God the Creator also derives from the Mosaic Law.[5] It seems to have gradually ceased in the Western Church after the fifth century, but it may still be found in a few places by way of custom.

Local statutes as well as laudable customs regarding tithes and first fruits are to be respected (c. 1502).

Begging or Collecting Alms. The Code distinguishes between the free-will offerings of the faithful and the offerings given in response to *requests.* Safeguarding the prescriptions of canons 621–624, private persons, whether lay or cleric, are forbidden to beg or to collect alms for any pious purpose or for any ecclesiastical institution except with the permission of the Holy See or of their own Ordinary as well as that of the local Ordinary of the place in which they wish to beg (c. 1503). *To beg, in the strict sense of the word,* means to go from door to door and to ask for alms for some pious purpose. This would include seeking information regarding the names of generous persons in a certain locality, making a list of them, and then calling upon them with a request for alms.

The following actions do not come under the prohibition of the canon: (1) asking help of those who are personally known to one, provided it is done with discretion; (2) collecting alms in a *church,* or at the meeting of some society, as such gifts are considered voluntary offerings; (3) going to certain homes at the invitation of the occupants; (4) visiting benefactors to thank them for previous benefactions or to bid them farewell, as is sometimes done by missionaries.

What about begging letters? Strictly speaking, begging letters do not come under the law, since in such begging there is no personal, oral request for alms. Custom, which is the best interpreter of law (c. 29), allows them. Besides there is less danger of abuse and embarrassment in a letter requesting alms than there is in a personal request for them. One can always toss letters into the wastebasket. If the receiver of a circular letter, which describes the usefulness of a certain good work that is being promoted, decides to send an alms, his gift is considered to be a free-will offering.

Those who resort to circular letters for the collection of alms for sundry pious purposes should be moderate and discreet in their re-

---

⁵ Num. 18:19.

quests for help, and should avoid all dramatic and exaggerated descriptions of their needs. It is a good rule to advise the faithful to pay no attention to circular letters asking for help, unless the sender is known to them, or his letter has the approval of his own Ordinary.

Private persons are forbidden to collect alms, that is, persons who have no special office which would entitle them to do so. Thus a parish priest has the right and duty, by reason of his office, to request alms for the various needs of the parish, and is explicitly empowered to do so (cc. 415, § 2, 5° and 630, § 4). Special rules for religious who wish to beg for alms will be found in canons 621-624. It is self-evident that alms given either freely or upon request must always be used for the purpose intended by the donor.

The *Cathedraticum.* The *cathedraticum* is a moderate tax to be paid annually to the Bishop in token of subjection by all churches and benefices subject to his jurisdiction as well as by lay confraternities. The amount is to be determined according to the norms laid down in canon 1507, § 1, unless it has already been determined by long standing custom **(c. 1504).**

A moderate tax. As early as the sixth century it was customary in Spain and Italy, on the occasion of the visitation of the Bishop, to pay him two *solidi* in honor of the episcopal see (*cathedra*). Hence, the name *cathedraticum.* In the Roman Synod of 1725, Benedict XIII decreed that it should not exceed two gold *solidi* or twenty *iulii,* about two dollars in our money. It was further decreed that the amount should be the same for all and should not vary from year to year.[6] The *cathedraticum* is to be paid not only by parish churches but by all churches, public oratories, and benefices subject to the jurisdiction of the Bishop. Hence the churches and chapels of exempt religious are not subject to this tax. Confraternities of lay persons erected by the authority of the Bishop must pay the *cathedraticum* provided they use their own churches. Simple pious associations which use the parish church are not subject to the tax.[7]

Although the *cathedraticum* is not subject to prescription (c. 1509, 8°), it need not be paid to the Vicar Capitular or to the Administrator during the vacancy of the Episcopal See.[8] While a Bishop is not obliged to insist on his right to the *cathedraticum* and need not require it if he wishes to remit it, he may nevertheless introduce it into his

---

[6] S. C. Conc., March 14, 1920; *AAS,* 12 (1920), 444; *Digest,* I, 719.
[7] *Ibidem.*
[8] S. C. Conc., Aug. 20, 1917; *AAS,* 9 (1917), 497; *Digest,* I, p. 719.

diocese even though it was never before required. The amount, however, must be determined by the Bishops of the Province and approved by the Holy See.

From what has been said above, it is evident that the use of the term *cathedraticum* to designate the tax levied by Bishops in the United States for the support of their dioceses is not accurate. More will be said about this tax under canon 1506.

Contributions of Various Kinds. Extraordinary contributions (called *tributa, exactiones*) are treated in canons 1505 and 1506. They are permitted under special circumstances: (1) seminary tax (cf. cc. 1355–1356); (2) pension on a benefice (c. 1429); (3) charitable subsidy. This latter consists of an extraordinary but moderate contribution required of all the *beneficiaries* (not of the benefices), whether secular or religious, for some special pressing need of the diocese (c. 1505). Pre-Code canonists offered the following as examples justifying a request for such charitable subsidy: the expenses of the Bishop's consecration, extraordinary necessary repairs on the cathedral, expenses of the Bishop's visit *ad limina*. It was supposed, however, that the ordinary income of the Bishop was not sufficient to cover these expenses.

The amount requested of each beneficiary should be moderate both absolutely and relatively to his income.

The Ordinary can exact no other contributions for the good of the diocese from churches, benefices, and other ecclesiastical institutions, even though they be subject to him, except in the act of foundation or consecration. No contribution can be exacted from Mass stipends, whether manual or founded (c. 1506).

By the act of foundation is meant the consent given by the Ordinary to build a church or institution on a certain piece of ground; by consecration is meant the consecration of a church, not the simple or solemn blessing of it.

The contribution exacted must be for the good of the diocese; for instance, an annual sum to be contributed for the support of the orphans or the seminary. It may be imposed *in perpetuum,* to be paid annually; or it may be imposed for a term of years only. Once imposed the Ordinary cannot increase it. This contribution may be imposed upon churches, public oratories, and public church institutions such as hospitals, provided that they are subject to the local Ordinary.

Method of taxation in force in the United States. The prevailing method of supporting the Bishop and the diocesan curia by means of a tax imposed upon each parish in proportion to its income is based upon the legislation of the Second Plenary Council of Baltimore (n. 100) which reads as follows:

"Since it is equitable and just that all the faithful of each diocese should contribute to the proper support of the Bishop who bears the burden and care of all, the Fathers assembled judged that this matter was to be treated in the Diocesan Synods in which the priests having the care of souls were to take counsel among themselves and agree on a certain pension to be given annually to their Ordinary, to be made up of a definite portion of the income of each church. Such an assignment and division, after being examined and approved by the Ordinary, shall be published as a diocesan law to be observed by all." This provision was approved without any change by the S. Congregation for the Propagation of the Faith.

This assessment on parish funds for the support of the Bishop has been popularly though incorrectly called the *cathedraticum,* as we have seen above. Here a problem presents itself. How can this assessment be reconciled with the prescriptions of canons 1505 and 1506, which not only make no provision for such an assessment but would seem to exclude it? Even before the Code such diocesan assessments were contrary to the common law to which the Church in the United States became subject in 1908, but they were approved by the Holy See as the only practical means of meeting the needs of the diocese. Since the same needs are present today, they may be continued as long as necessary unless the Holy See expressly prohibits them. This opinion is strengthened by the fact that as late as 1929 the S. Congregation of the Eastern Church approved this same method of parish assessments for the Greek-Ruthenian dioceses of the United States.[9]

As to the annual collections taken up in all dioceses of the United States for Peter's Pence, the Holy Land, the Indian and Negro Missions, the Catholic University, and in many dioceses for the support of the seminary, the orphans, diocesan high schools, and the like, they are covered by canons 1503, 415, § 2, 5°, and 630, § 4. Canon 1503 permits the local Ordinary to collect alms within the limits of his territory without having to obtain permission from anyone. Local pastors, both diocesan and religious, are empowered by canons 415

---

[9] *AAS,* 21 (1929), 154, art. 7; *Digest,* I, p. 9. Cf. Weinz, *Ius Decretalium,* III, n. 223, p. 224; Ayrinhac, *Administrative Legislation,* p. 402; Beste, *Introductio in Codicem,* Ed. 2, p. 728; Kremer, *Church Support in the United States,* p. 124.

and 630 to take up collections for the benefit of their parishioners. Now, the Ordinary is the immediate pastor of the entire diocese and enjoys this right in a higher degree. He can also demand that the clergy subject to him assist him in gathering these alms; and he may prescribe when such collections are to be taken up in the individual parishes, how they are to be announced, and what other details are to be observed concerning them.[10]

Stole Fees and Other Taxes. A tax may be defined as a fee (gratuity, remuneration) imposed by canon law to be given by the faithful to the curia or to the sacred ministers on the occasion of favors granted or of the sacred ministry exercised in their favor. Since this is a very delicate matter open to misunderstanding on the part of the faithful, it is prescribed that only a Provincial Council or the Bishops of the Province in a joint meeting may determine the amount of the taxes to be given for various acts of voluntary jurisdiction, or for the execution of rescripts of the Holy See, or on the occasion of the administration of the sacraments or sacramentals. These taxes must be *uniform* for the entire ecclesiastical Province. The list of taxes prescribed by the Bishops of the Province has no binding force unless it has been first approved by the Holy See (c. 1507, § 1).

The purpose of this legislation is twofold: first, to determine the maximum tax beyond which nothing may be demanded or exacted (which maximum must be uniform for all dioceses of the province);[11] second, to give the Holy See the opportunity to watch over all such taxes and to eliminate anything that might savor of simony or might give occasion of scandal to the faithful. Thus security in the matter of these taxes is established both for the ministers of the Church and for the faithful.

It is understood, of course, that the sacraments and sacramentals are never to be denied the faithful who are unable to pay the tax assessed (c. 463, § 4).[12] On the other hand, while it is forbidden to *demand* or *exact* a larger tax than that established, one may *accept* a larger amount *freely* and *spontaneously* offered, unless local legislation forbids it.

Regarding *funeral taxes,* the canon refers back to canon 1234 which prescribes that each Ordinary determine them with the consent of his chapter (diocesan consultors).

Regarding taxes for marriage dispensations, see canon 1056.

---

[10] Kremer, *Church Support in the United States,* p. 126.

[11] S. C. Conc., June 10, 1896, ad II; Dec. 11, 1920, *AAS,* 13 (1921), 351; *Digest,* I, p. 720.

[12] S. C. Conc., June 10, 1896, I, 2.

As to court fees (pro actibus iudicialibus) canon 1909 is to be observed **(c. 1507, § 2)**. This canon prescribes that they be determined by the Bishops of the Province, but does not require the approval of the Holy See.

Prescription. Prescription, as a means of acquiring (property) and of freeing oneself (from an obligation), is admitted by the Church in regard to church property according to the civil legislation of each respective nation. However, the reservations laid down in the following canons must be observed **(c. 1508)**.

Prescription is a peculiar mode either of acquiring ownership of property by possessing it for a period of time under certain prescribed conditions, or of freeing oneself from an obligation in the same way. The former is called *acquisitive* prescription; the latter, *liberative* or extinctive prescription.

Prescription is based mediately upon the natural law but owes its origin immediately to human law. Its foundation is the common good. It is governed immediately and in detail by the positive enactments of human law. Five conditions are generally required to establish prescription: (1) a thing that is prescriptible (c. 1509); (2) actual possession; (3) some kind of title; (4) time required by the law (cf. c. 1511); (5) good faith (cf. c. 1512).

1. *A thing that is prescriptible,* that is, the matter must be subject to prescription. All things, whether corporeal or incorporeal, movable or immovable, public or private, are *generally* prescriptible unless prohibited by positive law either absolutely, or relatively to certain times and persons.

Since the Church is a perfect society, she has the right to regulate the law of prescription in regard to her own property. Hence her laws are to be observed before all others. The civil laws of each nation regarding prescription are *canonized* only in so far as they are not opposed to the provisions of canon law as laid down in the Code.

The Code decrees that *the following are not subject to prescription* **(c. 1509):**

1°. *Whatever pertains to the divine law, whether natural or positive.* The reason for this is evident — no human law can annul the divine law. Thus property seized by theft or violence can never be acquired by prescription.

2°. *Things which can be obtained by apostolic privilege only.* Note the word *only.* An example would be the privilege sometimes granted to priests to administer confirmation and minor orders.

3°. *Spiritual rights which lay persons are not capable of receiving,* that is, *when there is question of prescription in favor of lay persons.* Thus a lay person is incapable of receiving jurisdiction or benefice in the Church (c. 118).

4°. *The certain and undoubted boundaries of ecclesiastical provinces, dioceses, parishes, vicariates and prefectures apostolic, prelatures and abbacies nullius.*

5°. *Mass stipends and their obligations.* The prohibition applies to manual as well as to founded Masses and applies both to the person who is obliged to give a stipend and to the person who is obliged to say Mass by reason of a stipend received.

6°. *A benefice without a title,* that is, without even a color of title to form a basis for the right to the benefice. If any kind of title is had, even though an invalid one, prescription is not forbidden.

7°. *The right of visitation and of obedience if the consequence would be that subjects can be visited by no prelate and are no longer subject to any prelate.*

8°. *Payment of the cathedraticum.* The reason for this is that the *cathedraticum* is paid as a token of subjection to the Bishop.

Prescription of sacred things. Sacred things, as defined by c. 1497, § 2, are such as have been destined for divine worship by consecration or benediction. They lose their consecration or blessing when they are so badly damaged or so much changed as to lose their original form and thus become useless for their purpose, or if they are used for unbecoming purposes or offered for sale publicly or at auction (c. 1305).

Sacred things are subject to a limited prescription. If they are owned by private persons, they may be prescribed by private persons, but not for profane uses. If, however, they have lost their consecration or blessing, they may be freely acquired for profane uses, but not for sordid uses (c. 1510, § 1).

Sacred things not owned by a private person but by an ecclesiastical moral person are not subject to prescription by a private person. They are, however, subject to prescription by another ecclesiastical moral person (c. 1510, § 2).

2 and 3. Possession and title in prescription. The Code has nothing to say about these two conditions which are always required for prescription; hence the conditions laid down by the civil law regarding them should be followed.

4. Time required for prescription. Time alone, no matter how long, can never be the efficient cause of rights. Yet by reason of positive law a certain amount of time is required as a *condition* for prescription. Here again the requirements of the civil law must be followed, unless canon law requires a different period.

The following requirements of canon law in regard to time must also be observed: For immovable things and for movable *precious* things, and for rights and actions real or personal, the space of one hundred years is required for prescription if they belong to the Holy See; thirty years, if they belong to some other ecclesiastical moral person (c. 1511). For all other property belonging to the Holy See or to ecclesiastical moral persons, the time required by the civil law will suffice for prescription. Temporal things not in the possession of a moral person, or not enjoying moral personality, such as pious causes, are likewise subject to the civil law in regard to the time necessary for prescription.

5. *Good faith and prescription.* Good faith is a judgment by which one prudently concludes that he justly possesses a thing as his own without any violation of the rights of another. In the strict sense, it is a judgment of *ownership* justly acquired; in the broad sense, it is the persuasion of lawful *possession*. Theologically and canonically speaking, possession of a thing which is lawful in conscience inasmuch as it excludes sin is sufficient to establish good faith.

No prescription is valid unless it is based upon good faith, not only at the beginning of possession, but throughout the entire time required for prescription (c. 1512). The principle laid down in the canon is merely a declaration of the natural law and is to be observed not only in regard to church property but in regard to all other things as well, even though it may not be required by the civil law. For a person who keeps a thing belonging to another without good faith does so with the consciousness of his obligation to restore it to its owner. Thus he sins; and that sin may not be rewarded even by the civil law. On the other hand the civil law should not be accused of favoring evil because it does not always require good faith for prescription. Various considerations of the common good may move the civil legislator to require less in the external forum and to allow the individual to follow his own conscience in the matter. Even St. Thomas admitted the problems involved.[13]

---

[13] "Ratio huius contrarietatis (inter ius canonicum et civile) est, quia alius est finis quem intendit civilis legislator, scilicet pacem servare et stare inter cives, quae impediretur si praescriptio non curreret; quicumque enim vellet posset venire et dicere: istud fuit meum quocumque tempore. Finis autem iuris canonici tendit in quietem Ecclesiae et salutem animarum." *Quodlib.* 12, art. 24.

Good faith is required not only at the beginning of possession, but *throughout the entire time* required for prescription. Nevertheless, if a person takes possession of a thing in good faith but later begins to doubt whether the thing belongs to another or not, he remains in good faith and may use prescription even though the doubt still remains; provided, however, that he made diligent inquiry to resolve the doubt. The reason for this is that *"in dubio melior est conditio possidentis."* It follows that one is not obliged to divest himself of a thing which he obtained in good faith merely because of an insoluble doubt which arises later on.

When there is question of moral persons, good faith must be had on the part of those individual persons who act in the name of the moral person.

Section 3: Gifts and Bequests for Pious Causes (cc. 1513–1517)

PRELIMINARY SURVEY

Definition of Terms
Who Can Make Such Gifts and Bequests (c. 1513, § 1)
Obligation of Heirs (c. 1513, § 2)
Fulfillment of Pious Wills (1514)
Ordinaries as Executors of Pious Wills (c. 1515)
Clerics and Religious as Trustees (c. 1516)
Changes in Last Wills and Testaments (c. 1517)

Definition of Terms. For a proper understanding of the five canons treating of pious causes it is necessary to have clear definitions of the terms used.

1. *Pious cause (causa pia)* is according to Molina[14] "anything that is done principally in consideration (*intuitu*) of God and a supernatural end — to merit grace or glory with God or in satisfaction for one's own or another's sins." The term includes all works which, either by reason of their direct purpose (*ex fine operis*) or by reason of the intention of the donor, are destined for a supernatural end. This supernatural end may be the worship of God and the honor of the saints or the spiritual or temporal welfare of one's neighbor. In this latter case, however, the motive of Christian charity must enter in; a motive of mere philanthropy will not suffice. It is well to note here that the

---

[14] *De iust. et iure,* d. 134.

work of purely lay associations, even though they are not established by ecclesiastical authority, are to be included under the term *pious causes* because of their supernatural motive, as, for example, the work of the Society of St. Vincent de Paul (see Sec. 1, Art. 3, *supra*).

Here are some examples of pious causes: the celebration of Holy Mass; the building of churches, monasteries, schools, orphanages, hospitals, homes for the aged, and their maintenance; promoting confraternities, associations for the promotion of the faith and good morals among youth, and other similar works.

The following are obviously not pious causes: little theaters; recreational centers intended only to give opportunity for physical exercise and merely social recreation; hospitals, orphanages, and schools which are evidently founded by reason of purely philanthropic motives. In case of doubt regarding the nature of the work itself, the matter will be determined by the intention of the donor. If he is a Catholic, the *presumption* will be in favor of a pious cause.

2. *Pious foundation* (*pia fundatio*) is a sum of money or its equivalent (goods which can be turned into money eventually) given in any way to a moral person in the Church with the obligation *in perpetuum,* or at least for a long time, *to use the income* to have Masses said, or for other well-defined ecclesiastical functions, or for the performance of certain works of piety and charity (c. 1544).

3. *Pious will* (*pia voluntas*) is any provision made for a pious cause.

4. *An act among the living* (*actus inter vivos*) in the present context means any donation or other contract by which ownership of property is transferred *irrevocably* to another for a pious cause. It becomes effective the moment it is accepted by the beneficiary. It is called *inter vivos* because ownership is transferred at once without any consideration of the death of the donor entering into the act.

5. *An act in consideration of death* (*actus mortis causa*) is a provision made for the transfer of property to take place *after the death* of the donor. This may take either of two forms:

a. *A donation in consideration of death* (*donatio mortis causa*) by which a gift of certain property is made during the lifetime of the donor, but subject to revocation on his part at any time before his death. While the beneficiary must accept it to give it effect, the ownership of the property is not transferred to him by the acceptance but only after the death of the donor; provided that the latter has not revoked it during his lifetime.

b. *Last will and testament* (*ultima voluntas*) is the final declaration of a person's intentions as to the disposition of his property that he wills to be made after his death. Hence a will is an *act,* not a contract, and it is essentially *revocable.* It requires no acceptance on the part of the beneficiary; it is valid even though it is made without his knowledge. It takes effect only after the death of the person who made it.

6. *Heir* (*heres*) a physical or moral person who alone or with others is entitled by law to a deceased person's estate, that is, to the sum total of his real and personal property together with all the legal obligations encumbering such property.

a. Inheritance (*hereditas*) is the property of a deceased person which passes to the heir upon his acceptance.

b. Necessary heir (*heres necessarius*) is one who by reason of civil law may not be excluded from at least a partial inheritance. Thus according to the civil law of certain European countries parents are obliged to leave a definite portion (one fourth, or one third, or even one half) of their property to their children. In most modern civil codes the widow is entitled to a portion (usually a third) of her deceased husband's property, but she may waive her portion in order to inherit under her husband's will.

c. Free heir (*heres voluntarius*) is one who becomes an heir by the free will of the testator (sometimes called a "legatee" or "devisee" in civil law).

d. Legal heir (*heres legalis*) is one who succeeds to the property of a person who dies intestate.

7. *Legacy* (*legatum*) is a specific gift (of property or money) made by last will and testament directly to a person, which property or money is to be taken from the estate and delivered by the heir or by the executor or administrator of the estate. Canonists dispute as to whether the *legatee* (*legatarius*) acquires a *ius ad rem* (merely a right to demand his legacy from the heir) or a *ius in re* (real ownership of the property still in the possession of the heir). In either case the heir has the obligation of transferring the property to the legatee.

8. *Trust* (*fideicommissum*) is the transfer of ownership of property to one person for the benefit of another. In canon law a trust may be established either by an act among the living, or by last will and testament.

Four things are required to establish a trust:

a. Property (*fideicommissum*) to be transferred to the trustee in order that it may be administered by him in favor of the beneficiary.

b. A *trustee* (*fiduciarius*), either a physical or a moral person (distinct from the beneficiary of the trust) to whom the ownership of the property is transferred with the obligation of administering it for the beneficiary.

c. A *beneficiary* (*fideicommissarius*), either a physical or a moral person or a pious cause for whose benefit the property is to be administered according to the will of the donor.

d. Actual transfer of ownership of property (*fiducia*) to the trustee so that he may administer the trust.

Hence if a sum of money is given to a cleric or a religious for a specific purpose, such as the building of a church or the purchase of vestments, this would not be a trust but a simple gift, since a trust implies a certain amount of administration of the property given in trust for the benefit of the third party.

Who Can Make Gifts and Bequests for Pious Causes? Any person who is free under the natural law as well as under canon law to dispose of his possessions can give them to pious causes, either by an act *inter vivos* or by an act *mortis causa* (c. 1513, § 1). The *natural law* requires only the free use of reason for the making of a pious will. Infants, insane persons, persons under the influence of strong drink or drugs, and persons acting under the influence of unjust fear, are barred by the natural law. Novices may not and cannot give away their property during their novitiate (c. 568), and professed religious in congregations may not do so during their lifetime (c. 583, § 1). The novice in a congregation, however, must make a will before taking his first vows (c. 569, § 3); and a religious professed of simple vows must give away all his property within the sixty days immediately preceding his profession of solemn vows (c. 581, § 1).

Obligation of Heirs. The *civil* law frequently restricts the rights of the individual regarding the disposition of his property, either by establishing disabilities (as in the case of minors and married women) or by requiring certain formalities for the transfer of property, especially in the case of last wills and testaments. The Church prescribes that, when a will is made in her favor, all the solemnities of the civil law be observed as far as that is possible. If, however, these solemnities have been omitted, the heirs are to be reminded (admonished) to carry out the will of the testator (c. 1513, § 2). The will of a testator regarding pious causes may be proved with certainty by any written document or even without one, provided his will is known through the testimony of two or three reliable witnesses (c. 1791, § 2).

The term "admonished" (*moneantur*) might at first sight seem to imply that the heirs have no strict obligation to carry out the bequests made in favor of pious causes if the will is invalid because it lacks the legal formalities (cf. c. 467, § 2); but an answer of the Code Commission[15] states that the term contains a *precept*, not a mere exhortation. This is in keeping with the common teaching of canonists (with but few exceptions) both before and after the Code and with the practice of the Roman Curia. Taken in its context, therefore, the answer of the Code Commission means not merely that the heirs must be *admonished* but rather that they have an *obligation in conscience* to carry out the provisions of a (civilly invalid) will regarding any bequest to pious causes.[16]

According to the common opinion of canonists, *necessary heirs* may always claim the portion to which they are entitled by law, even against pious causes. These latter are then to be provided for from the remaining portion of the estate.

Fulfillment of Pious Wills. The wishes of the faithful who give or leave their goods (property) to pious causes, whether by an act *inter vivos* or by one *mortis causa,* are to be carried out most diligently even regarding the manner of administering and spending the gifts, safeguarding only the rights of the Ordinary as laid down in canon 1515 (c. 1514). In this canon the Church enunciates a fundamental principle upon which she has always insisted, namely, the careful and exact carrying out of the wishes of the faithful who make bequests to pious causes. Undoubtedly the obligation is a grave one, both at law and in conscience.

Regarding the manner of administration, the donor may place certain restrictions about the investment of the money or property donated, or he may prescribe that one or another of his heirs be numbered among the administrators of the pious bequest.

Regarding the manner of spending or distributing money or property, limitations may be placed: (1) regarding *quantity,* i.e., a fixed amount of money or a specific piece of property; (2) regarding *place* — scholarships for boys of a certain parish, city, or diocese; (3) regarding *time,* as certain Masses to be said on fixed days. Any such determinations must be meticulously carried out "nor may the funds donated be diverted to other good works even though these seem to be better and more useful."[17] Only the Holy See, by reason of its power of

---

[15] February 17, 1930, *AAS,* 22 (1930), 196; *Digest,* I, p. 725.

[16] S. C. Conc., Dec. 20, 1828; *Fontes,* VI, p. 296, n. 4024; S. Poenit., Jan. 10, 1901; *Fontes,* n. 6447, VIII, p. 469.

[17] S. C. Prop. Fide, Instr. an. 1807; *Fontes,* VII, p. 216, n. 4688.

eminent domain, may allow a change in this matter for just reasons. Ordinaries may do so only by reason of special delegation of the Holy See.[18]

A private answer of the S. Congregation of the Council[19] given to an Ordinary in the United States says that in interpreting wills in which a sum of money is left for the celebration of Masses and in which nothing was said about the nature of the Masses, the beneficiaries may not interpret the mind of the testator in favor of *sung* Masses; nor may the beneficiary take from the legacy the sum of *two* dollars for low Masses when nothing is said in the will as to the number of Masses. If in either case peculiar circumstances seem to advise the contrary, recourse should be had to the S. Congregation for a proper interpretation of the mind of the testator.

Ordinaries as Executors of Pious Wills. *Ordinaries* (as defined in c. 198, § 1) are executors of all pious wills whether *mortis causa* or *inter vivos* (c. 1515, § 1). In last wills and testaments the testator himself usually appoints the executor, that is, the person who is to carry out his wishes after his death. Even in a gift *inter vivos,* the donor may appoint an executor. If this has been done, the Ordinary may not substitute another executor in place of the person appointed, nor may he personally undertake the administration of the pious will. His office is confined to giving assistance to the executor appointed and to fulfilling the duties enumerated in § 2 of this canon.

Under this law the Ordinary can and must carefully see to it, even by visitation, that pious wills are carried out; and delegated executors must give him an account upon completion of their trust (c. 1515, § 2). By delegated executors are meant those appointed either by the testator or donor, or by the civil law, or in default of either by the Ordinary himself. The right of visitation extends even to persons and institutes not governed directly by church law as in the case of a purely secular work to which a pious trust has been bequeathed or donated.

Any clauses contrary to this right of Ordinaries which may be added to last wills and testaments are to be considered as nonexistent (c. 1515, § 3).

Clerics and Religious as Trustees of Pious Causes. As soon as a cleric or religious has received property in trust (*fiducia*) for a pious cause, whether by donation (*inter vivos*) or by reason of a last will

---

[18] Conc. Trident., *Sess.* XXII, *de ref.,* c. 6; S. C. Conc., Apr. 23, 1927; *AAS,* 20 (1927), 363; *Digest,* I, p. 724.
[19] June 15, 1928; *Digest,* II, p. 206.

and testament, he must inform his Ordinary of his trust and indicate to him the nature and extent of the property involved, whether movable or immovable. In case the donor has expressly forbidden this, the cleric or religious may not accept the trust (c. 1516, § 1). Before the Code, canon law imposed this obligation on lay trustees as well.[20] Under the present law it suffices that they submit to his visitation and give him an account of their administration on completion of their trust (c. 1515, § 2).

The Ordinary must oblige the trustee to deposit the trust fund in a safe place and to invest it (if necessary). He must also carefully see to it that the trust is carried out according to the norms laid down in canon 1515 (c. 1516, § 2).

Trust funds given to a religious are under the jurisdiction of the local Ordinary, provided that such funds are intended for the benefit of churches, or of the inhabitants, or of pious causes of the place or of the diocese; in all other cases such trust funds are under the jurisdiction of the proper Ordinary of the religious (c. 1516, § 3). Parochial churches, schools, orphanages, and hospitals would be under the jurisdiction of the local Ordinary; churches of exempt religious, as well as houses of studies for members of an exempt institute, would be subject to the religious Ordinary. The Ordinary for religious who are not exempt would be the local Ordinary (see c. 198).

Changes in Last Wills and Testaments. Any reduction (*reductio*), restriction (*moderatio*), or change (*commutatio*) of last wills is reserved to the Holy See unless the person who makes the will expressly grants this power to the local Ordinary. In either case no change may be made except for a just and necessary cause (c. 1517, § 1).

By *reduction* is meant any diminution of the obligations imposed by a last will, as for instance in the number of Masses to be said or the number of free scholarships; by *restriction* is meant a more specific determination regarding secondary and accessory conditions, such as a *sung* Mass or a Mass to be said in a particular church; by *commutation* is meant a substitution of one obligation for another, as when money given to decorate a church is used for the support of the poor.

The Holy See exercises its power to make such changes through the Sacred Penitentiary in occult cases. In public cases this power is exercised through the Congregation which is competent to deal with the

---

[20] S. C. Conc., Aug. 9, 1909; *Fontes*, VI, p. 902, n. 4355.

matter, as, for instance, the Congregation of the Council, or the Congregation de Propaganda Fide, or the Congregation for Religious. In all cases, however, a just and necessary cause is required since the right of eminent domain does not give the sovereign the power arbitrarily to set aside the wishes of the faithful regarding the disposition of their possessions. However, a *necessary* cause is not synonymous with impossibility of fulfillment. A decidedly greater utility of the work substituted over that originally determined upon by the donor would be sufficient cause.

Interpretation of a pious last will is not the same as commutation. Since the Ordinary is the executor of all pious wills, he has the right to interpret them if necessary. This should be done by determining the exact wishes of the donor as expressed in the document establishing a foundation, or as expressed in his last will and testament even though it be invalid at civil law, or as determined from the testimony of reliable witnesses, and so on.

If the fulfillment of the obligations imposed has become impossible because the revenue has been diminished through no fault of the administrator, the local Ordinary may diminish the obligations provided that he take counsel with the interested parties and that he fulfill the wishes of the donor as far as that is possible. An exception is made in the case of Mass stipends; the reduction of these is always reserved to the Holy See exclusively (c. 1517, § 2). However, if the articles of foundation expressly permit the reduction of Mass obligations in the event of diminished revenue, the Ordinary may make the reduction.[21]

While the right to reduce obligations concerning Masses is reserved exclusively to the Holy See, still the power to do so may be *delegated* to the Ordinaries, as is actually the case in the quinquennial faculties.[22]

In conclusion it will be well to note that, generally speaking, the canons dealing with pious causes refer principally to such gifts and bequests as are to be expended directly, that is, where the capital itself is to be used for the furtherance of the pious cause. This is evident from canon 1515, § 2 which requires the executor to give an account to the Ordinary after his work is completed. Ordinary foundations, however, are not excluded but are implied in the terms *investment* (*collocatio*), *founder* (*fundator*), and *diminished revenues* (*imminuti reditus*) of canons 1516 and 1517. In such cases the foundation remains

---

[21] Code Com., July 14, 1922 ad ix; *AAS*, 14 (1922), 529; *Digest*, I, p. 726.
[22] See faculties granted by the S. Cong. Conc., *Digest*, II, p. 35.

lay property subject only to the vigilance of the Ordinaries according to canons 336, 344, 1515–1517. In *pious foundations,* however, that is, such as are given to a moral person in the Church (c. 1544), the property of the foundation becomes church property and is subject to all the provisions of the Code regarding church property.[23]

Summary of Principles Regarding Pious Causes

(Based on Resolution of S. C. Conc., April 23, 1927)

1. The term "pious will" includes all gifts made for a pious cause, both *inter vivos* and *mortis causa* (cc. 1513, 1515).

2. The fulfillment of "pious wills" is obligatory in conscience on the heirs even though in a particular case the legal formalities required by civil law have been omitted (c. 1513, § 2).

3. Fiduciary gifts may be made not only by last will and testament but also by acts *inter vivos* (c. 1516).

4. Property dedicated to a pious cause becomes strictly ecclesiastical property and is called a *pious foundation* only when given to a *moral person* in the Church (cf. cc. 1497, § 1; 1544). In all other cases the property remains lay property, even though a foundation has been established for the benefit of a pious cause.

5. Even lay property belonging to a pious cause is subject to the vigilance of Ordinaries according to cc. 336, 344, and 1515–1517.

6. Ordinaries, however, cannot change the terms of a will unless this authority has been expressly committed to them by the donor or founder (c. 1517, § 1).

Conclusion: Every *pious* foundation (c. 1544) is a pious cause; but not every pious cause is a pious *foundation.*

Section 4. Administration of Church Property (cc. 1518–1528)

PRELIMINARY SURVEY

Roman Pontiff Supreme Administrator (c. 1518)
Local Ordinary Guardian of Diocesan Property (c. 1519)
Diocesan Council of Administration (c. 1520)
Local Board of Administration (cc. 1521–1522)
Duties of Administrators of Church Property
    (cc. 1523–1528)

---

[23] S. C. Conc., Apr. 23, 1927; *AAS,* 20 (1928), 362; *Digest,* I, p. 724.

Roman Pontiff Supreme Administrator. *Administration of property* may be compared to the government of persons. Just as the proper function of government is the preservation of the well-being of persons in order to help them to their proper end in life, so the administration of property consists in preserving all temporal things which have been acquired and using them for their destined end. This function comprises three things: (1) the preservation and improvement of property which has been acquired; (2) the natural or artificial production of fruits or income from such property; (3) the useful application of such fruits or income to the proper persons.

The right of administration flows from the right of property. For the right of ownership includes the right to use, enjoy, and dispose of property — all of which imply acts of administration. In the case of the Supreme Pontiff the right of administration arises likewise from his power of jurisdiction. All church property is held by moral persons in the Church and moral persons have the status of minors in church law. Now the property of minors is subject to administration under special laws in every society. Hence it is not surprising to find various classes of administrators of church property in canon law: some immediate, others mediate; some independent, others subordinated and dependent.

By reason of his primacy of jurisdiction, the Roman Pontiff is the supreme administrator and dispenser (manager) of all church property (c. 1518). He regulates the administration of all such property by means of general laws and constantly exercises unremitting vigilance over it. He also reserves to himself — through the Roman Congregations — more important acts of administration, such as the alienation of church property worth more than $6,000 (gold) dollars.

In matters regarding property belonging to the Universal Church and to the Apostolic See, the Supreme Pontiff exercises his office of supreme administrator through the Roman Curia in matters regarding other church property, through the administrators of the individual moral persons in the Church according to the norms laid down in the Code of canon law. This does not mean, however, that the Roman Pontiff is the owner of all church property; but merely that he is its supreme guardian. As St. Thomas puts it: *"Res Ecclesiae sunt eius (Papae) ut principalis dispensatoris, non tamen sunt eius ut domini et possessoris."*[24]

Local Ordinary the Guardian of Diocesan Property. The local Ordi-

---

[24] *Summa*, 2-2ae, q. 100, art. 1, ad sept.

nary has the right and the duty of carefully watching over the administration of all church property in his territory which has not been withdrawn from his jurisdiction. Legitimate prescriptions which grant him greater rights remain in full force (c. 1519, § 1). The local Ordinary is the *immediate* administrator of all property which constitutes the episcopal benefice (*mensa episcopalis,* cf. cc. 1472 sqq.) as well as of any funds held in common (*massa communis*) for the benefit of the diocese as such. He is also the immediate administrator of all funds belonging to the diocesan seminary (cf. cc. 1357 and 1359). Together with the cathedral chapter (diocesan consultors in the United States, cf. c. 427) he administers immediately the property of the cathedral church (c. 1182, § 1). Our canon does not refer to these properties, but to others which have their own immediate administrators. The local Ordinary is to exercise careful and diligent vigilance over such administrators; but he may not take upon himself the immediate administration of any church property which by law has its own administrator.

Church property is withdrawn from the jurisdiction of the local Ordinary by way of special reservations or exemptions granted by the Holy See in single instances (cf. c. 63, § 1) or allowed by the law itself as in the case of property of exempt religious (cf. cc. 615 and 618, § 2, 1°).

Ordinaries shall take care to regulate everything that pertains to the administration of church property by enacting special statutes or instructions as occasion demands. In so doing they must keep within the limits of the common law and take into account the rights of various persons and legitimate customs and circumstances (c. 1519, § 2). Since each individual moral person in the present organization of the Church enjoys financial autonomy and has the administration of its own property, the Ordinary cannot dispose of such property. All administrative acts must be made in the name of the moral person. However, administrators of such property are subject to the direction and control of the local Ordinary and must obey whatever regulations he may make within the limits of the law (cf. cc. 485, 1182, 1476, 1491).

The Ordinary may, therefore, prescribe explicitly whatever is implicitly contained in the Code; or he may make provisions which are beyond (outside) but not contrary to those canons which deal with administration. He may not forbid or restrict that which is explicitly granted by the Code.

The Ordinary must also respect acquired rights (e.g., from the articles of a foundation) and other rights granted to individual administrators by the general law of the Church.

Diocesan Council of Administration. To help him fulfill this office (of vigilance) properly, the Ordinary shall establish in his episcopal city a council consisting of himself as president and two or more capable men who, as far as possible, should be expert in both the canon and the civil law. The Ordinary himself is to choose the members of this Council after taking the advice of his chapter (consultors) unless their appointment has already been provided for in some other equivalent manner by particular law or custom (c. 1520, § 1). In many dioceses of the United States by provision of the Ordinary the board of diocesan consultors (cf. cc. 423–428) likewise constitutes the board of administration prescribed by the present canon. For the functions of the board of administration see canons 1415, § 2; 1532; 1539, § 2; 1541, § 2; 1653, § 1.

Persons related to the Ordinary in the first or second degree of consanguinity or affinity are excluded from the office of administrator, that is, they may not be appointed as members of the board of administration. Only the Holy See can dispense from this rule (c. 1520, § 2). This regulation implies that laymen also may be members of the board of administration provided that they have the proper qualifications.

In all administrative acts of greater moment the local Ordinary shall not omit (fail, neglect) to hear the opinion of the board of administration. The members of the board, however, have only a consultative vote except in those cases in which their consent is expressly required by the common law (as in cc. 1532 and 1539) or by the articles of a foundation (c. 1520, § 3). The members of this board must take an oath in the presence of the Ordinary to fulfill their office well and faithfully (c. 1520, § 4).

The introduction of the diocesan council of administration into the common law of the Church does not in any way reflect upon the honesty or the ability of the local Ordinary. As compared with former times, modern administration of church property has become a complex matter demanding much time and attention; while the spiritual care of the diocese by itself is a task worthy of the local Ordinary's best efforts. Likewise, modern civil legislation in regard to property demands the counsel of experts who will be of great service to the local Ordinary in handling these difficult problems and help him to avoid mistakes which have been made occasionally in the past to the great disedification of the faithful.

Local Board of Administration. Besides the diocesan council or board of administration the local Ordinary must also appoint some prudent, capable men of good reputation to administer the property of any church or pious place for which the law or the articles of foundation have provided no administrator. After three years the Ordinary shall appoint others in their place unless local circumstances make this inadvisable **(c. 1521, § 1).**

Every moral person in the Church must have its own administrator who takes care of its property in the name of the Church. Such administrators are usually provided for by law, either by allowing the moral person to choose its own administrators, or by direct appointment (see cc. 1182; 1476; 1489, § 3). Our canon deals with churches and places which have not been provided with an administrator. The Ordinary is to appoint prudent and capable men, usually clerics, but laymen are not excluded. He may also allow the church or pious place to have a part in the administration. The term of office for these specially appointed administrators is *three* years, after which others are to be appointed in their place if this can be done conveniently. The Ordinary may, however, remove any of these administrators from office, even before the expiration of this three-year term, if he proves to be inefficient.

The entire administration of church property must always be done in the name of the Church and subject to the local Ordinary's right of visitation, his right of demanding an account from time to time, and his right of prescribing the mode of administration. This is especially the case when laymen are given a part in the administration either by reason of the title of foundation or by the free appointment of the local Ordinary **(c. 1521, § 2).**

Local administrators appointed according to the provisions of canon 1521 must observe the following provisions before assuming their office: (1) they must take an oath in the presence of the Ordinary or of the rural dean that they will fulfill their office faithfully and well; (2) they must make an accurate and distinct inventory which shall be signed by all the administrators and which shall include all immovable property, all precious movable objects, and all other things, with a description and evaluation of each; or they may accept an inventory previously made provided that they check it and indicate the things which have been lost as well as new things which have been acquired; (3) one copy of the inventory must be kept in the archives of the administration; and another, in the archives of the diocesan curia. Any change made in the patrimony in question must be recorded in both (c. 1522). Likewise, an inventory of all church furnishings that are either blessed or consecrated is prescribed in canon 1296, § 2.

Duties of Administrators of Church Property. As has been stated above, administrators are not the owners of church property but merely the guardians thereof; hence they are not free to conduct their administration independently but must observe the various regulations contained in canons 1523-1528.

The fundamental principle of all good administration is contained in and illustrated by canon 1523: Administrators of church property are obliged to fulfill their office with the care and diligence of a good *paterfamilias.* Hence they must observe the following:

1. Be *vigilant* that the church property entrusted to their care suffer no harm or perish in any way;

2. *Observe the regulations* of canon and civil law, as well as regulations imposed by a founder or donor or by legitimate authority;

3. *Collect the income* and fruits accurately and in due time, keep them in a safe place, and use them according to the mind of the founder or according to established laws or norms;

4. With the permission of the Ordinary, to lay out or use for the benefit of the Church (moral person) money which may be left over after all expenses are paid and which can be invested profitably;

5. *Keep well-ordered accounts* of receipts and expenditures;

6. *Keep in good order* in the archives or in a convenient safe *all documents and legal papers* upon which the rights and property of the moral person depend. Authentic copies of all such papers should be deposited in the archives or safe of the curia (diocesan or religious, as the case may be).

All Catholics, and especially clerics, religious, and the administrators of church property, must give workmen whom they employ an honest and just wage; they must see to it that such employees have leisure at suitable times to devote themselves to exercises of piety. They may by no means divert them from their family cares or from their efforts to save money; nor may they impose burdens upon them which are beyond their strength or which are unsuitable to their age and sex (c. 1524).

Comment on this miniature of the Church's social polity would be out of place here except, perhaps, to remind clerics and religious of their obligation to take the lead in carrying it out and thus affording a good example to the laity.

Notwithstanding any custom to the contrary, all administrators (whether clerics or laymen) of any church, even of a cathedral church, or of any pious place canonically erected (see c. 1489, § 1), or of a confraternity (see cc. 690 and 691) are obliged to give an account of their administration to the local Ordinary every year **(c. 1525, § 1).**

This canon is to be understood in the light of canon 1519, § 1. Hence, churches and church property in the possession of exempt religious are not here included (see c. 615) unless such property belongs to a parish attended by religious (cf. cc. 533, § 1, 4°; 535, § 3, 2°; 630, §§ 3 and 4; 1425). Pious places which have not been erected as a moral personality in the Church are not obliged to give this annual account to the local Ordinary since their property is not church property (see c. 1497, § 1). On the other hand, pious institutes which are noncollegiate moral persons must give the annual account, even though they be exempt (see c. 1492, § 1).

If by reason of particular law this annual account must be given to other designated persons, then the local Ordinary or his delegate must be admitted to the accounting; but any discharge or release (from this obligation) given to the administrators as regards the other designated persons does not release them from their obligation of giving the annual account to the local Ordinary **(c. 1525, § 2).**

This second paragraph of the canon is taken almost verbally from the Council of Trent.[25] Particular law in this case might arise either from the articles of a foundation or from civil law. In either case the annual account must be given to the local Ordinary also.

Litigation. Administrators shall not begin a lawsuit in the name of the Church, nor act as defenders in one, without having first obtained the written permission of the local Ordinary; or, in case of urgent necessity, at least the permission of the rural dean whose duty it will be to inform the Ordinary at once of the permission given **(c. 1526).** To defend the rights of the Church is in itself an act of ordinary administration. Still the legislator requires the previous permission of the local Ordinary, or at least that of the rural dean in urgent cases, because of the importance of the act and to restrain administrators from rushing into court.

---

[25] *Sess.* XXII, *de ref.,* c. 9.

The prohibition laid down in the canon applies only to church property subject to the jurisdiction of the local Ordinary. An administrator who goes into court contrary to the wish of his Ordinary is personally liable for any damages that may result from his action.[26]

Extraordinary expenditures. Unless they previously obtain permission from the local Ordinary, administrators act *invalidly* when they exceed the limitations and methods of ordinary administration (c. 1527, § 1). *Ordinary administration* includes whatever is necessary for the preservation of church property and whatever actions are required to collect the income from such property; also the payment of current bills and taxes, the making of ordinary repairs, and keeping an ordinary bank account. Ordinary acts of administration also include such acts as are to be done at fixed intervals (monthly, quarterly, annually) as well as those which are necessary for the customary transaction of business.

Extraordinary administration includes such acts as do not occur periodically and are of their nature of greater importance; for example, the various actions listed under the title of *contracts* (see section 5 below) and all acts for which the law requires for validity the permission of the Ordinary, e.g., investment of money in c. 1523, 4°. As a *directive norm* in this matter, the Instruction of the Sacred Congregation for the Propagation of the Faith approved for the dioceses of Holland on July 21, 1856, will prove helpful.[27] The following acts are there listed as exceeding the limits of ordinary administration:

1. To accept or to renounce an inheritance, legacy, donation, or foundation;

2. To purchase immovable property;

3. To sell, exchange, mortgage, or pawn immovable church property; or to subject it to any other servitude or burden, or to lease it for a period of *more than three years;*

4. To sell, exchange, mortgage, or divert in any other way from the place for which they are destined, objects of art, historical documents, or other movable property of *great importance;*

5. To borrow large sums of money as a (temporary) loan, or to make agreements and other onerous contracts;

6. To build, pull down, or rebuild in a new form any church building or to make extraordinary repairs upon them;

7. To establish a cemetery;

---

[26] S. C. Ep. et Reg., *Spoletana,* Nov. 29, 1850.
[27] *Fontes,* Vol. 7, p. 346, n. 4841.

8. To start or to suppress parochial institutions which are parish property;

9. To impose a *per capita* tax, to put on a drive (*collectas inducere*), or to give to others things belonging to the (parish) church;

10. To enter upon a lawsuit either as litigant or as defender.

Local Ordinaries, in or out of synod, may establish other norms for extraordinary expenditure; for instance, they may forbid pastors to spend more than a definite sum of money (say $500) for extraordinary expenses without the permission of the Bishop. It is evident, of course, that local Ordinaries can give permission for extraordinary acts of administration only in so far as they come within their own jurisdiction (see canons on contracts, section 5, below).

The Church (that is, the moral person) is not responsible for contracts entered into by administrators without the permission of the competent superior, except in such cases as, and to the extent to which, it has benefited by them (c. 1527, § 2). Administrators, therefore, should be careful not to overstep the limits of their office lest they be held personally responsible for their actions.

Cessation from office of administrator. Even though they be not obliged by reason of an ecclesiastical benefice or office, administrators who have either expressly or tacitly accepted their office and then relinquish it of their own accord in such manner that harm comes to the Church are themselves obliged to make restitution (c. 1528). The office of an administrator should come to an end either by the lapse of time prescribed by law, or by reason of the will of his superior who removes him from office or accepts his resignation.

Section 5. Contracts Regarding Church Property
(cc. 1529–1543)

PRELIMINARY SURVEY

Application of the Civil Law (c. 1529)
Conditions for Alienation (cc. 1530–1533)
Remedies for Irregular Alienation (c. 1534)
Gifts Made by Administrators (c. 1535)
Gifts Made to Rectors of Churches (c. 1536)
Loans of Church Property (c. 1537)
Mortgages and Debts (c. 1538)
Sale and Exchange of Sacred Things (cc. 1539–1540)
Leases of Church Property (cc. 1541–1542)
Interest on Loans (c. 1543)

Application of the Civil Law in Contracts. For centuries the Church had adopted and followed the Roman law regarding contracts, supplying certain corrections and modifications to meet her own needs. As the Roman law gradually gave way to the modern civil codes, the Church at first tolerated, then sanctioned, the use of the latter in the matter of contracts in individual countries. The Code finally *canonized* the civil law in this regard.

The prescriptions of local civil law concerning general or specific contracts, both named and unnamed, and concerning payments, shall be canonically observed in regard to ecclesiastical matters and shall have full canonical effect, unless such prescriptions are contrary to the divine law or unless the canon law decrees otherwise **(c. 1529).** Whatever, therefore, the civil law determines as necessary for a valid and licit contract, holds also in canon law: the capacity of persons to contract, proper matter for contract, consent and formalities required, cause and effect of contracts, the manner of fulfilling an obligation assumed, payment of debts and obligations (*solutiones*), etc.

Unless they are contrary to the divine law. Thus the sale of stolen goods is by divine law incapable of transferring a valid title as against the true owner.

Unless the canon law decrees otherwise. Such exceptions in the Code deal almost exclusively with the *alienation* of church property, though they also affect some other contracts. For example see canons 1479, 1495, § 2, 1513–1517, 1531, 1532, 1535–1537, 1540, 1542, 1543.

Regarding Money, Free Capital and Invested Capital

Money as such is intended primarily as a means of obtaining the necessities of life, and is considered a fungible. But it may also be used to produce income; and when it is permanently invested for this purpose it is classed with immovable property and becomes subject to the laws regarding alienation. Money obtained by gift, or as the income of church property, is considered *free capital* before it is invested. It may, therefore, be used to pay off debts or to purchase things without any permission from an ecclesiastical superior. But, as we have seen in canon 1523, 4°, it is the duty of the administrator of church property to invest all money not needed for current expenses. This act of investment, however, is considered an act of extraordinary administration and requires the consent of the ecclesiastical superior. Hence, the specific act of a superior is required to change *free capital* into *invested* capital. Until such an act has been placed, cash on hand is to be considered as free capital.

Money may be invested in many ways. It may be used to purchase real estate, which then becomes church property subject to all the laws regarding such property; it may be invested in stocks and bonds; or it may be put into a special fund for a specific purpose, such as the building of a church, or school, etc. Once it is permanently invested in any of these ways, it is said to be invested capital and becomes subject to all the laws regarding alienation.

Conditions for Alienation of Church Property. In the strict sense alienation means any act by which the direct ownership of property is transferred to another, as in the case of a gift, a sale, or an exchange. In a wider sense it includes any lawful act by which the use or usufruct of property, or some claim upon it, is given to another, though the naked ownership is retained. Under this head would come rentals, leases, mortgages, and the like. In the canons which follow alienation is to be understood in this wide sense and may be defined as any lawful act whereby the ownership of church property is transferred to another, or is exposed to the danger of loss, or is withdrawn from the direct possession of the Church for a considerable length of time, or, in general, any contract by which church property is placed in a less favorable condition by reason of burdens or obligations imposed upon it.

Alienation includes:

1. Any act by which title to property (ownership) is transferred to another, e.g., gifts, sale or exchange of property.

2. Any act which is a *preparation* for alienation, such as giving security, a mortgage (see 1538), an option, compromise, settlement.

3. Any act by which the use of property is transferred to another, as rental, a lease, and the like.

4. In general, any act by which church property is subjected to burdens either *in perpetuum* or for a long time, such as granting the use, the usufruct, or easements of various kinds.

Alienation does not include:

1. Spending money which is free capital (that is, not as yet formally invested nor reserved for formal investment) to pay debts or make purchases.

2. Loaning money at a moderate rate of interest.

3. The sale of old church furniture, including vestments, etc., in order to replace it with new furniture which is of equal value.[28]

4. The assumption of a mortgage already encumbering property which is purchased, since the mortgage is not put on church property, but rather the Church acquires partial ownership to property already encumbered by a mortgage.

5. The sale or exchange of immovable property given in lieu of money for the payment of debts, since such property represents money.

6. The spending of money for the purpose for which it was given by the donors.

7. The refusal to accept a gain, or a gift, since these acts do not alienate anything but are acts of mere nonacquisition. These are governed by c. 1536.

Safeguarding the prescriptions of canon 1281, § 1 (which require the permission of the Holy See for the alienation of notable relics and precious images), the following acts are required to alienate movable or immovable church property which has a permanent value and is not perishable: (1) a written appraisal of the property made by trustworthy experts; (2) a just cause, that is, urgent need, or evident usefulness for the Church, or piety; (3) permission of the legitimate superior without which the act of alienation is invalid (c. 1530, § 1).

Two conditions are required in order that property come under this law regarding alienation: (1) it must be *church* property, that is, it must belong to a *moral person in the Church.* Hence there is no question here of the private or personal possessions of individual clerics or religious. (2) It must be property *which can be preserved,* that is, property not consisting of fungible goods which by their nature are consumed in the first use of them. Such would be grain, fruits, wine, clothing, individual animals and their offspring. Money comes under this head as long as it has not been lawfully invested.

1. *Appraisal of property by experts.* Since the plural is used, there must be at least two.[29] The superior is the judge, both of their competency to pass judgment and of their trustworthiness (cf. c. 1795). The opinion of the experts is to be given in writing. Nothing more is required; hence, they are not required to give their opinions separately, or under oath. The appraisal of the experts should be given regarding the *present commercial value* of the property in question. This may best be done by indicating the lowest selling price (that is,

---

[28] S. S. C., July 12, 1919; *AAS,* 11 (1919), 418.
[29] "Pluralis enim locutio duorum saltem numero est contenta," Reg. 40, R.J. in VI°.

the price under which the property should not be sold) as well as the highest price which under present selling circumstances might possibly be obtained. In the petition to the competent superior for permission to alienate, the lowest selling price should be mentioned, since one may always take more, but may never alienate for less, than the price mentioned in the petition. The value put upon the property by public officials for the purpose of taxation may be taken as the appraisal of one expert, provided it is just and does not violate commutative justice.

2. *A just cause is required,* not for the validity of the alienation, as was the case in the law before the Code, but for its lawfulness. Three such causes are mentioned: *urgent need,* such as necessary repairs on church buildings, necessary payment of a debt which is due, the need of supporting the Church's ministers, or of providing the essentials for divine worship. If the need is not *urgent,* it should be met in some other way; as all forms of alienation are repugnant to the law. *Evident usefulness* for the Church (the moral person owning the property). *Evident* means that which is not doubtful and can be readily perceived. *Usefulness* implies some benefit derived and not mere absence of loss from the alienation. By *Church* is meant, as always in these canons, the moral person, as the diocese, the parish, the society. Hence, utility for an individual person or for some particular good work would not be a sufficient reason for alienating church property. The third just cause enumerated is *piety,* which term includes the spiritual and corporal works of mercy as well as all works for the honor of God.

3. *The legitimate superior* is defined in canons 534 and 1532.

To avoid all loss to the Church, other timely precautions that the superior may prescribe should not be omitted (**c. 1530, § 2**). The superior who grants the permission to alienate church property is to add precautions to those laid down in the law itself. These precautions may be made in *single instances* as each case may require, or they may be general precautions imposed by Ordinaries for all cases of alienation. The purpose of such precautions is to avoid loss or harm to the Church — either *material* loss because of foolish alienations, or *moral harm* which may arise from accusations made against the Church by reason of ignorance, carelessness, disregard of the civil laws, etc., on the part of administrators who alienate church property.

Property may not be alienated for a lower price than that indicated in the appraisal made by the experts (c. 1531, § 1).[30] Hence the advisability of getting a double estimate as suggested above. The lowest selling price would then be taken as the norm for the observance of this canon.

Alienation should be made by public auction, or at least the fact that alienation will take place should be made public, unless circumstances should dictate otherwise; and the property should be given, all things considered, to him who has offered the highest price (c. 1531, § 2).[31] Alienation of church property by way of public auction is not customary in the United States. Hence all the more need for observing the alternative laid down in the canon, that is, of making known the fact that church property is to be disposed of so that bids may be received from various prospective buyers. While ordinarily the property to be disposed of should be given to the highest bidder, still circumstances may arise in which this might not be advisable, as when property near a church might be used by the highest bidder for purposes not desirable in that vicinity, for instance, to build a dance hall.

Money received by way of alienation must be invested, carefully, safely, and usefully in favor of the Church (c. 1531, § 3). Hence such money *may not be spent*, unless permission to spend it was obtained at the time permission was granted to alienate the property. Obviously, permission to use the money acquired by alienation to pay off a debt would be implicitly granted when the reason for granting the alienation was the urgent need of paying said debt.

Permission of Legitimate Superior for Valid Alienation. In two cases the lawful superior whose permission is required for the validity of an alienation (c. 1530, § 1, 3°) is the Holy See itself: (1) when there is question of *precious* things; (2) when there is question of any kind of property worth *more* than 30,000 lire or francs (c. 1532, § 1).

In the case of precious things, namely, such as have a *notable* value by reason of art, history, or the material out of which they are made (cf. c. 1497, § 2; also c. 1281). According to many commentators, precious things have a notable value if they are worth *more* than 1000 lire or francs. This opinion was sustained in a case decided by the S. Congregation of the Council.[32]

In two cases, therefore, the permission of the Holy See must be obtained in order to alienate church property: (1) in the case of

---

[30] Code Com., Nov. 24, 1920; *AAS*, 12 (1920), 577; *Digest*, I, p. 729.
[31] S. C. Conc., July 19, 1919; *AAS*, 11 (1919), 416; *Digest*, I, p. 729.
[32] July 12, 1919; *AAS*, 12 (1920), 577; *Digest*, I, p. 728.

precious objects whose value *exceeds* 1000 lire or francs; (2) in the case of ordinary property whose value *exceeds* 30,000 lire or francs. What are the equivalent values in United States and English currency? The Code uses terms based upon the decimal system, and gives them the same value, "lire or francs." What kind of francs? French, Swiss, or Belgian? Evidently any of these. Now, the only case in which the Italian lira and the French, Swiss, and Belgian franc have the same value is in the case of gold coin. The makers of the Code evidently took the norms of the Latin Monetary Union as their own in determining money values. According to this Union, first entered into in Paris in 1865, and subsequently renewed from time to time in later years, these four countries agreed to issue gold coins having the same size, weight, and gold content, which would be received interchangeably in all four countries. On this basis alone can the French, Swiss, Belgian franc, and the Italian lira be said to be equivalent.

Now, the gold franc and lira was the equivalent to .193 of the gold dollar of the United States and Canada. In everyday life the dollar was considered as equivalent to five francs or lire; hence when the Code was promulgated, writers and commentators naturally put $6,000 gold dollars (and 1200 gold English pounds) as the equivalent of 30,000 gold francs or lire. This opinion, common to all canonists, that gold coin alone is the true and recognized unit of value is admitted *in practice* by the Roman Congregations. Hence we may state that in practice it is certain that $6,000 in gold (United States or Canadian money) and 1200 gold English pounds are the equivalent of 30,000 gold francs or lire; that 200 gold United States or Canadian dollars, or 40 gold English pounds are the equivalent of 1000 gold francs or lire. These are the two figures mentioned in our canon. All others can be estimated on the same basis.

On January 31, 1934, President Roosevelt, by Presidential Proclamation, reduced the gold content of the dollar, making its gold value only 59.06 per cent of the par established in 1900. In view of this substantial devaluation, the former gold dollar is worth 1.69 of the devaluated 59-cent dollar. Hence 6000 gold dollars may now be safely reckoned as equivalent to 10,000 fifty-nine-cent dollars; 200 gold dollars equal 335 fifty-nine-cent dollars.[33] For practical purposes, since the fifty-nine-cent dollar is only a temporary expedient, we shall henceforth give the equivalent values in gold (100-cent) dollars.

---

[33] Doheny, *Practical Problems in Church Finance,* p. 40 sqq.; Ellis, in *Periodica,* Vol. 27, p. 348.

When there is question of alienating a piece of property which is indivisible, such as a house, an organ, a chalice, a painting, there will be no difficulty in applying the law. Difficulties arise when various pieces of property are to be alienated. What rule is to be followed? The Code Commission has given us the rule.[34] The Commission was asked: "Whether in virtue of c. 1532, § 1, 2°, the permission of the Holy See is required in order to alienate at one transaction several pieces of church property belonging to the same person when the value of the articles taken together (*per modum unius*) is in excess of 30,000 lire or francs?" To this the Commission replied: "In the affirmative."

Pieces of property must be taken together (*per modum unius*) when they coalesce for the purpose of alienation. This may occur in three ways:

1. *By intention.* Once it is determined to alienate several pieces of property, their total joint value must be considered in reference to the permission needed, regardless of any time intervals between sales of individual pieces.

2. *By time.* When several independent pieces of property are alienated within a short space of time, these acts become morally one.

3. *By purpose,* that is, various items of property are alienated for the same purpose, e.g., it is decided to put up an addition to a building and there is no cash at hand. The estimated cost of the building is 5500 gold dollars and some church property is sold to meet the cost. Before the addition is finished, however, the actual cost runs to 6500 gold dollars. The permission of the Holy See would have to be obtained to alienate property in order to obtain the extra 1000 dollars since the total amount of property alienated in order to pay for the building is over 6000 gold dollars.

Alienations of church property made independently, which do not coalesce by reason of intention or time or purpose are to be judged individually in relation to the permission required.

If the property to be alienated, however, is divisible, then one must mention all parts already alienated in the petition for further alienation; otherwise the permission to alienate is invalid (c. 1532, § 4). Property may have a *physical* unity, as a piece of land, or a *moral* unity, as a herd of cattle, a library, a collection of rare coins. Such property would come under the term *divisible property* within the meaning of the canon.

---

[34] July 20, 1929; *AAS*, 21 (1929), 574; *Digest*, I, p. 731.

When the value of the property to be alienated is *more than* 1000 but *not over* 30,000 lire or francs (200 to 6000 gold dollars) the local Ordinary can give the necessary permission after obtaining the consent of the cathedral chapter (diocesan consultors), of the diocesan council of administration, and of the parties concerned (c. 1532, § 3). By *"parties concerned,"* here and throughout this chapter, is meant: the founder or patron of a church, benefice, pious institute, and the like; the beneficiary in regard to the property constituting his benefice; the collegiate person or moral body owning the property under consideration. Should the cathedral chapter (diocesan consultors) and the administrative council disagree, the Ordinary cannot supply the consent of either of these bodies.[35]

When the value of the property to be alienated *does not exceed* 1000 lire or francs (not over 200 gold dollars), the local Ordinary may give the necessary permission after *consulting* (*audito*) the council of administration (unless the matter be of small moment) and after obtaining the *consent* of the interested parties (c. 1532, § 2). While the consent of the diocesan council of administration is not required in this case, but only their advice (and even this may be omitted in matters of small moment, i.e., anything less than fifty dollars), the *consent* of the interested parties must always be obtained.

The prescriptions laid down in canons 1530 to 1532 are to be observed not only when there is question of alienation in the strict sense, but also when there is question of entering into any contract by reason of which the condition of the Church (moral person) may become less favorable (c. 1533). Included under this canon would be such contracts as the following: contracting debts and mortgages (specifically mentioned in canon 1538), annuity obligations, compromise or arbitration in financial matters, renunciation of active easements, allowing passive easements, acting as security for others, and all contracts of a similar nature. All such contracts are governed by the prescriptions of the canons just mentioned.

Remedies for Irregular Alienation. The Church (moral body) has a right to institute a personal action against anyone who has alienated church property without the required formalities, as well as against his heirs. If the alienation was invalid, it has a right to a real action against any possessor whatsoever, but the purchaser has the right to claim damages from the administrator who illegally transferred the property to him (c. 1534, § 1). The formalities required are: (1) eval-

---

[35] S.C.C., Jan. 14, 1922; *AAS*, 14 (1922), 160; *Digest*, I, p. 731.

uation by experts, (2) sale to the highest bidder, (3) for price determined by the experts, (4) a just cause, (5) the proper permission. The first four are required for a licit act; the fifth, for a valid act. If the act of alienation is merely illicit, ownership of the property is actually transferred and the Church no longer has a valid claim over it. Her only redress lies in a personal action against the administrator who unlawfully alienated the property. He can be obliged to compensate the Church for any damages ensuing from the unlawful contract. If the contract, however, is *invalid,* then the Church is still the legitimate owner of the property and she can demand its return from the person who actually holds it. This person, in turn, has a right to claim full compensation from the administrator who alienated the property invalidly.

If church property has been alienated *invalidly,* the administrator responsible for the alienation has a right to recover the property as has his superior and their respective successors in office. Finally, any cleric attached to the church (moral body) which has suffered the loss has a similar right (c. 1534, § 2).

Gifts Made by Administrators. Except for small and moderate gifts sanctioned by local custom, prelates and rectors shall not presume to make donations from the movable goods of their churches unless there be a just reason, such as remuneration or reward, piety, or christian charity; otherwise the donation may be revoked by their successors (c. 1535). Since prelates and rectors of churches (moral persons) are not the owners but only the administrators of church property, they have no right to give away any of that property. There is no question here of immovable property, since to give away such property would come under alienation forbidden by the preceding canons. Our canon treats of small gifts made from movable goods (money, fruits of the earth) which do not form a part of the invested capital of the Church.

If all the faithful, however, have an obligation to give alms occasionally, moral persons in the Church have a similar obligation according to their ability. Hence administrators of church property may give such small alms and moderate gifts as are sanctioned by local usage. This is considered part of their ordinary administration.

Exceptions in favor of larger gifts are made in three cases:

a. As a remuneration, that is, as a sign of gratitude to benefactors. Such gifts are not pure gifts, but are owed by reason of the title of gratitude; they must be proportioned to the merits of the benefactor and to the benefits received.

b. A sense of duty (pietas) toward superiors, relatives, one's country.

c. Christian charity toward the poor, the sick, orphans, etc.

In all these cases the donations made are not free gifts; but rather they are the fulfillment of an obligation. At times this may be a grave obligation, especially during public calamities, e.g., war, famine, or epidemic.

Gifts Made to Rectors of Churches. Unless the contrary is proved, it is to be presumed that donations made to rectors of churches, including those of religious, are made to the church **(c. 1536, § 1).** The reason for this presumption lies in the fact that ordinarily the pious intention of the donor is directed rather to some sacred act or to some public need than to the advantage of the person who performs the sacred act or cares for the public need. A contrary intention may be proved by the express will of the donor, or from the circumstances under which the donation was made.

A donation made to a church may not be refused by the rector or superior without the permission of his Ordinary **(c. 1536, § 2);** such a refusal made unlawfully gives rise to an action for restitution *in integrum* (see cc. 1687–1689), or to indemnity, according to losses sustained by the church **(c. 1536, § 3).** Although such a refusal of a donation made to a church would not be classed as an act of alienation and would be valid, still the rector or superior has no right to refuse a donation without the permission of his Ordinary. The reason for this seems to be that all gifts made to churches are considered as given to God, even before their acceptance. Therefore, they are pious wills; and canon 1515, § 1 makes the Ordinary the executor of all pious wills. The Ordinary in question is the major superior in the case of exempt clerical religious; in all other cases, the local Ordinary.

Since the refusal is not an invalid act, the loss thereby incurred may be recovered in one of two ways: (*a*) by an action for restitution *in integrum,* that is, the right of accepting the gift is restored (see cc. 1687–1689); or (*b*) by an action for indemnity if restitution has become impossible because the property has passed into other hands. An action for indemnity is a demand upon the party responsible for the unlawful refusal for full reparation of losses sustained.

A donation made to a church and lawfully accepted cannot be recalled because of ingratitude on the part of the prelate or rector **(c. 1536, § 4).** The reason is evident. The donation has been made to the church or moral person, not to the prelate or rector. *"Delictum personae non debet in detrimentum Ecclesiae redundare."*[36]

Note. For a study of the sources of canons 536, 1535, and 1536, especially *"Romanos Pontifices"* of Leo XIII, 8 May, 1881, read two decisions in a famous Manila case: Signatura Apostolica, April 6, 1920, *AAS,* XII (1920), 258; and S. R. Rota, August 16, 1921, *AAS,* 14 (1922), 239.

Loans of Church Property. Sacred things should not be lent for any use which is repugnant to their nature **(c. 1537).** In this canon there is question of granting the temporary use of sacred things without compensation (*commodatum*). The law does not forbid lending church property. It merely specifies that *sacred things* (i.e., things destined for divine worship by consecration or blessing — c. 1497, § 2) may not be lent if the borrower wants them for uses not in accordance with their sacred character (see c. 1150). Thus it would be licit to lend sacred vestments to another church for temporary use in divine services, but it would not be allowed to lend them for a theatrical performance.

Mortgaging Church Property and Contracting Debts. When for a lawful reason there is need to pledge or mortgage church property, or when there is question of contracting a debt, the superior who is to give the permission as determined by canon 1532 must first demand that all interested parties be consulted and he must see to it that such debts are paid as soon as possible **(c. 1538, § 1).** A *pledge* or *pawn* is any movable property which is transferred to the creditor as security for the payment of a loan. A *mortgage* is a lien upon land or other immovable property as security for a debt. *To contract a debt* means to borrow something, usually money, at interest. Our canon lays down the following norms for all three of these contracts: (*a*) the permission of the same superior is to be obtained as in the case of alienation (see canons 1532 and 1533); (*b*) all interested parties (for instance, the council of administration, or the superior of a religious community and his council) are to be consulted before granting the permission; (*c*) the superior who grants the permission must see to it that the debt is paid as soon as possible.

For this reason the Ordinary is to determine the amount of money which is to be set aside annually for the payment of the debt **(c. 1538, § 2).** A similar direction is prescribed for religious in canon 536, § 5.

---

[36] Reg. 76, R.J. in VI°.

The canon supposes that property already possessed by the Church is pledged or mortgaged. If property encumbered with a mortgage is purchased, the Church acquires less but does not alienate anything.

Sale and Exchange of Sacred Things. In the sale and exchange of sacred things no account of the consecration or blessing is to be taken in determining the price **(c. 1539, § 1).** Since both the sale and exchange of church property are forms of alienation, they come under the general laws given above. The point of the present canon is that it forbids taking any consideration of the consecration or blessing when determining the price of sacred things. To do so would constitute the sin of simony as defined in canon 727, § 1. We may recall here in passing that *indulgenced articles* lose their indulgences if they are sold (c. 924, § 2) even though their price is not increased on account of the indulgence.

Administrators may exchange negotiable securities payable to bearer (*tituli ad latorem*) for others which are more safe and productive, or at least equally safe and productive, provided that all appearance of business and trade be excluded. However, the consent of the Ordinary, of the diocesan council of administration, and of the interested parties is required **(c. 1539, § 2).** Under the old law any exchange of investments in negotiable papers was considered an act of alienation and was subject to all the regulations concerning alienations.[37] The Code, however, has taken into account the greater frequency of such changes of investment in modern business and considers such a change as an act of administration. Among such negotiable papers the most common are stocks and bonds. An administrator may therefore either exchange such stocks and bonds directly for other stocks or bonds, or he may sell them for cash and purchase others, provided that the following conditions are fulfilled: (*a*) He must avoid all appearance of making a business out of it and especially must avoid what is called speculation (see canon 142). (*b*) He must exchange his present stocks or bonds for such as are safer and more productive, or at least equally safe and equally productive. The safety of the investment must always be the primary consideration. (*c*) He must obtain the consent of his own Ordinary (for exempt clerical religious the major superior) and the consent of the diocesan council of administration (see canon 1520) and that of the interested parties.

Although the Code speaks only of "negotiable securities payable to

---

[37] S. C. Conc., Feb. 17, 1906; *Fontes,* VI, p. 833, n. 4328.

bearer" (*tituli ad latorem*) and says nothing of securities that are payable to definite individuals or moral persons (*tituli nominales*) the permission to exchange securities given in this canon should be applied to them as well.

Without a special permit of the local Ordinary immovable church property is not to be sold or leased to its administrator, nor to persons related to him in the first or second degree of consanguinity or affinity (c. 1540). To avoid endangering church property, as well as to close the door to possible abuses, it is forbidden to sell or lease church property either to the administrator himself, or to his relatives within the second degree of consanguinity or affinity. If in some special case it may seem to be useful to do so, a special permission of the local Ordinary must be obtained. While this canon does not appear to affect religious, yet it will be advisable for them to avoid selling or leasing their property to relatives of the religious, in order to protect their freedom of action, if for no other reason.

Leases of Church Property. A lease is a contract by which property, whether movable or immovable, is let to another for his use for a determined time at a specified price or rent. The contract may be considered from two angles: from the viewpoint of the person (*locator*) giving the use of his property to another for a specified rental the contract is a lease (*locatio*); from the viewpoint of the person (*conductor*) paying the rent and using the property, it is a renting (*conductio*).

Since a lease of church property is a partial or temporary alienation, it is subject, in part at least, to the laws regarding alienation.

In the leasing of real estate (*fundus*)[38] there should be a public announcement of the intention to lease and the contract should be awarded to the highest bidder unless particular circumstances suggest otherwise (c. 1531, § 2). Besides, the contract should clearly indicate the exact boundaries of the property, specify the nature of the cultivation or care expected, define the time and mode of payment of the rental (*canon*), and secure guarantees for the fulfillment of these conditions (c. 1541, § 1). In all leases it is forbidden to anticipate the payment of rentals beyond six months without the permission of the local Ordinary, who may grant such a permission in extraordinary cases provided he lays down suitable provisions to prevent loss or harm to the church (moral body) granting the lease (c. 1479).

---

[38] "*Fundi* appellatione omne aedificium et omnis ager continetur; sed in usu urbana aedificia *aedes*, rustica *villae*, dicuntur; locus vero sine aedificio in urbe *area*, rure *ager* appellatur: idumque ager cum aedificio *fundus* dicitur." Florent. Dig. 50, 16, 211.

In every lease of church property permission of the proper authority must be obtained as follows:

1. *From the Holy See,* if the value of the lease (annual rental) *exceeds* 30,000 lire or francs (6000 gold dollars), *and* the term of the lease runs *beyond nine years;*

2. *From the local Ordinary,* with the *consent* of the cathedral chapter (diocesan consultors), of the diocesan council of administration, and of the parties interested, in two cases: (*a*) when the value of the lease (annual rental) exceeds 30,000 lire or francs (6000 gold dollars) but the term of the lease does not run beyond nine years; (*b*) when the value of the lease (annual rental) lies between 1000 and 30,000 lire or francs (200 to 6000 gold dollars) but the term of the lease runs *beyond* nine years;

3. *From the local Ordinary,* after he has *consulted* the diocesan council of administration, and with the *consent* of the interested parties, if the value of the lease (annual rental) does not exceed 1000 lire or francs (200 gold dollars) and the term of the lease runs *beyond* nine years;

4. If the term of the lease does not run beyond nine years, and the value of the lease does not exceed 1000 lire or francs (200 gold dollars) the lawful administrator may give the lease after he has informed the Ordinary (*monito Ordinario*) (c. 1541, § 2; and c. 1532, §§ 2 and 3).

If church property is subjected to the contract of *emphyteusis,* the grantee cannot free himself from the obligation of paying the annual rental (*canonem redimere*) without the permission of the lawful ecclesiastical superior mentioned in canon 1532; if he does so with the proper permission, he must pay the Church a sum sufficient to yield at least the annual rental (c. 1542, § 1). In its original form, the contract called *emphyteusis* was a perpetual lease by which the owner of an uncultivated piece of land granted it to another, either in perpetuity or for a long term. The following conditions were attached to the grant: that the grantee should improve the land by building on it, planting it, or cultivating it; that he should pay an annual rent; that the grantee had the right to transfer the contract to others or transmit it by descent to his heirs; that the grantor should never re-enter possession of the land as long as the rent should be paid by the grantee or his assigns.[39] The Church adopted this form of contract from the Roman Law. It is still to be found in modern

---

[39] Bouvier, *Law Dictionary,* s.v. *emphyteusis.*

civil codes based upon the Roman law (France, Belgium, Italy) but in the form of a long-term lease of immovable property only. While practically unknown under that name in American law, it is closely akin to a ninety-nine-year lease.

Leaving the details of the contract to the determination of the civil law (c. 1529), the Code makes certain provisions regarding it. The grantee cannot free himself from the obligation of paying the annual rental (*canonem redimere*) without the permission of the competent superior, as in other matters of alienation, since such an act would transfer title to the property to him and thus would be a true alienation. Should the necessary permission be obtained, the grantee must make a cash settlement sufficient to yield interest in an amount at least equal to the annual rental.

The provisions of canon 1542, § 1 regarding the release from the obligation of paying the annual rental (*canonem redimere*) would seem to apply also to the redemption of annuities or other payments to the Church and to the extinction of annual payments from estates. In all cases in which such a redemption is permitted, if the payment be made in government (or other) securities, only the *actual* value (market value) of such securities is to be considered. The *nominal value* (face value) is not to be considered if that be less than their actual value.[40]

In the contract of *emphyteusis* on church property the grantee must be obliged to give all the necessary guarantees for the payment of the rent (*canon*) and for the fulfillment of the conditions inserted in the contract. Furthermore, a stipulation must be put in the contract that in case of conflict the parties shall settle their differences before an ecclesiastical court. It shall also be expressly stipulated that all improvements accrue to the property and not to the grantee (c. 1542, § 2).

Interest on Loans. When a fungible is given to another in such wise that it becomes his and is later to be returned only *in kind,* no profit may be derived by reason of the contract itself; but in such a loan it is not *per se* unlawful to make an agreement for the legal rate of interest (unless it is evident that the legal rate is exorbitant), or even for a higher rate, provided that there be a just and proportionate reason (c. 1543).

This canon deals with loans for consumption (*mutuum*). It contains three provisions:

---

[40] S.C.C., Jan. 23, 1923; *AAS*, 15 (1923), 513; *Digest*, I, p. 732.

1. One may never take interest on a loan for consumption by reason of the contract itself. The reason is evident, since in such a loan the ownership of the thing loaned is transferred and it is inseparable from its use which is not distinct from its substance. By returning the loan in kind, the borrower gives back as much as he has received. Hence there is no intrinsic title for profit in the loan itself.

2. In all loans for consumption, it is always allowed to make an agreement for the legal rate of interest provided such rate is not manifestly exorbitant. Such exorbitance would have to be determined with respect to all the circumstances of place, time, and persons.[41] Unless it is clear that the legal rate of interest is excessive, it is to be presumed that it is licit.

3. In certain cases one may agree upon a rate higher than the legal rate, provided such a rate is warranted by a just and proportionate cause.

While upholding the traditional teaching of the Church that in a loan for consumption (*mutuum*) there is no just cause for profit by reason of the contract itself, the present canon states implicitly that in modern times there is always present in such a loan some just reason for demanding the legal rate of interest and explicitly allows an even greater rate of interest provided there be just and proportionate reasons for demanding it. The canon, however, studiously avoids determining what these just reasons are, leaving that to Catholic moralists and economists to determine.

Section 6. Pious Foundations (cc. 1544–1551)

PRELIMINARY SURVEY

Notion of Pious Foundations (c. 1544)
Norms for Acceptance and Establishment (cc. 1545–1546)
Investment of Endowment (c. 1547)
Preservation of Documents (cc. 1548–1549)
Pious Foundations and Exempt Religious (c. 1550)
Release From Obligations of Pious Foundations (c. 1551)

Notion of Pious Foundation. By a pious foundation is meant any kind of property given to a moral person in the Church in any manner whatsoever with the obligation of using the annual income either for

---

[41] S. C. de Prop. Fide, instr. an. 1873; *Fontes*, VII, p. 442, n. 4880.

the celebration of Masses, or for carrying out certain defined ecclesiastical functions, or for the performance of some works of piety and charity. These obligations may be imposed *in perpetuum* or for a long time (c. 1544, § 1). Four elements are required for a pious foundation:

1. *Property to be kept,* that is, the property or money is not to be spent at once on pious works but is to be invested and the income used for such pious works. This property is called the *endowment* of the pious foundation. It may consist of any kind of property, money, stock and bonds, real estate.

2. *Property given to a moral person in the Church,* hence to a moral person already in existence. The foundation itself cannot be made a moral person. The moral person must be an ecclesiastical person, e.g., diocese, parish, religious house, etc., not a secular moral person such as the St. Vincent de Paul Society. Every moral person canonically erected in the Church enjoys the capacity of receiving pious foundations.

3. *Property given with an obligation in justice* to perform certain predetermined works of piety or charity.

4. *In perpetuum or for a long time,* at least forty years according to most authors. A foundation made for a shorter period of time will fall under the heading of a *pious trust* explained above.

The modern tendency, at least in the United States, is against *perpetual* foundations, especially for Masses, for many reasons. Hence it would be preferable to have the pious foundation made for a definite number of years — twenty-five, or forty, or at most fifty. Some diocesan statutes require this, and the faithful are informed that their wills will be thus interpreted.

A pious foundation is complete when it is *accepted* by the official representative of the moral person. It then has the nature of a bilateral contract *"do ut facias"* (c. 1544, § 2), which means that the moral person has an obligation arising from commutative justice to fulfill its part of the contract. Should the moral person fail to do so, even for a time, it has no right to the income of the endowment during that time.

Norms for Acceptance and Establishment. The local Ordinary has the right and the duty to lay down norms regarding the quantity below which a pious foundation may not be established, as well as norms for the proper distribution of the income of the foundation (c. 1545). Thus, if the founder has not determined the number of Masses to be said, the local Ordinary will determine it according to the amount laid down in the synodal decrees or determined by custom. If, on the other hand, the founder has determined the number of Masses but has not given an endowment sufficient to provide the stipend required by synodal decree, the matter shall be referred back to him if he is still living. If the founder does not wish to meet the requirements of the law, the local Ordinary may refuse to give his consent to the pious foundation. If the founder is dead, it may be possible to determine from the circumstances of the foundation that he wished rather to have Masses said at a certain place or on certain days without having them applied to his intentions. If this is not clear, the local Ordinary cannot reduce the number of Masses stipulated by the founder unless this power has been given to him in the articles of foundation (c. 1517, § 2); but he may accept the foundation conditionally, that is, upon condition that the Holy See will reduce the number of Masses requested to conform with the synodal stipend for founded Masses.

As to the norms for the distribution of the income of the foundation, the local Ordinary may and should establish such norms unless the founder himself has determined this distribution in detail.

When there is question of a pious foundation established in the churches of exempt religious, even though they be parochial churches, the major superior of the exempt religious institute is the Ordinary in question (c. 1550). Despite the fact that exempt religious are obliged to abide by the regulations of the local Ordinary in the matter of stipends for *manual* Masses (c. 831), the religious Ordinary may freely determine the amount of the endowment of a pious foundation, subject only to the requirements of the constitutions of his institute.

Norms for acceptance of pious foundations. Before a moral person may accept a pious foundation, it is required that the consent of the local Ordinary be obtained in writing. The local Ordinary is not to give his consent until he has duly ascertained that the moral person can fulfill not only the new obligation to be undertaken but also all obligations previously undertaken. He shall especially take care that the income corresponds to the obligations imposed, according to local standards (c. 1546, § 1). These requirements must be fulfilled for the licitness of the acceptance, not for its validity. It is the moral person who actually accepts the foundation, not the local Ordinary.

The patron of the church has no rights regarding the acceptance, establishment, and administration of a pious foundation (c. 1546, § 2).

Investment of Endowment. Money and movable goods assigned as an endowment for a pious foundation shall immediately be deposited in a safe place designated by the local Ordinary for the purpose of safeguarding them. This money, or the price of the movable goods, shall (according to the prudent judgment of the Ordinary after he has consulted the parties interested as well as the diocesan council of administration) forthwith be carefully and profitably invested for the benefit of the foundation with an explicit and individual mention of the obligation attached (c. 1547). As soon as the foundation has been accepted, the endowment, supposing that it consists of money or movable goods, is to be deposited in a safe place designated by the Ordinary. It is understood, of course, that movable goods are to be sold and their price deposited. Even though such movable goods happen to be precious articles within the definition of canon 1497, § 2 (such as jewels, works of art, and the like), they may be sold without permission of the Holy See since by the very nature of the contract the law requires that they be sold and converted into cash. Obviously such goods may be retained for a short time in order to insure their sale at a fair price. Immovable goods, such as real estate, buildings, etc., may be kept, provided they are producing revenue and there is no objection on the part of the founder.

After a study of the investment market has been made, these goods should be invested without delay in safe and profitable investments. The final decision rests with the Ordinary after he has first consulted the interested parties (the founder or his heirs, and the moral person to whom the foundation has been granted) as well as the diocesan council of administration (see c. 1520). The investment is to be made for the benefit of the moral person and an explicit mention of the obligations involved is to be made in the document of investment. Thus if the obligation of the foundation involves Masses to be said and scholarships for the Catholic education of youth, both obligations are to be mentioned and the amount of the income to be given to each is to be determined specifically, as well as the time during which the obligations are binding upon the moral person.

Preservation of Documents. All foundations, even those made *viva voce*, should be recorded in writing; and one copy of such records should be kept in the archives of the curia and the other in the archives of the moral person to whom the foundation pertains (c. 1548). While there is no prohibition against the establishment of a foundation *viva voce*, still the canon prescribes that the administrator of the moral person to whom a foundation is thus presented should draw up a written instrument recording the name of the founder, the amount received, the obligations assumed, and the date of acceptance. To this the Ordinary's written consent to the foundation should be added. In case the moral person is an exempt religious church, the second copy of the documents relating to pious foundations will be sent to the provincial curia, not to the diocesan curia.

Besides observing the prescriptions of canons 1514–1517 and 1525, every church shall have a list carefully drawn up of all the obligations incumbent upon it by reason of its pious foundations, and this list must be carefully preserved in a safe place by the rector of the church.

In addition to the book in which the rector of a church must enter all manual Masses according to canon 843, § 1, another book must be kept by the rector in which are recorded each individual obligation, whether perpetual or temporary, as well as the date on which the obligation was fulfilled, and the amount of income received, so that an exact account regarding all these obligations may be given to the local Ordinary (c. 1549).

In every church is to be here understood according to the meaning given the term in canon 1498, that is, every moral person whether diocesan or religious, for instance, a religious community. The prescriptions of the canon apply not only to founded Masses but to all pious foundations, hence to pious and charitable works.

Pious Foundations and Exempt Religious. When there is question of pious foundations in the churches of exempt religious, even though they be parochial churches, the rights and duties of the local Ordinary mentioned in canons 1545–1549 pertain exclusively to the major superior (c. 1550).[42]

Here again the term "church" is to be taken in the sense of moral person. For all pious foundations, therefore, in churches or institutions belonging to exempt religious, the Ordinary is the major superior who must approve and accept them, lay down conditions for their acceptance, watch over their administration and fulfillment of obligations, and receive reports concerning them. This applies to parochial churches also, provided they belong to the religious (see c. 1425, § 2); but it does not apply to parochial churches belonging to the diocese and committed to the care of religious.

Release From Obligations of Pious Foundations. The reduction of obligations incumbent upon pious foundations is reserved solely to

---

[42] Code Com., July 25, 1926; *AAS*, 18 (1926), 393; *Digest*, I, p. 699.

the Holy See, unless express provision to the contrary is provided in the articles of foundation; but the prescription of canon 1517, § 2 must be observed (c. 1551, § 1).

In general the law reserves to the Holy See the power of reducing the obligations incumbent on pious foundations. There are two exceptions: first, if the articles of a foundation expressly grant this power to the Ordinary, he may reduce any kind of obligation, including founded Masses;[43] second, when through no fault of the administrator the income of a pious cause has diminished in such a way that it no longer suffices for the full performance of the duties imposed. In this latter case, however, founded Masses are excluded and the conditions laid down in canon 1517, § 2 must be carried out.

An indult permitting the reduction of founded Masses may not be extended either to other Masses that are of obligation by reason of a contract or to other obligations incumbent upon a pious foundation (c. 1551, § 2).

Unless the contrary is evident, a general indult permitting the reduction of obligations incumbent upon pious foundations is so to be understood that the person receiving it is to reduce other obligations rather than founded Masses (c. 1551, § 3).

Local Ordinaries who possess an indult to reduce obligations of pious causes may use their faculty in favor of *regulars* who live in their diocese.[44]

We may be permitted to conclude the treatise on church property with a quotation from Father Vermeersch: "Although we are dealing with temporal things, we cannot sufficiently urge the careful observance of the canons regarding the administration of church property, The property of the Church demands our greatest care since her temporal possessions are directed to spiritual and apostolic purposes. Internal peace and tranquillity of soul on the part of administrators likewise demands this care lest at the end of life they be tortured by lamentable anxieties due to business matters less well done or regulated. Let us bear willingly the troublesome inconvenience of such administrations that we may bring forth fruit in patience (Luc. 8:13) and attain the end of our faith, the salvation of souls (1 Pet. 1:9)."[45]

---

[43] Code Com., July 14, 1922, ad XI; *AAS,* 14 (1922), 529; *Digest,* I, p. 726.
[44] Gasparri, *Tract. de SS. Eucharistia* I, n. 619; Many, *De Missa,* n. 78, 6.
[45] *Epitome Iuris Canonici* II, p. 609, n. 871.

QUESTIONS

1. Why has the Church the right to own property of all kinds? (C. 1495, § 1).

2. What is meant by the term "church" in these canons? (C. 1498).

3. How do you define "church property" or *"bona ecclesiastica"*? (C. 1497).

4. Are the personal possessions of a diocesan priest or of a religious with a simple vow of poverty considered as *church* property? (C. 1497).

5. How can the Church acquire property? (C. 1499, § 1).

6. In whom is the ownership of church property vested? (C. 1499, § 2).

7. What is meant by an administrator of church property?

8. What acts come under the term "ordinary administration"? "ordinary expenses"? (C. 1523).

9. What acts come under the term "extraordinary administration"? "extraordinary expenses"? (C. 1527, § 1).

10. What are the obligations of an administrator to give a financial account to his Ordinary? (C. 1525).

11. What limitations are put on prelates and rectors of churches regarding gifts to be made from church funds? (C. 1535).

12. What is meant by a pious foundation? (C. 1544).

13. What are the requirements of the Code for a pious foundation? (Cc. 1544–1547).

14. Who gives the necessary permissions for a pious foundation in a church of exempt religious? (C. 1550).

CASES

1. The Synthetic Rubber Company has built a plant in the town of St. Omer, thus doubling the population. As there is only one parish in the town the Bishop has decided to divide it and erect a new parish. He asks you to draw up a plan for the division of finances (c. 1500).

2. At the request of friends and relatives, Father Brown started the custom of blessing automobiles on the Feast of St. Christopher. The first year he blessed twelve; this year, the fifth, he blessed one hundred and fifty. Many of the devout clients of St. Christopher slip an alms into the hands of the attending altar boy, not wishing to embarrass Father Brown. These alms Father Brown considers to be stole fees and, consequently, his own personal property. What do you say? (C. 1507).

3. Father Brown, pastor of St. Mary's Church, is left a bequest of $1,000 by one of his parishioners, of which $500 is to provide Masses for the repose of his soul, the other $500 is for the parish school. The relatives of

the deceased, who had received less than they thought they should, were determined to break the will and advised Father Brown of their intention. In view of the fact that neither the stipends nor the bequest for the school meant anything to him personally, he not only refused to take any action but waived all claim to the bequest. Afterward Father Brown's conscience bothered him. He comes to you to find out whether he did wrong in waiving the bequest? If so, what are his present obligations? (Cc. 1536, §§ 1 and 3; 1513, 2).

4. Father Paul, a pastor, stated in his will: "I leave my entire library to my successor in this parish." After Father Paul's death, Father Peter took his place and his library. Now Father Peter receives notice from the Bishop that he is transferring him to another parish and Father Peter wishes to know whether he may take the library with him. What is your answer? Is the library church property? (C. 1513).

5. A wealthy parishioner died some time ago and left a substantial sum for various pious works of the parish in his will, which, unfortunately, lacked the formalities required by civil law. The man's two daughters and three sons had the will declared invalid and divided the estate among themselves. These children of the deceased are good Catholics but evidently have no intention of carrying out the will of their father in regard to his pious bequest. What should the pastor do? How should he handle the case? (C. 1513).

6. Father Pinchpenny has three boxes for offerings in his church: one before the statue of St. Anthony is labeled, "for the poor"; a second before the statue of the saintly Curé of Ars labeled, "for poor students for the priesthood"; the third before the statue of St. Jude has no label. Since the church is an old parish church in the business district with but a small number of parishioners left, Father Pinchpenny takes the money from these boxes each week to pay his expenses, "presuming," as he says, "the consent of heaven and the faithful." What do you say? (C. 1514.)

7. The diocese of X owns a valuable piece of property in the business section of the city. Forty years ago the Bishop then ruling the diocese gave a ninety-nine-year lease to a large insurance company which built its home office on the site. Now the company wishes to obtain complete ownership of the property. The Bishop asks you, his canonist, to suggest a settlement which is in accordance with canon law. (C. 1542).

8. Father Benignus has $50,000 belonging to the parish invested in real estate, the interest of which is put in the bank each year to provide a fund for the erection of a parochial high school. Wishing to help the war effort, Father Benignus has determined to sell the real estate and buy government bonds. He also wishes to exchange other bonds in which parish funds are invested for government bonds. What permission does he need for these changes of investment of parochial funds? (Cc. 1532 and 1539).

9. Father Jones received a donation of $800 for a set of new Stations

of the Cross for the parish church. Through good fortune he bought a set worth $800 for $500, as the company which made them was discontinuing that particular line. Father Jones takes the $300 to make up his salary which the church funds do not permit him to collect in full. What would you say about Father Jones's action? (C. 1514).

10. Mr. Goodheart, a pious but land-poor Catholic, offers fifty acres of ground to any Sisterhood which will come to his community and build an institution of higher learning so that children who have completed the parochial school course will not be obliged to go to the public high school for their further education. The Sisters of St. Giles accept the offer. The generous Catholics of the community collect the sum of $75,000 to build an academy, to which the Sisters add another $75,000 of their own. After twenty-five years the Sisters of St. Giles see fit to withdraw from the Goodheart community and are replaced by the Sisters of St. Ives, who agree to pay an annual rental of $500 for the property. Whose permission must be obtained for the lease? Who owns the property? What would you suggest as an equitable settlement in the case? (C. 1514).

11. Domatilla, a wealthy but pious lady, on her deathbed entrusted $100,000 to her niece, Alberta, the annual interest on which money was to be used for the benefit of a certain hospital which was in financial straits. In the course of years, however, the hospital has become well-to-do financially. The parish school near the hospital conducted by the same Sisters needs financial help very badly, and Alberta consults you about giving the annual income to the school rather than to the hospital. What would you tell her? Is the foundation in this case church property? (C. 1517).

12. A wealthy manufacturer who died recently left a number of shares in his company in favor of the pastor of St. Jude's parish with the following request: "I desire that the income of the shares be used for Masses for myself and family." The pastor, not wishing to be bothered with these annual Masses, sells the shares and has the Masses said for the deceased's intention according to the diocesan stipend. Did he do right? What should he have done? How should he have proceeded in this case? (C. 1514; 1544).

13. Titus inherits his father's estate under a will drawn up October 1, 1938. On January 1, 1945, he finds a later will made by his father and hidden away in an envelope which got stuck in back of a drawer. In this later will his father had assigned a legacy of $500 to the parish church. Is Titus bound to pay this legacy? (C. 1513).

14. A new state highway was routed along the edge of the parochial property of St. Jude's rural parish and cemetery. Using its right of eminent domain, the State has appropriated a strip of the property for this use and has compensated the parish by a cash payment of $25,000. Father Black, the pastor of St. Jude's, is delighted. "At last," says he, "we have $25,000

unencumbered cash with which to build our long needed parish hall and social center." He proceeds forthwith to lay plans to begin the building. You are the Bishop of the diocese. What would you tell Father Black? (C. 1531, § 3).

15. The city has gradually been encroaching upon the diocesan seminary grounds. A neighbor who owns property adjoining the seminary tells the rector that he has been offered $25,000 for his property by a real estate company that wishes to break it up into lots for housing purposes; but the neighbor wishes to give the Seminary the first chance to buy it for that price. The rector informs his board of administration and they unanimously agree to buy the property in order to insure the privacy required by the seminary. The next morning the rector goes to the bank, draws out $25,000, and buys the property. At recreation that noon, a lively controversy is started by one of the professors who claims that the permission of the Holy See was needed to buy the property. Another disagreed saying that this was not alienation but a necessary, or at least useful, act of administration. What do you say? (C. 1532; free capital or invested capital?).

16. Explain how the sum of 1000 and 30,000 lire or francs of canon 1532 are to be reckoned in dollars. Give reasons for your statements.

17. Due to the fact that many of his parishioners are working in war plants, Father White has been able to collect $50,000 to renovate the church and to get new pews and a new organ. Whose permission does he need to sell the old pews and the old organ? (Cc. 1530–1532).

18. A Mississippi Valley Cathedral Church has an old altar made by Christian Indians at which, according to tradition, Father Marquette said Mass on his historic trip of exploration with Joliet. The material value of the altar is not over $500. The Jesuit Fathers are eager to get possession of this altar. Whose permission is needed to sell it to them? (C. 1532, § 1, 1°).

Readings:

Augustine, *Canonical and Civil Status of Parishes in the United States* (St. Louis: Herder, 1926); Augustine, *Commentary on Canon Law,* Vol. VI, 549–617; Ayrinhac, *Administrative Legislation* (New York: Longmans, 1930), 378–464; Bartlett, *Tenure of Parochial Property in the United States,* C.U. (N. 31), 1926; Bouscaren, *Canon Law and Church Property,* Un. of Detroit Law Journal, Nov., 1944, 1–12; Brown, *Canonical Juristic Personality,* C.U. (N. 39), 1927; Cleary, *Canonical Limitations on Alienation of Church.Property,* C.U. (N. 100), 1936; Comyns, *Papal and Episcopal Administration of Church Property,* C.U. (N. 147), 1942; Doheny, Church Property: Modes of Acquisition, C.U. (N. 41), 1927; Doheny, *Practical Problems in Church Finance* (Milwaukee: Bruce, 1941); Fallon, "Alienation and Contracting of Debts," *Irish Ecclesiastical Review,* LI

(1938), 529–534; Fallon, "Cathedraticum," *ibid.*, LIII (1939), 301–303; Golden, *Parochial Benefices in the New Code*, C.U. (N. 10), 1925; Goodwine, *Right of the Church to Acquire Property*, C.U. (N. 131), 1941; Hannan, *The Canon Law of Wills*, C.U. (N. 86), 1934; Hannan, "The Canon Law of Wills," *The Jurist*, 4 (1944), 522–547; Heston, *Alienation of Church Property in the United States*, C.U. (N. 132), 1941; Heston, "The Element of Stable Capital in Temporal Administration," *The Jurist*, 2 (1942), 120–133; Kremer, *Church Support in the United States*, C.U. (N. 61), 1930; Stenger, *Mortgaging of Church Property*, C.U. (N. 169), 1942; Stenger, "*Observance of State Laws in Ecclesiastical Mortgages*," *The Jurist*, 4 (1944), 463–473; Woywod, "Temporal Goods of the Church," (a series of articles), *Homiletic and Pastoral Review*, XXIX and XXX (1929); Woywod, *Practical Commentary on the Code*, Vol. II (New York: Wagner, 1925), 165–196.

PART SEVEN: CRIMES AND PENALTIES

CHAPTER XX

CRIMES AND PENALTIES IN GENERAL

Section 1. Crimes in General (cc. 2195–2213)

PRELIMINARY SURVEY

Crime Defined (c. 2195)
Quality and Quantity (c. 2196)
Classification as to Publicity (c. 2197)
Another Division: Ecclesiastical, Civil, Mixed (c. 2198)
Imputability Arising From Malice and Culpability (c. 2199)
Malice Defined: When Presumed (c. 2200)
Causes Which Excuse Entirely or Diminish Imputability
  (cc. 2201–2206)
Causes Which Increase Guilt (cc. 2206–2208)
Co-operation in Crime: When Imputable (c. 2209)
Causes of Action Growing Out of Crime (c. 2210)
Liability for Damages (c. 2211)
Attempted Crime: Frustrated Crime (cc. 2212, 2213)

Scope and Purpose of This Treatise. A seminary course is necessarily very condensed in its treatment of the Church's penal law. The philosophical postulates, the · historical development, extended discussion of principles, and even some finer points which might have a practical bearing must be omitted. The chief aim is to give the student the knowledge which will enable him to deal properly with cases, especially reserved censures, in the confessional. Yet we cannot rush on to solutions of classified cases without understanding certain fundamental principles which alone can support reasonable conclusions. Cases become relatively simple when first principles of law are grasped at least in their fundamentals, whereas without this understanding the solution of reserved cases becomes merely a maze of meaningless technicalities. Hence the student will do well to take an interest in the principles of penal law, even though they may not appear to be immediately practical.

Crime. A crime or delict in ecclesiastical law means an external and morally imputable violation of law to which a canonical sanction, at least indeterminate, is attached **(c. 2195, § 1).** Unless the contrary appear, what is said of crimes applies also to violations of a precept to which a penal sanction is attached **(c. 2195, § 2).**

1. Not every sin is a crime. The Church, as a visible society, punishes by sanctions only certain *external* transgressions which disturb the social order.[1] Formerly, delict was a minor transgression, crime a graver one. This distinction is abolished by the Code.

2. The transgression must be *morally imputable;* otherwise there can be no real crime, and a penalty would be unjust. Moreover, in order to merit a penalty, the moral imputability must be *grave* (c. 2218, § 2). It may consist either in malice (*dolus*) or in culpable ignorance or negligence (*culpa*) (c. 2199).

3. It must be a violation of *law,* natural or ecclesiastical, or of a *precept.* A law proceeds from the power of jurisdiction, is for the common good, and *per se* permanent; a precept may proceed from jurisdiction or from dominative or domestic power, may be for the private good, may be limited in duration. But a precept with a penal sanction can proceed only from jurisdiction in the external forum. Hence the culpable violation of a precept lawfully imposed by a woman religious superior or even by a superior of nonexempt clerical religious, could not be a crime in the strict sense (cf. cc. 118, 501, § 1); nor could an ecclesiastical penalty in the strict sense be imposed for such violation.[2]

4. A violation of a law or jurisdictional precept will not constitute a crime unless *at least an indeterminate sanction* is attached to it (cf. c. 2217). This is the rule stated in canon 2195, but it must be considered in connection with canon 2222, § 1, which permits a superior to punish transgressions, even where no penalty was provided by law or precept, if the act gave scandal or was of special gravity. In other words, canon 2222 provides an indeterminate sanction for such violations and thus brings them within the definition of a crime as stated in canon

---

[1] We leave aside the question whether the Church *can* punish a merely internal act. In fact, she *does not*.

[2] Such violations would be juridically *private* misdeeds, subject to private or domestic penalties. Cf. A Coronata, IV, n. 1641.

2195. In general, the reading of forbidden books, though an external violation of law, is not a crime for want of a sanction. An exception is the special case provided for in canon 2318, § 1, which has a sanction. Omission of one's Easter duty is a sin (c. 859) but not a crime, because no sanction is provided.

5. Can a *moral person* be guilty of a crime? This question can be subtly debated;[3] but canon 2255, § 2 expressly states that a community (which is a collegiate moral person, c. 99) is in proper cases subject to the penalties of suspension and interdict, though never of excommunication; and canon 2274, § 1 speaks of a crime perpetrated by a community or college.

Quality and Quantity. The *quality* of a crime is derived from the object of the law; its *quantity* is measured not only by the gravity of the law which is violated but also by the greater or lesser imputability of the act and the greater or lesser damage which results from it (c. 2196). Crimes are distinguished according to kind (quality) in canons 2314–2414; the gravity (quantity) of the same specific crime varies according to imputability and resultant damage.

Classification as to Publicity. A crime is:

1. *Public,* if it is already commonly known or the circumstances are such as to lead to the conclusion that it can and will easily become so;

2. *Notorious in law,* after judgment by a competent judge which has become *res iudicata* (cf. c. 1902), or after confession by the culprit in open court according to canon 1750;

3. *Notorious in fact,* if it is publicly known and was committed under such circumstances that no maneuver can conceal nor any legal defense excuse it;

4. *Occult,* if not public; *materially* occult if the crime itself is hidden, *formally* occult if its imputability is hidden (c. 2197).

"Commonly known" (*divulgatum*) means known to the greater part of the inhabitants of a place or the members of a community; but this is not to be taken mathematically, but in prudent moral estimation. A crime may remain occult though known to a number of persons who are likely to keep it quiet, whereas it may be public though known to only a few who are sure to divulge it. It may be public in one place and occult in another, or may become occult even in the same place after a lapse of years.

---

[3] Roberti seems to hold the negative; *De Delictis et Poenis,* n. 73. *Contra,* Wernz-Vidal, *Ius Poenale,* n. 37; A Coronata, IV, n. 1642.

Ecclesiastical, Civil, Mixed. A crime which violates only the law of the Church is by its nature punishable only by ecclesiastical authority, which may call for the assistance of the secular arm if it deems it necessary or appropriate; a crime which violates only the civil law is punishable by the civil authority in its own right, except as provided in canon 120, though the Church is also competent in such cases by reason of the sin; a crime which violates the law of both the civil and ecclesiastical society is punishable by both powers (c. 2198).

Imputability. The character of a moral act which makes it attributable to a certain person is called imputability. The imputability of a crime depends on the malice (*dolus*) of the culprit or on his culpability (*culpa*) in being ignorant of the law or in failing to use due diligence; hence all causes which increase, diminish, or excuse from malice or culpability, automatically increase, diminish, or excuse from the imputability of a crime (c. 2199).

Malice here means the deliberate will to violate the law; opposed to it on the part of the mind is want of knowledge, on the part of the will, want of freedom (c. 2200, § 1). When an external violation of the law has been committed, malice is presumed in the external forum until the contrary is proved (c. 2200, § 2).

Culpability may be either culpable *ignorance* of the law (cf. c. 2202), or culpable *negligence* (cf. c. 2203). Although it is *per se* a lower degree of guilt than malice (c. 2203, § 1), yet it may be gravely imputable. Formerly a crime done with malice was called *delictum,* while the term *quasi delictum* was reserved for those done with mere culpability. These terms are retained by some authors.

Defects of Reason as Affecting Imputability. Persons who actually lack the use of reason are incapable of crime (c. 2201, § 1). Persons who are habitually insane, even though they have at times lucid intervals or appear sane in certain mental processes or acts, are nevertheless presumed to be incapable of crime (c. 2201, § 2). A crime committed in voluntary drunkenness has some imputability, but less than when the same crime is committed by one in full possession of his faculties, unless however the drunkenness was purposely produced in order to commit the crime or to provide an excuse; when a law is violated in involuntary drunkenness, imputability is entirely lacking if the drunkenness completely took away the use of reason; it is diminished if it did so only in part. The same is to be said of other similar mental disturbances (c. 2201, § 3). Weakness of mind diminishes but does not entirely remove the imputability of a crime (c. 2201, § 4).

Ignorance of the Law. The violation of a law which was not known is not imputed at all if the ignorance was inculpable; otherwise imputability is diminished more or less in proportion to the culpability of the ignorance (c. 2202, § 1). Ignorance of the penalty alone does not remove imputability, but diminishes it somewhat (c. 2202, § 2). What is said of ignorance applies also to inadvertence or mistake (c. 2202, § 3).

Culpable Negligence: Accident. If a person violates the law through the omission of due diligence, imputability is diminished in the measure to be determined by a prudent judge according to the circumstances; if the culprit foresaw the event and nevertheless failed to take the precautions to prevent it which any careful man would have taken, the culpability is close to malice (c. 2203, § 1). An accident resulting from chance, which could not be foreseen, or which though foreseen could not be prevented, is entirely free from imputability (c. 2203, § 2).

Nonage. Minority (cf. c. 88, § 1), unless the contrary appear, diminishes the imputability of a crime, and the more so the more closely it approaches infancy (c. 2204).

Force: Fear. Physical force which takes away all power to act completely excludes crime (c. 2205, § 1). Also fear which is even relatively grave, necessity, and even grave inconvenience usually excuse entirely from crime, if there is question of merely ecclesiastical laws (c. 2205, § 2). But if the act done is intrinsically wrong, or tends toward contempt of the faith or of ecclesiastical authority, or toward harm to souls, the causes mentioned in § 2 diminish but do not entirely remove the imputability of the crime (c. 2205, § 3). The circumstance of legitimate defense against an unjust aggressor, if due moderation be observed, entirely excuses from crime; otherwise it merely diminishes imputability; and the same is to be said of provocation (c. 2205, § 4).

Fear is said to be *relatively grave* when the evil feared, though not such in itself as to produce grave fear in a normally courageous person, is such as to produce it in the person in question in view of his or her character and circumstances. Such fear usually excuses entirely from imputability for violation of merely ecclesiastical laws. In order to have this effect, is it necessary that the fear be unjustly imposed by an external free agent? Authors commonly neglect this point. Since the law in this connection does not state that these circumstances are required, and penal laws are to be favorably interpreted, it is at least solidly probable that grave fear is a complete excuse even though not external and unjust.[4]

Exceptional cases, in which fear, necessity, or grave inconvenience do not entirely remove but merely diminish imputability are those where "the act is intrinsically wrong or tends toward contempt of the faith or of ecclesiastical authority, or harm to souls." The effect of fear in excusing from a penalty in such cases will be discussed later.

Heat of Passion. Passion, if voluntarily and deliberately aroused or nourished, rather increases imputability; otherwise passion diminishes imputability more or less in proportion to the heat of the passion; and it entirely removes imputability if it precedes and prevents all deliberation and consent (c. 2206).

Summary of Causes Which Entirely Remove Imputability.

1. *Want of use of reason;* this is *presumed* in those who are habitually insane, though they have lucid intervals (c. 2201);[5]

2. *Drunkenness* or use of intoxicating drugs, if involuntary and completely alienating the use of reason (c. 2201, § 3);

3. *Inculpable ignorance of the law* (not merely of the penalty); or inadvertence or error regarding it, without fault (c. 2202, §§ 1, 3);

4. Mere *accident* which could not be foreseen or prevented (c. 2203, § 2);

5. Overpowering *force* (c. 2205, § 1);

6. *Grave fear, necessity, or grave inconvenience, usually;* but in exceptional cases (cf. next paragraph, n. 6) these causes only diminish imputability (c. 2205, § 2);

7. *Self-defense,* or its equivalent, against unjust aggression, with due moderation (c. 2205, § 4);

8. *Uncontrollable passion* if it entirely alienated freedom (c. 2206).

Summary of Causes Which Diminish Imputability.

1. *Drunkenness,* etc., even though voluntary, provided it was not directly sought for the purpose of doing or excusing the crime (c. 2201, § 3);

---

[4] Supporting our view, cf. Genicot, *Theol. Mor.,* II, n. 607; Wernz-Vidal, *Ius Poenale,* n. 89. *Contra,* Michiels, *De Delictis et Poenis,* pp. 200, 206.

[5] It is disputed whether this presumption is *iuris simpliciter,* admitting proof to the contrary, or *iuris et de iure,* excluding such proof (cf. cc. 1825, 1826). Creusen (*Epit.,* I. C., III, n. 389) holds contrary proof admissible. It is also disputed whether the habitually insane who have lucid intervals are, during those intervals, bound by or free from other laws of the Church (cf. cc. 12, 88).

2. *Mental weakness* (c. 2201, § 4);

3. *Ignorance* (or inadvertence, error) regarding law, fact, or penalty, though culpable, but the more culpable it is the less it excuses (c. 2202);

4. *Culpable negligence;* but if the event was foreseen and due precautions neglected, the culpability closely approaches malice (c. 2203, § 1);

5. *Minority,* and the more as it approaches infancy (c. 2204);

6. *Grave fear, necessity, grave inconvenience* in special cases where, instead of excusing entirely as above, n. 6, they merely diminish guilt (c. 2205, § 3);

7. *Self-defense,* or its equivalent, when excessive force was used in repelling the assault, or the provocation was slight (c. 2205, § 4);

8. *Passion,* antecedent but not overpowering, excuses partially in proportion to its ardor (c. 2206).

Aggravating Circumstances. Besides other aggravating circumstances, a crime is more serious: (1) in proportion to the greater dignity of the person who commits the crime or who is offended by it; (2) because of the abuse of authority or office in committing the crime **(c. 2207).** Thus clerics are more severely punished than the laity for certain crimes, because of their greater dignity (cf. cc. 2323, 2346, 2354, 2358, 2359, etc.); the penalty for laying violent hands on sacred persons increases with their dignity (c. 2343).

Habitual or Repeated Crimes. A *recidivus* in law is one who after having been found guilty commits a crime of the same kind again in such circumstances, especially of time, that his pertinacity in an evil will can be prudently conjectured **(c. 2208, § 1).** One who several times commits a crime, even of a different kind, increases his guilt **(c. 2208, § 2).** In general the penalty is heavier (c. 2234). Examples: cc. 2408, 2414, 2183, 2184, 2185).

Summary of Causes Which Increase Guilt.

1. *Passion* deliberately excited or nourished (c. 2206);

2. *Aggravating circumstances* in general; especially the dignity of the culprit (because the scandal is then greater), the dignity of the person injured (since greater harm results), the abuse of authority or office (c. 2207);

3. *Repetition of crimes,* whether of the same or different kinds (c. 2208).

Co-operation: General Notions. Co-operation here means concurrence with another in a crime. It has various divisions and degrees.

It is:

a. Formal if the intention is shared explicitly or implicitly; *material* if only the external action;

b. Moral or *physical* according to the nature of the acts contributed to the crime. Advice is a moral contribution, carrying a ladder, a physical one. Moral co-operation is necessarily formal; physical may be either formal or material;

c. Complicity *before or in the act* (e.g., by preparing or taking part in it); or *after the act* (by aiding escape, concealing property or evidence, etc.);

d. Positive, consisting of some contributing act; or *negative,* mere failure to prevent.

Guilt of Co-operators in Crime. Persons who conspire to commit a crime and physically concur in it are all held equally guilty, unless circumstances increase or diminish the guilt of some or one of them (c. 2209, § 1). In a crime which by its nature requires an accomplice, each party has the same guilt unless the contrary is clear from the circumstances (c. 2209, § 2). Not only the one who commands a crime and who is thus the principal culprit, but also those who induce the commission of the crime or concur in it in any way, incur no less guilt, other things being equal, than the one who perpetrated it, if without their help the crime would not have been committed (c. 2209, § 3). But if their co-operation only made easier a crime which would have been committed even without their concurrence, it is less guilty (c. 2209, § 4). One who by timely retractation completely withdrew his influence toward the commission of the crime is freed from all imputability, even though the perpetrator nevertheless completed the crime for reasons of his own; if he did not completely withdraw his influence, the retractation diminishes but does not entirely remove culpability (c. 2209, § 5). One who concurs in a crime only by neglecting his duty incurs imputability proportionate to the obligation which he had to prevent the crime by doing his duty (c. 2209, § 6). Praise of the crime after its commission, sharing in its fruits, concealing and harboring the culprit, or other acts subsequent to the completion of the crime, may constitute new crimes, namely, if they are punished by a penalty in the law; but, unless before the crime there was an agreement with the criminal to perform those acts, they do not entail imputability for the crime (c. 2209, § 7).

Causes of Action Arising From Crime. A crime may give rise to both a penal or criminal action and a civil action (in the ecclesiastical court); the penal action has for its purpose to declare or inflict a penalty according to law and to exact satisfaction; the civil action is for damages. Both suits are governed by the general procedural canons of the Code (cc. 1552–1959); and the same judge in the criminal action may, at the request of the injured party, take up the civil action and pronounce judgment (cf. c. 2210).

Liability of Co-operators for Damages. All who concur in a crime in the ways mentioned in canons 2209, §§ 1–3, are held *in solidum* to make good all expenses and damages which anyone may have suffered from the crime, even though the judgment against them be only for proportionate payment (c. 2211). To be bound *in solidum* means, of course, that each one is liable to pay in full if the others do not pay their share. This rule applies only to *positive, necessary* co-operators (c. 2209, §§ 1–3).

Attempted and Frustrated Crimes. One who did acts or omissions which by their nature contribute to a crime, but who did not complete the crime, either because he changed his mind or because he lacked adequate means to complete it, commits an attempt at crime (c. 2212, § 1). When all acts or omissions which by their nature conduce to the crime and are sufficient to complete it are provided, but for some other reason beside the will of the agent, they fail to produce their effect, the attempt at crime is properly called a *frustrated crime* (c. 2212, § 2). Equivalent to a frustrated crime is the action of one who tried, but without effect, to induce another to commit a crime (c. 2212, § 3). An attempt at crime constitutes a true crime if it is legally punishable by a peculiar penalty (c. 2212, § 4).

Except as hereinafter provided in § 3, an attempt at crime has its own imputability, and this is the greater the more closely it approaches consummation, though it is less than that of a consummated crime (c. 2213, § 1). A frustrated crime is more culpable than a simple attempt at crime (c. 2213, § 2). One who freely desisted after having begun to commit a crime is free from all imputability if no damage or scandal resulted from the attempt (c. 2213, § 3).

Question. An attempted crime results in public or private harm, but is not completed. Is it a true crime? Let us suppose that there is no special law providing a peculiar penalty for the deed as far as it actually went. At first sight it would seem that canons 2212, § 4 and 2228 might be cited for the negative. However, Noval (*Ius Pontificium,* 1929, p. 118) and Creusen (*Epit.* ed. 4, III, n. 396) give good reasons for the affirmative. In fact all the elements of a crime according to canon 2195, including *sanctio indeterminata* are present. Certainly the *penalty of the completed crime* is not incurred (c. 2228); but canon 2235 does provide an indeterminate optional penalty *ferendae sententiae* (cf. c. 2217, 1°, *"verbis facultativis"*).

Section 2. Penalties in General (cc. 2214–2235)

PRELIMINARY SURVEY

General Right and Policy of the Church (c. 2214)
Ecclesiastical Penalty Defined (c. 2215)
Classifications (cc. 2216, 2217)
Circumstances to Be Considered in Applying Penalties
    (c. 2218)
Interpretation (c. 2219)
The Power to Impose Penalties (cc. 2220–2222)
Discretion in Imposing Penalties (c. 2223)
Multiplication of Penalties (c. 2224)
Formalities in Declaring Penalties (c. 2225)
The Subject of Penal Law (c. 2226)
Rulers, Cardinals, Bishops (c. 2227)
All Elements of Crime Must Be Present (c. 2228)
Excusing or Extenuating Causes for Penalties
    Latae Sententiae (c. 2229)
Persons Who Have Not Attained Puberty (c. 2230)
Penalties for Complicity or Co-operation (c. 2231)
Circumstances Excusing From Observance Before
    Declaratory Sentence (c. 2232)
Conditions for Imposing Penalties, Especially Censures
    (c. 2233)
Penalties for Several Crimes (c. 2234)
Penalties for Attempted and Frustrated Crimes (c. 2235)

Right and Policy of the Church. The Church has a constitutional and proper right, independent of any human authority, to coerce delinquents among her subjects by both spiritual and temporal penalties (c. 2214, § 1).

However, the caution voiced by the Council of Trent, *Sess*. XIII, *de ref., cap*. 1, must be kept in mind: "Bishops and other Ordinaries should remember that they are shepherds and not slave-drivers, and that they must so rule over their subjects as not to domineer over them but to love them as sons and brothers; they should endeavor by exhortation and admonition to deter them from wrongdoing lest they be obliged to administer due punishment after faults have been committed. Yet if through human frailty their subjects do wrong, they must observe the precept of the Apostle, and reprove, entreat, rebuke them in all patience and doctrine; for sympathy is often more effective for correction than severity, exhortation better than threats of punishment, kindness better than insistence on authority. If in view of the seriousness of a crime there be need of punishment, then they must combine authority with leniency, judgment with mercy, severity with moderation, to the end that discipline, so salutary and essential to public order, be maintained without asperity, and that those who have been punished may amend their ways, or, if they refuse to do so, that others may be deterred from wrongdoing by the salutary example of their punishment" (c. 2214, § 2).

Definition. An ecclesiastical penalty is a privation of some good for the correction of the culprit and for the punishment of the crime, inflicted by lawful ecclesiastical authority (c. 2215). The good of which the delinquent is deprived must, of course, be one which is under the control of the Church; for example, the sacraments, the right to assist at the Holy Sacrifice, indulgences, the right of patronage, temporal goods, reputation. Grace as such, merit as such are directly in the hands of God; these cannot be *directly* controlled by ecclesiastical penalties.

Classification as to Purpose. In the Church delinquents are punished: (1) by medicinal penalties, or censures; (2) by vindictive penalties; (3) by penal remedies and penances (c. 2216). The purpose of a censure is correction, hence it is called medicinal; the purpose of certain other penalties is satisfaction or expiation, they are called vindictive. We shall later have definitions of *censures* (c. 2241) and *vindictive penalties* (c. 2286), an enumeration of the principal *penal remedies* (c. 2306), and a description of and norms for *penances* (c. 2312).

Other Classifications. A penalty is said to be:

1. *Determinate,* if it is prescribed exclusively in the law or precept; *indeterminate,* if it is left to the prudent discretion of the judge or superior, either in preceptive or optional terms;

2. *Latae sententiae,* if a determinate penalty is so attached to the law or precept that it is incurred *ipso facto* upon commission of the crime; *ferendae sententiae,* if it has to be inflicted by a judge or superior;

3. *A iure,* if a determinate penalty is established by the law itself,

whether it be *latae* or *ferendae sententiae; ab homine,* if it is imposed by way of particular precept or by a judicial condemnatory sentence, even though it be established by the law; hence a penalty *ferendae sententiae* attached to the law, before a condemnatory sentence, is only *a iure,* after a condemnatory sentence, it is both *a iure* and *ab homine,* but is considered as *ab homine* **(c. 2217, § 1).**

A penalty is always understood to be *ferendae sententiae,* unless it is expressly stated to be *latae sententiae* or to be contracted *ipso facto* or *ipso iure,* or unless some other similar expressions are used (c. 2217, § 2).

Examples: the following expressions certainly designate a penalty *latae sententiae:* "*eo ipso,*" "*noverit se esse excommunicatum,*" "*habeatur tamquam excommunicatus*" (c. 2353), "*eum excommunicatio tenet*" (c. 2388, § 2), "*subiaceat excommunicationi,*" "*maneat excommunicatus.*" A penalty is certainly *ferendae sententiae* if the law says: "*excommunicetur,*" "*suspendatur,*" "*sub excommunicationis poena prohibemus.*" The extent and exercise of judicial discretion in applying penalties *ferendae sententiae,* or in declaring penalties *latae sententiae,* are explained in canon 2223.

Note on Penalties *Ab Homine.* The distinction between penalties *a iure* and *ab homine* is important in practice in connection with faculties to absolve from them; hence we must try to form a clear notion of what a penalty *ab homine* is. It is not easy to be certain of the scope of the definition of penalties *ab homine* which we have just taken from canon 2217. Let us look at several cases.

1. A penalty *ferendae sententiae* is provided by law for a certain crime; the crime is committed, and later a judicial sentence condemns the culprit to suffer the penalty. Such a penalty, after the sentence, is both *a iure* and *ab homine,* but is considered as *ab homine.* This is a clear case (c. 2217, § 1, 3°).

2. A penalty *ferendae sententiae* is threatened in a particular precept imposed by a lawful superior; the subject violates the precept, and later the superior inflicts the threatened penalty (extrajudicially). This case is exactly parallel to the first, except that there is question of a precept instead of a law, and an extrajudicial condemnation instead of a judicial one. This seems to be clearly a penalty *ab homine* under the terms of the same canon, "*si feratur per modum praecepti peculiaris.*"

3. A penalty *latae sententiae* is established by a particular precept, to be incurred *ipso facto* upon violation of the precept. For example,

a Bishop orders one of his priests to make a six-day closed retreat within a certain time, under pain of *ipso facto* suspension. When the precept is violated the penalty is incurred. Is this a penalty *ab homine?* The question is a delicate one, to which a final and certain answer can scarcely be given. The discussion is beyond the elementary scope of this work; but there are reasons favoring a negative answer, and for practical purposes this case may be classified as not a penalty *ab homine.*[6]

4. A penalty *ferendae sententiae* is threatened in a common precept (as opposed to a particular precept) by a lawful superior; or a penalty *latae sententiae* is established by a common precept, to be incurred *ipso facto* on violation of the precept. Neither of these cases can be classified as certainly *ab homine;* for practical purposes, therefore, they are not.

Circumstances to Be Considered in Applying Penalties. Penalties should be decreed with due proportion to the crime, taking into account imputability, scandal, and damage; hence not only the object and gravity of the law should be considered, but also the age, knowledge, education, sex, condition, and state of mind of the delinquent, the dignity of the person offended or of the delinquent himself, the end intended, the place and time of the crime, whether the delinquent acted under the influence of passion or grave fear, whether he repented of the crime and tried to avoid its evil consequences, and other such considerations (c. 2218, § 1). Not only whatever excuses from all guilt, but whatever excuses from grave guilt, likewise excuses from any penalty whether *latae* or *ferendae sententiae,* even in the external forum if the excuse is proved for the external forum (c. 2218, § 2). When mutual injuries have been inflicted they offset each other, unless one of the parties, because the injury done by him was greater, ought to suffer some penalty, mitigated according to the requirements of the case (c. 2218, § 3).

Interpretation. In penalties the more benign interpretation should be followed (c. 2219, § 1). But in case of doubt whether a penalty inflicted by a competent superior is just or not, the penalty must be observed in the external forum, except in the case of an appeal with suspensive effect (c. 2219, § 2). Except as provided in canon 2231

---

[6] We rely in part on the reasoning adduced by Michiels in *Ephemerides Theol. Lovan.,* 1927, p. 180, n. 613 sq., to which Creusen replied in *Nouvelle Revue Theol.,* 1928, 436 sq. See also *Irish Eccl. Rec.,* 1925, p. 523. Our *practical* conclusion here will be found consistent with another practical conclusion on a related question arising under canon 2245, § 4.

(regarding the penalties incurred by co-operators), it is not permitted
to extend penalties from person to person or from case to case, even
though the reason is the same or even stronger (c. 2219, § 3).

Power to Inflict Penalties. Those who have power to enact laws or
to impose precepts can also attach penalties to the law or the precept;
those who have only judicial power can only apply according to law
penalties lawfully established (c. 2220, § 1). The precepts here referred
to are *jurisdictional* precepts, proceeding from a true power of jurisdiction. The Vicar General, however, though he has true jurisdiction,
is expressly excluded from the power of inflicting penalties, unless he
has a special mandate (cf. c. 2220, § 2).

Those who have legislative power can, within the limits of their
jurisdiction, fortify a law with a suitable penalty or even make the
legal penalty more severe, not only in the case of a law enacted by
themselves or their predecessors, but also, if there is special reason for
such action, in the case of both the divine law and an ecclesiastical
law enacted by a superior power and in effect in the territory
(c. 2221).

Even though a law has no sanction attached to it, the legitimate
superior can, even without any previous threat of punishment, punish
its violation by a just penalty, if scandal was given or if the special
gravity of the transgression makes such action appropriate; otherwise
the culprit cannot be punished unless he was previously warned and
threatened with a penalty *latae* or *ferendae sententiae* in case of
transgression, and nevertheless violated the law (c. 2222, § 1).

Likewise the lawful superior, even though it is only probable that a
crime has been committed, or though penal action upon a crime which
was certainly committed is now barred by prescription, has not only
the right but also the duty not to promote a cleric whose fitness is not
certain, and, in order to prevent scandal, to forbid a cleric the exercise
of the sacred ministry, or even to remove him from office according
to law; and in this case these procedures are not considered penal
(c. 2222, § 2).

Norms for Applying Penalties (cc. 2223–2225). These will concern
more directly the ecclesiastical superiors and judges; we may note
here only a few of the more practical points. Canon 2223 explains very
nicely the discretion which is left to the judge when a penalty
ferendae sententiae is provided by the law "either in preceptive or
optional terms" (cf. c. 2217, § 1, 1°), or when there is question of
declaring a penalty *latae sententiae*. Canon 2224 regulates the judicial

discretion in cases of multiple penalties. If penalties are provided for an attempt at crime and for a frustrated crime, these penalties are not to be applied cumulatively with that for the completed crime (cf. c. 2224, § 3). If a penalty is declared or inflicted by a judicial sentence, the provisions of the canons governing the pronouncement of a judicial sentence are to be observed; if a penalty *latae* or *ferendae sententiae* is inflicted by way of particular precept, it should ordinarily be declared or imposed in writing or before two witnesses, and the reasons for the penalty should be indicated, except as provided in canon 2193 (regarding suspension *ex informata conscientia*) (c. 2225).

Procedure. Although procedure as such is not within the scope of this course, we must indicate some rather serious difficulties connected with the interpretation of canon 2225 taken in conjunction with several other canons of the Code, notably with canon 1933. In short, without concerning ourselves with the *details* of procedure, we do want to know at least *in what cases judicial procedure is required,* and on the other hand in what cases penalties may be declared or inflicted "by way of particular precept." The question is by no means easy to answer. Although we cannot answer it fully, we will indicate the knotty points and some opinions for their solution.

In general, judicial procedure is appropriate only for public crimes (c. 1933, § 1). In certain special cases the usual procedure is supplanted by special norms. Such cases are: nonresidence, concubinage, negligence in the pastoral office (cc. 2168–2185); suspension *ex informata conscientia* (cc. 2186–2194); the dismissal of male religious of solemn vows or of simple perpetual vows in a clerical exempt institute (c. 654 sq.). Moreover, special procedure, not strictly judicial, is provided for the dismissal of other religious (c. 649 sq.) and for the administrative removal and transfer of pastors (cc. 2142–2167).

Even in public crimes other than those governed by these special norms, certain penalties may be inflicted without the usual judicial trial. Our problem is to try to determine precisely in what cases this is true. Canon 1933, § 4 states: "Penance, penal remedy, excommunication, suspension, interdict, provided the crime is certain, can be inflicted also by way of precept without a judicial trial." This canon in connection with canon 2225 raises two grave questions. First, is this enumeration of penalties in canon 1933, § 4 exclusive, or can it be extended, and if so how far? Vindictive penalties are not mentioned. Hence, if the enumeration is exclusive, all vindictive penalties except suspension and interdict require the full judicial procedure. Yet it is the practice of many ecclesiastical authorities to inflict slight vindictive penalties without formal trial. Formal criminal proceedings are rare occurrences in diocesan tribunals. Second, is the enumeration of penalties in canon 1933, § 4 modified and restricted by canon 2225? To us, this latter canon seems to suppose rather than to determine in any way the distinction between the two classes of cases, those which require judicial procedure and those which do not. Many authors agree with this view; some, however, hold a different interpretation by insisting on the tense of the verb, *inflicta sit* in canon 2225. The text is: "Si vero poena latae vel ferendae sententiae *inflicta sit* ad modum praecepti particularis . . . " In view of the apparent purpose and context of this canon, we take this to mean: "If a penalty *latae* or *ferendae sententiae is inflicted* by way of particular precept . . . " It is true that this rendition does some violence to the verb *inflicta sit,* which is in a past tense; but the contrary view is subject to a greater difficulty. Those authors who hold that these words mean, "if a penalty *latae* or *ferendae sententiae has been* (antecedently) *established* by way of particular precept . . . " seem to us to do violence, not to the tense but to the radical meaning of the verb *inflicta sit.* This interpretation not only does violence to the literal text, but it attributes to canon 2225 an effect which seems to be entirely foreign to its setting and context, namely, to modify canon 1933, § 4, by limiting the cases in which a penalty can be inflicted by precept to those in which the penalty was also established by precept and not by law.

The practical importance of this rather subtle dispute will be apparent from a consideration of the various opinions. Remember the question: what are the penalties which can be inflicted (even in a public crime) by way of precept, that is, without judicial procedure?

1. Noval, A Coronata, and others answer: those penalties only which are enumerated in canon 1933, § 4 (the enumeration is exclusive), and those only if they were established by precept (the enumeration of canon 1933, § 4 is modified and restricted by canon 2225).[7]

2. Another opinion: those penalties only which are enumerated in canon 1933, § 4, whether they were established by precept or by law (the enumeration of canon 1933, § 4 is exclusive and is not restricted by canon 2225).

3. A third opinion attributed to Chelodi, Vermeersch-Creusen, Cappello, Michiels: all those penalties mentioned in canon 1933, § 4, which

---

[7] Cf. A Coronata, III, n. 1453.

were established by law, and moreover any other penalties which were established by precept.

4. Roberti: any penalty, whether established by law or by precept, may be applied or declared by way of precept, except those penalties for which formal judicial or other process is absolutely required by law. Roberti claims that this rule is in accord with the practice of diocesan authorities and of the Roman Curia, a consideration which, in matters of this kind, is entitled to considerable weight. He concludes by enumerating as follows the cases in which formal procedure is required.

Cases in Which Formal Procedure Is Required. 1. Deposition (c. 2303), perpetual privation of ecclesiastical dress (c. 2304), degradation (c. 2305), for all of which penalties canon 1576, § 1, 2° requires judicial procedure before a board of five judges.

2. Penal deprivation of (not administrative removal from) an irremovable benefice (c. 192, § 2), for which canon 1576, § 1, 1° requires judicial procedure before a board of three judges.

3. Cases reserved to the Holy Office (c. 1555, § 1).

4. The special cases governed by canons 2142–2194, namely: (a) the administrative removal of irremovable pastors (cc. 2147–2156); (b) the administrative removal of removable pastors (cc. 2157–2161); (c) the transfer of pastors (cc. 2162–2167); (d) penal action against nonresident clerics (cc. 2168–2175); (e) penal action against clerics for concubinage (cc. 2176–2181); (f) penal action against negligent pastors (cc. 2182–2185); (a) cases of suspension *ex informata conscientia* (cc. 2186–2194).

5. The dismissal of religious (cc. 649 sq., 654 sq.).[8]

In all other cases (even the rather severe vindictive penalty of obliging a cleric to reside in a house of penance outside the diocese, cf. cc. 2301, 2302) this opinion would allow the infliction of the penalty without *formal* procedure.

Who Are Held by Penalties. Whoever is bound by a law or precept is held by the penalty attached to the law or precept, unless he is expressly exempted (c. 2226, § 1). Although a later penal law modifies a prior one, yet if when the later law was enacted the crime had already been committed, the more favorable law is to be applied (c. 2226, § 2). If the later law repeals the former law or only the penalty, the penalty ceases immediately, except in the case of censures already contracted (c. 2226, § 3). For a censure once contracted is removed

---

[8] Cf. Roberti, *De Delictis et Poenis*, I, nn. 257–263.

only by absolution (c. 2248, § 1). A penalty holds the culprit everywhere, even though the superior's authority has lapsed, unless there is
express provision to the contrary (c. 2226, § 4).

Only the Roman Pontiff can inflict or declare a penalty in the case
of the persons mentioned in canon 1557, § 1 (c. 2227, § 1). Those
persons are: the heads of states, their sons or daughters or those who
have the immediate right of succession, Cardinals, Apostolic Legates,
and Bishops, even titular ones (c. 1557, § 1). Unless expressly mentioned, Cardinals are not subject to penal laws, nor are Bishops
(unless expressly mentioned) subject to *latae sententiae* penalties of
suspension and interdict (c. 2227, § 2).

A penalty established by law is not incurred unless the crime was
perfect in its kind according to the proper meaning of the words of
the law (c. 2228).

Excusing Causes. *Affected ignorance* either of the law or merely of
the penalty does not excuse from any *latae sententiae* penalty, even
though the law contain the special expressions mentioned in § 2
(c. 2229, § 1).

If the law contains the words: *praesumpserit, ausus fuerit, scienter,
studiose, temerarie, consulto egerit,* or other similar expressions which
require full knowledge and deliberation, any diminution of imputability, either on the part of the intellect or of the will, exempts from
penalties *latae sententiae* (c. 2229, § 2).

If the law does not contain such words or expressions:

1. *Ignorance* of the law or merely of the penalty, if crass or supine,
does not exempt from any *latae sententiae* penalty; if it is not crass
or supine, it excuses from medicinal but not from vindictive *latae
sententiae* penalties;

2. *Drunkenness, omission of due diligence, weakness of mind, the
impetus of passion,* if notwithstanding the diminution of imputability
the action is still gravely culpable, do not excuse from *latae sententiae*
penalties;

3. *Grave fear,* if the crime tends toward the contempt of the faith
or of ecclesiastical authority or toward the public harm of souls, by no
means exempts from *latae sententiae* penalties (c. 2229, § 3). This
language is very similar to that of canon 2205, § 3, regarding the effect
of grave fear on imputability. There is, however, a notable difference.
According to that canon, if the act is intrinsically wrong, grave fear
does not excuse from but merely diminishes imputability, whereas
the present canon, dealing with penalties, says nothing about acts

intrinsically wrong, but merely denies the benefit of grave fear as an excuse where the act tends toward contempt of the faith, etc. The Code Commission has replied that grave fear excuses from penalties *latae sententiae* even though the crime is intrinsically wrong and gravely culpable, provided it does not tend to the contempt of the faith or of ecclesiastical authority nor to the public harm of souls.[9] *Examples:* contempt of the faith — public apostasy (c. 2314); contempt of ecclesiastical authority — suing one's own Bishop in a civil court (c. 2341); public harm to souls — publishing books of heretics which promote heresy (c. 2318).

Even though a culprit, according to § 3, 1°, is not held by *latae sententiae* censures, this does not prevent his being punished in a proper case with some other suitable penalty or penance (c. 2229, § 4).

Persons Who Have Not Attained Puberty are excused from *latae sententiae* penalties, and should rather be corrected by educative penalties than by censures or grave vindictive penalties; but persons (who have attained puberty) who induce them to violate the law or who co-operate with them in crime in the ways mentioned in canon 2209, §§ 1–3, themselves incur the penalty established by law (c. 2230).

Although the age of puberty is clearly defined in the Code as 14 for males, 12 for females (c. 88, § 2), yet some authors, arguing chiefly from sources in the old law, contend that in penal matters the age is 14 for both sexes. This may be held as probable until the contrary is authentically declared; it would exempt girls under 14 from *latae sententiae* penalties.[10]

Brief Summary of Excuses and Exemptions.

1. Whatever excuses from mortal guilt excuses from all penalties (c. 2218, § 2).

2. From penalties *latae sententiae,* if the law has special expressions, any diminution of imputability on the part of the intellect or the will excuses (c. 2229, § 2).

3. Ignorance, neither affected nor crass, excuses from medicinal but not from vindictive penalties, even though the law has not the special expressions (c. 2229, § 3, 1°).

---

[9] Code Com., 30 Dec., 1937; *AAS,* 30, p. 73; *Digest,* II, p. 570. For acts that work public harm to souls, cf. McCoy, *Force and Fear in Relation to Delictual Imputability and Penal Responsibility* (Cath. U., 1944), pp. 97, 127. For acts involving contempt of the faith or of ecclesiastical authority, *ibid.,* pp. 92–96.

[10] Cf. V-C, *Epit.,* III, n. 424. Roberti, *De Delictis et Poenis,* n. 247, points out an argument for it from canon 1648, § 3.

4. Grave fear (not necessarily unjust and external) excuses from penalties *latae sententiae* even if the act was intrinsically wrong and gravely culpable, but not if it tends to the contempt of the faith or of ecclesiastical authority or to the public harm of souls (c. 2229, § 3, 3° and reply of Code Commission).

5. Persons before puberty are exempt from *latae sententiae* penalties, but their accomplices incur them (c. 2230); this exemption probably applies to girls up to 14.

6. Unless named, Cardinals are exempt from all penal laws, Bishops from suspension and interdict *latae sententiae,* but not from excommunication (c. 2227). Princes or rulers and their children or proximate expectant successors, Cardinals, and Bishops, even titular, and Papal Legates are exempt from all penalties except those inflicted or declared by the Roman Pontiff (c. 2227).

Penalties for Co-operators. If more than one co-operate to commit a crime, though only one is named in the law, those also who are mentioned in canon 2209, §§ 1–3 are bound by the same penalty unless the law provide otherwise; other co-operators are not so bound, but they are to be punished by some other just penalty according to the prudent judgment of the superior, unless the law provides a special penalty for them (c. 2231).

Observance of Penalty. A penalty *latae sententiae,* whether medicinal or vindictive, is *ipso facto* binding in both the internal and external forum, upon a delinquent who is conscious of the crime; but until a declaratory sentence has been passed the delinquent is excused from observing the penalty whenever he is unable to observe it without infamy, and in the external forum no one can exact from him its observance unless the crime is notorious, without prejudice however to the provision of canon 2223, § 4 (c. 2232, § 1). The canon cited provides that if an interested party requests it, or if the public good demands it, a sentence declaring a penalty should be issued; although in general such a declaration is left to the prudent discretion of the superior.

A declaratory sentence makes the penalty retroactive to the time when the crime was committed (c. 2232, § 2).

Infliction of Penalties. No penalty can be inflicted unless it is certain that a crime was committed and that its prosecution is not barred by prescription (c. 2233, § 1). Even though that is legally proved, if there is question of inflicting a censure, the culprit must be reprehended and warned to desist from contumacy according to canon

2242, § 3, and, if in the prudent judgment of the same judge or superior it seems fitting, a suitable time should be allowed him to comply; if the contumacy continues, the censure may be inflicted (c. 2233, § 2).

Plurality of Penalties. One who has committed several crimes should not only be punished more severely, but in a proper case, according to the prudent discretion of the judge, should moreover be put under surveillance or some other penal remedy (c. 2234).

Attempted or Frustrated Crime. A frustrated crime or an attempt at crime, if they are not punished by law as distinct crimes, can be punished by appropriate penalties according to the gravity of the case, except as provided in canon 2213, § 3 (c. 2235). The canon cited exempts from criminal imputability when the culprit voluntarily desisted and caused neither damage nor scandal.

Section 3. The Remission of Penalties (cc. 2236–2240)

PRELIMINARY SURVEY

Who Has Power to Remit Penalties (c. 2236)
Power of Ordinaries (c. 2237)
Invalidity of Remission Obtained Under Stress of Grave Fear (c. 2238)
Circumstances and Manner of Remission (c. 2239)
Limitation by Prescription (c. 2240)

The Power to Remit. The remission of a penalty, by absolution in the case of censures, by dispensation in the case of vindictive penalties, can be granted only by the one who imposed the penalty, or by his competent superior or successor, or by one to whom the power to remit it has been given (c. 2236, § 1). One who can exempt from the law can also remit a penalty attached to the law (c. 2236, § 2). A judge who applies *ex officio* a penalty established by his superior, cannot remit it after it is applied (c. 2236, § 3).

Absolution is an act of judicial jurisdiction; if the penitent is rightly disposed he has a right to it; once given it cannot be revoked; it is the *only* means of remitting censures (cf. c. 2248, § 1). *Dispensation,* on the other hand, is an act of voluntary jurisdiction; it is a favor, not a right; once given it can be revoked, because the obligation still exists radically in the law; it is *one* of the ways in which vindictive penalties may cease (cf. cc. 2226, § 3, 2289).

Power of Ordinaries. In *public* cases an Ordinary can remit all penalties *latae sententiae* which are established by the common law, except: (1) cases which have been brought into court; (this is done when summons has been completed or the party has made an appearance in court according to canon 1725, in either a civil or criminal action arising out of a crime according to canon 2210); (2) censures reserved to the Holy See; (3) penalties involving incapacity for benefices, offices, dignities, functions in the Church, active and passive voice or the privation thereof, or involving perpetual suspension, infamy of law, privation of the right of patronage and of a privilege or favor granted by the Holy See (**c. 2237, § 1**). The penalties mentioned under n. 3 are all vindictive penalties (cf. c. 2368).

In *occult* cases, without prejudice to canons 2254 (absolution from censures in urgent cases) and 2290 (dispensation from vindictive penalties in urgent cases), the Ordinary can personally or through another remit all penalties *latae sententiae* established by common law, except censures most specially or specially reserved to the Holy See (**c. 2237, § 2**).

Note on Jurisdiction for Remitting Penalties. In canon 2237 there is question of the extent of the power of Ordinaries to remit penalties; they are given power *over certain penalties* and not over others. But even as regards penalties over which they have power, there is another condition for valid absolution or dispensation, namely, jurisdiction *over the person* (c. 201, § 1). Hence, in order to get a complete picture of the power of Ordinaries, especially to absolve from reserved censures, we shall have to consider also canon 2253 which deals with that subject and specifies the persons whom the Ordinary can absolve. These two canons together will furnish the solution to some puzzling cases. We shall return to this subject in connection with canon 2253.

Effect of Force and Fear. The remission of a penalty is *ipso facto* invalid if it was extorted by force or grave fear (**c. 2238**). Here there is question only of fear unjustly produced.

Manner of Remission. A penalty can be validly remitted in favor of a person who is present or absent; it can be remitted absolutely or conditionally; in the external forum or only in the internal forum (**c. 2239, § 1**). The reason is that we are not here speaking of sacramental absolution. Although a penalty can be remitted even orally, still if the penalty was inflicted in writing, the remission should be in writing (**c. 2239, § 2**).

Prescription. As regards the barring of a penal action by prescription, the provision of canon 1703 is to be observed (c. 2240). The canon cited provides that the usual period of limitation is three years; special provision (5 or 10 years) is made for certain special classes of crime. Cases pertaining to the Holy Office follow the special rules of that tribunal (c. 1555, § 1).

CASES AND QUESTIONS

1. Can a Cardinal who holds no other office inflict ecclesiastical penalties? (C. 2220; V-C, *Epit.*, III, n. 411).

2. A seminarian who has taken quite an interest in canon law is suspected of misbehavior, which however cannot be proved. Because of this doubt of his fitness, his ordination is deferred. He claims that the penalty is unjust and "against canon law" (c. 2222, § 2).

3. A priest is discovered by his Bishop in the very act of committing a crime; no other person knows of it. Is the crime occult or public, notorious in fact or in law? (C. 2197; V-C, *Epit.*, III, n. 384).

4. Girl seduced, pregnant. Uncle advised her to procure abortion; doctor recommended well-known method; effect followed her action. Do the girl, the uncle, and the doctor incur the censure? (Cc. 2350, 2209, 2231; *Periodica*, Vol. 22, p. 140*, 171*).

5. Druggist confesses selling abortive drug; does not know whether effect followed or not. Does he incur the censure?

6. A defendant on trial for a crime claims he was ill at the time and under mental strain. Should this be considered? (Cc. 2201, § 4, 2218, § 1).

7. "Ignorance of the law is no excuse." To what extent does this axiom hold in the penal law of the Church? (C. 2202).

8. Against the declaration of the penalty for dueling (c. 2351) it is argued that the culprit was challenged publicly and that his reputation was at stake (cc. 2205, §§ 2, 3; V-C, *Epit.*, III, n. 389).

9. Is the penalty of canon 2371 *latae* or *ferendae sententiae*? (C. 2217, § 2). What about those of canons 2414, 2386, 2375, 2368, § 1?

10. Can an ecclesiastical penalty, e.g., excommunication, deprive a person of sanctifying grace? (Cc. 2215, 2241, § 1, 2257).

11. A man tries to persuade a woman to submit to an abortion; she refuses. Is the man guilty of the crime of abortion? Of any crime? Of the sin of abortion? (Cc. 2350, 2212, §§ 3, 4, 2213, § 1, 2235).

12. X incurs a censure *latae sententiae* established by episcopal law in the diocese of T. Later X claims that the censure no longer binds: (1) because he is now living in another diocese; (2) because the Bishop of T is dead (cc. 2226, § 4, 2248, § 1).

13. A penitent confesses keeping for a friend a book which was forbidden *nominatim* by Apostolic letter. What is the penalty? (C. 2318, § 1). He

admits that he knew the law but says he did it only for fear of offending his friend (c. 2229, § 2).

14. A girl 13 years old deliberately walks into the cloister of regulars, on a dare from a companion, 16, who stays outside. Do either or both incur the censure? (Cc. 2342, 2°, 2230, 2231).

15. A priest who is under suspension *a divinis* (c. 2279, § 2, 2°) for 30 days (vindictive penalty) finds himself in circumstances where he must either say Mass or suffer loss of reputation. He is in the state of grace. Can a simple confessor do anything to enable him to say Mass? (C. 2290). Could he say Mass without going to confession? (C. 2232).

16. Penitent confesses a sin to which a censure of excommunication *latae sententiae* reserved to the Bishop is attached by diocesan law. The confessor judges that this is a censure *ab homine* (c. 2217, § 1, 3°).

17. In an occult case can a Provincial of regulars by common law absolve his subject from an excommunication simply reserved to the Holy See? (Cc. 198, § 1, 2237, § 2).

18. Maud is a special nurse for Doctor Jones in his private hospital; administers anesthetic, handles instruments. Occasionally illicit operations for removal of nonviable fetus are performed. Does she incur the censure of canon 2350? (Cc. 2209, § 4, 2231).

19. Mrs. S. submitted to an abortion which proved effective; says she was terribly afraid, as the doctor told her another Caesarean would mean almost certain death. Knew of excommunication. Now thoroughly repentant. Was there a mortal sin? Censure? Can simple confessor absolve? (Cc. 2350, 2229, § 3, 3°; Genicot, *Theol. Mor.*, II, n. 607; Wernz-Vidal, *Ius Canonicum* VII, *Ius Poenale*, n. 89).

20. Mrs. Z., a midwife, occasionally practices craniotomy. Does she incur the censure of canon 2350? Can she be punished? (C. 2350, Cappello, *De Censuris*, n. 385, c. 2222, § 1).

Readings:

Esswein, *Extrajudicial Penal Powers of Ecclesiastical Superiors*, Cath. U., 1941; Connor, *The Administrative Removal of Pastors*, Cath. U., 1937; Murphy, *Suspension Ex Informata Conscientia*, Cath. U., 1932; Swoboda, *Ignorance in Relation to the Imputability of Delicts*, Cath. U., 1941; Eltz, *Co-operation in Crime*, Cath. U., n. 156; *The Jurist*, Vol. 4, p. 572 (Costello, on penal legislation of the Code); *Irish Ecclesiastical Record*: Vol. 26, p. 523 (Kinane, on reservation of an *ab homine* censure); Vol. 29, p. 293 (O'Neill, on ignorance of law or penalty); *Apollinaris*, 1931, p. 294 (Roberti, *quaenam poenae applicari possint per modum praecepti*); *Clergy Review*: Vol. 12, p. 340 (*impuberes*, and absolution from heresy); Vol. 17, p. 353 (*aetas pubertatis pro puellis in ordine ad poenas latae sententiae contrahendas*); *Periodica*: Vol. 22, pp. 140*, 171* (case on co-operation in abortion).

CHAPTER XXI

CENSURES IN GENERAL

PRELIMINARY SURVEY

Censure Defined (c. 2241)
Contumacy Defined (c. 2242)
When Is Censure Suspended by Appeal or Recourse (c. 2243)
Multiplication of Censures (c. 2244)
Reserved Censures (c. 2245)
Rules Governing Reservations (cc. 2246, 2247)
Absolution From Censures (cc. 2248–2250)
Effect of Absolution in Either Forum (c. 2251)
Absolution in Danger of Death (c. 2252)
Absolution in Ordinary Circumstances (c. 2253)
Absolution in Urgent Cases (c. 2254)

Censure. A censure is a penalty by which a person who is baptized, who has committed a crime, and who is contumacious, is deprived of certain spiritual goods or goods which are attached to spiritual ones, until, having desisted from contumacy, he is absolved **(c. 2241, § 1).** Censures, especially those which are *latae sententiae,* and most of all excommunication, should be inflicted only with restraint and great circumspection **(c. 2241, § 2).** Only a baptized person can be affected, since it is an ecclesiastical penalty, and baptism is the door to the Church (c. 87). Once incurred, a censure is removed only by absolution (c. 2248, § 1).

Contumacy. Only an external, grave, consummated crime joined with contumacy is punished by censure; but censure can be decreed against delinquents who are unknown **(c. 2242, § 1).** Contumacy in general means obstinate disregard of authority; but in penal law it has a technical meaning.

In the case of censures *ferendae sententiae,* one is contumacious if, notwithstanding the warnings mentioned in canon 2233, § 2, he does not desist from the crime, or refuses to do penance for it and to make due reparation of the damage and scandal; but to incur a censure *latae sententiae,* all that is needed is the transgression of the law or precept to which a *latae sententiae* penalty is attached, unless the culprit is excused from it by some legitimate reason (c. 2242, § 2). The *warning* required by this canon is *always necessary* before the infliction of a *censure ferendae sententiae,* even if there has been scandal or special gravity as contemplated by canon 2222, § 1. This will be clear from a careful reading of canons 2222, § 1, 2233, § 2, and 2242, § 2.

Contumacy is considered to have ceased when the culprit has really repented of the crime and has given or at least seriously promised to give satisfaction for the damage and scandal. Judgment regarding the existence of these conditions rests with the person of whom absolution is asked (c. 2242, § 3).

Censure, When Effective: When Suspended by Recourse or Appeal? We may summarize this matter by distinguishing the following cases:

1. A censure *latae sententiae* is incurred *ipso facto* on commission of a crime; it is immediately effective, and there is no recourse. Penance and absolution are the way out (c. 2217, § 1, 2°).

2. A censure *latae sententiae,* after having been so incurred, may moreover be declared *(sententia declaratoria).* This has further consequences as to its observance (cf. c. 2232, § 1); the culprit is no longer excused from its observance by danger of infamy. There is a right of appeal from the sentence, usually *in suspensivo,* i.e., with the effect of suspending the sentence until it is confirmed; but if the matter in question does not legally admit of an appeal or recourse *in suspensivo,* then the appeal has no suspensive effect. Moreover, even in appeals which have suspensive effect, it is only the *sentence* that is suspended pending the appeal; the *censure,* inasmuch as it was incurred *ipso facto* independently of the sentence appealed from, remains in effect.

3. A censure *ferendae sententiae* is inflicted by a condemnatory sentence; it is immediately effective, and there is an appeal only *in devolutivo,* without suspensive effect (cf. c. 2243, § 1). Or a censure *ferendae sententiae* is inflicted by a precept; it is immediately effective; recourse *in devolutivo* (cf. c. 2243, § 1).

4. A censure is threatened by a judgment or precept, either to be incurred *ipso facto* on violation of the judgment or precept or to be inflicted by another judgment or precept; there is an appeal or recourse, but without suspensive effect, unless the particular matter concerned admits of a suspensive appeal or recourse. Even then the appeal or recourse suspends only the censure, not the judgment or

precept from which it arose, unless the appeal or recourse was against the judgment or precept itself (cf. c. 2243, § 2). For example, if a precept amounted to the infliction of a vindictive penalty (e.g., prohibition to exercise the sacred ministry except in a certain church, as in canon 2298), a recourse duly taken *from that precept* would have a suspensive effect (c. 2287).

Multiple Censures. Not only different censures, but also a censure of the same kind may be multiplied in the same subject (c. 2244, § 1).

A censure *latae sententiae* is multiplied: (1) if different crimes, each involving a censure, are committed by the same action or by different actions; (2) if the same crime, which is punishable by censure, is repeated so that there are several distinct crimes; (3) if a crime, punishable with different censures by distinct superiors, is committed once or oftener (c. 2244, § 2). If the same crime is punishable by distinct superiors with the *same* censure, it is generally held that numerically distinct censures are incurred, if the intention of the superior to that effect is clear.[1]

A censure *ab homine* is multiplied if several precepts, or sentences, or distinct parts of the same precept or sentence, each inflict a censure on its own account (c. 2244, § 3).

Reservation of Censures. Reservation of a censure means the limitation of power to absolve from it to certain persons or classes of persons (cf. c. 893, §§ 1, 2). The purpose of such a reservation is the same as that of reservation of sins, that is, to emphasize the gravity of the offense, but the reservation of censures is governed by special rules (*ibid.*). Some censures are reserved, others nonreserved (c. 2245, § 1). A censure *ab homine* is reserved to the person who inflicted the censure or pronounced the sentence, or to his competent superior, successor, or delegate; of censures *a iure* some are reserved to the Ordinary, others to the Holy See (c. 2245, § 2). Of those reserved to the Holy See, some are reserved simply, others specially, others most specially (c. 2245, § 3). A censure *latae sententiae* is not reserved unless the law or precept expressly reserved it; and in doubt of law or fact the reservation is not binding (c. 2245, § 4).

This text raises two difficulties which may be illustrated by concrete cases.

1. A censure *ferendae sententiae* is contained in the law; upon commission of the crime sentence is passed by a judge applying the

---

[1] Cf. Ayrinhac, *Penal Legislation,* p. 93.

censure. To whom is this censure reserved, and who can remit it? It is certainly a censure *ab homine* (c. 2217, § 1, 3°). A censure *ab homine* is reserved to "the person who inflicted the censure or pronounced the sentence" (c. 2245, § 2), and the same person can remit it (c. 2253, 2°). Yet, a judge who applies *ex officio* a penalty established by his superior cannot remit it after it is applied (c. 2236, § 2). To reconcile all these provisions of the Code, it seems necessary to hold that in such case the censure, which is certainly *ab homine*, is reserved not to the judge but to the Ordinary.

2. A censure is threatened by a particular precept, to be incurred *ipso facto* on violation of the precept. Nothing is said in the precept about the censure being reserved. Is it reserved? We answer in the negative. This is a censure *latae sententiae*, and canon 2245, § 4 states that such a censure is not reserved without special mention. This conclusion is consistent with what we said in connection with canon 2217, § 1, 3°, namely, that such a censure is not *ab homine* (cf. p. 802). If it were held to be *ab homine*, then it would be more difficult to hold that it is not reserved; and authors who hold that it is *ab homine* have difficulty in explaining the canons which state without distinction that penalties *ab homine* are reserved. Though this question is difficult and much disputed, our solution is at least probable.[2] From a practical standpoint it may be followed, because "in doubt of law or fact a reservation is not binding" (c. 2245, § 4).

Regulations Regarding the Establishment of Reserved Censures. A censure should not be reserved except in view of the peculiar gravity of crimes and the necessity of protecting ecclesiastical discipline and curing the consciences of the faithful (c. 2246, § 1). A reservation of a censure is to be interpreted strictly (c. 2246, § 2). If a censure is already reserved to the Holy See, an Ordinary cannot establish for the same crime another censure reserved to himself (c. 2247, § 1).

Effect of Reservation of Censure on Power to Absolve From Sin. 1. *Territorial limitation.* The reservation of a censure in a particular territory is of no effect outside that territory, even though the culprit goes out of the territory for the express purpose of obtaining absolution (c. 2247, § 2). We have seen that a *censure* once incurred follows the culprit everywhere (c. 2226, § 4); but the *reservation* does not. Hence, outside the territory absolution is still needed, but a simple confessor

---

[2] For the beginning of a study of this disputed question, see V-C, *Epit.*, III, n. 442, 443, pp. 218, 219; Cappello, *De Censuris*, n. 68. For a fuller discussion, see Moriarty, *Extraordinary Absolution from Censures*, p. 91 sq.

can give it. A censure *ab homine,* however, is reserved everywhere (c. 2247, § 2).

2. *Reservation of sin "ratione censurae."* The reservation of a censure which impedes the reception of the sacraments involves the reservation of the sin to which that censure is attached; but if one is excused or absolved from the censure, the reservation of the sin ceases entirely (c. 2246, § 3). Excommunication, for example, is a censure which impedes the reception of the sacraments (cf. c. 2260, § 1), that is, it forbids their reception, but does not *de se* render them invalid.[3] If such a censure is moreover reserved, then, not all the sins which the penitent has on his conscience, but only the sin to which the reserved censure is attached, is reserved by reason of the censure. This means that, as long as the censure remains, that sin cannot be directly absolved by a simple confessor.

3. *Ignorance of the reservation on the part of the confessor.* If a confessor, ignorant of (or inattentive to or forgetful of) the reservation of a censure, absolves the penitent from the censure and sin, the absolution of the censure is valid, provided it be not a censure *ab homine* or one reserved most specially to the Holy See (c. 2247, § 3).

Absolution From Censure. Any censure, once contracted, is removed only by lawful absolution (c. 2248, § 1). From the moment when the culprit has desisted from contumacy according to canon 2242, § 3, absolution may not be denied; but the one who absolves can in a proper case impose a suitable vindictive penalty or penance for the crime (c. 2248, § 2). A censure, once it has been removed by absolution, does not revive, except in case an obligation which was imposed under pain of falling back into the censure has not been fulfilled (c. 2248, § 3).

Multiple Censures: Omission in Good Faith. If a person is under more than one censure, he can be absolved from one of them without receiving absolution from the others (c. 2249, § 1). One who asks absolution must mention all the cases; otherwise the absolution is valid only for the case mentioned; if, though only a particular absolution was asked, the absolution given was general, it is valid also for censures which were withheld from mention in good faith, except a censure most specially reserved to the Holy See, but it is not valid for those withheld in bad faith (c. 2249, § 2). This last provision *supposes that the confessor has the power* to absolve from the censures in question. It does not confer that power. Hence, if the censures,

---

[3] Cf. Cappello, *De Censuris,* n. 147.

whether mentioned or withheld in good faith, were reserved and the confessor had not the power *aliunde* to absolve from them, the general absolution would be ineffective as far as those censures are concerned. The usual formula of absolution is general as regards censures; hence, the present canon always applies to those censures which the confessor has power to absolve, except those most specially reserved.

Absolution From Sins Without Absolution From Censures: Formula. In the case of a censure which does not impede the reception of the sacraments, a subject who is properly disposed and has withdrawn from contumacy can be absolved from his sins without being absolved from the censure **(c. 2250, § 1).** The penitent must have desisted from contumacy, to be properly disposed. If this condition is fulfilled there is nothing to prevent his receiving valid absolution from all his sins even though the censure for any reason remain.

But in the case of a censure which impedes the reception of the sacraments, the subject cannot be absolved from his sins unless he has first been absolved from the censure **(c. 2250, § 2).** Let it be carefully noted that, though this canon uses the expression, *"nequit absolvi,"* this provision is not intended to affect the validity of the sacrament. This has already been noted in connection with canon 2260, § 1. Note that canon 2250, § 2 expresses a grave prohibition, not an invalidating clause.[4] The formula of absolution in confession first gives absolution from censures, then from sins. But if for any reason the absolution from the censure is invalid, or is not given at all, nevertheless, provided the penitent is rightly disposed, his sins will always be forgiven, *directly* in the case of sins which are *not reserved,* *indirectly* in the case of sins which are reserved either *ratione sui* or *ratione censurae.*

In the sacramental forum, absolution from censures is contained in the usual formula for absolution from sins as prescribed in ritual books; in the nonsacramental forum, it can be given in any way, but for absolution from excommunication it is proper as a rule to use the formula given in those same books **(c. 2250, § 3).**

Absolution in the Internal or External Forum. If absolution from a censure is given in the external forum, it affects both fora, if it is given only in the internal forum, the person so absolved may, in the absence of scandal, conduct himself as absolved even as regards

---

[4] Cf. Cappello, *De Sacramentis,* I, nn. 81 sq.; V-C, *Epit.,* III, n. 449; A Coronata, III, n. 1755, p. 170.

acts of the external forum; but unless the fact of absolution is proved or at least legitimately presumed in the external forum, the censure can be urged by the superiors of the external forum to whose authority the culprit may be subject, until absolution has been given in the external forum (c. 2251). Since the jurisdiction of a confessor is per se limited to the internal forum, some such provision as this was necessary. This canon delicately secures a certain freedom of external action for the culprit who has been sacramentally absolved, while at the same time safeguarding the authority of superiors in the external forum. When absolution has been given in the internal forum only, adequate proof of that fact has the same effect in the external forum as if the absolution had been given there. As to the manner of proof, the Sacred Penitentiary gave some interesting directions in connection with the Holy Year Jubilee in 1925.[5] Absolution is presumed in the external forum when it becomes publicly known that the culprit has gone to confession and made due satisfaction.[6]

Absolution From Reserved Censure in Danger of Death. Those who, being in danger of death, received from a priest who had no special faculty absolution from a censure *ab homine* or from one most specially reserved to the Holy See, are bound, after they have recovered from the danger, to have recourse, under pain of falling back into the censure, to the one who imposed the censure if it is a censure *ab homine,* to the Sacred Penitentiary or to a Bishop or other person who has the faculty, as provided in canon 2254, § 1, if it is a censure *a iure;* and to abide by their orders (c. 2252).

1. In danger of death (which need not be extreme, but merely solidly probable), all priests have power to absolve from all sins and censures, however reserved (c. 882). Our present canon mentions two cases only in which a recourse is necessary after the person recovers, namely, a censure *ab homine* and one most specially reserved to the Holy See. There is now a *third case* in which such recourse is necessary, namely, when a priest who has attempted marriage and is unable to separate, asks for absolution from the censure of canon 2388, § 1, in danger of death.[7]

2. Recourse is to be made *"ad normam c. 2254, § 1,"* that is, "within a month, at least by letter and through the confessor if this can be done without grave inconvenience."

---

[5] S. Paen., *Monita,* 31 July, 1924, V; *AAS,* 16, p. 337; *Digest,* I, p. 425.
[6] Noldin, *De Censuris,* n. 32.
[7] S. Paen., 18 Apr., 1936; *AAS,* 28, p. 242; *Digest,* II, p. 579.

3. The recourse, if the censure is *a iure,* is "to the Sacred Penitentiary or to a Bishop or other person who has the faculty." This language does not infer that Bishops usually have this faculty.[8]

4. The recourse must be made (in all *three* cases) under pain of falling back into the censure. While this obligation exists, it need not *always* be explicitly urged upon the penitent by the confessor; this should be done only when the confessor feels that it will not unduly disturb the penitent.

5. What if the penitent after recovery makes this recourse but fails to follow the injunctions given? Undoubtedly he is obliged to obey; otherwise the recourse would be meaningless. But does failure to do so revive the censure in the same way as failure to have recourse? Some doubt this because of the position of the words *eorumque mandatis parendi.* Extrinsically only we concede enough probability to this opinion to permit one to consider that the censure does not revive if recourse has been made but the injunctions given are not observed.[9] But the grave obligation to obey remains.

6. Though this canon does not expressly say so, the penitent who recovers from danger of death may, instead of having recourse according to the terms of this canon, go to a confessor who has faculties over the censure, and receive absolution without recourse as provided in canon 2254, § 2.[10]

Absolution in Ordinary Circumstances. Outside danger of death, the following can absolve:

1. From a nonreserved censure, in the sacramental forum, any confessor; outside the sacramental forum, whoever has jurisdiction over the culprit in the external forum;

2. From a censure *ab homine,* he to whom it is reserved according to canon 2245, § 2; and he can give absolution even though the culprit has transferred his domicile or quasi-domicile to another place;

3. From a censure reserved *a iure,* he who established it or to whom it is reserved, and their successors, competent superiors, or delegates. Hence, from a censure reserved to the *Bishop* or to the *Ordinary,* any Ordinary can absolve his subjects, and the local Ordinary can absolve even strangers (*peregrinos*); from a censure reserved to the Holy See, the Holy See or others who have obtained from the Holy See the power, general if the censure is simply reserved, special if it

---

[8] Code Com., 12 Nov., 1922; *AAS,* 14, p. 663; *Digest,* I, p. 846.
[9] Cf. Cappello, *De Censuris,* n. 117.
[10] Cf. Cappello, *De Censuris,* n. 118.

is specially reserved, and finally most special if it is most specially reserved, without prejudice to the provisions of canon 2254 (c. 2253). Combine this canon with canon 2237 to solve practical cases on ordinary absolution from reserved censures.

Absolution From Censures *Latae Sententiae* **in Urgent Cases.** In urgent cases, namely, if censures *latae sententiae* cannot be observed externally without danger of grave scandal or infamy, or if it is hard for the penitent to remain in the state of grave sin for such time as may be necessary in order that the competent superior may provide, then any confessor can, in the sacramental forum, absolve from the same, no matter how they are reserved, imposing, under pain of falling back into the censure, the obligation of having recourse within a month, at least by letter and through the confessor, if it can be done without grave inconvenience, without mentioning the name, to the Sacred Penitentiary or to a Bishop or other superior who has the faculty, and of fulfilling his injunctions (c. 2254, § 1).

Nothing prevents the penitent, even after he has received absolution as above, or even after he has had recourse to the superior, from going to another confessor who has the special faculty needed for his case, and obtaining absolution from him, repeating the confession at least of the crime with the censure; and when he has received absolution he is to receive instructions from the same confessor, without being obliged afterward to observe the other mandates which may come from the superior (c. 2254, § 2).

If in some extraordinary case this recourse is morally impossible, then the confessor himself, except in the case of absolution of the censure mentioned in canon 2367, can give absolution without the obligation above described, but he must prescribe what should be prescribed in such a case, and impose a suitable penance and satisfaction for the censure, so that if the penitent does not perform the penance and make the satisfaction within a suitable time which shall be prescribed by the confessor, he shall fall back into the censure (c. 2254, § 3).

Practical Notes. 1. This power is given to *confessors;* therefore jurisdiction to hear the confession of the person in question is required; and the power is given for the sacramental forum only.

2. The *circumstances* which constitute an urgent case are two, alternatively: "if censures *latae sententiae* cannot be observed externally without danger of grave scandal or infamy, *or* if it is a hardship for the penitent to remain in the state of grave sin for the time which

may be necessary in order that the superior may provide." In the first case, scandal or infamy, there is question evidently of a censure which is occult at least in the place where its external observance would be an occasion of scandal or infamy. In the second case the hardship must be felt by the penitent, with or without preparation by the confessor. To remain in the state of mortal sin even for one day is objectively a tremendous evil. If the penitent does not feel the hardship he must be disposed by exhortation and instruction until he does feel it, and only then can he be absolved, if the superior cannot be reached within one day. In special cases, a few hours might suffice.[11]

3. The object of the absolution is all censures *latae sententiae,* however reserved, saving the exception to be mentioned below (cf. n. 5). This is clear from the text: "tunc quilibet confessarius in foro sacramentali *ab eisdem,* quoquo modo reservatis absolvere potest." The words *ab eisdem* can grammatically refer to nothing else than *censurae latae sententiae.* Sins reserved *ratione sui* are not included: first, because the canon does not mention them; it mentions the "state of sin" as connected with censures; second, the extension of this canon by analogy to reserved sins is entirely unnecessary, since canon 900 expressly removes all reservations of sins whenever special faculties cannot be asked for without grave inconvenience to the penitent.[12] Moreover the clause *sub poena reincidentiae* is simply meaningless as applied to a forgiven *sin.*

4. Censures *latae sententiae* even though most specially reserved to the Holy See are certainly included.[13] The same may most probably be held of those reserved to the Holy Father in person,[14] except the case to be mentioned in n. 5.

5. The censure *latae sententiae* incurred under canon 2388, § 1, though only simply reserved to the Holy See by the Code, yet in the case of a priest who after the crime of attempted marriage is unable to effect a separation, cannot be absolved at all as an urgent case under this canon.[15]

6. The censure *latae sententiae* for false denunciation (specially

---

[11] Cf. Cappello, *De Censuris,* n. 124, 4; Moriarty, *Extraordinary Absolution from Censures,* p. 152.

[12] Cappello, *De Censuris,* n. 125, applies canon 2254 to reserved *sins* as such "*ex analogia iuris.*" But the analogy is here represented by a distinct provision of law, namely, canon 900. When we have given that canon its full effect, the analogy is exhausted.

[13] S. Paen., 21 Apr., 1921; *AAS,* 13, p. 239; *Digest,* I, p. 847.

[14] Cf. Moriarty, *Extraordinary Absolution from Censures,* pp. 178–184.

[15] S. Paen., 4 May, 1937; *AAS,* 29, p. 283; *Digest,* II, p. 580.

reserved to the Holy See by canon 2363) requires special consideration. It can be absolved under this canon only if the conditions named in canon 2363 have been fulfilled: "a qua *nequit ullo in casu absolvi*, nisi falsam denuntiationem formaliter retractaverit, et damna, si qua inde secuti sint, pro viribus reparaverit, imposita insuper gravi ac diuturna poenitentia, firmo praescripto canonis 894." Hence: (*a*) absolution can be given only after actual formal retractation and reparation; mere promise is not sufficient; (*b*) a grave and long penance must be enjoined;[16] (*c*) the sin remains reserved to the Holy See *ratione sui*, but this reservation would cease according to canon 900 if faculties could not be asked without grave inconvenience to the penitent.[17]

7. Are censures *ab homine* within the scope of this canon? A rather troublesome question. If there is question of a censure *latae sententiae*, we answer in the affirmative, because the canon makes no exception of them. However, it is disputed whether there can be such a thing as a censure *latae sententiae* which is *ab homine*. Some authors admit it in the case of a particular precept threatening a censure to be incurred *ipso facto* on violation. Such a censure is certainly *latae sententiae;* we found some reason as well as authority for holding that it is not *ab homine* (cf. c. 2217); but even if it is, it is included under this canon. If there is question of the usual censure *ab homine*, which is *ferendae sententiae* (cf. c. 2217, § 1, 3°) it is very difficult to bring it within the terms of the canon, which speaks only of *latae sententiae* censures. It is this alone which causes us to hesitate, and not at all the fact that such a censure is usually public.[18] There is nothing to prevent a public censure from being absolved in virtue of this canon, for, though the observance of a public censure would not usually cause scandal or infamy, yet the hardship to the penitent of remaining in the state of sin is equally grave for a public as for an occult censure. It is true that the absolution of a public censure in the sacramental forum creates a certain conflict between the internal and external forum, but this is not at all an unheard-of thing, and is satisfactorily provided for in practice by canon 2251. Even Cappello, who in former editions of his work *De Censuris* was very averse to admitting censures *ab homine* to the benefits of this canon 2254, now holds that they may be absolved under certain conditions.[19] And he is speaking evidently of censures

---

[16] As to the meaning of these and other expressions, cf. Cappello, *De Censuris*, n. 101.
[17] Cf. Code Com., 10 Nov., 1925; *AAS*, 17, p. 583; *Digest*, I, p. 415.
[18] Cf. Cappello, *De Censuris*, n. 133.
[19] Cf. Cappello, *De Censuris*, n. 133.

ferendae sententiae. One of the conditions he names, very properly, is that in that case the recourse should be to the person to whom the censure *ab homine* is reserved. These arguments seem to us to dispose of the objection that absolution of such censures should not be allowed because the censures are public. But what of our much more radical difficulty, namely, that the canon speaks only of censures *latae sententiae?* A possible solution seems to be the following. Ordinarily, the *casus urgentior* of canon 2254 will scarcely arise in connection with a *ferendae sententiae ab homine* censure. The circumstance of danger of scandal or infamy will not be present because the censure is *per se* public; the sudden necessity for absolution on the other ground (hardship to the penitent) is unlikely in a case which already supposes a degree of contumacy. For these reasons the canon does not mention censures *ferendae sententiae;* yet in an exceptional case (where the censure, though public, is not known in the particular place, or where the penitent can really be disposed by the confessor to feel the urgent need of absolution and to promise recourse to the superior) canon 2254 can be extended by necessity and analogy (cf. c. 20) to censures *ab homine* which are *ferendae sententiae.* This is substantially the opinion of Cappello, and is admitted in practice by a few others, though admittedly the weight of authority is against any application of canon 2254 to *ferendae sententiae* censures.[20] We think the minority opinion we have outlined is probable both on reasons and authority and therefore safe in practice.

8. Recourse by the confessor. If the penitent is a priest or other well-educated person with a permanent residence, the matter can be handled by mail as follows: the confessor, with the penitent's permission, writes to the Sacred Penitentiary (or other superior) stating the case, *reticito nomine,* and asking for *mandata* and permission to transmit them to the penitent, whose address he will have secured in advance. In due course the confessor (who has given his own true name and address) receives a letter from the Sacred Penitentiary, enclosing the *mandata* in an inner sealed envelope. Without reading them or breaking the seal, he sends these to the penitent.[21]

9. The moral impossibility of recourse is verified where the penitent is illiterate or so circumstanced that the confessor will be unable to

[20] Cf. Moriarty, *Extraordinary Absolution from Censures,* p. 188; Cappello, *De Censuris,* n. 133; A Coronata, *Institutiones Iuris Canonici,* IV, n. 1762, note 7.

[21] The formula for such recourse is given in Arregui, *Theol. Mor.,* n. 617, and also, with those for various other recourses, in Moriarty, *op. cit., Appendix I,* pp. 294-297; V-C, *Epit.,* III, n. 454, p. 228; Cappello, *De Censuris,* n. 131.

communicate with him later, even by mail. Not every case encountered in hearing confessions in a strange place will necessarily be of this type.

10. The penitent may afterward go to a privileged confessor according to paragraph 2, in which case he need neither make the recourse to the superior which was enjoined upon him, nor observe the *mandata* which he will receive from the superior in case he has already made the recourse.[22]

CASES AND QUESTIONS

1. A penitent confesses abortion but says he "did not intend to violate the law of the Church." The confessor judges that there was no contumacy and hence that no censure was incurred (cc. 2241, § 1, 2242, § 2).

2. A Bishop, claiming to act under canon 2222, § 1, inflicts an excommunication by way of precept, without previous warning, upon a priest whose grave misconduct has given great scandal. Is the action valid *in foro interno? In foro externo?* (Cc. 2233, § 2, 2242, § 2).

3. In an entirely private interview a Bishop says to one of his priests: "I forbid you under pain of *ipso facto* suspension to contribute any more articles to that paper." The priest has recourse by letter to the Sacred Congregation of the Council against this action, then he immediately contributes another article to the same paper, and then he consults you. Is he suspended? (Cf. c. 2243, § 2). May he continue to contribute to the paper pending the recourse? May he do so at least when out of the diocese, or after the Bishop's death? (C. 24).

4. X married a non-Catholic, with a dispensation from mixed religion. After the marriage by a priest he went through the ceremony again before a Protestant minister. Is he under one excommunication or two? (Cf. c. 2319 and *Conc. Balt. III,* n. 127; cc. 2244, § 2, 3°, 2247, § 1).

5. Y, living in Louisville, incurs an excommunication *latae sententiae* reserved to the Ordinary by diocesan law there. Later, while visiting in Cincinnati for a week, is he still under the excommunication? (C. 2226, § 4). Can he receive absolution from a simple confessor in Cincinnati? (C. 2247, § 2). What if the same excommunication is reserved by diocesan law also in Cincinnati? (Cf. *Digest,* I, p. 415). In the same case, if the same excommunication exists by distinct diocesan laws in both dioceses, if Y happens to meet his own Louisville pastor in Cincinnati, could he be absolved by him? (Cc. 873, § 1, 881, § 2).

6. A diocesan law establishes a censure of excommunication *ferendae sententiae.* X violates the law and the excommunication is inflicted by sentence. He then goes to another diocese and asks absolution In his con-

---
[22] Cf. V-C, *Epit.,* III, n. 454, p. 227.

fession he insists on the fact that no mention was made of the excommunication being reserved. What should the confessor do and why? (Cc. 2217, § 1, 3°; 2242, § 3; 2245, § 2 and 4; 2247, § 2).

7. X is under excommunication *latae sententiae* reserved to the Ordinary. Goes to confession. Are all his sins "reserved"? Is any one of them? (Cc. 2250, § 2, 2246, § 3).

8. Z, for a notorious crime, has incurred a *latae sententiae* excommunication which is public in the fullest sense, but not reserved. Now penitent, he seeks absolution. C, the simple confessor, asks himself whether he ought to absolve him in the sacramental forum from this public censure (c. 2242, § 3); and if so, whether he should warn him not to approach Communion publicly until he has made public reparation (c. 2251).

9. P, a priest, incurs the excommunication most specially reserved to the Holy See by canon 2367, § 1 (for absolving his accomplice *in peccato turpi*). Thoroughly repentant, he makes a good confession telling the whole thing, with other sins, to a supposedly learned confessor, who assures him that, since the sin with the accomplice was not consummated, the censure was not incurred, and so gives him absolution. After many years, learning that the confessor was mistaken, P is much worried as to the validity of the absolution: (1) of that sin; (2) of that censure; (3) of other grave sins confessed at the same time (cc. 2250, § 2; 2247, § 3; A Coronata, IV, p. 172, n. 1757). What would you tell him?

10. N has just been ordained, has no faculties. While he is visiting in a hospital, a patient asks to speak to him, makes a confession including a censure reserved *Ordinario a iure*. Bewildered, N asks a few questions, decides that the patient is at least probably in danger of death, absolves him from everything, saying nothing about recourse. Later he learns that the patient was not really in danger, though there was probable reason for believing that he was. Doubts about validity of absolution from the censure. (Cc. 2252, 209; Cappello, *De Censuris*, n. 118). What if he later learns that the patient was not even in probable danger but had deliberately deceived him? (*Ibid.*).

11. Father Distractus knowingly and without excuse has kept a book which is forbidden by name by Apostolic letter (c. 2318, § 1); now repentant, he carefully prepares his confession, but through distraction omits in good faith to mention this sin and censure. Realizing the omission later, he takes comfort in the thought that the confessor used the general formula. Since the censure was omitted in good faith, he reasons, it was surely absolved (c. 2249, § 2); and as for the sin, it was absolved *directly,* since it was reserved only *ratione censurae* (c. 2246, § 3). What do you say?

12. X is absolved in danger of death from a censure *ab homine;* after recovery he makes the recourse as enjoined by canon 2252, but neglects to perform the *mandata*. Does he fall back into the censure? Is he simply free?

13. V, a clerical exempt religious, is guilty of abortion, entirely occult. Doubts to which Ordinary the censure is reserved. He argues that both the Provincial and the Bishop are Ordinaries (c. 198, § 1); hence, that either could absolve in an occult case (c. 2237, § 2), or even in a public case (c. 2237, § 1). But then, "quilibet Ordinarius absolvere potest *suos subditos*" (c. 2253, 3°); he wonders whether he is a subject of the Bishop, at least for the purpose of absolution in the sacramental forum. Finally, knowing that the diocesan pagella gives faculties to absolve from censures *a iure* reserved to the Ordinary, he goes to a diocesan priest to confession. (C. 874, § 1; V-C, *Epit.*, III, n. 442, 2, p. 219, ed. 4).

14. A, an exempt clerical religious of simple perpetual vows, has been guilty of apostasy from religion (c. 644, § 1). Is he excommunicated? To whom is the excommunication reserved? (Cf. c. 2385). If he is later dismissed from the order, does the excommunication automatically cease? (Cf. c. 2248, § 1). Then who can absolve from it? Can the major superior do so despite the fact that the culprit is no longer his subject? (C. 201, § 1). Can the Ordinary of the place do so despite the fact that the excommunication was reserved to the major superior? (C. 2237, § 1, 2253, 3).[23]

15. Father X, confessor, says the excommunication of canon 2339 is not reserved. Hence, he feels free to absolve from it in the internal forum even outside confession (cf. c. 2253, 1°); and in confession under any circumstances (cf. cc. 2241, § 1; 2242, § 3).

16. A confessor in a priests' retreat gets a case of *absolutio complicis* (c. 2367); the penitent is deeply conscious of the hardship of remaining in sin, and there is no way to get the faculty quickly. Describe exactly what the confessor should do.

17. Penitent confesses having contracted marriage *coram ministro* (*Conc. Balt. III*, n. 127), both parties being Catholics (cc. 2319, § 1, 1°, 1063, § 1), with very grave public scandal in the community. The confessor wonders: (*a*) whether this provision of the Council of Baltimore is still in effect (c. 6); (*b*) if so, whether he can absolve from it *in casu urgentiori* under canon 2254, § 1, or should refuse absolution in order to avoid scandal and conflict with the external forum (c. 2251).

18. Father Innane, a simple confessor, knows little about reserved censures, and so, acting on the principle *"Ecclesia supplet"* which he remembers distinctly, he absolves indiscriminately from the following censures; (1) an excommunication reserved to the Ordinary by common law; (2) an excommunication reserved most specially to the Holy See; (3) an excommunication *ferendae sententiae* after condemnatory sentence was

---

[23] Our solution is to answer *this last question* in the affirmative; for the Ordinary of the place has both power over the censure (c. 2237) and jurisdiction over the person (c. 2253). In practice, however, the absolution should have been given by the major superior before the dismissal. If, after dismissal, the person is still bound by his vows (cf. c. 669, § 1), we think the major superior also retains jurisdiction over him for the purpose of absolving from this censure.

imposed. All the penitents were in good faith, well disposed, and made full confessions. Are they absolved of all their sins, directly or indirectly? Of all the censures? (Cf. cc. 2247, § 3; 2246, § 3; 2250, § 2).

19. A pastor has stolen parish funds, calumniated the Bishop, caused scandal in other ways. After several warnings have failed to produce any sign of amendment, the Bishop calls him in, and, in the presence of two officials of the Curia who write down the interview, inflicts upon him by way of precept a *suspensio a divinis* (c. 2279, § 2, 2°), stating the causes for such action (cf. cc. 2222, § 1, 2225). The pastor immediately has recourse to the Sacred Congregation of the Council by letter, attacking the penalty as contrary to law because imposed without trial. Having made this recourse, he continues to say Mass. What do you say of the *validity* of the Bishop's action? (Cf. c. 1933, § 4). Does the recourse suspend the penalty? (Cf. c. 2243, § 1).

20. Can a *latae sententiae* censure of suspension be absolved in virtue of canon 2254 on the ground that the penitent feels the hardship of remaining in the state of sin? (Cf. A Coronata, IV, n. 1762, p. 179; Moriarty, *Extraordinary Absolution from Censures,* p. 154).

Readings:

Dargin, *Reserved Cases According to the Code of Canon Law,* Cath. U., 1924; Moriarty, *The Extraordinary Absolution from Censures,* Cath. U., 1938; *Apollinaris* (1933), p. 341 (Roberti, *an censura latae sententiae per praeceptum constituta sit reservata*); *Irish Ecclesiastical Record,* Vol. 59, p. 273 (Fallon, on reservation of censure *latae sententiae* attached to particular precept).

CHAPTER XXII

EXCOMMUNICATION, INTERDICT, SUSPENSION: SUSPENSIO EX INFORMATA CONSCIENTIA

Section 1. Excommunication (cc. 2255-2267)

PRELIMINARY SURVEY

Kinds of Censures. Censures are: (1) excommunication; (2) interdict; (3) suspension **(c. 2255, § 1)**. Excommunication can affect only physical persons, and therefore if it is ever pronounced against a moral body, it is understood to affect the individuals who concurred in the crime; interdict and suspension can affect also the community as a moral person; excommunication and interdict can affect also lay persons, suspension, clerics only; interdict can affect also a place; excommunication is always a censure; interdict and suspension can be either censures or vindictive penalties, but in doubt they are presumed to be censures **(c. 2255, § 2)**.

Interdict and suspension are vindictive penalties when imposed for a determined time, e.g., six months, or *in perpetuum*, or *ad beneplacitum nostrum* (c. 2298, 2°); if no time limit is given, they are censures, for a censure must be absolved when contumacy ceases, regardless of time limits (c. 2248, § 2).

Divine Services: Legitimate Acts. In the canons which follow:

(1) the term *divine services* means functions of the power of order which by institution of Christ or of the Church pertain to divine worship and can be done only by clerics; (2) the term *legitimate ecclesiastical acts* means: to administer ecclesiastical property; to serve as judge, auditor, or referee (cf. cc. 1582, 1584), defender of the bond, promoter of justice (cf. c. 1586), promoter of the faith (i.e., in beatification proceedings, c. 2010), notary, chancellor, courier, bailiff, advocate or procurator in ecclesiastical trials; to act as godparents in baptism or confirmation; to vote in ecclesiastical elections; to exercise the right of patronage (c. 2256).

Excommunication. Excommunication is a censure by which one is excluded from the communion of the faithful, with the consequences which are enumerated in the following canons, and which cannot be separated (c. 2257, § 1). It is also called *anathema,* especially if it is inflicted with the solemnities described in the Roman Pontifical (c. 2257, § 2).

Vitandus and *Toleratus.* Some excommunicated persons are *vitandi,* others *tolerati* (c. 2258, § 1). No one is *vitandus* unless he has been excommunicated by name by the Holy See, and the excommunication has been publicly announced, and it is expressly stated in the decree or sentence that he is to be avoided, without prejudice to canon 2343, § 1, 1° (c. 2258, § 2). The canon cited declares anyone who lays violent hands on the Supreme Pontiff *ipso facto vitandus.*

Consequences: Privation of Right to Assist at Divine Services. Every excommunicated person *lacks the right* to assist at divine services, but not at the preaching of the word of God (c. 2259, § 1). If a *toleratus* assists passively, he need not be ejected; if a *vitandus* so assists, he must be ejected, or if that is impossible the services must be stopped if that can be done without grave inconvenience. From active assistance, which implies some participation in celebrating the divine services, not only a *vitandus* but any excommunicated person against whom there has been a declaratory or condemnatory sentence, or whose excommunication is otherwise notorious, should be kept away (c. 2259, § 2). We have italicized the expression *lacks the right,* because it seems worth while to note that the Code does *not* say such a person is *forbidden* to assist.[1] Many overlook this distinction, which is, however, fundamental in law. Some, with probable reason, hold that the two are equivalent here because a prohibition did exist in the old law.

---

[1] Cf. Ayrinhac, *Penal Legislation,* n. 115.

Reception of Sacraments, Sacramentals, Ecclesiastical Burial. Neither may an excommunicated person receive the sacraments, and after a declaratory or condemnatory sentence, not even sacramentals (c. 2260, § 1). As regards ecclesiastical burial, the provisions of canon 1240, § 1, 2° are to be observed (c. 2260, § 2). The canon cited merely states that persons under excommunication (or interdict) are deprived of ecclesiastical burial *after a declaratory or condemnatory sentence.*

Administration of Sacraments. An excommunicated person is forbidden licitly to consecrate or administer sacraments and sacramentals, except as follows (c. 2261, § 1). Except as provided in § 3, the faithful can for any just cause ask for sacraments or sacramentals of one who is excommunicated, especially if there is no one else to give them; and in such cases the excommunicated person so asked may administer them, and is not obliged to ask the reason for the request (c. 2261, § 2). But from an excommunicated *vitandus* or one against whom there is a declaratory or condemnatory sentence, the faithful may only in danger of death ask for sacramental absolution according to canons 882, 2252, and also for other sacraments and sacramentals in case there is no one else to administer them (c. 2261, § 3).

Summary. Let us put this matter into summary form.

1. A *toleratus* before sentence may administer any sacrament or sacramental on request.

2. A *toleratus* after sentence, or a *vitandus,* may only in danger of death administer: (*a*) sacramental absolution, even if another priest be present; (*b*) other sacraments or sacramentals, if there is no one else to administer them.

Indulgences, Suffrages, Public Prayers. An excommunicated person does not share in the indulgences, suffrages, public prayers of the Church (c. 2262, § 1). However, (1) the faithful are not forbidden to pray for him privately; (2) nor are priests forbidden to apply Masses for him privately, provided that scandal be avoided; but if he is a *vitandus,* Mass can be offered thus only for his conversion (c. 2262, § 2).

Legitimate Acts, Etc. An excommunicated person is excluded from legitimate ecclesiastical acts in the measure which is defined in the parts of the Code which deal respectively with various such acts; he cannot be a plaintiff in an ecclesiastical cause except as provided in canon 1654 (i.e., in general he is excluded, but even a *vitandus* or *toleratus* after sentence can be represented by proxy in proceedings aimed at avoiding spiritual harm, and can act *per se* in impugning the excommunication itself); he is forbidden to hold ecclesiastical offices or positions and to enjoy privileges which were granted him by the Church before his excommunication (c. 2263). He may be a defendant, and if summoned is bound to appear.[2]

Acts of Jurisdiction Illicit or Invalid. An act of jurisdiction of the external or internal forum placed by an excommunicated person is illicit; and if there has been a condemnatory or declaratory sentence, also invalid, except as provided in canon 2261, § 3 (i.e., it is valid and licit even after sentence in case the faithful in danger of death ask for absolution or, if no other minister is available, for other sacraments or sacramentals); otherwise (i.e., if there has been no sentence) the act is valid, and is even licit if it is asked for by the faithful according to canon 2261, § 2 (for any just cause) (c. 2264).

Summary. Acts of jurisdiction placed by:

1. A *toleratus* before sentence, are always valid, but are illicit unless asked for by the faithful;

2. A *toleratus* after sentence, or a *vitandus,* are invalid, except sacramental absolution asked for in danger of death.

Active and Passive Voice: Orders. Every excommunicated person: (1) is by law forbidden to elect, present, or nominate; (2) cannot obtain ecclesiastical dignities, offices, benefices, pensions, or any other position in the Church; (3) cannot be promoted to orders (c. 2265, § 1). But an act placed in violation of § 1, 1° or 2° is not void unless it was placed by a *vitandus* or by another excommunicated person after a declaratory or condemnatory sentence; if such a sentence has been passed, an excommunicated person is moreover incapable of validly obtaining any pontifical favor, unless in the papal rescript mention is made of the excommunication (c. 2265, § 2).

Fruits of the Benefice, Office, Etc., or Benefice or Office Itself. After a condemnatory or declaratory sentence, an excommunicated person is deprived of the fruits of a dignity, office, benefice, pension, or position which he may have in the Church; and a *vitandus* is deprived of the dignity, office, benefice, pension, or position itself (c. 2266).

Communication With *Vitandus* Forbidden. The faithful must avoid communication in profane matters with an excommunicated *vitandus,* except in the case of a husband or wife, parents, children, servants, subjects, and in general unless there is some reasonable excusing cause (c. 2267).

---

[2] Cf. Ayrinhac, *Penal Legislation*, n. 119.

Section 2. Interdict (cc. 2268-2277)

PRELIMINARY SURVEY

Definition and Classification (c. 2268)
Power to Impose: Effect (c. 2269)
Local Interdicts (cc. 2270–2273)
Personal Interdicts (cc. 2274, 2275)
Innocent Persons in a Local or Collective Interdict
  (c. 2276)
Interdict From Entry Into the Church (c. 2277)

Interdict: Nature and General Classifications. An interdict is a censure by which the faithful, while remaining in communion with the Church, are forbidden the use of certain sacred things which are enumerated in the canons which follow (c. 2268, § 1). The prohibition is imposed either directly by a *personal* interdict, when the use of those things is forbidden to the persons themselves, or indirectly by a *local* interdict, when their dispensation or reception is forbidden in certain places (c. 2268, § 2). The things forbidden by interdict are liturgical services, some of the sacraments, and Christian burial, but never preaching. Since interdict is usually a medicinal penalty, it is called a censure, but at times it may be a vindictive penalty, as when it is imposed for a definite time.[3]

Power to Impose: Effect. A general interdict, whether local, upon the territory of the diocese or country, or personal, upon the people thereof, can be imposed only by the Holy See or by its authority; but a general interdict upon a parish or the people of a parish, and particular interdict, whether local or personal, can be imposed also by a Bishop (c. 2269 § 1). A personal interdict follows the person everywhere; a local one is not effective outside the place interdicted, but in that place all persons, even though strangers or exempt, in the absence of a special privilege, must observe it (c. 2269, § 2).

Local Interdict. A local interdict, whether general or particular, does not forbid the administration of the sacraments and sacramentals to the dying, *servatis servandis,* but it forbids in that place any divine service or sacred rite, with the exceptions mentioned in § 2 of this canon and in canons 2271, 2272 (c. 2270, § 1). On Christmas, Easter, Pentecost, the Feasts of Corpus Christi and of the Assumption, a local

---

[3] A modern example of a personal interdict is reported in *La Documentation Catholique,* Vol. 35, p. 551.

interdict is suspended, and only the conferring of orders and the solemn nuptial blessing are forbidden (c. 2270, § 2).

General Local Interdict. If an interdict is local and general and the decree does not expressly provide otherwise: (1) clerics, provided they are not themselves under a personal interdict, are permitted to perform all divine services and sacred rites in any church or oratory, privately, behind closed doors, in a low voice, and without ringing of bells; (2) but in the cathedral, in parish churches, and in any church which is the only one in the town, and in these exclusively, it is permitted to celebrate one Mass, to keep the Blessed Sacrament, to administer baptism, the Holy Eucharist, penance, to assist at marriages without giving the nuptial blessing, to hold funerals but without any solemnity, to bless baptismal water and the holy oils, and to preach the word of God. But in these sacred functions singing and external display, the ringing of bells, and playing the organ or other musical instruments are forbidden; Holy Viaticum is to be brought to the sick privately (c. 2271).

Particular Local Interdict. In a local particular interdict, if an altar or chapel of some church is interdicted, no sacred service or rite is to be celebrated at that altar or in that chapel (c. 2272, § 1). If a cemetery is interdicted, the bodies of the faithful may indeed be buried there, but without any ecclesiastical rites (c. 2272, § 2). If the interdict is upon a certain church or oratory: (1) if it is a capitular church, and the Chapter is not interdicted, the provision of canon 2271, 1° is applicable (cf. preceding paragraph above), unless the decree prescribes that the conventual Mass may be celebrated and the canonical hours be recited in another church or oratory; (2) if it is a parish church, the provision of canon 2271, 2° is to be observed, unless the decree substitutes another church for it during the interdict (c. 2272, § 3).

Places Affected. If a city is interdicted, its suburbs are equally so, not excepting exempt places and the cathedral itself; if a church is interdicted, the interdict includes chapels which are connected with it, but not the cemetery; if a chapel is interdicted, the whole church is not affected, and when a cemetery is interdicted, the church adjacent to it is not affected, but all oratories erected in the cemetery itself are (c. 2273).

Personal Interdicts Upon a Collective Body. If a community or college has committed a crime, an interdict can be imposed either on the individuals who are guilty or on the community as such, or on both the guilty individuals and the community (c. 2274, § 1). In the first case, canon 2275 is observed (i.e., it is a personal interdict) (c. 2274, § 2). In the second case, the community or college cannot exercise any spiritual right which belongs to it (c. 2274, § 3). In the third case, the effects are cumulative (c. 2274, § 4).

Personal Interdict. Those who are under a personal interdict: (1) may not celebrate divine services nor assist at any, except at the preaching of the word of God; if they assist passively it is not necessary to eject them; but interdicted persons after a condemnatory or declaratory sentence, and those whose interdiction is otherwise notorious must be kept away from active assistance which involves any active participation in celebrating divine services; (2) are forbidden to administer or receive the sacraments and sacramentals, as provided in canons 2260, § 1 and 2261 (that is, they are forbidden to *receive* the sacraments, and after sentence also the sacramentals; they are permitted before sentence to *administer* both sacraments and sacramentals on request; but after sentence, only in danger of death, and, as to everything except sacramental absolution, only if there is no one else to administer them); (3) are bound by canon 2265 (which concerns ecclesiastical offices, etc., and promotion to orders); (4) are deprived of ecclesiastical burial according to canon 1240, § 1 (that is, only after sentence) (c. 2275).

Innocent Persons Under Interdict. One who is under a local interdict or an interdict imposed upon a community or college, without having been responsible for it, may, if he is not forbidden by any other censure and if he is properly disposed, receive the sacraments according to the foregoing canons without absolution from the interdict and without making any other satisfaction (c. 2276).

Interdict From Entry Into the Church. Interdict from entry into the church includes the prohibition to celebrate divine services in the church, or to assist at them, or to receive ecclesiastical burial; but if the person interdicted assists he need not be ejected, and if he is buried his body need not be removed (c. 2277).

Section 3. Suspension (cc. 2278-2285; 2186-2194)

PRELIMINARY SURVEY

Suspension Defined: General: From Office or Benefice
  (c. 2278)
Suspension From Office: Various Particular Suspensions
  (c. 2279)
Suspension From Benefice (c. 2280)
Suspension by Bishop: What Offices or Benefices Affected
  (c. 2281)
Suspension *Latae Sententiae* by Common Law: What Offices,
  Etc., Affected (c. 2282)
Additional Disabilities: Invalidity of Acts (c. 2283)
Sacraments, Sacramentals, Acts of Jurisdiction (c. 2284)
Suspension as Affecting Collective Body and Component
  Members (c. 2285)
General Summary of Suspension *Ex Informata Conscientia*
  (c. 2186–2194)

Suspension Defined: General: From Office or Benefice. Suspension is a censure by which a cleric is excluded from office or from benefice or from both (c. 2278, § 1). The effects of suspension also (that is, like those of interdict, unlike those of excommunication) can be separated; but, unless the contrary appear, *general* suspension includes all the consequences mentioned in the canons of this article (that is, canons 2278–2285); whereas suspension *from office* or *from benefice* includes only the effects respectively proper to each kind (c. 2278, § 2).

Suspension is applicable only to clerics (c. 2255, § 2). The special powers of clerics are those of *order* and *jurisdiction*. Acts of these powers are usually connected with an office or benefice, although acts of order are not necessarily so; yet, as we shall see (cf. c. 2279) acts of order also are impeded by suspension from office.

Suspension is usually a censure, but may be instead a vindictive penalty (when inflicted for a definite time independently of withdrawal from contumacy, as in canon 2298, 2°).

Suspension From Office. Suspension *from office* simply, without any added qualifications, forbids all acts of order and of jurisdiction, and also of mere administration, pertaining to the office, except the administration of the property of one's own benefice (c. 2279, § 1).

Various Particular Suspensions. Suspension:

1. *A iurisdictione* in general, forbids every act of jurisdiction for both fora, whether ordinary or delegated;

2. *A divinis,* forbids every act of the power of order which one receives either from sacred ordination or by privilege;

3. *Ab ordinibus,* (forbids) every act of the power of order received through ordination;

4. *A sacris ordinibus,* every act of the power of order received through ordination to sacred orders;

5. *A certo et definito ordine exercendo,* every act of the designated order, but the cleric so suspended is moreover forbidden to confer that order, to receive any higher order, and to exercise it should it have been received after the suspension;

6. *A certo et definito ordine conferendo,* forbids conferring that order, but not a lower or higher one;

7. *A certo et definito ministerio,* for example, from the ministry of hearing confessions, *vel officio,* for example, from a definite office with the care of souls, forbids every act of that particular ministry or office;

8. *Ab ordine pontificali,* every act of the power of episcopal order;

9. *A pontificalibus,* the exercise of pontifical acts as defined in canon 337, § 2, namely, sacred functions which according to liturgical books require the pontifical insignia, i.e., the crozier and miter (c. 2279, § 2).

Suspension From Benefice. Suspension *from benefice* deprives one of the fruits of the benefice, except the right to live in the house belonging to it, but not of the right to administer the property of the benefice, unless the decree or sentence of suspension expressly takes this power away from the suspended cleric and gives it to another (c. 2280, § 1). A beneficiary who, in spite of the suspension, appropriates the revenues of the benefice, is bound to restore them and can be forced to do so even by canonical sanctions if necessary (c. 2280, § 2).

What Offices or Benefices Are Affected. A *general* suspension or a suspension *from office,* or *from benefice,* affects all offices or benefices which the cleric has in the diocese of the superior who decrees the suspension, unless the contrary appear (c. 2281).

When Suspension Is by Common Law and *Latae Sententiae.* A local Ordinary cannot suspend a cleric from a particular office or benefice which he holds in another diocese; but a suspension *latae sententiae* established by the common law affects all offices or benefices in any diocese (c. 2282).

Effects of Suspension: Validity of Acts. What is provided by canon 2265 regarding excommunication applies also to suspension (c. 2283). That is to say:

1. Every suspended person: (*a*) is forbidden by law to elect, present,

or nominate; (*b*) cannot obtain ecclesiastical dignities, offices, benefices, or pensions, or any other position in the Church; (*c*) cannot be promoted to orders.

2. But an act placed in violation of § 1, (*a*) and (*b*) is not void unless it was placed by a suspended person after a declaratory or condemnatory sentence; if such a sentence has been passed, a suspended person is moreover incapable of validly obtaining any pontifical favor, unless in the papal rescript mention is made of the suspension.

Sacraments and Sacramentals: Acts of Jurisdiction. If a censure of suspension has been incurred which forbids the administration of sacraments and sacramentals, the provision of canon 2261 is to be observed (cf. p. 833); if one which forbids acts of jurisdiction in the external or internal forum, the act, e.g., sacramental absolution, is invalid if there has been a condemnatory or declaratory sentence, or if the superior expressly declares that he revokes the power of juris- diction itself; otherwise it is only illicit, and not even that if it was asked for by the faithful in accordance with canon 2261, § 2 (**c. 2284**).

Suspension Against a Collective Body. If a community or college of clerics has committed a crime, suspension can be imposed either on the individual guilty persons, or on the community as such, or on both the guilty persons and the community (**c. 2285, § 1**). In the first case, the canons of this article (i.e., cc. 2278-2285) apply (**c. 2285, § 2**). In the second case, the community is forbidden to exercise the spiritual rights which belong to it as a community (**c. 2285, § 3**). In the third case, the effects are cumulative (**c. 2285, § 4**). Spiritual rights are, for example, the right to vote as a body, to exercise the care of souls, the right to be consulted on appointments to benefices, rights of precedence, etc.

Appendix: A Summary of Suspension *Ex Informata Conscientia* (cc. 2186-2194)

Nature and History. This kind of suspension is a real penal suspension, subject to all the rules which we have just reviewed; it is merely distinctive in its procedure, and is governed moreover by these special canons 2186-2194, which are in the procedural part of the Code.

This special procedure dates remotely from the Council of Trent,[4] though it was there applied to a slightly different purpose. It is now designed to enable ecclesiastical superiors to inflict suspension extra- judicially, i.e., without the usual process of penal law, especially in

---

[4] *Sess.* XIV, c. 1, *de ref.*

cases of occult crimes where a judicial trial is impossible. A similar procedure had been instituted by Pope Lucius III[5] to enable superiors of regulars to refuse higher orders to such of their subjects as were guilty of occult crimes. An Instruction of the Sacred Congregation of Propaganda, of 20 Oct., 1884,[6] outlined the procedure and applied it to the suspension of clerics in mission countries. This procedure is now incorporated into the general law as one of several special procedures for special cases.[7]

Justification. At first sight it seems to be contrary to natural justice to deprive a cleric of a vested right and inflict a grave penalty upon him without trial. The only answer is to admit that this is an extraordinary remedy, to be used with extreme restraint, to be safeguarded by genuine precautions, but yet to hold that it is not contrary to justice when its use is required for the public welfare of the Church. The common good of the supernatural society established by Christ takes precedence of any purely private right, vested though it be. This remedy may be the only means in certain cases to deal with an astute occult criminal who is doing untold harm to the Church. It is safeguarded by being entrusted to Bishops under strict regulations, and with right of recourse to the Holy See. It is a fact that the S. C. of the Council, in its review of such cases, has frequently set aside suspensions thus decreed by Bishops, and has held them to reinstate the cleric in office, property, and reputation. The remedy can be and has been abused, but it is not necessarily against justice.[8]

Outline of Procedure. 1. Suspension *ex informata conscientia* is an *extraordinary remedy,* not to be used where the Ordinary can resort to the usual procedures of penal law without grave inconvenience. Its *scope is limited;* the Ordinary can impose in this way only suspension from office, total or particular (cf. c. 2186).

2. Even *warnings are not required;* the whole thing is done by simple decree, in accordance with these special rules (cf. c. 2187). However, *if the suspension is a censure,* it *cannot be inflicted* even in this way *without previous warning,* because of the general rule laid down in canon 2233, § 2. Hence, if it is imposed without warning, it must be treated as a vindictive penalty.[9]

---

[5] C. 5, X, I, 11.
[6] Gasparri-Serédi, *Fontes,* n. 4907, Vol. VII, p. 509.
[7] Cf. Murphy, *Suspension ex Informata Conscientia;* Cath. U. Canon Law Studies, n. 76 (1932).
[8] Cf. V-C, *Epit.,* III, n. 373; A Coronata, III, n. 1627.
[9] Cf. A Coronata, III, n. 1630, p. 560, notes 5–7.

3. The decree should be *in writing*, dated, should state that it is *ex informata conscientia* (though reasons are not given), and should state the time for which it is to last (it may not be inflicted *in perpetuum*) if it is inflicted as a vindictive penalty. It may also be inflicted as a censure, but then the culprit must be told the reason. If the suspension is partial, the prohibited acts must be clearly specified (cf. c. 2188).

4. *If another is put in the office* a salary is provided for him out of the revenues of the benefice. The suspended cleric can, in a recourse to higher authority, impugn the justice of this allowance, which is called a pension (cf. c. 2189).

5. The Ordinary who inflicts it *must have proof amounting to certainty* that the cleric committed a crime grave enough to merit it (cf. c. 2190).

6. The *cause is usually an occult crime* in the sense of canon 2197, 4°; it can never be a notorious crime; it may be a public crime only if one of the following cases is verified: (*a*) if solid and trustworthy witnesses exist but cannot be induced to testify in open court, nor is any other proof available for such a trial; (*b*) if the cleric is using intimidation or other means to prevent a fair trial; (*c*) if the civil law or grave danger of scandal prevent a trial (cf. c. 2191).

7. Suspension *ex informata conscientia* is valid if of several crimes *one only is occult* (cf. c. 2192).

8. It is left to the discretion of the Ordinary whether to *inform the culprit of the reason* for his suspension or not (unless it is a censure, in which case the reason must be made known to him, c. 2188, 2°); but he should use pastoral charity, so that if he tells him the reason, the penalty, accompanied by paternal admonitions, may serve not only for punishment but also for amendment (cf. c. 2193).

9. If the cleric takes a recourse (which is his right), the Ordinary *must send to the Holy See the proofs* which he has gathered, which prove that the cleric really committed a crime which can be punished by this extraordinary penalty (cf. c. 2194). The recourse will be *in devolutivo* only, if the suspension is a censure (cf. c. 2243, § 2 by way of analogy); if it is a vindictive penalty canon 2287 would seem to give the recourse a suspensive effect, though several authors may be cited for the contrary view.[10]

---

[10] A Coronata, III, n. 1636, p. 567, notes 1 and 2.

CASES AND QUESTIONS

1. What is the difference between a censure and a vindictive penalty? (Cf. c. 2216). Can an excommunication be either medicinal or vindictive? Is this also true of interdict and suspension? How can one tell whether these latter are censures or vindictive penalties? (Cf. cc. 2255, § 2, 2248, § 2). What practical difference does it make (Cf. cc. 2236, § 1, 2254, 2290).

2. Can you find divergent authorities as to whether an excommunicated person is excused from attendance at Mass on Sunday? (Cf. c. 2259; Lehmkuhl, *Theol. Mor.,* II, 55, nn. 890, 891; Cappello, *De Censuris,* n. 149; Ayrinhac, *Penal Legislation,* n. 115). Which opinion do you favor?

3. XY, a pastor, has incurred a *latae sententiae* excommunication from which he is not yet absolved. On Saturday afternoon he goes to the confessional, knowing that the usual crowd of penitents will be on hand, hears many confessions. Did he sin in doing this? (Cf. c. 2261, § 2; Cappello, *De Censuris,* n. 148).

4. Q, organist in St. Columban's church, incurs an excommunication *latae sententiae* for an occult crime; may he continue as organist and draw his salary? (Cc. 145, § 1, 2266). Later the crime becomes known and a declaratory sentence is pronounced; what do you say now? Finally upon commission of another graver crime, he becomes a *vitandus.* What now?

5. PQ, a priest with diocesan faculties, is under sentence of excommunication, but has appealed to a higher court. No one outside the Curia knows anything about it. Pending the appeal he hears confessions as usual in the church where he is a regular assistant pastor. Is this licit? Are the absolutions valid? (Cc. 2243, § 1, 2264, 209; V-C, *Epit.* III, n. 468, 6°).

6. Bradford, a Catholic, obtains a civil divorce from his lawful wife, and while she is still living, marries another woman civilly, 1928. Is the excommunication of *Conc. Balt. III,* n. 124 still in effect? (C. 6). Does it apply to this case?

7. A priest has been excommunicated by name by the Holy See and the decree is published in the *Acta Apostolicae Sedis.* Is he a *vitandus?* (C. 2258, § 2).

8. X, who was under excommunication *latae sententiae* for abortion, died without the sacraments. May he have ecclesiastical burial? (C. 2260, § 2).

9. Seminarian in discussion group: "If excommunication does not deprive one of grace, it seems to me to be of little effect on the soul; it is a purely external bond." What would you say? (Cc. 2260, 2257, 2262).

10. Father Severus, superior of a clerical nonexempt congregation, to Father Lassus, a priest of the same house, who is notoriously negligent in attendance at exercises: "If you are absent from choir this evening you will be *ipso facto* suspended *a divinis,* and the suspension will be reserved to me." Father Lassus is absent; is he suspended? (Cc. 2220, 501).

11. Is suspension a censure or a vindictive penalty? How would you

classify it in cases where it is inflicted for a definite time, or without specification of time and without warning? (Cc. 2233, § 2, 2248, § 2).

12. Does the infliction of a suspension always suppose a grave sin committed by the cleric? (C. 2218, § 2).

13. Is the remission of a suspension an act of jurisdiction? Voluntary or judicial? (Cc. 201, 2236, § 1). If it is a censure, must the person be present to receive the absolution? (C. 2239, § 1). Should absolution be given in the internal or external forum?

14. What form of absolution is used in absolving from a suspension? (C. 2250, § 3).

15. A pastor is suspended *a beneficio,* but nevertheless continues to take his salary. Is this all right? Must he make restitution? To whom? Is he excused from this if he is really poor? (C. 2280; A Coronata, IV, n. 1813, pp. 241, 242).

16. A priest has incurred a censure *latae sententiae* of suspension *a divinis* reserved to the Holy See under canon 2372; he feels that to abstain from saying Mass on a certain day would endanger his reputation. Is he excused from the censure by canon 2232, § 1? (Is this an occult case?)

17. A priest of a nonexempt congregation has been dismissed, after perpetual vows, for minor crimes (c. 671, 1°). Is he under censure? If the case is occult and the observance of the censure would endanger his reputation, may he disregard it? (C. 2232, § 1). Can he be absolved from it in an urgent case under canon 2254? Under canon 2290? If he is already excused from its observance by canon 2232, what advantage would he gain by receiving absolution?

18. A religious man in confession states: "My superior has suspended me." What is the first question to ask? (Cf. cc. 501, 2220, § 1).

19. The Provincial Superior of a clerical exempt institute suspends *a iurisdictione* one of his subjects who has been giving scandal after repeated warnings, and at the same time tells him that he withdraws all faculties which he has given him and that he is instructing the local superior to do the same. Later the suspended father, at the request of a pastor friend, hears confessions at the parish church, relying on the diocesan faculties which he obtained from the Bishop. Are the confessions valid? (C. 2284). Gravely illicit? (C. 2279, § 2, 1°).

20. A priest who is under suspension *a divinis* says Mass. Is this a sin? (C. 2279, § 2, 2°). Are there any penal consequences? (C. 985, 7°). Would this irregularity be incurred if the priest were excused under canon 2232, § 1? (C. 986).

21. Father X has been suspended *ab ordine subdiaconatus.* May he read the Epistle when saying low Mass privately? The reading of the Epistle is one of the functions of the subdeacon (c. 2279, § 2, 5°).

22. Father B, through malicious gossip, is rather widely suspected of giving scandal but is in fact innocent. His Bishop, a kindly man, realizes

that the loss of reputation is entirely undeserved, but says: "You are suspended until your reputation is restored; I can do nothing by way of transfer." Is this a case of *infamia facti?* (C. 2293). Is the suspension valid? (C. 2218, § 2).

23. Bishop places a recalcitrant priest under a personal interdict, and the matter becomes notorious everywhere. Priest leaves diocese. Can he say Mass? (Cc. 2269, § 2, 2275). Must he at least attend Mass on Sunday? (C. 2275). If he came to you to confession (simple confessor) what would you do? May you absolve him from his sins without absolving from the interdict? (C. 2275). Can you absolve from the interdict? (C. 2254). Who can? (Cf. 2236, § 1; Cappello, *De Censuris,* n. 478; A Coronata, IV, n. 1798).

24. Are there any interdicts *latae sententiae* in the Code? (Cc. 2332, 2339, 2338, § 3). Are they reserved? (*Ibid.*). Can an interdict be a censure *ab homine?* (C. 2217).

25. Bishop, acting *ex informata conscientia,* suspends one of his priests for six months without previous warning. He has in his secret archives sworn statements from three good witnesses which prove the priest guilty of a grave occult crime. The priest takes a recourse against the suspension, to the S. C. of the Council. Was this suspension validly imposed? (Cc. 2187, 2233, § 2). Is the priest suspended pending the recourse? (C. 2287; A Coronata, III, n. 1636). Would you hazard a conjecture as to the result of the recourse?

Readings:

Hyland, *Excommunication, Its Nature, Historical Development, and Effects,* Cath. U., 1928; *Australasian Catholic Record* (1935), p. 342 (Nevin, on suspension *ex informata conscientia*).

CHAPTER XXIII

VINDICTIVE PENALTIES: PENAL REMEDIES: PENANCES

Section 1. Vindictive Penalties (cc. 2286-2305)

PRELIMINARY SURVEY

General Provisions. *Vindictive penalties* are those which aim directly at the expiation of crime, so that their remission does not depend on the cessation of contumacy on the part of the culprit (c. 2286).

There is a right of *appeal or recourse in suspensivo* from the infliction of a vindictive penalty, unless the law expressly states the contrary (c. 2287). An appeal pertains to judicial procedure, a recourse is taken from an administrative decree.

Upon a first offense, except in the case of certain very grave penalties (degradation, deposition, privation of office or benefice), and unless punishment is necessary to repair scandal, it is left within the discretion of the judge to suspend the execution of the condemnatory sentence; but if the culprit commits another crime within three years, both are to be punished together (cf. c. 2288).

A vindictive penalty *ceases by expiation or dispensation* granted by the legitimate authority according to canon 2236 (cf. c. 2289).

Power of Confessor to Dispense in Urgent Cases. In urgent occult cases, if by observing a vindictive penalty *latae sententiae* the culprit would betray himself with loss of reputation and scandal, any confessor can, in the sacramental forum, suspend the obligation of observing it, imposing the burden of having recourse at least within a month by letter and through the confessor if this can be done without grave inconvenience, without mentioning names, to the Sacred Penitentiary or to a Bishop who has the faculties, and abiding by the mandates received from them (c. 2290, § 1). And if in an extraordinary case this recourse is impossible, the confessor himself can grant the dispensation on the same terms as are prescribed for absolution from censures in canon 2254, § 3 (c. 2290, § 2).

Practical Notes. Though this canon 2290 is analogous to canon 2254, it will be useful to note some important similarities and contrasts:

1. Both canons deal with urgent cases, but *each defines an urgent case in different terms:* in canon 2290 the only urgent case is one of necessity arising from danger of infamy or scandal; the hardship on the part of the penitent at remaining in the state of sin cannot be felt here, because the vindictive penalty never prevents him from being absolved from his sins if he is properly disposed.

2. Accordingly canon 2290 is *limited to occult cases,* since only in these can there be danger of infamy or scandal from observing the penalty; canon 2254 has no such limitation, implicit or explicit.

3. Both canons grant the power *to confessors and for the sacramental forum only:* both provide for a recourse, and in the same way, under pain of falling back into the penalty for failure to have recourse, or failure to fulfill the mandates.[1]

4. Another notable difference is that canon 2254 provides for *absolu-*

---

[1] The doubt, which we conceded on extrinsic grounds only, as to whether the culprit falls back into the censure for failure to observe the *mandata,* is suggested only in connection with canon 2252, in recourses after recovering from danger of death. It is not suggested in connection with either canon 2254 or canon 2290.

tion from censures, whereas canon 2290 provides, *not for dispensation* from the vindictive penalties, but, except where recourse is impossible, *only for suspension* of their observance. Since canon 2232 already provides that a culprit before sentence is excused from observing either a censure or a vindictive penalty with danger of infamy, one may ask what is gained by obtaining the suspension of a vindictive penalty under canon 2290, § 1. The answer is that in this latter case the culprit is entirely free from observing the penalty until the reply from the superior arrives; whereas in the former case he is free only as long as the observance would jeopardize his reputation.[2]

5. Though it is clear that irregularity even *ex delicto* is not strictly a vindictive penalty, some authors have extended the provisions of canon 2290 to the dispensation of such an irregularity (e.g., that of canon 985, 4°, incurred by abortion).[3] We admit that we cannot see any intrinsic probability in their opinion, especially as canon 990, § 2 exactly defines the power of confessors to dispense from irregularities and explicitly excludes the case we have given as an example. With somewhat better reason, other authors would apply canon 2232, § 1 to irregularities *ex delicto*.[4] It should be noted that these two opinions do not lead to quite the same practical result (cf. n. 4 above).

Common Vindictive Penalties. The principal vindictive penalties applicable to the faithful in general according to the gravity of the case are:

1. Local interdict upon a community or moral body, which is perpetual, or for a definite time, or to last during the will of the superior;

2. Interdict on the same terms, against entry into the church;

3. Penal suppression or transfer of an episcopal see or parish;

4. Infamy of law;

5. Privation of ecclesiastical burial according to canon 1240, § 1;

6. Privation of the sacramentals;

7. Privation or temporary suspension of a pension which is paid by the Church or from church property, or of some other ecclesiastical right or privilege;

8. Exclusion from the exercise of legitimate ecclesiastical acts;

9. Incapacity for ecclesiastical favors or positions in the Church

---

[2] Cf. A Coronata, IV, n. 1823, p. 252; V-C, *Epit.*, III, n. 491.
[3] Cf. Sabetti-Barrett, *Theol. Mor.*, ed. 1939, p. 1176, n. 187; Jorio, *Theol. Mor.*, III, p. 572.
[4] Cf. A Coronata, IV, n. 1723, p. 121; V-C, *Epit.*, III, n. 426, p. 211.

which do not require the clerical state, or for obtaining academic degrees by ecclesiastical authority;

10. Privation or temporary suspension of some position, faculty, or favor already obtained;

11. Privation of the right of precedence, or of active and passive voice, or of the right to use honorary titles, insignia, or dress, granted by the Church;

12. Pecuniary fines (c. 2291).

Summary of Further Provisions. The *penal suppression or transfer* of an episcopal see is reserved to the Holy See; that of a parish can be decreed by Ordinaries of places only after having consulted their Chapters (or diocesan consultors, c. 427) (cf. c. 2292).

Infamy is either *of law* or *of fact*. Infamy *of law* is the penalty of that name established by the common law for certain specified cases.[5] Infamy *of fact* is contracted when a person, either because of a crime he has committed or because of corrupt morals, has, in the judgment of the Ordinary, lost his good repute among upright and solid members of the faithful. Neither kind of infamy affects persons related to the culprit by consanguinity or affinity, except as provided in canon 2147, § 2, 3° (c. 2293). The canon cited provides that the bad repute of persons with whom a pastor is living, whether they be relatives or not, may be canonical reason for the removal of even an irremovable pastor, if such cohabitation impairs his own good repute.

Consequences of infamy of law are: the person is irregular according to canon 984, 5°; he is moreover incapable of obtaining ecclesiastical benefices, pensions, offices, and dignities, or of doing legitimate ecclesiastical acts, or of exercising any ecclesiastical right or function; and finally must be prevented from taking any part in the exercise of sacred functions (c. 2294, § 1).

Consequences of infamy of fact: the person must be held off from receiving orders according to canon 987, 7° (which mentions infamy of fact among the simple impediments), and from ecclesiastical dignities, benefices, and offices, and also from exercising the sacred ministry and from legitimate ecclesiastical acts (c. 2294, § 2).

Infamy of law ceases only by dispensation from the Holy See; *infamy of fact ceases* when in the judgment of the Ordinary, in view of all the circumstances and especially of a long-continued amendment of life, the culprit has regained his good repute in the eyes of upright and solid members of the faithful (c. 2295).

---

[5] Cf. for example, canons 2320, 2328, 2343, § 1, 2351, § 2, 2356, 2357.

Incapacity, if there is question of things for which capacity is established by the common law, can be inflicted as a penalty only by the Holy See. Supervening incapacity does not take away vested rights unless the penalty of deprivation is added to it (c. 2296).

The *money obtained from pecuniary fines* inflicted according to common law, if the same law makes no provision for its disposal, and money obtained from fines established or to be established by particular law, must be applied by Ordinaries of places for pious uses, and not to the profit of the episcopal or capitular benefice (c. 2297).

Vindictive Penalties Peculiar to Clerics. Vindictive penalties applicable to clerics only are:

1. Prohibition from exercising the sacred ministry except in a certain church;

2. Suspension when it is perpetual, or for a definite time, or during the will of the superior;

3. Penal transfer from an office or benefice actually held to another inferior one;

4. Privation of a right attached to a benefice or office;

5. Incapacity for all or some dignities, offices, benefices, or other positions proper to clerics;

6. Penal privation of benefice or office with or without a pension;

7. Prohibition to remain in a certain place or territory;

8. Precept to remain in a certain place or territory;

9. Temporary privation of ecclesiastical dress;

10. Deposition;

11. Perpetual privation of ecclesiastical dress;

12. Degradation (c. 2298).

Privation of Benefice, or of Special Ministry. If a cleric has an irremovable benefice, he can be penally deprived of it only in the cases specified in the law; if he has a removable one, other reasonable causes may suffice (c. 2299, § 1). Clerics who have benefices, offices, or dignities can also be forbidden for a certain time to exercise only a certain ministry connected with them, e.g., preaching, hearing confessions, etc. (c. 2299, § 2). A cleric cannot be deprived of the benefice or pension which was his title for ordination, unless his support is assured from other sources, except as provided in canons 2303 (deposition) and 2304 (perpetual privation of ecclesiastical dress) (c. 2299, § 3).

Scandal. If a cleric gives grave scandal and fails to amend after warning, and if the scandal cannot otherwise be removed, he can in the meantime be deprived of the right to wear ecclesiastical dress; this privation, while it lasts, includes the prohibition to exercise any ecclesiastical ministry, and the privation of clerical privileges (c. 2300).

Prescribed Residence Outside Diocese. The Ordinary cannot prescribe that a cleric live in a certain place outside his diocese, unless he has the consent of the Ordinary of the place, or unless it is a house for the punishment and correction of clerics not only of that diocese but also from outside, or unless it is an exempt religious house, in which case the consent of the superior of that house must be had (c. 2301).

Place of Residence Prescribed or Forbidden. The prescription to live and the prohibition from living in a certain place, and the placing of a cleric in a house of penance or in a religious house, especially if these penalties are to be of long duration, may be imposed only in grave cases, in which, according to the prudent judgment of the Ordinary, these penalties are necessary for the amendment of the cleric or the reparation of scandal (c. 2302).

Deposition. Without impairing either the obligations arising from orders received or the privileges of clerics, deposition imports suspension from office, and incapacity for all offices, dignities, benefices, pensions, and positions in the Church, as well as privation of those which the culprit already has, even though they constitute his title for ordination (c. 2303, § 1). But in this last case, if the cleric is really indigent, the Ordinary in his charity should try to provide for him as best he can, lest he be driven to mendicancy to the discredit of the clerical state (c. 2303, § 2). The penalty of deposition can be inflicted only in the cases specified in the law (c. 2303, § 3).

Further Measures Against Deposed Cleric. If a deposed cleric shows no signs of amendment, and especially if he continues to give scandal, and after warning fails to amend, the Ordinary can deprive him perpetually of the right to wear ecclesiastical dress (c. 2304, § 1). This privation entails the privation of clerical privileges and the cessation of the provision of canon 2303, §2, that is, the charitable subsidy in indigence (c. 2304, § 2).

Degradation. Degradation includes deposition, the perpetual privation of ecclesiastical dress, and the reduction of the cleric to the lay state (2305, § 1). This penalty can be inflicted only for a crime for which it is specified in the law, or if a cleric who has already been deposed and deprived of clerical dress, continues for a year to give grave scandal (c. 2305, § 2). It has two forms; one is *verbalis* or *edictalis*, which is inflicted by a mere sentence, but produces all its juridical effects immediately without execution; the other is *realis,* in which all the solemnities prescribed in the Roman Pontifical are observed (c. 2305, § 3).

Section 2. Penal Remedies and Penances (cc. 2306-2313)

PRELIMINARY SURVEY

Various Penal Remedies (c. 2306)
Admonition (c. 2307)
Reprehension (c. 2308)
Norms for Admonition and Reprehension (c. 2309)
The Next Step: Precept or Injunction With Threat of Penalty (c. 2310)
In Grave Cases or in Danger of Relapse: Surveillance (c. 2311)
Penances: Purpose and General Norm (c. 2312)
Enumeration of Principal Penances (c. 2313)

Penal Remedies. Penal remedies are: (1) admonition; (2) reprehension; (3) precept; (4) surveillance (c. 2306). This enumeration is not given as exclusive. An Instruction of the S. C. of Bishops and Regulars which dealt with this matter mentions also spiritual exercises.[6] These, however, are now classified among penances by canon 2313.

Admonition. If one is in the proximate occasion of committing a crime, or as a result of an investigation which has been made one is under grave suspicion of having committed one, the Ordinary should give him an admonition or warning, either personally or through a third person (c. 2307).

Reprehension. If one's conduct gives rise to scandal or grave disturbances of order, reprehension is called for, to be given by the Ordinary personally or through another or by letter, always adapted to the peculiar conditions of the person and fact concerned (c. 2308).

Publicity or Secrecy. Both admonition and reprehension may be public or secret (c. 2309, § 1). A public reprehension or admonition should be given either before a notary or before two witnesses or by letter, but in such wise that there be some documentary proof of the

---

[6] S. C. Ep. et Reg. 11 June, 1880, n. 4; Gasparri-Serédi, *Fontes,* n. 2005, Vol. IV, p. 1022, n. 4.

receipt and content of the letter (c. 2309, § 2). Public reprehension can be used only against a culprit who has been convicted of the crime or has confessed it; it is judicial if it is made by a judge sitting for the court, or by the Ordinary before a criminal trial (c. 2309, § 3). Judicial reprehension either takes the place of a penalty or is added to it, especially in the case of a *recidivus* (c. 2309, § 4). Admonition and reprehension, even when they are given secretly, must be proved by some document which is to be kept in the secret archives of the Curia (c. 2309, § 5). Either reprehension or admonition can be given once or oftener according to the judgment and prudence of the superior (c. 2309, § 6).

Precept. When admonitions or reprehensions have been given in vain, or when there is no hope that they will be effective, a precept is given, which should clearly state what the person must do or avoid, with a threat of penalty in case of disobedience (c. 2310).

Surveillance. If the gravity of the case makes it appropriate, and especially if the person is in danger of relapsing into the same crime, the Ordinary may put him under surveillance (c. 2311, § 1). Surveillance can also be used to increase the penalty, especially in the case of *recidivi* (c. 2311, § 2).

Penances. Penances in the external forum are imposed so that the culprit may either escape a penalty or receive absolution or dispensation from a penalty already incurred (c. 2312, § 1). A public penance should never be imposed for a crime or transgression which is occult (c. 2312, § 2). Penances should be regulated not so much by the quantity of the crime as by the contrition of the penitent, with due regard for the quality of persons and the circumstances of offenses (c. 2312, § 3).

Principal Penances. The principal penances are the precepts: (1) to recite certain prayers; (2) to make a pilgrimage or do other works of piety; (3) to observe a special fast; (4) to give alms for pious uses; (5) to make spiritual exercises for some days in a pious or religious house (c. 2313, § 1). The Ordinary may in his prudent discretion add to penances the penal remedies of admonition and reprehension (c. 2313, § 2).

Readings:

Conran, *The Interdict,* Cath. U., 1930; Rainer, *Suspension of Clerics,* Cath. U., 1937; Christ, *Dispensation from Vindicative Penalties,* Cath. U., 1944; Findlay, *Canonical Norms Governing the Deposition and Degradation of Clerics,* Cath. U., 1941.

CHAPTER XXIV

PENALTIES FOR PARTICULAR CRIMES

Section 1. Crimes Against the Faith and Unity of the Church
(cc. 2314-2319)

PRELIMINARY SURVEY

Apostasy, Heresy, Schism (c. 2314)
Suspicion of Heresy (c. 2315)
Co-operation in Heresy (c. 2316)
Teaching Condemned Doctrines (c. 2317)
Publishing, Etc., Certain Forbidden Books (c. 2318)
Crimes Connected With Marriage (c. 2319)

Plan of This Chapter. Penal statutes in general have the reputation of being full of technicalities; perhaps those of the Church are no exception. Consequently, for a *full* knowledge of these laws, many detailed questions should be raised, discussed, and solved in connection with almost every canon. However, a seminary textbook cannot attempt so ambitious a program. We shall give in this chapter only the substance of the canons pretty much as they are in the Code, with scarcely any comment. In a final chapter, which is scarcely more than a practical Appendix, we will resume the consideration of those crimes which seem to be of more practical interest, and summarize in a very condensed form the chief questions which concern them.[1]

Apostasy, Heresy, Schism. All apostates from the Christian faith, and all heretics and schismatics: (1) are *ipso facto* excommunicated; (2) if after due warning they fail to amend, they are to be deprived of any benefice, dignity, pension, office, or other position which they may have in the Church, they are to be declared infamous, and clerics, after a repetition of the warning, are to be deposed; (3) if they have joined a non-Catholic sect or publicly adhered to it, they are *ipso facto*

---

[1] The present chapter affords a *rapid general survey* of the particular penalties of the Code, which is certainly not without value. It is advisable not to delay on this chapter, but to read it carefully and quickly as a preparation for more detailed studies later.

infamous, and clerics, in addition to being considered to have tacitly renounced any office they may hold, according to canon 188, 4°, are, if previous warning proves fruitless, to be degraded (c. 2314, § 1).

Absolution from the excommunication mentioned in § 1, when it is to be given in the forum of conscience, is specially reserved to the Holy See. But if the crime of apostasy, heresy, or schism has been brought *in any way*, even by voluntary confession, into the external forum of the Ordinary of the place, the same Ordinary, but not the Vicar General without a special mandate, can, in virtue of his ordinary authority in the external forum, absolve the penitent, after the latter has legally made an abjuration, observing the other requirements of law; and the person so absolved can then be absolved from the sin by any confessor in the forum of conscience. The abjuration is regarded as legally made when it is made before the Ordinary of the place or his delegate and at least two witnesses (c. 2314, § 2).

Suspicion of Heresy. One who is suspected of heresy, and who after warning fails to remove the cause of suspicion, shall be barred from legitimate acts, and if he is a cleric he shall moreover, after a repetition of the warning has proved fruitless, be suspended *a divinis;* if one who is suspected of heresy does not amend his life within six full months from the time when the penalty was incurred, he shall be considered a heretic and be subject to the penalties for heresy (c. 2315).[2]

Co-operation in Heresy. One who spontaneously and with full knowledge helps in any way in the propagation of heresy, or who co-operates *in divinis* with heretics contrary to the provision of canon 1258, is suspected of heresy (c. 2316).

Teaching Condemned Doctrines. Those who obstinately teach or defend, either publicly or privately, a doctrine which has been condemned, though not as formally heretical, by the Holy See or by a General Council, are to be excluded from the ministry of preaching the word of God or of hearing sacramental confessions, and from teaching in any capacity, in addition to any other penalties which the condemnatory sentence may inflict or which the Ordinary, after due warning, may deem necessary to repair the scandal (c. 2317).

Publishing, Reading, Keeping Certain Specially Forbidden Books. Those who publish books of apostates, heretics, or schismatics, which propound apostasy, heresy, or schism, and likewise those who defend or who knowingly and without permission read or keep such books

---

[2] For cases in which suspicion of heresy is incurred *ipso facto*, cf. canons 2316, 2319, 2320, 2332, 2340, 2371.

or any others which have been forbidden by name by Apostolic letter, incur *ipso facto* an excommunication specially reserved to the Holy See, when the work is published (c. 2318, § 1).

Authors and publishers who without due permission cause to be printed books of Sacred Scripture or annotations or commentaries thereof, *ipso facto* incur an excommunication which is reserved to no one (c. 2318, § 2). On the permission required for such books, see canons 1385, § 1, 1° and 1391; on their prohibition without such permission, canon 1399, 5°.

Crimes Connected With Marriage. Catholics are under an excommunication *latae sententiae* reserved to the Ordinary: (1) who contract marriage before a non-Catholic minister contrary to canon 1063, § 1; (2) who contract marriage with an explicit or implicit agreement that all children or any child be educated outside the Catholic Church; (3) who knowingly presume to present their children to non-Catholic ministers to be baptized; (4) who, being parents or taking their place, knowingly present their children to be educated or trained in a non-Catholic religion (c. 2319, § 1).

Those mentioned in numbers 2-4 of the preceding paragraph are moreover suspect of heresy (c. 2319, § 2).

Section 2. Crimes Against Religion (cc. 2320–2329)

PRELIMINARY SURVEY

Profanation of the Sacred Species (c. 2320)
Saying Mass Twice in the Day or Without Fasting
    (c. 2321)
Simulation of Priestly Powers (c. 2322)
Blasphemy: Perjury (c. 2323)
Crimes Concerning Mass Stipends (c. 2324)
Superstition: Sacrilege (c. 2325)
False Relics (c. 2326)
Traffic in Indulgences (c. 2327)
Violating Graves (c. 2328)
Violating Churches or Cemeteries (c. 2329)

Profanation of the Sacred Species. One who throws away the sacred Species, or for any evil purpose steals them or keeps them, is suspect of heresy; incurs an excommunication *latae sententiae* most specially reserved to the Holy See; is *ipso facto* infamous, and if he is a cleric, is moreover to be deposed (c. 2320).

Saying Mass Twice or After Breaking the Fast. Priests who, contrary to the provisions of canons 806, § 1, and 808, presume to repeat Mass on the same day, or to celebrate it without fasting, are to be suspended from the celebration of Mass for a time to be determined by the Ordinary according to the circumstances of each case (c. 2321).

Simulation of Priestly Powers. One who has not been raised to the order of the priesthood: (1) if he simulates the celebration of Mass or receives sacramental confession, *ipso facto* incurs an excommunication specially reserved to the Holy See; and moreover, if a layman, he is to be deprived of any pension or position which he may have in the Church, and to be punished with other penalties according to the gravity of the offense; if a cleric, he is to be deposed; (2) if he usurps any other priestly function, he shall be punished by the Ordinary according to the gravity of the case (c. 2322).

Blasphemy: Perjury. Whoever has committed blasphemy or extrajudicial perjury, is to be punished according to the prudent discretion of the Ordinary, especially if he be a cleric (c. 2323).

Crimes Concerning Mass Stipends. Whoever has criminally violated the provisions of canons 827 (traffic in Masses), 828 (number of Masses to correspond to stipends), or 840, § 1 (integral transmission of stipends), shall be punished by the Ordinary according to the gravity of the case, not excluding in a proper case suspension, or privation of ecclesiastical benefice or office, or, in the case of lay persons, excommunication (c. 2324).

Superstition: Sacrilege. Whoever has practiced superstition or committed a sacrilege shall be punished by the Ordinary in proportion to the gravity of the fault, without prejudice to the penalties established by law against certain acts of superstition or sacrilege (c. 2325).

Falsification of Relics, Etc. One who manufactures false relics or who knowingly sells or distributes the same, or knowingly exposes them to the public veneration of the faithful, *ipso facto* contracts an excommunication reserved to the Ordinary (c. 2326).

Traffic in Indulgences. Those who traffic in indulgences are *ipso facto* punished by excommunication simply reserved to the Holy See (c. 2327).

Violation of Corpses or Graves. One who violates the bodies or graves of the dead, for the purpose of stealing or for any other evil purpose, shall be punished by a personal interdict, shall be *ipso facto* infamous, and if he be a cleric shall moreover be deposed (c. 2328).

Violation of Church or Cemetery. Violators of a church or cemetery, according to canons 1172 (which declares how a church is violated), and 1207 (which applies the same provisions to cemeteries), shall be punished by the Ordinary according to the gravity of the case, with the penalty of interdict from entry into a church, and other appropriate penalties (c. 2329).

Section. 3. Crimes Against Ecclesiastical Authorities, Persons, and Things (cc. 2330-2349)

PRELIMINARY SURVEY

Crimes Committed in Papal Elections. As regards the penalties established for the crimes which can be committed in the course of an election of a Supreme Pontiff, the Constitution of Pius XII, *Vacantis Apostolicae Sedis,* of 8. Dec., 1945, governs exclusively (c. 2330). There are nine such excommunications reserved *personally* to the Roman Pontiff, so that they can be absolved by no one else except in danger of death.[3]

Disobedience: Conspiracy. Those who obstinately fail to comply when the Roman Pontiff or their own Ordinary lawfully prescribes or forbids something, shall be punished according to the gravity of the fault, with suitable penalties, not excluding censures (c. 2331, § 1). Those who conspire against the authority of the Roman Pontiff or of his Legate, or of their own Ordinary, or against the lawful commands of the same, and likewise those who provoke subjects to such disobedience, shall be punished with censures or other penalties; and if they be clerics they shall be deprived of dignities, benefices, or other positions; if they be religious, they shall be deprived of active and passive voice and of office (c. 2331, § 2).

Appeal From Pope to General Council. All persons of whatever state, rank, or condition, even though they be king, Bishop, or Cardinal, who appeal from the laws, decrees, or mandates of the reigning Roman Pontiff to a universal Council, are suspect of heresy, and *ipso facto* contract an excommunication which is specially reserved to the Holy See; and universities, colleges, Chapters, or other moral persons of whatever name, who are guilty of the same offense, incur an interdict reserved in the same special way to the Holy See (c. 2332).

Recourse to the Civil Authority to Impede Communication of Papal Documents. Those who have recourse to the civil authority to impede letters or any documents whatever proceeding from the Holy See or from a Legate thereof, and those who directly or indirectly forbid the promulgation or execution of such documents, or who because of them injure or intimidate either the persons whom such letters or communications concern, or other persons, are *ipso facto* under excommunication specially reserved to the Holy See (c. 2333).

Interference With the Liberty, Rights, Jurisdiction of the Church. The following incur an excommunication *latae sententiae* specially reserved to the Holy See: (1) those who issue laws, mandates, or decrees contrary to the freedom or rights of the Church; (2) those who directly or indirectly impede the exercise of ecclesiastical jurisdiction either of the internal or external forum, and for this purpose have recourse to any lay authority (c. 2334).

---

[4] Cf. *AAS*, 38–65; Cappello, *De Censuris,* n. 565, p. 493.

Affiliation With Masonic or Similar Societies. Those who join a Masonic sect or other societies of the same sort, which plot against the Church or against legitimate civil authority, incur *ipso facto* an excommunication simply reserved to the Holy See (c. 2335).

Special Provisions for Clerics and Religious. Clerics who commit a crime mentioned in canons 2334, 2335 shall, in addition to the penalties provided in those canons, be punished either by suspension from or by deprivation of any benefice, office, dignity, pension, or position which they may have in the Church; and religious, by the privation of office and of active and passive voice, and by other penalties according to the constitutions (c. 2336, § 1).

Moreover clerics and religious who become members of a Masonic sect or other similar societies are to be reported to the Sacred Congregation of the Holy Office (c. 2336, § 2).

Inciting the People to Impede Ecclesiastical Jurisdiction. If a pastor, in order to interfere with the exercise of ecclesiastical jurisdiction, dares to provoke popular demonstrations, to encourage public petitions in his favor, to stir up the people by speech or writing, or do other things of the sort, he shall be punished according to the gravity of the fault in the prudent judgment of the Ordinary, even to the extent of suspension in a proper case (c. 2337, § 1).

The Ordinary shall punish in the same way any priest who, by whatsoever devices, arouses the people to prevent the priest who has been lawfully appointed pastor or administrator from entering the parish (c. 2337, § 2).

Violation of Censures, Etc. Those who without the required faculty presume to absolve from an excommunication *latae sententiae* which is most specially or specially reserved to the Holy See, *ipso facto* incur an excommunication simply reserved to the Holy See (c. 2338, § 1).

Those who give any aid or comfort to an excommunicated *vitandus*, in regard to the crime for which he was excommunicated; and likewise clerics who, with full knowledge and of their own accord, participate in divine services with such a person, or admit him to participate in divine services, *ipso facto* incur an excommunication simply reserved to the Holy See (c. 2338, § 2).

Those who knowingly celebrate or cause to be celebrated divine services in interdicted places, or who admit to the celebration of divine services when the latter are forbidden by censure, clerics who are excommunicated, interdicted, or suspended, after a declaratory or condemnatory sentence, incur *ipso facto* an interdict from entry into a church, until they shall have given proper satisfaction in the judgment of the one whose sentence they have disregarded (c. 2338, § 3).

Those who have given cause for a local interdict or an interdict upon a community or college are *ipso facto* under personal interdict (c. 2338, § 4).

Violation of Laws Regarding Christian Burial. Those who, in violation of canon 1240, § 1, dare to command or compel ecclesiastical burial to be given to infidels, apostates from the faith, heretics, schismatics, or others who are either excommunicated or interdicted, incur an excommunication *latae sententiae* reserved to no one; and those who of their own accord give ecclesiastical burial to the same, incur an interdict from entry into the church, reserved to the Ordinary (c. 2339).

Obduracy in Censures. One who, in a stubborn spirit, remains under censure of excommunication for a year, is suspect of heresy (c. 2340, § 1).

If a cleric remains under the censure of suspension for six months he is to be given a serious warning; and if he does not desist from contumacy after a month has elapsed from the time of warning, he shall be deprived of any benefices or offices which he may have in the Church (c. 2340, § 2).

Violation of the *Privilegium Fori*. If anyone, in violation of canon 120, dare to summon before a lay tribunal a Cardinal of the Holy Roman Church, or a Legate of the Holy See, or any other major official of the Roman Curia in connection with business pertaining to his office, or his own Ordinary, he incurs *ipso facto* an excommunication specially reserved to the Holy See; if he dare to summon in the same manner another Bishop, even merely titular, or an Abbot or Prelate *nullius,* or the highest superior of a religious institute approved by the Holy See, he incurs an excommunication *latae sententiae* simply reserved to the Holy See; finally, if, without having obtained the permission of the Ordinary of the place, he dare to summon in the same manner any other person who has the *privilegium fori,* the culprit, if a cleric, incurs *ipso facto* suspension from office reserved to the Ordinary; if a lay person, he shall be punished by his own Ordinary with suitable penalties according to the gravity of the case (c. 2341).

Violation of Papal Cloister. The following incur *ipso facto* an excommunication simply reserved to the Holy See: (1) persons of whatever class, condition, or sex who violate the cloister of nuns by entering their monastery without the required permission, and likewise those who introduce or admit such persons; and if the culprits are clerics they shall moreover be suspended for a time to be determined by the Ordinary according to the gravity of the fault; (2) women who violate the cloister of male regulars, and all others, whoever they are, who introduce or admit such females of whatever age; religious who are guilty of such introduction or admission shall moreover be deprived of any office they may have and of active and passive voice; (3) nuns who illegitimately leave the cloister in violation of canon 601 (c. 2342).

Violation of the *Privilegium Canonis*. Anyone who lays violent hands on the person of the Roman Pontiff (1) incurs an excommunication *latae sententiae* which is reserved most specially to the Holy See; and is *ipso facto vitandus;* (2) is *ipso iure* infamous; (3) if he is a cleric, he is to be degraded (c. 2343, § 1).

One who lays violent hands on a Cardinal of the Holy Roman Church or a Legate of the Roman Pontiff: (1) incurs an excommunication *latae sententiae* specially reserved to the Holy See; (2) is *ipso iure* infamous; (3) is to be deprived of any benefices, offices, dignities, pensions, and of any position which he may have in the Church (c. 2343, § 2).

One who lays violent hands on a Patriarch, Archbishop, or Bishop even though only titular, incurs an excommunication *latae sententiae* specially reserved to the Holy See (c. 2343, § 3).

One who lays violent hands on the person of any other cleric or of a religious of either sex is *ipso facto* under excommunication reserved to his own Ordinary, who may moreover in a proper case punish him with further penalties according to his prudent discretion (c. 2343, § 4).

Other Offenses Against Higher Clerics. Whoever, either directly or indirectly, in the public press, or in speech or writing, makes injurious attacks upon the Roman Pontiff, a Cardinal, a Legate of the Roman Pontiff, the Sacred Roman Congregations, the Tribunals of the Holy See and their major officials, or upon his own Ordinary, or stirs up opposition or animosity against their acts, decrees, decisions, or sentences shall be compelled by the Ordinary, not only at the instance of the injured party but even *ex officio,* and even by censures, to make satisfaction, or shall be punished by other appropriate penalties and penances, according to the gravity of the fault and the reparation required for the scandal (c. 2344).

Usurping the Rights or Property of the Roman Church. Those who, either personally or through others, usurp or withhold property or rights belonging to the Roman Church, shall be under an excommunication *latae sententiae* specially reserved to the Holy See; and if they be clerics they shall moreover be deprived of dignities, benefices, offices and pensions, and be declared ineligible for the same (c. 2345).

Confiscation and Appropriation of Church Property. If anyone presumes to appropriate to his own use and to usurp ecclesiastical property of any kind, movable or immovable, corporeal or incorporeal, either by personal action or through others, or to prevent the income of such property from being received by those to whom it legally belongs, he shall be under excommunication until he shall have made complete restitution of the property itself, shall have removed the obstacle which prevents the due reception of the income, and shall have obtained absolution from the Holy See; if he was a patron of the church or property concerned, he shall also be automatically deprived of the right of patronage; and a cleric who commits this crime or consents to the same shall moreover be deprived of all benefices, shall become incapable of obtaining any others, and at the discretion of his Ordinary shall be suspended from the exercise of his orders, even after he has made full satisfaction and obtained absolution (c. 2346).

Unlawful Alienation of Ecclesiastical Property. Without prejudice to the nullity of the act, and the obligation, which may be urged even by the infliction of censures, to restore the property unlawfully acquired and to make good the damages which may have been caused, one who shall presume to alienate ecclesiastical property or to consent to the alienation thereof, in violation of the provisions of canons 534, § 1 and 1532, shall suffer the following penalties: (1) if there is question of property whose value does not exceed one thousand francs, the culprit shall be punished by the lawful ecclesiastical superior with suitable penalties; (2) if there is question of property whose value is more than one thousand but less than thirty thousand francs, a patron (who is guilty of this offense) shall be deprived of the right of patronage; an administrator shall be deprived of that office; a religious superior or procurator shall be deprived of his office and of eligibility for other offices, in addition to other appropriate penalties to be inflicted by superiors; an Ordinary or other clerics who hold an office, benefice, dignity, or position in the Church shall pay twice the value of the property in favor of the church or pious cause which has suffered from the unlawful alienation; other clerics (thus guilty) shall be suspended for such time as the Ordinary may determine; (3) if the permission of the Holy See was required according to the provisions of those canons and was deliberately omitted, all those who are in any way guilty, either by alienating the property, or by receiving it, or by giving consent to the transaction, incur moreover an excommunication *latae sententiae* reserved to no one (c. 2347).

Neglect to Execute Pious Gifts or Legacies. One who has received a legacy or donation to a pious cause either by act *inter vivos* or by will, even in a fiduciary capacity, and who fails to carry out the donor's intention, is to be compelled to do so by the Ordinary, even by the infliction of a censure (c. 2348).

Refusing Legitimate Taxes or Contributions. Those who refuse to make contributions which are legally due according to canons 463, § 1 and 1507 shall be punished in the prudent discretion of the Ordinary until they comply with the law (c. 2349).

Section 4. Crimes Against Life, Liberty, Property, Reputation, and Morals (cc. 2350–2359)

PRELIMINARY SURVEY

Abortion: Suicide (c. 2350)
Dueling (c. 2351)
Duress as to Clerical or Religious Vocation or Profession (c. 2352)
Abduction (c. 2353)
Certain Special Crimes Against the Person, Liberty or Property (c. 2354)
Injuries to Another by Speech or Writing (c. 2355)
Bigamy (c. 2356)
Immorality: Adultery, Public Concubinage, Etc. (cc. 2357–2359)

Abortion. Those who procure abortion, not excepting the mother, incur, if the effect is produced, an excommunication *latae sententiae* reserved to the Ordinary; and if they be clerics they are moreover to be deposed (c. 2350, § 1).

Suicide. Those who make an attempt upon their own life, if death follows, are to be deprived of ecclesiastical burial according to canon

1240, § 1, 3°; otherwise, they are to be excluded from legitimate ecclesiastical acts, and if they be clerics, are to be suspended for such time as the Ordinary may determine, and removed from benefices or offices to which the care of souls either in the internal or external forum is attached (c. 2350, § 2).

Dueling. In addition to the provision of canon 1240, § 1, 4°, those who fight a duel, or simply challenge to a duel or accept such a challenge, or in any way co-operate in or encourage a duel, or who of set purpose are spectators at a duel and permit it, or do not as far as is in their power prevent it, whatever their dignity, incur *ipso facto* an excommunication simply reserved to the Holy See (c. 2351, § 1).

The principals and their seconds are moreover *ipso facto* infamous (c. 2351, § 2).

Compulsion to Embrace Clerical or Religious State. All persons, whatever be their dignity, who in any way compel either a man to embrace the clerical state, or a man or woman to enter a religious institute or to make a religious profession therein, either solemn or simple, perpetual or temporary, are *ipso facto* punished by excommunication reserved to no one (c. 2352).

Abduction. Whoever, for the purpose of marriage or of satisfying lust, abducts by force or fraud a woman who is unwilling, or abducts in any way a woman of minor age even though she be willing, if her parents or guardians are either ignorant of the fact or refuse their consent, shall be *ipso iure* excluded from legitimate ecclesiastical acts and shall moreover be punished by other penalties according to the gravity of the case (c. 2353).

Certain Special Crimes. A layman who has been legally found guilty of the crime of homicide, of abduction of a person of either sex who has not attained puberty, of selling a human person for slavery or for some other evil purpose, or of usury, rapine, qualified theft (i.e., theft accompanied by aggravating circumstances), or unqualified theft in a very grave matter, arson, or malicious destruction of property in a very notable degree, grave mutilation or wounding or assault, is *ipso iure* excluded from legitimate ecclesiastical acts and from any position he may have in the Church, and must moreover make good the damage (c. 2354, § 1).

A cleric who has committed any of the crimes mentioned in paragraph 1 shall be punished by an ecclesiastical court, according to the degree of his guilt, with penances, censures, the privation of office, benefice, and dignity, and in a proper case even with deposition; and one who is guilty of homicide shall be degraded (c. 2354, § 2).

Injuries by Speech or Writing, or Other Means. If anyone, not by direct action, but by speech or writing, or any other means, injure anyone or harm his reputation, he not only can be compelled according to canons 1618 and 1938 to give due satisfaction and to repair the damage, but may moreover be punished with appropriate penalties and penances, even to the extent of suspension or removal from office and benefice, in a proper case, where the culprit is a cleric (c. 2355).

Bigamy. Bigamists, that is, those who, in spite of the conjugal bond, attempt another marriage, even a so-called civil marriage, are *ipso facto* infamous; and if in spite of warning by the Ordinary, they continue in the illicit relation so begun, they are to be punished by excommunication or personal interdict according to the gravity of the case (c. 2356).

Immorality Committed by Lay Persons. Lay persons who have been legally found guilty of a crime of sexual immorality committed with a minor under sixteen years of age, or rape, sodomy, incest, pandering, are *ipso facto* infamous, besides being subject to other penalties which the Ordinary may deem proper to inflict (c. 2357, § 1).

Lay persons who have committed a public crime of adultery or are publicly living in concubinage, or who have been legally found guilty of other crimes against the sixth commandment of the Decalogue, shall be barred from legitimate ecclesiastical acts until they shall show signs of genuine repentance (c. 2357, § 2).

Immorality Committed by Clerics in Minor Orders. Clerics in minor orders, who are guilty of some crime against the sixth commandment, shall be punished according to the gravity of their guilt, even by dismissal from the clerical state if the circumstances of the crime seem to demand it, in addition to the penalties mentioned in canon 2357 if the latter are called for (c. 2358).

Clerics in Major Orders. Clerics in sacred orders, whether secular or religious, living in concubinage, when a previous admonition has proved fruitless, are to be compelled, by privation of the income of office, benefice, and dignity, to desist from the illicit relationship and to repair the scandal, and the provisions of canons 2176-2181 are to be observed (c. 2359, § 1).

If they have committed a crime against the sixth commandment with a minor under sixteen years of age, or have committed adultery, rape, bestiality, sodomy, pandering, or incest with any person related to them by consanguinity or affinity in the first degree, they shall be suspended, declared infamous, deprived of any office, benefice, dignity, or position which they may have, and in more serious cases, shall be deposed (c. 2359, § 2).

If they have committed any other crime against the sixth commandment, they are to be visited with appropriate penalties according to the gravity of the case not excepting the privation of office or benefice, especially if they are charged with the care of souls (c. 2359, § 3).

Section 5. Crimes of Falsification (cc. 2360–2363)

PRELIMINARY SURVEY

Forgery of Pontifical Documents (c. 2360)
Deliberate Falsehood or Omission in Petitions for Rescripts (c. 2361)
Forgery of Other Ecclesiastical Documents (c. 2362)
False Charges of Solicitation (c. 2363)

Forgery of Pontifical Documents. All persons who shall forge or falsify letters, decrees, or rescripts of the Holy See, or knowingly make use of such forged or falsified documents *ipso facto* incur an excommunication specially reserved to the Holy See (c. 2360, § 1).

Clerics who are guilty of the crime mentioned in § 1 shall moreover be punished by other penalties, which may go as far as privation of ecclesiastical benefice, office, dignity, and pension; religious are to be deprived of all offices which they have in their religious institute and of active and passive voice, in addition to other penalties which may be provided in their respective constitutions (c. 2360, § 2).

Deliberate Falsehood or Omission in Petitions for Rescripts. If anyone, in the petition to obtain a rescript from the Holy See or from the Ordinary of the place, through fraud or deceit withholds the truth or states a falsehood, he can be punished by his own Ordinary according to the gravity of the case, without prejudice to the provisions of canons 45 and 1054 (c. 2361).

Forgery or Falsification of Documents. Those who forge or falsify ecclesiastical documents or records whether public or private, and those who knowingly use such documents or records, shall be punished according to the gravity of the crime, without prejudice to the provision of canon 2406, § 1 (c. 2362).

False Accusation of Solicitation. If anyone, personally or through others, falsely makes to superiors a juridical accusation of solicitation against a confessor, he or she *ipso facto* incurs an excommunication specially reserved to the Holy See, from which he may in no case be absolved unless he shall have formally retracted the false accusation and repaired as far as possible the damages which may have ensued; and moreover a grave and long penance is to be imposed, and the provision of canon 894 observed (c. 2363).

Section 6. Crimes in the Administration or Reception of Orders and Other Sacraments (cc. 2364–2375)

PRELIMINARY SURVEY

Unlawful Administration of Sacraments (c. 2364)
Unlawful Administration of Confirmation (c. 2365)
Giving Absolution Beyond Jurisdiction (c. 2366)
Absolving an Accomplice *in Peccato Turpi* (c. 2367)
Solicitation (c. 2368)
Violation of the Seal (c. 2369)
Consecration of Bishop Without Apostolic Mandate
  (c. 2370)
Simony in Administration or Reception of Sacraments
  (c. 2371)
Receiving Orders From One Under Censure (c. 2372)
Unlawful Ordination (c. 2373)
Unlawful Reception of Orders (c. 2374)
Contracting Mixed Marriage Without Dispensation
  (c. 2375)

Unlawful Administration of Sacraments. A minister who dares to administer sacraments to persons who are forbidden either by divine or ecclesiastical law to receive them, shall be suspended from the administration of the sacraments for a time to be determined in the prudent discretion of the Ordinary, and shall be punished by other penalties according to the gravity of the fault, without prejudice to the special penalties provided by law against certain crimes of this class (c. 2364).

Unlawful Confirmation. A priest who, without having the faculty either by law or by grant from the Roman Pontiff, dares to administer the sacrament of confirmation, shall be suspended; if he has the faculty but dares to exceed its limits, he is *ipso facto* deprived of it (c. 2365).

Giving Absolution Beyond Jurisdiction. A priest who presumes to hear sacramental confessions without the required jurisdiction is *ipso facto* suspended *a divinis;* one who presumes to absolve from reserved sins is *ipso facto* suspended from hearing confessions (c. 2366).

Absolving an Accomplice *in Peccato Turpi*. One who absolves or pretends to absolve his accomplice in a sin of impurity *ipso facto* incurs excommunication most specially reserved to the Holy See; and this even in danger of death if another priest, though not approved for confessions, could without any grave consequence in the way of infamy or scandal hear the dying person's confession, except in the case where the dying person refuses to confess to another (c. 2367, § 1).

One does not escape this excommunication if he absolves or pretends to absolve an accomplice who omits to confess the sin of complicity, from which he (or she) has not been absolved, but omits it because he (or she) has been directly or indirectly induced to do so by the accomplice confessor (c. 2367, § 2).

Solicitation. One who commits the crime of solicitation mentioned in canon 904 shall be suspended from the celebration of Mass and from hearing sacramental confessions, or even according to the gravity of the crime be declared incapable of receiving them, be deprived of all benefices and dignities, active and passive voice, and be declared incapable of them all, and in more flagrant cases shall also be degraded (c. 2368, § 1).

Failure to Denounce. One of the faithful who, in violation of canon 904, knowingly fails to lodge an accusation within a month against the one by whom he was solicited, incurs an excommunication *latae sententiae* reserved to no one, and he should not be absolved until he has fulfilled this obligation or seriously promised to do so (c. 2368, § 2).

Violation of the Seal. A confessor who presumes to violate directly the seal of confession incurs an excommunication most specially reserved to the Holy See; one who does so indirectly is subject to the penalties mentioned in canon 2368, § 1 (c. 2369, § 1).

Whoever rashly violates the provision of canon 889, § 2 shall, according to the gravity of the case, be punished with a salutary penalty, which may be even excommunication (c. 2369, § 2).

Consecration of Bishop Without Apostolic Mandate. A Bishop who consecrates anyone as Bishop without an Apostolic mandate, contrary

to the provisions of canon 953, and the Bishops, or the priests acting
in their place, who assist as co-consecrators, and the one who is so
consecrated, are *ipso iure* suspended until the Holy See shall dispense
them (c. 2370).

Simony in Administration or Reception of Sacraments. All persons,
even those of episcopal dignity, who shall knowingly promote anyone
to orders through simony, or be so promoted themselves, or shall so
administer or receive other sacraments, are suspect of heresy; and
clerics moreover incur a suspension reserved to the Holy See (c. 2371).

Receiving Orders From One Under Censure. Those who presume
to receive orders from one who is excommunicated, or suspended, or
interdicted, after a declaratory or condemnatory sentence has been
passed upon him, or from a notorious apostate, heretic, or schismatic,
ipso facto incur a suspension *a divinis* reserved to the Holy See; one
who in good faith is ordained by any such person, is forbidden to
exercise the order so received until he shall be dispensed (c. 2372).

Unlawful Ordination. The following *ipso facto* incur a suspension
from conferring orders for one year, reserved to the Holy See:

1. Those who, in violation of the provision of canon 955, ordain
a subject not their own without dimissorial letters from the proper
Ordinary;

2. Those who, in violation of the provisions of canons 993, 4° and
994, ordain their own subject who has been elsewhere long enough to
contract a canonical impediment there;

3. Those who, in violation of the provisions of canon 974, § 1, 7°,
promote anyone to orders without a canonical title;

4. Those who, without a legitimate privilege, promote to orders,
even with dimissorial letters from his proper superior, a religious who
belongs to a religious community outside the territory of the one
who ordains, unless it is legitimately proved that it is one of the
exceptional cases mentioned in canon 966 (c. 2373).

Unlawful Reception of Orders. One who maliciously receives orders
without dimissorial letters or with false ones, or before reaching the
canonical age, or *per saltum,* is *ipso facto* suspended from the order
so received; one who does so without testimonial letters, or while he
is under censure, irregularity, or impediment, is to be punished with
severe penalties according to circumstances (c. 2374).

Contracting Mixed Marriage Without Dispensation. Catholics who
dare to contract a mixed marriage, even though it be valid, without
a dispensation from the Church, are *ipso facto* barred from legitimate

ecclesiastical acts and from the sacramentals, until they shall have obtained a dispensation from the Ordinary (c. 2375).

Section 7. Crimes Against the Obligations of the Clerical and Religious State (cc. 2376–2389)

PRELIMINARY SURVEY

Refusal to Take Junior Clergy Examination (c. 2376)
Obstinacy in Absence From Clerical Conferences (c. 2377)
Grave Negligence in Rites and Ceremonies (c. 2378)
Disregard of Law on Clerical Dress (c. 2379)
Unlawful Trading or Commerce (c. 2380)
Illegitimate Absence (c. 2381)
Grave Neglect of Parochial Duties (c. 2382)
Failure to Keep Parish Records (c. 2383)
Negligence in Duties of Canon Theologian and Penitentiary (c. 2384)
Apostasy From Religion (c. 2385)
Flight From Religion (c. 2386)
Fraudulent Religious Profession of Cleric (c. 2387)
Sacrilegious Marriages (c. 2388)
Grave Violation of Common Life by Religious (c. 2389)

Refusal to Take Junior Clergy Examination. Priests who, without being dispensed therefrom by the Ordinary and without a legitimate excuse, refuse to take the examination mentioned in canon 130, shall be compelled to do so by the Ordinary with appropriate penalties (c. 2376).

Obstinacy in Absence From Clerical Conferences. Priests who persistently violate canon 131, § 1 shall be punished by the Ordinary in his prudent discretion; and if they are religious confessors who have not the care of souls, he shall suspend them from hearing the confessions of seculars (c. 2377).

Grave Negligence in Rubrics and Ceremonies. Major clerics who in the sacred ministry gravely neglect the rites and ceremonies prescribed by the Church, and fail to amend after due warning, shall be suspended according to the gravity of the case (c. 2378).

Disregard of Law on Clerical Dress. Clerics who, in violation of canon 136, fail to wear ecclesiastical dress and the clerical tonsure, shall receive a grave admonition; after the lapse of a month without amendment, from the time of the warning, minor clerics fall *ipso iure* from the clerical state according to canon 136, § 3; major clerics, in addition to being held by canon 188, 7° (tacit renunciation of offices), are to be suspended from the orders they have received, and if they are notoriously leading a life foreign to the clerical state, and fail to amend after a second warning, then after three months from this second warning, they are to be deposed (c. 2379).

Unlawful Trade or Commerce. Clerics or religious who, personally or through others, engage in commerce or trading in violation of the provisions of canon 142, are to be visited with appropriate penalties by the Ordinary according to the gravity of the case (c. 2380).

Illegitimate Absence. One who has an office, benefice, or dignity, with the obligation of residence, and who is illegitimately absent: (1) is *eo ipso* deprived of all the income of his office or benefice in proportion to his illegitimate absence, and must turn over this income to the Ordinary, who shall distribute it to the church, or to some pious place, or to the poor; (2) shall be deprived of his office, benefice, dignity according to canons 2168-2175 (c. 2381).

Grave Neglect of Parochial Duties. If a pastor is gravely negligent in the administration of the sacraments, the care of the sick, the instruction of children and people, in preaching on Sundays and holydays, in the care of the parish church, of the Most Blessed Sacrament, of the holy oils, he shall be punished by the Ordinary according to canons 2182-2185 (c. 2382).

Failure to Keep Parish Records. A pastor who fails to make the entries in the parish books diligently according to law, or fails to preserve the said books carefully, shall be punished by his own Ordinary according to the gravity of the case (c. 2383).

Canon Theologian and Penitentiary. A canon theologian and canon penitentiary who are negligent in performing their duties shall be progressively dealt with by the Bishop through admonitions, the threat of penalties, the subtraction of part of the income and its assignment to the persons who take their place; if their negligence continues for a whole year after warning, they shall be punished by suspension from the benefice; and if for another six months, by privation of the benefice itself (c. 2384).

Apostasy From Religion. Without prejudice to the provisions of canon 646, a religious who is an apostate from religion *ipso iure* incurs an excommunication reserved to his own major superior, or, if it is a lay religious institute or one not exempt, reserved to the Ordinary of the place where he is staying; he is also barred from legitimate ecclesiastical acts, and deprived of all the privileges of his institute; and in case he returns he is perpetually deprived of active and passive voice, and should moreover be punished by his superiors according to the constitutions with other penalties according to the gravity of the case (c. 2385).

Flight From Religion. A religious who is a fugitive *ipso facto* incurs privation of any office he may have had in his institute, and, if he is in sacred orders, suspension reserved to his own major superior; and when he returns he is to be punished according to the constitutions, and if the constitutions make no provision for such punishment, the major superior shall inflict penalties according to the gravity of the case (c. 2386).

Fraudulent Religious Profession of Cleric. A religious cleric whose profession has been declared null because of fraud on his part, if he is in minor orders, is to be ejected from the clerical state; if he is in major orders, he is *ipso facto* suspended until the Holy See shall see fit to dispense him (c. 2387).

Sacrilegious Marriages. Clerics in sacred orders or regulars or nuns after a solemn vow of chastity, who shall presume to contract marriage even if only civilly, and all persons who shall presume to contract marriage even if only civilly with any of the aforesaid persons, incur an excommunication *latae sententiae* simply reserved to the Holy See; clerics moreover, if after warning they fail to amend within a time to be fixed in advance by the Ordinary according to circumstances, shall be degraded, without prejudice to the provisions of canon 188, 5° (c. 2388, § 1).

If there is question of the professed of simple perpetual vows in religious orders or congregations, all, as above provided, are under excommunication *latae sententiae* reserved to the Ordinary (c. 2388, § 2).

Grave Violation of Common Life. Religious who shall in a notable matter violate the law of the common life prescribed by the constitutions, are to receive a grave admonition, and if they fail to amend are to be punished even by privation of active and passive voice, and, if they are superiors, also by privation of their office (c. 2389).

Section 8. Crimes in the Conferring, Reception, and Laying Aside of Ecclesiastical Dignities, Benefices, and Offices
(cc. 2390–2403)

PRELIMINARY SURVEY

Interference With Freedom of Canonical Elections (c. 2390)
Election, Presentation, Nomination of Unworthy Candidate, Etc. (c. 2391)
Simony in Connection With Offices, Benefices, or Dignities (c. 2392)
Unlawful Conferring of Office, Etc. (c. 2393)
Unlawful Taking of Possession (c. 2394)
Accepting Office Not Vacant (c. 2395)
Retention of Two Incompatible Offices (c. 2396)
Cardinal Refusing to Take Oath (c. 2397)
Delay in Receiving Episcopal Consecration (c. 2398)
Dereliction of Office (c. 2399)
Resignation of Office to Lay Person (c. 2400)
Continuation in Office After Privation or Removal (c. 2401)
Failure of Abbot to Receive Blessing (c. 2402)
Omission of Profession of Faith (c. 2403)

Interference With Freedom of Canonical Elections. Those who in any way, personally or through others, interfere with the freedom of ecclesiastical elections, or who, after a canonical election, in any way molest either the electors or the person elected on account of the election, are to be punished in proportion to their guilt (c. 2390, § 1).

If the lay or secular power, in violation of the freedom guaranteed by canon law, presume to interfere unlawfully in an election which should be conducted by a college of clerics or religious, those electors who solicited or welcomed such interference are *ipso facto* deprived for that time of the right to elect; anyone who knowingly consented to his own election in this manner becomes *ipso facto* ineligible for the office or benefice in question (c. 2390, § 2).

Election, Presentation, Nomination of Unworthy Candidate, Etc. A college which knowingly elects an unworthy candidate is *ipso facto* deprived for that time of the right to proceed to a new election (c. 2391, § 1).

Individual electors who knowingly depart from the substantial form of an election can be punished by the Ordinary according to the gravity of the fault (c. 2391, § 2).

Clerics or lay persons who knowingly present or nominate an unworthy candidate are *ipso facto* deprived for that time of the right to present or nominate (c. 2391, § 3).

Simony. Without prejudice to the provisions of canon 729, those who commit the crime of simony in connection with any ecclesiastical offices, benefices, or dignities: (1) incur an excommunication *latae sententiae* simply reserved to the Holy See; (2) are *ipso facto* perpetually deprived of any right which they may have had to elect, present, or nominate; (3) if they are clerics, they are moreover to be suspended (c. 2392).

Unlawful Conferring of Offices, Etc. All who legitimately have the right to elect, present, or nominate, and who presume to confer the office, benefice, or dignity in disregard of the authority of the one to whom the right of confirmation or investiture belongs, are *ipso facto* deprived for that time of their right (c. 2393).

Unlawful Taking of Possession. Anyone who takes possession on his own authority of an ecclesiastical benefice, office or dignity, or who, after having been elected, presented, or nominated to the same, shall intrude himself into their possession, management, or administration before he has received the necessary letters of confirmation or investiture and has presented them to those to whom they should be presented according to law: (1) shall be *ipso facto* ineligible to the same and shall moreover be punished by the Ordinary according to the gravity of the case; (2) shall be compelled by suspension, privation of benefice, office, or dignity already obtained, and in a proper case also by deposition, to withdraw immediately after a previous warning from the occupation of the aforesaid benefice, office, or dignity, and from their management and administration; (3) the Chapters, communities, or other persons concerned, who shall admit any such candidate so elected, presented, or nominated, before he has presented his credentials, are *ipso facto* suspended from the right to elect, nominate, or present, subject to the pleasure of the Holy See (c. 2394).

Accepting Office Not Vacant. One who knowingly accepts an office, benefice, or dignity conferred upon him when it is not *de iure* vacant, and permits himself to be put in possession thereof, is *ipso facto* ineligible to acquire it thereafter, and is to be punished by other penalties in proportion to his guilt (c. 2395).

Retention of Two Incompatible Offices. A cleric who, after having obtained peaceful possession of an office or benefice which is incompatible with one which he already holds, shall presume to retain the prior one contrary to the provisions of canons 156 and 1439, is *ipso iure* deprived of both (c. 2396).

Cardinal Refusing to Take Oath. If anyone who has been raised to the dignity of the Cardinalate refuses to take the oath mentioned in canon 234, he is *ipso facto* forever deprived of that dignity (c. 2397).

Delay in Receiving Episcopal Consecration. If anyone who has been raised to the Episcopacy neglects to receive consecration within three months as provided by canon 333, he shall not receive the income, but it shall be applied to the maintenance of the cathedral church; and if thereafter he persist in the same negligence for another three months, he is *ipso iure* deprived of the Episcopacy (c. 2398).

Dereliction of Office. Major clerics who shall presume to abandon a charge committed to them by their own Ordinary without his permission, shall be suspended *a divinis* for a time to be fixed by the Ordinary according to circumstances (c. 2399).

Resignation of Office in Hands of Lay Person. A cleric who shall presume to resign an ecclesiastical office, benefice, or dignity into the hands of lay persons incurs *ipso facto* suspension *a divinis* (c. 2400).

Continuation in Office After Privation or Removal. Anyone who, in spite of legitimate deprivation or removal, persists in retaining an office, benefice, or dignity, or illegitimately contrives dilatory excuses for not giving it up, shall after due warning be compelled to do so by suspension *a divinis* and other penalties, not excepting deposition in a proper case (c. 2401).

Failure of Abbot to Receive Blessing. An Abbot or Prelate *nullius* who fails to receive the blessing as prescribed by canon 322, § 2, is *ipso facto* suspended from jurisdiction (c. 2402).

Omission of Profession of Faith. Whoever, contrary to the provisions of canon 1406, neglects without just cause to make the required profession of faith, shall be warned and given an appropriate time within which to comply; when that time has elapsed, the refractory party shall be punished even to the deprivation of office, benefice, dignity, or position; and in the meantime he shall not receive the income of the benefice, office, dignity, or position (c. 2403).

Section 9. Abuse of Ecclesiastical Power or Office
(cc. 2404–2414)

PRELIMINARY SURVEY

Abuse of Ecclesiastical Authority in General (c. 2404)
Tampering With Episcopal Documents (c. 2405)
Official Misfeasance or Malfeasance Regarding Episcopal or
Parochial Records (c. 2406)
Attempt to Bribe Officials (c. 2407)
Extortion (c. 2408)
Vicar Capitular Giving Dimissorial Letters Illegally
(c. 2409)
Violation of Rights of Ordinary Regarding Ordination of
Religious (c. 2410)
Illegal Admission to Noviceship or Religious Profession
(c. 2411)
Maladministration of Dowry: Failure to Notify Ordinary
of Admission or Profession (c. 2412)
Circumventing Canonical Visitor of Religious (c. 2413)
Impeding Liberty of Confession of Religious (c. 2414)

Abuse of Authority in General. Abuse of ecclesiastical authority shall be punished according to the prudent discretion of the lawful superior according to the gravity of the fault, without prejudice to the provisions of canons which establish a definite penalty for certain particular abuses (c 2404).

Tampering With Episcopal Documents. A Vicar Capitular and all other persons, whether members of the Chapter or not, who either personally or through others remove, destroy, conceal, or substantially alter any document pertaining to the episcopal Curia, *ipso facto* incur an excommunication simply reserved to the Holy See and are also liable to be punished by the Ordinary by deprivation of their office or benefice (c. 2405).

Official Misfeasance or Malfeasance Regarding Episcopal or Parochial Records. If anyone who is officially responsible for preparing, making entries in, and preserving documents or books of ecclesiastical Curiae or parochial registers, shall presume to falsify, alter, destroy, or conceal them, he shall be deprived of his office or be visited by the Ordinary with other grave penalties in proportion to his guilt (c. 2406, § 1).

Any such official who shall maliciously refuse to make out, transmit, or show the aforesaid records, documents, or books to one who legitimately asks for the same, or who shall in any manner prove false to his official duty, is subject to punishment at the discretion of the Ordinary according to the gravity of the case by privation of his office, or suspension from the same, or by fine (c. 2406, § 2).

Attempt to Bribe Officials. Whoever shall attempt by gifts or promises to induce Curial officials or any ecclesiastical functionaries, judges, advocates, or procurators, to any act or omission contrary to their official duty, shall be punished by a suitable penalty and be compelled to make good any damages that may have been caused (c. 2407).

Extortion. Those who raise the amount of the taxes which are prescribed by custom or legitimately approved according to canon 1507, or who exact anything more, shall be punished by a severe pecuniary fine, and *recidivi* shall be suspended or removed from office according to the gravity of the case, in addition to being obliged to make restitution of whatever they have unjustly received (c. 2408).

Illegal Dimissorial Letters. A Vicar Capitular who grants dimissorial letters for ordination contrary to the provisions of canon 958, § 1, 3°, is *ipso facto* suspended *a divinis* (c. 2409).

Violation of Rights of Ordinary Regarding Ordination of Religious. Religious superiors who, in violation of the provisions of canon 965–967, presume to send their subjects to be ordained by a Bishop other than their own local Ordinary, are *ipso facto* suspended from the celebration of Mass for one month (c. 2410).

Illegal Admission to Noviceship or Religious Profession. Religious superiors who admit an unfit candidate to the noviceship contrary to canon 542, or admit any candidate without the required testimonials, to the noviceship contrary to canon 544, or to the profession contrary to canon 571, § 2, shall be punished according to the gravity of their guilt, even to the extent of privation of their office (c. 2411).

Maladministration of Dowry: Failure to Notify Ordinary of Admission or Profession. The superioresses of religious women, even though exempt, shall be punished by the Ordinary of the place according to the gravity of their guilt, in a proper case even to the extent of privation of their office: (1) if, in violation of canon 549, they presume to spend in any way the dowries of the candidates whom they have received, subject always to the obligation mentioned in canon 551 (regarding the restoration or transfer of the dowry upon departure or transfer of the religious); (2) if, in violation of canon

552, they fail to notify the local Ordinary of the approaching admission of a candidate to the noviceship or profession (c. 2412).

Circumventing Canonical Visitor of Religious. Superioresses who, after a visitation has been announced, shall transfer any of their subjects without the Visitor's consent to another house, and likewise all religious women, whether superiors or subjects, who shall personally or through others, directly or indirectly, induce religious women to remain silent when questioned by the Visitor, or to dissimulate the truth in any way, or to be insincere in their statements, or who shall molest them under any pretext whatever because of the replies they made to the Visitor, shall be declared by the Visitor incapable of obtaining any office which involves the government of others, and superioresses shall be deprived of the office which they hold (c. 2413, § 1).

The provisions of the above paragraph apply also to religious institutes of men (c. 2413, § 2).

Impeding Liberty of Confession of Religious. A Superioress who acts in any way contrary to canons 521, § 3, 522, or 523 shall be warned by the Ordinary of the place; if she offends again she shall be punished by him with privation of her office, and he shall immediately notify the Sacred Congregation of Religious (c. 2414).

The Special Case of a Priest Who Has Attempted Marriage and Cannot Separate. A priest who attempts marriage is *ipso facto* under excommunication simply reserved to the Holy See, as we noted above in explanation of canon 2388, § 1. However, two later documents of the Sacred Penitentiary, approved by the Supreme Pontiff, have the effect of making this excommunication *most specially* reserved to the Holy See, in the case of a priest who has attempted marriage and is unable to effect a complete separation.[4]

Violating the "Secret of the Holy Office." This secret binds all persons in the Holy Office and all those in the Sacred Consistorial Congregation who treat of appointments of Bishops, erection of dioceses, etc., until those matters are lawfully published. The penalty for its violation is not mentioned in the Code; it is an *ipso facto* excommunication, which can be absolved outside of danger of death only by the Supreme Pontiff himself, to the exclusion even of the Cardinal Major Penitentiary.[5]

---

[4] S. Paen., 18 Apr., 1936; *AAS*, 28, p. 242; *Digest*, II, p. 579.
[5] Cf. A Coronata, *Institutiones*, I, n. 332.

The Censures of the Council of Baltimore. The Third Plenary Council of Baltimore enacted two *latae sententiae* excommunications which are still of some practical importance.

"We establish the penalty of excommunication, reserved to the Ordinary, to be incurred *ipso facto* by those who, after obtaining a civil divorce, dare to attempt marriage" (*Conc. Balt. III*, n. 124). Since *particular* penal laws not contrary to the Code are not abrogated by the Code, this penalty is still in effect in the United States.

"We likewise decree that Catholics who, outside their own diocese, in any State or Territory within the jurisdiction of the Bishops who are present or should be present at this Council, contract or attempt marriage before a minister of any non-Catholic sect, incur an excommunication reserved to the Bishop, from which however any of the aforesaid Ordinaries can absolve either personally or through a priest whom they delegate for this purpose. If the persons commit this crime in their own diocese, We enact that they be *ipso facto* bound by excommunication which is reserved to their own Ordinary unless they go to some other Bishop without the intention to evade the law" (*Conc. Balt. III*, n. 127). The words last quoted, expressing the manner in which this excommunication is reserved to the parties' own proper Bishop, seem to us to be contrary to the Code, and therefore now ineffective (cf. c. 2247, § 2). Consequently this crime, whether committed in one's own diocese or elsewhere within the territory described, results in an excommunication *latae sententiae* which is reserved to the Ordinary in the usual Code sense (cf. c. 2253, 3°). The excommunication itself is not contrary to the Code, and is consequently still in effect. It would apply to certain cases not reached with certainty by canon 2319, § 1, for example, to cases where *both parties* were Catholics.

Readings:

MacKenzie, *The Delict of Heresy, Its Commission, Penalization, Absolution,* Cath. U., 1932; Barry, *The Violation of Cloister,* Cath. U., 1942; Huser, *The Crime of Abortion in Canon Law,* Cath. U., 1942; Linahen, *De Absolutione Complicis in Peccato Turpi,* Cath. U., 1942; *The Jurist,* Vol. 4, p. 610 (Hannan, on profession of faith by converts); *Ecclesiastical Review:* Vol. 90, p. 623 and Vol. 91, p. 625 (Schaaf, on *absolutio complicis*); Vol. 94, p. 410 (Schaaf, on books proscribed by Apostolic Letter); *Irish Ecclesiastical Record,* Vol. 51, p. 300 (Fallon on violation of *privilegium canonis*); *Periodica,* Vol. 18, p. 165* (Cappello, on penalties for simony); Vol. 18, p. 161* (Arendt, on penalties for simony); Vol. 23, p. 55* (on absolution of heretics); Vol. 26, p. 501 (Lopez, on absolution from censure incurred by priest attempting marriage); Vol. 27, p. 32 (Lopez, on procedure of Holy Office in cases of solicitation).

CHAPTER XXV

SOME STUDY OUTLINES ON THE PRINCIPAL CENSURES *LATAE SENTENTIAE*

Plan of This Chapter. We have now taken the trouble to glance in a very summary way at the entire penal law of the Church. It may seem bewildering. We know that we cannot learn it all at once, nor carry all its details in our memory. Happily, no such superhuman effort is required of us at this time. We can learn the minimum essentials for ordinary confessional work now, and in time we can learn a great deal more, *if we use the right method.* The first step in a sound method is what we have already done, to look over the whole field. The next steps would seem to be the following: (1) to concentrate on the excommunications, suspensions, and interdicts which are *latae sententiae,* and make a *complete list* of them for ready reference and frequent repetition; (2) to *mark particularly those* which seem either especially important or most likely to occur unexpectedly in practice, and to make a *condensed outline* of these, if possible with some mnemonic scheme for remembering them; (3) to *study the censures which are on that special list* a little more fully than we have yet done; (4) finally, to *review,* if it can be done *in a synoptic manner, the principles* for dealing with reserved censures and sins in the confessional. Accordingly we divide this chapter into the following sections:

Section 1. Complete List of *Latae Sententiae* Censures

Section 2. Select List of *Latae Sententiae* Excommunications and Suspensions

Section 3. Study Outlines for Some Censures on the Select List

Section 4. Chart Illustrating Concrete Cases of Reserved Sins and Censures

Section 1. Complete List of *Latae Sententiae* Censures[1]

---

[1] *Some* of the *suspensions* here listed are vindictive penalties rather than censures, and are marked as such. The asterisk placed before the words designates certain crimes and penalties which will be collected in a special list later, as the most practical for study.

The following is a complete list of *latae sententiae* censures divided into three groups: Excommunications; Suspensions; Interdicts.

EXCOMMUNICATIONS

(The asterisk designates excommunications of greater importance, which are considered in Section 2, below.)

Canon	Brief Designation of Crime[2]	How Reserved
2314, § 1	*Apostasy, heresy, schism	a) *In foro conscientiae,* specially to Holy See b) *In foro externo,* to the Ordinary
2318, § 1	*Special books (publishing, defending, reading, keeping)	specially to Holy See
2318, § 2	*Scripture printed without permission (author; publisher)	*nemini*
2319, §§ 1–4	*Marriage before minister; (also non-Catholic education or baptism)	to the Ordinary
Conc. Balt. n. 127	*Marriage before minister in cases not covered by Code	to the Ordinary
Conc. Balt. n. 124	*Marriage after civil divorce	to the Ordinary
2320	*Profanation of sacred Species	most specially to Holy See
2322, 1°	Mass or confession without priestly orders	specially to Holy See
2326	Relics (falsification, sale, unlawful public exposition)	to the Ordinary
2327	Traffic in indulgences	simply to Holy See
2330	Crimes in papal election	most specially to Holy See (Document I)

---

[2] For a *full,* i.e., *accurate* designation, constant reference to the text of the Code is essential; for this reason the reference to the canon is given at the left.

2332	Appeal from Pope to Council	specially to Holy See
2333	Recourse to lay authority to impede papal documents	specially to Holy See
2334, 1°	Laws contrary to liberty or rights of Church	specially to Holy See
2334, 2°	Recourse to lay authority to impede ecclesiastical jurisdiction	specially to Holy See
2335	*Masonic societies	simply to Holy See
2338, § 1	Presuming to absolve from excommunication *l. s.* specially or most specially reserved	simply to Holy See
2338, § 2	Communication with *vitandus*	simply to Holy See
2339	Ordering or compelling ecclesiastical burial of excommunicated or interdicted person	*nemini*
2341	*Summoning higher Prelate before lay tribunal	specially to Holy See
2341	*Summoning Prelate lower than own Bishop before lay tribunal	simply to Holy See
2342	*Various violations of papal cloister	simply to Holy See
2343, § 1	*Laying violent hands on Roman Pontiff	most specially to Holy See
2343, §§ 2, 3	*Laying violent hands on Cardinal *et al.* down to titular Bishop	specially to Holy See
2343, § 4	*Laying violent hands on cleric or religious	to culprit's own Ordinary
2345	Usurping property or	

	rights of *Roman* Church	specially to Holy See
2346	Confiscation of church property	simply to Holy See
2347	Alienation without *beneplacitum*	*nemini*
2350	*Abortion	to the Ordinary
2351, § 1	Dueling	simply to Holy See
2352	Compulsion to clerical or religious state	*nemini*
2360, § 1	Forgery of papal documents	specially to Holy See
2363	*False accusation of solicitation	specially to Holy See
2367, §§ 1, 2	*Absolving *complex in peccato turpi*	most specially to Holy See
2368, § 2	*Failure to denounce for solicitation	*nemini*
2369, § 1	*Direct violation of seal	most specially to Holy See
2385	*Apostasy from religion	*a)* clerical exempt, to his own major superior
		b) lay or nonexempt, to Ordinary of place
2388, § 1	*Marriage with sacred orders or solemn vows (accomplices also)	simply to Holy See
2388, § 1 (*Dig.* 2, pp. 579, 580)	*Same in case of priest who cannot separate	most specially to Holy See
2388, § 2	*Marriage with simple perpetual vows	to Ordinary
2392	Simony in office, benefice, etc.	simply to Holy See
2405	Tampering with episcopal documents	simply to Holy See

SUSPENSIONS

Canon	Brief Designation of Crime	Nature and Reservation[3]
671, 1°	*Religious of perpetual vows dismissed for minor crimes	general, reserved to Holy See
2341	*Summoning cleric or religious before lay tribunal	from office, res. to Ordinary
2366	Presuming to hear confessions without jurisdiction	a divinis, not reserved
2366	Presuming to absolve from reserved sins	from hearing confessions, not reserved
2370	Consecrating Bishop without mandate	general, res. to Holy See
2371	Simony in reception or administration of sacraments	general, res. to Holy See
2372	Receiving orders from one under censure	a divinis, res. to Holy See
2373	Various illegal ordinations	from conferring orders (vindictive, 1 yr.), res. to Holy See
2374	Illegal reception of orders	from order so received, not reserved
2386	*Religious fugitive in sacred orders	general, res. to own major superior
2387	Religious in sacred orders, fraudulent profession	general (vindictive), res. to Holy See
2394, 3°	Chapter admitting official unlawfully in possession	from right to elect, etc. (vindictive), res. to Holy See
2400	Resigning office to lay person	a divinis, not reserved

---

[3] These suspensions are censures unless marked as vindictive penalties.

2402	Abbot or Prelate *nullius* failing to r e c e i v e blessing	from jurisdiction, n o t reserved
2409	Vicar Capitular illegally granting dimissorial letters	*a divinis,* not reserved
2410	Violating right of Ordinary in ordination of religious	from celebration of Mass (vindictive, 1 month), not reserved

INTERDICTS

Canon	Brief Designation of Crime	Nature and Reservation
2332	College appealing from Pope to Council	specially to Holy See
2338, § 3	Permitting divine services in interdicted place	from entry into church, not reserved
2338, § 4	Giving cause for local or collective interdict	personal, not reserved
2339	G i v i n g ecclesiastical b u r i a l to excommunicated or interdicted person	from entry into church, reserved to Ordinary

Excommunications *Latae Sententiae.* Let us now concentrate our attention on the excommunications *latae sententiae.* We present again the complete list of these excommunications, but now arranged in a synoptical chart and classified according to the manner of their reservation.

Section 2. Select List of *Latae Sententiae* Excommunications and Suspensions

Excommunications. From the complete list we have selected twenty-three excommunications *latae sententiae* (those which were marked with a star), which seem for various reasons most desirable to remember. They fall into five groups arranged in the order of their gravity as indicated by the severity with which they are reserved: (1) those reserved *most specially* to the Holy See (5); (2) those reserved *specially* to the Holy See (5); (3) those reserved *simply* to the Holy See (4); (4) those reserved *to the Ordinary* (7); (5) those *not reserved* (2).

Twenty-three Excommunications *Latae Sententiae*

Most specially reserved to the Holy See (5):

Profaning the Sacred Species (c. 2320)
Laying Violent Hands on the Roman Pontiff (c. 2343, § 1)
Absolving or Pretending to Absolve an Accomplice (c. 2367)
Direct Violation of the Seal (c. 2369, § 1)
Priest Having Attempted Marriage, Unable to Separate (c. 2388, § 1; *Digest,* 2, pp. 579, 580)

Specially reserved to the Holy See (5):

Apostasy, Heresy, Schism (*in foro conscientiae,* c. 2314)
Special Books (c. 2318, § 1)
Summoning Higher Prelate Before Lay Tribunal (c. 2341)
Laying Violent Hands on Higher Prelate (c. 2343, §§ 2, 3)
False Accusation of Solicitation (c. 2363)

Simply reserved to the Holy See (4):

Masonic Societies (c. 2335)
Summoning Lower Prelate Before Lay Tribunal (c. 2341)
Various Violations of Papal Cloister (c. 2342)
Attempting Marriage With Solemn Vows or Sacred Orders (c. 2388, § 1)

Reserved *to the Ordinary* (7):

Marriage (Mixed) Before Non-Catholic Minister (c. 2319, § 1)
Marriage Before Non-Catholic Minister (*Conc. Balt. III,* n. 127)
Marriage After Divorce (*Conc. Balt. III,* n. 124)

COMPLETE CHART OF EXCOM

1. Most Specially Reserved to the Holy See	2. Specially Reserved to the Holy See	3. Simply Reserved to the Holy See
	*Apostasy, Heresy, Schism in *foro conscientiae* (c. 2314, §§ 1, 2) *Books *specially* prohibited (c. 2318, § 1)	
*Profaning S a c r e d Species (c. 2320)	Mass, confession, without priestly orders (c. 2322, 1°)	Traffic in indulgences (c. 2327)
Crimes in election of Roman Pontiff (c. 2330)	Appeal to Council (c. 2332)	*Masonic societies (c. 2335)
	Recourse to lay power to impede papal documents (c. 2333)	Presuming to absolve from excom., special, most special (c. 2338, §1)
Violating secret of the Holy Office (*AAS,* 1–82 ; 9–232)	Laws against Church: Recourse to impede jurisdiction (c. 2334) *Summoning *higher* Prelate before lay tribunal (c. 2341)	Communication w i t h *vitandus* (c. 2338, § 2)
*Violent hands on Roman Pontiff (c. 2343, § 1)	*Violent hands on Cardinal to titular Bishop (c. 2343, §§ 2, 3) Usurping property or rights of *Roman* Church (c. 2345)	*Summoning *lower* Prelate before lay tribunal (c. 2341) *Violations of p a p a l cloister (c. 2342) Confiscation of church property (c. 2346)
		Dueling (c. 2351)
	Forgery of papal documents (c. 2360) *False accusation of solicitation (c. 2363)	
*Absolving complex *in peccato turpi* (c. 2367) *Direct violation of seal (c. 2369, § 1)		
*Priest who attempted marriage and cannot separate (c. 2388, § 1 and *Digest,* Vol. 2, p. 579, 580)		*Marriage attempt with sacred orders or solemn vows (c. 2388, § 1)
		Simony in offices, etc. (c. 2392)
		Tampering with episcopal documents (c. 2405)

*The cases which are considered most important are marked with an asterisk, with the key word in bold type.

MUNICATIONS *LATAE SENTENTIAE*

4. Reserved to the Ordinary by Common Law	5. Reserved to the Ordinary by Particular Law	6. Reserved to No One
Apostasy, Heresy, Schism — in *foro externo* (c. 2314)		
*Marriage (mixed) before minister (c. 2319, § 1, 1°)	*Marriage before minister (*Conc. Balt. III*, n. 127)	*Scripture books (author and publisher only) (c. 2318, § 2)
Non-Catholic education agreed on in marriage (§ 1, 2°)		
Presenting child for non-Catholic baptism (§ 1, 3°)	*Marriage after civil divorce (*Ibid.*, n. 124)	
Presenting child for non-Catholic education (§ 1, 4°)		
False relics (c. 2326)		
		Ordering ecclesiastical burial of excommunicated, etc. (c. 2339)
*Violent hands on cleric or religious (c. 2343, § 4)		
		Unlawful alienation of church property (c. 2347)
*Abortion (c. 2350, § 1)		Compulsion to clerical or religious state (c. 2352)
		*Failure to denounce for solicitation (c. 2368, § 2)
*Apostasy from religion (c. 2385)		
*Marriage with simple vows (c. 2388, § 2)		

Laying Violent Hands on Cleric or Religious (c. 2343, § 4)
Abortion (c. 2350)
Apostasy From Religion (c. 2385)
Marriage With Simple Perpetual Vows (c. 2388, § 2)

Not reserved (2):
Scripture Books (c. 2318, § 2)
Failure to Denounce for Solicitation (c. 2368, § 2)

Suspensions. These three seem worthy of special attention:

Three Suspensions *Latae Sententiae*

Religious of Perpetual Vows Dismissed for Minor Crimes (c. 671, 1°)
Summoning Cleric or Religious Before Lay Tribunal (c. 2341)
Religious in Sacred Orders a Fugitive From Religion (c. 2386)

How to Remember the Twenty-three Excommunications. We memorize telephone numbers without difficulty; 55472 is easy enough. That is our key number. Each digit represents the *number of excommunications in each class,* in descending order, beginning with those most specially reserved to the Holy See. Now all we need is a little system for memorizing the *excommunications themselves* in each group, by some significant word. Perhaps each student can work out his own system. Many are helped by beginning with initial letters. We might represent each excommunication by the initial letter of a word which will easily suggest the substance of the crime, thus:

Most specially reserved to the Holy See...	S	(Species)
(5)	V	(Violent)
	C	(Complex)
	S	(Seal)
	P	(Priest)
Specially reserved to the Holy See.......	A	(Apostasy)
(5)	B	(Books)
	L	(Lay tribunal)
	V	(Violent)
	F	(False)
Simply reserved to the Holy See........	M	(Masonic)
(4)	L	(Lay tribunal)
	C	(Cloister)
	M	(Marriage)

Reserved to the Ordinary.............M (Marriage)
        (7)   M (Marriage)
                        M (Marriage)
                        V (Violent)
                        A (Abortion)
                        R (Religious apostate)
                        M (Marriage)

Not reserved (or reserved to no one)....S (Scriptures)
        (2)   F (Failure to denounce)

Initials have been selected which will, after very slight practice, easily recall the significant word. For example, B stands exclusively for Books, L for Lay tribunal, P for Priest, R for Religious, V for Violent (laying violent hands on cleric in violation of the *privilegium canonis*). S is a symbol for three distinct words, Species, Seal, Scripture, but the first two will be easily remembered (as belonging to the excommunications most specially reserved). C represents two separate key words, Complex, and Cloister; A is for Apostate and Abortion. M, the first time it occurs, stands for Masonic, then throughout (5 times) for Marriage. The distinctions between the five excommunications connected with marriage are not difficult to remember. F stands for two distinct words, but the connection between the two excommunications helps to remember them; they are False (accusation of solicitation) and Failure (to denounce for solicitation).

Thus, if we can recall these initial letters in their distinct groups, it should be easy to name the excommunications in each group. One difficulty remains: a disconnected series of mere initials is hard to remember. Let us build a little sentence (perhaps the more foolish the better) for each group, to bring our key initials easily to mind. As far as possible, words will be used which suggest the real key word.

Class of excommunication	Mnemonic phrase
Most specially reserved to Holy See	Special Violent Complex Seizes Priest
Specially reserved to Holy See	Apostate Books Loom Violently False
Simply reserved to Holy See	Masons Lay Cloister Monument
Reserved to Ordinary	Married Men Move Violently About Religious Monastery
Not reserved	Scriptures (never) Fail

These five little sentences are easy to memorize; and they contain the key to the twenty-three most practical excommunications *latae sententiae*. We shall now study these same excommunications in slightly greater detail.

Section 3. Study Outlines for Excommunications of the Select List

Most Specially Reserved to the Holy See (5):

1. Profaning the Sacred Species (c. 2320). Two or three distinct crimes and distinct censures are possible under this canon:

a. To throw away;

b. To take away for a bad purpose;

c. To retain for a bad purpose.

In *b* and *c,* the bad purpose is an element of the crime, but it will be presumed from the unlawful withdrawal or retention. Stealing the ciborium but leaving the Hosts in good order is not "throwing away," and is not punished by excommunication. If the same person both takes away the Sacred Species for a bad purpose and retains them for a bad purpose, two censures are incurred (cf. c. 2244, § 1, § 2, 1°). This supposes, of course, that the *retention for a bad purpose* is sufficiently protracted to amount to an act distinct from the *taking for a bad purpose,* or is distinguished from it by a different bad purpose.[4]

2. Laying Violent Hands on the Roman Pontiff (c. 2343, § 1). The essence of this crime is sufficiently explained under canon 119, *privilegium canonis* (cf. p. 102).

3. Absolving or Pretending to Absolve an Accomplice *in Peccato Turpi* (c. 2367).

a. The *sin* in question is an external, grave, mutual sin of impurity, certain as to both parties. It may consist of words or acts; need not be consummated. Whether committed before or after priesthood makes no difference in this regard.

b. The *accomplice* may be any man, woman, or child who is guilty of the same sin, externally grave, with full consent on both sides.

c. If there is *no absolution nor pretense,* there is no censure. Hence, giving a mere blessing (to save penitent's reputation, e.g., when others

---

[4] See Vermeersch-Creusen, *Epit.,* III, n. 520; Cappello, *De Censuris,* n. 204, 3; A Coronata, IV, n. 1882; *contra,* Sole, *De Delictis et Poenis,* n. 335, 4, p. 241.

might observe) and telling the penitent that no absolution is being given, would not merit the censure.

d. If *penitent omits this sin,* without having been induced by the confessor to omit it — no censure, because no absolution nor pretense regarding this sin.

e. If the penitent *mentions this sin and absolution is given,* if there is necessity for confession and the penitent cannot without danger confess to another, and the penitent is warned that this sin must be repeated in another confession — probably no censure is incurred; other sins are forgiven directly, this one indirectly (Noldin, *De Censuris,* n. 55; Cappello, *De Censuris,* n. 170).

f. Indirectly inducing penitent to omit this sin includes case where confessor persuaded penitent beforehand that it was not mortal; hence penitent now omits it for that reason (Holy Office, 16 Nov., 1934, *AAS,* 26, p. 634, *Digest,* II, p. 578). Hence, in this case the censure is incurred.

g. Confessor *does not certainly recognize penitent* as accomplice; or, penitent does not now recognize confessor as her accomplice, and did not at any time recognize her accomplice as a priest — no censure.

h. If *this sin has already been absolved* — no censure.

4. Direct Violation of the Seal (c. 2369, § 1).

a. Though others also are bound by the seal (cf. c. 889, § 2), *only the confessor* incurs this penalty. He need not have faculties; it is sufficient that he be a priest and hears the confession.

b. Seal *applies to all matter* of sacramental confession whose revelation would be "in gravamen poenitentis et (*vel*) in odium sacramenti." Holds even after death of penitent, because "in odium sacramenti" would apply even then.

c. Confession is sacramental if made *in ordine ad absolutionem,* though absolution be not given.

d. Speaking to penitent outside confession, about confession matter, without his permission, is forbidden, but is not violation of the seal — no censure.

e. Violation is *direct* if it reveals both the sin and the person.

f. Because of the word "praesumpserit," any diminution of imputability on the part of intellect or will would excuse from this censure (cf. c. 2229, § 2).

5. Priest Who Has Attempted Marriage and Is Unable to Separate. This case is sufficiently clear from the two documents of the Sacred Penitentiary.

Specially Reserved to the Holy See (5)

1. Apostasy, Heresy, Schism (c. 2314).

a. Definitions of apostate, heretic, schismatic are given in canon 1325, § 2.

b. In all cases a requisite for the crime is an internal attitude *externally manifested.*

c. Pertinaciter (in definition of heretic) does not imply duration, nor violence; it simply means setting up one's own mind against the *known* mind of the Church. The denial or doubt must be externally manifested, and *formal,* i.e., subjectively a grave sin. Adherence to a non-Catholic sect is not necessary for this censure. On the other hand, many persons born and educated in heresy may be only material heretics; yet the practice is to absolve them from this censure if they were converted after puberty.

d. Reservation of this censure is twofold: it is specially reserved to the Holy See only if the absolution is given in the internal forum; after it has been brought *in any way* (by public or private accusation, or voluntary extrasacramental confession) into the external forum of the Ordinary, it is reserved to the Ordinary. Converts coming into the Church, by speaking of their religious affairs to a priest outside confession, have brought their censure (if any) to the external forum; and diocesan pagellas usually give priests the faculty of absolving from this censure in the external forum. Hence, the priest who receives a convert will give this absolution immediately after the abjuration or profession of faith; after which, the *censure* being removed for both fora (cf. c. 202, § 1), the confessor can then absolve from the *sin* without special faculties. Note that the abjuration, since it belongs to the external forum, must be capable of proof there. Hence, two witnesses are required. A new formula for the abjuration was approved shortly before 1942 by the Holy Office.[5] The words of the canon, "servatis servandis," include the following: make sure of validity of former baptism, give proportionate penance, demand reparation of scandal if any and denunciation of others formally guilty, exact promise to break off relations with sect. All this, however, within reason.

2. Special Books (c. 2318, § 1).

a. Note that *two distinct crimes* are punished by this section: *the*

---

[5] Cf. *Digest,* II, p. 182; *The Jurist,* Vol. 4 (1944), p. 610 sq.

first can be committed only by publishers, *the second* by those who defend, read, or keep certain books.

b. First crime: *publishers* of books of apostates, heretics, schismatics, which propound apostasy, heresy, or schism, incur the excommunication when the book is published for general circulation.

c. Second crime: persons who defend, or knowingly and without permission read or keep *the above books or books which are prohibited by name by Apostolic letter,* incur excommunication. Note:

1) *Books only* are mentioned here. The term in this connection *does not include* magazines, etc., since canon 1384, § 2 applies only to provisions *of that Title,* namely, canons 1384–1405. Hence the term here means only printed books, of some size, constituting a moral unit by reason of their content.

2) They must be *forbidden by name or title.* This is not the case when all works of a named author are condemned without naming the works.

3) They must be *forbidden by Apostolic letter,* i.e., a Bull, Brief, or Encyclical of the Roman Pontiff. This does not include a decree of the Holy Office, nor even an order of the Pope made public without any *letter.*

4) To *retain* (keep) means for a notable time, and does not include librarians unless book is kept in their room or home.

5) This censure would not affect a *Bishop* (c. 1401).

3. Summoning Higher Prelate Before Lay Tribunal (c. 2341).

4. Laying Violent Hands on Higher Prelate (c. 2343, §§ 2, 3).

5. False Accusation of Solicitation (c. 2363).

a. The accusation must be *against the confessor* as such for the crime of solicitation; whether the accusation be made in person or through others makes no difference.

b. It must be a *juridical* accusation made to the Ordinary of the place or to the Holy Office (c. 904). The Vicar General cannot proceed in such cases without special mandate; hence, an accusation lodged with him is not strictly juridical.

c. The accusation must be *false,* and knowingly so; hence a grave sin of slander.

d. Conditions for absolution: formal juridical retractation; reparation of damage as far as possible; grave and long penance (*gravis et diuturna;* as to meaning of these terms, cf. Cappello, *De Censuris,* nn. 101, 131).

e. Can this censure be absolved as an *urgent case* under canon

2254? Yes, *provided the condition* of actual retractation and reparation of damage as far as possible *has been actually fulfilled.* The promise to do so is not sufficient (cf. c. 2363; V–C, *Epit.,* III, n. 565).

Simply Reserved to the Holy See (4)

1. Masonic Societies (c. 2335).

a. The censure is *incurred* if the society is one which plots against Church or State, openly or secretly, whether members are secret or not, bound by oath or not. Cappello thinks Socialists are included. Communist party certainly is. Knights of Pythias, Odd Fellows, Sons of Temperance, are forbidden as intrinsically wrong, but not under censure (Holy Office, 20 June, 1895, 18 Jan., 1896).

b. Conditions for absolution: total withdrawal from the society, promise to have nothing to do with it and to *pay no more dues,* to repair scandal as far as possible, to turn over insignia, etc., to withdraw name from rolls as soon as this can be done without grave loss (Holy Office, 7 March, 1883; Gasparri-Serédi, *Fontes,* n. 1080, Vol. IV, p. 412).

c. In the case of the *Knights of Pythias, Odd Fellows, Sons of Temperance,* no censure has been incurred. The conditions for absolution of the *sin* are the same as above except that, to avoid grave loss, a person may continue paying dues. The confessor must refer each case to the Apostolic Delegate or to his Metropolitan (Holy Office, 18 Jan., 1896; *Ecclesiastical Review,* Vol. 14, p. 361).[6]

2. Summoning Lower Prelate Before Lay Tribunal (c. 2341).

3. Various Violations of Papal Cloister (c. 2342).

a. Three different crimes: the first, unlawful entering, introducing, or admitting to *cloister of nuns:*

1) *Papal* cloister, cf. c. 597, § 1 and Instruction of S. C. of Religious, in *Digest,* I, p. 314.

2) *Nuns* are women with solemn vows, not including those in institutes whose vows are solemn according to the constitutions but reduced to simple vows by indult (c. 488, 7°; V–C, *Epit.,* III, n. 541).

3) Whether person admitted be male or female makes no difference, but *age* may. Persons *under the age of puberty* are not held by the censure (c. 2230), but co-operators who have attained puberty are (for

---

[6] The following references may be of service: Cappello, *De Censuris,* n. 296 sq.; Sabetti-Barrett, pp. 1028–1031; *Conc. Balt. III,* n. 244 sq. and Appendix, p. 282 sq.; *Ecclesiastical Review,* Vol 1, pp. 125, 179; Vol. 13, p. 67; Vol. 14, p. 361; Vol. 49, p. 468; Ayrinhac-Lydon, *Penal Legislation,* p. 200.

introducing or admitting them). If, however, the person admitted were *under the age of reason,* they would not come under the terms of *this part* of the canon, as "clausuram violantes," and hence even those who admit them would commit no crime (cf. Cappello, *De Censuris,* n. 319, 4); but see *b.*

b. The second crime: females violating *cloister of male regulars,* and all persons (including superiors) who introduce or admit them, *of whatever age,* incur the censure. Under this provision, though, of course, an infant would incur no censure, anyone admitting a female infant would incur it.

c. The third: nuns after their profession unlawfully going out incur the censure. Here novices and even postulants are not included (cc. 540, § 3, 601, *Digest,* I, p. 314); nor are those who are under temporary vows before their solemn profession (Cappello, n. 323).

4. Attempting Marriage With Sacred Orders or Solemn Vows (c. 2388, § 1).

a. Three classes of persons incur this excommunication: religious after solemn vows; clerics after subdiaconate; persons attempting marriage with either.

b. Civil marriage is sufficient to incur the censure; but a *pretended* marriage, namely, one in which it is certain that there was no matrimonial consent, is not sufficient.[7]

c. Even *crass ignorance,* or *fear though not grave* would excuse, because of the word *praesumpserit* (cf. c. 2229, § 2).

d. The case of a *priest* who has incurred this censure and who is unable for the gravest reasons to cease from cohabiting under the same roof with the partner of his crime (though promising perfect chastity and removing the occasion of sin), and who seeks absolution in order to be admitted to the sacraments after the manner of laymen, is reserved to the Sacred Penitentiary in such a way that it amounts to a reservation *most specially* to the Holy See. It cannot be absolved in an urgent case in virtue of canon 2254, but only in danger of death, and then with the obligation of recourse to the Sacred Penitentiary in case of recovery. (Cf. Sacred Penitentiary, 18 Apr., 1936; *AAS,* 28, p. 242, *Digest,* II, p. 579; and 4 May, 1937; *AAS,* 29, p. 283, *Digest,* II, p. 580.)

---

[7] Cf. Chelodi, *Ius Poenale,* n. 102; Cappello, *De Censuris,* n. 355. The contrary opinion does not seem probable, since the case clearly presents neither a marriage nor an attempt at marriage.

Reserved to the Ordinary (7)

1. Marriage (Mixed) Before Non-Catholic Minister Against Canon 1063 (c. 2319, § 1).

a. This censure is incurred only *by the Catholic party* in a marriage with a non-Catholic, before a non-Catholic minister *as such;* it is not incurred if both parties are Catholics (because of a solidly probable opinion to that effect; cf. Cappello, *De Censuris,* n. 369, 4).

b. Is it incurred *if the non-Catholic party is unbaptized?* Disputed question. The affirmative answer is theoretically correct; however, some authors hold otherwise because of the mention in canon 1063 of the impediment of *mixed religion.* The answer to this argument is that canon 1071 makes the same provision for marriages where the impediment is disparity of cult. However, since the negative opinion is extrinsically probable, we may hold in practice that the censure is not incurred. But the censure of the Council of Baltimore would be incurred.

c. Canon 1063 says "before or after marriage before the Church"; *what if no Catholic marriage took place?* Most authors seem to hold that the censure is incurred anyway. It seems to us that there is a doubt of law, which should be sufficient to excuse from the censure.[8] However, the censure of the Council of Baltimore would apply in such a case (cf. n. 2, below).

2. Marriage Before Non-Catholic Minister (*Conc. Balt. III*, n. 127). This excommunication is incurred by Catholics who contract or attempt marriage before a minister of any non-Catholic sect. It is incurred even if both parties were Catholics, or if no Catholic marriage took place.

3. Marriage After Divorce (*Conc. Balt. III*, n. 124).

a. "Poenam excommunicationis statuimus Ordinario reservatam, ipso facto incurrendam ab eis qui, postquam divortium civile obtinuerint, matrimonium ausi fuerint attentare."

b. Because of the words *ausi fuerint,* any diminution of imputability would excuse from this censure (c. 2229, § 2).

c. Does the party who did not *obtain* the divorce, but who merely *marries a divorced person* incur the censure? Yes; as a positive necessary co-operator (cc. 2231, 2209, § 3).

---

[8] *Contra,* Cappello, *De Censuris,* n. 369, 3.

4. Laying Violent Hands on Cleric or Religious (c. 2343, § 4).

a. This means a *personal and real* (as opposed to a merely verbal) *injury,* e.g., to person, liberty, or dignity.

b. Shoot at one, hit another? *Disputatur.* St. Alphonsus (III, n. 628) cites Suarez for negative; makes negative probable, hence no censure, because of the doubt (cf. cc. 15, 2219, § 1).

c. Religious, even *lay* and *novice,* included (c. 614), but not postulant.

d. Excuses: anything that excuses from grave sin in the act concerned (c. 2218, § 2).

e. The censure is reserved *Ordinario proprio (percutientis).* But any Ordinary could absolve, provided the culprit be his subject at the time of the absolution; and any Ordinary of the place could absolve even a stranger (c. 2253, 3°).

f. This excommunication is incurred if the person violated is lower than a titular Bishop. For titular Bishops and persons of higher dignity up to the Roman Pontiff, the excommunication is *specially* reserved; for the Roman Pontiff, *most specially.*

5. Abortion (c. 2350).

a. Abortion is taken in its common meaning, the ejection of a living nonviable fetus. It must be directly intended. It does not include craniotomy or embryotomy because these are not commonly called simply abortion. As a consequence, these horrible crimes escape censure.

b. The *theoretical question as to the moment of the infusion of the human soul* is not considered. The censure is incurred any time after conception has certainly taken place.

c. Matre non excepta; but grave fear may and often does excuse her, even though guilt remain mortal (Code Commission, 30 Dec., 1937, *AAS,* 30, p. 73, *Digest,* II, p. 570). Fear *need not be extrinsic* and unjust, in order to excuse.

d. The *effect* must have taken place; i.e., the act placed for the purpose of procuring abortion must have certainly resulted in it.

e. Co-operators are held or not according to canons 2209 and 2231: moral *and* physical co-operation together — censure incurred; *mandans* — censure incurred; moral *or* physical co-operation "without which the crime would not have been committed" — censure incurred.

f. What if the guilty person repents and *comes to confession before the effect has taken place?* Ans.: He has not *yet* incurred the censure; hence he can be absolved from his sins, including this one, if properly disposed. If the effect follows thereafter, he will not *then* incur the censure, because then he is free from the sin.

g. What if he merely *repented sincerely before the effect,* but *confesses after it?* Ans.: Some, including St. Alphonsus (III, n. 395) hold that the censure is not incurred; this is at least extrinsically prob-able; in practice, no censure (cf. c. 2219, § 1, and Cappello, *De Censuris,* nn. 29, 386).

h. Is it necessary to incur the censure that the *fetus be alive* when ejected?

1) If the child is certainly dead before any attempt to eject it is made, there is no abortion, and no censure.

2) If the child is killed by embryotomy or craniotomy, an abomi-nable crime is committed, but it is not "abortion" in the common parlance, hence no censure is incurred.

3) If a living child is attacked and destroyed by any of the means which commonly go by the name of abortion (curetting the womb, drugs, compresses, etc.), it makes no difference whether the child died before being ejected or afterward. The difference between this case and n. 2 is that this is commonly called abortion, the other is not.

6. Apostasy From Religion (c. 2385).

a. Apostasy from religion is defined in canon 644, § 1.

b. It includes two elements: *factum et animus;* both must be *exter-nally manifest* in order that the censure be incurred.

c. The *reservation* is: (1) in a *clerical exempt* institute, to the culprit's *own major superior;* (2) otherwise, to the *Ordinary of the place* where he is staying, with or without domicile. As to absolution, cf. c. 2253, 3°.

7. Marriage With Simple Perpetual Vows (c. 2388, § 2).

a. Both the *party under vow* and the *person with whom* marriage is attempted or contracted, incur the censure.

b. Vows must be *perpetual,* though simple, in *either an order or a congregation.*

c. If such a religious *runs off with a person* of the other sex, dis-missal occurs *ipso facto;* but whether the religious is also released from his vows or not, depends on the constitutions (cc. 646, 669, § 1). If he is released from his vows at the time of the automatic dismissal, the party would not be under vows at the time of the subsequent marriage, and hence no censure would be incurred by the marriage.

d. The special expression *praesumentes* is carried over also into this part of the canon, with all its excusing force.

Reserved to No One (2)

1. Authors or Publishers Who Print Scripture Without Permission (c. 2318, § 2).

a. Only *authors and publishers* incur this censure. The works concerned are *books of Scripture* or *annotations* or *commentaries* thereof.

b. Publication is not required; the censure is incurred as soon as a notable number of copies (*sufficient* for publication, which is the danger guarded against) are *printed with a view to publication* by order of either authors or publishers (Cappello, *De Censuris,* n. 398, 3).

c. The *permission required* for books of Scripture or commentaries or annotations thereof may be given by any of three distinct Ordinaries: (1) the Ordinary of the author personally; (2) the Ordinary of the place of publication; (3) the Ordinary of the place of printing (c. 1385, § 2). If any of these permissions was validly obtained, the censure is not incurred.

d. There is question of *books,* a term which, *in the penal part of the Code,* retains its strict meaning and *does not include* magazines, leaflets, etc. (cf. c. 1384, § 2, *"sub hoc titulo"*).

2. Failure to Denounce for Solicitation (c. 2368).[9]

a. Solicitation means *direct inducing* to sin against the sixth commandment:

1) Man, woman, or child;

2) Whether induced to sin alone, with confessor, or with other person;

3) Whether the person so induced to sin be the penitent or some other person through the penitent;

4) The sin must be *grave,* and *certain;*

5) Although the law contains the words *temerario ausu* (Doc. V, § 1), yet canon 2229, § 2, with all its excuses *does not apply* here, because there is no question of a *latae sententiae* penalty, cf. c. 2368, § 1.

b. Connection with confession:

1) Either *in confession* (from beginning to absolution, even though absolution be not given);

2) Or *immediately before or after* confession;

3) Or *on the occasion of confession* (when the *penitent* intended to go);

4) Or *on pretext* of confession (on the part of the *confessor*);

[9] For a very full treatment of this difficult matter, cf. Cappello, *De Censuris,* nn. 421–461.

5) Or *in the place* of confession *and with pretense* of confession.

c. Denunciation is to be made *personally,* to the Ordinary of the place or his delegate. This obligation binds even if the penitent is unable to prove the charge. If the difficulties of making the accusation personally are extremely grave, it can be made by letter or through another person (cf. Arregui, *Theol. Mor.,* n. 656).

d. In general an *extremely grave* difficulty in making the accusation would excuse from the law entirely as long as the difficulty continues. Such difficulty may be purely private and need not concern the public welfare. But the mere fear of offending the person to be accused is not a sufficient excuse.

e. Not only the person solicited but all persons who know the fact with certainty (outside professional confidence) are obliged to lodge the accusation; but *only the person solicited is subject to this penalty* for failure to do so (c. 2368, § 2).

A CHART FOR SOLVING

GENERAL CLASS OF RESERVED CENSURE OR SIN TO WHICH THE CASE BELONGS:

1. Censure most specially reserved to the Holy See
2. Censure specially reserved to the Holy See
3. Censure simply reserved to the Holy See
4. Censure reserved to the Ordinary by common law
5. Censure reserved to the Ordinary by particular law
6. Censure reserved to no one
7. Censure *ab homine*
8. Sin reserved *ratione sui* to the Holy See (cf. c. 894)
9. Sin reserved *ratione sui* by the Ordinary to himself (cf. diocesan pagella)

CIRCUMSTANCES AFFECTING THE POWER TO ABSOLVE DIRECTLY WITHOUT SPECIAL FACULTIES:

(a) *Doubt* either of law or fact (cf., for reserved *sins and censures* c. 209; censures c. 2245, § 4)

(b) *Danger of death* (cc. 882, 2252)

(c) For censures *latae sententiae, urgent case, with* recourse (c. 2254, § 1)

(d) For censures *latae sententiae, urgent case, without* recourse (c. 2254, § 3)

(e) For *sins or* (probably) *censures reserved by Ordinaries to themselves*, if the confessor is a *pastor*, during the time allowed for the paschal precept, or a missionary during a mission (c. 899, § 3)

(f) For reserved *sins only*, if the penitent is either *confined to the house by illness*, or is making this confession *in preparation for marriage*, or if *special faculty to absolve has been asked and refused*, or in the judgment of the confessor cannot be asked without *grave inconvenience* to the penitent or without danger of violating the seal (c. 900, 1°, 2°); or in all cases where the confession is made *outside the particular territory* in which the reservation was established (c. 900, 3°)

(g) For reserved *censures*, in all cases where the confession is made outside the particular territory in which the reservation was established (c. 2247, § 2), *except* a censure *ab homine* (*ibid.*)

(h) *Ignorance* either of the *law* or the *penalty*, on the part of the *penitent* (c. 2229), with distinctions, however, regarding *affected* ignorance and *crass* ignorance, which that canon **makes**

(i) Ignorance of the *reservation of a censure*, on the part of the *confessor* (c. 2247, § 3)

(k) If the censure is omitted in good faith from the confession, but **the** confessor *has faculties to absolve from it*, and uses the general formula (c. 2249, § 2)

EXPLANATION OF THE CHART

In the accompanying chart (on the opposite page) we have arranged the *general classes of censures and sins* in *vertical columns* numbered from 1 to 9 to correspond with the classification at the head of this page. The *horizontal lines* intersecting the vertical columns, are designated by letters from (a) to (k), corresponding to the same letters on this page, which indicate *particular circumstances* which, according to the canons cited, might affect the power to absolve.

Thus, the *intersection* of column and line on our chart specifies a *concrete case*, i.e., a case of a certain *class*, occurring under specific *circumstances*.

Y (Yes) — Absolution can be given directly.

O (No) — Absolution cannot be given directly.

NOTE: In (k) there is question of a confessor who *has special faculties* to absolve from the censure or sin. In all the other cases there is question of a simple confessor who *has not special faculties*.

CONCRETE CASES

	1	2	3	4	5	6	7	8	9
(a) Doubt	Y	Y	Y	Y	Y	Y	Y	Y	Y
(b) Danger of death	Y[1]	Y	Y	Y	Y	Y	Y[1]	Y	Y
(c) Urgent case, with recourse	Y[2]	Y[3]	Y	Y	Y	Y	Y[4]	O[5]	O[5]
(d) Urgent case, without recourse	Y[6]	Y[3]	Y	Y	Y	Y	Y[4]	O[5]	O[5]
(e) Can. 899, § 3	O	O	O	O	Y	Y	O	O	Y
(f) Can. 900	O	O	O	O	O	Y	O	Y	Y
(g) Can. 2247, § 2	O	O	O	O	Y	Y	O	O	O
(h) Ignorance, penitent Can. 2229	Y	Y	Y	Y	Y	Y	Y	O[7]	O[7]
(i) Ignorance, confessor Can. 2247, § 3	O	Y	Y	Y	Y	Y	O	O	O
(k) Can. 2249, § 2	O	Y	Y	Y	Y	Y	Y	O[8]	O[8]

NOTES

[1] With obligation of recourse in case of recovery.

[2] Except the case of a married priest who cannot separate (*Canon Law Digest*, II, p. 580).

[3] One censure included here, namely, false accusation of solicitation, can be absolved even in an urgent case, only after formal retractation and reparation as far as possible has been made (can. 2363). The mere promise to make the retractation and reparation is not sufficient.

[4] See the discussion in the text (*Canon Law: A Text and Commentary*) as to absolving a censure *ab homine in casu urgentiori*. It is only exceptionally that it can be done, but the possibility is not entirely excluded.

[5] On this point, Cappello holds the contrary (*De Censuris*, n. 125); but we prefer to rely exclusively on canon 900 for absolution from reserved *sins* in urgent cases.

[6] Except *absolutio complicis* and the case of a *married priest unable to separate*.

[7] The contrary opinion cited by Arregui, n. 608, seems to us devoid of probability. (Cf. Genicot, *Theol. Mor.*, II, n. 345.)

[8] By a kind of analogy with the principle of canon 2249, § 2, if a penitent in good faith omits to mention a reserved *sin* when confessing to a priest who has faculties to absolve from that sin, though the sin is not directly absolved, yet, according to a probable and common opinion, the reservation is removed, so that the sin could afterward be absolved directly by a simple confessor (Genicot, *Theol. Mor.*, II, n. 350).

CASES AND QUESTIONS

1. Which of the following crimes are punished by a censure *latae sententiae:* heresy, profanation of the Sacred Species, blasphemy, solicitation, absolving one's *complex,* abortion, marrying before a civil officer, striking a religious novice, bringing civil suit against a priest, joining a Masonic society, apostasy from religion, illegally admitting novice to religious profession, flight from religion, dismissal from religion for minor crimes? (Try answering from memory; then consult complete list of *latae sententiae* censures.)

2. In the above list (n. 1), which penalties if any are reserved excommunications? How is each reserved?

3. State the censure *latae sententiae,* if any, whether it is reserved, and if so how, in the following crimes:

a. False accusation of solicitation; failure to denounce for solicitation;

b. Reading forbidden books in general; reading books by schismatic defending schism; as publisher causing printing of Scriptures without permission;

c. Absolving *complex in peccato turpi;* solicitation in confession;

d. Violation of papal cloister; of common or episcopal cloister;

e. Apostasy from faith; apostasy from religion; flight from religion in sacred orders;

f. Marriage (mixed) before non-Catholic minister; before civil officer; marriage of two Catholic parties before non-Catholic minister; marriage of divorced person; marriage with simple perpetual vows; marriage with solemn vows or sacred orders.

4. A confessor accused of solicitation admits the fact but claims that his ignorance of the law (though admittedly crass) should excuse him from the penalty in view of the words *"temerario ausu"* in the law (c. 2229, § 2).

5. Charles is dying; confesses he is a priest, an apostate from a regular order, and that he contracted marriage after departure from religion; is now separated (cc. 2385, 2388, § 1, 2252).

6. A religious superioress in a retreat confesses that she has consistently opposed the use of the "occasional" confessor by her subjects, by forbidding it and exacting an account about it of sisters who go out together. She is now repentant. Has she incurred any penalty? (Cc. 522, 2414).

7. First seminarian: "Penal laws not contained in the Code are simply revoked; just read canon 6, 5°." Second seminarian: "All the same, the excommunication enacted by the Council of Baltimore for marrying after obtaining a divorce is still in effect." Can you settle this controversy to the satisfaction of both?

8. Priest penitent is sure he incurred suspension *a divinis* for presuming

to hear confessions without jurisdiction. If so (cf. c. 2366), can a simple confessor absolve him from this suspension? What formula would he use? (C. 2250, § 3).

9. Religious superior has incurred suspension of canon 2410, comes to confession, penitent for this and other sins. Can simple confessor absolve him from his sins? What about this suspension? (Cc. 2286, 2236, § 1, 2290).

10. Sister confesses as follows: "Father, I'm in trouble. About two hours ago I took some money from the school athletics account and left the convent without permission, intending to take the train to Chicago and go back to my parents and never to return. I don't know why I came into this church, but here I am. Can you help me?" The confessor wonders whether she is an apostate from religion, and whether there is anything he can do about it (c. 644, § 1).

11. Marriage before a civil officer is a reserved *sin* (without censure) in the diocesan pagella. Confessor A absolves from it as a *casus urgentior* because it would take a day to obtain the faculty; confessor B, with the penitent's permission, asks for the faculty by phone, is refused, comes back to the confessional and absolves the penitent; confessor C absolves because he does not know about the reservation. Are these absolutions valid (directly)? (Cc. 900, 2°, 2247, § 3).

12. S, a pastor, is hearing confessions in his church during Easter week (cf. c. 859). He absolves: (*a*) from a sin and censure reserved by the Bishop to himself in the pagella (c. 899, § 3); (*b*) from formal heresy (c. 2314, § 2) in a case where the penitent is preparing for marriage. Are these absolutions directly valid? (C. 900, 1°; *Digest*, I, p. 415).

13. X confesses abortion; knew of the excommunication, but did not know it was reserved. Was the censure incurred? (Cc. 893, § 2, 2229, § 1; De Meester, *Compendium*, III, part 2, n. 1717).

14. Excited seminarian, on morning of examination *ad audiendas confessiones:* "Say, I thought there were only four excommunications most specially reserved. Isn't that right? Now I hear there are five. And what about those censures that are incurred in a conclave? And what is this 'secret of the Holy Office'?" Can you help inform him? (C. 2230; *Digest*, II, pp. 579, 580.)

15. A pastor, after being declared by sentence suspended from jurisdiction: (*a*) assists at a marriage in his parish; (*b*) hears confessions. Are the marriage and the absolutions valid? (Cc. 2279, § 2, 1°, 2284, 1095, § 1, 1°; Cappello, *De Matrimonio,* n. 662).

16. Have you any reliable method for recalling quickly the more important of the *latae sententiae* excommunications?

17. Are the suspensions of canons 2373 and 2387 censures or vindictive penalties? Reason for your answer?

simulation of consent, 506
stole fees, 524
through interpreter, 510
time, 535
under civil law, 406
unity, 400
use of, in doubt regarding validity, 429
of *vagi*, 421
venereal disease, 473
when baptism doubtful, 478
with unworthy Catholics, 464
with witnesses alone, 525
Married man impeded to orders, 381
Masonic societies: *outline*, 904
affiliation, 867
Masonry, books favoring, 729
Mass: after breaking fast, 864
excommunicated person and, 77
for excommunicated person, 860
funeral, when permitted, 629
Gregorian, 345
places for hearing, 635
in private oratories, 603
pro populo, 212, 213
pro sponsis, 529, 531
stipends, crimes concerning, 864
Master of novices, 266
Matrimonial cases: party who is guilty cause of nullity, standing in court, 506
report, 176
Matrimonial consent: 497
conditional, 510
continues till revoked, 515
in invalid marriage, 515
and knowledge or belief of nullity, 504
knowledge required, 498
must be genuine, 505
not affected by simple error, 502
presumed from external expression, 505
simulation, 506
Medal, scapular, 347
Membership in religious institute, 258
Mensa episcopalis, 185
Mental defects as irregularity, 375
Metropolitans: 169
indulgences, 328
powers, 170
Military chaplains: 191
faculties for scapulars, 347
marriage, 520
fast and abstinence, 640
Military service: of clerics: 118; in U. S., 104
impediment to orders, 381
Minister of Orders, 359
Minor cleric, reduction to lay state, 147

Minor impediment: dispensation, 451
to marriage, 438
Minors: imputability of crimes, 802
marriage, 423
rights of, 78
Missions in parishes, 695
Mixed marriage: contracted without dispensation, 877
no religious rites, 464
sacred rites forbidden, 532
Mixed religion impediment, 459
Modernism, oath against, 21, 734
Modesty in dress, report, 176
Monastic congregation, 232
Money, 772
Month, how reckoned, 44
Monuments, cemetery, 610
Morality, books attacking, 728
Moral persons: 86
acts of, 87
how constituted, 86
perpetuity of, 88
union with parish, 191
Mortgaging of church property, 782
Music and singing, 650
Mutilation as irregularity, 378

National parish, marriage, 520
Natural law: on marriage, 400
on reading, 712
Negligence, as basis of crime, 802
Negotiatio: forbidden to clerics, 119
penalty for clerics or religious, 879
Neophytes impeded to orders, 381
New devotions, 648
Non-Catholics: books of Sacred Scripture, 726
books treating professedly of religion, 728
burial in Catholic cemetery, 628
commended to Ordinaries and pastors, 695
co-operation in worship with, 646
discussions with, 685
ecclesiastical burial, 626
Nonconsummated marriage, 548
Nonresidents, when bound by laws, 27
Notaries, 182
Novices, funeral, 615
Noviceship: admission of diocesan cleric to, 100
failure to notify Ordinary, 885
illegal admission, 885
Novitiate: in religious institute, 259
for details *see* Religious novitiate
Nuns, 232
Nuptial blessing: 529, 535
liturgical summary, 531
not repeated, 585

failure to execute, 871
Pious will: 756
  administration of, 759
  executors of, 760
  fulfillment of, 759
Place of marriage, 535
Places in church, 649
Plenary councils, 170
Plenary indulgences, little treasury, 354
Polygamy, 400
Pontifical household, precedence, 93
Pontifical institute, 232
Pope: election of, 126, 154, 155
  crimes, 865
  see also Roman Pontiff
Portiuncula indulgence, 353
Posthumous child, origin of, 79
Postulantship in religious institute, 258
Postulation, 128
Poverty: simple vow of, 274
  solemn vow of, 275
**Practice of medicine or surgery as
  irregularity,** 379
Prayers: authority of Ordinary, 647
  for gaining indulgences, 340
Preachers for lay religious, 250
Preaching: 686, 689
  exempt religious, 691
  explanation of Gospel, 694
  by extradiocesan priests, 692
  faculty, permission, consent, 690
  in Lent and Advent, 694
  matter and manner, 695
  by Ordinary, 693
  by pastor, 693
  revocation of faculty or permission,
  692
  Sunday homily, 693
Precedence: 92, 93
  among Bishops, 174
  among parochial vicars, 225
  among prelates, 170
  among religious, 233
Precepts: particular, how effective, 36
  penal remedy, 860
Prefects Apostolic, 170
Prelacy, 96
Prelates: funeral, 614
  inferior, 172
  precedence among, 170
Prelates *nullius:* burial, 609
  indulgences, 328
Prescription: as applied to custom, 40
  barring penalty, 819
  of Church property, 752
  as foundation of privilege, 65
  when required for custom, 41
Presumed death of former spouse, 474
Presumption: of fatherhood, 540
  of ignorance, 30

of knowledge or ignorance, 500
of legitimacy, 540
of validity of marriage and baptism,
  403
Priest: attempting marriage, unable to
  separate, 886
  dispensing: from matrimonial impediments in danger of death, 441;
  "when all is ready for the wedding,"
  444
  having attempted marriage, unable to
  separate, *outline,* 901
  powers to dispense, 72
Priesthood, vocation, 697
Primates, 169
Privilege: of exemption for religious,
  291
  of faith, 564, 565
Privileged altar, 331
Privileges: 19
  of clerics: 102; how lost, 105
  communication of, 63
  definition and division of, 63
  expiration of, 67
  interpretation of, 66
  manner of acquiring, 63, 64
  norms for use of, 66
  renunciation of, 66
  use of, in external forum, 67
Privilegium canonis, 102
Privilegium competentiae, 105
Privilegium fori, 103
  penalties for violation, 868
Privilegium immunitatis, 104
Probabilism, applied to doubtful laws,
  29
Procedure, in suspension *ex informata
  conscientia,* 848
Processions: 663
  reserved function, 206
Procurator general of religious, 244
Profanation of Sacred Species, 863
Profession of faith: 733
  omission of, 883
Professional secret, and impediment to
  marriage, 420
Prohibition of books, 720
Promoter of justice, 182
Promulgation: of ecclesiastical laws, 23
  of interpretation of law, 32
Proof: of consecration or blessing, 591
  of simulated consent in marriage, 506
Proper Ordinary, how determined, 82
Proper pastor, how determined, 82
Property: acquirement of, by church,
  743
  administration of in church, 743
  alienation of: permission for, 746;
  irregular, remedy for, 779; unlawful,
  penalties for, 870

INDEX OF CANONS

Heavy type indicates pages on which canons receive principal treatment. Light face gives cross references.